Lecture Notes in Computer Science

# Lecture Notes in Artificial Intelligence 17131

Founding Editor

Jörg Siekmann

Series Editors

This was established in 1988 as a topical subseries of LNCS devoted to artificial intelligence. The editors are Wolfgang Wahlster (DFKI, Berlin), Zhi-Hua Zhou (Nanjing University), and Randy Goebel (University of Alberta, Edmonton).

For further information please contact lncs@springer.com.

Stefano Bistarelli · Marco Maratea ·
Francesco Santini
Editors

# AIxIA 2026 – Advances in Artificial Intelligence

XXIVth International Conference
of the Italian Association for Artificial Intelligence, AIxIA 2026
Perugia, Italy, October 6–9, 2026
Proceedings

Springer

*Editors*
Stefano Bistarelli
University of Perugia
Perugia, Italy

Marco Maratea
University of Calabria
Rende, Italy

Francesco Santini
University of Perugia
Perugia, Italy

ISSN 0302-9743 ISSN 1611-3349 (electronic)
Lecture Notes in Artificial Intelligence
ISBN 978-3-032-40773-3 ISBN 978-3-032-40774-0 (eBook)
https://doi.org/10.1007/978-3-032-40774-0

LNCS Sublibrary: SL7 – Artificial Intelligence



This Springer imprint is published by the registered company Springer Nature Switzerland AG
The registered company address is: Gewerbestrasse 11, 6330 Cham, Switzerland

# Preface

This volume contains the proceedings of the 24th International Conference of the Italian Association for Artificial Intelligence (AIxIA 2026), the primary scientific event of the Associazione Italiana per l'Intelligenza Artificiale (AIxIA). AIxIA is a nonprofit organization dedicated to promoting the advancement of Artificial Intelligence (AI) within academic, social, and production contexts. The association established the series of international conferences in 1991, initially organizing an event every two years, and then maintaining an annual schedule from 2015 onward. Over the years, the conference has visited many cities throughout the national territory, as reported in the LNCS proceedings of the various editions (https://link.springer.com/conference/aiia).

AIxIA 2026 was held in Perugia, Italy, during October 6–9, hosted by the University of Perugia at the Auditorium San Francesco, in the historic center of the city. The conference received 78 submissions for the regular research papers track. Each paper was reviewed in a single-blind process, in which the reviewers remained anonymous to the authors, by members of the Program Committee and by additional reviewers, with an average of 3.7 reviews per paper, and finally, 52 papers were accepted for publication in these proceedings and presented at the conference. Besides regular papers, the conference also received the submission of 15 discussion papers, i.e., position papers or extended abstracts of articles recently published in premier international conferences and journals related to AI. After a dedicated review process, 10 discussion papers were accepted for presentation at the conference.

AIxIA 2026 featured three invited talks, given by Francesca Toni (Imperial College London), Roberto Navigli (Sapienza University of Rome), and Alessandro Sperduti (University of Padua). The conference agenda also included two tutorials, by Eleonora Giunchiglia (Imperial College London) and Andrea Omicini (University of Bologna), and a panel titled "Per ELIZA (in occasione dei suoi sessant'anni)", with Oliviero Stock, devoted to the sixtieth anniversary of ELIZA.

Besides the main track, AIxIA 2026 encompassed a wide range of theoretical and applied AI aspects, with 20 workshops held alongside the conference and dedicated to specific topics, bringing together AI communities with related interests. In addition, the following collateral events were organized: a Doctoral Consortium, the AIxIA award ceremony, a panel with representatives of the industrial world, and two public events on the impact of AI on citizens and on enterprises.

We express our gratitude to the institutions and sponsors who supported AIxIA 2026, namely the Department of Mathematics and Computer Science of the University of Perugia, Intelligentiae, DLVSystem, Sviluppumbria, the FAIR project, Regione Umbria, and BUP, together with the institutions that granted their patronage: the University of Perugia, the City of Perugia, Confcommercio, Confartigianato Umbria, and Confindustria Umbria. We also thank the AIxIA Executive Board for its steadfast assistance, and the University of Perugia for granting us the opportunity to host the conference in its facilities. Moreover, we want to thank all authors for submitting high-quality research papers, and the members of the Program Committee and the additional reviewers for their efforts to produce fair and thorough evaluations of the submitted papers. Our heartfelt thanks also go to the Workshop Chairs, Marco Baioletti (University of Perugia) and Antonella Guzzo (University of Calabria), to the Tutorial Chairs, Andrea Formisano (University of Udine) and Carlo Taticchi (University of Perugia), and to the Doctoral Consortium Chairs, Stefano Ferilli (University of Bari) and Valentina Poggioni (University of Perugia), for their invaluable contributions in shaping an exciting program for AIxIA 2026. Finally, we would like to express our gratitude to all those who, in various capacities, contributed to the success of AIxIA 2026.

August 2026

Stefano Bistarelli
Marco Maratea
Francesco Santini

# Organization

## General Chair

| | |
|---|---|
| Stefano Bistarelli | University of Perugia, Italy |

## Program Committee Chairs

| | |
|---|---|
| Marco Maratea | University of Calabria, Italy |
| Francesco Santini | University of Perugia, Italy |

## Workshop Chairs

| | |
|---|---|
| Marco Baioletti | University of Perugia, Italy |
| Antonella Guzzo | University of Calabria, Italy |

## Tutorial Chairs

| | |
|---|---|
| Andrea Formisano | University of Udine, Italy |
| Carlo Taticchi | University of Perugia, Italy |

## Doctoral Consortium Chairs

| | |
|---|---|
| Stefano Ferilli | University of Bari, Italy |
| Valentina Poggioni | University of Perugia, Italy |

## Travel Grant Chairs

| | |
|---|---|
| Gabriele Costante | University of Perugia, Italy |
| Nicola Gigante | Free University of Bozen-Bolzano, Italy |

## Industry Liaison and Public Events Chairs

| | |
|---|---|
| Gabriella Cortellessa | National Research Council of Italy, Italy |
| Ivan Mercanti | University of Perugia, Italy |

## Publicity Chair

| | |
|---|---|
| Valentina Franzoni | University of Perugia, Italy |

## Local Arrangement Chairs

| | |
|---|---|
| Gabriele Costante | University of Perugia, Italy |
| Valentina Franzoni | University of Perugia, Italy |

## Web and Social Chairs

| | |
|---|---|
| Marco Cuccarini | University of Perugia, Italy |
| Chiara Luchini | University of Perugia, Italy |

## Proceedings Chairs

| | |
|---|---|
| Stefano Bistarelli | University of Perugia, Italy |
| Marco Maratea | University of Calabria, Italy |
| Francesco Santini | University of Perugia, Italy |

## Program Committee

| | |
|---|---|
| Carlo Adornetto | University of Calabria, Italy |
| Francesco Amigoni | Politecnico di Milano, Italy |
| Alessandro Artale | Free University of Bozen-Bolzano, Italy |
| Vincenzo Auletta | Università di Salerno, Italy |
| Marco Baioletti | Università degli Studi di Perugia, Italy |
| Pietro Baroni | University of Brescia, Italy |
| Roberto Basili | University of Roma Tor Vergata, Italy |
| Sebastiano Battiato | University of Catania, Italy |
| Elena Bellodi | University of Ferrara, Italy |

| | |
|---|---|
| Gloria Beraldo | CNR-ISTC, Italy |
| Stefano Berretti | University of Florence, Italy |
| Stefano Bistarelli | Università di Perugia, Italy |
| Domenico Bloisi | University of Basilicata, Italy |
| Stefano Borgo | CNR-ISTC, Italy |
| Stefano Cagnoni | University of Parma, Italy |
| Roberta Calegari | Alma Mater Studiorum–Università di Bologna, Italy |
| Francesco Calimeri | University of Calabria, Italy |
| Alberto Casagrande | Università degli Studi di Udine, Italy |
| Antonio Chella | Università di Palermo, Italy |
| Federico Chesani | University of Bologna, Italy |
| Alessandro Cimatti | Fondazione Bruno Kessler, Italy |
| Flavio S. Correa da Silva | University of São Paulo, Brazil |
| Stefania Costantini | Università degli Studi dell'Aquila, Italy |
| Claudio Di Ciccio | Utrecht University, The Netherlands |
| Francesco M. Donini | Università della Tuscia, Italy |
| Stefano Ferilli | Università degli Studi di Bari, Italy |
| Diodato Ferraioli | Università degli Studi di Salerno, Italy |
| Johannes K. Fichte | Linköping University, Sweden |
| Alberto Finzi | Università di Napoli Federico II, Italy |
| Fabio Fioravanti | University of Chieti-Pescara, Italy |
| Andrea Formisano | Università di Udine, Italy |
| Fabio Gasparetti | Roma Tre University, Italy |
| Marco Gavanelli | University of Ferrara, Italy |
| Massimiliano Giacomin | University of Brescia, Italy |
| Nicola Gigante | Free University of Bozen-Bolzano, Italy |
| Enrico Giunchiglia | Università degli Studi di Genova, Italy |
| Gianluigi Greco | University of Calabria, Italy |
| Davide Lanti | Free University of Bozen-Bolzano, Italy |
| Domenico Lembo | Sapienza University of Rome, Italy |
| Maurizio Lenzerini | Sapienza University of Rome, Italy |
| Nicola Leone | University of Calabria, Italy |
| Francesca Alessandra Lisi | Università degli Studi di Bari "Aldo Moro", Italy |
| Marin Lujak | University Rey Juan Carlos, Spain |
| Dario Malchiodi | University of Milan, Italy |
| Marco Maratea | Università della Calabria, Italy |
| Giuseppe Mazzotta | University of Calabria, Italy |
| Alessio Micheli | University of Pisa, Italy |
| Marina Mongiello | Politecnico di Bari, Italy |
| Marco Montali | Free University of Bozen-Bolzano, Italy |
| Aniello Murano | University of Naples Federico II, Italy |

| | |
|---|---|
| Angelo Oddi | CNR-ISTC, Italy |
| Andrea Orlandini | CNR-ISTC, Italy |
| Roberto Pirrone | Università degli Studi di Palermo, Italy |
| Valentina Poggioni | Università degli Studi di Perugia, Italy |
| Luigi Portinale | Università del Piemonte Orientale "A. Avogadro", Italy |
| Luca Pulina | University of Sassari, Italy |
| Riccardo Rasconi | CNR-ISTC, Italy |
| Francesco Ricca | University of Calabria, Italy |
| Fabrizio Riguzzi | University of Ferrara, Italy |
| Andrea Roli | University of Bologna, Italy |
| Marco Rospocher | Università degli Studi di Verona, Italy |
| Marco Roveri | University of Trento, Italy |
| Salvatore Ruggieri | Università di Pisa, Italy |
| Giuseppe Sansonetti | Roma Tre University, Italy |
| Francesco Santini | University of Perugia, Italy |
| Luigi Sauro | University of Naples Federico II, Italy |
| Domenico Fabio Savo | University of Bergamo, Italy |
| Enrico Scala | Università di Brescia, Italy |
| Francesco Scarcello | University of Calabria, Italy |
| Filippo Sciarrone | Universitas Mercatorum, Italy |
| Fabio Stella | University of Milano-Bicocca, Italy |
| Carlo Taticchi | Università degli Studi di Perugia, Italy |
| Mauro Vallati | University of Huddersfield, UK |
| Eloisa Vargiu | Cetaqua Water Technology Centre, Spain |
| Serena Villata | CNRS, France |

## Additional Reviewers

Alviano, Mario
Ballot, Gabriel
Bartucci, Simone
Bertagnon, Alessandro
Borroto, Manuel
Cauteruccio, Francesco
Cuteri, Andrea
De Benedictis, Riccardo
De Rose, Edoardo
Dovier, Agostino
Duca, Marco
Esposito, Andrea
Ferragina, Luca
Filice, Francesca
Foderaro, Elisa
Kabir, Mohimenul
Laboccetta, Luca
Magliocca, Francesco
Manna, Marco
Marangone, Edoardo
Marra, Piero
Maubert, Bastien
Pandolfo, Laura
Reale, Kristian
Tamantini, Christian

# Contents

# Designing AI-Mediated Higher Education: Course Design as Cognitive Governance

Giovanni Adorni[1(✉)], Daniele Zolezzi[1], and Daniele Scala[2]

[1] DIBRIS, University of Genoa, Viale F. Causa 13, 16145 Genoa, Italy
giovanni.adorni@unige.it, daniele.zolezzi@edu.unige.it
[2] DLCM, University of Genoa, P.za S. Sabina 2, 16124 Genoa, Italy
daniele.scala@edu.unige.it

**Abstract.** Generative AI is reshaping higher education by distributing reasoning and knowledge production across human and algorithmic actors. Although current responses emphasise AI literacy and responsible use, they offer limited guidance on governing cognitive delegation through course design.

Drawing on Cyber Humanities and distributed cognition, this paper introduces *Course Design as Cognitive Governance* and *Delegation-Aware Instructional Design* (DAID), a three-level framework linking delegation thresholds, epistemic learning outcomes, dialogic interaction, and governance-oriented assessment to preserve epistemic agency and reflective supervision.

The framework was initially operationalised through the redesign of a master's course in "AI for Digital Humanities", involving 25 students across three examination sessions and 1,125 prompts. Assessment triangulated artefacts, process traces, oral defence, and three lightweight indicators (MPI, DCRI, and PDVS). Exploratory findings showed positive associations between the indicators and expert judgements, while oral defence revealed reflective regulation not always visible in prompt logs. The study provides preliminary evidence of operational feasibility rather than general validation of educational effectiveness.

**Keywords:** Cognitive Governance · Generative AI in Higher Education · Delegation-Aware Instructional Design · Cognitive Delegation · Epistemic Agency

## 1 Introduction

Generative Artificial Intelligence (GenAI) is reshaping higher education: reasoning, writing, and knowledge production increasingly emerge through interaction with Large Language Models (LLMs). Unlike earlier technologies that mainly supported information access, generative systems can participate in problem framing, interpretation, decomposition, and validation [11,14,23]. Educational activity therefore increasingly unfolds within hybrid human-AI cognitive systems rather than solely within individual learners [13].


S. Bistarelli et al. (Eds.): AIxIA 2026, LNAI 17131, pp. 1–15, 2027.
https://doi.org/10.1007/978-3-032-40774-0_1

This transformation challenges universities' responsibility to cultivate reflective judgement, intellectual autonomy, and critical inquiry [6,7]. Current institutional responses primarily emphasise AI literacy, ethical use, and academic integrity [9,15]. Although necessary, these approaches provide only partial guidance for addressing cognitive offloading [17,20], erosion of epistemic agency, and the progressive outsourcing of reasoning [23].

The educational challenge is therefore not simply whether students use AI, but how learning environments regulate the distribution of cognitive activity between human and algorithmic actors. We therefore argue that universities should design hybrid human–AI learning ecosystems that preserve reflective supervision, epistemic visibility, and meaningful human responsibility.

Drawing on Cyber Humanities, Cyber Humanism, and distributed cognition, this paper frames higher education as a human–centred cognitive infrastructure in which instructional design shapes human–AI interaction [1]. We introduce *Cognitive Governance* as the pedagogical and institutional capacity to regulate AI-mediated cognition while preserving epistemic visibility, reflective accountability, and dialogic validation [2]. From this perspective, course design becomes a governance activity concerned with how cognition is distributed, delegated, supervised, and validated.

The paper makes four contributions: (i) it proposes *Delegation-Aware Instructional Design* (DAID) as a framework for regulating cognitive delegation; (ii) it introduces *epistemic learning outcomes* centred on reflective validation and human responsibility; (iii) it reconceptualises assessment as a governance infrastructure for preserving reasoning visibility; and (iv) it presents an initial empirical operationalisation through the redesign of an "AI for Digital Humanities" course.

Compared with AI literacy frameworks primarily concerned with competences for responsible AI use [9,15,19], the proposed approach focuses specifically on course design as a mechanism for governing cognitive delegation. The empirical study provides exploratory evidence of the framework's operational feasibility rather than a general validation of its educational effectiveness.

Section 2 presents the three-level framework, Sect. 3 reports its course-level operationalisation and empirical analysis, and Sect. 4 discusses broader implications and limitations.

## 2 Course Design as Cognitive Governance: A Three-Level Framework

Current AI literacy frameworks primarily address the competences required for the responsible and critical use of AI in education [9,15,19]. From the perspective adopted in this paper, however, AI-mediated higher education also raises a distinct instructional-design problem: how cognitive activities should be distributed, delegated, supervised, and validated across human and algorithmic actors. This section proposes a three-level framework that interprets course design as a form of *Cognitive Governance*, extending AI literacy through delegation-aware instructional design.

Within this framework, instructional design is not limited to organising content, learning activities, and assessment. It also regulates how responsibility for framing, reasoning, validation, and accountability is allocated within hybrid human–AI learning environments. The framework distinguishes: (i) a macro-level foundational stance, *Cognitive Governance*; (ii) a meso-level design framework, *Delegation-Aware Instructional Design*; and (iii) micro-level operational components through which governance principles are instantiated in learning activities and assessment. In practical terms, the box below summarises a four-step workflow for applying DAID, while Fig. 1 presents its three-level architecture and operational dimensions.

**Operationalising DAID**

**1. Define delegation thresholds** for cognitively consequential activities.
**2. Design governance-oriented activities** that preserve human framing, supervision, and validation.
**3. Collect epistemic traces** through prompt journals, decomposition logs, and reflective checkpoints.
**4. Triangulate assessment** across artefacts, process evidence, and oral defence.

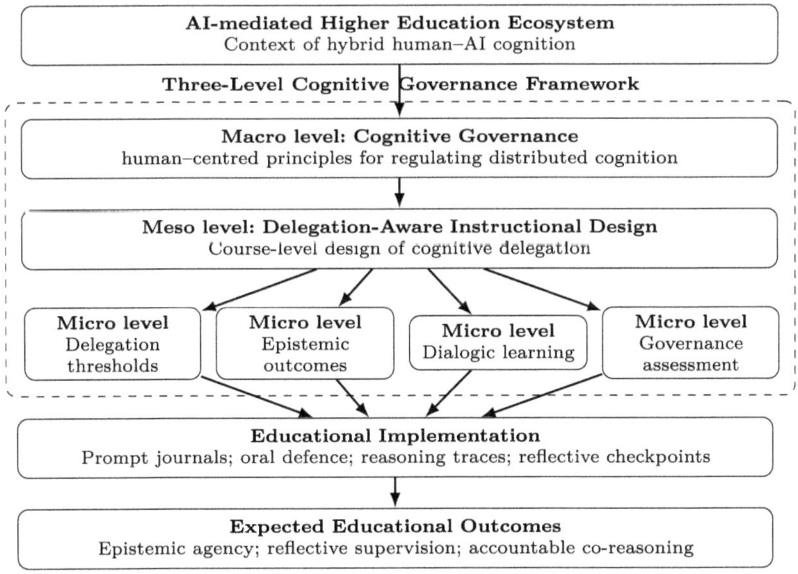


**Fig. 1.** Three-level Cognitive Governance framework and its operational implementation within AI-mediated higher education.

### 2.1 Macro-Level: Cognitive Governance as a Foundational Stance

From the perspective adopted in this paper, course design is embedded within a broader institutional and pedagogical stance that regulates how cognition is distributed between human and algorithmic actors. The macro level therefore does not prescribe individual learning activities; rather, it establishes the human-centred principles that guide subsequent instructional design decisions.

Within this perspective, every educational activity can be interpreted as implicitly regulating agency, responsibility, and epistemic accountability across hybrid cognitive systems [7,13]. In AI-mediated education, instructional design increasingly governs how cognitive effort is delegated, supervised, and made visible. Students rely on LLMs not only for low-level assistance but also for framing problems, decomposing tasks, and validating solutions [14,23], thereby redistributing cognitive agency across hybrid human–AI systems [13]. The educational challenge is therefore not whether cognitive delegation occurs, but how its boundaries are intentionally designed and governed.

Accordingly, *Cognitive Governance* provides the foundational principles and normative basis for course-level decisions about delegation, supervision, and assessment.

### 2.2 Meso-Level: Delegation-Aware Instructional Design Framework

*Delegation-Aware Instructional Design (DAID)* translates the principles of Cognitive Governance into course-level design decisions. Rather than prescribing specific teaching methods, DAID provides a governance-oriented framework through which instructors intentionally regulate how cognitive responsibilities are distributed between learners and AI systems during educational activities.

Operationally, DAID links four design dimensions—delegation thresholds, epistemic outcomes, dialogic interaction, and governance-oriented assessment—which are enacted through the workflow summarised above. Central to DAID are *delegation thresholds*: pedagogical boundaries beyond which AI support risks becoming cognitive substitution.

The delegation thresholds proposed in Table 1 are not intended as a normative taxonomy. Rather, they provide an illustrative design heuristic for reasoning about the degree of AI delegation that may be pedagogically appropriate for different cognitive activities. The categories are therefore relative to the intended learning outcomes, disciplinary context, learners' prior competence, and the forms of supervision and validation built into the course.

Not all forms of delegation have the same pedagogical implications. Delegating low-level procedural activities may reduce unnecessary cognitive load and support exploration, whereas delegating framing, interpretive judgement, or validation risks transforming cognitive support into cognitive substitution, potentially leading to *epistemic collapse*—the progressive disappearance of reflective supervision behind fluent AI-generated artefacts [20].

Accordingly, DAID also introduces *epistemic learning outcomes* that complement traditional knowledge- and skill-based objectives. These outcomes include reflective validation, dialogic reasoning, and AI orchestration—that is, the strategic coordination of AI support while preserving human intentionality and responsibility. Rather than replacing established models of metacognition and self-regulated learning, they extend them to distributed human–AI cognitive contexts [18,22,25].

**Table 1.** Illustrative Delegation Thresholds and Safeguards in AI-Mediated Learning

| Cognitive Activity | Suggested Delegation | Primary Epistemic Risk | Recommended Safeguard |
|---|---|---|---|
| Syntax support | High | Limited conceptual engagement | Learner review |
| Brainstorming | Moderate | Uncritical option adoption | Alternative comparison |
| Exploratory prompting | Moderate | Directionless exploration | Explicit task framing |
| Task decomposition | Limited | Loss of problem ownership | Learner-authored plan |
| Interpretive judgement | Minimal | Uncritical acceptance | Justification requirement |
| Validation of outputs | Minimal | False confidence in correctness | Independent verification |
| Epistemic accountability | None | Loss of responsibility | Oral or written defence |

### 2.3 Micro-Level: Operational Components of DAID

At the micro level, Delegation-Aware Instructional Design is operationalised through concrete pedagogical mechanisms that translate governance principles into everyday educational practice. Whereas the macro level establishes the institutional stance and the meso level defines course-level design decisions, the micro level specifies how learners and instructors interact with AI throughout learning and assessment activities. In this sense, it represents the operational implementation of Cognitive Governance.

**Dialogic Learning Design.** DAID operationalises Cognitive Governance by treating prompting not as command engineering but as the *dialogic regulation of reasoning*. Interaction becomes educationally meaningful when learners iteratively frame problems, negotiate interpretations, compare alternatives, and critically supervise AI-generated outputs rather than merely accepting them [16,23]. Building on Prompt-Based Learning and Natural Language Programming, prompting follows a structured cycle of problem framing, prompt formulation, evaluation, revision, and reflective validation [4]. From a dialogic perspective [5], understanding emerges through interaction; however, without explicit validation and reflection, dialogic prompting risks collapsing into cognitive outsourcing.

**Assessment as Governance Infrastructure.** Within DAID, assessment is no longer limited to evaluating final artefacts but becomes a governance mechanism through which instructors reconstruct reasoning trajectories and supervise cognitive delegation. Since fluent AI-generated outputs increasingly obscure the underlying reasoning process [10,23], assessment must preserve *epistemic visibility*—the possibility of reconstructing how learners framed problems, regulated delegation, validated outputs, and revised their interpretations [17,24]. This requires trace-based evidence such as prompt journals, decomposition logs, reasoning traces, iterative reformulations, and oral defence. Rather than functioning primarily as a mechanism for detecting misconduct, oral discussion becomes a dialogic space for demonstrating epistemic accountability and reflective supervision [5].

From an Artificial Intelligence perspective, the proposed framework can also be interpreted as a reference cognitive architecture for human–AI collaboration, specifying how cognitive responsibilities are intentionally distributed, delegated, supervised, and validated during AI-mediated problem solving. Although instantiated in this paper through the redesign of an "AI for Digital Humanities" course, the same governance principles are intended to be transferable across different disciplinary contexts and assessment formats while preserving the underlying human–centred logic of Cognitive Governance.

Section 3 presents the operational instantiation of this architecture through the redesign of an "AI for Digital Humanities" course, illustrating how these governance principles can be translated into instructional design, assessment, and reflective learning practices.

## 3 Empirical Implementation: Redesigning the "AI for Digital Humanities" Course

This section reports on the empirical operationalisation of the Cognitive Governance framework through a master's course redesign—"Artificial Intelligence for Digital Humanities" (6 ECTS) at the University of Genoa. The redesign spanned three examination sessions and explicitly adopted Delegation-Aware Instructional Design principles to regulate AI-mediated cognition, reflective supervision, and epistemic visibility during project-based learning.

### 3.1 Context and Two-Phase Architecture

The course blends foundational AI topics (search, knowledge representation, NLP, computer vision, ML) with Python labs and Digital Humanities projects [21]. Students come from heterogeneous humanities backgrounds with limited programming experience, making the course a useful site for examining how AI-mediated support can both scaffold and destabilise epistemic autonomy.

A two-phase cognitive architecture guided the redesign. The first phase emphasises *autonomous reasoning*: students develop problem framing, decomposition, and validation skills with limited AI use. This phase preserves epistemic grounding before introducing AI-mediated cognitive amplification. The second phase enables *AI-mediated co-reasoning*: LLMs act as dialogic partners—supporting brainstorming, critique, and iterative refinement—while students retain responsibility for supervision and validation.

### 3.2 Delegation-Aware Assignments and Assessment Model

To preserve epistemic visibility and make reasoning reconstructable, the course adopted delegation-aware assignments that required students to document how they regulated AI-mediated cognition. Specifically, students produced:

- **Prompt journals**: documenting interactions with generative systems, including revisions, validation decisions, and reflective prompting practices.
- **Decomposition logs and reasoning traces**: explicit representations of problem framing, planning, and solution decomposition.
- **Oral defence**: justifying methodological decisions, validation strategies, and AI delegation practices.

Assessment was designed as a governance-oriented triangulation framework integrating project artefacts, process documentation, and dialogic evaluation. A seven-dimensional rubric (C1–C7, 0–4) assessed problem comprehension and framing (goals, constraints, and assumptions), decomposition and strategy, technical implementation/co-design, verification and validation, critical discussion and reflection, autonomy and responsibility in the oral defence, and responsible AI use. The rubric provided the basis for expert judgement, while three lightweight process indicators, originally introduced in [3], supplied complementary trace-based evidence:

- *Metacognitive Prompting Index (MPI)*: explicit externalisation of four binary metacognitive functions—planning (P), monitoring (M), evaluation/validation (E), and reflection (R).
- *Delegation/Co-reasoning Index (DCRI)*: balance between delegation-oriented and co-reasoning prompts.
- *Problem Decomposition & Validation Score (PDVS)*: cumulative presence of explicit decomposition (PD1), verification or testing (PD2), and discussion of limitations or error analysis (PD3), on a 0–3 scale.

Together, the indicators operationalise cognitive delegation, reflective supervision, and epistemic visibility as partially observable process dimensions rather than direct estimates of learning outcomes. They were computed through prompt-level heuristic coding, aggregated at log level, and used to complement—not determine—project artefacts, rubric-based expert judgement, and oral defence. Table 2 summarises the assessment framework.

**Table 2.** Governance-Oriented Assessment Components

| Component | Governance Function |
|---|---|
| Prompt journals | Traceability of AI-mediated reasoning |
| Decomposition logs | Visibility of framing and planning |
| Oral defence | Reconstruction of intentionality |
| MPI, DCRI, PDVS | Metacognitive visibility, AI orchestration, structural validation |
| Rubric C1–C7 | Governance-oriented expert evaluation |

### 3.3 Empirical Study: Participants, Data, and Research Questions

**Participants.** Twenty-five students (17 F, 8 M) participated across two January 2026 sessions ($n = 7$ and $n = 15$) and one May 2026 session ($n = 3$). All students completed an individual AI-mediated project involving text classification, information extraction, or constraint satisfaction using GPT-4, Gemini, or Claude.

**Data Sources.**

1. Prompt journals (mean: 45 prompts per student; approximately 1,125 in total).
2. Rubric-based evaluation (C1–C7, 0–4) independently performed by two instructors ($\kappa = 0.78$).
3. Process indicators (MPI, DCRI, PDVS) extracted from prompt journals using the heuristic dictionaries described in [3]; a second coder independently analysed 20% of the logs ($\kappa = 0.81$).

**Research Questions.**

1. **RQ1.** Do MPI, DCRI, and PDVS capture meaningful variation in cognitive delegation and reflective supervision?
2. **RQ2.** How do these indicators relate to rubric-based expert judgements?
3. **RQ3.** Which qualitative patterns of cognitive delegation and human–AI co-reasoning emerge during AI-mediated project development?

### 3.4 Results

*Descriptive Statistics.* Table 3 shows the cohort-level distribution (N = 25). Students exhibited moderate metacognitive visibility (MPI mean 44.6), high co-reasoning orientation (DCRI 81.5), and relatively strong structural evidence (PDVS mean 2.1), with substantial individual variation. This variability cautions against uniform assumptions about delegation behaviour or epistemic supervision.

**Table 3.** Descriptive statistics (N = 25)

| Measure | Mean | SD | Min | Max |
|---|---|---|---|---|
| MPI (0–100) | 44.6 | 18.2 | 11.4 | 82.5 |
| DCRI (0–100) | 81.5 | 12.3 | 46.7 | 95.0 |
| PDVS (0–3) | 2.1 | 0.7 | 1.0 | 3.0 |
| C1–C7 total (0–28) | 23.1 | 3.4 | 16.0 | 28.0 |

*Correlations (RQ1, RQ2).* Spearman correlations (Table 4) indicate that MPI correlates moderately with total rubric score ($\rho = 0.52$, $p < 0.01$) and strongly with C5 (reflection) and C7 (responsible AI). DCRI correlates with C3 (co-design) and C7 ($\rho = 0.48, 0.61$). PDVS correlates strongly with C2 (decomposition, $\rho = 0.67$) and C4 (verification, $\rho = 0.59$). No indicator correlates perfectly with any rubric score, consistent with their intended complementary role as visibility measures rather than competence proxies.

**Table 4.** Spearman correlations between indicators and rubric criteria (N = 25)

| Criterion | MPI | DCRI | PDVS |
|---|---|---|---|
| C1 - Framing | 0.31 | 0.22 | 0.41* |
| C2 - Decomposition | 0.39* | 0.35 | **0.67**** |
| C3 - Co-design | 0.44* | **0.48*** | 0.38* |
| C4 - Verification | 0.40* | 0.41* | **0.59**** |
| C5 - Reflection | **0.58**** | 0.28 | 0.44* |
| C6 - Autonomy (oral) | 0.36 | 0.33 | 0.27 |
| C7 - Responsible AI | **0.62**** | **0.61**** | 0.39* |
| Total score | **0.52**** | **0.48*** | **0.53**** |

$*p < 0.05$, $**p < 0.01$ (two-tailed)

*Qualitative Patterns (RQ3).* Analysis of prompt logs and oral defence transcripts revealed three patterns:

- **High MPI** ($> 60$): explicit planning, monitoring, and reflective closure, defined here as explicit appraisal of lessons learned, limitations, trade-offs, or next steps. A substantial minority reached this level.
- **Low MPI** ($< 30$): may reflect internalised rather than absent metacognition. These students solved problems correctly and performed well orally, but their prompts were predominantly action-oriented. This reinforces MPI as a visibility index, not a competence measure.
- **Mixed DCRI (50–70)**: rare. Most students consistently used co-reasoning; a few delegation-dominant cases (DCRI $< 50$) were flagged during oral defence and prompted additional verification questions.

Using the evaluation model's classification [3], students fell into profiles A (mature intentional control), B (guided exploratory), C (assisted executive), or D (fragile/opportunistic). Most were A or B, indicating generally intentional AI orchestration within the two-phase architecture. Profile C combined correct outputs with fragile process documentation, requiring more structured oral defence. No student remained D after oral defence—some would have been classified as D based on logs alone—illustrating the compensatory role of oral assessment.

Cohort analysis led to two instructional changes: (i) a mandatory "validation plan" worksheet, responding to under-represented verification/testing (PD2) and discussion of limitations or error analysis (PD3); and (ii) explicit reflective-closure prompts, responding to sparse and unevenly distributed reflection-coded prompts (R-count: No. of prompts per student with $R = 1$; mean 5.2, SD 7.1).

The empirical study provides an initial operationalisation of Cognitive Governance, translating an abstract governance framework into observable indicators of cognitive delegation, reflective supervision, and epistemic visibility.

### 3.5 Interpretation and Design Considerations

The findings provide preliminary support for DAID's operational viability. MPI, DCRI, and PDVS captured variation in cognitive delegation while complementing expert judgement, and the high DCRI (81.5%) aligned with the course's dialogic framing of AI. Low MPI alongside strong oral performance shows that limited log visibility does not imply absent reflective regulation, supporting triangulation of traces, artefacts, and oral defence.

Validation-oriented prompting remained underrepresented: students often used AI for planning and generation, whereas reflection and explicit validation were less visible. In this cohort, reflective supervision was not consistently externalised without explicit scaffolding. These findings informed validation worksheets, reflective checkpoints, and clearer decomposition templates to strengthen epistemic visibility and cognitive governance.

For larger cohorts, learning analytics could flag recurrent patterns and cases for selective review, avoiding exhaustive log inspection. Although operationalised in project-based learning, DAID may also inform written examinations, including calculus, through task-specific delegation thresholds, visible intermediate reasoning, and explicit validation.

# 4 Discussion and Implications

The empirical implementation discussed in the previous section illustrates how governance-oriented approaches may help regulate cognitive delegation while preserving reflective supervision and epistemic accountability. Beyond the specific course redesign, the proposed framework raises broader implications for the role of instructors, the design of AI-native curricula, and the institutional governance of distributed human–AI cognition.

## 4.1 The Instructor as Cognitive Architect

Within the perspective adopted in this paper, university instructors can be understood not only as content experts or evaluators but also as designers and orchestrators of distributed cognition [6,8]. In AI-mediated educational ecosystems, this role involves regulating delegation thresholds, designing reflective checkpoints, preserving reasoning traceability, and supporting dialogic validation throughout inquiry processes.

From this perspective, we introduce the notion of the *cognitive architect*: an educator responsible for governing hybrid human–AI learning ecosystems. This role includes designing governance-aware learning activities, regulating acceptable forms of cognitive delegation, and supporting learners in critically negotiating AI-mediated cognition. Teaching can therefore be conceived as the construction of environments in which AI amplifies inquiry without replacing learners' responsibility for interpretation, justification, and validation.

This perspective complements faculty development approaches that primarily emphasise operational AI literacy. Governance-oriented competences such as reflective supervision, dialogic orchestration, and regulation of cognitive delegation are proposed as complementary capacities for preserving epistemic agency within AI-rich educational environments [9,15,17].

## 4.2 Governance-Aware Universities and AI-Native Curricula

If universities fail to intentionally regulate cognitive delegation, AI-mediated learning environments risk evolving into forms of *outsourced cognition*, where framing, interpretation, and validation are progressively externalised to algorithmic systems [20,23]. Under these conditions, higher education may preserve the appearance of productivity while weakening reflective inquiry and epistemic accountability.

The proposed framework complements emerging AI governance approaches by focusing not on regulating AI systems themselves, but on governing the human cognitive processes that emerge through interaction with them. From this perspective, governance becomes primarily an educational and epistemic responsibility rather than a purely technological one.

This perspective points towards the development of *AI-native curricula*: educational structures designed for hybrid human–AI cognition rather than for the simple integration of AI tools into traditional instructional models. In such curricula, delegation, validation, traceability, and reflective supervision become explicit design dimensions, helping instructors distinguish when AI-mediated support strengthens exploratory inquiry and when it risks cognitive substitution. At institutional level, this also suggests the need for governance-aware policies that address AI-mediated cognition as part of the broader digital transformation of higher education [12], rather than treating it only as a matter of academic misconduct.

### 4.3 Limitations and Future Work

The study is based on a single course implementation within one institutional context and involved a relatively small cohort. Its findings should therefore be interpreted as exploratory evidence of operational feasibility rather than as generalisable evidence of effectiveness. The absence of a control group further precludes causal claims about the effects of DAID on learning outcomes.

More broadly, governance-oriented approaches present important challenges. Process-oriented assessment may increase workload. Delegation thresholds vary across disciplines, and excessive proceduralisation may weaken reflective autonomy. Future work should evaluate the framework across broader disciplinary contexts, compare different implementation models, and explore partial automation of governance-oriented indicators while preserving human-in-the-loop validation.

## 5 Conclusions

This paper argues that integrating Generative AI into higher education calls for governance-oriented models that regulate AI-mediated cognition while preserving epistemic agency and human accountability. The challenge extends beyond AI adoption and literacy to governing how cognition is distributed, delegated, supervised, and validated within hybrid human–AI learning ecosystems.

Drawing on Cyber Humanities, Cyber Humanism, and distributed cognition, we introduced the overarching conceptual perspective of *Course Design as Cognitive Governance* and *Delegation-Aware Instructional Design* (DAID) as its course-level design framework.

The redesign of an "AI for Digital Humanities" course provided an initial illustration of how governance-oriented structures may support co-reasoning, reflective validation, and dialogic inquiry while limiting superficial delegation and epistemic opacity.

We also reframed the instructor as a *cognitive architect*, responsible for designing hybrid educational environments that sustain critical inquiry, reflective supervision, and human responsibility. From this perspective, universities can be understood as cognitive and civic infrastructures that shape how reasoning, interpretation, and accountability are organised within algorithmically mediated societies.

Although developed through one course redesign, DAID is intended as a transferable design perspective for governing human–AI cognition across diverse higher education contexts, rather than as a prescription of specific AI tools or pedagogical techniques. Its four design dimensions—delegation thresholds, epistemic learning outcomes, dialogic interaction, and governance-oriented assessment—provide a common structure that can be adapted to different disciplines, learning activities, and assessment formats.

Ultimately, higher education depends less on access to increasingly capable intelligent systems than on institutions' capacity to design human–centred cognitive ecosystems that sustain epistemic agency, critical judgement, and responsible participation.

## Ethics Statement and Generative AI Disclosure

**Ethics Statement.** This study retrospectively analysed educational data generated during regular course activities at the University of Genoa; all data were fully anonymised before analysis. After completion of assessment and grading, students provided verbal informed consent for the use of their prompt logs, project artefacts, assessment data, and oral-defence data for research and publication. Consent or refusal had no effect on their evaluation. In view of this retrospective, anonymised-data design, formal ethical review was not sought.

**Generative AI Disclosure.** During the preparation of this work, the authors used OpenAI's ChatGPT to support language revision, paraphrasing, grammar checking, and stylistic refinement. All AI-assisted outputs were critically reviewed, edited, and verified by the authors, who take full responsibility for the content of the publication.

## References

1. Adorni, G., Bellini, E., Torre, I.: Reclaiming agency through cyber humanism: a european agenda for ai, education and culture. In: Digital Humanism: First Interdisciplinary Science and Research Conference, DIGHUM 2025, pp. 407–420. Springer, Vienna (2025). https://doi.org/10.1007/978-3-032-11108-1_31
2. Adorni, G.: Human-centered AI in higher education: toward a shared framework for AI literacy and faculty development in the age of generative AI. In: Proceedings of Ital-IA 2026: 6th National Conference on Artificial Intelligence. CEUR Workshop Proceedings. CEUR-WS.org, Rome (2026). https://ceur-ws.org/
3. Adorni, G., Grosso, D.: From prompts to programmes: natural language programming as a metacognitive scaffold for genai-assisted problem solving. Digit. Libr. Perspect. **42**(1), 1–16 (2026). https://doi.org/10.1108/DLP-01-2026-0026
4. Adorni, G., Scala, D., Torsani, S.: Programming cognition with language: toward a dialogic architecture for ai-mediated learning. In: 2026 22nd International Conference on Information Technology Based Higher Education and Training (ITHET), pp. 1–10 (2026). https://doi.org/10.1109/ITHET69978.2026.11585082

5. Bakhtin, M.: The Dialogic Imagination: Four Essays. Univ. of Texas Press, Austin (1981)
6. Barnett, R.: The limits of competence: knowledge, higher education, and society. In: SRHE and Open University Press imprint, Society for Research into Higher Education & Open University Press (1994). https://books.google.it/books?id=ciBwQgAACAAJ
7. Barnett, R.: Realizing the university in an age of supercomplexity. In: Realizing the University in an Age of Supercomplexity, Society for Research into Higher Education & Open University Press (2000). https://books.google.it/books?id=bBdXAAAAYAAJ
8. Biggs, J., Tang, C.: EBOOK: teaching for quality learning at university. UK Higher Education OUP Humanities & Social Sciences Higher Education OUP, McGraw-Hill Education (2011). https://books.google.it/books?id=VC1FBgAAQBAJ
9. Cosgrove, J., Cachia, R.: Digcomp 3.0: European digital competence framework – fifth edition. Technical report, Publications Office of the European Union, Luxembourg (2025). https://data.europa.eu/doi/10.2760/0001149
10. Firat, M.: What chatgpt means for universities: perceptions of scholars and students. J. Appl. Learn. Teach. **6**(1), 1–22 (2023). https://doi.org/10.37074/jalt.2023.6.1.22
11. Floridi, L.: The Ethics of Artificial Intelligence: Principles, Challenges, and Opportunities. Oxford Academic (2023). https://doi.org/10.1093/oso/9780198883098.001.0001
12. Gutović, V., et al.: Higher Education Global Trends Report: Towards Inclusive, Equitable and Quality Higher Education in an Internationally Mobile Landscape. UNESCO, Paris (2026). https://doi.org/10.54674/IN.2026.94
13. Hutchins, E.: Cognition in the Wild. MIT Press, Cambridge (1995)
14. Kasneci, E., Sessler, K., Küchemann, S., et al.: Chatgpt for good? On opportunities and challenges of large language models for education. Learn. Individ. Differ. **103**, 102274 (2023). https://doi.org/10.1016/j.lindif.2023.102274
15. Miao, F., Cukurova, M.: Ai competency framework for teachers. Technical report, United Nations Educational, Scientific and Cultural Organization, Paris, France (2024). https://unesdoc.unesco.org/ark:/48223/pf0000391104
16. Mollick, E., Mollick, L.: Using AI to implement effective teaching strategies in classrooms: Five strategies, including prompts. SSRN Working Paper 4391243, The Wharton School (2023). https://doi.org/10.2139/ssrn.4391243
17. OECD: OECD Digital Education Outlook 2026: Exploring Effective Uses of Generative AI in Education. OECD Publishing, Paris, France (2026). https://doi.org/10.1787/062a7394-en
18. Panadero, E.: A review of self-regulated learning: six models and four directions for research. Front. Psychol. **8**, 422 (2017). https://doi.org/10.3389/fpsyg.2017.00422
19. Redecker, C.: European framework for the digital competence of educators: Digcompedu. Technical report, Publications Office of the European Union (2017). https://publications.jrc.ec.europa.eu/repository/handle/JRC107466
20. Risko, E., Gilbert, S.: Cognitive offloading. Trends Cogn. Sci.**20**(9), 676–688 (2016). https://doi.org/10.1016/j.tics.2016.07.002. pMID:27542527
21. Russell, S.J., Norvig, P.: Artificial Intelligence: A Modern Approach, 4th edn. Global Edition. Pearson, London (2021)
22. Schraw, G., Dennison, R.: Assessing metacognitive awareness. Contemp. Educ. Psychol. **19**(4), 460–475 (1994). https://doi.org/10.1006/ceps.1994.1033

23. Selwyn, N.: On the limits of artificial intelligence (ai) in education. Nordisk tidsskrift for pedagogikk og kritikk: Special Issue Artif. Intell. Educ. **10**, 3–14 (2024). https://doi.org/10.23865/ntpk.v10.6062
24. Werthner, H., Prem, E., Lee, E.A., Ghezzi, C. (eds.): Perspectives on Digital Humanism. Springer, Cham (2022). https://doi.org/10.1007/978-3-030-86144-5
25. Zimmerman, B.: Becoming a self-regulated learner: an overview. Theory Pract. **41**(2), 64–70 (2002). https://doi.org/10.1207/s15430421tip4102_2

# The Impact of Domain-Specific Knowledge in Legal AI: A Case Study on Italian Criminal Law

Renzo Alva Principe[1(✉)], Matteo Palmonari[1], Alberto Aimi[2,3], and Davide Romano[3]

[1] University of Milano-Bicocca, Milan, Italy
{renzo.alvaprincipe,matteo.palmonari}@unimib.it
[2] Università degli Studi eCampus, Novedrate, Italy
[3] Winfried, Milan, Italy
{alberto.aimi,davide.romano}@winfried.it

**Abstract.** In the domain of criminal law, establishing liability fundamentally depends on mapping a natural-language description of the facts onto the exact statutory charge (*rubrica imputativa*) and its mitigating or aggravating modifiers. Large Language Models (LLMs), with their broad semantic understanding, are a natural tool for this task, yet in such a specialized domain purely semantic matching or LLM-based classification struggles to tell apart cases that read alike but are legally distinct. We argue, and provide evidence, that well-structured domain knowledge can guide retrieval in ways that semantic similarity alone cannot. We study this in the retrieval of a statutory charge from a natural-language description, a core step in a vertical, professionally curated system for Italian criminal law with direct industrial application. We present a knowledge-aware retrieval pipeline built on a structured resource that distinguishes base offenses from complex and circumstantiated ones and uses an explicit mapping from each offense to its admissible circumstances, together with a query-reduction step that decomposes a query into its base-offense core and its circumstantial modifiers, routing each to the appropriate index. Results indicate that injecting this domain structure improves retrieval over strong purely semantic baselines.

**Keywords:** Legal information retrieval · Domain-specific knowledge · Query decomposition · Dense and sparse retrieval · Large Language Models · Italian criminal law

## 1 Introduction

In the domain of criminal law, legal qualification requires mapping a natural-language description onto the precise statutory charge (*rubrica imputativa*). This task is inherently compositional: a charge may consist of a single statutory provision or involve varied combinations of offenses and circumstances. Because


S. Bistarelli et al. (Eds.): AIxIA 2026, LNAI 17131, pp. 16–29, 2027.
https://doi.org/10.1007/978-3-032-40774-0_2

a purely text-based system lacks an understanding of which configurations are legally valid, providing computational support for this process remains a foundational challenge. This limitation is particularly evident in professionally curated, knowledge-based legal-tech architectures. The platform under study provides expert-validated metadata for a charge, but only after the user manually inputs the exact statutory provisions—thereby presupposing the very knowledge the practitioner seeks to discover. We cast this missing entry point as an information retrieval problem: given a natural-language query identifying a charge, the objective is to retrieve the precise provisions that constitute the applicable *rubrica imputativa*. The hardest cases are precisely these structured ones, where formal combinatorial knowledge is decisive.

Legal retrieval has progressed from lexical matching to dense retrieval over statutory text [1], and more recently to approaches that exploit the structure of legislation: its hierarchical organization [2] and the web of references among provisions [3,4], up to knowledge graphs of an entire code [5]. These methods model the *topology* of the law, how provisions nest within its divisions and cite one another, but not the *compositional* logic of a charge: which circumstances may legally attach to a given offense, and thus which combinations of provisions form a valid configuration. This knowledge is left uncaptured, and evaluation does not credit the joint recovery of a composite charge.

We argue, and provide evidence, that making this knowledge explicit fills the gap. We present **KMSR** (Knowledge-Guided Multi-Stage Retrieval), a pipeline built around the law's compositional structure that retrieves over a knowledge base encoding the law's offense-to-circumstance compatibility and applies a *query-reduction* step that routes each query to the appropriate index, so that retrieval ranges over admissible charges rather than raw text. The pipeline mirrors the sequence of qualification, first the offense, then its admissible circumstances, then the assembled charge, so that retrieval ranges over valid configurations rather than raw text. Evaluated on 350 queries from real users of the platform, annotated by legal experts, KMSR improves substantially over strong retrieval baselines, including lexical, semantic, and hybrid methods, with the clearest gains on the hardest cases, where the answer is a joint configuration of provisions and a partial match yields a wrong charge rather than a partially correct one.

We make the following contributions: **(i)** *KMSR*[1], a knowledge-guided multi-stage retrieval pipeline built around the law's compositional structure; **(ii)** a formulation of statutory charge retrieval as a compositional task, distinguishing flat from block-structured relevance, together with block-aware evaluation metrics; **(iii)** an evaluation on real, expert-annotated queries showing that explicit domain structure outperforms strong semantic baselines, localizing the gain on the compositional cases.

[1] https://github.com/Winfriedsrl/KMSR hosts code, prompts and the query set. The knowledge base is proprietary; any further release will be announced there.

## 2 Legal Background and Problem Formulation

We introduce the legal concepts underlying our task, describe the legal-tech system that grounds our approach, and formalize the retrieval problem.

### 2.1 Legal Qualification Process and the Structure of the Tatbestand

In criminal law, as in every legal domain, answering even a simple question begins with an act of *qualification*: recognizing, within a concrete factual situation, the factual requirements of the relevant legal norm (*fattispecie astratta* or, in German legal terminology, *Tatbestand*)—that is, the abstract set of facts whose occurrence triggers a specific legal consequence [6]. This step dictates all subsequent determinations, from the applicable penalty to the admissibility of wiretapping or the imposition of pre-trial detention, among other substantial and procedural determinations.

As is well known, this process is far from mechanical; rather, it represents the outcome of a complex cognitive process that cannot be reduced to the application of formal deductive logic [7]. Within the framework of this interpretive activity, the jurist is led to explore various *fattispecie astratte* weighing their consequences and prerequisites, and comparing them with the concrete facts under examination to arrive at the most pertinent conclusion [8].

A crucial phase in this mental process consists of retrieving information regarding the specific *fattispecie astratta* under analysis. More precisely, in the domain of criminal law, offenses and statutory circumstances constitute the primary examples of *Tatbestände* about which the practitioner seeks to obtain information. Offenses define the behaviors prohibited or mandated by the legal system and, on a technical level, can be described by a single provision (e.g., Art. 575 c.p.: "Whoever causes the death of a human being is punished...") or by multiple provisions interacting together (e.g., Arts. 56(1) and 575 c.p. regarding attempt). Statutory circumstances further qualify an offense, modifying its legal treatment (e.g., Art. 576(1) c.p.).

Offenses and statutory circumstances are contained in the Criminal Code and in other legislative acts distributed throughout the broader statutory framework. These legislative acts are organized into articles subdivided into paragraphs, which may further contain minimal syntactic units such as numbers, letters, or individual sentences.

When a charge is brought against an individual, it must contain, among other elements, "the clear and precise enunciation of the fact and the aggravating circumstances [...], with the indication of the relevant articles of the law" (Art. 417, paragraph 1, letter b, of the Code of Criminal Procedure)—that is, the articulation, through specific statutory provisions, of the *Tatbestand* the accused is alleged to have fulfilled. The indication of these violated provisions is commonly referred to as the *rubrica imputativa*.

However, the *rubrica imputativa* can also be expressed—and commonly is by practitioners—in natural language (e.g., *omicidio volontario*: Art. 575 c.p.;

*rapina impropria*: Art. 628(2) c.p.). Natural language can likewise express complex configurations derived from the combination of offenses and statutory circumstances (e.g., *lesioni personali tentate aggravate dalla recidiva semplice*: Arts. 56(1), 582(1) and 99(1) c.p.). These expressions act as a definitive bridge between the practitioner and the relevant provision, serving as an intermediate conceptual step in identifying the *fattispecie astratta* that governs a given case.

## 2.2 Bridging Natural Language and Knowledge Bases

Winfried[2] is an industry-grade, legal platform actively deployed in Italy, serving a professional user base that includes defense counsel, judges, and prosecutors. In its current deployment, the system provides deterministic access to curated legal data powered by a proprietary knowledge base; however, it strictly requires users to provide explicit structural references—such as specific articles, paragraphs, or the aforementioned minimal syntactic units—as their query input. Each unit is explicitly typed as either a base offense or a statutory circumstance, and the precise hierarchical and functional relationships between them are mapped. By formalizing these structural interdependencies, the platform enables the direct mapping of valid interactions between base offenses and their mitigating or aggravating modifiers (Fig. 1).

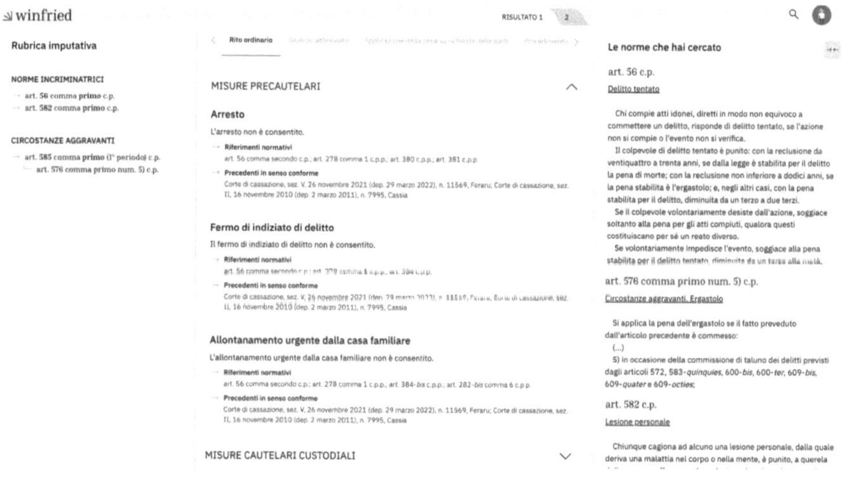


**Fig. 1.** Winfried's output for the *rubrica imputativa* "Artt. 56, 582, 585, 576 no. 5 c.p."

Historically, this design framed the task as information retrieval over *rubrica imputativa*: the user, possessing prior knowledge of the relevant norms, queries the system to ascertain their legal consequences. In the era of large language

---

[2] https://winfried.it/.

models, however, a natural-language interface has transitioned from a mere convenience to a primary necessity—representing precisely the capability that the system previously lacked. Indeed, the system does not yet allow users to input the *rubrica imputativa* in natural language, even though such expressions constitute the standard point of entry for legal practitioners in their daily work.

Two considerations place the knowledge base at the center of this unaddressed gap. First, the natural-language entry point can be provided only if a natural-language description is mapped onto the structured data it already encodes. Second, it grants deterministic access to legal information: where a purely generative system is probabilistic and susceptible to hallucinations, a curated knowledge base can constrain and ground it, pruning the space of possible answers to those the law actually admits. This is the core insight behind the present work: exploiting Winfried's structured knowledge to restrict the set of candidate answers returned to a user querying in natural language.

### 2.3 Problem Formulation

Let $\mathcal{P}$ be the set of provisions of the Italian Criminal Code, where each $p \in \mathcal{P}$ is an atomic statutory unit (an article, paragraph, or sub-unit). These provisions are categorized into *offenses* and *statutory circumstances*, each of which may consist of one or more units. A *rubrica imputativa* is defined as a formal composition of one base offense with zero or more circumstances, restricted exclusively to legally admissible combinations.

**Definition 1 (Statutory Charge Retrieval).** *Given a natural-language query $q$ identifying a* rubrica imputativa, *retrieve the complete list $\hat{\mathcal{R}}_q = (p_1, \ldots, p_k)$, where $\hat{\mathcal{R}}_q \subseteq \mathcal{P}$, of provisions that constitute it.*

Queries fall into two regimes. *Flat queries* identify a legal category with *independent* answers: *omicidio* maps to intentional, consensual, preterintentional, and negligent homicide (Arts. 575, 579, 584, 589 c.p.), each a valid but partial answer. *Block-structured queries* specify a charge that exists only as a *joint* configuration of provisions: *truffa aggravata dalla minorata difesa* requires *both* Art. 640(1) c.p. (fraud) *and* Art. 640(2)(2-ter) c.p. (aggravating circumstance), and a partial match is not partially correct but wrong. This distinction shapes both method (Sect. 4) and evaluation (Sect. 5.3).

## 3 Related Work

*Legal Information Retrieval and Statutory Article Retrieval.* Legal information retrieval is a broad and active field [14]. Within it, statutory article retrieval (SAR) targets the provisions relevant to a natural-language legal question: BSARD established a citizen-facing benchmark over Belgian law and showed that fine-tuned dense retrievers outperform lexical ones [1], and JuriFindIT recently extended SAR to Italian, additionally encoding explicit cross-article references

[4]. These works define the retrieval setting we build on, but take the individual provision as the unit and treat relevance as set-based, without modelling the compositional offense–circumstance structure that constitutes a charge.

*Structure-Aware Retrieval Over Legal and Normative Text.* A growing line injects the structure of the law into retrieval. G-DSR augments a dense retriever with a graph neural network over the hierarchical division structure of legislation [2]. LegisSearch builds on a property-graph knowledge base of Italian legislation, encoding cross-references and amendments, and couples it with universal embeddings and LLM query expansion [3], while Cerini et al. model the Italian Criminal Code itself as a hierarchy-and-reference graph as a basis for AI-assisted inference, though as a design proposal without retrieval evaluation [5]. The same intuition extends beyond legislation to technical standards: a Graph-RAG approach represents documents as units linked by parthood and citation edges and improves retrieval through neighbourhood smoothing and a graph re-ranker [10], and hybrid norm retrieval fuses knowledge-graph and textual signals [11]. All of these exploit the law's topology, how provisions nest and cross-reference one another, yet none encodes which circumstances an offense may legally carry, i.e. the compositional admissibility that defines a charge.

*Domain Specialization by Training.* An orthogonal way to bring domain knowledge to a model is to train it: continued pre-training and instruction tuning on legal corpora yield vertical legal LLMs, such as LegalMidm for Korean law [12] and the continued-pre-training adaptation of an open LLM to Italian law [13]. This bakes knowledge into parameters, where it is implicit and hard to inspect; we instead keep domain knowledge explicit in a knowledge base that retrieval ranges over. Across all these lines two gaps remain and motivate our work: retrieval is not guided by the offense–circumstance compatibility intrinsic to legal qualification, and evaluation does not credit the *joint* recovery of a composite charge. We address both, with a structure-guided pipeline and block-aware metrics.

## 4 Knowledge-Guided Multi-stage Retrieval

Treating the law as flat text forces a single retriever to recover, in one shot, passages that only jointly form a valid charge. KMSR (Knowledge-Guided Multi-Stage Retrieval) instead mirrors how a jurist proceeds: identify the offense, then the circumstances that may legally attach to it, and finally assemble the charge, injecting the domain knowledge of which circumstances are admissible for which offense directly into retrieval rather than leaving it to the model. Figure 2 shows the pipeline, read left to right: a reductor feeds two retrieval stages bridged by a mapper, whose candidates are pooled and then filtered and ordered by two LLM modules. Throughout, we trace the query *truffa aggravata dalla minorata difesa* (fraud aggravated by the victim's vulnerability), whose correct answer is fraud (Art. 640(1) c.p.) *together with* its special aggravating circumstance (Art. 640(2)(2-ter) c.p.).

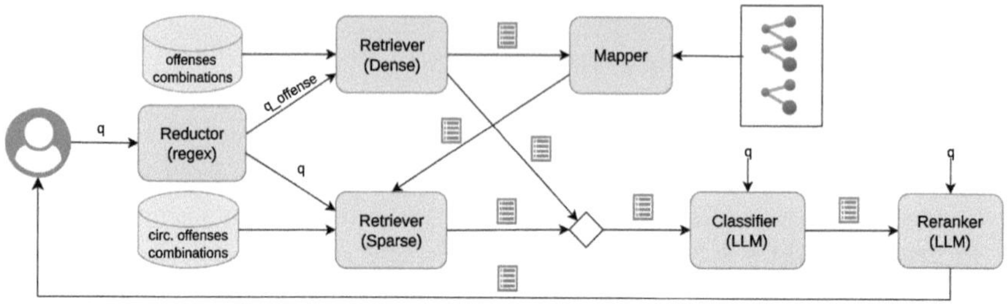


**Fig. 2.** Knowledge-Guided Multi-Stage Retrieval (KMSR).

*Knowledge-Structured Representation.* KMSR retrieves over two corpora of *structured units*, offense combinations and circumstantiated-offense combinations, each unit a candidate charge, paired with a *compatibility mapping* that records, for every offense, the circumstantiated combinations the code admits for it (the mapping feeding the mapper in Fig. 2). For our example the offense corpus contains fraud, the circumstantiated corpus charges such as fraud+vulnerability and fraud+against-the-State, and the mapping links fraud to exactly those admissible variants. Making this compositional structure explicit lets search range over admissible charges, so that domain knowledge, not surface similarity, governs which circumstances are eligible. This representation is the substrate on which every downstream module operates.

*Reductor.* The query reductor (left of Fig. 2) decomposes the user query $q$ into an offense-focused sub-query $q_{offense}$ and the full query $q$, routing $q_{\text{offense}}$ to the offense stage and $q$ to the circumstance stage and the two LLM modules. For our example $q_{\text{offense}} = \textit{truffa}$ while $q = \textit{truffa aggravata dalla minorata difesa}$. Feeding the offense stage only $q_{\text{offense}}$ keeps the circumstantial terms from diluting the base-offense match, while the circumstance stage still sees the full request.

*Offense Retriever.* The offense retriever, a *dense* retriever (top branch), searches the offense-combinations corpus with $q_{\text{offense}}$ and returns the top-$m$ candidate base offenses, establishing *what* crime is at issue before any circumstance is considered; for our query it surfaces fraud alongside neighbouring patrimonial offenses. We use a semantic matcher because offenses are phrased paraphrastically, through lay synonyms or descriptions of the conduct rather than statutory wording, so lexical overlap is unreliable here.

*Mapper.* The mapper replaces each of the $m$ candidate offenses with the circumstantiated combinations the code admits for it (for fraud: fraud+vulnerability, fraud+against-the-State, ..., never an illegal pairing), which becomes the search space of the next stage. This is the crux of KMSR: encoding the code's composition rules as an explicit lookup prunes a space otherwise dominated by legally impossible charges, turning an intractable search into a focused one and ensuring the model never entertains a charge the law does not allow.

*Circumstance Retriever.* The circumstance retriever, a *sparse* retriever (bottom branch), then searches *within* the admissible set using the full query $q$, returning the $n$ best circumstantiated combinations per candidate offense, a candidate set of order $m(1+n)$; for our query it ranks fraud+vulnerability first, matched on the phrase *minorata difesa*. We use a lexical matcher because circumstances hinge on precise, discriminative terms (*minorata difesa*, *armi*, *infraquinquennale*) whose exact presence is decisive.

*Candidate Pool.* The pool (the diamond in Fig. 2) merges the offense-level and circumstance-refined candidates, for our query both bare fraud and fraud+ vulnerability. Since some queries are answered at the offense level and others demand a specific circumstantiated charge, pooling keeps both granularities available rather than committing prematurely.

*LLM Classifier.* The classifier, reading $q$ with the pool, selects the $j$ charges that best answer it; for our query it keeps fraud+vulnerability and discards bare fraud and any wrong-circumstance variant. Judging whether a composite offense–circumstance configuration matches the request is a semantic decision that similarity scores cannot make alone, so the LLM removes the plausible-but-wrong candidates retrieval inevitably surfaces.

*LLM Reranker.* Finally, the selected charges from the LLM classifier are expanded into their constituent passages and passed to the LLM reranker which, again reading $q$, orders them into the final *top-k* passages; for our example it places Art. 640(1) and Art. 640 (2)(2-ter) c.p., the two passages of the charge, at the top. The deliverable is ranked passages, not charges: a charge spans several passages whose order matters, and completing each block as early as possible is exactly what the task rewards.

## 5 Experimental Setup

### 5.1 Dataset

*Ground Truth.* We evaluate on 350 real queries issued by paying users of the system and annotated by legal experts over the Italian Criminal Code, split by category into 120 flat, 227 block-structured and 3 mixed.

*Corpora.* The systems retrieve over four corpora in two families, raw legal text and knowledge-structured units. *All passages* (10,784) is the entire Criminal Code segmented into individual provision passages, the law as written with no task-specific structure; *restricted passages* (2,040) is the same passage-level text limited to the provisions defining the offenses and circumstances relevant to the task. *Offense combinations* (23,991) are units each a base offense, possibly a minimal composition such as an attempted offense, together forming the catalogue of chargeable offenses; *circumstantiated-offense combinations* (1,299,924) are units each a complete charge, a base offense paired with a legally valid set of circumstances, enumerating every valid configuration.

### 5.2 Baselines

A baseline follows the standard *retrieve-then-rerank* pipeline over the law as flat text: it retrieves the most relevant passages from a corpus and reranks them with an LLM. We vary two ingredients. The retrieval method is either *sparse* (BM25 keyword matching), *dense* (embedding similarity) or *hybrid* (Reciprocal Rank Fusion of the two). The corpus (Sect. 5.1) is either *all passages* or the *restricted* offense/circumstance subset. Crossing the three methods with the two corpora yields six baselines, all sharing KMSR's LLM reranker. They span the canonical retrieval paradigms and the two cheapest ways of injecting task knowledge, searching the whole code versus only the relevant provisions.

### 5.3 Metrics

We evaluate retrieval at the *passage* level. For a query $q$, let $\mathcal{R}_q$ be its set of relevant (ground-truth) passages and $\hat{\mathcal{R}}_q = (p_1, \ldots, p_k)$ the ranked list returned by the system. The three query categories demand different notions of relevance, so we tailor a metric to each: *flat queries* ask for a set of independent passages, *block-structured queries* for complete *blocks* (an offense/circumstance combination is relevant only if *all* its passages are retrieved together), and *mixed queries* combine both.

*Flat Queries.* Relevance is set-based, so we use standard passage-level recall and a binary NDCG [15] that rewards placing relevant passages near the top of the ranking.

*Block-Structured Queries.* The ground truth is a set of blocks $\mathcal{B}_q = \{b_1, \ldots, b_m\}$, each block $b$ a set of passages that must be recovered *jointly*; a partially retrieved block carries no credit. *Block recall* is the fraction of fully retrieved blocks, and *block AP* additionally rewards completing them early. For a fully retrieved block let its *completion rank* be $c(b) = \max_{p \in b} \operatorname{rank}(p)$, the position of its last retrieved passage, and let $c_{(1)} \leq c_{(2)} \leq \cdots$ be the completion ranks of the completed blocks in increasing order:

$$\text{BlockRecall} = \frac{|\{ b \in \mathcal{B}_q : b \subseteq \hat{\mathcal{R}}_q \}|}{m}, \qquad \text{BlockAP} = \frac{1}{Z} \sum_i \frac{i}{c_{(i)}}, \tag{1}$$

where $Z$ is the same sum for the ideal arrangement, in which every block is completed as early as possible and smaller blocks come first, so that BlockAP $\in [0, 1]$, equal to 1 for a perfect ranking.

*Aggregate Scores.* For a single number per system we average each query's score under the metric suited to its category. *Weighted Recall* uses flat recall for flat queries and block recall for block-structured ones (their average for mixed queries), and *Weighted Ranking* is defined analogously from NDCG and block AP; being averages over the whole set, both reflect the actual distribution of query types. All scores carry 95% confidence intervals from bootstrap resampling (1000 resamples).

### 5.4 Technical Details

KMSR retrieves $m$=30 candidate offenses with dense search and, for each, the $n$=10 best circumstantiated combinations with sparse search; the classifier selects $j$=20 charges, which are expanded into passages and reranked to the final $k$=10. The Reductor module is implemented using regular-expressions. The baselines instead retrieve the top 30 passages and rerank them to 10; their hybrid variant fuses the sparse and dense rankings with Reciprocal Rank Fusion ($k_{\mathrm{RRF}}$=60, fusion window 100). All systems share the same LLM (`gpt-5-mini`) for the reranker and classifier and, wherever dense retrieval is used, the same `text-embedding-3-large` embeddings.

## 6 Results

**Table 1.** Aggregate retrieval performance weighted over query types, with 95% bootstrap confidence intervals. Best in bold.

| Model | Passages Corpus | Weighted Recall | Weighted Ranking |
|---|---|---|---|
| Sparse Baseline | all | 0.421 [.371,.473] | 0.374 [.327,.421] |
| Dense Baseline | all | 0.437 [.386,.483] | 0.381 [.336,.424] |
| Hybrid Baseline | all | 0.478 [.424,.526] | 0.410 [.360,.453] |
| Sparse Baseline | restricted | 0.497 [.447,.549] | 0.436 [.389,.485] |
| Dense Baseline | restricted | 0.440 [.389,.487] | 0.398 [.352,.443] |
| Hybrid Baseline | restricted | 0.492 [.441,.541] | 0.432 [.385,.478] |
| KMSR: 2-stage map. | off./circ.off. comb. | 0.576 [.527,.625] | 0.474 [.429,.520] |
| + query reduction | off./circ.off. comb. | 0.615 [.564,.669] | 0.481 [.438,.523] |
| + LLM reranking | off./circ.off. comb. | **0.706** [.657,.753] | **0.625** [.582,.669] |

Table 1 and Fig. 3 report the results. The six baselines fall in a narrow band (Weighted Recall 0.42–0.50) with overlapping confidence intervals; the strongest is Sparse on the restricted corpus (0.497 Recall, 0.436 Ranking). KMSR reaches 0.706 Recall and 0.625 Ranking, a +0.21 (+42%) and +0.19 (+43%) gain over that baseline, with 95% intervals disjoint from every baseline. The build-up is monotone: structured two-stage retrieval with the mapping already reaches 0.576, query reduction 0.615, and the LLM reranker the final 0.706.

By query category (Fig. 3), we find no evidence of a difference on flat queries (flat recall $\approx$ 0.95, NDCG $\approx$ 0.90 for all three), whereas on block-structured queries KMSR (0.58 block recall, 0.47 block AP) more than doubles the baselines, with disjoint intervals.

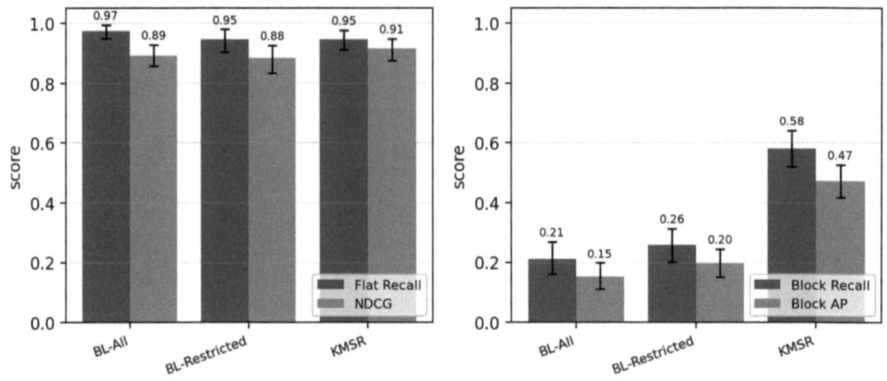


**Fig. 3.** Performance by query category (95% bootstrap CI). Left: flat queries (120), flat recall and NDCG. Right: block-structured queries (227), block recall and block AP. BL-All = Baseline All Passages; BL-Restricted = Baseline Restricted Passages.

## 7 Analysis and Discussion

*Retrieval Alone is Not the Lever.* The baselines' overlapping intervals (Table 1) do not support a ranking of the retrievers or the corpora; the single robust effect is the asymmetric impact of restricting the corpus. Restriction acts as a lexical-noise filter: in the heterogeneous all-passages corpus, term matching surfaces many on-vocabulary but off-topic passages, depressing the lexical signal, so once the corpus is confined to the relevant provisions exact term overlap becomes discriminative. This is why the sparse retriever jumps (+0.08, the only near-disjoint shift in the table) while the dense retriever, already robust to corpus size, filters implicitly and is essentially unaffected (0.437→0.440); the apparent reordering of the retrievers between corpora is evidence about the corpus, not about the retrievers.

*KMSR Separates, and Only Where Structure Matters.* KMSR is the only system whose intervals are disjoint from every baseline on both metrics, so its improvement cannot be attributed to sampling variability. A single-index retriever saturates around 0.50 Weighted Recall however it is configured, because it resolves the query against one flat view of the corpus; KMSR instead recovers the task's latent structure, querying the offense and circumstance indices with the split sub-queries, linking them through the domain mapping, and resolving the pool with the LLM modules. The per-category view (Fig. 3) shows the gain is entirely conditional on that structure: on flat queries, where a single provision answers the query, all systems are saturated and KMSR's added machinery neither helps nor hurts, and the whole improvement falls on block-structured queries. The Weighted build-up in Table 1 traces it to the components in turn: the domain mapping supplies the first, structural jump (without it the two-stage pool stays at 0.488, on par with the baselines), query reduction adds a targeted gain by isolating the circumstantial part of the query, and the LLM reranker contributes the largest ranking increment by ordering and completing blocks near the top (on block-structured queries alone the build-up runs $0.26 \rightarrow 0.38 \rightarrow 0.45 \rightarrow 0.58$, which is not shown for space reasons). Each component thus acts where the task is compositional and nowhere else.

*The Boundary of Explicit Knowledge.* KMSR's gains come from making domain knowledge explicit, and its ceiling is set by the same choice. Some distinctions cannot be recovered from surface text at all: in criminal dogmatics the boundary between a base offense and a statutory circumstance is not strictly fixed, since a configuration once treated as a qualified offense may be interpreted, or legislatively reclassified, as an autonomous offense, a separation widely held to lack any substantive ontological foundation [9]. Queries on this shifting boundary are intrinsically ambiguous, and no system, ours included, can resolve them from the query text alone; only an up-to-date formal encoding of the statutory framework can. This delimits the contribution rather than undercutting it: structured domain knowledge complements retrieval and large language models precisely where the task is compositional.

## 8 Conclusion and Future Work

We studied whether explicit domain knowledge still adds value alongside retrieval pipelines with large language models, on the retrieval of criminal-law charges from natural-language queries. KMSR makes the law's compositional structure explicit, through a knowledge base separating base from circumstantiated offenses, an offense-to-circumstance mapping, and a structure-guided query reduction, and improves substantially over strong retrieval baselines. The gain is concentrated on the compositional cases, with parity on the simpler ones, stems from the knowledge-guided composition as a whole, and is bounded by what the knowledge encodes rather than by retrieval. Structured domain knowledge thus complements, rather than competes with, large models where the task is knowledge-dependent.

Three future directions follow: (i) extend the system's input from natural language descriptions of a *rubrica imputativa* to natural-language description of the facts of the case (*fattispecie concreta*); (ii) ensure that the offense-to-circumstance mapping remains complete and systematically updated, since the knowledge base acts as the performance ceiling; (iii) add an uncertainty mechanism allowing the system to abstain when retrieval confidence falls below a set threshold.

**Acknowledgments.** The work has received funding from the European Union's Horizon Europe research and innovation programme under grant agreement No. 101189771 (DataPACT), and from the AI-PACT project (B47H22004460001), funded by the Italian Ministry of Enterprises and Made in Italy under the European Union Next Generation EU programme and the Italian PNRR.

**Disclosure of Interests.** The authors have no competing interests to declare that are relevant to the content of this article

## References


1. Louis, A., Spanakis, G.: A statutory article retrieval dataset in French. In: Proceedings of the 60th Annual Meeting of the Association for Computational Linguistics, vol. 1: Long Papers, pp. 6789–6803. Association for Computational Linguistics, Dublin (2022). https://doi.org/10.18653/v1/2022.acl-long.468
2. Louis, A., van Dijck, G., Spanakis, G.: Finding the law: enhancing statutory article retrieval via graph neural networks. In: Proceedings of the 17th Conference of the European Chapter of the Association for Computational Linguistics, pp. 2761–2776. Association for Computational Linguistics, Dubrovnik (2023). https://doi.org/10.18653/v1/2023.eacl-main.203
3. Colombo, A., Bernasconi, A., Bellomarini, L., Guiso, L., Michelacci, C., Ceri, S.: LegisSearch: navigating legislation with graphs and large language models. Artif. Intell. Law (2025). https://doi.org/10.1007/s10506-025-09482-6
4. Dalla Noce, N., Colla, D., Farhang Doust, S., De Mattei, L., Bacciu, D.: JuriFindIT: an Italian legal retrieval dataset. In: Findings of the Association for Computational Linguistics: EACL 2026, pp. 4223–4241. Association for Computational Linguistics (2026)
5. Cerini, S.Y., et al.: Graph-based modelling of the Italian Criminal Code as a knowledge base for AI-assisted inference. In: Joint National Conference on Cybersecurity (ITASEC & SERICS 2026). CEUR Workshop Proceedings, Cagliari (2026)
6. That many—if not all—normative propositions can be described as a deontic conditional has been recognized at least since Kelsen, Hans: Reine Rechtslehre. Studienausgabe der 1. Auflage 1934. Tübingen, p. 34 (2008)
7. That the application of law is nothing more than a logical subsumption under major premises [...] can no longer be seriously maintained by anyone. Larenz, Karl. Methodenlehre der Rechtswissenschaft, p. 154. Berlin/Heidelberg/New York (1975)
8. The most compelling account of the hermeneutic process: at least within the domain of criminal law, remains that of Hassemer, Winfried: Tatbestand und Typus. Untersuchungen zur strafrechtlichen Hermeneutik, Köln/Berlin/Bonn/München (1968)
9. Among many others, see: Romano, Mario: Commentario sistematico del codice penale, Milano, vol. I, p. 635 (2004)
10. Masoud, A., Arazzi, A., Germani, M., Nocera, S., A.: Exploring structural complexity in normative RAG with graph-based approaches: a case study on the ETSI standards (2026). arXiv:2604.09868
11. Wehnert, S., Padmanabhan, V., De Luca, E.W.: Hybrid legal norm retrieval: leveraging knowledge graphs and textual representations. In: Legal Knowledge and Information Systems (JURIX 2024). Frontiers in Artificial Intelligence and Applications. IOS Press (2024). https://doi.org/10.3233/FAIA241245
12. Jang, Y., et al.: LegalMidm: use-case-driven legal domain specialization for Korean large language model. In: 3rd Workshop on Data-centric Machine Learning Research (DATA-FM), ICLR 2026 (2026). arXiv:2604.25297
13. Valerio, F., Basile, P., de Gemmis, M.: Adapting a large language model to the legal domain: a case study in Italian. In: Proceedings of the Eighth Workshop on Natural Language for Artificial Intelligence (NL4AI 2024). CEUR Workshop Proceedings, vol. 3877. CEUR-WS.org (2024)
14. Sansone, C., Sperlí, G.: Legal information retrieval systems: state-of-the-art and open issues. Inf. Syst. **106**, 101967 (2022). https://doi.org/10.1016/j.is.2021.101967

15. Järvelin, K., Kekäläinen, J.: Cumulated gain-based evaluation of IR techniques. ACM Trans. Inf. Syst. **20**(4), 422–446 (2002). https://doi.org/10.1145/582415.582418

# Minimum-Cost Hyperedge Interventions for Consensus Reaching via Answer Set Programming

Vincenzo Auletta, Francesco Cauteruccio(✉), Diodato Ferraioli, and Grazia Ferrara

DIEM, University of Salerno, 84084 Fisciano, Italy
{auletta,fcauteruccio,dferraioli,grferrara}@unisa.it

**Abstract.** Consensus reaching in social network group decision making is usually studied over graph-based social structures, where edges represent pairwise trust, influence, or communication relations. However, many deliberation processes involve higher-order interactions, such as committees, discussion threads, panels, or temporary coalitions. We propose a hypergraph-based model for consensus intervention in which a moderator may activate candidate hyperedges representing group deliberation contexts. Each active hyperedge provides a plausible local compromise value, constrained by the initial opinion range of its members, and used to justify opinion revisions. We formalize the minimum-cost hyperedge intervention problem and give an Answer Set Programming encoding that jointly selects hyperedges, local compromise values, revised opinions, and revision justifications under structural and opinion-change costs. Preliminary experiments compare pairwise-only and higher-order interventions under a bridge-use moderation policy and different activation-cost regimes. Results show that the usefulness of hyperedges depends on group-deliberation costs: higher-order interventions reduce structural cost under sublinear and linear costs in our instances, whereas pairwise-only interventions are preferable under pairwise-sum coordination costs; nevertheless, hypergraph interventions consistently reduce revision cost.

**Keywords:** Answer Set Programming · Consensus Reaching · Social Network Group Decision Making · Hypergraphs · Opinion Management

## 1 Introduction

Group decision making studies (GDM) how a set of decision makers can express, aggregate, and revise their preferences in order to select one or more alternatives [1,13]. A central component of many group decision making models is the consensus reaching process (CRP), in which decision makers are supported in modifying their opinions so that the group reaches an acceptable level of agreement before a final selection is made. In social network group decision making


S. Bistarelli et al. (Eds.): AIxIA 2026, LNAI 17131, pp. 30–42, 2027.
https://doi.org/10.1007/978-3-032-40774-0_3

(SNGDM), the consensus process is influenced by social relations among decision makers, such as trust, influence, or communication links [11]. Existing approaches commonly represent these relations as graphs, whose nodes are decision makers and whose edges encode pairwise relations. This graph-based view is natural and has enabled a rich body of work on trust-based consensus models, opinion evolution, and opinion management [11]. Nevertheless, many real deliberation processes are not purely pairwise. A committee discussion, a project meeting, a group chat, a panel of domain experts, or a discussion thread can involve several decision makers at once. Such interactions may have effects that cannot be reduced to independent pairwise edges. For example, a decision maker may be willing to revise an opinion after discussing with a group of heterogeneous experts, even if no single expert would be sufficiently influential alone. Similarly, consensus may be facilitated by creating mixed deliberation groups that bridge otherwise polarized communities.

Hypergraphs provide a natural formalism for representing group deliberation contexts involving more than two decision makers [3,4]. In our model, a hyperedge does not encode a specific trust, influence, or communication semantics. Rather, it represents an untyped and undirected deliberation context, such as a committee, discussion thread, panel, or temporary coalition, that is available or may be activated by a moderator. Such contexts may be derived from, or constrained by, underlying social relations, but the present paper abstracts from their type and direction. This motivates the following question: given a group of decision makers whose opinions are not sufficiently close, which higher-order deliberation contexts should a moderator activate in order to reach consensus at minimum cost?

We address this question from a knowledge representation perspective. We introduce the *Minimum-Cost Hyperedge Intervention for Consensus Reaching* problem. The input consists of a set of decision makers, their initial opinions on a discrete scale, a set of candidate hyperedges, and costs associated with activating such hyperedges. The goal is to find an optimal feasible solution: selected hyperedges, local compromise values, revised opinions, and revision justifications satisfying the consensus constraints while minimizing structural and opinion-revision costs. Indeed, the problem is naturally combinatorial. A solution requires deciding which hyperedges to activate, which decision makers revise their opinions, which local compromise values are used, and whether the resulting final opinions satisfy the global consensus condition. Answer Set Programming (ASP) is well suited for this task because it supports declarative modeling of combinatorial search and optimization problems by means of rules, constraints, and weak constraints.

The contributions of this paper are as follows:

- we introduce a hypergraph-based view of consensus intervention in social network group decision making;
- we formalize the Minimum-Cost Hyperedge Intervention Problem based on local compromise and global consensus constraints;
- we provide an ASP encoding of the problem;

- we report preliminary experiments on synthetic instances comparing hypergraph interventions with pairwise-only interventions.

The remainder of the paper is organized as follows. Section 2 discusses related work. Section 3 provides the necessary background. Section 4 introduces the proposed problem. Section 5 presents the ASP encoding. Section 6 discusses a running example. Section 7 reports preliminary experiments, and Sect. 8 concludes the paper.

## 2 Related Work

We draw on three lines of research: consensus reaching in SNGDM, opinion dynamics on higher-order networks, and ASP for preference handling and combinatorial decision problems.

In SNGDM, a moderator supports decision makers connected by trust, influence, or communication relations in reaching an acceptable agreement level [1,11, 16,18,27]. Existing work studies trust-based consensus, opinion evolution, leadership, large-scale settings, and cost-aware consensus models [2,5,19,26,28,29]. These approaches typically assume a fixed graph of pairwise relations, whereas we make higher-order structural interventions part of the moderator's decision space.

Higher-order network research shows that many social interactions are better modeled by hypergraphs or simplicial complexes than by graphs [3,4]. This view has led to hypergraph and multi-body variants of bounded-confidence, Deffuant, Friedkin–Johnsen, and nonlinear consensus dynamics [6,17,20,21,23,25,30]. These works mainly study opinion evolution over a fixed higher-order topology; our problem is complementary, since the moderator must decide which higher-order deliberation contexts to activate.

On the methodological side, ASP is widely used for combinatorial search and optimization [12,14], and has been extended with several preference-handling frameworks, including ordered disjunction, qualitative preference semantics, ASPRIN, and possibilistic or abductive variants [7–9,22,24]. To the best of our knowledge, ASP has not been used to encode structural intervention problems on social hypergraphs, where deliberation contexts, local compromise values, final opinions, and revision justifications are optimized jointly.

## 3 Background

*Hypergraphs.* Hypergraphs generalize graphs by allowing an edge to connect more than two nodes. Formally, a hypergraph is a pair $\mathcal{G} = (D, \mathcal{H})$, where $D$ is a finite set of nodes and $\mathcal{H} \subseteq 2^D \setminus \{\emptyset\}$ is a set of hyperedges [4]. In our setting, nodes are decision makers and hyperedges are deliberation contexts, such as committees, discussion groups, or panels. We consider undirected hyperedges; directed hyperedges could model asymmetric group influence, but are left for future work.

*Answer Set Programming.* Answer Set Programming (ASP) is a declarative methodology for knowledge representation and reasoning based on stable model semantics [12,15]. In ASP, a problem is described by a logic program, and its answer sets correspond to solutions. A rule has the form

$$a \leftarrow b_1, \ldots, b_m,\ not\ c_1, \ldots, not\ c_n,$$

where $a$ is a head atom, $b_i$ are positive body atoms, and $not\ c_j$ are default-negated atoms. Rules without head atoms are integrity constraints, while facts are rules with empty body. Modern ASP systems following ASP-Core-2 also support choice rules, aggregates, arithmetic expressions, and optimization statements [10], which are essential for the encoding below.

## 4 Minimum-Cost Hyperedge Intervention

Let $D = \{d_1, \ldots, d_m\}$ be a set of decision makers and $V = \{0, \ldots, K\}$ a finite opinion scale. An initial opinion profile is a function $op : D \to V$. We deliberately use scalar opinions to isolate the higher-order intervention problem from richer preference representations. Let $\mathcal{H}$ be the set of already available hyperedges, representing existing deliberation contexts active at no additional cost. Let $\mathcal{C}$ be a set of candidate hyperedges that may be activated by a moderator, each with positive integer cost $cost(h)$. Thus, note that the topology in this paper is a topology of deliberation contexts, not a typed model of trust, influence, or communication relations. We call any set $S \subseteq \mathcal{C}$ a *candidate intervention*; it induces the active hyperedges $\mathcal{A} = \mathcal{H} \cup S$. A feasible solution is not determined by $S$ alone: it must also assign local compromise values $val(h) \in V$ to active hyperedges, a revised opinion profile $op' : D \to V$, and revision justifications satisfying the constraints below. To avoid unrealistic compromises, the local value of an active hyperedge must lie within the initial opinion range of its members. Denoting

$$\underline{op}(h) = \min_{d \in h} op(d), \qquad \overline{op}(h) = \max_{d \in h} op(d),$$

we require $\underline{op}(h) \leq val(h) \leq \overline{op}(h)$ for every active hyperedge $h$. We use a global consensus threshold $\epsilon$, requiring

$$\forall d_i, d_j \in D, \quad |op'(d_i) - op'(d_j)| \leq \epsilon,$$

and a local threshold $\lambda$, requiring that if $d$ is attributed to active hyperedge $h$, then

$$|op'(d) - val(h)| \leq \lambda.$$

The threshold $\epsilon$ is global because it constrains the final opinion profile as a whole, by bounding the distance between every pair of decision makers; $\lambda$ is local because it constrains only the compatibility between an individual revision and the compromise value of its justifying hyperedge. The structural intervention cost and revision cost are

$$C_H(S) = \sum_{h \in S} cost(h), \qquad C_R(op, op') = \sum_{d \in D} |op(d) - op'(d)|.$$

We first minimize $C_H(S)$, then, among structurally optimal solutions, minimize $C_R(op, op')$. Note that the range condition captures the assumption that a committee cannot produce a plausible compromise outside the span of its members' initial positions. Thus, mixed hyperedges may enlarge the feasible compromise interval, while homogeneous within-group hyperedges remain limited to the opinion range of their members.

**Definition 1 (Minimum-Cost Hyperedge Intervention).** *Given*

$$I = \langle D, V, op, \mathcal{H}, \mathcal{C}, cost, \epsilon, \lambda \rangle,$$

*a* feasible solution *consists of selected hyperedges* $S \subseteq \mathcal{C}$*, active hyperedges* $\mathcal{A} = \mathcal{H} \cup S$*, a local value assignment* $val : \mathcal{A} \to V$*, a revised profile* $op' : D \to V$*, and a justification function* $just : R \to \mathcal{A}$ *on* $R = \{d \in D \mid op'(d) \neq op(d)\}$*, such that:*

*(i) for every* $d \in R$*,* $d \in just(d)$*;*
*(ii) for every* $d \in R$*,* $|op'(d) - val(just(d))| \leq \lambda$*;*
*(iii) for every* $h \in \mathcal{A}$*,* $\underline{op}(h) \leq val(h) \leq \overline{op}(h)$*;*
*(iv) for every* $d_i, d_j \in D$*,* $|op'(d_i) - op'(d_j)| \leq \epsilon$*;*
*(v) the structural and revision costs are* $C_H(S)$ *and* $C_R(op, op')$*, respectively.*

*An* optimal solution *is a feasible solution that minimizes* $(C_H(S), C_R(op, op'))$ *lexicographically.*

A selected hyperedge represents an opportunity for local deliberation, not a constraint forcing all its members to adopt its local value. Only changed opinions require justification, and each revised decision maker is attributed to one active hyperedge, which identifies the deliberation context supporting the suggested revision. Compatibility with all active hyperedges an agent belongs to, as well as stronger participation semantics, are left for future work. This yields an explanation layer: the model returns both final opinions satisfying consensus and the context responsible for each revision. Additional moderation policies, such as requiring cross-group justifications, can be added declaratively by changing input facts or adding ASP rules. Moreover, the proposed ASP formulation is motivated by the combinatorial nature of the problem, since a solution must choose hyperedges, local values, final opinions, and justifications.

# 5 ASP Encoding

We encode an instance by input facts `agent(D)`, `value(V)`, `opinion(D,V)`, `existing(H)`, `candidate(H)`, `member(D,H)`, and `cost(H,C)`. Thresholds are constants `epsilon` and `local_thr`. The auxiliary predicate `dist(V1,V2,D)` gives $D = |V1 - V2|$ over the finite opinion scale. The optional bridge-use policy, introduced below, is activated by the fact `require_bridge` and uses `min_bridge_uses`.

```
{ selected(H) } :- candidate(H).
active(H) :- existing(H).
active(H) :- selected(H).

1 { local_value(H,V) : value(V) } 1 :- active(H).
1 { final_opinion(D,V) : value(V) } 1 :- agent(D).

min_initial(H,M) :- active(H),
    M = #min { V : member(D,H), opinion(D,V) }.
max_initial(H,M) :- active(H),
    M = #max { V : member(D,H), opinion(D,V) }.
:- local_value(H,V), min_initial(H,M), V < M.
:- local_value(H,V), max_initial(H,M), V > M.
```

**Listing 1.1.** Core choices

Listing 1.1 generates selected hyperedges, local values, and final opinions, and enforces the compromise-range condition.

```
revised(D) :- opinion(D,V0), final_opinion(D,V), V != V0.
covered(D) :- active(H), member(D,H).
:- revised(D), not covered(D).

1 { uses(D,H) : active(H), member(D,H) } 1 :- revised(D).

:- uses(D,H), final_opinion(D,V), local_value(H,VH),
   dist(V,VH,Delta), Delta > local_thr.
```

**Listing 1.2.** Revision detection and local justification

Revisions are detected by comparing initial and final opinions. Each revised decision maker must be covered by an active hyperedge and attributed to exactly one active hyperedge containing her. The attribution is valid only if the final opinion is within the local threshold of the hyperedge value (Listing 1.2).

```
consensus_violation(D1,D2) :-
    agent(D1), agent(D2), id(D1,I1), id(D2,I2), I1 < I2,
    final_opinion(D1,V1), final_opinion(D2,V2),
    dist(V1,V2,Delta), Delta > epsilon.

:- consensus_violation(D1,D2).
```

**Listing 1.3.** Global consensus constraint

Listing 1.3 enforces the global consensus condition by eliminating answer sets in which two final opinions are farther apart than `epsilon`.

```
#minimize { C@2,H : selected(H), cost(H,C) }.
revision_cost(D,C) :- opinion(D,V0), final_opinion(D,V), dist(V0,V,C).
#minimize { C@1,D : revision_cost(D,C) }.
```

```
bridge(H) :- active(H), member(D1,H), low_group(D1),
             member(D2,H), high_group(D2).
bridge_use(D,H) :- uses(D,H), bridge(H).
:- require_bridge,
   #count { D,H : bridge_use(D,H) } < min_bridge_uses.
```

**Listing 1.4.** Optimization and optional bridge-use policy

Lexicographic optimization uses priority `@2` for structural cost and `@1` for revision cost. Listing 1.4 also shows the optional bridge-use policy. A bridge hyperedge contains at least one member of each opinion group, encoded by `low_group/1` and `high_group/1`; when `require_bridge` is present, at least `min_bridge_uses` revision attributions must use bridge hyperedges. Indeed, this policy is only one example of a moderation policy; further constraints can be added declaratively without changing the core encoding.

## 6 An Example

Consider six decision makers $d_1, \ldots, d_6$ with initial opinions $(1, 2, 3, 8, 9, 10)$ on $\{0, \ldots, 10\}$. Decision makers $d_1, d_2, d_3$ form a low-opinion group and $d_4, d_5, d_6$ a high-opinion group. The existing hyperedges are $h_L = \{d_1, d_2, d_3\}$ and $h_R = \{d_4, d_5, d_6\}$. The candidates are $h_3 = \{d_3, d_4\}$ with cost 4, $h_4 = \{d_2, d_3, d_4, d_5\}$ with cost 3, and $h_5 = \{d_1, d_6\}$ with cost 5. We set $\epsilon = 3$, $\lambda = 1$, and require at least one revision to be justified by a bridge hyperedge.

The cheapest candidate bridge is $h_4$. One optimal answer set selects $h_4$, assigns local values $val(h_L) = 3$, $val(h_4) = 8$, and $val(h_R) = 8$, and returns the final opinion profile $(4, 4, 4, 7, 7, 7)$. The corresponding justifying hyperedges for $(d_1, \ldots, d_6)$ are

$$(h_L, h_L, h_L, h_R, h_4, h_R).$$

The maximum distance between final opinions is 3, the structural intervention cost is 3, and the total revision cost is 12. In particular, the answer set contains `selected(h4)` and `uses(d5,h4)`, so the selected bridge is actually used to justify a revision. The example also shows how the graph-based case is recovered by restricting candidates to size two, while larger hyperedges model group-level deliberation.

## 7 Preliminary Experimental Evaluation

In this section, we present a preliminary evaluation of our proposed encoding on a series of synthetic instances. Our aim is to understand when higher-order interventions are useful compared with pairwise-only interventions. We consider three research questions: *RQ1*, whether hyperedges reduce structural intervention cost; *RQ2*, how this advantage changes under different bridge-demand levels and hyperedge activation-cost regimes; and *RQ3*, what computational overhead is observed.

### 7.1 Experimental Settings

We compare two settings: a *pairwise-only* setting and a *hypergraph* setting. In the former, each candidate intervention connects one low-opinion and one high-opinion decision maker. In the latter setting, candidates have size between two and six and contain at least one member of each group. All other aspects of the encoding are identical.

For each instance, decision makers are split into two equal groups $L$ and $R$. Initial opinions for $L$ are sampled from $\{1, 2, 3\}$, and opinions for $R$ from $\{7, 8, 9\}$. Two existing hyperedges, $h_L = L$ and $h_R = R$, represent within-group deliberation contexts. Candidate hyperedges are sampled randomly. In all experiments, local compromise values are constrained to lie between the minimum and maximum initial opinions of the members of the corresponding active hyperedge.

We set $\epsilon = 3$, $\lambda = 1$, and use the bridge-use policy from Sect. 5. This policy requires some revisions to be justified by cross-group deliberation contexts, modeling settings in which numerical proximity alone is not considered sufficient. Without this policy, the optimizer may legitimately reach consensus using only existing within-group hyperedges, selecting no candidate bridge. That is, this kind of policy is introduced to study settings in which the moderator explicitly requires cross-group deliberation to support the revision process. The policy also creates a structural distinction between pairwise and higher-order interventions. If $b$ revisions must be justified by bridge hyperedges, then pairwise bridges can justify at most two such revisions each, whereas one bridge hyperedge of size $s \geq b$ can in principle justify all $b$. The experiments therefore study where this structural effect appears under different activation-cost regimes, and how it interacts with revision cost and solving time.

We consider three activation-cost regimes. The first is a *sublinear* regime,

$$cost_{\text{sub}}(h) = 2 + \left\lceil \frac{|h|}{2} \right\rceil + \theta,$$

which models economics of scale in group meetings. The second is a *linear* regime,

$$cost_{\text{lin}}(h) = 1 + |h| + \theta,$$

which models a per-participant cost. The third is a *pairwise-sum* regime,

$$cost_{\text{pair}}(h) = 2 + \frac{|h|(|h| - 1)}{2} + \theta,$$

which models coordination overhead growing with the number of pairwise interactions inside a group. In all cases, $\theta$ is uniformly sampled from $\{0, 1, 2\}$. The three regimes are normalized so that size-two hyperedges have the same base cost; hence differences in the results are due to the treatment of larger hyperedges, not to a different price for pairwise bridges.

We implemented the instance generator in Python 3.12, and we solved them with CLINGO 5.8.0 [14]. Each run had a 30-second timeout and was executed on a machine equipped with an Intel Xeon w7-3445 CPU and 64 GB of RAM. As

**Table 1.** Experimenting with increasing number of decision makers. Averages are computed over optimally solved instances. Best values in each comparable pair are reported in bold. Lower is better for costs, selected hyperedges, and time; higher is better for optimality

| $m$ | Setting | Opt. (%) | Struct. cost | Rev. cost | Sel. hyp. | Time (s) |
|---|---|---|---|---|---|---|
| 10 | Pairwise-only | **100.0** | 9.350 | 17.100 | 3.100 | 0.063 |
| 10 | Hypergraph | **100.0** | **5.150** | **16.600** | **1.050** | **0.028** |
| 20 | Pairwise-only | 10.0 | 15.000 | 34.500 | 5.000 | 12.544 |
| 20 | Hypergraph | **70.0** | **9.357** | **32.714** | **2.000** | **5.902** |
| 30 | Pairwise-only | 0.0 | – | – | – | – |
| 30 | Hypergraph | 0.0 | – | – | – | – |

measures, we report the percentage of instances solved to optimality, structural cost, revision cost, number of selected hyperedges, higher-order usage rate, and total solving time including grounding. The higher-order usage rate is the percentage of optimally solved instances in which the hypergraph setting selects at least one candidate hyperedge of size greater than two. The whole ASP encoding, the generator, and the instances are available in a GitHub repository[1].

### 7.2 Increasing Number of Decision Makers

In a first experiment, we vary $m \in \{10, 20, 30\}$. For each value of $m$ and each setting, we generate 20 instances. The bridge-use requirement is $\max(1, \text{round}(0.5\, m))$, so at least half of the decision makers must have revisions justified by cross-group deliberation contexts. We report the results in Table 1. For $m = 10$, both settings prove optimality on all instances. The hypergraph setting reduces average structural cost from 9.350 to 5.150, and the number of selected interventions from 3.100 pairwise bridges to 1.050 higher-order hyperedges on average. Revision cost is also lower, decreasing from 17.100 to 16.600. This supports *RQ1* on small instances: when several bridge uses are required, higher-order deliberation contexts can replace multiple pairwise interventions while preserving plausible local compromise values. For $m = 20$, the difference is also visible in terms of optimality proofs: the hypergraph setting solves 70.0% of the instances to optimality, compared with 10.0% for the pairwise-only setting. On optimally solved instances, hypergraph solutions also have lower structural cost, lower revision cost, and fewer selected interventions. For $m = 30$, neither setting proves optimality within the timeout. These results should therefore be read as preliminary evidence about the modeling tradeoff, not as a complete scalability study. Still, they indicate that the hypergraph intervention space can be computationally competitive in the tested instances, despite being richer than the pairwise-only one.

[1] https://github.com/finalfire/hyperedge-interventions-crp-asp.

**Table 2.** Experimenting with bridge-demand and activation-cost regimes for $m = 10$. Averages are computed over 20 optimally solved instances per configuration. *Pair cost* and *Hyper cost* report structural cost in the pairwise-only and hypergraph settings, respectively. *Pair rev.* and *Hyper rev.* report revision cost. *HO use* is the percentage of hypergraph instances in which at least one selected candidate hyperedge has size greater than two. Lower is better for costs

| Cost regime | $\rho$ | Pair cost | Pair rev. | Hyper cost | Hyper rev. | HO use (%) | Hyper time (s) |
|---|---|---|---|---|---|---|---|
| Sublinear | 0.2 | **3.600** | 16.950 | 4.200 | **16.150** | 85.0 | 0.022 |
| Sublinear | 0.4 | 6.000 | 17.050 | **4.100** | **16.200** | 100.0 | 0.017 |
| Sublinear | 0.6 | 9.100 | 17.650 | **5.050** | **16.950** | 100.0 | 0.020 |
| Linear | 0.2 | **3.600** | 16.950 | 4.650 | **16.200** | 80.0 | 0.015 |
| Linear | 0.4 | 6.000 | 17.050 | **5.100** | **16.250** | 100.0 | 0.016 |
| Linear | 0.6 | 9.100 | 17.650 | **7.050** | **16.950** | 100.0 | 0.020 |
| Pairwise-sum | 0.2 | **3.600** | 16.950 | 5.850 | **16.300** | 70.0 | 0.017 |
| Pairwise-sum | 0.4 | **6.000** | 17.050 | 8.000 | **16.350** | 90.0 | 0.017 |
| Pairwise-sum | 0.6 | **9.100** | 17.650 | 12.300 | **16.800** | 100.0 | 0.021 |

### 7.3 Cost-Regime and Bridge-Demand Sensitivity

In a second experiment, we fix $m = 10$ and vary both the bridge-use ratio $\rho \in \{0.2, 0.4, 0.6\}$ and the activation-cost regime. For each value of $\rho$, the requirement is $\max(1, \text{round}(\rho m))$ bridge attributions. For each instance identifier, we keep the same opinions, candidate hyperedges, and random noise values across cost regimes, changing only the cost formula. This makes the comparison isolate the effect of the cost model. All configurations are solved to optimality within the timeout.

The results are reported in Table 2. Under the sublinear regime, the pairwise-only setting is structurally cheaper at low bridge demand ($\rho = 0.2$), where one or few pairwise bridges are sufficient. As demand increases, the advantage shifts to the hypergraph setting: at $\rho = 0.4$, average structural cost decreases from 6.000 to 4.100, and at $\rho = 0.6$, from 9.100 to 5.050. This confirms the expected crossover under economies of scale, now under the additional constraint that each local compromise must lie within the initial opinion range of its members.

The same qualitative crossover also appears under the linear regime. Although larger hyperedges no longer benefit from a sublinear cost function, the hypergraph setting is still structurally cheaper for $\rho = 0.4$ and $\rho = 0.6$. This suggests that the advantage of higher-order interventions is not solely an artifact of the sublinear pricing model: when several bridge attributions are required, a single mixed deliberation context may still be preferable to multiple pairwise interventions.

The pairwise-sum regime gives a different picture. Since the cost of a hyperedge grows with the number of internal pairwise interactions, higher-order interventions are no longer structurally cheaper than the pairwise-only baseline. In this regime, pairwise-only solutions have lower structural cost for all tested bridge demands. Nevertheless, higher-order hyperedges are still selected frequently in the hypergraph setting, with HO usage increasing from 70.0% at $\rho = 0.2$ to 100.0% at $\rho = 0.6$. This shows that the encoding does not force higher-order interventions to be structurally preferable: when group coordination is expensive, their structural-cost advantage disappears.

Across all regimes, the hypergraph setting obtains lower average revision cost than the corresponding pairwise-only setting. This effect is not determined by the structural argument above, since revision cost depends on the interaction among final opinions, local compromise ranges, and available candidate hyperedges. The experiment therefore supports a more nuanced conclusion: higher-order interventions are structurally advantageous under sublinear and, in these instances, also linear meeting costs, but not under pairwise-sum coordination costs; however, they may still reduce the amount of opinion revision even when they are structurally more expensive. Average solving times remain below 0.1 seconds for all hypergraph configurations in this experiment, so the table mainly informs the modeling tradeoff rather than scalability.

## 8 Conclusion

In this paper, we proposed a declarative model for minimum-cost hyperedge interventions in consensus reaching. The model extends graph-based SNGDM by allowing a moderator to activate higher-order deliberation contexts represented as hyperedges. Each active hyperedge introduces a local compromise value constrained by the initial opinion range of its members, and revised opinions must be justified by active hyperedges. We provided an ASP encoding and preliminary synthetic experiments comparing hypergraph and pairwise-only interventions.

The results show that the usefulness of higher-order interventions depends on the activation-cost regime. Hypergraph interventions are structurally advantageous under sublinear and linear meeting costs in our instances, whereas pairwise-only interventions are preferable under pairwise-sum coordination costs. At the same time, the hypergraph setting consistently yields lower revision cost, suggesting that higher-order deliberation contexts may remain useful even when they are not structurally cheaper. In future work, we will address richer preference representations, iterative opinion evolution, stronger participation semantics, soft compromise penalties, and validation on real social decision-making data.

## References

1. Auletta, V., Fanelli, A., Ferraioli, D.: Consensus in opinion formation processes in fully evolving environments. In: Proceedings of the AAAI Conference on Artificial Intelligence (AAAI 2019), pp. 6022–6029. AAAI Press (2019)

2. Auletta, V., Ferraioli, D., Greco, G.: Optimal majority dynamics for the diffusion of an opinion when multiple alternatives are available. Theoret. Comput. Sci. **869**, 156–180 (2021)
3. Battiston, F., et al.: The physics of higher-order interactions in complex systems. Nat. Phys. **17**(10), 1093–1098 (2021)
4. Battiston, F.: Networks beyond pairwise interactions: structure and dynamics. Phys. Rep. **874**, 1–92 (2020)
5. Ben-Arieh, D., Easton, T.: Multi-criteria group consensus under linear cost opinion elasticity. Decis. Support Syst. **43**(3), 713–721 (2007)
6. Boccaletti, S., et al.: The structure and dynamics of networks with higher order interactions. Phys. Rep. **1018**, 1–64 (2023)
7. Brewka, G., Delgrande, J.P., Romero, J., Schaub, T.: asprin: Customizing answer set preferences without a headache. In: AAAI (2015)
8. Brewka, G., Delgrande, J.P., Romero, J., Schaub, T.: A general framework for preferences in answer set programming. Artif. Intell. (2023)
9. Brewka, G., Niemelä, I., Truszczyński, M.: Answer sets and qualitative decision making. Synthese **146**(1–2), 171–187 (2005)
10. Calimeri, F., et al.: Asp-core-2 input language format. Theory Pract. Logic Program. **20**(2), 294–309 (2020)
11. Dong, Y., et al.: Consensus reaching in social network group decision making: research paradigms and challenges. Knowl.-Based Syst. **162**, 3–13 (2018)
12. Erdem, E., Gelfond, M., Leone, N.: Applications of answer set programming. AI Mag. **37**(3), 53–68 (2016)
13. Ferraioli, D., Ventre, C.: Social pressure in opinion dynamics. Theor. Comput. Sci. **795**, 345–361 (2019)
14. Gebser, M., Kaminski, R., Kaufmann, B., Schaub, T.: Answer Set Solving in Practice. Morgan and Claypool (2012)
15. Gelfond, M., Lifschitz, V.: Classical negation in logic programs and disjunctive databases. N. Gener. Comput. **9**(3), 365–385 (1991)
16. Gong, Z., Ma, H., Lei, Q., Goh, M.: New consensus reaching process with minimum adjustment and feedback mechanism for large-scale group decision making problems under social trust networks. Eng. Appl. Artif. Intell. (2024)
17. Hickok, A., Kureh, Y., Brooks, H.Z., Feng, M., Porter, M.A.: A bounded-confidence model of opinion dynamics on hypergraphs. SIAM J. Appl. Dyn. Syst. **21**(1), 1–32 (2022)
18. Liu, P.: Consensus reaching for social network group decision making with ELICIT information: a perspective from the complex network. Inf. Sci. (2023)
19. Lu, Y.: Large-scale group decision consensus under social network: a chance-constrained robust optimization-based minimum cost consensus model. Expert Syst. Appl. (2024)
20. Majhi, S., Perc, M., Ghosh, D.: Dynamics on higher-order networks: a review. J. R. Soc. Interface **19**, 20220043 (2022)
21. Neuhäuser, L., Mellor, A., Lambiotte, R.: Multibody interactions and nonlinear consensus dynamics on networked systems. Phys. Rev. E **101**, 032310 (2020)
22. Nicolas, P., Garcia, L., Stéphan, I., Lefèvre, C.: Using possibilistic logic for modeling qualitative decision: ASP algorithms. Int. J. Approx. Reason. (2013)
23. Sahasrabuddhe, R., Neuhäuser, L., Lambiotte, R.: Modelling non-linear consensus dynamics on hypergraphs. J. Phys. Complexity **2**, 025006 (2021)
24. Schaub, T., Wang, K.: A semantic framework for preference handling in answer set programming. Theory Pract. Logic Program. **3**(4–5), 569–607 (2003)

25. Schawe, H., Hernández, L.: Higher order interactions destroy phase transitions in Deffuant opinion dynamics model. Commun. Phys. **5**, 32 (2022)
26. Wang, F., Yu, X., Mao, Y., Pedrycz, W.: Social network group decision making with minimum cost and maximum satisfaction consensus based on bargaining game. Inf. Fusion **123**, 103270 (2025)
27. Wu, P.: A consensus method in social network large-scale group decision making with interval information. Expert Syst. Appl. (2023)
28. Zhang, B.: Consensus mechanism with maximum-return modifications and minimum-cost feedback. Inf. Fusion (2020)
29. Zhang, H., Dong, Y., Xu, Y.: An overview on feedback mechanisms with minimum adjustment or cost in consensus reaching in group decision making: research paradigms and challenges. Inf. Fusion (2020)
30. Zhu, W.: A linear opinion dynamics model with higher-order interactions (2023). arXiv:2310.05689

# Influence Maximization on Partially Observable Social Networks with Graph Reconstruction

Vincenzo Auletta, Francesco Cauteruccio, Diodato Ferraioli(✉), Grazia Ferrara, Andrea Marino, and Rocco Gerardo Pizzulo

Università degli Studi di Salerno, Fisciano 84084, Italy
{auletta,fcauteruccio,dferraioli,grferrara,rpizzulo}@unisa.it,
a.marino120@studenti.unisa.it

**Abstract.** Influence Maximization (IM) is one of the most studied problems in social network analysis and involves selecting a set of $k$ users (seed set) from a social network to start an information diffusion and maximize the expected number of influenced users (influence spread). Despite its wide-ranging applications, from viral marketing to public health campaigns, the IM problem presents significant challenges since it has been proved to be NP-hard under most diffusion models. Moreover, real-world social networks are often only partially observable, with incomplete node and edge information due to privacy or data collection limitations.

To address this issue we propose an adaptive multi-round approach that uses techniques of graph reconstruction. Specifically, from an inferred Kronecker generative parameter matrix, we first estimate the missing part of the network, then compute a seed set that also takes into account the nodes not present in the partial graph. By starting the information diffusion from this seed set, the framework will be able to reach new nodes not initially observable, thus expanding its knowledge of the partial graph and being able to compute a more accurate generative parameter matrix at the next step. This iterative process continues until the framework converges to an accurate reconstruction of the full graph or achieves a desired influence spread. We experimentally evaluate this framework on both synthetic and real-world network topologies. Results highlight its effectiveness and show how it is often better with respect to a baseline adaptive approach that does not reconstruct the partial network.

**Keywords:** Influence Maximization · Seeding · Graph Generation

## 1 Introduction

In recent years, the widespread adoption of online social networks, capable of connecting millions of people around the world, has brought significant attention to the phenomenon of *information diffusion*. This process refers to how content shared on social platforms spreads through user interactions, often reaching a


S. Bistarelli et al. (Eds.): AIxIA 2026, LNAI 17131, pp. 43–56, 2027.
https://doi.org/10.1007/978-3-032-40774-0_4

large audience in a short time. It is easy to imagine that this phenomenon can be exploited to achieve various goals, such as during the 2010 Arab spring [13] or during the 2008 US presidential election [14]. This phenomenon has opened new avenues for various applications, especially in fields such as viral marketing [10,22], election manipulation [3,7], and public health campaigns [5,34,37].

In viral marketing, companies aim to promote products or services by selecting influential users who can maximize the spread of information throughout the network. Instead, in election manipulation, selection of influential users aims to promote a candidate in electoral campaigns. Similarly, in public health campaigns, identifying key individuals to disseminate information can help prevent disease outbreaks and protect vulnerable communities by ensuring that critical messages reach as many people as possible. The Influence Maximization (IM) problem arises within this context, focusing on identifying a limited subset of users, known as *seed set*, that can maximize the information diffusion across the network so to reach the largest possible number of people. This problem has been widely studied in the scientific community, leading to the development of numerous IM techniques that differ in efficiency and accuracy. However, all of these methods rely on the assumption that the full network topology is known, which is rarely valid in real-world scenarios. In practice, most social network data are collected from networks missing both users and relationships between them [19] due to several constraints. For example, resource limitations might restrict data collection to a specific geographic region or subset of users. This is further compounded by user-defined privacy settings, which can partially or completely obscure friendships, as demonstrated by the 2011 Facebook case in New York City, where 52.6% of users hid their friend lists [9]. This leads to incomplete data, making it challenging to apply traditional IM techniques effectively.

In this work, we relax the assumption of perfect knowledge of the topology by considering partial graphs, whose parts that are not directly observable are inferred using known results from the network completion problem.

*Our Contribution.* To address the IM problem in the partial observability scenario, we propose a novel framework that builds on key insights of the network completion problem. Partial observability forces us to choose seeds based only on the subgraph that we know. These choices can be largely suboptimal since we can miss nodes that are poorly relevant in the observable subgraph, but they may be central in the full but unknown graph.

To address this issue, we employ the KronFit algorithm [23] to infer missing edges and nodes based on the Kronecker graph model. The output of this algorithm is a parameter matrix which, when raised to a Kronecker power, generates self-similar networks that capture input graph properties. Hence, by inputting the partial subgraph that we know, we can construct an augmented graph that accounts for the unobservable portions of the network, ensuring that seed selection is guided by a more comprehensive view of the network structure.

How much should we enlarge our graph? Nodes of the augmented graph are only virtual, i.e., they do not really exist. Their role is to describe a probable structure of the full graph besides the partially known subgraph. Hence, adding too many virtual nodes can amplify the noise generated from the structure of the known subgraph not being a good sample of the structure of the full graph. On the other side, adding too few virtual nodes would cancel out the advantages of graph reconstruction. Hence, in this work we introduce a *dynamic thresholding* technique to optimize the balance between including virtual nodes and keeping robustness in the seed set. This adaptive mechanism adjusts the fraction of virtual nodes to consider based on the characteristics of each reconstruction iteration, minimizing the impact of reconstruction errors on influence spread.

Unfortunately, a seed selection algorithm applied on this augmented graph can choose as seeds nodes that are only virtual, i.e., that do not belong to the known component of the graph. Hence, a critical step in our methodology is the *devirtualization process*, which ensures that we limit seed selection to only those nodes included in the partially observable network.

While the advantage of graph augmentation can be limited in the single run, particularly depending on how good is the known sample, still this procedure can become more and more effective when the input graph becomes larger and thus more representative of the structure of the entire network. Hence, we consider an *adaptive multi-round* framework, in which multiple campaigns are executed with each campaign working with not only the initially known portion of the social network, but also with the nodes infected at the previous runs.

In order to confirm the effectiveness of our framework, we run preliminary simulations in both synthetic and real graphs, and compare our framework against an approach that does not use graph augmentation (i.e., it chooses seeds only based on the known nodes). We prove that our framework often provides an advantage with respect to this naive approach. We also show that in many settings the performance of our framework quickly approaches that of the algorithm that always chooses seeds based on the knowledge of the full graph.

## 2 Related Works

*Influence Maximization.* We use the standard *Influence Maximization* (IM) formalization, detailed in Sect. 3, given by Kempe, Kleinberg, and Tardos [17], who proved NP-hardness and showed that a greedy algorithm achieves a $(1 - 1/e)$-approximation guarantee thanks to the monotonicity and submodularity of the influence function. Subsequent work has focused on improving the scalability of this approach without sacrificing approximation guarantees: CELF [25] and CELF++ [11] exploit submodularity to prune redundant Monte Carlo simulations, while TIM/TIM+ [30] and IMM [29] use reverse-reachable-set sampling to obtain near-linear-time approximations with the same theoretical guarantee. In parallel, a separate line of work develops efficient heuristic seed selectors that forgo formal guarantees in exchange for speed, including degree centrality, PageRank-based selection, and VoteRank [28], which iteratively elects seeds through a voting procedure that discounts the neighborhoods of already-selected nodes. Comparative studies [28] show that, despite the absence of formal guarantees, these heuristics are often competitive with approximation algorithms on real-world networks, particularly when the priority is computational efficiency rather than worst-case optimality. We build on this observation by adopting

PageRank and VoteRank as our seed selectors, since their low computational cost is essential given that our framework must repeat seed selection at every iteration of the reconstruction loop.

*Influence Maximization under Uncertainty.* Several lines of work relax the assumption that the network and its parameters are fully known, but each relaxes a different piece of that assumption. Robust IM assumes the topology is fully observed but edge probabilities are only known to lie within bounded intervals, and seeks seed sets that perform well under worst-case parameter realizations [8]. Online IM assumes the topology is fully observed but edge probabilities are unknown and must be learned across repeated campaigns, typically through combinatorial bandit algorithms [15,21,35], even in adaptive setting [4]. Both lines of work, therefore, address parameter uncertainty while retaining full knowledge of the graph structure, which is the opposite of our setting.

Closer to our problem, a small number of works directly address topological incompleteness. Some works [5,16,32,37] perform IM on a small, queryable subgraph by adaptively selecting which nodes to probe before committing to a seed set, in the context of interventions for real-world field deployments. These methods assume access to an oracle that can be queried on demand; our setting differs in that we have no such oracle, and the only way to acquire new structural information is to run a diffusion campaign and observe its outcome.

*Network Completion and Graph Generative Models.* The network completion problem, introduced by Kim and Leskovec [18], asks for the most plausible reconstruction of the unobserved portion of a graph given a partial observation. Existing approaches fall into two broad families. Local link-prediction methods—including common neighbors, Adamic-Adar [1], and learned embedding approaches such as node2vec [12]—predict the presence of missing edges between already-known nodes, but cannot account for nodes that are entirely unobserved. Generative reconstruction methods, by contrast, model the graph as a sample from a parametric family and can therefore also generate plausible unobserved nodes alongside missing edges. The Kronecker graph model [26] and its associated fitting procedure, KronFit [23], belong to this second family and form the core reconstruction tool of our framework, as it requires no data beyond the single partial graph being completed. More recently, Tran et al. [33] propose DeepNC, which trains an autoregressive deep generative model (GraphRNN) on a corpus of structurally similar, largely-complete graphs and reports substantially lower reconstruction error than Kronecker-based completion; this gain, however, comes at the cost of requiring an external training corpus and a far more expensive per-fit procedure, neither of which is compatible with the repeated, self-contained reconstruction our framework performs at every iteration. Tran et al. [31] also apply Kronecker-based reconstruction to the related problem of community detection under partial observability, and identify the same trade-off between reconstruction coverage and injected noise that motivates our dynamic thresholding mechanism. To the best of our knowledge, generative graph reconstruction has not previously been used to drive seed selection in an influence maximization pipeline, which is the gap our work addresses.

## 3 Definitions

*Influence Maximization.* Let $G = (V, E)$ be a (possibly directed) network, with each edge $e$ having a probability $p_e \in [0, 1]$. Given a subset $S \subseteq V$ of vertices, the *Independent Cascade (IC)* diffusion model describes how information diffuses along the network. Specifically, it starts with the set of initially *active* (i.e., informed) nodes being $A_0 = S$, and at each discrete time step $t \geq 1$, it assumes that every $u \in A_{t-1}$, i.e., those nodes that have been recently activated, attempts to pass information along its outgoing edges $e = (u, v)$ leading to a non-active node $v$, with the tentative being successful only with probability $p_e$; in this case we say that $u$ infects $v$ and $v$ belongs to the set $A_t$ of vertices activated at time $t$. This diffusion process ends at the first time step $T$ such that $A_T$ is empty. The set of nodes activated during the diffusion process starting with seeds $S$ is $A(S) = \bigcup_{t=0}^{T-1} A_t$. Due to the stochastic nature of the diffusion process, we will focus on the expectation of this quantity, namely $\sigma(S) = \mathbb{E}[A(S)]$.

The problem of *Influence Maximization* with IC then consists in computing, given the network $G$, edge probabilities $p$, and a budget $B$, the set of seeds $S^*$ of size at most $B$ that maximizes the expected number of activated nodes, i.e., $S^* = \arg\max_{S:\, |S| \leq B} \sigma(S)$. Unfortunately, this problem is NP-hard [17]. An hill-climbing greedy algorithm, that starts with an empty seed set $S$ and iteratively inserts into $S$ the node $v$ providing the maximum marginal gain to the influence function $\sigma(\cdot)$, i.e., the one that maximizes $\sigma(S \cup \{v\}) - \sigma(S)$, returns a seed set that is able to infect at least a fraction $(1 - 1/e)$ of the number of nodes that would have been infected by the optimal seed set $S^*$.

Despite being polynomial time, this hill-climbing algorithm still turns out to require huge computational overhead. For these reasons, a lot of work has been devoted to design more-efficient approaches. While most of these are able to provide formal approximation guarantees (see Related Work section), we here focus mainly on heuristic-based influence maximization algorithms, that choose as seeds nodes maximizing some centrality measure such as *PageRank*, *VoteRank* and *Degree Centrality* [28]. These algorithms are extremely efficient, and this makes them suitable for the iterative nature of our framework. Moreover, it is well known that often the results of these heuristics are comparable with the ones of more complex (and more time-demanding) algorithms [2].

*Kronecker Graph Model.* The Kronecker graph model, introduced in [26], is based on a recursive construction and it creates self-similar graphs. The process begins with an *initiator* graph $K_1$, and it recursively computes larger graphs $K_2, K_3, \ldots$, through the *Kronecker product* of two matrices, defined as follows:

**Definition 1 (Kronecker product of matrices).** *Given $A \in \mathbb{R}^{m \times n}$ and $B \in \mathbb{R}^{m' \times n'}$, their Kronecker product $A \otimes B \in \mathbb{R}^{mm' \times nn'}$ is* $\begin{pmatrix} a_{11}B & \cdots & a_{1n}B \\ \vdots & \ddots & \vdots \\ a_{m1}B & \cdots & a_{mn}B \end{pmatrix}$.

From this definition, it is intuitive to understand that the Kronecker product of two graphs can be obtained as the Kronecker product of their adjacency matrices.

**Definition 2 (Kronecker product of graphs).** *If $G$ and $H$ are graphs with adjacency matrices $A(G)$ and $A(H)$ respectively, then the Kronecker product $G \otimes H$ is defined as the graph with adjacency matrix $A(G) \otimes A(H)$.*

**Definition 3 (Kronecker power).** *The $k^{th}$ power of $K_1$ is the matrix $K_1^{[k]}$ (abbreviated to $K_k$), such that $K_1^{[k]} = K_k = \underbrace{K_1 \otimes K_1 \otimes \cdots \otimes K_1}_{k \text{ times}} = K_{k-1} \otimes K_1$.*

Leskovec et al. [26] showed that this Kronecker power construction yields graphs with a range of desired properties. Nevertheless, its discrete nature still produces undesired effects: e.g., based on $K_1$, either the network is very sparse or very dense, with no chances of achieving networks whose degree distribution was in the middle among these two extremes.

To address this issue, Leskovec et al. [26] proposed a stochastic version of Kronecker graphs to eliminate this effect. The main idea is to relax the assumption that the entries of the adjacency matrix of the initiator graph take only binary values, allowing them to be within the interval $[0, 1]$. Kronecker-powering such initiator matrix we can now obtain a large stochastic adjacency matrix, where each entry gives the probability of a particular edge appearing in the graph. This stochastic adjacency matrix defines a probability distribution over all graphs. To obtain a graph, we sample an instance from this distribution by selecting individual edges, where each edge is selected independently with probability given by the entry of the large stochastic adjacency matrix.

**Definition 4 (Stochastic Kronecker graph).** *Let $\mathcal{P}_1$ be a $N_1 \times N_1$ probability matrix, i.e., the value $\Theta_{ij} \in \mathcal{P}_1$ denotes the probability that edge $(i, j)$ is present, with $\Theta_{ij} \in [0, 1]$; and let $\mathcal{P}_1^{[k]} = \mathcal{P}_k$ be the $k^{th}$ Kronecker power, where each entry $p_{uv} \in \mathcal{P}_k$ encodes the probability of an edge $(u, v)$. Then, to obtain an instance $K = R(\mathcal{P}_k)$ we include each edge (u,v) in $K$ with probability $p_{uv} \in \mathcal{P}_k$.*

While a deterministic Kronecker graph model would allow to immediately extend the observed graph, with a stochastic Kronecker graph model we would need to generate from the observed graph the initiator model. The approach that is commonly used to this aim is to find for the current observed graph $G$, the initiator model $\mathcal{P}$ that is more probable to generate $G$ as the outcome of the Stochastic Kronecker Graph construction. Specifically, Leskovec et al. [23] introduce *KronFit*, an algorithm that uses a maximum likelihood approach to find the initiator $\mathcal{P}_1$ that is more likely to outcome the given graph $G$ under the Stochastic Kronecker graph model. We will adopt this tool in our framework.

## 4 Our Algorithm

In this chapter we present KRONIM, a novel framework to maximize the influence spread over a partially observable social network. The framework begins with the reconstruction of the partial network using the KronFit algorithm [23], which estimates the hidden portions of the unobservable complete graph. This process

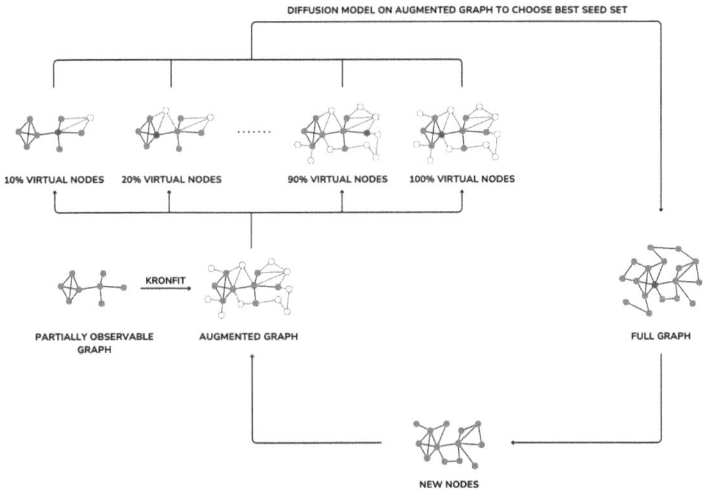


**Fig. 1.** KronIM framework

generates an initialization parameter matrix, which is then used to create an augmented graph containing *virtual nodes* that approximate the structure of the complete network. However, since these nodes are merely estimates, they could compromise the selection of seeds; so, to ensure robustness and reliability, the framework selects multiple seed sets on several graph instances that account for varying percentages of virtual nodes. Still, the computed seed sets cannot be used directly on the augmented graph since they could contain virtual nodes, so we also need a devirtualization process. At this point, the refined seed sets are tested on the augmented graph, which is used as a proxy of the ground truth to identify the set of seeds that achieves the best performance. Finally, this seed set is used to start a diffusion campaign on the complete unobservable network. The campaign allows in this way to enlarge the partial graph with the newly activated nodes and edges, providing a more solid base on which to perform the next step. Figure 1 provides a graphical representation of this framework, while we next dive in the details of each component of this framework.

*Graph Recovery.* The core of the KronIM framework lies in the graph reconstruction phase, during which we generate an augmented graph that models and extends the properties of the partial topology. To this aim, we will use the Stochastic Kronecker graph model discussed above. Namely, given at each time step $t$, we consider the adjacency matrix $A$ of the graph $G$ observed until $t$. Next by running the KronFit algorithm, we compute $\Theta$, i.e., (an approximation of) the most likely initiator model of $A$. Next, $\Theta$ is raised to the Kronecker power until the number of nodes in the resulting graph is greater than or equal to that of the complete graph (whose total size, or at least a close estimate, is assumed to be known). This process generates a stochastic adjacency matrix, denoted as $\Theta^k$. The augmented graph is then formed by placing the partial adjacency

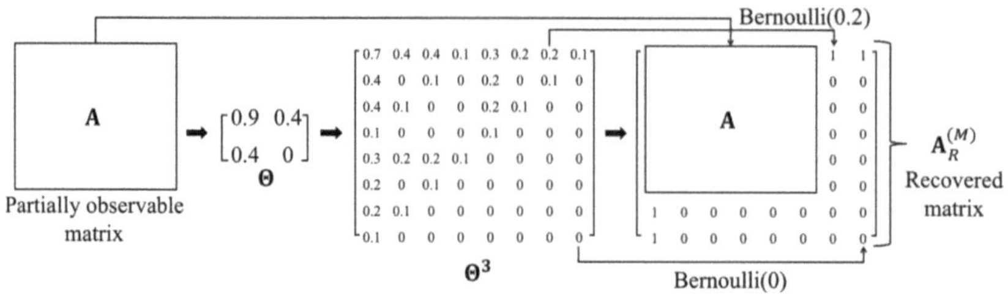


**Fig. 2.** Graph Recovery

matrix $A$ in the upper-left corner of $\Theta^k$, with Bernoulli trials conducted, with probabilities given by the entries of $\Theta^k$, to estimate and fill in the missing parts of the network. Figure 2 provides a graphical representation of this procedure.

*Influential Node Selection.* The additional nodes in the reconstructed graph are referred to as *virtual nodes* and, as highlighted in [31], including all of them in the partial network could lead to suboptimal results due to two main error sources. The first is related to the fitting of $\Theta$, while the other stems from random errors that occur during the Bernoulli series used to project a probabilistic value to zero or one. In particular, the second type of error, unlike the first, cannot be reduced as it is associated with a purely stochastic process. For this reason, the more recovered nodes we include, the higher the sum of errors. On the other hand, using just a very small portion of missing nodes is unlikely to provide benefits, since there is insufficient information. Following this discussion, it is therefore critical to determine the optimal fraction of virtual nodes to be added to the partial graph in order to achieve effective results. To this aim, we avoid fixing such a fraction in advance. Instead, we evaluate different fractions $p$ of virtual nodes to be added. For each such fraction, we compute a set $S_p$ of seeds and we evaluate how good $S_p$ performs on the graph returned by the graph recovery algorithm. We choose to add the fraction $p$ of virtual nodes that maximizes the performance of $S_p$, by breaking ties in favor of the smallest tied fraction. It is worth pointing out that selecting the virtual-node fraction on the reconstructed graph itself is a heuristic surrogate: the augmented graph is both the object we optimize over and the proxy against which we evaluate. We avoid evaluating candidate fractions directly on the real graph because every real diffusion could alter the observed context and would prevent a fair comparison across fractions, unless one adopts an online-learning scheme. However, the latter would pay a substantial exploration cost in the early rounds, thus offsetting the advantage of reconstruction. Our experiments below show that our heuristic approach yields consistent improvements across topologies and execution stages.

Once the percentage of virtual nodes to include has been set, it would be necessary to understand which of these virtual nodes to add. For this process, known as *influential node selection*, we rely on the concepts of connectivity and centrality and we apply two different stages of filtering. The first important aspect to underline is that if virtual nodes are not connected to the partial graph, they will not affect the computation of the seed set since they do not modify the properties of real nodes; so the first step is to select only virtual nodes that are connected to the known part of the graph.

Then, we adopt degree centrality as a second filter for virtual nodes, which measures the number of immediate neighbors of a node, to estimate their usefulness. In particular, virtual nodes (the ones connected to the partial graph) are sorted according to this centrality measure, and we construct several instances of reconstructed graphs including the desired percentage of these nodes.

*Seed Set Devirtualization.* For each graph configuration obtained during the influential node selection phase, the seed set is calculated and diffusion is simulated on the augmented graph, which acts as the ground truth. During the seed set computation, it could happen that a virtual node is selected. As already discussed, the existence of these nodes is just inferred, so it is impossible to select them as initial influencers; therefore, the computed seed sets are required to undergo a refinement process that substitutes any selected virtual node with a real one. This process is called *devirtualization*. We implemented it through a filtering procedure, in which virtual nodes are directly removed from the seed set and replaced with the first real nodes that were initially excluded from selection.

The implementation of the full process of virtual node filtering by connectivity, different percentage evaluation, virtual node selection by degree centrality, seed selection, and seed set devirtualization is available at https://gitlab.com/core_lab/thesis/kronim.git.

## 5 Experiments

*Experimental Protocol.* In order to experimentally evaluate the proposed KronIM framework and assess its effectiveness in influence maximization on partially observable graphs, we conducted a series of tests. In particular, we created partial graphs consisting of 55% of the original nodes, sampled using two different methods, enabling us to rigorously evaluate the performance of the framework under unbiased node selection conditions.

To highlight the advantages of reconstructing the partial network, we compared the performance of KronIM with an adaptive baseline approach that skips the reconstruction phase and directly applies influence maximization on the partial graph. Additionally, we provide a performance upper bound by comparing both KronIM and the baseline to the application of the seeding algorithm in the ideal case, where perfect knowledge of the underlying network is available.

The experimental protocol involved running 100 iterations of influence maximization for each of the two approaches under analysis. To obtain a reliable estimate of information spread across the network, we conducted 1000 simulations per iteration and, to ensure a robust influence spread, we set the seed budget $B$ to 2.5% of the total number of nodes in the network.

To assess the performance of the proposed framework and compare it with the baseline that omits network reconstruction, we adopt the *Mean Relative*

*Error* (MRE), defined as $\text{MRE} = \frac{1}{N}\sum_{i=1}^{N} \frac{|\min(\hat{y}_i - y_i, 0)|}{y_i}$, as the primary evaluation metric. In our specific case, the MRE measures the discrepancy between the number of nodes reached by each approach and the result achieved on the fully observable graph. By averaging these errors across all iterations, the MRE provides a concise yet comprehensive value that encapsulates the average deviation of each approach from the influence spread in the ideal full-knowledge case. A lower MRE indicates a more accurate replication of the influence propagation in the fully observable graph, and thus a major effectiveness of the method.

*Dataset.* The proposed framework was tested and evaluated on both real and synthetic social network topologies. For the synthetic social networks, it is crucial to ensure that they model the main characteristics common to the real ones, such as degrees following a power law distribution and the small world phenomenon. For this reason, synthetic networks were generated using several graph models.

**Affiliation Model.** [38] This model merges the preferential attachment approach [27], that allows to model scale-free networks, and the Watts-Strogatz approach [36], that allows to create small-world networks. In networks generated by this model, nodes do not decide to attach to other nodes, but they decide to affiliate to communities in a way that resembles the preferential attachment model, i.e., nodes tend to choose communities with many nodes. Once each node has been affiliated to communities, the model creates strong ties among nodes within the communities, and a fixed number of weak ties between communities that act as bridges. In particular, we generated a graph with 500 nodes and 50 communities, with a community affiliation probability of 10% and a maximum of 2 communities in which a node can participate. Within each community, the probability of a strong tie is 5%, while the number of out-community edges was set at 3.

**Configuration Model.** [6] The configuration model starts from the in-degree and out-degree sequences, where each entry represents the degree of a node, and generates a directed graph by randomly assigning edges to match the given degree sequences. In our experiments, we generated a degree sequence guaranteeing a degree distribution that agrees with a power law, and then we generated a graph of 500 nodes and 1764 edges.

**Kronecker Graph Model.** [23] This model generates self-similar networks by recursively applying Kronecker product on an initiator matrix. Once the produced matrix has enough nodes, the resulting stochastic matrix is used to establish the presence of edges among nodes (matrix indices). Networks generated by this model present a power-law degree distribution, small-world property and model hierarchical structure. In particular, we set the initiator matrix to $\Theta = [0.9, 0.7; 0.5, 0.2]$ as it resembles the typical initiator structure of the real networks analyzed in [23]. From this initiator, we generated a graph with 512 nodes and 1797 edges by kronecker powering it with $k = 9$.

The real network topologies used in this work have been Facebook and FilmTrust, both available on KONECT [20]. The choice of these networks is

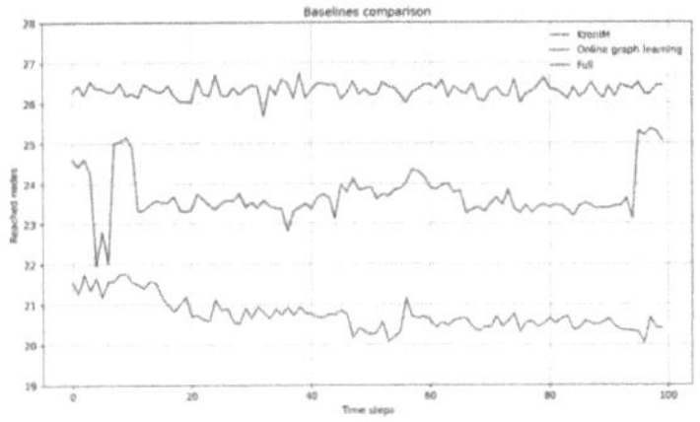


(a) Pagerank on Kronecker graph
MRE: **0.0995** (KronIM) vs 0.2116 (baseline)

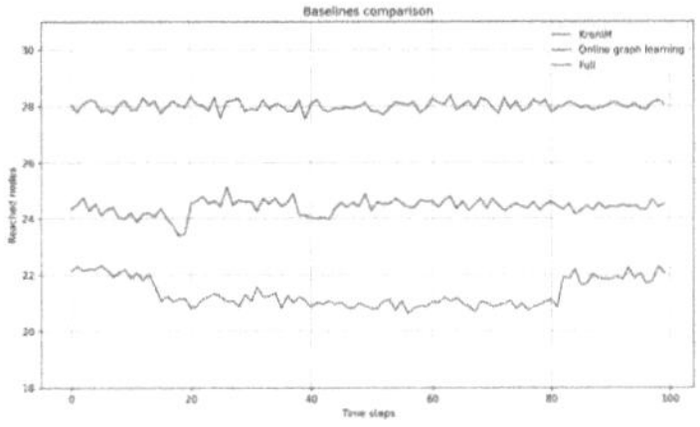


(b) Voterank on Kronecker graph
MRE: **0.1291** (KronIM) vs 0.2384 (baseline)

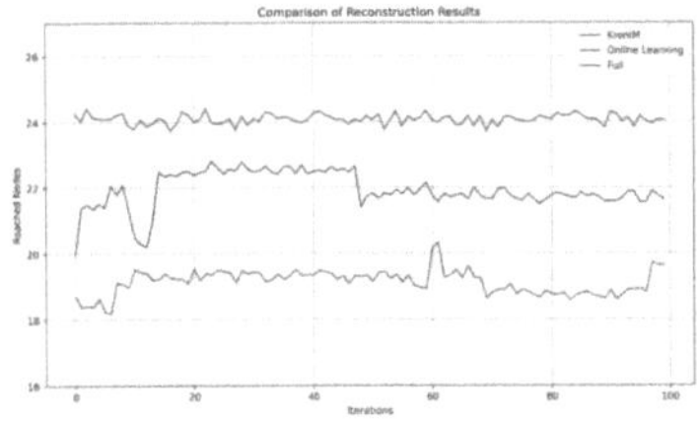


(c) Pagerank on Configuration Graph
MRE: **0.0893** (KronIM) vs 0.2058 (baseline)

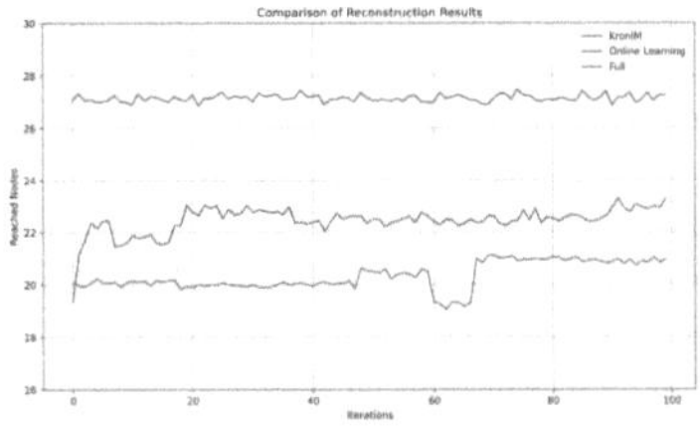


(d) Voterank on Configuration Graph
MRE: **0.1729** (KronIM) vs 0.2510 (baseline)

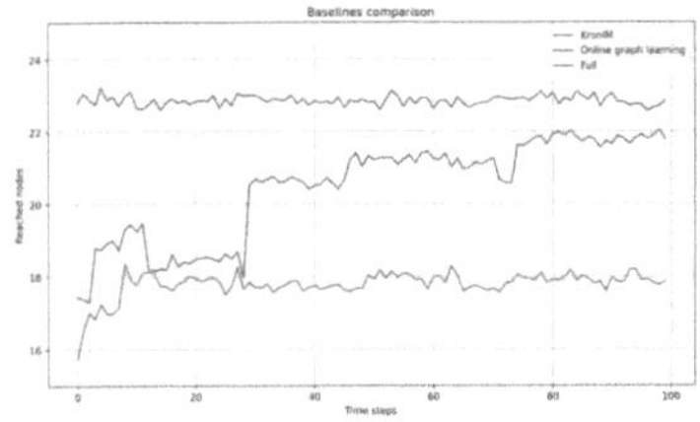


(e) Pagerank on Affiliation Graph
MRE: **0.1048** (KronIM) vs 0.2219 (baseline)

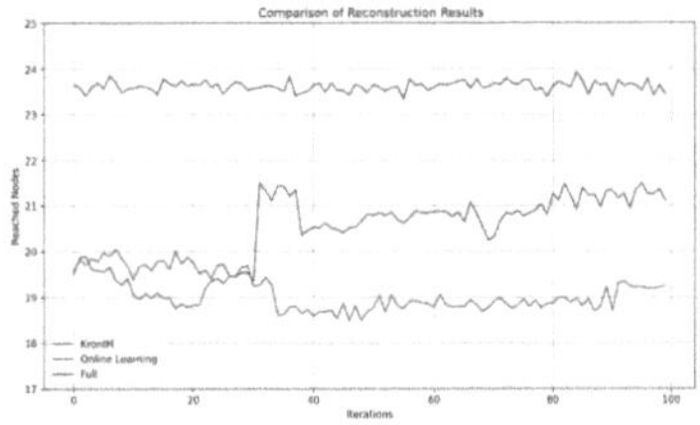


(f) Voterank on Affiliation Graph
MRE: **0.1358** (KronIM) vs 0.1897 (baseline)

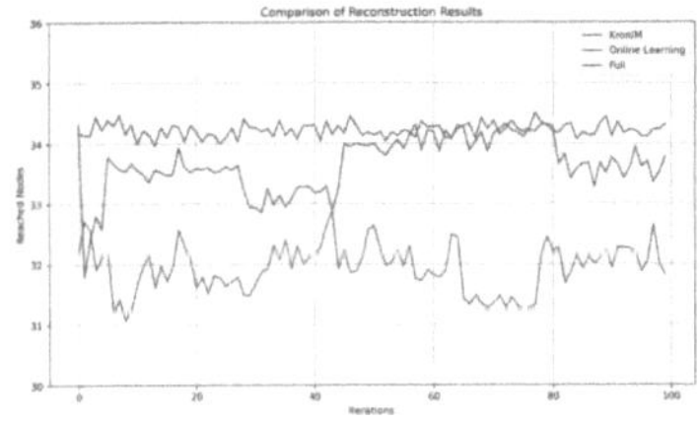


(g) Pagerank on FilmTrust Graph
MRE: **0.0171** (KronIM) vs 0.0668 (baseline)

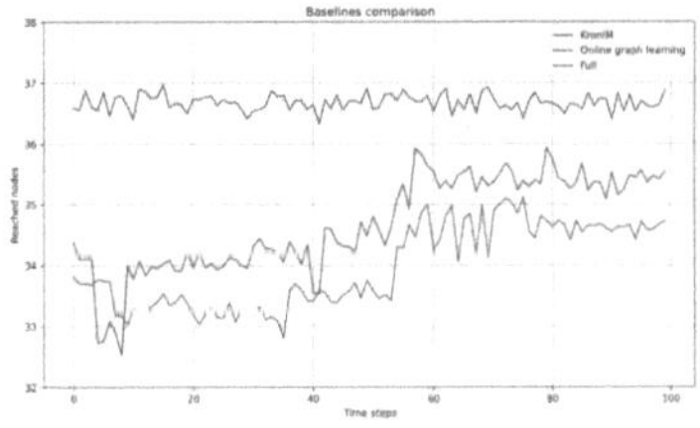


(h) Voterank on FilmTrust Graph
MRE: **0.0546** (KronIM) vs 0.0737 (baseline)

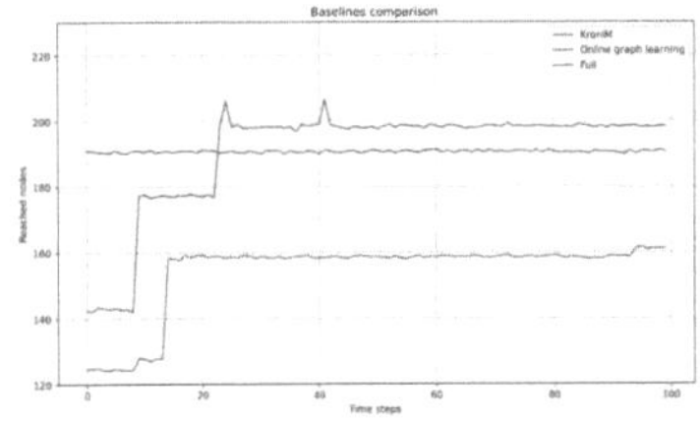


(i) Pagerank on Facebook Graph
MRE: **0.0328** (KronIM) vs 0.1921 (baseline)

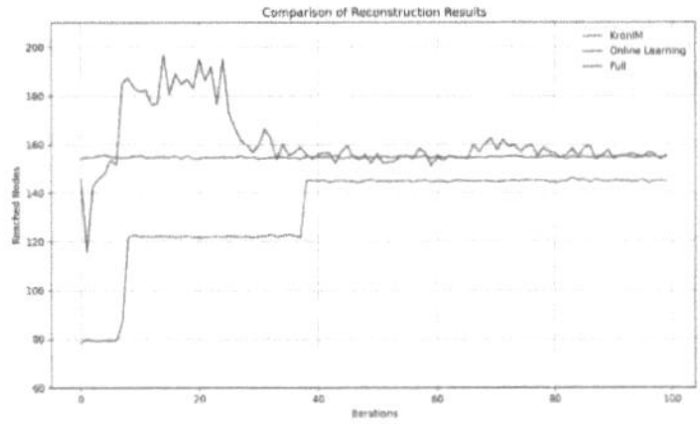


(j) Voterank on Facebook Graph
MRE: **0.0071** (KronIM) vs 0.1423 (baseline)

**Fig. 3.** Baseline comparison on different graphs

motivated mainly by their moderate size, that allows for meaningful results in a limited amount of time, so that multiple experiments can be run.

For each synthetic and real graph, a weight $w_e$ for each edge $e = (u, v)$ is chosen uniformly at random in the interval $[0, 0.1]$. Next, to generate the partially observable known graph, two main techniques, illustrated in [24], have been used:

*Results.* Below, we present the results obtained using PageRank and VoteRank for seed selection and random node selection as sampling technique to generate the partial graph. In this specific setting, our framework reduces the Mean Relative Error (MRE) of the baseline without reconstruction by approximately 50%, achieving an average approximation of approximately 90% to the ideal full-knowledge case. Other combinations of seed selection and sampling technique will show comparable results. Figure 3 highlights how our framework outperforms the baseline over the different graph structures on which it has been tested.

Results about the Facebook graph turn out to be even more interesting. Indeed, on this network, our framework is able to obtain even better results than simply applying heuristics on the completely observable graph.

## 6 Conclusions

The main contribution of this work is to introduce a framework to improve influence maximization performance when the network is only partially observable, that uses graph reconstruction tools. The performed experimental validation provided us very positive feedback on the proposed framework, by showing that the graph reconstruction effectively improves the performance of the influence maximization algorithm.

We acknowledge that our experiments are very preliminary, and that more detailed experiments should be done by considering, e.g., different graph topologies, different seed selection algorithms, different independent cascade probabilities, different filtering strategies for virtual seed selection, or different devirtualization approaches. Moreover, it would also be necessary to highlight how robust our framework is when embedded in environments returning weaker feedback. What happens, for example, when edge probabilities are not revealed and they are just estimated or they must be learned?

## References

1. Adamic, L.A., Adar, E.: Friends and neighbors on the web. Soc. Netw. **25**(3), 211–230 (2003)
2. Almazaydeh, L., Al Tawil, A., Shaban, A., Al-Qudah, R.: Heuristic centrality methods challenge greedy optimization in influence maximization. Sci. Rep. (2026)
3. Auletta, V., Carbone, F., Ferraioli, D.: Election manipulation in social networks with single-peaked agents. In: International Conference of the Italian Association for Artificial Intelligence, pp. 467–480. Springer (2023)

4. Auletta, V., Carbone, F., Ferraioli, D., Vinci, C.: Adaptive multi-round influence maximization with limited information. In: Dima, C., Ferrando, A., Malvone, V. (eds.) PRIMA 2025: Principles and Practice of Multi-Agent Systems. PRIMA 2025. LNCS, vol. 16366, pp. 187–204. Springer, Cham (2026). https://doi.org/10.1007/978-3-032-13562-9_14
5. Auletta, V., Ferraioli, D., Ferrara, G.: Influence maximization in unknown social networks: a contextual bandit approach. In: Dima, C., Ferrando, A., Malvone, V. (eds.) PRIMA 2025: Principles and Practice of Multi-Agent Systems. PRIMA 2025. LNCS, vol. 16366, pp. 224–231. Springer, Cham (2026). https://doi.org/10.1007/978-3-032-13562-9_14
6. Bollobás, B.: A probabilistic proof of an asymptotic formula for the number of labelled regular graphs. Eur. J. Comb. **1**(4), 311–316 (1980)
7. Castiglioni, M., Ferraioli, D., Gatti, N., Landriani, G.: Election manipulation on social networks: seeding, edge removal, edge addition. J. Artif. Intell. Res. **71**, 1049–1090 (2021)
8. Chen, W., Lin, T., Tan, Z., Zhao, M., Zhou, X.: Robust influence maximization. In: Proceedings of the 22nd ACM SIGKDD International Conference on Knowledge Discovery and Data Mining, pp. 795–804 (2016)
9. Dey, R., Jelveh, Z., Ross, K.: Facebook users have become much more private: a large-scale study. In: IEEE PerCom, pp. 346–352(2012)
10. Domingos, P., Richardson, M.: Mining the network value of customers. In: KDD, pp. 57–66 (2001)
11. Goyal, A., Lu, W., Lakshmanan, L.V.: Celf++ optimizing the greedy algorithm for influence maximization in social networks. In: WWW, pp. 47–48 (2011)
12. Grover, A., Leskovec, J.: Node2vec: scalable feature learning for networks. In: Proceedings of the 22nd ACM SIGKDD International Conference on Knowledge Discovery and Data Mining, pp. 855–864 (2016)
13. Howard, P.N., Duffy, A., Freelon, D., Hussain, M.M., Mari, W., Maziad, M.: Opening closed regimes: what was the role of social media during the arab spring? Available at SSRN, p. 2595096 (2011)
14. Hughes, A.L., Palen, L.: Twitter adoption and use in mass convergence and emergency events. Int. J. Emergency Manag. **6**(3–4), 248–260 (2009)
15. Iacob, A., Cautis, B., Maniu, S.: Contextual bandits for advertising campaigns: a diffusion-model independent approach. In: Proceedings of the 2022 SIAM International Conference on Data Mining (SDM), pp. 513–521. SIAM (2022)
16. Kamarthi, H., Vijayan, P., Wilder, B., Ravindran, B., Tambe, M.: Influence maximization in unknown social networks: learning policies for effective graph sampling. In: Proceedings of the 19th International Conference on Autonomous Agents and MultiAgent Systems, pp. 575–583 (2020)
17. Kempe, D., Kleinberg, J., Tardos, É.: Maximizing the spread of influence through a social network. In: KDD, pp. 137–146 (2003)
18. Kim, M., Leskovec, J.: The network completion problem: inferring missing nodes and edges in networks. In: Proceedings of the 2011 SIAM International Conference on Data Mining, pp. 47–58. SIAM (2011)
19. Kossinets, G.: Effects of missing data in social networks. Soc. Netw. **28**(3), 247–268 (2006)
20. Kunegis, J.: Konect: the koblenz network collection. In: WWW, pp. 1343–1350 (2013)
21. Lagrée, P., Cappé, O., Cautis, B., Maniu, S.: Algorithms for online influencer marketing. ACM Trans. Knowl. Discov. Data (TKDD) **13**(1), 1–30 (2018)

22. Leskovec, J., Adamic, L.A., Huberman, B.A.: The dynamics of viral marketing. ACM Trans. Web (TWEB) **1**(1), 5–es (2007)
23. Leskovec, J., Chakrabarti, D., Kleinberg, J., Faloutsos, C., Ghahramani, Z.: Kronecker graphs: an approach to modeling networks. J. Mach. Learn. Res. **11**(2) (2010)
24. Leskovec, J., Faloutsos, C.: Sampling from large graphs. In: KDD, pp. 631–636 (2006)
25. Leskovec, J., Krause, A., Guestrin, C., Faloutsos, C., VanBriesen, J., Glance, N.: Cost-effective outbreak detection in networks. In: KDD, pp. 420–429 (2007)
26. Leskovec, J., Chakrabarti, D., Kleinberg, J., Faloutsos, C.: Realistic, mathematically tractable graph generation and evolution, using kronecker multiplication. In: ECML PKDD, pp. 133–145 (2005)
27. Piva, G.G., Ribeiro, F.L., Mata, A.S.: Networks with growth and preferential attachment: modelling and applications. J. Complex Netw. **9**(1), cnab008 (2021)
28. Seyfosadat, S.F., Ravanmehr, R.: Systematic literature review on identifying influencers in social networks. Artif. Intell. Rev. **56**(Suppl 1), 567–660 (2023)
29. Tang, Y., Shi, Y., Xiao, X.: Influence maximization in near-linear time: a martingale approach. In: SIGMOD, pp. 1539–1554 (2015)
30. Tang, Y., Xiao, X., Shi, Y.: Influence maximization: near-optimal time complexity meets practical efficiency. In: SIGMOD, pp. 75–86 (2014)
31. Tran, C., Shin, W.Y., Spitz, A.: Community detection in partially observable social networks. ACM Trans. Knowl. Discov. Data (TKDD) **16**(2), 1–24 (2021)
32. Tran, C., Shin, W.Y., Spitz, A.: Im-meta: influence maximization using node metadata in networks with unknown topology. IEEE Trans. Netw. Sci. Eng. **11**(3), 3148–3160 (2024)
33. Tran, C., Shin, W.Y., Spitz, A., Gertz, M.: Deepnc: deep generative network completion. IEEE Trans. Pattern Anal. Mach. Intell. **44**(4), 1837–1852 (2020)
34. Valente, T.W., Pumpuang, P.: Identifying opinion leaders to promote behavior change. Health Educ. Behav. **34**(6), 881–896 (2007)
35. Vaswani, S., Kveton, B., Wen, Z., Ghavamzadeh, M., Lakshmanan, L.V., Schmidt, M.: Model-independent online learning for influence maximization. In: International Conference on Machine Learning, pp. 3530–3539. PMLR (2017)
36. Watts, D.J., Strogatz, S.H.: Collective dynamics of 'small-world' networks. Nature **393**(6684), 440–442 (1998)
37. Wilder, B., et al.: End-to-end influence maximization in the field. In: AAMAS, pp. 1414–1422 (2018)
38. Yang, J., Leskovec, J.: Community-affiliation graph model for overlapping network community detection. In: IEEE 12th International Conference on Data Mining, pp. 1170–1175. IEEE (2012)

# Declarative Verification of Binary Neural Networks

Damiano Azzolini(✉) and Riccardo Zese

University of Ferrara, Ferrara, Italy
{damiano.azzolini,riccardo.zese}@unife.com

**Abstract.** Neural Networks (NNs) have seen a tremendous spike in interest in recent decades due to the availability of efficient hardware, which has allowed practitioners to obtain impressive results across many research areas. However, the lack of interpretability of such models represents a weakness in tasks where requirements on the obtained results are needed. Thus, many researchers started investigating the field of NN verification, i.e., checking whether a NN satisfies certain properties. In this paper, we propose an answer set programming (ASP) encoding for convolutional and fully connected layers, together with three different properties. We run an experimental evaluation on binary NNs (BNNs, i.e., with binary weights and step activation function) of three different sizes to assess our approach. Overall, ASP can be considered a viable tool for BNN verification.

**Keywords:** Neural Network Verification · Answer Set Programming · Logic

## 1 Introduction

Neural Networks (NNs) [29] are state-of-the-art machine learning algorithms, with surprising accomplishments in many research areas. Despite their tremendous success, NNs lack interpretability. As a result, the field of NN verification has expanded greatly in the last decade [1,32,37]. The goal is to prove certain properties of the network under consideration. For example, one may be interested in computing the minimum number of pixels in an image to corrupt such that the classification produced by an NN changes [46], or reducing the size of the network but preserving the same outputs [35]. Many such properties require the exploration of a large solution space to compute the optimal solution.

Answer set programming (ASP) [13] is a logic-based language which excels at solving combinatorial problems and has been successfully adopted to solve a variety of tasks in many research areas [8,9,11,22,24,25]. Given the success of ASP, in this paper, we propose an ASP encoding for the fully-connected and convolutional layers. Then, we focus on binary NNs (whose weights and output are binary) and discuss three properties, namely robustness, reducibility, and compression. Lastly, we conduct an experimental evaluation on three networks


S. Bistarelli et al. (Eds.): AIxIA 2026, LNAI 17131, pp. 57–72, 2027.
https://doi.org/10.1007/978-3-032-40774-0_5

of increasing size. Overall, ASP confirms itself as an expressive and effective language for addressing NN verification.

The paper is structured as follows: Sect. 2 introduces the background on ASP and NN, Sect. 3 presents ASP encodings for fully connected and convolutional layers, Sect. 4 describes the properties considered and their ASP representation, Sect. 5 discusses the experimental evaluation, Sect. 6 surveys related work, and Sect. 7 concludes the paper.

# 2 Background

## 2.1 Answer Set Programming

Here, we focus only on the concepts used in this work. For a complete treatment, see, e.g., [15] for the syntax and [14,15,23,28] for the semantics.

*Syntax.* A *literal* $l$ is an atom $a$ or its negation (as failure) *not* $a$. Variables are denoted by uppercase letters (or _ for the *anonymous* variable) while constants are denoted by lowercase letters and numbers. We also consider *tuples* of the form $(a_0, \ldots, a_n)$ where each $a_i$ is an atom. The notation $a..b$ with $a, b \in \mathbb{N}, a < b$ denotes an interval and is expanded to every number $k \in [a, b]$. For example, $a(1..3)$ is expanded into $a(1)$, $a(2)$, and $a(3)$. An *aggregate literal* (aggregate, for short) is of the form $\#\{w_1 : a_1, \ldots, w_n : a_n\} \odot k$ where each $a_i$ is an atom, each $w_i$ is an integer, $k$ is an integer, and $\odot \in \{<, >, \leq, \geq, =, \neq\}$. Variables appearing only in aggregate literals are called *local*. A variable is *global* if it appears in at least one literal not involved in aggregation.

A *normal rule* $r$ is of the form $h \text{ :- } l_1, \ldots, l_n$ where $h$ is the *head* atom and the $l_i$s are *literals* (possibly aggregates) whose conjunction denotes the *body* (denoted with $B(r)$). A *constraint* is a rule with an empty head. A *fact* is a rule without body. A choice element $E$ is of the form $a : l_1, \ldots, l_n$ where $a$ is an atom and the $l_i$s are literals. Sometimes, the conjunction of literals can be omitted. A *choice atom* is of the form $\{E\}$ where $E$ is a choice element. Choice atoms are syntactic shortcuts that can be rewritten as normal rules. A *weak constraint* is an expression of the form $:\sim l_1, \ldots, l_n.[w@l, T]$ where each $l_i$ is a literal, $w$ is a term, and $T$ is a (possibly empty, and in this case is omitted) tuple of terms. With the notation *name/arity* we denote the atom (resp. head rule) with name *name* and arity (i.e., number of arguments) *arity*. We consider an answer set program (ASP, and we will use the same acronym to denote Answer Set Programming) as a finite set of normal rules and weak constraints.

*Example 1.* The following ASP contains some of the syntactical constructs presented above. Rules $r1/1$ and $r3/1$ have an aggregate with only local variables in the body, while rule $r2/1$ has an aggregate with a global variable.

```
a(1). a(2). {a(3)}. b(1,2). b(1,3). c((1,2)).
r0:- a(2).
r1(X):- X = #count{V : a(V)}.
r2(X):- a(Z), X = #count{V : b(Z,V)}.
r3(X):- X = #count{V : b(V,_)}.
```

*Semantics.* A program is *ground* if none of its rules contains variables. The grounding of a rule is obtained by replacing variables with constants in all possible ways. When global variables are involved, first, these are replaced with ground terms, then, local variables are expanded. An interpretation $I$ is a set of atoms. An atom (resp. literal) $a$ (resp. *not* $a$) is true in $I$ (denoted with $I \models a$) if $a \in I$ (resp. $a \notin I$). For an aggregate $A$, $I \models A$ if $(\sum_{i=1,\ldots,n \,\wedge\, I \models a_i} w_i) \odot k$. $I \models l_1, \ldots, l_n$ if, $\forall l_i$, $I \models l_i$. For a rule $r$ with head atom $h$, $I \models r$ if $h \in I$ and $I \models B(r)$. The semantics of ASP is based on the concept of *stable model* which, in turn, is based on the *reduct*. The reduct of a ground ASP $P$ w.r.t. an interpretation $I$, denoted with $P^I$, is obtained by removing from $P$ each rule $r$ such that $I \not\models B(r)$ and by replacing negative literals with their truth value w.r.t. $I$. $I$ is a *stable model* (also called *answer set*) of $P$ if $I \models P^I$ and is *minimal*, i.e., $\nexists J \subset I \mid J \models P^I$. The cost of an answer set $M$ is computed as $\sum_{(w,T) \in W} w$, where $W = \{(w,T) \mid :\sim b_1, \ldots, b_n, [w,T] \in P$, $w$ is a numeric constant, and $M \models b_1, \ldots, b_n\}$. An answer set is *optimal* if there are no other answer sets with lower cost.

*Example 2.* Example 1 has 2 answer sets, $M_0$ and $M_1$. Both contain the atoms $M = \{a(1), a(2), r0, b(1,2), b(1,3), r2(2), r2(0), r3(1), c((1,2))\}$. $M_0 = M \cup \{r1(2)\}$ and $M_1 = M \cup \{a(3), r1(3)\}$. If we add the weak constraint $:\sim r1(X).[X@1, X]$, $M_0$ has cost 2 while $M_1$ has cost 3, so only $M_0$ is optimal.

### 2.2 Neural Networks

In recent decades, Neural Networks (NNs) have become one of the most successful approaches to handle classification problems. This is mainly due to their ability to capture and represent complex relationships among the entities to be classified. The idea of NNs originally emerged from the attempt to mimic the behaviour of biological neurons and their interactions in the human brain. The first theoretical foundations were introduced by [39] and later led to the development of the first NN model, the Perceptron [44].

In general, an NN consists of a set of processing units, called *neurons*, arranged into layers. The input data are multiplied by a *weight matrix* and fed into the neurons of the first layer, which apply an *activation function* to produce an output. This output can be interpreted as a measure of the neuron's activation level. The same procedure is then applied iteratively across subsequent layers until the output layer is reached. The final layer produces a probability distribution over the target classes. More formally, given an input vector $x \in \mathbb{R}^d$, a fully connected layer computes $h = \sigma(Wx + b)$ where $W$ is a weight matrix, $b$ is a bias vector, and $\sigma(\cdot)$ is an activation function such as ReLU (i.e., $\text{ReLU}(x) = max(0, x)$). This architecture is commonly referred to as a Fully Connected (Deep) Neural Network, Artificial Neural Network, or Multilayer Perceptron. During training, this distribution is used to compute a *loss function* that quantifies the discrepancy between the predicted output and the true label. The network parameters are then updated accordingly.

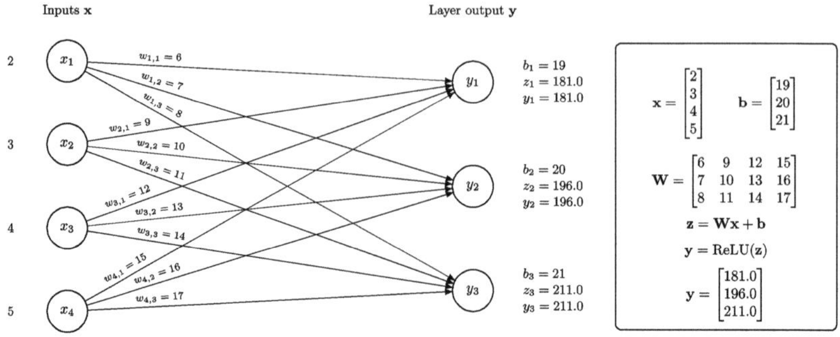


**Fig. 1.** Computation of the output of a fully connected layer.

*Example 3 (Fully-connected layer example).* Let us consider a fully connected layer containing 3 neurons and taking input from 4 neurons. Thus, it has a weight matrix $W \in \mathbb{R}^{3\times 4}$ and an activation function $\sigma = \text{ReLU}$. Figure 1 illustrates the computation of the values for the output layer.

Over time, NNs have also been extended to more advanced and structurally different models. Among these, Convolutional Neural Networks (CNNs) [36] have gained significant attention for tasks involving data with spatial and/or topological structure. In particular, they are designed to process inputs with a grid-like organization, such as images and time series. CNNs are composed of *convolutional layers* that apply convolution operations to the input in order to extract relevant features, typically followed by fully connected layers that perform classification using the extracted representations rather than the raw input.

The convolution between two functions $x$ and $w$ is denoted by $x * w$, where $x$ represents the input and $w$ the *kernel* (also known as *filter*). The result of the operation is commonly called a *feature map* (or simply a feature). A convolutional layer computes feature maps by sliding a kernel over the input and performing the weighted sum $y_{i,j} = \sigma\left(\sum_{u,v} K_{u,v} \cdot x_{i+u,j+v} + b\right)$ where $K$ represents the convolution kernel, and $(i, j)$ indexes spatial positions. The step size of this process is called *stride.* In practice, both the input and the kernel are typically tensors, i.e., multidimensional arrays, such as the 2D pixel grid of an image. The outcome of a convolution corresponds to the features extracted from the input data. Such representations are useful for classification and for detecting patterns in the data, largely independently of their position or scale. Finally, the last layers of a CNN are typically standard fully connected layers that carry out classification based on the extracted features. For this reason, a CNN can be viewed as composed of two main sub-networks: the first one performs feature extraction through convolutional operations, while the second one is a fully connected network that maps these features to the final class predictions.

*Example 4 (Convolutional layer example).* Consider a convolutional layer taking as input an image of size $3 \times 3$ with 2 channels, thus $X \in \mathbb{R}^{3\times 3\times 2}$. The layer has

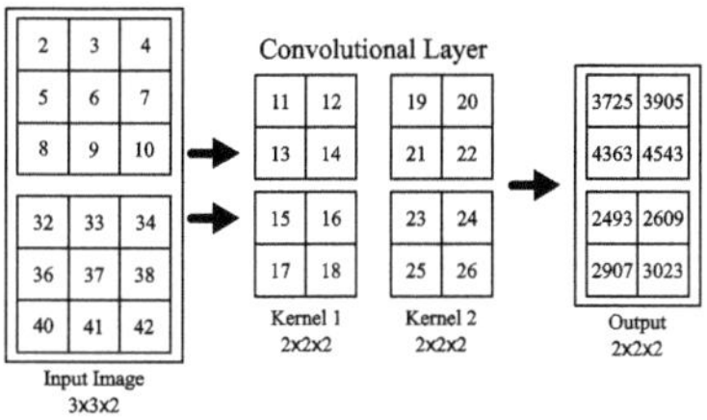


**Fig. 2.** Computation of the output of a convolutional layer.

two kernels of size $2 \times 2$, each spanning the two input channels, i.e., $K^{(1)}, K^{(2)} \in \mathbb{R}^{2\times2\times2}$. The output has size $2 \times 2$ and two channels, hence $Y \in \mathbb{R}^{2\times2\times2}$.

For each output channel $m \in \{1,2\}$ and spatial position $(i,j) \in \{1,2\} \times \{1,2\}$, the output is computed as $Y_{i,j,m} = \sigma\left(\sum_{c=1}^{2} \sum_{u=1}^{2} \sum_{v=1}^{2} K^{(m)}_{u,v,c}\right.$ $X_{i+u-1,j+v-1,c} + b_m)$ where $\sigma$ is the activation function (e.g., $\sigma$ = ReLU) and $b_m$ is the bias associated with kernel $m$. Figure 2 illustrates the computation of this convolutional layer.

Binary Neural Networks (BNNs) [48] are a special type of NN that operate on binary values. More precisely, a BNN is a function $f : \mathbb{N}^m \rightarrow \mathbb{N}^n$ where each layer considers as input tensor $\mathbf{x} \in \{0,1\}^m$, as output tensor $\mathbf{y} \in \{-1,1\}^n$, as weight matrix $\mathbf{w} \in \{-1,1\}^{m\times n}$, and as bias vector $\mathbf{b} \in \mathbb{Z}^n$, and maps $\mathbf{x} \mapsto \mathbf{y}$ as $\mathbf{y} = sign(\mathbf{w}^\top \mathbf{x} + \mathbf{b})$. That is, the output $y$ of a neuron is

$$y = \begin{cases} +1 \text{ if } \sum_{i=1}^{m} w_i x_i + b \geq 0 \\ -1 \text{ otherwise} \end{cases} \tag{1}$$

## 3 Convolutional and Fully Connected Layers Encodings

In this section, we propose ASP encodings for fully connected layers (Sect. 3.1) and convolutional layers (Sect. 3.2). As the summations involved in the different layers are recursive, the use of *recursive aggregates* [3] makes such encodings very compact and interpretable. We use atoms with the signature $w$(*LayerFrom*, *NodeFrom*, *LayerTo*, *NodeTo*, *Weight*) to denote the entry (*Weight*) at position [*NodeFrom*, *NodeTo*] in the weight matrix [*LayerFrom*, *LayerTo*].

### 3.1 Fully Connected Layer

The following snippet describes a fully connected layer:

```
output_fc(Layer,Node,Weight):-
    layer(Layer), Node = 0..n,
    K = #sum{ W, NF :
        w(Prev,NF,Layer,Node,WeightPrev),
        output(Prev,NF,Output),
```

```
        W = Output*WeightPrev },
    w(-1,-1,Layer,Node,Bias), Weight = K+Bias.
```

where *layer*/1 denotes the id of the current layer, $n$ is the number of nodes in the current layer, $output(L, N, O)$ represents the output $O$ of the node $N$ of the layer $L$, and -1 in the first two arguments of $w/5$ (i.e., *NodeFrom* and *NodeTo*) denote the bias value. To encode a step activation function (e.g., Eq. 1), we can add a line to *output_fc*/3 with $Weight \geq 0$ and replace the argument *Weight* with 1. For the case $< 0$, we can add another rule with *not output_fc*(*Layer*, *Node*, *1*) in the body instead of the aggregate and -1 instead of the *Weight* argument.

*Example 5.* Consider the fully connected layer with $n = 3$ of Example 3 modelled by the following atoms, together with $layer(4)$,

```
output(3,0,2). output(3,1,3). output(3,2,4). output(3,3,5).
w(3,0,4,0,6). w(3,1,4,0,9). w(3,2,4,0,12). w(3,3,4,0,15).
w(3,0,4,1,7). w(3,1,4,1,10). w(3,2,4,1,13). w(3,3,4,1,16).
w(3,0,4,2,8). w(3,1,4,2,11). w(3,2,4,2,14). w(3,3,4,2,17).
w(-1,-1,4,0,19). w(-1,-1,4,1,20). w(-1,-1,4,2,21).
```

By considering the previous encoding of *output_fc*/3, we obtain the following atoms in the answer set $\{output\_fc(4,0,181), output\_fc(4,1,196), output\_fc(4,2,211)\}$.

### 3.2 Convolutional Layer

Recall that a convolutional layer is defined by: 1) the number of filters $N$, denoted with the signature *n_filters*(*Layer*, $N$); 2) the stride $S$, denoted with the signature *stride*(*Layer*, $S$); 3) the kernel size $K$, denoted with the signature *kernel_size*(*Layer*, $K$) (we assume a squared kernel; non-squared can be similarly modelled); and 4) the input size $(X, Y)$, denoted with the signature *input_size*(*Layer*, $(X, Y)$). Then, we use the signature *kernel*(*Layer*, *Filter*, (*Channel*, $X$, $Y$), *Weight*) to specify weights.

The following snippet describes a convolutional layer:

```
output_conv(Layer, Filter, (X0,Y0), Value):-
    layer(Layer), Prev = Layer - 1, n_filters(Layer,NF),
    Filter = 0..NF-1, in_size(Layer,(SX,SY)), stride(Layer,
        S),
    kernel_size(Layer,KS), StepX = 0..((SX-KS)/S),
    StepY = 0..((SY-KS)/S), X = StepX*S, Y = StepY*S,
    #sum{ W, KX, KY, K, V, CH :
        kernel(Prev, Filter, (CH,KX,KY), K),
        output_conv(Prev, CH, (KX + X, KY + Y), V),
        W = K*V } = Value.
```

The input size (*input_size*/2) for a layer $L$ can be computed as

```
in_size(L,(S,S)):- layer(L), Prev = L-1,
    S = #count{X : output_conv(Prev, _, (X,_), _)}.
```

by assuming squared output. This can be easily extended to non-squared outputs by adding another aggregate in the body counting the number of $Y$s. As for the fully connected layer, the step activation function can be easily simulated (see Sect. 3.1).

*Example 6.* Consider the convolutional layer described in Example 4 and modelled by the atoms

```
layer(1). kernel_size(1,2). stride(1,1).
n_filters(1,2). in_size(1,(3,3)).
```

and the outputs (*oc*/4 instead of *output_conv*/4 and *k*/4 instead of *kernel_size*/4, for brevity) of the previous layers and kernel weights represented as

```
oc(0,0,(0,0),2). oc(0,0,(0,1),3). oc(0,0,(0,2),4).
oc(0,0,(1,0),5). oc(0,0,(1,1),6). oc(0,0,(1,2),7).
oc(0,0,(2,0),8). oc(0,0,(2,1),9). oc(0,0,(2,2),10).
oc(0,1,(0,0),32). oc(0,1,(0,1),33). oc(0,1,(0,2),34).
oc(0,1,(1,0),36). oc(0,1,(1,1),37). oc(0,1,(1,2),38).
oc(0,1,(2,0),40). oc(0,1,(2,1),41). oc(0,1,(2,2),42).
k(0,0,(0,0,0),11). k(0,0,(0,0,1),12). k(0,0,(0,1,0),13).
k(0,0,(0,1,1),14). k(0,0,(1,0,0),15). k(0,0,(1,0,1),16).
k(0,0,(1,1,0),17). k(0,0,(1,1,1),18). k(0,1,(0,0,0),19).
k(0,1,(0,0,1),20). k(0,1,(0,1,0),21). k(0,1,(0,1,1),22).
k(0,1,(1,0,0),23). k(0,1,(1,0,1),24). k(0,1,(1,1,0),25).
k(0,1,(1,1,1),26).
```

By considering the *output_conv*/4 (abbreviated with *oc*/4) predicate described above, we obtain the following atoms in the answer set { $oc(1,1,(0,0),3725)$, $oc(1,1,(0,1),3905)$, $oc(1,1,(1,0),4363)$, $oc(1,1,(1,1),4543)$, $oc(1,0,(0,0),2493)$, $oc(1,0,(0,1),2609)$, $oc(1,0,(1,0),2907)$, $oc(1,0,(1,1),3023)$ }.

## 4 Properties and Encodings

In the following, we recall the definitions of different metrics proposed in the literature. We focus on BNNs, i.e., NN with step activation functions and binary output. This allows us to leverage existing ASP solvers. However, note that the encodings of Sect. 3 are general and not limited to values in $\mathbb{Z}$.

### 4.1 Robustness

The instance-based robustness of a BNN w.r.t. an instance $x_i$ is the minimum number of bits of $x_i$ to flip in order to change its classification.

**Definition 1 (Instance-based Robustness [46]).** *Given a BNN* $f : \{-1, 1\}^m \rightarrow \{0, 1\}$ *and an instance* $x_i$*, the robustness of the classification of* $x_i$ *w.r.t.* $f$*,* $f(x_i)$*, is*

$$BNNROB(x_i, f) = \min_{x_j | f(x_j) \neq f(x_i)} ||x_i - x_j||$$

*where* $||a - b||$ *denotes the Hamming distance between the binary strings* $a$ *and* $b$*.*

*ASP Encoding.* We can encode and verify the robustness property via ASP as follows: first, we use the signature *output_/3* to encode the input values (for example, the pixels composing $x_i$). Then, we add

```
{flipped(0, N) : output_(0, N, _)}.
output(0, N, 1):- flipped(0, N), output_(0, N, 0).
output(0, N, 0):- flipped(0, N), output_(0, N, 1).
output(0, N, W):- output_(0, N, W), not flipped(0, N).
:- output(l,0,v).
```

The first line states that each input value can be flipped or not. The next two lines flip the value if *flipped/2* is true. Note that these two can be merged into one rule by using the absolute value, but we keep them separated for clarity. The fourth rule forwards the original input value if flipped is not selected. The constraint imposes that the classification should change, so the output value of the last layer of the network should be different from the real value, where $l$ is the identifier of the last layer and $v$ is the opposite of the expected value. Note that we assume one neuron in the last layer with output either 0 or 1. By adding the following weak constraint

```
:~ flipped(1,N). [1@1,N]
```

it is possible to minimize the number of input bits to flip.

## 4.2 Reducibility

Differently from robustness, the reducibility property requires comparing the output of two different (B)NNs. Informally, given two BNNs, $f_1$ and $f_2$, reducibility asks whether the two can be made equivalent by removing (i.e., set to 0) some weights. This problem is similar to the functional equivalence problem [35,45]. Given a BNN $f$ with weights $w$ and $w' \subseteq w$, we denote $f$ where the weights in $w \cap w'$ are set to 0 as $f|_{w'}$.

**Definition 2.** *Given two NNs* $f_1$ *and* $f_2$ *and an input set* $X$*, the reducibility problem is:*

$$BNNRED(f_1, f_2, X) = \min_{w' \subseteq w | \forall x \in X, f_1|_{w'}(x) = f_2(x)} |w'|.$$

*ASP Encoding.* To encode the reducibility property, we need to add to *output_fc/3* and *output_conv/4* two additional arguments, namely, an id representing the considered network and an id representing the considered image. Then, we should also add two atoms in the body that carry this information. Call them *nn_id/1* and *img_id/1*. Then, also the atoms representing the weights of the network should contain an additional argument, representing the network to which they refer. In the following, let us focus on *output_fc/3* (which is now *output_fc/5*), as the treatment for *output_conv/4* (now *output_conv/6*) is analogous. We use the signature *w_/6* to represent the original weights. The following snippet encodes the desired property:

```
{active(n1,Prev,NF,Layer,Node,Weight) : w_(n1,Prev,NF,Layer
    ,Node,Weight)}.
w(n1,Prev,NF,Layer,Node,Weight):- active(n1,Prev,NF,Layer,
    Node,Weight).
w(n1,Prev,NF,Layer,Node,0):- w_(n1,Prev,NF,Layer,Node,
    Weight), not active(n1,Prev,NF,Layer,Node,Weight).
```

The first line states that a weight may or may not be active. If it is active, then the considered weight is unchanged (second line), otherwise, the considered weight is 0 (third line). In addition to this, we need a set of hard constraint imposing that the output of the network must be a certain value on a given image. For example

```
:-  output(f2,imageId,outLayer,outNode,T0), output(f1,
    imageId,outLayer,outNode,T1), T0 != T1.
```

where the arguments are instantiated as needed. As before, we can add a weak constraint minimizing the number of active weights.

```
:~ active(n1,Prev,NF,Layer,Node,Weight).[1,Prev,NF,Layer,
    Node,Weight]
```

### 4.3 Network Compression

Given a dataset $X$, the network compression task requires minimizing the sum of the absolute values of the weights (i.e., to maximize the number of weights set to 0, inactive), but, at the same time, keeping the classification of the elements in $X$ unchanged. This problem is akin to the bit-flip attack [43] and network pruning [12].

**Definition 3.** *Given a NN $f_1$ and an input set $X$, the network compression problem is:*

$$COMPR(f_1, X) = \min_{w' \subseteq w \mid \forall x \in X, f_1|_{w'}(x) = f_1(x)} \sum_{w_k \subset w'} |w_k|.$$

The ASP encoding is similar to the one of reducibility, where instead of $f_2$ we must consider the original output (so we can also remove the id of the network from *active*/6). However, we need to add a constraint for each layer, imposing that at least one weight per layer survives (otherwise, the NN becomes disconnected). We can do so with:

```
:- #count{Layer,Prev,NF,Node,Weight : active(f1,Prev,NF,
    Layer,Node,Weight)}=0.
```

As before, the version for the convolutional layer is similar (just consider *kernel*/4 instead of *w*/6). Lastly, it is worth mentioning that it is possible with minimal modifications to remove entire neurons (or prefer the removal, via weak constraints), by setting all the incoming and outgoing weights to zero w.r.t. a given neuron.

## 5 Experimental Evaluation

To assess our ASP approach, we considered three network sizes, namely *small*, *medium*, and *large*. All three have input of size $28 \times 28$, two convolutional layers (call them $C_1$ and $C_2$, both with kernel size $3 \times 3$ and stride 2), a flatten layer (transforming a tensor into a vector), and a fully connected layer with 1 output neuron. The difference between the three networks is in the number of output channels of the two convolutional layers: 2 and 2 for both $C_1$ and $C_2$ for *small*, 2 and 4 for $C_1$ and $C_2$, respectively, for *medium*, and 4 and 8 for $C_1$ and $C_2$, respectively, for *large*. Overall, *small* has 127 weights, *medium* has 235 weights, and *large* has 613 weights. In our evaluation, we considered BNNs obtained from the previous three networks as follows. We trained them using Tensorflow and Keras on the MNIST dataset (provided by the same libraries) on images representing 0 and 1. Then, we binarize the weights to $-1$ and 1 and replace the activation functions with the step function (output 1 if input $> 0$, $-1$ otherwise for the convolutional layers and output 1 if input $> 0$, 0 otherwise for the fully-connected layer). Thus, internal layers operate on $\{-1, 1\}$ while the output layer maps the classification to $\{0, 1\}$. The final weights that we considered are for networks that maintain an accuracy greater than 95% after applying the previously described binarization.

The ASP models comprises the encoding of the convolutional layer of Sect. 3.2 and the encoding of the fully-connected layer of Sect. 3.1. For the flatten layer, we manually added rules of the form $output(Layer, Position, Value) :- output(Layer, (X, Y), Value)$, one for each pair $(X, Y)$, where $Value$ is pre-computed from the values considered for $X$ and $Y$. This can also be done in ASP, but we preferred pre-computing the results as 1) it is an operation which does not depend on the considered weights (but only from the size of the input image, which is fixed) and 2) introduces unnecessary overhead on the computation. We considered the first 100 test images from the MNIST dataset as inputs. The experiments were run on a machine with Rocky Linux 9.2 running at 3.7 GHz with a time limit of 1 h for each instance and a memory limit of 64 GB.

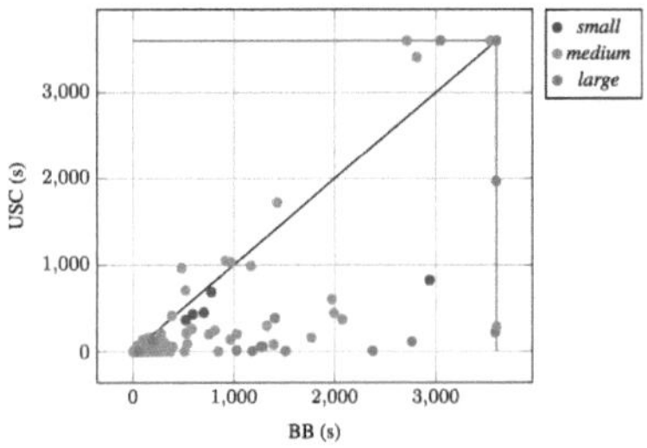


**Fig. 3.** Comparison between BB and USC for the robustness task.

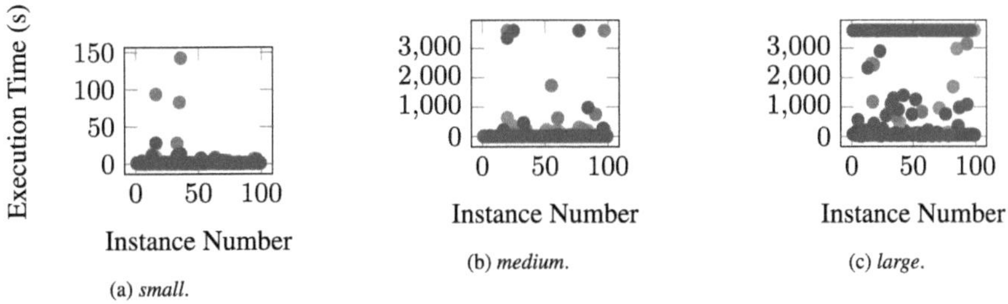


**Fig. 4.** Execution time for the robustness task by fixing to 1, 2, 3, and 4 the number of bits to flip.

We adopted clingo [27] and compared the *model-guided* (BB) [26] and *unsatisfiable core-guided* (USC) [7] algorithms. We also tried WASP [4]. However, we get a warning about possible wrong results due to recursive aggregates, so we did not consider it. Source code and datasets are available at the following link.

### 5.1 Results

**Robustness.** Figure 3 shows a scatter plot that compares the performance of BB and USC on the three networks. Overall, USC outperforms BB for most of the instances. For *small*, most of the points are concentrated close to the origin. For *medium*, both algorithms terminate within approximately 1000 s for the majority of the instances. Lastly, for *large*, only a handful of instances can be solved to the optimum within the time constraints. As, for larger networks, the optimality of the results requires an increasing amount of time and sometimes cannot be proven within the considered time limit, we run an alternative experiment on all three networks where we fixed the number of bits to flip to 1, 2, 3, and 4. To do so, we modified the choice rule of the encoding of Sect. 4.1 and impose a fixed size on the cardinality (for example, $2\{\mathit{flipped}(0, N) : \mathit{output\_}(0, N, \_)\}2$). Figure 4 shows the results. For *small*, most of the instances require a few seconds for all the desired numbers of flips. Among the 4 considered, flipping exactly 3 bits seem to be difficult for some (but few) instances, requiring sometimes more than 100 s. For *medium*, still most of the instances require a few seconds. Here flipping

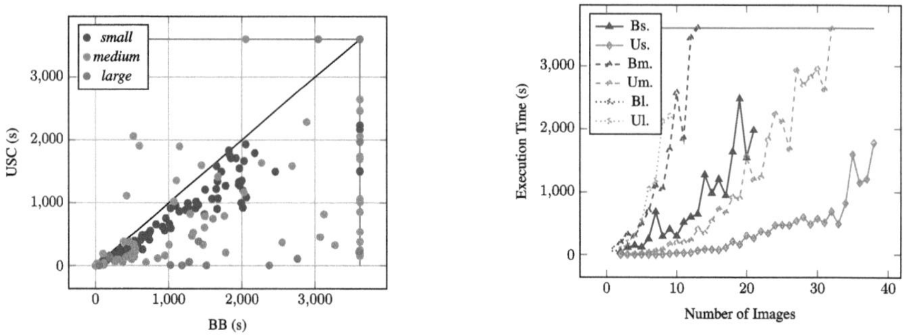


(a) BB vs. USC for the reducibility task.

(b) BB (B) vs USC (U) for the compression task on the three considered network (abbreviated with s, m, and l).

**Fig. 5.** Results on the reducibility and compression task.

exactly 3 and 4 bits seems to be very challenging for some inputs, requiring over 3000 s (but all terminate within the time limit). Lastly, for *large*, most instances still cannot be solved due to time limit. In all the cases, flipping only 1 bit always results in unsatisfiability, which can be quickly proven.

**Reducibility.** For each of the three networks, we iteratively increased the number of images to consider. For the Reducibility task, USC is more effective than BB (Fig. 5a). Overall, with USC on the *small* network, it is possible to consider all 100 images and solve the task in 38 min. For the *medium* network, USC is still better than BB, but it reaches timeout in some configurations. We note that in few cases the experiment considering $n$ images reaches timeout while that of $n+1$ terminates. For *large*, USC can only solve a handful of configurations, but still outperforms BB.

**Compression.** As for reducibility, we iteratively increase the number of images to consider. Also in this case, USC outperforms BB. For the *small* network, USC can consider up to 38 input images within the time limit, while BB stops at 21. A similar trend appears for the *medium*, where USC arrives at 32 while BB stops at 13. Lastly, for the *large* network, BB can solve the task with only 1 input image while USC up to 9.

Overall, USC has been shown to be more effective in addressing NN verification w.r.t. BB. For smaller networks, the global optimum can be found for all instances. When the size of the network increases, finding the optimal solution requires increasing resources and often cannot be computed within the considered time limits. Note that USC outputs only the optimal solution while BB keeps improving the results, so the latter can be used as a starting point to obtain sub-optimal solutions.

## 6 Related Work

There is a huge body of work on NN verification. Here, we focus only on a few of them. A general introduction can be found in [1,32,37]. The authors of [46] propose to evaluate the robustness of a BNN by compiling it into a circuit, leveraging the well-known knowledge compilation approach [18]. Differently, we do not need to compile the NN into an alternative form but rather encode it as an ASP. This also allows for a quick modification of the weights/structure of the network. Unfortunately, that paper does not include a link to the developed system. A similar discussion applies to the work by [40] which converts a NN into a SAT/MILP representation.

The compression task has similarities with pruning [20,31] (i.e., removing parameters to reduce the size of a network) and distillation [30] (i.e., the task of training a small network to mimic a larger one). These can be performed during the training and/or test phase. A survey can be found in [16]. The task we consider in Sect. 4.3 imposes that the classification of some input data should not change, rather than, say, a target accuracy. Furthermore, here we work in the discrete domain. The work in [41] focused on 2-layer fully connected NNs with ReLU activation function and proposed a theoretical framework to study symmetries. The approach discussed in [19] studied the minimal size of a shallow ReLU network to represent certain classes of functions and [42] addressed the functional problem, still at the theoretical level.

Few works considered ASP in the context of NN. The most similar to our approach is [34], where the authors propose an ASP encoding to model NNs. Their encoding is passed to the clingo[LPX] tool, which is an extension of the ASP solver clingo, which integrates a simplex solver. Differently, here we propose an ASP encoding with weak constraints. They focus on the multi layer perceptron only, while we also consider convolutional layers. Lastly, they consider only one type of explanation for NNs while here we discuss multiple ones. The approach of [2] proposes a preferential interpretation of Multilayer Perceptrons and conducts an experimental evaluation using ASP. Differently, in this paper we do not focus on providing interpretations of NN, but rather on verifying properties, also considering convolutional layers. Other approaches consider ASP as the symbolic component of a neuro-symbolic approach [47].

## 7 Conclusion

In this paper, we proposed ASP encodings for the convolutional and fully connected NN layers. Then, we considered three properties, namely robustness, reducibility, and compression, and also provided encodings for these. Lastly, we conducted an experimental evaluation on three BNNs of increasing sizes. The results show the effectiveness of ASP in solving such problems, although it suffers from increasing execution time. As future work, we plan to extend our evaluation to other properties, such as the (shortest) prime-implicant (PI) explanation [46]. However, being PI in $\Sigma_2^{\mathrm{P}}$ [33], it requires advanced ASP techniques such as saturation [17,21] or the adoption of alternative frameworks such as ASP(Q) [6,38]. Furthermore, it could also be interesting to adopt probabilistic ASP [10] to take into account the uncertainty in the output of a network. We conclude by noting that the presented encodings can be used as benchmarks for systems implementing recursive aggregates [3,5], as larger networks can be easily generated.

**Acknowledgments.** DA and RZ are members of the Gruppo Nazionale Calcolo Scientifico – Istituto Nazionale di Alta Matematica (GNCS-INdAM).

**Disclosure of Interests.** The authors have no competing interests to declare that are relevant to the content of this article.

## References

1. Albarghouthi, A.: Introduction to neural network verification. Found. Trends Programm. Lang. **7**(1–2), 1–157 (2021)
2. Alviano, M., Bartoli, F., Botta, M., Esposito, R., Giordano, L., Dupré, D.T.: A preferential interpretation of multilayer perceptrons in a conditional logic with typicality. Int. J. Approx. Reason. **164**, 109065 (2024)
3. Alviano, M., Dodaro, C., Fiorentino, S.: Model checker for recursive aggregates. In: Proceedings of the 22nd International Conference on Principles of Knowledge Representation and Reasoning, pp. 588–598 (2025). https://doi.org/10.24963/kr.2025/57, https://doi.org/10.24963/kr.2025/57
4. Alviano, M., Dodaro, C., Leone, N., Ricca, F.: Advances in WASP. In: Calimeri, F., Ianni, G., Truszczynski, M. (eds.) Logic Programming and Nonmonotonic Reasoning - 13th International Conference, LPNMR 2015, Lexington, KY, USA, September 27-30, 2015. Proceedings. LNCS, vol. 9345, pp. 40–54. Springer, Cham (2015). https://doi.org/10.1007/978-3-319-23264-5_5
5. Alviano, M., Faber, W., Gebser, M.: Rewriting recursive aggregates in answer set programming: back to monotonicity. Theory Pract. Logic Program. **15**(4–5), 559–573 (2015)
6. Amendola, G., Ricca, F., Truszczynski, M.: Beyond NP: quantifying over answer sets. TPLP **19**(5–6), 705–721 (2019). https://doi.org/10.1017/S1471068419000140
7. Andres, B., Kaufmann, B., Matheis, O., Schaub, TUnsatisfiability-based optimization in clasp. In: ICLP (Technical Communications). LIPIcs, vol. 17, pp. 211–221. Schloss Dagstuhl - Leibniz-Zentrum fur Informatik (2012)
8. Azzolini, D., Duca, M., Gallo, F., Ielo, A., Forti, S.: Application placement with constraint relaxation. Theory Pract. Log. Program. **25**(4), 437–454 (2025)
9. Azzolini, D., Forti, S., Ielo, A.: Continuous reasoning for adaptive container image distribution in the cloud-edge continuum. Clust. Comput. **28**(7), 461 (2025). https://doi.org/10.1007/s10586-025-05253-9
10. Azzolini, D., Riguzzi, F.: Probabilistic answer set programming with discrete and continuous random variables. Theory Pract. Log. Program. **25**(1), 1–32 (2025)
11. Baumeister, J., et al.: Towards industrial-scale product configuration. In: Dodaro, C., Gupta, G., Martinez, M.V. (eds.) Logic Programming and Nonmonotonic Reasoning. LPNMR 2024. LNCS, vol. 15245. Springer, Cham (2025). https://doi.org/10.1007/978-3-031-74209-5_6

12. Blalock, D., Gonzalez Ortiz, J.J., Frankle, J., Guttag, J.: What is the state of neural network pruning? Proc. Mach. Learn. Syst. **2**, 129–146 (2020)
13. Brewka, G., Eiter, T., Truszczynski, M.: Answer set programming at a glance. Commun. ACM **54**(12), 92–103 (2011)
14. Buccafurri, F., Leone, N., Rullo, P.: Enhancing disjunctive datalog by constraints. IEEE Trans. Knowl. Data Eng. **12**(5), 845–860 (2000)
15. Calimeri, F., et al.: ASP-Core-2 input language format. Theory Pract. Log. Program. **20**(2), 294–309 (2020)
16. Cheng, H., Zhang, M., Shi, J.Q.: A survey on deep neural network pruning: taxonomy, comparison, analysis, and recommendations. IEEE Trans. Pattern Anal. Mach. Intell. (2024)
17. Dantsin, E., Eiter, T., Gottlob, G., Voronkov, A.: Complexity and expressive power of logic programming. ACM Comput. Surv. **33**(3), 374–425 (2001)
18. Darwiche, A., Marquis, P.: A knowledge compilation map. J. Artif. Intell. Res. **17**, 229–264 (2002). https://doi.org/10.1613/jair.989
19. Dereich, S., Kassing, S.: On minimal representations of shallow relu networks. Neural Netw. **148**, 121–128 (2022)
20. Diffenderfer, J., Kailkhura, B.: Multi-prize lottery ticket hypothesis: Finding accurate binary neural networks by pruning a randomly weighted network (2021). arXiv:2103.09377
21. Eiter, T., Gottlob, G.: On the computational cost of disjunctive logic programming: propositional case. Ann. Math. Artif. Intell. **15**(3–4), 289–323 (1995)
22. Erdem, E., Gelfond, M., Leone, N.: Applications of answer set programming. AI Mag. **37**(3), 53–68 (2016)
23. Faber, W., Pfeifer, G., Leone, N.: Semantics and complexity of recursive aggregates in answer set programming. Artif. Intell. **175**(1), 278–298 (2011). https://doi.org/10.1016/j.artint.2010.04.002
24. Falkner, A.A., Friedrich, G., Schekotihin, K., Taupe, R., Teppan, E.C.: Industrial applications of answer set programming. KI-Künstliche Intelligenz **32**(2–3), 165–176 (2018)
25. Gamblin, T., Culpo, M., Becker, G., Shudler, S.: Using answer set programming for HPC dependency solving. In: SC, pp. 35:1–35:15. IEEE (2022)
26. Gebser, M., Kaminski, R., Kaufmann, B., Schaub, T.: Multi-criteria optimization in answer set programming. In: ICLP Technical Communications, pp. 1–10 (2011)
27. Gebser, M., Kaminski, R., Kaufmann, B., Schaub, T.: Multi-shot ASP solving with clingo. TPLP **19**(1) (2019). https://doi.org/10.1017/S1471068418000054
28. Gelfond, M., Lifschitz, V.: Classical negation in logic programs and disjunctive databases. N. Gener. Comput. **9**(3/4), 365–386 (1991)
29. Goodfellow, I., Bengio, Y., Courville, A.: Deep Learning. MIT Press, Cambridge (2016)
30. Hinton, G., Vinyals, O., Dean, J.: Distilling the knowledge in a neural network (2015). arXiv:1503.02531
31. Hoefler, T., Alistarh, D., Ben-Nun, T., Dryden, N., Peste, A.: Sparsity in deep learning: pruning and growth for efficient inference and training in neural networks. J. Mach. Learn. Res. **22**(241), 1–124 (2021)
32. Huang, X., et al.: A survey of safety and trustworthiness of deep neural networks: verification, testing, adversarial attack and defence, and interpretability. Comput. Sci. Rev. **37**, 100270 (2020)
33. Ignatiev, A., Narodytska, N., Marques-Silva, J.: Abduction-based explanations for machine learning models. In: Proceedings of the AAAI Conference on Artificial Intelligence, vol. 33, pp. 1511–1519 (2019)

34. Kaminski, R., Schaub, T., Romero, J., Razzaq, M.: Explaining artificial neural networks using answer set programming. In: Cerrato, M., Kalinauskaitė, D., Lukoševičius, M., Pechenizkiy, M., Šutienė, K. (eds.) Machine Learning and Principles and Practice of Knowledge Discovery in Databases. ECML PKDD 2024. CCIS, vol. 2559, pp. 3–18. Springer, Cham (2026). https://doi.org/10.1007/978-3-032-25305-7_1
35. Kurkova, V., Kainen, P.C.: Functionally equivalent feedforward neural networks. Neural Comput. **6**(3), 543–558 (1994)
36. LeCun, Y., et al.: Generalization and network design strategies. Connect. Perspect. **19** (1989)
37. Liu, C., Arnon, T., Lazarus, C., Strong, C., Barrett, C., Kochenderfer, M.J.: Algorithms for verifying deep neural networks. Found. Trends Optim. **4**(3-4) (2021). https://doi.org/10.1561/2400000035
38. Mazzotta, G., Ricca, F., Truszczynski, M.: Quantifying over optimum answer sets. TPLP **23**(4), 948–964 (2024). https://doi.org/10.48550/arXiv.2408.07697
39. McCulloch, W.S., Pitts, W.: A logical calculus of the ideas immanent in nervous activity. Bull. Math. Biophys. **5**(4), 115–133 (1943)
40. Narodytska, N., Kasiviswanathan, S., Ryzhyk, L., Sagiv, M., Walsh, T.: Verifying properties of binarized deep neural networks. In: Proceedings of the AAAI Conference on Artificial Intelligence, vol. 32 (2018)
41. Petzka, H., Trimmel, M., Sminchisescu, C.: Notes on the symmetries of 2-layer relu-networks. In: Proceedings of the Northern Lights Deep Learning Workshop, vol. 1, p. 6 (2020)
42. Phuong, M., Lampert, C.H.: Functional vs. parametric equivalence of ReLU networks. In: International Conference on Learning Representations (2020)
43. Rakin, A.S., He, Z., Fan, D.: Bit-flip attack: crushing neural network with progressive bit search. In: Proceedings of the IEEE/CVF International Conference on Computer Vision, pp. 1211–1220 (2019)
44. Rosenblatt, F.: The perceptron: a probabilistic model for information storage and organization in the brain. Psychol. Rev. **65**(6), 386 (1958)
45. Shen, G.: Exploring the complexity of deep neural networks through functional equivalence. In: Proceedings of the 41st International Conference on Machine Learning, pp. 44643–44664 (2024)
46. Shi, W., Shih, A., Darwiche, A., Choi, A.: On tractable representations of binary neural networks. arXiv:2004.02082 (2020)
47. Yang, Z., Ishay, A., Lee, J.: NeurASP: embracing neural networks into answer set programming. In: 29th International Joint Conference on Artificial Intelligence (IJCAI 2020) (2020)
48. Yuan, C., Agaian, S.S.: A comprehensive review of binary neural network. Artif. Intell. Rev. **56**(11), 12949–13013 (2023)

# Collective Decision-Making in Neural Monte Carlo Tree Search for Test Prioritization

Morena Barboni, Filippo Lampa(✉), Andrea Morichetta, and Andrea Polini

University of Camerino, Via Madonna delle Carceri 7, Camerino 62032, Italy
{morena.barboni,filippo.lampa,andrea.morichetta,andrea.polini}@unicam.it

**Abstract.** Neural Monte Carlo Tree Search often expresses exploitation, exploration, and auxiliary search biases through a single scalarized tree policy. This compression is convenient, but it can obscure whether distinct search objectives retain useful behavioral diversity or collapse into the same decision pattern once they share environmental feedback. We investigate this aspect in mutation-based test case prioritization, using ASCENT, an online Neural-MCTS framework, as a sparse-reward sequential benchmark. We replace its monolithic decision policy with a multi-agent committee that separates these search objectives and coordinates through the aggregation of action distributions. Trace analysis across five test-prioritization environments shows that the agents preserve non-redundant policy differentiation over long horizons rather than collapsing into a single strategy. Notably, this behavioral divergence depends on scale, such that small action spaces produce high agreement and larger spaces allow stronger divergence. While basic aggregation operators do not yet yield lower execution costs than the monolithic baseline, this separation creates an explicit, measurable coordination structure through which the interaction among otherwise entangled search objectives can be analyzed.

**Keywords:** Monte Carlo Tree Search · Multi-Agent Systems · Ensemble Decision-Making · Online Learning · Reinforcement Learning · Test Case Prioritization · Mutation Testing

## 1 Introduction

MCTS-based decision systems must decide not only which action currently appears valuable, but also how much search effort to allocate to uncertain, under-visited, or strategically diverse alternatives. In UCT and neural PUCT-style variants, this balance is typically controlled through a scalar exploration coefficient inside a single tree-selection rule [4,14]. While compact, this formulation entangles reward exploitation, visit-based exploration, and additional diversity-seeking heuristics before action selection. As a result, distinct search objectives are forced into a single compromise, and their individual contribution to the resulting search


S. Bistarelli et al. (Eds.): AIxIA 2026, LNAI 17131, pp. 73–86, 2027.
https://doi.org/10.1007/978-3-032-40774-0_6

behavior remains implicit. We study whether this compression can be relaxed by separating search control across specialized agents, using mutation-based test prioritization as a sparse-reward sequential benchmark built on ASCENT [3]. The resulting committee replaces the single decision policy with an Exploiter, an Explorer, and a Diversity agent, each maintaining private policy and search-tree statistics while sharing the same environment trajectory and value estimator. At each decision step, the agents communicate full probability distributions, which an aggregation module combines through arithmetic, geometric, weighted, or ordinal operators to produce the executed action and make role-specific agreement and disagreement observable at the decision boundary.

We evaluate the committee across five smart-contract systems, measuring aggregate performance alongside internal coordination dynamics via symmetric Kullback-Leibler divergence (SKL) and Spearman rank correlation ($\rho$). Tracking agent interactions in this way lays a foundation for a more explainable search process by externalizing intertwined search pressures and making their role-specific preferences, agreement, and disagreement directly measurable. Our core contributions are threefold: (i) we introduce a multi-agent Neural-MCTS architecture that decouples search control into heterogeneous agents with private tree statistics over a shared environment trajectory and value network; (ii) we implement a distributional aggregation interface at the decision boundary, through which complete agent action distributions over the candidate space are combined into a single executed action; and (iii) we provide an empirical characterization under sparse rewards showing that agents maintain distinct, non-converging policies throughout the run across all our test-prioritization environments, with scale-associated agreement patterns, although basic aggregation operators do not translate this behavioral variety into an optimization advantage over a monolithic baseline.

## 2 Background

### 2.1 Neural Monte Carlo Tree Search

Neural-MCTS maps sequential decisions onto a dynamically expanding tree structure evaluated via deep neural networks [14]. In an AlphaZero-style formulation, a dual-headed network $f_\theta(s)$ processes an environment state $s$ to output a policy vector $P(s, \cdot)$ representing prior probabilities over valid actions and a scalar value estimate $V(s)$ representing the expected cumulative reward. The engine runs forward tree simulations from the root using a Polynomial Upper Confidence Bound variant tailored for trees (PUCT) to select actions. Unexpanded leaf nodes are evaluated by $f_\theta$ to initialize child priors, and value estimates are backpropagated to update edge visit counts $N(s, a)$ and mean values $Q(s, a)$. In standard Neural-MCTS, executed actions are ultimately selected based on the finalized root visit distributions.

### 2.2 Distributional Coordination in Ensembles

Multi-agent and ensemble systems commonly aggregate local decisions through consensus averaging, voting, or linear combinations of model outputs [7,8,12]. Such interfaces are simple, but communicating only selected actions or scalar scores can discard the uncertainty structure encoded in full probability vectors, analogous to the information loss from replacing soft targets with hard labels [6]. In this work, we therefore use distributional coordination, where agents communicate complete probability mass functions over valid actions, allowing the distributions to be aggregated while preserving the information needed to measure cross-agent agreement at the decision boundary.

### 2.3 Mutation-Based Test Prioritization

Mutation testing evaluates test suite adequacy by injecting artificial faults (mutants) into the source code and checking whether the tests detect them. Since running the entire test suite against every mutant is expensive, mutation-based test prioritization aims, given a test suite $T$ and a set of mutants $M$, to order tests so that the killing ones are executed as early as possible, reducing the number of unnecessary executions [21]. ASCENT models this sequentially per mutant using online Neural-MCTS [3], where selecting an unexecuted test constitutes an action, and the search tree represents valid orderings without repetition. States are tuples $s = \{k, g, \sigma\}$ containing the current test index, target mutant, and partial test sequence, which is padded to a fixed-size vector $V$ where unexecuted indices are marked as $-1$. The sparse reward $R$ equals the number of test executions saved $(|T| - |\sigma|)$ if the latest test kills the mutant, and 0 otherwise. Rather than running multiple iterations per action, ASCENT preserves online efficiency by executing only a single tree simulation per step. To compensate for this limited budget, the search tree is preserved across mutants instead of being reset between episodes, allowing the framework to function as an online learner where statistics accumulated on earlier mutants directly guide subsequent prioritization decisions. Before networks are fully trained, the approach employs an initial warm-up phase relying on non-neural guidance, specifically, accumulated tree statistics and a kill-ranking heuristic. Once a rollout threshold is surpassed, neural policy and value predictions are integrated into the PUCT selection process. We preserve these environment dynamics and focus exclusively on evaluating committee-based variations within the internal selection mechanics.

## 3 Methodology

The committee separates exploitation, exploration, and diversity into specialized local search processes while preserving a single executed trajectory and a shared value-learning signal. We define the architecture in terms of private agent state, role-specific PUCT scoring, private search with shared execution, and aggregation of agent distributions. Figure 1 outlines the resulting architecture.

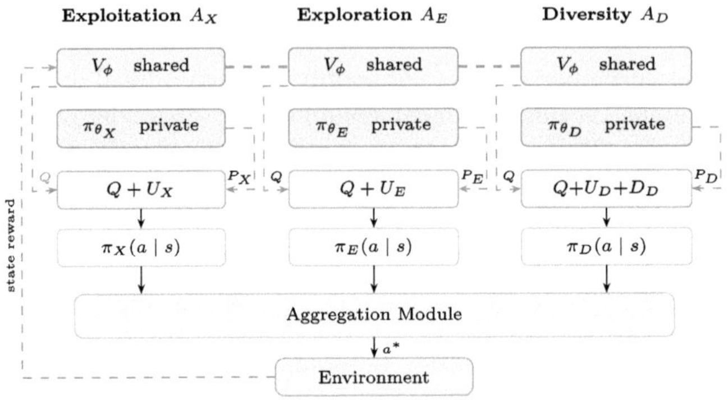


**Fig. 1.** Multi-agent Neural-MCTS committee architecture. Private policies produce agent-specific priors $P_i$, while the shared value network $V_\phi$ supports private action-value estimates $Q_i$. The aggregation module combines the resulting distributions $\pi_i(a \mid s)$ into a single executed action $a^*$.

### 3.1 Committee Architecture

Let $\mathcal{C} = \{A_X, A_E, A_D\}$ denote the committee, representing the Exploitation, Exploration, and Diversity agents, respectively. Each agent is modeled as $A_i = (\pi_{\theta_i}, V_\phi, \mathcal{T}_i)$, where $\pi_{\theta_i}$ is a private policy network, $\mathcal{T}_i$ is a private search tree, and $V_\phi$ is a value network shared across all agents. This partition decouples agent-specific action heuristics from global state estimation, allowing the private policies $\pi_{\theta_i}$ to assign role-specific priors to the same state. Conversely, because the committee operates over a single executed trajectory, all agents observe identical environment transitions and receive identical sequence pairs $(s, R)$. Retaining independent value estimators would replicate the same regression problem without informational gain; sharing $V_\phi$ eliminates this redundancy and limits computational overhead. Within each agent, node selection combines these signals: the shared $V_\phi$ supplies backed-up value estimates to $Q_i(s, a)$ with collective environmental knowledge, while the private $\pi_{\theta_i}$ provides the action prior $P_i(s, a)$ used to modulate the local exploration bonus.

### 3.2 Specialized Search Policies

Each agent performs independent MCTS simulations on its private tree $\mathcal{T}_i$. Let $N_i(s, a)$ be the visit count of edge $(s, a)$ in $\mathcal{T}_i$, $W_i(s, a)$ be the cumulative backed-up reward, and $N_i(s) = \sum_{b \in A(s)} N_i(s, b)$ be the total parent visits for valid actions $A(s)$. We define the smoothed action-value estimate as $Q_i(s, a) = \frac{W_i(s,a)}{1+N_i(s,a)}$ if $N_i(s, a) > 0$, and 0 otherwise, where the unit denominator offset acts as a zero-reward pseudo-count to damp early high-variance estimates. Node selection maximizes a finite PUCT-style score:

$$\mathrm{PUCT}_i(s, a) = Q_i(s, a) + U_i(s, a) + D_i(a), \tag{1}$$

where $D_i(a)$ is an optional diversity term, nonzero only for the Diversity agent. The prior-weighted exploration bonus is defined as

$$U_i(s,a) = c_i P_i(s,a) \frac{\sqrt{N_i(s)}}{1 + N_i(s,a)}, \tag{2}$$

where $c_i$ is the agent-specific exploration coefficient and $P_i(s,a)$ is the action prior. We preserve ASCENT's rollout-delay mechanism in the committee setting to handle untrained network states. Before the rollout threshold, the action prior is uniform, $P_i(s,a) = 1/|A(s)|$, and child expansion follows ASCENT's non-neural kill-ranking heuristic rather than policy network predictions. After the threshold, $P_i(s,a)$ is supplied by the private policy network $\pi_{\theta_i}$. The finite initialization and $1+N_i(s,a)$ denominator are deliberate, so that unvisited edges receive $Q_i(s,a) = 0$ and a bounded exploration bonus, rather than the maximal-priority treatment common in UCT implementations. This avoids forcing all agents through the same unseen actions during early search while damping high-variance early rewards. As private statistics, backed-up values, and diversity counts become non-uniform, the agents can develop differentiated search behavior. Strategic differentiation is controlled via role-specific parameterizations:

- **Exploitation Agent ($A_X$):** Uses a low exploration coefficient to focus search traversals heavily on accumulated rewards $Q_i(s,a)$, setting $D_X(a) = 0$.
- **Exploration Agent ($A_E$):** Uses an amplified exploration coefficient to bias lookahead selection towards low-visit branches, setting $D_E(a) = 0$.
- **Diversity Agent ($A_D$):** Uses a moderate exploration coefficient balancing reward and lookahead exploration, augmented by a session-scoped diversity bonus $D_D(a) = \frac{\delta}{1+f(a)}$, where $f(a)$ tracks the global execution count of test $a$ across all completed mutants and $\delta$ dictates the bonus scale.

### 3.3 Private Search, Shared Execution

During internal MCTS traversals, agents perform private, speculative expansions within their local trees $\mathcal{T}_i$, permitting diverse trajectory rollouts. After the agents complete their private simulations and the aggregation module selects a single action $a^*$, all agents advance their local root nodes to the child corresponding to $a^*$. The finalized trajectory $s_0 \xrightarrow{a_0^*} s_1 \xrightarrow{a_1^*} \ldots$, is shared by all agents, ensuring state alignment and stable value learning while preserving local search autonomy.

### 3.4 Distribution Aggregation

At each environment step, agent $A_i$ maps its local node statistics to a valid action probability distribution $\pi_i(a \mid s) = \mathrm{PUCT}_i(s,a)/\sum_{b \in \mathcal{A}(s)} \mathrm{PUCT}_i(s,b)$ over the remaining test candidates $\mathcal{A}(s)$. If all scores are zero, we fall back to the uniform distribution over $\mathcal{A}(s)$. Normalizing PUCT scores rather than visit counts preserves the current role-specific scoring signal, including the exploration coefficients and diversity bonus, instead of communicating only the accumulated topology of each private search tree. The aggregation module collects the ensemble distributions $\Pi = \{\pi_X, \pi_E, \pi_D\}$ and derives a unified decision using one of four aggregation operators ($m = |\mathcal{C}| = 3$):

- **Arithmetic Mean:** $\pi_C(a) = \frac{1}{m}\sum_{i=1}^{m} \pi_i(a)$, executing a linear combination where individual agents cannot unilaterally veto candidates.
- **Geometric Mean:** $\pi_C(a) = \left(\prod_{i=1}^{m} \pi_i(a)\right)^{1/m}$, where any agent assigning $\pi_i(a) \to 0$ drives $\pi_C(a) \to 0$, providing a soft veto mechanism. Zero probabilities are clipped to a small $\varepsilon$ to prevent unvisited node truncation.
- **Weighted Mean:** $\pi_C(a) = \sum_{i=1}^{m} w_i\, \pi_i(a)$ (where $\sum w_i = 1$), where weights $w_i$ adapt dynamically based on each agent's rolling reward efficiency within the episode context.
- **Borda Count:** An ordinal aggregation rule tracking candidate ranks $r_i(a)$ where lower ranks indicate higher preference. The Borda score is $B(a) = \sum_{i=1}^{m} r_i(a)$, selecting action $a^* = \arg\min_a B(a)$. This is robust to distributional scale differences but discards raw probability magnitudes.

For the continuous aggregators, the final executed action is $a^* = \arg\max_a \pi_C(a)$. Notably, rather than aggregating only after the full search completes, aggregation occurs after the agents' private simulations at every decision step, yielding the single action executed in the shared trajectory.

## 4 Evaluation

The work is implemented in a dedicated branch of the ASCENT [3] framework to ensure that the test environment, action spaces, and mutant distributions remain identical to those of the original implementation. The implementation and experimental configurations are publicly available on GitHub[1].

### 4.1 Experimental Configuration

Our approach was evaluated across five combinatorial optimization environments derived from open-source smart contracts: *BakerFi*, *Quadrata*, *SecondSwap*, *NextGeneration* (*NextGen*), and *THORWallet*. All experiments were executed on an NVIDIA A100 PCIe GPU with 40 GB of memory. To isolate the algorithmic impact of the committee design, all deep architectures, layer configurations, and training parameters preserve ASCENT defaults. We enforce a rollout threshold of 45 episodes to warm up the system before the neural policy and value networks replace the uniform action prior. To adapt to new mutant characteristics in real time, networks are updated after every episode (update delta $\Delta = 1$) by sampling batches of 40 experiences from a replay buffer whose maximum size matches the mutant set cardinality $|M|$ (storing one experience per mutant). Gradients are

[1] https://github.com/filippo-lampa/ASCENT/tree/multi-agent-prioritization.

computed independently for sampled experiences rather than in a single aggregate batch update, preserving network plasticity [11]. Both the policy and value components utilize single-hidden-layer feedforward neural networks with ReLU activations, optimized via the Adam optimizer. Each private policy network $\pi_{\theta_i}$ is trained independently at a learning rate of $10^{-4}$ using cross-entropy loss augmented by a 0.5 label smoothing factor. The shared value network $V_\phi$ is trained at a learning rate of $10^{-3}$ using an asymmetric mean squared error loss $\mathcal{L}_V = \frac{1}{N}\sum_{n=1}^{N} \alpha(y_n - \hat{y}_n)^2$ if $y_n < \hat{y}_n$ and $(y_n - \hat{y}_n)^2$ otherwise, where the penalty factor is set to $\alpha = 6.0$ to penalize value underestimations more heavily than overestimations, counteracting the sparse reward imbalance caused by surviving mutants. Individual committee agents use static, role-specific exploration coefficients: the Exploitation agent ($A_X$) uses $c_X = 0.5$, the Exploration agent ($A_E$) uses $c_E = 3.0$, and the Diversity agent ($A_D$) uses $c_D = 2.0$, augmented by an inverse-frequency session-wide diversity bonus with scale $\delta = 1.0$. We run five independent trials for each configuration to account for algorithmic stochasticity.

### 4.2 Results and Analysis

We evaluate the committee in terms of prioritization effectiveness and agent coordination. Effectiveness is measured by total tests executed on killable mutants and by mean tests-to-kill (TTK). Coordination is measured by symmetric Kullback-Leibler divergence, Spearman rank correlation, and agreement categories. Agreement is *full* if all agents rank the selected test first; *soft* if all place it in their top three but not all rank it first; *partial* if only some place it in their top three; and *none* otherwise. For two agents $A_i$ and $A_j$, step-level distributional separation is

$$\mathrm{SKL}_{ij}^t = \frac{1}{2}\left[\mathrm{KL}(\pi_i^t \,\|\, \pi_j^t) + \mathrm{KL}(\pi_j^t \,\|\, \pi_i^t)\right],$$

with probabilities restricted to the valid action set $A(s_t)$. Zero probabilities are clipped to a small $\varepsilon$ before computing SKL. Ordinal agreement is measured by Spearman's rank correlation $\rho_{ij}^t \in [-1, 1]$ between the rankings induced by $\pi_i^t$ and $\pi_j^t$. Table 2 reports, for each project and aggregation operator, the mean pairwise SKL and mean pairwise $\rho$ over the three agent pairs $\{(X,E),(X,D),(E,D)\}$, averaged over decision steps and independent trials. SKL and $\rho$ are complementary metrics, with SKL capturing distributional separation and $\rho$ capturing ordinal agreement between ranked test preferences.

### 4.3 Prioritization Performance

Table 1 shows that the best committee configuration reduces total test executions on killable mutants relative to random ordering across all systems, with reductions ranging from 33.9% on *NextGen* to 52.9% on *SecondSwap*. However, none of the committee variants outperforms monolithic ASCENT: the smallest gap occurs on *Quadrata* and the largest on *BakerFi*. Table 2 reports the aggregation-level results.

**Table 1.** Best committee variant versus random and ASCENT references. Values report the total tests executed on killable mutants.

| Project | Random | ASCENT | Committee | $\Delta$ random (%) |
|---|---|---|---|---|
| BakerFi | 322,161 | 130,052 | 173,292 | −46.2% |
| NextGen | 8,380 | 4,368 | 5,536 | −33.9% |
| Quadrata | 23,917 | 14,480 | 15,114 | −36.8% |
| SecondSwap | 16,472 | 7,108 | 7,753 | −52.9% |
| THORWallet | 484 | 276 | 296 | −38.8% |

Welch's $t$-tests ($n = 5$), using Arithmetic Mean as a representative reference, detect no significant TTK differences among Arithmetic, Geometric, and Weighted aggregation ($p \geq 0.09$); their confidence intervals also overlap substantially. These results provide no evidence that one continuous operator consistently dominates, and the small point-estimate differences may reflect run-to-run variability. In contrast, Borda Count performs significantly worse in every project ($p < 0.01$), with the strongest degradation on *NextGen*, *Quadrata*, and *SecondSwap*; it also remains the worst configuration on the smaller *THORWallet* system. The coordination results further suggest that stronger agreement is not necessarily associated with better prioritization. For example, Borda attains the highest Spearman correlation on *NextGen*, yet performs substantially worse than Weighted aggregation. Agreement therefore appears useful for characterizing cross-agent behavior, but not as a direct proxy for optimization quality.

*Interpreting the Performance Gap.* The primary purpose of the architectural separation is to expose and measure interactions among search objectives. We nevertheless hypothesized that aggregating differently biased search distributions at each decision step could produce a balanced behavior policy, while common environmental feedback would maintain a coherent executed trajectory. The results confirm that specialization remains observable, but do not show that it yields an optimization advantage. Distinct search biases may persist without being complementary in the states where each should dominate. One possible explanation concerns the aggregation operators, which combine preferences without identifying which agent may be most informative in a given state (arithmetic averaging may attenuate a strong minority preference, geometric aggregation may suppress an action assigned low probability by one agent, and Borda discards probability magnitudes). The resulting distribution may therefore represent an intermediate compromise without reproducing the exploration-exploitation balance obtained when these terms interact within a single calibrated PUCT policy. Credit assignment may also be diluted because only the aggregated action is executed, while the shared sparse reward provides neither counterfactual feedback for overridden proposals nor direct evidence of which agent contributed to a successful decision. Consequently, useful specialized proposals may receive no proposal-specific learning signal, and the aggregator receives little evidence

**Table 2.** Committee performance and decision agreement across five projects (five-trial means). TTK is reported as mean ± 95% CI half-width; arrows indicate the preferred direction.

| | | System Performance | | | Decision Agreement | | | |
|---|---|---|---|---|---|---|---|---|
| Project | Aggregation | Reward ↑ | Tests ↓ | TTK ↓ mean ± CI | Full+soft(%) | Partial(%) | Sym. KL↓ | Spearman$\rho$ ↑ |
| BakerFi | Arithmetic | 247.38 | 173292 | 92.62 ± 2.45 | 10.5 | 89.4 | 40.65 | 0.110 |
| | Geometric | 246.53 | 174882 | 93.47 ± 2.73 | 10.7 | 89.2 | 40.56 | 0.114 |
| | Weighted | 246.11 | 175668 | 93.89 ± 3.01 | 11.0 | 88.9 | 40.48 | 0.118 |
| | Borda | 95.00 | 458395 | 245.00 ± 15.27 | 7.8 | 4.6 | 41.20 | 0.095 |
| NextGen | Arithmetic | 36.85 | 5844 | 20.15 ± 2.25 | 22.2 | 76.0 | 34.54 | 0.235 |
| | Geometric | 36.91 | 5826 | 20.09 ± 1.64 | 27.8 | 71.4 | 33.27 | 0.249 |
| | Weighted | 37.91 | 5536 | 19.09 ± 1.41 | 28.1 | 69.9 | 32.55 | 0.266 |
| | Borda | 6.25 | 14718 | 50.75 ± 0.02 | 12.9 | 2.4 | 31.39 | 0.305 |
| Quadrata | Arithmetic | 68.48 | 15114 | 40.52 ± 1.01 | 29.6 | 69.7 | 31.43 | 0.304 |
| | Geometric | 68.12 | 15248 | 40.88 ± 2.69 | 28.8 | 70.6 | 32.46 | 0.279 |
| | Weighted | 67.73 | 15394 | 41.27 ± 0.99 | 28.3 | 71.0 | 31.71 | 0.288 |
| | Borda | 13.69 | 35551 | 95.31 ± 6.34 | 16.3 | 7.3 | 33.59 | 0.261 |
| SecondSwap | Arithmetic | 52.31 | 7861 | 16.69 ± 1.07 | 31.0 | 67.9 | 30.47 | 0.323 |
| | Geometric | 52.54 | 7753 | 16.46 ± 1.20 | 29.1 | 70.8 | 30.79 | 0.311 |
| | Weighted | 52.36 | 7837 | 16.64 ± 1.16 | 29.7 | 69.6 | 31.94 | 0.286 |
| | Borda | 19.55 | 23291 | 49.45 ± 4.43 | 18.5 | 6.1 | 29.62 | 0.346 |
| THORWallet | Arithmetic | 4.53 | 296 | 2.47 ± 0.30 | 78.4 | 20.1 | 10.61 | 0.673 |
| | Geometric | 4.33 | 320 | 2.67 ± 0.08 | 80.3 | 18.8 | 10.66 | 0.693 |
| | Weighted | 4.42 | 310 | 2.58 ± 0.12 | 74.5 | 23.9 | 11.34 | 0.672 |
| | Borda | 3.62 | 406 | 3.38 ± 0.21 | 59.0 | 30.9 | 17.81 | 0.487 |

about which role should dominate in a given state. Finally, the exploration coefficients and training configuration were inherited from monolithic ASCENT to isolate the architectural change; these settings may induce differentiation without producing well-calibrated complementarity. These explanations are neither mutually exclusive nor exhaustive, requiring targeted ablations to isolate their individual contributions.

## 4.4 Agreement Analysis

Our results reveal that agreement varies systematically with environment scale. *THORWallet*, the smallest environment, is the high-agreement case, with full+soft agreement between 59.0% and 80.3%, comparatively low SKL, and high Spearman correlation. Conversely, *BakerFi* exhibits predominantly partial agreement, SKL around 40.5, and Spearman correlation close to 0.11. Partial agreement also dominates in the intermediate projects under continuous aggregation, typically ranging from 69% to 76%. Borda behaves differently on *NextGen*, *Quadrata*, and *SecondSwap*, where partial agreement falls to 2.4%, 7.3%, and 6.1%, respectively, while full+soft agreement also remains limited. Many Borda selections therefore fall outside the agents' shared top-$k$ support, consistent with an ordinal rule that discards probability magnitudes. The smaller *THORWallet* action space limits this effect. Overall, the agreement metrics indicate that the

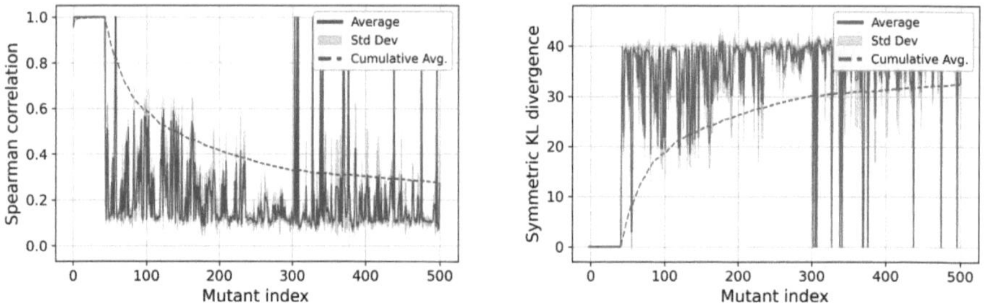


**Fig. 2.** *NextGen* under weighted aggregation: Spearman correlation (left) and SKL (right), showing local stability windows within long-run differentiation.

agents are not redundant. Policy collapse would produce high full/soft agreement, near-zero SKL, and Spearman correlation close to one. Instead, medium and large projects retain persistent partial agreement, elevated SKL, and low-to-moderate rank correlation. The committee therefore preserves overlapping candidate support without converging to identical preferences.

### 4.5 Temporal Patterns

The temporal traces for *NextGen* under weighted aggregation (Fig. 2) show recurring local re-synchronization within a broader differentiation trend, rather than a monotonic or strictly periodic pattern. After the rollout-delay horizon, shared non-neural guidance is replaced by neural inference, and agent preferences increasingly diverge under their specialized objectives. Spearman correlation nevertheless repeatedly rebounds, with elevated-correlation episodes occurring, for instance, around mutant indices $\approx$ 100, $\approx$220–240, and $\approx$ 480, before returning toward the $\approx$0.1–0.15 baseline. Beyond index $\approx$ 300, these rebounds become sharper, shorter, and more isolated. Because the running-average Spearman correlation continues to decrease while running-average SKL increases, these episodes indicate intermittent re-synchronization rather than global convergence. The *NextGen* top-$k$ logs support this interpretation. During the inspected warm-up prefix, mean SKL is approximately 0.09, mean $\rho$ is 0.998, and full agreement accounts for 97.8% of the steps. Post-warm-up, mean SKL rises to 39.8, mean $\rho$ falls to 0.11, and partial agreement reaches 85.9%. Thus, aggregation shifts from near-unanimity toward selection among specialized proposals.

## 5 Related Work

Our work intersects three research threads: Neural-MCTS extensions, ensemble and cooperative multi-agent search, and RL for test case prioritization.

### 5.1 Neural-MCTS and Adaptive Search

AlphaZero [14] established the canonical Neural-MCTS paradigm via a shared policy-value network. Our per-agent PUCT rule inherits its exploration coefficient $c_i$ from this formulation. While Silver et al. showed that $c_i$ shapes single-agent search, we show that it qualitatively drives inter-agent differentiation in a committee, turning a single-agent exploration parameter into explicit cross-agent search biases. Browne et al. [4] catalog single-agent diversity mechanisms (e.g., novelty bonuses, progressive widening). Our work externalizes diversity to a dedicated agent with a distributional interface, making it measurable at the aggregation level rather than embedded in a tree structure. SA-MCTS [15] tunes the exploration coefficient online for single-agent search. In our architecture, role-specific PUCT profiles remain fixed while private policies and tree statistics evolve. Therefore, our aim is not BAI-style optimal allocation, but to make the interaction among the three search pressures observable at each decision step. Finally, Wissow and Asai [18] show UCB1 struggles under scale-mismatched rewards, consistent with our PUCT-over-UCT choice.

### 5.2 Ensemble and Collective Search Architectures

Recent collective-MCTS methods for LLM reasoning, such as CoMCTS [20] and process-reward-guided ensembles [19], pool multiple generators at node expansion to improve reasoning paths. They differ from our work in two key ways: aggregation occurs at node-expansion rather than via step-level distribution aggregation, and they target LLM reasoning rather than sparse-reward sequential decisions. Crucially, neither measures nor exploits inter-agent disagreement as a signal. Decentralized cooperative planning [9] uses Decoupled-UCT for agents planning independent trajectories in a shared environment. Unlike our setting, these methods do not require multiple search processes to produce a single discrete action at each step, making aggregation central to our design. MADDPG [10] provides a centralized critic for agents acting in continuous spaces with independent rewards. Our setting diverges fundamentally: agents share a discrete action space and identical reward signals. Thus, our shared $V_\phi$ arises from observing the same transitions, not merely as a centralized training convenience.

### 5.3 Learning-Based Test Case Prioritization

Most ML-based TCP methods treat prioritization as an offline problem; for example, AnoLSTM-A [5] learns from historical metadata. RL formulations, including early model-free work [2,16] and modern variants with multi-objective rewards [13] or attention [17], frame TCP as a sequential decision problem. However, model-free RL requires intensive trial-and-error, hampering efficiency under tight budgets. For mutation testing, ASCENT [3] introduced single-agent Neural-MCTS for online, preprocessing-free prioritization. We use it as the benchmark for the committee architecture described in Sect. 3.

## 6 Threats to Validity

We assess internal, construct, and external threats to validity under the assumptions of the proposed multi-agent Neural-MCTS framework.

*Internal Validity.* The primary internal threat is credit assignment at the committee boundary [1]. Because only the aggregated action is executed, observed rewards cannot isolate individual agent contributions from cross-agent agreement or aggregation effects. Additionally, ASCENT settings were retained to isolate the architectural change but may be suboptimal for heterogeneous agents, so the performance gap may partly reflect configuration mismatch. Finally, training, mutant ordering, and policy updates add stochastic variation. Five trials mitigate this threat, but paired seeds and effect-size analyses would strengthen the evidence.

*Construct Validity.* Coordination metrics (SKL and Spearman $\rho$) serve as abstract proxies for multi-agent dynamics and are fundamentally blind to semantic structures within the action space. For example, we showed that low or negative $\rho$ with high SKL can still coexist with agreement on secondary or tertiary backup choices. A second threat is the computational overhead of multiple policy networks; sharing $V_\phi$ mitigates state-estimation redundancy, but the remaining footprint must be controlled via MCTS parameter tuning (e.g., increasing update interval $\Delta$, enlarging training batch sizes).

*External Validity.* Generalizability is bounded by the dimensionality and complexity of the target systems. For instance, THORWallet's high agreement may reflect its sparse mutant distribution and shorter decision horizon, which leave less room for the exploration, exploitation, and diversity pressures to diverge.

## 7 Conclusion and Future Work

This paper introduced a multi-agent committee for online Neural-MCTS test prioritization, separating exploitation, exploration, and diversity agents and evaluating it on ASCENT's sparse-reward benchmark [3]. Across five smart-contract systems, the committee yields substantial execution savings over random ordering but does not outperform monolithic ASCENT. The agents nevertheless avoid policy collapse, showing scale-dependent agreement and recurring local re-synchronization within a broader trend toward specialization. The remaining challenge is aggregation: current linear, geometric, and ordinal operators expose these coordination patterns but do not consistently convert specialization into lower execution cost.

Future work should develop credit-aware or meta-learned aggregation that uses local rewards and disagreement to adapt agent weights and balance consensus against high-confidence minority proposals, while comparing static aggregation with multi-agent argumentation. Ablations over agent roles, shared versus private components, and diversity-bonus decay on larger systems should clarify when specialization remains useful rather than collapsing into redundant consensus.

**Disclosure of Interests.** The authors have no competing interests to declare that are relevant to the content of this article.

## References


1. Albrecht, S.V., Christianos, F., Schäfer, L.: Multi-agent Reinforcement Learning: Foundations and Modern Approaches. MIT Press, Cambridge (2024)
2. Bagherzadeh, M., Kahani, N., Briand, L.: Reinforcement learning for test case prioritization. IEEE Trans. Softw. Eng. **48**(8), 2836–2856 (2021). https://doi.org/10.1109/TSE.2021.3054523
3. Barboni, M., Lampa, F., Morichetta, A., Polini, A.: Optimizing smart contract testing via neural-MCTS test prioritization. In: Knottenbelt, W., Ressi, D., Rossi, S., Tiezzi, F. (eds.) Blockchain Technology and Emerging Applications. Blocktea 2025. LNICS, Social Informatics and Telecommunications Engineering, vol. 669, pp. 19–36. Springer, Cham (2026). https://doi.org/10.1007/978-3-032-12335-0_2
4. Browne, C.B., et al.: A survey of Monte Carlo tree search methods. IEEE Trans. Comput. Intell. AI Games **4**(1), 1–43 (2012). https://doi.org/10.1109/TCIAIG.2012.2186810
5. Choudhury, T.K., Behera, M., Dash, S.K., Pani, S.K., Mishra, J.: AnoLSTM-A: a deep learning approach for test cases prioritization. Procedia Comput. Sci. **258**, 1793–1803 (2025). https://doi.org/10.1016/j.procs.2025.04.431
6. Hinton, G., Vinyals, O., Dean, J.: Distilling the knowledge in a neural network (2015). arXiv preprint arXiv:1503.02531
7. Kittler, J., Hatef, M., Duin, R.P.W., Matas, J.: On combining classifiers. IEEE Trans. Pattern Anal. Mach. Intell. **20**(3), 226–239 (1998)
8. Kuncheva, L.I.: Combining Pattern Classifiers: Methods and Algorithms. Wiley, Hoboken (2004)
9. Kurzer, K., Zhou, C., Zöllner, J.M.: Decentralized cooperative planning for automated vehicles with hierarchical Monte Carlo tree search. In: IEEE Intelligent Vehicles Symposium (IV), pp. 529–536 (2018). https://doi.org/10.1109/IVS.2018.8500712
10. Lowe, R., Wu, Y., Tamar, A., Harb, J., Abbeel, P., Mordatch, I.: Multi-agent actor-critic for mixed cooperative-competitive environments. In: Advances in Neural Information Processing Systems, vol. 30 (NeurIPS 2017), pp. 6380–6391 (2017)
11. Lyle, C., Zheng, Z., Nikishin, E., Pires, B.A., Pascanu, R., Dabney, W.: Understanding plasticity in neural networks. In: International Conference on Machine Learning, pp. 23190–23211. PMLR (2023)
12. Olfati-Saber, R., Fax, J.A., Murray, R.M.: Consensus and cooperation in networked multi-agent systems. Proc. IEEE **95**(1), 215–233 (2007)
13. Shi, T., Xiao, L., Wu, K.: Reinforcement learning based test case prioritization for enhancing the security of software. In: 2020 IEEE 7th International Conference on Data Science and Advanced Analytics (DSAA), pp. 663–672 (2020). https://doi.org/10.1109/DSAA49011.2020.00073
14. Silver, D., et al.: A general reinforcement learning algorithm that masters chess, shogi, and go through self-play. Science **362**(6419), 1140–1144 (2018)

15. Sironi, C.F., Liu, J., Winands, M.H.M.: Self-adaptive Monte Carlo tree search in general game playing. IEEE Trans. Games **12**(2), 132–144 (2020). https://doi.org/10.1109/TG.2018.2884768
16. Spieker, H., Gotlieb, A., Marijan, D., Mossige, M.: Reinforcement learning for automatic test case prioritization and selection in continuous integration. In: Proceedings of the 26th ACM SIGSOFT International Symposium on Software Testing and Analysis (ISSTA 2017), pp. 12–22 (2017). https://doi.org/10.1145/3092703.3092709
17. Su, Q., Li, X., Ren, Y., Qiu, R., Hu, C., Yin, Y.: Attention transfer reinforcement learning for test case prioritization in continuous integration. Appl. Sci. **15**(4), 2243 (2025). https://doi.org/10.3390/app15042243
18. Wissow, S., Asai, M.: Scale-adaptive balancing of exploration and exploitation in classical planning. In: Proceedings of the 27th European Conference on Artificial Intelligence (ECAI 2024) (2024)
19. Xu, L., Chi, Z., Yao, Y., Zhang, S., Liang, J.: Ensembling large language models with process reward-guided tree search for better complex reasoning (2024). arXiv preprint arXiv:2412.15797
20. Yao, H., et al.: Mulberry: empowering MLLM with o1-like reasoning and reflection via collective Monte Carlo tree search (2024). arXiv preprint arXiv:2412.18319
21. Zhang, L., Marinov, D., Khurshid, S.: Faster mutation testing inspired by test prioritization and reduction. In: Proceedings of the 2013 International Symposium on Software Testing and Analysis, pp. 235–245. ISSTA 2013, Association for Computing Machinery, New York, NY, USA (2013)

# Reconstruction Error Fingerprints for Few-Shot Neural Audio Codec Attribution

Luca Bindini(✉), Eleonora Ristori, Marco Lippi, and Paolo Frasconi

AI Lab, Department of Information Engineering, University of Florence,
Via di Santa Marta 3, 50139 Florence, Italy
{luca.bindini,eleonora.ristori,marco.lippi,paolo.frasconi}@unifi.it

**Abstract.** Modern music generation systems frequently rely on neural audio codecs or reconstruction backends to transform compact latent codes into waveforms. Previous work has shown that these reconstruction stages are highly informative for binary AI-generated music detection. In this paper, we study a complementary attribution question: given a reconstructed music excerpt, which codec family or codec configuration produced it? This problem is important because source attribution can support provenance analysis, auditing of generative pipelines, and diagnosis of reconstruction backends, while detection alone only answers whether an excerpt appears synthetic. To the best of our knowledge, existing work on AI-generated music has primarily addressed binary detection or text-to-music generator attribution, whereas neural audio codec attribution has not been systematically studied. Our approach builds on the frozen-decoder/source-specific encoder principle introduced for few-shot generative model attribution. A base autoencoder is pretrained on real music spectrogram patches, its decoder is frozen, and a compact encoder is trained for each candidate codec source. At inference time, selected patches are reconstructed by all source-specific encoder-decoder pairs, producing a vector of mean reconstruction errors that is classified by a linear support vector machine. We evaluate family-level attribution among Encodec, GriffinMel, and the LAC/DAC family, as well as model-level attribution among eight codec configurations, on a Free Music Archive (FMA)-based reconstruction benchmark. We further compare the autoencoder fingerprint with a full-spectrogram ResNet18 baseline motivated by machine-generated music detection. The results show a clear data-regime trade-off: autoencoder fingerprints are more data-efficient in the lowest-shot settings, while ResNet18 becomes stronger when hundreds of labelled examples per source are available.

**Keywords:** AI-generated music · neural audio codec attribution · few-shot learning

L. Bindini and E. Ristori—These authors contributed equally to this work.


S. Bistarelli et al. (Eds.): AIxIA 2026, LNAI 17131, pp. 87–99, 2027.
https://doi.org/10.1007/978-3-032-40774-0_7

## 1 Introduction

The rapid development of generative audio systems has made high-quality music synthesis accessible to a broad audience. Modern text-to-music and audio-continuation models, including systems based on discrete audio representations or neural audio tokens, can produce coherent musical excerpts containing instruments, vocals, rhythm, and production effects [4,6,7]. This progress creates artistic opportunities, but it also raises questions about authenticity, accountability, copyright, and provenance. Most technical work on AI-generated music focuses on detection: deciding whether an excerpt is human-made or machine-generated [1,3,11,15]. Detection is important, but it leaves open a second question: which technical source produced the generated or reconstructed sample?

This paper studies this second question in the context of neural audio codecs. Given a music excerpt known to belong to one of a set of reconstructed sources, the goal is to identify the codec family or configuration responsible for the reconstruction. The output is therefore not "real" or "fake", but a source label such as Encodec [5], GriffinMel based on Griffin–Lim reconstruction [8], LAC-labelled Descript Audio Codec (DAC) variants [10], or a specific configuration such as Encodec at 24 kbps. Real audio is used only to learn a shared reconstruction prior; it is not part of the attribution label space.

The attribution problem is relevant because many generative music systems decouple representation and generation. Neural audio codecs such as Encodec and DAC map waveforms into compact continuous or discrete codes and reconstruct waveforms through learned decoders [5,10]. A separate generative model then operates on the latent sequence rather than directly on raw audio [4,7]. Thus, even when the high-level generator is unknown, proprietary, or frequently updated, the final waveform may still carry artifacts from the codec or reconstruction backend. Afchar et al. [1] demonstrated the forensic relevance of this decoder-centric view by reconstructing Free Music Archive (FMA) tracks via multiple decoders and training classifiers to detect reconstruction artifacts.

Attribution is more demanding than detection. A binary detector can exploit any cue that separates original recordings from reconstructed audio. An attribution method must instead distinguish among multiple reconstructed sources while the musical content is controlled. This makes the task diagnostic: it asks whether codec-specific reconstruction artifacts remain separable from one another. Some recent work has considered attribution of text-to-music generators, notably FakeMusicCaps [3], and broader provenance mechanisms have been discussed for generative music [13]. However, to the best of our knowledge, no prior work systematically evaluates neural audio codec attribution where all classes share the same underlying musical content and differ primarily by codec backend.

The approach studied in this paper is based on the frozen-decoder/source-specific-encoder principle introduced by Bindini et al. [2] for few-shot generative image attribution. Their method trains a decoder on natural images, freezes it, and learns a compact encoder for each generative source; the vector of reconstruction errors obtained from all encoder-decoder pairs acts as a source fingerprint.

We transfer this principle to music spectrograms. The contribution is not to claim a new autoencoder architecture, but to test whether the same reconstruction-error fingerprinting principle is informative in a different signal domain and for a different forensic unit: neural audio codecs rather than visual generators.

We include a ResNet18 baseline [9] because Li et al. [12] report ResNet18 as a strong trade-off between in-domain and out-of-domain performance for machine-generated music detection from spectrogram-like representations.

In practical provenance analyses, the codec backend may be a relevant source of forensic evidence because modern music generators often rely on neural audio codecs or discrete audio tokenizers as their reconstruction stage [4,5,10]. When a newly observed backend, configuration, or deployment variant has to be analyzed, only a limited number of matched examples may be available, which motivates a few-shot attribution protocol rather than a large-scale supervised training setting. Therefore, the frozen-decoder design choice is especially attractive, because it uses a pretrained reconstruction prior, adds a new source by training only a compact encoder, and finally updates a lightweight classifier.

To summarize, the contributions of this paper are the following:

- We introduce few-shot neural audio codec attribution as a source attribution problem for AI-generated music analysis, addressing a setting in which codec-level source attribution has not been explored.
- We adapt the frozen-decoder/source-specific-encoder principle from few-shot image generator attribution to music spectrograms.
- We compare this lightweight reconstruction error fingerprint with a ResNet18 baseline, revealing a data-regime trade-off between low-shot reconstruction based attribution and higher data discriminative learning.

# 2 Related Work

## 2.1 AI Generated Music Detection

Synthetic media detection has been studied extensively for images, video, and speech [14,16–18]. Music is a distinct setting because excerpts may contain vocals, instruments, production effects, mixing, mastering, and compression. A detector trained on unrelated real and generated corpora may learn shortcuts such as genre, bitrate, loudness, or dataset origin rather than synthesis artifacts. Recent work has therefore started to build datasets and evaluation protocols specifically for machine-generated music detection [1,11,15].

Afchar et al. [1] proposed a controlled detection benchmark that mitigates confounding by reconstructing real Free Music Archive tracks through several decoders, including Encodec [5], Descript Audio Codec (DAC)-based variants [10], and GriffinMel/Griffin–Lim reconstruction [8]. The original and reconstructed versions share the same musical content, so classifiers are encouraged to learn reconstruction artifacts. Our work adopts the same decoder-centric motivation but changes the task: we do not decide whether a sample is real or reconstructed; we attribute reconstructed samples to their codec source.

### 2.2 Attribution and Provenance in AI-Generated Music

Attribution is related to but different from detection. Detection asks whether content is synthetic; attribution asks which source, generator, dataset, or transformation is responsible. In music, this distinction is important for provenance analysis, model auditing, copyright claims, licensing, and forensic investigation. FakeMusicCaps [3] explicitly addresses detection and attribution of synthetic music generated by text-to-music models. In parallel, provenance and attribution-by-design frameworks have been proposed to make generative music systems more transparent at training or inference time [13].

Our work focuses on a different attribution unit: the neural audio codec. This is useful when the high-level generator is unknown, unavailable, or frequently updated.

### 2.3 Frozen-Decoder Reconstruction Principles

Bindini et al. [2] showed that a frozen-decoder architecture can support few-shot attribution of image generators. Their method trains a decoder on natural images, freezes it, and learns a source-specific compact encoder for each generator. At inference, reconstruction errors across all source-specific encoder-decoder pairs form a low-dimensional source signature.

This paper adopts the same architectural principle while changing the domain and the scientific question. Images become spectrogram patches, visual generators become neural audio codec sources, and the attribution target becomes a codec family or codec configuration. Music spectrograms exhibit distinct local statistics compared to natural images, and codec artifacts are time-frequency phenomena rather than image synthesis artifacts.

## 3 Method

We consider an attribution problem in which each reconstructed excerpt belongs either to one of three codec families or to one of eight individual codec configurations. The goal is not to detect whether an excerpt is real or generated, but to assign the reconstructed excerpt to its source codec (Fig. 1).

### 3.1 Spectrogram Patch Representation

Each excerpt $x$ is transformed into a log-amplitude spectrogram $S(x)$. To use a compact convolutional reconstruction model, the spectrogram is divided into non-overlapping patches of size $64 \times 64$:

$$\mathcal{P}(x) = \{p_1, p_2, \dots, p_M\}. \tag{1}$$

Low-energy patches may contain limited source-specific information. We therefore select up to $P$ informative patches from each excerpt:

$$\mathcal{P}_P(x) \subseteq \mathcal{P}(x), \qquad |\mathcal{P}_P(x)| \leq P. \tag{2}$$

In our implementation, $P = 16$. If an excerpt yields fewer than $P$ non-overlapping patches, all available patches are used.

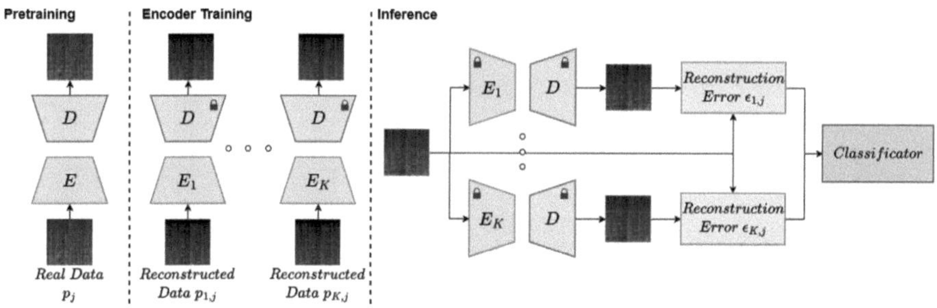


**Fig. 1.** Schematic of the reconstruction-error fingerprint. A decoder is pretrained on real spectrograms and frozen; each source-specific encoder is trained on reconstructed examples from one codec source. At inference, all encoder-decoder pairs reconstruct the same excerpt and their mean errors form the attribution fingerprint.

### 3.2 Shared Frozen Decoder

A base autoencoder $(E, D)$ is first trained on real music spectrograms: this step is source-agnostic and does not use reconstructed examples. The objective is

$$\min_{E,D} \mathbb{E}_{p\sim\mathcal{R}} \left[\|p - D(E(p))\|_2^2\right], \tag{3}$$

where $\mathcal{R}$ denotes the distribution of real spectrograms. After training, the decoder $D$ is frozen and shared by all source-specific encoders. Freezing the decoder is the central constraint inherited from the previous reconstruction-fingerprint architecture. It forces all encoders to reconstruct through the same learned spectrogram decoder. Without a common decoder, each source-specific autoencoder could freely adapt its own reconstruction space, making the errors less comparable and less interpretable as a source fingerprint.

### 3.3 Training Source-Specific Encoders

For each source $k \in \mathcal{F}$, we train a compact encoder $E_k$ while keeping $D$ fixed. Let $\mathcal{S}_k$ be the distribution of spectrogram patches reconstructed by source $k$. The training objective is

$$\min_{E_k} \mathbb{E}_{p\sim\mathcal{S}_k} \left[\|p - D(E_k(p))\|_2^2\right]. \tag{4}$$

The same inference architecture is used in both evaluation protocols. In family-level attribution, each encoder is trained on all configurations belonging to a family; for instance, the Encodec encoder uses Encodec-3, Encodec-6, and Encodec-24 examples. In model-level attribution, each encoder is trained on a single configuration. Thus, the method changes only in the definition of the source set $\mathcal{F}$.

### 3.4 Reconstruction-Error Fingerprints

At inference, every test excerpt is processed by all source-specific encoder–decoder pairs. For a selected patch $p_j \in \mathcal{P}_P(x)$, the reconstruction through source encoder $k$ is

$$\hat{p}_{k,j} = D(E_k(p_j)), \tag{5}$$

with patch reconstruction error

$$\epsilon_{k,j}(x) = \|p_j - \hat{p}_{k,j}\|_2^2. \tag{6}$$

The excerpt-level error for source $k$ is the mean over selected patches:

$$r_k(x) = \frac{1}{|\mathcal{P}_P(x)|} \sum_{p_j \in \mathcal{P}_P(x)} \epsilon_{k,j}(x). \tag{7}$$

The reconstruction-error fingerprint is the raw vector

$$\boldsymbol{r}(x) = [r_1(x), r_2(x), \ldots, r_K(x)]^\top \in \mathbb{R}^K. \tag{8}$$

This vector is the only representation used for attribution, by feeding a linear support vector classifier.

## 4 Experimental Protocol

### 4.1 Dataset and Sources

We use the reconstruction benchmark introduced by Afchar et al. [1]. In the benchmark, real tracks are passed through several audio decoders while preserving the underlying musical content. This property is important: attribution classes differ primarily by reconstruction backend rather than by song identity, artist, or genre.

We consider the eight configurations listed in Table 1: Encodec variants [5], GriffinMel variants based on Griffin–Lim reconstruction [8], and LAC-labelled Descript Audio Codec (DAC) variants [10]. They are grouped into three families for family-level attribution.

**Table 1.** Sources used in the attribution benchmark. The LAC/DAC row follows the benchmark naming and refers to LAC-labelled Descript Audio Codec (DAC) variants.

| Family | Individual configurations |
|---|---|
| Encodec | encodec24, encodec6, encodec3 |
| GriffinMel | griffin512, griffin256 |
| LAC/DAC | lac14, lac7, lac2 |

### 4.2 Few-Shot Protocol

We evaluate the methods in a few-shot regime by varying the number of training excerpts per source as $N \in \{5, 10, 20, 50, 100, 500\}$.

For family-level attribution, $N$ denotes the number of training examples per family. For model-level attribution, $N$ denotes the number of training examples per individual codec configuration. For each value of $N$, we perform five independent runs with the same seeds for the autoencoder fingerprint and ResNet18 baseline.

### 4.3 Autoencoder Fingerprint

The compact encoder contains two convolutional blocks with $3 \times 3$ kernels, ReLU activations, and $2 \times 2$ max-pooling, followed by a bottleneck convolution with 128 channels. The decoder is inherited from the real-spectrogram autoencoder and frozen during all source-specific training. Each source encoder is trained for 1000 epochs using Adam with learning rate $10^{-3}$ and mean squared error loss. For each excerpt, informative patches are selected and concatenated into a patch-level training set. During evaluation, final features are obtained by averaging patch errors. The downstream classifier is a linear SVC.

This model is included because the tiny-autoencoder strategy of Bindini et al. [2] is specifically designed for lightweight few-shot attribution. The base decoder provides a pretrained reconstruction prior, while each new source requires only a compact encoder. This makes the approach suitable for low-data regimes in which training a high-capacity end-to-end classifier may be unstable.

### 4.4 ResNet18 Baseline

To compare the reconstruction-error approach with a conventional discriminative model, we train a ResNet18 classifier [9] on whole spectrogram images. ResNet18 is selected because it has been used as a strong architecture for machine-generated music detection from spectrogram-like representations [12]. In our experiments, however, the model is not trained for binary detection: its final layer is replaced according to the number of attribution classes, and it is trained directly for family-level or model-level codec attribution. Spectrograms are resized to $224 \times 224$ and optimized with cross-entropy loss.

This architecture plays a complementary role to the autoencoder fingerprint. It tests whether a high-capacity supervised classifier can learn attribution cues directly from the full spectrogram when the number of labelled examples increases. This makes the comparison informative across data regimes: the autoencoder fingerprint is expected to be advantageous at low $N$, while ResNet18 may benefit more strongly from larger training sets.

### 4.5 Reproducibility Details

For both methods, all results are computed over the same five random seeds and the same training sizes. In family-level attribution, $N$ denotes the total number of training excerpts per family; in model-level attribution, $N$ denotes the number of training excerpts per individual codec configuration. The test split is kept fixed across all values of $N$. For the autoencoder fingerprint, reconstruction-error vectors are scaled using statistics estimated on the training split before fitting the linear SVC. The SVC regularization parameter is selected by cross-validation on the training data. For ResNet18, the final classification layer is replaced according to the number of attribution classes and the network is trained directly on resized whole-spectrogram inputs using cross-entropy loss. No real examples are included as attribution labels in either setting.

# 5 Results

## 5.1 Family-Level Attribution

Table 2 compares the autoencoder-based reconstruction-error fingerprints with ResNet18 in the family-level attribution setting. The reconstruction-error fingerprint is clearly more data-efficient in the lowest-shot regimes. At $N = 5$, it reaches 65.39% balanced accuracy, whereas ResNet18 remains close to chance at 33.30%. The same pattern holds at $N = 10$ and $N = 20$. At $N = 50$, the gap becomes small: the autoencoder fingerprint reaches 71.45% and ResNet18 reaches 68.89%.

The trend changes as more labelled examples become available. From $N = 100$ onward, ResNet18 becomes competitive and then clearly stronger, reaching 94.70% balanced accuracy at $N = 500$. In contrast, the autoencoder fingerprint saturates around 71–72%. The table shows the central trade-off: the autoencoder fingerprint provides a strong low-shot inductive bias, while ResNet18 exploits larger supervised training sets more effectively.

**Table 2.** Family-level attribution comparison. Results are reported as mean ± standard deviation over five independent runs. The best result for each $N$ is shown in bold.

| $N$ | Balanced accuracy (%) | | Weighted F1 (%) | |
|---|---|---|---|---|
| | AE fingerprint | ResNet18 | AE fingerprint | ResNet18 |
| 5 | **65.39 ± 1.50** | 33.30 ± 0.10 | **61.91 ± 1.55** | 21.45 ± 2.09 |
| 10 | **66.45 ± 1.20** | 33.94 ± 1.05 | **62.61 ± 1.50** | 24.69 ± 6.03 |
| 20 | **68.92 ± 1.77** | 46.19 ± 2.60 | **65.47 ± 2.29** | 46.89 ± 3.64 |
| 50 | **71.45 ± 0.69** | 68.89 ± 2.46 | **68.26 ± 0.85** | 65.66 ± 2.80 |
| 100 | 71.10 ± 2.01 | **72.47 ± 5.22** | 67.56 ± 2.92 | **71.62 ± 4.20** |
| 500 | 71.82 ± 1.06 | **94.70 ± 2.21** | 68.71 ± 1.21 | **94.51 ± 2.56** |

### 5.2 Model-Level Attribution

Table 3 reports the same comparison for model-level attribution among eight individual codec configurations. This task is substantially harder because configurations within the same family share reconstruction mechanisms and often differ mainly in bitrate or artifact intensity. The autoencoder fingerprint is again stronger in the lowest-shot regime: at $N = 5$, it reaches 31.31% balanced accuracy, compared with 14.63% for ResNet18. At $N = 20$, the autoencoder fingerprint still leads by approximately six percentage points.

At larger training sizes, the discriminative baseline overtakes the lightweight fingerprint. At $N = 100$, ResNet18 reaches 46.21% balanced accuracy, compared with 38.01% for the autoencoder fingerprint. At $N = 500$, ResNet18 reaches 68.62%, while the autoencoder fingerprint remains at 38.33%. This confirms that fine-grained attribution benefits strongly from additional supervised examples when a high-capacity classifier is available.

**Table 3.** Model-level attribution comparison. Results are reported as mean ± standard deviation over five independent runs. The best result for each $N$ is shown in bold.

| $N$ | Balanced accuracy (%) | | Weighted F1 (%) | |
|---|---|---|---|---|
| | AE fingerprint | ResNet18 | AE fingerprint | ResNet18 |
| 5 | **31.31 ± 0.78** | 14.63 ± 0.80 | **27.51 ± 0.96** | 10.96 ± 1.53 |
| 10 | **33.07 ± 0.90** | 24.76 ± 1.23 | **29.49 ± 1.66** | 23.68 ± 0.78 |
| 20 | **35.37 ± 0.36** | 29.33 ± 0.87 | **31.54 ± 0.63** | 28.20 ± 0.79 |
| 50 | **37.29 ± 0.41** | **37.29 ± 2.95** | 33.97 ± 0.53 | **36.27 ± 3.14** |
| 100 | 38.01 ± 0.69 | **46.21 ± 0.75** | 35.04 ± 0.98 | **45.67 ± 0.88** |
| 500 | 38.33 ± 1.12 | **68.62 ± 6.73** | 35.84 ± 0.96 | **68.21 ± 6.89** |

From a forensic perspective, these results suggest different operating regimes. Family-level attribution can provide a useful provenance cue even with very limited supervision, especially when the goal is to distinguish broad reconstruction backends. In contrast, configuration-level attribution should be interpreted more cautiously: although performance is above chance, the confusion patterns indicate that bitrate-level or variant-level decisions are not reliable enough to be used as standalone evidence in the most data-scarce regimes.

### 5.3 Confusion Analysis

Figure 2 shows model-level count confusion matrices for the autoencoder fingerprint at $N = 5$, $N = 10$, $N = 20$, and $N = 50$, aggregated over the five runs. Counts are shown rather than row-normalized percentages in order to make the absolute volume of errors explicit. At $N = 5$, predictions are concentrated on a few labels, especially `lac2` and `griffin256`. This reflects the limited evidence available to the source-specific encoders and to the final linear classifier.

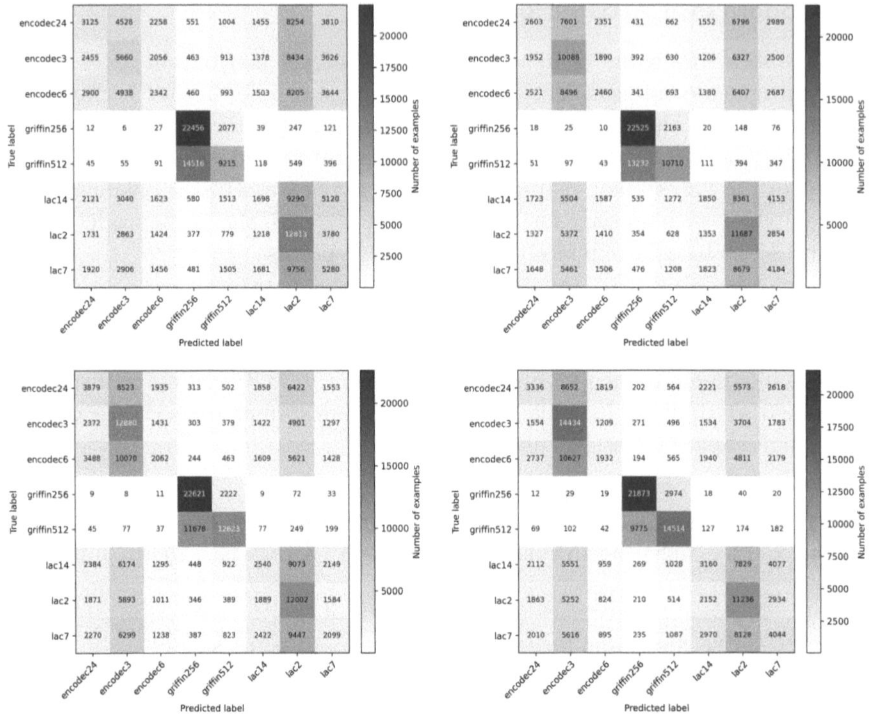


**Fig. 2.** Model-level confusion matrices for the autoencoder fingerprint using raw counts aggregated over five runs. Top row: $N = 5$ and $N = 10$. Bottom row: $N = 20$ and $N = 50$. GriffinMel configurations are comparatively separable, while Encodec and LAC/DAC configurations remain strongly entangled. The intermediate settings show that additional examples progressively strengthen some diagonal entries but do not remove the main Encodec–LAC/DAC ambiguity.

GriffinMel is already the most separable family, while Encodec and LAC/DAC configurations are strongly confused.

The intermediate regimes provide a clearer view of how the fingerprint evolves with additional examples. At $N = 10$ and $N = 20$, the matrices remain dominated by the same cross-family ambiguity between Encodec and LAC/DAC, but the prediction mass becomes less concentrated on a single class and several diagonal entries increase. In particular, `encodec3`, `griffin512`, and `lac14` become progressively more represented on the diagonal. This indicates that the reconstruction-error fingerprint does acquire additional configuration-specific information as the number of examples grows, even though the learned neural codecs remain difficult to separate.

At $N = 50$, predictions become less collapsed, although confusion between Encodec and LAC/DAC remains substantial. This explains why the autoencoder fingerprint is strong at family-level attribution but limited at fine-grained configuration attribution: many errors are between learned neural codec configurations that are acoustically and architecturally closer to one another than to GriffinMel.

Overall, the comparison supports a nuanced conclusion. The autoencoder fingerprint is preferable when the number of labelled examples is very small, because the pretrained decoder and source-specific encoders impose a strong reconstruction-based inductive bias. ResNet18 is preferable when the number of labelled examples becomes sufficiently large, because the full-spectrogram classifier can learn richer discriminative cues that are not restricted to the low-dimensional reconstruction-error vector.

## 6 Conclusion

We studied few-shot neural audio codec attribution using reconstruction-error fingerprints. The work adapts the frozen-decoder/source-specific-encoder principle from generative image attribution to music spectrograms and evaluates whether the resulting error vectors can identify codec families or individual codec configurations.

The comparison with ResNet18 reveals a clear data-regime trade-off. Autoencoder fingerprints are more effective when only a few examples are available, both at family level and at model level. This advantage is likely connected to the pretrained decoder and to the constrained source-specific encoders: the method does not have to learn a full discriminative representation from scratch for every few-shot setting. ResNet18, on the other hand, benefits more from larger labelled training sets and achieves higher performance when hundreds of examples per source are available, especially at $N = 500$.

From a forensic perspective, these results suggest different operating regimes. Family-level attribution can provide a useful provenance cue even with limited supervision, especially when the goal is to distinguish broad reconstruction backends. Model-level attribution should be interpreted more cautiously: although performance is above chance, the confusion patterns show that closely related neural codec configurations, especially Encodec and LAC/DAC variants, remain difficult to separate. Thus, configuration-level predictions should be understood as compact evidence of reconstruction similarity rather than as definitive forensic conclusions in isolation.

The study has three main limitations. First, the evaluation is restricted to reconstructed versions of the Free Music Archive benchmark, which provides strong content control but does not cover all real-world music-generation pipelines. Second, the candidate sources are limited to the codec families and configurations available in the benchmark. Third, all experiments are closed-set: every test excerpt is assumed to come from one of the candidate sources. Robustness to post-processing, unseen codecs, and end-to-end generators remains an important direction for future work.

These findings also suggest future methodological directions. Reconstruction-error fingerprints are useful when the forensic setting is data-scarce and lightweight adaptation is required. Full-spectrogram discriminative classifiers are promising when many labelled examples are available, but their weak low-shot behavior indicates that they may need better pretraining. Future work should therefore explore pretext tasks for ResNet-like models, such as masked spectrogram prediction, reconstruction, contrastive learning, or codec-aware self-supervision, so that discriminative networks can inherit some of the low-shot robustness currently provided by the autoencoder pretraining stage.

Overall, this study provides a controlled evaluation of codec attribution in AI-generated music and clarifies the scope of reconstruction-error methods in this domain. The results support the use of autoencoder fingerprints as lightweight low-shot attribution signals, while also showing that high-capacity discriminative models become preferable when larger labelled sets are available.

## References


1. Afchar, D., Meseguer-Brocal, G., Hennequin, R.: AI-generated music detection and its challenges. In: 2025 IEEE International Conference on Acoustics, Speech and Signal Processing, ICASSP 2025, Hyderabad, India, 6–11 April 2025, pp. 1–5. IEEE (2025). https://doi.org/10.1109/ICASSP49660.2025.10890655
2. Bindini, L., Bertazzini, G., Baracchi, D., Shullani, D., Frasconi, P., Piva, A.: Tiny autoencoders are effective few-shot generative model detectors. In: IEEE International Workshop on Information Forensics and Security, WIFS 2024, Rome, Italy, 2–5 December 2024, pp. 1–6. IEEE (2024). https://doi.org/10.1109/WIFS61860.2024.10810686
3. Comanducci, L., Bestagini, P., Tubaro, S.: Fakemusiccaps: a dataset for detection and attribution of synthetic music generated via text-to-music models. J. Imaging **11**(7), 242 (2025). https://doi.org/10.3390/jimaging11070242
4. Copet, J., et al.: Simple and controllable music generation. In: Oh, A., Naumann, T., Globerson, A., Saenko, K., Hardt, M., Levine, S. (eds.) Advances in Neural Information Processing Systems 36: Annual Conference on Neural Information Processing Systems 2023, NeurIPS 2023, New Orleans, LA, USA, 10–16 December 2023 (2023). http://papers.nips.cc/paper_files/paper/2023/hash/94b472a1842cd7c56dcb125fb2765fbd-Abstract-Conference.html
5. Défossez, A., Copet, J., Synnaeve, G., Adi, Y.: High fidelity neural audio compression. Trans. Mach. Learn. Res. **2023** (2023). https://openreview.net/forum?id=ivCd8z8zR2
6. Dhariwal, P., Jun, H., Payne, C., Kim, J.W., Radford, A., Sutskever, I.: Jukebox: a generative model for music. CoRR abs/2005.00341 (2020). https://arxiv.org/abs/2005.00341
7. García, H.F., Seetharaman, P., Kumar, R., Pardo, B.: Vampnet: music generation via masked acoustic token modeling. In: Sarti, A., et al. (eds.) Proceedings of the 24th International Society for Music Information Retrieval Conference, ISMIR 2023, Milan, Italy, 5–9 November 2023, pp. 359–366 (2023). https://doi.org/10.5281/zenodo.10265299
8. Griffin, D.W., Lim, J.S.: Signal estimation from modified short-time Fourier transform. In: IEEE International Conference on Acoustics, Speech, and Signal Processing, ICASSP 1983, Boston, Massachusetts, USA, 14–16 April 1983, pp. 804–807. IEEE (1983). https://doi.org/10.1109/ICASSP.1983.1172092

9. He, K., Zhang, X., Ren, S., Sun, J.: Deep residual learning for image recognition. In: 2016 IEEE Conference on Computer Vision and Pattern Recognition, CVPR 2016, Las Vegas, NV, USA, 27–30 June 2016, pp. 770–778. IEEE Computer Society (2016). https://doi.org/10.1109/CVPR.2016.90
10. Kumar, R., Seetharaman, P., Luebs, A., Kumar, I., Kumar, K.: High-fidelity audio compression with improved RVQGAN. In: Oh, A., Naumann, T., Globerson, A., Saenko, K., Hardt, M., Levine, S. (eds.) Advances in Neural Information Processing Systems 36: Annual Conference on Neural Information Processing Systems 2023, NeurIPS 2023, New Orleans, LA, USA, 10–16 December 2023 (2023). http://papers.nips.cc/paper_files/paper/2023/hash/58d0e78cf042af5876e12661087bea12-Abstract-Conference.html
11. Li, Y., Li, H., Specia, L., Schuller, B.: M6: multi-generator, multi-domain, multilingual and cultural, multi-genres, multi-instrument machine-generated music detection databases. Sci. Rep. **16**(1), 9237 (2026)
12. Li, Y., Sun, Q., Li, H., Specia, L., Schuller, B.W.: Explainable detection of machine generated music and early systematic evaluation. Sci. Rep. **16**, 13757 (2026). https://www.nature.com/articles/s41598-026-42133-7
13. Morreale, F., Hutiri, W., Serrà, J., Xiang, A., Mitsufuji, Y.: Attribution-by-design: ensuring inference-time provenance in generative music systems. CoRR abs/2510.08062 (2025). https://doi.org/10.48550/arXiv.2510.08062
14. Verdoliva, L.: Media forensics and deepfakes: an overview. IEEE J. Sel. Top. Signal Process. **14**(5), 910–932 (2020). https://doi.org/10.1109/JSTSP.2020.3002101
15. Vila, L.C., Sturm, B.L.T., Casini, L., Dalmazzo, D.: The AI music arms race: on the detection of AI-generated music. Trans. Int. Soc. Music. Inf. Retr. **8**(1) (2025). https://doi.org/10.5334/tismir.254
16. Wang, S., Wang, O., Zhang, R., Owens, A., Efros, A.A.: CNN-generated images are surprisingly easy to spot... for now. In: 2020 IEEE/CVF Conference on Computer Vision and Pattern Recognition, CVPR 2020, Seattle, WA, USA, 13–19 June 2020, pp. 8692–8701. Computer Vision Foundation/IEEE (2020). https://openaccess.thecvf.com/content_CVPR_2020/html/Wang_CNN-Generated_Images_Are_Surprisingly_Easy_to_Spot..._for_Now_CVPR_2020_paper.html
17. Wu, Z., et al.: Asvspoof: the automatic speaker verification spoofing and countermeasures challenge. IEEE J. Sel. Top. Signal Process. **11**(4), 588–604 (2017). https://doi.org/10.1109/JSTSP.2017.2671435
18. Zang, Y., Zhang, Y., Heydari, M., Duan, Z.: Singfake: singing voice deepfake detection. In: IEEE International Conference on Acoustics, Speech and Signal Processing, ICASSP 2024, Seoul, Republic of Korea, 14–19 April 2024, pp. 12156–12160. IEEE (2024). https://doi.org/10.1109/ICASSP48485.2024.10448184

# Extending DP-sr with Future Atoms: Declarative Scheduling of Future Events

Francesco Calimeri, Veronica De Bastiani, Luca Laboccetta(✉), Simona Perri, and Giorgio Terracina

DeMaCS, University of Calabria, Via P. Bucci, 87036 Rende, CS, Italy
{francesco.calimeri,luca.laboccetta,simona.perri, giorgio.terracina}@unical.it, veronica.debastiani@proton.me

**Abstract.** Stream Reasoning (SR) is increasingly relevant in scenarios requiring continuous reasoning over heterogeneous and highly dynamic data streams, often combined with large background knowledge bases. *DP*-sr is a purely declarative ASP-based framework for SR, featuring a rich language and a generalized architecture that decouples language support from the underlying ASP system. However, in its current form, *DP*-sr mainly supports reasoning over past and present observations, while many monitoring tasks also require forward-looking reasoning, such as scheduling delayed checks, reminders, or follow-up events. In this paper, we extend *DP*-sr with two future-oriented constructs: *future atoms*, which schedule the generation of atoms at future time points once triggering conditions hold, and the `in_future` operator, which allows reasoning on atoms that have already been scheduled by the program but not yet produced. The proposed constructs provide a direct and declarative way to model delayed effects and future checks, avoiding cumbersome encodings based on recursive state maintenance and backward-looking windows. We illustrate their modelling capabilities on representative SR scenarios and experimentally show that they improve both clarity and performance, especially under bursty streaming workloads.

**Keywords:** Stream Reasoning · Knowledge Representation and Reasoning · Answer Set Programming

## 1 Introduction

Stream Reasoning (SR) [17] combines continuous data processing with logical inference: it targets settings in which information arrives as an unbounded, rapidly evolving flow, and conclusions must be drawn on the fly by combining the incoming events with a substantial body of background knowledge. Such requirements are central to domains as diverse as Smart Cities, the Internet of Things (IoT), and Healthcare, where answers must be at the same time timely and accurate, and where a late or imprecise decision may have serious consequences.


S. Bistarelli et al. (Eds.): AIxIA 2026, LNAI 17131, pp. 100–114, 2027.
https://doi.org/10.1007/978-3-032-40774-0_8

The heterogeneity and sheer volume of data streams have, over the years, motivated a broad spectrum of SR proposals, developed within rather different research communities, ranging from Data Stream Management Systems (DSMS) and Complex Event Processing (CEP) to the Semantic Web and Knowledge Representation and Reasoning (KRR) [1,2,9,18,20,22,26–28]. Within KRR, Answer Set Programming (ASP) has been particularly successful: its purely declarative nature pairs high expressiveness with the ability to capture intricate scenarios in a compact and natural way. A milestone in bringing ASP to streams is LARS [4], which adds to ASP window operators and temporal modalities (such as "always", "sometimes" and "at"); since full LARS is intractable, the available engines target tractable fragments [3–5,19,30]. More recently, the *I-DLV-sr* system [12,14] couples the stream processor *Apache Flink* [15] with the incremental ASP reasoner *$\mathcal{I}$ncr-DLV2* [11]. Building on *I-DLV-sr*, and following the path of other domains where usable ASP tools enabled real-world applications [25], *DP*-sr [13] enriches the base language with additional modelling constructs and adopts a generalized architecture that decouples language support from the choice of a specific ASP engine, so that any reasoner complying with the ASP-Core-2 standard [10,21] can be used. This paper targets a further, so far missing, capability: reasoning not only about the past and present, but also about events expected to occur in the future. Window-based constructs only look back, whereas many monitoring tasks must also look forward, scheduling delayed checks, reminders, or follow-up events; with the existing language this can only be emulated awkwardly, by reaching back, time point by time point, to the past instants that encode the intended delay. Reasoning about the future is not new: metric and linear-time temporal logics offer future-time operators [23], also imported into ASP by temporal and metric-temporal extensions [6–8], and Complex Event Processing systems routinely schedule timers over events [16]. Our aim is more pragmatic: rather than a full temporal logic, we add two lightweight, directly executable constructs to an already deployed, Flink-based ASP stream reasoner.

The goal of this work is therefore to extend *DP*-sr [13] with two dedicated constructs that capture this behaviour declaratively:

- the *future atom*, a rule head annotated with a temporal delay, that schedules the generation of an atom at a future time point once its body is satisfied;
- the `in_future` operator, that allows a program to reason on the fact that an atom has been scheduled and will become true after a given amount of time, even before it is actually produced.

We illustrate these constructs on real-world SR scenarios with their *DP*-sr encodings, and report an experimental analysis of their performance.

The remainder of the paper is organized as follows. Section 2 recalls the background on *DP*-sr needed in the following and introduces the two new constructs, the future atom and the `in_future` operator, together with their semantics and their implementation. Section 3 reports and discusses our experimental evaluation. Finally, Sect. 4 draws some conclusions and outlines directions for future work.

## 2 Extending *DP*-sr with Future-Oriented Constructs

*DP*-sr [13,24] is a purely declarative framework for Stream Reasoning, rooted in the ASP-based stream reasoning line initiated by *I-DLV-sr* [12]. It combines Answer Set Programming with stream-oriented constructs, runs on top of the stream processor *Apache Flink* [15], and adopts an architecture that keeps language support independent of the underlying ASP engine. The formal syntax, semantics, and architecture of *DP*-sr are presented in [24]; here, we recall the relevant notions and focus on the future-oriented extension proposed in this work.

In *DP*-sr, data are observed over time as a *stream* $\Sigma = \langle S_0, \ldots, S_n \rangle$, where each set $S_i$ contains the ground atoms that hold at *time point* $i$, namely, the events observed at that instant. A program is a set of rules whose bodies are conjunctions of *streaming literals*. A streaming literal looks *backward* in time: rather than checking the current instant only, it inspects a window of past time points, defined relative to the current one, and tests whether the event of interest occurs there, e.g., always, at least, or at most a given number of times. Notably, standard ASP literals can be regarded as a special case of streaming literals, in which the evaluation is restricted to the current time point. In the base language, when the body of a rule holds at a time point $i$, its head atom is added to $S_i$ and becomes available for further reasoning.

To evaluate a program efficiently, *DP*-sr splits it into subprograms that can be processed separately, possibly in parallel. The splitting is driven by a *Stream Dependency Graph* (SDG), whose nodes are the predicates occurring in rule heads and whose arcs record the dependencies among them; an arc is labelled "<" when the dependency is *temporal*, that is, it goes through a non-degenerate streaming literal and hence relates different time points. We refer the reader to [12] for the formal definitions of the SDG and its use in program splitting.

The constructs recalled so far are designed to reason over present and previously observed data.

In the rest of this section we extend the language with two constructs that, instead, support *forward*-looking reasoning: the *future atom* (Sect. 2.1), which schedules the generation of an atom at a future time point, and the `in_future` operator (Sect. 2.2), which reasons about atoms that have already been scheduled for future generation but have not been produced yet. We then describe how the two constructs are realized in the system (Sect. 2.3), show them at work on a representative monitoring scenario (Sect. 2.4), and discuss their expressiveness and modelling convenience (Sect. 2.5).

### 2.1 Future Atoms

A *future atom* is a rule head equipped with a temporal delay, specifying that the derived atom has to be produced at a later time point rather than at the current one. A rule whose head contains a future atom has the following form:

$$h \ \texttt{after} \ \{d\} \ \texttt{:-} \ B.$$

where

- $h$ is an atom occurring in the head of the rule.
- $B$ is a conjunction of *DP*-sr streaming literals.
- $d \in \mathbb{N}^+$ is a delay expressed as a number of stream time points.

We call a rule whose head is a future atom a future-atom rule.

Intuitively, when the body $B$ is satisfied at a time point $i$, the atom $h$ is not made true immediately. Instead, its ground instance is scheduled and added to the stream at the future time point corresponding to $i + d$.

*Example 2.1.* Consider the following rule:

```
r1:  a(X) after {3} :- b(X).
```

If the event `b(7)` is true at time point $i$, the rule does not imply the derivation of `a(7)` at the current time point; instead, it causes a generation to be properly scheduled, so that `a(7)` will be generated at time point $i + 3$.

More formally, let $\Sigma = \langle S_0, \ldots, S_n \rangle$ be the input stream, and let $P$ be a *DP*-sr program extended with future atoms. At each time point $i$, the evaluation proceeds as in the standard *DP*-sr semantics, but over a stream already enriched with all atoms scheduled in previous time points and due at $i$.

Then, for every ground instance of a future-atom rule whose body holds at time point $i$ over the enriched stream, the corresponding ground instance of the head, denoted by $h_g$, is scheduled for time point $i + d$. When that time point is reached, the scheduled atom is added to the corresponding stream set, i.e., $S_{i+d} \leftarrow S_{i+d} \cup \{h_g\}$. From then on, $h_g$ participates in the evaluation of streaming literals and rules exactly like any other event in the stream.

Hence, the notions of backward observation, satisfaction of streaming literals, applicability of rules, and streaming model are preserved; the extension only adds a scheduling mechanism for rule heads whose effects are delayed.

*Safety.* The safety condition follows the standard *DP*-sr intuition: variables occurring in the scheduled head must be bound by positive body literals, so that the scheduled atom is ground when it is added to the stream at the future time point. For instance, the rule in Example 2.1 is safe because $X$ occurs in the positive body atom `b(X)`.

*Dependency Graph.* In order to deal with this new construct, the definition of the SDG (recalled above) is extended so as to treat a future atom as a temporal dependency. Let $q$ be the predicate of the scheduled head $h$ and let $preds(B)$ be the set of predicates occurring in the body $B$ of a future-atom rule. For every $p \in preds(B)$, the SDG contains an arc $(p, q)$ labelled with "<". All arcs induced by standard rules are still generated as in the base language. Consequently, future atoms are handled uniformly with other temporal dependencies during program splitting.

*Example 2.2.* Consider the program:

```
r2: b(X) :- c(X).
r3: d(X) after {5} :- b(X).
```

The standard rule $r_1$ induces the usual dependency from c to b, whereas the future-atom rule $r_2$ induces an arc from b to d labelled with "<". The label captures the fact that the derivation of d is temporally delayed with respect to the satisfaction of b.

## 2.2 The in_future Operator

Besides scheduling an atom for a later time point, it is sometimes useful to check whether an atom has already been scheduled for future generation, even before it is produced. For this purpose, *DP*-sr provides the *in_future* operator.

An in_future literal is a body literal of the form:

$$a \texttt{ in\_future } [d]$$

where:

- $a$ is a standard ASP atom
- $d \in \mathbb{N}^+$ is a number of time points.

As usual for streaming literals, an in_future literal may also occur under default negation. Intuitively, at time point $i$, a literal of the form $a$ in_future $[d]$ is satisfied by each scheduled ground atom that is an instance of $a$ and is due at some time point within the interval $[i, i + d]$.

*Applicability.* It is important to observe that this form of look-ahead is only defined for standard atoms $a$ whose predicate occurs in the head of at least one future-atom rule. Indeed, in_future does not predict future external inputs from the stream, nor future consequences of ordinary rules; rather, it queries explicit future scheduling information produced by future atoms. Thus, an expression of the form $a$ in_future $[d]$ is meaningful only when the predicate of $a$ occurs in the head of some future-atom rule. If this condition is not met, i.e., if the predicate of $a$ never occurs in the head of a future-atom rule, the system reports a warning.

*Dependency Graph.* As for the future atom, the definition of the SDG (recalled above) is extended accordingly: given a rule whose body contains a literal of the form $a$ in_future $[d]$, let $p$ and $q$ be, respectively, the predicates of $a$ and of the rule head $h$. Then, the SDG contains an arc $(p, q)$ labelled with "<". The label captures that the derivation of $h$ depends on temporal information associated with the future generation of $a$.

### 2.3 Implementation

*DP*-sr is realized as a Java system on top of the stream processor *Apache Flink* [15], which compiles each program into a dataflow of operators evaluated over the input stream. We refer the reader to [24] for the overall architecture and for the ASP back-ends supported during the evaluation; here we focus on how the two new constructs are realized.

In our implementation, *future atoms* are handled by a dedicated stateful *Flink* operator. The operator maintains a map from future time points to the set of ground atoms scheduled for those time points. Whenever the body of a future-atom rule is satisfied, the corresponding head atom is instantiated and inserted into this state with the proper future timestamp. At every time point, the operator retrieves the atoms scheduled for the current time point, emits them as stream facts, and removes them from the state.

So far, delays have been treated abstractly as numbers of time points. In the concrete language, the delay of a future atom, as well as the bound of an `in_future` literal, may also be written with a time unit, such as `msec`, `sec`, or `min`, with seconds assumed by default. Such expressions are normalized with respect to the program time unit before evaluation.

Moreover, the operator also materializes auxiliary atoms that make the scheduled future generation observable before the actual head atom is produced.

Consider a rule of the form $h$ `after` $\{d\}$ `:-` $B$., whose head is a future atom. Assume that, at time point $i$, a ground instance of the body $B$ is satisfied, and consider the corresponding ground instance of the head, call it $h_g$ (recall that $d$ is the delay, in time points). Then:

- for every offset $j$ such that $0 \leq j < d$, at every time point $i + j$, an auxiliary atom is produced stating that $h_g$ will become true after $d - j$ time points. Such auxiliary atoms are of the form `a_future_in`$r$`(t)`, where $h_g = a(\mathbf{t})$, $a$ is the predicate symbol of $h_g$, and $r = d - j$ is the *remaining delay.*
- the ground atom $h_g$ is produced at time point $i + d$.

For example, for the rule $b(X)$ `after` $\{2\}$ `:-` $B$., if $B$ holds at time point $i$ with $X = 7$, the operator produces:

$$\begin{aligned} i &\rightarrow \texttt{b\_future\_in2seconds(7)} \\ i+1 &\rightarrow \texttt{b\_future\_in1seconds(7)} \\ i+2 &\rightarrow \texttt{b(7)} \end{aligned}$$

As for the `in_future` construct, the implementation relies on the aforementioned generated auxiliary atoms. In particular, an expression of the form $b(X)$ `in_future` $[o]$ is evaluated as true at the current time point if the corresponding future atom head `b(X)` is true or there exists at least one auxiliary atom of the form `b_future_in`$r$`(X)` such that $1 \leq r \leq o$. Such atoms are internal to the workflow, they let the `future atom` and `in_future` operators communicate and are not exposed in the final answer stream.

## 2.4 Modelling Monitoring Tasks with Future-Oriented Constructs

In this section we show how a real-world SR problem can be modelled via *DP*-sr and, in particular, using the future-oriented constructs introduced in this paper. We consider a reasoning task from the *Maritime Monitoring* domain [29]; after briefly introducing the context, we present its encoding in *DP*-sr.

**Table 1.** Streaming and Background Events

| Streaming Event | Description |
|---|---|
| entersArea(V, A) | Vessel V enters area A |
| leavesArea(V, A) | Vessel V leaves area A |
| withinArea(V, A) | Vessel V is within area A |
| gapStart(V) | Vessel V stopped sending position signals |
| gapEnd(V) | Vessel V resumed sending position signals |
| vesselGapInArea(V,P) | Vessel V entered a communication gap while being in position category P, where P can be "nearPorts" or "farFromPorts" |
| **Background Event** | **Description** |
| areaType(A,T) | Area A is of Type T |
| vesselType(V,T) | Vessel V is of Type T |
| limitedArea(A) | Area A is a limited/protected area |

**Maritime Monitoring** Maritime surveillance systems are essential for maritime safety, quickly detecting real-time hazardous or illegal vessel activities. They use the Automatic Identification System (AIS), a tracking technology that combines VHF transceivers with GPS and navigation sensors such as gyrocompasses. This system delivers crucial vessel information and relies on coastal AIS base stations or satellites for positional data beyond land-based coverage. In this domain, we consider the following reasoning tasks:

- delayed area-stay detection;
- persistent communication-gap detection.

In the standard setting, these tasks are mainly oriented towards past and present information: at each time point, the system decides what currently holds by considering the current stream and previous observations. However, in several monitoring scenarios, it is also useful to explicitly schedule future checks.

These behaviours can be naturally expressed by means of *future atoms*. Rather than immediately deriving the target atom, a future atom schedules it at a later time point, allowing the program to separate the triggering condition from the delayed verification.

Streaming data come from GPS signals and concern events related to vessel position, communication status, etc. These streaming events, along with some necessary background events, are summarized in Table 1.

*Delayed Area-Stay Detection.* The first task concerns the recognition of vessels that are still inside a protected or limited area after a given amount of time. When a vessel enters a limited area, the system schedules a delayed check instead of immediately deriving an alert. If the vessel is still inside the same area when the check is produced, an alert is derived. Moreover, shortly before the delayed check expires, military vessels operating in the same area can be notified, so that they can start approaching the suspicious vessel before the possible alert is actually triggered.

```
r4: checkStay(Vessel,Area) after {2 min} :-
      entersArea(Vessel,Area),
      limitedArea(Area).

r5: alert(Vessel) :-
      checkStay(Vessel,Area),
      withinArea(Vessel,Area).

r6: militaryIntervention(MilitaryVessel,Vessel,Area) :-
      checkStay(Vessel,Area) in_future [30 sec],
      withinArea(Vessel,Area),
      withinArea(MilitaryVessel,Area),
      vesselType(MilitaryVessel,military).
```

Rather than being derived on entry, `checkStay(Vessel,Area)` is scheduled two minutes later; at that future time point the second rule derives the alert if the vessel is still within the same area. The third rule, in turn, uses `in_future` to notify the military vessels in the area shortly before a possible alert, namely when the scheduled check is due within the next thirty seconds.

*Persistent Communication-Gap Detection.* The second task concerns the recognition of persistent communication gaps. A vessel may temporarily stop sending AIS messages because of short transmission issues. Therefore, it may be useful not to derive an alert immediately when the gap starts, but only if the communication gap persists for a given amount of time.

This behaviour can be modelled by combining a future atom with the inertial generator of *DP*-sr [24]. The inertial generator is a modelling construct that maintains a generated atom across time points, starting from an initiating event and until a terminating event occurs. In this case, it is used to maintain the communication gap while it is active, whereas the future atom schedules a delayed check.

```
r7: #generate(communicationGap(Vessel,NearOrFarPorts);
          vesselGapInArea(Vessel,NearOrFarPorts):
          gapEnd(Vessel)).

r8: gapCheck(Vessel,NearOrFarPorts) after {5 min} :-
      vesselGapInArea(Vessel,NearOrFarPorts).

r9: gapAlert(Vessel,NearOrFarPorts) :-
      gapCheck(Vessel,NearOrFarPorts),
      communicationGap(Vessel,NearOrFarPorts).
```

The inertial generator derives and maintains `communicationGap(Vessel, NearOrFarPorts)` from when the vessel enters a gap until a matching `gapEnd (Vessel)` event; meanwhile, the future atom schedules `gapCheck(Vessel, NearOrFarPorts)` five minutes later, preserving the position category in which the gap started. When that check is generated, the last rule verifies whether `communicationGap(Vessel,NearOrFarPorts)` still holds: if so, the gap has persisted long enough and `gapAlert(Vessel,NearOrFarPorts)` is derived.

## 2.5 Future-Oriented Constructs Versus Base-Language Encodings

The proposed future-oriented constructs do not add expressive power in the strict sense, since their behaviour can be simulated by means of ordinary streaming rules. Their main advantage is rather that they provide a more direct and declarative way of expressing delayed derivations and look-ahead, in the natural direction that goes from a current condition to a future effect. We make this concrete on the same example that we later benchmark in Sect. 3: an atom `a(X)` that must be produced fifteen minutes after each `b(X)`, together with a look-ahead that detects when `a(X)` is about to be generated within the next five minutes.

*Emulating the Future Atom.* The future atom rule $r_1$ naturally states that `a(X)` must become true fifteen minutes after `b(X)` has been observed.

```
r10: a(X) after {15 min} :- b(X).
```

Without the construct, the same behaviour has to be encoded indirectly, by looking back at the exact past time point that should trigger the derivation: at the current time point, `a(X)` is derived whenever `b(X)` was observed exactly fifteen time points ago.

```
r11: a(X) :- b(X) in {15}.
```

The body of the rule $r_2$ inspects the single time point fifteen steps in the past and holds precisely when `b(X)` was observed there, regardless of whether `b(X)` also occurred at more recent time points.

*Emulating* `in_future`*.* A similar consideration applies to `in_future`: it can be simulated as well, by asking whether the body that scheduled the atom held in a suitable past interval, instead of whether the atom will hold in a future one. This is only possible for atoms produced by future atoms, though: ordinary rules derive their heads at the same time point as their bodies, and so carry no information about future generations. Using `in_future`, the look-ahead on the scheduled `a(X)` is written directly as:

```
r12:  in_future_5_min(X)  :- a(X) in_future [5 min].
```

stating that `in_future_5_min(X)` holds whenever the scheduled atom `a(X)` will be generated within the next five minutes. Without `in_future`, the same condition must be expressed by enumerating the past time points whose `b(X)` schedules an `a(X)` due within the next five minutes, namely those observed between ten and fifteen time points ago:

```
r13:  in_future_5_min(X)  :- b(X) in {10,11,12,13,14,15}.
```

Indeed, a `b(X)` observed $j$ time points ago schedules an `a(X)` that is due in $15-j$ minutes, so it falls within the next five minutes exactly when $10 \leq j \leq 15$. The programmer must therefore unfold the whole triggering interval by hand, whereas `in_future` expresses the same look-ahead directly, as a single forward-looking literal.

It is worth observing that this is a particularly simple and favourable case for the base-language encoding: the triggering condition is a single atom, the delay is fixed, and there is only one rule scheduling `a(X)`. Even in this setting, however, the emulation exposes low-level timing details that are implicit in the future-oriented constructs: the programmer has to know that `a(X)` is scheduled from `b(X)`, compute the relevant past offsets, and update the encoding whenever the delay or the look-ahead bound changes. With several future-atom rules scheduling the same predicate, the emulation must reconstruct all the corresponding triggering conditions, whereas `in_future` uniformly queries the scheduling information associated with that predicate.

Hence, both constructs let the programmer express temporal intentions in their natural direction, from a current condition to a future effect, rather than reconstructing them backward over past time points. They also keep scheduling and look-ahead explicit and statically checkable: future atoms create scheduled facts, and `in_future` queries them directly, allowing the system to warn when it is used on predicates that are not produced by future-atom rules. As we show in Sect. 3, this modelling advantage also has a performance counterpart: the base-language emulation repeatedly accesses and re-evaluates past facts, whereas the proposed operators rely on precomputed scheduling state.

# 3 Evaluation

As discussed in Sect. 2.5, both constructs can in principle be rewritten in the base language, so no expressiveness is strictly lost without them. This section shows that they are nonetheless convenient also for performance: we compare an encoding using the two constructs against an equivalent base-language emulation, measuring the per-time-point processing latency of both on streams of increasing size.

## 3.1 The Two Encodings

The benchmarked scenario is a minimal but representative combination of the two constructs: whenever an event b(X) is observed, a corresponding a(X) must be produced fifteen minutes later and, in the meantime, we want to detect when a(X) is about to be generated within the next five minutes.

With the native constructs, this is expressed by two short rules:

```
r14:  a(X) after {15 min} :- b(X).
r15:  in_future_5_min(X) :- a(X) in_future [5 min].
```

The future atom schedules a(X) fifteen minutes after each b(X), while the second rule derives in_future_5_min(X) exactly when a(X) has already been scheduled and is due within the following five minutes.

The same behaviour, without the two constructs, must be reconstructed from the past by directly accessing the time points that would trigger each derivation:

```
r16:  a(X) :- b(X) in {15}.
r17:  in_future_5_min(X) :- b(X) in {10,11,12,13,14,15}.
```

These are exactly the point-access encodings introduced in Sect. 2.5: the first rule reproduces the future atom and the second the in_future test. What matters for the experiment is one property of this emulation: unlike the native version, whenever the accessed time points fall on the burst delivered at time point 10, it must look up and re-evaluate all those b(X) facts, instead of reading precomputed scheduling state.

## 3.2 Experimental Setting

All experiments were carried out on an HP Victus 15, equipped with an Intel Core i7-13700H CPU (2.4–5.0 GHz) and 16 GB of DDR4 RAM, running Arch Linux. We ran both encodings over streams spanning 30 time points, one per minute, considering four input sizes, with 500, 1000, 1500 and 2000 b(X) facts, respectively. To stress the base-language emulation in a controlled way, all the b(X) facts are delivered together at time point 10, so that the base-language rules must look them all up together whenever their accessed time points reach time point 10. For each configuration we measured the per-time-point *processing latency*, that is, the time the system spends to evaluate each incoming time point. To account for measurement noise, every configuration was executed over ten independent runs, and we report, for each time point, the latency averaged over the ten runs. All the material needed to reproduce the experiments (encodings, input streams, and scripts) is publicly available.[1]

### 3.3 Results

Figure 1 reports the per-time-point latency of the two encodings, one panel per input size. For most of the stream the two encodings are cheap and nearly indistinguishable, staying low and flat up to time point 19. They separate between time points 20 and 25, when the facts delivered at time point 10 become ten to fifteen minutes old, so the scheduled `a(X)` is about to be due and is finally produced at time point 25: there the base-language emulation must look up and re-evaluate the whole burst and stays clearly above the native one, which only reads precomputed scheduling state. Both peak at time point 25 and then fall back to baseline. This gap widens with the input size: at the peak the base-language latency grows from about 0.05 s (500 facts) to about 0.11 s (2000), while the native encoding stays between about 0.04 and 0.06 s.

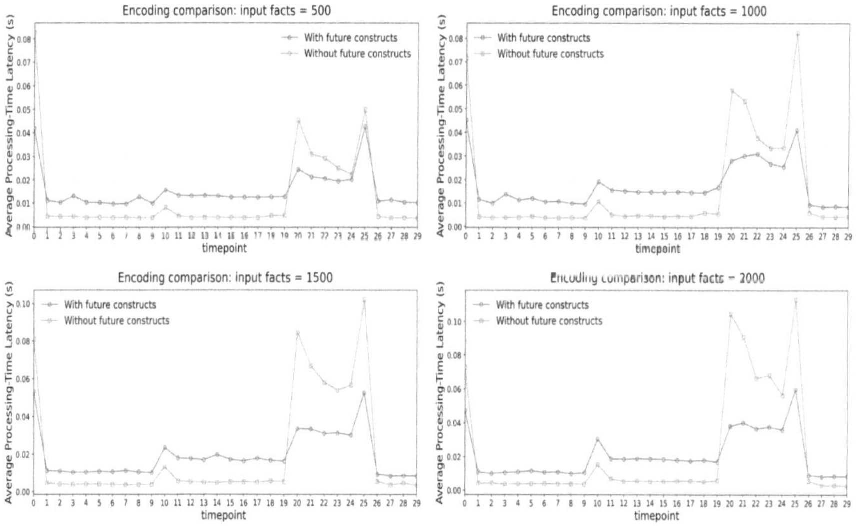


**Fig. 1.** Per-time-point processing latency, averaged over ten runs, of the encoding based on the native constructs (*With future constructs*) and of its base-language emulation (*Without future constructs*), over 30 time points and for 500, 1000, 1500 and 2000 input facts. All the `b(X)` facts are delivered at time point 10.

[1] https://github.com/Ronnie2603/Benchmark-Future-Constructs---DP-sr.

## 4 Conclusion

In this work we extended DP-sr with two future-oriented constructs: future atoms and the `in_future` operator. Future atoms declaratively schedule the generation of atoms at later time points, while `in_future` queries atoms that have already been scheduled. Together, they support forward-looking monitoring tasks, such as delayed checks, reminders, and follow-up events, without the indirect backward-looking encodings otherwise required. Our experiments show that this modelling advantage also improves performance under bursty workloads, by avoiding repeated re-evaluation of the same past facts. In future work, we plan to validate the constructs on larger benchmarks and to further enrich the language, for instance with temporal aggregations over future events.

## References

1. Anicic, D., Fodor, P., Rudolph, S., Stojanovic, N.: EP-SPARQL: a unified language for event processing and stream reasoning. In: Srinivasan, S., Ramamritham, K., Kumar, A., Ravindra, M.P., Bertino, E., Kumar, R. (eds.) Proceedings of the 20th International Conference on World Wide Web, WWW 2011, Hyderabad, India, 28 March–1 April 2011. pp. 635–644. ACM (2011). https://doi.org/10.1145/1963405.1963495
2. Barbieri, D.F., Braga, D., Ceri, S., Valle, E.D., Grossniklaus, M.: C-SPARQL: a continuous query language for RDF data streams. Int. J. Semantic Comput. **4**(1), 3–25 (2010). https://doi.org/10.1142/S1793351X10000936
3. Bazoobandi, H.R., Beck, H., Urbani, J.: Expressive stream reasoning with laser. In: d'Amato, C., et al. (eds.) ISWC 2017. LNCS, vol. 10587, pp. 87–103. Springer, Cham (2017). https://doi.org/10.1007/978-3-319-68288-4_6
4. Beck, H., Dao-Tran, M., Eiter, T.: LARS: a logic-based framework for analytic reasoning over streams. Artif. Intell. **261**, 16–70 (2018). https://doi.org/10.1016/J.ARTINT.2018.04.003
5. Beck, H., Eiter, T., Folie, C.: Ticker: a system for incremental ASP-based stream reasoning. Theory Pract. Log. Program. **17**(5-6), 744–763 (2017). https://doi.org/10.1017/S1471068417000370
6. Cabalar, P., Diéguez, M., Schaub, T., Schuhmann, A.: Metric temporal answer set programming over timed traces. In: Logic Programming and Nonmonotonic Reasoning (LPNMR 2022). LNCS, vol. 13416, pp. 117–130. Springer, Cham (2022). https://doi.org/10.1007/978-3-031-15707-3_10
7. Cabalar, P., Kaminski, R., Morkisch, P., Schaub, T.: telingo = ASP + time. In: Logic Programming and Nonmonotonic Reasoning (LPNMR 2019). LNCS, vol. 11481, pp. 256–269. Springer, Cham (2019). https://doi.org/10.1007/978-3-030-20528-7_19
8. Cabalar, P., Kaminski, R., Schaub, T., Schuhmann, A.: Temporal answer set programming on finite traces. Theory Pract. Logic Program. **18**(3–4), 406–420 (2018). https://doi.org/10.1017/S1471068418000297
9. Calbimonte, J.-P., Corcho, O., Gray, A.J.G.: Enabling ontology-based access to streaming data sources. In: Patel-Schneider, P.F., et al. (eds.) ISWC 2010. LNCS, vol. 6496, pp. 96–111. Springer, Heidelberg (2010). https://doi.org/10.1007/978-3-642-17746-0_7

10. Calimeri, F., et al.: ASP-core-2 input language format. Theory Pract. Log. Program. **20**(2), 294–309 (2020). https://doi.org/10.1017/S1471068419000450
11. Calimeri, F., Ianni, G., Pacenza, F., Perri, S., Zangari, J.: ASP-based multi-shot reasoning via DLV2 with incremental grounding. In: PPDP 2022: 24th International Symposium on Principles and Practice of Declarative Programming, Tbilisi, Georgia, 20–22 September 2022, pp. 2:1–2:9. ACM (2022). https://doi.org/10.1145/3551357.3551371
12. Calimeri, F., Manna, M., Mastria, E., Morelli, M.C., Perri, S., Zangari, J.: I-DLVsr: a stream reasoning system based on I-DLV. Theory Pract. Log. Program. **21**(5), 610–628 (2021). https://doi.org/10.1017/S147106842100034X
13. Calimeri, F., Mastria, E., Perri, S.: DP-SR: a purely declarative programming framework for stream reasoning (2024). https://sites.google.com/unical.it/dp-sr
14. Calimeri, F., Mastria, E., Perri, S., Zangari, J.: The stream reasoning system I-DLV-SR: enhancements and applications in smart cities. In: Governatori, G., Turhan, A. (eds.) Rules and Reasoning - 6th International Joint Conference on Rules and Reasoning, RuleML+RR 2022, Berlin, Germany, 26–28 September 2022, Proceedings. LNCS, vol. 13752, pp. 38–53. Springer, Cham (2022). https://doi.org/10.1007/978-3-031-21541-4_3
15. Carbone, P., Katsifodimos, A., Ewen, S., Markl, V., Haridi, S., Tzoumas, K.: Apache Flink™: stream and batch processing in a single engine. IEEE Data Eng. Bull. **38**(4), 28–38 (2015). http://sites.computer.org/debull/A15dec/p28.pdf
16. Cugola, G., Margara, A.: Processing flows of information: from data stream to complex event processing. ACM Comput. Surv. **44**(3), 15:1–15:62 (2012). https://doi.org/10.1145/2187671.2187677
17. Dell'Aglio, D., Valle, E.D., van Harmelen, F., Bernstein, A.: Stream reasoning: a survey and outlook. Data Sci. **1**(1-2), 59–83 (2017). https://doi.org/10.3233/DS-170006
18. Do, T.M., Loke, S.W., Liu, F.: Answer set programming for stream reasoning. In: Butz, C., Lingras, P. (eds.) AI 2011. LNCS (LNAI), vol. 6657, pp. 104–109. Springer, Heidelberg (2011). https://doi.org/10.1007/978-3-642-21043-3_13
19. Eiter, T., Ogris, P., Schekotihin, K.: A distributed approach to LARS stream reasoning (system paper). Theory Pract. Log. Program. **19**(5–6), 974–989 (2019)
20. Gebser, M., Grote, T., Kaminski, R., Schaub, T.: Reactive answer set programming. In: Delgrande, J.P., Faber, W. (eds.) LPNMR 2011. LNCS (LNAI), vol. 6645, pp. 54–66. Springer, Heidelberg (2011). https://doi.org/10.1007/978-3-642-20895-9_7
21. Gebser, M., Leone, N., Maratea, M., Perri, S., Ricca, F., Schaub, T.: Evaluation techniques and systems for answer set programming: a survey. In: Lang, J. (ed.) Proceedings of the Twenty-Seventh International Joint Conference on Artificial Intelligence, IJCAI 2018, Stockholm, Sweden, 13–19 July 2018, pp. 5450–5456. ijcai.org (2018). https://doi.org/10.24963/IJCAI.2018/769
22. Hoeksema, J., Kotoulas, S.: High-performance distributed stream reasoning using S4. In: Ordring Workshop at ISWC (2011)
23. Koymans, R.: Specifying real-time properties with metric temporal logic. Real-Time Syst. **2**(4), 255–299 (1990). https://doi.org/10.1007/BF01995674
24. Laboccetta, L., Mastria, E., Calimeri, F., Leone, N., Perri, S., Terracina, G.: Towards effective ASP-based stream reasoning: facilitate the reasoning over patterns of events. In: Bruni, A., Momigliano, A., Pradella, M., Rossi, M., Cheney, J. (eds.) Proceedings of the 26th International Symposium on Principles and Practice of Declarative Programming, PPDP 2024, Milano, Italy, 9–11 September 2024, pp. 18:1–18:12. ACM (2024). https://doi.org/10.1145/3678232.3678248

25. Leone, N., Ricca, F.: Answer set programming: a tour from the basics to advanced development tools and industrial applications. In: Faber, W., Paschke, A. (eds.) Reasoning Web 2015. LNCS, vol. 9203, pp. 308–326. Springer, Cham (2015). https://doi.org/10.1007/978-3-319-21768-0_10
26. Mileo, A., Abdelrahman, A., Policarpio, S., Hauswirth, M.: StreamRule: a non-monotonic stream reasoning system for the semantic web. In: Faber, W., Lembo, D. (eds.) RR 2013. LNCS, vol. 7994, pp. 247–252. Springer, Heidelberg (2013). https://doi.org/10.1007/978-3-642-39666-3_23
27. Pham, T., Ali, M.I., Mileo, A.: C-ASP: continuous ASP-based reasoning over RDF streams. In: Balduccini, M., Lierler, Y., Woltran, S. (eds.) Logic Programming and Nonmonotonic Reasoning - 15th International Conference, LPNMR 2019, Philadelphia, PA, USA, 3–7 June 2019. LNCS, vol. 11481, pp. 45–50. Springer, Cham (2019). https://doi.org/10.1007/978-3-030-20528-7_4
28. Le-Phuoc, D., Dao-Tran, M., Xavier Parreira, J., Hauswirth, M.: A native and adaptive approach for unified processing of linked streams and linked data. In: Aroyo, L., et al. (eds.) ISWC 2011. LNCS, vol. 7031, pp. 370–388. Springer, Heidelberg (2011). https://doi.org/10.1007/978-3-642-25073-6_24
29. Pitsikalis, M., Artikis, A., Dreo, R., Ray, C., Camossi, E., Jousselme, A.: Composite event recognition for maritime monitoring. In: DEBS, pp. 163–174. ACM (2019)
30. Ren, X., Curé, O., Naacke, H., Xiao, G.: BigSR: real-time expressive RDF stream reasoning on modern big data platforms. In: Abe, N., et al. (eds.) IEEE International Conference on Big Data (IEEE BigData 2018), Seattle, WA, USA, 10–13 December 2018, pp. 811–820. IEEE (2018). https://doi.org/10.1109/BIGDATA.2018.8621947

# UN-ASP: Handling Numerical Uncertainty in Answer Set Programming

Denise Angilica, Alessia Donata Camarda(✉), Giovambattista Ianni, and Simona Perri

University of Calabria, Rende, Italy
{denise.angilica,alessiadonata.camarda,giovambattista.ianni, simona.perri}@unical.it

**Abstract.** Reasoning over imprecise, uncertain, or arbitrarily rounded numerical information is a relevant challenge in knowledge representation and automated reasoning. In this paper, we propose UN-ASP, a rounding semantics for numerical values in Answer Set Programming (ASP). The semantics works in terms of abstracting uncertain numerical data into discrete sets of plausible values, while keeping the traditional ASP semantics. Plausible values can be selected within user-defined ranges and according to a given granularity. This allows the program to reason over alternative numerical approximations while preserving the discrete nature of ASP and exploiting existing ASP technology. Moreover, inconsistent scenarios possibly induced by alternative approximations are handled by relying on paracoherent semantics. We illustrate the approach on examples involving uncertain timestamps and spatial data, showing how UN-ASP can recover relevant inferences that would be lost under exact numerical matching or sharp rounding policies.

**Keywords:** Answer Set Programming · Uncertain data · Numerical uncertainty

## 1 Introduction

Answer Set Programming (ASP) [13] is a powerful declarative logic programming language widely used in fields such as artificial intelligence, scheduling, robotics, and digital forensics [1,10,11]. Data from the above domains often include numerical values that are subject to uncertainty, lack of precision, or are simply too fine-grained.

Dealing with this peculiar type of data can be problematic in logic-based languages, which are generally tailored at dealing with symbolic constants. Numeric values, such as timestamps or coordinates, are often dealt with simple rounding policies, which can suffer from semantic problems, both in terms of unexpected and/or missing infererences.

For instance, let us consider two numerical variables such as $x_1 = 10.49$ and $x_2 = 10.51$. Depending on the application at hand, one could desire to treat their


S. Bistarelli et al. (Eds.): AIxIA 2026, LNAI 17131, pp. 115–128, 2027.
https://doi.org/10.1007/978-3-032-40774-0_9

difference as negligible. However, on the one hand, an approach relying on exact equality of symbols, i.e. classical unification over symbolic terms, might treat such quantities as distinct; sharp rounding to the nearest, e.g. integer value, on the other hand, may arbitrarily separate the two values (like, e.g., rounding $x_1$ to $rx_1 = 10$ and $x_2$ to $rx_2 = 11$). Let us consider the ASP facts $boat_x(b_1, x_1)$ and $boat_x(b_2, x_2)$, together with the rule:

$$near(B_1, B_2) \text{ :- } boat_x(B_1, X), boat_x(B_2, X), B_1 \neq B_2.$$

Under standard logic programming semantics, the atom $near(b_1, b_2)$ is not derived, since unification requires $x_1 = x_2$. On the other hand, applying a simple rounding policy may still prevent the derivation, as the values might be mapped to distinct constants, or not, by pure chance. For instance, rounding to the nearest integer maps $y_1 = 10.09$ and $y_2 = 10.11$ to $ry_1 = ry_2 = 10$ while $rx_1 \neq rx_2$ as we have seen.

One may then consider relaxing constant equality by introducing a notion of approximate matching, where identity e.g. $x = y$ is substituted by $x \approx y \iff |x - y| < \epsilon$, i.e. numerical values are treated as equal whenever they are sufficiently close. However, such approaches introduce their own peculiarities. Note for instance, that $\approx$ is not a transitive operator (i.e. $x \approx y$ and $y \approx z$, does not necessarily imply $x \approx z$), while equality in logic programming is transitive, and this may lead to unintuitive behavior.

A rich and consolidated body of literature has addressed these issues in numerical reasoning through frameworks such as interval reasoning [5] and fuzzy numbers [12,20]. However, efficiently aligning such frameworks with the symbolic and grounding-based architecture of existing ASP solvers is far from obvious.

In this paper, we propose a rounding semantics, called *UN-ASP*, for handling uncertain numerical knowledge in ASP. UN-ASP can be seen as an abstraction of numerical values to sets of plausible roundings, thus changing input programs into an ordinary ASP program over discretized "plausible" values.

Remarkably, in UN-ASP, admissible approximations of numerical values are treated as simultaneously available possibilities.

Inconsistency caused by uncertainty is handled using an already established paracoherent semantics [3], which allows considering multiple (possibly conflicting) scenarios at once. This makes it possible to leverage state-of-the-art solvers while avoiding losing inferences due to sharp and arbitrary rounding. The key contributions of this work are the following:

- We formalize a new rounding semantics for uncertain numerical input data, which are abstracted to a range of simultaneous possibilities, whose range and density is a knowledge designer choice. A second, paracoherent semantics can be used for handling conflicting possibilities.
- The UN-ASP semantics paves the way to effective implementation, as it can be obtained by avoiding drastic changes in the unification semantics and/or variable identity; also, it is unnecessary to deal explicitly with new type of objects such as intervals or fuzzy numbers. To this end we provide a first illustrative implementation.

– We provide a qualitative analysis of the applicability of the proposed semantics to existing ASP encodings.

The paper is structured as follows. In Sect. 2, we introduce a running example to clarify the idea behind the new semantics. In Sect. 3, we formalize UN-ASP and describe its implementation. Section 4 discusses some technical issues regarding our semantics. Section 5 discusses the use of paracoherent reasoning for transformed programs that become incoherent. Section 6 overviews potential usages of UN-ASP in real-world scenarios. Lastly, in Sect. 7 we discuss related work and in Sect. 8 we outline the conclusions and possible future work. Our prototypical implementation can be found in the following repository: https://github.com/DeMaCS-UNICAL/UN-ASP.

## 2 Running Example: The Cake Dilemma

Consider a room with two doors, $d_1$ and $d_2$, each equipped with a sensor recording opening events together with their timestamps. A slice of cake is placed inside the room on a lifting sensor $ls$, which records the time at which the cake is removed. Two kids, Alice and Bob, are initially located behind doors $d_1$ and $d_2$, respectively. After a short time interval, both kids are found in the room and the cake has disappeared. The goal is to determine who may have eaten the cake. We assume that the sensors are only approximately synchronized, so recorded timestamps should not be interpreted as exact values. The scenario can be modeled in ASP as follows, using a 100-unit-per-hour temporal representation (e.g., the timestamp 11:30 corresponds to 1150):

$$
\begin{array}{l}
door(d_1).\ door(d_2).\ cake(ls).\ time(1100..1250).\\
log(d_1, 1198).\ log(d_2, 1204).\ log(ls, 1200).\\
inRoom(X, T_1) \text{ :- } time(T_1),\ door(X),\ log(X, T_2),\ T_2 \leq T_1.\\
suspect(X) \text{ :- } cake(C),\ inRoom(X, T_1),\ log(C, T_2),\ T_1 \leq T_2.\\
nonUniqueSuspect(X) \text{ :- } suspect(X),\ suspect(Y),\ X \neq Y.\\
culprit(X) \text{ :- } suspect(X),\ \texttt{not}\ nonUniqueSuspect(X).
\end{array}
$$

With these exact timestamps, Alice is derived as the only culprit since door $d_1$ is opened before the cake is lifted, whereas door $d_2$ is opened afterwards. However, this conclusion depends on treating timestamps as exact values. To account for synchronization uncertainty, one may associate each recorded timestamp with a finite set of admissible approximations, representing alternative plausible values. For instance, the value 1198 may be associated with $\{1180, 1190, 1200, 1210\}$, allowing the reasoning process to consider multiple plausible temporal configurations while preserving the discrete nature of ASP programs.

## 3 UN-ASP

In this section, we introduce UN-ASP, standing for ***UNcertain* ASP**, a rounding-based extension of Answer Set Programming for handling uncertain numerical knowledge. To model uncertainty, we apply a transformation of standard ASP programs. In particular, selected numerical arguments, occurring in atoms whose predicates are declared as uncertain, are replaced by finite sets of admissible approximations. We assume the usual syntax and semantics of ASP as background knowledge [7], and recall only the notation needed to define the transformation.

Let $\mathcal{C}$, $\mathcal{V}$, and $\mathcal{P}$ be pairwise disjoint finite sets consisting of constants, variables and predicate names, respectively. Each predicate symbol has a fixed arity and we denote by $p[i]$ the $i$-th argument position of $p$. A subset $\mathcal{P}_u \subseteq \mathcal{P}$ identifies the uncertain predicates, i.e., predicates whose numerical arguments may be subject to approximation. For each predicate $p \in \mathcal{P}_u$ with arity $n$, we denote by $I_p \subseteq \{p[1], \ldots, p[n]\}$ its set of uncertain argument positions. For each $p[i] \in I_p$, we introduce two rational values $\rho_{p[i]}, \sigma_{p[i]} \in \mathbb{Q}$. Intuitively, the former represents the radius of the range of admissible approximations for numerical terms occurring at position $p[i]$, while the latter represents its granularity.

Let $a = p(t_1, \ldots, t_n)$ be an atom over the predicate $p \in \mathcal{P}_u$. For each term $t_i$ occurring at position $p[i]$, we define the mapping $\mu(t_i)$ as follows:

$$\mu(t_i) = \begin{cases} \{k\sigma_{p[i]} \mid k\sigma_{p[i]} \in [t_i - \rho_{p[i]},\, t_i + \rho_{p[i]}),\ k \in \mathbb{Z}\} & \text{if } t_i \in \mathbb{Q} \text{ and } p[i] \in I_p \\ \{t_i\} & \text{otherwise.} \end{cases}$$

In other words, each numerical term occurring in an uncertain argument position is mapped to the multiples $k\sigma_{p[i]}$ of $\sigma_{p[i]}$ that fall within the approximation interval determined by $\rho_{p[i]}$. The upper bound of the interval is open to guarantee that, for fixed values of $\sigma_{p[i]}$ and $\rho_{p[i]}$, all uncertain terms occurring at the same argument position of the predicate $p$ generate sets of admissible approximations with equal cardinality.

Let $a = p(t_1, \ldots, t_n)$ be an atom over a predicate $p \in \mathcal{P}_u$. We define $\mu(a)$ as the set of all atoms $p(t'_1, \ldots, t'_n)$ such that $t'_i \in \mu(t_i)$ for each $i \in \{1, \ldots, n\}$.

*Example 1.* Consider again the Motivating Example in Sect. 2. Assume that the binary predicate $log$ belongs to $\mathcal{P}_u$ and that its second argument is uncertain, hence $log[2] \in I_{log}$. A knowledge designer, or an investigator, might choose to let $\sigma_{log[2]} = 10$ and $\rho_{log[2]} = 20$, as their reasonable approximation range and granularity. For instance, for the timestamp 1198, occurring in $log(d_1, 1198)$, we obtain $\mu(1198)$ by considering the interval $[1198 - 20, 1198 + 20) = [1178, 1218)$, and collecting the multiples of $\sigma_{log[2]} = 10$ falling within it, namely $\{1180, 1190, 1200, 1210\}$. By applying $\mu$ to the atoms with predicate $log$ we obtain the following new facts:

$$\begin{aligned} \{&log(d_1, 1180).\ log(d_1, 1190).\ log(d_1, 1200).\ log(d_1, 1210).\\ &log(d_2, 1190).\ log(d_2, 1200).\ log(d_2, 1210).\ log(d_2, 1220).\\ &log(ls, 1180).\ log(ls, 1190).\ log(ls, 1200).\ log(ls, 1210).\} \end{aligned}$$

As previously discussed, the discrete elements of $\mu$ range over a right-open interval to guarantee admissible approximation sets of fixed cardinality, for fixed $\rho$ and $\sigma$. Indeed, as can be observed from the example, if the upper bound were closed, the value 1200 would be mapped to $\{1180, 1190, 1200, 1210, 1220\}$, thus generating one additional approximation value with respect to 1198, which is mapped to $\{1180, 1190, 1200, 1210\}$. The Fig. 1 below provides a graphical representation of how the mapping $\mu$ is applied to our motivating example.

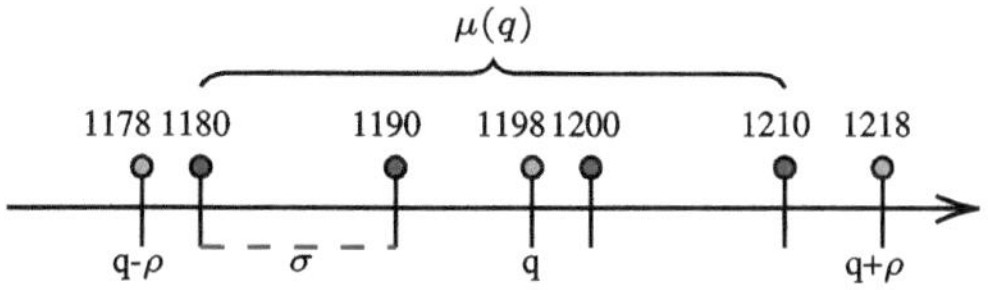


**Fig. 1.** Depiction of Example 1. The value $q$=1198 occurring at position $log[2]$ in $log(d_1, 1198)$ is approximated by considering $\rho_{log[2]} = 20$ and $\sigma_{log[2]} = 10$. The resulting set $\mu(1198)$ contains all admissible rounded values in the computed range.

The mapping $\mu$ extends to rules in the natural way. Given a rule $r$, $\mu(r)$ is the set of rules obtained by replacing each atom $a$ occurring in $r$ with an atom in $\mu(a)$. Note that, if the predicate of $a$ is not uncertain, then $\mu(a) = \{a\}$ and therefore $a$ is left unchanged. Otherwise, all admissible approximations of $a$ are considered.

*Example 2.* Consider the following rule: $r : a(123)$ :- $b(123, X)$. For $\rho_{b[1]} = 10$ and $\sigma_{b[1]} = 10$, we have that $\mu(r)$ is:

$$a(123) \text{ :- } b(120, X).$$
$$a(123) \text{ :- } b(130, X).$$

Then, given a program $P$, its uncertain version is defined as $\mu(P) = \bigcup_{r \in P} \mu(r)$. The uncertain answer sets of $P$ are then the standard answer sets of the transformed program $\mu(P)$, denoted as $AS(\mu(P))$. Thus, UN-ASP does not modify the answer set semantics itself: uncertainty is compiled away by the transformation, and the resulting program is evaluated as an ordinary ASP program. Notice that the Herbrand Universe and Base used for grounding are those induced by the transformed program $\mu(P)$.

*Example 3.* Let us consider again the program in Sect. 2 and apply the approximation mapping described in Example 1. The transformed program $\mu(P)$ admits an answer set containing, among others, the following atoms:

$$\{inRoom(d_1, 1180),\ inRoom(d_2, 1190),\ suspect(d_1),\ suspect(d_2),$$
$$nonUniqueSuspect(d_1),\ nonUniqueSuspect(d_2)\}.$$

By contrast, the original program admits an answer set containing:

$$\{inRoom(d_1, 1198),\ inRoom(d_2, 1204),\ suspect(d_1),\ culprit(d_1)\}.$$

The difference between the two cases is that, under the transformed program, the approximated timestamps make it possible to derive that both doors may have been opened before the cake was lifted. As a consequence, both children are classified as suspects, and no unique culprit can be concluded. In contrast, under the original program, the exact timestamps lead to deriving only one culprit.

### 3.1 Implementing UN-ASP

We implemented a prototype of UN-ASP on top of the DLV2 System [8,9]. The implementation realizes the mapping $\mu$ as a preprocessing rewriting of the input program. The user specifies which predicates and argument positions are considered uncertain by means of a set of directives with the following form:

$$\#uncertain\ p/a,\ i.\ rho = v_1,\ sigma = v_2.$$

Here, $p$ is the predicate name, $a$ is its arity, $i$ is the uncertain argument position, and $v_1$ and $v_2$ are the values assigned to $\rho_{p[i]}$ and $\sigma_{p[i]}$, respectively. If a predicate contains more than one uncertain argument position, each one must be explicitly specified using a dedicated directive, as described above. Given such a directive, the implementation rewrites the program in two steps. First, a fresh predicate $p\_r$ is introduced to collect the admissible approximations of the uncertain arguments. These values are computed using an *external atom* [2] that implements the mapping $\mu$, for the given choices of $\rho$ and $\sigma$. For instance, for the running example of Sect. 2, the directive:

$$\#uncertain\ log/2,\ 2.\ rho = 20,\ sigma = 10.$$

gives rise to the rule:

$$log\_r(X_1, N) \text{ :- } log(X_1, N_1),\ \&split\_number(N_1, 20, 10; N).$$

where the external atom $\&split\_number(N_1, 20, 10; N)$ builds the output of $\mu$ applied to the $N_1$ with $\rho = 20$ and $\sigma = 10$ variable and binds it to the $N$ variable. Second, all rules containing an uncertain predicate $p$ in the body are rewritten, replacing the occurrences of $p$ with the corresponding fresh predicate $p\_r$. In the running example, all occurrences of $log(X, T)$ used for reasoning are therefore replaced by $log\_r(X, T)$, whose second argument ranges over the admissible approximations of the original timestamp.

## 4 Technical Considerations

*Size of Grounded Uncertain Programs.* The transformation may introduce a combinatorial blow-up, since all combinations of admissible approximations have to be considered. In general, for each rule $r$ in the original program, we will have $O(m^k)$ new rules in the transformed program, for $m$ the maximum size of an application of $\mu$ and $k$ the number of uncertain attributes appearing in $r$. However, pending a future accurate assessment, we qualitatively expect that the number of uncertain numerical occurrences appearing in the same rule is typically small and fixed in practical encodings.

Therefore, for fixed uncertain attributes, and fixed $m$, the size of the transformed program grows linearly w.r.t. the size of the input program. In practice, depending on the choice of $\sigma$ and $\rho$, different numerical values may generate overlapping approximation sets, so that multiple original values collapse into the same rounded constants. Thus, the transformation does not necessarily increase the number of distinct numerical constants relevant for grounding. As an example, consider a road traffic monitoring system storing information in the form $log(time)$.

Suppose the dataset contains the facts $\{log(1000..1100)\}$, corresponding to 101 distinct timestamps, and we approximate $log[1]$ using $\rho_{log[1]} = \sigma_{log[1]} = 25$. Applying $\mu$ yields: $\{log(975)$, $log(1000)$, $log(1025)$, $log(1050)$, $log(1075)$, $log(1100)\}$, thus reducing the number of assertions from 101 to only 6.

*Disjunction, Choice Rules, and Possible Worlds.* In UN-ASP, admissible approximations of numerical values are treated as an abstraction of the original uncertain data and are made simultaneously available in the transformed program. Thus, the resulting program should not be interpreted as explicitly enumerating mutually exclusive possible worlds, where each uncertain observation is assigned exactly one admissible value. Rather, $\mu(P)$ represents an over-approximation of the consequences that may arise from the plausible rounded values induced by the input data.

An alternative semantics could encode admissible approximations by means of disjunctive assertions or choice rules, enforcing the selection of exactly one approximation for each uncertain numerical occurrence in each answer set. This would yield a scenario-based, or possible-world-style, interpretation of uncertainty. However, such an approach would dramatically increase the number of candidate answer sets, since the number of scenarios grows exponentially with the number of uncertain observations. For instance, if $m$ admissible approximations are generated for each of $k$ independent numerical observations, then up to $m^k$ alternative scenarios may have to be considered.

By contrast, UN-ASP deliberately avoids world enumeration. The transformed program compactly exposes all admissible rounded representatives to standard ASP reasoning, preserving the use of ordinary solvers and avoiding the combinatorial blow-up caused by selecting one approximation per observation. This comes with a semantic trade-off: a single answer set of $\mu(P)$ may combine consequences supported by different admissible approximations, even when these approximations would be mutually exclusive in a scenario-based semantics. We regard this behavior as intentional, since the goal of UN-ASP is not to reconstruct a single most plausible numerical world, but to recover inferences that are robustly or potentially supported under controlled numerical abstraction.

*Transitivity of Approximated Values Under UN-ASP.* As discussed in Sect. 1, approaches to numerical rounding based on approximate matching need to deal with the non-transitivity of the approximation relation: one may have $x \approx y$ and

$y \approx z$, but not necessarily $x \approx z$, unless $x, y$ and $z$ all pairwise fall within the distance $\epsilon$ of choice.

For instance, consider the following program $P$ with the predicate $boat_x \in \mathcal{P}_u$, with $boat_x[2] \in I_{boat\_x}$.

$$gathering \text{ :- } boat_x(B_1, X_1), boat_x(B_2, X_2), boat_x(B_3, X_3),$$
$$X_1 = X_2, X_1 = X_3, B_1 \neq B_2, B_1 \neq B_3, B_2 \neq B_3.$$

A rounding semantics based on syntactic replacement of equality with $\approx$ might just transform the above in $P_\epsilon$:

$$gathering \text{ :- } boat_x(B_1, X_1), boat_x(B_2, X_2), boat_x(B_3, X_3),$$
$$X_1 \approx X_2, X_1 \approx X_3, B_1 \neq B_2, B_1 \neq B_3, B_2 \neq B_3.$$

where, we recall, $x \approx y \iff |x - y| < \epsilon$. Now if we consider the set of facts $\{boat_x(b1, 100),\ boat_x(b2, 112),\ boat_x(b3, 122)\}$ with $\epsilon = 14$, we infer, using $P_\epsilon$, that *gathering* is true although $b1$ and $b3$ are 22 units apart, which is not a desirable inference.

To enforce a similar rounding diameter, we may set, under UN-ASP semantics, a granularity $\sigma_{boat\_x[2]} = 5$ and a radius $\rho_{boat\_x[2]} = \epsilon/2 = 7$. We can apply $\mu$ to numerical values obtaining $\mu(100) = \{95, 100, 105\}$, $\mu(112) = \{105, 110, 115\}$, and $\mu(122) = \{115, 120, 125\}$. Since the three approximated sets dot not share any rounded constant, $P$ does not infer *gathering* under UN-ASP semantics, as expected.

## 5 Paracoherent UN-ASP

The transformation introduced in Sect. 3 expands uncertain numerical values into sets of admissible approximations. While this allows the program to reason over alternative numerical reconstructions, some approximation-induced reconstructions may be incompatible with the constraints encoded in the program. As a consequence, the transformed program $\mu(P)$ may become incoherent, i.e., it may have no standard answer set.

*Example 4.* Let us consider again the running example and add the following rules:

$$someoneInRoom(T) \text{ :- } inRoom(X, T).$$
$$invalidScenario \text{ :- } cake(C),\ log(C, T),\ \texttt{not}\ someoneInRoom(T).$$
$$\text{:- } invalidScenario.$$

The predicate *invalidScenario* captures temporal reconstructions in which the cake is lifted while nobody is in the room. The integrity constraint excludes such reconstructions. Now consider the input facts: $\{log(ls, 1184),\ log(d_1, 1194),\ log(d_2, 1200)\}$. After applying $\mu$ with the same values of $\sigma$ and $\rho$ considered in Example 1, several admissible approximations are generated. In particular: $\mu(1194) = \{1180, 1190, 1200, 1210\}$, $\mu(1200) = \{1180, 1190, 1200, 1210\}$, $\mu(1184) = \{1170, 1180, 1190, 1200\}$. Among the atoms generated by the transformation, there are also approximations corresponding to the following reconstruction: $\{log(ls, 1170),\ log(d_1, 1180),\ log(d_2, 1180)\}$. In this configuration, the cake is lifted before either Alice or Bob enters the room. Then, *invalidScenario* is derived, thus violating the integrity constraint.

$$invalidScenario \text{ :- } cake(ls),\ log(ls, 1170), \texttt{not}\ someoneInRoom(1170).$$

At the same time, however, other admissible reconstructions would still allow deriving $suspect(d_1)$ and $suspect(d_2)$.

$$suspect(d_1) \text{ :- } cake(ls),\ inRoom(d_1, 1180),\ log(ls, 1190),\ 1180 \leq 1190.$$
$$suspect(d_2) \text{ :- } cake(ls),\ inRoom(d_2, 1180),\ log(ls, 1190),\ 1180 \leq 1190.$$

Therefore, the uncertainty transformation generates both meaningful and conflicting reconstructions, but the presence of incompatible ones makes $\mu(P)$ incoherent under standard answer set semantics.

To still extract meaningful information from transformed programs that become incoherent, we rely on the paracoherent semantics introduced in [3].

In our setting, the original program $P$ is first transformed into $\mu(P)$, and then $\mu(P)$ is further transformed into its paracoherent counterpart, denoted by $\mu(P)^k$. This post-processing step does not change the original encoding or the definition of $\mu$. Moreover, the auxiliary atoms introduced by the paracoherent transformation provide diagnostic information about the constraints involved in the inconsistency.

If $\mu(P)$ admits standard answer sets, the paracoherent models of $\mu(P)^k$, when restricted to the original vocabulary, coincide with the answer sets of $\mu(P)$. The only additional atoms are the auxiliary atoms introduced by the paracoherent transformation. If, instead, $\mu(P)$ has no standard answer set, the paracoherent models of $\mu(P)^k$ still provide meaningful information about the program, allowing UN-ASP to reason over approximation-induced reconstructions that would otherwise make the standard semantics fail.

*Example 5.* Let us apply the paracoherent semantics to the uncertain version of the Cake Dilemma extended with the rules introduced in Example 4. The resulting paracoherent model contains, among others, the atoms:

$$\{suspect(d_1),\ suspect(d_2),\ nonUniqueSuspect(d_1),\ nonUniqueSuspect(d_2),$$
$$invalidScenario,\ \#gap(\_\_constr613)\}$$

The atoms $suspect(d_1)$ and $suspect(d_2)$ show that the program still preserves meaningful deductions about the solution of the problem even if there exist some temporal reconstructions that violate the domain knowledge. The atom *invalidScenario*, together with a diagnostic atom such as $\#gap(\_\_constr613)$, indicates that the integrity constraint is involved in the inconsistency. Thus, paracoherent reasoning allows UN-ASP to preserve informative consequences even when some approximation-induced reconstructions make the transformed program incoherent under standard answer set semantics.

## 6 UN-ASP in Practice

To illustrate the use of UN-ASP on a more realistic setting, we consider a collision detection task over the Automatic Identification System (AIS) vessel data [16]. In maritime navigation, positioning and tracking data are collected using instruments that are subject to measurement noise, limited accuracy, and that often necessitate some rounding in order to deal with qualitative reasoning systems. This is especially relevant near ports or in heavy-traffic areas, where small errors in coordinates may affect the detection of potentially dangerous situations. We consider a decision-support setting in which maritime authorities need to detect possible spatial overlaps between vessels. Figure 2 illustrates how approximating vessel positions may affect the detection of spatial overlaps. For the sake of simplicity, we assume that longitude and latitude values represent linear coordinates over an Euclidean plane, and that all vessels have approximately the same physical size.

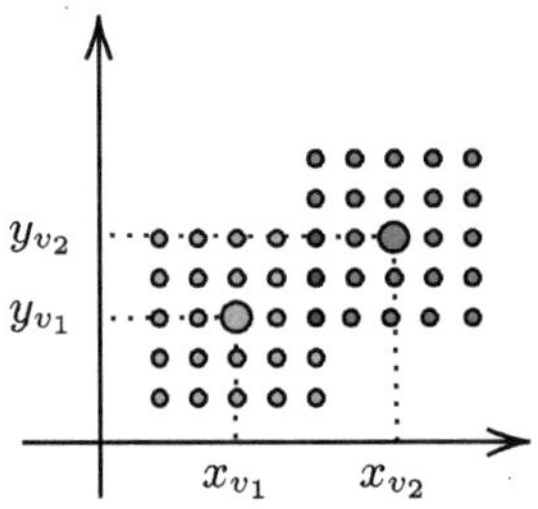


**Fig. 2.** Illustration of the abstraction mapping applied to vessel positions for two vessels, $v_1$ and $v_2$, and the resulting collision interpretation due to overlapping approximations.

Each vessel is described by a fact $vessel(V, Lon, Lat, T)$, reporting its longitude and latitude at time $T$. For instance, $vessel(22805, 38311, 42402, 684)$ places vessel 22805 at longitude 38311 and latitude 42402 at time 684.

*Modelling Spatial Overlap Without UN-ASP.* A vessel is not a point: to account for its physical extent (and for the noise affecting its reported position), one would normally surround each vessel with a rectangular bounding box and check whether boxes intersect. Without a notion of uncertainty, this must be modelled explicitly. One first materializes the four sides of every box from the reported coordinates and a half-size $H$ of the vessel,

$$box\_lat\_min(V, T, MinY) \text{ :- } vessel(V,, Y, T),\ MinY = Y - H.$$
$$box\_lat\_max(V, T, MaxY) \text{ :- } vessel(V,, Y, T),\ MaxY = Y + H.$$

(longitude bounds are analogous) and then tests, on *both* axes, the classical interval-intersection condition,

$$\begin{aligned}lat\_overlap(V1, V2, T) \coloneq\ & V1 < V2,\ box\_lat\_min(V1, T, Min1),\\ & box\_lat\_max(V1, T, Max1),\\ & box\_lat\_min(V2, T, Min2),\\ & box\_lat\_max(V2, T, Max2),\\ & Min1 \leq Max2,\ Min2 \leq Max1.\end{aligned}$$

plus an analogous rule for $lon\_overlap$ and a final rule combining the two. The intended meaning of the bounding box is genuinely simple, yet this encoding is verbose and error-prone: most of its rules are spent manufacturing interval endpoints and re-implementing interval arithmetic, which has little to do with the actual problem.

*Modelling Spatial Overlap with UN-ASP.* In UN-ASP, the bounding box is nothing but the uncertainty region around a coordinate: the interval $[Lat-H,\ Lat+H]$ is exactly "the latitude up to a half-width $H$". This is precisely what UN-ASP captures natively. It therefore suffices to declare the two numerical arguments of $vessel$ as uncertain, choosing the half-width parameter $\rho$ equal to the (common) vessel half-size and the granularity $\sigma$ accordingly:

$$\#uncertain\ vessel/4, 2.\ rho = 100,\ \ sigma = 100.$$
$$\#uncertain\ vessel/4, 3.\ rho = 100,\ \ sigma = 100.$$

As before, the choice of $\rho$ and $\sigma$ is driven by domain knowledge and by the requirements of the application designers. With this single declaration, UN-ASP maps each coordinate to its admissible rounded approximations, so that the physical extent of the vessels is already accounted for. Spatial overlap can be then reduced to a single rule, stating that two vessels overlap whenever they share a common rounded longitude $X$ *and* a common rounded latitude $Y$:

$$overlap(V1, V2) \coloneq vessel(V1, X, Y, T),\ vessel(V2, X, Y, T),\ V1 \neq V2.$$

The above do not require endpoints, and no interval comparisons: the uncertainty is encapsulated in $\rho$ and $\sigma$, while overlap is detected by plain unification over the shared rounded constants.
Consider again two vessels observed at the same time, $\{vessel(22805, 38311, 42402, 684),\ vessel(22801, 38265, 42375, 684)\}$. With the exact reported positions, $overlap(22801, 22805)$ is not derivable, and under standard ASP reasoning the two vessels are not classified as overlapping. By contrast, applying UN-ASP maps their coordinates to sets of plausible approximations,

$$\begin{aligned}\{&vessel(22805, 38300, 42400, 684),\ vessel(22805, 38300, 42500, 684),\\ &vessel(22805, 38400, 42400, 684),\ vessel(22805, 38400, 42500, 684),\\ &vessel(22801, 38200, 42400, 684),\ vessel(22801, 38300, 42400, 684),\\ &vessel(22801, 38200, 42300, 684),\ vessel(22801, 38300, 42300, 684)\}\end{aligned}$$

so that, in the, possibly unique, UN-ASP answer set of $P$ i.e. the answer set of $\mu(P)$, both vessels are approximated by the common longitude 38300 and latitude 42400. The rule above then derives $overlap(22801, 22805)$, identifying the two vessels as a potential spatial-overlap situation that exact numerical matching would have missed.

## 7 Related Work

Several approaches have been proposed to handle vagueness or uncertainty within
declarative formalisms [19]. These often deal with the degree of uncertainty of propositional values, such as in Probabilistic Logic programming [17], where uncertainty is generally dealt with by associating probabilities to facts or rules; a relatively recent proposal to introduce continuous numerical values following some probability distribution under the probabilistic answer set programming model has been introduced in [4]. One of the most popular approaches is fuzzy logic, in which uncertainty is modeled through degrees of truth, which has also been proposed under the ASP umbrella [6]. The fuzzy paradigm can be applied directly to numerical quantities, instead of propositional values: arithmetic operations in fuzzy number-based systems [12] could involve algebraic extensions that take these degrees into account and propagate them. While this allows for flexibility in representing uncertainty, fuzzy number-based systems introduce some implementation challenges, like e.g. dealing with fuzzy numbers of arbitrary shape, as each fuzzy number is represented by a membership function whose shape might vary after common arithmetic operations. Nonetheless, some recent attempt to use fuzzy numbers in a logic programming context exists [15].

Related ideas have also been explored in similarity-based and approximate reasoning frameworks [14,18]. However, these approaches often require specialized unification mechanisms and may introduce non-trivial semantic issues. Interval-based methods, which represent uncertain values as continuous ranges with operations defined over interval bounds, are closer to our approach [5].

## 8 Conclusion

In this paper, we introduced UN-ASP, a rounding semantics for handling numerical uncertainty in ASP. UN-ASP can be seen as an abstraction of uncertain numerical data to the nearest roundings: uncertain numerical values are mapped to finite sets of discretized plausible values, according to user-defined parameters controlling the approximation range and granularity. The resulting program remains an ordinary ASP program, thus allowing existing ASP technology to be used without modifying unification or introducing dedicated numerical solving machinery.

We also discussed how paracoherent reasoning can be combined with the proposed transformation when approximation-induced reconstructions make the transformed program incoherent under standard answer set semantics. The examples considered in the paper show that UN-ASP can recover relevant inferences that may be lost under exact numerical matching or sharp rounding policies.

As this is a preliminary contribution, several aspects still require further investigation. Future work includes studying scenario-based variants of the approach, for instance by using disjunctions or choice rules to select mutually exclusive approximations, extending the framework to richer classes of programs, and conducting a broader experimental evaluation of memory consumption and running times.

**Acknowledgments.** This work was partially supported by the AI4Nature and SINTESI projects, funded under the PNRIC 2021–2027 program (DM n.307/2025).

## References

1. Aker, E., Patoglu, V., Erdem, E.: Collaborative housekeeping robotics using answer set programming. In: SIU, pp. 1–4. IEEE (2013)
2. Alviano, M., et al.: The ASP system DLV2. In: Balduccini, M., Janhunen, T. (eds.) LPNMR 2017. LNCS (LNAI), vol. 10377, pp. 215–221. Springer, Cham (2017). https://doi.org/10.1007/978-3-319-61660-5_19
3. Amendola, G., Dodaro, C., Faber, W., Ricca, F.: Paracoherent answer set computation. Artif. Intell. **299**, 103519 (2021)
4. Azzolini, D., Riguzzi, F.: Probabilistic answer set programming with discrete and continuous random variables. Theory Pract. Log. Program. **25**(1), 1–32 (2025). https://doi.org/10.1017/S1471068424000437
5. Benhamou, F.: Interval constraint logic programming. In: Podelski, A. (ed.) TCS School 1994. LNCS, vol. 910, pp. 1–21. Springer, Heidelberg (1995). https://doi.org/10.1007/3-540-59155-9_1
6. Blondeel, M., Schockaert, S., Vermeir, D., Cock, M.D.: Fuzzy answer set programming: An introduction. In: Soft Computing: State of the Art Theory and Novel Applications. Studies in Fuzziness and Soft Computing, pp. 209–222. Springer, Cham (2013)
7. Calimeri, F., et al.: Asp-core-2 input language format. Theory Pract. Log. Program. **20**(2), 294–309 (2020)
8. Calimeri, F., Ianni, G., Pacenza, F., Perri, S., Zangari, J.: Forget and regeneration techniques for optimizing asp-based stream reasoning. In: PADL. LNCS, pp. 1–17. Springer, Cham (2024)
9. Calimeri, F., Ianni, G., Pacenza, F., Perri, S., Zangari, J.: ASP-based multi-shot reasoning via DLV2 with incremental grounding. Theory Pract. Log. Program. **25**(3), 281–303 (2025)
10. Costantini, S., De Gasperis, G., Olivieri, R.: Digital forensics and investigations meet artificial intelligence. Ann. Math. Artif. Intell. 193–229 (2019). https://doi.org/10.1007/s10472-019-09632-y
11. Dodaro, C., et al.: Operating room scheduling via answer set programming: improved encoding and test on real data. J. Log. Comput. **34**(8), 1556–1579 (2024)
12. Dubois, D., Prade, H.: Operations on fuzzy numbers. Int. J. Syst. Sci. **9**(6), 613–626 (1978). https://doi.org/10.1080/00207727808941724
13. Lifschitz, V.: Answer Set Programming. Springer, Cham (2019)
14. Medina, J., Ojeda-Aciego, M., Vojtáš, P.: Similarity-based unification: a multi-adjoint approach. Fuzzy Sets Syst. **146**(1), 43–62 (2004)
15. Paul, S., Ray, K.S., Saha, D.: Modeling uncertainty and imprecision in nonmonotonic reasoning using fuzzy numbers. CoRR abs/2001.01781 (2020). https://doi.org/10.48550/arXiv.2001.01781
16. Ray, C., Dréo, R., Camossi, E., Jousselme, A.L., Iphar, C.: Heterogeneous integrated dataset for maritime intelligence, surveillance, and reconnaissance. Data Brief **25**, 104141 (2019)

17. Riguzzi, F.: Foundations of Probabilistic Logic Programming: Languages, Semantics, Inference and Learning. River Publishers (2023)
18. Sessa, M.I.: Approximate reasoning by similarity-based SLD resolution. Theor. Comput. Sci. **275**(1–2), 389–426 (2002)
19. Straccia, U.: Managing uncertainty and vagueness in description logics, logic programs and description logic programs. In: Reasoning Web. LNCS, pp. 54–103. Springer, Cham (2008)
20. Zadeh, L.A., Aliev, R.A.: Fuzzy Logic Theory and Applications - Part I and Part II. WorldScientific (2018)

# F-ATOMIC: Reinterpreting Everyday Events Through Investigative Contexts

Alessia Donata Camarda(✉), Giovambattista Ianni, Simona Perri, and Antonio Rodofili

University of Calabria, Rende, Italy
{alessiadonata.camarda,giovambattista.ianni,simona.perri}@unical.it

**Abstract.** Building structured knowledge bases for commonsense reasoning can be time-consuming and expensive in terms of human effort. Thus, recent efforts have focused on automating the acquisition and generation of commonsense knowledge bases, aimed at supporting artificial intelligence systems. The advent of Large Language Models (LLMs) has significantly facilitated this process. In this paper, we propose **F-ATOMIC**, a forensic extension of the well-known $\text{ATOMIC}_{20}^{20}$ knowledge graph. F-ATOMIC reinterprets everyday events within investigative contexts, focusing on criminal or potentially malevolent scenarios. The resulting dataset contains 9 175 tuples spanning six macro-categories. Its main objective is to provide an initial forensic commonsense knowledge graph that can support symbolic and neurosymbolic approaches to digital forensic tasks. We also present a proof-of-concept application implemented in Answer Set Programming.

**Keywords:** Commonsense Reasoning · Digital Forensics · Neurosymbolic AI · Answer Set Programming · Knowledge Graphs

## 1 Introduction

General knowledge about the world and people's everyday life, the so called *Commonsense Knowledge* (CK), is usually taken for granted during speeches, discussions and interactions. CK represents one of the main sources that humans draw on when solving tasks in their everyday lives and beyond. However, computer systems do not possess CK unless it has been encoded previously and given as input to a system itself. This is a serious issue because it prevents systems from drawing conclusions that are obvious or easy for humans. For this reason, over the years there have been several efforts to encode common knowledge [8,18] with the aim of subsequently providing it as input to artificial intelligence systems. CK is typically represented through ontologies or knowledge graphs, i.e., graphs where the nodes represent entities and the arcs represent the relationships between those entities [22,23]. However, populating these data structures can be time-consuming and costly. Among other reasons, this has led to a gradual decline in interest. The advent of Large Language Models (LLMs) [25] has


S. Bistarelli et al. (Eds.): AIxIA 2026, LNAI 17131, pp. 129–142, 2027.
https://doi.org/10.1007/978-3-032-40774-0_10

significantly impacted the knowledge population process, making it increasingly easier, though not without risks: the knowledge retrieved from LLMs strongly depends on their training data, which is a problem in domain-specific contexts where the availability of information is usually reduced. Among these domains is digital forensics [2], i.e., the application of science to the identification, collection, examination, and analysis of data while preserving the integrity of the information and maintaining a strict chain of custody. More broadly, similar challenges also arise in investigative contexts where commonsense knowledge is required to interpret incomplete or ambiguous evidence. CK is implicitly applied in these contexts -for example, when we build deductions on the assumptions that a knife cannot be found in a bedroom- but case-related information is rarely disclosed. However, since forensic CK can be found in newspaper articles, interviews and other online sources used as LLM training data, it is in principle possible to go beyond the limited amount of labelled data available in this domain. To this end, we propose F-ATOMIC: a forensic extension of ATOMIC$^{20}_{20}$ [14]. F-ATOMIC is a dataset constructed by extracting latent knowledge from a pre-trained language model and filtering the generated tuples through an automated Multi-Judge evaluation process. The reliability of the automated filtering process was assessed through a manual evaluation conducted on a sample of tuples. Our main contributions can be summarized as follows.

- We augment ATOMIC$^{20}_{20}$ by reinterpreting selected everyday events within criminal or potentially malevolent scenarios, providing, to the best of our knowledge, the first event-centered dataset focused on forensic commonsense knowledge.
- We filter the generated tuples through an automated Multi-Judge evaluation process and assess its reliability through a manual evaluation conducted on a sample of tuples.
- We present a proof-of-concept example implemented in Answer Set Programming to illustrate how the dataset can be used in symbolic pipelines.

The paper is structured as follows. Section 2 provides an overview of the related work on which our study is based. Section 3 outlines knowledge extraction and validation methods in detail. Section 4 presents a proof-of-concept use case for criminal plan reconstruction using Answer Set Programming. Finally, Sect. 5 summarizes our contributions and future works.

The dataset, together with the code used to obtain it, is available at the following repository: https://github.com/Shadowz-git/forensic_atomic.

## 2 Related Work

Crowdsourcing was a facilitating factor for the generation of Common-Sense Knowledge Graphs (CSKGs) [22,23]. This method generally yielded fairly accurate CSKGs but with the introduction of some bias and noise. For instance, within ConceptNet, one can identify tuples, such as `Causes(listening to music, deafness)`, which are conceptually erroneous. It is not listening to music itself that can result in deafness; rather, it is incorrect listening habits. The advent of deep learning prompted endeavours to augment existing CSKGs through the refinement of models that have been pre-trained on the currently available knowledge [3,13,14]. However, the available information is consistently related to daily events and does not concentrate on specific domains, thus remaining of general purpose. In particular, these resources do not explicitly capture commonsense knowledge associated with criminal or investigative contexts. The advent of LLMs triggered a paradigm shift, given the possibility to extract from them a plethora of knowledge. LLMs have been employed in the context of populating ontologies with pre-existing schema [5], as well as deriving entities, associations, and properties, to populate novel schemes starting from textual and tabular data [11,19]. The CK extracted from LLMs has two main advantages. Firstly, it enables to extend the CSKGs we already possess. Secondly, it improves model performance on specific tasks, such as question and answering [26]. In addition, LLMs facilitate the conceptualization of existing knowledge and its re-instantiation, thereby enabling the creation of new, highly accurate tuples to be inserted into CSKGs [26]. In the forensic domain, ontologies were developed to formalize this type of knowledge [4,21,24]. However, even these ontologies lack the event-centered commonsense inferences that humans draw upon when interpreting actions, intentions, and possible consequences in investigative tasks. F-ATOMIC addresses this gap by reinterpreting everyday events within criminal or potentially malevolent scenarios and associating them with context-dependent commonsense inferences.

# 3 F-ATOMIC

This section describes the process used to construct and validate F-ATOMIC. Starting from a subset of events extracted from $\text{ATOMIC}_{20}^{20}$, we generated forensic reinterpretations through an LLM-based pipeline and subsequently assessed their quality through a multi-stage validation process. The overall workflow is illustrated in Fig. 1. The following subsections describe each phase in detail.

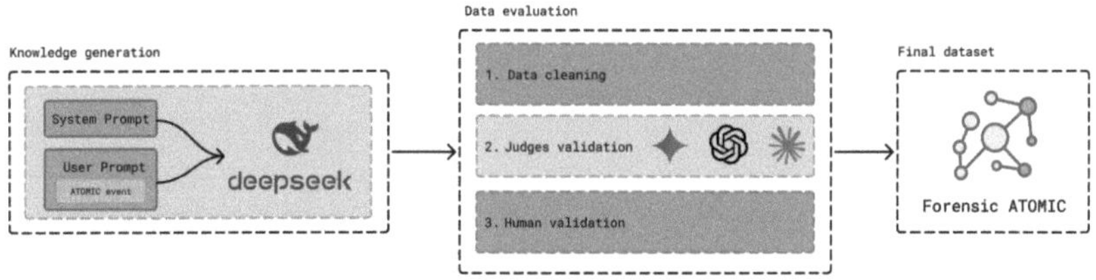


**Fig. 1.** The workflow of generation, automated validation, and human assessment of the F-ATOMIC dataset.

### 3.1 Knowledge Generation

We populated an event-centered graph containing information relating to social interactions in the criminal sphere, with a focus on everyday events that can be reinterpreted as potentially criminal in nature. ATOMIC$^{20}_{20}$ [14] was used as a starting CSKG because it already contains many events that could be interpreted from the forensic perspective. Indeed, we extracted a subset of ATOMIC by selecting events containing at least one of 116 predefined trigger words associated with potentially criminal activity, e.g., *steal*, *cut*, *buy*. 5,712 events were selected as input to the pipeline. F-ATOMIC also inherits 16 relations defined in ATOMIC$^{20}_{20}$, but their semantics are reinterpreted in a forensic context. Examples of such relations are: *xIntent*, capturing the actor's possible motivation behind the event; *xAttr*, describing the actor's possible traits as extracted from the event; *xEffect*, encoding the possible consequences the event has on the actor; and *oEffect*, encoding the possible consequences the event has on others or on third parties. The selected events and the relations to be populated were included in the system and user prompts provided to the LLM, which generated the new forensic knowledge. We chose to deploy DeepSeek V3.2 [7] as the *extractor* model because it allows us to strike a balance between performance and cost. Furthermore, it was selected because it maintained the output format (JSON) without introducing additional errors. The final prompt created for the model contained various pieces of information, including: the role assigned to the model, the task to be performed, the taxonomy of relevant categories, an explanation of the relationships to be populated, and some examples. In particular, to generate tuples that cover a wide range of cases, we introduced a taxonomy, shown in Table 1, of potential crimes that are of interest to us. The model was therefore tasked with generating tuples that fall within the context provided by the taxonomy.

**Table 1.** Forensic taxonomy used to guide the LLM into the criminal context.

| Category | Sub-categories |
|---|---|
| Violent Crimes | Assault, Homicide, Kidnapping, Robbery, Sexual Offense |
| Property Crimes | Theft, Burglary, Arson, Vandalism, Trespassing |
| Financial Crimes | Fraud, Money Laundering, Bribery, Tax Evasion |
| Cyber Crimes | Hacking, Phishing, Identity Theft, Online Harassment |
| Organized Crimes | Drug Trafficking, Racketeering, Weapon Smuggling |
| Public Order/Justice | Perjury, Obstruction of Justice, Disorderly Conduct |

The model was first asked to interpret each event as unambiguously illegal and, if possible, to generate a second interpretation matching a different category or subcategory, thus exploring a different physical, financial or digital angle. In other words, a single source event may correspond to a maximum of two tuples in F-ATOMIC, as we requested the model to generate a primary criminal interpretation and, when possible, an additional interpretation that is distinct from the first. This is especially important for ensuring diversity within the dataset, which would otherwise be skewed toward certain categories. Together with these special requests, the model was asked to generate a short text describing the context associated with the tuple; this text was stored in the *context* field.

To make the structure of F-ATOMIC explicit, Table 2 reports a compact example of a generated tuple. The tuple is associated with the source event *PersonX buys a car*, reinterpreted under the *Money Laundering* subcategory. Besides the source event, category, subcategory, and context, each tuple contains the values generated for the ATOMIC$^{20}_{20}$ relations in the corresponding forensic scenario. For readability, the table reports only a representative subset of the generated relations; the complete tuple includes the relations inherited from ATOMIC$^{20}_{20}$.

**Table 2.** Compact example of a tuple from F-ATOMIC for the event *PersonX buys a car* under the *Money Laundering* subcategory.

| Field | Value |
|---|---|
| Event | PersonX buys a car |
| Category | Financial Crimes |
| Subcategory | Money Laundering |
| Context | PersonX buys a car with illegally obtained funds to conceal the origin of the money. |
| *xIntent* | to conceal the origin of illicit funds; to create a seemingly legal asset from criminal proceeds |
| *xNeed* | a method to transfer the funds; a willing seller that does not ask probing questions |
| *xEffect* | illicit funds are converted into a tangible asset; PersonX appears to have legitimate wealth |
| *oEffect* | the dealership unwittingly facilitates a crime; the legitimate economy is contaminated |
| *isAfter* | PersonX identifies a suitable car to purchase |
| *HasSubEvent* | PersonX selects a vehicle; PersonX arranges payment in cash or structured deposits; PersonX takes possession of the car and title |
| *isBefore* | PersonX may sell the car to further layer the funds; law enforcement may trace the purchase back |

### 3.2 Data Cleaning

Tuples generated from the previous phase underwent a cleaning process. Specifically, tuples were discarded if the model failed to maintain context or if they contained filler words, such as "As an AI model, I cannot ...". The replies were also discarded if they contained non-Latin Unicode characters (such as Cyrillic) or invisible control characters. These preliminary results were also normalized to correct any misspelled category or subcategory names, for example, (sub)categories in plural form or with slightly modified versions of the names given in the taxonomy. Rather than discarding the entire tuple, we chose to correct these minor discrepancies. At the end of this process, we had 9,414 tuples.

### 3.3 Multi-judge Evaluation

Although the structural validation performed after the generation ensures the syntactic correctness of the data, the critical nature of the forensic domain requires an additional level of verification regarding the semantic consistency and investigative plausibility of the generated inferences. To address this need, we implemented a validation architecture based on the consensus of a triad of heterogeneous LLMs, the *Multi-Judge System*. This module queried three models belonging to different families, GPT-5 mini [20], Claude 4.5 Haiku [1], and Gemini 3.0 Flash Preview [12], with the aim of mitigating the biases and hallucinations inherent in each individual model under consideration. Each model acted as an independent judge to whom the original event, the criminal context, and the generated commonsense inferences were submitted. In particular, each judge was asked to focus on four aspects:

- Integrity: No empty required fields, gibberish, or corrupted text.
- Derivability: the category and/or subcategory must be plausibly derivable from a reasonable reading of the event text or from the *context* field. For neutral events, the 'context' field exists precisely to introduce a criminal scenario that the event text alone does not imply—this is expected and valid.
- Consistency: the relations *xIntent*, *xAttr*, and *xEffect* must not contradict the event.
- Proportionality: for events containing "accidentally" or "by mistake", xIntent must not describe an intentional aggressive act toward a person or object, even if imprecisely aimed. A precursor emotional state (e.g., *felt frustrated*) is acceptable; a precursor aggressive action (e.g., *to lash out*, *to hit*, *to throw*) is not.

The judges were provided with only some of the tuple fields, specifically: the event, the category, the subcategory, the context, and the *xIntent*, *xAttr*, *xEffect*, and *oEffect* relationships. This decision was made for two reasons: (i) to reduce costs, as sending and evaluating the complete tuple would significantly increase the number of tokens used, and (ii) because these fields are the most significant for determining whether the tuple truly falls within the forensic domain. Each judge assigned to each tuple a score on a scale of 0 to 100 and either approved or rejected the instance. Then, a tuple was included in the dataset if at least two out of three judges approved it and the average of these three scores was at least 60. If this did not occur, the tuple did not appear in the final dataset. The data analysis revealed that the Multi-Judge System acted as a significant filter, with a rejection rate ranging from 1.6% to 4.6% depending on the category of crime. The most frequent cases of rejection involve situations where the criminal interpretation is forced or overly abstract relative to the input event. This methodological rigour ensures that the dataset is less synthetic and more realistic, containing knowledge that can effectively be classified as commonsense. Following the Multi-Judge evaluation, the final version of the dataset comprises 9 175 tuples.

### 3.4 Data Understanding

A data understanding process was conducted after the Multi-Judge validation. As shown in Table 3, the resulting dataset is skewed predominantly toward financial crimes (31.5%) and organized crimes (22.6%). This predominance may be influenced by several factors, including the distribution of the selected source events, the filtering keywords, the taxonomy provided to the model, and the nature of the LLM pre-training data. Since LLMs are trained on vast datasets sourced from the web, including newspaper articles, investigative reports, and non-fiction literature, they may have internalized the frequency and relevance of such topics. At the subcategory level, the most frequent are *Fraud* (18.0%), *Drug Trafficking* (13.7%), and *Assault* (11.3%). Conversely, Cyber Crimes and Public Order events are less represented, suggesting that future extensions of the dataset should include targeted generation strategies to improve category balance.

**Table 3.** Distribution of macro-categories in the dataset.

| Crime Category | Instances | Percentage |
|---|---|---|
| Financial Crimes | 2.894 | 31.5% |
| Organized Crimes | 2.072 | 22.6% |
| Violent Crimes | 1.877 | 20.5% |
| Property Crimes | 1.254 | 13.7% |
| Cyber Crimes | 844 | 9.2% |
| Public Order/Justice | 234 | 2.6% |
| **Total** | 9 175 | 100.0% |

### 3.5 Human Evaluation

To better assess the quality of the augmented knowledge graph, several Google Forms were created to involve external annotators in the process of evaluating the dataset. These annotators included both students and individuals outside the affiliation institution of the authors of this paper, for a total of 12 participants. The volunteers who took part in the evaluation process came from a variety of backgrounds and, for the most part, had no prior experience of crowdsourcing activities. A sample of 550 tuples was randomly taken from the dataset evaluated by the Multi-Judge module, with an average of 25 events per form. Each form was filled by at least two different people. Human annotators were shown each event, its assigned forensic category and related inferences, as well as a document containing all the information needed to complete the form independently. The form description specified that the task was to determine whether the tuple made sense and reflected common human reasoning. In particular, each annotator should consider: (i) The clarity of the provided tuple. (ii) Whether the crime category can be inferred by commonsense from the context. (iii) Whether the outcomes are proportionate to the action. As with automated systems, human annotators were required to assign a score from 0 to 100 and indicate whether each tuple should be approved or rejected. A tuple was approved if the average score assigned by the annotators was at least 60 out of 100. The results of the comparison between human annotators and LLM evaluators, shown in Table 4, revealed a strong alignment, while also highlighting interesting differences in the granularity of the evaluations.

**Table 4.** Statistical summary of the comparative validation between human annotators and the Multi-Judge LLM evaluation framework. Scores are on a 0–100 scale; rates are percentages.

| Analyzed Metric | Value |
|---|---|
| Analyzed Sample | 550 tuples |
| Human Approval Rate | 88.7% |
| LLMs Approval Rate | 97.1% |
| **Decision Agreement** | **86.91%** |
| Average Human Score | 85.07 |
| Average LLM Score | 92.23 |
| Mean Absolute Error | 15.06 |
| Human agreement | 81.3% |

The most significant result is the 86.91% decision agreement rate: in a large majority of cases, the automated system and human annotators reached the same conclusion regarding the logical and forensic validity of the generated tuples. Although there is substantial agreement on whether to retain or discard a tuple, the average score assigned by LLMs (92.23) was higher than that assigned by humans (85.07), with a mean absolute error of 15.06 points. This discrepancy may reflect a phenomenon described in the literature as *algorithmic overconfidence* [16]: generative models may tend to assign high scores when they identify formal consistency. Human annotators, on the other hand, may apply a greater degree of "investigative doubt" or perceive subtle semantic issues that lead them to deduct points, even when they consider the commonsense inference generally acceptable.

The human evaluation was therefore used to assess the reliability of the automated validation process and did not alter the composition of the final dataset.

## 4 Criminal Plan Reconstruction Use Case

Our generated CSKG F-ATOMIC contains different semantic, emotional, and intentional interpretations of events in criminal contexts. This makes it a potentially useful resource for a wide range of tasks, such as intent prediction, victim effect prediction, context classification, and the generation of coherent criminal scenarios for training and educational purposes. As we are particularly interested in neurosymbolic and symbolic solutions, this section presents a proof-of-concept use case for criminal plan reconstruction using Answer Set Programming. The example illustrates how the context-dependent interpretations encoded in F-ATOMIC can provide background knowledge for reconstructing plausible criminal plans from incomplete observations.

*The Task.* It is rare for investigators to possess complete information regarding a criminal plan. Consequently, reconstructing criminal plans, namely, inferring by commonsense the most plausible and temporally consistent sequence of criminal activities in order to fill potential gaps in the available evidence, constitutes one of the primary tasks undertaken by law enforcement officers and investigators. In Artificial Intelligence, this particular task is commonly studied within the broader framework of plan recognition under temporal constraints [9,15]. Due to the requirements inherent in these scenarios, which involve incomplete knowledge, uncertainty, and temporal ordering of actions, there is a need to employ reasoning frameworks capable of managing these complexities. In recent years, Answer Set Programming (ASP) [10] has emerged as a suitable declarative paradigm for modelling reasoning tasks involving incomplete knowledge, default reasoning, and combinatorial search problems. Furthermore, ASP has proven to be an effective solution for forensic reasoning tasks [6], and in domains where reconstructing plans requires reasoning about temporal relations.

ASP programs consist of logical rules typically of the form `Head :- Body`, facts (rules without a body), hard constraints that restrict admissible solutions, and weak constraints that express preferences among answer sets. When weak constraints are used, the solver identifies the preferred answer sets according to the specified optimization criteria. All these elements are processed by an ASP solver that computes one or more *answer sets*, i.e., logically consistent solutions satisfying all rules and constraints. Knowledge derivation in ASP is performed by matching the atoms appearing in the body of a rule with the available facts. On the other hand, incomplete information is represented by default-negated atoms, which are assumed to be false whenever there is insufficient evidence to derive them. For a more comprehensive introduction to the syntax, semantics, and modelling techniques of ASP, the reader may refer to [17].

*Plan Reconstruction with F-ATOMIC.* We show how F-ATOMIC can play the role of a knowledge base encapsulating commonsense knowledge relating to crime, such as crime-specific plan templates or subcategory annotations that determine the most appropriate analysis of a given observation. Let us consider the event *PersonX buys a car*, whose relations are partially shown in Fig. 2. Thanks to F-ATOMIC, an investigator's observations can be situated within a criminal plan structure that depends on the criminal context. For instance, our CSKG contains two distinct entries for the event *PersonX buys a car*, one under the subcategory *Money Laundering* and one under the subcategory *Theft*. Under the MONEY LAUNDERING reading, the *isAfter* relation indicates that PersonX previously identified a suitable car to purchase, the *HasSubEvent* relation specifies that payment was arranged in cash or through structured deposits, and *xWant* reveals that the actor intends to potentially resell the vehicle for clean money. Under the THEFT reading, the same relations tell a completely different story: the *isAfter* field records that a car was stolen by another person and offered to PersonX, *HasSubEvent* describes a price negotiation with the seller/thief, and *xWant* reflects the intention to sell it quickly for a profit. It is this disambiguation that makes F-ATOMIC a useful resource: it provides the background knowledge needed to distinguish between plans involving several possible criminal scenarios, based on different subcategory annotations.

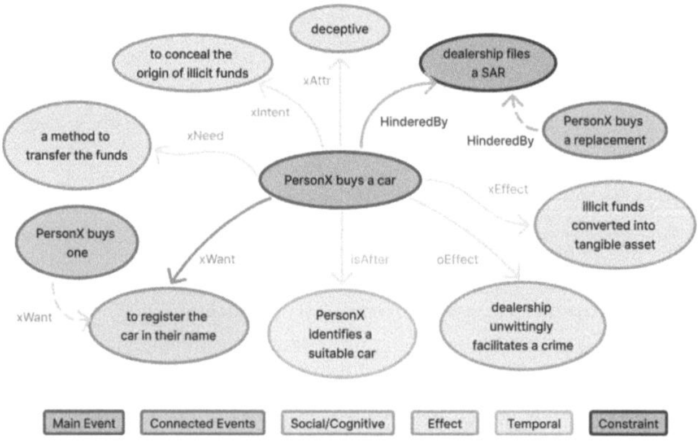


**Fig. 2.** Commonsense relations associated with the event *PersonX buys a car* under the *Money Laundering* reading, organised by node category.

Each event entry in our knowledge graph provides information that can support the construction of a partial plan structure. While *isAfter* and *isBefore* directly encode temporal relations, *HasSubEvent* and *xWant* provide additional events that can be organised into a plausible plan. Focusing on the *Money Laundering* reading, we manually derive a possible ordering from the relations associated with the selected event, as reported in Table 5.

**Table 5.** Possible criminal plan for the event PersonX buys a car, reconstructed from Forensic ATOMIC temporal relations.

| Step | Event | Source relation |
|---|---|---|
| 1 | PersonX identifies a suitable asset | *isAfter* of the main event |
| 2 | PersonX buys a car | main event |
| 3 | PersonX selects a vehicle | *HasSubEvent* of the main event |
| 4 | PersonX arranges payment | *HasSubEvent* of the main event |
| 5 | PersonX takes possession of the car | *HasSubEvent* of the main event |
| 6 | PersonX registers the car in their name | *xWant* of the main event |
| 7 | PersonX may resell the car | *isBefore* of the main event |

This plan is represented in ASP via the predicate `before`, which encodes the partial ordering of steps and enables reasoning about the main event.

```
before(px_identifies_suitable_asset, buys_car).
before(px_selects_vehicle, buys_car).
before(px_selects_vehicle,
       px_arranges_payment_in_cash_or_structured_deposits).
before(px_arranges_payment_in_cash_or_structured_deposits,
       px_takes_possession_of_car_and_title).
before(px_takes_possession_of_car_and_title,
       to_register_car_in_own_name).
before(to_register_car_in_own_name,
       px_may_sell_car_to_further_layer_funds).
```

Let us now consider the evidence the investigator actually possesses. This information, represented through the predicate `observed`, collects all the confirmed observations on which the reconstruction operates. Our goal is to abduce the smallest set of additional steps that are required to make the observations coherent with the F-ATOMIC plan template. To do this, for each unobserved event that is part of the plan template, we hypothesize that it occurred (guess phase). Then, we require each event included in the reconstructed plan to be supported by its predecessors: whenever an event belongs to the plan, every preceding step specified by the template must be either observed or abduced (check phase). Finally, given the fact that we could potentially generate plans where almost all the steps are abduced rather than observed, we use a weak constraint to minimize the number of hypothetical steps.

```
possible_plan_step(E) :- before(E, _).
possible_plan_step(E) :- before(_, E).
{ inferred(E) } :- possible_plan_step(E), not observed(E).
```

```
in_plan(E) :- observed(E).
in_plan(E) :- inferred(E).
:- in_plan(B), before(A,B), not observed(A), not inferred(A).
:~ inferred(E). [1@1,E]
```

Suppose the investigator has confirmed that PersonX bought a car, arranged the payment, and took possession of it, but has no evidence for the earlier or later steps in the plan.

```
observed(buys_car).
observed(px_arranges_payment_in_cash_or_structured_deposits).
observed(px_takes_possession_of_car_and_title).
```

The solver would produce the following optimal answer set:

```
in_plan(px_identifies_suitable_asset).                % inferred
in_plan(buys_car).                                    % observed
in_plan(px_selects_vehicle).                          % inferred
in_plan(px_arranges_payment_in_cash_or...).           % observed
in_plan(px_takes_possession_of_car_and_title).        % observed
```

The answer set shows two abduced steps: `px_identifies_suitable_car` and `px_selects_vehicle`, which are necessary antecedents of the observed events. The potential resale and registration steps are not abduced, since no subsequent observation demands their presence. Clearly, the plan follows the *Money Laundering* template from our knowledge graph. Under the *Theft* template the solver would load a completely different `before/2` chain, producing an entirely different set of abduced steps. The dataset is therefore what makes the reconstruction crime-specific.

## 5 Conclusion and Future Work

Commonsense represents one of the main sources that humans draw on when solving everyday and domain-specific tasks. Thanks to large language models, populating knowledge bases has become easier, even in domains where knowledge is scarce or hard to find. In this paper, we present F-ATOMIC, a forensic adaptation of the known ATOMIC model. F-ATOMIC was generated by querying an LLM and filtering through an automated Multi-Judge module, whose reliability was assessed through a manual evaluation conducted on a sample of tuples. The CSKG can potentially support various tasks, such as intent prediction, fine-tuning smaller models, and plan reconstruction. In this paper, we illustrated its use through a proof-of-concept example for criminal plan reconstruction. Extracting knowledge from LLMs reduces the need for repetitive calls to various models and provides a readily available knowledge base. However, there are still some challenges that need to be addressed in order to make this dataset more comprehensive and accurate. We will focus on these issues in the future.

- The tuple generation process could be extended with a second round using the conceptualized and re-instantiated dataset presented by [26], which leverages the CANDLE framework. This would enable us to increase the number of tuples and improve the coverage of the existing crime categories.
- Currently, manual validation has been performed on a subset of the entire dataset. Tools like Mechanical Turk could be used to validate and clean the entire dataset, removing any events or relationships that do not conform to our criteria.
- The dataset can be used to fine-tune smaller models and generate criminal cases and scenarios that, after expert validation, could support police training and educational activities.

**Acknowledgments.** This work was partially supported by the AI4Nature and SINTESI projects, funded under the PNRIC 2021–2027 program (DM n.307/2025).

## References

1. Anthropic: Claude 4.5 haiku (2026). https://www.anthropic.com/claude
2. Årnes, A.: Digital Forensics. Wiley, Hoboken (2017)
3. Bosselut, A., Rashkin, H., Sap, M., Malaviya, C., Celikyilmaz, A., Choi, Y.: Comet: commonsense transformers for automatic knowledge graph construction. In: Proceedings of the 57th Annual Meeting of the Association for Computational Linguistics, pp. 4762–4779 (2019)
4. Casey, E., Barnum, S., Griffith, R., Snyder, J., van Beek, H.M.A., Nelson, A.: Advancing coordinated cyber-investigations and tool interoperability using a community developed specification language. Digit. Investig. **22**, 14–45 (2017)
5. Ciatto, G., Agiollo, A., Magnini, M., Omicini, A.: Large language models as oracles for instantiating ontologies with domain-specific knowledge. Knowl. Based Syst. **310**, 112940 (2025)
6. Costantini, S., De Gasperis, G., Olivieri, R.: Digital forensics and investigations meet artificial intelligence. Ann. Math. Artif. Intell. **86**(1–3), 193–229 (2019)
7. DeepSeek-AI: Deepseek-v3 technical report (2024). https://arxiv.org/abs/2412.19437
8. Doug Lenat: Cyc technology (1995). https://cyc.com/
9. Fagundes, M.S., Meneguzzi, F., Bordini, R.H., Vieira, R.: Dealing with ambiguity in plan recognition under time constraints. In: AAMAS, pp. 389–396. IFAAMAS/ACM (2014)
10. Gelfond, M., Lifschitz, V.: The stable model semantics for logic programming. In: ICLP/SLP, pp. 1070–1080. MIT Press (1988)
11. Gómez, S.A., Fillottrani, P.R.: Leveraging large language models for ontology-based data access: a preliminary analysis. In: XXX Congreso Argentino de Ciencias de la Computación (CACIC) (La Plata, 7 al 11 de octubre de 2024) (2024)
12. Google: Gemini 3.0 flash preview (2026). https://deepmind.google/technologies/gemini/
13. Guan, X., Cao, J., Cao, B., Gao, Q., Liu, B.: Multi-hop commonsense knowledge injection framework for zero-shot commonsense question answering. Expert Syst. Appl. **298**, 129806 (2026)

14. Hwang, J.D., et al.: (comet-) atomic 2020: on symbolic and neural commonsense knowledge graphs. In: AAAI, pp. 6384–6392. AAAI Press (2021)
15. Kautz, H.A., Allen, J.F.: Generalized plan recognition. In: AAAI, pp. 32–37. Morgan Kaufmann (1986)
16. Li, Q., Cui, L., Kong, L., Bi, W.: Exploring the reliability of large language models as customized evaluators for diverse NLP tasks. In: COLING, pp. 10325–10344. Association for Computational Linguistics (2025)
17. Lifschitz, V.: Answer Set Programming. Springer, Cham (2019)
18. Miller, G.A.: Wordnet: a lexical database for English. Commun. ACM **38**(11), 39–41 (1995)
19. Oarga, A., Hart, M., Bran, A.M., Lederbauer, M., Schwaller, P.: Scientific knowledge graph and ontology generation using open large language models. In: Neurips 2024 Workshop Foundation Models for Science: Progress, Opportunities, and Challenges (2024)
20. OpenAI: GPT-5 technical overview (2026). https://openai.com/
21. Park, H., Cho, S.H., Kwon, H.-C.: Cyber forensics ontology for cyber criminal investigation. In: Sorell, M. (ed.) e-Forensics 2009. LNICST, vol. 8, pp. 160–165. Springer, Heidelberg (2009). https://doi.org/10.1007/978-3-642-02312-5_18
22. Sap, M., et al.: Atomic: an atlas of machine commonsense for if-then reasoning. In: Proceedings of the AAAI Conference on Artificial Intelligence, vol. 33, pp. 3027–3035 (2019)
23. Speer, R., Chin, J., Havasi, C.: Conceptnet 5.5: an open multilingual graph of general knowledge. In: Proceedings of the AAAI Conference on Artificial Intelligence, vol. 31 (2017)
24. Syed, Z., Padia, A., Finin, T., Mathews, M.L., Joshi, A.: UCO: a unified cybersecurity ontology. In: AAAI Workshop: Artificial Intelligence for Cyber Security. AAAI Technical Report, vol. WS-16-03. AAAI Press (2016)
25. Vaswani, A., et al.: Attention is all you need. In: NIPS, pp. 5998–6008 (2017)
26. Wang, W., et al.: CANDLE: iterative conceptualization and instantiation distillation from large language models for commonsense reasoning. In: ACL (1), pp. 2351–2374. Association for Computational Linguistics (2024)

# Re-evaluating Out-of-Distribution Learning in Drug Discovery

Francesco Capria, Alessio Micheli, and Domenico Tortorella(✉)

Department of Computer Science, University of Pisa, 56127 Pisa, Italy
f.capria@studenti.unipi.it,
{alessio.micheli,domenico.tortorella}@unipi.it

**Abstract.** Tanimoto similarity is widely used to define chemical novelty and out-of-distribution (OOD) learning regimes in drug discovery, yet it fails to capture the underlying mechanisms of dataset shift. In this work, we apply explainability techniques on machine learning models to investigate the nature of distribution shifts across training, validation, and test sets. Our analysis reveals that OOD scenarios arise from distinct sources, including class-prior shift, covariate shift in molecular fingerprints, and concept shift in the input-target relationship—factors not reflected by purely similarity-based metrics. By leveraging model explanations, we show that splits constructed using Tanimoto thresholds are insufficient to characterize the type of shift present at test time. This explains why OOD validation, as often currently implemented, does not lead to improved OOD generalization in practice. Our findings highlight the importance of diagnosing shift types using interpretable methods and suggest that robustness can only be achieved by developing and applying strategies tailored to the specific nature of the dataset shift.

**Keywords:** Machine Learning · Drug Discovery · Out-of-Distribution · Dataset Shift · XAI

## 1 Introduction

Drug discovery critically depends on the transition from hit identification to lead optimization, where initial candidate molecules from high-throughput or virtual screening are refined to improve potency, selectivity, and pharmacokinetic properties [7]. In this context, machine learning has become an essential tool, particularly for virtual screening, by enabling rapid prediction of molecular activity across vast chemical libraries and significantly reducing experimental costs and time [3,5]. However, these models are typically trained on limited and biased datasets, which makes their application to novel chemical scaffolds or unexplored regions of chemical space inherently an out-of-distribution (OOD) problem. As drug discovery naturally requires extrapolation beyond known compounds, the success of machine learning approaches hinges on their ability to


S. Bistarelli et al. (Eds.): AIxIA 2026, LNAI 17131, pp. 143–154, 2027.
https://doi.org/10.1007/978-3-032-40774-0_11

generalize under distributional shifts. Consequently, improving OOD generalization is crucial for ensuring that computational predictions remain reliable when identifying new hits and optimizing leads in real-world discovery pipelines.

However, OOD generalization is a major challenge in machine learning, arising when models encounter data that differs from their training distribution. In such settings, models often fail because they rely on superficial correlations rather than robust, underlying patterns [9]. This leads to unreliable and overconfident predictions when faced with novel inputs, domain shifts, or previously unseen scenarios. Developing models that can generalize beyond their training data remains difficult, as it requires capturing stable, invariant relationships while recognizing and adapting to distributional changes.

Out-of-distribution (OOD) scenarios can arise from different types of distributional shifts, including changes in prior probabilities (label distributions), covariates (input features), or the underlying relationship between inputs and outputs (concept shift) [8]. In this work, we assess the validity of out-of-distribution (OOD) model selection for well-established molecular fingerprint-based drug discovery models in hit identification tasks constructed to assess generalization to new molecules with low Tanimoto similarity, a requirement for patentability of new molecular compounds [14]. To investigate why this approach does not guarantee OOD generalization on such benchmarks, we apply explainable artificial intelligence (XAI) methods to characterize the types of distributional shifts.

## 2 Background

### 2.1 Drug Discovery

The central goal of drug discovery is to identify molecules that interact with a biological target and can be developed into safe and effective drugs. Since the chemical space of small molecules is extremely large, exhaustive experimental screening is infeasible, and early-stage campaigns rely on computational methods to prioritize promising compounds. In hit identification, this means discovering active molecules, or hits, that can serve as starting points for subsequent optimization of potency, selectivity, and pharmacokinetic properties [7].

Machine learning models support this process by learning structure-activity relationships from existing data and prioritizing compounds for experimental testing [6]. However, their practical value depends on whether predictions are made in regions of chemical space supported by the training data. This idea is captured by the *applicability domain*, defined as the region of the input space in which a predictive model is expected to be reliable [10]. Predictions within this domain can be regarded as interpolation and are generally more reliable, whereas predictions outside it correspond to extrapolation and should be treated with caution.

### 2.2 Dataset Shift

Supervised learning typically assumes that training and test data are drawn from the same joint distribution $P(X, Y)$ over inputs $X$ and labels $Y$. In practice, this assumption is often violated: the training distribution may differ from the deployment distribution $Q(X, Y)$. This phenomenon is known as *dataset shift* and is a major cause of performance degradation on out-of-distribution data [8,11]. Since the joint distribution can be factorized either as $P(X, Y) = P(Y|X)P(X)$ or as $P(X, Y) = P(X|Y)P(Y)$, different types of dataset shift can be distinguished according to which factor changes [8]:

**Prior probability shift** occurs when the marginal label distribution changes from $P(Y)$ to $Q(Y)$, while the class-conditional distribution remains stable, $P(X|Y) = Q(X|Y)$.
**Covariate shift** occurs when the marginal input distribution changes from $P(X)$ to $Q(X)$, while the conditional distribution $P(Y|X)$ remains stable.
**Concept shift,** or conditional shift, occurs when the conditional distribution changes from $P(Y|X)$ to $Q(Y|X)$, while the marginal input distribution $P(X)$ remains unchanged.

These types of distribution shift are not mutually exclusive and can occur in combination. Different combinations may lead to qualitatively different generalization failures, which is why characterizing the nature of the shift is important for understanding out-of-distribution behavior.

## 3 Materials and Methods

### 3.1 Chemical Fingerprints

Molecules are often represented using binary Extended-Connectivity Fingerprints (ECFPs), a class of circular fingerprints widely used to encode molecular structure [12]. ECFPs iteratively encode circular atomic environments around each atom. We use ECFP4 fingerprints, implemented as Morgan fingerprints with radius 2. This means that the largest encoded environments extend up to two bonds from the central atom, while the suffix "4" denotes the corresponding diameter. The resulting environment identifiers are hashed and folded into a fixed-length binary vector of $d = 1024$ bits [12,14]. Since this mapping is not necessarily one-to-one, distinct atomic environments may activate the same bit. Consequently, an individual ECFP4 bit does not necessarily represent a unique chemical substructure.

Given two molecules represented by binary fingerprints $\boldsymbol{x}, \boldsymbol{x}' \in \{0, 1\}^d$, chemical similarity is commonly quantified using the *Tanimoto similarity*, one of the standard similarity coefficients for binary molecular fingerprints [1]. It is defined as the ratio between the number of bits active in both fingerprints and the number of bits active in at least one of them:

$$\mathcal{S}(\boldsymbol{x}, \boldsymbol{x}') = \frac{|\boldsymbol{x} \cap \boldsymbol{x}'|}{|\boldsymbol{x} \cup \boldsymbol{x}'|}. \tag{1}$$

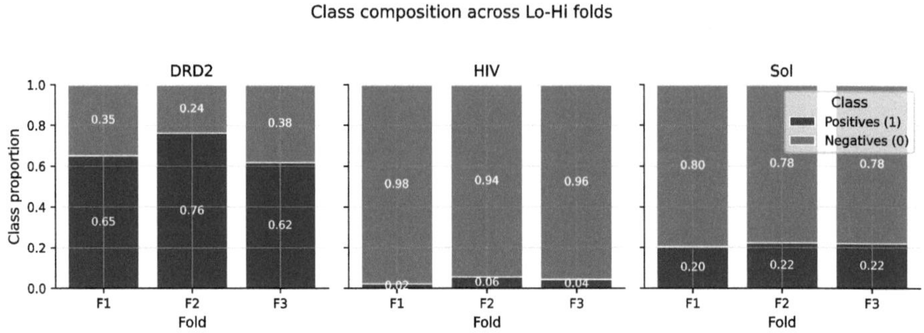


**Fig. 1.** Class composition across the three chemically separated outer folds for DRD2-Hi, HIV-Hi, and Sol-Hi in the Lo-Hi benchmark. Bars report the fraction of positive and negative molecules in each fold. HIV-Hi is strongly imbalanced, with only about 2–6% positives across folds, whereas DRD2-Hi is much less imbalanced.

The Tanimoto similarity ranges from 0, when the fingerprints share no active bits, to 1, when they are identical. This similarity measure is also known as *Jaccard* similarity or intersection-over-union (IoU) similarity.

### 3.2 Hit Identification Tasks

Hit identification aims to discover active molecules that are both correctly predicted and sufficiently novel with respect to the training compounds [7,14]. Random and scaffold splits often fail to enforce such novelty, leaving many test molecules structurally similar to the training ones. The Lo-Hi benchmark addresses this limitation by constructing chemically separated splits for hit-identification tasks: every test molecule is required to have ECFP4 Tanimoto similarity below 0.4 to every training molecule [14]. This threshold is adopted in Lo-Hi as a practical novelty criterion motivated by expert assessments of molecular structural similarity [4,14]. The resulting splits therefore enforce evaluation on structurally dissimilar molecules and operationally define an out-of-distribution (OOD) setting in chemical space.

This construction induces more than one form of distribution shift in the taxonomy introduced above [8]. By enforcing low ECFP4 Tanimoto similarity between training and test molecules, the Lo-Hi split is intended to induce covariate shift in molecular fingerprint space. At the same time, the class composition varies across datasets and folds, as shown in Fig. 1, introducing a prior-probability shift component. Thus, the resulting OOD setting is not only a chemically separated evaluation regime, but a combination of structural covariate shift and class-prior shift.

**Datasets.** We evaluate our approach on three binary tasks from the Lo-Hi benchmark [14]:

- `DRD2-Hi` concerns activity against the dopamine receptor D2;
- `HIV-Hi` is derived from antiviral screening data for inhibition of HIV replication;
- `Sol-Hi` addresses aqueous solubility, a relevant physicochemical property in early compound prioritization.

**Split Construction.** For each dataset, Lo-Hi provides three chemically separated folds [14]. In each outer split, one fold is held out as the final OOD test set, and the remaining two are used as the selection set. Within this selection set, we compare two validation strategies for model selection:

- In *OOD holdout validation*, the two folds are kept separate: one is used for inner training and the other for validation, so that chemical separation is preserved during model selection.
- In *random-shuffle validation*, the same outer-training molecules are instead pooled and randomly partitioned into inner training and validation sets using the same validation proportion as the corresponding OOD holdout split, yielding an in-distribution validation setting.

In both cases, the selected configuration is refit on the full outer training set and evaluated on the same held-out OOD test fold.

### 3.3 Explainable Learning Models

We employ three interpretable models trained on ECFP4 fingerprints: a Decision Tree, a Logistic Regression classifier, and a Linear SVM. These models are chosen because their decision rules can be inspected directly in fingerprint feature space, allowing us to study which molecular patterns each model emphasizes [6].

For each model, we extract a feature-level explanation, defined as a relevance score over fingerprint bits: impurity-based tree feature importance for the Decision Tree [2], the magnitude of the learned coefficients for Logistic Regression, and the magnitude of the learned weight vector for the Linear SVM. In all cases, these scores induce a ranking of fingerprint features according to their contribution to the model decision.

We use these rankings to analyze which fingerprint features drive the predictions and to assess whether the learned activity-relevant features remain stable across validation protocols and OOD test folds.

# 4 Experiments and Discussion

## 4.1 Fitting the Training Distribution and OOD Generalization Gap

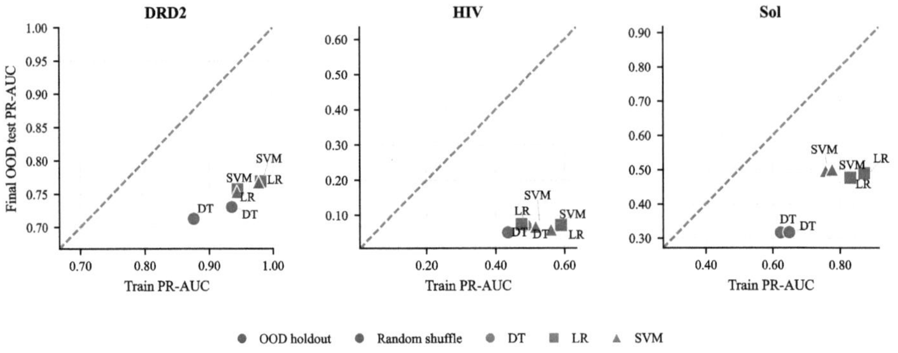


**Fig. 2.** Train PR-AUC versus Final OOD Test PR-AUC for DRD2, HIV and Sol datasets. Each point corresponds to a model (DT, LR or SVM) trained under either the OOD holdout (blue) or Random shuffle (red) validation protocol. The dashed diagonal line represents perfect agreement between training and test performance. (Color figure online)

Before analyzing the effect of the internal validation protocol, we first verify whether the selected models are able to fit the training distribution. Following the Lo-Hi benchmark, we have adopted PR-AUC (area under the precision-recall curve), a metric well suited to imbalanced binary classification settings [13,14]. Figure 2 compares train PR-AUC with final OOD test PR-AUC, while Table 1 reports training, inner-validation, and final test scores.

Consistently, train PR-AUC is higher than final OOD test PR-AUC across tasks and models. The difference is moderate for DRD2, where training scores range from 0.876–0.981 and test scores remain around 0.713–0.769. The difference is larger for solubility, where linear models achieve up to 0.872 on train but only 0.477–0.500 on test. Overall, HIV is more difficult, yet the same pattern holds: train scores remain above the very low final OOD test scores (0.05–0.07).

This suggests that poor out-of-distribution (OOD) performance is not chiefly due to an inability to fit the training data. Instead, the learned rules capture patterns that are useful within the training distribution, but which transfer only partially, or not at all, to chemically distinct test sets.

**Table 1.** Train, inner-validation, and final OOD test PR-AUC across Hi tasks. Values are mean ± standard deviation across outer folds. OOD holdout preserves chemical separation in the inner validation split, whereas random shuffle creates an in-distribution validation split.

| Dataset | Model | Protocol | Train PR-AUC | Val PR-AUC | Test PR-AUC |
|---|---|---|---|---|---|
| DRD2 | DT | OOD holdout | $0.876 \pm 0.033$ | $0.766 \pm 0.082$ | $0.713 \pm 0.068$ |
| | | Random shuffle | $0.935 \pm 0.013$ | $0.877 \pm 0.033$ | $0.731 \pm 0.111$ |
| | LR | OOD holdout | $0.944 \pm 0.035$ | $0.751 \pm 0.099$ | $0.757 \pm 0.100$ |
| | | Random shuffle | $0.981 \pm 0.010$ | $0.910 \pm 0.027$ | $0.769 \pm 0.108$ |
| | SVM | OOD holdout | $0.943 \pm 0.047$ | $0.738 \pm 0.100$ | $0.753 \pm 0.109$ |
| | | Random shuffle | $0.978 \pm 0.005$ | $0.906 \pm 0.025$ | $0.768 \pm 0.105$ |
| HIV | DT | OOD holdout | $0.435 \pm 0.117$ | $0.151 \pm 0.024$ | $0.051 \pm 0.030$ |
| | | Random shuffle | $0.487 \pm 0.094$ | $0.336 \pm 0.076$ | $0.070 \pm 0.053$ |
| | LR | OOD holdout | $0.475 \pm 0.126$ | $0.140 \pm 0.016$ | $0.074 \pm 0.038$ |
| | | Random shuffle | $0.590 \pm 0.093$ | $0.412 \pm 0.075$ | $0.071 \pm 0.037$ |
| | SVM | OOD holdout | $0.561 \pm 0.072$ | $0.104 \pm 0.023$ | $0.059 \pm 0.024$ |
| | | Random shuffle | $0.517 \pm 0.131$ | $0.375 \pm 0.078$ | $0.067 \pm 0.039$ |
| Sol | DT | OOD holdout | $0.624 \pm 0.115$ | $0.385 \pm 0.011$ | $0.317 \pm 0.022$ |
| | | Random shuffle | $0.649 \pm 0.145$ | $0.392 \pm 0.037$ | $0.317 \pm 0.024$ |
| | LR | OOD holdout | $0.830 \pm 0.125$ | $0.502 \pm 0.034$ | $0.477 \pm 0.049$ |
| | | Random shuffle | $0.872 \pm 0.036$ | $0.581 \pm 0.021$ | $0.490 \pm 0.047$ |
| | SVM | OOD holdout | $0.758 \pm 0.035$ | $0.479 \pm 0.036$ | $0.497 \pm 0.039$ |
| | | Random shuffle | $0.777 \pm 0.003$ | $0.572 \pm 0.012$ | $0.500 \pm 0.043$ |

### 4.2 Is OOD Validation in Model Selection Effective?

We now investigate whether the internal validation protocol used for model selection affects final OOD generalization. Figure 3 compares the mean inner validation PR-AUC with the mean final OOD test PR-AUC for the two protocols. Points below the dashed diagonal line indicate that inner validation overestimates final OOD test performance.

A clear pattern emerges across the three tasks. Random-shuffle validation, which constructs an in-distribution validation set, yields substantially higher inner-validation scores than OOD holdout validation: around 0.88–0.91 versus 0.74–0.77 on DRD2, 0.34–0.41 versus 0.10–0.16 on HIV, and 0.57–0.58 versus 0.49–0.50 on Solubility for the linear models.

However, these higher validation scores do not translate into higher final OOD test performance. On DRD2, both protocols achieve similar test PR-AUC scores of around 0.71–0.78 despite the large difference in validation scores. On HIV, all points lie below the diagonal, with final OOD test PR-AUC remaining low and virtually unchanged at around 0.06 0.08 for both protocols. On Solubility, the

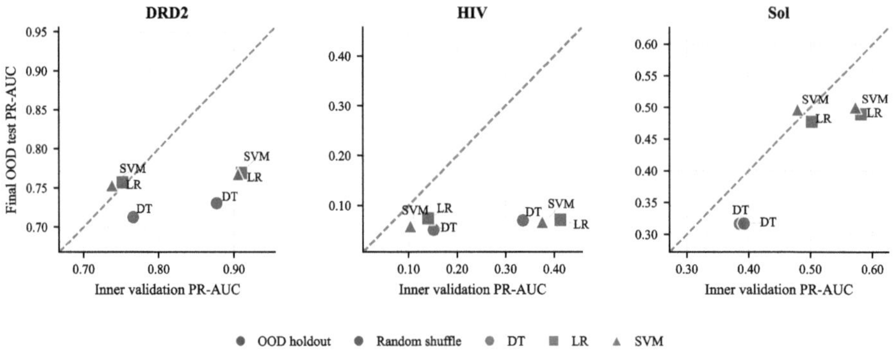


**Fig. 3.** Comparison of inner-validation and final OOD test PR-AUC across the three Hi tasks (DRD2, HIV, and Solubility). Each point shows the mean performance across outer folds for one model and validation protocol. Blue points indicate OOD holdout validation and red points indicate random-shuffle validation. Marker shapes denote the model type (circle: Decision Tree, square: Logistic Regression, triangle: Linear SVM). The dashed diagonal line represents perfect agreement between validation and test performance. (Color figure online)

inflated validation scores of random-shuffle validation likewise do not result in any improvement in final test performance for the linear models.

Overall, OOD holdout validation provides lower and more conservative estimates, indicating that chemically separated validation folds reduce the optimism of in-distribution model selection. Nevertheless, within the considered tasks and models, this more realistic protocol does not systematically improve final OOD test performance. A Tanimoto-defined OOD holdout is useful as a diagnostic validation setting, but is not sufficient by itself to ensure better final OOD generalization.

### 4.3 Detecting Concept Shift via XAI Analysis

Having shown in Sect. 4.2 that internal OOD validation does not systematically improve final OOD test performance, we analyze whether the selected models learn stable and separable decision rules. For each model and outer fold, we retain up to the top-100 activity-relevant ECFP4 features with non-zero relevance scores. We measure rule stability through the mean pairwise Jaccard overlap across folds. We then assess class separability in the restricted feature space by computing nearest opposite-class Tanimoto similarity both within the test fold and from test to training molecules. Exact-collision rates quantify the fraction of molecules that become identical to an opposite-class neighbor under the selected features. Tables 2 and 3 report the results, with OOD-holdout values followed by random-shuffle values in parentheses.

**Table 2.** Rule-stability diagnostic in the activity-relevant feature space. We report the mean pairwise Jaccard similarity of important ECFP4 features between models selected across different folds, using up to the top-100 non-zero relevance features. Lower values indicate that different chemically separated folds lead the model to rely on different fingerprint features, consistent with representation-level concept instability. Each cell shows the value in the OOD validation setting, followed by the value in the random-shuffle validation setting in parentheses.

| Dataset | Model | Top-feature similarity |
|---|---|---|
| DRD2 | DT | 0.02 (0.07) |
| DRD2 | LR | 0.15 (0.13) |
| DRD2 | SVM | 0.11 (0.13) |
| HIV | DT | 0.06 (0.08) |
| HIV | LR | 0.17 (0.17) |
| HIV | SVM | 0.10 (0.14) |
| Sol | DT | 0.12 (0.14) |
| Sol | LR | 0.27 (0.31) |
| Sol | SVM | 0.36 (0.33) |

*Rule Instability Across Folds.* The Jaccard overlap is low for all tasks and models (between 0.02 and 0.36), indicating that features relevant to activity change substantially across chemically separated folds. This is consistent with representation-level concept instability, since different folds result in different learned input-target rules in fingerprint space. This instability is evident under both validation protocols, suggesting that replacing random shuffle validation with an OOD holdout does not resolve the issue.

*Distinguishability of Learned Representations.* As discussed in Sect. 2.2, covariate shift refers to changes in the input distribution $P(X)$ between the training and test data. In our setting, the Lo-Hi split creates a structural shift in the ECFP4 fingerprint space by enforcing a chemical separation between the two sets of data. We therefore ask whether the learned, model-selected representation still preserves class distinguishability under this shift. Opposite-class collisions provide a means of diagnosing this: exact collisions occur when molecules with different labels share the same selected-bit representation. We report this metric in Table 3.

On HIV, exact collisions are prevalent across models and protocols, with Exact Cross values ranging from 12.1% to 32.2%, indicating that molecules of different classes often become indistinguishable in the selected feature space. This is consistent with the low PR-AUC observed in Sect. 4.2. In the HIV Decision Tree, some exact collisions arise from opposite-class pairs where neither molecule activates a selected bit. These pairs collapse to the all-zero vector in the restricted selected-feature space, not in the full ECFP4 fingerprint, and therefore lie outside the support of the learned rule. On DRD2, the linear models keep

Exact Cross close to zero, never exceeding 2.0%, whereas the Decision Tree under OOD selection reaches 32.8%, suggesting that its restricted representation is too coarse to preserve class separability. On Solubility, exact collisions are negligible overall ($\leq 1.5\%$), with Exact Cross equal to 0% for the linear models. Therefore, the limited OOD generalization is better explained by feature instability than by opposite-class indistinguishability.

Overall, these results are consistent with a concept shift at the representation level: the selected ECFP4 features are unstable across chemically separated folds and, in some cases, collapse opposite-class molecules into identical restricted representations. Because this instability appears to be related to the combination of the chosen models and the ECFP4 feature space, simply changing the validation splitting strategy is unlikely to solve the problem. This provides a plausible mechanistic explanation for why OOD-holdout validation does not systematically improve final OOD generalization.

**Table 3.** Feature-space separability diagnostic in the selected activity-relevant representation. $\mathcal{S}_{\text{cross}}$ is the mean nearest opposite-class Tanimoto similarity from test to training molecules in the selected activity-relevant feature space. *Test collisions* and *training-test collisions* report the percentage of molecules with an identical nearest opposite-class neighbor ($\mathcal{S} = 1$) within the test fold and from test to training molecules, respectively. Higher exact-collision rates indicate that molecules of opposite classes become indistinguishable under the model-selected representation. Each cell shows the value in the OOD validation setting, followed by the value in the random-shuffle validation setting in parentheses.

| Dataset | Model | Cross-classsimilarity $\mathcal{S}_{\text{cross}}$ | Test collisions (%) | Training-test collisions (%) |
|---|---|---|---|---|
| DRD2 | DT | 0.74 (0.59) | 40.7 (19.9) | 32.8 (1.2) |
| DRD2 | LR | 0.56 (0.53) | 16.1 (20.2) | 0.7 (0.6) |
| DRD2 | SVM | 0.58 (0.54) | 16.1 (23.8) | 1.4 (2.0) |
| HIV | DT | 0.67 (0.70) | 29.3 (32.9) | 28.3 (32.2) |
| HIV | LR | 0.52 (0.52) | 18.0 (16.1) | 13.6 (12.1) |
| HIV | SVM | 0.58 (0.57) | 23.2 (17.5) | 23.5 (16.8) |
| Sol | DT | 0.59 (0.63) | 0.7 (1.5) | 0.1 (1.4) |
| Sol | LR | 0.46 (0.46) | 0.3 (0.5) | 0.0 (0.0) |
| Sol | SVM | 0.49 (0.49) | 0.0 (0.0) | 0.0 (0.0) |

## 5 Conclusion

In this work, we investigated the limitations of current out-of-distribution (OOD) evaluation practices in drug discovery, focusing on settings constructed using Tanimoto similarity thresholds. While such benchmarks are intended to approximate covariate shift—where test molecules differ from training data in feature space but share the same underlying structure–activity relationship—our analysis reveals a more problematic reality. The imposed shifts are often so extreme that they no longer preserve the original input–target relationship, effectively inducing concept shift rather than pure covariate shift. As a result, models are evaluated in regimes where generalization is not only difficult but, in many cases, fundamentally ill-posed.

This observation has important implications for the notion of applicability domain in cheminformatics. Traditionally, the applicability domain is understood as the region of chemical space in which a model can be expected to make reliable predictions, based on its training data. However, when OOD evaluation pushes models far beyond this domain—into regions characterized by qualitatively different structure–activity relationships—the resulting performance degradation may reflect a mismatch between training and test tasks rather than a failure of generalization alone. In this sense, current OOD benchmarks can conflate the model's inability to extrapolate with the absence of a learnable signal under severe distributional shift.

These findings suggest the need to rethink how OOD scenarios are defined and used in drug discovery. Rather than constructing splits that maximize dissimilarity without preserving meaningful predictive structure, OOD settings should be designed to reflect realistic generalization challenges—where learning remains possible, albeit non-trivial. This may involve more nuanced control over the type and magnitude of distribution shift, ensuring that evaluation protocols probe model robustness under covariate variations without collapsing into concept shift. Ultimately, advancing this field will require designing evaluation frameworks that reflect realistic generalization scenarios, where models are challenged but still able to discover patterns that are both learnable and practically relevant for drug discovery.

**Acknowledgments.** Research partly supported by:Project DEEP-GRAPH, funded by the Italian Ministry of University and Research, PRIN 2022 (project code: 2022YLRBTT, CUP: I53C24002440006);Project PAN HUB, funded by the Italian Ministry of Health (POS 2014–2020, project ID: T4-AN-07, CUP: I53C22001300001); PNRR, PE00000013 - "FAIR - Future Artificial Intelligence Research" - Spoke 1, funded by European Commission under the NextGeneration EU programme.

## References

1. Bajusz, D., Rácz, A., Héberger, K.: Why is Tanimoto index an appropriate choice for fingerprint-based similarity calculations? J. Cheminform. **7**(1), 1–13 (2015). https://doi.org/10.1186/s13321-015-0069-3
2. Breiman, L., Friedman, J.H., Olshen, R.A., Stone, C.J.: Classification and Regression Trees. Wadsworth International Group, Belmont (1984)
3. Ferreira, F.J.N., Carneiro, A.S.: AI-driven drug discovery: a comprehensive review. ACS Omega **10**(23), 23889–23903 (2025). https://doi.org/10.1021/acsomega.5c00549

4. Franco, P., Porta, N., Holliday, J.D., Willett, P.: The use of 2D fingerprint methods to support the assessment of structural similarity in orphan drug legislation. J. Cheminform. **6**(1), 1–10 (2014). https://doi.org/10.1186/1758-2946-6-5
5. Gangwal, A., Lavecchia, A.: Explainable AI methods for drug discovery: a survey of interpretability, metrics and mechanistic insight. Comput. Sci. Rev. **61**, 100943 (2026). https://doi.org/10.1016/j.cosrev.2026.100943
6. Jiménez-Luna, J., Grisoni, F., Schneider, G.: Drug discovery with explainable artificial intelligence. Nat. Mach. Intell. **2**(10), 573–584 (2020). https://doi.org/10.1038/s42256-020-00236-4
7. Keserű, G.M., Makara, G.M.: Hit discovery and hit-to-lead approaches. Drug Discov. Today **11**(15–16), 741–748 (2006). https://doi.org/10.1016/j.drudis.2006.06.016
8. Moreno-Torres, J.G., Raeder, T., Alaiz-Rodríguez, R., Chawla, N.V., Herrera, F.: A unifying view on dataset shift in classification. Pattern Recogn. **45**(1), 521–530 (2012). https://doi.org/10.1016/j.patcog.2011.06.019
9. Nagarajan, V., Andreassen, A., Neyshabur, B.: Understanding the failure modes of out-of-distribution generalization. In: Proceedings of the 9th International Conference on Learning Representations (2021). https://openreview.net/forum?id=fSTD6NFIW_b
10. Netzeva, T.I., et al.: Current status of methods for defining the applicability domain of (quantitative) structure-activity relationships: the report and recommendations of ECVAM workshop 52. Altern. Lab. Anim. **33**(2), 155–173 (2005). https://doi.org/10.1177/026119290503300209
11. Quiñonero-Candela, J., Sugiyama, M., Schwaighofer, A., Lawrence, N.D.: Dataset Shift in Machine Learning. MIT Press, Cambridge (2008). https://doi.org/10.7551/mitpress/9780262170055.001.0001
12. Rogers, D., Hahn, M.: Extended-connectivity fingerprints. J. Chem. Inf. Model. **50**(5), 742–754 (2010). https://doi.org/10.1021/ci100050t
13. Saito, T., Rehmsmeier, M.: The precision-recall plot is more informative than the ROC plot when evaluating binary classifiers on imbalanced datasets. PLoS ONE **10**(3), e0118432 (2015). https://doi.org/10.1371/journal.pone.0118432
14. Steshin, S.: Lo-Hi: practical ML drug discovery benchmark. In: Advances in Neural Information Processing Systems, vol. 36, pp. 64526–64554. Curran Associates, Inc. (2023). https://doi.org/10.52202/075280-2816. datasets and Benchmarks Track

# Machine Learning-Based Graph Coarsening for Public Transport Scheduling

Samuela Carosi[1], Andrea Cardia[2], Francesca Del Lungo[1], Francesco Geraci[1], and Lorenzo Sarti[1(✉)]

[1] Hitachi Mobility Multimodal Solutions - Hitachi Rail, Lucca, Florence, Italy
{samuela.carosi,francesca.dellungo,francesco.geraci, lorenzo.sarti}@hitachirail-maior.com

[2] Dipartimento di Informatica, University of Pisa, Pisa, Italy
andrea.cardia@phd.unipi.it

**Abstract.** Public transport operators face increasing pressure to optimize vehicle and crew scheduling under tighter budgets. This optimization problem can be modeled using a set partitioning formulation and solved through Column Generation, a well-established Operations Research technique. However, its computational cost becomes prohibitive for large-scale instances, limiting the ability to explore multiple planning scenarios.

In this paper, we present an ML-based Graph Coarsening approach developed to reduce the computational time of Column Generation-based scheduling algorithms while preserving solution quality.

The core idea is to leverage a binary classifier to reduce the size of the pricing graph explored by the Column Generation when generating vehicle and crew duties.

More specifically, given a pricing graph whose nodes represent trips and arcs represent feasible connections between trips that may belong to the same duty, a Random Forest classifier is trained to predict whether adjacent trips can be aggregated into valid duty subsequences. Merging the selected nodes before the Column Generation optimization process yields a reduced graph that enables significantly faster pricing iterations while preserving solution quality with limited degradation.

Experiments on real-world crew scheduling instances show very promising results: computation times are dramatically reduced while maintaining solution quality equivalent to that achieved by the standard Column Generation algorithm.

The proposed method has been validated on benchmark datasets from two transit operators, demonstrating improved scalability and computational efficiency. This work contributes to the growing field of hybrid Machine Learning and Operations Research approaches and provides practical insights into the deployment of such techniques in industrial scheduling systems.


S. Bistarelli et al. (Eds.): AIxIA 2026, LNAI 17131, pp. 155–168, 2027.
https://doi.org/10.1007/978-3-032-40774-0_12

**Keywords:** Graph Coarsening · Machine Learning · Crew Scheduling · Column Generation · Combinatorial Optimization

# 1 Introduction

**Transportation Outlook.** The increasing costs of energy and labor, limited operational resources, demand variability, and the need to rapidly evaluate alternative scenarios have made public transportation scheduling a highly complex decision-making activity. As a result, transport operators and agencies are increasingly required to produce operational plans that are efficient, robust, and adaptable. In this context, transportation planning is typically organized as a sequence of tightly interconnected optimization problems that include route planning, timetabling, Vehicle Scheduling, Crew Scheduling, and, finally, rostering. Although integrated formulations have been proposed for combining multiple planning stages [6,7], their computational complexity grows rapidly with the number of interacting decisions, resources, and operational constraints. As a result, large-scale real-world applications are often organized as a hierarchical planning process, where each stage is solved separately using specialized optimization techniques.

From an optimization perspective, the Vehicle Scheduling Problem (VSP) and the Crew Scheduling Problem (CSP) are particularly relevant, as they involve selecting mutually compatible activities under temporal, spatial, operational, and regulatory constraints, resulting in feasible schedules and duties, respectively. Although the proposed graph coarsening framework is conceptually applicable to both CSP and VSP, in the rest of this document we will focus on the CSP problem. This choice is motivated by both computational and practical considerations. Furthermore, VSP and CSP share the same high-level set partitioning structure and are both commonly solved using the same algorithmic techniques, and from an industrial perspective, crew-related costs usually represent a major component of the overall operating cost.

In practical applications, the number of feasible duties grows exponentially with the number of trips, making compact formulations based on the explicit enumeration of all alternatives computationally prohibitive.

**Column Generation.** A classical modeling approach for these problems relies on Set Partitioning formulations, while Column Generation (CG) is a well-established technique for solving the linear relaxation of such models when the number of *columns* (i.e., feasible schedules or duties) is too large to be handled explicitly [10].

CG starts from a restricted subset of columns and iteratively solves a Restricted Master Problem (RMP). The dual information obtained from the RMP is used to compute the reduced costs, which define the objective function of the associated Pricing Problems (PPs), whose purpose is to generate new columns with negative reduced cost that improve the solution. When no improving column can be found, the RMP solution is optimal for the linear relaxation of the full problem. In the presence of integrality requirements, as in the VSP and in the CSP, CG is commonly embedded within Branch-and-Price (B&P) frameworks [2] or combined with variable-fixing heuristics [10,12].

In transportation applications, the PP is commonly formulated as a Shortest Path Problem with Resource Constraints (SPPRC). In the pricing graph, nodes represent activities, trips, or temporal events, while arcs represent feasible transitions between consecutive activities. In the CSP setting, for example, nodes correspond to driver tasks and each path represents a feasible duty. Resources encode operational constraints such as working time, shift duration, cumulative driving time, break requirements, idle times. Labeling algorithms and dynamic programming techniques have long represented the state of the art for solving such problems [11,14], owing to their ability to handle complex resource structures. However, the PP is often NP-hard and must be solved repeatedly throughout the CG process. Consequently, even moderate improvements in PP solution times can lead to substantial reductions in overall computational effort. This aspect is particularly critical in practical applications, where planners must explore alternative scenarios, adjust parameters, compare operational strategies, and rapidly react to changes in input data or planning regulations. The present work addresses precisely this challenge by proposing a graph coarsening approach aimed at accelerating the solution of the PP.

**Machine Learning And Related Works.** A large body of literature has investigated methods for accelerating CG, with particular emphasis on the pricing phase. Existing approaches range from traditional optimization techniques to methods leveraging recent advances in Machine Learning (ML). Even if the former continue to be actively developed to improve CG performance [15], the latter have attracted considerable attention as promising tools for supporting Combinatorial Optimization (CO) algorithms [9]. Rather than replacing optimization procedures, ML models can learn costly decisions or heuristics from historical data and subsequently accelerate their execution [3]. For example, in [20,21], the authors show how supervised ML techniques can significantly reduce the computational effort required to solve the linear relaxation of VSP, CSP, and Vehicle Routing Problem.

*ML for RMP Enhancement.* Within this research area, a first family of approaches focuses on the RMP by improving the selection of columns to be added during CG. In [20], they use ML techniques to select, among all columns generated at each CG iteration, those to be added to the RMP. This perspective has been also extended by formulating column selection as a sequential decision-making problem and addressing it through Reinforcement Learning (RL) and graph-based representations of the optimization model [8]. Such approaches are particularly suitable when multiple negative reduced-cost columns are available, as adding all of them may slow down the reoptimization of the RMP.

*ML for Dual Information and Guidance Learning.* A second family of ML-based approaches seeks to learn auxiliary information used by CG, such as bounds, dual variables, or stabilization parameters [9,16,24]. In [25], the authors exploit the similarity between successive PP instances by learning an upper bound on their optimal value, which is used to reduce the search space and accelerate the pricing phase without affecting the exactness of the branch-and-price framework.

*ML for PP Reduction and Acceleration.* The research direction most closely related to the present work is the use of ML to directly reduce the complexity of the PP. Rather than acting only on generated columns, these methods aim to shrink the pricing search space itself by identifying promising arcs, connections, or subgraphs. In [21] the authors propose a supervised classifier for arc selection in SPPRC instances arising within CG. In the context of crew scheduling and rostering, [22] introduce a neural network that filters the most promising pairings to include in the subproblem associated with each crew member. Recent contributions such as [13] highlight a growing shift toward neural models capable of explicitly exploiting the graph structure of pricing problems. Lu et al. combine CG and Graph Neural Networks (GNNs) with attention mechanisms to reduce the number of paths explored during pricing in an integrated rider trip planning and crew scheduling problem [18]. Similarly, RL-based approaches have been employed to select pricing heuristics and construct reduced networks for Vehicle Routing Problems with Time Windows (VRPTW) and crew scheduling applications [26], or even to directly generate negative reduced-cost columns without relying entirely on labeling procedures [1].

The present work belongs to this latter research stream on ML-based pricing graph reduction. The proposed approach performs a graph coarsening step prior to the execution of CG by aggregating adjacent nodes representing compatible trips whenever a supervised classifier predicts that they are likely to belong to the same feasible operational sequence. The learned model neither replaces the PP nor alters the underlying set partitioning formulation. Instead, it operates directly on the pricing graph representation, reducing its size through the creation of supernodes while preserving an interpretable operational semantics suitable for integration into industrial VSP and CSP decision-support systems.

The paper is organized as follows. Section 2 presents the CSP and its set-partitioning formulation. Section 3 introduces the proposed machine-learning-based graph coarsening approach for accelerating the pricing phase within the CG framework. Sections 4 and 5 report the experiments and their computational results on real-world instances. Finally, Sect. 6 concludes the paper and discusses directions for future research.

## 2 Problem Description

In the CSP setting, a *duty* represents a sequence of trips assigned to a single driver during a working day. The CSP consists of constructing a set of feasible duties that collectively cover all the trips contained in a given timetable while minimizing the overall operating cost.

Let $T$ denote the set of trips to be covered and let $D$ be the set of all feasible duties. For each duty $d \in D$, let $c_d$ be its associated cost, and let $a_{td}$ be a coefficient equal to 1 if duty $d$ covers the trip $t$, and 0 otherwise.

The CSP can then be formulated as the following Set Partitioning Problem:

$$\Big\{ \min \sum_{d \in D} c_d x_d : \sum_{d \in D} a_{td} x_d = 1 \ \forall t \in T, \quad x_d \in \{0,1\} \ \forall d \in D \Big\}.$$

The binary variable $x_d$ assumes value 1 if duty $d$ is selected in the final solution and 0 otherwise. The set partitioning constraints ensure that each trip is covered exactly once. Although the formulation is compact, solving the CSP remains challenging, as the number of feasible duties grows exponentially with the number of trips, rendering complete enumeration computationally impractical for realistic instances.

In many CSP applications, the PP can be modeled on a directed graph $G = (V, E)$, where each node $v \in V$ represents a trip and each arc $(v_i, v_j) \in E$ represents a feasible connection between two trips. An arc exists only if the corresponding trips satisfy all temporal, spatial, and operational compatibility requirements. A path in $G$ therefore corresponds to a feasible duty, while the cost and resource consumption associated with the path reflect the characteristics of the corresponding driver schedule. Under this representation, the PP can be formulated as a SPPRC, where the objective is to identify a path with minimum reduced cost while satisfying all the duty feasibility requirements.

In practice, the computational effort of CG is largely dominated by the repeated solution of the PP, making it the computational bottleneck of the algorithm. For this reason, improving the efficiency of the PP is often the key factor in accelerating the overall algorithm. The remainder of this work focuses precisely on this component.

## 3 Methodology

Let's call $G$ the *input graph* associated with the current instance of the PP. We aim to construct a *reduced graph* $G'$ such that solving the problem on $G'$ yields a solution whose cost is equivalent, or very close, to that obtained on the original graph, while reducing computational time.

**Graph Coarsening via Machine Learning.** We propose a graph reduction preprocessing stage that reduces the size of the input graph $G$ while preserving essential structural properties.

Graph coarsening is a dimensionality-reduction technique that builds a sequence of progressively smaller graphs, by aggregating vertices into supernodes and edges into superedges, while attempting to preserve key structural properties of the original graph [5,17].

Formally, let $G = (V, E)$ be the input graph. Our goal is to construct a coarsened graph $G' = (V', E')$ where $|V'| < |V|$ and there is a surjective map $\pi : V \to V'$ which we call the *vertex map*. So, for each node $v' \in V'$ all nodes $\pi^{-1}(v') \subset V$ are mapped to the super-node $v'$ in the reduced graph $G'$ [5].

We define the vertex mapping through a binary classification model. Let $F(v_i, v_j) \in \mathbb{R}^d$ denote the feature vector of the arc $(v_i, v_j) \in E$. We train a classifier $f_\theta : F(v_i, v_j) \to \{0, 1\}$ parameterized by $\theta$ on a labeled dataset derived from known optimal or near-optimal solutions, where the label $y_{ij} = 1$ if trips $v_i$ and $v_j$ appear consecutively in the same duty, and $y_{ij} = 0$ otherwise.

At inference time, we do not discretize the model output into hard binary labels. Instead, we exploit the continuous predicted probability $P(v_i, v_j) = f_\theta(F(v_i, v_j)) \in [0, 1]$, interpreted as the model's confidence that trips $v_i$ and $v_j$ should be paired. A configurable threshold $\tau \in [0, 1]$ then determines the candidate set $C_\tau = \{(v_i, v_j) \in E : P(v_i, v_j) \geq \tau\}$.

This design decouples the training objective from the operational decision boundary: the model is trained under a standard binary classification objective, while $\tau$ can be adjusted at deployment time without retraining, allowing control over the trade-off between coarsening aggressiveness and the preservation of solution quality.

A positive prediction above the threshold implies that $v_i$ and $v_j$ are candidates for aggregation into a supernode $v' \in V'$. The supernode $v'$ inherits the incoming edges of the head node $v_i$ and the outgoing edges of the tail node $v_j$; all internal edges (outgoing from $v_i$ and incoming to $v_j$) are absorbed into the supernode and removed from $E'$. Sequences of more than two nodes are constructed by chaining consecutive pairs, producing supernodes that aggregate longer subsequences of trips. Compared to directly fixing predicted arcs, the proposed supernode construction yields computational benefits for SPPRC-based pricing algorithms and improves heuristic performance by avoiding partially infeasible paths that would otherwise fail at intermediate nodes, leading to a more stable label propagation.

**Training Data.** Training data are generated using historical instances for which baseline solutions have been computed by a column generation algorithm[1]. For each solved instance, we labeled every pair of trips $(v_i, v_j)$ as positive if it appears in a duty in the optimal solution, negative otherwise.

A filtering step on the training set data retains only the groups of pairs (grouped by the origin trip) that contains at least one pair labeled as optimal, and at least a non optimal one. This eliminates trivial or final-duty instances from the training set.

Each pair $(v_i, v_j)$ is characterized by a feature vector $\mathbf{x}_{ij} \in \mathbb{R}^d$ encoding both individual trip attributes and relational properties. Specifically, the feature set captures temporal attributes, such as departure and arrival times, break times between trips, as well as total driving and working times; origin- and destination-based temporal statistics, including the minimum, maximum, and mean duration percentages across arcs sharing the same origin or destination; and graph connectivity information, such as the number of outgoing arcs from the origin node and the number of incoming arcs to the destination node.

[1] The algorithm is a column generation approach combined with variable-fixing heuristics.

*Class Imbalance.* The datasets exhibit significant class imbalance, with non-optimal arcs outnumbering optimal ones by a ratio from 4:1 to 10:1. A targeted downsampling strategy is applied: for each origin-trip group, only the $k = 3$ non-optimal pairs with the shortest destination-trip duration are retained alongside all optimal arcs. This design follows the principle of *informed undersampling* [19]: by preserving hard negatives (those temporally closest to viable alternatives), the strategy refines the decision boundary while discarding easily distinguishable examples that provide negligible discriminative information [23]. The group-level application ensures that the sampling respects the combinatorial structure of the scheduling problem.

**Classifier.** We used a Random Forest classifier [4] as the predictive model $f_\theta$. This choice is motivated by the characteristics of our application and data. Random Forests generally perform well on heterogeneous tabular feature spaces without requiring extensive hyperparameter tuning or feature normalization, which is particularly suitable for our mixed feature set, comprising both temporal and structural attributes. In addition, their ensemble nature provides robustness against overfitting, an important property in our setting, where training data are obtained from a limited number of scheduling instances and may display distributional variability across transit agencies. A further advantage is their interpretability: feature-importance measures allow domain experts to verify that the learned pruning policy reflects operationally meaningful patterns rather than spurious correlations. More broadly, our assumption is not specific to Random Forest itself, but to the use of a supervised learning model capable of guiding graph reduction effectively; however, Random Forest offers a robust compromise between predictive accuracy, stability, and tuning effort.

To avoid information leakage, we employ a group-aware train/test split based on the origin trip identifier, using a 90/10 partition. This guaranties that all arcs associated with the same origin trip are assigned exclusively to either the training or the test set, ensuring a more reliable evaluation.

## 4 Experiments

**Experimental Setup.** The predictive pruning policy is implemented using a Random Forest classifier with 100 trees, balanced class weights, and unrestricted tree depth. This configuration was selected to provide a robust yet simple experimental setting without extensive hyperparameter tuning. Balanced weighting mitigates class imbalance, while unrestricted depth allows the model to capture complex nonlinear relationships among the classifiers. Preliminary experiments with depth-constrained trees consistently yielded worse predictive performance, supporting the final choice.

All experiments were conducted on a Linux server equipped with an AMD EPYC 7J13 64-Core Processor, 32 GB of RAM and no GPU.

**Datasets.** We evaluated our approach on real-world graph datasets derived from transport networks. Table 1 shows the datasets used for both training and test purposes. Each dataset models a regional transport network, where nodes correspond to individual trips connecting two locations, and edges encode the feasibility of sequencing trips. In particular, two trips are considered connected with an edge if the destination of the first trip coincides with the origin of the second one and if the pair of trips respects the problem rule sets.

This dataset was chosen for its realistic structure, its sparsity, and its heterogeneous connectivity patterns, which make it suitable for evaluating graph coarsening techniques.

The dataset was collected from real-world scenarios, using anonymous input data kindly provided by Hitachi customers.

**Table 1.** Benchmark datasets. For each dataset, the nodes (trips), the edges of the input graph and finally the duties generated from the standard CG (S-CG) algorithm are reported. All the datasets are disjoint. Those identified by the same letter come from the same transportation company.

| Name | Nodes | Edges | Duties |
|---|---|---|---|
| A - Large (A-L) | 2,023 | 1,627,237 | 275 |
| A - Medium (A-M) | 1,315 | 719,468 | 175 |
| B - Medium (B-M) | 1,150 | 532,264 | 130 |

**Evaluation Metrics.** To assess the effectiveness of the graph reduction policy, we consider two metrics: solution cost variation and pricer speedup. A negative cost variation indicates a deterioration in solution quality; since the goal of graph coarsening is to accelerate pricing without significantly affecting the final solution, this metric quantifies the quality loss induced by pruning. In our experiments, a cost variation of 1% is adopted as the maximum acceptable threshold.

The computational benefit is measured through the pricer speedup, defined as $PS = t_{OR}/t_{ML}$, where $t_{ML}$ is the pricing time under the learned reduction policy and $t_{OR}$ is the pricing time of the reference solver. Values greater than one indicate faster pricing. Together, these metrics evaluate the trade-off between computational efficiency and solution quality.

**Experimental Comparisons.** For each company, we compare four variants of the column generation solver. The first is the standard solver that does not use the binary classifier to prune the graph, denoted as S-CG, which serves as the reference configuration. The second is R-CG, where graph reduction is performed randomly: each candidate pair is assigned a random value in $[0, 1]$, and the pair is aggregated whenever this value falls below a given threshold. This setting provides a baseline to quantify the effect of graph pruning alone, independently of any learned policy. The third and fourth variants are based on a Random Forest binary classifier. In the third variant (M1-CG), the classifier is trained on historical data from a given company and evaluated on separate data from the same company. In contrast, in the fourth variant (M2-CG), the classifier is trained on historical data from one company and evaluated on data from a different company.

For each reduced variant, we report results over multiple classification thresholds $\tau$ (see Sect. 3), in order to characterize the full trade-off between computational efficiency and solution quality.

## 5 Results

**Random Forest Evaluation.** To assess the predictive performance of the Random Forest classifier, we considered the standard binary classification metrics: Accuracy, Precision, Recall, F1-score, and the Area Under the ROC Curve (AUC). Since the datasets are imbalanced, with relatively few positive examples, accuracy alone is not sufficient to assess the model quality. In this setting, precision is particularly important, as false positives should be minimized to ensure that graph reduction does not compromise solution quality. By contrast, lower recall is less critical, as false negatives primarily limit the achievable reduction and the associated computational gains. For this reason, the most relevant indicators are Precision and, more generally, the F1-score and AUC, which provide a more robust view of classifier performance.

**Table 2.** Performance of the Random Forest classifier across training and test datasets. Models trained on A-L and A-M were tested on datasets from the same company, whereas the model trained on B-M was also evaluated on A-L and A-M to assess transferability across companies.

| Training | Test | Accuracy | Precision | Recall | F1 | AUC |
|---|---|---|---|---|---|---|
| A-L | A-L | 0.981 | 0.965 | 0.968 | 0.966 | 0.995 |
| | A-M | 0.781 | 0.597 | 0.951 | 0.734 | 0.881 |
| A-M | A-M | 0.946 | 0.904 | 0.931 | 0.917 | 0.984 |
| | A-L | 0.830 | 0.854 | 0.486 | 0.620 | 0.870 |
| B-M | B-M | 0.966 | 0.951 | 0.948 | 0.949 | 0.983 |
| | A-L | 0.847 | 0.727 | 0.741 | 0.734 | 0.878 |
| | A-M | 0.748 | 0.560 | 0.958 | 0.707 | 0.893 |

Table 2 shows the Random Forest performance across all training–test dataset combinations. Models evaluated on datasets belonging to the same company achieve consistently strong results. In particular, the models trained and tested on A-L and A-M attain high values for all performance metrics, with Precision above 0.90 and AUC values close to 1, indicating excellent discriminative capability. A different behavior emerges when the model trained on B-M is used to handle datasets from other companies. Although performance decreases when the model is applied across companies, it still achieves reasonable predictive performance, albeit with a different balance between recall and precision. Overall, the results confirm that models trained on data from the target company provide the best performance. Nevertheless, the cross-company experiments suggest that a model trained on a different dataset can still capture useful patterns and may represent a viable starting point when insufficient training data are available for a new company. Interestingly, although the cross-company model exhibits lower predictive performance, the results reported in the next paragraph indicate that this degradation does not translate into a significant loss in the effectiveness of the Column Generation algorithm, which maintains similar or even better speed-up factors and solution quality. A possible interpretation is that the relatively simpler regulatory constraints, of the B-M case, compared with those of A-L and A-M, leads the model to generate a set of candidate pairings that is more robust and therefore better suited to support the optimization procedure. Further experiments will be required to validate this hypothesis.

**Impact of ML-Based Reduction on Speedup and Solution Quality.** The effectiveness of ML-based column filtering depends on both the reduction threshold and the origin of the training data. Table 3 reports the results in terms of computational speedup and solution quality (Costs) for company-specific (M1-CG) and cross-company (M2-CG) classifiers across all tested datasets.

**Table 3.** Results across datasets. Time (in minutes), speedup and solution cost variation (%) are reported for M1-CG and M2-CG under different thresholds. Bold values represent the best threshold configurations.

| Test set | CG | M1-CG | | | | M2-CG | | | |
|---|---|---|---|---|---|---|---|---|---|
| | | Train | Time | Speedup | Cost% | Train | Time | Speedup | Cost% |
| A-L | S-CG | - | 138.01 | - | - | - | - | - | - |
| | $\tau$ 0.95 | A-M | 136.38 | 1.01 | 0.00 | B-M | 82.67 | 1.68 | 0.02 |
| | $\tau$ 0.90 | A-M | 112.36 | 1.23 | 0.04 | B-M | 60.66 | 2.30 | 0.07 |
| | $\tau$ 0.80 | A-M | 75.48 | 1.83 | −0.04 | B-M | 37.10 | **3.72** | **−0.63** |
| | $\tau$ 0.70 | A-M | 63.57 | 2.17 | 0.03 | B-M | 28.83 | 4.75 | −1.01 |
| | $\tau$ 0.60 | A-M | 52.36 | **2.64** | **−0.31** | B-M | 23.70 | 5.91 | −1.77 |
| A-M | S-CG | - | 62.08 | - | - | - | - | - | - |
| | $\tau$ 0.95 | A-L | 52.74 | 1.19 | −0.02 | B-M | 35.20 | 1.78 | 0.00 |
| | $\tau$ 0.90 | A-L | 47.88 | 1.31 | 0.01 | B-M | 22.45 | **2.78** | **−0.58** |
| | $\tau$ 0.80 | A-L | 31.82 | **1.96** | **−0.60** | B-M | 12.46 | 5.01 | −1.15 |
| | $\tau$ 0.70 | A-L | 15.88 | 3.94 | −1.06 | B-M | 6.68 | 9.36 | −1.76 |
| | $\tau$ 0.60 | A-L | 8.80 | 7.10 | −1.76 | B-M | 5.69 | 10.99 | −1.77 |

Additionally, Figs. 1 and 2 compare two configurations on datasets A-L, and A-M reporting both the percentage reduction in the cost of the solution and the pricer speedup as the ML threshold becomes more aggressive, from the standard S-CG algorithm to $\tau = 0.60$ (overall speedups are omitted from both the tables and figures, as they closely match pricer speedups). The orange plot represents the random aggregation R-CG used as a baseline for graph reduction. In green and blue the performance of the M1-CG and M2-CG algorithms with different thresholds depicted, respectively.

Figure 1 highlights a clear trade-off between efficiency and quality as the reduction threshold $\tau$ becomes more aggressive from 0.95 to 0.60. As expected, all reduced variants speed up the pricer w.r.t. the reference S-CG, but they differ substantially in how much the solution quality is preserved. The random reduction baseline R-CG is consistently the weakest, indicating that sparsification alone is not sufficient; without an informed selection policy, many useful columns are removed too early, which harms the final solution.

By contrast, M1-CG, trained on data from the same company, is the most robust in terms of solution quality: the cost remains essentially unchanged up to $\tau = 0.80$, and the degradation is still limited at more aggressive thresholds, while speedup increases up to about 2x (with only minimal degradation of solution quality, while a 4x speedup is achieved at $\tau = 0.70$). M2-CG, trained on a different company, delivers the largest computational gains, reaching nearly 6x speedup at $\tau = 0.60$, with only a moderate loss in solution quality compared to R-CG.

Overall, the figures suggest two main findings: first, learned graph reduction generally outperforms random pruning; second, company-specific training appears preferable when solution quality is the priority, whereas cross-company training remains an attractive option when the main goal is maximizing computational acceleration with acceptable quality loss.

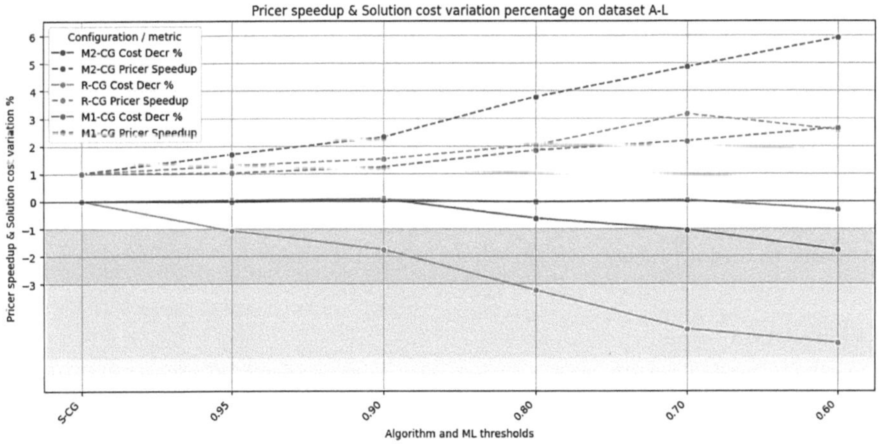


**Fig. 1.** Comparison of pricer speed up and solution cost variation percentage on dataset A-L with algorithms S-CG, R-CG, M1-CG and M2-CG with different thresholds.

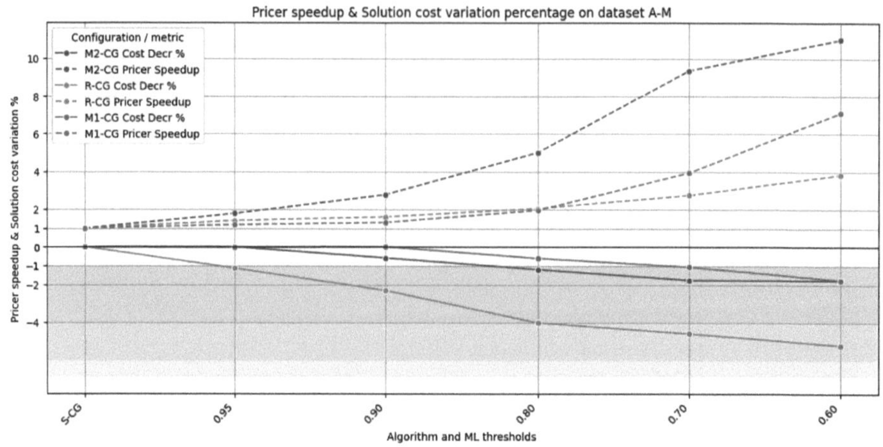


**Fig. 2.** Comparison of pricer speed up and solution cost variation percentage on dataset A-M with algorithms S-CG, R-CG, M1-CG and M2-CG with different thresholds.

## 6 Conclusions

In this paper, we proposed a machine-learning-based graph coarsening approach to accelerate the pricing phase of Column Generation for the Crew Scheduling Problem. Experiments on real-world instances demonstrate significant speedups while preserving solution quality with limited degradation, confirming that learned graph reduction substantially outperforms random reduction. Additional experiments and analyses are required to investigate why the cross-company approach, where the binary classifier is trained on data from another company, achieve better results w.r.t. the company-specific alternative.

Finally, since the optimal prediction threshold can vary from instance to instance, a natural extension of this work is a dynamic graph-switching strategy inspired by [21]. Such a mechanism would adapt the graph representation during optimization, starting from aggressive reductions in early iterations, gradually expanding the graph when improving columns become harder to generate, and reverting to a more restrictive threshold when too many are produced.

## References

1. Abouelrous, A., Bliek, L., Gabor, A.F., Wu, Y., Zhang, Y.: Reinforcement learning for solving the pricing problem in column generation for routing. Oper. Res. Perspect. **15**, 100364 (2025). https://doi.org/10.1016/j.orp.2025.100364
2. Barnhart, C., Johnson, E.L., Nemhauser, G.L., Savelsbergh, M.W.P., Vance, P.H.: Branch-and-price: column generation for solving huge integer programs. Oper. Res. **46**(3), 316–329 (1998). https://doi.org/10.1287/opre.46.3.316
3. Bengio, Y., Lodi, A., Prouvost, A.: Machine learning for combinatorial optimization: a methodological tour d'horizon. Eur. J. Oper. Res. **290**(2), 405–421 (2021). https://doi.org/10.1016/j.ejor.2020.07.063

4. Breiman, L.: Random forests. Mach. Learn. **45**(1), 5–32 (2001). https://doi.org/10.1023/A:1010933404324
5. Cai, C., Wang, D., Wang, Y.: Graph coarsening with neural networks. In: International Conference on Learning Representations (2021). https://openreview.net/forum?id=uxpzitPEooJ
6. Carosi, S., Frangioni, A., Galli, L., Girardi, L., Vallese, G.: A matheuristic for integrated timetabling and vehicle scheduling. Transp. Res. Part B: Methodol. **127**, 99–124 (2019). https://doi.org/10.1016/j.trb.2019.07.004
7. Carosi, S., Frangioni, A., Galli, L., Girardi, L., Vallese, G.: A tool for practical integrated time-table design and vehicle scheduling in public transport systems. In: Dell'Amico, M., Gaudioso, M., Stecca, G. (eds.) A View of Operations Research Applications in Italy, 2018. ASS, vol. 2, pp. 207–217. Springer, Cham (2019). https://doi.org/10.1007/978-3-030-25842-9_16
8. Chi, C., Aboussalah, A.M., Khalil, E.B., Wang, J., Sherkat-Masoumi, Z.: A deep reinforcement learning framework for column generation. In: Advances in Neural Information Processing Systems, vol. 35, pp. 9633–9644 (2022). https://doi.org/10.52202/068431-0700
9. Demelas, F.: Machine Learning for Lagrangian Relaxation. Ph.D. thesis, Université Sorbonne Paris Nord, Villetaneuse, France (2025). https://lipn.univ-paris13.fr/%7Edemelas/Manuscript_Final.pdf
10. Desaulniers, G., Desrosiers, J., Solomon, M.M.: Column Generation. GERAD 25th Anniversary Series, Springer, New York (2005). https://doi.org/10.1007/0-387-25486-2
11. Desrochers, M., Desrosiers, J., Solomon, M.M.: A new optimization algorithm for the vehicle routing problem with time windows. Oper. Res. **40**(2), 342–354 (1992). https://doi.org/10.1287/opre.40.2.342
12. Feillet, D.: A tutorial on column generation and branch-and-price for vehicle routing problems. 4OR **8**(4), 407–424 (2010). https://doi.org/10.1007/s10288-010-0130-z
13. Gerbaux, J., Desaulniers, G., Cappart, Q.: A machine-learning-based column generation heuristic for electric bus scheduling. Comput. Oper. Res. **173**, 106848 (2025). https://doi.org/10.1016/j.cor.2024.106848
14. Irnich, S., Desaulniers, G.: Shortest path problems with resource constraints. In: Desaulniers, G., Desrosiers, J., Solomon, M.M. (eds.) Column Generation, pp. 33–65. Springer, New York (2005). https://doi.org/10.1007/0-387-25486-2_2
15. Kletzander, L., Mannelli Mazzoli, T., Musliu, N., Van Hentenryck, P.: Integrating column generation and large neighborhood search for bus driver scheduling with complex break constraints. J. Artif. Intell. Res. **85**, 44:1–44:37 (2026). https://doi.org/10.1613/jair.1.19027
16. Kraul, S., Seizinger, M., Brunner, J.O.: Machine learning-supported prediction of dual variables for the cutting stock problem with an application in stabilized column generation. INFORMS J. Comput. **35**(3), 692–709 (2023). https://doi.org/10.1287/ijoc.2023.1277
17. Loukas, A., Vandergheynst, P.: Spectrally approximating large graphs with smaller graphs. In: Dy, J., Krause, A. (eds.) Proceedings of the 35th International Conference on Machine Learning. Proceedings of Machine Learning Research, vol. 80, pp. 3237–3246. PMLR (2018). https://proceedings.mlr.press/v80/loukas18a.html
18. Lu, J., Ye, T., Chen, W., Van Hentenryck, P.: Boosting column generation with graph neural networks for joint rider trip planning and crew shift scheduling. Transp. Res. Part E: Logistics Transp. Rev. **202**, 104281 (2025). https://doi.org/10.1016/j.tre.2025.104281

19. Mani, I., Zhang, I.: kNN approach to unbalanced data distributions: a case study involving information extraction. In: Proceedings of the ICML 2003 Workshop on Learning from Imbalanced Data Sets. Washington, DC (2003)
20. Morabit, M., Desaulniers, G., Lodi, A.: Machine-learning-based column selection for column generation. Transp. Sci. **55**(4), 815–831 (2021). https://doi.org/10.1287/trsc.2021.1045
21. Morabit, M., Desaulniers, G., Lodi, A.: Machine-learning-based arc selection for constrained shortest path problems in column generation. INFORMS J. Optim. **5**(2), 191–210 (2023). https://doi.org/10.1287/ijoo.2022.0082
22. Quesnel, F., Wu, A., Desaulniers, G., Soumis, F.: Deep-learning-based partial pricing in a branch-and-price algorithm for personalized crew rostering. Comput. Oper. Res. **138**, 105554 (2022). https://doi.org/10.1016/j.cor.2021.105554
23. Shrivastava, A., Gupta, A., Girshick, R.: Training region-based object detectors with online hard example mining. In: 2016 IEEE Conference on Computer Vision and Pattern Recognition, pp. 761–769. IEEE (2016). https://doi.org/10.1109/CVPR.2016.89
24. Sugishita, N., Grothey, A., McKinnon, K.: Use of machine learning models to warmstart column generation for unit commitment. INFORMS J. Comput. **36**(4), 1129–1146 (2024). https://doi.org/10.1287/ijoc.2022.0140
25. Václavík, R., Novák, A., Šůcha, P., Hanzálek, Z.: Accelerating the branch-and-price algorithm using machine learning. Eur. J. Oper. Res. **271**(3), 1055–1069 (2018). https://doi.org/10.1016/j.ejor.2018.05.046
26. Xu, K., Shen, L., Liu, L.: Enhancing column generation by reinforcement learning-based hyper-heuristic for vehicle routing and scheduling problems. Comput. Ind. Eng. **206**, 111138 (2025). https://doi.org/10.1016/j.cie.2025.111138

# Efficient Masked Decoding for Sign Motion Generation with Hand-Aware Token Refinement

Francesco Cassini(✉), Emanuele Musumeci, and Vincenzo Suriani

Diag, Sapienza University of Rome, Rome, Italy
francesco.cassini@gmail.com, {musumeci,suriani}@diag.uniroma1.it

**Abstract.** Generating sign language motions from text requires coherent body movement and precise hand articulation. Existing token-based sign generators can encode motion as latent streams, through Vector Quantization (VQ). Autoregressive (AR) decoding is computationally expensive and, due to its sequential nature, complicates local correction of uncertain hand states. This work investigates whether inference efficiency can be improved through parallel decoding while keeping the anatomical token representation, codebooks and VQ decoder fixed. Using a 3-stage pipeline, we first generate motion streams through iterative masked decoding using a token length estimate from the input text; we then refine low-confidence hand tokens at inference time; finally, we mitigate hand gesture ambiguity by selecting among top-$k$ candidates using pose-aware features. Experiments conducted on the CSL-Daily and Phoenix-2014T datasets show improvements in three of four pose metrics over the AR baseline and lower measured end-to-end generation time.

**Keywords:** Sign language generation · Non-autoregressive decoding · Motion tokens · Hand refinement

## 1 Introduction

Text-to-sign motion generation approaches for sign language usually map written sentences to articulated sign sequences. In this class of methods, linguistic information is distributed across posture, arm movement, hand configuration, orientation and timing, making hand errors more prominent and hard to correct without negatively affecting the accuracy of full-body motion. *Token-based modeling*, one of the main classes of approaches, encodes sign sequences as discrete motion tokens organized by anatomical region [1,9,10]. SOKE [1] is a representative example: it uses separate body, left hand and right hand Vector Quantized (VQ) streams and generates them autoregressively from text, so decoding cost grows with sequence length. Keeping the tokenizer and VQ decoder fixed, our pipeline generates body and hand token streams in parallel and then refines only uncertain hand tokens. Our contributions are (Fig. 1):


S. Bistarelli et al. (Eds.): AIxIA 2026, LNAI 17131, pp. 169–182, 2027.
https://doi.org/10.1007/978-3-032-40774-0_13

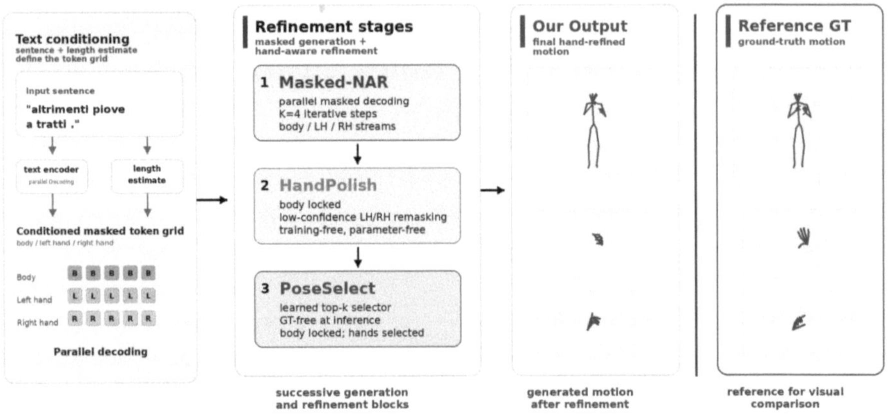


**Fig. 1.** Our proposed pipeline: input text and its length estimate condition the parallel decoding during inference. Hand motion is then refined based on the overall body pose.

- **3-stage hand-aware masked generation**. The first *masked non-AR decoding (Masked-NAR)* stage targets the cost of sequential decoding, generating anatomical streams in parallel through masked non-AR decoding. All token positions are refined in a fixed number of parallel iterations rather than decoded sequentially. The second *HandPolish* stage targets hand gesture generation errors: low-confidence hand tokens are regenerated at inference time while the body stream remains fixed, improving hand articulation without disturbing the rest of the motion. The third "*PoseSelect*" stage targets hand configuration ambiguity: a learned selector chooses among top-$k$ alternative hand tokens at inference time, reducing geometric hand error.
- **Controlled and reproducible evaluation.** We evaluate geometric accuracy, test-loop efficiency, measured GPU energy and motion vitality both for the native generation benchmark and the hand refinement benchmark.

The code to reproduce the experiments is available at: https://github.com/francescocassini/efficient-masked-sign-motion-hand-refinement

## 2 Related Work

*Discrete Sign Tokens and Masked Generation.* Approaches based on discrete sign tokens usually rely on sequence modeling, i.e. predicting ordered motion token streams over time, while preserving anatomical structure. SOKE [1] is the closest architectural reference: it maps signing motion to body, left hand and right hand VQ token streams and generates them autoregressively from text. T2S-GPT [19] similarly frames sign language production as autoregressive generation over learned discrete motion codes, using dynamic vector quantization and token durations. Other systems extend tokenized sign generation through gloss-to-pose discrete diffusion (G2P-DDM [16]), masked diffusion over part-wise tokens

(MaDiS [7]), gloss-level temporal conditioning (GLOS [8]), progressive regional refinement (SignPR [9]) and broader multimodal tokenization (M3T [10]). This family provides a fixed anatomical representation, but generation is often tied to sequential decoding or to global token prediction; our work keeps the same representation fixed and isolates whether parallel decoding and local hand token refinement can improve efficiency and geometric hand accuracy.

*Alternative Generation Routes.* Recent systems pursue alternative sign-generation routes through continuous or flow modeling rather than editable VQ token streams. SignSparK uses sparse keyframes with conditional flow matching [11], SignFlow models one-to-many generation with flow matching and optimal transport [12] and iterative latent refinement studies latent generation in a continuous pose space [13]. These systems address global motion generation by redesigning the generator or latent trajectory; our comparison instead keeps the anatomical body/LH/RH token interface shared with SOKE-AR and tests whether improvements can be obtained without replacing the underlying representation.

*Hand-Specific Refinement and Evaluation.* Manual articulation is a central difficulty in sign generation and several recent methods address hands or regional structure explicitly. Bensabath et al.'s [14] trains HandMDM for text-conditioned 3D hand motion, while HandX [18] studies bimanual hand motion and hand-focused metrics. In sign generation, Stable Signer [17] introduces a hand gesture rendering expert meanwhile SignPR and GLOS include regional or part-aware refinement mechanisms. We focus on a post generation token space variant of this problem: the proposed refinement stage edits only low confidence hand tokens while keeping body fixed, and the subsequent selector learns to choose among top-$k$ hand token candidates. Jiang et al.'s [15] shows that pose distance, embedding based and back-translation metrics capture different aspects of sign quality. This distinction matters in our refinement setting: a selector may reduce the hand component of Procrustes-Aligned Joint Position Error (PA-hand) while suppressing motion vitality. We therefore report PA-JPE with speed/GT and tstd/GT, the generated-to-reference ratios of motion speed and temporal standard deviation, as vitality rather than semantic indicators.

## 3 Method

The method operates on an anatomical token representation of sign motion. Each output sequence is represented as three synchronized streams of discrete Vector Quantized (VQ) tokens corresponding to body, left hand and right hand motion. This tokenizer is inherited from the SOKE setup [1]: it is a pre-trained VQ tokenizer/decoder that quantizes continuous signing motion into stream-specific codebook indices and reconstructs full-body pose sequences from the predicted body, left hand and right hand tokens. The tokenizer and decoder are kept fixed across all experiments; the proposed changes affect only token generation and

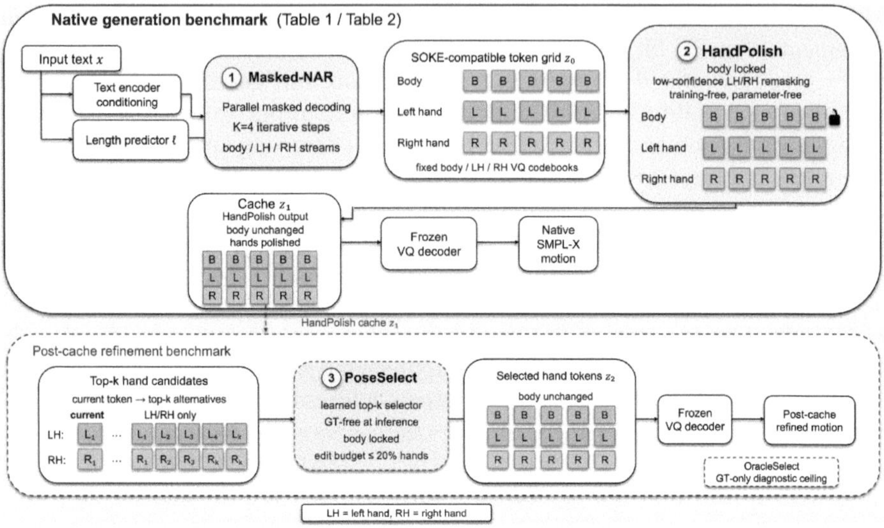


**Fig. 2.** Overview of the pipeline: Masked-NAR parallel generation, HandPolish training-free hand-token refinement and PoseSelect learned selection over top-k hand candidates, with OracleSelect serving as a diagnostic upper bound over the same candidate set.

token refinement. Figure 2 shows the architecture. A text encoder and a dataset text length estimator condition a triple-stream token grid for body, left and right hand. Masked-NAR fills this grid with parallel iterative decoding; HandPolish then refines only low-confidence hand positions while locking the body stream. PoseSelect is drawn separately: it resolves top-$k$ hand token alternatives after HandPolish and is evaluated separately from the native generation benchmark.

***Masked-NAR.*** Masked-NAR is the non-AR generator. It reuses the pre-trained SOKE tokenizer and VQ decoder [1] without updating them and replaces left-to-right token generation with masked iterative decoding over the same three anatomical streams. Let $\mathcal{S} = \{B, L, R\}$ denote body, left hand and right hand. For a sentence $x$ from dataset $d$, token length is estimated from text:

$$\hat{T} = \mathrm{clip}(\mathrm{round}(a_d + b_d u_d(x)), T_{\min}, T_{\max}),$$
$$(z_B, z_L, z_R) = G_\theta(x, \hat{T}), \qquad \hat{y} = D_{\mathrm{VQ}}(z_B, z_L, z_R). \tag{1}$$

Here $u_d(x)$ is a dataset-dependent text-unit count, $a_d, b_d$ are fitted length coefficients, and $T_{\min}, T_{\max}$ are length bounds. Generator $G_\theta$ produces stream-specific token sequences $z_s = (z_{s,1}, \ldots, z_{s,\hat{T}})$, with $z_{s,t} \in \{1, \ldots, V_s\}$ for codebook size $V_s$. Separate prediction heads keep body, left-hand and right-hand tokens inside their own vocabularies, while all positions and streams are predicted in parallel.

Training uses BERT style token corruption [4]: selected positions are masked, randomly replaced by valid stream tokens or kept unchanged and the model is trained with stream restricted cross-entropy. At inference, following masked parallel decoding [5,6], all streams are initialized from the estimated length and refined for $K = 4$ iterations, selected from iteration counts of 4, 6, 8, 10 and 12 because it was the fastest setting, achieved the lowest PA-body and nearly matched the best PA-hand:

$$z_{s,t}^0 = \texttt{[MASK]}, \quad t = 1, \ldots, \hat{T}, \qquad p_{s,t}^k = p_\theta(\cdot \mid x, z^{k-1}).$$

Positions selected for new decodings are sampled from a temperature-scaled top-$k$ distribution, restricted to the stream codebook. After each iteration, temporal confidence is computed jointly from body, left and right hand token probabilities:

$$c_t^k = \frac{1}{3}\left(c_{B,t}^k + c_{L,t}^k + c_{R,t}^k\right).$$

Here $c_{s,t}^k$ is the probability assigned at iteration $k$ to the sampled token of stream $s$ at position $t$, and $c_t^k$ averages this confidence across the three anatomical streams. A cosine schedule then selects the least confident temporal positions for another prediction step. All token updates are parallel across time positions and anatomical streams. The same probabilities provide the confidence signals used by the hand refinement stages.

***HandPolish.*** HandPolish reuses Masked-NAR probabilities for hand only remasking while freezing the generated body tokens. It identifies low confidence hand positions and predicts them again with the same generator, following the intuition of iterative masked refinement methods [5,6] and masked sign-generation models [7,16], but constraining edits to the manual streams. It is applied after Masked-NAR and does not train a separate hand-refinement network. Let $z^0 = (z_B^0, z_L^0, z_R^0)$ be the token grid produced by Masked-NAR with estimated length $\hat{T}$. HandPolish defines a sequence of refined token grids $z^1, z^2, z^3$, where the body stream is an invariant: $\forall j, z_B^j = z_B^0$ Only the left-hand and right-hand streams may be selected for correction. For a manual stream $s \in \{L, R\}$, token confidence is the maximum probability assigned by the Masked-NAR head under the current partially fixed token grid:

$$c_{s,t}^j = \max_{v \in \{1,\ldots,V_s\}} p_\theta(v \mid x, z^{j-1}).$$

Here $v$ ranges over the valid codebook of stream $s$, and $c_{s,t}^j$ summarizes generator confidence about the current hand token at position $t$. At each polishing pass $j$, HandPolish selects the least confident positions independently for each hand:

$$M_s^j = \mathrm{Lowest}_{\max(1, \lfloor \rho_j \hat{T} \rfloor)}\left(\{c_{s,t}^j\}_{t=1}^{\hat{T}}\right), \qquad s \in \{L, R\}.$$

$M_s^j$ is the set of hand positions selected for correction in stream $s$, and $\rho_j$ controls the fraction of positions considered at pass $j$. We use a decreasing polishing schedule $\rho = (0.25, 0.15, 0.08)$: the first pass is broad, later passes are more conservative. Selected hand positions are updated by a stream-wise argmax, keeping $\hat{T}$ fixed and avoiding additional sampling variance.

HandPolish differs from a continuous residual pose refiner: it does not add offsets to SMPL-X features and keeps the sequence inside the discrete VQ manifold, editing only uncertain hand tokens with the same stream-specific codebooks as the base generator. Its effect depends on the confidence structure of the base Masked-NAR checkpoint.

***PoseSelect.*** PoseSelect is the learned component of the refinement stack. It chooses among discrete hand token alternatives proposed by a dedicated candidate network instead of regressing a continuous hand pose correction, keeping edits inside the discrete VQ manifold. PoseSelect is separated from the native generator. After generation, the three token streams, their per-stream confidences and the estimated length are saved to disk; this saved output is referred to as the cache, and PoseSelect operates on it. The selector is trained from offline oracle labels but, at inference, sees only features that can be computed from the cache and the candidate tokens. Candidate proposals come from a hand token editor $q_\psi$, a lightweight transformer trained to predict replacement hand tokens from the cached token streams, their confidences and the input text. Let $\bar{z}$ denote the token grid produced by the final HandPolish pass ($\bar{z} = z^3$). For a hand stream $s \in \{L, R\}$ and position $t$, the candidate set contains the current token and the top-$k$ refinement proposals:

$$C_{s,t} = \{\bar{z}_{s,t}\} \cup \mathrm{TopK}_{v \in \{1,\ldots,V_s\}} q_\psi(v \mid x, \bar{z}).$$

$C_{s,t}$ is the candidate set for hand stream $s$ at position $t$; $V_s$ is the stream specific codebook, and $q_\psi(v \mid x, \bar{z})$ is the probability that the editor assigns to token $v$ given the text and the HandPolish refined grid. In the reported experiments, $k = 5$. The original token is included so that PoseSelect can keep the HandPolish output when none of the alternatives appears better.

PoseSelect scores candidates with inference-available feature groups: token identity/rank, confidence, gain style scores, position/change flags and decoded geometry/vitality descriptors. We write these features as $F_{s,t,i}$ for candidate $i$. PoseSelect predicts a distribution over the candidate set and selects

$$\hat{i}_{s,t} = \arg\max_i \pi_\phi(i \mid F_{s,t,1}, \ldots, F_{s,t,k+1}), \qquad \tilde{z}_{s,t} = C_{s,t}[\hat{i}_{s,t}].$$

$F_{s,t,i}$ denotes the inference available features for candidate $i$, $\pi_\phi$ is the learned selector distribution, $\hat{i}_{s,t}$ is the selected candidate index and $\tilde{z}$ is the token grid produced by PoseSelect; the body stream is frozen exactly as in HandPolish ($\tilde{z}_B = \bar{z}_B$). We also use an edit budget. With budget $b = 0.20$, at most a bounded fraction of manual positions is changed:

$$|\{(s,t) : \tilde{z}_{s,t} \neq \bar{z}_{s,t},\ s \in \{L, R\}\}| \leq b\, 2\hat{T}.$$

A preliminary sweep over edit budgets of 0.10, 0.20 and 0.30 selected 0.20 as the best trade-off between PA-hand and motion vitality.

Training supervision is offline: an oracle evaluates the top-$k$ candidates against the ground-truth pose and identifies the locally best candidate:

$$i^*_{s,t} = \arg\min_i d_{\text{hand}} \left( D_{\text{VQ}}(\tilde{z} \text{ with } C_{s,t}[i]), y_{\text{GT}} \right).$$

Here $D_{\text{VQ}}$ decodes the candidate edited token grid, $y_{\text{GT}}$ is the reference motion and $d_{\text{hand}}$ measures the hand pose error used only to construct offline oracle labels. The selector $\pi_\phi$ is trained to reproduce the oracle choice $i^*_{s,t}$ with a cross-entropy objective, plus an auxiliary regression term that predicts the error reduction of each candidate; both are used only during training. At inference, ground truth pose, tokens and errors are not available and PoseSelect ranks candidates using the inference available features alone: it can therefore be used at inference time without any ground truth (deployable), although it is not parameter free. OracleSelect instead applies the oracle rule above at evaluation time and serves only as a diagnostic upper bound.

# 4 Experimental Setup

***Datasets and Representation.*** The approach is evaluated on CSL-Daily [2] and RWTH-PHOENIX-Weather 2014T [3] (hereafter Phoenix-2014T), two continuous sign language benchmarks that provide videos aligned with sentence level text. CSL-Daily contains Chinese Sign Language sentences about daily life, while Phoenix-2014T contains German Sign Language weather broadcasts. After dataset construction, filtering and removal of samples without a valid text and motion pair, the full test benchmark contains 1818 samples: 1176 from CSL-Daily and 642 from Phoenix-2014T. Efficiency measurements use the first 200 samples of each dataset. These subsets are called CSL-200 and Phoenix-200.

All methods produce the three token streams $(z_B, z_L, z_R)$ and are evaluated only after the VQ decoder $D_{\text{VQ}}$, maps these streams back to a pose sequence.

***Comparison.*** The evaluation has two parts. The first part, the native generation benchmark compares SOKE-AR, Masked-NAR and Masked-NAR + HandPolish within a single evaluation pipeline that shares dataset, VQ decoding and metric implementation. The second part instead evaluates hand token selection applied after Masked-NAR and HandPolish have produced the full sequence. Every selection method starts from the same HandPolish caches introduced in the Method section, so all methods edit identical inputs. This setting is referred to as the "*post-cache benchmark*": it compares the unmodified cache, GainEdit, PoseSelect and OracleSelect, all operating on the candidate sets defined in the Method section. GainEdit is a learned editing baseline built on the same candidate network as PoseSelect: a regressor, trained to predict the expected reduction in hand error, ranks the positions and the top ranked replacement tokens are applied under the same edit budget. OracleSelect applies the oracle rule at evaluation time and serves as a diagnostic upper bound.

***Metrics.*** The main pose metric is the "*Procrustes-Aligned Joint Position Error*" computed after "*Dynamic Time Warping temporal alignment*" (DTW-PA-JPE), reported separately for body and hands. PA-body measures global pose accuracy after temporal and Procrustes alignment, while PA-hand aggregates the articulation error of the left and right hand. The left hand and right hand components, PA-LH and PA-RH, are inspected separately when the aggregate value could hide an asymmetry between the two hands; the main tables report PA-hand. For hand token refinement, PA-hand alone is insufficient: a method that chooses among alternative hand tokens can lower the geometric error by systematically preferring static, low motion candidates, suppressing motion amplitude and temporal variation. The post-cache benchmark therefore also reports two motion vitality indicators. Speed/GT is the ratio between the mean displacement of consecutive pose frames, $\frac{1}{T-1}\sum_{t=2}^{T}\|y_t - y_{t-1}\|_2$, of the generated sequence and that of the ground truth (GT) sequence; tstd/GT is the analogous ratio of the temporal standard deviation of the pose trajectory, averaged over pose dimensions. Values closer to one indicate dynamics closer to the reference. Since pose-based evaluation captures only part of sign quality [15], these ratios expose oversmoothing and loss of motion vitality that PA-JPE alone would not reveal. Efficiency is measured on the end-to-end test loop: total runtime over 200 samples, throughput, speedup relative to SOKE-AR and GPU energy per sample. The hardware and the energy sampling procedure belong to the evaluation protocol and are described in the next subsection.

***Protocols.*** The main benchmark uses the 1818 effective test samples with five independent evaluation runs (replicas) per method, with batch size 4. Masked-NAR and the learned refiners were trained and all evaluations were performed on one NVIDIA RTX 4090; HandPolish is training free. Dataset construction, exact DTW alignment, VQ decoding and the PA-JPE implementation are shared across all methods. Masked-NAR and HandPolish use the inference time sequence length estimated from text. The efficiency protocol uses three replicas on Phoenix-200 and CSL-200 and includes generation, VQ decoding, exact DTW metrics and prediction saving. GPU energy is estimated by sampling the board power with `nvidia-smi` during the test loop and integrating the sampled power over time.

PoseSelect is evaluated in two settings: we first verify the selector on a clean split with disjoint training, validation and test caches of 25491, 1596 and 1818 samples, respectively; no sample appears in more than one cache. The selector checkpoint is chosen on the validation cache and evaluated on a test cache never used for PoseSelect training. The second setting, referred to as R5 because it aligns the five replicas of the main protocol, applies PoseSelect to five regenerated HandPolish caches with 1818 samples per replica. The post-cache comparison in the results section uses this setting. The controlled sweep below selects the HandPolish schedule used for full evaluation (Table 1 and Fig. 3).

**Table 1.** HandPolish schedule selection on Phoenix-200. All variants use the same checkpoint, seed and 200 samples; lower PA-hand is better. Aggressive is selected for full evaluation because it gives the best PA-hand with two seconds of overhead.

| Setting | Schedule | PA-hand | Time/200 |
|---|---|---|---|
| Masked-NAR | – | 1.4497 | 39 s |
| Light | 10% | 1.4378 | 40 s |
| Balanced | 15% → 8% | 1.4268 | 41 s |
| Aggressive | 25% → 15% → 8% | **1.4094** | 41 s |

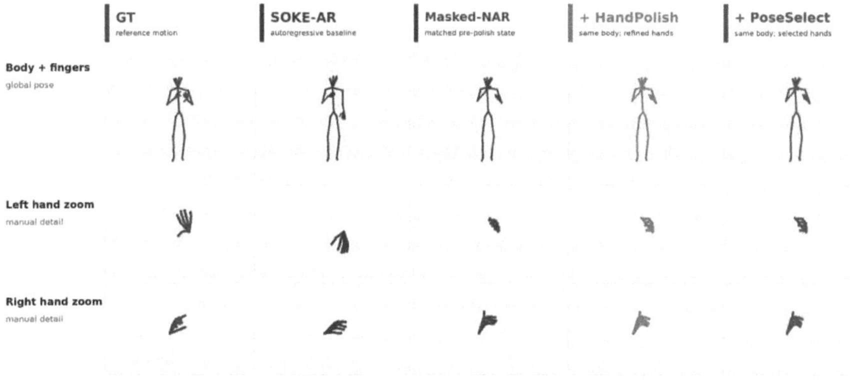


**Fig. 3.** Qualitative comparison on a single test sequence frame. Rows show the full-body pose with articulated fingers (top) and views of the left and right hands (middle, bottom). Columns, from left to right, show the ground-truth reference, the SOKE-AR baseline, Masked-NAR before HandPolish, Masked-NAR after HandPolish and the final PoseSelect output. Both refinement stages edit only hand tokens; therefore, the body pose in the last three columns is identical by construction and differs only in the hand regions.

## 5 Results and Analysis

The evaluation addresses three aspects: whether masked parallel decoding can replace SOKE-AR in the same token space without degrading pose quality; whether a refinement operator that edits only hand tokens while keeping body tokens fixed recovers residual hand articulation; whether the efficiency advantage of non-AR decoding remains visible when the evaluation covers the full test loop rather than only the forward pass of the Masked-NAR generator.

***Main Pose Accuracy.*** Table 2 reports the main pose benchmark on the full CSL-Daily and Phoenix-2014T effective test set; a lower value is better. Results are averaged over five replicas and reported with 95% confidence intervals. The table includes two Masked-NAR configurations with different roles. *Masked-NAR (direct)* is the checkpoint that provides the strongest direct comparison against

SOKE-AR. *Masked-NAR (HandPolish base)* is the checkpoint to which HandPolish is applied; reporting it as a separate configuration isolates the effect of polishing from the differences between the two checkpoints. SOKE-AR decodes deterministically from a single pre-trained checkpoint, so repeated replicas produce identical values and its confidence interval is zero.

**Table 2.** Main PA-JPE results on the CSL-Daily + Phoenix-2014T benchmark (1,818 effective samples, five replicas, 95 percent confidence intervals). Lower is better; each method is reported at its best operating point, whose role is described in the Results and Analysis section.

| Method | CSL body | CSL hand | PHX body | PHX hand |
|---|---|---|---|---|
| SOKE-AR | $9.6791 \pm 0.0000$ | $\mathbf{1.8732 \pm 0.0000}$ | $8.0912 \pm 0.0000$ | $1.6491 \pm 0.0000$ |
| Masked-NAR (direct) | $9.1851 \pm 0.0502$ | $1.8869 \pm 0.0056$ | $6.9940 \pm 0.0429$ | $1.4045 \pm 0.0047$ |
| Masked-NAR (HandPolish base) | $8.7414 \pm 0.0226$ | $1.9343 \pm 0.0019$ | $6.8017 \pm 0.0307$ | $1.4031 \pm 0.0013$ |
| Masked-NAR + HandPolish | $\mathbf{8.7329 \pm 0.0223}$ | $1.8867 \pm 0.0013$ | $\mathbf{6.7983 \pm 0.0306}$ | $\mathbf{1.3555 \pm 0.0037}$ |

**Table 3.** End-to-end test-loop efficiency on Phoenix-200 and CSL-200 (three replicas, one NVIDIA RTX 4090; protocol described in the Experimental Setup section). Energy is estimated from board level `nvidia-smi` power samples.

| Dataset | Method | Time 200 | ms/sample | Speedup | J/sample | Ratio |
|---|---|---|---|---|---|---|
| Phoenix | **SOKE-AR** | $71.62 \pm 0.63$ s | $358.10 \pm 3.15$ | 1.000× | $77.74 \pm 0.46$ | 1.000 |
| Phoenix | **Masked-NAR** | $34.93 \pm 0.35$ s | $174.65 \pm 1.75$ | 2.051× | $18.37 \pm 0.10$ | 0.236 |
| Phoenix | **Masked-NAR + HandPolish** | $\mathbf{35.41 \pm 0.25}$ s | $\mathbf{177.05 \pm 1.25}$ | **2.023×** | $\mathbf{19.73 \pm 0.09}$ | **0.254** |
| CSL | **SOKE-AR** | $63.12 \pm 0.24$ s | $315.60 \pm 1.20$ | 1.000× | $72.12 \pm 0.16$ | 1.000 |
| CSL | **Masked-NAR** | $36.15 \pm 0.08$ s | $180.75 \pm 0.40$ | 1.746× | $18.89 \pm 0.04$ | 0.262 |
| CSL | **Masked-NAR + HandPolish** | $\mathbf{36.49 \pm 0.21}$ s | $\mathbf{182.45 \pm 1.05}$ | **1.730×** | $\mathbf{19.92 \pm 0.10}$ | **0.276** |

Masked-NAR (direct) improves over SOKE-AR on three of the four reported pose metrics. On CSL-Daily, PA-body decreases from 9.6791 to 9.1851. On Phoenix-2014T, PA-body decreases from 8.0912 to 6.9940 and PA-hand from 1.6491 to 1.4045. The exception is CSL PA-hand, where SOKE-AR remains slightly better at 1.8732 versus 1.8869. Applied to its base checkpoint, the polishing stage improves all metrics, with the main effect on hand articulation: CSL PA-hand improves from 1.9343 to 1.8867 and Phoenix PA-hand from 1.4031 to 1.3555, corresponding to relative improvements of about 2.46% and 3.39%, respectively; PA-body changes only slightly. HandPolish does not edit body tokens, so small changes in the body metrics are indirect: DTW computes one temporal alignment for the full sequence. Editing hand tokens shifts this alignment and, through it, the body error. Benefits are tied to the base checkpoint: on the stronger Masked-NAR checkpoint used for the comparison, the same polishing procedure does not improve hand PA-JPE.

***End-to-End Efficiency.*** Table 3 reports the complete test loop on Phoenix-200 and CSL-200, including generation, VQ decoding, exact DTW metrics and prediction saving. Masked-NAR + HandPolish achieves end-to-end speedups of 2.023 fold on Phoenix-200 and 1.730 fold on CSL-200, adding only 0.48 and 0.34 s over Masked-NAR. It uses 25.4% and 27.6% of SOKE-AR GPU-board energy under the stated protocol.

**Table 4.** Post-cache hand-token refinement over matched HandPolish caches (five aligned replicas). Lower PA-JPE is better; speed/GT and tstd/GT closer to one indicate stronger motion vitality. OracleSelect is a non-deployable ground-truth ceiling.

| Dataset | Method | PA-body | PA-hand | Speed/GT | Tstd/GT |
|---|---|---|---|---|---|
| CSL | **HandPolish cache** | $8.3125 \pm 0.0199$ | $1.8072 \pm 0.0012$ | $0.772 \pm 0.001$ | $0.611 \pm 0.000$ |
| CSL | + **GainEdit** | $8.2962 \pm 0.0200$ | $1.6908 \pm 0.0018$ | $0.734 \pm 0.001$ | $0.586 \pm 0.002$ |
| CSL | + **PoseSelect** | $\mathbf{8.2931 \pm 0.0200}$ | $\mathbf{1.6854 \pm 0.0017}$ | $\mathbf{0.767 \pm 0.001}$ | $\mathbf{0.634 \pm 0.001}$ |
| CSL | + **OracleSelect** | $8.2966 \pm 0.0224$ | $1.5802 \pm 0.0021$ | $0.751 \pm 0.001$ | $0.613 \pm 0.001$ |
| Phoenix | **HandPolish cache** | $6.7732 \pm 0.0272$ | $1.3519 \pm 0.0032$ | $0.546 \pm 0.002$ | $0.588 \pm 0.002$ |
| Phoenix | + **GainEdit** | $6.7662 \pm 0.0270$ | $\mathbf{1.3127 \pm 0.0023}$ | $0.455 \pm 0.001$ | $0.509 \pm 0.002$ |
| Phoenix | + **PoseSelect** | $\mathbf{6.7631 \pm 0.0273}$ | $1.3127 \pm 0.0023$ | $\mathbf{0.522 \pm 0.001}$ | $\mathbf{0.578 \pm 0.002}$ |
| Phoenix | + **OracleSelect** | $6.7650 \pm 0.0305$ | $1.2498 \pm 0.0015$ | $0.513 \pm 0.002$ | $0.559 \pm 0.002$ |

**Table 5.** Runtime overhead of post-cache variants (240 samples after 16 warmup), with final hand VQ decoding but without full-sequence generation, metrics and saving.

| Variant | sec/sample | sample/s | peak CUDA MB | J/sample |
|---|---|---|---|---|
| GainEdit | 0.004415 | 226.48 | 259.1 | 0.246 |
| PoseSelect | 0.084813 | 11.79 | 259.1 | 3.722 |

***Hand-Token Refinement.*** Table 4 evaluates hand token refinement in the post-cache benchmark, where all methods start from the same matched HandPolish caches; these values are therefore not numerically comparable with the native HandPolish row of Table 2. PoseSelect improves PA-hand over the matched HandPolish caches on both datasets: by 6.74% on CSL-Daily and 2.90% on Phoenix-2014T. Compared with GainEdit, PoseSelect is slightly better on CSL-Daily and tied on Phoenix-2014T in PA-hand, while preserving higher speed/GT and tstd/GT on both datasets. Selecting a hand refiner by PA-hand alone would hide this trade-off. OracleSelect reaches a PA-hand of 1.5802 on CSL-Daily and 1.2498 on Phoenix-2014T, indicating that better inference-time candidate selection remains possible. OracleSelect is a diagnostic upper bound and is not deployable.

***PoseSelect Overhead.*** Table 5 reports the runtime of deployable refinement variants over 240 measured samples after 16 warmup samples, including the final hand VQ decoding. PoseSelect is slower than GainEdit (84.813 vs. 4.415 ms per sample), with similar peak CUDA memory. This additional runtime is the cost of the behavior in Table 4: equal or better PA-hand with higher motion vitality.

## 6 Discussion

With retrieval and duration fixed, shuffling equal length texts changed outputs by 34.7–37.5% of normal GT error. This confirms text sensitivity, not semantic correctness. Within an editable VQ token setting, the post-cache results indicate that reductions in hand error must be read together with motion vitality: token-level selection keeps edits on the VQ manifold, yet it can still trade motion amplitude for geometric accuracy. GainEdit and OracleSelect frame this comparison: the former is deployable but tends to reduce vitality, whereas the latter is a diagnostic ceiling over the same candidate set. The relevant trade-off is therefore joint: hand PA-JPE, motion vitality and runtime must be interpreted together. With the SOKE tokenizer and VQ decoder kept unchanged, Masked-NAR improves three of the four reported pose metrics over SOKE-AR and reduces the end-to-end test-loop time. HandPolish improves its matched Masked-NAR configuration, while PoseSelect improves hand-token selection over the cached outputs and preserves more motion vitality than GainEdit, at the cost of higher post-cache runtime.

***Limitations.*** The scope of these claims is bounded by the evaluation protocol. SOKE-AR and Masked-NAR are compared through the best-overall checkpoints preserved by the same selection rule during their respective training runs. However, since the split monitored during development coincided with the effective test split, a fully blind protocol, with checkpoints frozen on a separate validation split and a single final test evaluation, remains future work. The learned components of the hand refinement benchmark, PoseSelect and GainEdit, were instead trained and evaluated on disjoint train, validation and test caches. PoseSelect requires no ground truth at inference but is evaluated as a selector over HandPolish caches, not as a native generation method. DTW-PA-JPE, speed/GT and tstd/GT assess geometry and vitality; without back-translation or signer evaluation, semantic correctness and comprehensibility remain unverified. Energy measurements cover GPU-board power only [15].

## 7 Conclusions

We proposed text-to-sign motion generation based on the SOKE tokenizer, with anatomical streams and a frozen latent decoder, testing whether parallel decoding and post-hoc hand token editing improve efficiency and geometric hand accuracy with an unchanged representation. The 3-stage pipeline pairs Masked-NAR, a length-conditioned masked non-AR generator, with two hand-only refinements:

HandPolish, a training-free remasking of low-confidence hand tokens over a frozen body stream and PoseSelect, a learned selector over top-$k$ hand-token candidates using inference-time features. On CSL-Daily and Phoenix-2014T, Masked-NAR improved three of the four reported pose metrics over SOKE-AR. The Masked-NAR + HandPolish pipeline achieved an end-to-end test-loop speedup of up to 2.02-fold and reduced measured GPU-board energy to 25.4–27.6 percent of SOKE-AR under the stated protocol. HandPolish improved hand articulation on its matched checkpoint, and PoseSelect lowered hand PA-JPE while preserving more motion vitality than a gain-based baseline, indicating that hand error and vitality must be read jointly. Future work includes signer-centered semantic assessment, faster PoseSelect inference and richer non-manual representations.

**Disclosure of Interests.** The authors have no competing interests to declare.

## References


1. Zuo, R., Potamias, R.A., Ververas, E., Deng, J., Zafeiriou, S.: Signs as tokens: a retrieval-enhanced multilingual sign language generator. In: ICCV (2025)
2. Zhou, H., Zhou, W., Qi, W., Pu, J., Li, H.: Improving sign language translation with monolingual data by sign back-translation. In: CVPR (2021)
3. Camgoz, N.C., Hadfield, S., Koller, O., Ney, H., Bowden, R.: Neural sign language translation. In: CVPR (2018)
4. Devlin, J., Chang, M.W., Lee, K., Toutanova, K.: BERT: pre-training of deep bidirectional transformers for language understanding. In: NAACL-HLT (2019)
5. Ghazvininejad, M., Levy, O., Liu, Y., Zettlemoyer, L.: Mask-predict: parallel decoding of conditional masked language models. EMNLP-IJCNLP (2019)
6. Chang, H., Zhang, H., Jiang, L., Liu, C., Freeman, W.T.: MaskGIT: masked generative image transformer. In: CVPR (2022)
7. Zuo, R., Potamias, R.A., Sun, Q., Ververas, E., Deng, J., Zafeiriou, S.: MaDiS: taming masked diffusion language models for sign language generation. arXiv preprint arXiv:2601.19577 (2026)
8. Lee, T., Nam, H., Moon, G., Lee, K.M.: GLOS: sign language generation with temporally aligned gloss-level conditioning. arXiv preprint arXiv:2506.07460 (2025)
9. Liu, X., et al.: SignPR: a progressive vector-quantized diffusion framework for sign language production. In: CVPR (2026)
10. Symeonidis-Herzig, A., Low, J., Mercanoglu Sincan, O., Bowden, R.: M3T: discrete multi-modal motion tokens for sign language production. arXiv preprint arXiv:2603.23617 (2026)
11. Low, J., Symeonidis-Herzig, A., Ivashechkin, M., Mercanoglu Sincan, O., Bowden, R.: SignSparK: efficient multilingual sign language production via sparse keyframe learning. In: ECCV (2026)
12. Khan, N., Wu, B., Tan, S., Ishi, C.T., Nakadai, K.: SignFlow: end-to-end sign language generation for one-to-many modeling using conditional flow matching. In: ICMI (2025)
13. Kiziltepe, T., Tasyurek, S.M., Keles, H.Y.: Iterative latent refinement for robust non-autoregressive sign language production. In: ICCV Workshops (2025)

14. Bensabath, L., Petrovich, M., Varol, G.: Text-driven 3D hand motion generation from sign language data. arXiv preprint arXiv:2508.15902 (2025)
15. Jiang, Z., et al.: Meaningful pose-based sign language evaluation. WMT (2025)
16. Xie, P., Zhang, Q., Peng, T., Tang, H., Du, Y., Li, Z.: G2P-DDM: generating sign pose sequence from gloss sequence with discrete diffusion model. In: AAAI (2024)
17. Fang, S., Feng, Y., Zhong, H., Zhang, Y., Metaxas, D.N.: Stable signer: hierarchical sign language generative model. arXiv preprint arXiv:2512.04048 (2025)
18. Zhang, Z., et al.: HandX: scaling bimanual motion and interaction generation. In: CVPR (2026)
19. Yin, A., Li, H., Shen, K., Tang, S., Zhuang, Y.: T2S-GPT: dynamic vector quantization for autoregressive sign language production from text. In: ACL (2024)

# An Online and Explainable Active Learning Framework for Adaptive Machine Learning Models Under Concept Drift

Gabriele Nicolò Costa[1(✉)], Alessandra De Paola[1], Salvatore Drago[2], Pierluca Ferraro[1], and Giuseppe Lo Re[1]

[1] Department of Computer Engineering, University of Palermo, Palermo, Italy
{gabriele.costa03,alessandra.depaola,pierluca.ferraro,giuseppe.lore}@unipa.it

[2] IMT School for Advanced Studies, Lucca, Italy
salvatore.drago@imtlucca.it

**Abstract.** In recent years, adaptive Machine Learning models have been increasingly adopted in online and streaming settings, where data distributions evolve over time due to concept drift. In such scenarios, models must continuously adapt to maintain high predictive performance, while Active Learning strategies are commonly employed to select informative samples under limited labeling budgets. However, state-of-the-art online frameworks still face several challenges in achieving high performance with limited labeling costs, guaranteeing transparency into the active learning and adaptation processes, and distinguishing newly emerging concepts from those previously observed that recur over time. To address these limitations, this paper proposes an Online and Explainable Active Learning framework (OnEAL) for adaptive Machine Learning models operating in concept drift scenarios, such as cybersecurity applications. The proposed approach leverages model explanations to guide sample selection and continuously tracks feature importance over time, improving adaptability and interpretability while enabling the detection of recurring concepts. Experimental results show that OnEAL outperforms traditional Active Learning strategies, particularly under very limited labeling budgets. Furthermore, the explainability modules provide insights into the evolving behavior of the model and the features driving its decisions, supporting explanation-driven concept drift analysis.

**Keywords:** Machine Learning · Active Learning · Online Learning · Explainable AI · Concept Drift · CyberSecurity

## 1 Introduction and Related Work

The widespread adoption of connected devices such as IoT devices [1,29], online services [14], and automated monitoring systems has led to the continuous generation of large volumes of data, requiring Machine Learning (ML) models to


S. Bistarelli et al. (Eds.): AIxIA 2026, LNAI 17131, pp. 183–197, 2027.
https://doi.org/10.1007/978-3-032-40774-0_14

operate over streams whose statistical properties change over time due to a phenomenon known as concept drift [13,35]. Formally, given a data-generating process that follows a distribution $P_t(X, y)$ at time $t$ [28], *concept drift* occurs whenever $P_t(X, y) \neq P_{t+1}(X, y)$ [22], violating the stationarity assumption made in traditional ML settings [7,15] and causing the performance of static models to degrade over time. *Online Learning* addresses this issue through adaptive algorithms that continuously update their internal structure in response to incoming data, including incremental decision trees such as Hoeffding Adaptive Trees (HAT) [8], ensemble methods such as Adaptive Random Forests (ARF) [20], and online frameworks such as Learn++.NSE [17], all designed to preserve predictive performance under changing conditions [4,18]. However, a challenge in deploying adaptive ML models is the availability of labeled data at runtime: obtaining annotations from human experts is resource-intensive, making it infeasible to label every incoming instance and thus imposing a strict *query budget* constraint [9].

Active Learning (AL) frameworks address this challenge by strategically selecting the most informative samples for annotation, minimizing labeling cost while preserving model performance [33]. Proposed query strategies range from *Random Sampling*, which selects instances uniformly, to *Uncertainty Sampling* [25] and its variants *Margin* and *Entropy Sampling*, which target instances with the lowest prediction confidence, nearest the decision boundary, or with the highest predictive entropy, respectively. Under concept drift, such strategies are especially valuable, as samples from the emerging distribution are critical for timely model adaptation [27,36]. These challenges are particularly critical in the Cybersecurity application domain, such as Network Intrusion and Threat Detection scenarios [2,37], where data distributions shift continuously due to both novel zero-day attacks and change in benign activities [16]. In this domain, novel attack patterns may be systematically underrepresented with constrained annotation budgets [24,34], preventing models from learning newly emerging data distributions. Nevertheless, the lack of transparency in both the sample selection mechanism and the underlying model's decisions remains a challenge for adaptive ML within AL frameworks, hindering practical adoption in domains such as Cybersecurity [6]. Explainable Artificial Intelligence (XAI) addresses this gap by providing interpretable explanations and tracking how they evolve over time [11]. SHAP [30] has emerged as a consolidated method based on cooperative game theory, providing both local and global interpretability, and in recent works its application has been extended to incremental learning settings, where explanation stability across model updates becomes paramount [21]. Despite these advances, existing AL strategies for streaming environments still operate within the feature space, without exploiting the reasoning of the underlying model to guide sample selection. Furthermore, existing work integrating XAI into AL has mainly used explanations to justify individual queries rather than to continuously characterize how the stream itself evolves [23,32]. Moreover, integrating XAI within AL pipelines is particularly valuable under concept drift, where explanation-aware selection can clarify why an instance was queried and whether emerging decision patterns resemble previously observed ones, reducing annotation ambiguity and supporting operator understanding of model adaptation [19].

To address these limitations, this paper proposes an Online and Explainable Active Learning Framework, or OnEAL, for adaptive Machine Learning models operating in streaming environments under concept drift. The OnEAL framework consists of three main modules. First, the Online AL module exploits explanations computed by the underlying adaptive ML models to identify and query the most informative samples under a limited labeling budget. Second, the Explainer module provides insights into the features that most influence model predictions, improving the transparency of the decision-making process. Third, the Concept Analyzer module leverages these explanations to assess whether the concept observed in a given online batch resembles previously encountered data distributions, thereby supporting annotators in labeling newly arriving samples. Experimental results demonstrate that OnEAL enables adaptive ML models to better cope with evolving data distributions, particularly under constrained query budgets. The framework effectively identifies informative samples from emerging concepts, facilitating faster and more accurate adaptation to distribution changes. Furthermore, the Explainer and Concept Analyzer modules provide valuable insights into the relationship between new and historical data distributions while continuously tracking the features that drive model decisions, enhancing both interpretability and concept evolution analysis.

The remainder of this paper is organized as follows. Section 2 introduces the OnEAL framework, detailing its modules and working mechanisms. Section 3 shows the experimental evaluation that leads to final conclusions in Sect. 4.

## 2 OnEAL Framework

As illustrated in Fig. 1, the OnEAL framework comprises three main modules: the Online Active Learning module, the Explainable module, and the Concept Analyzer module, which interact with an adaptive online ML model. The framework is designed for data stream environments, where data arrive in batches and the underlying data distribution may evolve over time. The adaptive Online ML model performs predictions on incoming data and is continuously updated as newly labeled samples become available. To manage annotation costs efficiently, the Online Active Learning module selects the most informative instances for labeling according to a predefined query budget. Unlike traditional active learning approaches, this module leverages XAI techniques to guide sample selection: explanations computed for incoming instances are analyzed to identify samples whose explanation patterns significantly deviate from the expected behavior observed so far. Such samples are considered potentially informative, as they may represent previously unseen data, emerging concepts, or shifts in the underlying distribution. These instances are then submitted for annotation and used to update the adaptive online ML model. Following each update, the Explainable and Concept Analyzer modules provide complementary insights into the

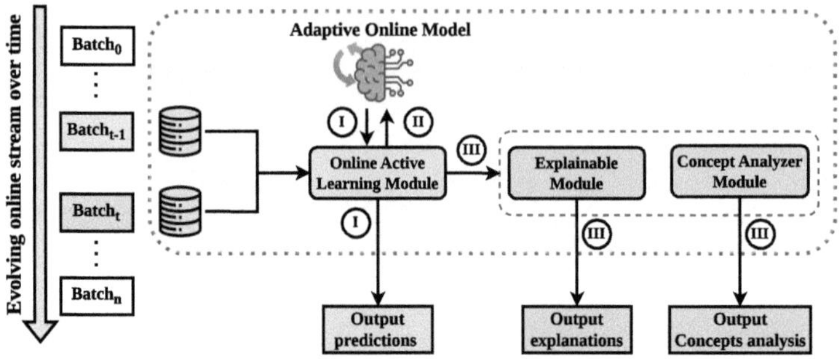


**Fig. 1.** OnEAL framework. For each incoming batch, the Online Active Learning module performs inference using an adaptive online ML model (step I) and updates the model according to an active learning query strategy (step II). Subsequently, the Explainable module provides explanations for the instances selected for labeling, as well as for the changes induced in the adaptive online ML model by the update process, meanwhile the Concept Analyzer module detects potential concepts that have reappeared from past observations (step III).

learning process. The Explainable module analyzes changes in feature importance before and after retraining to assess how newly acquired knowledge affects the model, by quantifying the effectiveness of each update. The Concept Analyzer module instead compares explanations of incoming samples with those of previously observed data (reference batches) to identify potential concept evolution, recurrence, or emergence of new concepts. Together, these modules allow the framework to monitor learning stability, evaluate the contribution of newly labeled samples, and detect domain shifts caused by concept drift, while also making model updates more transparent and interpretable for human analysts.

Finally, OnEAL is designed as a general-purpose and model-agnostic framework, allowing the adaptive online ML model to be instantiated with a wide range of ML algorithms capable of incremental updates or periodic retraining as new labeled samples become available. Furthermore, the framework supports the integration of appropriate XAI algorithms associated with the underlying ML model, enabling the generation of model explanations that are employed by the Explainable and Concept Analyzer modules.

The remainder of this section is organized as follows. Section 2.1 describes the XAI-driven active learning strategy and sample selection process. Section 2.2 details the Explainable module and how explanations support understanding of both active learning decisions and model adaptation over time. Section 2.3 details the Concept Analyzer module and its role in comparing evolving distributions with previous ones.

## 2.1 Online Active Learning Module

The Online Active Learning module, whose workflow is illustrated in Fig. 2, comprises an algorithm consisting of seven steps operating on a sequence of

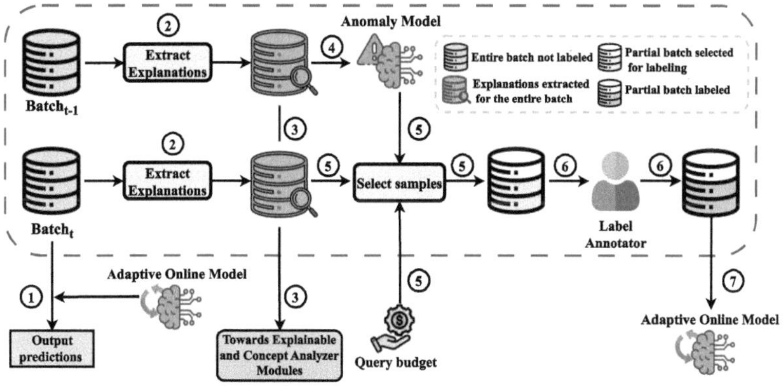


**Fig. 2.** Workflow of the Online Active Learning module.

unlabeled data batches within a streaming environment. When the algorithm receives a new batch of data, it identifies the most informative samples by analyzing their explanatory patterns, queries their labels according to a predefined budget and uses the acquired labels to update the adaptive model. This process is repeated for each new batch of data, enabling continuous and selective label acquisition as the underlying data distribution evolves. Let $B_t$ denote the current unlabeled batch arriving at time $t$, and let $f_t$ be the adaptive model trained on labeled data up to batch $B_{t-1}$. Upon the arrival of a new batch, the model first performs inference on all samples in $B_t$ (step 1). An XAI method is then applied to both $B_t$ and $B_{t-1}$ using $f_t$ (step 2), producing two sets of explanations: $\mathbf{\Phi}^{t-1} = \text{Explanations}(f_t, B_{t-1})$ and $\mathbf{\Phi}^t = \text{Explanations}(f_t, B_t)$, where each row of $\mathbf{\Phi}$ corresponds to the explanation vector of a sample. These explanations are forwarded to the other modules for further analysis (step 3). To identify potentially informative instances, $\mathbf{\Phi}^{t-1}$ is used to train an anomaly detection model $A(\cdot)$ (step 4), which learns the distribution of explanation patterns observed in recent data. For each explanation vector $\phi_i^t \in \mathbf{\Phi}^t$, an anomaly score is computed as: $s_i = A(\phi_i^t)$. A high anomaly score indicates that an explanation deviates from previously observed patterns, suggesting changes in the data distribution such as unseen data or emerging concepts. Samples are then ranked by anomaly score, and the top-ranked instances are selected according to a predefined query budget, forming the query set $\mathcal{Q}_t \subseteq B_t$ (step 5). This explanation-driven selection strategy is one of the core contributions of the OnEAL framework: rather than operating in the feature or prediction space, it selects samples directly in the explanation space, allowing it to detect instances whose decision-making patterns differ significantly from previous batches and to prioritize samples more likely to capture distribution changes and concept drift. Finally, $\mathcal{Q}_t$ is forwarded to an annotator for labeling (step 6), and the newly labeled samples are used to update the adaptive online model (step 7), enabling continuous adaptation to evolving data distributions while maintaining high predictive performance over time.

### 2.2 Explainable Module

During streaming evaluation, XAI explanations are computed for each batch both before and after updating the adaptive online ML model. The Explainable module plays a dual role: identifying the features most affected during retraining by analyzing variations in feature importance, and assessing the impact of each update by measuring the similarity between explanations obtained before and after retraining. Formally, let $\mathbf{\Phi}^t_{pre}$ and $\mathbf{\Phi}^t_{post}$ denote the explanations computed before and after the model update at batch $B_t$. These explanations are aggregated at the batch level into global feature importance vectors, $\mathbf{I}^t_{pre} = g(\mathbf{\Phi}^t_{pre})$ and $\mathbf{I}^t_{post} = g(\mathbf{\Phi}^t_{post})$, where $g(\cdot)$ aggregates the local explanations into a single per-feature importance score by computing the mean absolute value across all samples in the batch. The stability of the retraining process is quantified through the Temporal Stability Similarity ($TSS$) score:

$$TSS^t = \cos\left(\mathbf{I}^t_{post}, \mathbf{I}^t_{pre}\right). \tag{1}$$

Higher values indicate that the update preserved the decision-making process of the adaptive model, while lower values suggest a substantial change in the features driving its predictions.

### 2.3 Concept Analyzer Module

The Concept Analyzer module takes two inputs for each batch: pre and post updating explanations from the Online Active Learning module, and the TSS score from the Explainable module. While high TSS values indicate stable updates, significant peaks signal substantial changes potentially associated with the emergence of new concepts. To detect such events, the module monitors the TSS stream using an Exponentially Weighted Moving Average (EWMA). Whenever a peak is detected, the corresponding post-update explanation is stored as a reference concept, formally $\mathbf{ref}^t = \mathbf{I}^t_{post} = g\left(\mathbf{\Phi}^t_{post}\right)$, where $t$ denotes the batch at which the peak occurs.

The reference concept is then compared with the global feature importance vector obtained from the pre-update explanations of each future batch $j \geq t$, namely $\mathbf{I}^j_{pre} = g\left(\mathbf{\Phi}^j_{pre}\right)$, to track its temporal evolution through the Temporal Concept Similarity ($TCS$) score:

$$TCS^j = \cos\left(\mathbf{ref}^t, \mathbf{I}^j_{pre}\right), \qquad j \geq t. \tag{2}$$

High TCS values indicate that the feature importance pattern associated with the reference concept remains consistent over time, whereas lower values suggest progressive divergence, potentially reflecting the emergence of novel concepts or shifts in the underlying data distribution.

## 3 Experimental Evaluation

This section presents the experimental evaluation of OnEAL across datasets, adaptive ML models, and query budgets. Section 3.1 describes the experimental

**Table 1.** REFINE parameters used to generate a streamed version of the X-IIoTID dataset with induced gradual concept drift. $K$ denotes the spatial bias (that is, the ratio between benign and malicious samples), while *Offline* and *Online* indicate the numbers of samples used for offline initialization and online evaluation, respectively. *Drift Interval* is reported as [start, stop] within the online portion of the stream, and *Slope* controls the drift rate.

| K | Size | Offline | Online | Drift Interval | Slope |
|---|---|---|---|---|---|
| 0.5 | 120000 | 30000 | 90000 | [30000, 60000] | 1.0 |

setup, while Sect. 3.2 reports the results of the Online Active Learning, Explainable, and Concept Analyzer modules.

### 3.1 Experimental Setup

As a case study, OnEAL is applied to a ML-based network intrusion detection system (NIDS) that monitors traffic from heterogeneous devices to detect anomalies resulting from attacks. In this context, concept drift is caused by the continuous emergence of new devices and attack patterns, requiring the system to adapt while keeping labeling costs low and decision-making transparent. While this case study focuses on network intrusion detection, the OnEAL framework is general-purpose and applicable to any domain in which adaptive learning models must handle concept drift.

The experimental evaluation is performed on the X-IIoTID dataset [5], which captures the heterogeneity of industrial IoT (IIoT) environments by integrating network traffic and host-level observations across multiple devices, protocols, and operational contexts. This dataset introduces significant behavioral variability, making it suitable for evaluating adaptive online ML models under evolving conditions, including zero-day attacks and newly introduced devices, leading to concept drift in both malicious and benign data distributions. The dataset was collected over four months; data from the first two months were used for offline training, while data from the remaining two months were reserved for online evaluation. However, the dataset lacks ground-truth drift annotations, typically requiring drift to be inferred from drops in online performance. To address this limitation, a streamed version with induced gradual concept drift is also used for the experimental evaluation, generated via the REFINE framework [12]. REFINE is a modular framework that produces streaming versions of real-world datasets with explicit drift annotations and controlled class distributions through a spatial bias parameter regulating the proportion of benign and malicious samples. Concept generation and drift stream parameters are reported in Table 1.

Furthermore, OnEAL framework is evaluated using different online adaptive ML algorithms widely adopted for handling non-stationary data streams, introduced in Sect. 1: Adaptive Random Forest (ARF) [20], Hoeffding Adaptive Tree (HAT) [8], and Learn++.NSE [17]. In addiction, Isolation Forest (IF) [26] is employed as Anomaly Model within the Online Active Learning module, as explained in Sect. 2.1.

**Table 2.** Comparison between OnEAL and active learning strategies (AL-S) on the X-IIoTID dataset. $S1$, $S2$, and $S3$ denote Uncertainty, Margin, and Entropy Sampling, respectively. Results are reported as AUT scores for Accuracy (Acc.), F1-score (F1), and Recall (Rec.) across query budgets ($q$) and ML models. $BL$ denotes the 0% baseline, and $FL$ the 100% full-label upper bound.

| | | *ARF* | | | *HAT* | | | *Learn++.NSE* | | |
|---|---|---|---|---|---|---|---|---|---|---|
| $q$ | AL-S | Acc. | F1 | Rec. | Acc. | F1 | Rec. | Acc. | F1 | Rec. |
| 0.0 | BL | 55.17 | 43.31 | 22.86 | 37.21 | 28.70 | 10.84 | 55.61 | 46.85 | 33.99 |
| 0.05 | S1 | 85.77 | 78.11 | 71.95 | 83.65 | 71.16 | 66.12 | 75.84 | 60.29 | 61.60 |
| | S2 | 86.99 | 79.09 | 73.32 | 80.75 | 62.92 | 58.23 | 69.73 | 54.70 | 54.60 |
| | S3 | 81.06 | 69.84 | 64.34 | 62.00 | 45.01 | 24.23 | 73.00 | 65.31 | 66.42 |
| | **EAL** | **94.14** | **89.35** | **82.72** | **85.45** | **78.96** | **74.87** | **86.69** | **74.92** | **67.48** |
| 0.10 | S1 | 92.08 | 85.44 | 79.78 | 71.57 | 59.66 | 49.72 | 72.09 | 61.35 | 65.61 |
| | S2 | 89.82 | 82.45 | 79.36 | 77.30 | 68.01 | 58.54 | 80.17 | 67.72 | 59.64 |
| | S3 | 91.17 | 84.09 | 78.21 | 68.14 | 50.26 | 35.51 | 78.72 | 66.00 | 65.41 |
| | **EAL** | **94.21** | **89.38** | **82.85** | **85.37** | **78.13** | **67.72** | **85.11** | **79.37** | **74.81** |
| 0.20 | S1 | 93.50 | 89.23 | 85.49 | 84.38 | 73.41 | 70.49 | 80.69 | 67.73 | 67.85 |
| | S2 | 90.83 | 83.91 | 82.77 | 76.64 | 66.47 | 62.52 | 85.27 | 76.09 | 72.89 |
| | S3 | 94.23 | **90.63** | 86.88 | 72.48 | 58.37 | 43.13 | 84.58 | 73.36 | 73.47 |
| | **EAL** | **94.62** | 90.58 | **87.53** | **88.63** | **80.71** | **80.71** | **92.63** | **88.99** | **83.78** |
| 1.0 | FL | 93.89 | 90.19 | 87.28 | 85.02 | 75.93 | 75.24 | 93.10 | 88.65 | 82.97 |

### 3.2 Experimental Results

Experiments use an evaluation window of $W = 10\,000$ samples, with SHAP [30] employed as the XAI method for explanation computing. For each online learning model, OnEAL is compared against three established AL strategies (Sect. 1): Uncertainty, Margin, and Entropy Sampling, alongside the proposed XAI-driven AL query strategy. Three query budgets are considered, $q \in \{0.05, 0.10, 0.20\}$, plus two reference scenarios: a no-update baseline ($q = 0.0$) ($BL$) and a full-label ($FL$) upper bound ($q = 1.0$). Performance is evaluated using the Area Under Time (AUT) metric [31], computed for Accuracy, F1-score, and Recall. AUT-based results for the standard and streamed X-IIoTID scenarios are reported in Table 2 and Table 3, respectively.

On X-IIoTID in Table 2, HAT and Learn++.NSE outperform other AL strategies in terms of AUT(F1) and AUT(Recall), while ARF consistently outperforms even FL in terms of AUT(F1) and AUT(Accuracy). A similar behavior

**Table 3.** Comparison between OnEAL and active learning strategies (AL-S) on the streamed X-IIoTID dataset. $S1$, $S2$, and $S3$ denote Uncertainty, Margin, and Entropy Sampling, respectively. Results are reported as AUT scores for Accuracy (Acc.), F1-score (F1), and Recall (Rec.) across query budgets ($q$) and ML models. $BL$ denotes the 0% baseline, and $FL$ the 100% full-label upper bound.

| | | *ARF* | | | *HAT* | | | *Learn++.NSE* | | |
|---|---|---|---|---|---|---|---|---|---|---|
| $q$ | AL-S | Acc. | F1 | Rec. | Acc. | F1 | Rec. | Acc. | F1 | Rec. |
| 0.0 | BL | 71.94 | 68.79 | 90.77 | 74.44 | 71.07 | 93.57 | 76.06 | 73.58 | 95.61 |
| 0.05 | S1 | 96.24 | 96.23 | 97.16 | 72.69 | 71.96 | 61.69 | 92.23 | 92.16 | 94.50 |
| | S2 | 95.99 | 95.99 | 97.04 | 77.75 | 76.76 | 62.53 | 92.60 | 92.57 | 95.82 |
| | S3 | **96.55** | **96.53** | **97.84** | 70.80 | 65.05 | 44.48 | 92.25 | 92.04 | 93.69 |
| | **EAL** | 96.48 | 96.48 | 97.31 | **89.89** | **89.71** | **84.52** | **94.05** | **94.03** | **96.15** |
| 0.10 | S1 | **97.25** | **97.24** | **97.75** | 74.95 | 73.93 | 61.37 | 93.57 | 93.55 | 91.97 |
| | S2 | 96.63 | 96.63 | 96.70 | 77.92 | 76.28 | 63.15 | 91.21 | 91.08 | 87.47 |
| | S3 | 97.08 | 97.07 | 97.67 | 66.93 | 63.44 | 41.09 | 90.23 | 90.05 | 85.38 |
| | **EAL** | 96.16 | 96.15 | 96.65 | **93.51** | **93.50** | **91.23** | **95.94** | **95.93** | **97.93** |
| 0.20 | S1 | 97.33 | 97.32 | 97.85 | 83.19 | 83.02 | 79.39 | 82.40 | 79.51 | 79.70 |
| | S2 | **97.37** | **97.36** | **97.91** | 83.11 | 82.25 | 74.61 | 91.07 | 90.95 | 86.82 |
| | S3 | 97.04 | 97.03 | 97.17 | 79.30 | 78.87 | 66.96 | 85.68 | 85.21 | 81.83 |
| | **EAL** | 97.03 | 97.03 | 97.77 | **89.93** | **89.89** | **84.67** | **94.36** | **94.35** | **95.95** |
| 1.0 | FL | 97.88 | 97.87 | 98.39 | 95.21 | 95.20 | 94.65 | 96.07 | 96.05 | 97.57 |

is observed in the streamed setting in Table 3, where OnEAL demonstrates even stronger robustness: for HAT, consistent improvements emerge across all query budgets, with a particularly notable gap at $q = 0.1$. Learn++.NSE yields the best overall results for OnEAL, further confirming its effectiveness under more challenging streaming conditions. However, ARF's performance under OnEAL remains stable across query budgets and close to the FL upper bound, though it does not consistently outperform the best traditional AL strategy, unlike the results observed for HAT and Learn++.NSE, suggesting a narrower margin for explanation-driven selection with this model. Moreover the comparison between the two datasets further reveals that traditional AL strategies (Uncertainty and Margin) are relatively stable on the standard dataset but less consistent in the streamed one. OnEAL, instead, maintains stable and high performance across both settings, suggesting strong robustness to distribution shifts. This is further confirmed by Fig. 3 and Fig. 4, where OnEAL consistently achieves a higher mean and lower standard deviation across both models and query budgets. Regarding the relationship between query budget and performance, although increasing $q$ generally improves results for all adaptive ML models, OnEAL achieves strong performance even under strict labeling constraints, often matching or exceeding traditional strategies at higher budgets. Furthermore, Fig. 5 reports the online streaming evaluation under a strict query budget ($q = 0.05$), using ARF on X-

IIoTID and Learn++.NSE on the streamed scenario. Results show that OnEAL closely matches the FL and consistently surpasses the BL strategies, demonstrating the capability of the Online Active Learning module to effectively identify the most informative instances.

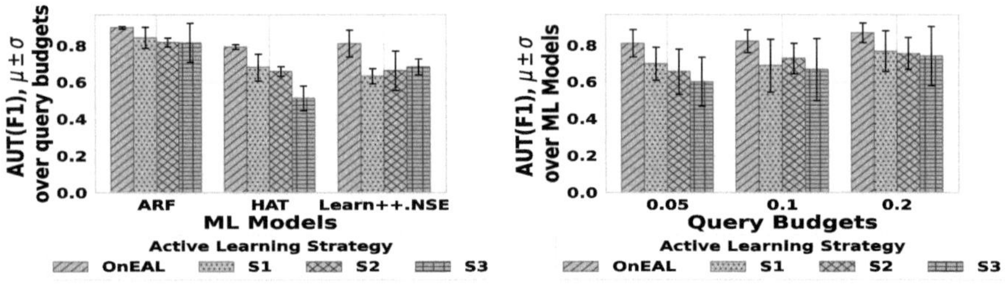


(a) ML models across query budgets. (b) Query budgets across ML models.

**Fig. 3.** Mean and std of AUT(F1) for AL strategies and OnEAL on X-IIoTID, aggregated across models and query budgets. $S1$, $S2$, $S3$ denote Uncertainty, Margin, and Entropy Sampling, respectively.

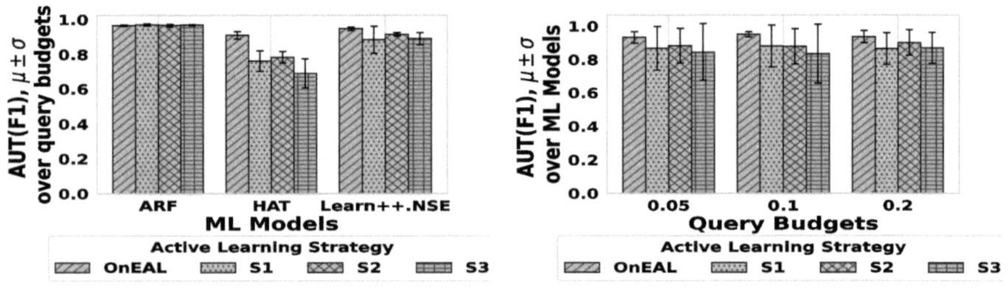


(a) ML models across query budgets. (b) Query budgets across ML models.

**Fig. 4.** Mean and std of AUT(F1) for AL strategies and OnEAL on streamed X-IIoTID, aggregated across models and query budgets. $S1$, $S2$, $S3$ denote Uncertainty, Margin, and Entropy Sampling, respectively.

Building upon the results obtained with ARF on the X-IIoTID dataset and Learn++.NSE on the streamed X-IIoTID scenario under a strict query budget of $q = 0.05$, the same experimental setting is adopted to evaluate the Explainable and Concept Analyzer modules. Starting from the Explainable module, Fig. 6 reports the top 10 features exhibiting the highest variation in SHAP values before and after each adaptive model updating at each batch $t$ for both datasets. These deltas indicate how the contribution of individual features to the predictions of the model changes after updating on new incoming data, and

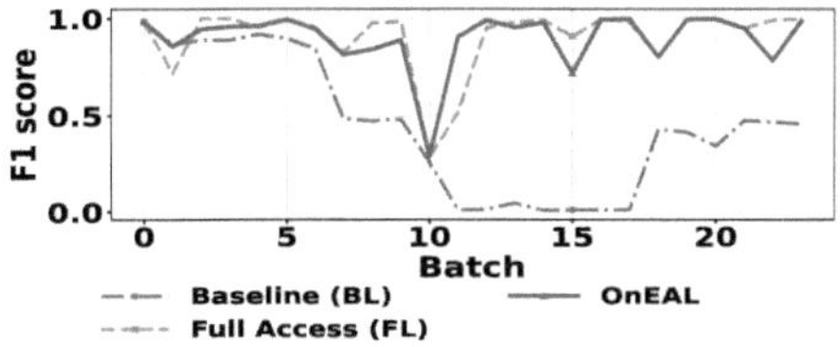


(a) ARF model on X-IIoTID.

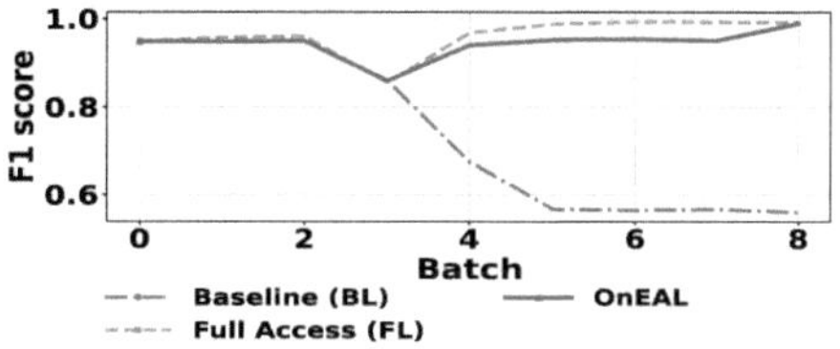


(b) Learn++.NSE on streamed X-IIoTID.

**Fig. 5.** Online streaming evaluation under a low query budget ($q = 0.05$). (a) ARF on X-IIoTID and (b) Learn++.NSE on the streamed X-IIoTID scenario. Curves compare OnEAL with a no-query baseline (BL) and a full-label (FL) upper bound.

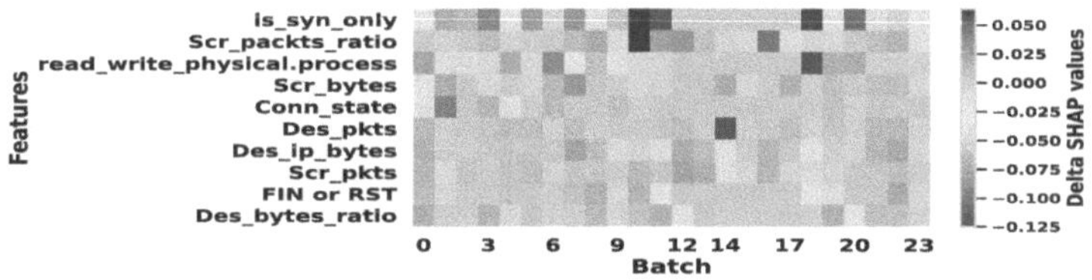


(a) ARF model on X-IIoTID.

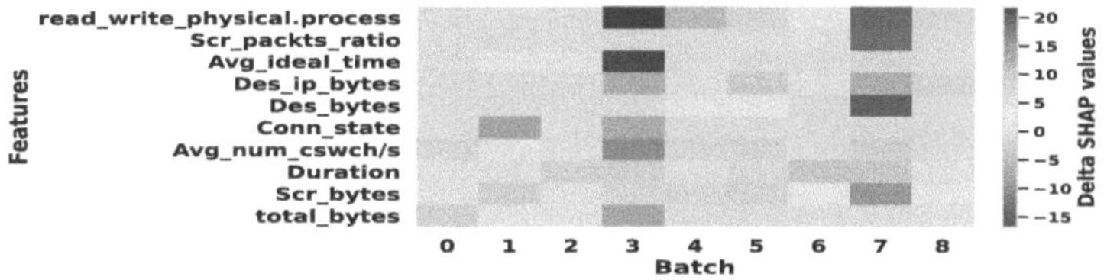


(b) Learn++.NSE on streamed X-IIoTID.

**Fig. 6.** Top 10 features with the highest variation in SHAP values before and after each model update for both datasets.

results show that the model progressively modifies its decision-making behavior. Specifically, the largest SHAP variations are consistently observed near the peaks of the TSS score reported in Fig. 7a and Fig. 8a, suggesting that periods of increased instability in model performance correspond to stronger shifts in feature importance; that is, the model is not only experiencing a drop in predictive stability but is also restructuring its internal decision logic. Furthermore, these peaks align with the performance degradations observed in the online evaluation reported in Fig. 5. This result reveals a strong correlation between fluctuations in predictive performance and variations in explanation patterns, indicating that both reflect the impact of concept drift on the underlying data distribution. Moreover, the Concept Analyzer module provides additional insight into these dynamics: Fig. 7a and Fig. 8a report peak deviations in concept-related metrics, while Fig. 8a and Fig. 8b show the TCS scores computed over selected reference batches. Overall, this analysis supports a deeper interpretation of the temporal behavior of the data stream. In the first dataset (Fig. 8a), explanations in following periods appear similar to those observed in the initial batches, suggesting a potential recurrence of previously seen concepts. This interpretation is further investigated using the streamed version of the dataset with induced concept drift: once a gradual drift begins at the third batch, the similarity between current explanations and early reference explanations progressively decreases, indicating that previously observed concepts no longer reappear and that the model increasingly relies on different feature importance. During the drift phase, explanations reflect a distinct and evolving concept, separated from earlier patterns. Finally, in the last batches, once the transition phase has ended, explanation patterns change again, marking the completion of the drift process and the emergence of a new concept.

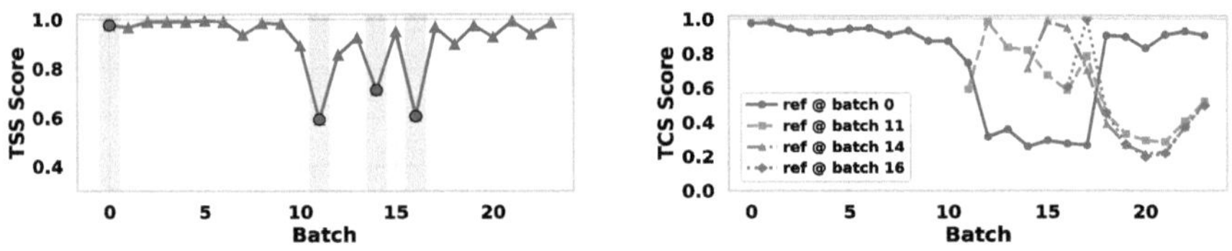


(a) TSS score (b) TCS score

**Fig. 7.** Results from the Explainable module (a) and the Concept Analyzer module (b) on X-IIoTID using ARF model with $q = 0.05$.

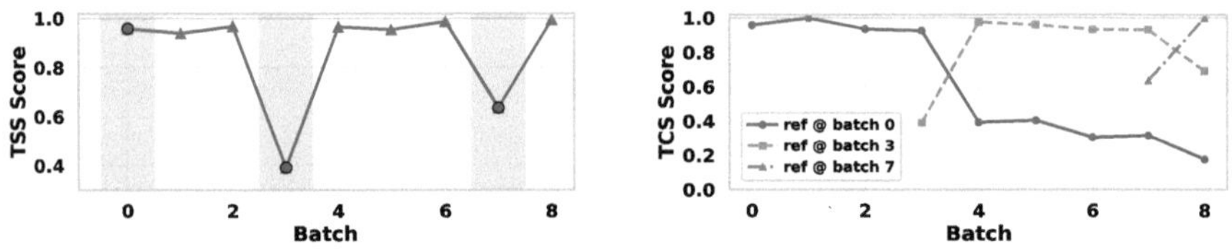


(a) TSS score (b) TCS score

**Fig. 8.** Results from the Explainable module (a) and the Concept Analyzer module (b) on streamed X-IIoTID using ARF model with $q = 0.05$.

## 4 Conclusions and Future Work

This paper proposes an online, explainable active learning framework for adapting machine learning models under concept drift. Unlike traditional approaches, it leverages XAI explanations from the underlying adaptive ML model at each streaming batch both to select the most informative samples and to interpret the behavior of the model over time. Experimental results show that OnEAL outperforms standard AL frameworks, especially with a limited query budget associated, while the explanations offer meaningful insight into update stability and into how newly emerging concepts relate to previously observed distributions. Future work will extend the framework with a triggering mechanism that queries for labels only upon the emergence of a new concept, thereby reducing annotation cost beyond what a fixed query budget allows. Enabling such a mechanism requires equipping OnEAL with a memory of previously identified concepts, rather than relying solely on the previous batch, so that genuinely novel concepts can be distinguished from recurring ones. This extension is a consequence of the Explainable and Concept-Analyzer modules already integrated within the framework: by continuously tracking changes in feature importance and measuring the similarity between incoming concepts and this concept memory, these modules would provide the necessary signals to determine when acquiring new labels is informative and when, conversely, the underlying distribution remains stable enough to skip annotation altogether. Finally, future work will analyze the performance of OnEAL to other domains affected by concept drift, such as distributed reputation systems [3], social network security [10].

## References


1. Agate, V., et al.: Population protocols for adaptive event dissemination with autonomous agents in vehicular networks. In: Proceedings of the 17th International Conference on Agents and Artificial Intelligence (ICAART), pp. 640–647 (2025)
2. Agate, V., De Paola, A., Drago, S., Ferraro, P., Lo Re, G.: Enhancing IoT network security with concept drift-aware unsupervised threat detection. In: 2024 IEEE Symposium on Computers and Communications (ISCC), pp. 1–6. IEEE (2024)
3. Agate, V., De Paola, A., Lo Re, G., Morana, M.: A simulation software for the evaluation of vulnerabilities in reputation management systems. ACM Trans. Comput. Syst. (TOCS) **37**(1–4), 1–30 (2021)
4. Agate, V., Drago, S., Ferraro, P., Lo Re, G.: Anomaly detection for reoccurring concept drift in smart environments. In: 2022 18th International Conference on Mobility, Sensing and Networking (MSN), pp. 113–120. IEEE (2022)
5. Al-Hawawreh, M., Sitnikova, E., Aboutorab, N.: X-iiotid: a connectivity-agnostic and device-agnostic intrusion data set for industrial internet of things. IEEE Internet Things J. **9**(5), 3962–3977 (2021)
6. Arrieta, A.B., et al.: Explainable artificial intelligence (xai): concepts, taxonomies, opportunities and challenges toward responsible ai. Inf. fusion **58**, 82–115 (2020)
7. Augello, A., De Paola, A., Lo Re, G.: Resource-aware federated learning for malware detection on smart devices. In: 2026 IEEE International Conference on Smart Computing (SmartComp), pp. 48–55 (2026). https://doi.org/10.1109/SmartComp69968.2026.00019
8. Bifet, A., Gavalda, R.: Adaptive learning from evolving data streams. In: International Symposium on Intelligent Data Analysis, pp. 249–260. Springer, Cham (2009)
9. Cacciarelli, D., Kulahci, M.: Active learning for data streams: a survey. Mach. Learn. **113**(1), 185–239 (2024)

10. Concone, F., Lo Re, G., Morana, M., Ruocco, C.: Twitter spam account detection by effective labeling. In: CEUR Workshop Proceedings, vol. 2315 (2019)
11. Costa, G.N., De Paola, A., Drago, S., Ferraro, P., Lo Re, G.: An heuristic and explainable unsupervised concept drift detector. In: 2026 IEEE International Conference on Smart Computing Workshops and Other Affiliated events (SmartComp Companion), pp. 61–66. IEEE (2026)
12. Costa, G.N., De Paola, A., Drago, S., Ferraro, P., Lo Re, G.: REFINE: robust evaluation framework for IDS under concept drift in dynamic environments. In: Proceedings of the 18th International Conference on Agents and Artificial Intelligence (ICAART), vol. 2, pp. 1835–1846 (2026)
13. De Paola, A., Drago, S., Ferraro, P., Lo Re, G.: HOIDS: concept drift aware hybrid online intrusion detection system. J. Netw. Comput. Appl. **254** (2026). https://doi.org/10.1016/j.jnca.2026.104556
14. De Paola, A., Ferraro, P., Imperiale, S., Lo Re, G.: Optimized decision-making in physical retail stores through an adaptive hybrid system. In: LNNS, vol. 1598, pp. 299 – 309 (2026). https://doi.org/10.1007/978-3-032-04160-9_27
15. Ditzler, G., Roveri, M., Alippi, C., Polikar, R.: Learning in nonstationary environments: a survey. IEEE Comput. Intell. Mag. **10**(4), 12–25 (2015)
16. Drago, S., Lorusso, M., Ferraro, P., De Paola, A., Lo Re, G.: Online framework for intrusion detection systems with explainable concept drift detection and adaptation phases. In: CEUR Workshop Proceedings, vol. 4198, CEUR-WS (2026)
17. Elwell, R., Polikar, R.: Incremental learning of concept drift in nonstationary environments. IEEE Trans. Neural Networks **22**(10), 1517–1531 (2011)
18. Gama, J., Žliobaitė, I., Bifet, A., Pechenizkiy, M., Bouchachia, A.: A survey on concept drift adaptation. ACM Comput. Surv. (CSUR) **46**(4), 1–37 (2014)
19. Ghai, B., Liao, Q.V., Zhang, Y., Bellamy, R., Mueller, K.: Explainable active learning (xal) toward AI explanations as interfaces for machine teachers. Proc. ACM Hum. Comput. Interact. **4**(CSCW3), 1–28 (2021)
20. Gomes, H.M., et al.: Adaptive random forests for evolving data stream classification. Mach. Learn. **106**(9), 1469–1495 (2017)
21. Haug, J., Braun, A., Zürn, S., Kasneci, G.: Change detection for local explainability in evolving data streams. In: Proceedings of the 31st ACM International Conference on Information & Knowledge Management, pp. 706–716 (2022)
22. Hinder, F., Vaquet, V., Hammer, B.: One or two things we know about concept drift—a survey on monitoring in evolving environments. part a: detecting concept drift. Front. Artif. Intell. **7**, 1330257 (2024)
23. Jia, S., Li, Z., Chen, N., Zhang, J.: Towards visual explainable active learning for zero-shot classification. IEEE Trans. Visual Comput. Graph. **28**(1), 791–801 (2021)
24. Jordaney, R., et al.: Transcend: detecting concept drift in malware classification models. In: 26th USENIX Security Symposium (USENIX security 17), pp. 625–642 (2017)
25. Lewis, D.D., Catlett, J.: Heterogeneous uncertainty sampling for supervised learning. In: Machine Learning Proceedings, pp. 148–156. Elsevier (1994)
26. Liu, F.T., Ting, K.M., Zhou, Z.H.: Isolation forest. In: 8th IEEE International Conference on Data Mining, pp. 413–422. IEEE (2008)
27. Losing, V., Hammer, B., Wersing, H.: Incremental on-line learning: a review and comparison of state of the art algorithms. Neurocomputing **275**, 1261–1274 (2018)
28. Lu, J., Liu, A., Dong, F., Gu, F., Gama, J., Zhang, G.: Learning under concept drift: a review. IEEE Trans. Knowl. Data Eng. **31**(12), 2346–2363 (2018)
29. Lu, Y., Da, X., L.: Internet of things (IoT) cybersecurity research: a review of current research topics. IEEE Internet Things J. **6**(2), 2103–2115 (2018)

30. Lundberg, S.M., Lee, S.I.: A unified approach to interpreting model predictions. In: Advances in Neural Information Processing Systems, p. 30 (2017)
31. Pendlebury, F., Pierazzi, F., Jordaney, R., Kinder, J., Cavallaro, L.: {TESSERACT}: eliminating experimental bias in malware classification across space and time. In: 28th USENIX Security Symposium (2019)
32. Phillips, R., Chang, K.H., Friedler, S.A.: Interpretable active learning. In: Conference on Fairness, Accountability and Transparency, pp. 49–61. PMLR (2018)
33. Settles, B.: Active learning. Synth. Lect. Artif. Intell. Mach. Learn. **18**, 1–111 (2012)
34. Vaarandi, R., Guerra-Manzanares, A.: Network ids alert classification with active learning techniques. J. Inf. Secur. Appl. **81**, 103687 (2024)
35. Webb, G.I., Hyde, R., Cao, H., Nguyen, H.L., Petitjean, F.: Characterizing concept drift. Data Min. Knowl. Disc. **30**(4), 964–994 (2016)
36. Žliobaitė, I., Bifet, A., Pfahringer, B., Holmes, G.: Active learning with drifting streaming data. IEEE Trans. Neural Netw. Learn. Syst. **25**(1), 27–39 (2013)
37. Žliobaitė, I., Pechenizkiy, M., Gama, J.: An overview of concept drift applications. In: Big Data Analysis: New Algorithms for a New Society, pp. 91–114 (2015)

# A Probabilistic Package for Explainable Action Selection in Resource-Aware Cooperative Agents

Stefania Costantini and Valentina Pitoni(✉)

Department of Information Engineering, Computer Science and Mathematics, University of L'Aquila, L'Aquila, Italy
{stefania.costantini,valentina.pitoni}@univaq.it

**Abstract.** Cooperative multi-agent systems often have to choose among feasible actions that are equivalent with respect to a goal but differ in reliability, preference, and resource consumption. We extend the epistemic logic L-DINF with a conservative probabilistic package that adds probability measures over epistemic alternatives, success probabilities for physical actions, and acceptance thresholds. The package supports probabilistic explicit belief, probabilistic executability, and probability-aware instances of the original action selector. We prove well-definedness, conservativity, operational reduction, reliability preference property, and soundness of explanation records. A health-care scheduling scenario and a controlled synthetic simulation compare deterministic and probabilistic selectors through ablations, sensitivity analysis, calibration, and scalability considerations. The result is a lightweight explainable layer for risk-aware action selection in resource-aware cooperative agents.

**Keywords:** Multi-agent systems · Epistemic logic · Reasoning under uncertainty · Action selection · Explainable AI

## 1 Introduction

Cooperative multi-agent systems are increasingly used to model settings in which autonomous components reason, coordinate, and act on behalf of individual or collective goals. In such systems, an action is rarely selected by executability alone. A feasible action may be outside the current role of an agent, consume too many resources, or be functionally acceptable but unreliable in the current circumstances. A clinic may prefer an in-person consultation, but a teleconsultation may be more likely to be accepted by a patient living at a long distance; a robot may prefer a short route, but a longer one may be safer; a service agent may choose between several providers that are equivalent for the user but differ in expected availability.

The logic of inferable, L-DINF, was introduced as an epistemic framework for resource-bounded cooperative agents [9–11]. It distinguishes background knowledge from explicit beliefs and represents reasoning through mental actions that


S. Bistarelli et al. (Eds.): AIxIA 2026, LNAI 17131, pp. 198–211, 2027.
https://doi.org/10.1007/978-3-032-40774-0_15

update the working memory of agents. Later work emphasized the modular semantics of the framework and introduced packages for costs, budgets, roles, preferences, equivalence classes of physical actions, and action selection [12]. This modular organization is crucial for the present paper: the epistemic core remains unchanged, while practical aspects of agent behaviour are represented by optional packages.

The research gap addressed here is not simply that L-DINF lacks probabilities. Several families of approaches address uncertainty, including probabilistic epistemic logics, probabilistic BDI systems, and decision-theoretic models such as MDPs and POMDPs. However, these approaches do not usually provide, in the same symbolic layer, an explicit account of inferential belief formation, mental actions, physical actions, roles, resources, preferences, equivalence among actions, and a human-readable justification of why one feasible substitute was selected instead of another. Conversely, deterministic L-DINF captures the symbolic and organizational constraints but cannot express that one enabled and affordable action is riskier than another. This paper aims to fill this specific gap by adding a conservative probability layer to L-DINF without turning it into a monolithic stochastic planner.

We add a probabilistic package consisting of probability measures over epistemic alternatives, success probabilities for physical actions, and thresholds used to decide when a belief or action is reliable enough for deliberation. The original language is preserved, while new probabilistic constructs are available only when uncertainty has to be considered. This makes the extension conservative: the non-probabilistic interpretation of previous L-DINF formulas is not changed by the presence of the probability package.

The contribution is fourfold. First, we define probabilistic explicit belief and probabilistic executability as conservative extensions of the L-DINF semantics. Second, we instantiate the original selector by a parametric score combining reliability, preference, and cost, and we distinguish hard-threshold and soft-reliability variants. Third, we prove basic formal properties, including reduction to the deterministic behaviour under suitable assumptions and a reliability preference property when reliability is the discriminating factor. Fourth, we complement the formal development with a health-care scenario and a controlled simulation study with explicit baselines, ablation variants, metrics, sensitivity analysis, calibration guidelines, and complexity discussion.

The paper is organized as follows: Sect. 2 discusses related work; Sect. 3 recalls the fragment of L-DINF needed for the extension; Sect. 4 introduces the running health-care scenario; Sect. 5 defines the probabilistic package; Sect. 6 presents probabilistic executability and the probability-aware selector; Sect. 7 proves formal properties; Sect. 8 describes explanation generation; Sect. 9 develops the numerical case study; Sect. 10 reports the simulation, sensitivity, calibration, and scalability analysis; Sect. 11 presents the dynamic update package; Sect. 12 discusses limitations and concludes.

## 2 Related Work

Classical work on belief, awareness, and limited reasoning distinguishes what an agent implicitly knows from what it explicitly considers [16], possibly considering epistemic attitudes and resource-bounded reasoning [3,4,24]. L-DINF belongs to this tradition but provides a constructive account of explicit belief, where mental actions may bear costs and executability conditions.

Concerning knowledge and probability, foundational probabilistic epistemic logics provide languages and semantics for degrees of belief over epistemic alternatives [17–19], while more recent work studies conditional probability in epistemic settings [15]. Unlike these general formalisms, our proposal connects probability measures to the existing L-DINF structures for explicit inferential beliefs, mental actions, roles, resources, action equivalence, and local action selection.

Probabilistic dynamic epistemic logic studies probability updates after events or observations [6]. This is close to L-DINF because L-DINF already has mental actions and action records. Here we deliberately isolate a static package first; dynamic aspects are defined as a further layer. Probabilistic BDI research addresses uncertain beliefs, plan selection, and verification under uncertain outcomes [2,5,25]. The difference with the present work is that the selected (alternative) action must satisfy the symbolic L-DINF structure: equivalence to the intended action, role enabling, affordability, and explicit policy-based optimality.

A natural comparison is with MDPs and POMDPs [7,22,27], that optimize policies over belief states for long-horizon stochastic planning. Our proposal is narrower: it is a local and explainable layer for choosing among feasible equivalent actions. Its strength is that explanations are produced from the same semantic objects used for selection: equivalence, executability, role enabling, affordability, threshold satisfaction, and score comparison.

Recent work in symbolic and neuro-symbolic AI [20] has emphasized the role of explicit representations and reasoning mechanisms in supporting transparency and explainability [26,28]. In our framework, explanations are intrinsic, since they are derived directly from the semantic objects involved in action selection rather than from a separate post-hoc module.

## 3 Background: The L-DINF Framework

Let $Agt$ be a set of agents, $Grp$ a set of groups, $Atm_A$ a set of physical actions, and $Res = \{r_1, \ldots, r_\ell\}$ a finite set of resources. Resource availability is represented by vectors such as $(r_1 : n_1, \ldots, r_\ell : n_\ell)$. For two vectors $r$ and $t$, $r \leq t$ holds when every component of $r$ is not greater than the corresponding component of $t$. This order is used to check whether the cost of a physical action is covered by the available budget.

The language contains formulas for explicit belief $\mathsf{B}_i\varphi$, background knowledge $\mathsf{K}_i\varphi$, action execution, past action records, executability, intention, preference, action equivalence, and mental-action updates. Mental actions include learning a perceived formula, inferring consequences from background knowledge, closing beliefs under conjunction, and revising beliefs when a contradiction is detected. Thus the framework does not treat belief as an opaque state: it records the inferential operations through which an agent acquires or changes explicit beliefs.

The core of an L-DINF model is

$$\mathcal{C}_M = (W, N, \mathcal{R}, V, S).$$

Here $W$ is a set of worlds, $\mathcal{R} = \{R_i\}_{i \in Agt}$ contains one epistemic equivalence relation per agent, $V$ is the valuation for atomic propositions, and $S$ records performed physical actions. The neighbourhood function $N$ represents explicit beliefs extensionally: $N(i, w) \subseteq 2^{R_i(w)}$ is a family of truth sets corresponding to propositions that agent $i$ keeps in working memory at $w$. If $R_i(w) = \{v \mid wR_iv\}$, then

$$M, w \models \mathsf{B}_i\varphi \quad \text{iff} \quad \|\varphi\|^M_{i,w} \in N(i, w),$$

where $\|\varphi\|^M_{i,w} = \{v \in R_i(w) \mid M, v \models \varphi\}$. Background knowledge is interpreted by the usual S5-style clause

$$M, w \models \mathsf{K}_i\varphi \quad \text{iff} \quad M, v \models \varphi \text{ for every } v \in R_i(w).$$

Thus $N(i, w)$ models what is explicit in working memory, while $R_i(w)$ models the situations compatible with background knowledge.

The remaining components are packages. Mental actions are governed by an executability function $E$, a budget $B_1$, and a cost function $C_1$. Physical actions are governed by an executability function $A$, a budget $B_2$, and a cost function $C_2$. Roles are represented by $H$, where $H(i, w)$ is the set of actions that agent $i$ is enabled to perform on behalf of its group. Preferences are represented by $P(i, w, \varphi_A)$. Equivalence of physical actions is represented by $Q(\varphi_A, w)$, the equivalence class of $\varphi_A$ at $w$. The selector $F$ chooses an action from the equivalence class of an intended action.

In the deterministic framework, if agent $i$ intends $\varphi_A$, the selector may return $\psi_A \in Q(\varphi_A, w)$ provided that $\psi_A \in A(i, w) \cap H(i, w)$ and $C_2(i, \psi_A, w) \leq B_2(i, w)$. The selected action is therefore equivalent to the intended action, executable, role-enabled, and affordable. All packages satisfy epistemic invariance conditions, for instance $wR_iv \Rightarrow A(i, w) = A(i, v)$, and similarly for roles, budgets, costs, preferences, and equivalence classes. The probability package introduced below follows the same design principle.

The selector is deliberately local: once reasoning has produced an intention, it filters equivalent actions by executability, role enabling, and affordability, and then chooses a feasible substitute. The probabilistic package preserves this pipeline and adds reliability information; it does not solve a full planning problem.

## 4 Running Scenario

We use a health-care scheduling scenario as a running example. A patient needs a first consultation. A mediator agent coordinates the request on behalf of a clinic, represented as a group of agents. The group contains a doctor agent, an administrative agent, and a telemedicine support agent. The intended physical action is a local in-person consultation. However, the clinic may satisfy the same abstract goal by different means: a local visit, a teleconsultation, a partner-clinic visit, or a remote triage followed by later scheduling.

The four actions are not identical, but they are equivalent with respect to the goal of providing a first clinical contact. They differ in resources, preference, and reliability. A local visit is highly preferred by the patient, but may have low probability of success when the doctor is overbooked. A teleconsultation requires network support but may be more affordable for the patient. A partner-clinic visit consumes less local doctor time but may be less preferred. Remote triage consumes fewer resources and can be useful as a fallback, but it may be clinically weaker than a complete consultation.

The deterministic L-DINF selector available so far can check that each action is in an equivalence class, that the agent or the group is enabled to perform it, and that the resources are available. What it cannot express is the fact that the success probability of the teleconsultation is higher than that of the local visit. This is the kind of situation targeted by the proposed probabilistic package. The scenario will be revisited in Sect. 9, where numerical data are used to compare policies and generate explanations.

## 5 A Probabilistic Package

We make the extension explicit at the model level. Let $M$ be an ordinary L-DINF model with core part and packages for mental actions, physical actions, roles, costs, budgets, preferences, equivalence classes, and selection.

**Definition 1 (Probabilistic L-DINF model).** *A probabilistic L-DINF model is a structure*

$$M^{\mathsf{prob}} = (M, \mathcal{P}_M^{\mathsf{prob}}), \qquad \mathcal{P}_M^{\mathsf{prob}} = (\mu, \rho, \theta),$$

*where $M$ is a L-DINF model, $\mu(i, w)$ is a probability measure on the epistemic alternatives $R_i(w)$, $\rho(i, w, \varphi_A) \in [0, 1]$ is the success probability of physical action $\varphi_A$ when performed by agent $i$ at world $w$, and $\theta(i, w) \in [0, 1]$ is the acceptance threshold used by $i$ at $w$, i.e., the minimum success probability accepted by agent $i$ for performing an action. The package is epistemically invariant:*

$$wR_iv \Rightarrow \mu(i, w) = \mu(i, v),$$
$$wR_iv \Rightarrow \rho(i, w, \varphi_A) = \rho(i, v, \varphi_A),$$
$$wR_iv \Rightarrow \theta(i, w) = \theta(i, v).$$

The invariance clauses say that two worlds indistinguishable for the background knowledge of an agent cannot differ with respect to the probabilistic information available to that agent. In finite models, every truth set is measurable. In the general case, we assume that truth sets of formulas belong to the sigma-algebra on which $\mu(i, w)$ is defined. The values of $\mu$, $\rho$, and $\theta$ may be supplied by a domain expert, estimated statistically from action records, or learned by an external module. The logic does not prescribe their origin; probabilities can be estimated from empirical observations, action records, or external predictive modules, while the framework specifies how they interact with beliefs and actions.

For $q \in [0, 1]$, probabilistic explicit belief is defined by

$$M, w \models \mathsf{B}_i^{\geq q}\varphi \quad \text{iff} \quad \mu(i, w)(\|\varphi\|_{i,w}^{M}) \geq q.$$

The thresholded form is the abbreviation $\mathsf{B}_i^{\theta}\varphi \equiv \mathsf{B}_i^{\geq \theta(i,w)}\varphi$. This operator does not replace the ordinary neighbourhood-based belief operator. It adds a graded test that can be used when the agent must decide whether the support for a formula is sufficient for action.

A mental action may use the probabilistic test in two conservative ways. It may add an ordinary explicit belief only when $\mu(i, w)(\|\varphi\|_{i,w}^{M}) \geq \theta(i, w)$, or it may add the formula $\mathsf{B}_i^{\geq q}\varphi$ itself to the working memory. The second option avoids turning uncertain support into categorical belief and is useful when later explanations must mention the degree of support. In both cases, the original neighbourhood semantics remains available.

The success-probability component $\rho$ is deliberately attached to physical actions rather than to action formulas in the abstract. This reflects the practical nature of the package: success may depend on the agent, the world, and the action. A teleconsultation performed by one clinic agent may be more reliable than the same action performed by another agent, because the former has better technical resources or availability. The threshold $\theta$ plays a different role. It expresses the minimum reliability level accepted by the agent or by the domain policy. It may be high in safety-sensitive domains and lower in exploratory or low-risk settings.

## 6 Probabilistic Executability and Selection

Probabilistic executability strengthens ordinary executability with a reliability requirement. For a physical action $\varphi_A$ and a bound $q$, we define

$$M, w \models can\_do_i^{\geq q}(\varphi_A)$$

iff all the following conditions hold: $\varphi_A \in A(i, w) \cap H(i, w)$, $C_2(i, \varphi_A, w) \leq B_2(i, w)$, and $\rho(i, w, \varphi_A) \geq q$. When no explicit bound is supplied, the default value is $q = \theta(i, w)$. For a group $G$, the definition is lifted existentially:

$$M, w \models can\_do_G^{\geq q}(\varphi_A) \quad \text{iff} \quad \exists i \in G \text{ such that} \quad M, w \models can\_do_i^{\geq q}(\varphi_A).$$

Thus, the group can probabilistically perform an action when at least one enabled member can perform it with sufficient reliability.

The original L-DINF selector $F$ is not replaced. We define probabilistic instantiations of it. The following definitions isolate the feasible domain and the two selection variants.

**Definition 2 (Feasible candidates).** *For an agent $i$, a world $w$, and an intended action $\varphi_A$, the ordinary feasible candidate set is*

$$Cand_i^w(\varphi_A) = \{\psi_A \mid \psi_A \in Q(\varphi_A, w),\\ \psi_A \in A(i,w) \cap H(i,w),\\ C_2(i, \psi_A, w) \le B_2(i,w)\}.$$

*The thresholded candidate set is*

$$Cand_i^{w,\ge q}(\varphi_A) = \{\psi_A \in Cand_i^w(\varphi_A) \mid \rho(i,w,\psi_A) \ge q\}.$$

Let $P_{\max} > 0$ be a normalization constant for preferences and let

$$norm(i,w,\psi_A) = \frac{\sum_{j=1}^{\ell} C_{2,j}(i,\psi_A,w)}{\sum_{j=1}^{\ell} B_{2,j}(i,w)}$$

be the normalized cost of $\psi_A$. The sums range over the $\ell$ resource-vector components, assumed to be expressed in comparable normalized units. Given a policy $\pi = (\lambda_\rho, \lambda_P, \lambda_C)$, the score is

$$score_i^{w,\pi}(\psi_A) = \lambda_\rho \rho(i,w,\psi_A) + \lambda_P \frac{P(i,w,\psi_A)}{P_{\max}}\\ - \lambda_C norm(i,w,\psi_A).$$

**Definition 3 (Soft probabilistic selector).** *If $Cand_i^w(\varphi_A) \neq \emptyset$, the soft selector is*

$$F_{\pi,\mathsf{soft}}^{\mathsf{prob}}(i,w,\varphi_A) = \arg \max_{\psi_A \in Cand_i^w(\varphi_A)} score_i^{w,\pi}(\psi_A).$$

Note that reliability is not used as a filter, but as a component of the score.

**Definition 4 (Hard probabilistic selector).** *If $Cand_i^{w,\ge q}(\varphi_A) \neq \emptyset$, the hard selector is*

$$F_{\pi,\mathsf{hard}}^{\mathsf{prob}}(i,w,\varphi_A) = \arg \max_{\psi_A \in Cand_i^{w,\ge q}(\varphi_A)} score_i^{w,\pi}(\psi_A).$$

*When no explicit $q$ is provided, $q = \theta(i,w)$.*

If the thresholded set is empty, the selector returns no action, and the system must invoke a fallback, a relaxation policy, or an escalation (e.g., a human decision).

In both variants, ties are broken by choosing first the action with maximal success probability, then the one with minimal normalized cost, and finally the first action according to a fixed total order on action names. When the variant is clear from context, we write simply $F_\pi^{\mathsf{prob}}$.

The policy $\pi$ is not part of the logical truth definition. It is an explicit design parameter. A reliability-oriented policy assigns a dominant weight to

$\lambda_\rho$, a resource-preserving policy increases $\lambda_C$, and a preference-oriented policy increases $\lambda_P$. This separation is important for explainability: the selected action can be justified not only by the data in the model but also by the declared decision attitude used by the agent.

The group case can be represented without changing the individual selector. For a group $G$, define the set of feasible agent-action pairs

$$Cand_G^w(\varphi_A) = \{(i, \psi_A) \mid i \in G,\ \psi_A \in Cand_i^w(\varphi_A)\}.$$

The group selector chooses the pair $(i, \psi_A)$ with maximal $score_i^{w,\pi}(\psi_A)$, using the same tie-breaking rule. This makes explicit both what action is selected and which group member is responsible for executing it.

## 7 Formal Properties

The following properties make explicit the behaviour of the package. They are intentionally simple, because the extension is designed as a conservative and inspectable layer over the existing L-DINF semantics.

**Proposition 1 (Well-definedness).** *Assume that the candidate set used by* $F_\pi^{\mathsf{prob}}$ *is finite and non-empty, that* $P_{\max} > 0$, *and that* $\sum_{j=1}^{\ell} B_{2,j}(i,w) > 0$. *Then* $F_\pi^{\mathsf{prob}}(i, w, \varphi_A)$ *returns a unique action in the candidate set.*

*Proof.* The score is a real-valued function on a finite non-empty set, so at least one maximizer exists. If the maximizer is unique, it is selected. Otherwise, the tie-breaking rule compares success probability, then cost, and finally a fixed total order. Hence exactly one action is returned.

**Proposition 2 (Conservativity).** *Let* $\alpha$ *be a formula or executability condition of the original L-DINF language that does not contain probabilistic operators or probabilistic executability tests. For every world* $w$, *the truth of* $\alpha$ *in the probabilistic extension is the same as in the underlying L-DINF model.*

*Proof.* The new functions $\mu$, $\rho$, and $\theta$ occur only in the clauses for $\mathsf{B}_i^{\geq q}\varphi$, $\mathsf{B}_i^{\theta}\varphi$, and $can\_do_i^{\geq q}(\varphi_A)$. All original clauses are unchanged.

**Proposition 3 (Threshold monotonicity).** *For* $q_1 \leq q_2$, *every candidate admitted by the hard selector at threshold* $q_2$ *is also admitted at threshold* $q_1$. *Consequently,* $can\_do_i^{\geq q_2}(\varphi_A)$ *implies* $can\_do_i^{\geq q_1}(\varphi_A)$.

*Proof.* Every action with success probability at least $q_2$ also has success probability at least $q_1$; the other feasibility conditions are identical.

**Proposition 4 (Operational reduction).** *Assume that* $\lambda_\rho = 0$, *that all feasible candidates have equal normalized cost, and that the deterministic L-DINF selector* $F$ *chooses a* $P$*-maximal feasible action in the equivalence class. Then the soft probabilistic selector and* $F$ *return the same action, up to the same deterministic tie-breaking order.*

*Proof.* Under the stated assumptions, the reliability and cost terms do not affect comparisons between candidates. The score is an increasing transformation of $P(i, w, \psi_A)$. Hence the set of score maximizers coincides with the set of preference maximizers used by the deterministic selector. If the same tie-breaking order is adopted, the returned action is the same.

**Proposition 5 (Reliability preference property).** *Let $\psi_A$ and $\chi_A$ be two feasible candidates with equal preference and equal normalized cost. If $\lambda_\rho > 0$ and $\rho(i, w, \psi_A) > \rho(i, w, \chi_A)$, then $score_i^{w,\pi}(\psi_A) > score_i^{w,\pi}(\chi_A)$. Hence the probabilistic selector prefers the more reliable action whenever reliability is the only discriminating factor.*

*Proof.* The preference and cost terms cancel out. The difference between the scores is $\lambda_\rho(\rho(i, w, \psi_A) - \rho(i, w, \chi_A))$, which is positive by assumption.

**Proposition 6 (Explanation soundness).** *If $F_\pi^{\mathsf{prob}}(i, w, \varphi_A) = \psi_A$, then $\psi_A$ is equivalent to the intended action, executable and role-enabled, affordable with respect to $B_2$, and has maximal score among the candidates admitted by the chosen variant.*

*Proof.* The first three clauses follow from membership in the candidate set. The maximality clause follows from the argmax definition and the tie-breaking rule.

## 8 Explanation Generation

By Proposition 6, the selector can return a sound explanation record together with the selected action. We make this object explicit.

**Definition 5 (Explanation record).** *If $F_\pi^{\mathsf{prob}}(i, w, \varphi_A) = \psi_A$, an explanation record is a tuple*

$$\begin{aligned} Expl(i, w, \varphi_A, \psi_A) = (&\varphi_A, \psi_A, Q(\varphi_A, w), \\ &Cand_i^w(\varphi_A), \mathbf{variant}, q, \pi, \\ &C_2(i, \psi_A, w), B_2(i, w), \\ &\rho(i, w, \psi_A), P(i, w, \psi_A), \\ &score_i^{w,\pi}(\psi_A), \mathbf{Rejected}). \end{aligned}$$

*where* **variant** *records whether the hard or soft selector was used, $q$ is the threshold when applicable, and* **Rejected** *stores, for each non-selected candidate, the values that made it lose the comparison.*

The record is sound because each field corresponds to a semantic condition used in the selection process. Here explainability means that the decision is traceable and faithful to the declared probabilities, preferences, costs, thresholds, and policy weights; it does not imply that these numerical parameters are automatically justified, since their origin and validation remain domain-dependent.

**Table 1.** From an explanation record to a human-readable justification.

| Record component | Human-readable explanation fragment |
|---|---|
| $\varphi_A$ | The original intention is to obtain a medical consultation. |
| $\psi_A$, $Q(\varphi_A, w)$ | The selected action is an equivalent realization of the intended goal. |
| Feasibility evidence | The action is executable, role-enabled, and affordable under the current budget. |
| $\rho(i, w, \psi_A) \geq q$ | Its estimated reliability is above the required acceptance threshold. |
| $P, C_2, \pi, score$ | Preference, cost, policy weights, and score justify the final ranking. |
| Rejected alternatives | Other equivalent actions obtained lower scores or failed the threshold test. |

Table 1 shows how the record can be rendered into a concise human-readable justification without a separate explanation engine.

In the health-care scenario, the system may state that `teleconsultation` was selected instead of `local_visit` because both actions realize the same consultation goal, the selected action is feasible and affordable, its reliability satisfies the threshold, and its score is higher under the current policy. The rejected action can also be explained contrastively: although it has higher preference, its lower success probability leads to a lower score.

## 9 Health-Care Case Study

Consider the clinic group introduced above. The mediator agent $m$ intends to perform $a_1$, a local in-person consultation. At world $w$, the equivalence class is

$$Q(a_1, w) = \{a_1, a_2, a_3, a_4\},$$

where $a_2$ is a teleconsultation, $a_3$ is a partner-clinic visit, and $a_4$ is remote triage followed by scheduling. The resources are doctor time $dt$, administrative time $adm$, network support $net$, and transport support $tr$. Let

$$B_2(m, w) = (dt : 10, adm : 8, net : 6, tr : 5), \qquad P_{\max} = 10.$$

Table 2 gives the data and the scores under a reliability-oriented policy $\pi_R = (100, 10, 20)$ and a preference-oriented policy $\pi_P = (30, 60, 10)$.

Under $\pi_R$, $F^{\mathsf{prob}}_{\pi_R}(m, w, a_1) = a_2$. The teleconsultation is not the most preferred action, but it has the highest success probability and obtains the maximal score. Under $\pi_P$, $F^{\mathsf{prob}}_{\pi_P}(m, w, a_1) = a_1$. Thus, the same feasible equivalence class produces different choices under different declared policies. The hard-threshold version with $q = 0.80$ also returns $a_2$, as it is the only action above threshold.

**Table 2.** Consultation actions and scores under two policies.

| Act. | Meaning | Cost | Pref. | $\rho$ | $\pi_R$ | $\pi_P$ |
|---|---|---|---|---|---|---|
| $a_1$ | Local visit | 9 | 9 | 0.66 | 68.79 | 70.70 |
| $a_2$ | Teleconsultation | 9 | 7 | 0.88 | 88.79 | 65.30 |
| $a_3$ | Partner clinic | 8 | 5 | 0.79 | 78.48 | 50.94 |
| $a_4$ | Remote triage | 6 | 6 | 0.70 | 71.86 | 54.93 |

The case study illustrates the role of the probabilistic package. Probability does not replace the symbolic structure of L-DINF. Equivalence, roles, and budgets still define the candidate set. Probability only refines the choice among candidates. Moreover, the policy is visible: changing the weights changes the result in a predictable way. This is important when a system must be audited or configured by a domain expert.

## 10 Simulation, Sensitivity, and Scalability

The worked example illustrates a single decision. To inspect repeated behaviour, we use a controlled synthetic simulation. The aim is not clinical validation, but a stress test of the selection mechanism under parameterized uncertainty. Each episode generates an equivalence class of eight feasible actions, each with a preference value in $[0, 10]$, a four-dimensional resource cost within budget, and a success probability sampled from a beta distribution with small perturbations. The selectors choose before the stochastic outcome is observed. We compare deterministic preference-only and cost/preference selectors, a hard-threshold probabilistic selector, the soft weighted selector, and ablation variants removing reliability, preference, or cost.

The metrics are expected success, normalized preference, normalized cost, risk exposure, and utility $100\rho + 10P/P_{\max} - 20norm$. Table 3 reports averages over 5000 episodes. In the synthetic setting considered here, probabilistic selectors tend to reduce risk exposure and improve expected success with respect to deterministic baselines. The price reflects a lower mean preference, as expected, because the selector balances willingness with reliability and resource consumption. The ablations show that reliability is necessary to reduce risk, preference is necessary for user-aligned choices, and cost is necessary to avoid resource-heavy selections.

Sensitivity to the policy parameters is reported in Table 4. Here $\lambda_P = 30$ and $\lambda_C = 20$ are fixed, while $\lambda_\rho$ varies. Increasing $\lambda_\rho$ improves expected success and reduces risk, but progressively moves selection away from the most preferred action. The trade-off is therefore explicit and configurable, rather than hidden inside an opaque heuristic.

The threshold $\theta$ is a reliability gate: higher values filter unreliable actions but may increase fallback cases. It should encode a domain requirement, while

**Table 3.** Controlled simulation: selectors, baselines, and ablations.

| Selector/policy | Succ. | Pref. | Cost | Risk | Utility |
|---|---|---|---|---|---|
| Preference-only | 0.653 | 0.953 | 0.297 | 0.691 | 68.90 |
| Cost/preference | 0.650 | 0.942 | 0.256 | 0.694 | 69.29 |
| No reliability ablation | 0.652 | 0.932 | 0.245 | 0.689 | 69.62 |
| No preference ablation | 0.918 | 0.512 | 0.274 | 0.017 | 91.21 |
| No cost ablation | 0.913 | 0.612 | 0.338 | 0.020 | 91.09 |
| Soft probabilistic | 0.911 | 0.589 | 0.281 | 0.019 | 91.35 |
| Hard, $q = 0.80$ | 0.912 | 0.586 | 0.285 | 0.014 | 91.38 |

**Table 4.** Sensitivity to the reliability weight $\lambda_\rho$, with $\lambda_P = 30$ and $\lambda_C = 20$.

| $\lambda_\rho$ | Succ. | Pref. | Cost | Risk | Utility |
|---|---|---|---|---|---|
| 0 | 0.652 | 0.932 | 0.245 | 0.689 | 69.62 |
| 20 | 0.757 | 0.907 | 0.253 | 0.433 | 79.68 |
| 40 | 0.815 | 0.856 | 0.270 | 0.248 | 84.69 |
| 60 | 0.849 | 0.800 | 0.269 | 0.135 | 87.52 |
| 80 | 0.872 | 0.748 | 0.279 | 0.080 | 89.10 |
| 100 | 0.884 | 0.722 | 0.286 | 0.050 | 89.95 |

$\lambda_\rho$, $\lambda_P$, and $\lambda_C$ tune the decision attitude; $\rho$ may come from observed frequencies, expert elicitation, or predictive models. If $k = |Q(\varphi_A, w)|$ and $r = |Res|$, the additional local overhead is $O(kr)$, or $O(|G|kr)$ for groups, assuming that the equivalence class and underlying L-DINF structures are already available. These bounds exclude construction and model checking of the complete epistemic model. Evaluating $\mathsf{B}_i^{\geq q}\varphi$ may require $O(|R_i(w)|)$ once the truth set is known, or less with symbolic representations.

## 11 Dynamic Update from Action Records

Action records provide a basis for calibrating reliability without changing the modular architecture. For each pair $(i, \varphi_A)$, assume $\mathrm{Beta}(\alpha_{i,\varphi_A}, \beta_{i,\varphi_A})$, where the parameters count successes and failures. After an outcome, a mental update action increments the appropriate parameter and the selector uses $\rho(i, w, \varphi_A) = \alpha_{i,\varphi_A}/(\alpha_{i,\varphi_A} + \beta_{i,\varphi_A})$. Thus, $\mathrm{Beta}(8, 2)$ changes from 0.80 to $9/11 \simeq 0.82$ after a success or $8/11 \simeq 0.73$ after a failure. Since estimates may be imperfect, an explanation may also report the score margin as an indication of decision stability.

Thresholds may also be adapted explicitly. If the hard candidate set is empty under urgency or scarcity, a mental action may temporarily relax $\theta$; the explanation record must report this exceptional risk-taking.

## 12 Discussion, Limitations, and Conclusions

We introduced a conservative probabilistic package for L-DINF supporting risk-aware and traceable local action selection while preserving its modular architecture. Formal properties, a case study, and simulation illustrate the explicit balance among reliability, preference, cost, and risk. Explanations are faithful to the structures and declared parameters governing selection, rather than generated post hoc.

The proposal does not address long-horizon POMDP planning. Its scalar resource aggregation is transparent and lightweight, but real resources may be non-commensurable or interdependent. Future work will consider richer aggregation and update policies, collective preferences, realistic scenarios, and ASP [8,21,23] and DALI [1,13,14] prototypes.

## References

1. AI4AQ Research Group: AAAI-DISIM-UnivAQ/DALI2. Zenodo (2026). https://doi.org/10.5281/zenodo.19858727
2. Archibald, B., Sevegnani, M., Xu, M.: Modelling and verifying BDI agents under uncertainty. Sci. Comput. Program. 103254 (2024)
3. Balbiani, P., Fernández-Duque, D., Lorini, E.: A logical theory of belief dynamics for resource-bounded agents. In: Proceedings of the 15th International Conference on Autonomous Agents and Multiagent Systems (AAMAS 2016), pp. 644–652. ACM (2016)
4. Balbiani, P., Fernández-Duque, D., Lorini, E.: The dynamics of epistemic attitudes in resource-bounded agents. Stud. Logica. **107**(3), 457–488 (2019)
5. Bauters, K., McAreavey, K., Liu, W., Hong, J., Godo, L., Sierra, C.: Managing different sources of uncertainty in a BDI framework in a principled way with tractable fragments. J. Artif. Intell. Res. **58**, 731–775 (2017)
6. van Benthem, J., Gerbrandy, J., Kooi, B.: Dynamic update with probabilities. Stud. Logica. **93**(1), 67–96 (2009)
7. Boutilier, C., Dean, T., Hanks, S.: Decision-theoretic planning: structural assumptions and computational leverage. J. Artif. Intell. Res. **11**, 1–94 (1999)
8. Brewka, G., Eiter, T.M.T.: Answer set programming: Special issue. AI Mag. **37**(3) (2016)
9. Costantini, S., Formisano, A., Pitoni, V.: An epistemic logic for multi-agent systems with budget and costs. In: Logics in Artificial Intelligence – 17th European Conference, JELIA 2021. Lecture Notes in Computer Science, vol. 12678, pp. 101–115. Springer, Cham (2021)
10. Costantini, S., Formisano, A., Pitoni, V.: Cooperation among groups of agents in the epistemic logic L-DINF. In: RuleML+RR 2022. Lecture Notes in Computer Science, vol. 13752, pp. 280–295. Springer, Cham (2022)
11. Costantini, S., Formisano, A., Pitoni, V.: An epistemic logic for formalizing group dynamics of agents. Interact. Stud. **23**, 391–426 (2023)
12. Costantini, S., Formisano, A., Pitoni, V.: Preference management in epistemic logic L-DINF. In: Proceedings of the 38th Italian Conference on Computational Logic (CILC 2023). CEUR Workshop Proceedings. CEUR-WS.org (2023)

13. Costantini, S., Tocchio, A.: A logic programming language for multi-agent systems. In: JELIA 2002. LNAI, vol. 2424, Springer, Cham (2002)
14. Costantini, S., Tocchio, A.: The DALI logic programming agent-oriented language. In: JELIA 2004. LNAI, vol. 3229, Springer, Cham (2004)
15. Dautovic, S., Doder, D., Ognjanovic, Z.: Reasoning about knowledge and conditional probability. Int. J. Approximate Reasoning **163**, 109037 (2023)
16. Fagin, R., Halpern, J.Y.: Belief, awareness, and limited reasoning. Artif. Intell. **34**, 39–76 (1987)
17. Fagin, R., Halpern, J.Y.: Reasoning about knowledge and probability. J. ACM **41**(2), 340–367 (1994)
18. Fagin, R., Halpern, J.Y., Megiddo, N.: A logic for reasoning about probabilities. Inf. Comput. **87**(1–2), 78–128 (1990)
19. Fagin, R., Halpern, J.Y., Moses, Y., Vardi, M.Y.: Reasoning About Knowledge. MIT Press, Cambridge (1995)
20. d'Avila Garcez, A.S., Gori, M., Lamb, L.C., Serafini, L., Spranger, M., Tran, S.N.: Neural-symbolic computing: an effective methodology for principled integration of machine learning and reasoning. J. Appl. Logics - IfCoLog J. **6**(4), 611–632 (2019)
21. Gelfond, M.: Answer sets. In: van Harmelen, F., Lifschitz, V., Porter, B.W. (eds.) Handbook of Knowledge Representation, Foundations of Artificial Intelligence, vol. 3, pp. 285–316. Elsevier (2008). https://doi.org/10.1016/S1574-6526(07)03007-6
22. Kaelbling, L.P., Littman, M.L., Cassandra, A.R.: Planning and acting in partially observable stochastic domains. Artif. Intell. **101**(1–2), 99–134 (1998)
23. Lifschitz, V.: Answer Set Programming. Springer, Heidelberg (2019)
24. Lorini, E.: Reasoning about cognitive attitudes in a qualitative setting. In: Logics in Artificial Intelligence - 16th European Conference. JELIA 2019, pp. 726–743. LNCS, Springer, Cham (2019)
25. Ma, J., Liu, W., Hong, J., Godo, L., Sierra, C.: Plan selection for probabilistic BDI agents. In: IEEE 26th International Conference on Tools with Artificial Intelligence, pp. 83–90. IEEE (2014)
26. Miller, T.: Explanation in artificial intelligence: insights from the social sciences. Artif. Intell. **267**, 1–38 (2019)
27. Puterman, M.L.: Markov Decision Processes: Discrete Stochastic Dynamic Programming. Wiley, Hoboken (1994)
28. Zhang, X., Sheng, V.S.: Neuro-symbolic ai: Explainability, challenges, and future trends. arXiv preprint arXiv:2411.04383 (2024). https://doi.org/10.48550/arXiv.2411.04383

# MARIO: Interpretable Machine Learning for Length-of-Stay Stratification from Longitudinal Administrative Health Records

Danilo Croce[1(✉)], Vania Ferrari[2], Michele Bisogno[1], Massimiliano Andrea Vitali[3], Daniele Di Giovanni[1], Maria Vittoria Marabello[2], Giuseppe Liotta[1], and Roberto Basili[1]

[1] University of Roma Tor Vergata, Rome, Italy
croce@info.uniroma2.it
[2] Exprivia S.p.A., Molfetta, Italy
[3] Policlinico Tor Vergata, Rome, Italy

**Abstract.** Hospital length of stay is a key variable for bed management, discharge planning and hospital resource allocation. Anticipating whether a patient is likely to experience a short or prolonged stay can support clinical-organizational coordination, but requires predictive models that are accurate, transparent and usable in realistic hospital-planning settings. We present MARIO, an interpretable machine learning framework that capitalizes on routinely collected hospital discharge records to support length-of-stay stratification in everyday hospital planning activities. MARIO represents each patient through a longitudinal sequence of hospitalization episodes and stratifies the target admission according to whether the stay is expected to last fewer than 10 days or at least 10 days. The model is driven by a patient-centric feature representation that combines demographic information, admission context, primary diagnosis, early procedures, previous hospitalizations, historical length-of-stay patterns, recency of hospital use and complexity indicators. MARIO adopts an intrinsically interpretable linear model: each prediction can be decomposed into feature-level contributions, making it possible to identify which patient-level signals most strongly affect the predicted outcome. Experiments on a large real-world anonymized dataset show 81.9% accuracy, with a substantial fraction of errors occurring near the 10-day decision threshold. The resulting explanations populate a decision-support interface that presents both the predicted length-of-stay class and the main readable motivations behind it, helping hospital operators inspect the evidence underlying the model output.

**Keywords:** Length of stay prediction · Interpretable machine learning · Clinical decision support · Administrative health records


S. Bistarelli et al. (Eds.): AIxIA 2026, LNAI 17131, pp. 212–225, 2027.
https://doi.org/10.1007/978-3-032-40774-0_16

# 1 Introduction

Hospital length of stay (LOS) is a key variable for hospital organization, bed management and discharge planning. Being able to anticipate whether a patient will require a short or prolonged stay can help hospitals plan resources, manage beds and coordinate discharge processes more effectively. This is particularly relevant in contexts where prolonged hospitalizations reduce bed availability, delay patient flow and may contribute to emergency department crowding and boarding [2]. In European healthcare systems, LOS is also influenced by broader organizational factors, such as healthcare-system structure, resource availability and reimbursement models [7], as well as by patient complexity, chronic conditions and recurrent hospital use [17]. For these reasons, LOS prediction has received increasing attention in the machine-learning literature. Several studies have explored predictive models for hospital admission, emergency department overcrowding, boarding, and hospital or emergency department LOS [10,11,14,16]. Other works have addressed short-vs-long LOS classification in specific clinical settings, such as COVID-19 hospitalization [13]. Overall, these studies show that routinely collected clinical and administrative data can be used to support more proactive hospital planning. However, the practical use of LOS prediction models in hospital workflows requires more than predictive accuracy. In bed management and discharge planning, a prediction is useful only if it can be inspected, related to concrete patient-level evidence, and understood by the operator who must use it. For example, knowing that a patient is predicted to require a prolonged stay is more useful if the system can also show that the prediction is supported by previous long hospitalizations, recent recurrent admissions, age-related factors, or combinations of past diagnoses and current admission information. Such explanations can help hospital operators focus their attention, verify the available evidence, and make more informed organizational decisions. This motivates the design of predictive systems that are not only effective, but also readable and explainable.

In this paper, we present MARIO, an interpretable machine-learning framework for hospital LOS stratification from anonymized Italian hospital discharge records collected at Policlinico Tor Vergata, a large Italian university hospital. The name MARIO originates from the broader project *Modello di Analisi del Rischio di uso Improprio dei servizi Ospedalieri*; in this work, we focus on its use for short-vs-prolonged stay stratification. The framework represents each patient as a longitudinal sequence of hospitalization episodes and predicts whether a target admission is likely to result in a stay shorter than 10 days or in a prolonged stay of at least 10 days. The data are derived from the Italian *Schede di Dimissione Ospedaliera* (SDO)[1], and are processed in anonymized form. MARIO builds a patient-centric representation that combines different sources of evidence. First, it uses general demographic and admission-related information available for the current hospitalization. Second, it reconstructs the patient's previous hospital history from past discharge records, including previ-

[1] In English: *Hospital Discharge Records.*

ous admissions, historical LOS patterns, recency of hospital use and indicators of accumulated complexity. Third, it can incorporate initial evidence from the current admission, such as diagnostic information associated with the target admission and procedures observed in the first two days of hospitalization. In this way, the prediction is not based on an isolated hospitalization record, but on a structured view of the patient trajectory. The predictive component is based on an intrinsically interpretable linear model. This choice is intentional: in a hospital planning scenario, the ability to inspect the evidence supporting a prediction is as important as the prediction itself. Since the prediction score can be decomposed into feature-level contributions, MARIO can identify which patient-level signals most strongly affect the predicted outcome. These signals can then be translated into readable motivations for a decision-support interface. Experiments on a real-world anonymized dataset show that MARIO achieves 81.9% accuracy in short-vs-long stay prediction, improving over a majority-class baseline. Error analysis further distinguishes borderline mistakes around the 10-day decision threshold from clearly prolonged stays predicted as short, the latter representing the most critical errors from an operational perspective. This distinction is relevant in practice, because not all errors have the same operational impact. The contributions are: (i) a patient-centric representation of longitudinal records; (ii) an interpretable linear model; (iii) an evaluation on real-world anonymized data with ablation and error analysis; and (iv) a decision-support interface with readable model-derived motivations.

## 2 Related Work

Hospital length of stay (LOS) is a central indicator for hospital organization, bed management and patient flow. Prolonged stays and delayed discharges may reduce ward capacity, slow down patient turnover and contribute to emergency department crowding and boarding. Previous studies have analyzed prolonged emergency department length of stay as an organizationally relevant phenomenon [2], while work on frequent users highlights the impact of recurrent access, chronic conditions and complex patient histories on emergency and hospital services [3,15]. At a broader level, LOS is also affected by healthcare-system organization, resource availability and reimbursement models, as shown by comparative analyses of long-term LOS trends across European countries [7]. These works motivate LOS prediction not only as a clinical modelling problem, but also as a tool for hospital planning and resource coordination.

Machine-learning methods have increasingly been applied to hospital-flow management and LOS prediction, including admission prediction, boarding and demand forecasting, emergency department LOS estimation, and short-vs-long stay classification in specific clinical settings [4,10,11,13,14,16]. Overall, this literature shows that routinely collected hospital data can support predictive models for patient-flow and LOS-related tasks. However, the operational use of LOS prediction models requires more than predictive accuracy. When predictions support bed management, discharge planning or prioritization, users need to inspect the patient-level evidence behind the output. This requirement is consistent with the broader literature on explainable and interpretable AI in healthcare, where explainability involves not only technical transparency but also clinical, ethical, legal and user-centered dimensions [1]. Moreover, model explanations should not be confused with causal justifications: in medicine, the distinction between explainability and human-centered understanding is crucial [8]. For decision-support systems, this implies that predictions should be auditable and connected to evidence available for the individual patient.

MARIO is positioned at the intersection of LOS prediction, interpretable machine learning and hospital decision support. Like previous LOS prediction studies, it uses routinely collected hospital data to stratify patients according to expected length of stay. Its distinctive aspect is the integration of patient-centric longitudinal modelling with an intrinsically interpretable classifier whose feature-level contributions can be translated into readable motivations for hospital operators. In this sense, MARIO moves beyond aggregate performance evaluation and focuses on how administrative hospital data can be transformed into inspectable predictive evidence for everyday planning workflows.

## 3 MARIO: An Interpretable Pipeline for LOS Stratification

MARIO is an interpretable machine-learning pipeline for hospital length-of-stay stratification from anonymized Italian discharge records. For each target admission, it predicts whether the stay will be short, i.e., fewer than 10 days, or prolonged, i.e., at least 10 days. The pipeline reconstructs each patient's longitudinal history from SDO flows and uses sparse, patient-centric features for prediction and dashboard-oriented explanation. Its key assumption is that admissions should be interpreted within the patient trajectory, allowing previous hospital use, LOS patterns, diagnoses, procedures and accumulated complexity to inform the prediction.

### 3.1 From SDO Flows to Patient-Centric Records

The input data are derived from Italian *Schede di Dimissione Ospedaliera* (SDO), originally organized as discharge-level flows. In the MARIO pipeline, the original information is distributed across three main sources: demographic information, clinical and administrative information, and departmental information. These flows are processed through an anonymization procedure that removes direct identifiers and generates a stable pseudonymous patient identifier, allowing records belonging to the same patient to be reconnected without exposing the original identity. In addition, all dates within each hospitalization episode are shifted by the same random offset of one or two days. This reduces the possibility of re-identifying hospitalizations from external temporal information, exactly preserving the internal temporal relations of each episode (including its LOS) and approximately preserving the relative temporal structure across episodes in the patient history. Diagnostic codes are also generalized by removing the last digit, thus reducing clinical granularity while retaining diagnostic-family information useful for stratification. After anonymization, the discharge-level records are transformed into a patient-centric longitudinal representation. Each patient is represented as one structured record containing demographic information and an ordered list of hospitalization episodes: $P = \langle e_1, e_2, \ldots, e_n \rangle$, where each episode $e_i$ corresponds to one admission. The temporal ordering of episodes is essential: it allows MARIO to distinguish what belongs to the previous history of the patient from what describes the target admission to be classified. This transformation is central to the pipeline. The original SDO data are naturally episode-centric, while the predictive task requires patient-level continuity. MARIO turns administrative hospital flows into a longitudinal registry suitable for descriptive analysis and predictive modelling. Given a patient history $P$ and a target episode $e_i$, MARIO constructs a supervised example $(x_i, y_i)$, where $x_i$ is the feature vector describing the patient and the target admission, and $y_i$ is the LOS class associated with the target episode. The binary target is defined as:

$$y_i = \begin{cases} \textit{short}, & \text{if } LOS(e_i) < \tau, \\ \textit{long}, & \text{if } LOS(e_i) \geq \tau, \end{cases}$$

with $\tau = 10$ days. This value was selected as a pragmatic operational threshold agreed with the hospital stakeholders, since stays beyond 10 days were regarded as more likely to require explicit bed-management, discharge-planning or transfer-coordination attention. The target LOS is used only to define the supervised label during training and evaluation; sensitivity analyses over alternative thresholds and ordinal LOS bands are left to future work.

### 3.2 Patient-Centric Feature Representation

The feature vector $x_i$ is designed to make the patient history readable by both the classifier and the human operator. MARIO does not rely on a small set of raw numerical variables. Instead, it transforms the available SDO information into a high-dimensional sparse vector of mostly Boolean indicator features. Each feature corresponds to a simple question about the patient, the target admission or the previous hospitalization history. The feature is set to 1 when the corresponding condition is true, and to 0 otherwise. For example, a feature may indicate whether the primary diagnosis of the target admission belongs to a given ICD diagnostic family, whether the same diagnostic family was observed in the previous hospitalization, or whether it occurred at least once in the last three hospitalizations. Other features encode utilization patterns, such as whether the patient has been hospitalized more than $k$ times in the past, with different values of $k$ generating different indicators. In this way, recurrent hospital use, diagnostic recurrence and previous complex trajectories can be represented explicitly. Numerical variables are converted into interpretable bins. Age, for instance, is not used as a single continuous value, but is mapped into age-group indicators. Similarly, previous LOS values can be discretized into categories representing short, intermediate or prolonged stays. This binarized representation makes heterogeneous information comparable within the same sparse vector and allows each active feature to be interpreted as a concrete patient-level signal.

The feature space is organized into the following families:

- **Demographic profile.** These features describe non-identifying patient characteristics derived from the anonymized demographic section, including age group, sex, citizenship status, civil status and education level when available.
- **Admission context.** These features describe the organizational conditions under which the target hospitalization starts, including admission regime, admission modality, admission priority, admitting unit, trauma-related indicators, planned or unplanned admission information, day of week, month of admission and weekend admission.
- **Primary diagnosis.** The primary diagnosis of the target admission is represented through generalized ICD-9-CM code prefixes [12]. This allows the model to exploit diagnostic information at different levels of granularity, from broad diagnostic families to more specific diagnostic groups, consistently with the anonymization procedure applied to the original codes.
- **Early procedures.** Procedures observed within the first two days of the target admission are encoded through hierarchical procedure-code prefixes and procedure-family indicators. These features provide an early signal of diagnostic or therapeutic intensity, care complexity and resource use.
- **Previous hospital use.** These features summarize the patient's prior use of hospital services, including the number of previous hospitalizations, admissions in recent temporal windows, time elapsed since the last hospitalization, recurrent admissions and the distribution of previous episodes over the reconstructed history.
- **Historical LOS patterns.** These features capture the patient's previous resource-consumption profile, including LOS categories of previous hospitalizations, maximum and average historical LOS, LOS of the most recent admissions and indicators of previous prolonged stays among recent episodes.
- **Longitudinal clinical complexity.** These features summarize the accumulated clinical and procedural complexity observed before the target admission. They include recurring diagnostic and procedure families, the diversity of diagnosis-code and procedure-code prefixes in the patient history, overlaps between current-admission codes and previously observed codes, repeated hospital use, recent readmission patterns, and combinations of historical utilization with current-admission evidence.

Overall, the representation provides a structured approximation of routinely available administrative and early clinical evidence. Its purpose is not to encode the complete clinical state of the patient, but to make heterogeneous information usable by the classifier and interpretable as patient-level evidence.

### 3.3 Linear Prediction and Dashboard-Oriented Explanations

MARIO adopts a linear One-vs-All classifier trained on sparse feature vectors[2]. This choice is aligned with the structure of the data: the representation contains many categorical, hierarchical and temporal indicators, most of which are inactive for any single patient. Linear large-margin models are well suited to this setting, since they scale efficiently with the number of examples and active features in high-dimensional sparse spaces [5,9], while remaining directly inspectable. For each class $c$, the classifier learns a weight vector $w_c$. Given an input vector $x$, the score assigned to class $c$ is:

$$s_c(x) = w_c^\top x = \sum_{j=1}^{d} w_{c,j} x_j.$$

The class scores correspond to signed margins produced by the linear classifiers. In the binary setting considered here, the scores express how strongly the example is assigned to the short-stay or prolonged-stay side of the learned decision functions. These scores can be inspected directly as margins, or normalized through a softmax transformation to obtain a pseudo-probability distribution over the two classes. This normalized score is not intended as a calibrated probability; rather, it provides the operator with an additional indication of how clear or uncertain the model decision is.

The linear formulation also provides a direct explanation mechanism. Since the score is additive, each active feature contributes to the class score. For a feature $x_j$, its contribution to class $c$ is: $\gamma_{c,j}(x) = w_{c,j} x_j$. Positive contributions increase the score of a class, while negative contributions decrease it. Therefore, the same computation that produces the prediction also identifies the active features that most strongly influence the class scores. In the dashboard, MARIO primarily displays the features that provide the strongest evidence for the predicted class. The learned weights can also be inspected at a global level. For a given class $c$, the magnitude $|w_{c,j}|$ indicates how strongly feature $j$ participates in the separation learned by the classifier. Features with weights close to zero have little discriminative effect for that class, while features with larger positive or negative weights are more influential in separating short and prolonged stays.

The displayed motivations are derived from the actual feature contributions used to compute the prediction, but are reorganized into semantic groups that are easier to inspect, such as diagnosis, early procedures, admission context, previous hospitalizations, historical LOS, demographic profile and complexity indicators. The output combines the predicted class, class scores, ranked feature contributions and readable dashboard motivations. These explanations represent predictive evidence rather than causal statements and are intended to support human inspection and planning.

[2] The task is binary in this work, but the One-vs-All formulation can be naturally extended to multi-class LOS stratification over multiple duration ranges; this extension is left for future work.

# 4 Experimental Evaluation

The evaluation is based on anonymized SDO records collected at Policlinico Tor Vergata over the period January 2023–June 2025. After excluding Day Hospital and access episodes, the patient-centric registry contains 18,295 patients and 42,823 ordinary hospitalization episodes. We consider a binary LOS stratification task: a target admission is labelled as *short* if $LOS < 10$ days and as *long* otherwise.

**Table 1.** Predictive performance and primary-diagnosis ablation.

| Setting | Model | Primary diag. | Test cases | Accuracy |
|---|---|---|---|---|
| All admissions | Majority-class baseline | – | 4,187 | 67.8% |
| | MARIO | Yes | 4,187 | 81.9% |
| | MARIO | No | 4,187 | 81.1% |
| With history | MARIO | Yes | 2,408 | 80.7% |
| | MARIO | No | 2,408 | 79.5% |

The evaluation uses the feature representation described in Sect. 3. Procedures from the target admission are restricted to those observed within the first 48 h, while the primary diagnosis is associated with the target admission and is not subject to this temporal window. We use deterministic patient-level splits, so that all episodes of the same patient belong to the same partition. All models were trained using the KeLP learning platform [6]. The linear One-vs-All classifiers were trained using the Dual Coordinate Descent (DCD) algorithm [9] with $L_2$-loss and no bias term. The regularization parameter was selected on the validation set from $C \in \{0.05, 0.1, 0.5, 1, 5, 10\}$ by maximizing macro-F1. The final experimental cohort is obtained after excluding non-ordinary admissions and applying target-construction criteria aligned with the intended hospital-planning scenario. In particular, short stays ending with voluntary discharge or death are excluded, while short stays followed by transfer to another acute-care facility or to another internal hospital unit are relabelled as prolonged-care trajectories. After these criteria, the corresponding split contains 33,462 training examples, 3,884 validation examples and 4,187 test examples.

## 4.1 Predictive Performance and Ablation Results

Table 1 summarizes the main experimental results. The main operational setting includes all target admissions, including first admissions for patients with no previous hospitalization history. In this setting, MARIO reaches 81.9% accuracy, improving the majority-class baseline by 14.1 percentage points and reducing the relative error by 43.7%. When primary-diagnosis features are removed, accuracy decreases only slightly, from 81.9% to 81.1%. This suggests that the

**Table 2.** Confusion matrix of the selected MARIO configuration.

| Actual class | Predicted short | Predicted long |
|---|---|---|
| Short stay | 2,532 | 308 |
| Long stay | 450 | 897 |

**Table 3.** Correct predictions and error categories for binary LOS stratification with threshold $LOS \geq 10$ days. Percentages do not sum exactly to 100 due to rounding.

| Outcome | N | % of test set |
|---|---|---|
| Correct predictions | 3,429 | 81.9% |
| Short → Long, with $LOS < 8$ | 241 | 5.8% |
| Borderline errors, with $8 \leq LOS \leq 12$ | 258 | 6.2% |
| Long → Short, with $LOS > 12$ | 259 | 6.2% |
| Total | 4,187 | 100.0% |

model does not rely on primary diagnosis alone, but exploits a broader combination of patient-level and admission-level signals. The second setting considers only target admissions for patients with at least one previously recorded hospitalization. This setting is not directly comparable in coverage, since the test set is smaller, but it is useful to verify whether the same trend holds when longitudinal history is always available. Also in this case, removing primary-diagnosis features produces a limited but consistent drop, from 80.7% to 79.5%.

### 4.2 Class-Level Behaviour and Error Distribution

The confusion matrix of the selected operational configuration is reported in Table 2. The model correctly classifies 3,429 out of 4,187 test hospitalizations, including 2,532 short stays and 897 prolonged stays. The confusion matrix shows an asymmetric behaviour between the two classes. Short stays are the majority class in the test set, with 2,840 cases out of 4,187, while prolonged stays account for 1,347 cases. Consequently, short stays are recognized more frequently than prolonged stays. This behaviour is expected in an early LOS stratification setting, since some hospitalizations become prolonged because of clinical or organizational events that emerge during the course of the admission, such as complications, delayed diagnostic or therapeutic procedures, transfer issues, discharge-planning difficulties or changes in clinical conditions. Beyond overall accuracy, short stays achieve 84.9% precision, 89.2% recall and 87.0% F1, while prolonged stays achieve 74.4% precision, 66.6% recall and 70.3% F1. The resulting balanced accuracy is 77.9%, with a macro-F1 of 78.6%.

This motivates an error analysis that goes beyond global accuracy and considers where errors occur with respect to the 10-day decision threshold. The overall error rate of MARIO is 18.1%, corresponding to 758 misclassified cases. However, these errors have different operational meanings depending on the true

LOS value. Errors close to the 10-day threshold are less clear-cut than errors far from the threshold: a patient discharged after 9 days and a patient discharged after 10 or 11 days may be similar from a clinical-organizational perspective, although they fall into different binary classes. Table 3 decomposes the test set into correct predictions and three error categories. Short stays with $LOS < 8$ predicted as long correspond to conservative overestimations. Borderline errors with $8 \leq LOS \leq 12$ occur around the decision threshold and partly reflect the discretization of an intrinsically continuous outcome. The most critical errors are long stays with $LOS > 12$ predicted as short, since they correspond to missed prolonged hospitalizations.

Overall, this decomposition shows that the residual error is not homogeneous. A substantial fraction of mistakes occurs near the threshold, where the binary distinction between short and prolonged stay is intrinsically borderline. The main operational risk is concentrated in the last error row of Table 3, namely long stays with $LOS > 12$ predicted as short. These cases correspond to clearly prolonged hospitalizations that are not identified by the model and therefore represent the most relevant underestimation errors for hospital planning. Future improvements should not only target global accuracy, but specifically reduce this category of false short-stay predictions.

## 5 MARIO in Use: From Prediction to Decision Support

MARIO exposes its output through a prototype decision-support interface for clinical-organizational workflows. The interface combines the predicted LOS class, a prediction score, a comparison with similar historical hospitalizations, and the main readable motivations extracted from the model.

**Operational Scenario.** In the intended scenario, MARIO is used during the early phases of hospitalization to support bed-management and discharge planning activities. For each admitted patient, the system provides an estimated LOS class, distinguishing between short and prolonged stay. The prediction is not intended to replace clinical judgement, but to provide an early organizational signal that can help operators identify cases requiring further inspection. Figure 1 shows the patient-level dashboard. In the example, MARIO predicts a short stay for an elderly female patient admitted to orthopedics and traumatology with a primary diagnosis related to a humerus fracture. The upper part of the interface reports the predicted LOS class, the admission date and the prediction score, together with the LOS distribution observed in a cohort of similar historical hospitalizations. This cohort-based view shows that most similar cases were discharged within 5–10 days, providing an immediate contextual reference for the model output. The same view also presents the main model-derived motivations. In this case, the highlighted signals include the primary diagnosis, the admitting unit, the ordinary admission regime, the acute admission type, the absence of previous hospitalizations, and demographic or temporal factors. These motivations summarize, at a glance, the patient-level and admission-level evidence that the model considered relevant for the prediction. The dashboard therefore acts as an inspection layer: it does not replace the clinical record, but helps users identify which pieces of information may deserve attention when interpreting the predicted LOS class.

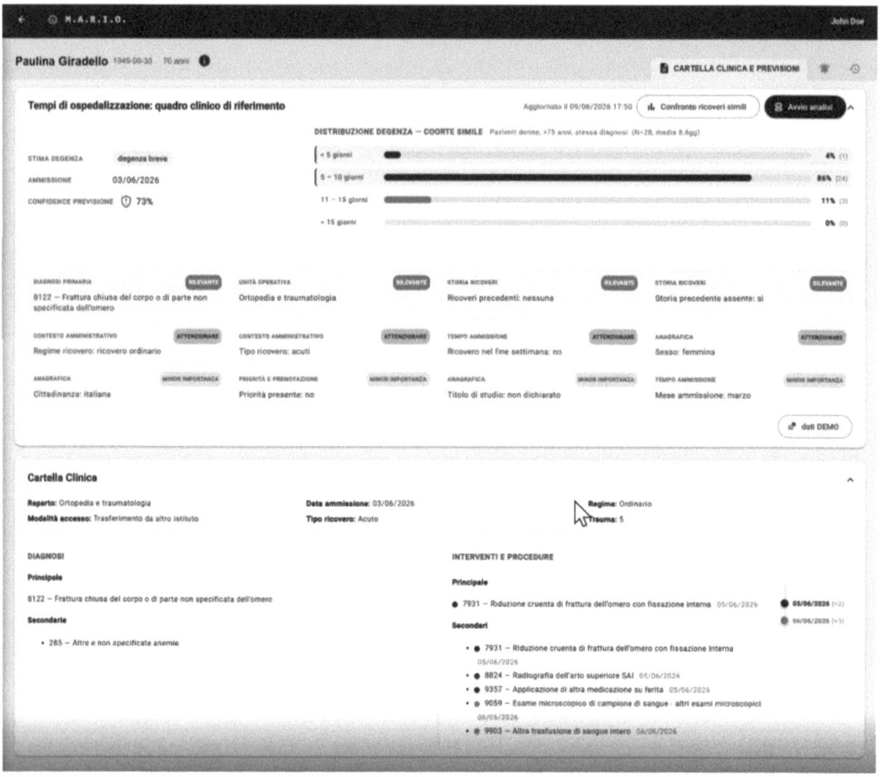


**Fig. 1.** Patient-level decision-support dashboard showing the predicted LOS class, prediction score, cohort-based contextualization, readable motivations, and access to the clinical record. The figure presents a synthetic record and contains no real patient data.

**Cohort-Based Contextualization.** The cohort-based panel compares the current patient with historical hospitalizations selected according to relevant patient and admission characteristics, such as diagnosis, gender and age group. The resulting LOS distribution is not used as a substitute for the classifier. Rather, it provides a descriptive reference frame that helps the operator understand whether the model output is coherent with similar past cases and with the hospital's previous experience.

**Readable Model Motivations.** The central part of the dashboard presents the main motivations behind the prediction. These motivations are derived from the feature-level contribution analysis of the linear classifier. Technical feature identifiers are mapped into readable clinical-organizational signals and grouped into categories such as primary diagnosis, admitting unit, admission context, previous hospitalizations, demographic information and temporal admission features. The interface also indicates the relative relevance of each motivation, allowing the operator to distinguish stronger evidence from weaker contextual signals. For example, the dashboard may highlight the role of the primary diagnosis, the admitting unit, the absence or presence of previous hospitalizations, admission regime, demographic factors or temporal admission characteristics. The objective is not to provide a causal explanation of LOS, but to show which patient-level signals the model used to support its prediction.

**Inspection of the Clinical Record.** The lower part of the interface gives access to the clinical evidence available for the selected hospitalization. It reports admission information, diagnosis codes, procedures and previous hospital-related information in a format that can be inspected together with the prediction and its motivations. This design keeps the model output connected to the underlying patient record: the operator can move from the predicted class, to the model-derived motivations, and then to the original clinical-administrative evidence. Overall, the prototype illustrates how MARIO can be integrated into a human-in-the-loop decision-support workflow. The system produces an early LOS stratification, contextualizes the prediction through similar historical cases, exposes the main model-derived motivations and allows inspection of the patient-level evidence. The final assessment remains under the responsibility of the healthcare professional, while MARIO supports prioritization, transparency and organizational awareness.

## 6 Conclusion and Future Work

We presented MARIO, an interpretable framework that transforms anonymized SDO records into patient-centric trajectories and predicts LOS classes through sparse, readable features. Its linear predictions are decomposed into feature-level contributions and presented through a decision-support dashboard. Experiments on real-world anonymized hospital discharge records show that MARIO improves over a majority-class baseline and achieves 81.9% accuracy in short-vs-long stay classification. The error analysis shows that residual errors have different operational meanings: a substantial fraction occurs around the 10-day decision threshold, while a similarly sized group consists of clearly prolonged hospitalizations predicted as short. The latter cases represent the main operational risk for hospital planning. This distinction is important because, in hospital-planning workflows, different error types may have different practical consequences. Several limitations remain. The current formulation reduces LOS prediction to a binary stratification problem based on a fixed threshold and does not capture the full ordinal or continuous nature of hospitalization duration. Moreover, administrative discharge records provide broad and routinely available information, but only approximate the complete clinical and organizational context of the patient. In particular, they do not fully represent social and care-continuity factors that may influence discharge timing, such as living conditions, availability of family or professional caregivers, social isolation, frailty, and access to post-acute or community-based support. The evaluation is retrospective and single-center, and therefore does not establish generalizability across hospitals, departments, countries or organizational settings. Moreover, the dashboard is presented as a prototype and has not yet been evaluated through a formal user study with clinical or organizational users.

Future work will focus on three directions. First, we plan to move beyond binary classification by exploring ordinal or multi-class LOS stratification and calibrated risk scores. Second, we will investigate additional feature families and learning strategies to reduce critical underestimations, particularly clearly prolonged stays predicted as short. Third, we aim to incorporate social and territorial-care information, when available and ethically appropriate, to better capture non-clinical factors affecting discharge. A prospective evaluation with clinical and organizational users will also assess the usefulness, readability and actionability of the dashboard explanations in real hospital-planning workflows.

**Acknowledgments.** This research was co-funded by the Italian National Complementary Plan (PNC), PNC-I.1 "Iniziative di ricerca per tecnologie e percorsi innovativi in ambito sanitario e assistenziale", Ministerial Decree No. 931 of 6 June 2022, initiative "DARE – DigitAl lifelong pRevEntion", grant code PNC0000002, CUP: B53C22006470001, B53C22006510001, and B53C22006260001.

## References

1. Amann, J., Blasimme, A., Vayena, E., Frey, D., Madai, V.I., consortium, P.: Explainability for artificial intelligence in healthcare: a multidisciplinary perspective. BMC Med. Inform. Decis. Making **20**(1), 310 (2020). https://doi.org/10.1186/s12911-020-01332-6
2. Beczek, A., Vámosi, M.: Prevalence of prolonged length of stay in an emergency department in urban Denmark: a retrospective health records repository review. J. Emerg. Nurs. **48**(1), 102.e1–102.e12 (2022). https://doi.org/10.1016/j.jen.2021.08.005
3. Bertoli Avella, A.M., et al.: Frequent users of the emergency department services in the largest academic hospital in the netherlands: a 5-year report. Eur. J. Emergency Med. **24**(2), 130–135 (2017). https://doi.org/10.1097/MEJ.0000000000000314
4. Blanco, J., Ferreras, M., Cosido, O.: Predictive modeling of hospital emergency department demand using artificial intelligence: a systematic review. Int. J. Med. Inform. **207**, 106215 (2026). https://doi.org/10.1016/j.ijmedinf.2025.106215
5. Fan, R.E., Chang, K.W., Hsieh, C.J., Wang, X.R., Lin, C.J.: Liblinear: a library for large linear classification. J. Mach. Learn. Res. **9**, 1871–1874 (2008)
6. Filice, S., Castellucci, G., Croce, D., Basili, R.: Kelp: a kernel-based learning platform. J. Mach. Learn. Res. **18**(191), 1–5 (2018). http://jmlr.org/papers/v18/16-087.html
7. Golinelli, D., Sanmarchi, F., Toscano, F., Bucci, A., Nante, N.: Analyzing the 20-year declining trend of hospital length-of-stay in European countries with different healthcare systems and reimbursement models. Int. J. Health Econ. Manage. **24**(3), 375–392 (2024). https://doi.org/10.1007/s10754-024-09369-0

8. Holzinger, A., Langs, G., Denk, H., Zatloukal, K., Müller, H.: Causability and explainability of artificial intelligence in medicine. WIREs Data Min. Knowl. Discovery **9**(4), e1312 (2019). https://doi.org/10.1002/widm.1312. https://wires.onlinelibrary.wiley.com/doi/abs/10.1002/widm.1312
9. Hsieh, C.J., Chang, K.W., Lin, C.J., Keerthi, S.S., Sundararajan, S.: A dual coordinate descent method for large-scale linear SVM. In: Proceedings of the 25th International Conference on Machine Learning, ICML 2008, pp. 408–415. ACM, New York (2008). https://doi.org/10.1145/1390156.1390208
10. Jain, R., Singh, M., Rao, A.R., Garg, R.: Predicting hospital length of stay using machine learning on a large open health dataset. BMC Health Serv. Res. **24**, 860 (2024). https://doi.org/10.1186/s12913-024-11238-y
11. King, Z., et al.: Machine learning for real-time aggregated prediction of hospital admission for emergency patients. NPJ Digit. Med. **5**, 104 (2022). https://doi.org/10.1038/s41746-022-00649-y
12. Ministero della Salute: Il manuale ICD-9-CM (2011). https://www.salute.gov.it/new/it/tema/assistenza-ospedaliera/il-manuale-icd9cm. Accessed 20 June 2026
13. Olivato, M., Rossetti, N., Gerevini, A.E., Chiari, M., Putelli, L., Serina, I.: Machine learning models for predicting short-long length of stay of covid-19 patients. Procedia Comput. Sci. **207**, 1232–1241 (2022). https://doi.org/10.1016/j.procs.2022.09.179
14. Ricciardi, C., et al.: Evaluation of different machine learning algorithms for predicting the length of stay in the emergency departments: a single-centre study. Front. Digit. Health **5**, 1323849 (2024). https://doi.org/10.3389/fdgth.2023.1323849
15. van Tiel, S., et al.: Systematic review of frequent users of emergency departments in non-us hospitals: state of the art. Eur. J. Emergency Med. **22**(5), 306–315 (2015). https://doi.org/10.1097/MEJ.0000000000000242
16. Vural, O., Ozaydin, B., Booth, J., Lindsey, B.F., Ahmed, A.: Deep learning-based forecasting of boarding patient counts to address emergency department overcrowding. Informatics **12**(3), 95 (2025). https://doi.org/10.3390/informatics12030095
17. Zaboli, A., et al.: The impact of chronic conditions on emergency department length of stay. Int. Emerg. Med. (2025). https://doi.org/10.1007/s11739-025-04080-5

# AiDER: Auditing and Document Evaluation via Rule Compilation and Small Language Models – An Education Case Study

Valerio Crocetti[1,2](✉), Elia Pacioni[1,3], Aldo Franco Dragoni[2], Michael Ignaz Schumacher[1], and Davide Calvaresi[1]

[1] HES-SO Valais-Wallis, 3960 Sierre, Switzerland
{valerio.crocetti,elia.pacioni,michael.schumacher, davide.calvaresi}@hevs.ch

[2] Università Politecnica delle Marche, 60131 Ancona, Italy
a.f.dragoni@univpm.it

[3] University of Extremadura, 06800 Mèrida, Spain

**Abstract.** Reviewing documents against natural-language requirements is hard when those requirements demand interpretation, contextual evidence, and non-trivial judgment. It is even harder when the review is to be automated reliably and made auditable. In domains like education, where teaching materials must align with pedagogical models and evolving expectations, including the rise of Large Language Models (LLMs), such decisions cannot be reduced to mechanical checks. When an LLM assigns a verdict directly, interpretation, evidence selection, and judgment collapse into a single opaque step, making errors hard to localize and outcomes hard to audit.

AiDER separates interpretation from judgment under a deliberate 2B-4B parameter constraint. Each natural-language requirement is compiled into an executable Common Expression Language (CEL) rule, and static analysis of that rule produces a bounded-evidence scaffold that constrains what the model may extract from the document. The verdict is then computed deterministically by applying the rule to the extracted evidence (no LLM call at this step), yielding an inspectable trace from requirement to rule, rule to evidence, and evidence to verdict.

We evaluate AiDER on four small models (Gemma 4 and Qwen3.5, at 2B and 4B) under three compilation strategies: human-written reference rules, direct compilation, and validation-loop repair. The evaluation uses 200 requirement-document pairs from a higher-education course pack. Across three performance dimensions (syntactic validity, semantic fidelity, and document-level agreement), direct compilation often yields valid but semantically divergent rules, whereas validation-driven repair substantially improves both validity and fidelity across all four models. An ablation shows that the static scaffold alone encodes most of the extraction intent: LLM-generated extraction contracts add little when the rule is well-specified, but matter more when it is ambiguous.


S. Bistarelli et al. (Eds.): AIxIA 2026, LNAI 17131, pp. 226–240, 2027.
https://doi.org/10.1007/978-3-032-40774-0_17

**Keywords:** rule compilation · pedagogical review · small language models · neuro-symbolic AI · hybrid AI · auditable AI

# 1 Introduction

The rapid progress of Generative Artificial Intelligence (GenAI) has sparked interest in automating review tasks long regarded as matters of human judgment. In many domains, documents must be checked against requirements stated in natural language (e.g., policies, guidelines, quality criteria, or institutional expectations). Such requirements are easy to state but difficult to implement/audit.

The problem is acute in higher education. Course materials do more than describe a course; they make intended learning outcomes, teaching activities, assessment expectations, and students' responsibilities explicit. This view of course materials as explicit design artifacts aligns with constructive alignment, which treats outcomes, instruction, and assessment as one design problem [2], and with work on educative curriculum materials [11].

Many such requirements cannot be reduced to mechanical checks. A reviewer may need to judge whether assessment criteria are sufficiently explicit to guide students, whether feedback opportunities are meaningfully built into the course, or whether a policy provides students with a clear basis for action. These judgments must be grounded in the document's content. However, they also require interpreting how that evidence functions in context—a challenge that grows when requirements are course- or institution-specific or tied to a particular pedagogical approach.

Recent work has begun to use Large Language Models (LLMs) to support the evaluation and design of educational materials. Studies of document-level pedagogical evaluation target lesson plans or K-12 instructional materials, where models prove more reliable on explicit, textually grounded features than on high-inference pedagogical criteria [17,20]. In higher education, related work examines LLM support for generating and evaluating course materials, including syllabi, assessments, and slides [35]. However, in most model-assisted review settings, criterion interpretation, evidence selection, and final judgment remain coupled in a single model-mediated process [4]. This entanglement makes the review hard to audit: when a verdict is wrong, it is difficult to tell whether the failure stems from misunderstanding the requirement, selecting weak evidence, or applying an inconsistent decision rule.

To make such reviews auditable, we present AiDER[1], a Small Language Model (SLM) framework that separates interpretation from judgment. AiDER requires each requirement to be represented as a rule in a restricted domain-specific language (DSL) based on the Common Expression Language (CEL) [7]. Static analysis of the compiled condition yields an evidence scaffold that asks the model to extract only the evidence needed to verify the rule. The model,

[1] Source code and replication materials are available at https://github.com/HISTLab-hevs/AiDER.

therefore, does not decide whether the requirement is satisfied; given the evidence, the binary verdict follows deterministically from executing the compiled condition. The resulting trace is inspectable by construction (each requirement to its rule, each rule to its evidence, and each verdict to that evidence), and failures are easier to diagnose, since errors in compiling rules, extracting evidence, and reaching a verdict can be analyzed separately.

We target 2B-4B class models that can be deployed on-premises. Educational materials are valuable intellectual property, and institutional policies may forbid sharing internal documents with third-party cloud LLMs. Although we evaluate AiDER in education, the pipeline is designed for auditable, requirement-based document review more broadly; however, its transferability to other domains is not evaluated in this study. Since these models may generate non-executable CEL rules, AiDER uses compilation errors as feedback in a repair loop to iteratively correct invalid rules. In turn, our work characterizes the reliability of rule compilation through three aspects: (a) the SLMs' ability to compile natural-language requirements into executable and sound CEL rules; (b) the effect of validation-driven repair on rule validity and fidelity; and (c) the impact of the resulting rules on document-level verdicts, including the contribution of model-generated extraction guidance.

To study these aspects, we instantiated AiDER on 200 applicable requirement-document pairs from instructional PDFs, comparing human reference rules, direct LLM-compiled rules, and validation-loop repair to trace how executable formalizations affect document-level verdicts. We also conducted a scaffold-only ablation to isolate the contribution of model-generated extraction guidance beyond the statically derived evidence scaffold.

The remainder of the paper is organized as follows: Sect. 2 reviews related work; Sect. 3 presents the methodology; Sect. 4 reports the results; and Sects. 5 and 6 discuss limitations and conclude the paper.

## 2 Related Work

Recent works explore whether LLMs can evaluate educational artifacts against pedagogical criteria. Hauk and Soujon [17] analyze written lesson plans and show the difficulty of obtaining reliable judgments on criteria that require pedagogical interpretation beyond explicit document features, while Li et al. [20] introduce SciEval, where models evaluate K-12 science instructional materials by producing rubric-aligned scores and supporting evidence. In higher education, Yao et al. [35] examine LLM-generated course materials, including syllabi, assessments, and slides, showing that course-material quality can itself become an object of model-supported evaluation. Broader work on LLM-assisted educational assessment also emphasizes the importance of explicit rubrics, operational criteria, and human refinement in model-supported evaluation workflows [6,12]. Across these settings, a recurring limitation is that model-based evaluation often couples evidence identification, criterion interpretation, and verdict assignment in a single model-mediated step.

The same concern appears in legal and compliance-oriented document review, where recent systems move beyond direct document-level prompting by introducing structured intermediate steps. Narendra et al. [26] propose a template-to-contract comparison pipeline that extracts key concepts from legal templates and checks their entailment in contracts through NLI/LLM-based reasoning. Sun et al. [31] propose a RAG-based compliance-checking framework that combines layered reasoning with eventic graphs for regulatory information. These approaches show that structuring review before assigning a decision has benefits, but their decisions still rely on entailment or retrieval-augmented reasoning over intermediate representations. AiDER takes a different approach: whether the requirement is given directly as a CEL rule or compiled from natural language, the rule defines the evidence scaffold and the decision logic. The model extracts structured, traceable evidence, but the final verdict is produced by deterministic rule evaluation.

Our approach also relates to semantic parsing and neuro-symbolic AI. Semantic parsing frames the problem as mapping natural language into executable logical forms, making interpretation checkable through formal representations [21]. Recent LLM-based systems extend this idea by translating natural-language problems into symbolic programs while relying on deterministic execution for inference. For example, Logic-LM translates reasoning problems into symbolic formulations and uses a solver to perform the final inference [29], while Crocetti and Dragoni [9] translate natural-language problems into executable Prolog [18] code and refine invalid programs through execution feedback. Similarly, Mensfelt et al. [25] introduce PrologMCP, which exposes Prolog through the Model Context Protocol (MCP)[2] as a reusable, stateful tool interface for LLM agents, supporting solver-backed inference through a translate-run-inspect-repair loop. More broadly, survey work on hybrid AI motivates combining data-driven and rule-based components to support reliability and transparency, while noting that evaluation and explanation practices remain fragmented [28]. AiDER integrates these principles into an auditable pipeline for requirement-based document review under a small-model constraint.

## 3 Methodology

AiDER replaces the single opaque verdict with a chain of inspectable steps. The remainder of this section first formalizes the review task, then describes the pipeline and compilation methods, and finally instantiates the setup in the higher-education case study.

### 3.1 Task Formalization

Let $\mathcal{R} = \{r_i\}_{i=1}^{m}$ be a set of pedagogical requirements, $\mathcal{D} = \{d_j\}_{j=1}^{n}$ a corpus of instructional documents, and $\mathcal{T} = \{t_h\}_{h=1}^{q}$ the set of document types, such

[2] https://modelcontextprotocol.io/docs/getting-started/intro.

as slides, assessments, syllabi, and rubrics. The functions $\theta$ and $\gamma$ associate each requirement $r_i$ with its single applicable type $\theta(r_i) \in \mathcal{T}$, and each document $d_j$ with its non-empty set of document types $\gamma(d_j) \subseteq \mathcal{T}$, respectively. Each document is represented as an ordered page sequence (Definition 1).

$$d_j = (p_{j1}, p_{j2}, \ldots, p_{j\ell_j}) \tag{1}$$

The review task is restricted to type-compatible requirement-document pairs (Definition 2).

$$\mathcal{A} = \{(r_i, d_j) \in \mathcal{R} \times \mathcal{D} \mid \theta(r_i) \in \gamma(d_j)\} \tag{2}$$

For each $(r_i, d_j) \in \mathcal{A}$, the goal is to assign a binary verdict $y_{ij} \in \{0, 1\}$, where $y_{ij} = 1$ indicates that $d_j$ satisfies $r_i$, and $y_{ij} = 0$ indicates that it does not. Pairs outside $\mathcal{A}$ are not evaluated.

### 3.2 Pipeline Architecture

AiDER operates in five phases illustrated in Fig. 1. Phases PH1, PH3, and PH4 involve LLM inference, while PH2 and PH5 are deterministic. In PH1, the model compiles each natural-language requirement $r_i$ into an executable CEL rule, combining all sub-requirements into a single compound condition using the evidence functions in Table 2. In PH2, the compiled rule is statically analyzed to recover all evidence item kinds and field paths without any LLM calls, producing an *evidence scaffold* that bounds what the extractor may emit. In PH3, the model reads the scaffold and produces per-kind and per-field *extraction instructions* that are constrained to the scaffold's kinds and fields. Together, the scaffold and these instructions form the *extraction specification.* In PH4, each document $d_j$ is processed in page batches, and the model returns structured *evidence items* carrying a kind, a verbatim evidence quote, and a field map. In PH5, the aggregated evidence items are evaluated deterministically against the compiled CEL rule, yielding the binary verdict $y_{ij} \in \{0, 1\}$ without an LLM call.

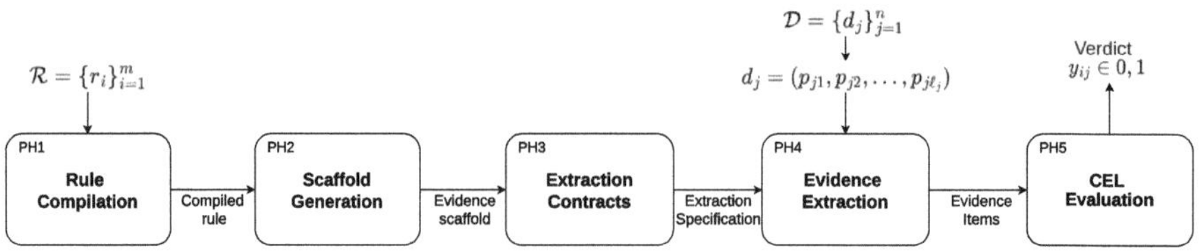


**Fig. 1.** Overview of the AiDER pipeline.

### 3.3 Rule Compilation Methods

Figure 2 illustrates the three methods for obtaining CEL rules. Let $\rho_i$ denote a compiled rule for requirement $r_i$, and let valid$(\rho_i) \in \{0, 1\}$ denote the deterministic validation procedure that checks whether the generated rule is syntactically well-formed and compatible with the restricted rule interface.

Under *Reference rules*, the human-written rule $\rho_i^\star$ associated with each requirement $r_i$ is loaded directly and used as the reference formalization against which generated rules are assessed.

Under *Direct compilation*, the model translates each natural-language requirement into a candidate rule in a single attempt (Eq. 3):

$$\tilde{\rho}_i = \mathrm{LLM}_{T_0}(r_i) \tag{3}$$

Equation 4 represents the resulting compiled rule:

$$\hat{\rho}_i^{\text{direct}} = \begin{cases} \tilde{\rho}_i, & \text{if valid}(\tilde{\rho}_i) = 1 \\ \perp, & \text{otherwise} \end{cases} \tag{4}$$

where $\perp$ denotes a compilation failure.

Under *Validation-loop compilation*, invalid rules enter a bounded repair loop initialized with $\rho_i^{(0)} = \tilde{\rho}_i$. At iteration $k$, the model is given the previous invalid rule and the corresponding validation error, and produces a repaired candidate as illustrated in Eq. 5:

$$\rho_i^{(k)} = \mathrm{Repair}_{T_k}\left(r_i, \rho_i^{(k-1)}, \epsilon_i^{(k-1)}\right) \tag{5}$$

where $\epsilon_i^{(k-1)}$ is the validation error from the previous attempt. The model temperature is raised across repair attempts as $T_k = T_0 + k \cdot \Delta T$, with $k = 1, \ldots, 5$, $\Delta T = 0.1$, resulting in repair temperatures from 0.1 to 0.5 [9]. The loop returns the first valid repaired rule (if one exists) or $\perp$ otherwise.

### 3.4 Dataset and Rule Corpus

We evaluated AiDER on open-access *Business Communications 2* course pack [24], a first-year undergraduate course at Coast Mountain College. The course spans 13 weeks and covers professional communication strategies, including bad-news delivery, informational reports, persuasive messages, and presentation design. The corpus contains 15 unique PDFs. Because some PDFs belong to multiple document types, the applicable-type counts are 8 slide decks, 6 assessment documents, 5 rubrics, and 1 syllabus.

We defined 40 human-written rules, distributed evenly across the four document types, to serve as a reference formalization. The rules' design was inspired by literature on AI-aware assessment design [8,22], peer instruction and active learning [10,13], syllabus design and tone [5,16,30], constructive alignment [2], formative assessment and feedback [14,27], cognitive-load reduction in multimedia learning [23], and rubric design [3]. The resulting benchmark set is designed

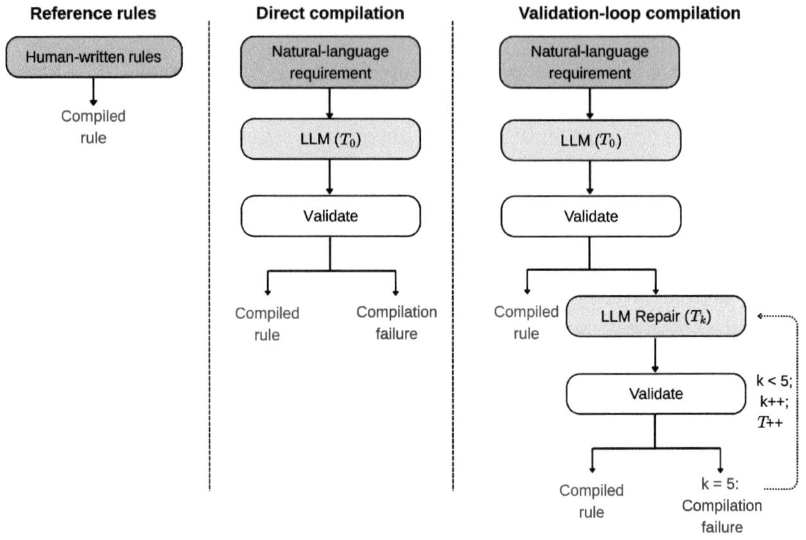


**Fig. 2.** Overview of the three compilation methods tested.

to cover common pedagogical concerns while exercising a diverse range of condition structures.

For each reference rule, we also defined a paired natural-language requirement request, written in plain English and without formal notation. Table 1 shows one reference rule and its paired natural-language request. Applicability is determined by matching each requirement to the corresponding document type. This type-matching procedure yielded $|\mathcal{A}| = 200$ applicable requirement-document pairs in the evaluated corpus.

**Table 1.** Example of a reference rule and its paired natural-language requirement.

| Document type | Natural-language requirement | Reference rule |
|---|---|---|
| Assessment | At least one grading criterion should be stated explicitly enough that students understand how their work will be evaluated. | `item_count_where("grading_criterion", "normalized.is_explicitly_stated", "==", "true") >= 1` |

AIDER's rule language is deliberately restricted to a fixed CEL interface. The interface exposes seven custom functions over extracted evidence items, covering item counts, existence checks, distinct-value counts, filtered counts and ratios, monotonic ordering checks, and group-level coverage checks. Human-written reference rules and model-compiled rules are therefore expressed through the same executable vocabulary. Table 2 lists the supported signatures.

This fixed set of functions makes each rule statically inspectable. Since evidence item kinds and field paths appear explicitly as function arguments, they can be recovered deterministically from the CEL condition. These elements define an evidence scaffold that constrains what the model must retrieve before any extraction instructions are generated.

**Table 2.** The seven custom functions in AiDER. `kind` selects the evidence kind; `path` (and `o_path`/`v_path` the ordering/value keys, `grp`/`fp` the grouping/filter keys) is a field path that must begin with `normalized.`; `op`/`val` form a filter predicate `field op val`; `dir` ∈ {`non_decreasing`, `strictly_increasing`}; supported operators: `==`, `!=`, `>`, `>=`, `<`, `<=`, `in`, `not_in`.

| # | Signature | Returns |
|---|---|---|
| 1 | item_count(kind) | int |
| 2 | item_exists(kind) | bool |
| 3 | item_distinct_count(kind, path) | int |
| 4 | item_count_where(kind, path, op, val) | int |
| 5 | item_ratio_where(kind, path, op, val) | float |
| 6 | item_ordered(kind, o_path, v_path, dir) | bool |
| 7 | item_all_groups_have(kind, grp, fp, op, val) | bool |

## 4 Results

We evaluated four models under the intentional 2B-4B parameter constraint: Gemma-4-E4B-it, Gemma-4-E2B-it [15], Qwen3.5-2B, and Qwen3.5-4B [34]. Each model was assessed under the three configurations reported in Fig. 2. Each model was run three times; all tables report mean ± sample standard deviation over these runs. All inference calls in the AiDER pipeline were served locally with vLLM [19], on a single NVIDIA DGX Spark workstation[3].

All models were run with sampling temperature $T_0 = 0$ and *constrained decoding* enabled. Constrained decoding restricts token sampling at each step to tokens permitted by the target JSON schema, so the model can emit only output that conforms to the expected structure [32]. The validation error returned to the repair loop (Sect. 3.3) is therefore always a CEL compilation error.

We turned off thinking mode across all runs. In preliminary experiments, the smaller Qwen models, in particular, tended to enter reasoning loops when thinking was active, exhausting the token budget within the <think> block and returning empty content.

For document-level evaluation, we employed Claude Opus 4.8 [1] as a fixed external LLM judge, following the LLM-as-a-judge evaluation protocol [36]. The judge is not part of the AiDER pipeline; it was used only to obtain a stable reference signal for evaluation. For each applicable pair, the judge received the

[3] https://www.nvidia.com/en-us/products/workstations/dgx-spark/.

document, the human reference rule description, and the condition. The resulting reference verdict was therefore anchored to the reference formalization and held constant across all runs. Consequently, generated rules may be penalized when they encode a reasonable alternative interpretation that differs from the human-written rule. Since the latter is fixed, differences across models in the reference-rule condition reflect extraction quality rather than variation in rule content.

*Evaluation Metrics.* From the rule perspective, we report the validation pass rate and three fidelity metrics relative to the human-reference rule. Evidence-kind Jaccard measures overlap in the evidence item kinds used by the two rules. Clause F1 compares executable structure by decomposing CEL conditions into clauses and scoring each clause by its best-matching counterpart in the other condition, using the mean Jaccard over rule function, evidence kind, and field paths. Cosine similarity, computed with BGE-small-v1.5 [33], captures semantic proximity but not executable equivalence. Failed compilations received a score of 0 on all rule-fidelity metrics. From the document perspective, we report Cohen's $\kappa$ and Matthews Correlation Coefficient (MCC) against the fixed judge reference over all applicable requirement-document pairs. When compilation failed, and no verdict could be produced, the missing verdict was treated as maximal disagreement with the judge by assigning the opposite label. Negative agreement values therefore reflect both wrong verdicts and unrecovered compilation failures under this penalty. In the extraction-guidance Ablation, $\Delta\kappa$ and $\Delta$MCC denote the gain of the complete extraction specification over the scaffold-only setting. Together, these metrics allowed us to analyze the three aspects outlined in Sect. 1.

## Compilation Quality

Table 3 reports compilation along two axes: whether a rule executes (Valid%) and how closely it matches the reference (Kind J., Cl. F1, Cosine). Under direct compilation, the 4B models compile most rules correctly, but validity and fidelity differ by model. Gemma-4-E4B-it leads on both, whereas Qwen3.5-4B approaches its validity yet trails sharply on evidence-kind Jaccard: its rules execute but rest on different evidence. The ordering Cosine > Kind J. $\geq$ Cl. F1 holds for every model, since cosine rewards rough semantic agreement while Kind J. demands an exact match of evidence kinds. A valid rule that reads closely to the reference can still select the wrong evidence, which is the component that determines what a rule actually checks and whose effect surfaces in the document-level results.

**Table 3.** Rule-compilation quality under direct and validation-loop compilation.

| | *Direct compilation* | | | | *Validation-loop compilation* | | | |
|---|---|---|---|---|---|---|---|---|
| Model | Valid% | Kind J. | Cl. F1 | Cosine | Valid% | Kind J. | Cl. F1 | Cosine |
| Gemma-4-E4B-it | **86.7**$\pm$3.8 | **.611**$\pm$.05 | **.408**$\pm$.02 | **.761**$\pm$.04 | **95.8**$\pm$1.4 | **.702**$\pm$.02 | **.462**$\pm$.01 | **.841**$\pm$.01 |
| Qwen3.5-4B | 79.2$\pm$1.4 | .412$\pm$.00 | .326$\pm$.00 | .701$\pm$.01 | 95.0$\pm$0.0 | .438$\pm$.00 | .365$\pm$.00 | .840$\pm$.00 |
| Gemma-4-E2B-it | 36.7$\pm$1.4 | .108$\pm$.01 | .104$\pm$.01 | .315$\pm$.01 | 56.7$\pm$2.9 | .250$\pm$.00 | .188$\pm$.01 | .490$\pm$.03 |
| Qwen3.5-2B | 67.5$\pm$2.5 | .216$\pm$.06 | .212$\pm$.02 | .582$\pm$.02 | 89.2$\pm$2.9 | .320$\pm$.02 | .294$\pm$.01 | .772$\pm$.03 |

**Table 4.** Decomposition of compilation validity into first-attempt and repair-recovered rules, out of 40. Final valid equals initial valid plus recovered rules.

| Model | Recovered | Unrecovered | F. Valid |
|---|---|---|---|
| Gemma-4-E4B-it | 3.7$\pm$1.2 | 1.7$\pm$0.6 | **38.3**$\pm$0.6 |
| Qwen3.5-4B | 6.3$\pm$0.6 | 2.0$\pm$0.0 | **38.0**$\pm$0.0 |
| Gemma-4-E2B-it | 8.0$\pm$1.0 | 17.3$\pm$1.2 | 22.7$\pm$1.2 |
| Qwen3.5-2B | 8.7$\pm$0.6 | 4.3$\pm$1.2 | 35.7$\pm$1.2 |

### Repair Effects

The validation loop lifts both axes (Table 3, right): three of the four models exceed 89% validity, and fidelity rises across the board. The two 4B models, however, expose a limit of repair. Their cosine becomes nearly identical, while Qwen3.5-4B's evidence-kind Jaccard stays far below Gemma-4-E4B-it's (.438 vs .702): repair closes the semantic gap between them but not the gap in the evidence each rule requests, so Qwen's reliance on different evidence kinds is a stable trait rather than a repairable error. Table 4 locates the remaining failures: Gemma-4-E2B-it still leaves almost half of its initially invalid rules invalid after repair, whereas Qwen3.5-2B leaves only a small fraction. Repair, therefore, makes natural-language rules far more usable by recovering validity. Still, the evidence a rule targets is set at the first compilation and changes little afterward, which bounds how much repair can help downstream.

### Document-Level Behavior

Table 5 reports agreement against the judge. The *Reference rules* column isolates extraction. It is the pipeline's strongest result: with a well-specified rule, three of the four models reach moderate to substantial agreement (up to $\kappa = .686$), and Gemma-4-E2B-it's score nearly matches Qwen3.5-4B's, so even a small model extracts evidence well once the rule is sound. Agreement drops for rules generated from natural language, and the negative values for the 2B models reflect the design penalty, since every failed compilation is scored as maximal disagreement. The two 2B models swap ranks between the settings: under reference rules Gemma-4-E2B-it leads (.534 vs .323) as the stronger extractor, but once the rule has to be created, the order reverses (.066 vs −.328), because Gemma-4-E2B-it's frequent compilation failures are penalized while Qwen3.5-2B compiles reliably enough to stay positive despite weaker extraction.

## Ablation: Scaffold-Only Versus Guided Extraction

The ablation evaluates whether LLM-generated extraction instructions provide useful guidance once the scaffold has already defined the admissible evidence types and fields. We compared the complete extraction specification with a scaffold-only variant, restricting the comparison to pairs associated with valid compiled rules under both extraction settings. Compilation failures were therefore excluded, so the values are not directly comparable to Table 5.

**Table 5.** End-to-end verdict agreement against the judge reference, pooled over 200 pairs.

| | *Reference rules* | | *Direct* | | *Validation-loop* | |
|---|---|---|---|---|---|---|
| Model | $\kappa$ | MCC | $\kappa$ | MCC | $\kappa$ | MCC |
| Gemma-4-E4B-it | **.686**$\pm_{.04}$ | **.697**$\pm_{.04}$ | **.246**$\pm_{.04}$ | **.246**$\pm_{.04}$ | **.336**$\pm_{.03}$ | **.344**$\pm_{.03}$ |
| Qwen3.5-4B | .539$\pm_{.03}$ | .543$\pm_{.03}$ | .028$\pm_{.05}$ | .028$\pm_{.05}$ | .276$\pm_{.03}$ | .282$\pm_{.03}$ |
| Gemma-4-E2B-it | .534$\pm_{.01}$ | .559$\pm_{.01}$ | −.504$\pm_{.05}$ | −.506$\pm_{.05}$ | −.328$\pm_{.12}$ | −.336$\pm_{.12}$ |
| Qwen3.5-2B | .323$\pm_{.03}$ | .323$\pm_{.03}$ | −.228$\pm_{.08}$ | −.228$\pm_{.08}$ | .066$\pm_{.04}$ | .073$\pm_{.05}$ |

The scaffold already captures much of the extraction intent. Additional instructions add little to human-written reference rules, where the scaffold is well-specified, and can even hurt weaker models such as Qwen3.5-2B. Their benefit is clearer with natural-language-compiled rules, where the scaffold is derived from imperfect model-generated conditions, leaving more room for disambiguation. The pattern is therefore consistent across methods: the statically derived scaffold carries most of the extraction intent on its own, and model-generated extraction contracts pay off mainly when the underlying rule is weak or underspecified. Once the scaffold is already well-formed, they become redundant or even counterproductive (Table 6).

**Table 6.** Extraction guidance ablation: per-method gain from LLM-generated extraction contracts vs. the judge reference.

| | *Ref. rules* | | *Direct* | | *Repair* | |
|---|---|---|---|---|---|---|
| Model | $\Delta\kappa$ | $\Delta$MCC | $\Delta\kappa$ | $\Delta$MCC | $\Delta\kappa$ | $\Delta$MCC |
| Gemma-4-E4B-it | **.045**$\pm_{.04}$ | **.040**$\pm_{.03}$ | **.085**$\pm_{.05}$ | .058$\pm_{.06}$ | .038$\pm_{.02}$ | .013$\pm_{.02}$ |
| Qwen3.5-4B | .001$\pm_{.02}$ | −.002$\pm_{.02}$ | .035$\pm_{.05}$ | .035$\pm_{.04}$ | .001$\pm_{.01}$ | .000$\pm_{.01}$ |
| Gemma-4-E2B-it | −.039$\pm_{.01}$ | −.040$\pm_{.01}$ | .052$\pm_{.14}$ | **.089**$\pm_{.19}$ | .058$\pm_{.01}$ | **.122**$\pm_{.05}$ |
| Qwen3.5-2B | −.181$\pm_{.03}$ | −.194$\pm_{.03}$ | .080$\pm_{.13}$ | .086$\pm_{.14}$ | **.078**$\pm_{.03}$ | .085$\pm_{.02}$ |

## 5 Limitations

The results of this study should be read in light of the evaluation's scope and design choices. The evaluation was designed as a focused case study in one higher-education setting. It used one course pack, with 15 PDFs, 40 requirements, and 200 applicable requirement-document pairs. This setting was useful for studying AiDER's behavior in detail, but it does not demonstrate how the framework would perform across many courses, institutions, or document types. Future work should therefore test the approach on larger and more diverse collections.

The human-written CEL rules served as reference rules, but they are not the only way to express each requirement. Indeed, some pedagogical requirements can be interpreted in more than one reasonable way. For this reason, the rule-level metrics indicate how close the generated rules are to our reference rules, rather than proving that a single rule is the only correct interpretation. Similarly, the document-level judge provides a consistent reference signal, but its proprietary nature limits strict reproducibility; future work should therefore include expert human review.

Overall, AiDER reduces the role of model-based judgment, but it still depends on LLM outputs in some parts of the pipeline. In particular, the model is used for rule compilation, extraction guidance, and evidence extraction. Errors in these steps can still affect the final verdict, even though the verdict itself is computed deterministically. The rule interface is also intentionally limited to keep the system inspectable and easy to validate. Extending the interface while preserving auditability and benchmarking runtime remain future work.

## 6 Conclusion

We introduced AiDER, a framework for auditable, requirement-based document review, which we evaluated here on teaching materials under a small-model constraint. Its central design choice is to separate interpretation from judgment: requirements are compiled into executable CEL rules, rules induce bounded evidence scaffolds, and verdicts are obtained through deterministic rule execution over extracted evidence.

The results show that syntactic validity, semantic fidelity, and document-level agreement are distinct dimensions of the same auditability problem. The 4B models can already produce valid rules, but these may still define a different evidence scaffold or decision boundary from the intended reference formalization. Given a well-specified rule, even small models can extract sufficient evidence to produce reliable deterministic verdicts, which is the clearest sign that the design works. Validation-driven repair improves validity and fidelity jointly, yet its end-to-end benefit is scale-dependent: the 4B models recovered measurable document-level agreement, whereas the 2B models remained limited even after repair. At the document level, the binding constraint for generated rules is therefore rule semantics rather than executability. Finally, the extraction-guidance ablation shows that the statically derived scaffold already encodes most of the extraction intent, with model-generated guidance adding value primarily when the compiled rule is imperfect.

Overall, the findings support treating pedagogical review as a formalization and evidence problem rather than as a direct model-judgment task. AiDER does not remove the need for expert rule design or human oversight. Still, by making rules and evidence inspectable, it traces each failure to a specific stage rather than to a single opaque verdict. Future work should scale the evaluation to more courses and institutions, complement LLM-based judgment with expert human review, explore heterogeneous setups that pair a stronger model for compilation with a small model for extraction, and extend the DSL without compromising static analysis.

**Acknowledgments.** This work was supported by the HES-SO R&I Mind the Gap: Adapting Higher Education to the Age of AI (MTG, 140012/RI-PSTRAT25-06), HES-SO RCSO ISNet Hybrid Ai foR ReIlable perSonalized cOachiNg (HARRISON) grant, Swiss AI Initiative (a0138).

## References

1. Anthropic: Claude opus 4.8 system card (2026). https://www.anthropic.com/claude-opus-4-8-system-card, model system card. Accessed 02 June 2026
2. Biggs, J.: Enhancing teaching through constructive alignment. High. Educ. **32**(3), 347–364 (1996). https://doi.org/10.1007/BF00138871
3. Brookhart, S.M.: How to create and use rubrics for formative assessment and grading. ASCD, Alexandria, VA (2013)
4. Chiang, C.H., Chen, W.C., Kuan, C.Y., Yang, C., Lee, H.y.: Large language model as an assignment evaluator: Insights, feedback, and challenges in a 1000+ student course. In: Proceedings of the 2024 Conference on Empirical Methods in Natural Language Processing, pp. 2489–2513. Association for Computational Linguistics, Miami (2024). https://doi.org/10.18653/v1/2024.emnlp-main.146. https://aclanthology.org/2024.emnlp-main.146/
5. Chickering, A.W., Gamson, Z.F.: Seven principles for good practice in undergraduate education. AAHE Bull. **39**(7), 3–7 (1987)
6. Chu, Y., Li, H., Yang, K., Copur-Gencturk, Y., Tang, J.: LLM-based automated grading with human-in-the-loop. In: 2025 IEEE International Conference on Teaching, Assessment, and Learning for Engineering (TALE), pp. 1–8. IEEE, Macao (2025). https://doi.org/10.1109/TALE66047.2025.11346771
7. Common Expression Language: Common expression language (2026). https://cel.dev/. Accessed 25 May 2026
8. Cotton, D.R.E., Cotton, P.A., Shipway, J.R.: Chatting and cheating: ensuring academic integrity in the era of ChatGPT. Innov. Educ. Teach. Int. **61**(2), 228–239 (2024). https://doi.org/10.1080/14703297.2023.2190148
9. Crocetti, V., Dragoni, A.F.: Bridging large language models and logic programming. In: 2025 IEEE International Conference on Metrology for eXtended Reality, Artificial Intelligence and Neural Engineering (MetroXRAINE), pp. 1066–1071. IEEE (2025). https://doi.org/10.1109/MetroXRAINE66377.2025.11340308
10. Crouch, C.H., Mazur, E.: Peer instruction: ten years of experience and results. Am. J. Phys. **69**(9), 970–977 (2001). https://doi.org/10.1119/1.1374249

11. Davis, E.A., Krajcik, J.S.: Designing educative curriculum materials to promote teacher learning. Educ. Res. **34**(3), 3–14 (2005). https://doi.org/10.3102/0013189X034003003
12. Emirtekin, E.: Large language model-powered automated assessment: a systematic review. Appl. Sci. **15**(10), 5683 (2025). https://doi.org/10.3390/app15105683
13. Freeman, S., et al.: Active learning increases student performance in science, engineering, and mathematics. Proc. Natl. Acad. Sci. U.S.A. **111**(23), 8410–8415 (2014). https://doi.org/10.1073/pnas.1319030111
14. Gibbs, G., Simpson, C.: Conditions under which assessment supports students' learning. Learn. Teach. High. Educ. **1**, 3–31 (2005)
15. Google DeepMind: Gemma 4 model card (2026). https://ai.google.dev/gemma/docs/core/model_card_4. Accessed 28 May 2026
16. Harnish, R.J., Bridges, K.R.: Effect of syllabus tone: students' perceptions of instructor and course. Soc. Psychol. Educ. **14**(3), 319–330 (2011). https://doi.org/10.1007/s11218-011-9152-4
17. Hauk, D., Soujon, N.: How reliable are large language models in analyzing the quality of written lesson plans? A mixed-methods study from a teacher internship program. Comput. Educ. Artif. Intell. **10**, 100538 (2026). https://doi.org/10.1016/j.caeai.2025.100538
18. Körner, P., et al.: Fifty years of Prolog and beyond. Theory Pract. Logic Program. **22**(6), 776–858 (2022). https://doi.org/10.1017/S1471068422000102
19. Kwon, W., et al.: Efficient memory management for large language model serving with PagedAttention. In: Proceedings of the 29th Symposium on Operating Systems Principles, SOSP '23, pp. 611–626. Association for Computing Machinery, Koblenz (2023). https://doi.org/10.1145/3600006.3613165
20. Li, Z., et al.: SciEval: a benchmark for automatic evaluation of K–12 science instructional materials (2026). https://doi.org/10.48550/arXiv.2604.25472. arXiv preprint arXiv:2604.25472
21. Liang, P.: Learning executable semantic parsers for natural language understanding. Commun. ACM **59**(9), 68–76 (2016). https://doi.org/10.1145/2866568
22. Lodge, J.M., et al.: Assessment reform for the age of artificial intelligence. Technical report, Tertiary Education Quality and Standards Agency (2023). https://www.teqsa.gov.au/guides-resources/resources/corporate-publications/assessment-reform-age-artificial-intelligence, published 23 November 2023
23. Mayer, R.E., Moreno, R.: Nine ways to reduce cognitive load in multimedia learning. Educ. Psychol. **38**(1), 43–52 (2003). https://doi.org/10.1207/S15326985EP3801_6
24. McMurray, K.: Business communications 2. Course pack, BCcampus Open Collection (2020). https://collection.bccampus.ca/course-pack/cntcnGgB/, curated and designed by Karen McMurray; course based on BENG 150; released through the BCcampus Open Online Courses Project in 2021; CC BY 4.0 except where otherwise noted; accessed 2026-05-27
25. Mensfelt, A., Prabhakaran, A., Haret, A., Trencsenyi, V., Stathis, K.: PrologMCP: a standardized prolog tool interface for LLM agents (2026). https://doi.org/10.48550/arXiv.2606.14935. arXiv preprint arXiv:2606.14935
26. Narendra, S., Shetty, K., Ratnaparkhi, A.: Enhancing contract negotiations with LLM-based legal document comparison. In: Proceedings of the Natural Legal Language Processing Workshop 2024, pp. 143–153. Association for Computational Linguistics, Miami (2024). https://doi.org/10.18653/v1/2024.nllp-1.11. https://aclanthology.org/2024.nllp-1.11/

27. Nicol, D.J., Macfarlane-Dick, D.: Formative assessment and self-regulated learning: a model and seven principles of good feedback practice. Stud. High. Educ. **31**(2), 199–218 (2006). https://doi.org/10.1080/03075070600572090
28. Pacioni, E., Coman, A.C., Calvaresi, D., Manzo, G., Schumacher, M.I.: Agent-based hybrid AI models and technologies: a systematic literature review. IEEE Access **14**, 21148–21166 (2026). https://doi.org/10.1109/ACCESS.2026.3661027
29. Pan, L., Albalak, A., Wang, X., Wang, W.: Logic-LM: empowering large language models with symbolic solvers for faithful logical reasoning. In: Findings of the Association for Computational Linguistics: EMNLP 2023, pp. 3806–3824. Association for Computational Linguistics, Singapore (2023). https://doi.org/10.18653/v1/2023.findings-emnlp.248. https://aclanthology.org/2023.findings-emnlp.248/
30. Parkes, J., Harris, M.B.: The purposes of a syllabus. Coll. Teach. **50**(2), 55–61 (2002). https://doi.org/10.1080/87567550209595875
31. Sun, J., Luo, Z., Li, Y.: A compliance checking framework based on retrieval augmented generation. In: Proceedings of the 31st International Conference on Computational Linguistics, pp. 2603–2615. Association for Computational Linguistics, Abu Dhabi (2025). https://aclanthology.org/2025.coling-main.178/
32. Willard, B.T., Louf, R.: Efficient guided generation for large language models (2023). https://doi.org/10.48550/arXiv.2307.09702. arXiv preprint arXiv:2307.09702
33. Xiao, S., Liu, Z., Zhang, P., Muennighoff, N., Lian, D., Nie, J.Y.: C-pack: packed resources for general Chinese embeddings. In: Proceedings of the 47th International ACM SIGIR Conference on Research and Development in Information Retrieval, pp. 641–649. Association for Computing Machinery (2024). https://doi.org/10.1145/3626772.3657878
34. Yang, A., et al.: Qwen3 technical report (2025). https://doi.org/10.48550/arXiv.2505.09388. arXiv preprint arXiv:2505.09388
35. Yao, H., Xu, W., Turnau, J., Kellam, N., Wei, H.: Instructional agents: reducing teaching faculty workload through multi-agent instructional design. In: Proceedings of the 19th Conference of the European Chapter of the Association for Computational Linguistics, vol. 1: Long Papers, pp. 4087–4109. Association for Computational Linguistics, Rabat (2026). https://doi.org/10.18653/v1/2026.eacl-long.191. https://aclanthology.org/2026.eacl-long.191/
36. Zheng, L., et al.: Judging LLM-as-a-judge with MT-Bench and chatbot arena. In: Advances in Neural Information Processing Systems, vol. 36, pp. 46595–46623. Neural Information Processing Systems Foundation (2023). https://doi.org/10.52202/075280-2020. https://proceedings.neurips.cc/paper_files/paper/2023/hash/91f18a1287b398d378ef22505bf41832-Abstract-Datasets_and_Benchmarks.html

# Optimizing Input Representations for Word-in-Context: A Controlled Ablation Study

Claudio Daloiso(✉), Francesca Fallucchi, Manuel Gozzi, and Alessandro Ligi

Department of Engineering Sciences, Guglielmo Marconi University, 00193 Rome, Italy
claudio.daloiso.1994@gmail.com, {f.fallucchi,a.ligi}@unimarconi.it, m.gozzi@studenti.unimarconi.it

**Abstract.** The Word-in-Context (WiC) task requires deciding whether a target word carries the same meaning in two different sentential contexts. When fine-tuning Transformer encoders, a common and intuitive choice is to mark the target word with special tokens, on the assumption that this helps the model locate the relevant span. We test that assumption with a controlled $2 \times 2$ factorial ablation on SuperGLUE WiC, separating explicit target-span marking (span highlighting) from a lexical prefix that prepends the target word, and decompose the prefix to isolate the lemma from the part-of-speech (POS) tag. The design is evaluated on DeBERTa-large and RoBERTa-large with 5-fold cross-validation on the union of training and development splits ($N = 6066$), using McNemar's test, Holm–Bonferroni correction and bootstrap confidence intervals. Span highlighting provides no benefit and significantly degrades DeBERTa-large (removing the markers improves out-of-fold accuracy by 2.26 pp, $p_{\text{Holm}} < 0.001$), consistent with prior observations in relation extraction that in-vocabulary markers can match or outperform newly introduced special tokens. The lexical prefix significantly improves both backbones when markers are absent. Since the SuperGLUE WiC release exposes no usable POS field, the decomposition contrasts the target lemma against a constant control, and on RoBERTa-large the lemma is the active component. The contribution is a controlled, statistically grounded quantification of input-formatting choices frequently adopted without separate verification.

**Keywords:** Word-in-Context · Transformer Encoders · Span Highlighting · Ablation Study · Natural Language Processing

## 1 Introduction

Word-sense discrimination is a long-standing problem in computational linguistics: a word may take on different meanings depending on its context. The distributional view of meaning, summarised by Firth's dictum that one shall know


S. Bistarelli et al. (Eds.): AIxIA 2026, LNAI 17131, pp. 241–254, 2027.
https://doi.org/10.1007/978-3-032-40774-0_18

a word by the company it keeps [14], holds that the surrounding context rather than the word form in isolation determines the intended sense. The Word-in-Context (WiC) dataset operationalises this view as a binary task: given two sentences and a shared target word, a model must decide whether the word carries the same meaning in both contexts [1]. WiC was subsequently incorporated into SuperGLUE [2].

With the rise of Transformer encoders such as BERT, RoBERTa, and DeBERTa [3–5], sentence-pair classification tasks are typically addressed through supervised fine-tuning. Beyond the choice of backbone, the way the input is represented can also influence performance. A natural choice for WiC is to mark the target word with special tokens, for example "Do you want to come over to my <TW>place </TW> later?", on the intuition that explicit markers help the model focus on the relevant span. This strategy (span highlighting) is closely related to marking techniques used in relation extraction and other semantic tasks. Yet the special tokens are not part of the model's original pre-training distribution and must be learned during fine-tuning; moreover, their effect can be conflated with other signals such as a prefix prepending the target word. This motivates the central question: does explicit span highlighting genuinely improve WiC, or does the useful signal mainly come from a lexical prefix?

To answer this, we pose three research questions. First, does explicit span highlighting improve WiC over an otherwise identical input, or is it unnecessary or even harmful (RQ1)? Second, does a lexical prefix improve WiC, and does it interact with span highlighting (RQ2)? Third, within the prefix, is the active component the target lemma or the part-of-speech tag (RQ3)?

We address these questions with a $2 \times 2$ factorial ablation that separates span marking from the lexical prefix, and further decompose the prefix into its lemma and part-of-speech components. Throughout, the architecture is held constant by design: every condition uses the same backbone and the same standard sequence-classification head, so only the surface form of the input varies. A span-aware component—span pooling, a token-weighted loss, or an attention bias—would alter model and input together and confound the contrast this study isolates; such variants are a follow-up (Sect. 7). Our study contributes a controlled ablation of target-span marking and a lexical prefix on SuperGLUE WiC, evaluated on DeBERTa-large and RoBERTa-large under a frozen training configuration with 5-fold cross-validation on $N = 6066$ examples, together with a statistical analysis based on McNemar's test, Holm–Bonferroni correction, and bootstrap confidence intervals, and an error analysis of the headline effect.

Our main results are clear-cut. Span highlighting provides no benefit and significantly degrades DeBERTa-large (a 2.26 pp drop, $p_{\mathrm{Holm}} < 0.001$), whereas the lexical prefix significantly improves both backbones when markers are absent (up to +2.18 pp on RoBERTa-large). The target lemma, not the part-of-speech tag, carries the signal, and the effect of the markers is diffuse rather than concentrated on an identifiable subset.

The remainder of the paper is organised as follows. Section 2 reviews related work, Sect. 3 describes the data, input conditions, models and evaluation protocol, and Sect. 4 reports the per-condition results, the statistical analysis and the error analysis. Sections 5, 6 and 7 discuss the findings, state the limitations and conclude.

## 2 Related Work

WiC was introduced by Pilehvar and Camacho-Collados as a benchmark for context-sensitive representations of word meaning [1], and included in SuperGLUE as a challenging test of contextual lexical discrimination [2]. A relevant caveat for any input-side study is that WiC does not test context and target word symmetrically: Liu et al. [16] probe lexical-semantic datasets with masked inputs and find that WiC-style tasks exhibit a strong context bias, with models able to exploit dataset regularities. This matters for our work, because it means that a lexical anchor on the target word is not trivially expected to help, and that any benefit deserves explicit measurement rather than assumption.

These tasks are typically addressed by fine-tuning Transformer encoders: BERT introduced bidirectional pre-training with masked language modeling [3], RoBERTa improved the pre-training procedure [4], and DeBERTa introduced disentangled attention between content and position [5]. In WiC these models are used as cross-encoders, where the two sentences are concatenated and the target word is not automatically privileged, which motivates explicit localization or lexical signals.

Marking the target span is a familiar device in adjacent tasks. In relation extraction, *Matching the Blanks* demonstrated that entity-centric representations based on marked spans are effective [8], and, more directly relevant to our question, Zhou and Chen [12] systematically compare marking variants and distinguish between markers that introduce *new special tokens* and markers that reuse *in-vocabulary punctuation*; the punctuation-based variant, which adds no out-of-distribution tokens, is a strong baseline. This distinction directly anticipates our finding for WiC: when a marker is realised through tokens that the model has never seen in pre-training, the benefit of marking is not guaranteed. Within WiC and adjacent tasks, XL-LEXEME highlights the target word in a bi-encoder for lexical semantic change [9], and participants in the MCL-WiC shared task used signals on the target word in multilingual settings [10,11]; crucially, these systems *assume* highlighting to be beneficial and do not evaluate the contribution of the marking against a baseline without it. Our ablation addresses precisely this open question in the cross-encoder setting: the question is not whether to mark the target, but whether marking is necessary when compared to a simple lexical prefix. A related idea is the lexical anchor: GlossBERT prepends WordNet gloss definitions to the input context for word sense disambiguation [13], showing that an anchor placed before the sentence can guide the model toward the relevant word; unlike the prefix studied here, it relies on external sense inventories rather than the target lemma alone.

Overall, prior work motivates our study but does not isolate the contribution of span highlighting and lexical prefixing under a controlled protocol; Table 1 summarises this positioning. To the best of our knowledge, no prior work jointly isolates span highlighting and a lexical prefix in a $2 \times 2$ factorial ablation on SuperGLUE WiC, nor decomposes the prefix into lemma and POS components. We do not claim to introduce target marking, nor that newly initialized markers can underperform—an effect already documented in relation extraction [12]; our contribution is to establish it, under statistical control, in the WiC cross-encoder setting and to contrast marking against a lexical prefix.

**Table 1.** Representative prior work. Mark. = target/span marking; Pref. = lexical prefix; 2×2 = controlled factorial ablation.

| Work | Task | Method | Mark. | Pref. | 2×2 | Difference from our work |
|---|---|---|---|---|---|---|
| WiC [1] | WiC dataset | baselines | No | No | No | Defines the task; does not study input formatting |
| SenseBERT [7] | WiC | supersense pre-training | No | No | No | Modifies pre-training; ours is input-side only |
| Matching the Blanks [8] | relation extr. | entity markers | Yes | No | No | Marker usefulness in RE; we test on WiC |
| Zhou & Chen [12] | relation extr. | marker variants | Yes | No | No | Compares punctuation vs special-token markers in RE; we test marking vs a prefix on WiC |
| XL-LEXEME [9] | WiC/LSCD | SBERT + target highlight | Yes | No | No | Bi-encoder; does not ablate marking; no 2×2 |
| MCL-WiC [10,11] | MCL-WiC | signal on target word | Yes | No | No | Multilingual; we isolate it against the prefix |

# 3 Methodology

## 3.1 Task and Data

A WiC example is a quadruple $(s_1, s_2, w, y)$, where $s_1$ and $s_2$ are two sentences, $w$ is the target word present in both, and $y \in \{0, 1\}$ indicates same-sense usage. The model learns $f(s_1, s_2, w) \rightarrow y$. The dataset provides $w$ in its base form (the `word` field), which we refer to as the target lemma throughout. When fine-tuning a cross-encoder, the two sentences are concatenated with separator tokens, but $w$ is not explicitly privileged. We study two input-augmentation strategies:

- **Span highlighting** (a positional signal): the target occurrence in each sentence is wrapped with the special tokens <TW> and </TW>. These tokens are added to the tokenizer and their embeddings are learned from scratch during fine-tuning; they do not belong to the model's pre-training vocabulary.

- **Lexical prefix** (a lexical anchor): the target word (the dataset `word` field) is prepended to each sentence in the form `word (POS):`. This signal reuses in-vocabulary tokens and provides an explicit lexical cue without introducing new symbols.

**Table 2.** Six input conditions: four core (2×2 design) and two decomposition conditions.

| Condition | Span | Prefix type | Example |
|---|---|---|---|
| `full` | Yes | word + POS | `place (noun): ...my <TW>place</TW> later?` |
| `no_highlight` | No | word + POS | `place (noun): ...my place later?` |
| `no_prefix` | Yes | none | `...my <TW>place</TW> later?` |
| `plain` | No | none | `...my place later?` |
| *Prefix decomposition conditions:* | | | |
| `word_only` | No | word only | `place: ...my place later?` |
| `pos_only` | No | POS only | `(noun): ...my place later?` |

The two signals are not equivalent: markers introduce new tokens, whereas the prefix reuses in-vocabulary tokens.

We use the SuperGLUE version of WiC: 5,428 training, 638 development, and 1,400 test examples with hidden labels. At the time of writing, we could not obtain an official test-set score because no active official submission route was available to us; all results are on labelled data. Since our contribution is a within-backbone comparison under an identical protocol, this does not affect the validity of the contrasts.

### 3.2 Input Conditions and Prefix Decomposition

Table 2 shows the six input conditions. The four core conditions form the 2×2 factorial design; two additional conditions decompose the prefix. For the conditions with span highlighting, the tokens `<TW>` and `</TW>` are added to the tokenizer as special tokens and the embedding matrix is resized: the marker vectors are therefore initialized from scratch and learned entirely during fine-tuning.

The prefix has the surface form `word (POS):`. We verified the availability of the POS attribute directly in the data: the official SuperGLUE WiC release does not include a part-of-speech field. Across all 7,466 records (training, development, and test), no instance carries a POS attribute, so every example in our labelled pool resolves to the default tag *noun*. Consequently, the POS component of the prefix is a constant token that carries no lexical-class information, and the prefix is effectively lexical—it anchors the target lemma. The two decomposition conditions `word_only` and `pos_only` make this explicit: the former prepends only the lemma (`word:`); the latter prepends only the constant POS tag (`(noun):`), and thus acts as a negative control.

### 3.3 Models and Training

We evaluate `microsoft/deberta-large` [5] and `roberta-large` [4]. The hyperparameters (Table 3) were tuned once on DeBERTa-large with Optuna [15] and then kept frozen across all conditions and both backbones; within-backbone comparisons are fully comparable, while absolute cross-backbone comparisons must be interpreted with caution since RoBERTa-large was not tuned separately. No early stopping is used, to keep the training budget constant across conditions. Training is performed in FP32 for numerical stability with DeBERTa's disentangled attention mechanism.

The search space covered only the parameters governing how far and how fast the encoder departs from its pre-trained state—learning rate, warmup ratio, weight decay, hidden and attention dropout, label smoothing—since architectural choices lie outside an input-side study. Freezing the resulting configuration is itself part of the design. Because the markers `<TW>` and `</TW>` enter the model as freshly initialized embeddings, the marked conditions are more sensitive than the unmarked ones to the learning rate and the warmup schedule in particular. Tuning each condition separately would let every arm absorb part of that sensitivity into its own search, so a residual difference could be attributed to unequal tuning effort rather than to the input format; a single frozen configuration removes this degree of freedom.

**Table 3.** Main training configuration, kept frozen across all conditions and backbones.

| Parameter | Value |
|---|---|
| Backbones | `microsoft/deberta-large`, `roberta-large` |
| Max sequence length | 128 |
| Epochs | 4 |
| Precision | FP32 |
| Effective batch size | 16 |
| Learning rate | $8.6557 \times 10^{-6}$ |
| Weight decay | 0.0384 |
| Warmup ratio | 0.0760 |
| Hidden dropout | 0.0935 |
| Attention dropout | 0.0666 |
| Label smoothing | 0.0209 |
| Selection metric | accuracy |

### 3.4 Evaluation Protocol

An initial analysis on the development set ($n = 638$) suggested the trends reported below but had limited statistical power: under per-seed McNemar tests with Holm correction only the prefix effect on DeBERTa-large reached significance. We therefore adopt as our main analysis a 5-fold cross-validation (CV) on the union of training and development splits ($N = 6066$), which increases statistical power at the cost of comparability with the official splits (see Sect. 6). A single, fixed stratified cross-validation split[1] is reused across all conditions and backbones, so that the out-of-fold (OOF) prediction vectors remain paired and McNemar's test applies. For each fold, the best checkpoint is selected by held-out-fold accuracy; this is standard practice in cross-validation and introduces at most a small optimistic bias on absolute accuracy, while the within-fold paired contrasts are much less exposed to this bias, since the same selection strategy applies identically to all conditions within each fold. Execution order does not affect results because every run starts from a freshly initialized model with its own seed. Holm–Bonferroni correction is applied to the family of all 7 contrasts per backbone (4 factorial + 3 decomposition), as detailed in Table 5.

**Table 4.** Cross-validated OOF accuracy and F1 (5-fold, $N = 6066$), with mean ± std over folds and delta vs. `full`.

| Backbone | Condition | Acc. (%) | F1 (%) | Δ vs. full (pp) |
|---|---|---|---|---|
| DeBERTa-large | `full` | 78.55 ± 0.76 | 78.54 ± 0.75 | +0.00 |
| | `no_highlight` | 80.81 ± 1.58 | 80.77 ± 1.60 | +2.26 |
| | `no_prefix` | 78.52 ± 1.70 | 78.48 ± 1.70 | −0.03 |
| | `plain` | 79.29 ± 0.83 | 79.27 ± 0.84 | +0.74 |
| | `word_only` | 79.67 ± 1.60 | 79.63 ± 1.63 | +1.12 |
| | `pos_only` | 80.20 ± 1.36 | 80.16 ± 1.38 | +1.65 |
| RoBERTa-large | `full` | 77.37 ± 1.21 | 77.28 ± 1.22 | +0.00 |
| | `no_highlight` | 77.88 ± 1.14 | 77.83 ± 1.17 | +0.51 |
| | `no_prefix` | 76.66 ± 1.01 | 76.57 ± 0.98 | −0.71 |
| | `plain` | 75.70 ± 1.32 | 75.60 ± 1.34 | −1.67 |
| | `word_only` | 77.53 ± 1.40 | 77.48 ± 1.42 | +0.16 |
| | `pos_only` | 75.95 ± 1.19 | 75.82 ± 1.27 | −1.42 |

## 4 Experimental Results

### 4.1 Per-Condition Accuracy

Table 4 reports the 5-fold cross-validated accuracy and F1 for each condition. Two patterns are visible at the descriptive level. First, removing span highlighting does not hurt and on DeBERTa-large clearly helps: `no_highlight` achieves 80.81% OOF accuracy, 2.26 pp above `full`. Second, the prefix is beneficial: on both backbones `no_highlight` (prefix, no markers) is substantially above `plain` (no augmentation). Figure 1 visualises these results.

[1] The split uses a fixed random seed to ensure reproducibility across all runs.

## 4.2 Statistical Analysis of the Contrasts

Table 5 reports all 7 contrasts per backbone (4 factorial + 3 decomposition). Holm correction is applied to the family of all 7 contrasts per backbone jointly. Figure 2 gives a forest-plot view of the four core contrasts.

Span highlighting does not improve either backbone and significantly harms DeBERTa-large. On DeBERTa-large, `full` vs. `no_highlight` is $-2.26$ pp (CI $[-3.20, -1.30]$, $p_{\mathrm{Holm}} < 0.001$): adding the markers lowers accuracy significantly. On RoBERTa-large the same contrast is $-0.51$ pp and non-significant. In no setting does highlighting yield a statistically robust improvement.

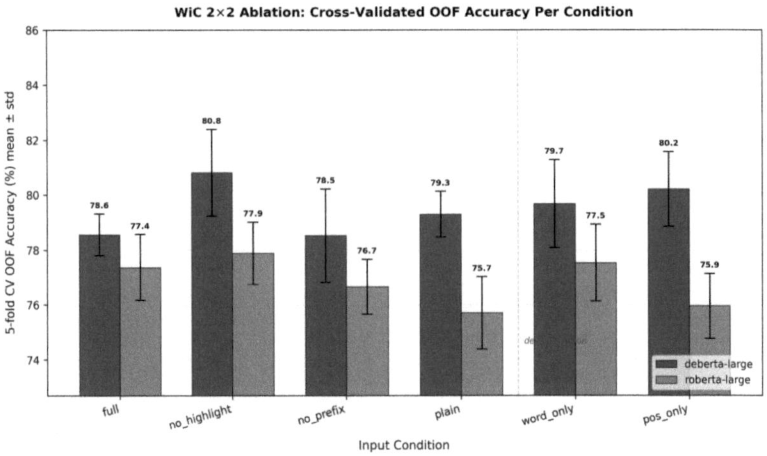


**Fig. 1.** Cross-validated OOF accuracy per input condition (5-fold, $N = 6066$), mean ± std over folds. The dashed vertical line separates the four core $2 \times 2$ conditions from the two prefix-decomposition conditions.

The lexical prefix significantly improves both backbones when span markers are absent. The `no_highlight` vs. `plain` contrast (prefix added, no markers) is positive and significant on both: $+1.52$ pp (CI $[+0.68, +2.34]$, $p_{\mathrm{Holm}} = 0.003$) on DeBERTa-large and $+2.18$ pp (CI $[+1.17, +3.15]$, $p_{\mathrm{Holm}} < 0.001$) on RoBERTa-large. An interaction is also present: the `full` vs. `no_prefix` contrast (prefix with highlighting) is non-significant on both backbones, suggesting that the markers partly mask the benefit of the prefix. The prefix is most useful when highlighting is absent.

The lemma, not the constant POS tag, drives the prefix effect on RoBERTa-large. On RoBERTa-large, `word_only` vs. `plain` is $+1.83$ pp ($p_{\mathrm{Holm}} = 0.001$); `pos_only` vs. `plain` is $+0.25$ pp (non-significant); `word_only` vs. `pos_only` is $+1.58$ pp ($p_{\mathrm{Holm}} = 0.006$). Since the POS tag is a constant (*noun*), this is the expected pattern of a negative control: the lemma carries the signal and the constant tag does not. These RoBERTa-large decomposition contrasts are

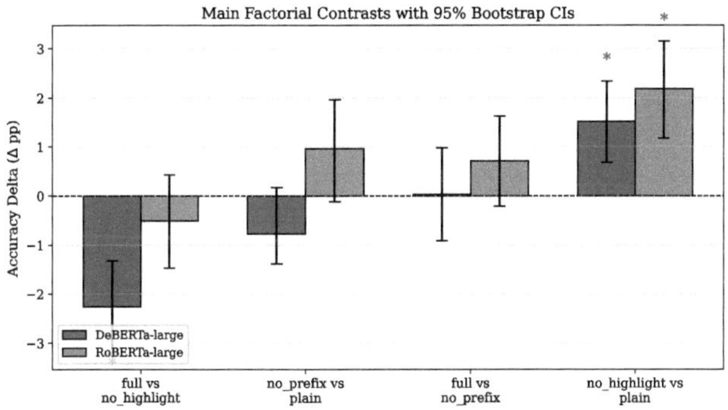


**Fig. 2.** Main factorial contrasts with 95% bootstrap confidence intervals (5-fold CV, $N = 6066$). For each contrast, $\Delta = \text{acc}(A) - \text{acc}(B)$ in percentage points; negative bars indicate that condition $B$ is more accurate. Asterisks mark contrasts that remain significant after Holm–Bonferroni correction ($p_{\text{Holm}} < 0.05$).

**Table 5.** Cross-validated contrasts (5-fold, $N = 6066$). Holm correction is applied to all 7 contrasts per backbone jointly. A checkmark in the Sig. column marks $p_{\text{Holm}} < 0.05$.

| Backbone | Contrast | Δ Acc. (pp) | 95% CI (pp) | $p_{\text{Holm}}$ | Sig. |
|---|---|---|---|---|---|
| DeBERTa-large | `full` vs. `no_highlight` | −2.26 | [−3.20, −1.30] | < 0.001 | ✓ |
| | `no_prefix` vs. `plain` | −0.77 | [−1.71, +0.16] | 0.456 | |
| | `full` vs. `no_prefix` | +0.03 | [−0.91, +0.97] | 0.972 | |
| | `no_highlight` vs. `plain` | +1.52 | [+0.68, +2.34] | 0.003 | ✓ |
| | `word_only` vs. `plain` | +0.38 | [−0.46, +1.24] | 0.808 | |
| | `pos_only` vs. `plain` | +0.91 | [+0.10, +1.71] | 0.159 | |
| | `word_only` vs. `pos_only` | −0.53 | [−1.35, +0.33] | 0.706 | |
| RoBERTa-large | `full` vs. `no_highlight` | −0.51 | [−1.45, +0.45] | 0.602 | |
| | `no_prefix` vs. `plain` | +0.96 | [−0.12, +1.96] | 0.308 | |
| | `full` vs. `no_prefix` | +0.71 | [−0.21, +1.63] | 0.419 | |
| | `no_highlight` vs. `plain` | +2.18 | [+1.17, +3.15] | < 0.001 | ✓ |
| | `word_only` vs. `plain` | +1.83 | [+0.86, +2.77] | 0.001 | ✓ |
| | `pos_only` vs. `plain` | +0.25 | [−0.66, +1.17] | 0.619 | |
| | `word_only` vs. `pos_only` | +1.58 | [+0.61, +2.51] | 0.006 | ✓ |

listed in Table 5. On DeBERTa-large no decomposition contrast reaches significance after Holm correction; in particular `pos_only` has a numerically higher delta than `word_only` on that backbone (+0.91 vs. +0.38 pp), which prevents a definitive claim. We therefore state the lemma finding as confirmed on RoBERTa-large only.

The 5-fold CV pools the official training and development splits and re-partitions them at random; because WiC reuses sentences and target words across examples, absolute OOF accuracy is not directly comparable to the official development or test sets, nor to leaderboard figures such as SenseBERT's 72.1% test accuracy [7]. For this reason we make no claim of leaderboard positioning and rely throughout on the within-fold paired contrasts, which remain valid since any distribution effect applies equally to all conditions on each fold.

For orientation, published accuracies on the official WiC test set place the BERT baseline of the SuperGLUE paper at 69.5% and the human estimate at 80.0% [2], with SenseBERT at 72.1% [7]. We deliberately do not tabulate our own accuracies alongside them, since the two quantities are computed on different data under different protocols. They do, however, indicate the regime at stake: the 7.9 pp separating the strongest of these systems from human performance is the headroom an input-side intervention competes for, and the 2.26 pp degradation caused by span markers consumes more than a quarter of it, in the wrong direction.

**Table 6.** Prediction agreement between `full` and `no_highlight` on DeBERTa-large (5-fold OOF, $N = 6066$). *Recovered* examples are classified correctly by `no_highlight` but not by `full`; *lost* examples are the opposite.

| | `no_highlight` correct | `no_highlight` wrong |
|---|---|---|
| `full` correct | 4398 | 367 (lost) |
| `full` wrong | 504 (recovered) | 797 |

### 4.3 Error Analysis

To understand *how* span highlighting changes predictions, rather than only its effect on aggregate accuracy, we examine the primary contrast on DeBERTa-large, `full` vs. `no_highlight`, at the level of individual out-of-fold predictions. Table 6 reports the agreement between the two conditions over the $N = 6066$ pooled examples.

Removing the markers recovers 504 examples while losing 367, a net gain of 137 correct predictions. This net difference corresponds exactly to the +2.26 pp out-of-fold gap reported in Sect. 4.2 (Table 5): the headline effect is the residual of two sizable, partially offsetting flows rather than a uniform shift.

We then tested whether the recovered and lost cases differ along simple, interpretable dimensions: we binned the relative position of the target word in each sentence as early, middle, or late, and flagged examples in which the target form occurs more than once. Neither feature separates the two groups: the position distributions are close (for instance, recovered cases have an early-position target in the first sentence 56.0% of the time against 50.1% for lost cases, with no comparable gap in the second sentence), and target repetition is negligible in both groups (below 1%). The effect of the markers is therefore diffuse rather than concentrated on an identifiable subset of examples.

Qualitatively, the discordant cases are ordinary polysemy pairs in both directions. A representative recovered example is *Roll out the paper.* vs. *The drawer rolled open.* (gold label: different senses), which `no_highlight` separates correctly and `full` does not; lost cases are of the same nature in the opposite direction. We did not identify a consistent linguistic property distinguishing when the markers help from when they hurt; this absence is itself informative, consistent with the special tokens perturbing the representation broadly rather than interfering with a specific phenomenon.

## 5 Discussion

The results challenge the intuitive assumption that explicitly marking the target word improves WiC: span highlighting yields no benefit on either backbone and significantly degrades DeBERTa-large. A plausible explanation concerns the nature of the signals. Span highlighting introduces special tokens absent from pre-training, initialized from scratch and learned on a small dataset; the lexical prefix instead reuses in-vocabulary tokens and provides an explicit lexical anchor. This reading is consistent with evidence from relation extraction, where Zhou and Chen [12] report that markers built from in-vocabulary punctuation can match or outperform markers that introduce new special tokens. Our results extend this observation to the WiC cross-encoder setting and quantify it with statistical control.

The decomposition sharpens this picture on RoBERTa-large. Since the SuperGLUE WiC release exposes no POS field, `pos_only` is a constant prefix acting as a negative control: it does not improve over `plain`, while `word_only` does and significantly outperforms `pos_only`, confirming that the benefit is lexical rather than an artifact of prepending any token. This is non-trivial given that WiC is known to carry a strong context bias [16], under which a target-side cue is not guaranteed to help. On DeBERTa-large the decomposition is inconclusive—`pos_only` numerically exceeds `word_only`, though neither contrast is significant—consistent with the encoder benefiting from any short prefix as a position cue, largely independent of its lexical content; separating this from a genuine part-of-speech effect would require the populated POS field the release lacks. An interaction reinforces the picture: the prefix helps most when highlighting is absent, suggesting the markers can interfere with the lexical anchor.

The error analysis in Sect. 4.3 both sharpens and bounds this interpretation. The 2.26 pp out-of-fold advantage of `no_highlight` is not a uniform improvement: removing the markers changes the prediction on roughly 14% of examples (504 recovered and 367 lost), and the reported figure is the net of these two flows. Crucially, the recovered and lost subsets are not separable by target position or by repetition of the target form, and we could not isolate a linguistic regime in which the markers are systematically harmful. This is consistent with the mechanism we propose: the out-of-vocabulary markers, initialized from scratch and learned on a small dataset, perturb DeBERTa-large's disentangled content–position attention broadly rather than disrupting a localized phenomenon. It also tempers any stronger reading: because the change is diffuse and partially self-cancelling, we characterise span highlighting as a net liability for this backbone, not as a targeted failure mode.

This interpretation is deliberately cautious: we have not analysed attention maps or conducted causal interventions, so we do not claim that the model literally looks at the prefix. A feature-attribution analysis quantifying which input regions drive the prediction would complement the accuracy-based evidence reported here, and is planned as a next step.

## 6 Limitations

No official test-set score was obtainable, as no active official submission route was available to us at the time of writing. The hyperparameters were tuned on DeBERTa-large and transferred to RoBERTa-large; within-backbone contrasts are valid, but absolute cross-backbone comparisons are not principled. The SuperGLUE WiC release exposes no POS field (verified across all 7,466 records), so we could not assess a genuine lexico-syntactic prefix; testing a real POS signal would require the original WiC distribution, which encodes a noun/verb distinction, or an external tagger. Relatedly, the design does not separate whether the benefit of the prefix arises from improved target localization, from easier optimization during fine-tuning, or from both. Checkpoint selection is based on held-out-fold accuracy, which may introduce a small optimistic bias on absolute OOF accuracy; the paired within-fold contrasts are much less exposed, since the same strategy applies identically to all conditions in each fold. Finally, the study covers only two encoder backbones, both used in a cross-encoder configuration; whether the same input-formatting effects hold for bi-encoder architectures—such as the one used by XL-LEXEME [9], where each context is encoded independently—remains an open question.

## 7 Conclusion and Future Work

We presented a controlled ablation of span highlighting and a lexical prefix for the Word-in-Context task, together with a prefix decomposition. Across a 5-fold cross-validation on two large encoders ($N = 6066$), span highlighting provided no benefit and significantly degraded DeBERTa-large, while the lexical prefix significantly improved both backbones when markers are absent; on RoBERTa-large the lemma, not the constant POS tag, is the active component, and the degradation caused by markers is diffuse rather than localized. The contribution is methodological: statistically grounded evidence on input-design choices often treated as implementation details.

Several directions remain open: submitting to the official test set once the platform is restored, and training on the full labelled pool (train + dev) as is standard after cross-validation; moving beyond passive marking by emphasizing the span through token-weighted losses or an attention bias, and re-initializing the `<TW> </TW>` embeddings from existing vocabulary tokens to test whether cold-start initialization is the source of the degradation; using the POS annotation of the original WiC distribution, or an external tagger, to assess a genuine lexico-syntactic prefix; extending to other tasks such as named-entity recognition; and including DeBERTa-v3 [6] to test whether the results generalize beyond masked-language-modeling pre-training.

**Acknowledgments.** The authors thank the supervisors and academic staff involved in the refinement of this work.

**Disclosure of Interests.** The authors have no competing interests to declare that are relevant to the content of this article.

## References

1. Pilehvar, M.T., Camacho-Collados, J.: WiC: the word-in-context dataset for evaluating context-sensitive meaning representations. In: Proceedings of NAACL-HLT 2019, pp. 1267–1273 (2019). https://doi.org/10.18653/v1/N19-1128
2. Wang, A., et al.: SuperGLUE: a stickier benchmark for general-purpose language understanding systems. In: Advances in NeurIPS, vol. 32, pp. 3261–3275 (2019)
3. Devlin, J., Chang, M.W., Lee, K., Toutanova, K.: BERT: pre-training of deep bidirectional transformers for language understanding. In: Proceedings of NAACL-HLT 2019, pp. 4171–4186 (2019). https://doi.org/10.18653/v1/N19-1423
4. Liu, Y., et al.: RoBERTa: a robustly optimized BERT pretraining approach (2019). arXiv:1907.11692
5. He, P., Liu, X., Gao, J., Chen, W.: DeBERTa: decoding-enhanced BERT with disentangled attention. In: International Conference on Learning Representations (ICLR) (2021)
6. He, P., Gao, J., Chen, W.: DeBERTaV3: improving DeBERTa using ELECTRA-style pre-training with gradient-disentangled embedding sharing. In: International Conference on Learning Representations (ICLR) (2023). arXiv:2111.09543
7. Levine, Y., et al.: SenseBERT: driving some sense into BERT. In: Proceedings of ACL 2020, pp. 4656–4667 (2020). https://doi.org/10.18653/v1/2020.acl-main.423
8. Baldini Soares, L., FitzGerald, N., Ling, J., Kwiatkowski, T.: Matching the blanks: distributional similarity for relation learning. In: Proceedings of ACL 2019, pp. 2895–2905 (2019). https://doi.org/10.18653/v1/P19-1279
9. Cassotti, P., Siciliani, L., De Gemmis, M., Semeraro, G., Basile, P.: XL-LEXEME: WiC pretrained model for cross-lingual lexical semantic change. In: Proceedings of ACL 2023 (Short Papers), pp. 1577–1585 (2023). https://doi.org/10.18653/v1/2023.acl-short.135
10. Martelli, F., Kalach, N., Tola, G., Navigli, R.: SemEval-2021 task 2: multilingual and cross-lingual word-in-context disambiguation (MCL-WiC). In: Proceedings of SemEval-2021, pp. 24–36 (2021). https://doi.org/10.18653/v1/2021.semeval-1.3
11. Gupta, R., Mundra, J., Mahajan, D., Modi, A.: MCL@IITK at SemEval-2021 task 2: multilingual and cross-lingual word-in-context disambiguation using augmented data, signals, and transformers. In: Proceedings of SemEval-2021, pp. 511–520 (2021). https://doi.org/10.18653/v1/2021.semeval-1.62
12. Zhou, W., Chen, M.: An improved baseline for sentence-level relation extraction In: Proceedings of AACL-IJCNLP 2022 (Short Papers), pp. 161–168 (2022)

13. Huang, L., Sun, C., Qiu, X., Huang, X.: GlossBERT: BERT for word sense disambiguation with gloss knowledge. In: Proceedings of EMNLP-IJCNLP 2019, pp. 3507–3512 (2019). https://doi.org/10.18653/v1/D19-1355
14. Firth, J.R.: A synopsis of linguistic theory, 1930–1955. In: Studies in Linguistic Analysis, pp. 1–32. Blackwell, Oxford (1957)
15. Akiba, T., Sano, S., Yanase, T., Ohta, T., Koyama, M.: Optuna: a next-generation hyperparameter optimization framework. In: Proceedings of 25th ACM SIGKDD International Conference on Knowledge Discovery and Data Mining, pp. 2623–2631 (2019). https://optuna.org
16. Liu, Q., McCarthy, D., Korhonen, A.: Measuring context-word biases in lexical semantic datasets. arXiv:2112.06733 (2021)

# Realizability Check for Pure Past Linear Temporal Logic on Finite Traces

Giuseppe De Giacomo[1], Sebastiano Dissegna[2], Marco Roveri[2(✉)], and Shufang Zhu[3]

[1] Department of Computer Science, University of Oxford, Oxford, UK
giuseppe.degiacomo@cs.ox.ac.uk
[2] Department of Information Engineering and Computer Science, University of Trento, Trento, Italy
{sebastiano.dissegna,marco.roveri}@unitn.it
[3] School of Computer Science and Informatics, University of Liverpool, Liverpool, UK
shufang.zhu@liverpool.ac.uk

**Abstract.** Pure-Past Linear-time Temporal Logic on finite traces ($\text{PPLTL}_\text{F}$) is an emerging formalism adopted in many fields of Artificial Intelligence (AI). It is as expressive as Linear-time Temporal Logic on finite traces ($\text{LTL}_\text{F}$), but it is exponentially more succinct. In this paper, we study the realizability check problem for $\text{PPLTL}_\text{F}$. We develop a symbolic backward search approach to the full-fledged $\text{PPLTL}_\text{F}$ realizability check. We implement the algorithm and perform an empirical experimental analysis on randomly generated $\text{PPLTL}_\text{F}$ formulas. We also compare our approach with the state-of-the-art $\text{LTL}_f$ synthesis tools Nike and SyftMax on equivalent formulas. The overall results show that our approach has merits and is promising.

## 1 Introduction

There has been significant attention in the research community directed towards synthesis [11,20] for realizing a specification $\varphi$ formulated in Linear-time Temporal Logic over finite traces ($\text{LTL}_\text{F}$) [15]. Synthesis consists of finding an agent strategy that generates a trace that, regardless of the (counter)strategy chosen by the environment, satisfies $\varphi$.

Pure-Past Linear-time Temporal Logic on finite traces ($\text{PPLTL}_\text{F}$) [8] has proved to be a quite effective formalism adopted in many fields of Artificial Intelligence [4,8]. The formulas in $\text{PPLTL}_\text{F}$ refer only to the present and past interpretations of their propositions. $\text{PPLTL}_\text{F}$ is as expressive as $\text{LTL}_\text{F}$ but is exponentially more succinct than it [8] (the best known translation algorithm requires $3EXPTIME$). However, the Alternating Finite-state Automaton (AFA) and the Deterministic Finite-state Automaton (DFA) corresponding to a $\text{PPLTL}_\text{F}$ formula can be computed in linear time and in single exponential time, respectively, directly from the formula [8]. $\text{PPLTL}_\text{F}$ synthesis is EXPTIME-complete [8]. These results have been exploited in the setting of deterministic planning domains with $\text{PPLTL}_\text{F}$ goals [4].


S. Bistarelli et al. (Eds.): AIxIA 2026, LNAI 17131, pp. 255–265, 2027.
https://doi.org/10.1007/978-3-032-40774-0_19

In this paper, we make the following contributions. First, we build a symbolic DFA for a PPLTL$_F$ formula $\varphi$ using the approach discussed in [8]. Second, we devise a symbolic algorithm that resembles the one used for strong planning [7] to compute the winning states for an adversarial reachability game on the DFA and show how to use it to solve the PPLTL$_F$ realizability problem. Third, we implement the algorithm with BDDs [5] in two tools: i) a naive C++ implementation (referred to BASE-LINE hereafter), and, ii) another implementation within the NUSMV model checker [6]. Finally, we performed an experimental analysis that compared BASE-LINE and NUSMV with the latest LTL$_F$ synthesis tools on equivalent random PPLTL$_F$ and LTL$_F$ formulas. We also performed a more extensive analysis by increasing the temporal depth of the formulas and the number of atomic propositions. The results show that our approach is viable and that NUSMV scales better than the naive BASE-LINE.

## 2 Background

**PPLTL$_F$ Basics.** Pure-Past Linear-time Temporal Logic on finite traces (PPLTL$_F$) [8] is the counterpart of Pure-Past Linear-time Temporal Logic (PPLTL) [17], which is interpreted over finite traces rather than on infinite traces like PPLTL. The formulas in PPLTL$_F$ refer only to the present and past interpretations of their propositions. It is as expressive as Linear-time Temporal Logic on finite traces (LTL$_F$), but it is exponentially more succinct [8].

**Syntax.** Given a finite set $\mathcal{P}$ of atomic propositions, PPLTL$_F$ is defined by:

$$\varphi := p \mid \neg\varphi_1 \mid \varphi_1 \wedge \varphi_2 \mid \mathbf{Y}\,\varphi_1 \mid \varphi_1\,\mathbf{S}\,\varphi_2$$

where, $p \in \mathcal{P}$ is an atom; $\wedge$ (And) and $\neg$ (Not) are Boolean connectives, $\mathbf{Y}$ (*Yesterday*) and $\mathbf{S}$ (*Since*) are temporal connectives. We use the usual abbreviations $\bot \equiv p \wedge \neg p$, $\top \equiv \neg\bot$, $\mathbf{Z}\,\varphi \equiv \neg\mathbf{Y}\,\neg\varphi$ (*Weak yesterday*), $\varphi_1 \vee \varphi_2 \equiv \neg(\neg\varphi_1 \wedge \neg\varphi_2)$, $\mathbf{O}\,\varphi \equiv (\top\,\mathbf{S}\,\varphi)$ (*Once*), and $\mathbf{H}\,\varphi \equiv \neg\,\mathbf{O}\,\neg\varphi$ (*Historically*). Hereafter $\boldsymbol{subf}(\varphi)$ denotes the set of subformulas of $\varphi$. A formula $\varphi$ is a *proper temporal formula* if and only if the top-level operator is a temporal operator.

**Semantics.** PPLTL$_F$ formulas are evaluated over *histories*, which are finite nonempty traces, defined as a sequence $\tau = s_o, .., s_n$, where each $s_i$ is a propositional interpretation over the alphabet $2^P$. With $len(\tau)$ we denote the length $n+1$ of $\tau$. The subtrace $\tau_{i,j}$ with $0 \le i \le j \le n$ can be obtained from a trace $\tau$ starting at position $i$ and ending at position $j$. The satisfaction relation $\tau, i \models \varphi$, which states that $\varphi$ holds in position $i$ is defined as follows:

- $\tau, i \models p$ if and only if $len(\tau) \ge 1$ and $p \in s_i$ (for $p \in \mathcal{P}$);
- $\tau, i \models \neg\varphi$ if and only if $\tau, i \not\models \varphi$;
- $\tau, i \models \varphi_1 \wedge \varphi_2$ if and only if $\tau, i \models \varphi_1$ and $\tau, i \models \varphi_2$;
- $\tau, i \models \mathbf{Y}\,\varphi$ if and only if $i \ge 1$ and $\tau, i-1 \models \varphi$;
- $\tau, i \models \varphi_1\,\mathbf{S}\,\varphi_2$ if and only if there exists $k$, with $0 \le k \le i < len(\tau)$ such that $\tau, k \models \varphi_2$ and for all $j$, with $k < j \le i$ we have that $\tau, j \models \varphi_1$.

A $\text{PPLTL}_\text{F}$ formula $\varphi$ is said to be *true* in $\tau$, written $\tau \models \varphi$, given $l = len(\tau)$, if and only if $\tau, l-1 \models \varphi$, that is, $\varphi$ holds in the very last state of history.

**Previous Normal Form.** Dually to the forward case [9], $\text{PPLTL}_\text{F}$ formulas can be rewritten into present and past components, aka Previous Normal Form(PNF) [4] by recursively applying the $\boldsymbol{pnf}(\cdot)$ defined as follows:

- $\boldsymbol{pnf}(p) = p$, where $p \in \mathcal{P}$;
- $\boldsymbol{pnf}(\neg\varphi) = \neg\boldsymbol{pnf}(\varphi)$;
- $\boldsymbol{pnf}(\varphi_1 \wedge \varphi_2) = \boldsymbol{pnf}(\varphi_1) \wedge \boldsymbol{pnf}(\varphi_2)$;
- $\boldsymbol{pnf}(\mathbf{Y}\,\varphi) = \mathbf{Y}\,\varphi$;
- $\boldsymbol{pnf}(\varphi_1\,\mathbf{S}\,\varphi_2) = \boldsymbol{pnf}(\varphi_2) \vee (\boldsymbol{pnf}(\varphi_1) \wedge \mathbf{Y}(\varphi_1\,\mathbf{S}\,\varphi_2))$.

$\boldsymbol{pnf}(\cdot)$ can be trivially extended to handle the other connectives. The formulas in PNF have proper temporal subformulas appearing only in the scope of the $\mathbf{Y}$ operator, and the formulas in the form $\mathbf{Y}\,\psi$ in $\boldsymbol{pnf}(\varphi)$ are such that $\psi \in \boldsymbol{subf}(\varphi)$.

**Theorem 1.** **( [4]).** *Every $\text{PPLTL}_\text{F}$ formula $\varphi$ can be converted into its PNF form in linear time to the size of the formula; the resulting formula is equivalent to $\varphi$.*

**$\text{PPLTL}_\text{F}$ Realizability.** The problem of $\text{PPLTL}_\text{F}$ realizability is described as a tuple $(\varphi, \mathcal{X}, \mathcal{Y})$, where $\varphi$ is a $\text{PPLTL}_\text{F}$ formula such that $P = \mathcal{X} \cup \mathcal{Y}$, and $\mathcal{X}$, $\mathcal{Y}$ are two disjoint sets of variables controlled by the environment and the agent, respectively. Sometimes, for simplicity, we do not explicitly mention $\mathcal{X}$ and $\mathcal{Y}$ if they are clear from the context.

**Definition 1.** *The* realizability problem $(\varphi, \mathcal{X}, \mathcal{Y})$ *aims to answer whether there exists an agent strategy $g : (2^{\mathcal{X}})^* \rightarrow 2^{\mathcal{Y}}$ such that for an arbitrary infinite sequence $\tau = X_0, X_1, ... \in (2^{\mathcal{Y}})^\omega$, we can find a $k \geq 0$ such that $\tau^k \models \varphi$ where $\tau^k = (X_0 \cup g(\epsilon)), (X_1 \cup g(X_0)), ..., (X_k \cup g(X_0, ..., X_{k-1}))$. If such a strategy does not exist, then $\varphi$ is unrealizable.*

$\text{PPLTL}_\text{F}$ realizability can be performed by computing the reverse Alternating Finite-state Automaton (AFA) for $\varphi$, computing the Deterministic Finite-state Automaton (DFA) for the reversed AFA for $\varphi$, and then synthesizing a winning strategy for an adversarial reachability game on the DFA [8]. $\text{PPLTL}_\text{F}$ synthesis is EXPTIME-complete, which is exponentially better than for $\text{LTL}_\text{F}$ [15] and LTL over infinite traces [20].

## 3 PPLTL Realizability

In this section, we first show how to build a symbolic representation of the DFA for a $\text{PPLTL}_\text{F}$ realizability problem $(\varphi, \mathcal{X}, \mathcal{Y})$, and then we show an algorithm to compute the winning states of the adversarial reachability game on the DFA (hereafter, for simplicity, we refer to as the DFA game) and use it to solve the realizability problem.

**Definition 2.** *The* syntactic closure $CL_\varphi$ *of a PPLTL$_F$ formula* $\varphi$ *in PNF form is inductively defined as follows:* $\varphi \in CL_\varphi$, $\psi \in CL_\varphi$ *and* $\psi$ *is not of the form* $\neg\chi$ *implies* $\neg\psi \in CL_\varphi$, $\neg\psi \in CL_\varphi$ *implies* $\psi \in CL_\varphi$, $\psi_1 \wedge \psi_2 \in CL_\varphi$ *implies* $\psi_1, \psi_2 \in CL_\varphi$, $\mathbf{Y}\,\psi \in CL_\varphi$ *implies* $\psi \in CL_\varphi$, $\psi_1 \,\mathbf{S}\, \psi_2 \in CL_\varphi$ *implies* $\psi_1, \psi_2 \in CL_\varphi$.

The cardinality of $CL_\varphi$ is linear in the size of $\varphi$.

We remark that $CL_\varphi$ could not be replaced by $\boldsymbol{subf}(\varphi)$. Let us consider a PPLTL$_F$ formula $\varphi$, $CL_\varphi$ denotes the syntactic closure of $\varphi$, while $\boldsymbol{subf}(\varphi)$ denotes the set of *all formulas* (including sub-formulas) of $\varphi$. Take $\varphi = \psi_1 \,\mathbf{S}\, \psi_2$ for example, $CL_\varphi = \{\psi_1 \,\mathbf{S}\, \psi_2, \neg(\psi_1 \,\mathbf{S}\, \psi_2), \psi_1, \neg\psi_1, \psi_2, \neg\psi_2\}$, while $\boldsymbol{subf}(\varphi) = \{\psi_1 \,\mathbf{S}\, \psi_2, \psi_1, \psi_2\}$.

**Algorithm 1:** *Check_Realizability*$(\varphi, \mathcal{X}, \mathcal{Y})$

**Input**: $(\varphi, \mathcal{X}, \mathcal{Y})$, the realizability problem
**Output**: *realizable* a Boolean value

1 $\phi := \boldsymbol{pnf}(\varphi)$;
2 $A_\phi :=$ BUILDDFA$(\phi)$;
3 **return** CHECKREALIZABILITY$(A_\phi, \mathcal{X}, \mathcal{Y})$;

**Definition 3.** *Given a PPLTL$_F$ formula* $\varphi$ *in PNF form on a set of Boolean variables* $\mathcal{P}$, *we define the function* $\boldsymbol{syst}(\varphi)$ *to return a formula that evaluates the truth value of* $\varphi$ *given the propositional interpretations at current and previous instants of the propositional atoms of* $\varphi$ *as follows:*

- $\boldsymbol{syst}(p) = p$, *where* $p \in \mathcal{P}$ *is a Boolean variable;*
- $\boldsymbol{syst}(\neg\varphi) = \neg\boldsymbol{syst}(\varphi)$;
- $\boldsymbol{syst}(\varphi_1 \wedge \varphi_2) = \boldsymbol{syst}(\varphi_1) \wedge \boldsymbol{syst}(\varphi_2)$;
- $\boldsymbol{syst}(\mathbf{Y}\,\varphi) =$ "$\mathbf{Y}\,\varphi$", *where* "$\mathbf{Y}\,\varphi$" $\notin \mathcal{P}$ *is a fresh Boolean variable representing the truth of* $\mathbf{Y}\,\varphi$.

**Symbolic DFA.** Given a PPLTL$_F$ formula $\varphi$ in PNF form over Boolean variables $\mathcal{P}$, we can obtain a symbolic DFA $A_\varphi = \langle \mathcal{P}, Q, q_0, T, q_f \rangle$ in linear time on the size of the formula as follows:

- $Q = \{\text{"}\mathbf{Y}\,\psi_i\text{"} \mid \mathbf{Y}\,\psi_i \in CL_\varphi\} \cup \{Final\}$;
- $q_0 = \neg Final \wedge \bigwedge_{\mathbf{Y}\,\psi_i \in CL_\varphi} \neg\text{"}\mathbf{Y}\,\psi_i\text{"}$;
- $T = (\bigwedge_{\mathbf{Y}\,\psi_i \in CL_\varphi} (\boldsymbol{syst}(\psi_i) \leftrightarrow \boldsymbol{syst}'(\mathbf{Y}\,\psi_i)) \wedge (Final' \leftrightarrow (Final \vee \boldsymbol{syst}(\varphi))))$;
- $q_f = Final$.

Where $\boldsymbol{syst}'(\cdot)$ introduces a fresh Boolean variable "$\mathbf{Y}\,\psi_i$"$'$ (*primed version*) for each variable "$\mathbf{Y}\,\psi_i$" such that $\mathbf{Y}\,\psi_i \in CL_\varphi$, and $Final'$ is a fresh Boolean variable representing the prime version of $Final$. The states of the DFA $A_\varphi$ consist of all possible complete assignments to the variables in $Q$. A generic Boolean formula $\psi$ on the variables $Q$ is such that its models (complete satisfying assignments to the variables in $Q$, making $\psi$ true) represent the corresponding states of the DFA. Thus, $\bot$ denotes the empty set of states, while $\top$ denotes all the possible states of the automaton. Intuitively, we expect that in the initial state, all the $\mathbf{Y}\,\psi_i \in CL_\varphi$ evaluate as false, and thus the "$\mathbf{Y}\,\psi_i$" are false to capture this. Similarly, $Final$ initially is false. $T$ is a formula that encodes the transition function of the DFA $A_\varphi$, i.e., we can move from a state $q$ to a state $q'$, if the state $q'$ "agrees on the past" of the formulas in state $q$. For example, if $q \models \psi$, then $q' \models$ "$\mathbf{Y}\,\psi$" must be valid. Moreover, $T$ also encodes the transition into the accepting state (if in the previous state "$\mathbf{Y}\,\varphi$" holds, or if we are already in the accepting state and we remain there). Notice that $q_0$ is a formula over the $Q$ variables. $T$ is a formula over the variables $Q$, $Q'$, and $\mathcal{P}$.

**Realizability Algorithm.** The algorithm for solving a realizability problem for a PPLTL$_\mathrm{F}$ formula $\varphi$ is described in Algorithm 1. First, we compute the equivalent PNF formula $\phi$ for $\varphi$ using the $\boldsymbol{pnf}(\cdot)$ function. Then we call the function BUILDDFA which computes the symbolic DFA for $\varphi$ as discussed previously. Finally, we call the function CHECKREALIZABILITY which is responsible for solving the DFA game and answer whether the original PPLTL$_\mathrm{F}$ realizability problem is realizable.

**Algorithm 2:** *CheckRealizability($A_\phi, \mathcal{X}, \mathcal{Y}$)*

**Input**: $A_\phi = \langle \mathcal{P}, Q, q_0, T, q_f \rangle$, the symbolic DFA
**Input**: $\mathcal{X}, \mathcal{Y}$ the enviroment and agent variables resp.
**Output**: *realizable* a Boolean value
1 $OldWin := \bot$;
2 $Win := q_f$;
3 $realizable := FALSE$;
4 **while** ($Win \neq OldWin$ ***and not*** $realizable$) **do**
5     $OldWin = Win$;
6     $Win :=$ STRONGPREIMAGE($A_\phi, \mathcal{X}, \mathcal{Y}, Win) \vee OldWin$;
7     **if** $(q_0 \wedge \neg Win) == false$ **then**
8         $realizable := TRUE$;
9 **return** $realizable$;

The function CHECKREALIZABILITY is described in Algorithm 2. Intuitively, the algorithm performs a backward least fixpoint computation starting from the final state $q_f$ by applying the STRONGPREIMAGE operator that computes the one backward step winning states from a set of winning states and accumulates them. The least fixpoint terminates when the initial state is included in the set of winning states computed so far ($q_0 \wedge \neg Win = false$, line 7) or when STRONGPREIMAGE does not add any new winning state ($Win \neq OldWin$, line 4).

The STRONGPREIMAGE is defined as follows.

$$\text{StrongPreImage}(A_\phi, \mathcal{X}, \mathcal{Y}, Win) = \exists \mathcal{Y}.\forall \mathcal{X}.\forall Q'.(T(Q, \mathcal{X}, \mathcal{Y}, Q') \rightarrow Win[Q'/Q]) \quad (1)$$

$Win$ is a formula over $Q$ variables, and with $Win[Q'/Q]$ we denote the parallel substitution of each variable in $Q$ with the corresponding primed variable in $Q'$. In this formulation of the game, the agent plays first, and then the environment plays.[1] Intuitively, it computes all the automaton states $q$ such that there is a choice for the agent ($\mathcal{Y}$) that for any move of the environment ($\mathcal{X}$) following the automaton transition relation we end up in a winning state $q'$ (satisfying $Win$). The following theorem guarantees that StrongPreimage is monotonic.

**Theorem 2.** *Let* $A_\phi = \langle \mathcal{P}, Q, q_0, T, q_f \rangle$ *be the symbolic DFA constructed as above,* $Win_1$ *and* $Win_2$ *be two formulas over* $Q$ *such that* $Win_2 \rightarrow Win_1$*, we have that* $\text{StrongPreimage}(A_\phi, \mathcal{X}, \mathcal{Y}, Win_2) \rightarrow \text{StrongPreimage}(A_\phi, \mathcal{X}, \mathcal{Y}, Win_1)$.

*Proof.* Trivial consequence of Eq. 1. □

**Theorem 3.** *Algorithm 2 eventually terminates.*

*Proof.* Trivial consequence of Theorem 2 and of the Tarski theorem for the computation of the least fixpoint with a monotonic function over a finite set of states. □

**Theorem 4.** *Algorithm 2 returns true iff there is a winning strategy for the agent in the DFA game* $A_\phi$*, false otherwise.*

*Proof.* (Sketch) Eq. 1 computes all the automaton states $q$ such that there is a choice for the agent ($\mathcal{Y}$) that for any move of the environment ($\mathcal{X}$) following the automaton transition relation we end up in a winning state $q'$ (satisfying $Win$). Algorithm 2 starts from the winning states (satisfying $q_f$) and applies Eq. 1 until the winning states include the initial states of the DFA (the specification is realizable since there is a strategy for the agent to reach $q_f$ regardless of the environment), or a fixpoint has been reached (the specification is therefore unrealizable). □

These results allow us to conclude that Algorithm 1 eventually terminates and is correct.

**Corollary 1.** *Algorithm 1 eventually terminates, and returns true iff the* $PPLTL_F$ *realizabilty problem* $(\varphi, \mathcal{X}, \mathcal{Y})$ *is realizable, false otherwise.*

The proof is a direct consequence of the following facts: i) $\phi = \boldsymbol{pnf}(\varphi)$ builds an equivalent formula; ii) $A_\phi$ is the DFA recognizing $\phi$ (thus also $\varphi$); iii) $\text{CheckRealizability}(A_\phi, \mathcal{X}, \mathcal{Y}, q_f)$ terminates and returns true if the DFA game admits a winning strategy for the agent (Theorem 4).

**Theorem 5.** *The* $PPLTL_F$ *realizability problem is EXPTIME-complete.*

*Proof.* (Sketch) Computation of the symbolic DFA for a $\text{PPLTL}_\text{F}$ formula is EXPTIME [8]. Indeed, the states in the symbolic DFA are complete assignments to the state variables in $Q$ (hence, exponentially many assignments), and the number of state variables in $Q$ is linear in the size of a formula $\text{PPLTL}_\text{F}$.

[1] We remark that it is also possible to consider the case where the environment plays first, and then the agent plays.

Consequently, the symbolic DFA construction takes an exponential time in the size of the PPLTLf formula. Algorithm 2 is linear. It has been shown in [8] that solving planning with Fully Observable Planning Domain (FOND) for $\text{PPLTL}_\text{F}$ goals is EXPTIME-complete in the size of the $\text{PPLTL}_\text{F}$ formula, which can be considered as a special case of $\text{PPLTL}_\text{F}$ realizability. We thus conclude that $\text{PPLTL}_\text{F}$ realizability is EXPTIME-complete. □

# 4 Related Works

To our knowledge, this is the first work that addresses the problem of realizability specifically for $\text{PPLTL}_\text{F}$. The complexity of this problem in its general case ($\text{LTL}_\text{F}$ and LTL synthesis) is known to be $2EXPTIME$. In order to reduce it, usually only some specific fragments of LTL are considered. This is the case

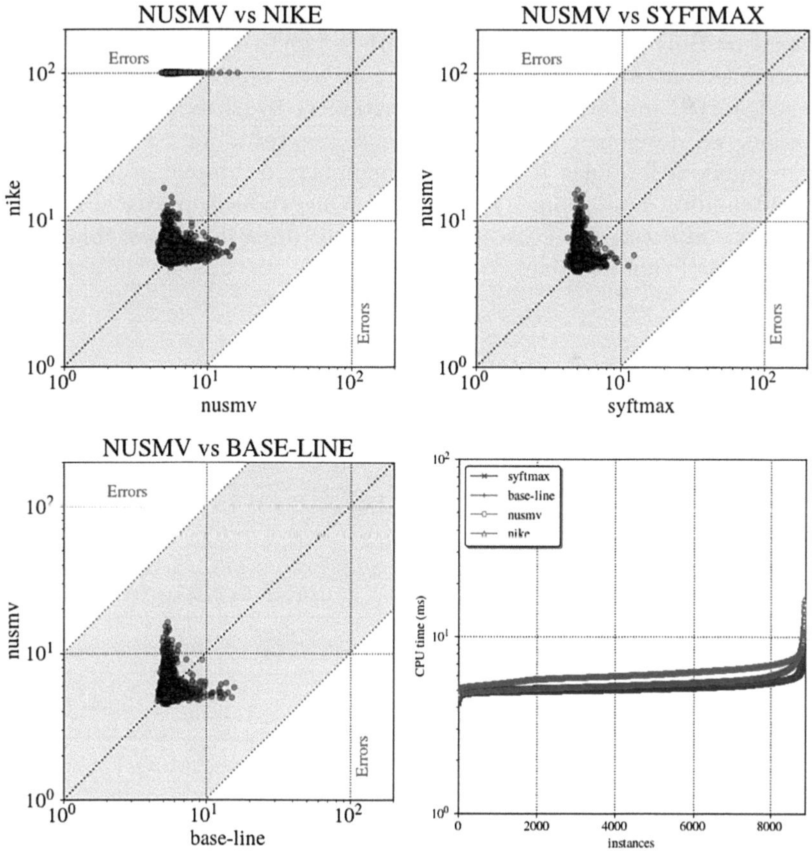


**Fig. 1.** Experimental results for a data set of 10k $\text{PPLTL}_\text{F}$ formulas of temporal depth 2 and average size of $|P|$ equals 2.18. Time is in milliseconds (ms). In the scatter plots, red is used for unrealizable, while blue for realizable. The lower right plot is the survival plot for this set of experiments. (Color figure online)

of [3,12,22] where safety-LTL specifications are addressed. Other works worth mentioning are [8] showing the advantages and proving the expressivity of this logic, and [4] to face the problem of planning for Temporally Extended Goals with goals expressed in $\mathrm{PPLTL_F}$ where the previous normal form is introduced. The last work that has been of great inspiration for this is [7], where Strong Planning is addressed through symbolic techniques. Realizability for $\mathrm{PPLTL_F}$ can also be performed with state-of-the-art $\mathrm{LTL}_f$ realizability checkers such as NIKE [10] or SYFTMAX [23] by computing for a given $\mathrm{PPLTL_F}$ formula $\varphi$ an equivalent $\mathrm{LTL_F}$ $\varphi'$ using the approach discussed in [8]. However, all of these approaches face a 3EXPTIME complexity blow-up to build the equivalent $\mathrm{LTL_F}$ formula.

## 5 Experimental Analysis

We implemented Algorithm 1 within the NUSMV symbolic model checker [6] leveraging on Binary Decision Diagrams (BDDs) [5] to encode the symbolic DFA and to implement Algorithm 2. Moreover, we also implemented BASE-LINE, a C++ naive BDD implementation of Algorithm 1. To perform the experimental evaluation, we developed a random formula generator for $\mathrm{PPLTL_F}$ that can generate random formulas with different numbers of atomic propositions and different temporal depths. Since the generator can produce unsatisfiable $\mathrm{PPLTL_F}$ formulas, we also run the BLACK solver [13] to discard unsatisfiable formulas (that are trivially unrealizable). Whenever possible, we compare the performance

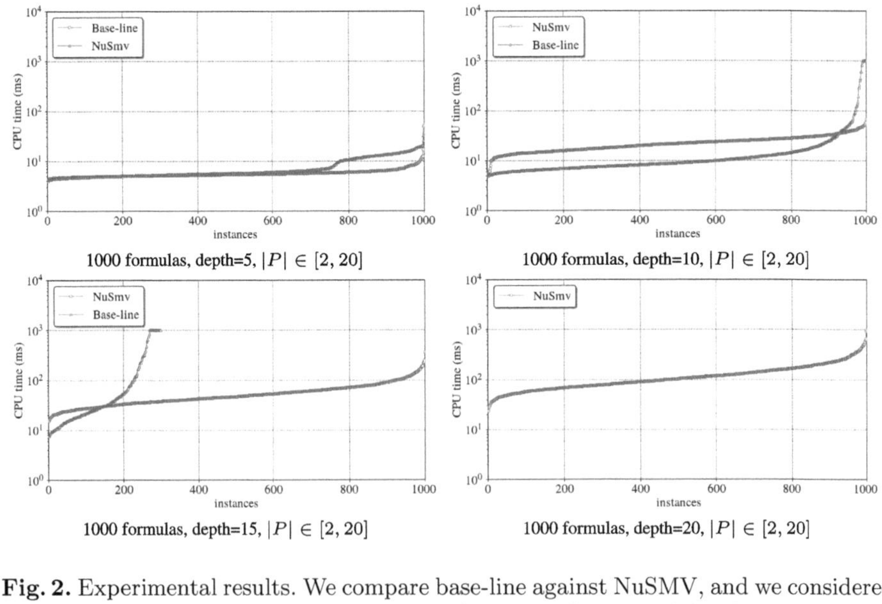


**Fig. 2.** Experimental results. We compare base-line against NuSMV, and we considered four dataset each consisting of 1k $\mathrm{PPLTL_F}$ formulas of temporal depths: 5, 10, 15, 20 with $|P|$ in the range [2,20]. Time is in milliseconds (ms).

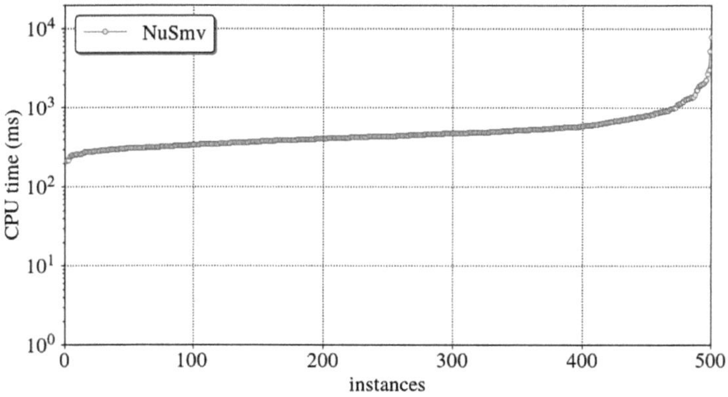


**Fig. 3.** Search time (ms), temporal depth 2, and average $|P| = 54$.

of our implementations in NuSMV and in Base-line with the state-of-the-art $\text{LTL}_\text{F}$ synthesis tools Nike and SyftMax. For this comparison, the random formula generator follows the patterns discussed in [14] to compute the equivalent $\text{LTL}_\text{F}$ formulas. All experiments were carried out on a laptop equipped with an Intel (R) Core (TM) i7-13700H and 32 GB of RAM. The program was executed in the WSL environment using a Python script. The code and all the experiments are available at https://github.com/sebdisdv/NuSMVPPLTLfSynth.

To compare NuSMV with Nike, Base-line, and SyftMax, a data set of 10k $\text{PPLTL}_\text{F}$ formulas of temporal depth 2 and average size of $|P|$ equals 2.18 was created along with their future equivalent counterpart. The results are reported in Fig. 1 (time is in milliseconds (ms)). The results show that in these small formulas the four tools have very similar performance. NuSMV, Base-line, and SyftMax always agree on the answer, while there are 1148 unrealizable cases where Nike gave realizable as answer (reported as an error in the graph).[2]

Then to evaluate the scalability of our solution we created four datasets of 1k $\text{PPLTL}_\text{F}$ formulas of temporal depths: 5, 10, 15, 20 with $|P|$ in the range [2,20], and one with an average $|P|$ of 54, but of temporal depth 2. For all of these experiments, the memory limit was the natural limit of the machine on which the experiments were run. We did not test with Nike and SyftMax since the generation of equivalent $\text{LTL}_\text{F}$ formulas was too demanding using the patterns, and it required the 3EXPTIME conversion that we did not implement in the random formula generator. The results (survival plots) are plotted in Fig. 2. Although for formulas of depth 5 the performances of NuSMV and Base-line are similar, moving at depth 10 NuSMV was able to solve the same number of problems of Base-line but faster. Increasing further the temporal depth to 15, Base-line was only able to solve 220 instances, while it run out of memory in all the other cases. For the cases of temporal depth 20, Base-line always

[2] We manually checked many of these cases and concluded that Nike provided a wrong answer.

went memory-out, while NuSMV succeeded in solving all the problems. The cases with an average $|P|$ of 54 and a temporal depth of 2 were solved only by NuSMV (see Fig. 3).

## 6 Conclusions and Future Work

In this paper, we develop a symbolic algorithm for the $\text{PPLTL}_\text{F}$ realizability check. The experiments show that on small formulas our tools are effective on equivalent $\text{LTL}_\text{F}$ formulas w.r.t. state-of-the-art tools. The implementation of NuSMV also scales well on larger formulas.

The approach can be extended in different directions. First, implementation-wise, we may consider optimizations of StrongPreimage to leverage optimizations typical of model checking like, e.g. conjunctive partitioning [16,18,19]. We can also consider extending the work to i) consider best-effort synthesis under multiple environment specifications [1], ii) maximally permissive strategies [21], and iii) dominant strategies [2]. We leave these for future work.

## References


1. Aminof, B., De Giacomo, G., Lomuscio, A., Murano, A., Rubin, S.: Synthesizing best-effort strategies under multiple environment specifications. In: KR, pp. 42–51 (2021)
2. Aminof, B., De Giacomo, G., Rubin, S.: Reactive synthesis of dominant strategies. In: AAAI, pp. 6228–6235. AAAI Press (2023)
3. Bansal, S., De Giacomo, G., Di Stasio, A., Li, Y., Vardi, M.Y., Zhu, S.: Compositional safety LTL synthesis. In: VSTTE, vol. 13800, pp. 1–19, Springer, Cham (2022)
4. Bonassi, L., De Giacomo, G., Favorito, M., Fuggitti, F., Gerevini, A.E., Scala, E.: Planning for temporally extended goals in pure-past linear temporal logic. In: ICAPS, pp. 61–69. AAAI Press (2023)
5. Bryant, R.E.: Binary decision diagrams. In: Handbook of Model Checking, pp. 191–217. Springer, Cham (2018)
6. Cimatti, A., et al.: NuSMV 2: an OpenSource tool for symbolic model checking. In: Brinksma, E., Larsen, K.G. (eds.) CAV 2002. LNCS, vol. 2404, pp. 359–364. Springer, Heidelberg (2002). https://doi.org/10.1007/3-540-45657-0_29
7. Cimatti, A., Pistore, M., Roveri, M., Traverso, P.: Weak, strong, and strong cyclic planning via symbolic model checking. Artif. Intell. **147**(1–2), 35–84 (2003)
8. De Giacomo, G., Di Stasio, A., Fuggitti, F., Rubin, S.: Pure-past linear temporal and dynamic logic on finite traces. In: IJCAI, pp. 4959–4965. ijcai.org (2020)
9. Emerson, E.A.: Temporal and modal logic. In: Handbook of Theoretical Computer Science, Volume B: Formal Models and Sematics (B), pp. 995–1072, Elsevier and MIT Press (1990)
10. Favorito, M.: Efficient algorithms for LTL_f synthesis. In: EUMAS, Lecture Notes in Computer Science, vol. 14282, pp. 540–546, Springer, Cham (2023)
11. Finkbeiner, B.: Synthesis of reactive systems. In: Dependable Software Systems Engineering, NATO Science for Peace and Security Series - D: Information and Communication Security, vol. 45, pp. 72–98. IOS Press (2016)

12. Geatti, L.: Temporal Logic specifications: expressiveness, satisfiability and realizability. Ph.D. thesis, University of Udine (2022)
13. Geatti, L., Gigante, N., Montanari, A.: BLACK: a fast, flexible and reliable LTL satisfiability checker. In: OVERLAY@GandALF, CEUR Workshop Proceedings, vol. 2987, pp. 7–12, CEUR-WS.org (2021)
14. Geatti, L., Montali, M., Rivkin, A.: Foundations of reactive synthesis for declarative process specifications. In: AAAI, pp. 17416–17425. AAAI Press (2024)
15. Giacomo, G.D., Vardi, M.Y.: Synthesis for LTL and LDL on finite traces. In: IJCAI, pp. 1558–1564. AAAI Press (2015)
16. Jin, H.S., Kuehlmann, A., Somenzi, F.: Fine-grain conjunction scheduling for symbolic reachability analysis. In: Katoen, J.-P., Stevens, P. (eds.) TACAS 2002. LNCS, vol. 2280, pp. 312–326. Springer, Heidelberg (2002). https://doi.org/10.1007/3-540-46002-0_22
17. Lichtenstein, O., Pnueli, A., Zuck, L.: The glory of the past. In: Parikh, R. (ed.) Logic of Programs 1985. LNCS, vol. 193, pp. 196–218. Springer, Heidelberg (1985). https://doi.org/10.1007/3-540-15648-8_16
18. Moon, I., Hachtel, G.D., Somenzi, F.: Border-block triangular form and conjunction schedule in image computation. In: FMCAD, Lecture Notes in Computer Science, vol. 1954, pp. 73–90. Springer, Cham (2000)
19. Moon, I., Kukula, J.H., Ravi, K., Somenzi, F.: To split or to conjoin: the question in image computation. In: DAC, pp. 23–28. ACM (2000)
20. Pnueli, A., Rosner, R.: On the synthesis of a reactive module. In: POPL (1989)
21. Zhu, S., De Giacomo, G.: Synthesis of maximally permissive strategies for $\text{LTL}_f$ specifications. In: IJCAI, pp. 2783–2789 (2022)
22. Zhu, S., Tabajara, L.M., Li, J., Pu, G., Vardi, M.Y.: A symbolic approach to safety LTL synthesis. In: HVC 2017. LNCS, vol. 10629, pp. 147–162. Springer, Cham (2017). https://doi.org/10.1007/978-3-319-70389-3_10
23. Zhu, S., Tabajara, L.M., Li, J., Pu, G., Vardi, M.Y.: Symbolic $\text{LTL}_f$ synthesis. In: IJCAI, pp. 1362–1369 (2017)

# Cross-Document Neural Re-ranking via Query-Induced Subgraphs

Andrea Giuseppe Di Francesco[1,2](✉), Christian Giannetti[1,3], Federico Siciliano[4], Nicola Tonellotto[5], and Fabrizio Silvestri[1]

[1] Sapienza University of Rome, Rome, Italy
{difrancesco,giannetti,fsilvestri}@diag.uniroma1.it
[2] ISTI-CNR, Pisa, Italy
[3] University of Cambridge, Cambridge, UK
[4] Istituto Nazionale di Geofisica e Vulcanologia, Rome, Italy
federico.siciliano@ingv.it
[5] University of Pisa, Pisa, Italy
nicola.tonellotto@unipi.it

**Abstract.** Neural re-rankers typically score query-document pairs independently, neglecting cross-document context within the retrieved candidate set. We propose Graph Neural Re-Ranking (GNRR), a framework that extracts a sparse, query-induced subgraph from a pre-computed semantic corpus graph and applies Graph Neural Networks (GNN) to propagate cross-document signals. Unlike self-attention re-rankers, which scale quadratically with the number of candidates ($\mathcal{O}(K^2)$), GNRR achieves $\mathcal{O}(c \cdot K)$ online complexity, where $c$ is the fixed corpus graph degree and $K$ the candidate set size. We evaluate five GNN operators within this framework and find that architecture choice substantially affects generalization to harder queries: the GCN variant is the only one that consistently improves over TCT-ColBERT across all three TREC benchmarks. On TREC-DLHard, the most challenging evaluation benchmark, GNRR achieves +5.2% relative AP over TCT-ColBERT and +9.0% AP over a self-attention re-ranker. Notably, self-attention re-ranking *degrades* AP on DLHard (−3.5% versus TCT-ColBERT), suggesting that sparse corpus-graph structure provides a complementary re-ranking signal that dense self-attention fails to capture. Efficiency analysis shows that GNN models require fewer parameters and lower per-query latency at $K = 1000$ than self-attention, with linear rather than quadratic scaling in candidate set size. Code to reproduce our experiment is available at https://github.com/difra100/Graph-Neural-Re-Ranking-via-Corpus-Graph.

**Keywords:** Neural Re-Ranking · Graph Neural Networks · Corpus Graph

---

A. G. Di Francesco and C. Giannetti—Equal contribution.


S. Bistarelli et al. (Eds.): AIxIA 2026, LNAI 17131, pp. 266–278, 2027.
https://doi.org/10.1007/978-3-032-40774-0_20

# 1 Introduction

Modern information retrieval systems typically follow a two-stage pipeline: an initial retrieval step (e.g., BM25 [25] or dense retrieval [11]) generates a set of candidate documents, which is refined by a neural re-ranking model (e.g., a transformer-based scorer [14,27]) to produce the final ranking. Despite their effectiveness, most neural re-rankers score each query-document pair independently, discarding relationships among candidates in the retrieved set [19,32].

Capturing cross-document context is desirable but costly. Prior work [21–23] employs self-attention mechanisms over the candidate set, treating documents as a permutation-invariant set [13,21]. However, self-attention incurs quadratic cost $\mathcal{O}(K^2)$ in the number of documents, limiting its applicability in latency-constrained settings. Moreover, as our experiments show, self-attention re-ranking can *degrade* performance on difficult queries where relevant documents rank low among predominantly non-relevant candidates.

We take a different approach. Rather than attending to all candidate pairs, GNRR builds a sparse, query-induced subgraph from the retrieved top-$K$ documents using a pre-computed semantic corpus graph [16] and applies lightweight Graph Neural Networks to propagate cross-document signals. GNN message passing costs $\mathcal{O}(c \cdot K)$ online, where $c$ is the fixed corpus graph degree, linear in $K$ compared to $\mathcal{O}(K^2)$ for self-attention. Because the corpus graph is pre-computed offline, the online overhead is substantially reduced compared to dense attention-based approaches.

Our contributions are as follows:

- We propose GNRR, a re-ranking framework that applies GNN-based propagation over query-induced subgraphs to capture cross-document interactions at $\mathcal{O}(c \cdot K)$ online cost (linear in $K$ for fixed graph degree $c$), comparing favorably to the $\mathcal{O}(K^2)$ complexity of self-attention-based re-rankers.
- We introduce a mechanism to extract query-specific subgraphs from a large pre-computed corpus graph, enabling efficient offline-online separation.
- We provide a comprehensive empirical comparison of five GNN architectures against self-attention baselines across three TREC benchmarks with varying difficulty profiles. GNN-based re-ranking is uniquely robust on the hardest benchmark (DLHard), outperforming self-attention re-ranking by up to +9.0% AP while requiring linear rather than quadratic computation. We additionally report a detailed inference-time efficiency analysis.

# 2 Related Work

Transformer-based re-rankers such as MonoBERT [19], ColBERT [11], and TCT-ColBERT [14] produce high-accuracy relevance scores but treat candidates independently.

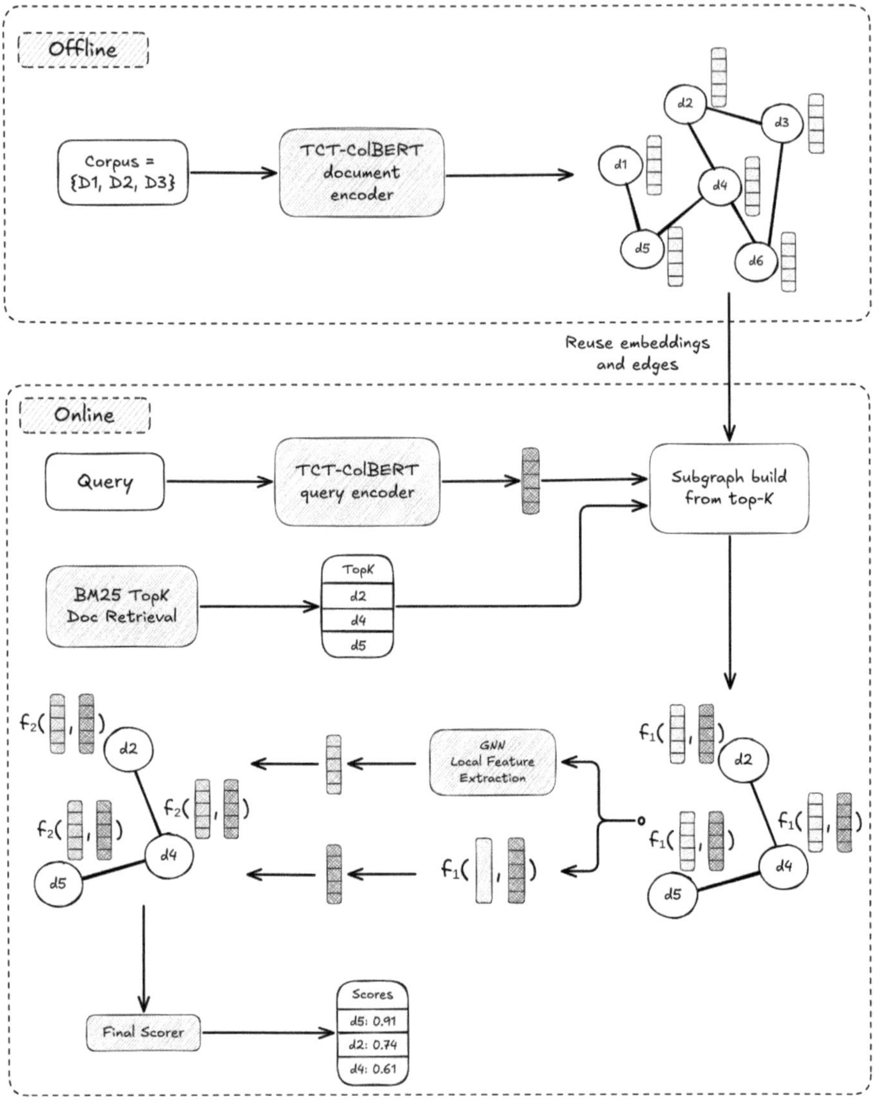


**Fig. 1.** GNRR pipeline ($K = 3$ example). *Offline*, TCT-ColBERT encodes the entire corpus and connects each document to its $c$ nearest semantic neighbors, building corpus graph $\mathcal{G}$ once for reuse across all queries. At query time, BM25 retrieves the top-$K$ candidates and TCT-ColBERT encodes the query; the candidate set determines a query-induced subgraph of $\mathcal{G}$, reusing offline document embeddings, while the query embedding flows into node feature construction. Concretely, $f_1$ combines the query and document embeddings into a per-candidate node feature; a GNN then propagates cross-document signals over the subgraph; and $f_2$ merges the GNN output with the original node feature before a final linear scorer produces the ranking.

*Set-Based Re-ranking.* SetRank [21] and related works [22,23] apply self-attention over the full candidate set to capture inter-document dependencies. While effective, these methods incur $\mathcal{O}(K^2)$ cost and, as we show, can be fragile on harder query sets where relevant documents are sparsely distributed.

*Graph-Based Representations in IR.* PageRank [20] exemplifies how document link structure can propagate importance signals. More recently, MacAvaney et al. [16] proposed Graph-based Adaptive Re-ranking (GAR), a retrieval framework that leverages a pre-computed semantic corpus graph to expand the initial candidate pool. GAR traverses the graph to add documents that are semantically related to the initially retrieved candidates, substantially improving retrieval recall.

GNRR differs fundamentally: GAR augments the *retrieval* stage, while GNRR uses corpus graph structure during *re-ranking*.

GNNs address this gap by jointly learning representations and propagating relevance signals across graph structure [8,28]. GNNs have been applied to ranking in several settings: custom PageRank from labeled examples [26], global ranking from pairwise comparisons [5,10], node importance in networks [15,24], and web resource ranking [7]. Intra-document word graphs have also been used for relevance matching [4,33]. Cross-document structure for re-ranking has been explored in multi-hop QA [18] where graphs are dynamically constructed per-question over reasoning chains; differently, we target general-purpose passage re-ranking using a static, pre-computed corpus graph built once offline and reused across queries. See [31] for a broader survey of graph-based re-ranking approaches. To our knowledge, no prior work applies GNN-based propagation over query-induced subgraphs from a pre-computed corpus graph for general-purpose document re-ranking.

## 3 Methodology

GNRR incorporates document-document relationships into neural re-ranking through three stages: (i) offline corpus graph construction, (ii) retrieval and query-induced subgraph extraction, and (iii) GNN-based re-ranking. Figure 1 illustrates the full pipeline.

**Corpus Graph.** Given a document corpus $\mathcal{C}$, we construct an offline semantic corpus graph $\mathcal{G} = (\mathcal{C}, \mathcal{E})$ where each document $d \in \mathcal{C}$ is a node and edges $(d_i, d_j) \in \mathcal{E}$ connect each document to its $c$ nearest neighbors by cosine similarity in the TCT-ColBERT embedding space, ensuring fixed-degree sparsity. Although this offline construction is computationally expensive, it is performed only once and amortized across all queries. We follow the construction procedure of [16].

**Retrieval and Subgraph Extraction.** Given a query $q$, BM25 [25] retrieves the top-$K$ documents $\mathcal{C}_q \subseteq \mathcal{C}$. From $\mathcal{G}$, we extract the query-induced subgraph retaining only retrieved nodes and edges between them:

$$\mathcal{G}_q = (\mathcal{C}_q, \mathcal{E}_q), \quad \mathcal{E}_q = \{(d_i, d_j) \in \mathcal{E} \mid d_i, d_j \in \mathcal{C}_q\}. \tag{1}$$

Connectivity is bounded by construction: $|\mathcal{E}_q| \leq c \cdot K$. Each node $d_i$ is assigned feature vector $\mathbf{x}_i = f_1(\mathbf{z}_q, \mathbf{z}_{d_i})$, with $f_1 = \odot$ (element-wise product) and $\mathbf{z}_q, \mathbf{z}_{d_i} \in \mathbb{R}^m$ denoting query and document embeddings from TCT-ColBERT. The resulting feature matrix $\mathbf{X}_q \in \mathbb{R}^{|\mathcal{C}_q| \times m}$ encodes query-document relevance per node.

**Re-ranking.** The GNN operates over $\mathcal{G}_q$ to propagate cross-document signals. Each feature vector is augmented with the document's BM25 score to retain lexical relevance as an explicit feature. The input $\mathbf{X}'_q \in \mathbb{R}^{|\mathcal{C}_q| \times (m+1)}$ is processed by the GNN:

$$\mathbf{H}_{q,\text{GNN}} = \text{GNN}(\mathbf{X}'_q, \mathbf{A}_q), \tag{2}$$

where $\mathbf{A}_q$ is the adjacency matrix of $\mathcal{G}_q$ and the hidden dimension is $m'$. The GNN output is merged with the original features by concatenation ($f_2 = \|$):

$$\mathbf{H}_q = f_2\left(\mathbf{H}_{q,\text{GNN}}, \mathbf{X}_q\right). \tag{3}$$

A linear scorer $\phi_\theta$ maps each row of $\mathbf{H}_q$ to a scalar relevance score, producing the final re-ranking:

$$\pi_q = \text{ARGSORT}(\phi_\theta(\mathbf{H}_q)). \tag{4}$$

*Complexity.* By construction $|\mathcal{E}_q| \leq c \cdot K$, so GNN message passing costs $\mathcal{O}(c \cdot K)$ for fixed corpus graph degree $c$. This scales linearly with $K$, compared to $\mathcal{O}(K^2)$ for self-attention over the same candidate set.

# 4 Experimental Setup

We address three research questions:

**RQ1.** Does modeling cross-document interactions via GNNs improve re-ranking over a strong transformer baseline?
**RQ2.** How does GNN-based re-ranking compare to self-attention re-ranking in terms of effectiveness and efficiency?
**RQ3.** How much does the GNN branch itself contribute to the observed gains?

## 4.1 Datasets

We use the MS MARCO passage ranking corpus [1] (8.8M documents). We use 14,994 queries for training and 200 queries for validation, both drawn from the MS MARCO training split. We evaluate on three standard test sets: TREC-DL19, TREC-DL20 [3], and TREC-DLHard [17].

- **DL19**: 43 queries, average 215 relevance judgments per query.
- **DL20**: 54 queries, average 211 relevance judgments per query.
- **DLHard**: 50 difficult queries, partially relabeled from DL19/DL20, targeting topics that challenge neural ranking models.

### 4.2 Models

We compare the following pipelines:

- **BM25** [25]: lexical-based retrieval baseline.
- **TCT-ColBERT** [14]: transformer-based re-ranker on top of BM25 (primary baseline).
- **Self-Attention**: a multi-layer Transformer encoder applied to the full BM25 candidate set features (same $f_1$ as GNRR), trained with LambdaRank. This is an $\mathcal{O}(K^2)$ set-based re-ranker and serves as the direct efficiency comparison to GNRR.
- **GAR** [16]: graph-augmented retrieval using the same pre-computed corpus graph to expand BM25 candidates. GAR operates at the *retrieval* stage (not re-ranking) and is included as a reference for corpus-graph-aware performance.
- **GNRR variants**: GNRR instantiated with GCN [12], GraphSAGE [9], GAT [29], GIN [30], and SignedConv [6] as the GNN operator, all trained over the semantic corpus graph.

We report four standard IR metrics: Average Precision (AP), Reciprocal Rank (RR), Precision at rank 3 (P@3), and nDCG@10 (nG@10) with relevance$\geq$ 2.

### 4.3 Training

All variants are trained with LambdaRank [2]. Training runs for up to 100 epochs with early stopping on validation nDCG@10 (patience 7). The TCT-ColBERT encoder remains frozen. We report results averaged over 3 random seeds.

### 4.4 Hyperparameters

We set the corpus graph neighborhood size to $c = 16$ and $K = 1000$. TCT-ColBERT produces embeddings of dimension $m = 768$. We tune $L \in \{1, 2, 3\}$ and $m' \in \{64, 128\}$ on the validation set. All the hyperparameters and model checkpoints are available in our code repository.

## 5 Results

### 5.1 GNN Re-Ranking vs. TCT-ColBERT (RQ1)

Table 1 shows that GNN re-ranking improves over TCT-ColBERT for the most effective architectures, with variation across models and benchmarks. GCN is the only architecture that improves AP across all three benchmarks: +5.8% on DL19, +3.8% on DL20, +5.2% on DLHard, with consistent nDCG@10 gains of +2.5%, +2.2%, and +3.5% respectively. GraphSAGE improves AP on DL19 (+0.9%) but degrades AP on DLHard (−3.0%); it improves nDCG@10 (+1.6%) and P@3 (+4.0%) on DLHard. GAT gains +2.6% AP on DL19 but degrades AP on DLHard (−4.8%), while improving nDCG@10 (+0.8%) and P@3 (+4.0%)

**Table 1.** Re-ranking on TREC-DL19, DL20, and DLHard using TCT-ColBERT features ($K = 1000$). Self-Attention and all GNRR variants are independent re-rankers applied on top of frozen TCT-ColBERT representations. Best score per column in **bold**. $^{*}$ and $^{**}$ indicate a significant t-test at 0.1 and 0.05 levels respectively.

| Pipeline | DL19 | | | | DL20 | | | | DLHard | | | |
|---|---|---|---|---|---|---|---|---|---|---|---|---|
| | AP | RR | P@3 | nG@10 | AP | RR | P@3 | nG@10 | AP | RR | P@3 | nG@10 |
| BM25 | 0.286 | 0.642 | 0.473 | 0.480 | 0.293 | 0.619 | 0.463 | 0.494 | 0.147 | 0.422 | 0.240 | 0.274 |
| +TCT-ColBERT | 0.430 | 0.843 | 0.667 | 0.685 | 0.453 | 0.817 | 0.691 | 0.680 | 0.230 | 0.538 | 0.353 | 0.373 |
| +Self-Attention | 0.431 | 0.844 | 0.674 | 0.686 | 0.454 | 0.827 | **0.704** | 0.684 | 0.222 | 0.529 | 0.340 | 0.368 |
| +GCN | **0.455**$^{**}$ | **0.858** | 0.713 | **0.702**$^{*}$ | **0.470**$^{**}$ | **0.840** | 0.673 | **0.695**$^{*}$ | **0.242** | **0.559** | **0.367** | **0.386** |
| +GraphSAGE | 0.434 | 0.850 | **0.729** | 0.689 | 0.454 | 0.837 | 0.667 | 0.685 | 0.223 | 0.531 | **0.367** | 0.379 |
| +GAT | 0.441 | 0.852 | 0.698 | 0.690 | 0.453 | 0.826 | 0.685 | 0.682 | 0.219 | 0.542 | **0.367** | 0.376 |
| +GIN | 0.449$^{*}$ | 0.853 | **0.729** | 0.691 | 0.455 | 0.793 | 0.642 | 0.675 | 0.215 | 0.490 | 0.333 | 0.357 |
| +SignedConv | 0.426 | 0.828 | 0.698 | 0.675 | 0.445 | 0.813 | 0.685 | 0.676 | 0.218 | 0.509 | 0.353 | 0.366 |

**Table 2.** Effect of improved retrieval recall on re-ranking. GAR augments BM25 candidates with semantic-graph-neighbor documents; GNRR re-rankers (trained on BM25 pools) are applied to the GAR-enlarged pool without retraining, using the same semantic corpus graph as during training. Best per column in **bold**.

| Pipeline | DL19 | | | | DL20 | | | | DLHard | | | |
|---|---|---|---|---|---|---|---|---|---|---|---|---|
| | AP | RR | P@3 | nG@10 | AP | RR | P@3 | nG@10 | AP | RR | P@3 | nG@10 |
| BM25 | 0.286 | 0.642 | 0.473 | 0.480 | 0.293 | 0.619 | 0.463 | 0.494 | 0.147 | 0.422 | 0.240 | 0.274 |
| +TCT-ColBERT | 0.430 | 0.843 | 0.667 | 0.685 | 0.453 | **0.817** | **0.691** | 0.680 | 0.230 | **0.538** | 0.353 | 0.373 |
| GAR | 0.440 | 0.833 | 0.667 | 0.696 | 0.447 | 0.815 | 0.685 | 0.680 | **0.233** | 0.532 | 0.353 | **0.373** |
| +GCN | 0.427 | 0.816 | 0.674 | 0.698 | 0.443 | 0.804 | 0.642 | 0.666 | 0.219 | 0.503 | 0.340 | 0.357 |
| +GraphSAGE | 0.431 | 0.815 | 0.698 | 0.697 | 0.432 | 0.790 | 0.667 | 0.664 | 0.220 | 0.501 | **0.360** | 0.356 |
| +GAT | **0.444** | 0.833 | **0.721** | **0.705** | **0.458** | 0.808 | 0.679 | **0.681** | 0.229 | 0.495 | **0.360** | 0.368 |
| +GIN | 0.429 | 0.790 | 0.674 | 0.676 | 0.421 | 0.777 | 0.617 | 0.616 | 0.200 | 0.456 | 0.320 | 0.325 |
| +SignedConv | 0.419 | **0.844** | 0.682 | 0.686 | 0.413 | 0.788 | 0.642 | 0.654 | 0.212 | 0.498 | 0.353 | 0.348 |

there. GIN gains +4.4% AP on DL19 but degrades on DLHard (−6.5% AP). SignedConv falls below TCT-ColBERT across all three benchmarks.

On DLHard, GCN is the only architecture that improves AP, raising it from 0.230 to 0.242 (+5.2%) alongside nDCG@10 gains of +3.5%. GAT improves nDCG@10 (+0.8%) and P@3 (+4.0%) on DLHard but not AP (−4.8%); GIN degrades across all DLHard metrics (−6.5% AP); SignedConv degrades AP, RR, and nDCG@10 on DLHard, with P@3 flat at 0.353. These results suggest that the choice of GNN aggregation scheme substantially influences generalization to harder query distributions.

### 5.2 GNN vs. Self-Attention (RQ2)

*Effectiveness.* Table 1 reveals an asymmetry between GCN and self-attention re-ranking across benchmarks. On DL19, self-attention improves by +0.2% AP over

TCT-ColBERT; GCN achieves +5.8% AP on the same benchmark. On DL20, self-attention gains +0.2% AP; GCN gains +3.8% AP, with smaller gains from other variants. On DLHard, self-attention degrades TCT-ColBERT by −3.5% AP (0.222 vs. 0.230) and −1.3% nDCG@10. GCN is the only method that improves AP on DLHard, achieving +5.2% over TCT-ColBERT and +9.0% over self-attention (0.242 vs. 0.222).

We attribute this asymmetry to structural regularization: the sparse corpus graph constrains information flow to semantically similar document pairs, while the full $K \times K$ attention matrix over predominantly non-relevant candidates amplifies noise in hard-query settings. The GNN restricts information flow to corpus-graph neighbors, filtering irrelevant cross-document interactions by construction.

**Table 3.** Inference efficiency at $K = 1000$. Latency averaged over DL19 queries on NVIDIA RTX 3090 Ti (GNN forward pass + subgraph extraction; TCT encoding excluded).

| Method | Complexity | Params | ms/query |
|---|---|---|---|
| Self-Attention | $\mathcal{O}(K^2)$ | 363.9K | 37.3 |
| GNRR+GCN | $\mathcal{O}(c \cdot K)$ | 279.6K | 34.2 |
| GNRR+GraphSAGE | $\mathcal{O}(c \cdot K)$ | 160.2K | 32.8 |
| GNRR+GAT | $\mathcal{O}(c \cdot K)$ | 246.8K | 34.3 |
| GNRR+GIN | $\mathcal{O}(c \cdot K)$ | 123.5K | 32.4 |
| GNRR+SignedConv | $\mathcal{O}(c \cdot K)$ | 295.7K | 35.2 |

*Inference Efficiency (Table 3).* GNN models are faster and smaller than self-attention: at $K = 1000$, GNN latency is 5–13% lower (32–35 ms vs. 37.3 ms) with up to 66% fewer parameters (GIN: 124K vs. 364K). The advantage grows with $K$: self-attention cost scales as $\mathcal{O}(K^2)$, so doubling $K$ quadruples its cost while GNN cost grows as $\mathcal{O}(c \cdot K)$ and remains linear. GCN achieves better DLHard effectiveness (+5.2% AP) at lower computational cost than self-attention.

### 5.3 Sensitivity to Candidate Distribution

All experiments presented so far use candidate pools initially retrieved by BM25. To assess whether GNRR depends on the distribution of BM25 candidates and to evaluate its complementarity with retrieval-enhancement methods such as GAR, we conduct an additional experiment. [16] introduced the semantic corpus graph as a mechanism for increasing the recall of the top-1000 retrieved candidates. The key intuition is that documents that are semantically similar to relevant documents may themselves be relevant. Their results show that improving candidate recall at the retrieval stage can enhance downstream re-ranking performance by recovering relevant documents that BM25 fails to retrieve.

Table 2 examines what happens when GNRR re-rankers (trained on BM25 candidate pools) are applied to GAR-augmented pools without retraining, using the same semantic corpus graph as during training. GAR raises DL19 AP from 0.430 to 0.440 (+2.3%) and nDCG@10 from 0.685 to 0.696 over the BM25+TCT-ColBERT baseline through retrieval-stage candidate expansion alone.

The five GNRR architectures respond differently to this distribution shift. GCN, GIN, GraphSAGE, and SignedConv all degrade AP relative to GAR alone across all three benchmarks, consistent with out-of-distribution failure: these models were trained to re-rank BM25 candidate pools and their fixed, non-adaptive aggregation schemes do not transfer directly to the larger, more diverse candidate distribution produced by GAR. GAT is the exception on DL19 and DL20. Its attention mechanism can adaptively reweight neighbors at test time, improving AP over GAR alone by +0.9% on DL19 (0.444 vs. 0.440) and +2.5% on DL20 (0.458 vs. 0.447); GAT also records the best nDCG@10 on both benchmarks. On DLHard, all five architectures degrade, suggesting that the shift in candidate distribution is particularly challenging on harder queries regardless of aggregation scheme.

These results carry two messages. First, attention-based aggregation generalizes more broadly across candidate distributions than fixed isotropic GNN operators. Second, retrieval and re-ranking stages must be jointly trained when the candidate source changes; re-training GNRR on GAR-augmented pools is a natural direction for future work.

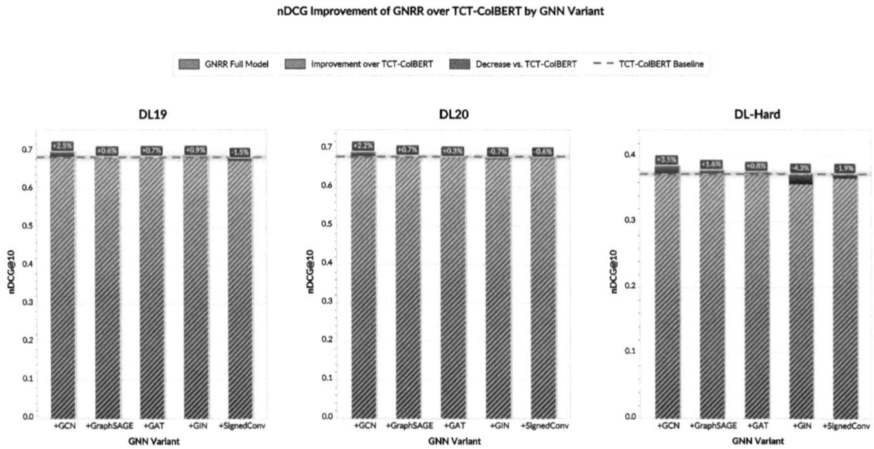


**Fig. 2.** nDCG@10 improvement of each GNRR variant over the TCT-ColBERT baseline on DL19, DL20, and DLHard. Green caps denote gains; bordeaux caps denote degradation. The dashed line marks the baseline (zero improvement). (Color figure online)

### 5.4 GNN Branch Contribution (RQ3)

To isolate the contribution of graph propagation, we perform an ablation in which the GNN branch output $\mathbf{H}_{q,\mathrm{GNN}}$ is replaced by a zero vector at inference time, removing all graph-derived information while leaving the rest of the model unchanged.

Figure 2 reports the relative change in nDCG@10 when the GNN branch is reactivated. GCN yields the largest and most consistent gains, improving nDCG@10 by +2.5% on DL19, +2.2% on DL20, and +3.5% on DLHard. GraphSAGE and GAT provide smaller improvements, while SignedConv offers little benefit.

These results indicate that graph-based message passing contributes useful ranking information beyond individual query-document representations. The particularly strong gains on DLHard suggest that cross-document signals are most valuable for difficult queries.

## 6 Conclusions

This paper introduced GNRR, a re-ranking framework that captures cross-document interactions by extracting a sparse, query-induced subgraph from a pre-computed semantic corpus graph and applying a GNN over transformer-based representations. Unlike self-attention re-rankers with $\mathcal{O}(K^2)$ cost, GNRR requires only $\mathcal{O}(c \cdot K)$ online computation, linear in the candidate set size for fixed corpus graph degree $c$.

Comparison with self-attention re-ranking reveals that GCN is the only method in our evaluation that improves AP on harder query sets: on TREC-DLHard, GCN achieves +5.2% AP over TCT-ColBERT and +9.0% AP over self-attention, whereas self-attention re-ranking *degrades* below the TCT-ColBERT baseline on the same set. Efficiency analysis shows that GCN achieves these gains with fewer parameters and lower per-query latency at $K = 1000$ than self-attention, with a theoretical linear vs. quadratic scaling advantage as $K$ grows.

These results suggest that sparse inter-document structure via pre-computed corpus graphs is a viable and computationally efficient mechanism for improving neural re-ranking, with particular value for difficult retrieval scenarios.

#### Limitations and Future Work

Results across architectures are mixed on DL20: GCN gains +3.8% AP while most other variants are flat or below TCT-ColBERT, suggesting that the benefit of graph propagation depends on the aggregation scheme. Future work includes: (1) heterogeneous graph structures encoding multiple relation types; (2) joint training with the dense encoder; (3) adaptive graph construction per query; and (4) scaling the corpus graph neighborhood size and studying its interaction with re-ranking quality. The gap between GAR and GNRR (re-ranking) also suggests that combining the two approaches through joint training is a natural direction.

**Generative AI Usage Disclosure.** Generative AI tools were used for debugging assistance and language editing only. Conceptualization, methodology, experimental design, analysis, and manuscript writing were conducted entirely by the authors.

**Funding Information.** This work was supported by the EVOLVE project, "A Fluid Framework for Dynamic Agentic AI Systems" (Sapienza Università di Roma), and partially supported by the FoReLab and CrossLab projects (Departments of Excellence) and by the NVIDIA Academic Grants Program 2026. This research was conducted as part of the ENRESFOOD project, funded under the FutureFoodS partnership. The project is co-funded by the Austrian Science Fund (FWF; 10.55776/KIN4661525), The Dutch Ministry of Agriculture, Fisheries, Food Security and Nature (BO-43-219-026), the Italian Ministry of University and Research (MUR), the German Federal Ministry of Research, Technology and Space (031B1717), and the European Union's Horizon Europe research and innovation programme via FutureFoodS, the European Partnership for a Sustainable Future of Food Systems, co-funded under Grant Agreement No. 101136361.

**Disclosure of Interests.** The authors have no competing interests to declare that are relevant to the content of this article.

## References

1. Bajaj, P., et al.: Ms marco: a human generated machine reading comprehension dataset (2018)
2. Burges, C., Ragno, R., Le, Q.: Learning to rank with nonsmooth cost functions. In: Schölkopf, B., Platt, J., Hoffman, T. (eds.) Advances in Neural Information Processing Systems, vol. 19. MIT Press (2006). https://proceedings.neurips.cc/paper_files/paper/2006/file/af44c4c56f385c43f2529f9b1b018f6a-Paper.pdf
3. Craswell, N., Mitra, B., Yilmaz, E., Campos, D., Voorhees, E.M., Soboroff, I.: Trec deep learning track: reusable test collections in the large data regime (2021)
4. Cui, H., Lu, J., Ge, Y., Yang, C.: How can graph neural networks help document retrieval: a case study on cord19 with concept map generation (2022)
5. Damke, C., Hüllermeier, E.: Ranking structured objects with graph neural networks. In: Soares, C., Torgo, L. (eds.) DS 2021. LNCS (LNAI), vol. 12986, pp. 166–180. Springer, Cham (2021). https://doi.org/10.1007/978-3-030-88942-5_13
6. Derr, T., Ma, Y., Tang, J.: Signed graph convolutional network (2018)
7. Ergashev, U., Dragut, E., Meng, W.: Learning to rank resources with GNN. In: Proceedings of the ACM Web Conference 2023, pp. 3247–3256 (2023)
8. Gilmer, J., Schoenholz, S.S., Riley, P.F., Vinyals, O., Dahl, G.E.: Neural message passing for quantum chemistry (2017)
9. Hamilton, W.L., Ying, R., Leskovec, J.: Inductive representation learning on large graphs. In: Proceedings of the 31st International Conference on Neural Information Processing Systems. NIPS 2017, pp. 1025–1035. Curran Associates Inc., Red Hook, NY, USA (2017)
10. He, Y., Gan, Q., Wipf, D., Reinert, G.D., Yan, J., Cucuringu, M.: Gnnrank: learning global rankings from pairwise comparisons via directed graph neural networks. In: international conference on machine learning, pp. 8581–8612. PMLR (2022)
11. Khattab, O., Zaharia, M.: Colbert: Efficient and effective passage search via contextualized late interaction over bert (2020)

12. Kipf, T.N., Welling, M.: Semi-supervised classification with graph convolutional networks (2017)
13. Lee, J., Lee, Y., Kim, J., Kosiorek, A., Choi, S., Teh, Y.W.: Set transformer: a framework for attention-based permutation-invariant neural networks. In: International Conference on Machine Learning, pp. 3744–3753. PMLR (2019)
14. Lin, S.C., Yang, J.H., Lin, J.: Distilling dense representations for ranking using tightly-coupled teachers (2020)
15. Liu, C., Cao, T., Zhou, L.: Learning to rank complex network node based on the self-supervised graph convolution model. Knowl.-Based Syst. **251**, 109220 (2022)
16. MacAvaney, S., Tonellotto, N., Macdonald, C.: Adaptive re-ranking with a corpus graph. In: Proceedings of the 31st ACM International Conference on Information & Knowledge Management. CIKM 2022, ACM (2022). https://doi.org/10.1145/3511808.3557231
17. Mackie, I., Dalton, J., Yates, A.: How deep is your learning: the dl-hard annotated deep learning dataset (2021)
18. Nie, P., Zhang, Y., Ramamurthy, A., Song, L.: Answering any-hop open-domain questions with iterative document reranking (2021). https://arxiv.org/abs/2009.07465
19. Nogueira, R., Yang, W., Cho, K., Lin, J.: Multi-stage document ranking with bert (2019)
20. Page, L., Brin, S., Motwani, R., Winograd, T.: The pagerank citation ranking: bringing order to the web. Technical report 1999-66, Stanford InfoLab (1999)
21. Pang, L., Xu, J., Ai, Q., Lan, Y., Cheng, X., Wen, J.: Setrank: learning a permutation-invariant ranking model for information retrieval. In: Proceedings of the 43rd international ACM SIGIR conference on research and development in information retrieval, pp. 499–508 (2020)
22. Pasumarthi, R.K., Zhuang, H., Wang, X., Bendersky, M., Najork, M.: Permutation equivariant document interaction network for neural learning to rank. In: Proceedings of the 2020 ACM SIGIR on International Conference on Theory of Information Retrieval, pp. 145–148 (2020)
23. Pobrotyn, P., Bartczak, T., Synowiec, M., Białobrzeski, R., Bojar, J.: Context-aware learning to rank with self-attention. arXiv preprint arXiv:2005.10084 (2020)
24. Qu, H., Song, Y.R., Li, R., Li, M.: GNR: a universal and efficient node ranking model for various tasks based on graph neural networks. XXPhys. A **632**, 129339 (2023)
25. Robertson, S.E., Walker, S., Jones, S., Hancock-Beaulieu, M.M., Gatford, M.: Okapi at TREC-3. In: Proceedings of the Third Text REtrieval Conference (TREC-3) (1994)
26. Scarselli, F., Yong, S.L., Gori, M., Hagenbuchner, M., Tsoi, A.C., Maggini, M.: Graph neural networks for ranking web pages. In: The 2005 IEEE/WIC/ACM International Conference on Web Intelligence (WI 2005), pp. 666–672. IEEE (2005)
27. Vaswani, A., et al.: Attention is all you need. In: Advances in Neural Information Processing Systems, vol. 30 (2017)
28. Veličković, P.: Everything is connected: graph neural networks. Curr. Opin. Struct. Biol. **79**, 102538 (2023). https://doi.org/10.1016/j.sbi.2023.102538
29. Veličković, P., Cucurull, G., Casanova, A., Romero, A., Liò, P., Bengio, Y.: Graph attention networks (2018)
30. Xu, K., Hu, W., Leskovec, J., Jegelka, S.: How powerful are graph neural networks? (2019)

31. Zaoad, M.S., Zawad, N., Ranade, P., Krogman, R., Khan, L., Holt, J.: Graph-based re-ranking: emerging techniques, limitations, and opportunities (2025). https://arxiv.org/abs/2503.14802
32. Zhan, J., Mao, J., Liu, Y., Zhang, M., Ma, S.: Repbert: Contextualized text embeddings for first-stage retrieval (2020). https://arxiv.org/abs/2006.15498
33. Zhang, Y., Zhang, J., Cui, Z., Wu, S., Wang, L.: A graph-based relevance matching model for ad-hoc retrieval (2021)

# A Structural Survey of Coordination Patterns in LLM-Based Multi-agent Systems

Nicola Esposito, Giuseppe Aniello, Giuseppe Gambino, Ciro Panariello, Domenico Alfano(✉), and Roberto Abbruzzese

Eustema S.p.A, Rome, Italy
{n.esposito,g.aniello,g.gambino,c.panariello, d.alfano,r.abbruzzese}@eustema.it

**Abstract.** LLM-based multi-agent systems (MAS) are one of the most active areas of generative AI, with a fragmented landscape of coordination patterns—sequential pipelines, routing schemes, Supervisor–Worker hierarchies, iterative feedback loops, decentralized swarms—and their hybrid compositions. Architectural choices are often driven by framework familiarity rather than by a systematic comparison of the structural properties distinguishing one pattern from another. This paper surveys LLM-based MAS architectures from a topology-centered perspective, focusing on the distribution of control, the flow of information, and the interaction among agents. We distil five base coordination patterns and a hybrid composition rule, and introduce a matrix organised along four analytical dimensions—Observability, Autonomy, Scalability, Token Efficiency—derived from recurring concerns in prior work on agent evaluation and benchmarking and articulated into twelve sub-characteristics coded on an ordinal three-level scale. The matrix is a synthesis tool, not a prescriptive scoring, showing how different coordination patterns privilege different properties. From the coding, two structural hypotheses emerge—an inverse relationship between observability and autonomy, and a coupling between scalability and the attribution of decisions and failures to identifiable agents—alongside one empirically documented trade-off that the coding makes structurally explicit: the widening of coordination overhead with autonomy. The contribution is methodological: a structured vocabulary connecting classical multi-agent systems theory with the emerging practice of LLM-based Agentic AI.

**Keywords:** Coordination Patterns · Agent Architecture · Multi-Agent Systems · LLM Agents · Agentic AI

## 1 Introduction

Large Language Models (LLMs) cannot by themselves act on the external world, verify their output, or revise a plan; AI Agent designs overcome these limits by


S. Bistarelli et al. (Eds.): AIxIA 2026, LNAI 17131, pp. 279–293, 2027.
https://doi.org/10.1007/978-3-032-40774-0_21

embedding an LLM in systems with tool use, planning, reflection, and memory [1,2]. As task complexity grows, single agents degrade—contexts broaden and specialization is lost—and Multi-Agent Systems (MAS), in which specialized agents collaborate sequentially, hierarchically, or in a distributed fashion, are the natural response. MAS are not new: a thirty-year tradition rooted in Wooldridge and Jennings [3] and Stone and Veloso [4] formalized agents as autonomous rational entities, standardized communication through FIPA-ACL [5], and produced foundational results on coordination models [6], agent-oriented methodologies [7,8], and organizational frameworks [9,10]. What is new in LLM-based MAS is the nature of the constituent agents: general-purpose reasoners driven by natural language. Coordination happens through natural-language hand-offs rather than codified protocols, specialization emerges from prompt design, and the cost of execution is dominated by token consumption. The rapid spread of LLM-based MAS has produced a proliferation of patterns documented as engineering building blocks, in surveys [1,14], and in decentralized, layered, and hybrid variants [12,13]. No architecture is superior in absolute terms: a pattern's structural properties depend on its coordination topology—the distribution of control, the flow of information, the locality of decisions, and the visibility of state. Recent empirical work shows that a substantial share of failures concerns organizational design and inter-agent coordination rather than individual agent capability [15], yet architectural decisions are still driven mostly by non-structural factors and the literature compares architectures narratively, with no shared vocabulary for structural properties—in sharp contrast with the formal languages of classical MAS [5,6,9]. This paper addresses that gap through a focused, topology-centered survey, narrower and complementary to broader maps of the field [14,16]. Rather than cataloguing every LLM-agent application, it concentrates on sources that make control, information flow, and interaction structure sufficiently explicit to support architectural comparison. We identify recurring coordination patterns, define minimal reference models organized along control centralization and flow dynamics, and compare them against four analytical dimensions: Observability, Autonomy, Scalability, Token Efficiency. The resulting matrix is the analytical core of the paper: descriptive rather than prescriptive, making structural assumptions and costs explicit before implementation-specific benchmarking, so that subsequent work can validate, refine, or challenge individual assignments. The paper makes four contributions: a topology-centered taxonomy of five base coordination patterns—pipeline, router, hierarchical, iterative feedback loop, decentralized/swarm—together with a hybrid composition rule that reads a system's profile off its base components, all organized by control centralization and flow dynamics rather than by framework or domain; an operationalization of the four dimensions into twelve sub-characteristics coded on an ordinal three-level scale with an explicit decision rule; three row-level regularities (observability–autonomy, token efficiency–autonomy, scalability–attribution) presented as conjectures to be operationalized rather than universal laws; and a mapping of recurrent coordination failures and evaluation concerns onto structural properties that practitioners can inspect before selecting an architecture.

## 2 Related Work

**Classical Multi-agent Systems.** The foundations were laid in the 1990s by Wooldridge and Jennings [3] and Stone and Veloso [4]; FIPA-ACL standardized speech-act communication [5]. The European community contributed coordination models (A&A, tuple centres) [6], agent-oriented software engineering (Gaia, Tropos) [7,8], and normative organizational MAS (Dignum's framework, JaCaMo) [9,10]; the structural classification of organizational paradigms—hierarchies, coalitions, teams, federations and markets—was systematised by Horling and Lesser [11] and remains the closest pre-LLM antecedent of the topology-centred reading we propose. This literature establishes that structural properties can be studied independently of agent reasoning. Direct transfer to LLM-based MAS is however undermined by the natural-language hand-offs, prompt-conditioned role behavior, and per-message token cost that current systems routinely involve; we therefore adopt the classical structural perspective but re-operationalize it around the control, information-flow, observability, and cost characteristics salient when the agents are LLM-based.

**LLM-Based Agents and Architectural Patterns.** ReAct established the alternation of reasoning and acting [2], Toolformer autonomous tool invocation [21], and Reflexion verbal reinforcement and reflective revision [22]. Multi-agent settings produced Multi-Agent Debate [23,24], Mixture-of-Agents [12], AgentNet's decentralized evolutionary coordination [13], and generative-agents societies [25]; frameworks such as AutoGen [26], MetaGPT [27], and CAMEL [28] made these mechanisms accessible, while vendor engineering reports consolidated the Supervisor–Worker pattern in production [1,29]. These works are useful for identifying concrete coordination mechanisms, but their limit is that they generally introduce or optimize one configuration at a time, and their architectural descriptions are entangled with prompts, tools, models, and framework abstractions; consequently they do not provide a common basis for comparing what follows from the coordination structure itself. Our survey abstracts recurring reference models from these implementations and evaluates them with a single set of topology-oriented criteria.

**Surveys, Benchmarks, and Failure Analyses.** Existing surveys position the LLM-MAS field along different primary axes: Guo et al. [14] along application domain and individual-agent profile, Han et al. [16] along open challenges spanning agent-world, agent-agent and agent-human interaction, and Yan et al. [37] along communication structure and protocols. Each treats topology as one dimension among many, but none operationalizes the pattern-by-property comparison that follows from a topology-centred lens, and the closest pre-LLM antecedent—the organizational-paradigm taxonomy of Horling and Lesser [11]—predates the natural-language, prompt-conditioned, token-priced regime that defines current LLM-MAS. A more recent taxonomy by Tran et al. [38] classifies LLM-MAS along collaboration mechanisms (actors, types, structures, strategies) and is the closest contemporary work to ours; we differ in operationalizing the comparison along a ternary structural-cost scale, so that collaboration mechanisms become the architect's input to the requirement profile rather than the unit of comparison itself. Benchmarks such as AgentBench [30], SWE-bench [31], WebArena [32], and coordination-oriented suites [19] measure end-to-end behavior, but outcomes jointly reflect model, prompts, tools, framework, and architecture, leaving the structural source of a trade-off implicit. Failure analyses such as Cemri et al. [15] identify recurring coordination breakdowns but only after systems are instantiated, providing no pre-implementation method for comparing topologies. Coordination failures account for a substantial share of MAS breakdowns [15] and architectural choices materially affect cost, reproducibility, and reliability [17,18]: architectural choice is thus a high-leverage decision made without a shared structural vocabulary, which the present survey supplies while leaving performance claims to benchmarks. Unlike existing surveys that classify systems by domain or mechanism, our matrix answers a different question: given a coordination topology, which structural properties are obtained for free, which only at implementation cost, and which only by changing the topology.

## 3 Survey Scope and Source Selection

This work is a focused structural survey conducted through purposive, theory-driven sampling—explicitly not an exhaustive or PRISMA-style review. Its unit of analysis is the coordination architecture: a recurring arrangement specifying how control is allocated, how information moves, how decisions are localized, and how agent roles interact. The search targeted literature exposing these structural choices rather than literature selected by application domain or task performance; the criteria below state the selection so that it can be scrutinized and reproduced. The analysis did not begin from a fixed list of query terms but from the structural concepts themselves. An initial core of 12 sources—recent surveys, benchmark and failure-analysis papers, and primary works introducing recurrent architectures—was expanded through backward and forward citation chaining [12–20,23–29,36,37,39,40] into a working corpus of about 30 candidate systems, by starting from a work that made a control or information-flow structure explicit and following its references and citing papers to locate systems committing to the same or neighbouring structures. Sampling was guided by saturation at the level of topology: the last 8 candidates examined instantiated already identified structures without requiring a new macro-pattern, and we therefore stopped at the five base coordination patterns and the hybrid composition rule reported in Sect. 4. The procedure is descriptive, not a claim of bibliographic completeness. A source was included when it (i) instantiated or analyzed a system with multiple LLM-based agents or functionally distinct roles, and (ii) described the architecture sufficiently to identify the allocation of control, the communication path, or the runtime flow of intermediate state. Classical MAS sources were retained when they supplied structural concepts; framework and vendor reports were included only as evidence that a pattern exists in practice. We excluded application papers treating the MAS as a black box, base-model or prompting studies, and framework variants that changed implementation details without changing control or information flow. Single-agent work was excluded unless it defined a recurrent control structure later instantiated through distinct agent roles, in which case it served as an architectural antecedent. The final corpus of about 30 candidates condenses into the five base coordination patterns and the hybrid composition rule, representing recurring topological alternatives rather than every published system. The selection and abstraction involve interpretive judgment, mitigated—not eliminated—by fixing the unit of analysis, stating inclusion and exclusion rules in advance, and coding reference models rather than individual papers; we return to coder dependence in Sect. 7. The synthesis rested on two organizing axes defined here. *Control centralization* concerns where decision authority resides: at the centralized extreme a single component holds the global view and directs the others, while at the decentralized extreme authority is distributed across peers with no privileged coordinator. *Flow dynamics* concerns how control and information move: at the static extreme the path is a fixed, acyclic sequence of hand-offs set at design time, while at the dynamic extreme it is decided at runtime through state-dependent branching and recurrent feedback. Candidate systems were positioned on these axes and grouped by shared minimal control and communication commitments; each group was then reduced to a minimal reference model containing only the roles, edges, state dependencies, and control transitions its definition requires. These reference models, not particular frameworks, are the objects coded in the comparison matrix.

## 4 A Taxonomy of MAS Architectures

This section presents five base coordination patterns and a hybrid composition rule, derived from the source-selection procedure above and positioned along the two axes defined in Sect. 3, control centralization and flow dynamics. The categories are coordination patterns and reference models rather than mutually exclusive labels for every implementation; systems that combine their minimal commitments are treated as hybrids. Each pattern is described at the level of abstraction at which it makes a single coordination commitment—Pipeline isolates flow, Router dispatch, Hierarchical vertical authority, Iterative Loop temporal feedback, Swarm peer decentralization, Hybrid composition. The heterogeneity of levels is by design: each pattern isolates one coordination dimension and leaves the others free—which is also why patterns can co-occur and nest, a router sitting within a hierarchy or a hierarchy containing a loop. We therefore group them not as instances of a single formal type but as recurring coordination patterns, each defined by the structural commitments it makes about the distribution of control, the flow of information, and the interaction among agents; the matrix codes those commitments. The five base patterns are coded in the comparison matrix (Sect. 5); the hybrid composition rule is illustrated by the example below, but does not carry a column of its own. A hybrid has no profile of its own, inheriting its properties cell by cell from the patterns it composes, and a given label (e.g. Planner Executor) admits many compositions with different cell values. Assigning it a single column would either duplicate its constituents' values or impose an arbitrary choice among them, so we treat hybrids as compositions read off the five base patterns.

**Sequential Pipeline.** The most linear pattern: the process is decomposed into predefined micro-tasks in strict unidirectional order, each agent receiving its predecessor's output (procedural determinism). Strengths: structural clarity, isolated testability, a trace coinciding with the ordered intermediate outputs. Limitations: rigidity, fragility (one failed stage blocks the chain), no parallelism, error propagation.

**Router.** A central node dispatches each request to the most appropriate specialized agent; the router may be an LLM, an embedding comparator, a classifier, or a rule engine. Strengths: flexibility to input variety and horizontal scalability—specialists are added by registration. Limitations: single point of failure, and no combination of multiple agents' expertise on cross-functional inputs.

**Hierarchical.** A Supervisor holds the global view and coordinates Workers with vertical skills and tools; it evaluates partial results, reformulates the plan, and maintains coherence. The pattern excels in state management and dynamic planning at the cost of the Supervisor's centrality. Variants include the classic Supervisor–Worker configuration [1,29]; ReWOO, which plans upfront and executes tool calls in parallel, trading adaptivity for token savings [33]; and Orchestrated MAS, which modularizes central control into planning, execution-control, and quality-management units.

**Iterative Feedback Loop.** An iterative feedback loop is treated as an architectural pattern when recurrent, state-dependent feedback is the principal coordination mechanism, not a local detail or fixed repetition count. Its minimal reference model has at least two functionally distinct roles: a producer/actor generating an action or artifact, and an observer/evaluator externalizing an assessment into coordination state. At iteration $t$, this state determines the iteration $t+1$ decision; execution terminates on an explicit stopping condition. The resulting directed cycle gives the pattern a topological signature even when both roles are realized by the same underlying LLM at different turns. A simple retry or fixed for-loop without externalized feedback is therefore not classified as this pattern. Variants include ReAct's Thought–Action–Observation alternation [2], Evaluator–Optimizer with structured feedback driving refinement [22,34], and context-restart loops that mitigate long-context degradation [35] by restarting the acting component while preserving structured external state [34].

**Decentralized and Swarm.** No central coordinator: peer agents collaborate through direct negotiation or codified handoffs, and coordination is emergent. The pattern maximizes resilience and adaptability; the challenge is converging to the global objective while preserving accountability. Variants: the strict peer-to-peer Swarm with handoff logic [13], and Stochastic Multi-Agent Consensus, where parallel agents' outputs are aggregated by voting, clustering, or a judge [23,24].

**Hybrid.** Hybrids combine different coordination logics in one system—determinism where rigor is required, autonomy where flexibility is needed—at the cost of systemic complexity. Examples: Multi-Agent Debate (Evaluator–Optimizer plus peer deliberation) [23,24], Planner–Executor (iterative loop plus hierarchical planning), and the Society Architecture of persona-driven agents [25].

## 5 A Structural Comparison Matrix for MAS Architectures

**Rationale.** End-to-end performance does not explain which structural properties make an architecture fragile, expensive, or hard to reproduce; framework-level evaluations show that architectural choices alone substantially affect latency, accuracy, reproducibility, and cost [17,18]. The matrix is therefore a structural comparison tool distinguishing properties induced by the coordination topology from those that depend on implementation. Its four dimensions correspond to four recurring evaluation concerns: Observability, because MAS behavior must be inspectable through traces and failure attribution [15,18,20]; Autonomy, because planning, reflection, and adaptation distinguish agentic execution from static workflows [2,22,36]; Scalability, because coordination protocols determine behavior as agents and dependencies grow [19,37]; Token Efficiency, because in LLM-based MAS coordination has a direct computational footprint [29,39,40]. These four are not an exhaustive account of architectural quality but the concerns most consistently recurring across agent evaluation, benchmarking, and failure analysis [15,18,19,36]; we treat them as four complementary lenses on coordination structure. Table 1 summarises which evaluation axes are treated as primary concerns across six representative surveys and benchmarks of LLM-based agents: each of the four dimensions we adopt is a primary axis in at least two of them, whereas the less frequent concerns are primary in at most one. Characteristics such as security, privacy, human oversight and latency are deliberately left outside the present scope because they are deployment- and policy-dependent rather than topology-induced: a hierarchy can be secure or insecure, and an iterative loop can be human-supervised or fully autonomous, without changing its coordination topology.

**Coding Scale.** Each cell records how a coordination pattern relates to a sub-characteristic on an ordinal three-level scale, defined by a single operational criterion—the structural cost of obtaining the property. *2 (Structurally intrinsic)*: the property follows from the pattern's minimal reference model (Sect. 4) itself, holding independently of model, prompts, or tooling for any implementation that conforms to that model. *1 (Conditional)*: the topology does not entail the property but admits it through a mechanism added within the same structure (e.g. per-stage retry, an inserted critic agent, context summarization), obtainable at implementation cost without changing the topology. *0 (Absent)*: the property cannot be obtained without altering the topology itself, so providing it would

**Table 1.** Evaluation axes treated as a primary (•), secondary (○), or absent (–) concern across six representative surveys and benchmarks of LLM-based agents. Each of the four dimensions adopted here is a primary axis in at least two sources, whereas the characteristics left outside the scope are primary in at most one.

| Evaluation axis | Cemri [15] | Han [16] | Ma [18] | Zhu [19] | Yehudai [36] | Yan [37] |
|---|---|---|---|---|---|---|
| Observability | • | – | • | ○ | • | ○ |
| Autonomy | ○ | • | – | • | • | – |
| Scalability | – | ○ | ○ | • | ○ | • |
| Token Efficiency | – | ○ | • | – | ○ | • |
| Security | – | ○ | – | – | ○ | ○ |
| Privacy | – | – | – | – | – | – |
| Human oversight | – | – | – | – | – | – |
| Latency | – | – | • | – | – | – |

turn the pattern into a different one (e.g. adding runtime replanning to a strict pipeline makes it hierarchical).

**Observability.** Extent to which behavior can be inspected, reconstructed, and audited [18,20]. *Accountability*: attribution of decisions and artifacts to an identifiable component [15,20]. *Trace Complexity*: whether the execution path can be followed without combinatorial branching [18]. *Rationale Externalization*: whether the topology requires reasoning to be exposed as inter-agent artifacts (ReAct's verbalized Thought, debate critiques, ReWOO's plan) rather than confined to intra-agent state.

**Autonomy.** Ability to operate adaptively without every step statically defined [3,36]. *Dynamic Planning*: decomposing goals and revising plans at runtime [2]. *Reflection*: internal critique, revision, or verification [22]. *Failure Recovery*: recovering from local failures through retry, fallback, reassignment, or replanning [15,18,41].

**Scalability.** Effectiveness as agents, parallel tasks, and dependencies increase [19,37]. *Parallelism*: intra-task concurrency—independent subtasks proceeding simultaneously (request-level throughput is not credited) [29]. *Modularity*: adding, replacing, or specializing agents without redesigning the coordination structure [27]. *Absence of Bottlenecks*: no coordinator, shared state, hub, or serial stage whose delay or failure gates downstream progress [19,37].

**Token Efficiency.** Computational footprint induced by the topology, distinct from implementation-level optimization [39,40]. *Context Locality*: avoidance of repeatedly injecting history, global state, or intermediate reasoning into subsequent calls [29,39]. *Communication Overhead*: avoidance of coordination traffic (handoffs, negotiation, voting) not directly constituting task work [37,40]. *Redundancy Cost*: avoidance of duplicated work—overlapping reasoning or revalidation of results produced elsewhere [39,40].

**Table 2.** Structural comparison of the five scored patterns under the ternary support scale: 2 = structurally intrinsic (entailed by the pattern's reference model), 1 = conditional (obtainable by an implementation mechanism within the same topology), 0 = absent (obtainable only by altering the topology).

| Dimension | Sub-characteristic | Pipe. | Router | Hier. | Iter. | Swarm |
|---|---|---|---|---|---|---|
| Observability | Accountability | 2 | 2 | 2 | 2 | 1 |
| | Trace Complexity | 2 | 2 | 1 | 1 | 0 |
| | Rationale Externalization | 1 | 1 | 2 | 2 | 1 |
| Autonomy | Dynamic Planning | 0 | 0 | 2 | 2 | 2 |
| | Reflection | 0 | 0 | 1 | 2 | 2 |
| | Failure Recovery | 1 | 1 | 2 | 2 | 2 |
| Scalability | Parallelism | 0 | 0 | 2 | 0 | 2 |
| | Modularity | 2 | 2 | 2 | 1 | 2 |
| | Absence of Bottlenecks | 0 | 0 | 0 | 0 | 2 |
| Token Efficiency | Context Locality | 2 | 2 | 1 | 1 | 1 |
| | Communication Overhead | 2 | 2 | 1 | 2 | 1 |
| | Redundancy Cost | 2 | 2 | 2 | 1 | 1 |

**Scope of the Scored Set.** The matrix scores the five patterns whose coordination topology fixes a single structural profile. The Hybrid category is excluded from the scored set for the structural reason given in Sect. 4: denoting the composition of two or more of these patterns at distinct layers of a system, it has no profile of its own and is read off its constituents.

**Why Three Levels.** Binary present/absent coding would conflate properties the topology precludes with those it accommodates through a local mechanism, erasing the distinction between hard constraint and cheap add-on. A finer scale would require a structural calibration metric that does not exist, reintroducing the implementation-dependent judgment the matrix excludes.

## 6 Applying the Matrix to the Surveyed Patterns

The matrix of Sect. 5 is read against the five scored patterns. Each cell is justified by the coordination topology alone and verifiable against Table 2; rather than restate every value, we highlight the cells whose level is not self-evident.

**Pipeline.** The strict unidirectional order makes every artifact attributable and the trace coincide with the ordered outputs (Observability intrinsic), and intrinsically avoids all three efficiency costs, since each stage sees only its predecessor's output. Rigidity precludes dynamic planning and reflection (= 0); rationale externalization and failure recovery are only conditional (= 1), reachable by making a stage emit its justification or retry. Stages are replaceable (Modularity

= 2), but serial execution gates progress (Parallelism, Absence of Bottlenecks = 0).

**Router.** One dispatch plus one specialist invocation give intrinsic attribution and a one-hop trace, and the per-request single message keeps all efficiency costs intrinsic. The routing decision is a label, so rationale externalization is conditional (= 1), as is re-dispatch after a failed call (Failure Recovery = 1); planning and reflection are precluded (= 0). Specialists register independently (Modularity = 2), but every request traverses the hub and none parallelizes within it (Parallelism, Absence of Bottlenecks = 0).

**Hierarchical.** The Supervisor's vantage makes Worker outputs attributable and plans/delegation rationale-bearing (both intrinsic), and the Supervisor intrinsically replans and reassigns on failure. Branching delegation makes the executed path diverge from the plan, replayable only under instrumentation (Trace Complexity = 1), and structured critique requires an added Evaluator role (Reflection = 1). Workers parallelize disjoint subtasks and are added independently (Parallelism, Modularity = 2), but all coordination passes through the Supervisor (Absence of Bottlenecks = 0); re-injected global state and delegation-and-report traffic are reducible but not intrinsically avoided (Context Locality, Communication Overhead = 1), while disjoint decomposition limits duplication (Redundancy Cost = 2).

**Iterative Loop.** Steps are attributable (Accountability = 2) and ReAct's Thoughts and the Evaluator's feedback intrinsically externalize the loop's reasoning, while revision, critique, and retry make the Autonomy column intrinsic. The open cycle count and accumulating context demote trace containment and context locality to conditional (= 1), the latter the long-context degradation regime [35] mitigable by windowing. Cycles are serialized and the loop monolithic (Parallelism, Absence of Bottlenecks = 0; Modularity = 1), with minimal intrinsic coordination traffic (= 2) but regenerated outputs across cycles (Redundancy Cost = 1).

**Swarm.** Decentralization makes the path genuinely combinatorial—the one observability property the structure precludes (Trace Complexity = 0)—and diffuses responsibility, though per-agent provenance logging restores attribution at implementation cost (Accountability = 1), as can a justification required of each hand-off (Rationale Externalization = 1). Distributed planning, peer critique, and reassignment on failure are all intrinsic (Autonomy column = 2), as are all three scalability conditions, including the unique absence of bottlenecks. The price is efficiency: state propagation, negotiation traffic, and deliberately duplicated consensus work are each reducible through codified hand-offs but not intrinsically avoided (Token Efficiency rows = 1).

### 6.1 Three Recurring Trade-Offs

The row profiles of the five scored patterns exhibit three recurring couplings between sub-characteristics. The first and the third (observability vs autonomy, scalability vs attribution) are hypotheses generated by the proposed coding, since their dimensions, operational definitions and level assignments are all products of the coding rather than of independent measurement; the second (token efficiency vs autonomy) is instead an empirically documented trade-off [39,40] that the coding makes structurally explicit. All three are stated below as order relations verifiable cell by cell against Table 2 and open to refutation by independent re-coding or measurement.

**Observability and Autonomy.** Every pattern that intrinsically plans or recovers (Hierarchical, Iterative, Swarm) drops below intrinsic trace containment: Trace Complexity falls to 1 where a central vantage survives and to 0 under full decentralization (Swarm). Runtime modification of control flow thus demotes trace containment by at least one level. Attribution follows a separate threshold: Accountability stays intrinsic (2) where a Supervisor or single loop context persists and is demoted only to conditional (1) under full decentralization, since provenance can still be instrumented.

**Token Efficiency and Autonomy.** This trade-off is documented empirically by token-distribution analyses [39,40] and production reports [29]; our coding makes structurally explicit how the cost is distributed across the Token Efficiency rows rather than concentrated in one, and which topological features pay for it. Every pattern with intrinsic Dynamic Planning has Context Locality demoted to 1, since runtime planning re-injects global state, recoverable by summarization only at implementation cost; every pattern with intrinsic Reflection (Iterative, Swarm) has Redundancy Cost demoted to 1, since critique is regeneration unless cached; and distributing control across agents adds coordination traffic, demoting Communication Overhead to 1 for Hierarchical and Swarm. The cost of autonomy is therefore not an undifferentiated tax but a widening of coordination overhead paid in three specific currencies—context propagation, duplicated work, and coordination traffic—which are the three components identified by [39,40], with long-context degradation [35] providing additional support for the Context Locality demotion.

**Scalability and Attribution.** The only pattern with intrinsic absence of bottlenecks (Swarm) is also the only one whose Accountability is demoted to conditional (1) rather than eliminated: removing the centralizing or serializing element removes the structural vantage for assignment but leaves provenance instrumentable. Conversely, every pattern retaining intrinsic attribution does so through such an element (chain, dispatch node, Supervisor, single context), each of which sets Absence of Bottlenecks to 0—a one-level exchange of attribution for bottleneck-freedom, consistent with coordination-protocol analyses [19,37].

### 6.2 Discussion

**Diagnostic Use.** Cemri et al. [15] report that a substantial share of MAS failures concerns organizational design and inter-agent coordination, distributed across specification, system design, inter-agent misalignment, and task verification, with no single category forming a majority. The matrix complements that taxonomy structurally: attribution failures map onto Accountability, runaway cost onto Token Efficiency, degradation under growth onto Absence of Bottlenecks, missing verification onto Reflection. Given an observed failure, a practitioner reads the corresponding cell for the adopted pattern: a 0 marks a structural tendency that no prompting will remove; a 1, a property the structure does not provide by itself but an explicit mechanism can supply; only a 2 makes it intrinsic.

**For Practitioners and Research.** Read row-wise, the matrix is a checklist of what a pattern does not provide for free: adopting Supervisor–Worker [1,29] means budgeting for trace reconstruction and context propagation; adopting a pipeline for knowledge-intensive processing [42,43] buys traceability and cost control at the price of runtime adaptivity. The matrix does not make these decisions; it prices them. Because each cell is an explicit claim, it generates falsifiable expectations testable by token-distribution studies [39,40], coordination benchmarks [19] and observability frameworks [18,20]; violations would localize which operational definitions need revision.

**Continuity with Classical MAS.** Characterizing MAS structurally, independently of agent reasoning, continues the classical tradition [6,7,9], where the tensions between centralized control and robustness and between decentralization and accountability already have antecedents. Token Efficiency is the genuinely new dimension: classical coordination assumed messages of negligible cost, whereas here every coordination message is a priced reasoning act.

## 7 Conclusions, Limitations, and Future Work

We characterized recurrent LLM-based multi-agent architectures through minimal reference models and a comparison matrix of four dimensions and twelve sub-characteristics, coded on an ordinal three-level scale whose decision rule makes every assignment inspectable and contestable. The matrix surfaced three recurring row-level couplings: autonomy versus trace containment and attribution, and scalability versus attribution, presented as hypotheses induced by the coded models rather than universal properties; and the widening of coordination overhead with autonomy, an empirically documented trade-off [39,40] that the coding makes structurally explicit. The contribution is methodological: a vocabulary in which coordination patterns can be named, compared cell by cell, and connected to both classical MAS theory and current LLM-agent practice. The principal limitation is the methodological status of the coding: the assignments are analytical judgments made by the authors, without an independent coding round, inter-rater reliability measurement, or empirical validation—Section 6 illustrates the vocabulary, it does not validate it—and the trade-offs of Sect. 6.1 are consequently hypotheses generated by the coding, not findings established against external evidence. The decision rule and the three-level scale reduce ambiguity and separate hard constraints from properties obtainable at implementation cost, but they neither eliminate coder dependence nor escape the discretization of properties that may vary continuously, so a finer re-coding could shift individual cells. Scope is bounded further by the saturation-oriented source selection, which targets recurrent coordination patterns rather than bibliometric completeness; the hybrid pattern remains unscored; the evidentiary basis mixes peer-reviewed work with preprints, vendor reports, and framework documentation [1,29,41], used to attest that patterns exist rather than to validate claims; and the four dimensions omit security, privacy, and human-oversight characteristics. These limitations define the future work. The most direct line is empirical operationalization, associating each sub-characteristic with measurable proxies testable on current infrastructure [17–20,39] and thereby converting the row-level hypotheses into falsifiable predictions; methodological hardening through multi-coder application and inter-rater reliability would address the coder dependence noted above; and compositional scoring of hybrids, together with further dimensions such as security, privacy, and human oversight, would extend the matrix's coverage.

## References


1. Anthropic: Building effective agents. Anthropic Engineering (2024). https://www.anthropic.com/engineering/building-effective-agents
2. Yao, S., et al.: ReAct: synergizing reasoning and acting in language models. In: Proceedings of the 11th International Conference on Learning Representations (ICLR), Kigali, Rwanda (2023). arXiv:2210.03629
3. Wooldridge, M., Jennings, N.R.: Intelligent agents: theory and practice. Knowl. Eng. Rev. **10**(2), 115–152 (1995)
4. Stone, P., Veloso, M.: Multiagent systems: a survey from a machine learning perspective. Auton. Robot. **8**(3), 345–383 (2000)
5. Foundation for Intelligent Physical Agents: FIPA ACL message structure specification. FIPA Standard SC00061G, Geneva, Switzerland (2002). http://www.fipa.org/specs/fipa00061/
6. Omicini, A., Ricci, A., Viroli, M.: Artifacts in the A&A meta-model for multi-agent systems. Auton. Agent. Multi-Agent Syst. **17**(3), 432–456 (2008)
7. Zambonelli, F., Jennings, N.R., Wooldridge, M.: Developing multiagent systems: the Gaia methodology. ACM Trans. Softw. Engi. Methodol. **12**(3), 317–370 (2003)
8. Bresciani, P., Perini, A., Giorgini, P., Giunchiglia, F., Mylopoulos, J.: Tropos: an agent-oriented software development methodology. Auton. Agent. Multi-Agent Syst. **8**(3), 203–236 (2004)
9. Dignum, V.: A model for organizational interaction: Based on agents, founded in logic. Ph.D. dissertation, SIKS Dissertation Series 2004-1, Utrecht University, Utrecht, The Netherlands (2004)
10. Boissier, O., Bordini, R.H., Hübner, J.F., Ricci, A., Santi, A.: Multi-agent oriented programming with JaCaMo. Sci. Comput. Program. **78**(6), 747–761 (2013)
11. Horling, B., Lesser, V.: A survey of multi-agent organizational paradigms. Knowl. Eng. Rev. **19**(4), 281–316 (2004)
12. Wang, J., Wang, J., Athiwaratkun, B., Zhang, C., Zou, J.: Mixture-of-Agents enhances large language model capabilities. In: Proceedings of the 13th International Conference on Learning Representations (ICLR), Singapore (2025). arXiv:2406.04692

13. Yang, Y., et al.: AgentNet: decentralized evolutionary coordination for LLM-based multi-agent systems. arXiv preprint arXiv:2504.00587 (2025)
14. Guo, T., et al.: Large language model based multi-agents: a survey of progress and challenges. In: Proceedings of the 33rd International Joint Conference on Artificial Intelligence (IJCAI), Jeju, South Korea (2024). arXiv:2402.01680
15. Cemri, M., et al.: Why do multi-agent LLM systems fail? arXiv preprint arXiv:2503.13657 (2025)
16. Han, S., Zhang, Q., Yao, Y., Jin, W., Xu, Z., He, C.: LLM multi-agent systems: challenges and open problems. arXiv preprint arXiv:2402.03578 (2024)
17. Orogat, A., Rostam, A., Mansour, E.: Understanding multi-agent LLM frameworks: a unified benchmark and experimental analysis. arXiv preprint arXiv:2602.03128 (2026)
18. Ma, T., et al.: MAESTRO: multi-agent evaluation suite for testing, reliability, and observability. arXiv preprint arXiv:2601.00481 (2026)
19. Zhu, K., et al.: MultiAgentBench: evaluating the collaboration and competition of LLM agents. In: Proceedings of the 63rd Annual Meeting of the Association for Computational Linguistics (ACL), Vienna, Austria, pp. 8580–8622 (2025)
20. Dong, L., Lu, Q., Zhu, L.: AgentOps: enabling observability of LLM agents. arXiv preprint arXiv:2411.05285 (2024)
21. Schick, T., et al.: ToolFormer: language models can teach themselves to use tools. In: Advances in Neural Information Processing Systems (NeurIPS), New Orleans, LA, USA, vol. 36 (2023). arXiv:2302.04761
22. Shinn, N., Cassano, F., Berman, E., Gopinath, A., Narasimhan, K., Yao, S.: Reflexion: language agents with verbal reinforcement learning. In: Advances in Neural Information Processing Systems (NeurIPS), New Orleans, LA, USA, vol. 36 (2023). arXiv:2303.11366
23. Du, Y., Li, S., Torralba, A., Tenenbaum, J.B., Mordatch, I.: Improving factuality and reasoning in language models through multiagent debate. In: Proceedings of the 41st International Conference on Machine Learning (ICML), Vienna, Austria (2024). arXiv:2305.14325
24. Liang, T., et al.: Encouraging divergent thinking in large language models through multi-agent debate. In: Proceedings of the Conference on Empirical Methods in Natural Language Processing (EMNLP), Miami, FL, USA (2024). arXiv:2305.19118
25. Park, J.S., O'Brien, J.C., Cai, C.J., Morris, M.R., Liang, P., Bernstein, M.S.: Generative agents: interactive simulacra of human behavior. In: Proceedings of the 36th Annual ACM Symposium on User Interface Software and Technology (UIST), San Francisco, CA, USA (2023)
26. Wu, Q., et al.: AutoGen: enabling next-gen LLM applications via multi-agent conversation. In: Proceedings of the 1st Conference on Language Modeling (COLM), Philadelphia, PA, USA (2024). arXiv:2308.08155
27. Hong, S., et al.: MetaGPT: meta programming for a multi-agent collaborative framework. In: Proceedings of the 12th International Conference on Learning Representations (ICLR), Vienna, Austria (2024). arXiv:2308.00352
28. Li, G., Hammoud, H.A.A.K., Itani, H., Khizbullin, D., Ghanem, B.: CAMEL: communicative agents for 'mind' exploration of large language model society. In: Advances in Neural Information Processing Systems (NeurIPS), New Orleans, LA, USA, vol. 36 (2023). arXiv:2303.17760
29. Anthropic: How we built our multi-agent research system. Anthropic Engineering (2025). https://www.anthropic.com/engineering/multi-agent-research-system

30. Liu, X., et al.: AgentBench: evaluating LLMs as agents. In: Proceedings of the 12th International Conference on Learning Representations (ICLR), Vienna, Austria (2024). arXiv:2308.03688
31. Jimenez, C.E., et al.: SWE-bench: can language models resolve real-world GitHub issues? In: Proceedings of the 12th International Conference on Learning Representations (ICLR), Vienna, Austria (2024). arXiv:2310.06770
32. Zhou, S., et al.: WebArena: a realistic web environment for building autonomous agents. In: Proceedings of the 12th International Conference on Learning Representations (ICLR), Vienna, Austria (2024). arXiv:2307.13854
33. Xu, B., Peng, Z., Lei, B., Mukherjee, S., Liu, Y., Xu, D.: ReWOO: decoupling reasoning from observations for efficient augmented language models. arXiv preprint arXiv:2305.18323 (2023)
34. Zhang, Q., et al.: Agentic context engineering: evolving contexts for self-improving language models. arXiv preprint arXiv:2510.04618 (2025)
35. Liu, N.F., Lin, K., Hewitt, J., Paranjape, A., Bevilacqua, M., Petroni, F., Liang, P.: Lost in the middle: how language models use long contexts. Trans. Assoc. Comput. Linguist. **12**, 157–173 (2024)
36. Yehudai, A., et al.: Survey on evaluation of LLM-based agents. arXiv preprint arXiv:2503.16416 (2025)
37. Yan, B., et al.: Beyond self-talk: a communication-centric survey of LLM-based multi-agent systems. arXiv preprint arXiv:2502.14321 (2025)
38. Tran, K.-T., Dao, D., Nguyen, M.-D., Pham, Q.-V., O'Sullivan, B., Nguyen, H.D.: Multi-agent collaboration mechanisms: a survey of LLMs. arXiv preprint arXiv:2501.06322 (2025)
39. Wang, Q., Tang, Z., Jiang, Z., Chen, N., Wang, T., He, B.: AgentTaxo: dissecting and benchmarking token distribution of LLM multi-agent systems. In: ICLR 2025 Workshop on Foundation Models in the Wild, Singapore (2025)
40. Zhang, G., et al.: Cut the crap: an economical communication pipeline for LLM-based multi-agent systems. In: Proc. 13th Int. Conf. on Learning Representations (ICLR), Singapore (2025). arXiv:2410.02506
41. LangChain: Fault tolerance. LangGraph Documentation (2025). https://docs.langchain.com/oss/python/langgraph/fault-tolerance
42. Petroni, F., et al.: KILT: a benchmark for knowledge intensive language tasks. In: Proceedings of Conference of the North American Chapter of the Association for Computational Linguistics (NAACL) (2021)
43. Lewis, P., et al.: Retrieval-augmented generation for knowledge-intensive NLP tasks. In: Advances in Neural Information Processing Systems (NeurIPS), vol. 33 (2020)

# Fuzzy Behavior Trees

Luca Ferragina[1], Ilenia Galati[1(✉)], Lorena Gullone[1], Francesco Scarcello[1], and Muhammad Asaf[1,2]

[1] DIMES Department, Unical, via P. Bucci 41C, 87036 Rende, CS, Italy
{luca.ferragina,ilenia.galati,lorena.gullone, francesco.scarcello,muhammad.asaf}@unical.it
[2] Artémat s.r.l., Via P. Bucci, Cubo 41C, 87036 Rende, CS, Italy

**Abstract.** Behavior Trees (BTs) are a widely adopted framework for modeling and executing intelligent agent behaviors in robotics, video games, and autonomous systems. Their popularity stems from their modularity, reusability, scalability, and clear hierarchical structure, which facilitate the design and maintenance of complex decision-making processes. Despite these advantages, standard BTs rely on crisp logical conditions and deterministic execution rules, making them inherently limited when operating in environments characterized by uncertainty, imprecision, incomplete information, or gradual transitions between behavioral states. To address these limitations, we introduce Fuzzy Behavior Trees (FBTs), a novel extension of Behavior Trees grounded in fuzzy logic. FBTs replace the binary evaluation mechanisms of traditional BTs with fuzzy reasoning, enabling the representation and processing of uncertain and graded information. In particular, our approach is based on a recently introduced fuzzy logic language that combines ASP with the ability to reason on qualitative fuzzy labels. We define the semantics of FBTs, describe their execution model, and present an illustrative example that highlights how fuzzy reasoning can be seamlessly incorporated into existing BT architectures.

**Keywords:** Fuzzy Logic · Behavior Tree · Answer Set Programming

## 1 Introduction

Behavior Trees (BTs) originated in the video game industry as a modular and scalable alternative to Finite State Machines for controlling non-player characters [14,15,23], and have since become a widely adopted framework for modeling and executing intelligent agent behavior in robotics and autonomous systems [6,13]. A BT decomposes a complex task into a hierarchy of reusable components: internal control-flow nodes (Sequence, Fallback, Parallel, and Decorator) orchestrate the execution of leaf nodes (Conditions, which query the world state, and Actions, which act upon it). Execution is driven by a periodic tick signal that traverses the tree from the root, with each active node returning one of three statuses, Success, Failure, or Running, to its parent. This design endows


S. Bistarelli et al. (Eds.): AIxIA 2026, LNAI 17131, pp. 294–308, 2027.
https://doi.org/10.1007/978-3-032-40774-0_22

BTs with modularity, reactivity, and a readable, inspectable control flow, and formal analyses have shown that they subsume earlier switching architectures, such as finite state machines, decision trees, and subsumption architectures, in terms of scalability and reusability [6,12].

To illustrate these standard semantics, consider a simple, deterministic combat scenario from a video-game (Fig. 1). An autonomous agent must decide whether to engage an enemy or fall back to an alternative behavior. The tree is rooted in a Fallback node, whose first child is a Sequence node encoding the engagement logic: the agent first checks whether it is *Healthy* or not (Condition); it then enters a loop (Decorator) that repeatedly tries to acquire a target through a nested Fallback, which succeeds if either an enemy is visible and *Selected* (Condition) or if a subsequent search procedure succeeds. Once a target is secured, it executes the *Fight* action. If any step fails, for instance if the agent is not healthy, the Sequence fails and the root fallback node (?) routes its execution to its second child, which is another behavior tree modeling some alternative behavior.

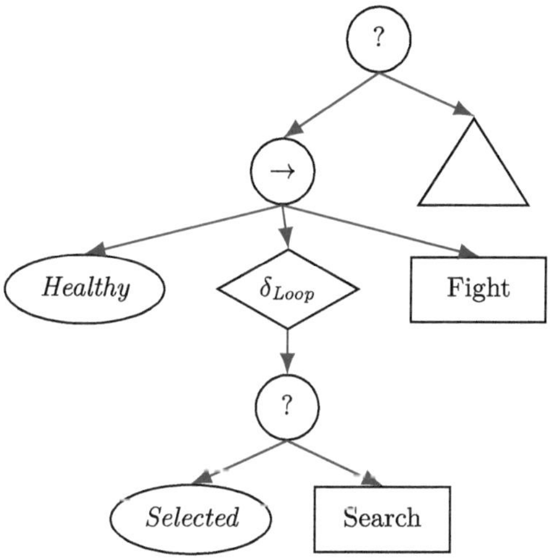


**Fig. 1.** A classical, deterministic (sub) Behavior Tree for a simple video-game scenario.

This crisp logic is highly readable and modular, but standard BTs rely on deterministic execution rules that struggle in environments characterized by uncertainty, incomplete information, or gradual transitions between behavioral states. Perceptual and operational categories, such as *obstacle nearby*, *corridor safe enough*, or the *tactical advantage*, lack sharp natural boundaries. Encoding them as hard thresholds yields brittle behavior, where negligible variations in a continuous observation (e.g., fluctuating partial visibility) can flip a condition's outcome and trigger abrupt behavioral switches. For instance, in the above example, the agent may have a certain degree of healthiness, which can be enough or not also depending on the enemy strength. In this case we usually reason by adopting qualitative labels such as high, low, medium, and so on. This mismatch between values (and the qualitative way we look at them) and the rigid symbolic decision structures has been identified as a central obstacle well beyond the BT setting, highlighting the need for a framework that is capable of handling graded uncertainty.

Fuzzy logic [32] offers the classical remedy to this problem, replacing binary truth with graded membership degrees $\mu \in [0,1]$. Linguistic terms such as *low*, *medium*, and *high* are formalized as overlapping fuzzy sets [33], logical connectives are generalized by $t$-norms and $t$-conorms [17], and the resulting inference machinery has a long record of application in control and autonomous robot navigation [21,26,27].

The integration of uncertainty management into rule-based reasoning has evolved from quantitative extensions of classical logic programming to fuzzy and neuro-symbolic frameworks. Early approaches introduced attenuation factors to model graded deduction [8], while Fuzzy Logic Programming later provided truth-functional semantics based on fuzzy operators [1,7,24,30]. Related developments extended fuzzy reasoning to more structured formalisms, including Description Logics and Answer Set Programming (ASP). In fuzzy Description Logics, vagueness is represented through membership functions and fuzzy operators while preserving decidability [5,20,29]. In fuzzy ASP, propositions are associated with truth degrees in $[0,1]$, generalizing stable-model semantics through suitable choices of t-norms and implication operators [2,16].

Further work investigated the interaction between fuzzy answer sets, negation, inconsistency, and minimality. For instance, non-stratified negation and inconsistency-tolerant fuzzy ASP have shown that graded truth and non-monotonic reasoning can coexist, although they introduce additional semantic complexity [4,25]. Other approaches, such as Fuzzy Linguistic Logic Programming, shifted the focus from numerical truth degrees to linguistic terms, enabling a form of reasoning closer to natural language [19]. More recently, Fuzzy Datalog has been extended with arbitrary t-norms and existential rules, while retaining favorable data-complexity properties [18].

Complementarily, neuro-symbolic AI has explored the integration of learning-based perception with symbolic reasoning under uncertainty. Systems such as *DeepProbLog*, *NeurASP*, and *SLASH* combine neural predictions with probabilistic or answer-set reasoning [22,28,31].

Existing attempts to bring this machinery into Behavior Trees, however, have remained shallow. Most integrations confine fuzzy inference to individual leaf nodes within an otherwise crisp tree [13]: graded evidence is defuzzified locally and cannot cross node boundaries, influence composite-node evaluation, or affect behavioral selection at the structural level. A step beyond the leaf level was taken in the LUMI Agents [3], where Sequence and Selector nodes aggregate child satisfaction degrees through $t$-norms and $t$-conorms; yet even there, fuzziness is restricted to the numerical propagation of status values. Note that the present work is intended as a response to the limitations of the basic first concept proposed in LUMI, with the goal of becoming the main framework for plan execution within the broader LUMI agent framework.

In the aforementioned approaches, graded knowledge remains a transient by-product of the tick: it is never stored, shared among nodes, reasoned over declaratively, or used to drive structural execution decisions such as reconsidering an earlier choice. Moreover, the formal foundations of graded tree execution, including semantic consistency across multiple linguistic labels, the interaction of graded truth with the Running status, and the computational properties of tick evaluation, have been left largely unspecified.

In this paper, we introduce *Fuzzy Behavior Trees* (FBTs), a novel extension of Behavior Trees that embeds fuzzy reasoning directly into the execution semantics of the tree. The framework is grounded in Answer Set Programming (ASP) [10, 11], and specifically in a recently introduced fuzzy label-based extension of ASP (FLASP), in which every predicate carries a finite set of linguistic labels and data-driven membership functions ground input atoms in numerical observations, possibly produced by machine learning components, as demonstrated in an industrial quality-control pipeline [9]. This design provides a basis for neuro-symbolic systems that combine data-driven learning with interpretable symbolic reasoning. Two features of the language are pivotal for our purposes. First, its $\gamma$-propagation mechanism supports principled transitions from graded to Boolean truth within the declarative semantics, without the need for external defuzzification steps. Second, the existence of multiple answer sets provides a powerful non-deterministic way of modeling complex problems, as in standard ASP. On the other hand, there are deterministic tractable fragments for which the answer set is unique and computable in polynomial time.

In an FBT, every node except Actions carries a fuzzy program evaluated over a shared knowledge base, and the success it reports to its parent is determined by the existence of a fuzzy answer set for that program, rather than by a simple Boolean aggregation of its children's outcomes; when a program admits several answer sets, the execution engine can behave in a non-deterministic way. Classical BTs are recovered exactly when node programs are restricted to their base cases, making FBTs a conservative generalization of the standard formalism. We formally define the semantics of FBTs, describe their execution model, and show how this BT framework connects symbolic behavioral modeling and fuzzy-logic reasoning.

The remainder of the paper is organized as follows. Section 2 recalls the label-based fuzzy Answer Set Programming language on which FBTs are built. Section 3 presents the formal definition of Fuzzy Behavior Trees and their execution model. Section 4 develops an illustrative example, and Sect. 5 concludes with a discussion and directions for future work.

## 2 Preliminaries: The FLASP Language

We build on the fuzzy Answer Set Programming language FLASP, which couples symbolic rules written over linguistic labels with numerically grounded membership functions. We briefly sketch the main properties of FLASP here, and we refer to [9] for further details.

Each predicate $p$ comes with a triple $\langle \Lambda_p, \mathrm{M}_p, \Sigma_p \rangle$, where $\Lambda_p$ is a finite set of *linguistic labels* (e.g. *low*, *medium*, *high*), $\mathrm{M}_p$ a family of *membership functions*, one per label, and $\Sigma_p$ a collection of *S-norms*. A *fuzzy interpretation* $\mathcal{I}\colon \mathcal{B}_\Pi \to [0,1]$ assigns a truth degree to each ground atom $p(\mathbf{c};\ell)$, in the labeled Herbrand base $\mathcal{B}_\Pi$. A fuzzy literal is either a positive atom or a negated atom $\neg_\mathcal{N} p(\mathbf{x};\ell)$, where $\mathbf{x}$ is a term tuple and $\mathcal{N}$ is a fuzzy negator. Rules have the form $h \leftarrow b_1 \otimes \cdots \otimes b_m$, where body literals are combined through a t-norm $\otimes$, while multiple rules with the same head are aggregated through an s-norm $\oplus$. For EDB (input) predicates, each label is equipped with a membership function $\mu_\ell : D \to [0,1]$ mapping numerical observations to graded facts. For IDB (derived) predicates, we do not have an explicit representation of membership functions, but we specify an admissible combinations of label degrees, through a truth profile $\gamma_p \subseteq [0,1]^{\Lambda_p}$. The all-zero profile is always admissible, to model the fact that the given atom $p$ is entirely false (all its labels have truth-value 0).

For instance, the leftmost part of Fig. 3 shows the labels *low* and *high* of the atom `able_to_fight`. The profile shown in this figure models their semantic connection. In this case, it is represented as a parametric curve $\gamma_p : [0,1] \to [0,1]^{\Lambda_p}$ that expresses the functional co-dependency between the labels. Note, for instance, that simultaneously large truth-values for both *low* and *high* are not allowed. Moreover, if the truth-value for *high* is small, in this case below 0.65, the profile says that *low* must be greater than 0. We will use this feature of FLASP programs in Sect. 4.

*Semantics.* An interpretation $\mathcal{I}$ is *consistent* if $\big(\mathcal{I}(p(\mathbf{c};\ell))\big)_{\ell\in\Lambda_p} \in \gamma_p$ for every atom. For a ground rule $r$ with head $h$, $\mathcal{I}(B(r))$ is obtained by applying the t-norm $\mathcal{T}$ to the interpretation of all body literals, and $\mathcal{I}(R_h) = \mathcal{S}_h\{\mathcal{I}(B(r)) \mid r \in R_h\}$, where $R_h$ is the set of rules with head $h$ and $\mathcal{S}_h$ is the s-norm associated with the head predicate to aggregate contributions from the different rules defining it. Trivially, $\mathcal{I}(\emptyset) = 0$.

Then, a *model* of $\Pi$ is a *consistent* interpretation $\mathcal{I}$ such that, for every atom $h$, $\mathcal{I}(h) \geq \mathcal{I}(R_h)$. An interpretation $\mathcal{I}$ for a program $\Pi$ is said to be *minimal* w.r.t. a given set of interpretations $W$, if there exists no other interpretation $\mathcal{I}' \in W$ $(\mathcal{I}' \neq \mathcal{I})$, such that $\mathcal{I}'(\bar{p}) \leq \mathcal{I}(\bar{p})$, for every ground atom $\bar{p}$. An interpretation $\mathcal{I}$ is called a minimal model of $\Pi$, if it is minimal w.r.t. the set of all models of $\Pi$.

It is easy to see that a program may have many minimal models, even infinitely many, or no model at all. We focus on those models, called *tight*, that are "maximally feasible", because all atoms have a maximal set of labels with a *critical* value, meeting rule-induced bounds or profile-induced bounds exactly, so that no degree can be lowered without losing model-hood. That tightness and minimality are complementary: minimality forbids jointly lowering a profile, whereas tightness avoids infinite sets of possibly incomparable models.

A *fuzzy answer set* (FAS) [9] is a tight minimal model of the reduct obtained by replacing each negated body literal $\neg_\mathcal{N} b$ with the constant $\mathcal{N}(\mathcal{I}(b))$. A program may admit several answer sets or none, the latter signaling a semantic inconsistency. For $\gamma$-monotone acyclic programs, there is a unique least answer set computable in polynomial time. In general, the language is more expressive (and more complex, NP-hard), and may admit multiple answer sets.

We extend FLASP with *true (strong) negation*, which lets a node retract a fact from the knowledge base by deriving its strong negation, giving behaviors a declarative way to update the shared knowledge during execution.

## 3 Fuzzy Behavior Trees

We define an FBT as a tree whose root is represented by a tuple of the form described below, and each of its children (if any) is itself an FBT.

**Definition 1 (Fuzzy Behavior Tree).** *A* Fuzzy Behavior Tree *(FBT) $n$ is recursively defined as a tuple*

$$n = \langle \mathcal{C}_n, t_n, \sigma_n, P_n, \mathrm{KB}_n, \Pi_n \rangle,$$

*where:*

- $\mathcal{C}_n$ *is a finite, ordered (possibly empty) list of* children, *each of which is itself an FBT node;*
- $t_n \in \{Sequence, Fallback, Parallel, Decorator, Reasoner, Action\}$ *is the node type; Reasoner and Action nodes are leaves ($\mathcal{C}_n = \emptyset$), and Decorator nodes have exactly one child;*
- $\sigma_n \in \{S, F, R, I\}$ *is the node status, indicating whether $n$ is currently running (R) or inactive (I), has terminated successfully (S), or has terminated with failure (F); initially, $\sigma_n = I$;*
- $P_n$ *is a finite set of predicate symbols, each equipped with a* FLASP *triple $\langle \Lambda_p, \mathrm{M}_p, \Sigma_p \rangle$, that identify the knowledge* declared *at $n$ and shared with the whole subtree rooted at $n$. We denote by $P_{\to n}$ the union of $P_n$ with the sets $P_m$ of all ancestors $m$ of $n$; this is the shared signature visible at $n$. In addition, $n$ may use a set $L_n$ of* local *predicates, visible only at $n$. We require each predicate symbol to be declared at most once along any root-to-leaf path;*
- $\mathrm{KB}_n$ *is the knowledge base accessible to the node: a finite set of graded facts over the signature $P_{\to n} \cup L_n$;*
- $\Pi_n$ *is a* FLASP *program over $P_{\to n} \cup L_n$ that allows $n$ to reason over and update its knowledge base. For Action nodes, which interact with the environment (e.g., through actuators and sensors) and whose status is not determined by logical satisfiability, we assume that $\Pi_n$ is only used to provide the results of the performed action in terms of facts added to (or retracted from)* $\mathrm{KB}_n$.

### 3.1 Semantics

Let FBT be a behavior tree.

Execution starts by ticking the root node of FBT. Whenever a node $\mathrm{n} = \langle \mathcal{C}_n, t_n, \sigma_n, P_n, \mathrm{KB}_n, \Pi_n \rangle$ is ticked, it executes the procedure associated with its type $t_n \in \{\mathit{Sequence}, \mathit{Fallback}, \mathit{Parallel}, \mathit{Reasoner}, \mathit{Action}, \mathit{Decorator}\}$: The program $\Pi_n$ is evaluated over the knowledge base $\mathrm{KB_n}$ (that is, we look for Fuzzy Answer Sets of $\Pi_n \cup \mathrm{KB_n}$), and its status changes from $I$ to $R$ if there is a FAS, or to $F$ if there is no FAS. If $\mathcal{C}_n$ is not empty, it will tick some child, say $n'$, to run. Whenever $n'$ ends its execution with the success status $S$, $\Pi_n$ is executed again over the knowledge base $\mathrm{KB_n}$ (if it has been updated after $n'$), then it continues its execution according to the semantics of its type $t_n$. We require that children ending in a failure (i.e., no fuzzy answer sets) do not modify $\mathrm{KB}_n$; that is, failing nodes have no side effects, except for irreversible action nodes.

Moreover, unlike standard Behavior Trees, here the outcome of a parent node is not obtained by simply aggregating the success or failure returned by its children. In fact, $n$ may fail at some early stage if its program $\Pi_n$ becomes inconsistent with respect to the current knowledge base. That is, $n$ is able to detect possible reasons to fail that are logically implied by complex outcomes of the processed children, even if each single child apparently succeeded with its planned task. Eventually, the status of $n$ will change from $R$ to either $S$ (success) or $F$ (failure).

We next describe the behavior of the different node types.

**Sequence Node.** A *Sequence* node $n$ ticks its children from left to right. As in standard BTs, if a child $n'$ is running, the node waits until it completes its execution. If $n'$ ends with a failure (state $F$, no Fuzzy Answer Set exists), then the sequence node $n$ ends with a failure too; otherwise $n$ executes $\Pi_n$ over the (possibly updated) knowledge base $\mathrm{KB_n}$, and if this evaluation finds a FAS, it continues with the next child, if any.

We point out that an important feature of the proposed framework is the dynamic program instantiation: the atoms computed by $n$ according to the updated knowledge base at each step are leveraged to prepare the execution of the next child. For instance, in a robotic application, depending on the exploration made by one child behavior-tree, we may "configure" some actions in the subsequent child that are tailored to a very specific physical area related to such an exploration. Technically, the FLASP program of the subsequent child is grounded over completely different worlds, focusing on those fragments of the research space identified by the models computed in previous children.

Then, the semantics of the sequence node $n$ is the following: $n$ fails whenever, after executing the child $n' \in \mathcal{C}_n$ in the sequence, either $n'$ fails or there is no possible ways for the nodes up to $n'$ of satisfying $n$. That is, there is no sequence of answer sets for these nodes such that the evaluation of $\Pi_n$ over the knowledge base $\mathrm{KB_n}$ obtained after the execution of $n'$ has an answer set.

Note that when FLASP programs are non-deterministic, that is, when they have multiple (feasible) answer sets, this feature allows us to describe very complex tasks in a quite natural declarative way, differently from the highly operational approach of standard behavior trees.

**Fallback (or Selector) Node.** A *Fallback* node $n$ ticks its children from left to right. If a child $n'$ is running, the node waits to complete its execution. If $n'$ ends with a failure (status $F$, no Fuzzy Answer Set exists), then $n$ continues with the next child, if any. Otherwise, in case of success, $n$ executes $\Pi_n$ over the (possibly updated) knowledge base $\mathrm{KB_n}$, and if this evaluation finds a FAS, it ends with status $S$; otherwise it ends with status $F$.

Then, the semantics of the fallback node $n$ is the following: $n$ fails whenever, for each child $n' \in \mathcal{C}_n$, either $n'$ fails, or there is no answer set computed by $n$ that satisfies $n$. That is, there is no way to get an answer set for the evaluation of $\Pi_n$ over the knowledge base $\mathrm{KB_n}$ obtained after the execution of $n'$.

**Reasoner Node.** A *Reasoner* node is a leaf node whose purpose is purely inferential. It has no children and does not execute actions in the external environment. When ticked, it evaluates its fuzzy program $\Pi_n$ over $\mathrm{KB}_n$. If $\Pi_n$ admits at least one fuzzy answer set, the node returns $S$; otherwise, it returns $F$. When $\Pi_n$ is restricted to crisp (Boolean) predicates and deterministic programs (e.g. stratified ASP programs without choice rules), this node recovers the role of a classical BT condition leaf. In the general setting, however, it can also produce graded conclusions and multiple admissible reasoning contexts, which may be exploited by a parent node in a non-deterministic way.

**Action Node.** An *Action* node $n$ is a leaf node associated with an executable behavior in the environment. Unlike the other node types, its status is not determined by the satisfiability of a fuzzy program, but by the correct execution of its specific action (for instance, obtaining information from sensors). After termination, its status is set to either $S$ or $F$. A node action usually updates the knowledge base, by writing atoms that represent its outcome.

Actions can be non-deterministic in general, and we distinguish among reversible and non-reversible actions. With respect to the former type, we usually require that they provide no effects on the knowledge base after a failure. However, non-reversible actions may change the knowledge base even in case of failure (because of non-reversible changes in the environment that are modeled in the common knowledge base).

**Parallel Node.** A *Parallel* node $n$ ticks all its children within the same execution step and does not impose a left-to-right ordering. It is similar to the sequence node, but it is not required that all children end with a success status. In classical BTs, these nodes have a parameter $m$ and ends with a success whenever at least $m$ children succeeded. However, in our more general context, the decision depends only on the execution of $\Pi_n$ over the knowledge base $\mathrm{KB}_n$ updated by the children that end their execution (which of course may well implement the standard BT policy).

**Decorator Node.** A *Decorator* node $n$ has exactly one child and, as in standard BTs, it manipulates the status returned by its child according to a predefined policy, and may selectively tick the child. Classical examples include the *Inverter*, which swaps status $S$ and $F$; *Repeat*/*Loop*, which re-ticks the child a given number of times or until a target status is reached; *Max-k-Tries*, which lets the child fail at most $k$ times before returning $F$ without further ticks; and *Timeout*, which returns $F$ if the child is still running after a prescribed time budget.

Overall, these node types show that the FBT framework preserves the familiar structure of standard Behavior Trees while enriching them with declarative reasoning over a shared knowledge base.

*Remark 1 (Conservative Extension of BTs).* For every classical Behavior Tree $T$, there exists an FBT $\mathcal{T}$ whose execution (and output) is the same as $T$.

*Proof (Sketch).* Let $T$ be a classical Behavior Tree and let $\mathcal{T}$ be its encoding as an FBT constructed preserving the topology of $T$ and replacing each node as follows.

- Every internal node (Sequence, Fallback and Parallel) is associated with the empty program $\Pi_n = \emptyset$.
- Every Condition node testing a Boolean condition $c$ is encoded as a Reasoner node whose program consists of the integrity constraint $\leftarrow \neg c$.
- Every Action node is encoded by the corresponding FBT action node, preserving its execution and status.
- Every Decorator node is encoded by the corresponding FBT decorator node, preserving its execution and status.

The resulting FBT behaves exactly as the original BT. For internal nodes, the empty program is always satisfiable; consequently, their execution depends solely on the status returned by their children, exactly as in classical Behavior Trees. Moreover, Reasoner nodes succeed precisely when the corresponding Boolean condition holds, while Action nodes preserve the original execution semantics. Consequently, every tick produces the same sequence of node activations and the same execution status as in the original Behavior Tree.

Remark 1 shows that the proposed framework is a conservative extension of classical Behavior Trees. Hence, standard BTs are recovered as a special case, while more expressive node programs enable reasoning over crisp or fuzzy knowledge, supporting graded decisions, multiple fuzzy answer sets, and, when appropriate, non-determinism.

To clarify the working principles of FBTs, in the following, we present an illustrative example that shows how fuzzy reasoning is embedded within the execution of the tree and determines the resulting behavior.

# 4 An Illustrative Example: An FBT for Combat Decision-Making

As an illustrative scenario, consider an autonomous agent embodied as a non-player character acting in a game environment. Its decision loop is fed by a perception layer: the game engine produces numerical estimates of task-relevant features of the surrounding entities, such as their visibility, health conditions, or size. Among the detected entities, the agent must commit to a single target and assess whether that target can plausibly be defeated under the current conditions; following a cautious combat doctrine, it engages only targets that it could fight effectively *both* in close-quarters combat *and* at range. The interest of the scenario lies in the crisp go/no-go decision that must be distilled from uncertain, heterogeneous graded evidence (strength, size, health, ammunition levels).

The predicates that define the signature for the common knowledge base $P_{(\rightarrow)}$ at the sequence node $(\rightarrow)$ are the following:

- the (crisp) predicates derived directly from the game environment, namely: `player`, `enemy`, `myself`, `distance`, and `visible`;
- the fuzzy predicates with measures provided by the game engine and mapped into input (EDB) predicates through suitable membership functions, that is, `health`, `shield_level`, `size`, `physical_strength`, and `gun_ammunition`;

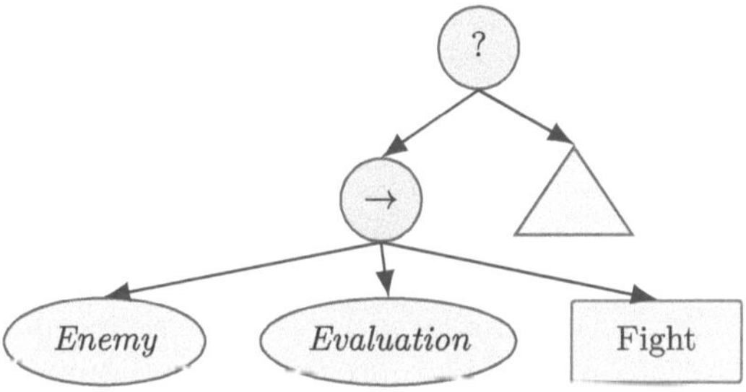


**Fig. 2.** Structure of the FBT employed in the example. Reasoner nodes (green ellipses) evaluate FLASP programs over the shared knowledge base, the Action node (orange rectangle) interacts with the environment, and the gray triangle denotes an alternative-behavior subtree. (Color figure online)

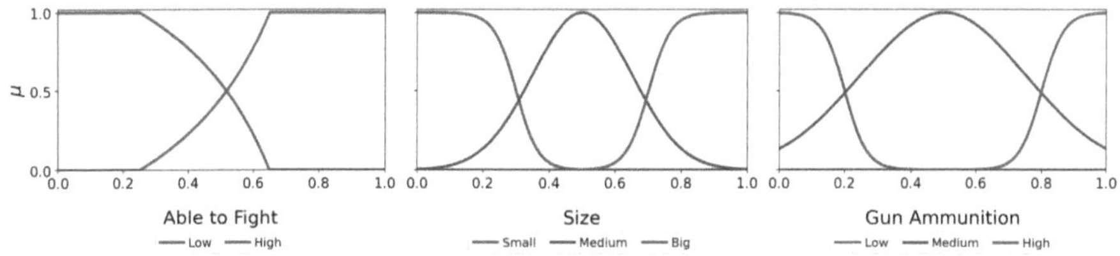


**Fig. 3.** Membership functions of the predicates `able_to_fight`, `size`, and `gun_ammunition`. Values along the x-axis are normalized to the range $[0, 1]$.

- `selected`, `close_lead`, `ranged_lead`, and `able_to_fight`, which are IDB predicates derived by the children and consumed by the Sequence node (predicates used within a single child only, such as the graded advantages, remain local to it).

In particular, the EDB contains atoms of the form $\texttt{player}(ID, H, D, P, F, A)$, $\texttt{enemy}(ID)$, and $\texttt{myself}(ID)$, where $ID$ is a unique identifier (of an enemy or of the player in action, `enemy` and `myself` only mark roles), and $H$, $D$, $P$, $F$, $A$ are its health, size, protection (armor), physical strength, and ammunition scores.

Throughout the example we use the Gödel operators, min for the t-norm and max for the s-norm, and the Łukasiewicz negator $\mathcal{N}(x) = 1 - x$ for the negation; recall that the `crisp` label only has Boolean 0–1 values, and it is omitted for the sake of presentation for predicates behaving in the classical way. That is, when the fuzzy label is not specified in some atom, it means that the `crisp` (Boolean) label is the only one used for it.

### 4.1 FLASP Programs

The Sequence node ($\Pi_{\rightarrow}$, Table 1) decides whether it is reasonable to start fighting, leveraging the knowledge derived from its child nodes. The constraint ensures that a FAS is obtained—thereby declaring the partial success of the node—only if it is possible to proceed with the action *Fight*. Then, the final success of the node will be determined by the actual outcome of this Action.

In particular, $\texttt{able\_to\_fight}(; high)$ is cautiously determined by the minimum truth value between the two possible attack modes, so that the agent is capable of fighting the selected enemy $E$ in either situation. Whenever the truth-value of $\texttt{able\_to\_fight}(; high)$ is small enough, we automatically obtain $\texttt{able\_to\_fight}(; low) > 0$ by means of the profile $\gamma_{\texttt{able\_to\_fight}}$ (see the leftmost plot in Fig. 3), which fires the constraint and causes the node to fail.

Furthermore, before the children's evaluation completes, all labels of the atom `able_to_fight` are zero (the all-zero profile is always admissible), leaving the constraint idle and allowing the node to stay consistent while its information is incomplete. Once the evaluation has committed its assessment, a decision can be made. Notably, because the children's behavior is non-deterministic, the Sequence fails only if *every* choice of the enemy $E$ in the children leads to the triggering of the constraint. Conversely, the node proceeds when the feasibility degree lies beyond the overlap region (0.65 in Fig. 3).

**Table 1.** FLASP rules for $\Pi_{\rightarrow}$ program in the FBT.

| |
|---|
| $\leftarrow \texttt{able\_to\_fight}(; low)$ |
| $\texttt{able\_to\_fight}(; high) \leftarrow \texttt{close\_lead}(E; high) \odot \texttt{ranged\_lead}(E; high)$ |

Consider now the first child, in charge of enemy selection, whose reasoning is presented in Table 2. This is a standard choice that fails only if no enemy is visible.

**Table 2.** Rules for $\Pi_{Enemy}$ program to identify and select a visible enemy.

| | |
|---|---|
| $\texttt{selected}(E) \leftarrow$ | $\texttt{enemy}(E) \odot \texttt{visible}(E) \odot \neg\, \texttt{ineligible}(E)$ |
| $\texttt{ineligible}(E') \leftarrow$ | $\texttt{enemy}(E) \odot \texttt{enemy}(E') \odot E' \neq E \odot \texttt{selected}(E)$ |
| $\texttt{enemy\_selected} \leftarrow$ | $\texttt{selected}(E)$ |
| $\leftarrow$ | $\neg\texttt{enemy\_selected}$ |

Given the committed target $E$, the second Reasoner ($\Pi_{Evaluation}$, Table 3) assesses the tactical situation. Specifically, a *close-quarters lead* (`close_lead`) holds if either the agent boasts high health and shields against a weakened target, or if the agent enjoys superior physical strength and better shielding than $E$. Conversely, a *ranged lead* (`ranged_lead`) is established when $E$ is large and poorly shielded, while the agent possesses abundant ammunition and adequate shields. The derived leads directly determine the feasibility of the respective attack modes. This program is deterministic and never fails: it is the *quality* of the committed degrees that decides the fate of the parent. Since all rules are guarded by $\texttt{selected}(E)$, grounding is confined to the committed target (dynamic program instantiation, Sect. 3).

**Table 3.** $\Pi_{Evaluation}$ program.

| | |
|---|---|
| $\texttt{close\_lead}(E; \mathit{high}) \leftarrow$ | $\texttt{player}(E, H, \_, P, \_, \_) \odot \texttt{selected}(E) \odot$ |
| | $\texttt{myself}(\mathit{ID}') \odot \texttt{player}(\mathit{ID}', H', \_, P', \_, \_) \odot$ |
| | $\texttt{health}(H'; \mathit{high}) \odot \texttt{shield\_level}(P'; \mathit{high}) \odot$ |
| | $\texttt{health}(H; \mathit{low}) \odot \texttt{shield\_level}(P; \mathit{medium})$ |
| $\texttt{close\_lead}(E; \mathit{high}) \leftarrow$ | $\texttt{player}(E, \_, \_, P, F, \_) \odot \texttt{selected}(E) \odot$ |
| | $\texttt{myself}(\mathit{ID}') \odot \texttt{player}(\mathit{ID}', \_, \_, P', F', \_) \odot$ |
| | $\texttt{physical\_strength}(F'; \mathit{high}) \odot$ |
| | $\texttt{physical\_strength}(F; \mathit{low}) \odot$ |
| | $\texttt{shield\_level}(P'; \mathit{medium}) \odot \texttt{shield\_level}(P; \mathit{low})$ |
| $\texttt{ranged\_lead}(E; \mathit{high}) \leftarrow$ | $\texttt{myself}(\mathit{ID}') \odot \texttt{player}(\mathit{ID}', \_, \_, P', \_, A') \odot$ |
| | $\texttt{player}(E, \_, D, \_, F, \_) \odot \texttt{selected}(E) \odot \texttt{size}(D; \mathit{big}) \odot$ |
| | $\texttt{distance}(E, \mathit{ID}'; \mathit{far}) \odot \texttt{gun\_ammunition}(A'; \mathit{high}) \odot$ |
| | $\texttt{shield\_level}(P'; \mathit{medium})$ |

## 5 Conclusion

We introduced Fuzzy Behavior Trees, which embed fuzzy reasoning directly into the execution semantics of BTs: building on FLASP, nodes evaluate fuzzy programs over a shared, hierarchically scoped knowledge base, and their success is decided by the existence of fuzzy answer sets rather than by a simple Boolean aggregation of children's statuses. As the example of Sect. 4 shows, this knowledge-mediated criterion lets a node fail for reasons only logically implied by the combined outcomes of its children, even when each child succeeded; and it can replace hand-coded retry loops with declarative non-determinism. Since classical BTs are recovered exactly when node programs are restricted to their base cases (Remark 1), FBTs can be adopted incrementally within existing BT designs. Several directions remain open: on the theoretical side, we plan to characterize the complexity of tick evaluation beyond the tractable fragments; on the practical side, we are developing an execution engine integrating membership functions learned from perceptual data; we plan to evaluate FBTs in games and robotics, comparing them against existing BT extensions [13], toward interpretable behavior architectures that unify symbolic control flow, graded uncertainty, and learned perception.

## References


1. Achs, Á., Kiss, A.: Fuzzy extension of datalog. Acta Cybern. **12**(2), 153–166 (1995). https://cyber.bibl.u-szeged.hu/index.php/actcybern/article/view/3454
2. Alviano, M., Peñaloza, R.: Fuzzy answer sets approximations. Theory Pract. Log. Program. **13**(4–5), 753–767 (2013). https://doi.org/10.1017/S1471068413000471
3. Asaf, M., Guarasci, P., Laurito, D., Longo, D.M., Mendicelli, A., Scarcello, F.: Lumi agents: a fuzzy BDI framework for intelligent agents. In: Proceedings of the 2nd Workshop on Green-Aware Artificial Intelligence (2025)
4. Blondeel, M., Schockaert, S., Vermeir, D., Cock, M.D.: Fuzzy answer set programming: an introduction. In: Yager, R.R., Abbasov, A.M., Reformat, M.Z., Shahbazova, S.N. (eds.) Soft Computing: State of the Art Theory and Novel Applications, Studies in Fuzziness and Soft Computing, vol. 291, pp. 209–222. Springer, Cham (2013). https://doi.org/10.1007/978-3-642-34922-5_15
5. Bobillo, F., Straccia, U.: fuzzydl: an expressive fuzzy description logic reasoner. In: IEEE International Conference on Fuzzy Systems (IEEE World Congress on Computational Intelligence), pp. 923–930. IEEE (2008)
6. Colledanchise, M., Ögren, P.: Behavior Trees in Robotics and AI: An Introduction. CRC Press, Boca Raton (2018)
7. Ebrahim, R.: Fuzzy logic programming. Fuzzy Sets Syst. **117**(2), 215–230 (2001). https://doi.org/10.1016/S0165-0114(98)00300-5
8. van Emden, M.H.: Quantitative deduction and its fixpoint theory. J. Log. Program. **3**(1), 37–53 (1986). https://doi.org/10.1016/0743-1066(86)90003-8
9. Ferragina, L., Galati, I., Gullone, L., Scarcello, F.: Applying answer set programming with fuzzy membership functions: a case study (2026). https://arxiv.org/abs/2607.03550
10. Gelfond, M., Lifschitz, V.: The stable model semanticsfor logic programming. In: 5th Conference on Logic Programming, pp. 1070–1080

11. Gelfond, M., Lifschitz, V.: Classical negation in logic programs and disjunctive databases. N. Gener. Comput. **9**(3), 365–385 (1991)
12. Ghzouli, R., Berger, T., Johnsen, E.B., Dragule, S., Wąsowski, A.: Behavior trees in action: a study of robotics applications. In: Proceedings of the 13th ACM SIGPLAN International Conference on Software Language Engineering, pp. 196–209 (2020)
13. Iovino, M., Scukins, E., Styrud, J., Ögren, P., Smith, C.: A survey of behavior trees in robotics and ai. Robot. Auton. Syst. **154**, 104096 (2022)
14. Isla, D.: Managing complexity in the halo2 ai. In: Game Developer's Conference Proceedings (2005)
15. Isla, D.: Building a better battle. In: Game developers conference, san francisco, vol. 32 (2008)
16. Janssen, J., Schockaert, S., Vermeir, D., De Cock, M.: General fuzzy answer set programs. In: International Workshop on Fuzzy Logic and Applications, pp. 352–359. Springer, Cham (2009)
17. Klement, E.P., Mesiar, R., Pap, E.: Triangular Norms, vol. 8. Springer, Heidelberg (2013)
18. Lanzinger, M., Sferrazza, S., Walega, P.A., Gottlob, G.: Fuzzy datalog∃ over arbitrary t-norms. In: Bjørner, N.S., Heule, M., Voronkov, A. (eds.) LPAR 2024: Proceedings of 25th Conference on Logic for Programming, Artificial Intelligence and Reasoning, Port Louis, Mauritius, May 26-31, 2024. EPiC Series in Computing, vol. 100, pp. 426–444. EasyChair (2024). https://doi.org/10.29007/CNGW
19. Le, V.H., Liu, F., Tran, D.K.: Fuzzy linguistic logic programming and its applications (2009). https://doi.org/10.1017/S1471068409003779
20. Lukasiewicz, T., Straccia, U.: Managing uncertainty and vagueness in description logics for the semantic web. J. Web Semant. **6**(4), 291–308 (2008)
21. Mamdani, E.H., Assilian, S.: An experiment in linguistic synthesis with a fuzzy logic controller. Int. J. Man Mach. Stud. **7**(1), 1–13 (1975)
22. Manhaeve, R., Dumancic, S., Kimmig, A., Demeester, T., Raedt, L.D.: Neural probabilistic logic programming in deepproblog. Artif. Intell. **298**, 103504 (2021). https://doi.org/10.1016/J.ARTINT.2021.103504
23. Mateas, M., Stern, A.: A behavior language for story-based believable agents. IEEE Intell. Syst. **17**(4), 39–47 (2002)
24. Medina, J., Ojeda-Aciego, M., Vojtáš, P.: A procedural semantics for multi adjoint logic programming. In: Portuguese Conference on Artificial Intelligence, pp. 290–297. Springer, Cham (2001)
25. Van Nieuwenborgh, D., De Cock, M., Vermeir, D.: Fuzzy answer set programming. In: Fisher, M., van der Hoek, W., Konev, B., Lisitsa, A. (eds.) JELIA 2006. LNCS (LNAI), vol. 4160, pp. 359–372. Springer, Heidelberg (2006). https://doi.org/10.1007/11853886_30
26. Ross, T.J.: Fuzzy Logic With Engineering Applications. Wiley, Hoboken (2005)
27. Saffiotti, A.: The uses of fuzzy logic in autonomous robot navigation. Soft. Comput. **1**(4), 180–197 (1997)
28. Skryagin, A., Stammer, W., Ochs, D., Dhami, D.S., Kersting, K.: Neural-probabilistic answer set programming. In: Kern-Isberner, G., Lakemeyer, G., Meyer, T. (eds.) Proceedings of the 19th International Conference on Principles of Knowledge Representation and Reasoning, KR 2022, Haifa, Israel, July 31 - August 5, 2022 (2022). https://proceedings.kr.org/2022/48/
29. Straccia, U.: Reasoning within fuzzy description logics. J. Artif. Intell. Res. **14**, 137–166 (2001)

30. Vojtás, P.: Fuzzy logic programming. Fuzzy Sets Syst. **124**(3), 361–370 (2001). https://doi.org/10.1016/S0165-0114(01)00106-3
31. Yang, Z., Ishay, A., Lee, J.: Neurasp: embracing neural networks into answer set programming. In: Bessiere, C. (ed.) Proceedings of the Twenty-Ninth International Joint Conference on Artificial Intelligence, IJCAI 2020, pp. 1755–1762. ijcai.org (2020). https://doi.org/10.24963/IJCAI.2020/243
32. Zadeh, L.: Fuzzy sets. Inf. Control **8**, 338–353 (1965)
33. Zadeh, L.A.: The concept of a linguistic variable and its application to approximate reasoning–i. Inf. Sci. **8**(3), 199–249 (1975)

# Design of an Ontological Model to Transfer Clinical Knowledge into Autonomous Robots

Elisa Foderaro[1(✉)], Alessandro Umbrico[1], Francesca Fracasso[1], Alberto Olivares-Alarcos[2], Domenico Massimo Pisanelli[1], Guillem Alenyà[2], Gabriella Cortellessa[1], Andrea Orlandini[1], and Antonio Andriella[2]

[1] CNR - Institute of Cognitive Sciences and Technologies, Rome, Italy
elisafoderaro@cnr.it
[2] CSIC-UPC, Institut de Robòtica i Informàtica Industrial, Barcelona, Spain

**Abstract.** As robots are increasingly deployed in real-world assistive and healthcare settings, they must adapt their behavior to users' cognitive, physical, and emotional characteristics while pursuing long-term assistive objectives. Achieving such adaptation requires robust representations of human-related knowledge that can support both reactive interaction and deliberative decision-making. However, existing approaches often rely on application-specific user models that limit reusability and fail to provide an explicit semantic connection between human features, assistive goals, and robot behaviors. This paper presents an ontological model designed to transfer human-centered knowledge into autonomous robotic systems. The ontology provides a unified semantic representation of human needs, cognitive and physical capabilities, and states, bridging the gap between highly abstract foundational ontologies and domain-specific user models. By serving as a common knowledge layer for human-centered cognitive robotic architectures, the model is intended to support the integration of short-term adaptation and long-term planning, enabling personalized, context-aware, and clinically informed interactions.

**Keywords:** Ontology · Human Modeling · Adaptive Interaction · Socially Assistive Robotics

## 1 Introduction

The increasing reliability of robot platforms and the availability of computational resources are pushing the use of robotic agents outside the lab in unstructured environments, raising challenges concerning their relationships with humans and explicit/implicit social norms. The multidisciplinary field of Human-Robot Interaction (HRI) investigate methodologies and technologies enhancing human awareness, adaptability, trustworthiness, and social acceptance of robotic solutions [6,13,25]. In contexts where humans and robots interact over extended


S. Bistarelli et al. (Eds.): AIxIA 2026, LNAI 17131, pp. 309–322, 2027.
https://doi.org/10.1007/978-3-032-40774-0_23

periods, robots are expected to possess decision-making skills built upon sound human modeling. Indeed, to tailor robot interactions on the specific needs of human users and the relevant social context, robots must be equipped with sophisticated reasoning capabilities that take into account, for instance, human perspectives [23], affective conditions [27], cognitive states [2], and norms and expectations [5].

Consider, for instance, cognitive stimulation interventions, where a socially interactive robot supports older adults experiencing mild cognitive decline. In such contexts, the robot must deliver exercises aligned with long-term therapeutic goals while continuously adapting its behavior to the user's engagement, emotional state, and cognitive workload. Similarly, in physical rehabilitation scenarios [29], robots assist patients by guiding exercises, monitoring performance, and adapting activities according to the patient's motor abilities, fatigue level, and recovery progress (See Fig. 1). In both cases, effective assistance emerges from the combination of long-term goal-oriented reasoning and short-term reactive adaptation during interaction. Since assistive needs can vary depending on the health condition of the user, the stage of the clinical pathway, and the objectives defined by the clinicians, rich models of human states and needs are necessary to coherently guide both the long- and the short-term interaction between an assistive robot and a user.

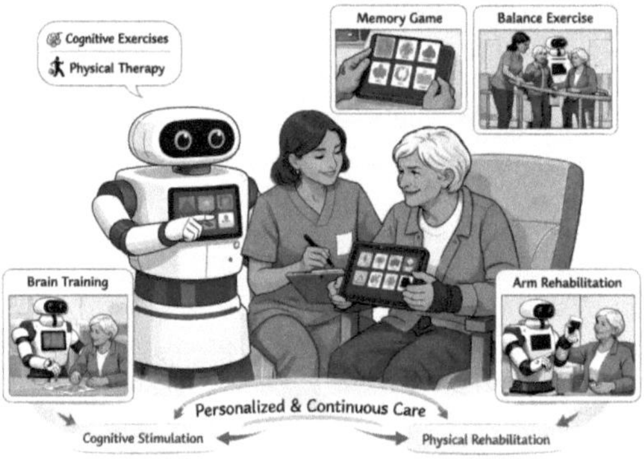


**Fig. 1.** Physical and Cognitive assistance through robotic interaction.

Several researchers have addressed the issue of adapting robot behaviors to user models [14,31], focusing also on combined short- and long-term perspectives [19,20]. However, a uniform and well-structured representation of "human features" that encompass health conditions, personal preferences, and physical/cognitive capabilities [22,30], and their direct implications for reasoning processes is still missing. Existing approaches typically treat short-term adaptation and long-term planning separately and often rely on application-specific user models that limit reusability across clinical domains. To the best of our knowledge, there is no explicit semantic framework that systematically relates human functioning qualities to robot goals, tasks, and interaction strategies.

This work addresses this gap by proposing an ontological model that holistically characterizes human features across cognitive, physical, and contextual dimensions, bridging abstract foundational ontologies and practical human modeling requirements of HRI. In doing so, our ontology offers a foundational core for human-centered cognitive architectures that integrate reactive (short-term) and deliberative (long-term) planning to support personalized, continuous, and context-aware interactions.

## 2 Holistic Modeling of Human Qualities

Addressing the variability and heterogeneity of assistive scenarios requires considering several features when designing adaptive assistive behaviors. First, assistive robots must account for a variety of human-related factors, including cognitive abilities, physical capabilities, emotional states, and personal preferences. These factors influence not only what type of assistance should be provided, but also how the interaction should be carried out. Second, assistive behaviors must balance functional objectives (e.g., completing a task or exercise) with interaction qualities such as engagement, trust, comfort, and acceptance. Finally, adaptive interaction requires integrating long-term reasoning, supporting therapeutic or assistive goals over time, with short-term reasoning that enables dynamic adaptation to the user's current state and context.

The combination of ontologies with robot controllers has been investigated to evaluate action opportunities [7], support cultural and social awareness [5, 10], and realize cognitive processes such as perspective taking, goal reasoning, and proactive adaptation [3,23,32]. Although such works rely on human-related models, a uniform semantics capturing the wide variety of health-related needs and features is missing. This is in part due to the high variability of application scenarios and in part to the large number of "user-related variables" that may affect assistance and interactions. As a result, researchers have typically defined their "own" application-specific models. A user model for assistive applications should account for "clinical perspective" and capture user-related knowledge in a formalism compliant with existing clinical standards.

In this regard, the International Classification of Functioning, Disability and Health (ICF) proposed by the World Health Organization (WHO)[1] provides a well-established framework for characterizing human functioning from a multi-dimensional perspective. The ICF framework is organized into four main categories. *Body Functions* concern the physiological functions of the human body (e.g., hearing and seeing), as well as mental functions from both cognitive (e.g., attention and memory) and emotional (e.g., mood) perspectives. *Activities and Participation* concern the capabilities of a person to execute tasks and engage in life situations, including communication, mobility, self-care, etc. *Environmental Factors* concern external aspects that directly or indirectly affect the user's functioning. *Body Structures* concern the anatomical parts of the body, such as organs, limbs, and their components.

[1] https://www.who.int/standards/classifications/.

Other researchers have considered ICF. The works [15,21] propose a robot-based assessment of users' skills to characterize the level of daily assistance needed. The work [16] integrates ICF semantics into the ACT-R cognitive architecture [1] to simulate the behavior of users with different needs. Such works primarily rely on a taxonomical representation of human features, lacking a semantics suitable for advanced and contextual reasoning. In this context, we do not limit the use of ICF to its taxonomic representation of human functioning. Rather, we integrate this framework into a domain ontology based on well-established foundational theory [9] to characterize heterogeneous *human features* and support *contextual framing* of human states.

### 2.1 Foundational Representation of Human Qualities

From an ontological perspective, the ICF taxonomy can be interpreted as a structured vocabulary of human qualities, understood as aspects of functioning that characterize a person's health condition, each associated with a level of functioning. The integration of the ICF taxonomy into a foundational semantics is the representational ground for the holistic model designed to *frame* human states at different abstraction levels and coherently contextualize short- and long-term interactions. Specifically, in this work, the ICF taxonomy is integrated into an ontological model grounded on DUL[2], a lightweight version of DOLCE[9].

According to the foundational structure of DUL/DOLCE, human modeling adopts the ontology pattern `Object-Quality-Region` to flexibly characterize the qualities of physical objects (e.g., a person) and their measurements. Each `PhysicalObject` is associated with a set of `Quality`, each of which captures a specific aspect of the object and persists for as long as the object exists. Each `Quality` is then mapped to a `Region`, which provides a structured representation of the space within which that quality can be interpreted. While the association between an object and its qualities remains stable over time, the mapping between qualities and their corresponding regions may evolve, allowing the model to track different measurements and account for changing interpretations of the attributes (and object state).

The concept `dul:Person` represents an agentive human individual and is specialized in `Patient` to describe any individual receiving assistive or rehabilitative support from the robotic system. Each individual of `Patient` is associated with one or more instances of `HumanFunctioningQuality`, a subclass of `dul:Quality`. This class serves as the root element of the integrated ICF taxonomy, describing the functioning of `Patient`. Each `HumanFunctioningQuality` is associated with a `HumanFunctioningRegion` (subclass of `dul:Region`), which also serves as the root of the ICF qualifiers defining the associated representational space of quality individuals.

The concept `ICFFunctioningRegion` (subclass of `HumanFunctioning Region`) implements the ICF qualifier scale, which quantifies the degree of impairment as follows: (i) the value 0 denotes `NoImpairment` (0–4%); (ii)

[2] DOLCE+DnS UltraLite - http://ontologydesignpatterns.org/ont/dul/DUL.owl.

the value 1 denotes `MildImpairment` (5–24%); (iii) the value 2 denotes `ModerateImpairment` (25–49%); (iv) the value 3 denotes `SevereImpairment` (50–95%); (v) the value 4 denotes a `CompleteImpairment` (96–100%) and; (vi) the values 8 and 9 represent the impossibility of measuring a quality (not specified and not applicable, respectively). Figure 2 shows the high-level structure resulting from applying the DOLCE pattern to the modeling of human functioning.

Following this pattern, an individual of `Patient` (e.g., `p#1`) is associated with several types of `HumanFunctioningQuality` individuals (e.g., `q#1`, `q#2`, ..., `q#n`). The distinction between qualities and regions is key to modeling dynamic health states. The individual `q#1` will always refer to the same functional quality of the particular patient `p#1` while the associated region can change to reflect his/her clinical progress or decline. The history of these updates can be preserved to support reasoning over the longitudinal patient evolution, but this aspect is outside the scope of the present work and will be addressed in future developments.

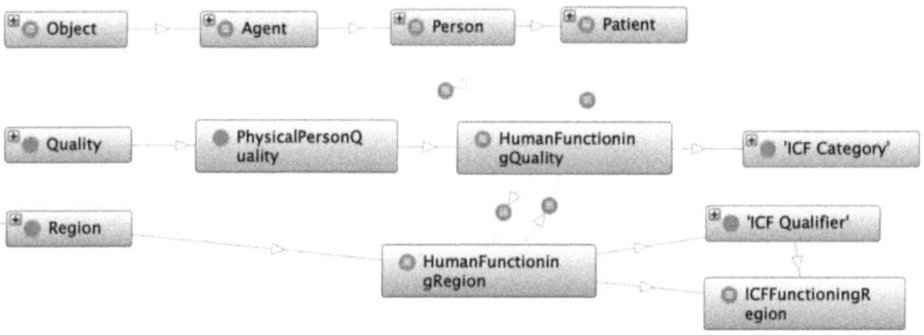


**Fig. 2.** DOLCE pattern applied to the modeling of ICF human qualities.

## 2.2 ICF Qualities and Beyond

The concept `HumanFunctioningQuality` characterizes any aspect of humans that is relevant according to the ICF taxonomy. As such, this concept is expanded into four concepts corresponding to the main ICF categories: (i) `BodyFunction (b)`; (ii) `Activities and Participation (d)`; (iii) `Environmental Factors (e)`; (iv) `BodyStructure (s)`. Each concept is further specialized into concepts representing increasingly specific aspects. As an example, the concept `BodyFunction (b)` is further decomposed into `MentalFunction (b1)` and, among others, `SensoryFunction (b2)`. The former concerns qualities like `Attention (b140)`, or `Memory (b144)`, etc. The latter concerns sensory-related qualities such as `Seeing (b210)`, `Hearing (b230)`, or `Pain (b280)`. The taxonomy supports higher levels of detail where needed. For example, `Memory (b144)` can be specialized into `ShortTermMemory (b1440)`, `LongTermMemory (b1441)`, or `Retrieval of memory (b1442)`, etc. This depth can be expanded or collapsed depending on the assistive needs.

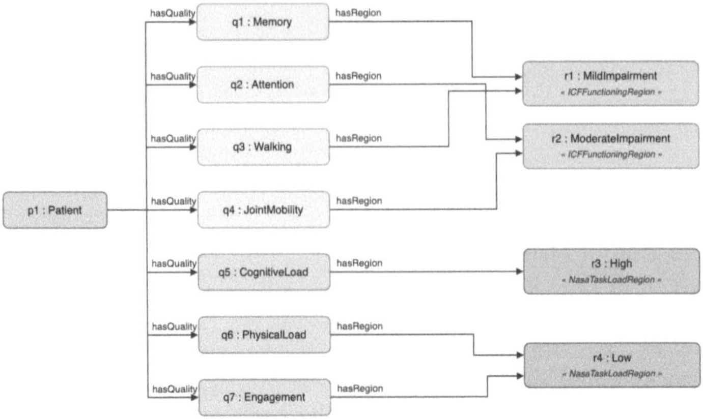


**Fig. 3.** Ontology-compliant description of a human with qualities and regions.

Under `Activities and Participation (d)`, the ontology captures a person's ability to execute tasks and engage in life situations. Examples include `Communication (d3)`, `Mobility (d4)`, and `SelfCare (d5)`, among others. The class `SelfCare (d5)` covers activities such as `Washing oneself (d510)`, `Dressing (d540)`, and `Eating (d550)`. These qualities are particularly relevant in rehabilitation contexts, where functional independence in daily activities is a primary clinical target. These qualities describe health needs suitable for long-term planning of assistance, since they would determine the stimulation needs of rehabilitation and clinical objectives. Some of these qualities, such as `Seeing (b210)` or `Hearing (b230)` are relevant to short-term planning also and might characterize general interaction preferences affecting action execution (e.g., prefer vocal interaction over text and touch when impairments of `Seeing` are reported).

In addition to ICF variables, there are additional qualities that must be considered to monitor and adapt the interactions. As an example, aspects measured by the NASA Task Load Index (NASA-TLX) [18] were integrated into the proposed ontology as additional qualities through dedicated taxonomical structures. To this aim, the ontology defines under `HumanFunctioningQuality` the concepts `Workload`, `Engagement` and `Performance`. Again, these concepts are further specialized into a taxonomical structure to support increasing levels of detail if necessary. For example, the concept `Workload` is specialized in `CognitiveLoad`, `PhysicalLoad`, and `TemporalLoad`. Similarly, the concept `Engagement` is specialized in `EmotionalState` and `AttentionLevel`.

The resulting ontological model (TBox) thus integrates multiple taxonomical qualities under the root concept `HumanFunctioningQuality`, enabling a uniform interpretation and correlation of different scales. As a note, whenever an assistive scenario requires aspects that are not yet represented, additional human qualities can be introduced under `HumanFunctioningQuality`, following established clinical knowledge and domain expert recommendations, without altering the underlying ontological structure. Figure 3 shows an example of a knowledge graph (ABox) modeling a concrete human instance with associated functioning qualities and measured levels of functioning, organized according to the ontological model. Note that measures concerning non-ICF qualities are expressed using a dedicated regional space (e.g., `NasaTaskLoadRegion`).

# 3 Putting Human Semantics in the Loop

The ontological model provides a shared semantic representation of human features that can be exploited by reasoning (decision-making) processes operating across different temporal scales. The ontological model enables human-centered personalization and adaptation by *framing user knowledge* at different levels of abstraction to provide the contextual subset of knowledge necessary to the related decision-making processes. Long-term reasoning focuses on stable qualities, suitable for supporting task selection and planning. Short-term reasoning instead relies on more dynamic qualities suitable for adapting the execution of (planned) actions. Considering the representative scenario in Fig. 1, the section discusses how the ontology enables a unified reasoning process in which human functioning qualities are consistently interpreted to bridge long-term planning and short-term interaction within a shared semantic framework.

## 3.1 Assessing ICF-Based Semantics Against Clinical Screening

Variables related to slow-changing user characteristics can be defined on the basis of clinician input. In particular, standard screening procedures are used to directly integrate clinical knowledge into the system. Such procedures usually rely on a set of standardized assessment scales, such as the Barthel Index [24] and the Functional Independence Measure (FIM) [26], each providing a scale-specific record over specific functional domains for each patient. To obtain a uniform semantic representation independent of the adopted assessment instrument, items from a set of standardized scales are mapped to the ICF categories embedded in the proposed model. Then, raw scores are converted into the appropriate ICF qualifier level (0–4).

Whenever a conversion procedure between an assessment scales and the ICF qualifiers was already available and validated in the literature, that mapping was adopted (e.g., for the FIM [34]). Otherwise, items are linked to the most appropriate ICF categories following the methodology proposed by Cieza et al. [11,12]. If an item encompasses different constructs, the information in each construct was individually linked, as in [28]. The adopted methodology follows established clinical practice, and its systematic validation involving clinical experts will be carried out as part of future work. The complete mapping between each item and the corresponding ICF category is publicly available on GitHub[3].

[3] https://github.com/pstlab/AIxIA26.

**Table 1.** Links between first-level ICF categories of body functions and activities and participation and assessment scales frequently used in rehabilitation

| ICF categories | FIM | BI | FAT | BBT | 9HPT | MI | BBS | TC | PC | FAC | WT |
|---|---|---|---|---|---|---|---|---|---|---|---|
| Body Functions | 3 | 2 | | | | 7 | | | | 1 | 1 |
| Activities and Participation | 19 | 12 | 2 | 4 | 4 | | 14 | 1 | 1 | 1 | 1 |

FIM, Functional Independence Measure; BI, Barthel Index; FAT, Frenchay Arm Test; BBT, Box and Block; 9HPT, Nine Hole Peg Test; MI, Motricity Index; BBS, Berg Balance Scale; TC, Trunk Control Assessment; PC, Postural Control Assessment; FAC, Functional Ambulation Categories; WT, Walking Tests.

Table 1 shows the distribution of the items from a set of assessment scales across the first-level ICF categories. The result is a patient-specific instantiation of the ontological model in which each `Patient` individual is associated with a set of `HumanFunctioningQuality` instances, each linked to an `ICFFunctioningRegion` representing the measured level of functioning through an ICF qualifier. This uniform representation provides the foundation for the inference mechanisms that support both long-term rehabilitation planning and short-term adaptation of system interactions.

### 3.2 From Level of Impairment to Clinical Objectives

The patient-specific profile provides a structured description of the individual's functional status, allowing for the translation of this knowledge into clinically relevant objectives that can explicitly support the rehabilitation. To this end, the concept of `TherapeuticGoal` is introduced in the ontology as a specialization of `dul:Goal`. `TherapeuticGoal` is further decomposed into more specialized classes, such as `AmbulationRecovery`, `FallsRiskPrevention`, or `MemorySkillsImprovement`. Each concept represents a clinical objective to be pursued by the `Patient`. Each patient is associated with one or more `TherapeuticGoal`(s) inferred from their functional profile.

The association between patient profiles and therapeutic goals is dynamically inferred with logical rules integrated into the ontology through the Semantic Web Rule Language (SWRL). Each rule specifies a pattern over one or more `HumanFunctioningQuality` instances and their associated impairment levels, and infers the corresponding `TherapeuticGoal`(s). This enables rehabilitation objectives to be automatically derived from clinical assessment data while maintaining an explicit and interpretable representation of the underlying decision criteria. Table 2 illustrates representative reasoning patterns supported by the ontology. In the rules, $Q$ denotes the `hasQuality` relation linking a patient to a quality, $R$ denotes the `hasRegion` relation between a quality and a region, and $CV$ denotes the `hasCardinalValue` property associating each region with its corresponding integer ICF qualifier value, ranging from 0 (`NoImpairment`) to 4 (`CompleteImpairment`), as introduced in Sect. 2.1.

Finally, TherapeuticGoal individual names are abbreviated for readability (e.g., mem_impr for MemorySkillsImprovement).

**Table 2.** Examples of rules inferring TherapeuticGoal individuals from patient profiles

| Rule | Formal specification |
|---|---|
| $R_1$ | $\forall p, q, r$ Patient$(p) \wedge Q(p,q) \wedge$ b144.MemoryFunctions$(q) \wedge R(q,r) \wedge CV(r) \geq 1 \rightarrow$ hasTherapeuticGoal$(p,$ mem_impr$)$ |
| $R_2$ | $\forall p, q, r$ Patient$(p) \wedge Q(p,q) \wedge$ d5.SelfCare$(q) \wedge R(q,r) \wedge CV(r) \geq 2 \rightarrow$ hasTherapeuticGoal$(p,$ adl_ind_impr$)$ |
| $R_3$ | $\forall p, q, r$ Patient$(p) \wedge Q(p,q) \wedge$ d450.Walking$(q) \wedge R(q,r) \wedge CV(r) \geq 3 \rightarrow$ hasTherapeuticGoal$(p,$ ambulation_recov$)$ |
| $R_4$ | $\forall p, q, r$ Patient$(p) \wedge Q(p,q) \wedge$ d450.Walking$(q) \wedge R(q,r) \wedge 1 \leq CV(r) \leq 2 \rightarrow$ hasTherapeuticGoal$(p,$ gait_ss_impr$)$ |
| $R_5$ | $\forall p, q_1, r_1, q_2, r_2$ Patient$(p) \wedge Q(p,q_1) \wedge$ d450.Walking$(q_1) \wedge R(q_1,r_1) \wedge 1 \leq CV(r_1) \leq 3 \wedge Q(p,q_2) \wedge$ d415.MaintainingBodyPosition$(q_2) \wedge R(q_2,r_2) \wedge CV(r_2) \geq 2 \rightarrow$ hasTherapeuticGoal$(p,$ falls_prevention$)$ |

$Q(p,q) \equiv$ hasQuality$(p,q)$, $R(q,r) \equiv$ hasRegion$(q,r)$, $CV(r) \equiv$ hasCardinalValue$(r)$.

Some objectives are inferred whenever an impairment is detected, regardless of its severity. For example, rule $R_1$ infers MemorySkillsImprovement whenever Memory presents at least MildImpairment level. Indeed, even mild memory deficits may require targeted intervention. The level of impairment would rather influence the intensity and frequency of the intervention. Other objectives exploit the ontology's hierarchy. For example, $R_2$ infers ActivitiesOfDailyLivingIndependenceImprovement whenever any quality subsumed by SelfCare, exhibits a ModerateImpairment level or higher. As a consequence, the same rule automatically applies to activities such as dressing, washing, or eating without requiring separate rules for each specific activity.

The same quality may activate different objectives, depending on the level of impairment. For example, Walking distinguishes between the objective of recovering ambulation, i.e., AmbulationRecovery, and the objective of improving or preserving walking ability, i.e., GaitSpeedSafetyImprovement, respectively $R_3$ and $R_4$. Other therapeutic goals depend on the simultaneous presence of multiple functional conditions. For example, $R_5$ infers FallsRiskPrevention only when impaired balance coexists with preserved walking ability, capturing a clinically meaningful risk profile that cannot be identified by considering either quality in isolation.

These examples show how the proposed explicit semantic rules enable the robot to interpret a patient's functioning profile at a higher level of abstraction, transforming standardized clinical observations into explicit rehabilitation objectives. In cases where a patient's functional profile does not match any existing rule pattern, no therapeutic goal is inferred. However, the ontology is designed to accommodate additional rules to cover previously unrepresented conditions. By encoding clinical knowledge into ontological inference rules, the proposed model supports reasoning that is intended to reflect the decision criteria adopted during rehabilitation planning. This provides a semantic connection between standardized clinical assessment and long-term assistive planning in which every inferred objective can be traced back to the patient's observed functional conditions and the rules that generated it.

### 3.3 Ontology Validation

The ontology has been defined in OWL [4], using Protégé[4], and is publicly available on GitHub. Validation was performed in two complementary steps. First, the ontology was checked for logical consistency using the HermiT reasoner[17], which classified the ontology without identifying any unsatisfiable classes, confirming the logical soundness of the schema. Second, since rules contain numerical SWRL builtins (e.g., `greaterThan`), the 28 SWRL rules were executed via the SWRLAPI/Drools rule engine. The execution completed successfully, producing a consistent set of inferred axioms with no errors or non-termination, confirming the correctness and absence of circular dependencies among the rules.

## 4 Towards the Integration of Semantic Human Modeling with Short-/Long-Term Adaptation

The proposed ontological model and associated reasoning mechanisms constitute the semantic foundation of an envisaged cognitive architecture integrating (human-aware) short- and long-term planning and execution. To bridge clinical objectives and robot behavior, the ontology introduces two additional concepts: `TherapeuticPlan` and `AssistiveTask`. `TherapeuticPlan`, defined as a specialization of `dul:Plan`, represents a structured rehabilitation intervention addressing one or more inferred `TherapeuticGoals`. Each plan is related to its therapeutic objectives. In turn, a `TherapeuticPlan` is composed of one or more `AssistiveTasks`, defined as specializations of `dul:Method` representing concrete exercises or assistive activities contributing to the achievement of the associated therapeutic goals.

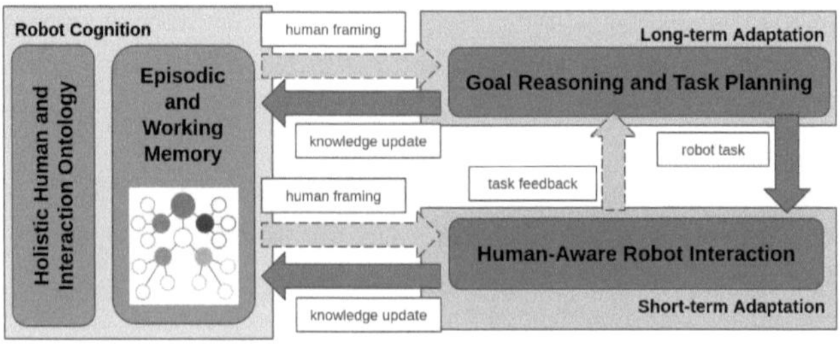


**Fig. 4.** Cognitive architecture for short-/long-term adaptive interaction.

[4] https://protege.stanford.edu/.

Figure 4 shows the main cognitive processes of the framework, highlighting the role of the ontology in the control flow. The architecture entails *slow* (deliberative) and *fast* (reactive) reasoning [8,33] to personalize and adapt interactions through shared human-centered semantics. The envisaged architecture pursues knowledge-driven robotic assistance by tailoring short- and long-term planning to the patient's specific needs. The two processes work at different time scales and synergically pursue the same assistive goal, but they query the knowledge graph under a different *framing*, i.e., they consider different (sub)sets of the ontological qualities to make decisions about: (i) *what* goal and actions to plan for (long-term); (ii) *how* and *when* to execute planned actions (short-term).

**Table 3.** Qualitative relevance of human functioning qualities for long-term (LT) and short-term (ST) reasoning in general cognitive stimulation and physical rehabilitation scenarios.

| Quality | Cognitive stimulation | | Physical rehabilitation | |
|---|---|---|---|---|
| | LT | ST | LT | ST |
| Memory | +++ | + | + | + |
| Attention | ++ | +++ | + | ++ |
| Cognitive load | + | +++ | + | + |
| Engagement | + | +++ | + | ++ |
| Physical load | – | + | + | +++ |
| Performance | – | + | ++ | +++ |
| Joint mobility | – | – | +++ | ++ |
| Walking | – | – | +++ | ++ |

Recalling the scenarios depicted in Fig. 1, Table 3 shows the different impact of ontological human qualities on the decisional processes for long-term (LT) and short-term (ST) planning. These are illustrative expert assumptions and are intended as a preliminary reference to be refined through future validation with clinical data. In the case of cognitive stimulation, LT planning would construct a `TherapeuticPlan` whose `AssistiveTask` instances target memory reinforcement and attention maintenance, for instance through orientation exercises or structured recall activities. During execution, ST planning would monitor interaction-related qualities such as `CognitiveLoad`, `Engagement`, and `Attention`. Changes in the measurements of these interaction-related qualities would trigger reactive reasoning processes to adapt the execution of the ongoing `AssistiveTask`. For example, when the estimated `CognitiveLoad` exceeds a given threshold, or the estimated `Engagement` falls below a given threshold, the execution of the current task should be adapted by reducing its difficulty or modifying the execution modality.

Similarly, in the case of physical rehabilitation, LT planning would construct a `TherapeuticPlan` whose `AssistiveTask` instances target gait recovery or mobility improvement, based on the level of impairment detected on `Walking` and `JointMobility` qualities. During execution, ST planning monitors interaction-related qualities such as `PhysicalLoad` and `Performance`, which are measured through sensory feedback. Changes in the measurements of these qualities reflect the evolving physical state of the patient (tracked through updates in the associated regions), enabling adaptations.

For example, when `PhysicalLoad` exceeds a given threshold, the system could reduce execution speed, introduce rest periods, or temporarily suspend the activity. Such adaptations enable the system to maintain safety and effectiveness while continuously adapting to the patient's evolving physical state.

## 5 Final Remarks and Future Works

The work introduces an ontological model to foster the practical use of human models within HRI applications. Grounded in the ICF framework and the DOLCE foundational ontology, the proposed model provides a structured semantic representation of human functioning qualities, impairment levels, interaction-related characteristics, and rehabilitation objectives. By linking these factors to robot goals, tasks, and interaction modalities, the ontology is intended to support human-centered reasoning by adapting action selection and execution. This enables developers to move beyond ad-hoc user representations and to design systems capable of coherent personalization and adaptation over time. Future work concerns the integration of the ontology with the envisaged cognitive framework. Experimental validation will be conducted in assistive scenarios such as cognitive stimulation and physical rehabilitation, evaluating the impact of the proposed model on personalization, adaptability, and user experience. Moreover, particular attention will be devoted to assessing whether the proposed semantic inference mechanisms effectively capture clinically meaningful rehabilitation objectives and support personalized planning and adaptive robot behavior during prolonged human-robot interaction.

**Acknowledgments.** CNR authors are supported by Cleverness (FOE 2020) under Grant DUS.AD016.133. Authors acknowledge the use of generative AI tools to assist in the graphical layout and visual refinement of selected figures and tables and a general grammar check. All the scientific content, experimental design, and rationale were conceived, developed, and validated by the authors.

**Disclosure of Interests.** The authors have no competing interests to declare that are relevant to the content of this article.

## References

1. Anderson, J.R., Matessa, M., Lebiere, C.: ACT-R: a theory of higher level cognition and its relation to visual attention. Hum.-Comput. Interact. (1997)

2. Andriella, A., Falcone, G., Rossi, S.: Enhancing robot assistive behaviour by mentalising user intent and beliefs with reinforcement learning. Int. J. Soc. Robot. (2025)
3. Andriella, A., Torras, C., Alenyà, G.: Short-term human-robot interaction adaptability in real-world environments. Int. J. Soc. Robot. (2020)
4. Antoniou, G., van Harmelen, F.: Web Ontology Language: OWL. Springer, Heidelberg (2004)
5. Awaad, I., Kraetzschmar, G.K., Hertzberg, J.: The role of functional affordances in socializing robots. Int. J. Soc. Robot. (2015)
6. Baraka, K., et al.: Human-interactive robot learning: definition, challenges, and recommendations. J. Hum.-Robot Interact. (2025)
7. Beßler, D., Porzel, R., Pomarlan, M., Beetz, M., Malaka, R., Bateman, J.: A formal model of affordances for flexible robotic task execution. In: ECAI. Proceedings of the 24th European Conference on Artificial Intelligence (2020)
8. Booch, G., et al.: Thinking fast and slow in AI. Proceedings of the AAAI Conference on Artificial Intelligence, vol. 35, no. 17, pp. 15042–15046 (2021)
9. Borgo, S., et al.: DOLCE: a descriptive ontology for linguistic and cognitive engineering. Appl. Ontol. (2022)
10. Bruno, B., et al.: Knowledge representation for culturally competent personal robots: requirements, design principles, implementation, and assessment. Int. J. Soc. Robot. (2019)
11. Cieza, A., et al.: Linking health-status measurements to the international classification of functioning, disability and health. J. Rehabil. Med. (2002)
12. Cieza, A., Fayed, N., Bickenbach, J., Prodinger, B.: Refinements of the ICF linking rules to strengthen their potential for establishing comparability of health information. Disabil. Rehabil. (2019)
13. Cortellessa, G., Benedictis, R.D., Fracasso, F., Orlandini, A., Umbrico, A., Cesta, A.: AI and robotics to help older adults: revisiting projects in search of lessons learned. Paladyn J. Behav. Robot. (2021)
14. De Benedictis, R., Umbrico, A., Fracasso, F., Cortellessa, G., Orlandini, A., Cesta, A.: A dichotomic approach to adaptive interaction for socially assistive robots. User Model. User-Adap. Inter. (2023)
15. Filippeschi, A., et al.: Towards skills evaluation of elderly for human-robot interaction. In: 27th IEEE International Symposium on Robot and Human Interactive Communication (RO-MAN) (2018)
16. García-Betances, R.I., Cabrera-Umpiérrez, M.F., Ottaviano, M., Pastorino, M., Arredondo, M.T.: Parametric cognitive modeling of information and computer technology usage by people with aging- and disability-derived functional impairments. Sensors (2016)
17. Glimm, B., Horrocks, I., Motik, B., Stoilos, G., Wang, Z.: Hermit: an owl 2 reasoner. J. Autom. Reason. (2014). https://doi.org/10.1007/s10817-014-9305-1
18. Hart, S.G., Staveland, L.E.: Development of NASA-TLX (task load index): results of empirical and theoretical research. In: Advances in Psychology. Human Mental Workload, North-Holland (1988)
19. Irfan, B., Ramachandran, A., Spaulding, S., Glas, D.F., Leite, I., Koay, K.L.: Personalization in long-term human-robot interaction. In: 14th ACM/IEEE International Conference on Human-Robot Interaction (HRI) (2019)
20. Kidd, C.D., Breazeal, C.: Robots at home: understanding long-term human-robot interaction. In: IEEE/RSJ International Conference on Intelligent Robots and Systems (2008)

21. Kostavelis, I., et al.: Understanding of human behavior with a robotic agent through daily activity analysis. Int. J. Soc. Robot. (2019)
22. Lastrico, L., et al.: Expressing and Inferring Action Carefulness in Human-to-Robot Handovers. In: 2023 IEEE/RSJ International Conference on Intelligent Robots and Systems (IROS) (2023)
23. Lemaignan, S., Warnier, M., Sisbot, E.A., Clodic, A., Alami, R.: Artificial cognition for social human-robot interaction: an implementation. Artif. Intell. (2017)
24. Mahoney, F.I., Barthel, D.W.: Barthel index. Maryland State Med. J. (1965)
25. Ostrowski, A.K., Zhang, J., Breazeal, C., Park, H.W.: Promising directions for human-robot interactions defined by older adults. Front. Robot. AI (2024)
26. Ra, K., Granger, C.V., Hamilton, B.B., Fs, S.: The functional independence measure: a new tool for rehabilitation. Adv. Clin. Rehabil. (1987)
27. Ramirez Duque, A.A., Lindsay, A., Foster, M.E., Petrick, R.P.A.: A lightweight artificial cognition model for socio-affective human-robot interaction. In: Proceedings of the 2024 ACM/IEEE International Conference on Human-Robot Interaction. Association for Computing Machinery (2024)
28. Schepers, V., Ketelaar, M., Van de Port, I., Visser-Meily, J., Lindeman, E.: Comparing contents of functional outcome measures in stroke rehabilitation using the international classification of functioning, disability and health. Disabil. Rehabil. (2007)
29. Schneider, S., Kummert, F.: Comparing robot and human guided personalization: adaptive exercise robots are perceived as more competent and trustworthy. Int. J. Soc. Robot. (2021)
30. Sciutti, A., Sandini, G.: Interacting with robots to investigate the bases of social interaction. In: IEEE Trans. Neural Syst. Rehabil. Eng. (2017)
31. Siva, S., Zhang, H.: Robot perceptual adaptation to environment changes for long-term human teammate following. Int. J. Robot. Res. (2022)
32. Umbrico, A., Cesta, A., Cortellessa, G., Orlandini, A.: A holistic approach to behavior adaptation for socially assistive robots. Int. J. Soc. Robot. (2020)
33. Umbrico, A., De Benedictis, R., Fracasso, F., Cesta, A., Orlandini, A., Cortellessa, G.: A mind-inspired architecture for adaptive HRI. Int. J. Soc. Robot. (2023)
34. Umemori, S., et al.: Development of a conversion table linking functional independence measure scores to international classification of functioning, disability, and health qualifiers: Insights from a survey of healthcare professionals. In: Healthcare. MDPI (2024)

# Contextual Knowledge Conflicts in RAG Systems with a Recipe Dataset

Ejdis Gjinika(✉), Luca Putelli, Mattia Chiari, Alessandro Pagani, Ivan Serina, and Alfonso Emilio Gerevini

Università degli Studi di Brescia, Via Branze 38, Brescia, Italy
{ejdis.gjinika,luca.putelli,mattia.chiari,alessandro.pagani, ivan.serina,alfonso.gerevini}@unibs.it

**Abstract.** In Retrieval Augmented Generation (RAG) systems, Large Language Models (LLMs) elaborate different documents to provide an useful answer to the users' requests. However, in many real-world domains (such as medical studies, or changing laws) there is no guarantee that the documents contain concordant information, causing a knowledge conflict. In this work, we aim to evaluate the behaviour of RAG systems, based on several LLMs by providing them discordant information. In particular, we consider culinary recipes. In this particular food domain, a dish can be prepared in different ways and different ingredients, according to alternative culinary traditions and personal preferences, all equally valid. We aim to verify whether RAG systems maintain their property of retrieving the right information, and how the generation process is influenced by the presence of several possible variants, characterizing whether they rely on one of them, combine them or provide erroneous answers. The code and data used in this work are publicly available at https://github.com/ejdisgjinika/rag-conflicts-recipe.

**Keywords:** Knowledge Conflicts · RAG · LLMs · LLMs for Food

## 1 Introduction

Recently, Retrieval Augmented Generation (RAG) has emerged as a prominent approach to improve the factual reliability of Large Language Models (LLMs) by grounding text generation on external documents [13]. In a standard RAG pipeline, documents are segmented into smaller textual units (chunks), encoded into dense vector representations, and stored in a database. Given a user query, the system retrieves the chunks that are most relevant to the query and provides them to the LLM as supporting context for response generation. Indeed, although modern LLMs exhibit remarkable capabilities across a wide range of tasks, their behaviour remains difficult to fully control and interpret: even in the RAG framework, they may generate factually inaccurate responses, rely on unsupported assumptions, or produce outputs in which external evidence conflicts with their internal knowledge [1].


S. Bistarelli et al. (Eds.): AIxIA 2026, LNAI 17131, pp. 323–337, 2027.
https://doi.org/10.1007/978-3-032-40774-0_24

According to the taxonomy introduced in [28], RAG systems deal with two types of knowledge: parametric knowledge and contextual knowledge. Parametric knowledge refers to the knowledge acquired by the model during training, while contextual knowledge corresponds to the information provided at inference time through the input context. The interaction between these two types of knowledge may give rise to knowledge conflicts, for instance when contextual information is inconsistent with the model's parametric knowledge. Similarly, *inter-context conflicts* arise when contextual knowledge contains contradictory information. Such conflicts are not merely theoretical: they routinely arise in real-world RAG applications across high-stakes domains such as medicine and law [9,12,16]. Consequently, understanding how RAG systems behave in the presence of conflicting contextual information is an interesting research challenge.

In this work, we focus on a specific and underexplored case: contextual sources that diverge yet are *all equally valid*, so that no single source can be deemed incorrect. In particular, we study RAG behavior in the food recipe domain, where multiple variants of the same dish naturally differ in their ingredients, quantities, or preparation steps. These variants emerge from regional adaptations or personal preferences, and each one of them is a legitimate variant of the same dish, with no unique ground truth. This setting is well suited to studying how RAG systems deal with conflicting information for two reasons. First, we deal with a real-world problem and its related dataset, in which conflicts are intrinsic to the domain rather than artificially injected (for instance, as in [28]). Second, we force the LLM to generate only the ingredient lists. This way, the answers are verifiable algorithmically, simply by checking lexically the ingredient names. Our analysis focuses on to ingredient divergences across variants of the same dish. In our experimental evaluation, we create a controlled evaluation setting to measure how RAG systems based on LLMs behave when the retrieved context offers several legitimate alternatives, characterizing whether and when they rely on a single variant, combine multiple variants, or generate invalid content. We define appropriate metrics based on the Jaccard Index, calculated over sets of ingredients, and we examine different embedding models and 12 open-source LLMs with sizes ranging from 0.8B to 26B parameters.

## 2 Related Work

As described in [28], knowledge conflicts in RAG can be divided in *context-memory conflicts*, where retrieved evidence contradicts the model's parametric knowledge, and *inter-context conflicts*, where retrieved sources contain conflicting, or even contradictory, information. For the first category, a line of work studies the effect of imperfect retrieval. Cuconasu et al. [4] analyze the retrieval stage and show the detrimental effect of irrelevant documents on generation. Wang et al. [23] propose a framework for consolidating parametric and contextual knowledge according to reliable sources. Another inconsistency arises when retrieved evidence contradicts the model's parametric knowledge. Several approaches mitigate such conflicts at generation time: Zhang et al. [31] deal with model conflicts at fact level to keep generation context-faithful, while Huo et al. [10] perform fine-grained comparisons rather than contrasting sources side by side. Wu et al. [26] inject conflict signals through multi-stage learning to make generation more robust to inconsistent evidence. Complementary behavioural analyses report two recurring biases: models tend to over-rely on their parametric knowledge rather than the retrieved context [21], while an *authority bias* leads them to trust user-provided input over retrieved evidence [14]. A parallel line of research tries to quantify the impact of conflicts: Wang et al. [25] find that LLMs can detect conflicting evidence yet struggle to produce the correct answer once a conflict is present; Zeng et al. [30] contribute a fact-checking benchmark that stress-tests RAG robustness against misleading retrievals.

Analysing inter-context conflicts, Sun et al. [20] create a framework that labels and re-ranks chunks to favour mutually supportive evidence. Crucially, this treats divergence as something to resolve, assuming at most one source is correct. More similarly to our work, into which retrieved sources diverge yet are all equally valid, the authors of [17] introduce a benchmark to study effects of conflicts in RAG scenario, demonstrating that even simple conflicts can substantially affect LLMs behavior. Another evaluation of LLM behaviour in the presence of different types of contextual knowledge conflicts is presented in [3]. However, a major difference from our work is that their evaluation is conducted manually, while we chose a specific domain and dataset for a totally deterministic study. Regarding applications of LLMs in the food domain [32], recent studies have been conducted for combining food ontologies with LLMs and RAG systems [2], or for ingredient substitution [19]. However, significant limitations for dietary assessment and recipe-nutrition mappings have been described in [7].

## 3 Knowledge Conflicts Evaluation

In this work, we evaluate how LLMs behave within a RAG framework when the retrieved context contains multiple variants of the same entity, each individually valid but collectively divergent, in the food domain. In our setup, shown in Fig. 1, the user requests the ingredient list for a specific dish to a RAG system. The system formulates its answer based on a vectorial database containing several recipes but, most importantly, with different variants of the same dish, each with their own ingredients. We analyse the answer provided by the RAG system, investigating whether it draws on one specific variant, it combines elements across different variants, or even if it introduces new ingredients absent from every version of the dish. An important characteristic of our work is that we can evaluate the returned ingredient lists lexically, simply by checking the names of each ingredient and comparing them with the different variants.

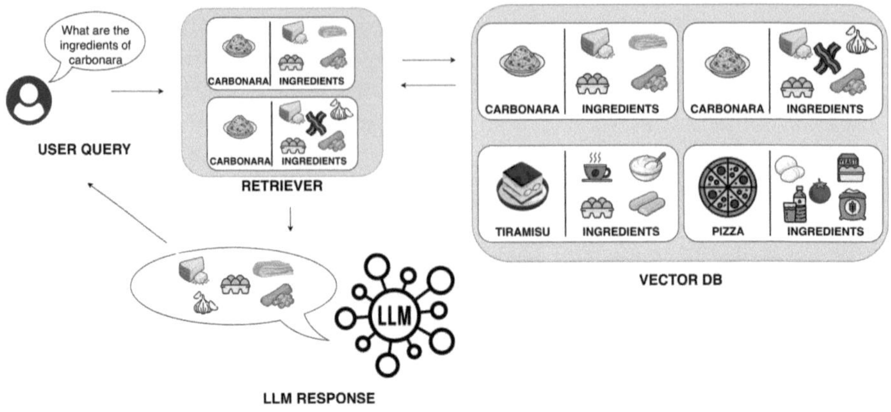


**Fig. 1.** Evaluation framework. The user asks the ingredients of a specific dish, and the LLM-based RAG system answers after retrieving different variants of the same dish.

### 3.1 Dataset and Vectorial Database

To build the RAG vector database for our experimental evaluation, we relied on the Kaggle dataset "*Food.com - Recipes and Reviews*".[1] The dataset contains 522,000 recipes, including multiple variants of the same dish. Throughout this paper, we use the term dish to denote the final food item identified by a specific name (e.g., tiramisu), independently of its particular recipe variants. To construct our final corpus, and consequently our vectorial database, we considered only those dishes associated with between three and six distinct recipes. Then, we randomly selected 400 dishes and their associated variants. Although each recipe in the Food.com dataset includes 28 attributes including the dish name, preparation instructions, cooking time, and additional metadata, we retained only the dish name and the list of ingredients, discarding all other fields. The vector database was then populated with all recipes corresponding to the selected 400 dishes. For each recipe, we created a textual chunk containing its ingredient list, structured as the sentence *"The ingredients of* {`dish_name`} *are: ..."*, followed by the ingredients. Please note that ingredient names are lemmatized and checked for spelling mistakes. We also remove quantities, punctuation and eventual stop words.

### 3.2 Evaluation Framework and Metrics

As illustrated in Fig. 1, our experimental evaluation follows a standard RAG workflow, which is made by two main phases: the **Retrieval** phase, and the **Generation** phase [13]. In our context, the user asks the RAG system the ingredients of a specific dish. Given this request, in the Retrieval phase the system first retrieves from the vectorial database the textual chunks that are most

[1] https://www.kaggle.com/datasets/irkaal/foodcom-recipes-and-reviews, licensed under CC0: https://creativecommons.org/publicdomain/zero/1.0/.

semantically similar to the user query, by computing an appropriate similarity metric. In our experiments, we set the number of chunks to retrieve as the number of variants of the dish; although in real-world application this simplified scenario may not be totally correct, still it can be useful to conduct a preliminary evaluation and model comparison. The retrieved chunks are then combined with the original query and a system prompt to form the input context provided to the RAG model. The system prompt instructs the model on the expected output format, requiring the ingredients to be returned as a semicolon-separated list. It also indicates that the answer should be solely based on the retrieved context, explicitly forbidding fact correction or answers based on the parametric knowledge. Finally, in the generation phase, the LLM processes the retrieved context and generates the ingredient list for the dish.

We then compare the generated list with the ingredient list of each available variant of that dish in order to analyse the behaviour of the RAG system under conflicting retrieved evidence. This setting, named **RAG vs Variants**, is particularly informative because the retrieved context may combine information from multiple recipe variants, whereas the final output may also be influenced by recipe-related knowledge encoded in the model parameters [32].

To quantify the overlap between two sets of ingredients, and therefore the similarities between the generated answer and the recipe variants, we adopt the Jaccard Index, also known as Intersection over Union. By definition, given two sets of ingredients $A$ and $B$, we compute $J$ as:

$$J(A,B) = \frac{|A \cap B|}{|A \cup B|}$$

This metric yields a score in the range $[0, 1]$. A value of 1 indicates that the two sets have the same elements, whereas a value of 0 indicates that the sets share no elements. Note that if there are any duplicated ingredients, these are removed from this calculation.

Given that we deal with different variants of a dish, our comparison is made several times, calculating different Jaccard Index values. Therefore, considering $n$ variants of a dish, we calculate the maximum and average values of $J$ ($J_{max}$ and $J_{mean}$) as follows:

$$J_{max} = \max_{i\in[1,n]} J(G, V_i), \quad J_{mean} = \frac{1}{n}\sum_{i=1}^{n} J(G, V_i)$$

into which $G$ is the ingredient list generated by the RAG system and $V_i$ are the $n$ different variants of the dish.

Finally, we designed another test case, called **LLM vs Variants**. Since the LLMs encode parametric knowledge, in this task we aim to evaluate how much information about the recipes is captured by this knowledge. In this setting, the Large Language Model (LLM) has to answer to the user's prompt, without any context. Next, we compare the list of ingredients generated by the model with the variants in our dataset. This comparison is performed exactly as in the RAG vs Variants task.

## 4 Experimental Setup and Results

We evaluate 12 language models spanning five families and covering a range of parameter scales from 0.8B to 26B parameters. From Meta's Llama 3.2 [8] we include the 1B and 3B models. From Google's Gemma family we evaluate the 1B, 4B, and 12B variants of Gemma 3, together with the dense 26B variant of Gemma 4 [22]. From Mistral AI's Ministral [15] we include the 3B, 8B, and 14B variants, and from the Qwen 3.5 family [29] the 0.8B, 2B, and 4B variants. This selection is designed to assess whether models size and architectural choices influence the behaviour of the generation model when exposed to divergent retrieved context.

All models are deployed through the Ollama framework using the default quantization for each model. During inference, we set each model's temperature at its default value. All experiments were run on a single MIG instance of an NVIDIA A100 GPU with 40 GB of VRAM. For the retrieval phase, we use FAISS (Facebook AI Similarity Search) [5,11] as vector database, using the inner product as similarity metric. For the indexing structure, we use IVFFlat (Inverted File Index). For computing the embedding vectors, we considered three different models: two BGE models for the English language (bge-base-en-v1.5 and bge-large-en-v1.5) [27] and a multilingual-e5-large model [24].

### 4.1 Results for the Retrieval Phase

Our first experiment was conducted to test the retrieval capabilities of the RAG systems considering three different embedding models, in the context of our recipe dataset. As a test set, we use 100 different dishes and their variants. The results are available in Table 1. As we can see, all three models lead to good performance, with the worst results obtained using multilingual-e5-large model. By using this model, the RAG retrieves all the correct variants for 86 dishes out of 100. However, both monolingual models reach higher results, and especially bge-base-en-v1.5 which makes the RAG system select all the correct cases in 99 dishes, with only one error. Interestingly, using a slight bigger version of the model (bge-large-en-v1.5, which produces vectors of size 1024 instead of 768 produced by the base model) provides worse results, with 10 dishes presenting incorrect chunks, 3 of them with more than one variant not correctly identified. Consequently, we adopted bge-base-en-v1.5 as the default embedding model used in all our further experiments.

**Table 1.** Retrieval evaluation over 100 queries. *Exact*: all reference chunks retrieved; *One mistake* and *Two or more mistakes*: number of incorrect chunks retrieved.

| Model | Exact | One mistake | Two or more mistakes |
|---|---|---|---|
| bge-base-en-v1.5 | 99 | 0 | 1 |
| bge-large-en-v1.5 | 90 | 7 | 3 |
| multilingual-e5-large | 86 | 9 | 5 |

**Table 2.** Comparison of $J_{max}$ and $J_{mean}$ scores of **LLM vs Variants** and **RAG vs Variants** tasks evaluated against the reference chunks, across all tested models. For both metrics we indicate the average and the standard deviation, calculated across all our test instances.

| Model | Size | LLM vs Variants | | RAG vs Variants | |
|---|---|---|---|---|---|
| | | $J_{max}$ | $J_{mean}$ | $J_{max}$ | $J_{mean}$ |
| Qwen 3.5 | 0.8B | 0.17(8) | 0.13(7) | 0.70(25) | 0.39(9) |
| Gemma 3 | 1B | 0.23(9) | 0.17(7) | 0.82(16) | 0.41(6) |
| Llama 3.2 | 1B | 0.27(9) | 0.22(7) | 0.84(18) | 0.40(8) |
| Qwen 3.5 | 2B | 0.26(10) | 0.20(8) | 0.60(15) | 0.41(6) |
| Ministral 3 | 3B | 0.31(10) | 0.24(8) | 0.73(20) | 0.40(7) |
| Llama 3.2 | 3B | 0.27(9) | 0.20(8) | 0.82(18) | 0.37(7) |
| Qwen 3.5 | 4B | 0.29(11) | 0.22(8) | 0.54(10) | 0.39(5) |
| Gemma 3 | 4B | 0.31(10) | 0.24(8) | 0.64(18) | 0.37(6) |
| Ministral 3 | 8B | 0.31(10) | 0.24(8) | 0.56(13) | 0.40(6) |
| Gemma 3 | 12B | 0.31(10) | 0.23(8) | 0.52(9) | 0.37(5) |
| Ministral 3 | 14B | 0.32(10) | 0.25(8) | 0.55(9) | 0.40(6) |
| Gemma 4 | 26B | 0.35(11) | 0.27(8) | 0.68(20) | 0.41(6) |

### 4.2 Results of the Generation Phase

After assessing the effectiveness of the retrieval phase of our RAG system, we then evaluate how the presence of conflicting contextual information impact the generation phase. As we described in Sect. 3.2, considering a specific dish we compare the ingredient list provided by the LLM with the ones reported in the dish variants in our dataset, and we calculate the Jaccard Index. In Table 2 we report the results, in terms of $J_{max}$ and $J_{mean}$ (both calculated as the average values across all our test set of 400 dishes) for the two test cases: **LLM vs Variants**, into which no RAG is present and we simply ask different LLMs for the ingredient lists, and **RAG vs Variants**, into which the answer is based on the context (i.e. the variants) retrieved by the RAG system.

Analysing the performance for the **LLM vs Variants** task, we can see that all our considered models are not particularly good in providing ingredients for a specific dish. In fact, even considering $J_{max}$, i.e. the Jaccard Index calculated with the most similar variant, most of the models identify between 20% and 30% of ingredients. However, there is quite variability across different dishes, with a standard deviation of about 10% for all considered models. Results are even lower in terms of $J_{mean}$, with most models sharing between 20% and 25% of ingredients with all the dishes. As one might expect, larger models achieve a higher $J_{max}$ and $J_{mean}$ value compared to smaller models, with the best results obtained by the largest model, Gemma 4 26B, which achieves 0.35 and 0.27, respectively in terms of $J_{max}$ and $J_{mean}$. Conversely, the worst performance are obtained by the smallest model Qwen 3.5 0.8B. Considering the other models,

Ministral 3 3B obtains quite good results, with 0.31 in terms of $J_{max}$ and 0.24 in terms of $J_{mean}$, even higher the definitely bigger Gemma 3 12B. The observed phenomenon suggests that models with a higher number of parameters encode more knowledge, as expected.

Considering the **RAG vs Variants** evaluation, first we can see that all considered LLMs obtain better results, with respect to the LLM vs Variants task, both in terms of $J_{max}$ and $J_{mean}$. The increase is particularly evident for smaller models, which benefit more by providing the retrieved variants in context. For instance, Gemma 3 1B obtains a remarkable 0.82 in terms of $J_{mean}$, whereas the same metric obtained without the RAG framework is only 0.23.

By analysing the results reported in Table 2 considering the model sizes, we can highlight more interesting findings, that denote how different models can have a very different behaviour. In fact, as we can see by analysing $J_{mean}$ although on average all models can identify about 40% of the ingredients across all the different variants, $J_{max}$ depends strongly from the model and its size. Even if larger models obtain an $J_{max}$ always higher than 0.5, revealing how more than half of the ingredients are shared between the LLM output and the most similar variant, these results are definitely lower than those obtained by the smaller models (Qwen 3.5 0.8B, Gemma 3 1B, Llama 3.2 1B, Ministral 3 3B, and Llama 3.2 3B), which obtain an $J_{max}$ higher than 0.7. The best results are obtained by Llama 3.2 1B, with an $J_{max}$ of 0.84. For many dishes, the tendency of these models is to select one specific variant and to output its ingredients. In several cases, as it can be seen by analysing the standard deviation, which is always higher than 0.15 in all four models, the $J_{max}$ value is in fact very close to 1, indicating a perfect overlap between the LLM output and one variant. Clearly, selecting one variant leads a quite lower $J_{mean}$, since different variants have different ingredients. Instead, models with a lower $J_{max}$, and especially Qwen 3.5 4B (0.54), Ministral 3 8B (0.56), Gemma 3 12B (0.52), and Ministral 3 14B (0.55) show a different behaviour into which they try to combine the information spread across the retrieved variants to produce a more cohesive response, rather then simply report the ingredients. Considering the standard deviation, we can see that this behaviour is mostly consistent across different dishes.

As we can see from Fig. 2, which shows the $J_{max}$ trend of the models among their number of parameters, this change of behaviour is mostly due to size. A consistent pattern is observed across models with fewer than 3 billion parameters: these models achieve higher $J_{max}$ values relative to larger models. An exception can be found for Qwen 3.5 2B, which achieves a lower value although it has less than 3B parameters. A second pattern consists of models that range from 4B to 14B. These models achieve $J_{max}$ below around 0.5 and 0.6, denoting that they adhere less strictly to one single recipe variant. An exception is represented by Gemma 4 26B that has a nearly-high value despite his 26B parameters.

### 4.3 Ingredient Lists Analysis

To gain deeper insight into the quality of models' responses and into their behaviour, as introduced in the previous section, we analyse when the LLMs

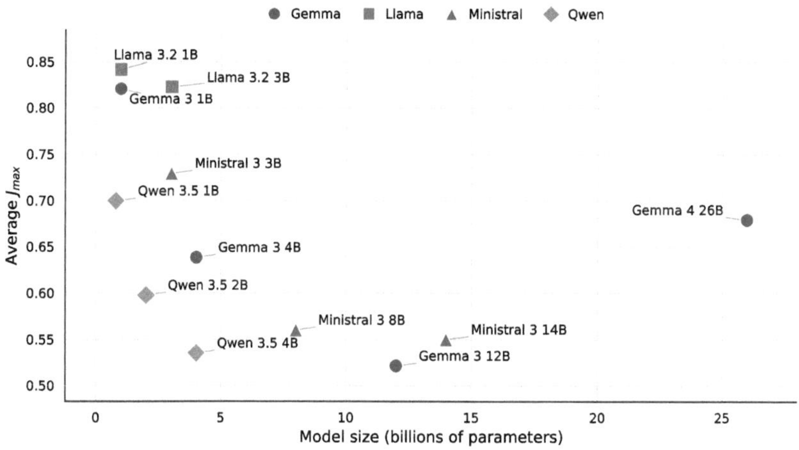


**Fig. 2.** $J_{max}$ on the RAG vs Variants task (on the y-axis) plotted against models size in billions of parameters (on the x-axis).

output an ingredient list which perfectly (or near perfectly) matches one specific variant. We define a *perfect match* when the comparison between the LLM output and the variant produces an a Jaccard Index exactly equal to 1. Similarly, we consider a *near-perfect match* when the comparison produces a $J \geq 0.8$.

Results are available in Fig. 3 for all the models we evaluated. The highest value of perfect matches is achieved by Llama 3.2 1B with a value of 36% followed by Qwen 3.5 0.8B with 27% and Gemma 3 1B with 26%. Notably, these three models correspond to the smallest models considered in this study. However, they achieve the best performance in terms of producing perfect responses and faithfully following the context provided for a single recipe. The notable exception is Gemma 4 26B with a perfect match ratio of 25% despite being the largest model evaluated. This suggests a stronger ability to exploit contextual information compared to models with far fewer parameters. Focusing on models having with between 2–3B parameters generally exhibit lower perfect-match ratios than their 1B counterparts, with values ranging from 7% to 14%. However, models in the 4–14B range show an even sharper drop, with perfect-match ratios below 1%. A similar tendency emerges considering near-perfect matches, though less pronounced. The highest near-perfect match ratio is 12%, achieved by Llama 3.2 3B, followed by Llama 3.2 1B with 8% and Gemma 3 1B with 6%. Notably, for most models the gain over perfect matches is marginal, suggesting that responses tend to be either highly faithful to the provided context or fall well below the 0.8 threshold, with few cases in between.

Another experiment we conducted is to measure the quality of the LLM outputs, verifying whether they present duplicate ingredients, which are clearly an error. The results, for all LLMs considered, are available in Fig. 4. In particular, in blue we indicate the percentage of duplicate ingredients across all our test set, and in orange we indicate the percentage of responses with at least one duplicate

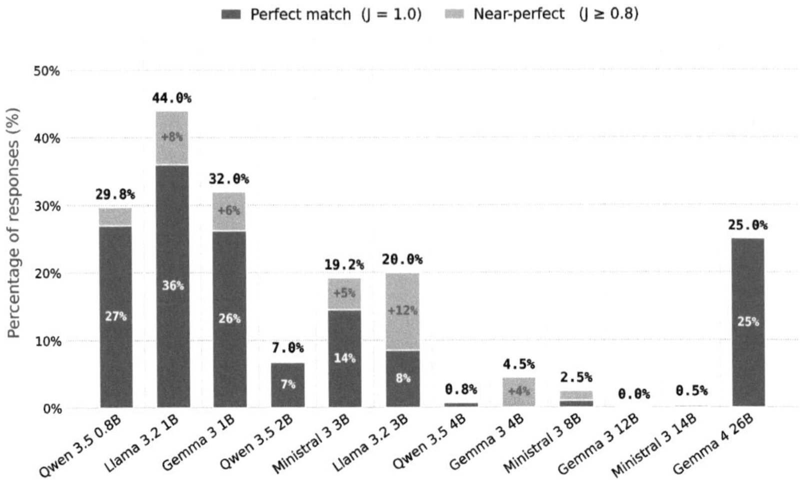


**Fig. 3.** Percentage of perfect (in blue) and near-perfect matches (in light blue) in comparing ingredient lists provided by the RAG system, considering different LLMs, with recipe variants. (Color figure online)

ingredient. For all models, the percentage of duplicate ingredients is quite modest, remaining below 12%. The worst results is obtained by Qwen 3.5 4B with a value of 11.4%, followed by Gemma 3 12B (9.7%) and Ministral 3 8B (8.7%). In general, the models with more than 4B parameters produce an higher overall number of duplicates ingredients compared to the smaller models with less than 4B. However, the share of responses with at least one duplicate ingredient is definitely higher, exceeding 50% for the majority of models. Again, larger models show a higher tendency to produce responses that contain at least one duplicate ingredient compared to smaller models, especially those with more than 4 billion parameters. The worst result is obtained by Gemma 3 12B, with 87.2%. Smaller models, such as Gemma 3 1B and Llama 3.2 1B obtain definitely better results. In particular, the latter obtains a remarkable 8.8%, with an overall number of only 0.7% ingredients duplicated.

More generally, the results of these two experiments highlight the tendency of larger models to try to synthetize the retrieved context and combine the different variants into a unique answer, rather than simply selecting one variant and copying its ingredients. However, this can generate implausible combinations, with duplicated ingredients.

### 4.4 Error Analysis

Finally, we evaluate how our considered LLMs are faithful to the retrieved context, by analysing whether they generate ingredients which were not present in the original recipe variants. More specifically, we call such ingredients as Ingredients Out-of-Context (OOC). Similarly, we define a Response Out-of-Context

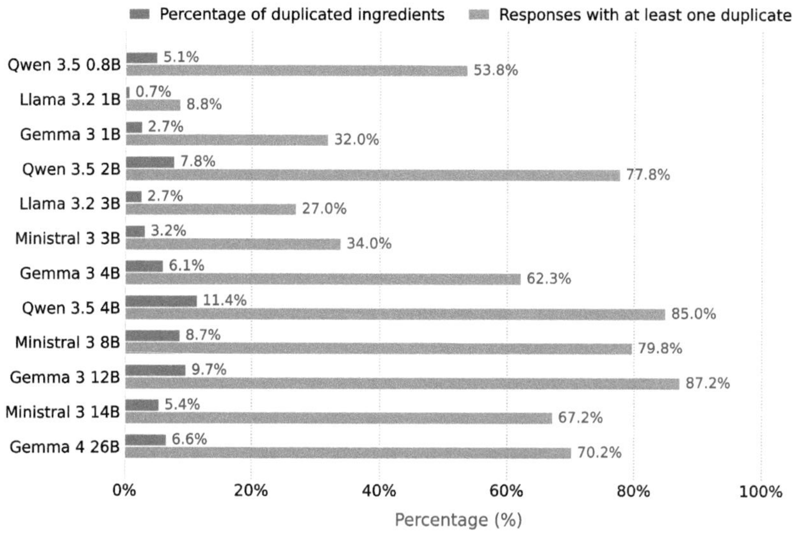


**Fig. 4.** Percentage of duplicated ingredients (in blue), and percentage of answers with at least one duplicated ingredients (in orange), for each considered model. (Color figure online)

**Table 3.** Analysis of out-of-context (OOC) ingredients across models. *Responses OOC* indicates the percentage of RAG responses containing at least one ingredient not found in the retrieved context. *Ingredients OOC* reports the raw count of OOC ingredients, the total number of ingredients in the model responses, and their ratio.

| Model | Size | Responses OOC | Ingredients OOC | | |
|---|---|---|---|---|---|
| | | | #OOC | Total | % |
| Qwen 3.5 | 0.8B | 10.5% | 109 | 9483 | 1.1% |
| Gemma 3 | 1B | 5.8% | 27 | 6735 | 0.4% |
| Llama 3.2 | 1B | 19.0% | 102 | 4792 | 2.1% |
| Qwen 3.5 | 2B | 12.0% | 91 | 13 801 | 0.7% |
| Llama 3.2 | 3B | 2.0% | 8 | 6129 | 0.1% |
| Ministral 3 | 3B | 22.8% | 124 | 7628 | 1.6% |
| Gemma 3 | 4B | 1.2% | 5 | 11 206 | 0.0% |
| Qwen 3.5 | 4B | 9.8% | 44 | 14 527 | 0.3% |
| Ministral 3 | 8B | 34.8% | 239 | 13 319 | 1.8% |
| Gemma 3 | 12B | 6.2% | 25 | 15 430 | 0.2% |
| Ministral 3 | 14B | 28.0% | 183 | 13 553 | 1.4% |
| Gemma 4 | 26B | 11.8% | 97 | 12 158 | 0.8% |

(Response OOC) as a model response which contains at least one Ingredient OOC. The results are available in Table 3.

Out of 400 test instance, the Responses OOC percentage vary widely across models (from 1.2% obtained by Gemma 3 4B to 34.8% obtained by Ministral 3 8B), indicating different levels of context faithfulness. Interestingly, there is no clear relationship between parameter count and this metric. Within the Llama 3.2 family, the largest model shows a markedly lower Responses OOC rate (19.0% at 1B vs. 2.0% at 3B), whereas Ministral 3 exhibits the opposite trend, with OOC rates increasing from 3B to 8B before partially recovering at 14B. Gemma 3 shows no monotonic behaviour across its models. However, it is quite clear that the Gemma 3 and Llama 3.2 models perform best.

We next examine the results reported in the Ingredients OOC column of Table 3. The first important results is that Ingredients OOC, are only a small fraction of the total ingredients generated (at most 2.1%). In particular, it is noteworthy that Gemma 3 4B generated only 5 ingredients OOC out of more than 11,000, whereas Llama 3.2 generates only 8 out of more than 6,000. However, this is valid even for the worst performing models in terms of Responses OOC. For instance, Ministral 3 models exhibit the higher Responses OOC rate (34.8% for the 8B model, 28.0% for 14B, and 22.8% for the 3B), yet their Ingredients OOC ratio remain very low (all between 1.4 and 1.8%) indicating that OOC ingredients, when present, constitute only a marginal fraction of the total predicted ingredients. Considering the Llama 3.2 family, the drop in Responses OOC from 1B to 3B is mirrored at the ingredient level, with the Ingredients OOC ratio falling from 2.1% to 0.1%. Gemma 3, despite showing variable Responses OOC rates across its variants, consistently achieves among the lowest Ingredients OOC ratios. All these results suggest that all our models are definitely faithful to the context, and that Ingredients OOC are only a sporadic introduction of isolated extraneous items.

## 5 Conclusions and Future Work

In this work, we investigated the behaviour of RAG-based systems in the presence of multiple, equally valid and conflicting information. More specifically, we considered a real-world domain and we evaluated how RAG systems retrieve ingredients from different variants of the same dish, analysing whether RAG systems tend to privilege a single retrieved variant, merge ingredients across different sources, or even generate inconsistent output. Our results, obtained across a range of open-source LLMs, highlight different strategies depending on the models. In fact, smaller models tend to select a single variant and generate its ingredients, whereas larger models tend to combine ingredients from different variants. However, they often produce duplicate and out-of-context ingredients.

As future work, we aim to expand our evaluation framework in more complex and nuanced scenarios, such as medicine [18] and law [12]. Moreover, we aim to understand how models select, merge, or reinterpret retrieved evidence (perhaps also using probing tasks and other Explainable AI techniques [6,32]), in order to build more transparent and reliable RAG pipelines. This can be performed by letting the model generate a more complex answer (explaining eventual inconsistencies) and by not forcing the model to output a strict list.

**Acknowledgements.** This work was carried out while Ejdis Gjinika was enrolled in the *Italian National Doctorate on Artificial Intelligence* run by Sapienza University of Rome in collaboration with Università degli Studi di Brescia.

## References

1. Alansari, A., Luqman, H.: Large language models hallucination: a comprehensive survey. Comput. Sci. Rev. **61**, 100970 (2026). https://doi.org/10.1016/J.COSREV.2026.100970
2. Bagozi, A., Bianchini, D., Garda, M., Melchiori, M., Rula, A.: Ontology-enhanced RAG for a personalised and sustainable food advisory system. Data Knowl. Eng. **164**, 102579 (2026). https://doi.org/10.1016/J.DATAK.2026.102579
3. Cattan, A., et al.: Dragged into conflicts: Detecting and addressing conflicting sources in search-augmented LLMs (2025). https://arxiv.org/abs/2506.08500
4. Cuconasu, F., et al.: The power of noise: redefining retrieval for RAG systems. In: Yang, G.H., Wang, H., Han, S., Hauff, C., Zuccon, G., Zhang, Y. (eds.) Proceedings of the 47th International ACM SIGIR Conference on Research and Development in Information Retrieval, SIGIR 2024, Washington DC, USA, 14–18 July 2024, pp. 719–729. ACM (2024). https://doi.org/10.1145/3626772.3657834
5. Douze, M., et al.: The faiss library (2024)
6. Gjinika, E., Arici, N., Putelli, L., Gerevini, A.E., Serina, I.: An analysis on how pre-trained language models learn different aspects. In: Polignano, M., Musto, C., Pellungrini, R., Purificato, E., Semeraro, G., Setzu, M. (eds.) Proceedings of the 5th Italian Workshop on Explainable Artificial Intelligence, Co-located with the 23rd International Conference of the Italian Association for Artificial Intelligence, Bolzano, Italy, 26–27 November 2024. CEUR Workshop Proceedings, vol. 3839, pp. 28–41. CEUR-WS.org (2024). https://ceur-ws.org/Vol-3839/paper2.pdf
7. Gjorgjevikj, A., et al.: Large language models in food and nutrition science: opportunities, challenges, and the case of foodyLLM. Curr. Res. Food Sci. **12**, 101351 (2026)
8. Grattafiori, A., et al.: The LLaMA 3 herd of models (2024). https://arxiv.org/abs/2407.21783
9. Hindi, M., Mohammed, L., Maaz, O., Alwarafy, A.: Enhancing the precision and interpretability of retrieval-augmented generation (RAG) in legal technology: a survey. IEEE Access **13**, 46171–46189 (2025). https://doi.org/10.1109/ACCESS.2025.3550145
10. Huo, N., et al.: Micro-act: mitigate knowledge conflict in question answering via actionable self-reasoning. In: Che, W., Nabende, J., Shutova, E., Pilehvar, M.T. (eds.) Proceedings of the 63rd Annual Meeting of the Association for Computational Linguistics (Volume 1: Long Papers), ACL 2025, Vienna, Austria, 27 July–1 August 2025, pp. 18550–18574. Association for Computational Linguistics (2025). https://aclanthology.org/2025.acl-long.909/
11. Johnson, J., Douze, M., Jégou, H.: Billion-scale similarity search with GPUs. IEEE Trans. Big Data **7**(3), 535–547 (2019)

12. Kalra, R., et al.: HyPA-RAG: a hybrid parameter adaptive retrieval-augmented generation system for AI legal and policy applications. In: Kumar, S., Balachandran, V., et al. (eds.) Proceedings of the 1st Workshop on Customizable NLP: Progress and Challenges in Customizing NLP for a Domain, Application, Group, or Individual (CustomNLP4U), pp. 237–256. Association for Computational Linguistics, Miami, Florida, USA (Nov 2024). https://doi.org/10.18653/v1/2024.customnlp4u-1.18, https://aclanthology.org/2024.customnlp4u-1.18/
13. Lewis, P., et al.: Retrieval-augmented generation for knowledge-intensive NLP tasks. In: Larochelle, H., Ranzato, M., Hadsell, R., Balcan, M., Lin, H. (eds.) Advances in Neural Information Processing Systems 33: Annual Conference on Neural Information Processing Systems 2020, NeurIPS 2020, 6–12 December 2020, Virtual (2020). https://proceedings.neurips.cc/paper/2020/hash/6b493230205f780e1bc26945df7481e5-Abstract.html
14. Li, Y., et al.: LLMs trust humans more, that's a problem! Unveiling and mitigating the authority bias in retrieval-augmented generation. In: Che, W., Nabende, J., Shutova, E., Pilehvar, M.T. (eds.) Proceedings of the 63rd Annual Meeting of the Association for Computational Linguistics (Volume 1: Long Papers), ACL 2025, Vienna, Austria, 27 July–1 August 2025, pp. 28844–28858. Association for Computational Linguistics (2025). https://aclanthology.org/2025.acl-long.1400/
15. Liu, A.H., et al.: Ministral 3. arXiv preprint arXiv:2601.08584 (2026)
16. Ng, K.K.Y., Matsuba, I., Zhang, P.C.: Rag in health care: a novel framework for improving communication and decision-making by addressing LLM limitations. NEJM AI **2**(1), AIra2400380 (2025). https://doi.org/10.1056/AIra2400380
17. Pham, Q., Ngo, H., Luu, A.T., Nguyen, D.Q.: Who's who: large language models meet knowledge conflicts in practice. In: Al-Onaizan, Y., Bansal, M., Chen, Y. (eds.) Findings of the Association for Computational Linguistics: EMNLP 2024, Miami, Florida, USA, 12–16 November 2024. Findings of ACL, vol. EMNLP 2024, pp. 10142–10151. Association for Computational Linguistics (2024). https://doi.org/10.18653/V1/2024.FINDINGS-EMNLP.593
18. Putelli, L., Gerevini, A.E., Lavelli, A., Mehmood, T., Serina, I.: On the behaviour of BERT's attention for the classification of medical reports. In: Musto, C., Guidotti, R., Monreale, A., Semeraro, G. (eds.) Proceedings of the 3rd Italian Workshop on Explainable Artificial Intelligence co-located with 21th International Conference of the Italian Association for Artificial Intelligence(AIxIA 2022), Udine, Italy, 28 November–3 December 2022. CEUR Workshop Proceedings, vol. 3277, pp. 16–30. CEUR-WS.org (2022). https://ceur-ws.org/Vol-3277/paper2.pdf
19. Senath, T., Athukorala, K., Costa, R., Ranathunga, S., Kaur, R.: Large language models for ingredient substitution in food recipes using supervised fine-tuning and direct preference optimization. Nat. Lang. Process. Journal **12**, 100177 (2025)
20. Sun, X., Chen, J., Zhou, B., Kuo, M.J.: ConRAG: contradiction-aware retrieval-augmented generation under multi-source conflicting evidence. J. Adv. Comput. Syst. **4**, 50–64 (2024). https://doi.org/10.69987/JACS.2024.40705
21. Tan, H., Sun, F., Yang, W., Wang, Y., Cao, Q., Cheng, X.: Blinded by generated contexts: how language models merge generated and retrieved contexts when knowledge conflicts? In: Ku, L., Martins, A., Srikumar, V. (eds.) Proceedings of the 62nd Annual Meeting of the Association for Computational Linguistics (Volume 1: Long Papers), ACL 2024, Bangkok, Thailand, 11–16 August 2024, pp. 6207–6227. Association for Computational Linguistics (2024). https://doi.org/10.18653/V1/2024.ACL-LONG.337
22. Team, K., et al.: Kimi-VL technical report. arXiv preprint arXiv:2504.07491 (2025)

23. Wang, F., Wan, X., Sun, R., Chen, J., Arik, S.Ö.: Astute RAG: overcoming imperfect retrieval augmentation and knowledge conflicts for large language models. In: Che, W., Nabende, J., Shutova, E., Pilehvar, M.T. (eds.) Proceedings of the 63rd Annual Meeting of the Association for Computational Linguistics (Volume 1: Long Papers), ACL 2025, Vienna, Austria, 27 July–1 August 2025, pp. 30553–30571. Association for Computational Linguistics (2025). https://aclanthology.org/2025.acl-long.1476/
24. Wang, L., Yang, N., Huang, X., Yang, L., Majumder, R., Wei, F.: Multilingual e5 text embeddings: a technical report. arXiv preprint arXiv:2402.05672 (2024)
25. Wang, Y., et al.: Resolving knowledge conflicts in large language models. In: First Conference on Language Modeling (2024). https://openreview.net/forum?id=ptvV5HGTNN
26. Wu, H., Wang, C., Sun, C., Lu, C., Zhang, Z., Chen, Y.: Conflict-aware RAG: multi-stage learning with conflict signals for robust retrieval-augmented generation. In: Hacid, H., Maarek, Y., Bonchi, F., Guy, I., Yilmaz, E. (eds.) Proceedings of the ACM Web Conference 2026, WWW 2026, Dubai, United Arab Emirates, originally scheduled for 13–17 April 2026, rescheduled for 29 June–3 July 2026, pp. 2114–2125. ACM (2026). https://doi.org/10.1145/3774904.3792289
27. Xiao, S., Liu, Z., Zhang, P., Muennighoff, N.: C-pack: Packaged resources to advance general Chinese embedding (2023)
28. Xu, R., et al.: Knowledge conflicts for LLMs: a survey. In: Al-Onaizan, Y., Bansal, M., Chen, Y. (eds.) Proceedings of the 2024 Conference on Empirical Methods in Natural Language Processing, EMNLP 2024, Miami, FL, USA, 12–16 November 2024, pp. 8541–8565. Association for Computational Linguistics (2024). https://doi.org/10.18653/V1/2024.EMNLP-MAIN.486
29. Yang, A., et al.: Qwen3 technical report. arXiv preprint arXiv:2505.09388 (2025)
30. Zeng, L., Gupta, R., Motwani, D., Zhang, Y., Yang, D.: Worse than zero-shot? A fact-checking dataset for evaluating the robustness of rag against misleading retrievals. In: Belgrave, D., et al. (eds.) Advances in Neural Information Processing Systems, vol. 38. Curran Associates, Inc. (2025). https://proceedings.neurips.cc/paper_files/paper/2025/file/ed25c00ff6900989116d3ba5d607d33d-Paper-Datasets_and_Benchmarks_Track.pdf
31. Zhang, Q., et al.: FaithfulRAG: fact-level conflict modeling for context-faithful retrieval augmented generation. In: Che, W., Nabende, J., Shutova, E., Pilehvar, M.T. (eds.) Proceedings of the 63rd Annual Meeting of the Association for Computational Linguistics (Volume 1: Long Papers), ACL 2025, Vienna, Austria, 27 July–1 August 2025, pp. 21863–21882. Association for Computational Linguistics (2025). https://aclanthology.org/2025.acl-long.1062/
32. Zhou, L., et al.: Does mapo tofu contain coffee? probing LLMs for food-related cultural knowledge. In: Chiruzzo, L., Ritter, A., Wang, L. (eds.) Proceedings of the 2025 Conference of the Nations of the Americas Chapter of the Association for Computational Linguistics: Human Language Technologies (Volume 1: Long Papers), pp. 9840–9867. Association for Computational Linguistics, Albuquerque (2025). https://doi.org/10.18653/v1/2025.naacl-long.496, https://aclanthology.org/2025.naacl-long.496/

# Preserving Assistive Identity Across Embodiments: A Knowledge-Driven AI Agent for Neurorehabilitation

Ludovica La Monica[1,2](✉), Gloria Beraldo[1], Viviana Bonci[3], Marianna Capecci[3], Maria Gabriella Ceravolo[3], Elisa Foderaro[1], Marcello Tascioni[1], Alessandro Umbrico[1], Andrea Orlandini[1], and Gabriella Cortellessa[1]

[1] CNR - Institute of Cognitive Sciences and Technologies, Rome, Italy
ldvc.lamonica@gmail.com
[2] Università Campus Bio-Medico di Roma, Rome, Italy
[3] Università Politecnica delle Marche, Ancona, Italy

**Abstract.** Neurological rehabilitation requires continuous and personalized support to address patients' evolving needs. While therapy sessions constitute a fundamental component of rehabilitation programs, patients often experience extended periods of inactivity and limited stimulation outside supervised activities. Although modern interacting devices like smartphones, tablets, and social robots can help bridge this gap, they are typically deployed as isolated tools, resulting in fragmented interactions that fail to preserve continuity, personalization, and contextual awareness. This paper presents a Migratable AI framework in which an intelligent agent maintains a persistent identity, memory, and assistive role while seamlessly operating across multiple embodiments. The framework combines structured patient knowledge with AI-driven dialogue generation to provide personalized interactions tailored to the rehabilitation context. A prototype has been preliminarily assessed in a hospital setting, focusing on feasibility, workflow integration, usability of the tablet-based embodiment, and technical responsiveness of the dialogue services.

**Keywords:** Personalized and Adaptive Interaction · Migratable Artificial Intelligence · Socially Assistive Robotics

## 1 Introduction

Patients with neurological conditions often undergo extended rehabilitation programs in which physical, cognitive, and emotional needs evolve. Addressing these needs is essential to support functional recovery but also to foster autonomy, adherence to therapy, motivation, and emotional well-being. In hospital rehabilitation settings, scheduled therapy sessions represent only parts of the patient's daily routine. Between therapy sessions, patients spend substantial amounts of time without structured activities or therapeutic supervision. These "inactive


S. Bistarelli et al. (Eds.): AIxIA 2026, LNAI 17131, pp. 338–352, 2027.
https://doi.org/10.1007/978-3-032-40774-0_25

periods" are typically spent waiting for scheduled treatments, staying in their hospital room, or moving between care settings, with limited opportunities for meaningful physical, cognitive, or social interaction. As a result, patients may experience reduced environmental stimulation and social isolation, which can negatively influence motivation and engagement in the rehabilitation process. For older adults, these conditions might also contribute to confusion, disorientation, and a decline in cognitive and emotional well-being.

Assistive technologies, including social robots, tablet-based interfaces, and AI-driven interaction systems, have been increasingly investigated as tools to complement clinical practice [1,2]. Telerehabilitation and mobile health systems have been used to promote self-management, motivation, and engagement outside direct clinical supervision [3]. In parallel, socially assistive robots have been explored as rehabilitation coaches able to provide instructions, motivational prompts, and personalized feedback during therapy-related activities [4]. However, most existing systems are designed as standalone services tightly bound to a specific embodiment, device, and context of use. As a result, when patients move across environments (e.g., from hospital to home or between different locations within the hospital), they may experience fragmented clinical support rather than a continuous relationship that preserves memory, context, and personalization [5,6]. To address this challenge, *migratable* Artificial Intelligence (AI) is introduced as an assistive paradigm in which an AI agent can operate through different physical embodiments while preserving its memory, role, and continuity of interaction with the patient [7]. The agent is therefore no longer bound to a specific physical device (i.e., *embodiment*) and interacting context. Rather, it follows the assisted user by *migrating* its intelligence over different physical devices (tablet, smartphone, TV, social robots), deployed in different social contexts (home, hospital room, hospital gym) [7].

Notably, such migration requires separating the assistive intelligence into two interconnected perspectives. The patient's health conditions, needs, preferences, and clinical goals remain persistent across embodiments, while each embodiment defines the available physical capabilities, interaction modalities, and social constraints that shape the delivered support. This introduces a fundamental challenge: although the clinical goals remain stable over time, the concrete activities through which such goals can be pursued may vary significantly depending on the available embodiment and environmental conditions. As a reference scenario, an in-hospital neuro-rehabilitation setting is considered where stimulation personalization and continuity could positively impact the quality and speed of the recovery process [8]. A migratable agent is conceived that can move between a social robot, supporting activities in the gym, and a tablet application, interacting with patients in their room, while maintaining a coherent assistive identity and objectives.

The system enables personalized interactions across different embodiments by combining a structured representation of patient information and clinical goals with LLM-based dialogue generation. This supports interactions grounded in the patient's history, current condition, and therapeutic context, under clinician supervision to ensure appropriateness for rehabilitation. The current prototype includes the two target embodiments, namely the TIAGo robot and the tablet-based application, together with the shared patient representation and the knowledge-driven dialogue services. The preliminary assessment reported in this paper focuses on feasibility, workflow integration, usability of the tablet-based embodiment, and technical responsiveness of the dialogue services. The full longitudinal migration protocol, involving systematic alternation between robot and tablet, is currently being integrated and will be evaluated in the ongoing clinical study.

## 2 Agent Migration and Identity Cues

Agent migration refers to the ability of an intelligent agent to move across different physical or virtual embodiments while preserving continuity in its interaction with the user. Early work on agent migration explored transitions between devices such as computers, mobile robots, and virtual agents, showing that migration can extend the agent's operational capabilities across different environments and interaction modalities [9,10]. Related ideas also emerged in ambient intelligence research, where conversational services were distributed across physical spaces and interaction devices. In this direction, the DELCA project introduced DisEmbodied Location-specific Conversational Agents, or "Ghosts", as context-specific conversational agents available through audio, mobile devices, and ambient displays [11]. Although DELCA was not framed as Migratable AI, it anticipated relevant issues concerning agent-mediated assistance across locations, recognizable interaction cues, and adaptation to the available devices and environmental context. Recent studies have focused on migratable AI and multi-embodiment interaction, emphasizing the importance of preserving the agent's memory and cognitive state during transitions [12,13].

Compared with previous approaches, the proposed framework focuses on a clinically grounded form of migration in which the agent's continuity is not limited to transferring an interface or a conversational state across devices. Rather, continuity is supported by a structured patient representation, clinical goals, interaction history, and embodiment capabilities, which together guide how the same assistive identity is expressed in different rehabilitation contexts. This distinguishes the proposed system from earlier multi-device or ambient-agent approaches, where the emphasis was mainly on context-dependent access to services, visual continuity, or user perception of migration, rather than on knowledge-driven personalization within a clinical pathway.

A central issue in the migration is whether users perceive the agent as the same entity after the transition. Previous studies have shown that changes in embodiment can disrupt this perception, especially when the agent moves between forms with different appearances, expressive capabilities, or interaction modalities [14,15]. Identity cues are the perceptual, behavioral, and knowledge-based elements that allow users to recognize an agent across embodiments. *Perceptual cues* include visual appearance, voice, and recurring ways of introducing itself. *Behavioral cues* concern interaction style, timing, gestures, and conversational patterns. *Knowledge-based cues* concern the agent's ability to remember previous interactions, user preferences, shared goals, and contextual information. Together, these cues support the perception of a persistent agent across multiple contexts and devices mediating the interaction [12,16].

In assistive and rehabilitation contexts, preserving identity cues is particularly relevant because the interaction is expected to unfold over time and to remain coherent with the user's evolving needs, therapeutic goals, and daily experience. Migratable AI is here applied to a hospital-based neuro-rehabilitation pathway, where patients follow extended rehabilitation programs after neurological events, such as stroke [7,8]. The proposed system combines two complementary embodiments into the daily routine: a social robot used in the rehabilitation gym and a tablet application used in the patient's room.

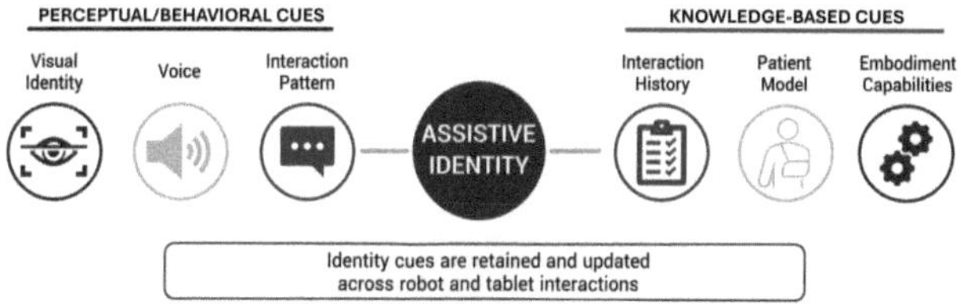


**Fig. 1.** Elements structuring the *identity* of a migratable agent.

Figure 1 shows how identity cues are instantiated in the neuro-rehabilitation scenario by the system. Perceptual and behavioral cues are conveyed through the agent's visual appearance, voice, communication style, and self-introduction, helping patients recognize the same agent across robot-mediated interactions in the rehabilitation gym and tablet-mediated interactions in their room. Knowledge-based cues are represented through a shared knowledge structure that is updated throughout the rehabilitation pathway. This structure integrates information about the patient, the rehabilitation process and goals, past interactions, user preferences, and the capabilities of the available embodiments. It also stores patient state information collected over time, such as mood, fatigue, pain, sleep quality, and perceived effort.

This shared structure allows the same assistive identity to be expressed differently according to the active embodiment and context. The robot can support embodied presence, voice-based interaction, gestures, and motor-assessment-related activities in the gym. In contrast, the tablet can support structured interviews, touch-based answers, daily check-ins, and personalized messages in the patient's room.

## 3 Migratable AI Architecture

The design of the envisaged Migratable system raises technical challenges that go beyond the usual agent-centric intelligent control [17–19]. Critical to the effective maintenance of the *agent identity* across migrations is the ability to separate/decouple the *intelligence* from the physical entities "materializing" the agent. Namely, the system must manage a non-deployed intelligence, maintaining the human-centric (personalized) knowledge across interactions. At the same time, the system must track several physical devices that represent the means by which the necessary stimuli and monitoring activities are implemented. Importantly, the system must tailor the assistance not only to the patient's specific needs, but also to the specific capabilities of the embodiment available in a given context. Consequently, assistive tasks must be scheduled according to the capabilities of the active embodiment and the context in which it is operating.

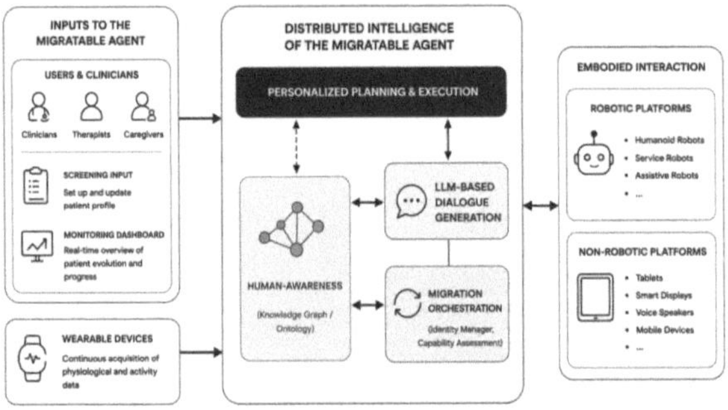


**Fig. 2.** Architecture overview of the Migratable System.

Figure 2 shows the main components that implement the functionalities of the migratable system. The left column concerns the input data provided by the clinicians to the migratable agent to initialize the personalization and the *awareness*. Specifically, the agent is fed with patient data from standard clinical procedures to determine his/her health conditions and needs, as well as rehabilitation objectives. An additional source of data is represented by the integrated wearable devices (e.g., the Garmin Vivosmart 4) that produce physiological data along with the rehabilitation path. Dedicated interfaces allow clinicians to monitor the agent's knowledge of the health state of the patient and the progression of the rehabilitation.

The central column shows the internal structure of the distributed intelligence component. It encapsulates the embodiment-free modular AI services that together contribute to the definition and maintenance of the identity cues necessary to personalize the interaction with the patient, contextualize the goal and the stimuli provided through the available embodiments. Specifically, the proposed migratable intelligence pursues a knowledge-driven approach to semantically interpret the health state of a patient, personalized clinical objectives, manage the migration process, and dynamically adapt planned stimuli/interactions to the heterogeneous capabilities of active embodiments, environmental context, and patient feedback. The right column then concerns the physical embodiments materializing the agents and enabling the actual interaction with the patient. Each embodiment is characterized by a limited set of capabilities that determine a specific *interface* between the agent and the patient. The types of stimulation, perception, and feedback implemented and collected through each embodiment are not the same. While perception cues like voice, interaction style, and appearance are kept constant across embodiments, the actual shape of the interaction and type of information/knowledge exchange with the patient could change. In this regard, the tablet and the social robot (TIAGo) have different capabilities (e.g., tactile vs voice interaction) and therefore employ dedicated interfaces and interaction services to support contextualized stimulation and monitoring.

### 3.1 Distributed Intelligence

Independent of the available embodiments and interaction contexts, the *distributed intelligence* component encapsulates delocalized modular AI services that together support the perception and knowledge-based cues characterizing the identity of the migratable agent.

**Migration Orchestration.** A central aspect is the capability of autonomously deciding when and where (i.e., in which embodiment) to migrate the agent and its intelligence. There could be multiple factors guiding the migration and the selection of the embodiment for the user. There could be various environments and social contexts in which embodiments are deployed. Similarly, multiple embodiments can be deployed in the same environment, opening up a multitude of choices. In the considered scenario, there are two social contexts and environments: the patient's room and the gym where rehabilitation exercises take place. Two distinct embodiments are deployed in these two environments: the tablet in the patient's room and the TIAGo robot in the gym. There is a 1:1 correspondence between environments and embodiments, and the migration orchestration might leverage the repetitive structure of the patient rehabilitation program within the structure. Given the physical distribution, only one embodiment can be activated to interact with the patient at a time. Consequently, the migration process is *reactively* triggered by the embodiment itself every time the tablet or the TIAGo is activated by the user. The migration process is necessary to contextualize personalization of modular AI services based on the capabilities of the active platform and to shape the resulting interaction.

**Human Awareness.** Regardless of the specific embodiment used, the agent must *understand* the health needs of a patient. Also, the agent must contextualize the patient's knowledge with the interaction capabilities of the embodiments and plan suitable stimulation and monitoring actions, according to their availability in time and space. To this end, the designed architecture integrates an ontology-based semantic description of the health needs of patients with the interaction capabilities of known embodiments [20] and plans person-to-person and adaptive interactions accordingly [21]. Representation capabilities are based on the International Classification of Functioning, Disability and Health (ICF)[1], which provides a well-established framework for characterizing human functioning from a multidimensional perspective.

From an ontological perspective, the ICF taxonomy can be interpreted as a structured vocabulary of *human qualities*, understood as aspects of functioning that characterize a person's health condition, each associated with a level of functioning. The ICF framework is integrated into an ontological model that extends DOLCE [22] with an ICF-based taxonomical description of human qualities. The integration of a standard vocabulary like ICF into a well-established theoretical formalism, like DOLCE, allows the migratable agent to understand health conditions and needs of patients and reliably exchange knowledge with clinicians. According to DOLCE, the modeling of human users follows the ontological pattern `Object-Quality-Region`. Each `PhysicalObject` is associated with a set of `Quality`, each of which captures a specific aspect of the object and persists for as long as the object exists. Each `Quality` is associated with a `Region`, which provides a representational space for measuring the qualities.

Although the association between an object and its qualities remains stable over time, the mapping between qualities and their corresponding regions may evolve, accounting for changes in the interpretation (or measurement) of the state of the "attached" physical entity. This pattern thus structures the ICF qualitative characterization of the functioning of assistive users. As such, the ICF framework is integrated into DOLCE semantics as a taxonomical description of `Quality` characterizing the "functioning" of patients.

**LLM-Based Dialogue Generation.** The integration of a Large Language Model (LLM) within the system architecture has been driven by the need to achieve a natural and socially flexible interaction across different embodiments, while maintaining control over the dialogue content [23]. To this aim, the architecture does not fully delegate the management of the conversation to the LLM. Rather, it uses its generative capabilities to build a coherent and contextualized conversational identity, realizing an assistive agent aware of the patient's clinical history and the rehabilitation path. Knowledge-driven prompting guides the LLM by dynamically structuring the conversational context according to knowledge cues. The semantic model is used to flexibly extract values and trends of human qualities collected by the agent. The *framing* extracted for a particular patient (e.g., trend of cognitive impairments, stress, or sleep behavior) within a desired temporal window (e.g., 1 day, 1 week, or more) is thus used to construct a *personalized prompt* which is passed to the LLM to generate controlled but personalized interaction text (verbalized through the embodiment).

[1] https://www.who.int/standards/classifications/international-classification-of-functioning-disability-and-health.

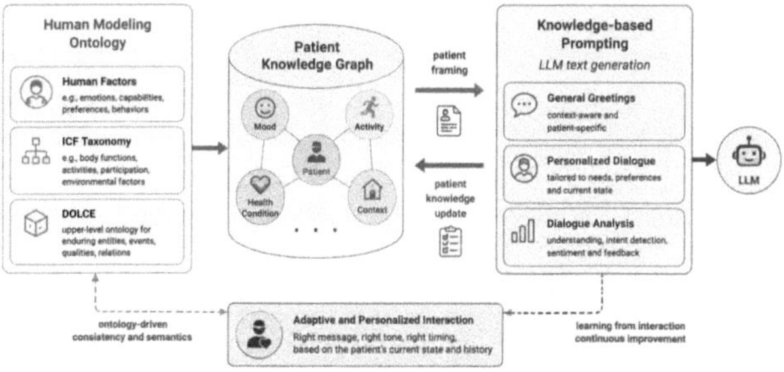


**Fig. 3.** Knowledge-driven prompting for contextual and personalized interactions.

Figure 3 shows the knowledge-driven prompting that contextualizes three LLM-based services integrated into the system. The first service generates a *general greeting* addressed to the collective environment (e.g., the whole rehabilitation gym), without any personal references. The second service manages a *personalized dialogue*, including personalized greetings, contextual reformulation of questions, and stateful dialogue generation, by constructing an iterative textual context from structured data collected during past interactions. This context is injected into the prompt together with precise behavioral instructions, ensuring identity consistency and narrative continuity across sessions. Specifically, the history of each dialogue turn is persistently stored into the backend and incrementally used to keep the memory of the conversation consistent. The third service implements *dialogue information extraction* to further enrich knowledge cues by extracting health-related parameters from the (unstructured) dialogue. To this end, the prompt is enriched with the list of ontological classes, together with their descriptions (intended meaning) and related measures. The analysis produces JSON-formatted data that contains a list of extracted values (or null) for each class in the prompt.

### 3.2 Embodied Interaction

The services supporting the interaction are tailored to two types of embodiment as shown in Fig. 4: a TIAGo social robot; a tablet-based application showing a virtual avatar of the TIAGo to recall its "physical shape" [7]. The modular services, presented in the previous sections, realizing the intelligence of the migratable agent, are deployed differently into each embodiment, according to the associated capabilities. The robot is suited for embodied, vocal, and sensor-supported interaction in the gym, whereas the tablet application supports structured self-reporting, visual communication, and repeated bedside assessment.

Both embodiments acquire and reuse information allowing the migratable agent to adapt its behavior according to the available platform, the current context, and the evolving rehabilitation pathway. Specifically, the TIAGo robot provides personalized verbal instructions, introduces therapy-related activities, and sustains short dialogues about the patient's stay and recovery. In addition,

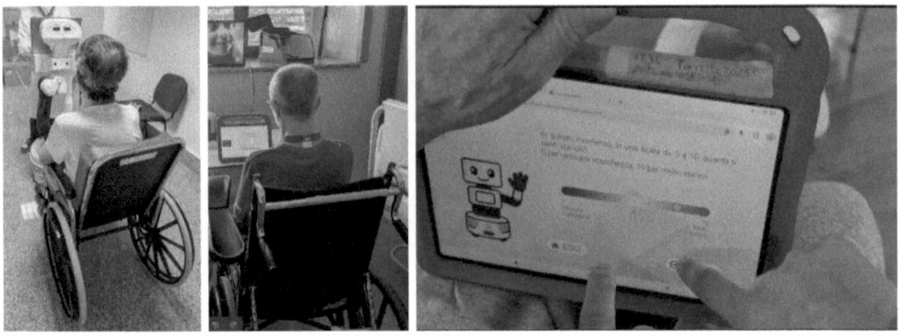

**Fig. 4.** (Left) A patient interacting with the TIAGo robot in the gym of the hospital. (Right) The same patient interacting with the virtual TIAGo on the tablet app developed inside the proposed system in his room.

the robot can exploit its onboard sensing capabilities (RGB-D camera, LiDAR, speaker, and microphone) to support motor-assessment by measuring motion parameters of the patient [8]. The tablet embodiment, with a dedicated application, provides assistance in the patient's room, where visual and touch-based interactions are more suitable. The patient-facing interface presents a virtual representation of TIAGo, delivers personalized introductory messages, and administers structured interviews through graphical components such as buttons, scales, and touch-based response elements.

The tablet application also includes an operator-facing interface supporting the clinical and technical management of the protocol. Through this interface, the operator can create and initialize the patient profile, associate the patient with the rehabilitation protocol, enter or update relevant clinical information, and access the data collected during the interaction. This component connects the patient-facing interaction with the shared patient representation, allowing the personalized dialogue to be grounded in structured and updated information.

**Table 1.** Human-modeling attributes collected through robot interaction.

| Attribute | Semantic description |
|---|---|
| Mood | Current emotional state used to adapt interaction style |
| Physical condition | Overall perceived physical well-being |
| Sleep quality | Quality of the previous night's sleep |
| Meal consumption | Whether the patient has eaten |
| Food appreciation | Satisfaction with meals |
| Time orientation | Ability to recognize the current day |
| Weather perception | Awareness of current weather conditions |
| Pain location | Presence of pain and interested body area |
| Pain intensity | Self-reported pain severity |
| Rehabilitation appreciation | Enjoyment of rehabilitation activities |
| Rehabilitation fatigue | Fatigue caused by rehabilitation |
| Physiotherapy appreciation | Physiotherapy Satisfaction and perceived usefulness |
| Speech therapy appreciation | Speech therapy Satisfaction and perceived usefulness |

**Table 2.** Human-modeling attributes collected through tablet interaction.

| Information dimension | Semantic description |
|---|---|
| Emotional profile | Serenity, anxiety, sadness, and related emotional indicators |
| Physical condition | General physical well-being and fatigue perception |
| Sleep quality | Sleep quality and night awakenings |
| Pain profile | Presence, intensity, location, timing, and communication of pain |
| Nutrition | Meal consumption, food appreciation, and swallowing-related issues |
| Temporal orientation | Recognition of the current day and weather awareness |
| Rehabilitation feedback | Perceived enjoyment, usefulness, and fatigue associated with therapy |
| Social support | Interactions with relatives, clinicians, and other patients |
| Loneliness | Perceived isolation and lack of companionship |
| Hospital experience | Perception of the ward and healthcare staff |
| Lifestyle engagement | Availability of pleasant or distracting activities |
| Clinical pathway | Medical visits and communication of relevant symptoms |

Regardless of the embodiment, both types of interaction follow a consistent three-phase structure: a personalized greeting, a core monitoring/training task, and a final farewell. However, during the core phase, the physical robot asks open-ended questions, whereas the tablet interface administers standardized scales for the patient to answer. Furthermore, the actual (sub)set of patient information gathered during the interaction changes according to the different capabilities and features of the developed interfaces. Table 1 and Table 2 summarize the information acquired through, respectively, the TIAGo robot and the tablet, deployed in the hospital facility. Both embodiments leverage the described LLM-based service to personalize and tailor the interaction content to patients. The continuous update of the interaction content for both embodiments is guaranteed by the incrementally refined knowledge cues of the distributed intelligence, which integrates also physiological data from the associated wearable devices.

## 4 The System at Work: Preliminary Assessment

A deployment and evaluation protocol was designed to assess the feasibility of introducing the proposed Migratable AI system within the daily routine of the neuro-rehabilitation unit. The protocol follows the structure in Fig. 5 and is organized around a two-week interaction period, including initial, intermediate, and final assessments, and recurring daily interactions.

At Day 0 the patient is introduced to the system and to the available devices, including the wearable sensor used for physiological and activity monitoring during the study. During the interaction period, the activities follows a recurring daily structure. In the morning, the patient interacts with the social robot in the rehabilitation gym. In the afternoon, the patient interacts with the tablet application in the room. This interaction enables the collection of repeated patient reported information while supporting continuity between the room and gym

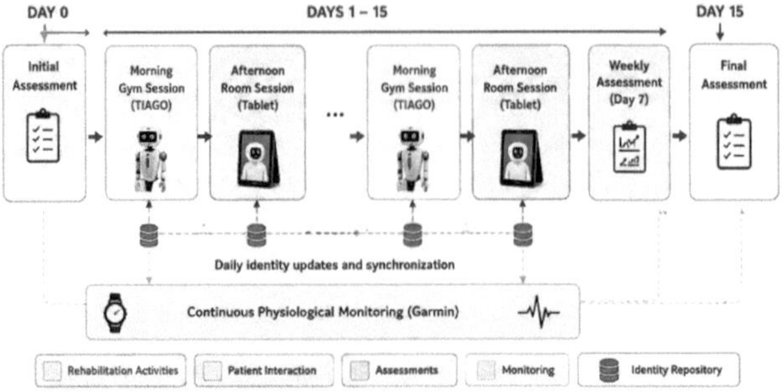


**Fig. 5.** Structure and temporal unfolding of the interaction protocol.

settings. Standardized clinical assessments are performed at the beginning, during, and at the end of the intervention to monitor progress, complemented by physiological data collected through the wearable device.

### 4.1 Preliminary Patient and Clinician Feedback

A preliminary feasibility evaluation was conducted to assess prototypes of some architectural components in the hospital rehabilitation setting. The evaluation focused specifically on the tablet-based application and on its integration into the daily clinical routine. The aim was not to assess clinical effectiveness, but to collect early feedback on usability, acceptability, and the perceived adequacy of the interaction. The preliminary evaluation involved two patients admitted to the neuro-rehabilitation unit. After the interaction through the tablet embodiment, patients completed usability and technology-acceptance questionnaires, including items related to perceived usefulness, ease of use, comfort, clarity of feedback, and willingness to continue using the system. Patients described the application as pleasant to use and reported that the length of the interaction was acceptable. During informal feedback, one relevant aspect emerged: the tablet-mediated interaction appeared to provide a useful degree of distance, allowing patients to express their opinions more freely, especially when commenting on therapies and daily activities. This suggests that the application may support the collection of patient-reported information in a way that feels less judgmental than direct face-to-face reporting. The questionnaire responses were consistent with this qualitative feedback. Given the very limited sample size, no quantitative conclusions can be drawn. However, the collected answers suggested a generally positive perception of the system in terms of usefulness, comfort, and clarity of feedback. From a clinical perspective, the tablet embodiment was considered feasible within the ward routine. The structured interview was perceived as a potentially useful tool to collect repeated information about mood, fatigue, pain, sleep, perceived effort, and satisfaction with rehabilitation activities. Recruitment is currently ongoing, and future work will include a comprehensive evaluation of the complete system with a larger cohort of patients. This preliminary evaluation does not yet assess whether patients perceive the robot and tablet embodiments as manifestations of the same assistive agent. The preservation of assistive identity across embodiments will be specifically investigated in the ongoing longitudinal study, where patients will systematically interact with both embodiments across the rehabilitation routine.

### 4.2 Scalability of Semantic Patient Framing

In addition to the preliminary user evaluation, a technical assessment was conducted to investigate the scalability and responsiveness of the proposed semantic patient framing framework. This framework continuously contextualizes LLM prompts with semantic patient knowledge retrieved from the ontology-based patient model. Since the amount of contextual information may increase over time as additional observations and clinical data become available, the primary objective of this evaluation is to assess whether the dialogue services remain responsive while progressively enriching the patient representation. The evaluation considered six experimental configurations obtained by varying the number of semantic patient attributes (1, 5, 10, and 20) and the length of the retrieved patient history (1, 3, and 7 days). For each configuration, greeting generation, multi-turn dialogue, personalized question generation, text-to-speech synthesis, and complete end-to-end interaction were executed repeatedly.

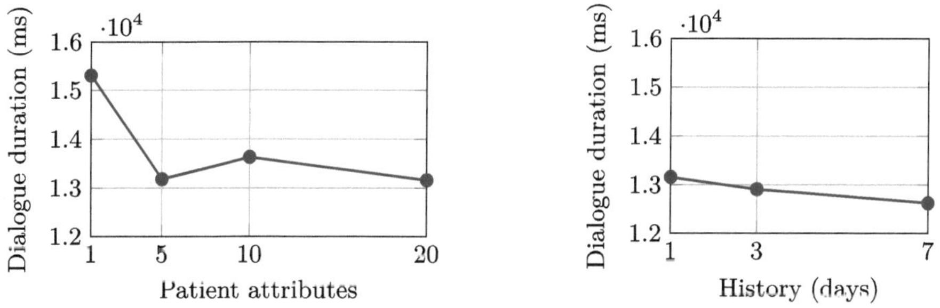


(a) Increasing semantic attributes. (b) Increasing retrieved history.

**Fig. 6.** Scalability of semantic patient framing. The duration of a complete dialogue session remains substantially constant while increasing both the number of semantic patient attributes and the amount of retrieved clinical history.

Figure 6 summarizes the results. Increasing either the number of semantic attributes or the amount of retrieved patient history does not produce a measurable increase in dialogue duration. The average duration remains approximately constant across the tested configurations (12.6–13.5 s), suggesting that, within the tested range, enriching the prompt with additional semantic patient information does not introduce a measurable latency increase. Table 3 reports the main performance indicators. Individual dialogue turns require approximately

1.5 s, independently of the contextual information provided to the LLM. Greeting generation takes approximately 1.4 s, while personalized question generation takes less than 0.8 s. The average end-to-end interaction latency is approximately 3.2 s. The most demanding operation concerns the dialogue analysis with the extraction of structured information from the acquired conversation. However, this operation is executed offline, and it does not affect fluency and perceived responsiveness.

**Table 3.** Summary of dialogue service performance.

| GreetingLatency | DialogueTurn | QuestionGeneration | DialogueAnalysis | TTSSynthesis | End-to-EndLatency[a] |
|---|---|---|---|---|---|
| ~1.4 s | ~1.5 s | 0.6–0.8 s | ~5.2 s | ~0.4 s | ~3.2 s |

[a] Given by the Greeting Latency or Question Generation + Dialogue Turn + TTS Synthesis.

These results should be interpreted as a preliminary technical assessment of the responsiveness of the dialogue services under increasing semantic context. They support the feasibility of using knowledge-driven patient framing during interaction, while the evaluation of the complete migration process and of identity preservation across embodiments remains part of the ongoing longitudinal study.

## 5 Conclusions and Future Work

This paper presents the design and preliminary implementation of a Migratable AI framework supporting continuous and personalized assistance in neurorehabilitation through multiple embodiments. The proposed architecture combines ontology-based patient modeling with knowledge-driven LLM prompting to preserve a coherent assistive identity while adapting the interaction to the patient's clinical profile and the capabilities of available embodiments. Preliminary results support the feasibility of the implemented components, with positive feedback on the tablet-based interaction and responsive dialogue services under increasing semantic context. Ongoing work focuses on the complete integration of the proposed architecture within the rehabilitation ward and on a longitudinal field study involving patients and clinicians following the presented protocol. The planned evaluation will investigate not only the usability and acceptability of the individual embodiments, but also whether preserving a continuous assistive identity across them improves continuity of care, patient engagement, and adherence to rehabilitation. More broadly, we envision Migratable AI as a step toward persistent AI assistants accompanying users across heterogeneous devices while maintaining a coherent identity, memory, and personalization.

**Acknowledgments.** CNR authors are supported by Cleverness (FOE 2020) under Grant DUS.AD016.133. Authors acknowledge the use of generative AI tools to assist in the graphical layout and visual refinement of selected figures and tables and a general grammar check. All the scientific content, experimental design, and rationale were conceived, developed, and validated by the authors.

**Disclosure of Interests.** The authors have no competing interests to declare that are relevant to the content of this article.

## References

1. Fiorini, L., et al.: Evaluating the interplay between emotional impact and usability of a technology-based socialization service in aged care: an Italian and Portuguese user study. Int. J. Med. Inform. **200**, 105913 (2025)
2. Ostrowski, A.K., Zhang, J., Breazeal, C., Park, H.W.: Promising directions for human-robot interactions defined by older adults. Front. Robot. AI **11** (2024)
3. Matamala-Gomez, M., et al.: The role of engagement in teleneurorehabilitation: a systematic review. Front. Neurol. **11**, 354 (2020)
4. Lee, M.H., Siewiorek, D.P., Smailagic, A., Bernardino, A., Bermudez i Badia, S.: Design, development, and evaluation of an interactive personalized social robot to monitor and coach post-stroke rehabilitation exercises: Mh lee et al. User Model. User-Adapt. Interact. **33**(2), 545–569 (2023)
5. Pani, J., et al.: Identifying and evaluating factors influencing technology adoption: a multi-pilot study within the Pharaon project. Int. J. Med. Inform. **206**, 106179 (2026)
6. Cortellessa, G., De Benedictis, R., Fracasso, F., Orlandini, A., Umbrico, A., Cesta, A.: AI and robotics to help older adults: revisiting projects in search of lessons learned. Paladyn J. Behav. Robot. **12**(1), 356–378 (2021)
7. La Monica, L., et al.: Towards the implementation of a migratable AI system to support patient rehabilitation. In: Cortellessa, G., De Benedictis, R., Fracasso, F., Orlandini, A., Umbrico, A. (eds.) Ambient Assisted Living, pp. 205–220. Springer, Cham (2026)
8. Beraldo, G., et al.: Introducing a socially interacting robot in clinical rehabilitation practice. In: 2025 34th IEEE International Conference on Robot and Human Interactive Communication (RO-MAN), pp. 449–454 (2025)
9. Imai, M., Ono, T., Etani, T.: Agent migration: communications between a human and robot. In: IEEE SMC 1999 Conference Proceedings. 1999 IEEE International Conference on Systems, Man, and Cybernetics (Cat. No. 99CH37028), vol. 4, pp. 1044–1048. IEEE (1999)
10. Holz, T., Dragone, M., O'Hare, G.M.P.: Where robots and virtual agents meet: a survey of social interaction research across Milgram's reality-virtuality continuum. Int. J. Soc. Robot. **1**, 83–93 (2009)
11. Hartmann, M.: Interfacing Ambient Intelligence. Ph.D. thesis, IT University of Copenhagen, Copenhagen, Denmark. Ph.D. thesis, Department of Digital Aesthetics and Communication (2005)
12. Tejwani, R., Moreno, F., Jeong, S., Park, H.W., Breazeal, C.: Migratable AI: Effect of identity and information migration on users' perception of conversational ai agents. In: 2020 29th IEEE International Conference on Robot and Human Interactive Communication (RO-MAN), pp. 877–884. IEEE (2020)
13. Bransky, K., Sweetser, P., Caldwell, S., Fletcher, K.: Mind-body-identity: a scoping review of multi-embodiment. In: Proceedings of the 2024 ACM/IEEE International Conference on Human-Robot Interaction, pp. 65–75 (2024)

14. Paulo, F., Gomes, A., Sardinha, E.M., Segura, H., Cramer, A., Paiva: migration between two embodiments of an artificial pet. Int. J. Humanoid Rob. **11**(01), 1450001 (2014)
15. Aylett, R., et al.: Do i remember you? Memory and identity in multiple embodiments. In: 2013 IEEE RO-MAN, pp. 143–148. IEEE (2013)
16. Koay, K.L., Syrdal, D.S., Walters, M.L., Dautenhahn, K.: A user study on visualization of agent migration between two companion robots. In: Proceedings of the 13th International Conference on Human-Computer Interaction, HCII 2009 (2009)
17. Moro, C., Nejat, G., Mihailidis, A.: Learning and personalizing socially assistive robot behaviors to aid with activities of daily living. J. Hum.-Robot Interact **7**(2) (2018)
18. Beraldo, G., De Benedictis, R., Cesta, A., Fracasso, F., Cortellessa, G.: Toward AI-enabled commercial telepresence robots to combine home care needs and affordability. IEEE Robot. Autom. Lett. **8**(10), 6691–6698 (2023)
19. Andriella, A., Torras, C., Alenyà, G.: Short-term human-robot interaction adaptability in real-world environments. Int. J. Soc. Robot. **12**(3), 639–657 (2020)
20. Sorrentino, A., et al.: Personalizing care through robotic assistance and clinical supervision. Front. Robot. AI **9** (2022)
21. De Benedictis, R., Umbrico, A., Fracasso, F., Cortellessa, G., Orlandini, A., Cesta, A.: A dichotomic approach to adaptive interaction for socially assistive robots. User Model. User-Adapt. Interact. **33**(2) (2023)
22. Borgo, S., et al.: DOLCE: a descriptive ontology for linguistic and cognitive engineering. Appl. Ontol. **17**(1), 45–69 (2022)
23. Tamantini, C., Umbrico, A., Fracasso, F., Beraldo, G., Cortellessa, G., Orlandini, A.: Adapting virtual agent interaction style with reinforcement learning to enhance affective engagement. Front. Digit. Health **7** (2026)

# Towards a Plausibility Metric for Contrastive Explanations in Automated Planning

Francesco Leofante[1,3], Pietro Fronza[2,3], and Marco Roveri[2,3](✉)

[1] Department of Computing, Imperial College London, London, UK
f.leofante@imperial.ac.uk

[2] Department of Information Engineering and Computer Science, University of Trento, Trento, Italy
pietro.fronza@alumni.unitn.it, marco.roveri@unitn.it

[3] School of Computer Science and Informatics, University of Liverpool, Liverpool, UK

**Abstract.** We study the problem of evaluating the plausibility of Contrastive Explanations (CEs) in automated planning. We introduce the first known notion of plausibility for this setting and present an associated quantitative metric. We then propose an algorithm to compute this metric using planning as SMT encodings and projected model counting. We implement these ideas in a software prototype and use it to evaluate our proposed metric on a range of problems from the planning literature.

## 1 Introduction

Explainable AI Planning (XAIP) [8,11] plays an important role in building trust, both in planners and in the plans they produce [5,10,21,32,33]. In particular, Contrastive Explanations (CEs) have emerged as a promising framework to improve the transparency of planning systems [15,19,20]. Given a plan, the aim of a CE is to answer user questions that compare two alternative courses of actions, with a focus on their (potentially counter-intuitive) differences. Examples of CE for XAIP are given in [20] and are shown in Table 1. The same authors also proposed an approach to generating CEs for planning problems. Given a planning problem $\Pi$, a plan $\pi$ for $\Pi$, and a contrastive question $Q$ on $\pi$, they compute an explanation in two steps. First, the question $Q$ is compiled into $\Pi$, thus obtaining a new planning problem $\Pi'$. Then a new plan $\pi'$ for $\Pi'$ is computed, if one exists. Ultimately, the comparison between $\pi$ and $\pi'$ is used to answer the contrastive question and explain the decision of the automated planner (e.g. "$a$ was used instead of $b$ because it led to a shorter plan").

A limitation of existing proposals to solve this explanation problem is that the whole explanation process is based on a single alternative $\pi'$ to the original plan $\pi$. The *local* scope of this explanation may not capture the deeper interactions between the properties of a planning task $\Pi$ and the alternative action


S. Bistarelli et al. (Eds.): AIxIA 2026, LNAI 17131, pp. 353–364, 2027.
https://doi.org/10.1007/978-3-032-40774-0_26

**Table 1.** Contrastive questions from [20].

| | |
|---|---|
| Q1 | Why is action $a$ not used in the plan, rather than being used? |
| Q2 | Why is action $a$ used in the plan, rather than not being used? |
| Q3 | Why is action $a$ used in state $s$, rather than action $b$? |
| Q4 | Why is action $a$ not performed before (after) action $b$, rather than $a$ being performed after (before) action $b$? |

sequence suggested by $Q$. Consider, for instance, a scenario where CEs are used to explain the decisions of a logistic robot operating in a dynamic environment. Assume now that constraining $\Pi$ under $Q$ results in a new problem $\Pi'$ that admits only one solution $\pi'$. This drastic reduction in the number of possible solutions can have severe implications on *plausibility* of CE, whereby the course of action suggested by $Q$ is not likely to be encountered with high probability. Although this does not affect the validity of a CE, explanations that hide this information may unintentionally mislead the user into thinking that the alternative action sequence is better than the one found by the planner.

*Our Contribution.* To mitigate this risk, we propose a novel quantitative metric to assess the plausibility of a CE. We quantify plausibility by comparing the number of valid plans that can be obtained following the original course of action (as computed by the planner) and the alternative suggested by the user. Concretely, we start from the approach of [20] and present a novel logical formalisation of contrastive questions into *contrastive axioms.* We then derive a formal notion of *support for a planning task*, which aims to characterise the space of solutions before and after the contrastive question posed by the user. Using our notion of support we derive a novel plausibility metric for CEs, informally stating that the higher the support, the more plausible an explanation is. We then give a procedure to compute the proposed plausibility metric leveraging Planning as satisfiability encodings [17] and (projected) model counting [2]. Finally, we evaluate this procedure on a range on planning problems taken from the literature. Crucially, we demonstrate the applicability of our approach to both classical and numeric planning problems, demonstrating the versatility of our appraoch as well as the effectiveness of the metric here proposed.

*Related Work.* Several techniques have been proposed to generate explanations for planning problems; see, e.g. [8] for a recent survey. One of the most popular XAIP strategies is the use of CEs [15,19,20], which are favoured for a number of properties, including their intelligibility [7] and alignment with human reasoning [28]. Although the plausibility of explanations has been the subject of several studies within Explainable ML [1,18,22], none of the existing approaches for explaining planning problems has investigated this dimension. Plausibility is deemed to be a fundamental requirement for building trustworthy human-AI partnerships and the absence of studies on the plausibility of CEs for planning is a concern. Our aim is to fill this literature gap and lay the formal foundations for a broader study of the plausibility of CEs in planning. In particular, we draw inspiration from [29], where model counting techniques are used to evaluate the quality of explanations for machine learning models. Our approach relies on similar ideas and leverages them to define a novel plausibility metric for planning problems, which is currently missing.

## 2 Background

*SAT, SMT and Related Model Counting Problems.* A *formula* $\varphi$ is a Boolean combination of propositional *variables* $\mathcal{V} = \{v_1, \ldots, v_n\}$. A formula is in Conjunctive Normal Form (CNF) if it is a conjunction of *clauses*, the clause being a disjunction of literals. A *literal* $l_i$ is a variable $v_i$ or its complement $\neg v_i$. An *assignment* is a mapping from variables to $\{\bot, \top\}$. Given an assignment, a clause is satisfied iff at least one of its literals is assigned $\top$. The Boolean Satisfiability problem (SAT) [6] consists in determining whether there exists an assignment that satisfies all clauses in $\varphi$. If one such assignment exists, then $\varphi$ is said to be *satifiable*, and the assignment is called a *model* of $\varphi$. Satisfiability Modulo Theories (SMT) [3] generalizes SAT to the problem of deciding the satisfiability of a first-order formula $\varphi$ with respect to some decidable theory $\mathcal{T}$. Examples include the theory of real numbers, integers, and the theories of data structures.

Given a CNF formula $\varphi$, the Model Counting problem (#SAT) [13] consists in counting the number of satisfying models for $\varphi$, which we denote by $\mathcal{C}(\varphi, \mathcal{V})$. Projected Model Counting (#∃SAT) [2] specializes #SAT to only count the number of solutions of $\varphi$ with respect to a given set of projection variables $\mathcal{P} \subseteq \mathcal{V}$, denoted by $\mathcal{C}(\varphi, \mathcal{P})$. These problems have also been considered in the SMT setting, for which a host of techniques have been proposed (see, e.g. [9,12,26,27].

*Automated Planning.* A *planning task* is a tuple $\Pi = \langle \mathcal{V}, A, I, G \rangle$ where $\mathcal{V} \subseteq \mathbb{B} \cup \mathbb{Q}$ is a finite set of *state variables*, $A$ is a finite set of *actions*, $I$ is an *initial state* and $G$ is a *goal condition.* A *partial state* $s$ is a mapping of a subset of variables $vars(s) \subseteq \mathcal{V}$ to values in their respective domains. We write $s[v]$ to denote the value of variable $v$ in the partial state $s$. A *state* is a partial state where $vars(s) = \mathcal{V}$. $I$ is a state and $G$ is a partial state. *Goal states* are states $s$ for which $G \subseteq s$. Each action $a \in A$ is a pair $(pre_a, eff_a)$, where $pre_a$ and $eff_a$ are partial states that define *preconditions* and *effects* of $a$, respectively. An action $a$ is *applicable* in state $s$ if $pre_a \subseteq s$. The successor state $s[\![a]\!]$ that results from the application of $a$ in $s$ is defined as $s[\![a]\!][v] = eff_a[v]$ if $v \in vars(eff_a)$ and $s[\![a]\!][v] = s[v]$ otherwise. A (valid) *plan* $\pi = \langle a_1, \ldots, a_n \rangle$ is an action sequence inducing a state sequence $S = \langle s_0, \ldots, s_n \rangle$ with $s_0 = I$, $G \subseteq s_n$ and for each $i = \{1, \ldots, n\}$, $a_i$ is applicable in $s_{i-1}$ and $s_i = s_{i-1}[\![a_i]\!]$. The length of the plan $\pi$ is denoted by $< (\pi) = n$.

*Planning as SMT.* Planning as satisfiability [17,30] is a framework to solve a planning task $\Pi = \langle \mathcal{V}, A, I, G \rangle$ by encoding plans of bounded length as the solutions of a logical formula, SMT in our case. A *state-based* SMT encoding of $\Pi$ for a given *horizon* $n$ uses *(i)* $n$ variable sets $A_1, \ldots, A_n$, where each $A_i$ consists of a unique variable $a_i$ for each action $a \in A$, and *(ii)* $n+1$ copies $\mathcal{V}_0, \ldots, \mathcal{V}_n$ of the state variable set $\mathcal{V}$. We let $I_i$ and $G_i$ be the formulas obtained from $I$ and $G$ after replacing each $v \in \mathcal{V}$ with the corresponding $v_i \in \mathcal{V}_i$. We also let $T_{i-1,i}$ be a formula describing how actions executed in the $i$th step of a plan affect states, i.e. $T_{i-1,i}$ enforces that each action implies its preconditions over $\mathcal{V}_{i-1}$ and its effects over $\mathcal{V}_i$. $T_{i-1,i}$ is also used to encode *explanatory frame axioms* and *mutual exclusion axioms* (we refer the reader to [30] for more details). The former axioms ensure that the variables not affected by actions do not change their values; the latter axioms specify the execution semantics for the actions in each set $A_i$. Here, we require that exactly one action be executed at a time. Then, the bounded planning problem for the horizon $n$ and task $\Pi$ is encoded by $\Pi_n = I_0 \wedge \bigwedge_{i=1}^{n} T_{i-1,i}^{n} \wedge G_n$. By construction, $\Pi_n$ is satisfiable iff there exists a plan $\pi_n$ within the horizon $n$, which can be extracted from the model of $\Pi_n$. In the following, we will refer to $\Pi_n$ as the Planning as SMT encoding of $\Pi$ for the horizon $n$.

*Contrastive Explanations (CEs).* CEs have been the subject of previous studies in the planning literature [15,19,20]. We rely on the formalization presented in [20], which we report in the following.

**Definition 1 ([20]).** *An* explanation problem *is a tuple $\mathcal{E} = \langle \Pi, \pi, Q \rangle$ where $\Pi$ is a planning task, $\pi$ is a plan for $\Pi$ and $Q$ is a contrastive question on $\pi$.*

A solution to $\mathcal{E}$ is another plan $\pi'$ calculated as follows. First, $Q$ is compiled into $\Pi$, resulting in a new (constrained) planning task $\Pi'$ such that any plan $\pi'$ for $\Pi'$ is also a valid plan for $\Pi$. Then, a planner is called on $\Pi'$ to generate a concrete $\pi'$. A *contrastive explanation* for $\mathcal{E}$ is generated by presenting $\pi$ and $\pi'$ to the user, with their differences highlighted.

## 3 Towards a Novel Plausibility Metric

As mentioned in the Introduction, the local scope of CEs may not capture important information about the planning problem. This is common across local explanation methods in XAI [14]. In the following, we propose a new metric that expands the scope of a CE towards providing a more holistic account of the interactions between $\Pi$ and the contrastive question $Q$.

### 3.1 Defining Our Metric

We begin by proposing a new compilation of a contrastive question $Q$ rooted in formal logic. Following existing treatments of CEs in philosophy [25], our aim is to produce a compilation in which the distinction between the course of action that occurred (*fact*) and its alternative (*foil*) is explicit in the encoding. We formalise these ideas below, where we assume that an explanation problem is given and formulate contrastive axioms as propositional formulae over the actions in $\pi$.

**Definition 2.** *Consider an explanation problem* $\mathcal{E} = \langle \Pi, \pi, Q \rangle$ *with* $< (\pi) = n$. *A* contrastive axiom $\varphi_Q = \langle \varphi_{fact}, \varphi_{foil} \rangle$ *for a question* $Q \in \{Q1, \ldots, Q4\}$ *is defined as:*

**(1)** $\varphi_{Q1} = \langle \bigwedge_{i=1}^{n} \neg a_i, \bigvee_{i=1}^{n} a_i \rangle$;
**(2)** $\varphi_{Q2} = \langle \bigvee_{i=1}^{n} a_i, \bigwedge_{i=1}^{n} \neg a_i \rangle$;
**(3)** $\varphi_{Q3} = \langle a_i \wedge \neg b_i, \neg a_i \wedge b_i \rangle$, *for some* $s_i$, $i \in \{1, n\}$;
**(4)** $\varphi_{Q4} = \langle a_i \wedge b_{i+1}, b_i \wedge a_{i+1} \rangle$, *for some* $s_i$, $i \in \{1, n-1\}$;

*over boolean propositions* $a_i, b_i$ *for actions* $a, b \in \pi$.

Our aim is to use contrastive axioms to evaluate the support, and ultimately the plausibility, of a given course of action. To this end, we formalise the concept of support below.

**Definition 3.** *Given a planning task* $\Pi = \langle \mathcal{V}, A, I, G \rangle$. *Let* $\sigma_n = \langle a_1, \ldots, a_n \rangle$, $a_i \in A$, *denote an arbitrary action sequence of length* $n$. *Then, the* support of $\Pi$ *is defined as* $\text{supp}(\Pi, n) = \{\sigma_n \in A^n \mid \sigma_n$ *is valid,* $\langle s_0, \ldots, s_n \rangle$ *is the state sequence induced by* $\sigma_n, s_0 = I, G \subseteq s_n\}$.

Intuitively, the support of a planning task $\Pi$ for a given horizon $n$ is defined as the number of valid plans of length $n$. Following Definition 3, we instantiate two specialised notions of support that are crucial for contrastive reasoning.

**Definition 4.** *Given the explanation problem* $\mathcal{E} = \langle \Pi, \pi, Q \rangle$ *with* $< (\pi) = n$. *Let* $\varphi_Q = \langle \varphi_{fact}, \varphi_{foil} \rangle$ *be a contrastive axiom for* $Q$. *We define* fact support *as* $\text{supp}_{fact}(\Pi, n) = \{\sigma_n \in \text{supp}(\Pi, n) \mid \sigma_n \models \varphi_{fact}\}$ *and* foil support *as* $\text{supp}_{foil}(\Pi, n) = \{\sigma_n \in \text{supp}(\Pi, n) \mid \sigma_n \models \varphi_{foil}\}$.

We are now ready to define the plausibility metric that is central to this work.

**Definition 5.** *Consider an explanation problem* $\mathcal{E} = \langle \Pi, \pi, Q \rangle$ *with* $< (\pi) = n$. *Let* $\varphi_Q = \langle \varphi_{fact}, \varphi_{foil} \rangle$ *be a contrastive axiom for* $Q$. *The* plausibility metric $\mathcal{P}$ *is:*

$$\mathcal{P} = \frac{|\text{supp}_{foil}(\Pi, n)|}{|\text{supp}_{fact}(\Pi, n)|} \tag{1}$$

Intuitively, $\mathcal{P}$ measures how the number of valid plans in $\Pi$ varies when the two contrastive alternatives in $Q$ are enforced. When $\mathcal{P} > 1$, then the alternative course of action suggested by $Q$ has a higher number of supporting plans, suggesting that it may be more plausible. On the other hand, when $\mathcal{P} \leq 1$, we can infer that the new course of action is at most as plausible as the old one.

**Observation 1.** *We note that a probabilistic formulation of* $\mathcal{P}$ *could be obtained by measuring the fraction of valid plans that can be obtained under* $\varphi_{foil}$ *(resp.* $\varphi_{fact}$*) among the total number of solutions admitted by* $\Pi$*. Intuitively, this alternative formulation describes the probability of obtaining a valid plan if a course of action (foil or fact) was followed.*

Computing $\mathcal{P}$ requires to enumerate all possible solutions of a (constrained) planning problem, and planners based on heuristic search are not suited for solving this task exactly. Therefore, we propose a novel solution that draws on recent advances in computational logic. We note that the use of formal logic constitutes a major point of divergence with respect to previous approaches [20].

### 3.2 Computing $\mathcal{P}$

Our main idea is to compute the plausibility metric using a logical representation of $\mathcal{E}$, based on the Planning as SMT paradigm. Within this framework, we can formulate the problem of computing the support of a planning task $\Pi$ as a #∃SAT problem. In fact, computing support only requires counting assignments to propositional action variables, effectively disregarding theory variables introduced in other parts of the SMT formula.

**Proposition 1.** *Given a planning task* $\Pi$*, let* $\Pi_n$ *be the corresponding Planning as SMT encoding for an horizon* $n$*, and let* $\mathcal{P} = \{A_1, \ldots, A_n\}$ *be the subset of variables appearing in* $\Pi_n$ *that pertain to actions in* $\Pi$*. Then,* $\text{supp}(\Pi, n) = \mathcal{C}(\Pi_n, \mathcal{P})$.

*Proof.* Following Definition 3, $\text{supp}(\Pi, n)$ is the set of all valid plans $\pi$ for $\Pi$ such that $< (\pi) = n$. If $\text{supp}(\Pi, n) \neq \mathcal{C}(\Pi_n, \mathcal{P})$, then $\Pi$ admits at least one valid plan $\pi^*$ such that $< (\pi^*) = n$ but $\pi^* \not\models \Pi_n$. However, this is impossible, as $\Pi_n$ captures all and only valid plans of length $n$. □

Proposition 1 establishes a link between the support of a planning task and the problem of counting the models of its corresponding Planning as SMT encoding, projected on action variables only. This result can be used to calculate the plausibility metric $\mathcal{P}$ as follows.

**Definition 6.** *Consider an explanation problem* $\mathcal{E} = \langle \Pi, \pi, Q \rangle$ *with* $< (\pi)$*. Let* $\Pi_n$ *be the Planning as SMT encoding of* $\Pi$ *with action variables* $\mathcal{P} = \{A_1, \ldots, A_n\}$ *for the horizon* $n$*. Furthermore, let* $\varphi_Q = \langle \varphi_{fact}, \varphi_{foil} \rangle$ *be the contrastive axiom obtained from* $Q$ *for the horizon* $n$*. The plausibility metric* $\mathcal{P}$ *can be computed as:*

$$\mathcal{P} = \frac{\mathcal{C}(\Pi_n \wedge \varphi_{foil}, \mathcal{P})}{\mathcal{C}(\Pi_n \wedge \varphi_{fact}, \mathcal{P})} \tag{2}$$

Definition 6 gives an operational definition of the plausibility metric $\mathcal{P}$, which can be readily implemented using tools and algorithms for Planning as SMT and projected model counting.

# 4 Experimental Results

In Sect. 3 we laid the theoretical foundations of a novel metric that allows us to reason about the plausibility of CEs. In this section, we demonstrate the utility thereof by reporting two experiments:

- in Sect. 4.1 we demonstrate how our metric can be used to analyse the plausibility of CEs in practice;
- in Sect. 4.2 we present numerical results demonstrating the wider applicability of our solution across a set of benchmarks taken from the planning literature.

The Python prototype used for these experiments, as well as additional experimental details, can be found in the supplementary material. Our experiments leverage the OMTPlan [23] tool to generate SMT formulas encoding planning problems. To ease our experimental analysis, we implemented a general model counting algorithm that is able to directly process SMT formulas generated by OMTPlan. More details about this algorithm can be found in the appendix. All experiments were carried out on a machine running Linux, equipped with 112 CPUs, 28 cores per socket Intel(R) Xeon(R) 2.20 GHz, and 256 Gb of RAM. We used a timeout of 3600 s and no memory limit.

## 4.1 Case Study: The Gripper Domain

This case study aims to demonstrate how our proposed metric can be used in practice. We focus on a modified version of the GRIPPER domain[1] summarised below. A complete PDDL formalisation is included in the additional material.

*Domain Description.* A `robot` with two grippers, `left` and `right`, has to transport two `balls` from `RoomA` to `RoomB`. The robot initially does not hold anything, modelled by the predicates `free(left)` and `free(right)`. Furthermore, both grippers are fully operational, modelled by the predicated `not-broken(left)` and `not-broken(right)`. Both robot and balls are located in `RoomA`, modelled by the predicates `at(robot,RoomA)`, `at(ball1,RoomA)` and `at(ball2,RoomA)`. The robot can perform four actions: `move(?room1,?room2)`, to move from one room to another; `pick(?ball,?room,?gripper)`, to pick up a ball from a room provided that the corresponding gripper is operational and empty; `drop(?ball,?room,?gripper)`, to drop the ball in a room provided that the gripper is operational, thus emptying the gripper. Finally, the robot can execute an action `drop-both` to simultaneously drop both balls when both grippers are operational.

*Inspecting a Plan.* Given the domain described above, assume that the following plan is obtained:

[1] https://ipc98.icaps-conference.org/.

```
Step 1: (pick ball2 roomA left)
Step 2: (move roomA roomB)
Step 3: (drop ball2 roomB left)
Step 4: (move roomB roomA)
Step 5: (pick ball1 roomA right)
Step 6: (move roomA roomB)
Step 7: (drop ball1 roomB right)
```

Upon inspecting the plan, the user may formulate the following questions: **(Q1)** Why was the action `drop-both` not used? **(Q2)** Why was the action `(drop ball2 roomB left)` used? **(Q3)** Why was the action `(move roomA roomB)` executed in step 2 instead of `(pick ball1 roomA right)`? **(Q4)** Why was the action `(move roomA roomB)` not performed before the action `(drop ball2 roomB left)`?

*Evaluating Plausibility.* We then instantiated our procedure to evaluate the support of each course of action. We built the Planning as an SAT encoding of the gripper domain using an horizon $n = 7$, which corresponds to the number of actions contained in the original plan. Two formulas are obtained for each contrastive question, encoding $\varphi_{fact}$ and $\varphi_{foil}$ respectively. Then, using a timeout of 1 h, we ran the projected model counting procedure to count the number of models admitted by each formula, and observed the following results. For **Q1**, the course of action suggested by the plan (i.e., not using the `drop-both` action) was supported by 3620 solutions, compared to the 604 solutions obtained for the alternative proposed by the user. Ultimately, this leads to a plausibility value $\mathcal{R} = 0.17$, which informs the user of the fact that using the action `drop-both` decreases the plausibility of encountering the suggested course of action. On the contrary, with **Q2** we observe a fact support of 592 as opposed to a foil support of 3632 which yields $\mathcal{R} = 6.14$. This informs the user that replacing the `(drop ball2 roomB left)`, maybe using the right gripper instead, would not compromise the chances of achieving the desired goal. Similar results are again observed for **Q3**, where a foil support of 692 compared to a fact support of 120 suggests that indeed replacing the action `(move roomA roomB)` with `(drop ball2 roomB left)` would result in improved plausibility ($\mathcal{R} = 5.77$). Finally, the results obtained for **Q4** show a foil support of 0, thus informing the user that the proposed order of actions renders the planning problem unsolvable within the given horizon.

### 4.2 Scalability

We performed additional experiments to assess the scalability of our approach. We considered 5 classical planning domains, as well as 5 domains containing numerical features. The former are taken from early editions of the IPC[2], whereas the latter are from [24,31]. The latter were chosen to demonstrate the wide

[2] https://www.icaps-conference.org/competitions/.

applicability of our approach, extending beyond classical planning. Indeed, our procedure only counts solutions with respect to the set of (boolean) action variables contained in a planning problem and can therefore be seamlessly applied to more expressive domains. For each domain considered, we selected three instances and generated a plan $\pi$ using the OMTPlan planner [23] for each. Then, for each plan, we produced four random contrastive questions following the templates of Table 1 and generated an encoding as described in Sect. 3 using an horizon equal to $< (\pi)$. We then measured the support and plausibility of each of the resulting combinations. Table 2 reports the average time (s) per axiom and the number of timeouts that occurred during the execution of these experiments. As we can observe, the scalability of our approach varies across domains. In particular, the highest number of timeouts occurs in the classical planning domain. This can be explained by considering the size of these planning problems, which is on average considerably larger than the numeric ones. In such cases, the worst-case complexity of model counting (#P) becomes apparent and leads to a higher number of timeouts. However, numeric domains show good overall performance, demonstrating the practical applicability of our approach.

**Table 2.** Execution time (s) of our procedure. T/O is set to 1hr.

| Domain | Q1 | | Q2 | | Q3 | | Q4 | |
|---|---|---|---|---|---|---|---|---|
| | avg time (s) | T/O | avg time (s) | T/O | avg time (s) | T/O | avg time (s) | T/O |
| airport | 1217.47 | 1 | 1217.61 | 1 | 1217.52 | 1 | 1217.61 | 1 |
| depot (classical) | 3600 | 3 | 3600 | 3 | 3600 | 3 | 3600 | 3 |
| driverlog | 2544.09 | 2 | 2546.99 | 2 | 2456.00 | 2 | 2444.96 | 2 |
| gripper | 3600 | 3 | 3600 | 3 | 3600 | 3 | 3600 | 3 |
| hiking | 3600 | 3 | 3600 | 3 | 3600 | 3 | 3600 | 3 |
| depot (numerical) | 2795.94 | 2 | 2803.04 | 2 | 2753.83 | 2 | 2628.81 | 2 |
| counters | 179.69 | 0 | 182.18 | 0 | 99.86 | 0 | 27.42 | 0 |
| gardening | 19.34 | 0 | 18.36 | 0 | 17.25 | 0 | 16.48 | 0 |
| rover | 2339.44 | 1 | 2380.29 | 0 | 576.45 | 1 | 404.91 | 0 |
| sec-clearance-sdac | 15.09 | 0 | 14.97 | 0 | 14.43 | 0 | 14.61 | 0 |

## 5 Conclusions

We presented the first approach to quantifying the plausibility of contrastive explanations for planning problems. We introduced the concept of plan support to this end; we then proposed a procedure to quantify plan support using Planning as SMT encodings and projected model counting. Our results are encouraging and open up several avenues for future research. First, we intend to investigate solutions to improve scalability. To this end, we believe it would be interesting to explore applications of approximate model counters to our setting. As our initial evaluations also included SMT formulas, we decided to leverage a general-purpose counting procedure. However, we have reasons to believe that modern counting algorithms could lead to considerable speed-ups, especially in the context of classical planning tasks that only feature propositional variables. For planning problems requiring theory variables, we believe it would be interesting to to investigate approximation schemes based on top-k planning algorithms [16], which could be leveraged to efficiently sample the solution space and obtain probabilistic guarantees of plausibility. Finally, we would be interested in exploring the applicability of our notions to counterfactual explanations for planning problems, such as those as recently discussed in [4].

# A Pseudocode

**Algorithm 1.** contrastive_questions

```
Input: (horizon, axiom, action1, action2, step)
solver = new ContrastiveSolver(axiom, action1, action2, step)
action_list = List()
for i in range(horizon) do
    for action in encoder.action_variables[i].items() do
        action_list.append(action)
    end for
end for
fact_solver = solver.get_fact_encoding()
fact_support = MODEL_COUNTING(fact_solver, action_list)
if len(fact_support) ≠ 0 then
    foil_solver = solver.get_foil_encoding()
    foil_support = MODEL_COUNTING(foil_solver, action_list)
    plausibility = len(foil_support)/len(fact_support)
else
    print "Fact support is empty, something went wrong"
end if
```

**Algorithm 2.** MODEL_COUNTING

```
function MODEL_COUNTING(solver, initial_terms)
    function ALL_SAT_REC(solver, terms)
        if solver.check() == sat then
            model = solver.model()
            yield m
            for i in range(|terms|) do
                solver.push()
                fix i^th term with its opposite model value
                fix all terms before i^th term to model value
                yield from ALL_SAT_REC(solver, terms[i+1:])
                solver.pop()
            end for
        end if
    end function
    yield from ALL_SAT_REC(solver, initial_terns)
end function
```

## References


1. Artelt, A., Hammer, B.: Convex density constraints for computing plausible counterfactual explanations. In: Proceedings of ICANN 2020. Lecture Notes in Computer Science, vol. 12396, pp. 353–365. Springer (2020)
2. Aziz, R.A., Chu, G., Muise, C.J., Stuckey, P.J.: #∃sat: projected model counting. In: Proceedings of SAT 2015. Lecture Notes in Computer Science, vol. 9340, pp. 121–137. Springer (2015)
3. Barrett, C.W., Sebastiani, R., Seshia, S.A., Tinelli, C.: Satisfiability modulo theories. In: Handbook of Satisfiability - Second Edition. Frontiers in Artificial Intelligence and Applications, vol. 336, pp. 1267–1329. IOS Press (2021)
4. Belle, V.: Counterfactual explanations as plans. In: Proceedings of ICLP 2023. EPTCS, vol. 385, pp. 339–352 (2023)
5. Bercher, P., et al.: Plan, repair, execute, explain - how planning helps to assemble your home theater. In: Proceedings of ICAPS 2014. AAAI (2014)
6. Biere, A., Heule, M., van Maaren, H., Walsh, T. (eds.): Handbook of Satisfiability - Second Edition. Frontiers in Artificial Intelligence and Applications, vol. 336. IOS Press (2021)
7. Byrne, R.M.J.: Counterfactuals in explainable artificial intelligence (XAI): evidence from human reasoning. In: Proceedings of IJCAI 2019, pp. 6276–6282. ijcai.org (2019)
8. Chakraborti, T., Sreedharan, S., Kambhampati, S.: The emerging landscape of explainable automated planning & decision making. In: Proceedings of IJCAI 2020, pp. 4803–4811. ijcai.org (2020)
9. Chistikov, D., Dimitrova, R., Majumdar, R.: Approximate counting in SMT and value estimation for probabilistic programs. In: Tools and Algorithms for the Construction and Analysis of Systems - 21st International Conference, TACAS 2015, Held as Part of the European Joint Conferences on Theory and Practice of Software, ETAPS 2015, London, UK, 11–18 April 2015. Lecture Notes in Computer Science, vol. 9035, pp. 320–334. Springer (2015) ¡error l="304" c="Invalid command: paragraph not started." /¿
10. Eifler, R., Cashmore, M., Hoffmann, J., Magazzeni, D., Steinmetz, M.: A new approach to plan-space explanation: analyzing plan-property dependencies in oversubscription planning. In: Proceedings of AAAI 2020, pp. 9818–9826. AAAI Press (2020)
11. Fox, M., Long, D., Magazzeni, D.: Explainable planning. CoRR, abs/1709.10256 (2017). http://arxiv.org/abs/1709.10256
12. Fredrikson, M., Jha, S.: Satisfiability modulo counting: a new approach for analyzing privacy properties. In: Joint Meeting of the Twenty-Third EACSL Annual Conference on Computer Science Logic (CSL) and the Twenty-Ninth Annual ACM/IEEE Symposium on Logic in Computer Science (LICS), CSL-LICS 2014, Vienna, Austria, 14–18 July 2014, pp. 42:1–42:10. ACM (2014)
13. Gomes, A.S., Selman, B.: Model counting. In: Handbook of Satisfiability. Frontiers in Artificial Intelligence and Applications, 2nd edn., vol. 336, pp. 993–1014. IOS Press (2021)
14. Guidotti, R., Monreale, A., Ruggieri, S., Turini, F., Giannotti, F., Pedreschi, D.: A survey of methods for explaining black box models. ACM Comput. Surv. **51**(5), 93:1–93:42 (2019)
15. Hoffmann, J., Magazzeni, D.: Explainable AI planning (XAIP): overview and the case of contrastive explanation (extended abstract). In: Reasoning Web. Explainable Artificial Intelligence. Lecture Notes in Computer Science, vol. 11810, pp. 277–282. Springer (2019)

16. Katz, M., Sohrabi, S., Udrea, O., Winterer, D.: A novel iterative approach to top-k planning. In: Proceedings of ICAPS 2018, pp. 132–140. AAAI Press (2018)
17. Kautz, H.A., Selman, B.: Planning as satisfiability. In Proceedings of ECAI 1992, pp. 359–363. Wiley (1992)
18. Kenny, E.M., Keane, M.T.: On generating plausible counterfactual and semi-factual explanations for deep learning. In: Proceedings of AAAI 2021, pp. 11575–11585. AAAI Press (2021)
19. Kim, J., Muise, C., Shah, A., Agarwal, S., Shah, J.: Bayesian inference of linear temporal logic specifications for contrastive explanations. In: Proceedings of IJCAI 2019, pp. 5591–5598. ijcai.org (2019)
20. Krarup, B., Krivic, S., Magazzeni, D., Long, D., Cashmore, M., Smith, D.E.: Contrastive explanations of plans through model restrictions. J. Artif. Intell. Res. **72**, 533–612 (2021)
21. Krarup, B., Smith, D., Long, D., Coles, A.: Explaining plan quality differences. In: Proceedings of ICAPS 2024. AAAI Press (2024)
22. Laugel, T., Lesot, M.-J., Marsala, C., Renard, X., Detyniecki, M.: The dangers of post-hoc interpretability: unjustified counterfactual explanations. In: Proceedings of IJCAI 2019, pp. 2801–2807. ijcai.org (2019). https://doi.org/10.24963/ijcai.2019/388
23. Leofante, F.: OMTPlan: a tool for optimal planning modulo theories. J. Satisf. Boolean Model. Comput. **14**(1), 17–23 (2023)
24. Leofante, F., Giunchiglia, E., Ábrahám, E., Tacchella, A.: Optimal planning modulo theories. In: Proceedings of IJCAI 2020, pp. 4128–4134. ijcai.org (2020)
25. Lipton, P.: Contrastive explanation. Roy. Inst. Philos. Suppl. **27**, 247–266 (1990)
26. Luu, L., Shinde, S., Saxena, P., Demsky, B.: A model counter for constraints over unbounded strings. In: ACM SIGPLAN Conference on Programming Language Design and Implementation, PLDI 2014, Edinburgh, United Kingdom, 09–11 June 2014, pp. 565–576. ACM (2014)
27. Ma, F., Liu, S., Zhang, J.: Volume computation for Boolean combination of linear arithmetic constraints. In: Automated Deduction - CADE-22, 22nd International Conference on Automated Deduction, Montreal, Canada, 2–7 August 2009. Lecture Notes in Computer Science, vol. 5663, pp. 453–468. Springer (2009)
28. Miller, T.: Explanation in artificial intelligence: insights from the social sciences. Artif. Intell. **267**, 1–38 (2019)
29. Narodytska, N., Shrotri, A.A., Meel, K.S., Ignatiev, A., Marques-Silva, J.: Assessing heuristic machine learning explanations with model counting. In: Proceedings of SAT 2019. Lecture Notes in Computer Science, vol. 11628, pp. 267–278. Springer (2019)
30. Rintanen, J.: Planning and SAT. In: Handbook of Satisfiability. Frontiers in Artificial Intelligence and Applications, 2nd edn., vol. 336, pp. 765–789. IOS Press (2021)
31. Scala, E., Haslum, P., Magazzeni, D., Thiébaux, S.: Landmarks for numeric planning problems. In: Proceedings of IJCAI 2017, pp. 4384–4390. ijcai.org (2017)
32. Sreedharan, S., Chakraborti, T., Kambhampati, S.: Handling model uncertainty and multiplicity in explanations via model reconciliation. In: Proceedings of ICAPS 2018, pp. 518–526. AAAI Press (2018)
33. Sreedharan, S., Srivastava, S., Smith, D.E., Kambhampati, S.: Why couldn't you do that? Explaining unsolvability of classical planning problems in the presence of plan advice. CoRR abs/1903.08218 (2019)

# Bound-Aware Heuristic Discovery with Large Language Models: A 15-Puzzle Case Study

Xiaojia Li[1], Csaba Kiss[2], Roland Molontay[2], and József Pintér[2](✉)

[1] Carleton College, Northfield, MN, USA
lil4@carleton.edu

[2] Department of Stochastics, Institute of Mathematics, Budapest University of Technology and Economics, Budapest, Hungary
{kisscs,molontay}@math.bme.hu, pinterj@edu.bme.hu

**Abstract.** Designing effective heuristics remains a central question in heuristic search and planning, especially when optimality requirements can be relaxed. We introduce a framework that uses large language models (LLMs) to synthesize lightweight, executable, and interpretable heuristics under empirical per-instance solution-cost constraints. Candidate programs are generated offline, evaluated with a fixed no-reopening A* search procedure, and retained only if they satisfy a specified cost-ratio bound on a discovery set. We evaluate the framework on Korf's 15-puzzle benchmark, a controlled testbed with known optimal solution costs. Several synthesized heuristics achieve lower normalized unique generated-node counts than nearby WA*-MDLC configurations; the best case yields approximately 2.26× fewer generated nodes and a 6.73× wall-clock speedup at comparable held-out cost ratios. These results suggest that LLM-guided synthesis can discover simple, interpretable heuristics that improve search efficiency under empirical solution-quality constraints and complement traditional weighted-search approaches. The method provides practical empirical validation on discovery instances, while all-state bounded-suboptimality guarantees remain outside its scope.

**Keywords:** heuristic search · bounded-suboptimal search · large language models · heuristic discovery · 15-puzzle · program synthesis

## 1 Introduction

Heuristic search underpins planning, combinatorial puzzles, and other large state-space problems where exhaustive optimal search is impractical [11,14], and the heuristic that guides the search largely determines performance. When strict optimality is unnecessary, bounded-suboptimal methods exploit the relaxed requirement, typically by modifying node ordering, queue management, or termination while using a supplied heuristic. Weighted A*, for instance, inflates


S. Bistarelli et al. (Eds.): AIxIA 2026, LNAI 17131, pp. 365–377, 2027.
https://doi.org/10.1007/978-3-032-40774-0_27

an admissible base heuristic, bounding the returned cost under the standard assumptions [5,16,21]. Such methods take the heuristic as given rather than synthesizing a new heuristic program for each quality regime.

This motivates a complementary direction: once optimality is relaxed, the heuristic need not be admissible and its structure can be adapted to the target regime. Yet heuristic design remains largely manual. We ask whether program synthesis with large language models (LLMs) can explore this design space, using empirical per-instance cost-ratio constraints to limit quality degradation during discovery.

Recent work shows that LLMs can discover executable programs through evaluation-driven search, including FunSearch [17], Evolution of Heuristics [13], and ReEvo [22], and can generate heuristic functions for classical planning, selected by empirical training performance [2]. None, however, formulate heuristic generation as a constrained discovery problem in which every accepted candidate must satisfy a per-instance solution-cost-ratio bound.

We introduce an LLM-guided framework for heuristic discovery under empirical solution-cost-ratio constraints. We treat the heuristic as the object of optimization: candidate programs are generated offline by an LLM and evaluated with a fixed no-reopening A* search, each required to satisfy per-instance cost-ratio constraints on a training set, with final quality measured only as an observed held-out ratio. This enables empirical exploration of inadmissible designs but provides no theorem-level guarantee for all states. We use the 15-puzzle as a controlled benchmark because its standard instances and known optimal costs make empirical suboptimality measurable; the broader aim is lightweight heuristic synthesis for relaxed-quality search and planning.

On Korf's 15-puzzle benchmark, the discovered heuristics produce encouraging results: in most settings, they require fewer normalized unique generated nodes than nearby WA*-MDLC configurations at comparable solution-cost ratios. These results provide preliminary evidence that optimizing heuristic-program structure can yield useful efficiency-quality trade-offs; they do not support a definitive dominance claim.

The contributions of this work are as follows:

- We introduce an LLM-guided framework for automatically proposing executable heuristic functions under empirical solution-quality constraints.
- We report a 15-puzzle case study showing that LLM-discovered lightweight heuristics can match WA*-MDLC and often reduce generated-node counts at comparable observed empirical cost ratios.
- We qualitatively analyze recurring structural patterns in synthesized heuristics, including weighted Manhattan-style terms, conflict penalties, and local blocking or trap penalties.

## 2 Background and Related Work

*Human-Designed Heuristics.* Classical heuristic search relies on manually designed heuristics derived from problem abstractions. Early work formalized admissible heuristics for A*, which guarantee optimality under nonnegative edge costs and appropriate duplicate handling [6,14]. For sliding-tile puzzles, more informative admissible heuristics such as Linear Conflict and Pattern Databases substantially reduce search effort relative to Manhattan distance [3,12]. When optimality is relaxed, designers often use inadmissible heuristics that trade quality for speed, e.g. through heuristic inflation [16] or learned combinations of heuristic signals [18]. Such designs are typically hand-built and rely on domain knowledge, so it remains unclear how heuristic structure should adapt when explicit quality limits are acceptable.

*Bounded-Suboptimal Search.* Bounded-suboptimal search lets solutions exceed the optimal cost by a controlled factor. Weighted A* inflates an admissible base heuristic and, under the standard assumptions, bounds the returned cost relative to optimal [5,16,21]; uniform weighting can be conservative, motivating more aggressive variants [21]. Related methods such as $A^*_\epsilon$ and optimistic search alter node-expansion priorities and add verification or termination mechanisms [15,21]. Across this line of work, search control is modified while heuristic information is treated as supplied rather than synthesized [20,21], so little work asks how the heuristic structure itself might change under relaxed optimality.

*Automated Heuristic Discovery.* Earlier work explored automated heuristic design via genetic programming, genetic algorithms, bootstrapped learning, and learned heuristic combinations [4,9,10,18]. More recently, LLM-based frameworks such as FunSearch, Evolution of Heuristics, and ReEvo generate and iteratively refine executable programs through evaluation-driven search [13,17,22], and LLMs have been used to generate heuristic functions for classical planning, selected by empirical training performance [2]. None of these methods enforce a strict per-instance solution-cost-ratio bound as an acceptance criterion. In contrast, we frame heuristic discovery as a constrained program-synthesis problem in which candidates are filtered by per-instance cost-ratio bounds on training instances.

## 3 Problem Setting and Method

We consider deterministic shortest-path problems with a finite state space $\mathcal{S}$, actions $\mathcal{A}$, a deterministic transition function, and non-negative action costs, solved from a start state $s_0$ to a goal $s_g$. Given a heuristic $h : \mathcal{S} \to \mathbb{R}_{\geq 0}$, we run a fixed no-reopening A* graph search [6] with node priority

$$f(n) = g(n) + h(n), \tag{1}$$

where $g(n)$ is the cost from $s_0$ to $n$; the search and tie-breaking rules stay fixed across experiments, so performance differences reflect the heuristic alone.

We use the classic 15-puzzle as a controlled benchmark: a $4 \times 4$ board with 15 tiles and one blank, unit-cost moves, and $16!/2 \approx 10^{13}$ reachable states [3,11,12]. It provides standard instances and known optimal costs, making empirical sub-optimality measurable. We deliberately restrict attention to lightweight state-evaluation heuristics and exclude PDBs, learned value networks, and large pre-computed tables.

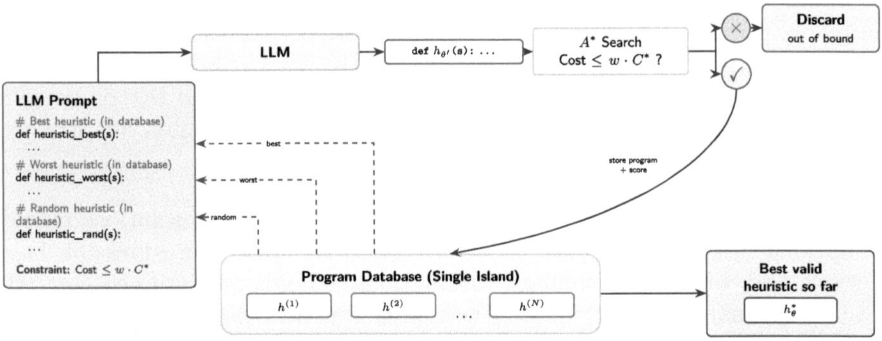


**Fig. 1.** Single island bounded suboptimal heuristic discovery loop. Each round, the LLM proposes one candidate heuristic, which is evaluated under the cost bound $w \cdot C^*$. Valid candidates are stored and used to form future prompts via best, worst, and random exemplars. Invalid candidates are discarded. The output is the best valid heuristic found so far: the valid candidate with the lowest average normalized unique generated-node count.

### 3.1 Overview

We treat heuristic design as an optimization problem while fixing the search algorithm: we explore the space of heuristic programs and keep candidates that minimize search effort subject to a training-set cost-ratio constraint. Reported quality is therefore an empirical held-out measurement.

Figure 1 illustrates one island of the discovery loop. At each iteration an LLM proposes a candidate program from previously evaluated examples, and a fixed no-reopening A* search evaluates it on the training instances. Candidates that satisfy the empirical bound are stored with their statistics; violators are rejected, though their records may persist in island histories to encourage prompt diversity. The LLM thus acts purely as a proposal mechanism: the deterministic search makes all evaluation and selection decisions.

### 3.2 Empirical Bound Constraint

Solution quality is measured relative to the optimal cost $C^*$. For a returned solution of cost $C$, the cost ratio is

$$\rho = \frac{C}{C^*}, \tag{2}$$

and $\rho \leq w$ means the solution is within the target ratio $w$. Weighted A* enforces such a bound through the search procedure itself [5,16,21]; here, $w$ is a discovery-time constraint on candidate heuristics. On a fixed training set $\mathcal{I}_{\text{train}}$, a candidate $h$ is valid only if

$$\frac{C_i(h)}{C_i^*} \leq w \qquad \forall i \in \mathcal{I}_{\text{train}}, \tag{3}$$

where $C_i(h)$ is the cost of A* with $h$ on instance $i$ and $C_i^*$ the optimal cost; a violation on even one training instance rejects the candidate. Optimal costs are used only offline, to normalize quality as $C/C^*$ (optimizing raw solution length would conflate instance difficulty), and running a discovered heuristic does not require $C^*$. Because the constraint is enforced only on discovery instances, it is an empirical training constraint, not a theoretical guarantee: we report final quality as the maximum observed ratio $\rho_{\max}$ on a disjoint held-out test set $\mathcal{I}_{\text{test}}$.

### 3.3 Heuristic Representation and Design Space

Each candidate is an explicit executable program defining a function $h_\theta : \mathcal{S} \rightarrow \mathbb{R}_{\geq 0}$ that maps a state to a non-negative estimate, where $\theta$ is the program's syntactic structure. Programs receive the raw puzzle state; we do not supply Manhattan distance, linear conflict, corner heuristics, pattern databases, or other classical components as primitives, although a program may recompute such quantities. The prompt includes a simple Manhattan-style example only to fix the expected output format. We target a lightweight class: prompts ask for finite, non-negative, self-contained state-evaluation heuristics that avoid lookahead, external memory, and large precomputed tables. We enforce these restrictions through prompting, robust evaluation, and manual inspection of the final programs, which access no pattern databases, learned value networks, or large precomputed structures at search time (a few use small constant-size lookup tables for local tile distances). Fuller automated verification is left to future work.

### 3.4 Constrained Evaluation and Selection

For a fixed bound $w$, discovery seeks a program $\theta$ that minimizes search effort on the training instances subject to the cost constraint:

$$\begin{aligned} \min_{\theta} \quad & \frac{1}{|\mathcal{I}_{\text{train}}|} \sum_{i \in \mathcal{I}_{\text{train}}} \text{Nodes}_{\text{norm}}(A^*, h_\theta)_i \\ \text{subject to} \quad & \frac{C_i(h_\theta)}{C_i^*} \leq w \quad \forall i \in \mathcal{I}_{\text{train}}. \end{aligned} \tag{4}$$

Here $\text{Nodes}_{\text{norm}}(A^*, h_\theta)_i$ is the unique generated-node count of A* with $h_\theta$ on instance $i$, divided by the IDA*($h_{\text{MD}}$) count reported by [11].

The per-instance constraint discourages heuristics that achieve a low average by erring badly on a few instances. Final evaluation uses only the disjoint test set $\mathcal{I}_{\text{test}}$, so $\rho_{\max}$ there measures empirical generalization rather than a worst-case guarantee.

### 3.5 Multi-island Evolutionary Dynamics

To prevent premature convergence and encourage broad exploration of the heuristic design space, the framework maintains multiple island populations. Each round is synchronous: one proposal per island is generated and evaluated before the next round begins. Every eight rounds, islands are ranked by their best valid heuristic, and the lower-ranked islands are refilled with a small number of elite programs from the surviving islands. This cull-and-refill mechanism is intended to preserve diversity while allowing successful heuristic patterns to propagate across the search process.

## 4 Experimental Setup

### 4.1 Benchmark Instances

All experiments use Korf's 100-instance 15-puzzle benchmark [11], a standard evaluation suite [8,19]. We use one fixed split: 15 randomly chosen instances form the discovery/training set (used both to score candidate search effort and to enforce the cost-ratio constraint) and the remaining 85 form the held-out set on which all reported cost ratios and generated-count comparisons are computed. Evaluating robustness across multiple splits remains future work.

### 4.2 Baseline Heuristics and Normalization

Search effort is normalized relative to the supplied IDA* reference counts using Manhattan Distance ($h_{\text{MD}}$) [11]. A normalized generated-count ratio of 1.0 corresponds to the reference IDA*($h_{\text{MD}}$) generated count for the same instance.

The primary comparison is Weighted A* with Manhattan Distance plus Linear Conflict (WA*-MDLC), a standard sliding-tile enhancement [12]. More powerful 15-puzzle methods exist, such as pattern databases (PDBs) [3] and neural solvers such as DeepCubeA [1], but they rely on large memory, offline training, or precomputation and thus occupy a different computational regime.

### 4.3 Cost Bound Settings

Performance is evaluated across several values of the bound parameter $w$, which specifies the maximum allowed solution cost ratio as in Equation (3). Smaller values enforce near-optimal solutions, whereas larger values allow more aggressive heuristics that trade solution quality for reduced search effort.

Within our framework the bound is enforced empirically during discovery on the training instances, and the resulting maximum observed solution-cost ratio is reported on the disjoint test set. In the baseline comparison, WA*-MDLC and the LLM-discovered heuristics are both plotted using the observed held-out $\rho_{\max}$ measured on the same test instances.

### 4.4 Evaluation Protocol

All methods use the same graph-search procedure. OPEN is maintained as a priority queue and CLOSED records previously expanded states. For each generated state, the best-known path cost ($g$-value) is retained. Expanded states are not reopened, and the goal test is performed only when a node is selected from OPEN. Ties are broken in FIFO order by insertion time.

A* with a discovered heuristic uses priority $f(n) = g(n) + h(n)$. WA* uses priority $f_W(n) = g(n) + Wh_{\mathrm{MDLC}}(n)$. Because the synthesized heuristics are generally inadmissible, A* with these heuristics does not guarantee optimal solutions under this protocol. Solution quality is therefore measured using observed solution-cost ratios relative to reference optimal solution costs.

Search efficiency uses the same unique generated-node convention as the discovery objective normalized by the IDA*($h_{\mathrm{MD}}$) reference counts, keeping evaluation aligned with the optimized quantity.

### 4.5 Implementation Details and Reproducibility

During heuristic discovery, the framework samples from Gemini 2.5 Pro, Gemini 2.5 Flash, and Gemini 2.5 Flash Lite. Model selection is randomized across iterations to increase proposal diversity rather than to favor any particular model. The models operate purely as offline proposal mechanisms within the same evaluation procedure.

Heuristic discovery follows an island-based evolutionary process with 8 islands and 23 proposal rounds, yielding 184 evaluated candidate programs per discovery run. Islands are culled and refilled every 8 rounds. The current study evaluates the core combination of LLM proposal, empirical training-set filtering, island-based search, and held-out evaluation on a fixed 15/85 split.

## 5 Experimental Results

This section compares the retained LLM-discovered heuristics with WA*-MDLC on Korf's 15-puzzle benchmark. Unless otherwise stated, search effort is measured by the arithmetic mean of normalized unique generated-node counts, denoted by $\mu_{\mathrm{nodes}}$, and solution quality is measured by the maximum observed solution-cost ratio, denoted by $\rho_{\max}$, over the held-out evaluation instances.

Because our workflow reserves instances for discovery, we avoid comparing held-out results against full-benchmark baseline numbers [7,11,21], which would conflate method performance with the evaluated instance set; all WA*-MDLC and discovered-heuristic results below use the same 85 held-out instances.

### 5.1 Comparison with WA*-MDLC

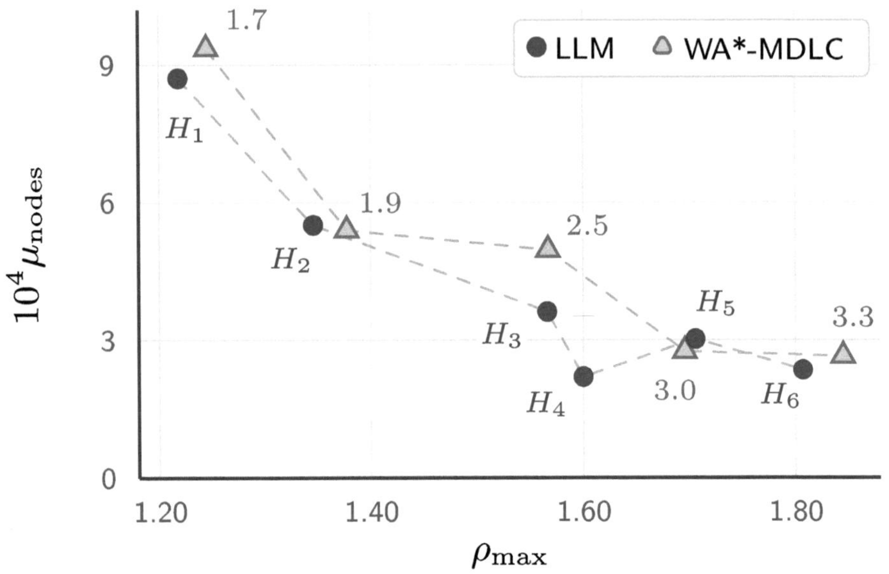


**Fig. 2.** Held-out 15-puzzle comparison under the unique generated-node convention. Blue circles show retained LLM-discovered heuristics; red triangles show selected WA*-MDLC weights, labeled by their weight parameter $w$. (Color figure online)

Figure 2 presents an efficiency–quality comparison between the retained LLM-discovered heuristics and selected WA*-MDLC weights. Both methods are evaluated on the same held-out Korf instances, and all x-values correspond to observed maximum solution-cost ratios on this held-out set.

Table 1 lists each retained heuristic's discovery-time cost-ratio bound; the runtime-speedup column reports the wall-clock ratio between the nearest WA*-MDLC point in $\rho_{\max}$ and that heuristic, measured by sequential execution on the same held-out instances. Note that wall-clock time is not determined solely by the number of unique generated nodes, since it also reflects repeated state generation, OPEN/CLOSED operations, and heuristic-evaluation overhead.

Under the unique generated-node convention, the results are mixed but encouraging. At observed cost ratios around 1.56–1.60, two discovered heuristics need fewer unique generated nodes than the nearby WA*-MDLC configuration ($W = 2.5$), by about 1.37× and 2.26×. At lower cost ratios the picture is less clear, with several heuristics roughly tied with or worse than nearby WA*-MDLC points, so we do not claim uniform dominance. Overall, LLM-discovered heuristics produce competitive points in the efficiency-quality plane and often improve on nearby WA*-MDLC configurations.

**Table 1.** Held-out performance under the unique generated-node convention. For $H_1$–$H_6$, $w$ is the discovery-time cost-ratio bound; for WA*-MDLC, $w$ is the WA* weight. Runtime speedup is measured against the nearest WA*-MDLC point in $\rho_{\max}$.

| Method | $w$ | $\rho_{\max}$ | $10^4\mu_{\text{nodes}}$ | Time speedup |
|---|---|---|---|---|
| $H_1$ | 1.25 | 1.218 | 8.711 | 2.78× |
| $H_2$ | 1.35 | 1.346 | 5.509 | 1.67× |
| $H_3$ | 1.45 | 1.566 | 3.616 | 1.47× |
| $H_4$ | 1.55 | 1.600 | 2.198 | 6.73× |
| $H_5$ | 1.75 | 1.706 | 3.023 | 2.55× |
| $H_6$ | 1.65 | 1.807 | 2.350 | 2.56× |
| WA*-MDLC | 1.7 | 1.245 | 9.362 | – |
| WA*-MDLC | 1.9 | 1.377 | 5.396 | – |
| WA*-MDLC | 2.5 | 1.567 | 4.966 | – |
| WA*-MDLC | 3.0 | 1.696 | 2.752 | – |
| WA*-MDLC | 3.3 | 1.844 | 2.651 | – |

### 5.2 Relation to Search-Control Methods

We compare against WA*-MDLC because it is a lightweight, directly comparable search-control baseline; Optimistic Search, other WA* variants, and combinations of synthesized heuristics with stronger search control are relevant but out of scope here, and we leave them to future work. The distinction matters: WA* and Optimistic Search modify node-expansion order and may offer formal guarantees, whereas we change the heuristic used by a fixed search procedure, so our quality claim is empirical rather than a theoretical bound.

## 6 Discovered Heuristics

The retained programs go beyond simple rescalings of Manhattan distance. Across $H_1$–$H_6$, the LLM builds interpretable heuristic estimators by recombining a small set of recurring structural motifs. We describe the six retained examples below, where $\lfloor\cdot\rfloor$ denotes flooring to an integer.

*$H_1$: Corner/Edge/Center Weighted Conflict.*

$$H_1(s) = \Big\lfloor \textstyle\sum_{t\neq 0} w(t)\mathrm{MD}_t(s) + 3.4\,\mathrm{LC}(s)\Big\rfloor,$$

where $\mathrm{MD}_t$ is the Manhattan distance of tile $t$, LC a linear-conflict term, and the weight $w(t)$ is 1.85 for corner-goal, 1.70 for edge-goal, and 1.55 for interior tiles, prioritizing geometrically constrained tiles within the familiar Manhattan-plus-conflict form.

*$H_2$: Trap and Endgame Penalty.*

$$H_2(s) = \big\lfloor \tfrac{7}{4}\big(\mathrm{MD}(s) + 4\mathrm{LC}(s) + 4\mathrm{Trap}(s) + 6D(s) + 5E(s)\big)\big\rfloor.$$

Trap($s$) counts misplaced tiles whose neighbors are all solved tiles, $D(s)$ detects late-game deadlocks, and $E(s)$ penalizes misplaced last-row tiles once the first three rows are largely solved, emphasizing boards that look near-solved under Manhattan distance but are hard to finish.

*$H_3$: Row-Weighted Conflict.*

$$H_3(s) = \Big\lfloor 1.5\big( \textstyle\sum_{t \neq 0} w_r(t)\mathrm{MD}_t(s) + 3.5\,\mathrm{LC}_{\mathrm{row}}(s) \\ + 3.0\,\mathrm{LC}_{\mathrm{col}}(s) + 5\,\mathrm{Corner}(s)\big)\Big\rfloor.$$

The row weights are $(2.0, 1.8, 1.5, 1.2)$ from top to bottom, row conflicts are penalized slightly more than column conflicts, and Corner($s$) flags incorrect corner tiles blocked by already-correct neighbors.

*$H_4$: Swap-and-Corner Conflict.*

$$H_4(s) = \big\lfloor 2.58\big(\mathrm{MD}(s) + 2\mathrm{LC}(s) + 4\mathrm{Swap}(s) + 5\mathrm{Corner}(s)\big)\big\rfloor.$$

Swap($s$) detects adjacent reversed pairs (e.g. $(2, 1)$ or $(6, 5)$, horizontal or vertical). More aggressive than the others, it produced one of the strongest efficiency–quality trade-offs in our held-out evaluation (Table 1).

*$H_5$: Blank-Guided Weighted Conflict.*

$$H_5(s) = \lfloor 2.8\,\mathrm{MD}(s) + 5.6\,\mathrm{LC}(s)\rfloor + \mathrm{LMBP}(s) + \mathrm{BIP}(s).$$

LMBP($s$) is the Manhattan distance from the blank to the goal of the highest-index misplaced tile, and BIP($s$) penalizes solved tiles adjacent to the blank, adding blank-position information to the usual displacement and conflict terms.

*$H_6$: Quadratic Row-Prioritized Conflict.*

$$H_6(s) = \Big\lfloor \tfrac{1}{10}\big( \textstyle\sum_{t \neq 0} \big(a_t\mathrm{MD}_t(s) + 4\mathrm{MD}_t(s)^2\big) \\ + 125\mathrm{LC}(s) + 5\big)\Big\rfloor.$$

The coefficients $a_t$ are $27, 17, 12, 10$ for tiles 1–4, 5–8, 9–12, and 13–15: a row-prioritized weighted Manhattan heuristic with a quadratic distance term and a strong conflict correction.

Overall, these programs are creative and interpretable. They reuse recognizable puzzle ideas while adding nontrivial weightings, local-configuration penalties, and blank- or corner-prioritized corrections. They serve as search accelerators and human-readable design hypotheses, exposing concrete structural features that could be studied, refined, or folded into hand-designed heuristics.

## 7 Limitations and Conclusion

We presented evidence that LLM-guided synthesis can discover new heuristic structure for relaxed-quality search. On Korf's 15-puzzle, the workflow generates candidate programs offline, screens them with empirical per-instance cost-ratio constraints, and evaluates them on held-out instances. The resulting lightweight heuristics are competitive with WA*-MDLC and achieve lower unique generated-node counts in parts of the efficiency-quality plane at comparable held-out cost ratios. The workflow can introduce new conditional terms and penalties, exploring heuristic structure as well as parameters. It trains no policy or value network and leaves a symbolic heuristic usable in a standard search procedure.

The study is deliberately limited: it uses one fixed discovery/evaluation split and one set of generated candidates, with a lightweight baseline and no comparison to pattern databases or learned solvers. These choices limit claims about robustness and state-of-the-art 15-puzzle performance. The quality guarantee is empirical: the constraint is enforced only on discovery instances and we report observed held-out ratios. Settings without known optimal costs will need alternative validation, such as incumbent-based objectives, bounded-cost search, or teacher heuristics.

The present study evaluates the complete discovery pipeline as a whole and does not isolate the individual contributions of model mixing, exemplar feedback, island evolution, or the empirical cost-ratio filter. Component-wise ablations and robustness analyses across independent runs and discovery/test splits are left for future work.

These results position heuristic-function synthesis as a complement to search-control relaxation rather than a replacement. Natural next steps are to test robustness across multiple splits and independent runs, add ablations against coefficient tuning and the cost-ratio filter itself, and move from this controlled puzzle benchmark toward planning domains, where heuristic design remains a central and largely manual challenge.

**Acknowledgments.** Csaba Kiss has been supported by the Cooperative Doctoral Programme of the National Research, Development, and Innovation Fund. The work of Roland Molontay has been supported by the János Bolyai Research Scholarship of the Hungarian Academy of Sciences and by NKFIH 142169 research grant. József Pintér is funded by Project No. KDP-IKT-2023-900-I1-00000957/0000003 with support provided by the Ministry of Culture and Innovation of Hungary from the National Research, Development and Innovation Fund, financed under the KDP-2023 funding scheme. Roland Molontay is also supported by the National Research, Development, and Innovation Fund through the OTKA Grant PD-142585.

During the preparation of this manuscript, the authors used ChatGPT to assist with language and structural editing. All outputs were reviewed and verified by the authors, who take full responsibility for the content.

**Data Availibility Statement.** All code, complete prompts, executable heuristic programs, evaluation scripts, per-instance results, and reproduction instructions are available at https://github.com/Lee-Li-404/15Puzzle_Search.

**Disclosure of Interests.** The authors have no competing interests to declare that are relevant to the content of this article.

## References


1. Agostinelli, F., McAleer, S., Shmakov, A., Baldi, P.: Solving the Rubik's cube with deep reinforcement learning and search. Nat. Mach. Intell. **1**(8), 356–363 (2019)
2. Corrêa, A.B., Pereira, A.G., Seipp, J.: Classical planning with LLM-generated heuristics: challenging the state of the art with python code. Adv. Neural Inf. Process. Syst. **38**, 42070–42108 (2025). https://proceedings.neurips.cc/paper_files/paper/2025/hash/3bf4b55960aaa23553cd2a6bdc6e1b57-Abstract-Conference.html
3. Culberson, J.C., Schaeffer, J.: Pattern databases. Comput. Intell. **14**(3), 318–334 (1998). https://doi.org/10.1111/0824-7935.00065
4. Elyasaf, A., Zaritsky, Y., Hauptman, A., Sipper, M.: Evolving Solvers for FreeCell and the Sliding-Tile Puzzle. In: Proceedings of the International Symposium on Combinatorial Search, vol. 2, no. 1, pp. 189–190 (2011)
5. Fickert, M., Gu, T., Ruml, W.: New results in bounded-suboptimal search. In: Proceedings of the AAAI Conference on Artificial Intelligence, vol. 36, no. 9, pp. 10166–10173 (2022)
6. Hart, P.E., Nilsson, N.J., Raphael, B.: A formal basis for the heuristic determination of minimum cost paths. IEEE Trans. Syst. Sci. Cybern. **4**(2), 100–107 (1968)
7. Hasan, D.O., Aladdin, A.M., Talabani, H.S., Rashid, T.A., Mirjalili, S.: The fifteen puzzle-a new approach through hybridizing three heuristics methods. Computers **12**(1), 11 (2023)
8. Hatem, M., Burns, E., Ruml, W.: Solving large problems with heuristic search: general-purpose parallel external-memory search. J. Artif. Intell. Res. **62**, 233–268 (2018)
9. Hauptman, A., Elyasaf, A., Sipper, M., Karmon, A.: GP-rush: using genetic programming to evolve solvers for the rush hour puzzle. In: Proceedings of the 11th Annual Conference on Genetic and Evolutionary Computation, GECCO 2009, pp. 955–962. Association for Computing Machinery, New York (2009). https://doi.org/10.1145/1569901.1570032
10. Jabbari Arfaee, S., Zilles, S., Holte, R.C.: Learning heuristic functions for large state spaces. Artif. Intell. **175**(16), 2075–2098 (2011)
11. Korf, R.E.: Depth-first iterative-deepening: an optimal admissible tree search. Artif. Intell. **27**(1), 97–109 (1985)
12. Korf, R.E., Taylor, L.A.: Finding optimal solutions to the twenty-four puzzle. In: Proceedings of the Thirteenth National Conference on Artificial Intelligence, AAAI 1996, vol. 2. pp. 1202–1207. AAAI Press, Portland (1996)
13. Liu, F., et al.: Evolution of heuristics: towards efficient automatic algorithm design using large language model. In: Proceedings of the 41st International Conference on Machine Learning, ICML 2024, Vienna, Austria, vol. 235, pp. 32201–32223 (2024)
14. Pearl, J.: Heuristics: Intelligent Search Strategies for Computer Problem Solving. Addison-Wesley Pub. Co., Inc., Reading (1984). https://www.osti.gov/biblio/5127296
15. Pearl, J., Kim, J.H.: Studies in Semi-Admissible Heuristics. IEEE Trans. Pattern Anal. Mach. Intell. **PAMI-4**(4), 392–399 (1982). https://doi.org/10.1109/TPAMI.1982.4767270, https://ieeexplore.ieee.org/document/4767270
16. Pohl, I.: Heuristic search viewed as path finding in a graph. Artif. Intell. **1**(3), 193–204 (1970)
17. Romera-Paredes, B., et al.: Mathematical discoveries from program search with large language models. Nature **625**(7995), 468–475 (2024)

18. Samadi, M., Felner, A., Schaeffer, J.: Learning from multiple heuristics. In: Proceedings of the 23rd National Conference on Artificial Intelligence, AAAI 2008, vol. 1, pp. 357–362. AAAI Press, Chicago (2008)
19. Sturtevant, N.R., Shperberg, S., Felner, A., Chen, J.: Predicting the Effectiveness of Bidirectional Heuristic Search. In: Proceedings of the International Conference on Automated Planning and Scheduling, vol. 30, pp. 281–290 (2020)
20. Thayer, J.T., Ruml, W.: Bounded suboptimal search: a direct approach using inadmissible estimates. In: Proceedings of the Twenty-Second International Joint Conference on Artificial Intelligence - Volume One, IJCAI 2011, pp. 674–679. AAAI Press, Barcelona (2011)
21. Thayer, J.T., Ruml, W.: Faster than weighted a*: an optimistic approach to bounded suboptimal search. In: ICAPS, pp, 355–362 (2008)
22. Ye, H., et al.: ReEvo: large language models as hyper-heuristics with reflective evolution. Adv. Neural. Inf. Process. Syst. **37**, 43571–43608 (2024)

# LLM Inference on NVIDIA GB200 NVL72: A Cross-Architecture Experimental Analysis

Luca Lussu[1], Erion Islamay[1], and Fabrizio Montecchiani[2(✉)]

[1] E4 Computer Engineering, Scandiano, Italy
{luca.lussu,erion.islamay}@e4company.com
[2] Department of Engineering, University of Perugia, Perugia, Italy
fabrizio.montecchiani@unipg.it

**Abstract.** Large Language Model inference is increasingly constrained by memory movement rather than raw computational throughput, making the evaluation of next-generation hardware platforms a critical problem for both researchers and practitioners. At the same time, recent frontier models have introduced different paradigms, including sparse Mixture-of-Experts, State Space Models, recurrent linear-attention mechanisms, and hybrid architectures, whose interaction with emerging hardware platforms remains poorly understood.

In this paper, we present an end-to-end experimental analysis of NVIDIA's GB200 NVL72 platform for frontier LLM inference. We evaluate seven state-of-the-art models spanning diverse architectural families. Experiments are conducted on a production Kubernetes cluster using one node of the platform equipped with four Blackwell SM100 GPUs. Three representative serving workloads are considered, targeting long-context agentic interactions, maximum throughput, and sustained decode stress. Our results show that, despite substantial architectural differences, all evaluated models ultimately converge toward a memory-bound decoding regime, suggesting that reducing memory movement is more critical for inference efficiency than increasing computational throughput.

**Keywords:** LLM Serving · GB200 NVL72 · Cross-architecture analysis

## 1 Introduction

The rapid evolution of Large Language Models (LLMs) has fundamentally transformed the landscape of AI systems. While early generations of LLMs were largely based on dense Transformer architectures, recent developments have introduced a broad range of alternative architectural paradigms, including sparse Mixture-of-Experts (MoE) models [25], State Space Models (SSMs) [7], recurrent linear-attention mechanisms [17,31], and hybrid architectures [21] that combine multiple computational primitives within the same network. This architectural diversification has important implications for inference systems. Different architectures exhibit distinct computational characteristics, memory-access


S. Bistarelli et al. (Eds.): AIxIA 2026, LNAI 17131, pp. 378–392, 2027.
https://doi.org/10.1007/978-3-032-40774-0_28

patterns, KV-cache requirements, and communication behaviors. Understanding how such architectures interact with contemporary hardware platforms has therefore become a key challenge for the design of efficient serving infrastructures.

At the same time, NVIDIA Blackwell introduces a new generation of AI accelerators designed for large-scale inference workloads [23]. Specifically, the GB200 NVL72 platform (GB200 for short) combines Blackwell SM100 GPUs, HBM3e memory, NVLink 5, and Grace CPUs connected through NVLink-C2C. While NVIDIA reports substantial theoretical improvements in throughput and memory bandwidth compared with previous Hopper-based systems, empirical evidence regarding the behavior of real-world LLM workloads on GB200 remains limited and existing studies provide only a partial picture. Several works investigate the energy efficiency of LLM inference on H100-class hardware [6,16,20,26], while others focus on analytical projections for future Blackwell systems [4] or kernel-level microbenchmarks [11].

This gap is particularly relevant because recent architectural innovations are explicitly designed to address some of the bottlenecks that dominate LLM inference. These include Multi-head Latent Attention [8], linear-time and state-space designs such as Lightning Attention [17] and Mamba-2 [7], Gated DeltaNet [31], and sparse MoE [25]. Whether these diverse architectural innovations translate into measurable serving advantages on Blackwell-based platforms remains largely unexplored. The study is therefore guided by the following research questions:

**RQ1:** How does throughput scale across different LLM architectures on GB200?
**RQ2:** Is inference on GB200 primarily compute-bound or memory-bound?

To address these questions, we conduct a comprehensive empirical study of LLM inference on GB200. Our benchmark suite includes seven frontier models spanning diverse architectural families and evaluates them under three representative serving scenarios: long-context agentic, maximum throughput, and sustained decode-intensive workloads. We complement traditional latency and throughput metrics with scheduler-level telemetry and hardware-level measurements. To the best of our knowledge, this is the first empirical study comparing multiple frontier LLM architectures on a production NVIDIA GB200 NVL72 platform.

The remainder of the paper is organized as follows. Section 2 recalls the notions used throughout the paper and summarizes related work on LLM inference benchmarking and architectural diversity. Section 3 describes the hardware platform, software stack, and evaluated models. Section 4 details the benchmark scenarios, collected metrics, and experimental procedure. Section 5 addresses RQ1 by analyzing throughput scalability across architectures. Section 6 addresses RQ2 by analyzing the memory-system behavior of GB200 inference. Section 7 discusses the main limitations of the study and concludes the paper.

## 2 Background and Related Work

*Background.* LLM inference proceeds in two phases with different computational characteristics [1]. In the prefill phase, the model processes the entire input prompt in a single forward pass, a compute-intensive operation dominated by large matrix multiplications. In the decode phase, one token is generated per request at each decoding step. Since each step requires re-reading the model weights from GPU memory, decoding is typically limited by memory bandwidth rather than by computational throughput. [29]. The attention keys and values of the tokens already processed are stored in the KV cache to avoid their recomputation. Since the KV cache shares GPU memory with the model weights and grows with context length and with the number of concurrent requests, it also limits how many requests can be served concurrently [14]. Quantization stores weights, and optionally the KV cache, in low-precision formats such as MXFP4 [24,30], NVFP4 [2], FP8 and AWQ 4-bit [15], reducing the data transferred per decoding step. Its benefit depends on serving-runtime kernels that operate directly on the quantized format [9,32]. In the next paragraphs, we briefly summarize two research directions that are fundamental for our work: inference benchmarking and architectural innovations for LLMs.

*LLM Inference Benchmarking and Energy Efficiency.* The rapid deployment of LLMs has motivated extensive research on the performance and energy characteristics of inference systems. Chen et al. [4] introduced the *1/W Law*, an analytical model relating token-generation efficiency to context-window size and providing projections for future accelerator platforms. Large-scale benchmarking initiatives such as ML.ENERGY [5] and subsequent studies have expanded the evaluation of inference efficiency across multiple hardware platforms and serving workloads. Other works have investigated token-level energy consumption, latency-throughput trade-offs, and the relative contribution of prefill and decode phases during inference [6,12,16,20,26]. The introduction of the Blackwell architecture has stimulated early performance analyses of its computational capabilities. Existing studies primarily consist of kernel-level microbenchmarks measuring Tensor Core throughput, memory bandwidth, and low-level execution characteristics [11]. More recently, preliminary evaluations have appeared for consumer-grade Blackwell GPUs, comparing FP4 and BF16 inference on desktop hardware [13]. While valuable, these studies do not provide an end-to-end characterization of frontier LLM serving workloads on GB200 platforms.

*Architectural Diversity in Modern LLMs.* Recent frontier models have significantly expanded the design space of architectures. Sparse Mixture-of-Experts approaches [3] activate only a subset of parameters for each generated token, reducing computational cost while preserving model capacity. Multi-head Latent Attention architectures [8] compress KV-cache representations through latent-space projections, substantially reducing memory requirements. Hybrid State Space Models such as Mamba-2 [7,10] replace part of the attention mechanism with recurrent state updates, while Gated DeltaNet [31] and Lightning

Attention [17] introduce alternative forms of linear-time sequence processing. Although these approaches are increasingly adopted in state-of-the-art models, comparative studies evaluating their serving behavior under identical hardware and software conditions remain limited.

**Table 1.** Hardware configuration of the evaluated GB200 node.

| Component | Specification | Component | Specification |
|---|---|---|---|
| GPU Architecture | Blackwell SM100 | Power Cap | ~1200 W/GPU |
| GPUs per Node | 4 | GPU–GPU Link | NVLink 5 (1800 GB/s) |
| GPU Memory | 192 GB HBM3e | CPU | NVIDIA Grace ARM64 |
| GPU Memory BW | ~8 TB/s/GPU | CPU–GPU Link | NVLink-C2C (900 GB/s) |

## 3 Experimental Setup

This section describes the hardware platform, software stack, and evaluated models used throughout the experimental analysis.

*Hardware Platform.* Experiments were conducted on one node of a production NVIDIA GB200 NVL72 cluster. The node is equipped with four Blackwell SM100 GPUs and two NVIDIA Grace ARM64 CPUs, with each Grace CPU paired with two GPUs through NVLink-C2C; the four GPUs are interconnected through fifth-generation NVLink. The platform provides high-bandwidth HBM3e memory and a fully integrated CPU–GPU architecture designed for large-scale AI workloads. Table 1 summarizes the main hardware characteristics. For single-GPU experiments, each model was deployed on an individual GPU. Multi-GPU experiments used all four GPUs of the node through tensor parallelism.

*Software Stack.* The cluster runs Kubernetes 1.34.4 and uses vLLM 0.18.0 as the serving engine. End-to-end serving metrics, for instance output throughput and time-to-first-token (TTFT), are collected using the `vllm bench serve` benchmarking framework. Hardware telemetry is collected through NVIDIA Data Center GPU Manager (DCGM), while vLLM scheduler and KV-cache metrics are obtained from the Prometheus endpoint exposed by vLLM and used for diagnostic analysis. vLLM automatically selects optimized execution kernels depending on model architecture and quantization format. The deployment therefore includes multiple backend implementations supporting sparse MoE routing, linear-attention mechanisms, State Space Models, and standard Transformer layers.

*Evaluated Models.* The benchmark includes seven frontier models spanning five architectural families. All seven models use sparse MoE feed-forward layers and differ primarily in their sequence-mixing mechanism. GPT-OSS 120B [25] follows a conventional Transformer-based sparse MoE design. Nemotron-3-Super [22] is a hybrid Mamba-2 model [21] that combines state-space layers with a small fraction of attention layers. Qwen3-Coder-Next [27] and Qwen3.5 [28] belong to the Gated DeltaNet family, which interleaves recurrent linear-attention layers with periodic full-attention layers and routes their feed-forward computation through sparse MoE experts; Qwen3.5 is evaluated in two sizes, 122B and 397B. Kimi K2.5 [19] employs MLA [8] to reduce KV-cache requirements. MiniMax M2.5 [18] is based on Lightning Attention [17], a recurrent constant-memory alternative to standard attention. The first four models (GPT-OSS 120B, Nemotron-3-Super, Qwen3-Coder-Next, and Qwen3.5-122B) fit in a single GPU (TP=1), while the remaining three (Kimi K2.5, MiniMax M2.5, and Qwen3.5-397B) require all four GPUs of a node (TP=4). Table 2 summarizes the evaluated models.

**Table 2.** Evaluated models and key architectural mechanisms.

| Model | Key Mechanism | Quantization | Active Params. | TP |
|---|---|---|---|---|
| GPT-OSS 120B | MoE | MXFP4 | 5B | 1 |
| Nemotron-3-Super 120B | Mamba-2 hybrid | NVFP4+FP8 | 12B | 1 |
| Qwen3-Coder-Next | Gated DeltaNet | AWQ 4-bit | 3B | 1 |
| Qwen3.5 122B | Gated DeltaNet | NVFP4 | 10B | 1 |
| Kimi K2.5 | Multi-head Latent Att. | NVFP4+FP8 | ~32B | 4 |
| MiniMax M2.5 | Lightning Attention | NVFP4+FP8 | 10B | 4 |
| Qwen3.5 397B | Gated DeltaNet | NVFP4+FP8 | 17B | 4 |

## 4 Benchmark Methodology

This section describes the scenarios in terms of workload used for the experiments, the collected metrics, and the experimental procedure.

*Scenarios and Datasets.* To evaluate different aspects of serving behavior, we consider three representative workloads, summarized in Table 3. All experiments were executed using the `vllm bench serve` benchmarking framework. **S1 (Agentic Workload)** simulates realistic agent-based interactions with long contexts and partial prefix reuse: it replays a fixed, pre-generated dataset (loaded in `custom` mode) in which each ~60k-token request shares an identical hand-authored ~12k-token system-prompt prefix, followed by a variable suffix of real user turns from ShareGPT. By construction, this shared prefix accounts for ~20% of each request's input tokens, yielding a ~20% KV-cache hit rate that reflects the cross-request prefix reuse characteristic of agentic LLM serving [33], and stresses both the prefill and decode phases while exercising KV-cache management. **S2 (Maximum Throughput)** uses balanced, fixed input and output lengths (1k/1k) and progressively increases concurrency to identify the maximum achievable throughput of each deployment. **S3 (Decode Stress)** minimizes prefill cost and emphasizes long decoding (0.5k/8k input/output), making it particularly suitable for studying memory-bandwidth utilization and latency under sustained generation. Unlike S1, scenarios S2 and S3 use synthetic prompts generated in `random` mode (`--dataset-name random`). Across all scenarios, decoding is greedy (`temperature=0`) and uses `--ignore-eos` to enforce the target output length, ensuring comparable token counts across models; reproducibility is ensured by the static dataset in S1 and a fixed seed (42) in S2 and S3.

**Table 3.** Benchmark workloads.

| Scenario | Input | Output | Concurrency range |
|---|---|---|---|
| S1 Agentic Workload | 60k | 1k | 1–96 (TP = 1)/1-192 (TP = 4) |
| S2 Maximum Throughput | 1k | 1k | 1–1000 (both TP = 1 and TP = 4) |
| S3 Decode Stress | 500 | 8k | 1–192 (TP = 1)/1-256 (TP = 4) |

*Collected Metrics.* The evaluation combines application-level, scheduler-level, and hardware-level metrics. At the application level, we monitor the following metrics: Output throughput - TPT (tokens/s); Time-To-First-Token - TTFT (ms); Time-Per-Output-Token - TPOT (ms); Inter-Token-Latency - ITL (ms); End-to-End request latency - E2E (ms). At the scheduler level, we collect the number of running requests, the number of queued requests, the KV-cache utilization, and preemption events. At the hardware level, we monitor the DRAM activity (%), the Tensor Core activity (%), and the GPU clock frequency (MHz). While only a subset of these metrics are reported in the paper in the interest of space, we used all metrics to analyze and interpret the results of the experiments.

*Experimental Procedure.* For single-GPU configurations (TP = 1), each model was deployed on a dedicated GPU. Multi-GPU experiments used tensor parallelism across four GPUs interconnected through NVLink (TP = 4). For every concurrency level, benchmark outputs were combined with Prometheus telemetry and DCGM measurements. Hardware metrics were sampled throughout the execution and aggregated over the entire benchmark duration.

## 5 Throughput Scalability

This section addresses RQ1 by analyzing how inference throughput and latency scale across model architectures in different workload scenarios.

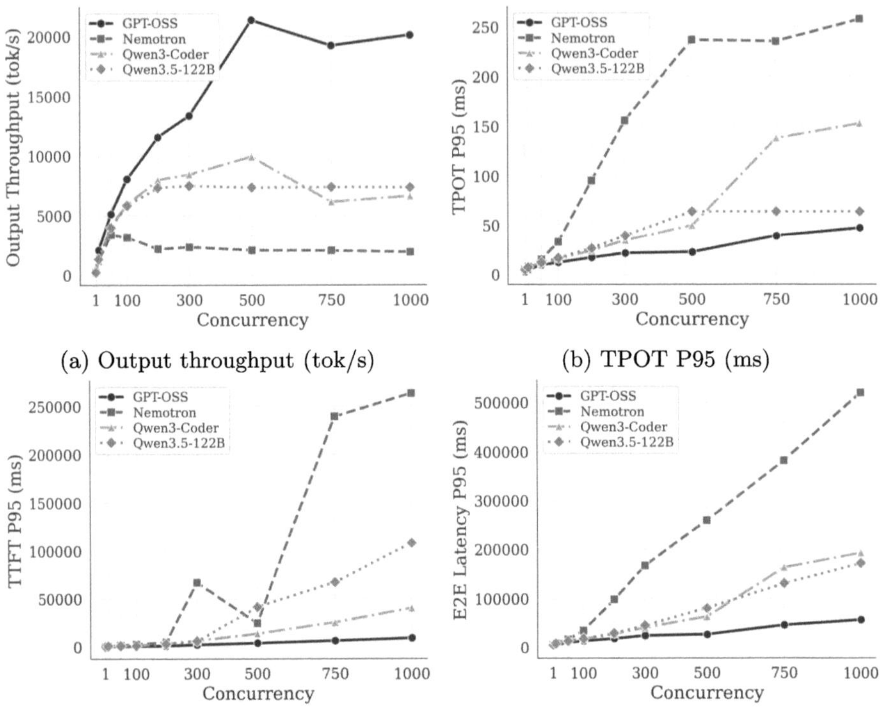


(a) Output throughput (tok/s) (b) TPOT P95 (ms)

(c) TTFT P95 (ms) (d) E2E P95 (ms)

**Fig. 1.** Single-GPU (TP=1) results for S2 (Maximum Throughput).

*Single-GPU Throughput.* Table 4 reports the metrics achieved for each scenario at a fixed per-scenario concurrency level (S1: 96, S2: 500, S3: 192). Figure 1 instead charts the metrics across all concurrency values over S2, the most interesting scenario concerning RQ1.

GPT-OSS 120B achieves the highest single-GPU throughput, reaching 21,369 tok/s in the maximum-throughput workload (S2) and 9,008 tok/s in the decode stress workload (S3). This behavior is explained by the combination of three factors: sparse MoE execution, a low number of active parameters per token, and an execution path that is well optimized for Blackwell through native MXFP4 kernels and the vLLM Model Runner V2 pipeline. The Qwen models exhibit competitive but lower throughput. Qwen3-Coder-Next benefits from a very small number of active parameters, but its AWQ-based execution path does not fully exploit Blackwell FP4 Tensor Core support. Qwen3.5-122B uses community NVFP4 quantization and achieves more stable behavior at high concurrency, but its larger number of active parameters increases memory traffic during decoding. Nemotron-3-Super reaches substantially lower throughput than the other single-GPU models in scenario S2. This behavior is not fully explained by model size or active parameter count alone and is associated with an architecture-specific

**Table 4.** Summary for R1. Best and worst values are highlighted independently for each scenario. TPT stands for throughput; latencies are P95.

| Model | TPT (tok/s) | TPOT (ms) | TTFT (ms) | ITL (ms) | E2E (s) | TP |
|---|---|---|---|---|---|---|
| **Scenario S1 (96 concurrent requests)** | | | | | | |
| GPT-OSS 120B | 676 | 74.5 | 118.3 | 213.1 | 147.6 | 1 |
| Nem.-3-Super 120B | 679 | 124.7 | 114.5 | 212.6 | 144.2 | 1 |
| Qwen3-Coder-Next | 554 | 154.9 | 139.3 | 278.9 | 177.9 | 1 |
| Qwen3.5 122B | 427 | 151.3 | 201.3 | 260.2 | 233.9 | 1 |
| Kimi K2.5 | 325 | 43.8 | 269.1 | 283.1 | 306.5 | 4 |
| MiniMax M2.5 | 996 | 109.1 | 51.3 | 202.9 | 139.0 | 4 |
| Qwen3.5 397B | 832 | 152.1 | 69.2 | 228.9 | 179.3 | 4 |
| **Scenario S2 (500 concurrent requests)** | | | | | | |
| GPT-OSS 120B | 21,369 | 22.8 | 3.8 | 46.0 | 26.4 | 1 |
| Nem.-3-Super 120B | 2,087 | 237.0 | 24.4 | 272.8 | 258.6 | 1 |
| Qwen3-Coder-Next | 9,925 | 49.6 | 13.6 | 283.4 | 62.6 | 1 |
| Qwen3.5 122B | 7,340 | 63.7 | 41.3 | 322.7 | 80.1 | 1 |
| Kimi K2.5 | 6,452 | 97.4 | 34.7 | 197.2 | 106.0 | 4 |
| MiniMax M2.5 | 16,742 | 28.9 | 4.8 | 62.4 | 33.4 | 4 |
| Qwen3.5 397B | 11,086 | 44.6 | 11.0 | 213.1 | 55.2 | 4 |
| **Scenario S3 (192 concurrent requests)** | | | | | | |
| GPT-OSS 120B | 9,008 | 18.4 | 0.8 | 22.8 | 147.6 | 1 |
| Nem.-3-Super 120B | 3,673 | 48.1 | 3.3 | 58.7 | 386.0 | 1 |
| Qwen3-Coder-Next | 7,425 | 20.9 | 2.9 | 24.4 | 168.5 | 1 |
| Qwen3.5 122B | 6,989 | 22.7 | 2.8 | 26.2 | 182.2 | 1 |
| Kimi K2.5 | 3,974 | 52.3 | 94.6 | 34.5 | 419.7 | 4 |
| MiniMax M2.5 | 9,865 | 18.3 | 0.9 | 22.2 | 146.8 | 4 |
| Qwen3.5 397B | 8,445 | 21.6 | 2.7 | 24.4 | 175.7 | 4 |

latency anomaly observed under medium-to-high concurrency in the maximum-throughput and in the decode stress workloads. Inspection of scheduler telemetry and hardware counters did not reveal corresponding increases in DRAM utilization, suggesting the anomaly originates from the serving implementation rather than memory saturation.

Overall, the single-GPU results show that total parameter count is a poor predictor of inference throughput. Instead, throughput is primarily determined by the number of active parameters, the memory traffic generated during decoding, the quantization format, and the maturity of the serving runtime path.

*Multi-GPU Throughput.* Table 4 reports the metrics achieved for each scenario at the same fixed per-scenario concurrency levels (S1: 96, S2: 500, S3: 192). Figure 2 charts the metrics obtained across all concurrency values over scenario S2.

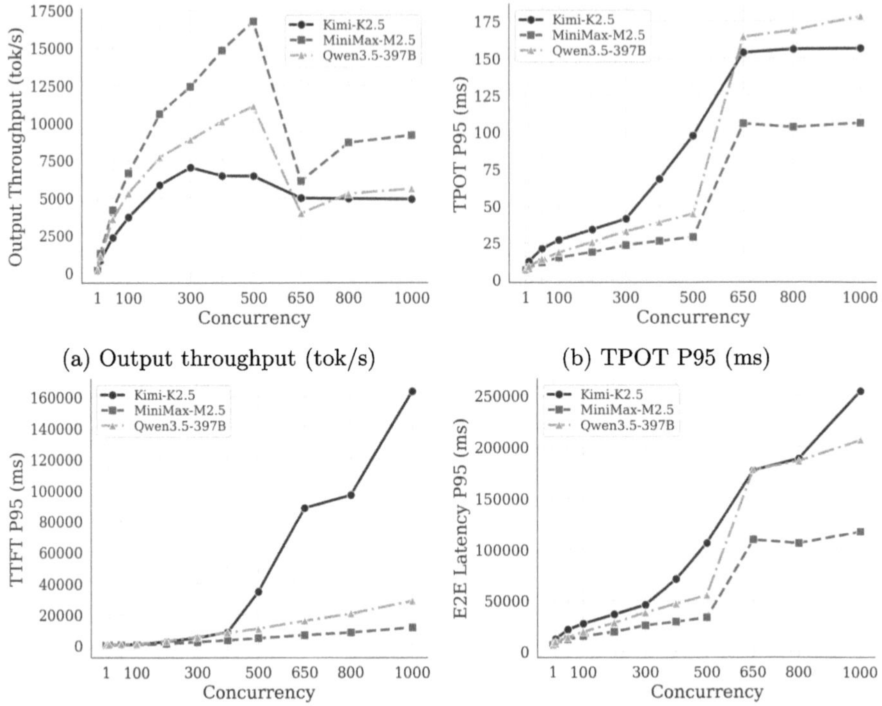


(a) Output throughput (tok/s)
(b) TPOT P95 (ms)
(c) TTFT P95 (ms)
(d) E2E P95 (ms)

**Fig. 2.** Multi-GPU (TP = 4) results for S2 (Maximum Throughput).

Among the multi GPU models, MiniMax M2.5 achieves the highest throughput, reaching 16,742 tok/s in the maximum throughput workload (S2) and 9,865 tok/s in the decode stress workload (S3). MiniMax M2.5 is also the most compact model in the TP = 4 group with 230B total and 10B active parameters, yielding a 31GiB per GPU weight footprint, against 55GiB for Qwen3.5-397B and 139GiB for Kimi K2.5 which already favours throughput. Beyond its smaller size, its Lightning Attention architecture replaces most attention layers with recurrent, constant-memory updates, making each decoding step lighter and allowing the model to sustain higher concurrency than the other TP=4 deployments. Kimi K2.5, despite using MLA to reduce KV-cache footprint, is limited by its much larger active parameter count. Qwen3.5-397B benefits from the same Gated DeltaNet family as the smaller Qwen models but shows lower throughput than MiniMax under sustained decode stress (S3), suggesting that recurrent linear-attention mechanisms do not provide uniform benefits across implementations and model scales.

These results indicate that tensor parallelism alone does not determine performance. The effectiveness of multi-GPU inference depends on the interaction between architectural design, active parameter count, memory footprint, quantization format, and runtime kernel support.

## 6 Memory-System Behavior

This section addresses RQ2 by analyzing whether LLM inference on GB200 is primarily compute-bound or memory-bound.

*Hardware Utilization.* Figures 3 and 4 summarize the observed hardware utilization. Across all tested models and workloads, GB200 inference is consistently memory-bound: every operating point in the figures lies below the balanced diagonal, with DRAM activity exceeding Tensor Core activity. Reporting time-averaged DCGM counters per concurrency level, decode-dominated workloads keep Tensor Core activity below 9% while DRAM activity rises with concurrency up to ~59%; only the prefill-heavy agentic regime (S1) is compute-leaning, reaching ~28%, yet still memory-bound.

The low Tensor Core utilization does not indicate that the platform is underused. Rather, it reflects the intrinsic structure of autoregressive decoding. At each decoding step, the model generates a single token per sequence and must repeatedly access model weights, KV-cache entries, routing metadata, and activation buffers. This results in low arithmetic intensity and makes memory bandwidth the dominant limiting factor. We also remark that the GPU clock stays stable at 2062 MHz over all experiments.

*Evidence of Memory-Bound Decoding.* The decode stress workload (S3) provides the clearest evidence of memory-bound behavior. In this scenario, input prompts are short while outputs are long, reducing the relative contribution of the prefill phase and emphasizing sustained token generation.

Throughput increases with concurrency until the memory system reaches an effective saturation point. Beyond that point, additional concurrency primarily increases latency rather than throughput. This pattern is visible across architectures, despite their different computational primitives.

Sparse MoE models reduce memory traffic by activating only a subset of experts per token. Lightning Attention reduces memory pressure by replacing most attention layers with recurrent state updates. MLA reduces KV-cache footprint through latent projections. Gated DeltaNet and Mamba-2 reduce the frequency or cost of full attention operations. Despite these differences, all models converge toward the same fundamental bottleneck: memory movement during decode.

*Interaction Between Architecture and Memory Traffic.* The results suggest three recurring factors influencing inference efficiency on GB200. First, active parameter count matters more than total parameter count. Sparse models with large total capacity can outperform smaller models when only a small fraction of parameters is accessed per token. Second, KV-cache footprint has a direct impact

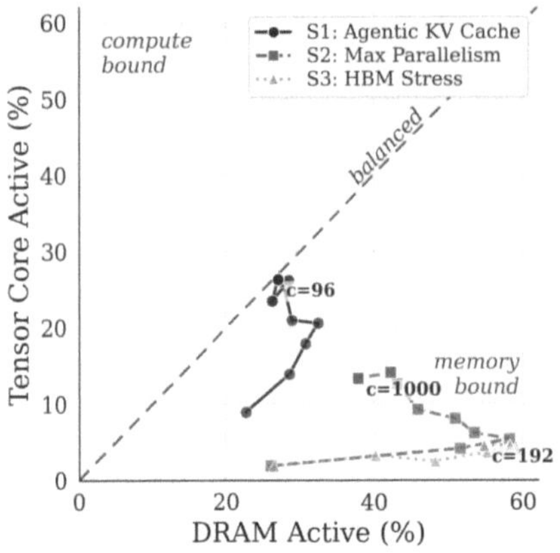


(a) GPT-OSS 120B

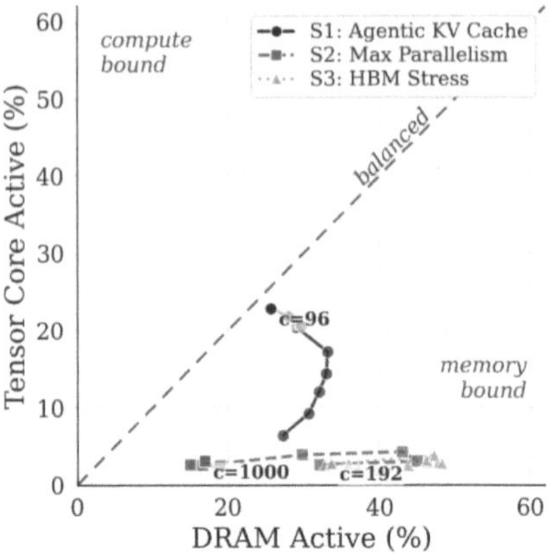


(b) Nemotron-3-Super 120B

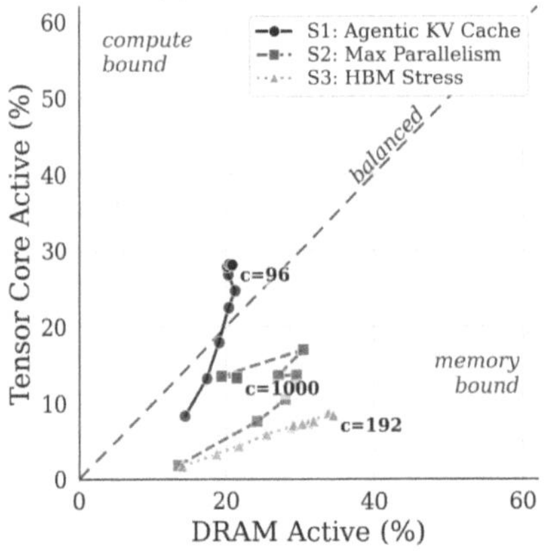


(c) Qwen3-Coder-Next

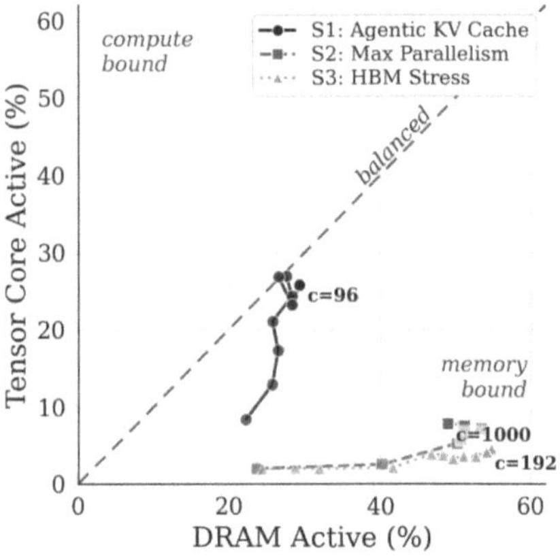


(d) Qwen3.5 122B

**Fig. 3.** Single-GPU (TP = 1) hardware utilization: time averaged DRAM vs. Tensor Core activity per concurrency level.

on scalability. Architectures that reduce or compress the KV cache can sustain higher concurrency before scheduler queues or cache pressure dominate latency. Third, runtime maturity is critical. Hardware support for FP4 arithmetic does not automatically translate into higher end-to-end throughput unless the serving engine can map model operations onto optimized kernels.

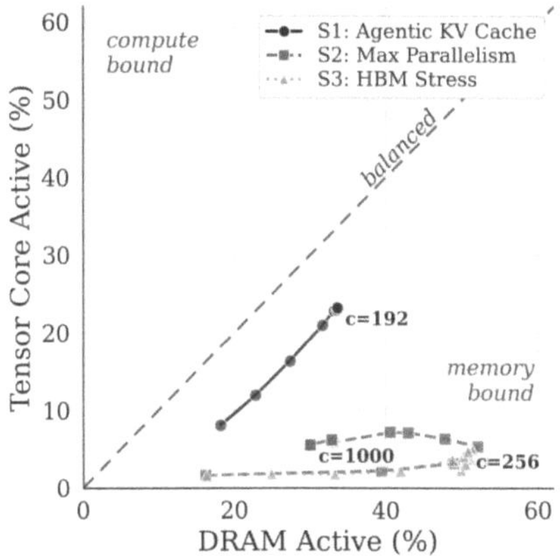


(a) Kimi K2.5

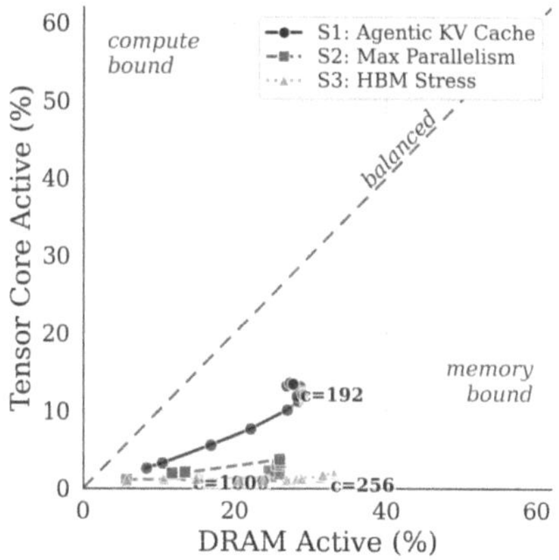


(b) MiniMax M2.5

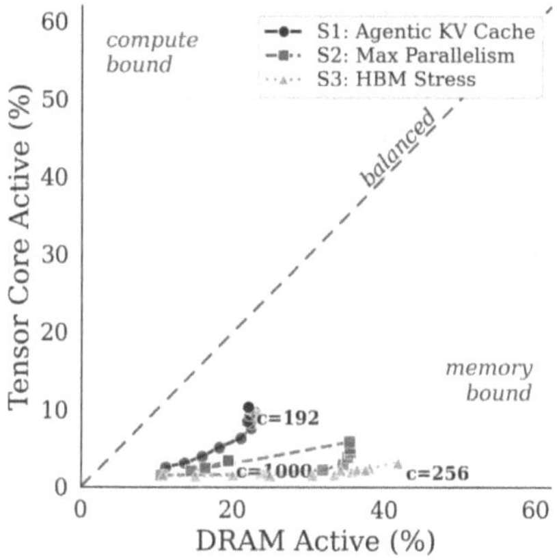


(c) Qwen3.5 397B

**Fig. 4.** Multi-GPU (TP = 4) hardware utilization: time averaged DRAM vs. Tensor Core activity per concurrency level.

# 7 Limitations and Conclusions

*Limitations.* This study has several limitations that should be considered when interpreting the results. First, all experiments were conducted using a single serving framework, namely vLLM. Although vLLM is widely adopted and provides highly optimized implementations for modern LLM inference, different serving systems may lead to different observed performance characteristics. Second, the benchmark suite includes only a limited set of frontier models. While the selected models cover a diverse range of architectural paradigms, the results cannot necessarily be generalized to all existing implementations of these architectural families. Furthermore, the evaluated models are released with different quantization formats and runtime implementations, including MXFP4, NVFP4, FP8, and AWQ variants. Consequently, the observed performance differences reflect the combined effect of architectural design, quantization strategy, and serving-runtime maturity. While this setup accurately represents real-world deployment conditions, it does not allow these factors to be fully disentangled. Third, the evaluation is performed on a GB200-based platform and therefore reflects the interaction between the considered models and the hardware-specific optimizations available on the Blackwell architecture.

*Conclusions.* The persistence of memory-bound decoding on GB200 has broader implications for accelerator and serving-system design. Blackwell substantially increases theoretical compute capability [11], but LLM decoding does not fully exploit this compute peak because the bottleneck lies primarily in memory movement. In this sense, GB200 shifts but does not eliminate the central bottleneck of LLM inference. From these results, three lessons follow for practitioners deploying LLMs on Blackwell-class hardware: (i) Nominal model size is a poor predictor of throughput – in our experiments, three models of the same nominal size ($\approx 120B$) differ by a factor of ten ($\approx 2k$ against $\approx 21k$ tok/s). Throughput is instead determined by architectural properties, namely the number of active parameters and the memory traffic generated during decoding, together with the maturity of the runtime path. (ii) All models converge toward a memory-bound decoding regime on GB200. This confirms on Blackwell the memory bottleneck of large-batch LLM inference reported in earlier work [29]: the generational increase in compute raises the ceiling without changing which resource is binding. (iii) Hardware capabilities translate into performance gains only when supported by mature runtime implementations and optimized kernels [9,32].

In future work, we aim to extend the analysis to energy efficiency and to a controlled study isolating the effect of individual quantization formats for a fixed model architecture.

## References


1. Agrawal, A., et al.: Taming throughput-latency tradeoff in LLM inference with Sarathi-Serve. In: OSDI 2024, pp. 117–134. USENIX Association (2024)
2. Alvarez, E., et al.: Introducing NVFP4 for efficient and accurate low-precision inference. NVIDIA Developer Technical Blog (2025). https://developer.nvidia.com/blog/introducing-nvfp4-for-efficient-and-accurate-low-precision-inference/
3. Cai, W., Jiang, J., Wang, F., Tang, J., Kim, S., Huang, J.: A survey on mixture of experts in large language models. IEEE Trans. Knowl. Data Eng. **37**(7), 3896–3915 (2025). https://doi.org/10.1109/TKDE.2025.3554028
4. Chen, H., Liu, X., Liu, Y., Jiang, J., He, B., Liu, X.: The 1/w law: an analytical study of context-length routing topology and gpu generation gains for LLM inference energy efficiency. arXiv preprint arXiv:2603.17280 (2026)
5. Chung, J.W., et al.: The ML.ENERGY benchmark: toward automated inference energy measurement and optimization. In: Advances in Neural Information Processing Systems (NeurIPS), Datasets and Benchmarks Track (2025). https://openreview.net/forum?id=CXqq2v6qUv
6. Chung, J.W., Wu, R., Ma, J.J., Chowdhury, M.: Where do the joules go? Diagnosing inference energy consumption. arXiv preprint arXiv:2601.22076 (2026)

7. Dao, T., et al.: Transformers are SSMs: generalized models and efficient algorithms through structured state space duality. In: Berkenkamp, F. (ed.) Forty-First International Conference on Machine Learning, ICML 2024. Proceedings of Machine Learning Research, vol. 235, pp. 10041–10071. PMLR/OpenReview.net (2024)
8. DeepSeek-AI: DeepSeek-V3 technical report. arXiv preprint arXiv:2412.19437 (2024)
9. Frantar, E., Castro, R.L., Chen, J., Hoefler, T., Alistarh, D.: MARLIN: mixed-precision auto-regressive parallel inference on large language models. In: Proceedings of the 30th ACM SIGPLAN Annual Symposium on Principles and Practice of Parallel Programming (PPoPP), pp. 239–251. ACM (2025). https://doi.org/10.1145/3710848.3710871
10. Gu, A., Dao, T.: Mamba: linear-time sequence modeling with selective state spaces. In: Conference on Language Modeling (COLM) (2024). https://openreview.net/forum?id=tEYskw1VY2
11. Jarmusch, A., Chandrasekaran, S.: Microbenchmarking NVIDIA's Blackwell architecture: an in-depth architectural analysis. arXiv preprint arXiv:2512.02189 (2025)
12. Kakolyris, A.K., Masouros, D., Vavaroutsos, P., Xydis, S., Soudris, D.: throttLL'eM: predictive GPU throttling for energy efficient LLM inference serving. In: 2025 IEEE International Symposium on High Performance Computer Architecture (HPCA), pp. 1363–1378. IEEE (2025). https://doi.org/10.1109/HPCA61900.2025.00103
13. Knoop, J., Holtmann, H.: Private LLM inference on consumer Blackwell GPUs: a practical guide for cost-effective local deployment in SMEs. arXiv preprint arXiv:2601.09527 (2026)
14. Kwon, W., et al.: Efficient memory management for large language model serving with PagedAttention. In: Proceedings of the 29th Symposium on Operating Systems Principles (SOSP), pp. 611–626. ACM (2023). https://doi.org/10.1145/3600006.3613165
15. Lin, J., et al.: AWQ: Activation-aware weight quantization for on-device LLM compression and acceleration. In: MLSys 2024, vol. 6, pp. 87–100 (2024)
16. Maliakel, P.J., Ilager, S., Brandic, I.: Characterizing LLM inference energy-performance tradeoffs across workloads and GPU scaling. arXiv preprint arXiv:2501.08219 (2025)
17. MiniMax: MiniMax-01: Scaling foundation models with lightning attention. arXiv preprint arXiv:2501.08313 (2025)
18. MiniMax AI: MiniMax-M2.5 (model card) (2026). https://huggingface.co/MiniMaxAI/MiniMax-M2.5
19. Moonshot AI: Kimi-K2.5 (model card) (2026). https://huggingface.co/moonshotai/Kimi-K2.5
20. Niu, C., et al.: TokenPowerBench: benchmarking the power consumption of LLM inference. In: Proceedings of the AAAI Conference on Artificial Intelligence (AAAI), vol. 40, pp. 32582–32590 (2026). https://doi.org/10.1609/AAAI.V40I38.40535
21. NVIDIA: Nemotron-H: a family of accurate and efficient hybrid Mamba-transformer models. arXiv preprint arXiv:2504.03624 (2025)
22. NVIDIA: NVIDIA nemotron 3: efficient and open intelligence. arXiv preprint arXiv:2512.20856 (2025)
23. NVIDIA Corporation: NVIDIA blackwell architecture technical brief (2024). https://resources.nvidia.com/en-us-blackwell-architecture. Accessed 06 June 2026

24. Open Compute Project: OCP microscaling formats (MX) specification, version 1.0 (2023). https://www.opencompute.org/documents/ocp-microscaling-formats-mx-v1-0-spec-final-pdf
25. OpenAI: gpt-oss-120b & gpt-oss-20b model card (2025). https://arxiv.org/abs/2508.10925
26. Pronk, K., Zhao, Q.: Benchmarking energy efficiency of large language models using vLLM. arXiv preprint arXiv:2509.08867 (2025)
27. Qwen Team: Qwen3-Coder-Next technical report. arXiv preprint arXiv:2603.00729 (2026)
28. Qwen Team: Qwen3.5: Towards native multimodal agents (2026). https://qwen.ai/blog?id=qwen3.5, model card: Qwen3.5-122B-A10B, Qwen3.5-397B-A17B
29. Recasens, P.G., et al.: Mind the memory gap: unveiling GPU bottlenecks in large-batch LLM inference. In: 2025 IEEE 18th International Conference on Cloud Computing (CLOUD), pp. 277–287 (2025). https://doi.org/10.1109/CLOUD67622.2025.00036
30. Rouhani, B.D., Zhao, R., More, A., Hall, M., Khodamoradi, A.: Microscaling data formats for deep learning. arXiv preprint arXiv:2310.10537 (2023)
31. Yang, S., Kautz, J., Hatamizadeh, A.: Gated delta networks: improving mamba2 with delta rule. In: The Thirteenth International Conference on Learning Representations (ICLR) (2025). https://openreview.net/forum?id=r8H7xhYPwz
32. Ye, Z., et al.: FlashInfer: efficient and customizable attention engine for LLM inference serving. In: Proceedings of Machine Learning and Systems (MLSys) (2025)
33. Zheng, L., et al.: SGLang: efficient execution of structured language model programs. In: Advances in Neural Information Processing Systems (NeurIPS 2024), vol. 37 (2024)

# AGoT: A Reasoning Framework for LLM Agents

Mattia Matteini(✉), Marco Raggini, Giovanni Ciatto, and Andrea Omicini

Department of Computer Science and Engineering (DISI), Alma Mater Studiorum—Università di Bologna, Via dell'Università 50, 47522 Cesena, FC, Italy
{mattia.matteini,giovanni.ciatto,andrea.omicini}@unibo.it, marco.raggini2@studio.unibo.it

**Abstract.** Modern Large Language Models (LLMs) exhibit structural limitations that reduce their reliability – such as opaque reasoning processes and limited exploration of alternative solution paths – which prompt engineering techniques such as Chain of Thoughts (CoT) can address only partially. This paper introduces an *Agentic* Graph of Thoughts (AGoT), which extends the Graph of Thoughts (GoT) prompting technique to an agentic framework. In AGoT, LLM-powered agents leverage a *dynamically-constructed* graph to record their reasoning, possibly including generation, tool invocation, self-evaluation, and tool-crafting steps. Agents can explore multiple reasoning paths, possibly backtracking and extending the graph as needed, while making their reasoning process more explicit and inspectable. AGoT supports dynamic tool use and crafting: new tools can be autonomously generated at runtime when no available tool can solve the problem. We evaluate our approach on the Hendrycks MATH benchmark, comparing the proposed architecture against a Zero-Shot CoT baseline across three different Gemini models. Results suggest that AGoT can make reasoning more robust, as the multi-path exploration and tool-crafting mechanisms help agents recover from incorrect reasoning steps and address a wider variety of problems.

**Keywords:** Agentic AI · Large Language Models · Graph of Thoughts · Prompt Engineering

## 1 Introduction

A central challenge for Large Language Models (LLMs) is that their reasoning process is often implicit, fragile, and difficult to control. When a model produces a wrong intermediate step, a purely linear generation process offers limited support for detecting the error, revising earlier decisions, reusing valid partial results, or invoking external computational resources when the model's internal reasoning is insufficient.


S. Bistarelli et al. (Eds.): AIxIA 2026, LNAI 17131, pp. 393–406, 2027.
https://doi.org/10.1007/978-3-032-40774-0_29

This issue is typically addressed by making reasoning more explicit. Chain of Thoughts (CoT) prompting encourages an LLM to produce intermediate reasoning steps before giving an answer [12]. Tree of Thoughts (ToT) approaches extend this idea by exploring multiple reasoning branches and by allowing search over partial solutions [13]. Graph of Thoughts (GoT) further generalises this perspective by representing LLM-generated thoughts as vertices in a graph, with edges capturing dependencies among them [1], enabling richer reasoning patterns than chains or trees, including aggregation, refinement, and feedback loops.

However, existing GoT-style approaches remain primarily framed as prompting or reasoning-structure design techniques. In particular, applying GoT to a new task typically requires the designer to specify, at least implicitly, how thoughts should be generated, transformed, evaluated, and combined. This limits the applicability of graph-based reasoning in autonomous LLM agents, where the reasoning process evolves at runtime in response to intermediate results, tool outputs, failures, and new sub-problems. Conversely, agentic approaches such as ReAct [14] interleave reasoning and action, allowing LLMs to interact with tools or environments, yet they usually represent execution as a linear trajectory rather than as an explicit graph recording alternative branches, failed attempts, reusable intermediate states, and dependencies among reasoning steps.

Inspired by the graph-based abstraction of GoT, we propose *Agentic* Graph of Thoughts (AGoT), a graph-based reasoning framework for tool-augmented LLM agents. Not just a prompting technique, AGoT adapts GoT to an agentic setting: the reasoning process is represented as an evolving execution graph that records the agent's goals, intermediate reasoning steps, tool invocations, evaluations, backtracking decisions, and final answer. Therefore, the graph works not just as a representation of generated thoughts, but also as a runtime memory and control structure for an autonomous reasoning agent.

The key idea is to separate the general reasoning logic from the concrete reasoning trace produced for a particular problem. AGoT uses a reusable control structure to guide the agent through general phases of problem solving, while dynamically constructing an execution graph for each input instance. Thus, the agent can keep track of its attempts, identify the need for external tools, evaluate intermediate results, recover from unsuccessful branches, and extend its operational capabilities via tool use and crafting.

Accordingly, in this paper we *(i)* introduce AGoT, an agentic reasoning framework expanding GoT towards a tool-augmented autonomous agent setting; *(ii)* define a graph-based execution model for agent reasoning; *(iii)* integrate tool use and tool crafting into the reasoning process; and *(iv)* evaluate the proposed framework on mathematical tasks from the MATH benchmark [3], comparing it against a tool-augmented Zero-Shot CoT baseline.

## 2 Background

### 2.1 Prompt Engineering for Reasoning

A major line of work has studied how to improve the reasoning capabilities of LLMs by making intermediate reasoning steps explicit. Chain of Thoughts (CoT) prompting encourages a model to produce a sequence of intermediate steps before returning the final answer [12]. This simple mechanism has been shown to improve performance on mathematical, symbolic, and commonsense reasoning tasks. Variants such as Self consistency CoT (CoT-SC) further improve robustness by sampling multiple reasoning chains and selecting an answer by aggregation or voting [11].

Tree of Thoughts (ToT) methods generalise this idea from a single sequence to a branching search process [13]. Instead of committing to one chain of reasoning, ToT maintains multiple partial solutions, evaluates them, and expands promising branches. This enables exploration, pruning, and backtracking, thereby addressing some limitations of purely linear reasoning.

Graph of Thoughts (GoT) further extends this progression by representing thoughts as vertices in a graph and dependencies among thoughts as edges [1]. This allows richer transformations than chains or trees, including aggregation, refinement, and feedback loops. However, existing GoT-style approaches are primarily framed as prompting or thought-transformation frameworks. In practice, they typically require the human designer to specify how thoughts are generated, transformed, combined, and evaluated for a given task. This makes them powerful but also task-dependent: the structure of the reasoning process is often designed before execution rather than constructed by an autonomous agent while solving a problem.

### 2.2 Agentic Systems

Another line of work studies LLMs as agents that interact with external tools and environments. In this context, the model is not only asked to generate an answer, but also to decide which actions to take and how to incorporate observations into subsequent reasoning. An important approach is ReAct: it interleaves reasoning traces and actions, allowing an LLM to reason about a task while querying external sources or interacting with an environment [14]. Related work has explored LLMs as planners, embodied agents, tool users, and decision-making systems [10,15,16].

These approaches are relevant because they shift the role of the LLM from text generator to interactive problem solver. Tool-augmented agents can overcome knowledge limitations by using calculators, search engines, code interpreters, APIs, databases, or simulators. This is particularly important for tasks that require exact computation, external information, or actions whose results cannot be reliably inferred from the model's internal knowledge alone.

### 2.3 Self-evaluating Reasoning

An interesting line of research concerns self-evaluation, critique, and correction in LLM reasoning. Several methods use LLMs not only to generate candidate solutions, but also to evaluate, refine, or repair them. LLM-as-a-judge methods use a language model as an evaluator of generated outputs [2]. This technique can improve scalability and explainability while reducing the amount of direct human involvement required in the evaluation process, yet remains affected by verbosity and self-enhancement biases. Reflection-based approaches allow agents to analyze their own failures and use this feedback in subsequent attempts [9]. Self-refinement methods iteratively improve an answer by alternating between generation, feedback, and revision [7].

These methods address an important weakness of direct generation: an LLM may produce plausible but incorrect intermediate steps, and errors can propagate if they are not detected. Evaluation and correction mechanisms provide a way to interrupt this process. They can identify low-quality reasoning states, trigger revision, or guide the model toward alternative solution paths.

# 3 The AGoT Framework

This section presents AGoT, an agentic reasoning framework inspired by the GoT graph-based abstraction [1]. Rather than producing yet another prompting framework, we aim at extending graph-structured reasoning towards autonomous, tool-augmented agency. We first identify the actual problem addressed by our framework along with the requirements to satisfy, then we delve into the details of how AGoT works by combining a *static graph* – which defines the admissible control flow of the reasoning process –, and a *dynamic graph*—which records the concrete execution produced for a specific problem instance.

## 3.1 Problem Statement and Requirements

We assume the existence of an agent $\mathcal{A}$, controlling an LLM $\mathcal{M}$ by means of request–response interactions $q_1, r_1, q_2, r_2, \ldots$. To support its reasoning, we assume the agent can invoke external tools from a pool of tools $\mathcal{T}$ as part of its execution—we denote the *initial* set of tools as $\mathcal{T}_0$, assuming that as execution progresses, the agent may craft new tools and extend $\mathcal{T}$. Finally, we assume that the agent is *reactive* w.r.t. human users, – hence remaining idle until a new goal is submitted by the user –, and *proactive* w.r.t. the LLM and the tools—hence being able to invoke the LLM and the tools, and manage their responses, without requiring human intervention. Along this line, the common workflow consists of a user submitting a goal to the agent, and the agent interacting with the LLM and the tools to produce a final answer for the user.

Under these assumptions, given some user-provided input goal $g$, we focus on the problem of letting $\mathcal{A}$ construct a dynamic execution graph $G_e$ that records the *reasoning process* leading to a final answer $a$. The execution graph should make the intermediate reasoning states explicit, including: tool invocations, self-evaluations, failures, backtracking decisions, crafted tools, as well as intermediate and final responses produced during execution.

We identify four requirements that any method addressing this problem should satisfy: (**R1**) the method should construct the execution graph $G_e$ *dynamically*, without requiring the user to specify a problem-specific reasoning graph in advance; (**R2**) the execution graph should be *explicit* – i.e. external w.r.t. the LLM, and inspectable – and include at least one successful reasoning path from $g$ to $a$, and possibly many failed or incomplete paths; (**R3**) while exploring reasoning steps leading from $g$ to $a$, in order to steer the reasoning process and create intermediate/final results, the agent $\mathcal{A}$ should be able to either *(i)* query the LLM $\mathcal{M}$ or *(ii)* invoke external tools from $\mathcal{T}$ and use their outputs; (**R4**) similarly, the agent $\mathcal{A}$ should be able to generate and register new tools at runtime when the available tools in $\mathcal{T}$ are insufficient, without requiring manual intervention. In the remainder of this section, we describe how these requirements are addressed via a static state-machine (the 'static' graph), aimed at building the 'dynamic' graph ($G_e$), and the execution mechanisms that connect them.

### 3.2 Static Graph: The Agent's State Machine

AGoT models agents' behaviour as a state machine, which is represented as a static directed graph. Its purpose is to specify the admissible phases of an agentic reasoning process and the transitions among them. In this sense, the static graph acts as a general-purpose workflow metamodel.

Formally, the static graph is defined as $G_s = (S, T)$, where $S$ is the set of possible workflow states and $T \subseteq S \times S$ is the set of admissible transitions. Each state in $S$ corresponds to a general phase of reasoning (see Fig. 1a), such as problem initialisation, tool-oriented reasoning, tool invocation, response evaluation, backtracking, or tool crafting.

*Initialisation.* Agents start in state `__start__`, where they wait for user-provided inputs. Upon receiving some input $g$, they transition to the `goal` state, which aims at storing $g$ and initialising the first runtime node of the dynamic graph, namely a **Goal Node** (cf. Sect. 3.3). From this state, the agent will automatically transition to the `tool_reasoning` state, hence exploring the next admissible reasoning step.

*Reasoning and Tool Usage.* In the `tool_reasoning` state, the agent analyses the last goal $g$ operationally and reasons about how to address it without solving it directly. This is where multiple **Reasoning Nodes** are generated in the dynamic graph, each representing one potential action to take. Then, the agent transitions into the `tool_call` state, where it selects and executes one action, either by invoking a tool or by producing a solution without tool support. In either case, the dynamic graph is updated with new nodes representing the tool invocation and its output, or the produced solution. In any case, execution then transitions to the `response_evaluation` state, where the candidate response is automatically evaluated (see next paragraph).

Finally, the `reasoning_mode` state addresses the situation where $g$ is too complex and needs decomposition into smaller sub-problems—possibly leading to new **Goal Nodes** in the dynamic graph.

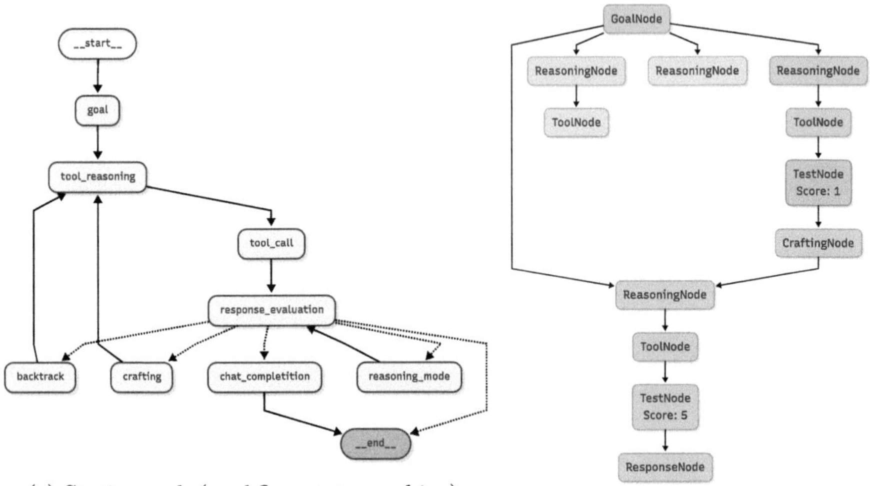


(a) Static graph (workflow state machine).

(b) Execution graph (end of run).

**Fig. 1.** Figure 1a shows the reusable workflow state machine. Continuous lines represent deterministic transitions, while dashed lines represent conditional transitions. Figure 1b shows a dynamic execution graph instantiated for a specific problem. Green nodes represent visited nodes, red nodes indicate failed validation, and gray nodes represent unexplored alternatives. (Color figure online)

*Evaluation.* The `response_evaluation` state evaluates a candidate response via the LLM-as-a-judge mechanism. This implies generating **Test Nodes** in the dynamic graph to assess the quality of the candidate response. The evaluation determines whether the response can be accepted, whether the agent should backtrack, or whether execution should enter the crafting phase because the current toolset is insufficient.

*Recovery and Extension.* The `backtrack` and `crafting` states implement runtime adaptation. The `backtrack` state is reached when the current reasoning path is judged inadequate; it stores feedback and redirects execution toward an alternative path. The `crafting` state is reached when the system identifies a missing operational capability; it triggers a new tool generation and makes it available to the following reasoning steps.

*Fallback and Termination.* The `chat_completion` state provides a fallback response when structured reasoning paths are exhausted. The `__end__` state terminates execution once an answer is accepted or a fallback response is produced.

### 3.3 Dynamic Graph: A Memory of the Reasoning Process

Agent reasoning consists of a dynamic execution graph $G_e$ being constructed at runtime for a specific input problem. Unlike the static graph, which is task-independent, the dynamic graph stores the actual reasoning trajectory produced by the agent. It records which reasoning steps were taken, which tools were invoked, which paths failed, which tools were crafted, and which candidate answer was eventually accepted.

We define the dynamic graph as $G_e = (N, E)$, where $N$ is the set of runtime nodes and $E$ is the set of directed execution edges (see Fig. 1b). Each node $n \in N$ is represented as $n = (id_n, \tau_n, \rho_n, \pi_n)$, where $id_n$ is a unique identifier, $\tau_n \in S$ is the corresponding static-graph state, $\rho_n$ is the node status, and $\pi_n$ is a state-specific payload. The status $\rho_n$ can indicate, for example, whether the node is open, resolved, failed, or accepted. The payload $\pi_n$ stores the information required by the corresponding state, such as a prompt, a reasoning trace, a tool call, an evaluation score, judge feedback, or a crafted tool definition.

Each edge $e \in E$ connects two runtime nodes and is defined as $e = (n, n', h)$, where $n$ is the source node, $n'$ is the target node, and $h$ is the message history propagated along that transition. The message history provides the context used by the LLM in subsequent reasoning steps. When needed, the framework can modify this history to steer the next node, for example by adding judge feedback after a failed evaluation or by informing the agent that a newly crafted tool is now available.

Nodes and arcs in the dynamic graph are created at runtime as governed by the transitions of the state machine defined by the static graph. Each node has a type, corresponding to some particular aspect of the reasoning process. A **Goal Node** stores the problem to solve. A **Reasoning Node** stores the reasoning process generated by the LLM. A **Tool Node** stores the selected tool, the tool prompt, and the corresponding result. A **Test Node** stores the evaluation of a candidate result. A **Backtrack Node** stores feedback generated by the judge so that subsequent paths can avoid the same failure. A **Crafting Node** stores the generated tool definition and the checks performed before registration. Finally, a **Response Node** stores an evaluated candidate answer and its explanation.

For example, if the agent attempts to solve a mathematical problem, invokes an existing calculator tool, receives an inadequate result, and then crafts a specialised helper function, then the dynamic graph records each of these steps as distinct nodes. The failed tool path remains in the graph, while the crafted tool becomes available to later reasoning nodes. This is the mechanism by which AGoT supports graph-tracked reasoning and path exploration, addressing requirement R2.

### 3.4 Execution, Agents, and Evaluation

Execution proceeds by instantiating runtime nodes according to the static graph. At each step, the current node receives the relevant message history, performs its state-specific operation, stores its output in the dynamic graph, and selects the next admissible state. At a high level, the execution loop is as follows: 1. initialise the dynamic graph with a **Goal Node**; 2. select the next admissible state according to the static graph; 3. execute the corresponding agentic operation; 4. store the produced output in a new runtime node; 5. evaluate the output; 6.

accept the response, backtrack, craft a new tool, or continue reasoning; 7. terminate when an answer is accepted or fallback generation is reached. Several states are implemented through specialised agents. Each agent follows a local two-state loop composed of a `model` state and a `tools` state. In the `model` state, the LLM decides whether to generate a direct response or invoke a tool—addressing requirement R3. If a tool is invoked, execution enters the `tools` state; the tool output is then returned to the `model` state so that the agent can continue reasoning or produce a response. This local agent loop is used by dynamic graph nodes that require agentic LLM calls, such as `tool_reasoning` and `tool_call`.

Response evaluation is performed by an LLM-as-a-judge. The judge receives the candidate answer along with the relevant reasoning history, and evaluates *(i)* response format, *(ii)* answer correctness, and *(iii)* quality of the explanation. The judge assigns a solution score $s \in [0, 5]$ and an estimated problem complexity $c \in \{1, \ldots, 5\}$. The candidate response is accepted when $s \geq 5.5 - 0.5 \cdot c$. The threshold is therefore adaptive: more complex problems may accept a slightly lower score, whereas simpler problems require a stricter evaluation. If the candidate answer fails the threshold, the judge feedback is stored in the dynamic graph and used to determine the next step—either backtracking or tool crafting.

### 3.5 Tool Crafting

Tool crafting is the mechanism through which AGoT extends its operational capabilities at runtime. It is triggered when the current reasoning path identifies a missing capability that cannot be satisfied by the available toolset $\mathcal{T}$. This may happen during tool-oriented reasoning, when the agent recognises that no existing tool is adequate, or during response evaluation, when the judge determines that failure is due to a missing computational operation rather than to a merely incorrect reasoning step.

The crafting process happens when `crafting` state in static graph is reached. At the same time, a new **Crafting Node** is created in the dynamic graph, which stores the generated tool definition. This mechanism addresses requirement R4. At the same time, the current implementation treats crafted tools as runtime artifacts whose quality depends on the underlying model. As discussed in the experimental section, malformed or unnecessary tools may still be produced, making tool validation and refinement important directions for future work.

## 4 Experiments

This section provides an initial empirical evaluation of AGoT on mathematical reasoning tasks. The goal is not to claim general superiority over all agentic reasoning systems in mathematics. However, mathematical tasks represent a good testbed for evaluating the effectiveness of multiple-path reasoning, backtracking, tool use, and runtime tool crafting.

We compare AGoT against a *Tool-Augmented Zero-Shot Chain-of-Thought* [5] baseline, abbreviated as Zero-Shot CoT+Tools. The baseline uses the same language model backbone and has access to the same initial toolset as AGoT. This comparison therefore isolates the effect of the proposed orchestration layer and runtime capability extension from the mere availability of external tools. All experiments were conducted using Gemini models, namely `gemini-2.5-flash`, `gemini-2.5-flash-lite`, and `gemini-3.1-flash-lite`, as the core language model backbones. The temperature was fixed to 1.0 for all runs. Each approach was evaluated twice on 50 tasks, and the two runs were averaged. Framework code and experiments are available on GitHub[1].

### 4.1 Benchmark and Metrics

We evaluate the framework on the MATH benchmark [3], a dataset designed to assess mathematical problem solving, which contains 12,500 competition-style problems across seven mathematical disciplines and multiple difficulty levels. In our experiments, we report results for six category groups: Algebra, Counting and Probability, Geometry, Intermediate Algebra, Number Theory, and Precalculus. MATH is appropriate for initial evaluation for three reasons. First, its problems require multi-step reasoning, making it suitable for testing whether an execution framework can manage intermediate reasoning states. Second, many problems benefit from exact symbolic or numerical computation, allowing us to observe when the agent invokes available tools or attempts to craft new ones. Third, the benchmark provides reference answers, enabling objective accuracy evaluation.

We report three classes of metrics. *Accuracy* measures the percentage of tasks where the final answer matches the benchmark solution after answer extraction. We also report the *execution error rate*, defined as the percentage of runs that fail because of system-level execution errors rather than incorrect mathematical reasoning. *Resource consumption* measures the efficiency cost of the framework: we report the average wall-clock time required to produce a final answer and the token consumption of each approach, computed as the sum of input and output tokens. *Tool behaviour* measures how often the system relies on external operational capabilities: we report the number of tool invocations and crafted tools. For Zero-Shot CoT+Tools, tool invocation counts refer to calls to the initial toolset only; crafted tools are marked as not applicable because the baseline approach cannot generate new tools. For AGoT, tool invocation counts include calls made during execution, while crafted-tool counts record tools generated and registered at runtime.

### 4.2 Results

As shown in Table 1, the effect of AGoT is strongly model-dependent. With Gemini 2.5 Flash, accuracy improves from 82.83% to 91.17%. With Gemini 3.1 Flash Lite, accuracy improves from 61.50% to 82.50%. By contrast, with Gemini 2.5 Flash Lite, accuracy decreases from 86.83% to 69.17%. These results suggest

[1] https://github.com/MarkRagg/GoT.

**Table 1.** Aggregate MATH benchmark results by model and approach. Token consumption is computed as input plus output tokens.

| Model | Approach | Accuracy | Avg. Time (s) | Avg. Tokens |
|---|---|---|---|---|
| Gemini-2.5-flash-lite | AGoT | 69.17% | 116.49 | 2,216,983.33 |
| Gemini-2.5-flash-lite | Zero-Shot CoT+Tools | **86.83%** | 11.30 | 194,334.17 |
| Gemini-2.5-flash | AGoT | **91.17%** | 92.67 | 1,319,468.33 |
| Gemini-2.5-flash | Zero-Shot CoT+Tools | 82.83% | 14.62 | 210,479.17 |
| Gemini-3.1-flash-lite | AGoT | **82.50%** | 29.58 | 526,093.33 |
| Gemini-3.1-flash-lite | Zero-Shot CoT+Tools | 61.50% | 6.51 | 239,340.00 |

that the proposed framework is beneficial only when the underlying model is sufficiently capable of following instructions, using feedback, and deciding when tool crafting is appropriate.

Across the aggregate rows in Table 1, AGoT yields a modest average accuracy improvement of 3.9 percentage points. However, this improvement comes with a substantial efficiency cost. The average runtime of AGoT is roughly 4.5 to 10.3 times as long as that of Zero-Shot CoT+Tools, depending on the model. Token consumption shows the same trend, reflecting the additional model calls required by graph construction, evaluation, backtracking, and tool management.

**Table 2.** Execution errors and tool-use/crafting statistics.

| Model | Approach | Errors | Tool Invocations | Crafted Tools |
|---|---|---|---|---|
| Gemini-2.5-flash-lite | AGoT | 2.83% | 4926.5 | 22 |
| Gemini-2.5-flash-lite | Zero-Shot CoT+Tools | **1.83%** | 327.5 | N/A |
| Gemini-2.5-flash | AGoT | **1.33%** | 1428.5 | 413 |
| Gemini-2.5-flash | Zero-Shot CoT+Tools | 5.83% | 329 | N/A |
| Gemini-3.1-flash-lite | AGoT | **0.00%** | 704 | 50 |
| Gemini-3.1-flash-lite | Zero-Shot CoT+Tools | 35.50% | 2052 | N/A |

Table 2 provides a complementary view of execution robustness. The mean execution error rate decreases from 14.4% with Zero-Shot CoT+Tools to 1.4% with AGoT. This reduction is explained by the high error rate observed for Gemini 3.1 Flash Lite in the baseline. The result suggests that AGoT can be more robust to execution failures, even when the accuracy benefit is not uniform across models.

The tool statistics also expose an important limitation. More tool crafting does not necessarily imply better reasoning. For instance, Gemini 2.5 Flash crafts many more tools than the other models, suggesting that its crafting policy may be overly permissive rather than genuinely beneficial. Conversely, Gemini 2.5

Flash Lite rarely crafts tools effectively, suggesting that weaker models may not reliably identify missing capabilities or generate usable tool definitions. These observations indicate that tool-crafting policies require additional calibration and validation.

Category-level accuracy for all three models is reported in Fig. 2.

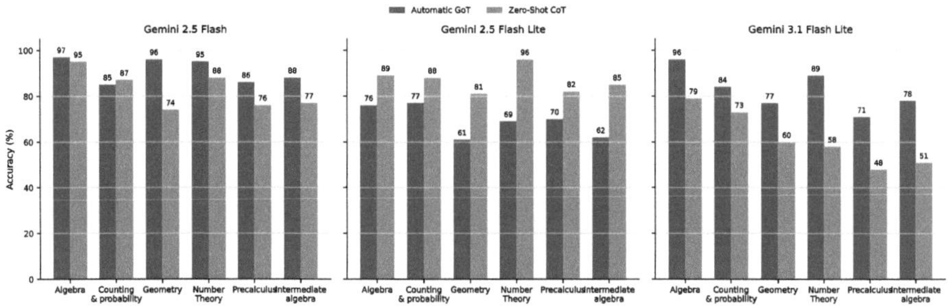


**Fig. 2.** Category-level MATH accuracy for AGoT and the Zero-Shot CoT+Tools baseline across all evaluated Gemini models. The graph shows that AGoT improves accuracy for models capable of handling and crafting tools properly, but can reduce accuracy if models do not use tools effectively.

### 4.3 Error Analysis and Tool Crafting

The most frequent non-mathematical issue concerns final-answer formatting. The MATH benchmark expects answers in a `\boxed{answer}` format. Although the structured output expected by the execution framework is generally respected, lighter models sometimes omit the benchmark-specific format. When this happens, the mathematical answer may still be correct, but additional manual inspection is required to verify equivalence with the reference answer.

A second recurring issue concerns the `divide_complexity` tool. This tool is intended to decompose a complex problem into independent subtasks. In practice, the independence constraint is not always respected: the model sometimes produces two equivalent or mutually dependent subtasks rather than a meaningful decomposition. This weakens the benefit of decomposition and can lead to redundant reasoning paths. A stricter validator for subtask independence would likely improve the reliability of this component.

The models also differ in their tool-crafting behaviour. Gemini 2.5 Flash Lite rarely decides to craft a new tool and often rejects the crafting request. Gemini 2.5 Flash shows the opposite behaviour, frequently generating new functions, sometimes unnecessarily. Gemini 3.1 Flash Lite produces the most reliable crafted tools among the evaluated models: its generated functions generally respect the requested constraints and include appropriate comments. Across all models, the main failure mode is the generation of incorrectly formatted functions, especially in tasks requiring structured inputs such as lists or tuples.

Overall, these observations qualify the quantitative results. AGoT can improve robustness and accuracy for sufficiently capable models, but its effectiveness depends on model-sensitive behaviours: using judge feedback appropriately, and crafting tools only when a missing capability is detected.

### 4.4 Threats to Validity and Limitations

The present evaluation has three main limitations. First, the comparison is restricted to a tool-augmented Zero-Shot CoT baseline. This baseline is useful for isolating the effect of graph-based orchestration and tool crafting, but it is not a comprehensive comparison against stronger agentic baselines such as ReAct-style systems or task-specific GoT implementations. Second, MATH evaluates multi-step mathematical reasoning, but it does not fully exercise tasks where graph aggregation, branch merging, and reuse of intermediate states are central. Third, tool crafting is evaluated through observed execution behaviour, but not through a separate benchmark specifically designed to test the correctness, reusability, and safety of generated tools. Broader evaluation should therefore include stronger agentic baselines, tasks where graph structure is intrinsically useful, and dedicated measurements of crafted-tool quality.

## 5 Conclusion

This paper presents AGoT, an agentic graph-based reasoning framework for tool-augmented LLM agents inspired by the GoT prompt engineering technique. Rather than treating graph-structured reasoning only as a prompting pattern, the proposed framework uses a reusable static graph to define the admissible control flow of reasoning and a dynamic execution graph to record the concrete reasoning trajectory produced for each problem instance. This execution graph makes explicit the agent's intermediate reasoning states, tool invocations, response evaluations, backtracking decisions, crafted tools, and final answer.

The experimental evaluation on the MATH benchmark provides initial evidence that AGoT can achieve high robustness and accuracy when used with sufficiently capable base models. Compared with a Tool-Augmented Zero-Shot CoT baseline, AGoT improves accuracy for Gemini 2.5 Flash and Gemini 3.1 Flash Lite, while decreasing accuracy for Gemini 2.5 Flash Lite. This suggests that benefits depend on the model's ability to follow agentic instructions, exploit judge feedback, and decide when runtime tool crafting is appropriate.

At the same time, the evaluation highlights some limitations. AGoT increases runtime, token consumption, and tool-management complexity. Moreover, the quality of crafted tools varies across models, and the judge component remains limited by the reasoning ability of the model used for evaluation. Future work is likely to include *(i)* comparing the framework against stronger agentic baselines, *(ii)* evaluating it on tasks that force dynamic graph expansion, and *(iii)* improving tool specification for better crafting and usage.

## References


1. Besta, M., et al.: Graph of thoughts: solving elaborate problems with large language models. In: Wooldridge, M.J., Dy, J.G., Natarajan, S. (eds.) Proceedings of the 38th AAAI Conference on Artificial Intelligence, vol. 38, no. 16: AAAI-24 Technical Tracks 16, pp. 17682–17690. AAAI Press (2024). https://doi.org/10.1609/AAAI.V38I16.29720
2. Gu, J., et al.: A survey on LLM-as-a-judge. Innov. **7**(6), 101253:1–101253:30 (2026). https://doi.org/10.1016/j.xinn.2025.101253
3. Hendrycks, D., et al.: Measuring mathematical problem solving with the MATH dataset. In: Vanschoren, J., Yeung, S. (eds.) Proceedings of the Neural Information Processing Systems Track on Datasets and Benchmarks 1 (NeurIPS Datasets and Benchmarks 2021), pp. 1304–1314 (2021). https://datasets-benchmarks-proceedings.neurips.cc/paper/2021/hash/be83ab3ecd0db773eb2dc1b0a17836a1-Abstract-round2.html
4. 11th International Conference on Learning Representations, ICLR 2023. OpenReview.net, Kigali, Rwanda (2023). https://openreview.net/group?id=ICLR.cc/2023/Conference
5. Kojima, T., Gu, S.S., Reid, M., Matsuo, Y., Iwasawa, Y.: Large language models are zero-shot reasoners. In: Koyejo et al. [6], pp. 22199–22213 (2022). https://doi.org/10.52202/068431-1613
6. Koyejo, S., Mohamed, S., Agarwal, A., Belgrave, D., Cho, K., Oh, A. (eds.): Advances in Neural Information Processing Systems 35: 36th Conference on Neural Information Processing Systems (NeurIPS 2022) (2022). https://doi.org/10.52202/068431
7. Madaan, A., et al.: Self-refine: iterative refinement with self-feedback. In: Oh et al. [8], pp. 46534–46594 (2023). https://doi.org/10.52202/075280-2019
8. Oh, A., Naumann, T., Globerson, A., Saenko, K., Hardt, M., Levine, S. (eds.): Advances in Neural Information Processing Systems 36: 37th Conference on Neural Information Processing Systems (NeurIPS 2023) (2023). https://doi.org/10.52202/075280
9. Shinn, N., Cassano, F., Gopinath, A., Narasimhan, K., Yao, S.: Reflexion: language agents with verbal reinforcement learning. In: Oh et al. [8], pp. 8634–8652 (2023). https://doi.org/10.52202/075280-0377
10. Song, C.H., Wu, J., Washington, C., Sadler, B.M., Chao, W.-L., Su, Y.: LLM-Planner: few-shot grounded planning for embodied agents with large language models. In: IEEE/CVF International Conference on Computer Vision, ICCV 2023, Paris, France, 1–6 October 2023, pp. 2986–2997. IEEE (2023). https://doi.org/10.1109/ICCV51070.2023.00280
11. Wang, X., et al.: Self-consistency improves chain of thought reasoning in language models. In: ICLR 2023 [4] (2023). https://openreview.net/forum?id=1PL1NIMMrw
12. Wei, J., et al.: Chain-of-Thought prompting elicits reasoning in large language models. In: Koyejo, et al. [6] (2022). https://doi.org/10.52202/068431-1800
13. Yao, S., et al.: Tree of thoughts: deliberate problem solving with large language models. In: Oh, et al. [8], pp. 11809–11822 (2023). https://doi.org/10.52202/075280-0517
14. Yao, S., et al.: ReAct: synergizing reasoning and acting in language models. In: ICLR 2023 [4] (2023). https://openreview.net/forum?id=WE_vluYUL-X

15. Yuan, S., et al.: EASYTOOL: enhancing LLM-based agents with concise tool instruction. In: Chiruzzo, L., Ritter, A., Wang, L. (eds.) 2025 Conference of the Nations of the Americas Chapter of the Association for Computational Linguistics: Human Language Technologies, NAACL 2025, vol. 1: Long Papers, pp. 951–972. Association for Computational Linguistics, Albuquerque (2025). https://doi.org/10.18653/V1/2025.NAACL-LONG.44
16. Zhai, Y., et al.: Enhancing decision-making for LLM agents via step-level q-value models. In: Walsh, T., Shah, J., Kolter, Z. (eds.) 39th AAAI Conference on Artificial Intelligence, 37th Conference on Innovative Applications of Artificial Intelligence, 15th Symposium on Educational Advances in Artificial Intelligence, AAAI 2025, pp. 27161–27169. AAAI Press, Philadelphia (2025). https://doi.org/10.1609/AAAI.V39I25.34924

# Reliability Before Validity: Stability and Sensitivity of LLM Risk-Pattern Selection for AI Deployment Risk Assessment

Gareth McConomy[1](✉), Raymond Bond[1], David H. Glass[1], Jun Liu[1], and Holly Toner[2]

[1] School of Computing, Ulster University, Belfast, Northern Ireland, UK
mcconomy-g@ulster.ac.uk

[2] Kainos plc, Belfast, Northern Ireland, UK

**Abstract.** A growing line of work uses large language models (LLMs) to match a free-text description of an AI deployment against a fixed library of named risk patterns, framing risk identification as a case-based-reasoning (CBR) task within AI-governance pipelines. The approach is promising, but its selections must first be reliable, and no operational oracle is available: domain experts frequently disagree, so there is no stable ground truth to recover. We therefore take a reliability-precedes-validity stance and measure reproducibility, stability, and sensitivity rather than correctness. We compare four arms (unstructured, chain-of-thought, holistic CBR, and a deterministic formal CBR scorer) across four LLMs and ten cases, probing each method with meaning-preserving paraphrases and meaning-altering edits, scored by top-10 set-membership overlap with bootstrap CIs; with ten cases this is a characterisation, not a powered test. We find that (i) instability is distributed across the detection and scoring stages, with scoring often the larger source and the split model-dependent; (ii) the unstructured arm is the most reproducible yet the least sensitive, the configuration a stability-only metric would reward; (iii) only the two CBR arms that use the detection labels are stable *and* sensitive, indicating that structure is what buys sensitivity; and (iv) the holistic and formal scorers are a statistical tie in sensitivity at this scale, the formal one adding determinism and auditability but trading stability through the coarseness of its scores. We make no claim about correctness, which is out of scope by design.

**Keywords:** Large language models · Case-based reasoning · AI risk assessment · Reliability · Reproducibility · Stability · Sensitivity

## 1 Introduction

A growing line of research proposes using large language models (LLMs) to identify the risks of an AI deployment by matching a free-text description


S. Bistarelli et al. (Eds.): AIxIA 2026, LNAI 17131, pp. 407–420, 2027.
https://doi.org/10.1007/978-3-032-40774-0_30

of the deployment against a library of named risk patterns, a case-based-reasoning (CBR) task [1–5]. Each pattern is a named, recurring way an AI deployment can cause harm, defined by a short list of *enabling conditions*: observable features of a deployment that make that risk more likely. As a route to AI governance [6,7] the approach is promising but not yet established: before such a tool can be relied upon in practice, its selections must be *reliable*. We treat reliability as comprising three measurable properties: *reproducibility* (repeating the same case yields the same selection), *stability* (rewording the case without changing its meaning leaves the selection unchanged), and *sensitivity* (a material, risk-relevant change to the case does change the selection). Reliability is distinct from *accuracy* (whether the selected risks are the right ones), which we do not address. Whether such selections are reliable is not obvious, because LLM outputs shift under semantically irrelevant input changes [12,16]; establishing it is the question we take up.

What makes this setting unusual is that reliability cannot be replaced by a correctness check. For AI-risk assessment no operational oracle is available: governance-mapping work from the MIT AI Risk Repository [8,9] reports that LLM risk-coverage judgements frequently disagree with human consensus, and expert reviewers with one another. Where experts do not converge, validity is contested and costly to adjudicate rather than simply recoverable, so we take a reliability-precedes-validity stance: before asking whether a selection is *right*, we ask whether the process is reproducible, stable, and sensitive, the properties measurable without an oracle.

We study four selection *methods*, which we call *arms* (A1–A4), over a fixed library of 86 AI-risk patterns and ten deployment cases, across four LLMs, probing each with meaning-preserving paraphrases (stability) and meaning-altering edits (sensitivity), read on a stability $\times$ sensitivity plane with bootstrap CIs. Because two arms share a condition-detection stage (an LLM step that labels each pattern's enabling conditions PRESENT, PARTIAL, or ABSENT) and differ only in their scorer, the design also localises where instability forms. With $n = 10$ cases this is a characterisation, not a powered test.

*Aim, Research Questions, and Objectives.* Our *aim* is to characterise the *reliability* (not the accuracy) of LLM risk-pattern selection for AI deployment, and to localise where any unreliability arises. Three research questions follow. **RQ1**: how reproducible and stable is each method under repetition and meaning-preserving rewording? **RQ2**: is each method sensitive to genuine, risk-relevant changes in the case, or merely stable because it does not react to content? **RQ3**: when a method is unstable, does the instability arise in the condition-detection stage or in the scoring stage? Our objectives are to (i) define expert-free reliability measures that need no ground truth; (ii) compare four methods across four LLMs and ten cases under both perturbation types; and (iii) attribute instability to a pipeline stage.

## 2 Related Work

*LLM Inconsistency and Paraphrase Sensitivity.* That LLM outputs vary under semantically irrelevant input changes (paraphrase, reordering, formatting) is well documented, from perturbation-based behavioural testing [13] to enterprise perturbation benchmarks [12]. We claim no contribution on this general phenomenon; we take it as our premise and focus on *where* in a structured pipeline the instability forms.

*Stability and Sensitivity.* The most closely related work distinguishes an output's stability under meaning-preserving change from its sensitivity to meaning-altering change. Riasat [14] separates stability, correctness, sensitivity, and validity, arguing internal consistency is an insufficient proxy for correctness; Pirouzkhah et al. [15] study semantics-preserving perturbations for code revision; Kostíc et al. [16] show meaning-preserving perturbations destabilise LLM scores and rankings; RobustFlow [17] is closest but targets workflow *generation* and remedies instability by training. We adopt this framing as background: it differs in object (general reasoning, code, workflow generation) and in assuming or training for ground truth, whereas we evaluate case-based risk-pattern selection where no operational oracle is available, characterising reliability rather than training for it.

*CBR with LLMs.* The combination of case-based reasoning [18,19] with LLMs is an active area [4,5], but is typically quality-framed, validated against ground truth or human alignment, and does not, to our knowledge, decompose instability by pipeline stage; our use is reliability-oriented, not quality-claiming.

*The No-Oracle Premise.* Our no-oracle premise follows governance practice: the MIT AI Risk Repository [8,9] reports that LLM risk-coverage assessments frequently disagree with human consensus, and expert reviewers with one another, so no stable ground truth exists to recover. Validity is not thereby unattainable, merely contested and costly to adjudicate; a multi-expert layer remains future work. The regime is familiar: metamorphic testing addresses exactly this oracle problem, checking relations between outputs under controlled input transformations [10], as our paired probes do; validating LLM generative-agent systems without ground truth is likewise open [11].

*Gap.* We are not aware of prior work at this intersection: CBR risk-pattern selection for AI-deployment governance, in a no-oracle setting, with stage-localised instability. The constituent ideas, cited above, are not ours.

## 3 Method

Figure 1 summarises the design. We measure the *reliability* (reproducibility, stability, and sensitivity) of LLM risk-pattern selection, not its correctness. There

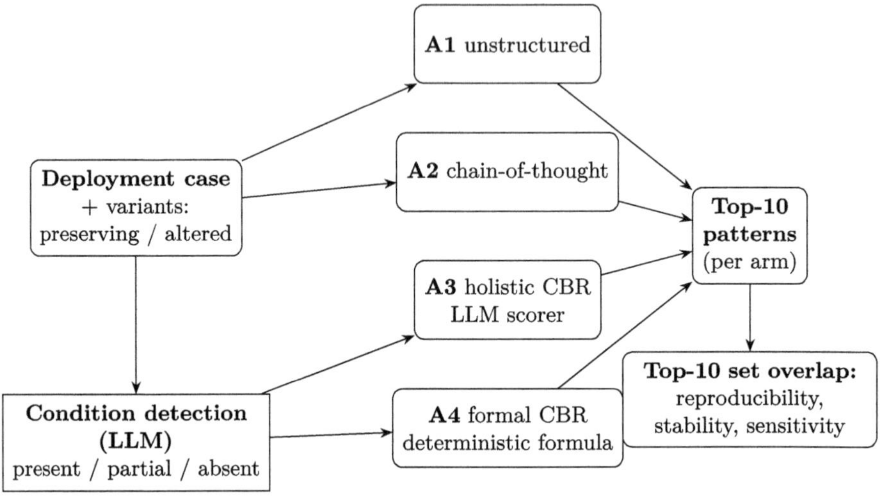


**Fig. 1.** Experimental pipeline. A deployment case, with its meaning-preserving and meaning-altering variants, is processed by four selection arms. A1 and A2 read the full pattern library directly; A3 and A4 instead use a shared condition-detection stage and differ only in their scorer (holistic LLM judgement vs. a deterministic formula), the single-variable contrast in the design. Each arm returns its top-10 patterns; selections are compared by top-10 set-membership overlap to measure reproducibility, stability under rewording, and sensitivity under content change.

is no expert, no answer key, and no recall metric anywhere in the design; validity is out of scope by construction, because no oracle for case–pattern applicability exists even in principle (Sect. 1). Every quantity we report is a property of how the *selection process* behaves under repetition and input perturbation.

### 3.1 Materials: A Fixed Pattern Library and Ten Fresh Cases

All four arms operate over one fixed library of **86** AI-risk patterns (identifiers P2–P87; P1 is absent, which is immaterial). Each pattern carries a short list of *enabling conditions*: between three and five per pattern (mean 3.92), 337 condition slots in total, each a brief textual label such as "Safety-Critical Operational Domain." The enabling conditions are the unit the detection stage classifies and the substrate of the formal scorer. They are graded, compensatory evidence, not individually necessary or jointly sufficient: the formal scorer averages their satisfied weights, so more satisfied conditions raise a pattern's applicability. For example, pattern P3 (Automation-Induced Skill Degradation Under Reduced Practice) carries enabling conditions such as "Routine Tasks Suitable for Automation" and "Skills Are Perishable Without Practice"; the detection stage decides, for a given case, whether each is PRESENT, PARTIAL, or ABSENT. The library is the identical shared input for every arm, model, and perturbation variant; there is no pre-retrieval or candidate shortlist, and each arm ranks over the whole 86-pattern space.

The ten deployment cases are fresh, span three domains (finance ×3, health ×3, public sector ×4), run 809–998 words each, and carry no annotations or answer key. They were authored by a separate LLM (Sect. 3.8) distinct from every LLM under test, so none is evaluated on text it wrote. One finance case, for instance, describes a building society extending a self-trained loan-underwriting engine from small-business loans to larger commercial mortgages, with loan officers increasingly reluctant to override it; full input and output traces are in the linked repository.

### 3.2 The Shared Condition-Detection Stage

Two of the four arms (A3 and A4) use a shared condition-detection step. For a given case text, the LLM under test (not a separate detector) classifies every enabling condition of every pattern as PRESENT, PARTIAL, or ABSENT, with a short ($\leq$ 15 word) quoted evidence span justifying each label. Labels are keyed by the integer pair (`pattern_id`, `condition_index`), which is the only join key; the condition text is copied through for human audit only.

Crucially, detection is **re-run on every repeat and variant**, never cached: its instability is part of what the dependent arms' reliability measures, and fixing it would make the formal arm appear falsely perfect; it is a measured quantity, not noise to remove.

### 3.3 The Four Arms

Each arm selects and ranks the top $K = 10$ patterns for a case; Table 1 summarises each arm's input and processing. The arms differ in the reasoning scaffold placed between the case and the ranking.

**Table 1.** The four arms. Every arm outputs a ranked top-10 of the same 86 patterns.

| Arm | Input | Processing |
|---|---|---|
| A1 unstructured | library + case | one LLM call selects and ranks; no scaffold |
| A2 chain-of-thought | library + case | A1 plus a generic step-by-step instruction |
| A3 informal CBR | labels + case | LLM holistically scores and ranks, weighing labels as evidence; no fixed formula |
| A4 formal CBR | labels only | deterministic similarity function (Sect. 3.4); no further LLM call |

A3 and A4 differ in exactly one variable, the scorer (LLM holistic judgement vs. a deterministic function) applied to identical labels: the only single-variable contrast in the design. A1 and A2 are whole-library baselines; that comparison is not fully controlled, since the structured arms receive an additional detection pass (extra decomposition and computation), so their advantage is the effect of the detection-plus-scoring package, not prompt wording alone (Sect. 6).

### 3.4 The Formal Similarity Function (A4)

For a case and a pattern with enabling conditions of detected statuses $s_1, \ldots, s_N$, the formal score is the normalised mean of status weights

$$\text{sim}(\text{case}, \text{pattern}) = \frac{1}{N} \sum_{i=1}^{N} w(s_i),$$

where $w(\text{PRESENT}) = 1.0$, $w(\text{PARTIAL}) = 0.5$, $w(\text{ABSENT}) = 0.0$, and any condition lacking a detected label defaults to ABSENT. Patterns are ranked by descending score, with ties broken by ascending integer `pattern_id`. The function is fully deterministic and emits a per-condition evidence trace, giving A4 a mechanically reconstructible audit trail; it is an ordered weighted averaging (OWA) aggregation [20] at orness 0.5 (neutral), with the OWA generalisation a pluggable seam not exercised here. The coarse status set collapses many scores into ties, so we report tie frequency and lean on the content-sensitivity probe (Sect. 3.5) rather than rank order alone.

### 3.5 Reliability Dimensions and the Set-Overlap Metric

All measurement is automated; no human grades any output. We characterise three expert-free dimensions:

1. **Reproducibility** (*same input, same output?*): agreement across three identical repeats of a method on an unchanged case (e.g. ask one model to select for the same case three times and check whether the top-10 patterns stay the same).
2. **Stability** (*reworded input, same output?*): invariance of the selection under meaning-preserving rewordings of the case (same facts, different wording).
3. **Sensitivity** (*materially changed input, changed output?*): the selection *should* move under a genuine, risk-relevant change to the case (e.g. removing human oversight). This guards against *inert stability*: a method that looks consistent only because it barely reacts to anything.

To compare two top-$K$ selections we use a **set-membership overlap** metric: the membership overlap $|A \cap B|/K$ of the two top-10 *sets* and its complement $\Delta = 1 - |A \cap B|/K$. We avoid ordered rank correlation, which would credit A4's arbitrary-but-stable identifier tiebreak as genuine stability; set overlap counts only membership churn.

From this we derive three change quantities per arm and model: *noise* $\Delta$ (run-to-run change on the unchanged original), *preserving* $\Delta$ (paraphrase variant vs.

original), and *altered* $\Delta$ (content-altered variant vs. original). We summarise stability as $1 - \text{presv}\Delta$ and sensitivity as $\text{altrd}\Delta - \text{presv}\Delta$ (movement under content change in excess of movement under mere rewording). The desired ordering is $\text{altrd}\Delta \geq \text{presv}\Delta \geq \text{noise}\Delta$. Sensitivity so measured is necessary, not sufficient: it certifies that an arm *responds* to risk-relevant change, not that the response is *appropriate*, which only expert judgement could certify.

### 3.6 Stage Decomposition: Localising Where Instability Forms

The matched A3/A4 pair localises instability to a stage. A4's scorer is deterministic, so *all* of A4's instability is inherited from detection. Pinning the labels and re-running only the holistic A3 scorer isolates **scoring-stage** instability, so comparing fixed-label against detection-varying A3 partitions A3's instability between the two stages. A **coherence rule** keeps this clean: in repeat $r$ of a (model, case, variant), A3 and A4 use detection repeat $r$; A1 and A2 never touch detection.

### 3.7 Perturbation Design

For each case a separate LLM generates six perturbation variants of the case text. **Four are meaning-preserving** (every fact, number, and named entity held fixed, only the wording changed) and drive stability: *stylistic_rewrite* (different register and word choice), *structural_reorder* (same content, reordered), *lossless_summary* ($\approx$ 25% shorter, every fact kept), and *detail_elaboration* ($\approx$ 25% longer, no new facts). **Two are content-altered** and drive the sensitivity probe: *altered_1* makes one autonomy change (e.g. removing a human override) and *altered_2* one change to domain, affected population, or stakes, so a governance assessment *should* reach a different conclusion; the model states the change explicitly.

### 3.8 Models, Parameters, and Run Protocol

Four co-equal LLMs are evaluated under test: `gpt-4o`, `gemini-2.5-pro`, `grok-4`, and `deepseek-chat` (a non-reasoning model). A fifth, separate LLM (`claude-sonnet-4-6`) authors the cases and generates all perturbations and is never placed under test. The LLM arms run at deployment temperature 0.3; $K = 10$.

We collect three identical repeats of the unchanged original per (model, arm), two repeats on each preserving variant, and three repeats on each altered variant, across all 10 cases and 4 models, every call logged. Confidence intervals come from a **nonparametric bootstrap that resamples the 10 cases** [21] ($B = 2000$, 95% percentile); we report bootstrap CIs rather than null-hypothesis tests.

# 4 Results

All reliability quantities below are top-10 set-membership overlaps over the full run of 2,720 arm units (480 originals plus 2,240 perturbation units; no failed units). Throughout we report *relative*, not absolute, reproducibility: even on unchanged text and the most stable arm, roughly a fifth of the top-10 churns from one run to the next.

## 4.1 Detection-Stage Reproducibility

Before any scorer is applied, the shared detection stage is itself only partially reproducible. Across three identical repeats, 80.0–85.9% of (case, pattern, condition) labels are identical all three times (gemini 80.0, gpt-4o 80.8, grok 81.4, deepseek 85.9); most movement is PARTIAL-boundary wobble, with hard PRESENT↔ABSENT flips rarer and concentrated in gemini (7.0% vs. 1.4–3.4% elsewhere). Across models only 59.9% of cells are unanimous (4/4). So the detection stage is itself a real instability source, present before either CBR scorer runs and measured by the stage decomposition rather than discarded as noise.

## 4.2 Where Instability Forms: Reproducibility Decomposition

Pinning the detection labels and re-running only the holistic A3 scorer lifts A3's top-10 reproducibility for every LLM (Table 2, "A3 fixed" > "A3 vary"), confirming detection is a genuine but not dominant instability source. It contributes an estimated 33–56% of A3's top-10 instability and the holistic scorer the rest; even with labels frozen, A3 reproducibility reaches only 0.81–0.89. The split is model-dependent: instability is distributed across both stages, not localised to either.

**Table 2.** Reproducibility decomposition: mean top-10 set overlap across three identical repeats, by model. "A4 (det-var)" is the deterministic formal arm (all its variance inherited from detection); "A3 vary" lets detection move, "A3 fixed" pins detection to one repeat's labels. The final column is the detection stage's estimated share of A3's total top-10 instability.

| model | A1 | A2 | A4 (det-var) | A3 vary | A3 fixed | detect. share |
|---|---|---|---|---|---|---|
| gpt-4o | .783 | .643 | .750 | .683 | .813 | 41% |
| gemini | .823 | .787 | .707 | .747 | .830 | 33% |
| grok | .800 | .817 | .710 | .740 | .887 | 56% |
| deepseek | .783 | .660 | .810 | .747 | .887 | 55% |

### 4.3 Stability and Sensitivity Across the Four Arms

Table 3 reports the three change quantities per arm (model-averaged) and Fig. 2 plots all 16 (arm, model) points with bootstrap CIs. Two arms satisfy the desired ordering altrd$\Delta$ $\geq$ presv$\Delta$ $\geq$ noise$\Delta$: A3 and A4, the label-based arms (those that score patterns from the detection labels). A1 is stable but barely moves under content; A2 inverts the ordering, the signature of degenerate stability.

Sensitivity is a *paired* quantity: the per-case difference altrd$\Delta$ − presv$\Delta$, read from its own bootstrap interval, not inferred from whether the marginal CIs in Table 3 overlap. The four-arm model-averaged paired sensitivity headline (bootstrap 95% CI, resampling the 10 cases) is: A1 +1.2 pts $[+0.2, +2.2]$; A2 −0.3 pts $[-1.6, +1.1]$; A3 +4.8 pts $[+3.5, +6.3]$; A4 +4.6 pts $[+2.2, +6.7]$. A3 and A4 exclude 0 and are roughly four times A1's; A1 clears 0 only slightly; A2 straddles 0.

**Table 3.** Per-arm change quantities, **averaged across the four LLMs** (top-10 set-membership change $\Delta$ in %, with bootstrap 95% CIs resampling the 10 cases, $B = 2000$): noise$\Delta$ (run-to-run on the original), presv$\Delta$ (paraphrase vs. original), altrd$\Delta$ (content-altered vs. original). Stability margin = presv$\Delta$−noise$\Delta$ (smaller is more stable); sensitivity margin = altrd$\Delta$−presv$\Delta$ (larger is more sensitive). These are model-averaged figures and mask per-model structure: in particular A3 and A4 are null on grok; see Fig. 2 for the per-model resolution.

| arm | noise$\Delta$ [95%CI] | presv$\Delta$ [95%CI] | altrd$\Delta$ [95%CI] | stab. margin | sens. margin |
|---|---|---|---|---|---|
| A1 | 20.2 [18.6,21.8] | 20.0 [18.1,21.9] | 21.2 [19.0,23.2] | −0.2 | +1.2 |
| A2 | 27.3 [23.2,31.1] | 27.9 [25.1,30.7] | 27.6 [24.6,30.5] | +0.6 | −0.3 |
| A3 | 27.1 [23.9,29.9] | 27.1 [24.3,29.6] | 31.9 [28.8,34.9] | +0.0 | +4.8 |
| A4 | 25.6 [22.6,28.6] | 28.6 [26.5,30.7] | 33.2 [30.7,35.4] | +3.0 | +4.6 |

Per model, only A3 and A4 have sensitivity CIs that exclude 0, and only on the three non-grok models, where their sensitivity runs roughly +4 to +6 points (Fig. 2); on grok both straddle 0 (+2.3% and +2.6%), so weak sensitivity here is an LLM property, not an arm property. Every A1 and A2 cell straddles 0. These results *indicate* that structure, which uses the condition labels, is what buys sensitivity, while the unstructured and CoT baselines do not reliably move under content change.

### 4.4 The Unstructured Baseline is Stable but Minimally Sensitive

A1 is the most stable arm (model-averaged preserving overlap ~80%) yet only minimally sensitive to content. Its model-averaged per-case sensitivity is +1.2 pts, bootstrap 95% CI $[+0.2, +2.2]$: the interval clears 0, so A1 is not strictly inert, but the effect is barely above zero and roughly a quarter of the ~ 5 pt sensitivity of the structured arms. A stability-only metric would have ranked A1 best; the sensitivity probe *characterises* it instead as stable but only weakly content-sensitive: the stability trap.

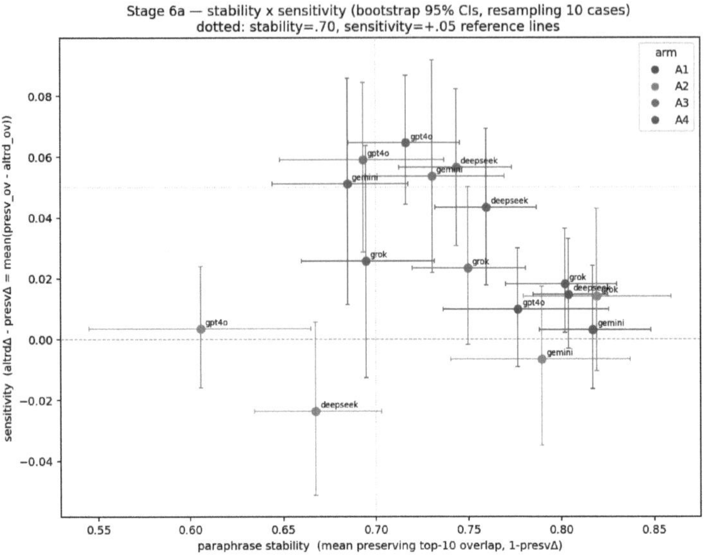


**Fig. 2.** Stability × sensitivity across the 16 (arm, model) points. The $x$-axis is stability (mean overlap under meaning-preserving rewording); the $y$-axis is sensitivity (altrd$\Delta$−presv$\Delta$); bars are bootstrap 95% CIs (resampling the 10 cases). Only the label-based arms A3 and A4 have sensitivity CIs clear of 0, and only on gpt-4o, gemini, and deepseek; grok is the weak-sensitivity model for both A3 and A4.

### 4.5 A4's Stability Gap is Genuine Score Coarseness, not a Tiebreak Artefact

A4 is the least stable arm under rewording (stability margin +3.0 pts, Table 3). Its coarse three-level scores produce heavy ties: the rank-10 cutoff falls inside a group of patterns sharing one score in 680/680 (100%) of runs, so which tied patterns fill the final slots is settled by the identifier tiebreak. The extra churn is not mere tiebreak shuffling: 75.4% of preserving-variant swaps are genuine own-score movement (the pattern's own score changed under rewording), and the tie-cut share matches rerun noise (24.6% vs. 25.6%); it is paraphrase moving coarse scores across boundary tiers, coarseness-brittleness of the formal scorer, not a tiebreak artefact. Per LLM, the mean number of the 10 top slots fixed by score rather than the identifier tiebreak is 8.0 on grok and 7.1 on gpt-4o, but only 1.4 on gemini, whose PRESENT-heavy detection saturates the score so that the top-10 is mostly identifier order.

### 4.6 Holistic vs Formal Scorer: A Statistical Tie in Sensitivity

The matched A3/A4 pair (identical labels, scorer the only difference) lets us ask whether the holistic or the formal scorer is more content-sensitive. The per-model bootstrap CI on the sensitivity difference (A4−A3) straddles 0 on every model (point estimates −1.3% to +0.6%), so at $n = 10$ the two scorers are statistically indistinguishable in sensitivity. We therefore do not crown a scorer: both are sensitive; the formal one adds determinism and a mechanical audit trail but trades stability via its coarseness (Sect. 4.5). A qualitative check (unscored) confirms face validity: across the 20 altered variants, the patterns entering and leaving the top-10 track the stated change.

# 5 Discussion

Stated directly: explicit condition detection makes selection responsive to substantive change; the deterministic scorer buys auditability, not sensitivity, and cedes stability through coarse scores and ties.

*Stability Alone is a Trap.* A reliability metric built on reproducibility alone would have been actively misleading here: A1, the unstructured baseline, is the most stable arm yet barely moves under genuine content change (Sect. 4.4), so a stability-only evaluation would have crowned the arm that engages least with the case. Any reliability assessment therefore needs a sensitivity probe alongside its stability measure; without one, the inert configuration scores best.

*Structure Buys Sensitivity.* Only the two arms that use the shared condition-detection labels (A3, A4) reach the stable-and-sensitive region, on three of the four LLMs (Sect. 4.3); the unstructured and chain-of-thought baselines, which see the same library and case but no detection step, do not reliably move under content change: the condition-detection scaffold, not the extra CoT instruction, forces engagement with case content. We do not claim the structured arms select *better* patterns, only that they respond to content where the unstructured arm is almost inert.

*Where to Invest: Detection, Not the Scoring Mathematics.* The stage decomposition (Sect. 4.2) spreads instability across both stages, the holistic scorer often the larger source; yet replacing it with a deterministic function does *not* improve sensitivity (the A3↔A4 tie, Sect. 4.6) and adds tie-brittleness (Sect. 4.5). Effort is better spent stabilising the shared condition-detection input than elaborating the scoring mathematics, which buys auditability but neither sensitivity nor stability.

*Model-Dependence: No Universal Best Pairing.* No single (arm, model) pairing dominates: the label-based arms are sensitive on gpt-4o, gemini, and deepseek but null on grok (weak sensitivity is a property of the LLM, not the arm), while gemini's detection saturates the formal scorer into tie-degeneracy; model choice is not separable from mechanism.

*Practitioner Implications.* In practice: prefer the structured, label-based pipeline over freehand prompting when sensitivity matters; treat the top-10 as a *shortlist for human attention*, not a ranking (membership churns ~20–33%, and within-tie order is a tiebreak artefact); use the output as a thinking aid, not an oracle; and check sensitivity to content change, not just run-to-run reproducibility.

## 6 Limitations

Several limitations bound these results. With $n = 10$ cases this is a *characterisation, not a powered test*: the bootstrap intervals are wide and per-cell (arm × model) results are indicative, not conclusive. There is no oracle by design: we measure reliability, not validity (no ground truth, expert panel, or recall metric enters anywhere), so a stable or sensitive arm is not thereby accurate. A single fixed 86-pattern library and one governance framing bound transfer to other libraries, domains, or framings. Reported reproducibility is relative: "stable" means "no worse than the noisy baseline." A single separate LLM authored both the cases and the perturbations, bounding ecological validity; though disjoint from every LLM under test, an independent or human-authored source would strengthen the design, in particular human checks that preserving rewrites preserve and altering edits alter only what is intended. The arm comparison is not fully controlled: the structured arms receive an extra detection pass, so their advantage reflects that whole package, not scaffold wording alone. Finally, sensitivity rests on a sparse two-point gradient per case (one autonomy change, one domain/population/stakes change) against a three-repeat noise floor: enough to characterise whether an arm responds to content, but not to map the response surface densely.

## 7 Conclusion and Future Work

We brought the stability-versus-sensitivity lens to CBR AI-risk-pattern selection where no operational oracle is available, and added a stage-localisation method attributing pipeline instability to detection or scoring. Across four arms, four LLMs, and ten cases: reproducibility alone is misleading, only the label-based CBR arms are both stable and sensitive, instability is distributed across detection and scoring, and the two scorers tie in sensitivity, the formal one buying auditability at the cost of stability. None of this speaks to correctness, which remains out of scope.

Future work has two tracks. First, the deferred *fusion* direction (combining the holistic and formal scorers, or structured and unstructured arms) has a prerequisite: a fuller sensitivity response surface than the present two-point contrast, e.g. by Monte Carlo sampling of the perturbation space; even a dense surface shows that a method *is* sensitive, not that its sensitivity is *appropriate*. Second, validation at scale: more cases, an independent or human-authored case and perturbation source, and, once validity is in scope, a multi-expert study relating reliability to correctness.

**Acknowledgments.** This work was undertaken as part of a PhD funded by Kainos plc.

**Data Availibility Statement.** Pattern library, cases, perturbations, run logs, and analysis code: https://github.com/ggmcconomy/Ai_stability_testing.

**Disclosure of Interests.** The authors have no competing interests to declare. For completeness: this work forms part of a PhD funded by Kainos plc, and one author (H. Toner) is employed by Kainos plc.

**Declaration on Generative AI.** The authors used Claude (Anthropic) for literature synthesis during knowledge-graph construction, manuscript drafting and language editing, and case-study development; generative AI was excluded from the experiments themselves.

## References

1. McConomy, G., Bond, R., Glass, D., Liu, J., Toner, H.: Augmenting large language models with causal risk patterns for AI deployment risk assessment. In: Proceedings of IEEE ICAD 2026 (2026). (to appear)
2. McConomy, G., Bond, R., Glass, D., Liu, J., Toner, H.: Bridging causal reasoning and fuzzy calibration for trustworthy AI risk assessment. In: Proceedings of FLINS-ISKE 2026 (2026). (to appear)
3. McConomy, G., Bond, R., Glass, D., Liu, J., Toner, H.: Layer-appropriate augmentation for human-AI risk assessment: integrating case-based reasoning with fuzzy calibration. In: Proceedings of HHAI 2026 (2026). (to appear)
4. Gan, W., Dao, M.-S., Zettsu, K.: Case-based reasoning augmented large language model framework for decision making in realistic safety-critical driving scenarios (2025). arXiv:2506.20531
5. Bach, K., et al.: Case-based reasoning meets large language models: a research manifesto for open challenges and research directions. Working paper, hal-05006761 (2025)
6. National Institute of Standards and Technology: Artificial Intelligence Risk Management Framework (AI RMF 1.0). NIST AI 100-1 (2023)
7. European Parliament and Council of the European Union: Regulation (EU) 2024/1689 laying down harmonised rules on artificial intelligence. Artificial Intelligence Act). Official Journal of the European Union (2024)
8. MIT AI Risk Initiative: Mapping the AI governance landscape: April 2026 update. airisk.mit.edu (2026)
9. Slattery, P., et al.: The AI risk repository: a comprehensive meta-review, database, and taxonomy of risks from artificial intelligence (2024). arXiv:2408.12622
10. Xie, X., Ho, J.W.K., Murphy, C., Kaiser, G., Xu, B., Chen, T.Y.: Testing and validating machine learning classifiers by metamorphic testing. J. Syst. Softw. **84**(4), 544–558 (2011)
11. Adornetto, C., et al.: Generative agents in agent-based modeling: overview, validation, and emerging challenges. IEEE Trans. Artif. Intell. **6**(12), 3165–3183 (2025)
12. Bogavelli, T., Bamgbose, O., Gauthier Melançon, G., Riols, F.: Evaluating robustness of large language models in enterprise applications: benchmarks for perturbation consistency across formats and languages (2026). arXiv:2601.06341

13. Ribeiro, M.T., Wu, T., Guestrin, C., Singh, S.: Beyond accuracy: behavioral testing of NLP models with CheckList. In: Proceedings of 58th Annual Meeting of the Association for Computational Linguistics, pp. 4902–4912 (2020)
14. Riasat, N.: When stability fails: hidden failure modes of LLMs in data-constrained scientific decision-making. In: ICLR 2026 Workshop (I Can't Believe It's Not Better) (2026). arXiv:2603.15840
15. Pirouzkhah, S., Serbout, S., Bacchelli, A.: Consistent or sensitive? Automated code revision tools against semantics-preserving perturbations (2026). arXiv:2602.14595
16. Kostić, B., Fallon, C., Risch, J., Löser, A.: Same meaning, different scores: lexical and syntactic sensitivity in LLM evaluation (2026). arXiv:2602.17316
17. Xu, S.: RobustFlow: towards robust agentic workflow generation (2025). arXiv:2509.21834
18. Aamodt, A., Plaza, E.: Case-based reasoning: foundational issues, methodological variations, and system approaches. AI Commun. **7**(1), 39–59 (1994)
19. López de Mántaras, R., et al.: Retrieval, reuse, revision and retention in case-based reasoning. Knowl. Eng. Rev. **20**(3), 215–240 (2005)
20. Yager, R.R.: On ordered weighted averaging aggregation operators in multicriteria decision making. IEEE Trans. Syst. Man Cybern. **18**(1), 183–190 (1988)
21. Efron, B., Tibshirani, R.J.: An Introduction to the Bootstrap. Chapman & Hall, New York (1993)

# A Peer-to-Peer Platform for Lifelong Learning in Dynamic Human-AI Agent Communities

Stefano Melacci[1], Christian Di Maio[1,3(✉)], Tommaso Guidi[1,2], and Marco Gori[1]

[1] University of Siena, Siena, Italy
{stefano.melacci,marco.gori}@unisi.it, christian.dimaio@phd.unipi.it, tommaso.guidi@unifi.it
[2] University of Florence, Florence, Italy
[3] University of Pisa, Pisa, Italy

**Abstract.** The lifelong learning research community often relies on simulated data streams derived from static, offline datasets without directly experiencing real-world environments where learning machines continuously develop and interact with others. In order to bridge this gap, this paper introduces UNaIVERSE (https://unaiverse.io), an open-source, decentralized peer-to-peer platform designed for agents (whether human or artificial) that adapt over time. UNaIVERSE enables authentic lifelong learning through live-streamed interactions within dynamic communities of human and artificial agents. At the core of the platform are "Worlds", i.e., autonomous ecosystems where agents learn and specialize through interaction-driven processes rather than fixed data collections. UNaIVERSE allows agents to acquire and refine skills as a direct consequence of sustained social interaction, facilitating the study of emergent behaviors and continuous adaptation in a truly multi-agent setting with streaming data. The peer-to-peer architecture naturally induces open-world, non-stationary settings where agents may arrive, depart, and migrate across Worlds at any time, offering a flexible playground for rigorous investigations and bridging the gap between isolated continual learning benchmarks and grounded, interaction-rich learning environments. This paper describes several use cases that are not intended as full-fledged experimental evaluations, but rather as illustrations of the design space that UNaIVERSE opens up for lifelong learning research.

**Keywords:** Decentralized AI · Lifelong Learning · Human-AI Co-evolution

## 1 Introduction

Research on lifelong and continual learning has made considerable progress over the last decade, producing algorithms that mitigate catastrophic forgetting [19,44], architectures with explicit memory mechanisms [8,37,39], replay


S. Bistarelli et al. (Eds.): AIxIA 2026, LNAI 17131, pp. 421–437, 2027.
https://doi.org/10.1007/978-3-032-40774-0_31

techniques [32], and benchmarks that simulate non-stationary data streams from static collections [22]. Yet a fundamental tension persists: the data streams used for experimentation in (semi) supervised continual learning are almost always derived from fixed, offline datasets that are shuffled, split, or replayed to mimic temporal dynamics. When considering the continual reinforcement learning case [17], the notion of acting in a dynamic environment becomes prominent, and the previous statement is less supported, since there exist specific simulators to directly interact with [27]. Relying on pre-collected interactions is convenient and reproducible, but it misses several properties of real-world lifelong learning: genuine non-stationarity arising from an evolving environment, whose dynamics are not fully known in advance (hence interactions cannot be pre-collected), open-world conditions where new classes, tasks, and even new learners may appear at any time, and social interaction among heterogeneous agents with complementary competences. Recent analyses have questioned whether benchmark-level conclusions transfer to more realistic settings [44]. This gap between isolated benchmarks and ecologically grounded learning goes beyond lifelong learning, and it has been recognized across multiple sub-communities. In (non-lifelong) reinforcement learning, the gap between simulators and deployment remains a known bottleneck [3], despite the existence of live simulators [2,14]; in federated learning, the complexity of real-world agent heterogeneity is seldom captured by synthetic partitions [16].

The recently promoted Collectionless AI perspective [13] pushes the argument further: if the ultimate goal is to build agents that learn and evolve from temporal interactions rather than from curated collections, then the research infrastructure itself must move beyond collection-centric pipelines. This paper is inspired by such motivation, and it introduces UNaIVERSE (https://unaiverse.io) an open-source, decentralized peer-to-peer platform whose primary purpose is to provide the lifelong learning community with a principled infrastructure for studying adaptation, forgetting, and emergent specialization in settings that go beyond local simulation. UNaIVERSE organizes agents into "Worlds", i.e., communities governed by explicit norms that regulate agent interactions, assign roles, and structure temporal dynamics through finite-state automata. Data are exchanged as *live streams* over a peer-to-peer network; agents can join and leave Worlds at any time, creating genuinely open-world, non-stationary conditions by design. UNaIVERSE is indeed a multi-agent platform, but, unlike many existing solutions, it is fully agent-agnostic. Existing models of different types can be easily wrapped and exposed or exploited for experimentation, beyond LLMs. Recent live benchmarking suites [52] and conceptual frameworks [4] stress the role of LLMs and multi-agent systems in lifelong learning. UNaIVERSE generalizes the multi-agent approach without being tied to LLMs, used either as orchestrators or as the core of the agent.

The contribution of this paper is two-fold. On one hand, it promotes a message to the lifelong learning community and, more generally, machine learning community, to encourage the switching toward more advanced and realistic benchmarking conditions. On the other hand, it describes a platform to support such a message, describing use-cases and scenarios that can help the community to expand the scope of its research in lifelong and continual learning, hence going beyond proposing a bare position, but indeed showcasing a real tool. As a result, the contribution is architectural and infrastructural, not algorithmic. We do not propose new continual learning methods nor claim state-of-the-art results on existing benchmarks. Instead, we describe the design rationale and the main components of UNaIVERSE and map its features to open problems in lifelong learning. The accompanying code and examples are publicly available.[1]

## 2 Related Work

A core motivation behind UNaIVERSE is the gap between the complexity of natural ecosystems and the constrained environments used in AI research: popular lifelong learning benchmarks mimic non-stationarity in a synthetic, deterministic way, while agentic AI platforms relegate multi-agent interaction to the rigid orchestration of narrow tasks [18]. UNaIVERSE bridges this gap with non-stationarity that emerges from open-ended social dynamics.

**Continual and Lifelong Learning Benchmarks.** A large body of work evaluates continual learning algorithms on benchmarks derived from static datasets, such as Split-CIFAR, Split-MNIST, and permuted variants [19,44]. CORe50 [22] added temporal correlations, and later work proposed task-free and online settings [12]. These benchmarks share a structural limit: non-stationarity is fixed by the dataset splits rather than emerging from the environment, and the learner works in isolation, with no interaction with other agents and no open-ended task discovery. UNaIVERSE moves from synthetic to emergent, socially-driven non-stationarity, where data distributions shift as the communities evolve.

**Platforms for Agentic AI.** The landscape of frameworks for building AI agents is growing rapidly (a structured comparison is given in Table 1). Orchestration frameworks such as CrewAI, n8n, LangChain/Graph, Dify, and Eliza OS simplify the development of individual LLM-based agents and their integration with external services [29,43]. Concurrently, Multi-Agent System (MAS) frameworks like AutoGen, MetaGPT, and ChatDev have introduced mechanisms for agents to collaborate via role-playing [15,28,47]. However, these systems target isolated, developer-defined objectives (e.g., writing a module or analyzing a dataset): they do not model persistent communities of interacting agents, nor open-ended social dynamics or temporal evolution. Decentralized platforms like Coral [11] and NANDA [30] distribute computation but lack the community architectures, rule enforcement, and role fluidity of UNaIVERSE. Existing MAS platforms are also almost exclusively LLM-centric, while UNaIVERSE is strictly model-agnostic and natively interfaces LLM agents, RL policies, symbolic algorithms, and human-in-the-loop clients. It acts as a universal wrapper: agents built with any framework in Table 1 participate as nodes within its Worlds.

[1] https://github.com/orgs/collectionlessai/.

**Table 1.** Comparing agent-oriented platforms. Most build individual agents; UNaIVERSE models *communities* of interacting agents and is compatible with all listed frameworks (⋆). *Model Agnostic*: wraps any model, not only LLM providers. *Emergent Social Dyn.*: roles and interaction graph change at runtime (join, leave, promote, migrate). *Decentralized/Peer-to-peer*: no central orchestrator or relay. *Privacy*: encrypted messages, locally verified tokens, no central data accumulation.

| SOLUTION | Simplified Dev. of Agents | Fully Model Agnostic | Integration w/ Apps | Decentralized Platform | Emergent Social Dyn. | Peer-to-peer Network | Privacy Constr. |
|---|---|---|---|---|---|---|---|
| Cerebrum | ✓ | ✗ | ✓ | ✓ | ✗ | ✗ | ✓ |
| Dify | ✓ | ✗ | ✓ | ✗ | ✗ | ✗ | ✗ |
| CrewAI | ✓ | ✗ | ✓ | ✗ | ✗ | ✗ | ✗ |
| Eliza OS | ✓ | ✗ | ✓ | ✗ | ✗ | ✗ | ✗ |
| LangChain/Graph | ✓ | ✗ | ✓ | ✗ | ✗ | ✗ | ✗ |
| n8n | ✓ | ✗ | ✓ | ✗ | ✗ | ✗ | ✗ |
| Coral Ecosystem | ✓ | ✗ | ✓ | ✓ | ✗ | ✗ | ✓ |
| NANDA | ✓ | ✗ | ✓ | ✓ | ✗ | ✗ | ✗ |
| AutoGen | ✓ | ✗ | ✓ | ✗ | ✗ | ✗ | ✗ |
| MetaGPT | ✓ | ✗ | ✓ | ✗ | ✗ | ✗ | ✗ |
| ChatDev | ✓ | ✗ | ✓ | ✗ | ✗ | ✗ | ✗ |
| UNaIVERSE | ✓⋆ | ✓ | ✓⋆ | ✓ | ✓ | ✓ | ✓ |

**Open-Ended Multi-agent Environments.** A parallel line of work builds simulated worlds explicitly designed to expose agents to persistence, population scale, and open-endedness. Neural MMO [34,35] pioneered massively multi-agent persistent ecosystems, showing that larger populations magnify exploration and induce niche formation. Later sandboxes (MineDojo [9], Crafter [14], Craftax [23], MiniHack [31]) combine procedural generation with long-horizon skill acquisition, while POET [45] showed open-ended co-evolution of environments and agent policies, and TwinMarket [49] let agents' actions drift the environment itself. These environments have been extremely valuable for studying emergent behavior, but they remain *simulator-centric*: agents and dynamics are bundled inside a single engine, the set of participants is controlled by the experimenter, and the protocol is ultimately another form of pre-specified, if procedurally generated, stream. UNaIVERSE takes a complementary perspective: rather than shipping a pre-built virtual world, it provides the connective tissue (a peer-to-peer substrate with Worlds, roles, and live streams) on top of which simulators like Neural MMO or MineDojo can be exposed as agents or World backends, while also admitting heterogeneous learners and human participants they were not designed to host.

**Federated and Decentralized Continual Learning.** Federated Continual Learning (FCL) [46,48] studies the integration of distributed training with non-stationary local streams, and has identified phenomena such as *spatial-temporal catastrophic forgetting*, where spatial heterogeneity across clients exacerbates temporal forgetting during aggregation [50]. Related efforts address dynamic client participation, asynchronous updates, and model-heterogeneous collaboration without a shared dataset [36]. Still, FCL inherits the federated assumption of a shared task and a coordinated aggregation schedule, with clients seen as passive data silos rather than interacting agents with their own goals. UNaIVERSE relaxes these assumptions: peers are autonomous, may not share a task, exchange live streams rather than gradient updates, and are coordinated by FSA-encoded norms rather than a central aggregator. FCL methods can still be deployed *within* a World, but the platform presupposes no particular aggregation protocol.

**Multi-agent Continual Reinforcement Learning and Emergent Communication.** Continual Reinforcement Learning, surveyed in the single-agent case [1,17], is now being extended to multiple agents [51], where standard remedies fail to preserve role assignments and coordination protocols as policies adapt [40]. Emergent-communication work studies how agents learn interaction protocols under partial observability [20,26], but within single centralized training setups rather than open, live communities. UNaIVERSE is complementary: it offers an infrastructural level at which role-based interaction, long-lived channels, and open membership can be observed over realistic time scales, to study how learned coordination survives agent churn, migration, and learner heterogeneity.

**Lifelong LLM-Based and Embodied Social Agents.** LLM-powered agents have revived interest in memory, self-improvement, and social learning as ingredients of lifelong behavior, with benchmarks for sequential skill acquisition and episodic recall [10,52], embodied frameworks exploring theory of mind and cultural transmission [21,41], position pieces toward agents as dynamic processes [4], and collective learning at the edge [33]. UNaIVERSE generalizes this on two axes: its model-agnostic design lets artificial and human agents coexist in one World, and time and membership are first-class, so agents join, leave, and migrate carrying knowledge across Worlds.

## 3 The UNaIVERSE Platform

This section briefly describes the main components of UNaIVERSE. The reader can access it at https://unaiverse.io and find, examples, extended descriptions, and technical information at https://docs.unaiverse.io.

### 3.1 Architecture Overview

**Authenticated P2P Agents and Worlds.** UNaIVERSE is an authenticated peer-to-peer network where multiple agents "live". Each node hosts either an agent or a World, where Worlds are communities of agents organized around shared goals and governed by explicit rules. Agents live in one World at a time and can migrate between Worlds, dynamically reshaping the communities (Fig. 1)[2]. Every node is fully autonomous once authenticated on the network. The authentication is performed by an entry point that issues time-limited authentication tokens, which are appended to every message and can be verified autonomously by any recipient to confirm the sender's identity. The entry point plays no role in relaying agent-to-agent communication, which flows directly over the P2P mesh. The network supports multiple transport protocols (HTTPS, QUIC-UDP, WebRTC-UDP) and automatically selects the most appropriate one for each connection, adapting to firewalls and NAT configurations.

**Main Components.** A researcher can wrap any model (a classifier, a predictor, a symbolic module) into an agent in a few lines of code, by declaring such a model to be the *processor* of the agent (i.e., its computational core, detailed in Sect. 3.2) and specifying the input/output data types, so that it exchanges data only with compatible agents. Data is shared by *live streams*, where every sample carries a timestamp, a source identifier, and a data type that uniquely identify it. Every agent supports a set of default *actions* (Python methods returning True/False – process data, learn from data, engage another agent, disconnect, send action-requests to other agents, etc.): the ones that are about making predictions and learning directly involve the agent's processor, hence they depend on its specific implementation, while some other actions open up multi-agent interaction (send action-request).[3] When an agent joins a World, it gets a role and an additional set of World-specific actions, that depend on the assigned role. The way these actions are triggered, and what-can-be-done-and-when is modeled by a Finite State Automaton (FSA) that is still part of the joined World. The FSA models the so-called *behavior* of the agent (detailed in Sect. 3.2), and it is fully crafted by the World designer, together with the additional World-specific actions. Every agent, independently of its structure, becomes compliant with the World it enters by inheriting all the just mentioned elements. Differently, what it learns stays in its model parameters and carries over to the next World.

**Human and Artificial Agents.** UNaIVERSE treats human and artificial agents in the same way: humans use a placeholder for the processor (since the processor is basically the human brain) and only need an interface to provide their perceptual data, while obeying the same FSAs and actions as their artificial counterparts. Human agents join UNaIVERSE through a web browser, which serves as the interface for exploring Worlds and interacting with other agents. Artificial agents are instantiated through a Python interface distributed as a PyPI package (`pip install unaiverse`). When the agent (being it human or not) joins a World, the World's FSA and World-specific additional actions are

[2] The platform also supports direct agent-to-agent communication outside any World, generalizing standard Web interactions in a peer-to-peer fashion.

[3] The learning facilities currently assume a PyTorch model, but custom learning actions can be written for other model types.

dynamically sent and applied through a hot-swap mechanism, without requiring any action from the agent's owner. Due to the hot-swap, every artificial agent based on pre-existing models can be turned into a UNaIVERSE agent that participates in the social dynamics of a World, without any other extra effort. UNaIVERSE does not expose a centralized `step(action)` → `observation` interface as found in single-agent RL environments. Each agent communicates asynchronously with peers, and is governed by the role-specific FSA. There is no global environment loop: non-stationarity and open-world conditions emerge from the infrastructure itself rather than being encoded in a simulator.

**Example.** As a concrete example, a PyTorch Convolutional Neural Network (CNN) is plugged into an agent by setting it as the processor of the agent, and by declaring a stream of images as input and a stream of labels as output; on joining a World (Sect. 4.1) it inherits a role and an expected behavior (FSA and actions), with no specific extra code written by the CNN's owner.

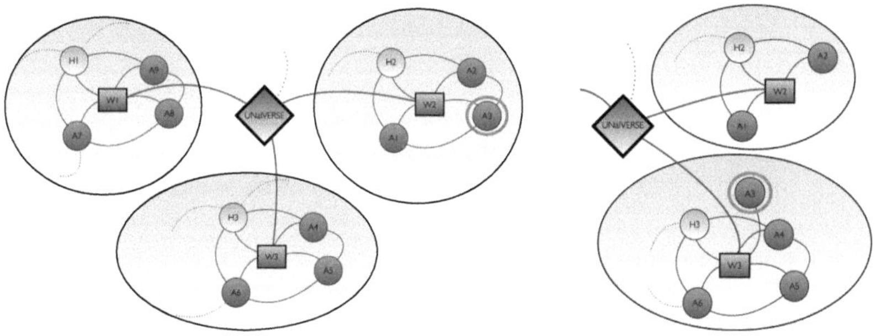

(a) UNaIVERSE is composed of Worlds: communities governed by a `World` agent.

(b) Agents live in one World at a time but can migrate, inheriting new behaviors. Here, A3 migrated from W2 to W3.

**Fig. 1.** Overview of UNaIVERSE (W: World; H: human agent; A: artificial agent). Each World is managed by a dedicated World agent (red node) that assigns roles, tracks membership, and enforces interaction norms. Agents belong to one World at a time and communicate directly over the P2P mesh. (Color figure online)

All the components described in this section are implemented and available in the current release of the platform (`pip install unaiverse`); the open directions discussed in Sect. 5 are the only parts left for future work.

### 3.2 Agents: Behavior and Processor

Every agent in UNaIVERSE is structured around two primary modules: a *behavior* and a *processor* module (Fig. 2a).

**Behavior.** The behavior module determines what an agent can and cannot do at each moment. It is built around a Finite State Automaton (FSA), provided by the World that the agent joins, and a custom policy that manages concrete action selection. States represent the agent's current condition; transitions are labeled with actions that return success or failure. A policy selects among the available outgoing transitions, and the agent transitions to a new state when an action succeeds. Some transitions can be disabled by default and enabled only when another agent explicitly requests them (by sending an action-request), modeling social interactions that emerge from the community dynamics (see Sect. 3.3).

**Processor.** The processor is the computational core of the agent. It takes input data from a source stream, processes it, and produces output data that populate its output stream. A processor can be any callable Python object: a neural network, a symbolic reasoner, a rule-based system, or a combination thereof. UNaIVERSE makes no assumptions on the internal model of each agent, which is a deliberate design choice to support the widest possible range of research approaches. When the processor implements a learnable model (for instance, a PyTorch module), it can be paired with an optimizer and loss functions, enabling online learning directly driven by the data received from the interaction streams.

**Capabilities.** Every agent comes with a set of basic actions (e.g., calling the processor on incoming stream data to produce predictions, or triggering a learning step that consumes a labeled sample from a stream and updates the model parameters), which are inherited from a shared base class. Joining a World augments this action set with World-specific actions defined by the World creator. The FSA of the behavior module can then exploit this extended action set, where each edge of the FSA is paired with an action. If the action returns True, the transition is performed, otherwise the policy function selects a new one.

### 3.3 Worlds: Communities, Roles, and Interactions

**Communities and Roles.** A World in UNaIVERSE can be understood as a special agent with governance duties. It is responsible for keeping track of the community members, assigning roles to newcomers, collecting statistics about the participants, and enforcing the norms of the community (Fig. 2b-2c). Roles are central to the design of a World. Each role carries a specific FSA that governs the agent's behavior within that community. For example, a World designed for supervised learning might define the roles of TEACHER and STUDENT: the teacher's FSA structures the delivery of labeled data through a sequence of lectures and exams, while the student's FSA governs listening, learning, and examination phases. The assignment of roles can follow different criteria (round-robin, profile-based, random) and is fully customizable by the World creator. Building a World requires: defining an agent class with the actions that will be available to the agents joining the World; defining the World class (a special agent), including the role-assignment logic; and a JSON file per role, describing

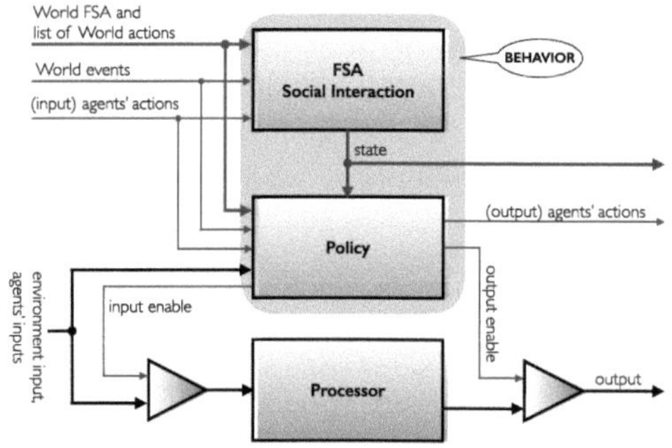


(a) Architecture of every agent. The main components are *behavior* (FSA + policy) and *processor*. The behavior controls when and how the processor is activated, and agents interact through output/input events.

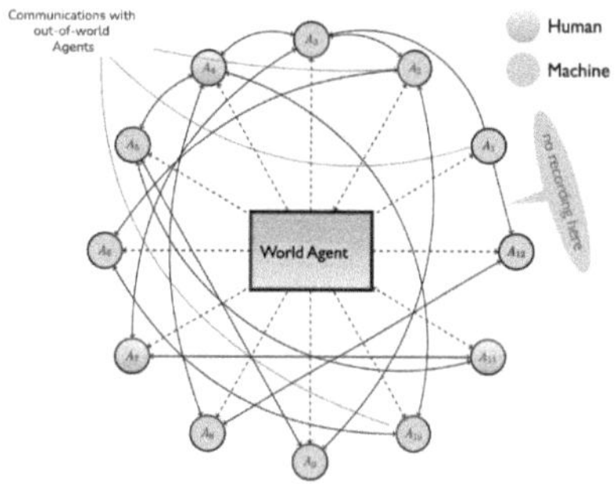


(b) A World governs humans and machines through a P2P network.

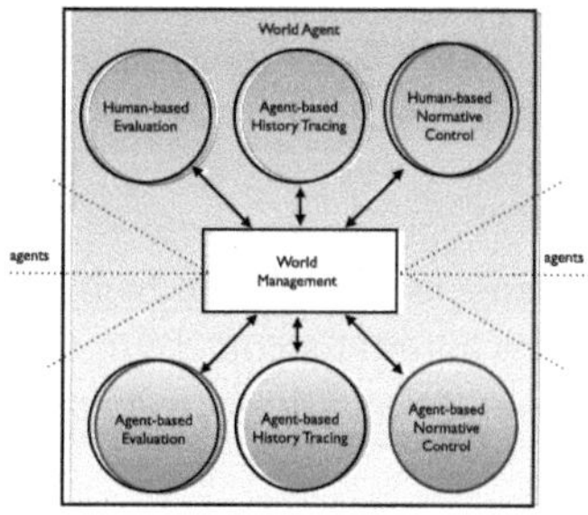


(c) Structure of the World agent, including evaluation and history.

**Fig. 2.** Agent and World architecture. (a) Structure of a UNaIVERSE agent, showing the behavior module (FSA and policy) that governs when the processor is activated. (b) A World manages a community of human and artificial agents over the P2P network. (c) Internal modules of the World agent.

the FSA for that role. In the current version of the platform, FSAs are designed by the World creator. Whether FSAs can be learned or evolved through agent interaction is an open research direction that the platform is designed to support (see Sect. 4), but is not implemented at the platform level yet. The same FSAs can also be generated programmatically from Python code.

**Interactions Among Agents.** The interaction between a pair of agents, A and B, is mediated through the FSA mechanism. When A needs something from B, it executes a special action in its own FSA that sends the request to B over the network. This request tells B which of its own actions should be executed, and B runs that action locally. When B completes the requested operation, it sends a confirmation back to A. In continual learning, it is typical to deal with multi-step actions, i.e., actions that process a stream of data samples. Learning from a stream implies that the learning action is triggered once, and it keeps consuming samples from the stream until a stopping condition is met. Prediction follows the same pattern, with the processor being called once per incoming sample until the stream ends. This convention is not enforced by the platform but is offered as a design pattern. Developers are free to structure interactions differently. The key property is that interactions are always expressed as transitions in the agents' FSAs, making them transparent and traceable. Since each agent maintains its own FSA state and executes transitions independently, the interaction mechanism scales with the number of active connections per agent rather than with the total World population. The World agent tracks membership and assigns roles but does not relay data between peers, which communicate directly over the mesh.

### 3.4 Time and Streams

**Time.** Every agent is equipped with a clock whose frequency can be customized. At each clock cycle, the agent checks network connections, processes incoming messages, and advances its FSA until a blocking configuration is reached, where an action cannot be performed because streamed data is missing, or because it is waiting for a request from another agent. This discrete-time model accommodates heterogeneous temporal granularities: an agent processing video frames may operate at a higher clock rate than one handling symbolic queries.

**Streams.** Data exchanges are virtualized through the notion of *streams*. Every agent creates streams through which the outputs of its processor are shared with connected agents, and from which inputs to the processor are taken. A stream stores only one sample at a time, which is overwritten when a new sample arrives. This design enforces an online processing discipline that is inherently aligned with the collectionless perspective: agents must process each sample as it arrives, without the ability to store and replay past data from the stream itself. Communication over the P2P network is encrypted, and every message carries an authentication token that can be verified by the recipient without contacting any server. Two types of message exchange are supported: direct messages (one-to-one) and pubsub messages (broadcasting within a World through the P2P mesh).

## 4 UNaIVERSE in Lifelong Learning Research

The design of UNaIVERSE was not driven by any single learning algorithm or benchmark, but several of its architectural properties map directly onto challenges that the lifelong learning community has identified as critical [19,42]. This section makes this mapping explicit. We stress that the paragraphs below do not claim that UNaIVERSE solves any of these problems: each one points to a research direction that the platform makes possible to study under conditions that standard benchmarks cannot reproduce.

**Non-stationarity by Construction.** In most continual learning benchmarks the distribution shifts at pre-defined task boundaries [19,44], a synthetic non-stationarity that fails to capture the gradual, multi-causal drift of real-world deployment [25]. In UNaIVERSE, non-stationarity arises organically: agents join and leave Worlds, the composition of the community changes, the data streams produced by other agents evolve as those agents learn. This form of non-stationarity is more realistic and harder to anticipate, providing a testing ground for algorithms that must cope with unpredictable distribution shifts. It thus enables what the authors of [42] called a key desideratum: moving beyond task-boundary-driven protocols toward settings where distribution change is a property of the environment, not of the experimental design.

**Open-World Conditions.** The peer-to-peer architecture naturally supports open-world settings: agents with unseen capabilities can join at any time and others can leave, so the set of tasks, classes, and partners is not fixed in advance, which is hard to simulate with static benchmarks. Mundt et al. [25] argued that open-world recognition, active learning, and continual learning are interdependent facets of one problem. UNaIVERSE realizes this vision by construction: an agent that enters a new World must simultaneously adapt to different streams (open-world recognition), eventually decide whether and how to engage and adapt its policy (active learning), and integrate new knowledge without overwriting previously acquired skills (continual learning).

**Streaming Data and Online Learning.** The stream-based data exchange in UNaIVERSE enforces an online learning discipline: every sample is consumed upon arrival and immediately overwritten. This aligns with the collectionless perspective [13] and provides a realistic protocol for evaluating forward-only learning algorithms [6,24]. The distributed communication model proposed by UNaIVERSE makes it natively suitable for studying online continual learning, a setting identified as increasingly relevant for on-device learning and real-time adaptation, yet underrepresented in the current benchmark ecosystem [42].

**Table 2.** Social learning scenario. A student with a randomly initialized CNN joins and lives in the World for a given time (50 labeled MNIST samples per class for lectures, 20 for exams, 100 unlabeled for the best student; error rate reported). Subscript $t$: teacher lectures; $b$: best-student lectures.

| Living Time ($s$) | #Lectures | Initial Error | Final Error |
|---|---|---|---|
| 90.0 | $6_t + 6_b$ | 0.93 | 0.26 |
| 180.0 | $13_t + 13_b$ | 0.93 | 0.14 |

### 4.1 Illustrative Scenarios

The scenarios presented in this section are intended as illustrations of the design space that UNaIVERSE opens for lifelong learning research (code available at https://github.com/collectionlessai/unaiverse-examples). They should not be interpreted as experimental evaluations or claims of methodological novelty. Their purpose is to show how the platform's features translate into concrete research settings that are difficult or impossible to replicate with standard benchmarks. This list is not intended to be exhaustive, and the platform is designed to support a wide range of additional scenarios.

**Social Learning.** The first scenario we consider focuses on a social learning scheme in a low-supervision regime. A TEACHER agent delivers a series of lectures, each consisting of a live stream of labeled mini-batches for classification purposes, followed by an exam. The teacher streams unlabeled mini-batches and each STUDENT agent returns its predicted labels, identifies the best-performing student and shares additional unlabeled batches with it. This student then predicts labels for the shared data and streams the resulting self-labeled batches to the other students, who learn from them. The scenario illustrates several lifelong learning themes: online learning from a stream, semi-supervised dynamics driven by social interaction, and the emergence of a knowledge hierarchy (best student becomes an auxiliary teacher). Table 2 summarizes this World on MNIST (per-class budget in the caption; teaching in 2 rounds, batch size 32). A student with a randomly initialized CNN joins and learns through sustained interaction: living there longer yields better results, and agents can join or leave asynchronously while others keep living in the World. The new agent joins a pre-existing community and improves solely through the social interactions structured by the World, without any teaching code, which is inherited when it joins. A natural next step is studying cross-World transfer in case a student agent migrates to a different World and apply its learned representations in a new context, carrying knowledge in its model parameters while adapting to a different community of peers.

**Continual, Class-Incremental Learning.** Focusing on class-incremental experiences, we propose a World where a TEACHER agent delivers lectures about three animal classes (albatross, cheetah, giraffe) from ImageNet [7]. For each class, 40 images are used for teaching and 10 disjoint images are reserved for evaluation, for a total of 120 teaching and 30 evaluation samples, streamed one class at a time across separate lectures. STUDENT agents are convolutional-network-equipped learners that learn online from the stream. After all lectures, students are evaluated on all three classes simultaneously, measuring classification error rate on the held-out evaluation set. The challenge is catastrophic forgetting: each lecture covers only one class, showing no data from the others, so agents must retain earlier knowledge without replay. Two agent configurations are compared: one with a vanilla CNN, and one whose classification head includes

Continual Neural Units [37,39], which are designed to mitigate forgetting. The best-performing student can be promoted to a new teacher role, introducing a social mechanism for knowledge consolidation and transfer.

**Collectionless Learning.** Another scenario we describe pushes toward the collectionless end of the spectrum [13], considering two variants of cases in which an agent "listens" to a data stream and is asked to learn from it on the fly. In the first variant, a TEACHER agent streams the Wikipedia definition of "cat" token by token, and a STUDENT agent must learn to reproduce the definition by predicting the next token, without backpropagation through time and without storing past tokens. The student is implemented with a linear state-space model [38] and operates in a strictly forward manner. In the second variant, agents are put to the test on the demanding task of learning from really long sequences [6]. Here the task is reformulated under the Collectionless principles and taken to the limit to obtain "Perpetual Generation" [5], where the agent is asked to learn online to track a signal, relying solely on the supervision and without input, while also being able to keep generating it after the reference signal is no longer provided. The teacher provides scalar signal examples with conditioning information, and the student learns to reproduce and generalize them (including generalizing descriptive properties such as amplitude) using a learning scheme based on Optimal Control and Hamiltonian dynamics [24]. Both scenarios illustrate a research direction native to UNaIVERSE: learning from a single stream of data, without any opportunity to revisit past samples.

## 5 Conclusions

This paper presented UNaIVERSE, a peer-to-peer platform for decentralized human-AI communities, and argued for its use in lifelong learning research, since its non-stationary, open-world, interaction-driven environments complement static benchmarks. We proposed research scenarios to inspire future work, stressing that the design space extends well beyond the cases shown here, and invite the community to contribute new Worlds. Open directions include adversarial robustness in multi-agent communities and systematic benchmarks of latency, fault tolerance, and throughput at scale, so far tested only with small communities. UNaIVERSE is open-source and the code is available at https://github.com/orgs/collectionlessai/, while the platform is live at https://unaiverse.io/.

**Acknowledgments.** This study was partly supported by the University of Siena (Piano per lo Sviluppo della Ricerca - PSR 2024, F-NEW FRONTIERS 2024), under the project "TIme-driveN StatEful Lifelong Learning" (TINSELL). The acknowledgment is extended to Rete SAIHUB (Siena, Italy), which, jointly with the Italian Ministry of University and Research (DM 117/2023, PNRR, Missione 4, Componente 2, Investimento 3.3), funded the scholarship of Christian Di Maio.

**Disclosure of Interests.** The UNaIVERSE platform described in this paper is open-source and freely available to the research community. The authors declare the following competing interest: UNaIVERSE S.r.l. is a spin-off company of the University of Siena, and all the authors of this paper are co-founders of the company. The research presented here was carried out within the authors' academic affiliations.

## References

1. Abel, D., Barreto, A., Van Roy, B., Precup, D., van Hasselt, H., Singh, S.: A definition of continual reinforcement learning. Adv. Neural Inf. Process. Syst. **36**, 50377–50407 (2023). https://doi.org/10.52202/075280-2192
2. Albrecht, J., et al.: Avalon: a benchmark for rl generalization using procedurally generated worlds. Adv. Neural. Inf. Process. Syst. **35**, 12813–12825 (2022)
3. Baker, B., et al.: Emergent tool use from multi-agent autocurricula. In: International Conference on Learning Representations (ICLR 2020) (2020). https://openreview.net/forum?id=SkxpxJBKwS
4. Bhatti, P., Shaikh, Z.A., Zaman, F.U.: Designing inclusive ai for aging populations: a conceptual agentic framework for lifelong learning. VFAST Trans. Softw. Eng. **14**(1), 90–107 (2026)
5. Casoni, M., Guidi, T., Melacci, S., Betti, A., Gori, M.: Perpetual generation: online learning of linear state-space models from a single stream. In: Senn, W., et al. (eds.) Artificial Neural Networks and Machine Learning – ICANN 2025, pp. 533–544. Springer, Cham (2026). https://doi.org/10.1007/978-3-032-04558-4_43
6. Casoni, M., Guidi, T., Tiezzi, M., Betti, A., Gori, M., Melacci, S.: Pitfalls in processing infinite-length sequences with popular approaches for sequential data. In: Suen, C.Y., Krzyzak, A., Ravanelli, M., Trentin, E., Subakan, C., Nobile, N. (eds.) Artificial Neural Networks in Pattern Recognition, pp. 37–48. Springer, Heidelberg (2024). https://doi.org/10.1007/978-3-031-71602-7_4
7. Deng, J., Dong, W., Socher, R., Li, L.J., Li, K., Fei-Fei, L.: Imagenet: a large-scale hierarchical image database. In: 2009 IEEE Conference on Computer Vision and Pattern Recognition, pp. 248–255 (2009). https://doi.org/10.1109/CVPR.2009.5206848
8. Ermis, B., Zappella, G., Wistuba, M., Rawal, A., Archambeau, C.: Memory efficient continual learning with transformers. Adv. Neural. Inf. Process. Syst. **35**, 10629–10642 (2022)
9. Fan, L., et al.: MineDojo: building open-ended embodied agents with internet-scale knowledge. Adv. Neural Inf. Process. Syst. **35**, 18343–18362 (2022). https://proceedings.neurips.cc/paper_files/paper/2022/hash/74a67268c5cc5910f64938cac4526a90-Abstract-Datasets_and_Benchmarks.html
10. Fan, S., et al.: If an LLM were a character, would it know its own story? Evaluating lifelong learning in LLMs. In: Liakata, M., Moreira, V.P., Zhang, J., Jurgens, D. (eds.) Proceedings of the 64th Annual Meeting of the Association for Computational Linguistics, vol. 1: Long Papers, pp. 35846–35858. Association for Computational Linguistics (2026). https://doi.org/10.18653/v1/2026.acl-long.1659. https://aclanthology.org/2026.acl-long.1659/
11. Georgio, R.J., Forder, C., Deb, S., Rahimov, A., Carroll, P., Gürcan, Ö.: Coral protocol: open infrastructure connecting the internet of agents (2025). https://doi.org/10.48550/arXiv.2505.00749. http://arxiv.org/abs/2505.00749

12. Gori, M., Lippi, M., Maggini, M., Melacci, S., Pelillo, M.: *En Plein Air* visual agents. In: Murino, V., Puppo, E. (eds.) ICIAP 2015. LNCS, vol. 9280, pp. 697–709. Springer, Cham (2015). https://doi.org/10.1007/978-3-319-23234-8_64
13. Gori, M., Melacci, S.: Position paper: collectionless artificial intelligence. In: 2025 International Joint Conference on Neural Networks (IJCNN), pp. 1–8. IEEE (2025). https://doi.org/10.1109/IJCNN64981.2025.11228186. https://ieeexplore.ieee.org/abstract/document/11228186
14. Hafner, D.: Benchmarking the spectrum of agent capabilities. In: International Conference on Learning Representations (ICLR 2022) (2022). https://openreview.net/forum?id=1W0z96MFEoH
15. Hong, S., et al.: MetaGPT: meta programming for a multi-agent collaborative framework. In: The Twelfth International Conference on Learning Representations, ICLR 2024, Vienna, Austria, 7–11 May 2024. OpenReview.net (2024). https://openreview.net/forum?id=VtmBAGCN7o
16. Kairouz, P.: Advances and open problems in federated learning. Found. Trends Mach. Learn. (2021)
17. Khetarpal, K., Riemer, M., Rish, I., Precup, D.: Towards continual reinforcement learning: a review and perspectives. J. Artif. Intell. Res. **75**, 1401–1476 (2022)
18. La Malfa, E., et al.: Large language models miss the multi-agent mark. Adv. Neural Inf. Process. Syst. **38** (2025). https://proceedings.neurips.cc//paper_files/paper/2025/hash/cc14cadd13ca5a13ba899cb49351c139-Abstract-Position_Paper_Track.html
19. Lange, M.D., et al.: A continual learning survey: defying forgetting in classification tasks. IEEE Trans. Pattern Anal. Mach. Intell. (2021). https://doi.org/10.1109/TPAMI.2021.3057446. http://arxiv.org/abs/1909.08383
20. Li, T., et al.: Applications of multi-agent reinforcement learning in future internet: a comprehensive survey. IEEE Commun. Surv. Tutor. **24**(2), 1240–1279 (2022). https://doi.org/10.1109/COMST.2022.3160697
21. Lică, M., Shirekar, O., Colle, B., Raman, C.: Mindforge: empowering embodied agents with theory of mind for lifelong cultural learning. In: Advances in Neural Information Processing Systems (NeurIPS 2025) (2025). https://arxiv.org/abs/2411.12977
22. Lomonaco, V., Maltoni, D.: Core50: a new dataset and benchmark for continuous object recognition. In: Levine, S., Vanhoucke, V., Goldberg, K. (eds.) Proceedings of the 1st Annual Conference on Robot Learning. Proceedings of Machine Learning Research, vol. 78, pp. 17–26. PMLR (2017)
23. Matthews, M., et al.: Craftax: a lightning-fast benchmark for open-ended reinforcement learning. In: Proceedings of the 41st International Conference on Machine Learning, vol. 235, pp. 35104–35137. PMLR (2024). https://proceedings.mlr.press/v235/matthews24a.html
24. Melacci, S., Betti, A., Casoni, M., Guidi, T., Tiezzi, M., Gori, M.: A unified framework for neural computation and learning over time. In: Proceedings of of the ECAI Workshop on Machine Learning Meets Differential Equations: From Theory to Applications, vol. 277, pp. 71–95. PMLR (2025)
25. Mundt, M., Hong, Y., Pliushch, I., Ramesh, V.: A wholistic view of continual learning with deep neural networks: forgotten lessons and the bridge to active and open world learning. Neural Netw. **160**, 306–336 (2023)
26. Pi, Y., et al.: Applications of multi-agent deep reinforcement learning communication in network management: a survey (2024). https://arxiv.org/abs/2407.17030

27. Powers, S., Xing, E., Kolve, E., Mottaghi, R., Gupta, A.: Cora: benchmarks, baselines, and metrics as a platform for continual reinforcement learning agents. In: Conference on Lifelong Learning Agents, pp. 705–743. PMLR (2022)
28. Qian, C., et al.: ChatDev: communicative agents for software development. In: Ku, L.W., Martins, A., Srikumar, V. (eds.) Proceedings of the 62nd Annual Meeting of the Association for Computational Linguistics, vol. 1: Long Papers, pp. 15174–15186. Association for Computational Linguistics (2024). https://doi.org/10.18653/v1/2024.acl-long.810. https://aclanthology.org/2024.acl-long.810/
29. Rama, B., Mei, K., Zhang, Y.: Cerebrum (AIOS SDK): a platform for agent development, deployment, distribution, and discovery. In: Proceedings of the 2025 Conference of the Nations of the Americas Chapter of the Association for Computational Linguistics: Human Language Technologies (System Demonstrations), pp. 135–142. Association for Computational Linguistics (2025). https://doi.org/10.18653/v1/2025.naacl-demo.14. https://aclanthology.org/2025.naacl-demo.14
30. Raskar, R., et al.: Beyond dns: unlocking the internet of ai agents via the nanda index and verified agentfacts. arXiv preprint arXiv:2507.14263 (2025)
31. Samvelyan, M., et al.: MiniHack the planet: a sandbox for open-ended reinforcement learning research. In: NeurIPS D&B (2021)
32. Smith, J.S., et al.: Adaptive memory replay for continual learning. In: Proceedings of the IEEE/CVF Conference on Computer Vision and Pattern Recognition, pp. 3605–3615 (2024)
33. Soltoggio, A., et al.: A collective AI via lifelong learning and sharing at the edge. Nat. Mach. Intell. **6**(3), 251–264 (2024)
34. Suarez, J., Du, Y., Isola, P., Mordatch, I.: Neural MMO: a massively multiagent game environment for training and evaluating intelligent agents (2019). https://arxiv.org/abs/1903.00784
35. Suarez, J.: The Neural MMO platform for massively multiagent research. In: NeurIPS Datasets and Benchmarks (2021)
36. Tang, S.: DeLAMA: decentralized and lifelong-adaptive multi-agent collaborative learning (2024). arXiv:2403.06535
37. Tiezzi, M., Becattini, F., Marullo, S., Melacci, S.: Memory head for pre-trained backbones in continual learning. In: Conference on Lifelong Learning Agents, pp. 179–197. PMLR (2025)
38. Tiezzi, M., Casoni, M., Betti, A., Guidi, T., Gori, M., Melacci, S.: Back to recurrent processing at the crossroad of transformers and state-space models. Nat. Mach. Intell. **7**(5), 678–688 (2025)
39. Tiezzi, M., Marullo, S., Becattini, F., Melacci, S.: Continual neural computation. In: Joint European Conference on Machine Learning and Knowledge Discovery in Databases, pp. 340–356. Springer, Heidelberg (2024). https://doi.org/10.1007/978-3-031-70344-7_20
40. Tomilin, T., et al.: Meal: a benchmark for continual multi-agent reinforcement learning. In: International Conference on Machine Learning (ICML 2026) (2026). https://arxiv.org/abs/2506.14990, to appear
41. Tziafas, G., Kasaei, H.: Lifelong robot library learning: bootstrapping composable and generalizable skills for embodied control with language models. In: 2024 IEEE International Conference on Robotics and Automation (ICRA), pp. 515–522 (2024). https://doi.org/10.1109/ICRA57147.2024.10611448
42. Verwimp, E., et al.: Continual learning: applications and the road forward. Trans. Mach. Learn. Res. (2024). https://arxiv.org/abs/2311.11908
43. Walters, S., et al.: Eliza: a Web3 friendly AI agent operating system (2025). https://doi.org/10.48550/arXiv.2501.06781. http://arxiv.org/abs/2501.06781

44. Wang, L., Zhang, X., Su, H., Zhu, J.: A comprehensive survey of continual learning: theory, method and application. IEEE Trans. Pattern Anal. Mach. Intell. **46**(8), 5362–5383 (2024)
45. Wang, R., Lehman, J., Clune, J., Stanley, K.O.: POET: open-ended coevolution of environments and their optimized solutions. In: Proceedings of the Genetic and Evolutionary Computation Conference (GECCO 2019), pp. 142–151. ACM (2019). https://doi.org/10.1145/3321707.3321799
46. Wang, Z.: Federated continual learning for edge-AI: a comprehensive survey (2024). arXiv:2411.13740
47. Wu, Q., et al.: AutoGen: enabling next-gen LLM applications via multi-agent conversations. In: First Conference on Language Modeling (COLM 2024) (2024). https://openreview.net/forum?id=BAakY1hNKS
48. Yang, X., Yu, H., Gao, X., Wang, H., Zhang, J., Li, T.: Federated continual learning via knowledge fusion: a survey. IEEE Trans. Knowl. Data Eng. **36**(8), 3832–3850 (2024)
49. Yang, Y., et al.: Twinmarket: a scalable behavioral and social simulation for financial markets. In: Advances in NeurIPS, vol. 38, pp. 63469–63519. Curran Associates (2025)
50. Yu, H.: Handling spatial-temporal data heterogeneity for federated continual learning via tail anchor. In: CVPR (2025)
51. Yuan, L., Li, L., Zhang, Z., Zhang, F., Guan, C., Yu, Y.: Multiagent continual coordination via progressive task contextualization. IEEE Trans. Neural Netw. Learn. Syst. **36**(4), 6326–6340 (2025). https://doi.org/10.1109/TNNLS.2024.3394513
52. Zheng, J., et al.: Lifelongagentbench: evaluating llm agents as lifelong learners. arXiv preprint arXiv:2505.11942 (2025)

# An Ontology-Grounded Knowledge Graph Framework for Personalized and Explainable Emotional Support in Conversational Systems

Maria Grazia Miccoli(✉), Mauro Carlucci, Berardina De Carolis, Giuseppe Palestra, and Stefano Ferilli

University of Bari, Bari, Italy
m.miccoli@phd.uniba.it

**Abstract.** In the context of user modeling and personalization, effective emotional support requires going beyond affect detection to incorporate the situational context that elicits it, in line with appraisal-based theories of emotion. This paper presents a framework for personalized emotional support in conversational systems, designed to operate across everyday and sensitive contexts. The framework models the relationships between emotions and situations, extracts emotional and contextual cues from user messages, queries an ontology-grounded knowledge graph to identify suitable coping strategies, filters them according to the user's situation, and generates empathic responses through a context-aware Large Language Model. The knowledge graph is dynamically updated with newly acquired user-related information, enabling the system to adapt over time. Unlike purely data-driven approaches, recommendations are derived from explicit knowledge and reasoning paths, enabling traceability, interpretability, and explainability, addressing a key limitation of LLM-only solutions. An application scenario illustrates the complete interaction flow, from user input to a justified coping-strategy recommendation. A persona-based evaluation, assessing appropriateness and safety of selected strategies across diverse user profiles,highlights the potential of the proposed approach for explainable and personalized emotional support, showing consistent alignment with established coping guidelines.

**Keywords:** Affective Computing · Conversational System · Knowledge Graph · Explainability · Trust

## 1 Introduction

In everyday life, emotional support plays a central role in fostering well-being and constructive coping during periods of stress or negative affect [4,6]. From a psychological perspective, emotional responses are not triggered directly by


S. Bistarelli et al. (Eds.): AIxIA 2026, LNAI 17131, pp. 438–451, 2027.
https://doi.org/10.1007/978-3-032-40774-0_32

external events, but arise from how individuals evaluate and interpret their situations. According to appraisal-based theories of emotion [3], individuals first assess the significance of a situation (*primary appraisal*) and then evaluate available resources and constraints to cope with it (*secondary appraisal*). The resulting *coping strategies*, namely cognitive, emotional, and behavioral responses to manage perceived demands [23], are deeply shaped by personal context, past experiences, and situational constraints, and cannot be meaningfully selected without modeling these factors explicitly.

Conversational agents have emerged as a promising means to deliver emotional support at scale [7,8]. Recent advances in Large Language Models (LLMs) have enabled agents capable of simulating empathic dialogue and active listening. However, existing systems largely rely on generalized text patterns or black-box generation mechanisms, offering limited transparency into *why* specific coping strategies are suggested and no guarantees about their contextual feasibility [2]. Without an explicit representation of why a situation is stressful and what resources are available, a conversational system cannot provide recommendations that are both personalized and traceable. While recent hybrid approaches combine knowledge graphs with LLM-based generation to improve the appropriateness of strategies [24,25], they rely on generic commonsense resources and do not maintain a persistent, structured model of the individual user, leaving key dimensions of personalization, safety constraints, and explainability unaddressed.

This paper addresses the following research question: *How can a conversational system deliver personalized and explainable emotional support by grounding its recommendations in an explicit, inspectable representation of the user's situation and constraints, rather than relying solely on the implicit patterns learned by a language model, while preserving conversational fluency?*

To address this question, we propose an ontology-grounded knowledge graph framework for personalized emotional support in conversational systems that advances the state of the art along four axes:

- **Longitudinal Personalization:** It instantiates a user-specific knowledge graph grounded in appraisal theory, modeling the current emotional state alongside past experiences, personal interests, and situational context, enabling long-term user tracking.
- **Operationalized Secondary Appraisal:** It maps physical symptoms and conditions as explicit semantic constraints, dynamically pruning coping strategies that are contextually inappropriate or unsafe for a given user.
- **Explainability-by-Construction:** Every recommendation corresponds to an inspectable reasoning path in the knowledge graph, which naturally supports both positive justifications and *why-not* explanations for discarded strategies.
- **Safety-Driven Architecture:** A hybrid Graph-RAG paradigm confines all decision-making within a symbolic Graph Layer under local user control, employing an LLM-as-a-Judge validation step before an external LLM generates the final response.

We validate the framework through a persona-based simulation with 50 synthetic user profiles, designed to cover diverse emotional contexts and combinations of constraints, to rigorously assess the safety and consistency of the constraint-filtering mechanism. This choice is intentional: deploying immature conversational systems to real users in sensitive emotional contexts carries concrete risks of harm. Verifying safety and reasoning correctness via simulation is a necessary ethical precondition for any future human-subject evaluation. We acknowledge that a direct quantitative comparison with LLM-only baselines on our specific pipeline remains an open direction, which we address in the discussion alongside other limitations.

The remainder of this paper is organized as follows. Section 2 reviews related work. Section 3 describes the ontology design and knowledge graph implementation. Section 4 describes the system architecture and an end-to-end conversational scenario. Section 5 discusses validation results, current limitations, and future directions.

## 2 Background and Motivation

The integration of emotional support into conversational AI requires modeling complex relationships between individual context, cognitive evaluations, and behavioral outcomes. This section contextualizes our work within the landscape of emotion ontologies and affect-aware conversational agents.

### 2.1 Ontological Modeling of Emotions and Coping

Ontologies provide a formal framework to represent affective phenomena beyond simple polarity. In their comprehensive survey, Park and Storey [17] categorize emotion ontologies into discrete, dimensional, and process-based models, highlighting a persistent lack of rich contextual structures and reusable standards. While clinical ontologies such as the Mental Health Ontology (MHO) [10] focus on diagnostic reasoning, general-purpose models often restrict emotions to isolated classification labels, as in DEGARI [14] or EmotiNet [1]. More expressive *Hybrid Process Ontologies* explicitly model the generative cycle of emotions from triggering events to behavioral intentions, as in HEO [9] and SenticNet-based frameworks [5]. Our framework positions itself within this class, while extending it along dimensions that remain underexplored in prior work.

The theoretical grounding of our emotional representation draws on Plutchik's structural model [19], which provides a principled taxonomy of primary emotions, their oppositional relations, intensity levels, and compositional combinations. Crucially, in our architecture Plutchik's categories are not used as isolated classification labels: they represent the affective outcomes of the *primary appraisal* phase in Lazarus and Folkman's framework [3], i.e., the emotional result of evaluating a situation's significance with respect to personal goals and resources. This integration anchors the emotional representation in a process-oriented theory rather than a purely taxonomic one.

For coping strategies, we adopt Lazarus and Folkman's distinction between problem-focused and emotion-focused coping [3], refined through the behavioral dimensions of the COPE-NVI inventory [22]. Alternative frameworks such as Roseman's appraisal-based emotion theory [20,21], and Haidt's moral emotion model [11] offer complementary perspectives, particularly on social and moral emotions; however, they are less directly operationalizable as actionable coping triggers in everyday support scenarios, which is the primary focus of our work. The appraisal process underlying coping activation is further informed by Kobasa's notion of hardiness [12], emphasizing commitment and perceived control as individual resources.

We note that the proposed ontology is designed as a *domain-specific* model optimized for personalized coping-strategy recommendation, rather than as a general-purpose upper ontology. Alignment with top-level ontologies, which would support broader interoperability, is left as future work. Physical symptoms and conditions are integrated as explicit semantic constraints representing the *secondary appraisal* phase [3], dynamically pruning coping recommendations based on physical viability.

### 2.2 Affect-Aware Conversational Systems

Conversational companions have increasingly been deployed to deliver automated well-being interventions. Rule-based and specialized systems such as Woebot [7] and Tess [8] leverage cognitive behavioral therapy (CBT) protocols to assist users experiencing anxiety or stress. In narrative medicine, systems such as CArEN [15] and a conversational agent for obesity prevention [18] utilize standardized coping patterns to guide user interactions.

While effective within narrow operational bounds, these agents face critical limitations from a user modeling perspective: they rely on predefined logic or black-box generative models, offering no guarantees about contextual safety and no visibility into *why* a specific coping recommendation is produced. Crucially, they do not operationalize Lazarus and Folkman's *secondary appraisal* [3], the evaluation of available options under specific physical and situational constraints, leaving a key dimension of personalized support unaddressed.

Recent work has begun to close this gap: hybrid architectures combining knowledge graphs with LLM-based generation have been shown to significantly outperform purely generative LLM baselines in strategy appropriateness and consistency [24,25]. However, these approaches rely on generic commonsense resources and do not maintain a persistent, structured model of the individual user, leaving key dimensions of longitudinal personalization, feasibility-aware filtering, and explainability unaddressed. Our framework advances this direction by introducing all four axes described in Sect. 1.

## 3 Ontology Design

The ontology is conceived as an explicit user model for emotional support: it captures how individuals experience situations, the resources they can rely on, and the constraints that limit the feasibility of coping actions. Following an incremental design process [16], development proceeds through domain definition, entity and relationship modeling, logical representation, and knowledge base implementation.

### 3.1 Domain Definition and Theoretical Grounding

The domain encompasses everyday emotionally significant situations where personalized and traceable coping recommendations are required. Emotional states are represented following Plutchik's structural model [19], which provides a principled taxonomy of emotions, intensity levels, oppositional and compositional relations. As discussed in Sect. 2, Plutchik's categories serve as the affective outcomes of the primary appraisal phase rather than as isolated classification labels.

Coping strategies operationalize Lazarus and Folkman's framework [3], distinguishing problem-focused from emotion-focused approaches, and are further characterized along the behavioral dimensions of the COPE-NVI inventory [22] (active coping, planning, distancing, self-control, assumption of responsibility, positive reappraisal). Both adaptive strategies, supporting long-term well-being, and maladaptive strategies, providing short-term relief at potential cost, are represented in the knowledge graph. Maladaptive strategies are never proactively recommended: they are retained in the graph exclusively to support *why-not* explanations and to enable the Judge-LLM to explicitly flag and suppress them during the safety validation step. The appraisal process is further informed by Kobasa's notion of hardiness [12]. Physical symptoms and conditions are modeled as explicit feasibility constraints operationalizing the secondary appraisal stage.

### 3.2 Entity and Relationship Modeling

The user model comprises eight core entities, formally specified with their attributes and value domains in Table 1: **Person**, anchor of the model; **Situation**, active emotionally significant circumstance, characterized by context and perceived threat level; **Experience**, archived past events that modulate current appraisal; **Emotion**, affective outcome of appraisal; **Coping Strategy**, adaptive or maladaptive behavioral response; **Interest**, personal preferences enabling meaningful strategy selection; **Symptom** feasibility constraint carrier, characterized by severity and chronicity; and **Condition**, higher-level context for one or more symptoms.

A key design choice is a *state-transition mechanism*: the active *Situation* node remains fixed for the duration of an interaction and, once the interaction concludes, is detached and re-instantiated as an *Experience* node, preserving longitudinal memory without overwriting the user's history and enabling the system to track recurring situational patterns over time.

Relationships operationalize the cognitive flow of appraisal and coping, as illustrated in Fig. 1. The core reasoning chain is: `Situation/Experience` → causes `Emotion` → triggers `Coping Strategy` → manages `Emotion`, with rules encoded declaratively as typed graph relations rather than as a separate rule engine. Personalization is introduced via `hasInterestIn` (linking Person to Interest, which also `triggers` strategies) and `hasExperience` (linking Person to past Experiences). Safety enforcement is governed by `reducesResourcesFor`, connecting active `Symptom` nodes to `Coping Strategy` nodes with a reduction level (partial, significant, or complete). Oppositional and compositional relations between emotions (`hasOpposite`, `composes`) support nuanced affective reasoning beyond isolated labels.

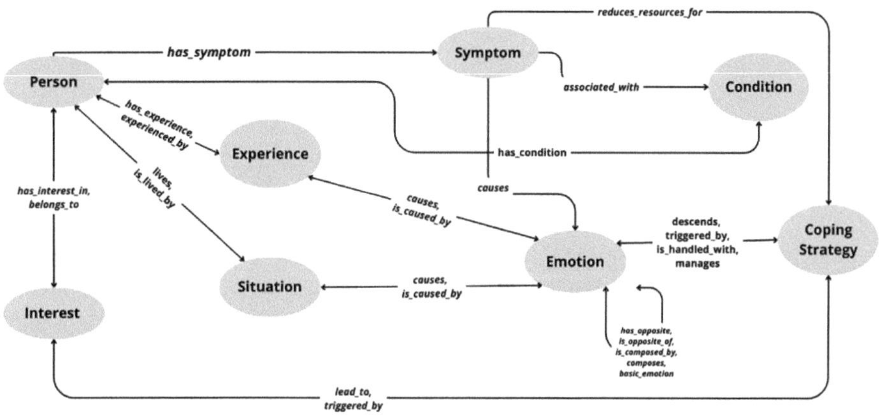


**Fig. 1.** Visual representation of the ontology structure, showing how situations, emotions, and personal context lead to coping strategies, constrained by symptoms and conditions.

### 3.3 Knowledge Base Implementation

The ontology is operationalized as a local Neo4j knowledge graph[1], which forms the core of the system's knowledge base. The graph was constructed manually by the authors, populating domain knowledge from the psychological frameworks cited in Sect. 3.1. The resulting knowledge base comprises 32 emotions (organised according to Plutchik's structural model [19], comprising 8 primary emotions, their intensity variants, and compositional combinations), 30 coping strategies (20 adaptive, 10 maladaptive), 15 symptoms, 6 conditions, 40 situations, 38 experiences, and 36 interests, connected by 263 typed relationships across 11 relation types. Graph integrity was verified through unit tests targeting node constraints and relationship propagation. User-specific nodes (Person, Situation, Experience, Symptoms, Interests) are asserted incrementally at runtime from conversational inputs. This separation between static domain knowledge and dynamic user data preserves maintainability and keeps all personal

[1] https://neo4j.com.

information under local user control. Given an emotional state and situational context, the system aggregates candidate coping strategies via three parallel graph queries: **(i) emotion-based reasoning**, retrieving adaptive strategies associated with the detected emotion; **(ii) interest-based reasoning**, mapping the user's active interests to contextually aligned coping activities; **(iii) experience- and context-aware reasoning**, retrieving strategies that proved viable in past Experiences of similar context. The union of the three result sets is filtered through active `reducesResourcesFor` edges. Strategies with a `complete` reduction level are hard-excluded from the candidate set; those with `partial` reduction level are retained but annotated with a cautionary flag. From the resulting candidate set, a strategy is selected uniformly at random and forwarded, together with its constraint parameters and any cautionary annotations inherited from the filtering step, to the safety verification layer, where the Judge-LLM [13] confirms contextual coherence before response generation. No further ranking is applied prior to this selection; the uniform random draw is a deliberate design choice to avoid over-fitting recommendations to a narrow subset of strategies. Note that randomness is confined to the final selection among an already personalized and safety-filtered candidate set, not to the personalization or safety mechanisms themselves. Safety enforcement is fully delegated to the deterministic symbolic layer: the Judge-LLM operates exclusively over a pre-filtered candidate set from which harmful strategies have already been removed, and cautionary-flagged strategies are surfaced to the user with an explicit contextual warning.

## 4 Application Scenario and Interaction Flow

The ontology-driven user model is operationalized within a Python-based conversational framework that decouples deterministic symbolic decision-making from linguistic realization. The system integrates the local Neo4j knowledge graph with `Gemini-2.0-Flash`[2], accessed via its free-tier API, for natural language processing tasks. Gemini-2.0-Flash was selected for its low-latency generation, support for structured JSON-schema output constraints, and suitability for academic prototyping without requiring specialized infrastructure. The LLM is invoked with temperature set to 0 for all extraction and validation tasks, ensuring deterministic structured outputs; temperature is set to 0.7 for the final empathetic response generation. The same model is retained for the Judge role for consistency with the extraction layer and for its reliable structured JSON output under low-temperature settings, which simplifies schema validation of the safety assessment. An architectural overview is provided in Fig. 2.

### 4.1 Conversational Agent Architecture

User interaction initiates via free-text input. The execution pipeline flows through four sequential layers:

[2] https://cloud.google.com/vertex-ai/generative-ai/docs/models/gemini/2-0-flash.

**Table 1.** Ontology entities with attributes and admissible value domains. The eight *context categories* used across Situation, Experience, and Interest were selected pragmatically to cover common everyday domains, rather than derived from a formal context taxonomy

| Entity | Attributes | Value domains |
|---|---|---|
| Person | id, name, age, origin, gender, gender identity, sexual orientation, religion, job role, political orientation | – |
| Experience | description, context, emotional load | *context* ∈ {academic, work, family, romantic, friendship, health, leisure, other}; *load* ∈ {positive, negative, neutral, traumatic} |
| Situation | description, context, perceived threat level | *context* ∈ {academic, work, family, romantic, friendship, health, leisure, other}; *threat* ∈ {low, medium, high} |
| Emotion | name, intensity level | *intensity* ∈ {low, medium, high} |
| Coping Strategy | description, focus, type, induced behavior | *focus* ∈ {problem, emotion}; *type* ∈ {adaptive, maladaptive}; *behavior* ∈ {active coping, planning, distancing, self-control, assumption of responsibility, positive reassessment} |
| Symptom | name, severity, chronicity | *severity* ∈ {mild, moderate, severe}; *chronicity* ∈ {acute, chronic} |
| Condition | name, category | *category* ∈ {physical, psychological, other} |
| Interest | description, context | *context* ∈ {sporting, relational-social, family, work, academic, leisure, art-culture, technology, other} |

1. **Information Extraction Layer.** The raw user message is processed by the LLM under strict JSON-schema constraints, extracting: active emotional states and intensity, context-bound situations and perceived threat level, physical symptoms when articulated, and relevant interests or past experiences.The extraction prompt explicitly enumerates the ontology's entity types and value domains, constraining the LLM's output space to valid cate-

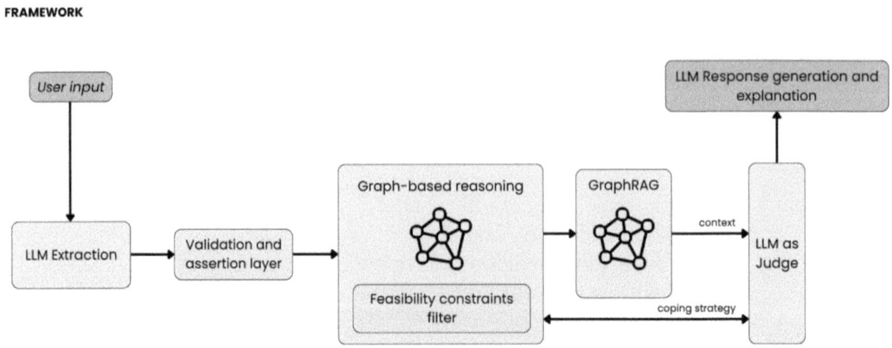


**Fig. 2.** Architecture of the ontology-grounded conversational framework, illustrating LLM-based extraction, graph-based reasoning with feasibility constraints, GraphRAG grounding, and safety-aware response generation with an end-to-end example.

gories rather than free-form labels. Outputs are validated against the ontology schema before assertion; extraction failures (e.g., missing required fields or out-of-domain values) trigger a clarification request to the user rather than propagating malformed data downstream.

2. **Graph Ingestion Layer.** Validated entities are incrementally asserted into the local Neo4j graph. If an active *Situation* node already exists, it is detached and re-instantiated as an *Experience* node, preserving longitudinal memory under local user control. Crucially, only structured semantic payloads (not raw user messages) are transmitted to the external LLM, limiting exposure of sensitive personal content to the API.
3. **Deterministic Reasoning Layer.** Candidate coping strategies are aggregated via the three parallel graph pathways described in Sect. 3.3 and filtered through active `reducesResourcesFor` constraints, which hard-exclude unsafe strategies and annotate partially constrained ones. All decision-making at this stage is entirely local and deterministic.
4. **Safety Verification and Generation Layer.** A GraphRAG pipeline packages the selected strategies, blocked alternatives with their constraint parameters, and a structured reasoning trace into a prompt payload for an LLM-as-a-Judge [13] component. The Judge evaluates the selected strategy against the user's full contextual profile (explicitly considering active symptoms, conditions, and sensitive personal attributes as guardrails) and verifies its contextual coherence. Where cautionary flags are present, the Judge determines whether to surface the strategy accompanied by an appropriate warning. Since all unsafe strategies have already been deterministically excluded at the reasoning layer, the Judge's role is coherence verification and tone calibration, not safety filtering. The validated strategy then proceeds to response generation, where the LLM produces the final empathetic and explainable natural language response.

### 4.2 End-to-End Interaction Flow

Consider a user reporting work-related stress: *"Today I feel really anxious, I have too much to do at work."* The extraction layer produces: `Emotion = anxiety (intensity = high)`; `Situation = "work overload" (context = work, threat = high)`; `Experience = previous deadline pressure (context = work, load = negative)`; `Interest = "writing" (context = leisure)`. The reasoning layer activates three pathways: high-intensity anxiety maps to adaptive strategies such as *Deep Breathing*; the leisure interest maps writing to *Journaling*; the archived work experience maps recurring stress to *Time Management Planning*. No feasibility constraints are active, so all three candidates are forwarded to the Judge-LLM, which validates them; strategies, such as *Go For A Run*, are absent from this candidate set as they are not linked to the active interest or experience paths in this scenario, not because they are unsafe. The generation module produces:

> *"I'm sorry you're feeling overwhelmed at work. Because this situation is causing strong anxiety and you enjoy writing, journaling could help you organise your thoughts and regain focus. If you'd like, we can also look at other ways to manage your workload."*

In contrast, consider the same user reporting the same work-related stress, but with an added health dimension: *"Today I feel really anxious, I have too much to do at work. On top of that, I've had a terrible headache all day from staring at the screen, and I think I'm running a fever."* The extraction layer additionally identifies: `Symptom = headache (severity = moderate, chronic = false)`; `Symptom = mild fatigue (severity = mild, chronic = false)`. The active `reducesResourcesFor` edges associated with these symptoms apply `complete` exclusions to physically demanding strategies such as *Go for a run* and *Reorganise your workspace*. Cognitively intensive alternatives such as *Make a to-do list* and *Time Management Planning* are retained in the candidate set but annotated with a significant cautionary flag, as sustained concentration may worsen the headache. The feasible candidate set therefore includes *Listen to calming music*, *Meditate for 10 min*, and *Talk to a therapist* as unconstrained candidates, alongside *Make a to-do list* and *Time Management Planning* as flagged alternatives. A strategy is selected uniformly at random from the full set and forwarded to the Judge-LLM, which validates the selection. So the generation module produces:

> *"I'm sorry you're feeling so overwhelmed, and I can imagine how much harder everything feels when you're also dealing with a headache and a fever. Rather than pushing through more tasks, I'd suggest listening to some calming music for a few minutes — it requires no effort and can help ease both the anxiety and the physical tension. Please also make sure to rest; your body is telling you it needs a break."*

The contrast between the two cases illustrates the core contribution of the framework: the same situational context produces different candidate sets and different responses depending on the user's active health constraints, with safety enforcement operating deterministically at the graph level before any language generation occurs.

### 4.3 Validation and Performance

To verify functional correctness, safety enforcement, and reasoning robustness prior to any human deployment, the framework was evaluated on 50 synthetic user personas. Each profile was instantiated with a randomized configuration of one to three physical symptoms drawn from the 15-symptom ontology, covering both acute and chronic severity levels, and spanning all eight situational contexts.

The validation protocol targeted two dimensions: (i) *graph integrity*, unit tests verified that relationships among symptoms, conditions, and coping strategies were correctly instantiated and that the `reducesResourcesFor` edges propagated constraint signals correctly; (ii) *safety layer robustness*, a dedicated suite of 20 scenarios (10 safe and 10 unsafe) evaluated the Judge-LLM's ability to intercept unsafe or hallucinated advice. Coherence Frequency, defined as:

$$\text{Coherence Frequency} = \frac{\text{Correct Classifications}}{\text{Total Scenarios}} \times 100\%$$

yielding a Coherence Frequency of 85%, above the 80% acceptability threshold established for the prototype stage. A finer-grained characterization of error types and an independent validation of the Judge-LLM against human-annotated ground truth are left to future work.

Across all 50 test cases, the reasoning engine correctly excluded every strategy contraindicated by active symptoms. We note that, given the deterministic nature of the reasoning engine and the manually validated graph structure, full constraint adherence is an expected property of a correctly implemented system rather than an empirical discovery; the value of this evaluation lies in verifying the absence of implementation bugs and confirming the correct propagation of constraint signals across the full persona space. Notably, several personas were deliberately instantiated with symptom combinations severe enough to block all graph candidates, verifying that in such cases the system correctly returns no recommendation rather than hallucinating unsafe alternatives. Out-of-domain entities surfacing during extraction (i.e., values not present in the graph at query time) are intercepted by the schema validator and either rejected or asserted as new nodes, ensuring that the reasoning layer always operates on a consistent graph state.

As a representative example, a persona characterized by extreme fatigue and psychomotor retardation (User 14), when queried for sadness management, correctly received *"Write in a journal"* rather than physically demanding alternatives such as *"Go for a run"* or *"Reorganise your workspace"*, which were blocked by active `reducesResourcesFor` edges with severity `complete`.

Graph query latency remained consistently below 20 ms on consumer hardware (AMD Ryzen 7 4800H, 16 GB RAM), confirming that the symbolic reasoning layer introduces negligible overhead for real-time conversational interaction.

We acknowledge two limitations of this evaluation. First, the 50-persona simulation was deliberately scoped to verify functional correctness and safety enforcement rather than recommendation quality; it does not quantitatively measure personalization quality, perceived empathy, user trust or long-term engagement beyond feasibility filtering; a comparison against LLM-only baselines on strategy appropriateness metrics is left to future work, where the empirical advantage of hybrid approaches documented in the literature [24,25] will be verified on our specific pipeline. Second, the evaluation does not involve real users; as stated in Sect. 1, this is an intentional precondition for safe deployment, prioritizing verification of system stability before any human-subject exposure, rather than an oversight.

## 5 Discussion and Conclusion

This work introduces a hybrid, knowledge-driven framework for explicit user modeling in emotional support conversational systems. By grounding an ontology in appraisal theory and instantiating it as a persistent, user-specific knowledge graph, the architecture moves beyond surface-level affect classification toward contextualized, multi-path reasoning over emotions, situations, past experiences, interests, and physical constraints. Unlike purely generative approaches, every recommendation and every exclusion of infeasible alternatives is deterministically traceable to explicit paths within the knowledge graph, establishing explainability-by-construction and enabling structural *why-not* explanations prior to natural language generation. The state-transition mechanism, by which active `Situation` nodes are archived as `Experience` nodes once fixed for the duration of an interaction, further supports coherent longitudinal memory and the detection of recurring situational patterns over time.

*Ethical Considerations.* Sensitive personal attributes (gender identity, sexual orientation, religion, political orientation) are modeled exclusively as guardrails for the Judge LLM, preventing stereotyping responses without influencing strategy selection. All personal data remains stored locally; the external LLM receives only structured semantic payloads. Future deployment with real users would require ethics review and informed consent.

*Limitations and Future Work.* Several limitations remain. Reliance on an external LLM for extraction, also reused for judging, introduces correlated misclassification risk only partly mitigated by schema validation, while the final generation step remains susceptible to instruction-following failures despite acting on a pre-validated strategy. Context categories (Table 1) were chosen pragmatically rather than grounded in a formal taxonomy, and the ontology's current scale may limit coverage of less common situational or clinical profiles. Evaluation was limited to simulated constraint adherence, deferring recommendation appropriateness, empathic quality, user trust, and longitudinal consistency to planned human studies; the Neo4j Community Edition deployment also lacks multi-user clustering, and alignment with top-level ontologies is left open. Future work will replace the external LLM with lightweight task-specific components, benchmark against LLM-only baselines on appropriateness and safety violation rates [24,25], run empirical studies on empathy and trust, and extend the ontology to wider contextual and multi-modal inputs.

**Acknowledgments.** We acknowledge partial financial support under the National Recovery and Resilience Plan, Mission 4, Component 2, Investment 1.1, Call for tender No. 1409 published on 14.9.2022 by the Italian Ministry of University and Research (MUR), funded by the European Union – NextGenerationEU– Project Title SISTER – CUP No.: H53D23010440001 - Grant Assignment Decree No. P2022K5WFC.

**Disclosure of Interests.** The authors have no competing interests to declare that are relevant to the content of this article.

## References

1. Balahur, A., Hermida, J.M., Montoyo, A.: Building and exploiting emotinet, a knowledge base for emotion detection based on the appraisal theory model. IEEE Trans. Affect. Comput. **3**(1), 88–101 (2011)
2. Bickmore, T.W., Picard, R.W.: Establishing and maintaining long-term human-computer relationships. ACM Trans. Comput.-Hum. Interact. (TOCHI) **12**(2), 293–327 (2005)
3. Biggs, A., Brough, P., Drummond, S.: Lazarus and Folkman's psychological stress and coping theory. In: The Handbook of Stress and Health: A Guide to Research and Practice, pp. 349–364 (2017)
4. Burleson, B.R.: Emotional support skills. In: Handbook of Communication and Social Interaction Skills, pp. 569–612. Routledge (2003)
5. Cambria, E., Grassi, M., Hussain, A., Havasi, C.: Sentic computing for social media marketing. Multimedia Tools Appl. **59**(2), 557–577 (2012)
6. Cohen, S., Wills, T.A.: Stress, social support, and the buffering hypothesis. Psychol. Bull. **98**(2), 310 (1985)
7. Fitzpatrick, K.K., Darcy, A., Vierhile, M.: Delivering cognitive behavior therapy to young adults with symptoms of depression and anxiety using a fully automated conversational agent (Woebot): A randomized controlled trial. JMIR Mental Health **4**(2), e19 (2017). https://doi.org/10.2196/mental.7785
8. Fulmer, R., Joerin, A., Gentile, B., Lakerink, L., Rauws, M.: Using psychological artificial intelligence (Tess) to relieve symptoms of depression and anxiety: randomized controlled trial. JMIR Mental Health **5**(4), e64 (2018). https://doi.org/10.2196/mental.9782
9. Grassi, M.: Developing HEO human emotions ontology. In: Fierrez, J., Ortega-Garcia, J., Esposito, A., Drygajlo, A., Faundez-Zanuy, M. (eds.) BioID 2009. LNCS, vol. 5707, pp. 244–251. Springer, Heidelberg (2009). https://doi.org/10.1007/978-3-642-04391-8_32
10. Hadzic, M., Chen, M., Dillon, T.S.: Towards the mental health ontology. In: IEEE International Conference on Bioinformatics and Biomedicine, pp. 284–288. IEEE (2008)
11. Haidt, J., et al.: The moral emotions. Handb. Affect. Sci. **11**(2003), 852–870 (2003)
12. Kobasa, S.C.: Stressful life events, personality, and health: an inquiry into hardiness. J. Pers. Soc. Psychol. **37**(1), 1 (1979)

13. Li, H., et al.: LLMs-as-judges: a comprehensive survey on LLM-based evaluation methods (2024). https://arxiv.org/abs/2412.05579
14. Lieto, A., Pozzato, G.L., Zoia, S., Patti, V., Damiano, R.: A commonsense reasoning framework for explanatory emotion attribution, generation and re-classification. Knowl.-Based Syst. **227**, 107166 (2021)
15. Miccoli, M.G., De Carolis, B.N., Palestra, G., Toma, A.: Enhancing digital narrative medicine through emotion analysis in conversational agents. In: Proceedings of the 33rd ACM Conference on User Modeling, Adaptation and Personalization, pp. 290–294 (2025)
16. Noy, N.F., McGuinness, D.L., et al.: Ontology development 101: a guide to creating your first ontology. Technical Report. KSL-01-05, Stanford Knowledge Systems Laboratory (2001)
17. Park, E.H., Storey, V.C.: Emotion ontology studies: a framework for expressing feelings digitally and its application to sentiment analysis. ACM Comput. Surv. **55**(9) (2023). https://doi.org/10.1145/3555719
18. Perla, L., et al.: Creating narrative-based adaptive learning environments for health: an exploratory study on AI conversational agents for obesity prevention. Sport e Didattica Inclusiva **9**(1), (2025). Giornale Italiano di Educazione alla Salute
19. Plutchik, R.: The multifactor-analytic theory of emotion. J. Psychol. **50**(1), 153–171 (1960)
20. Roseman, I.J.: Appraisal determinants of emotions: constructing a more accurate and comprehensive theory. Cogn. Emot. **10**(3), 241–278 (1996)
21. Roseman, I.J.: A model of appraisal in the emotion system. In: Appraisal Processes in Emotion: Theory, Methods, Research, pp. 68–91 (2001)
22. Sica, C., et al.: Coping orientation to problems experienced-nuova versione italiana (COPE-NVI): uno strumento per la misura degli stili di coping. Psicoterapia Cognitiva e Comportamentale **14**(1), 27 (2008)
23. Wechsler, B.: Coping and coping strategies: a behavioural view. Appl. Anim. Behav. Sci. **43**(2), 123–134 (1995)
24. Yang, H., Hong, J., Jo, S., Oh, H.: Sage: self-retrieval-augmented generative llm for emotional support conversation. Expert Syst. Appl. **313**, 131524 (2026)
25. Zhong, L., et al.: Cognitive policy-driven llm for diagnosis and intervention of cognitive distortions in emotional support conversation. arXiv preprint arXiv:2604.17178 (2026)

# Rob-LAPI(S)$^2$: Robotic Language-to-Action Planning via Iterative Schema Synthesis

Emanuele Musumeci[1(✉)], Abdel Hakim Drid[2], Daniele Nardi[1], and Vincenzo Suriani[1]

[1] Sapienza University of Rome, Rome, Italy
{musumeci,nardi,suriani}@diag.uniroma1.it
[2] Mohamed Khider University of Biskra, Biskra, Algeria
abdelhakim.drid@univ-biskra.dz

**Abstract.** Translating natural language (NL) instructions into formal symbolic plans is a fundamental challenge in AI planning. While Large Language Models (LLMs) offer language understanding, benchmarks show that 96% of LLM-generated PDDL parses correctly yet only 25% is semantically valid, revealing a gap between syntactic fluency and semantic correctness that external validators alone cannot close. We introduce Rob-LAPI(S)$^2$, a domain-agnostic pipeline that iteratively elicits and refines PDDL domain and problem files from NL, guided by symbolic validator diagnostics and static reachability analysis, without injecting any ground-truth structured knowledge. We evaluate Rob-LAPI(S)$^2$ on seven standard IPC planning domains, reaching 96% average symbolic validity and 73% ground-truth executability under simulator-grounded evaluation, a systematic *validation gap* that reveals the limits of formal self-consistency as a proxy for real executability. On household benchmarks (VirtualHome, AlfWorld) it achieves 90% and 55% task success from purely NL. Code: https://github.com/EmanueleMusumeci/Rob-LAPIS.

**Keywords:** PDDL synthesis · LLM planning · neuro-symbolic planning · task planning

## 1 Introduction

Autonomous planning agents operating exclusively over natural language (NL) specifications face a critical issue: in complex settings where tacit knowledge is required to correctly reconstruct the planning domain, a representation gap emerges between planning self-consistency and real-world executability of the computed plan. For example, a household service robot told to *"put the mug in the fridge"* must locate the mug, plan a navigation and manipulation sequence, and execute it. Even in this trivial case, the planning domain has to explicitly represent the robot's capabilities and the environment's affordances so that the resulting actions are both formally sound and physically realizable. Classical


S. Bistarelli et al. (Eds.): AIxIA 2026, LNAI 17131, pp. 452–465, 2027.
https://doi.org/10.1007/978-3-032-40774-0_33

planners handle such problems once the domain is formally specified; the bottleneck is translating verbal instructions and perceived states into a symbolic description a planner can accept. Direct LLM-as-planner approaches sacrifice formal correctness [25]: reliable self-verification requires external validators [8].

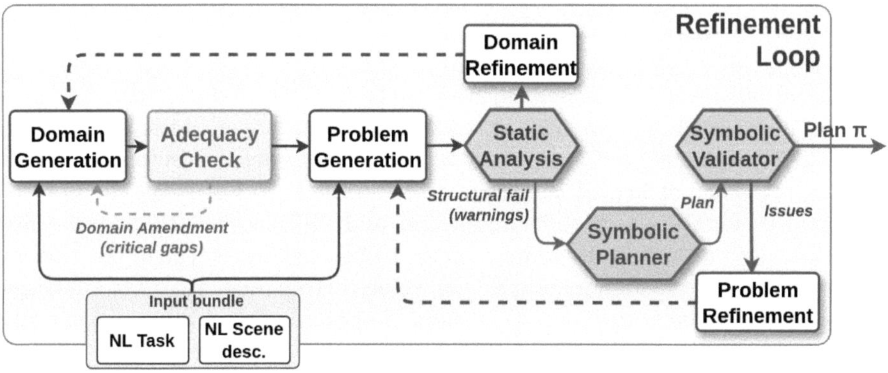


**Fig. 1.** The Rob-LAPI(S)$^2$ neuro-symbolic grounding loop. NL task and scene descriptions are synthesized into formal PDDL models (domain $\mathcal{D}$ and problem $\mathcal{P}$) by an LLM. The problem's `:init` block is derived from the scene description and *locked* during refinement: only predicate definitions and action schemas are amended. A symbolic backend (FastDownward/VAL) and $h^2$ static analysis provide iterative feedback, ensuring the final plan is formally sound.

Rob-LAPI(S)$^2$ takes a different path: assuming the robot's *action domain* is implicitly known (e.g., as a fixed skill repertoire or a NL description of the available environment affordances), an LLM can synthesize the *problem* file from verbal instructions and scene descriptions. Using NL as an intermediate representation modality (i.e. between the simulated environment and the LLM) keeps the system compatible with various perception frameworks. Our pipeline adds a metacognitive refinement loop: the LLM reads diagnostic traces from symbolic validators, identifies logical errors, and auto-regressively corrects the symbolic model until a valid plan is found. We evaluate **Rob-LAPI(S)$^2$** across seven standard IPC domains and two benchmarks in the household service robotics domain, VirtualHome and AlfWorld. Closing the loop between LLM synthesis and symbolic validation lets Rob-LAPI(S)$^2$ ground task plans in embodied environments. Contributions:

- **A general NL-to-PDDL synthesis pipeline.** Rob-LAPI(S)$^2$ iteratively elicits and refines PDDL domain and problem files from NL, guided by symbolic validation and static reachability analysis. It is domain-agnostic.
- **Validation gap.** An empirical characterisation of the gap between symbolic self-consistency and ground-truth executability across IPC and household benchmarks; on VirtualHome and AlfWorld the pipeline reaches parity with

ground-truth-domain baselines without expert-authored PDDL, surpassing them on individual task types.

Implementation available at https://github.com/EmanueleMusumeci/Rob-LAPIS.

## 2 Background

A *classical planning task* is defined as a tuple $\Pi = \langle F, A, I, G \rangle$, where $F$ is a finite set of propositions (*fluents*), $A$ is a set of *actions*, $I \subseteq F$ is the initial state, and $G \subseteq F$ is the assigned goal. Each action $a \in A$ is defined by preconditions $pre(a) \subseteq F$, a set of logical conjuncts to be evaluated as true on the current state in order for the action to be applicable, and effects $\mathit{eff}(a)$, partitioned into $\mathit{eff}^+(a)$, which correspond to adding fluents to be considered true in the current state after executing action $a$ and $\mathit{eff}^-(a)$ which corresponds instead to subtracting them. A *plan* $\pi = \langle a_1, \ldots, a_n \rangle$ is *valid* if applying the actions sequentially from $I$ yields a state $s_n \supseteq G$, with each $a_i$ applicable in its predecessor state.

In the Planning Domain Definition Language (PDDL) [14], a planning task is specified by two constructs: a *domain* $\mathcal{D}$ that declares types, predicates, and action schemas with lifted parameters, and a *problem* $\mathcal{P}$ that declares objects, the initial state $I$, and goal $G$. Given $\mathcal{D}$ and $\mathcal{P}$, a planner grounds the schemas into proposition-level actions and searches for $\pi$. A symbolic validator independently checks that $\pi$ is valid with respect to $\mathcal{D}$ and $\mathcal{P}$, or analyzes the input constructs to identify grounding or formal issues (i.e. syntax errors).

Rob-LAPI(S)$^2$ addresses the problem of correctly synthesizing a PDDL domain and problem from a NL specification: given an input NL task $t$ and a scene description $s$, produce $\mathcal{D}$ and $\mathcal{P}$ such that a classical planner can find a valid plan $\pi$. This requires bridging ambiguous linguistic descriptors and the strict predicate logic requirements of PDDL.

## 3 Related Work

**PDDL Synthesis.** Translating NL into formal PDDL bridges informal requirements with classical planning [4]. Direct LLM-as-planner approaches, which auto-regressively emit action sequences, produce plans that read plausibly but often contain misnamed symbols or actions with no counterpart in the domain. Planetarium [25] quantified this gap: 96% of LLM-generated PDDL parses, yet only 25% is semantically valid; LLM-Modulo [8] argues LLMs cannot reliably self-verify without external sound verifiers. Neuro-symbolic pipelines therefore elicit an intermediate formal model before grounding a plan: NL2Plan [3] uses a 6-step extraction to synthesize domain and problem from minimal text; LLM+P [13] assumes a ground-truth domain and translates instructions into problem files; ISR-LLM [24] refines problems against ground-truth domains under validator feedback; Planning in the Dark [7] avoids expert intervention via a schema library and semantic validation. Others translate first to Answer

Set Programming before compiling to PDDL, or apply multi-agent validator feedback [10]. Tooling [23] and a recent survey [21] reflect a growing ecosystem, and formal validators remain critical for robust deployment [22].

**Language Models in Robot Task Planning.** In embodied settings the additional challenge is grounding language into environments with a varied range of affordances. SayCan [1] grounds action proposals in pre-trained robotic affordances; Code-as-Policies [12] generates executable Python for embodied control. Neither yields formal PDDL that a classical planner can verify or optimise [5]. In household simulators [18,19], modular methods such as BUTLER [16] and FILM [17] generalize across tasks but rely on black-box policies or hardcoded heuristics rather than synthesising symbolic models. Recent neuro-symbolic work includes Thought of Search [9], which has LLMs write Python search code, and PDDL2NL [20], which runs in the opposite direction, converting PDDL to NL for the LLM to solve. Rob-LAPI(S)$^2$ instead extracts the full symbolic model, domain and problem, from the environment's NL state, with symbolic validation guiding autoregressive refinement through VAL [6].

## 4 Methodology

We formalize PDDL synthesis as finding a mapping $f : (t, s) \to (\mathcal{D}, \mathcal{P})$ solvable by a classical planner. From the two NL inputs, a task instruction $t$ and a scene description $s$, a normalized entity inventory is extracted to align with the simulator's symbolic state; in a realistic deployment this description would come from a vision-language perception layer. The pipeline is shown in Fig. 1. Both $\mathcal{D}$ and $\mathcal{P}$ are generated from NL that captures preconditions and effects semantically, without exposing predicate names or type signatures. Scene descriptions are short, third-person factual assertions, not free-form narrative:

> *"The agent is currently in the bedroom. In the home office, there is a couch with a television and a remote control nearby. The couch is positioned next to the television, and the remote control is resting by the couch. The television is plugged in but switched off. The television appears clean."*

**Adequacy Check.** Verifies that the generated domain has the expressive power to represent the observed world. It uses a 3-step Chain-of-Thought: *predicate extraction* lists the predicate signatures of $\mathcal{D}$; *observation mapping* matches each observed fact in $s$ against them, classifying gaps as *Critical* (required for planning) or *Irrelevant* (visual or spatial detail); *domain amendment* then adds any missing predicates to $\mathcal{D}$ and re-starts synthesis. Following this, a *schema-injection* step then extracts type, predicate, and constant definitions from $\mathcal{D}$ and injects them into the problem-generation prompt. This prevents predicate hallucination and type mismatches without flooding the prompt.

**Static Analysis.** Given $\mathcal{D}$ and $\mathcal{P}$, a static analysis gate detects problems guaranteed to be unsolvable through three failure modes: *unfixable preconditions*, required by actions but produced by no effect; *unreachable actions*, whose preconditions cannot be satisfied from $I$ and the effect graph; and *missing goal support*, where no effect can satisfy a goal fluent. These three checks are realised by the CPDDL $h^2$ reachability analysis [2]; if an unsolvable state is identified, the specific unreachable preconditions are included in the refinement prompt. Warnings from this analysis are passed to the Domain Refinement step, as shown in Fig. 1, and activate corrective components of the refinement prompts. Static analysis presupposes a syntactically well-formed model: it operates on the parsed domain and problem, so a specification that fails to parse is routed directly to refinement on the parser's own diagnostic.

The adequacy check identifies *predicate coverage gaps*: properties observable in the scene that cannot be expressed with the current predicate set. These gaps are definitional shortcomings of the domain, not of the initial-state description: adding a missing predicate requires amending the domain's `(:predicates)` block (and potentially the affected action schemas), not the problem file. Furthermore, the `:init` lock (see Sect. 4) explicitly forbids additions to the initial state unless they are grounded in the scene description, so amending the problem is not a valid response to a coverage gap.

**Symbolic Refinement.** If static analysis raises no warning, the system proceeds to plan generation. On planner failure the *symbolic validator* identifies syntax problems and its diagnostics are passed to Problem Refinement; Rob-LAPI(S)$^2$ collects errors and warnings into structured feedback over a predefined number of refinement cycles, each inner iteration run up to 3 times until validation succeeds. Diagnoses identifying domain-level errors in the FastDownward log trigger *Domain Refinement* first, so the correction budget is not spent on a structurally invalid domain. We use UnifiedPlanning [15] to parse PDDL and interface with the backends. The problem's initial state is locked in the prompt: the LLM may not add facts to `:init` unless supported by the environment description, preventing it from "solving" errors by hallucinating world-state shortcuts, a main cause of failure. The ground-truth simulator is consulted only after the refinement loop (Sect. 5), except in the Sim-Rob-LAPI(S)$^2$ configuration described next.

**Ground-Truth Evaluation.** To separate semantic errors from symbol name mismatches with the ground-truth simulator, we introduce an oracled scenario, *Sim-Rob-LAPI(S)*$^2$ (Table 1, last column), which grounds the problem's object inventory and initial state directly in the simulator's state, and replays every VAL-valid plan against the simulator *inside* the refinement loop, feeding any validation error back as a diagnostic. The domain is still synthesized, so this isolates semantic divergence from naming mismatch. Every other configuration skips this binding, which is why they report 0% ground-truth runnability: a naming failure, not a physical-plausibility one (Fig. 2).

(a) AlfWorld: Initial State (b) AlfWorld: Heating Object (c) AlfWorld: Goal Achieved

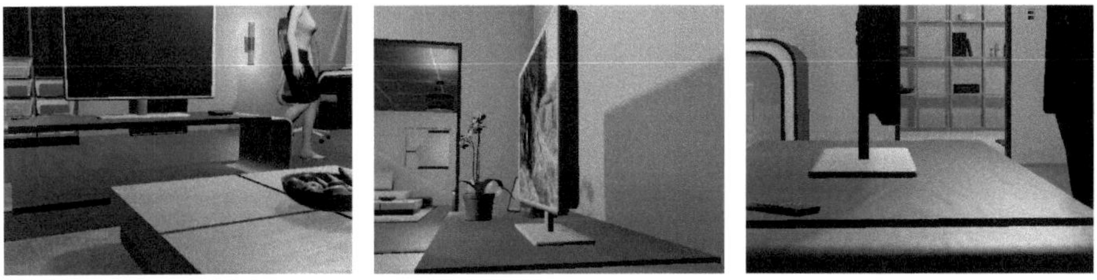

(d) VirtualHome: Initial State (e) VirtualHome: Turning on TV (f) VirtualHome: Goal Achieved

**Fig. 2.** Key frames from successful executions in AlfWorld and VirtualHome. Rob-LAPI(S)$^2$ synthesizes the planning domain and problem from NL descriptions and executes the resulting plans in the AlfWorld ((a), (b) and (c)) and VirtualHome ((d), (e) and (f)) simulated environments.

**Prompting.** Generation prompts include explicit constraints (to improve compatibility with the symbolic backends), requiring hierarchical types to be avoided and effects to remain pure STRIPS, while enforcing the exact predicate signatures and object identifiers from the schema-injection step. The `:init` lock policy is enforced as an explicit prompt clause forbidding additions to `(:init)` and any modifications made by the LLM to the init block are restricted to a predefined list of allowed objects. Prompts differ by stage: domain generation sees only the NL description of the entities, their states and relations, and the goals, with no ground-truth PDDL shown unless an experiment explicitly targets problem generation alone; problem generation additionally receives the generated domain (or the ground-truth domain where the experiment requires it) and a normalized entity inventory; refinement reuses these inputs augmented with planner and validator diagnostics, static-analysis output, and the LLM's previous PDDL.

**Spatial Relation Disambiguation.** Spatial predicates such as `inside`, `next-to`, and `on-top-of` carry structurally distinct argument roles depending on whether the subject is a character or an object (e.g., a character can be *inside* a room, while an object is *on-top-of* a surface). When the domain is synthesized from NL, separate LLM calls for domain and problem generation can independently choose different predicate argument orders, causing *domain/problem predicate drift*. To address this without injecting ground-truth schemas, the NL description is augmented with a disambiguation paragraph that clarifies which participant fills which role, and the problem generation and refinement prompts include an explicit rule requiring that only declared predicate names and signatures are used.

**Embodied environment identifier normalization.** Some environments encode auxiliary information (e.g., object coordinates) directly in symbolic identifiers, making them opaque to NL-based generation. In such cases, the pipeline strips the auxiliary suffix from object identifiers before generation (`apple_2_25_1` $\rightarrow$ `apple_1`), while inheriting location names verbatim from the scene description (e.g., `CounterTop_1`). After planning, generated object names are resolved to the simulator's identifiers by matching on (object type, shared location), preserving evaluation fairness by avoiding any injection of ground-truth structured data.

# 5 Evaluation

## 5.1 Experimental Setup

All experiments are conducted using Claude 4.6 Sonnet as an LLM backend. The symbolic planner used is FastDownward [5] wrapped in UnifiedPlanning [15], which is also used for parsing PDDL. VAL [6] is used as a symbolic validator, while CPDDL [2] is used for the static analysis.

**Baselines.** We compare against two representative pipelines over the IPC benchmark. *LLM+P* [13] translates NL goals into PDDL problem files against a ground-truth domain, then defers to a classical planner; it does not synthesize domains. *NL2Plan* [3] extends this by synthesizing both domain and problem through a six-stage extraction pipeline, at substantially higher token cost. We adopt these as the most direct competitors of Rob-LAPI(S)$^2$. Due to the extremely high costs of running a whole benchmark with the NL2Plan architecture, we decided to perform a full run only on the two IPC domains with, respectively, the best and the worst ground-truth runnability for Rob-LAPI(S)$^2$ (Blocksworld and Storage; Table 1, last column).

**Benchmarks.** We evaluate on two testbeds. A first set of tests is conducted over the same selection of the IPC domains used in the evaluation of LLM+P [13] (Blocksworld, Floortile, Tyreworld, Storage, Barman, Grippers, Termes), providing a controlled classical baseline. As Tantakoun et al. [21] caution, IPC domains are likely within LLM training data, so we treat IPC as a controlled-validity benchmark rather than a generalization test. Every configuration in Table 1 uses the same backend on the same domains, so any advantage given from the presence of task examples in the original training dataset applies to all scenarios alike, while our claims concern the *contrasts* between scenarios (with vs. without adequacy check; synthesized vs. ground-truth domain), not absolute scores. The validation gap itself argues against faithful recall: a model reproducing canonical IPC formalizations would score near-100% ground-truth executability, not 73%. For this reason, a second set of tests uses embodied tasks, where we use the Embodied Agent Interface (EAI) benchmark [11], standardizing 20 household activities over the VirtualHome [18] simulator, and the AlfWorld [19] testing environment, which couples textual interaction with the AI2-Thor physics engine.

**Fairness Guarantees.** The synthesized PDDL is produced exclusively from NL inputs; the ground-truth PDDL plays no role in domain and problem generation. It is consulted only at evaluation time, except in experiments explicitly targeting problem generation in isolation, and in the simulator-grounded Sim-Rob-LAPI(S)$^2$ configuration of Sect. 4, whose object inventory and initial state are grounded in the simulator by construction.

*Hypotheses.* Our experiments test three claims. **H1**: iterative refinement with validation and static reachability raises success rates beyond single-pass generation. **H2**: symbolic self-consistency does not imply ground-truth executability, so a meaningful fraction of formally valid plans fail in the simulator. **H3**: when the LLM writes both domain and problem, predicate naming stays internally consistent, avoiding the coupling errors that arise when adapting to an externally defined schema. To prevent the LLM from copying PDDL structures from the simulator's internal state, all ground-truth scene representations are converted into plain-text narrative, constrained to the normalized entity vocabulary (e.g., "apple_1 is inside the fridge"). The system must extract the symbolic PDDL problem solely from this unstructured text, so that success rates reflect semantic reasoning rather than structural pattern matching. Object names are normalized symbolic identifiers (e.g. `apple_1`); perception noise, alias drift and hallucinated entities are out of scope. We assume a perception backend returns a stable entity inventory, framing Rob-LAPI(S)$^2$ as a symbolic-planning contribution decoupled from perception, in line with prior LLM-based neuro-symbolic planners [1,13]. The ground-truth problem PDDL is consulted only at evaluation time, to align token variants (e.g. `on-table` with `ontable`) and, in AlfWorld, to resolve action arguments against the simulator's identifiers, leaving plan structure intact.

## 5.2 Experimental Results

For each problem instance, the pipeline attempts to synthesize a domain/problem pair and a plan; this can fail outright if the LLM produces PDDL a classical planner cannot solve within budget, or if VAL flags it as inconsistent even when a plan is returned (mistyped parameters, ungrounded predicates). We call an instance **self-consistent** (reported as `VAL`) when this generate-plan-validate loop succeeds: a plan is found, and VAL confirms it is valid with respect to the same domain and problem pair the planner was given. Self-consistency is therefore a property of the generation process, not a tautology of planner search: a large share of the failures reported below occur precisely because no self-consistent triple is produced. **Ground-truth runnability** (GT) is a strictly independent second check: the same plan is replayed in a simulator instantiated from the ground-truth domain and problem. A plan can be self-consistent yet fail this check whenever the semantics of the elicited domain, while internally coherent, diverge from the real rules of the environment. The gap between the two is a measure of semantic correctness, and is the focus of our evaluation.

**IPC Domains.** Table 1 reports 20 problems per domain over the 7 IPC domains used by LLM+P. Gray columns denote configurations consuming the ground-truth domain (LLM+P and **GT-**Rob-LAPI(S)$^2$); LLM+P is evaluated both few-shot, as in the original paper, and zero-shot, for comparability with the zero-shot Rob-LAPI(S)$^2$. The Rob-LAPI(S)$^2$ columns report domain-and-problem synthesis without (Dom.) and with (Adq.) the adequacy check and schema injection, and the last column reports self-consistency and ground-truth runnability. It should be noted that the adequacy check compensates for semantic underspecification in the NL descriptions of the IPC domains, while it is unnecessary in embodied settings where the scene graph is a complete closed-world observation and representational gaps are caught by symbolic validation. Compared to NL2Plan [3], Rob-LAPI(S)$^2$ reaches 100% vs. 95% on Blocksworld while being faster (8.9 s vs 325 s on average) and 19× cheaper.

**Table 1.** IPC benchmark results. Baselines that consume a ground-truth domain are marked with '*'. *GT-Rob-LAPI(S)*$^2$ feeds the ground-truth domain directly into the pipeline, while *Rob-LAPI(S)*$^2$ synthesizes it from scratch (Dom. = without adequacy check, Adq. = with adequacy check). Only Sim-Rob-LAPI(S)$^2$ produces plans that are runnable in the ground-truth simulator, all other configurations achieve 0% ground-truth runnability and are therefore not shown in that column. For Sim-Rob-LAPI(S)$^2$, scores are reported as A/B, where A is the symbolic self-consistency (%) and B is the ground-truth runnability (%).

| Domain | *LLM+P** | | *NL2Plan* | GT-Rob-LAPI(S)$^2$ * | | Rob-LAPI(S)$^2$ | | Sim-Rob-LAPI(S)$^2$ |
|---|---|---|---|---|---|---|---|---|
| | Few* | Zero* | 325s | Few* | Zero* | Dom. | Adq. | VAL / GT |
| Blocksworld | 100* | 80* | 95 | 100* | 100* | 100 | 100 | 100/90 |
| Floortile | 100* | 45* | – | 90* | 90* | 90 | 85 | 100/75 |
| Tyreworld | 95* | 90* | – | 95* | 75* | 75 | 90 | 100/45 |
| Storage | 100* | 90* | 25 | 100* | 75* | 100 | 100 | 100/35 |
| Barman | 95* | 0* | – | 80* | 0* | 50 | 100 | 100/90 |
| Grippers | 100* | 100* | – | 100* | 100* | 100 | 100 | 100/90 |
| Termes | 100* | 95* | – | 100* | 95* | 100 | 100 | 100/85 |
| **Avg** | 99* | 71* | – | 95* | 76* | 85 | 96 | 100/73 |

Evaluating within the generated-domain setting, where the adequacy check is the only varying factor (Dom. vs. Adq. in Table 1), the check is decisive on

Barman (50% → 100%) and Tyreworld (75% → 90%), leaves the other four domains unchanged at 100%, and costs five points on Floortile (90% → 85%), for a net average gain of eleven points (85% → 96%). This supports **H1**: iterative symbolic feedback recovers domains that generation alone cannot handle, and **H3**: synthesizing domain and problem jointly is more robust than adapting to an external PDDL convention, whose coupling errors refinement alone cannot fix. A notable result deserving clarification is LLM+P zero-shot's 0% on Barman despite being seeded with the ground-truth domain. Barman involves multi-ingredient cocktail mixing with complex ordered preconditions; without few-shot demonstrations, the LLM consistently produces problems with incorrect fluent assignments that a classical planner cannot solve. The iterative refinement loop in Rob-LAPI(S)$^2$ compensates for this (50% without adequacy check, 100% with), confirming that the feedback mechanism, not the domain specification, is the critical differentiator on structurally complex domains. Our results reveal a *validation gap*: 100% self-consistent plans (sound under VAL) translate into only 73% actual executability in the ground-truth environment. This confirms **H2** and motivates the need for simulation-in-the-loop feedback for reliable robotic deployment.

**Table 2.** Overall success rates on robotic benchmarks. The (GT) variant uses the ground-truth domain; (Syn) generates it. VAL% is self-consistency, GT% runnability in the ground-truth simulator. Time is per task over 20 trials; Refs. is mean refinement iterations; tokens are totals over the 20 trials (∼ approximate).

| Benchmark | VAL (%) | GT (%) | Time (s) | Refs. | Tokens in/out |
|---|---|---|---|---|---|
| VirtualHome (GT) | 100 | 100 | 12 | 0.2 | ∼49k/∼8k |
| VirtualHome (Syn) | 90 | 90 | 41 | 0.3 | ∼101k/∼39k |
| AlfWorld (GT) | 55 | 55 | 302 | 1.9 | 803k/275k |
| AlfWorld (Syn) | 55 | 55 | 149 | 1.7 | ∼385k/∼190k |

**VirtualHome.** We evaluate Rob-LAPI(S)$^2$ on 20 household tasks from the EAI benchmark [11], covering 20 activity types (e.g. "*Browse internet*", "*Watch TV*", "*Cook food*"). Table 2 reports the results over the household benchmarks. With the 488-line EAI domain provided, Rob-LAPI(S)$^2$ synthesizes correct problems and valid plans for all 20 tasks (Table 2). In the (Syn) experiments no ground-truth domain is provided, so Rob-LAPI(S)$^2$ synthesizes both domain and problem from NL. The dominant failure mode is the domain/problem predicate drift described in Sect. 4, mitigated there without injecting ground-truth schemas. Rob-LAPI(S)$^2$ reaches 18/20 (90%), succeeding on 18 of the 20 tasks solved by the ground-truth baseline; the two failures (*Cook_some_food*, *Wash_hands*) stem from a missing initial fluent that the refinement prompts could not surface.

**AlfWorld.** AlfWorld poses a stronger grounding challenge: unlike VirtualHome's semantic names, its coordinate-encoded identifiers (e.g. `apple_2_25_1`) are opaque to NL generation. The identifier normalisation and post-hoc matching of Sect. 4 resolve this without injecting ground-truth. We evaluate 20 trials from the AlfWorld training split, also in this case in both (GT) and (Syn) variants. Also in this case, all symbolically self-consistent plans are confirmed runnable in a simulator initialized with the ground-truth domain. Table 3 breaks performance down per task. Both configurations reach 11/20 (55%), but through complementary failure patterns: domain synthesis inverts `pick_cool` (2/3 → 3/3) and improves `pick_heat` (0/3 → 1/3), while `pick_two_obj_and_place` drops to 0/3. When the domain is generated, the LLM encodes appliance-state preconditions as semantically expressive fluents (e.g. a fridge of type `cooling-appliance` in state `closed`) that can be populated directly from the NL scene, avoiding latent dependencies that require deduction: 3/3 on `pick_cool` and 1/3 on `pick_heat`, against 2/3 and 0/3 under the ground-truth domain. The ground-truth `alfred.pddl` instead encodes preconditions over latent fluents (`coolable`, `heatable`, `sliceable`) that exist in the simulator but are never surfaced in NL. Since the `:init` lock forbids inventing them, the LLM must infer them, succeeding when the attribute is strongly entailed by domain semantics (refrigeration transfers cleanly, hence 2/3 on `pick_cool`) and failing when the inference is weaker (`pick_heat`, 0/3). The opposite asymmetry shows up on tasks that require a clear discrimination of object properties through proper assignment of PDDL types: `alfred.pddl` maintains a separation between movable objects and receptacles that the LLM tends to flatten into a single"`physical-object`" type, complicating the grounding of actions tied to receptacle objects and producing a 0/3 failure on `pick_two_obj_and_place` when the domain is generated. A richer expert type system would improve robustness to this problem.

**Table 3.** AlfWorld breakdown by task type. (GT) uses the ground-truth `alfred.pddl` action domain; (Syn) generates it from NL.

| Task Type | Rob-LAPI(S)$^2$ (GT) | | Rob-LAPI(S)$^2$ (Syn) | |
|---|---|---|---|---|
| | VAL | GT | VAL | GT |
| look_at_obj_in_light | 4/5 | 4/5 | 3/5 | 3/5 |
| pick_and_place_simple | 1/3 | 1/3 | 2/3 | 2/3 |
| pick_clean_then_place_in_recep | 2/3 | 2/3 | 2/3 | 2/3 |
| pick_cool_then_place_in_recep | 2/3 | 2/3 | 3/3 | 3/3 |
| pick_heat_then_place_in_recep | 0/3 | 0/3 | 1/3 | 1/3 |
| pick_two_obj_and_place | 2/3 | 2/3 | 0/3 | 0/3 |
| **Overall %** | 55% | 55% | 55% | 55% |

This parity, with its asymmetric pattern, also rules out the LLM having hallucinated the state description to simplify the task: it would then beat the ground-truth baseline rather than fail cleanly on `pick_two_obj_and_place`.

**Cost of the Refinement Loop.** Table 2 reports the cost profile of each configuration. Refinement is rarely invoked when grounding is straightforward and dominates the budget otherwise: VirtualHome converges in 0.2–0.3 iterations per task (12–41 s, roughly 49–101k input tokens); AlfWorld needs 1.7–1.9 iterations (149–302 s, 385–803k input tokens). Cost scales with grounding difficulty, not plan length. On IPC, where refinement is seldom needed, Rob-LAPI(S)$^2$ averages 8.9 s per task against NL2Plan's 325 s. The loop is bounded by a fixed refinement-cycle budget, so worst-case cost per task is capped.

## 6 Discussion

On IPC, the refinement loop reaches 96% average self-consistency across 140 problems; the Barman recovery of Sect. 5.2 shows that meta-cognitive symbolic feedback drives real auto-regressive improvement in symbolic model elicitation.

In the embodied benchmarks instead, the gap between the domain generation benchmark and the ground-truth one is mainly due to an incorrectly modeled initial state. This asymmetry reflects the evaluation interface, not the domains. Because the NL barrier withholds the simulator's identifier space, comparing a plan against ground truth needs an entity-resolution step binding generated symbols to simulator identifiers, exactly the binding a deployed system needs between perception and actuation. The embodied benchmarks perform it by default (Sect. 4), so VAL and GT track closely; on IPC only Sim-Rob-LAPI(S)$^2$ applies it, so other configurations report 0% from naming mismatch alone. AlfWorld (Sect. 5.2) shows that for an LLM the hardest part is not synthesizing PDDL from scratch but adapting to a pre-existing expert schema. When Rob-LAPI(S)$^2$ writes the domain itself, every precondition an action requires is representable in the generated problem file, due to the expressivity of the tokens it picks as domain fluents. Forced onto a ground-truth domain, the system often cannot populate the latent fluents (object temperatures, appliance states) that the expert domain requires but the NL description never mentions: recovering them demands deduction, which the inductive next-token objective does not support. Counter-intuitively, internal semantic consistency matters more than conformance to an external schema.

*Limitations.* Rob-LAPI(S)$^2$ assumes that scene descriptions are available in long-form NL. A fully deployed system would require a perfect perception layer (or an unusually patient human user) to convert 3D scene graphs into NL. Beyond perception, the open challenges are (a) eliciting tacit physical knowledge that NL descriptions tend to omit, and (b) integrating elicited models with pre-existing symbolic knowledge bases without the coupling errors observed when the ground-truth domain is provided; a curated seed library of common household operators would lighten the burden on domain elicitation, but any vocabulary the LLM must conform to is a smaller instance of the same coupling problem, so a hybrid seeded and domain-agnostic synthesis would have to demonstrate that the seed does not reintroduce that cost. Two further limitations concern the refinement loop: it runs for a fixed budget rather than an adaptive criterion, without detecting stagnation (repeated failure to shrink the diagnosed error set) to stop early; and it cannot distinguish an incorrectly elicited model from a genuinely unsolvable instance, since both surface identically as a planner or static-analysis failure and are treated as repairable until the budget is exhausted.

## 7 Conclusion

Iterative LLM-based PDDL generation, guided by symbolic and semantic feedback, grounds robotic instructions in formal plans. On VirtualHome and AlfWorld, domain generation from NL reaches parity with expert-authored baselines by keeping the symbolic vocabulary consistent, trading task-type-specific gains against losses.

This work shows that a structured description of the environment's initial state and transition rules suffices for an LLM to produce a sound symbolic model without injecting ground-truth structured information. The validation gap is nonetheless wide: 100% symbolic consistency on the IPC tasks corresponds to only 73% runnability under the simulator-grounded configuration of Sect. 4. Bridging it requires diagnostic feedback from *both* symbolic validators and simulated execution traces inside the refinement loop.

**Disclosure of Interests.** The authors have no competing interests to declare that are relevant to the content of this article.

## References

1. Ahn, M., Brohan, A., Brown, N.: Do as I can, not as I say: grounding language in robotic affordances. In: Conference on Robot Learning (CoRL) (2022)
2. Fišer, D.: cpddl (2025). https://doi.org/10.5281/zenodo.16423301
3. Gestrin, E., Singhal, V., Hoffman, G., Chamberland, S.: NL2Plan: robust LLM-driven planning from minimal text. In: Proceedings of the AAAI Conference on Artificial Intelligence (2025)
4. Ghallab, M., Nau, D., Traverso, P.: Automated Planning: Theory and Practice. Morgan Kaufmann (2004)
5. Helmert, M.: The Fast Downward planning system. J. Artif. Intell. Res. **26**, 191–246 (2006)
6. Howey, R., Long, D., Fox, M.: VAL: Automatic plan validation, continuous effects and mixed initiative planning using PDDL. In: Proceedings of the IEEE International Conference on Tools with Artificial Intelligence (ICTAI), pp. 294–301 (2004)
7. Huang, S., Lipovetzky, N., Cohn, T.: Planning in the dark: LLM-symbolic planning pipeline without experts. In: Proceedings of the AAAI Conference on Artificial Intelligence (2025)
8. Kambhampati, S., et al.: LLMs can't plan, but can help planning in LLM-Modulo frameworks. In: Proceedings of the International Conference on Machine Learning (ICML) (2024)

9. Katz, M., Kokel, H., Srinivas, K., Sohrabi, S.: Thought of search: planning with language models through the lens of efficiency. Adv. Neural Inf. Process. Syst. (NeurIPS) (2024)
10. Malfa, L., E.: An end-to-end planning framework with agentic LLMs and PDDL. arXiv preprint arXiv:2512.09629 (2025)
11. Li, M., et al.: Embodied agent interface: benchmarking llms for embodied decision making. Adv. Neural Inf. Process. Syst. **37** (2024)
12. Liang, J., et al.: Code as policies: language model programs for embodied control. In: IEEE International Conference on Robotics and Automation (ICRA) (2023)
13. Liu, B., et al.: LLM+P: empowering large language models with optimal planning proficiency. In: IEEE/RSJ International Conference on Intelligent Robots and Systems (IROS), pp. 5258–5265 (2023)
14. McDermott, D., et al.: Pddl—the planning domain definition language. Technical Report. CVC TR-98-003/DCS TR-1165, Yale Center for Computational Vision and Control (1998)
15. Micheli, A., Bit-Monnot, A., Roger, G., Scala, E., et al.: Unified planning: modeling, manipulating and solving ai planning problems in python. SoftwareX **29** (2025). https://doi.org/10.1016/j.softx.2024.102012
16. Micheli, V., Fleuret, F.: BUTLER: achieving task-generalization with natural language instructions via semantic goal conditioned hierarchical policies. In: Workshop on Language and Reinforcement Learning (LaRL) (2021)
17. Min, S.Y., Jayaraman, D., Gupta, A., Bisk, Y.: FILM: following instructions in language with modular methods. In: International Conference on Learning Representations (ICLR) (2022)
18. Puig, X., et al.: VirtualHome: simulating household activities via programs. In: CVPR (2018)
19. Shridhar, M., Yuan, X., Côté, M.A., Bisk, Y., Trischler, A., Hausknecht, M.: ALFWorld: aligning text and embodied environments for interactive learning. In: International Conference on Learning Representations (ICLR) (2021)
20. Stein, K., Fišer, D., Hoffmann, J., Koller, A.: Automating the generation of prompts for LLM-based action choice in PDDL planning. In: Proceedings of the International Conference on Automated Planning and Scheduling (ICAPS) (2025)
21. Tantakoun, M., Muise, C., Zhu, X.: Llms as planning formalizers: a survey for leveraging large language models to construct automated planning models. In: Findings of the Association for Computational Linguistics: ACL 2025, pp. 25167–25188 (2025)
22. Vallati, M., Barták, R., Chrpa, L., McCluskey, T.L., Petrick, R.P.A.: Knowledge engineering for planning and scheduling in the LLM era. In: Proceedings of the International Conference on Automated Planning and Scheduling (ICAPS), vol. 35, pp. 391–395 (2025)
23. Wang, J., et al.: PDDL-GenAI: a plugin for LLM-based support in planning domain modeling. In: ICAPS Demo Track (2025)
24. Zhu, Z., Jiao, R., Peng, N.: ISR-LLM: iterative self-refined large language model for long-horizon sequential task planning. In: IEEE International Conference on Robotics and Automation (ICRA) (2024)
25. Zuo, M., Lipkin, A., Stone, P., Tellex, S.: Planetarium: a rigorous benchmark for translating text to structured planning languages. In: Proceedings of the Conference of the North American Chapter of the Association for Computational Linguistics (NAACL) (2025)

# LLM-Based Source Code Compression via Thresholded Symbol Ranking

Angelo Nardone[1(✉)] and Paolo Ferragina[1,2]

[1] Department of Computer Science, University of Pisa, Pisa, Italy
angelo.nardone@phd.unipi.it, paolo.ferragina@santannapisa.it
[2] Scuola Superiore Sant'Anna, Pisa, Italy

**Abstract.** We study the problem of lossless compression of source code, motivated by the storage demands of large-scale software archives, such as Software Heritage (https://www.softwareheritage.org/). General-purpose compressors (e.g., `zstd`, `bzip2`) offer a good trade-off between compression ratio and speed, but fail to exploit all special regularities inherent in source code. Recent approaches leverage Large Language Models (LLMs) within Shannon's symbol-ranking framework, relying on a scheme in which the predicted rank can grow arbitrarily. While effective at reducing space, this setting incurs significant throughput degradation, and leaves open the question whether it is necessary to explicitly encode all ranks. In this work, we introduce LLM-based compressors deploying two novel symbol-ranking variants that bound predictions to the top-$T$ ranks ($T = 1$ or 63), with out-of-threshold symbols stored as exceptions and compressed jointly with the rank stream via general-purpose compressors. We conduct the first large-scale evaluation of LLM-based source code compression across 30 model variants spanning 19 base LLMs, including general-domain, code-specialized, and quantized models. Our $T$-bounded approach outperforms prior LLM-based compressors both in compression ratio (up to 37% relative improvement) and compression throughput (40% faster). Compared to general-purpose compressors (e.g., `zstd`, `bzip2`), we obtain up to 82% relative compression gain but at a lower speed, thus offering a new trade-off point in the compression-speed spectrum. We also show that these gains are stronger on source code than on natural language, suggesting an interesting indication, namely that source code exposes regularities captured by LLMs but missed by general-purpose exact-match-based compressors. We conclude by commenting on open problems that offer theoretical and practical avenues of research.

**Keywords:** Lossless compression · Source code compression · Large language models · Symbol ranking · Algorithms

## 1 Introduction

Data compression is a cornerstone of modern computing, reducing storage, bandwidth, and memory pressure while improving cache efficiency [29]. This is especially critical for lossless compression, which guarantees exact reconstruction in


S. Bistarelli et al. (Eds.): AIxIA 2026, LNAI 17131, pp. 466–480, 2027.
https://doi.org/10.1007/978-3-032-40774-0_34

domains where fidelity is essential, such as textual data, databases, and source code. The need for efficient lossless source-code compression is amplified by the rapid growth of software repositories: platforms such as GitHub and GitLab now host hundreds of millions of projects, and in 2024 alone GitHub reported more than 100 million new projects and nearly 1 billion contributions [18].

This growth affects large-scale archival infrastructures such as the *Software Heritage Archive (SWH)*, launched by INRIA and UNESCO to collect, preserve, and provide universal access to publicly available source code – an effort essential for long-term archival, reproducibility, and for providing a reliable codebase for AI model training. While efficient methods exist for compressing the Merkle DAG underpinning SWH's infrastructure [17,27], the main challenge lies in compressing the source-code files themselves – commonly referred to as *blobs*. These constitute the overwhelming majority of SWH's storage footprint and are currently compressed independently with `gzip`-based tools, a strategy that fails to capture redundancies across files. Several approaches have been proposed to address this limitation: [6] showed that compressing files jointly via proper ordering and large-context-window compressors can partially exploit such redundancies, yet at the cost of expensive reorderings and with moderate compression gains.

These limitations motivate new approaches to source-code compression. Since LLMs are effective at modeling sequences, capturing long-range dependencies, and predicting upcoming tokens [12], we investigate their use as predictors within Shannon's *symbol-ranking* framework [33]. Our goal is twofold: to assess whether LLM-based symbol ranking can improve compression ratio while retaining practical throughput, thus bringing such techniques closer to deployment in large-scale archives, and to advocate for lossless compression as a principled, task-agnostic lens to study and compare foundation models.

**State of the Art.** Lossless compression via symbol ranking has a long history [33]. Early implementations include the Move-to-Front (MTF) compressor [4] and Prediction by Partial Matching (PPM) [9,10,16,22,26]. A major step forward was the Burrows-Wheeler Transform (BWT) [8], refined by Fenwick [15], which, with MTF and RLE, underpins widely used compressors (e.g., `bzip2` [32]).

The connection between language modeling and compression has long been established [24,31], and the rise of neural networks has revitalized this perspective. Early neural compressors, such as *DeepZip* [19] and *NNCP* [3], combined RNN/LSTM-based prediction with Arithmetic Coding, achieving interesting compression ratios at very high computational cost. With the advent of Transformers [36], LLM-based approaches emerged as strong candidates for lossless compression. *LLMZip* [35] was among the first to exploit LLMs for compression, considering both Symbol Ranking, combined with `zlib`, and Arithmetic Coding driven by LLM-predicted probability distributions. *FineZip* [25] explicitly builds on *LLMZip*, adding parameter-efficient fine-tuning (LoRA) and dynamic context windows; consistently with *LLMZip*, it considers both Symbol Ranking with `bzip2` and Arithmetic Coding, with the latter slightly improving compression but being much slower. *AlphaZip* [28] focused on smaller models to improve throughput, pairing Symbol Ranking with `gzip` or Brotli. Finally, Delétang et al. [12] conducted a broader study of foundation models of different sizes – Chinchilla (70B, 7B, 1B), LLaMA 2 (7B), and vanilla Transformers (3.2M, 800K, 200K) – combined with Arithmetic Coding, showing that they can act as effective compressors for diverse data types, including English text, images and videos, while highlighting trade-offs involving model size, context length, tokenization, and computational cost.

All these works share a common principle: leveraging a (neural) predictor to assign ranks by decreasing predicted likelihood and encoding them via a general-purpose compressor [1,13,30,32], or directly feeding predicted probabilities into Arithmetic Coding [37]. In both cases, every symbol is assigned a rank or probability, corresponding to Shannon's unbounded setting ($T = \infty$) – no threshold is applied to separate high-confidence predictions from rare symbols. While surpassing general-purpose compressors in compression ratio, both approaches suffer from very low throughput, preventing their use in real-world scenarios, and leave open the question about the impact of $T$ on the final compression ratio.

**Our Contribution.** In this work, we investigate LLM-based lossless compression for source code, with the following key contributions.

– *Novel Symbol-Ranking Pipelines.* We revisit *symbol ranking for text compression*, introduced by Shannon in his 1951 work [33], and employ LLMs to generate context-driven rankings of the top-$T$ most probable symbols. Shannon formalized three prediction schemes: (i) guessing only the most likely symbol ($T = 1$), with a yes/no outcome and symbol revelation upon error; (ii) scanning the full ranked list until the correct symbol is found ($T = \infty$); and (iii) a thresholded variant that stops after $T$ incorrect guesses and reveals the symbol. We revisit this *thresholded* scheme and propose LLM-based variants focusing on two configurations ($T = 1$ and $T = 63$), comparing them against the unbounded setting ($T = \infty$) of prior work [12,25,28,35] and showing that thresholding enables relevant trade-offs between compression ratio and throughput.

– *Comprehensive Model Evaluation.* We benchmark 30 model variants across 19 base LLMs – including code-specialized, general-domain, and quantized models, ranging from 120M to 3B parameters – assessing predictive quality, compression performance, and runtime in the most extensive study to date. For each model, we analyze parameter count, memory footprint, and the impact of code specialization and quantization. Our framework reveals broader trends absent from prior work, which considered at most 3 models of largely varying sizes: specialized code models achieve the best compression, while smaller or quantized models optimize throughput. We also shed new light on scaling laws [21]: larger models consistently improve compression ratio, but at the cost of proportionally lower throughput, highlighting a fundamental trade-off between model capacity and practical efficiency.

– *Measured Gains.* Our $T$-bounded strategies achieve up to 37% relative compression gain and 40% faster throughput over the unbounded approach ($T =$

$\infty$) adopted in prior work [25,28,35], and up to 68% relative compression gain over general-purpose compressors on reordered archives [6], rising to 82% when compressing individual files. Although throughput remains lower than that of general-purpose compressors, our pipeline operates on individual files (unlike [6]), making parallelization trivial and improving random access to compressed files.

– *Source-Code Compression.* While prior LLM-based compression literature focused exclusively on natural language corpora or images, we are the first to evaluate this approach on source code – a setting of growing importance, as already motivated. This context was previously explored by Boffa et al. [6] using only general-purpose compressors and costly global reorderings over large archives. We show that LLM-based compressors squeeze source code more than natural language, thus suggesting that source code contains regularities that elude general-purpose compressors but are well captured by LLMs.

These findings indicate that LLM-based symbol-ranking combined with thresholding and lightweight or quantized models represent a promising path toward practical and scalable source-code compression, particularly suited for cold backup scenarios where compression ratio takes priority over speed, paving the way for new pipelines, LLM-specialized models, and novel strategies to reduce costly LLM-inference calls – challenges that we discuss at the end of the paper.

## 2 Theoretical Background

**General-Purpose Compressors.** We use three general-purpose lossless compressors, both as baselines and as backends in our LLM-based pipelines. They cover two major and complementary families: *dictionary-based* compression algorithms, represented by `zstd` (which extends the LZ77 paradigm with strong entropy coding [11,14]), and *block-sorting* compression algorithms, represented by `bzip2` [8,32] and `bzip3` [34]. We exclude statistical encoders (e.g., Arithmetic Coding) since prior LLM-based compression studies [25,35] show that they substantially increase runtime, reducing overall throughput.

**Symbol-Ranking Text Compression.** The idea of *symbol-ranking text compression* originates from Shannon's seminal 1951 paper on the entropy of English text [33]. In his experiments, human subjects were asked to predict the next character of a sequence, producing a ranked list of symbols according to their likelihood. Shannon formalized three prediction methods: (i) guessing only the most likely symbol ($T = 1$), receiving a yes/no feedback and, in case of error, returning also the correct symbol; (ii) continuing to guess the correct symbol by scanning their ranked list (by decreasing likelihood), until it is found, thereby recording its rank position ($T = \infty$); and (iii) a hybrid approach, where guessing proceeds as in the previous method but stops after a fixed threshold $T$ of wrong guesses, at which point the correct symbol is revealed.

**Definition 1 (Symbol Ranking).** *Let $S = (s_1, \ldots, s_n)$ be a string over an alphabet $\Sigma$. For each position $i$, let $W_i$ denote its* context *(for example, the* *last k symbols). A* predictor *associates with* $W_i$ *a probability distribution over* $\Sigma$, *yielding an ordered list* $\Sigma_{W_i} = (\sigma_0, \dots, \sigma_{|\Sigma|-1})$, *where* $\mathbb{P}(\sigma_0 \mid W_i) \geq \cdots \geq \mathbb{P}(\sigma_{|\Sigma|-1} \mid W_i)$. *The* rank *of the correct next symbol* $s_i$ *is then defined as*

$$Rank(s_i \mid W_i) = j \iff s_i = \sigma_j. \tag{1}$$

*The* symbol ranking *transformation maps* $S$ *into a sequence of integers (ranks)* $R = (r_1, \dots, r_n)$, *where* $r_i = Rank(s_i \mid W_i)$.

**Definition 2 (Symbol Ranking with Exceptions).** *Let* $S$ *and* $W_i$ *be as above, and let a predictor associate with each* $W_i$ *a probability distribution over* $\Sigma$, *yielding the ordered list* $\Sigma_{W_i}$ *as in Definition 1. Fix a threshold* $T \in \mathbb{N}$. *For each position* $i$, *the output symbol* $r_i$ *is*

$$r_i = \begin{cases} Rank(s_i \mid W_i), & \text{if } Rank(s_i \mid W_i) \leq T, \\ ESC, & \text{otherwise}, \end{cases} \tag{2}$$

*where* $Rank(s_i \mid W_i)$ *is defined as in Eq.* (1), *and* `ESC` *is an escape symbol. In the case of* `ESC`, *the true symbol* $s_i$ *is stored in a side list* $E$. *The output of* symbol ranking with exceptions *is thus the pair* $(R, E)$, *where* $R$ *is the sequence of ranks/escapes and* $E$ *is the list of (symbol) exceptions.*

Shannon's three methods derive from the definitions: the first to Definition 2 with $T = 1$, the second to Definition 1 (equivalently, Definition 2 with $T = \infty$), and the third to Definition 2 with any finite $T > 1$.

It is important to stress that symbol ranking is not a compression algorithm per sé, but a *transform* producing a sequence of integers with a skewed distribution. These can then be efficiently encoded using general-purpose compressors (e.g., `zstd`, `bzip2`, or `bzip3`). The effectiveness of the method ultimately depends on the quality of the predictor. In particular, the more *skewed* the predicted distributions are, the more tokens fall into low ranks, which directly corresponds to lower entropy and thus higher compressibility. It goes without saying that the predictor must be *deterministic* to ensure full reversibility of the compression process, and thus preserve the lossless property in the decompression stage.

**LLM-Based Predictors and Proposed Pipeline.** The connection between language modeling and compression has long been recognized [24,31]. Recent works have reinforced this link, showing that accurate next-token prediction implies efficient compression. Once text is tokenized – with tokens corresponding to the symbols to be compressed – LLMs can generate *"precise"* probability distributions over the next token given a context, making them ideal predictors for symbol-ranking compression. The key advantage of LLMs resides in the fact that, thanks to neural-network processing and the more recent Attention Mechanism [36], the *k-long context* used to estimate symbol probabilities is not matched *exactly*, as in PPM-like approaches (cf. [9,10,16,22,26]), but may be *fuzzily and weightly matched*, thus offering a much higher precision in the estimate.

In the Introduction, we discussed early neural approaches. All these works – whether they explicitly adopt a symbol-ranking pipeline [25,28,35] or feed predicted probabilities into a statistical compressor [12,25,35] – rely solely on the approach described in Definition 1 (i.e., $T = \infty$): no threshold is applied to separate high-confidence predictions from rare symbols, leaving unexplored the impact of bounding $T$ on both compression ratio and throughput. These studies consistently show that LLM-based predictors outperform general-purpose compressors in compression ratio, but still suffer from extremely low throughput. Furthermore, most of them evaluate only a single model, and even the most systematic study [12] considers just three models with largely varying sizes, without systematically analyzing which architectural or training factors most influence compression performance across models of comparable scale. Finally, while [12] extends compression experiments to images and video, all these works focus exclusively on classical text corpora, leaving source code – a setting of growing importance, as motivated in the Introduction – entirely unexplored.

**Our Proposal.** We address the limitations of prior work along three complementary directions. First, we extend the symbol-ranking framework by implementing all three of Shannon's methods (Definitions 1 and 2), introducing for the first time a thresholded pipeline ($T$-bounded). Second, we benchmark 30 model variants spanning 19 base architectures on source code – the first large-scale LLM-based compression study on this domain – advocating for compression as a task-agnostic lens to compare foundation models. Third, we show that LLMs capture source-code regularities beyond the reach of general-purpose compressors, achieving compression ratios surpassing those on natural language.

Methodologically, the first pipeline reproduces the unbounded setting ($T = \infty$) of prior work [12,25,28,35]; the second – introduced here – applies a rank threshold $T$, replacing out-of-threshold tokens with an escape symbol stored in a side list. Both pipelines share a unified architecture optimized for throughput. Each file is processed independently in an *offline setting*, making the pipeline parallelizable across GPUs. Within each file, we use a *dynamic context window* growing up to a fixed maximum $M$; longer windows are split with zero stride, ensuring coverage without overlap. Input sequences are processed in batches of size $B$, enabling parallel rank computation across multiple sequences on GPU.

Finally, the ranked and escaped sequences are compressed using general-purpose lossless compressors – i.e., `zstd`, `bzip2`, and `bzip3` – selected for their balance between compression effectiveness and speed. Statistical encoders such as Arithmetic Coding were deliberately excluded, as prior studies [25,35] showed that their runtime penalties outweigh the modest compression gains.

## 3 Experimental Setup

All experiments were conducted on an NVIDIA DGX H100 server with 8×H100 GPUs (80 GB each), dual Intel Xeon Platinum CPUs, and 2 TiB of RAM, running Ubuntu 22.04. The implementation was developed in Python/PyTorch, with pretrained models accessed via the Hugging Face ecosystem. This setup enabled medium/large-scale LLMs to be tested efficiently under realistic conditions.

**Datasets.** We conduct our experiments on *source-code corpora* derived from the Stack-Edu collection [2,20], curated from The Stack v2 [5,23], namely the StarCoder2 training corpus. Stack-Edu provides *SWH identifiers* (SWHIDs) enabling us to fetch the corresponding files directly from the Software Heritage archive. This choice is motivated by three main reasons: (i) it ensures that our experiments are conducted on code that already forms part of the Software Heritage Archive, offering a realistic scenario aligned with our goal of designing compression algorithms for this infrastructure; (ii) it guarantees high-quality code aligned with the training corpora of modern LLMs; and (iii) it provides full reproducibility, since the data are publicly accessible.

**Two-Phase Evaluation Strategy.** To avoid long experiments, we adopt a strategy based on a proper dataset design (see Sect. 4), as described below:

– In *Phase One* (exploratory analysis), we construct a $\sim$ 60 MB mixed-language dataset by uniformly sampling $\sim$ 10 MB of source code for each of six representative programming languages: Python, C, C++, C#, Java, and JavaScript. This smaller dataset allows us to evaluate all 30 LLMs in terms of both predictive accuracy and runtime efficiency, without the computational burden of large-scale experiments. The goal is to identify promising models while discarding those that show poor accuracy or excessive runtime.

– In *Phase Two* (in-depth analysis), we focus only on the most promising models and therefore build larger, per-language datasets of approximately $\sim$ 100 MB each, for the same six programming languages used in Phase One, amounting to nearly $\sim$ 600 MB in total. This design enables a detailed language-specific evaluation of the complete compression pipeline. To ensure comparability across datasets, the average file size was constrained to approximately 3KB per file.

**Models.** The choice of prediction model is critical, as it directly affects both rank accuracy and runtime performance. Except for `CodeT5`, all models considered are of the decoder-only type. Decoder-only architectures are naturally suited to our task, as they are designed for autoregressive generation: given a context, they estimate the probability distribution of the next token – the same required for rank computation. Encoder-only and encoder–decoder models are less effective for prediction and were thus only marginally included.

Most tested models fall in the small/mid-scale range (1–3B parameters), reflecting practical runtime constraints. Two larger representatives, `LLaMA-3.1-8B` and `Mistral-7B-v0.3`, are included to cover widely adopted LLM families. Overall, we evaluate 30 variants from 19 base architectures, many considered for the first time in a lossless compression setting. A schematic summary is provided in Table 1, reporting parameter count and code specialization or quantization. For several families, multiple variants are included (e.g., different precisions or code-specific fine-tuning), allowing us to assess how these design choices affect both compression performance and the broader predictive capabilities of the models.

**Table 1.** Evaluated models. *Qnt* denotes quantized models; *Code* denotes code-specialized models. Bold entries denote those selected for the in-depth evaluation.

| Model | Par. | Qnt. | Code | Model | Par. | Qnt. | Code |
|---|---|---|---|---|---|---|---|
| **StarCoder2-3B (4bit)** | 3B | Yes | Yes | **Llama-3.2-1B (4bit)** | 1.23B | Yes | No |
| StarCoder2-3B (8bit) | 3B | Yes | Yes | Llama-3.2-1B | 1.23B | No | No |
| **StarCoder2-3B (bf16)** | 3B | No | Yes | Llama-3.2-3B (4bit) | 3.21B | Yes | No |
| StarCoder2-3B (fp32) | 3B | No | Yes | Llama-3.2-3B | 3.21B | No | No |
| DeepSeekCoder-1.3B | 1.3B | No | Yes | Llama-3.1-8B (4bit) | 8B | Yes | No |
| **DeepSeekCoder-1.3B AWQ** | 1.3B | Yes | Yes | Llama-3.1-8B | 8B | No | No |
| CodeGemma-2B | 2.5B | No | Yes | Mistral-7B | 7B | No | No |
| **CodeGemma-2B AWQ** | 2.5B | Yes | Yes | Mistral-7B (4bit) | 7B | Yes | No |
| Gemma-2-2B | 2.6B | No | No | Qwen3-1.7B | 1.7B | No | No |
| **Gemma-2-2B (4bit)** | 2.6B | Yes | No | **UniXcoder-base** | 0.13B | No | Yes |
| SmolLM3-3B | 3B | No | No | CodeT5-base | 0.22B | No | Yes |
| Granite-2B | 2B | No | No | GPT-2 small | 0.124B | No | No |
| Granite-Code-3B | 3B | No | Yes | GPT-2 medium | 0.355B | No | No |
| **Granite-Code-3B (4bit)** | 3B | Yes | Yes | GPT-2 large | 0.774B | No | No |
| **Phi-2** | 2.7B | No | No | GPT-2 xl | 1.5B | No | No |

## 4 Experimental Results

In this section, we follow the two-phase evaluation strategy mentioned above.

### 4.1 Phase One (Exploratory Analysis)

In this first phase, we evaluate all 30 LLMs on a 60 MB multilingual code dataset (see Sect. 3), focusing on predictive accuracy – captured by the rank distribution – and throughput, without performing actual compression. All models use a unified pipeline ($T = \infty$, Definition 1) with fixed $B = 32$ and $M = 512$, selected through preliminary experiments as the configuration maximizing GPU efficiency within memory constraints.

**Prediction Results.** From a predictive standpoint, most models exhibit highly skewed rank distributions: rank 0 accounts for about 70–80% of occurrences, while the first 63 ranks cover 95–98%. In particular, code-specialized LLMs such as `StarCoder2`, `DeepSeekCoder`, `GraniteCode`, and `CodeGemma` achieve the skewest rank profiles. Among all evaluated models, two clear outliers emerge: `CodeT5`, whose encoder–decoder architecture results in very poor rank accuracy (cf. Fig. 1(a)), and `UniXcoder` together with the `GPT-2` family, which are the only other models falling below the ranges reported above (i.e., 70–80% and 95–98%). In particular, the `GPT-2` family exhibits poor results across all evaluated metrics (e.g., number of tokens, mean, variance), whereas `UniXcoder` maintains values comparable to those of other models. Consequently, `CodeT5` and all `GPT-2` variants are excluded from the following in-depth experimental Phase Two, while `UniXcoder` is retained as a lightweight baseline.

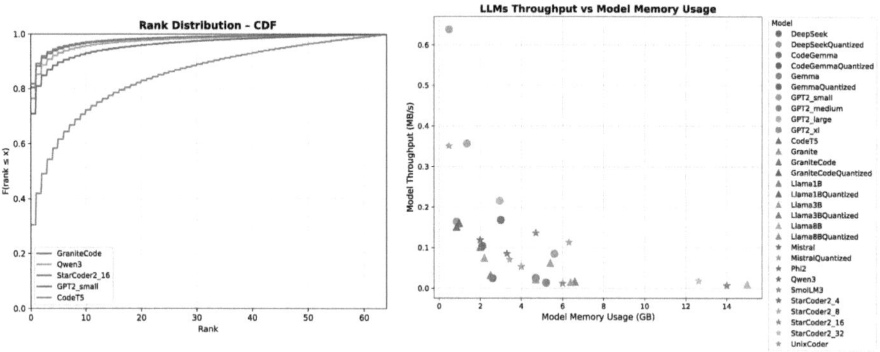


(a) Rank prediction CDF.

(b) Throughput vs. memory.

**Fig. 1.** Exploratory analysis. (a) CDF of rank predictions for models, highlighting the weak predictive accuracy of `CodeT5`. (b) Throughput versus memory usage, showing the inverse relation between model size and inference speed.

**Time Results.** Execution-time measurements confirm that throughput constitutes the main bottleneck. Even the fastest models reach at most ~0.6 MB/s, while the majority cluster around or below 0.1 MB/s. A negative correlation emerges between GPU memory footprint and throughput (Fig. 1(b)): larger models, such as `Llama-8B` and `Mistral`, exhibit slower processing rates (i.e., they occur at the rightmost corner). To balance predictive accuracy and speed, we define a selection threshold of 0.1 MB/s and retain only those models that satisfy this throughput constraint and the predictive-quality filter discussed above.

**Conclusions.** The first-phase analysis sheds light on scaling laws [21]: larger models improve prediction quality, but reduce throughput, exposing a capacity–efficiency trade-off. The nine selected LLMs – highlighted in bold in Table 1 – are predominantly quantized, with `StarCoder2-3B (bf16)` as the non-quantized exception. They form the basis of the second experimental phase, where we evaluate the full compression pipeline and the proposed thresholded strategies.

### 4.2 Phase Two (In-Depth Analysis)

In this second phase, we move to a complete compression evaluation – focusing on compression ratio and throughput – across six language-specific datasets, each containing 100 MB (see Sect. 3). We first benchmark general-purpose compressors (`zstd`, `bzip2`, `bzip3`) directly on the datasets as baselines, then integrate them within the two symbol-ranking pipelines of Sect. 2.

**Methodology.** As baselines, we apply `zstd`, `bzip2`, and `bzip3` without LLM involvement, under both *fast* and *high-compression* settings. Each compressor is tested in two configurations: (i) files compressed independently; (ii) files reordered by inverted path names and aggregated into a `.tar` archive, following [6].

For the symbol-ranking pipelines, we keep the same configuration used in Phase One, namely $B = 32$ and $M = 512$. The known pipeline (Definition 1, $T = \infty$) records each token's exact rank as a 32-bit integer and compresses the resulting stream with the baseline compressors. The new pipeline (Definition 2) instantiates Shannon's first method with $T = 1$ and his third method with $T \in \{3, 7, 15, 31, 63, 127, 255\}$. Ranks are encoded in $\lceil \log_2(T+1) \rceil$ bits, while exceptions are stored separately as 32-bit integers; both streams are then compressed with the same baseline compressors. Consistently with Phase One, $T = 63$ emerges as the best configuration for Shannon's third method.

**Results on General-Purpose Compression Baselines.** Unless otherwise stated, baseline results refer to the archive-based configuration, which achieves the best compression. As expected, `zstd-3` delivers the highest throughput ($\approx$40 MB/s) but also the worst compression, while higher compression level (i.e., `zstd-12` and `zstd-22`) improves compression ratio at the cost of speed. `bzip2` shows nearly identical throughput across the various compression levels, with minor gains in compression for `bzip2-9`. In contrast, `bzip3` offers the best speed–compression trade-off and is therefore adopted as the strongest baseline.

**LLM Pipeline Comparison.** Across all pipelines, models, and datasets, the execution-time breakdown shows that *rank computation* (i.e., the LLM forward pass), together with tokenization, is the dominant bottleneck, accounting for more than 99% of the total runtime. As a consequence, throughput is determined by the choice of the model rather than by the downstream compressor, and we can focus on the configurations that achieve the best compression.

Our second pipeline, which introduces a rank threshold $T$, improves over the conventional unbounded approach of the first pipeline ($T = \infty$). With $T = 1$ (Shannon's first method), throughput improves by up to 40%, at the cost of a small compression loss. In contrast, $T = 63$ (Shannon's third method) achieves both higher throughput and better compression than $T = \infty$. This is due to two factors: (i) more than 95% of tokens fall within the top-63 predictions, keeping the exception list small, and (ii) ranks require only 6 bits instead of 32. Overall, the $T = 63$ pipeline yields up to 37% additional compression gain and up to 40% throughput improvement over $T = \infty$ across configurations – the latter matching $T = 1$, since extracting top-1 and top-63 predictions is practically time equivalent. These results identify $T = 63$, combined with `bzip3-default` or `zstd-22`, as the most effective LLM-based configuration, which we adopt for the final comparison against general-purpose compressors.

From the model perspective, consistent patterns emerge across all configurations. As expected, the `StarCoder` family achieves the strongest compression, while the smallest model, `UniXcoder`, maximizes throughput at the cost of weaker compression. Models around 1B parameters – in particular `Llama3.2-1B` and `DeepSeekCoder` – offer the best speed–compression trade-off; remarkably without requiring code specialization in the case of `Llama3.2-1B`.

**LLM Pipelines vs. General-Purpose Compressors.** Across all experiments, LLM pipelines compress better than general-purpose compressors, but with significantly lower throughput. Figure 2 illustrates this trade-off by comparing our best configuration – the $T = 63$ pipeline with `bzip3-default` and representative LLMs – against strong general-purpose compressors in the tar-based setting. In all datasets, the two families occupy distinct regions in the throughput–compression plane: general-purpose compressors cluster in the *upper-right*, offering very high throughput but weaker compression, whereas LLM-based pipelines lie in the *lower-left*, achieving better compression at cost of one–two orders of magnitude lower speed.

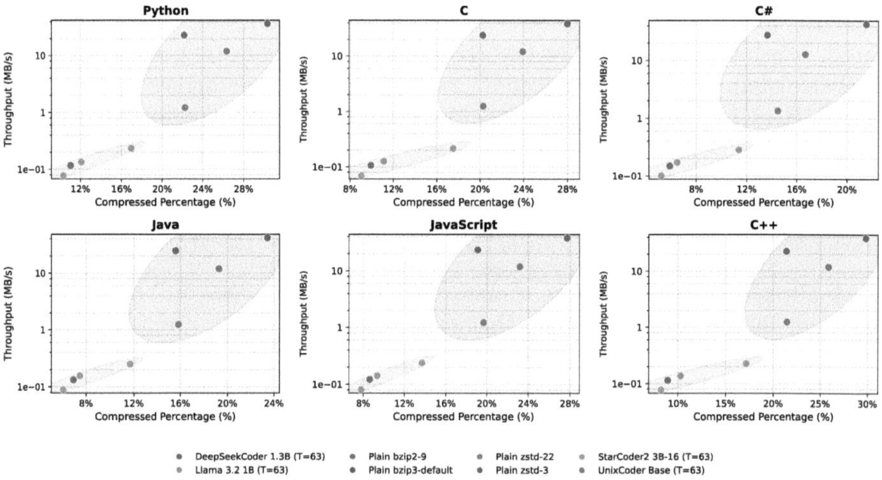


**Fig. 2.** Throughput (log scale) versus compressed percentage for the best LLM-based pipeline ($T = 63$ with `bzip3-default`) and general-purpose lossless compressors (`zstd-22`, `zstd-3`, `bzip-9`, `bzip3`) in the tar-based setting.

Quantitatively, the best LLM configuration reduces compressed size by up to 68% compared to the strongest baselines. This improvement is significant because our LLM-based method operates on single files (or even partial files, depending on the context window), which makes parallelization trivial. In contrast, general-purpose compressors exploit inter-file similarities by first sorting them (by reversed filename, as in [6]) and applying them with large context windows: hence they incur the cost of computing those reorderings for large source-code collections, such as in Software Heritage. When general-purpose compressors are instead applied to individual files, the best LLM configuration reduces compressed size by up to 82%. Notably, under both baselines, even `UniXcoder`, which yields the weakest compression among our selected LLMs, still outperforms the strongest general-purpose compressors (see Fig. 2). The remaining model-level trends are consistent with the previous analysis.

As far as decompression throughput is concerned, we mention that it is a few KB/s slower than compression. This indicates that current LLM-based symbol-ranking schemes still require throughput improvements before becoming competitive for real-world applications. Nonetheless, our results point to a promising direction, especially when combined with lighter architectures or new schemes that reduce costly LLM predictions, also considering that our pipelines can be parallelized across batches. Further future directions are discussed in Sect. 5.

**Text Compression vs. Source Code Compression.** As a final comparison, Table 2 contrasts the gains obtained by LLM-based compressors on English text and source code. For text, we use the raw compression results reported by Delétang et al. [12] on enwik9 with Transformer 800K, Chinchilla-1B, and LLaMA 2 (see Table 1 of [12]), and normalize them against `zstd-22` for a fair comparison. For source code, we report our average gains over the six language-specific datasets using `UniXcoder`, `Llama3.2-1B`, and `DeepSeekCoder`, again normalized against `zstd-22`. We consider the two scenarios discussed above: files compressed individually, or reordered by inverted path names and packed with `tar` [6].

**Table 2.** Compression gains of LLM-based compressors on English text [12] and source code (this work). Our results are averaged across six languages.

| Work | Data | Method | Model | Params | Mode | Gain |
|---|---|---|---|---|---|---|
| Delétang et al. [12] | English text | Arithmetic coding | Transformer-like | 800K | one file | 0.99× |
| | | | Chinchilla | 1B | one file | 1.90× |
| | | | Llama2 | 7B | one file | 2.59× |
| This work | Source code | Symbol ranking (`zstd-22`) | UniXcoder | 0.13B | collection | 1.89× |
| | | | Llama-3.2-4bit | 1B | collection | 3.04× |
| | | | DeepSeekCoder-AWQ | 1.3B | collection | 3.29× |
| | | | UniXcoder | 0.13B | sorted coll. | 1.18× |
| | | | Llama-3.2-4bit | 1B | sorted coll. | 1.90× |
| | | | DeepSeekCoder-AWQ | 1.3B | sorted coll. | 2.35× |

It is easy to observe that LLM-based compression yields larger gains on source code than on English text. It is striking that at comparable model scales, source-code gains are consistently higher: `DeepSeekCoder` nearly matches the gain of LLaMA 2 despite being much smaller, and the advantage becomes even larger when source-code files are compressed individually. These results suggest that source code exposes structural regularities that are well captured by LLMs but less effectively exploited by general-purpose compressors such as `zstd-22`.

## 5 Conclusions and Future Works

Building on Shannon's symbol-ranking framework, we conducted the first systematic study of LLM-based compression on source-code corpora, and proposed new approaches that yield relative compression gains up to 37% and throughput improvements up to 40% over existing LLM-based methods, while also surpassing general-purpose compressors by up to 82% in relative compression gain, yet remaining slower.

**Future Works.** Despite these advances, throughput remains the limitation of LLM-based compressors. Future work can be divided into three directions. The first concerns pipeline refinements, aimed at reducing the cost of LLM inference: (i) *parsing-based preprocessing* (e.g., Prefix-Free Parsing [7]) to eliminate redundancy before rank computation, and thus reducing the number of LLM-inference steps; (ii) *skipping the first tokens*, where prediction is known to be inaccurate; (iii) dedicated handling of *flat probability distributions*, where rank computation offers little benefit; and (iv) *parallel processing* of batches to improve throughput.

A second direction concerns the extension to *larger datasets* and the development of specialized models for compression: (i) *distillation* of large into lightweight models; (ii) *hardware-aware optimizations*, such as bfloat16 inference or quantization. Finally, a third direction is a deeper analysis of the structural properties that make source code more compressible than natural language.

**Acknowledgments.** The work of Paolo Ferragina was supported by the Alfred P. Sloan Foundation with the grant #G-2025-25193 (https://sloan.org). The authors express their sincere gratitude to the reviewers for their detailed comments and suggestions that significantly improved the submitted manuscript, and Vittorio Romano for his continuous assistance with SoBigData.it HPC infrastructure.

**Disclosure of Interests.** The authors have no competing interests to declare that are relevant to the content of this article.

## References

1. Alakuijala, J., et al.: Brotli: a general-purpose data compressor. ACM Trans. Inf. Syst. (TOIS) **37**(1), 1–30 (2018)
2. Allal, L.B., Lozhkov, A., Bakouch, E., Blázquez, G.M., Penedo, G.: SmolLLM2: when smol goes big - data-centric training of a small language model. arXiv preprint arXiv:2502.02737 (2025)
3. Bellard, F.: Lossless data compression with neural networks (2019). https://bellard.org/nncp/nncp.pdf
4. Bentley, J.L., Sleator, D.D., Tarjan, R.E., Wei, V.K.: A locally adaptive data compression scheme. Commun. ACM **29**(4), 320–330 (1986)
5. BigCode: The stack v2 (2024), software repository at Hugging Face: https://huggingface.co/datasets/bigcode/the-stack-v2
6. Boffa, A., et al.: On the compressibility of large-scale source code datasets. J. Syst. Softw. **227**, 112429 (2025)

7. Boucher, C., Gagie, T., Kuhnle, A., Langmead, B., Manzini, G., Mun, T.: Prefix-free parsing for building big BWTs. Algorithms Mol. Biol. **14**(1), 13 (2019)
8. Burrows, M., Wheeler, D.J.: A block-sorting lossless data compression algorithm. Technical report, Digital Equipment Corporation, Systems Research Center (1994)
9. Cleary, J.G., Teahan, W.J.: Unbounded length contexts for PPM. Comput. J. **40**(2–3), 67–75 (1997)
10. Cleary, J.G., Witten, I.H.: Data compression using adaptive coding and partial string matching. IEEE Trans. Commun. **32**(4), 396–402 (1984)
11. Collet, Y.: Zstandard compression and the application/zstd media type (2021), rFC 8878. Internet Engineering Task Force
12. Delétang, G., et al.: Language modeling is compression. In: International Conference on Learning Representations, vol. 2024, pp. 14165–14181 (2024)
13. Deutsch, P., Gailly, J.L.: Rfc1950: Zlib compressed data format specification version 3.3 (1996)
14. Facebook: Zstandard (Zstd): Fast real-time compression algorithm (2025), software repository
15. Fenwick, P.: Block sorting text compression - final report. Technical report, University of Auckland (1996)
16. Ferragina, P.: Pearls of Algorithm Engineering. Cambridge University Press (2023)
17. Fontana, T., Vigna, S., Zacchiroli, S.: Webgraph: the next generation (is in rust). In: Companion Proceedings of the ACM Web Conference, pp. 686–689 (2024)
18. GitHub: News and insights (2025). https://github.blog/news-insights/. Accessed 28 Oct 2025
19. Goyal, M., Tatwawadi, K., Chandak, S., Ochoa, I.: Deepzip: lossless data compression using recurrent neural networks. arXiv preprint arXiv:1811.08162 (2018)
20. HuggingFaceTB: Stack-edu dataset (2025), dataset available via Hugging Face
21. Kaplan, J., et al.: Scaling laws for neural language models. arXiv preprint arXiv:2001.08361 (2020)
22. Lelewer, D.A., Hirschberg, D.S.: Streamlining context models for data compression. In: Proceedings of the Data Compression Conference, p. 91 (1991)
23. Lozhkov, A., et al.: StarCoder 2 and The Stack v2: The next generation. arXiv preprint arXiv:2402.19173 (2024)
24. Mahoney, M.V.: Fast text compression with neural networks. In: Proceedings of the 13th International Florida Artificial Intelligence Research Society Conference (FLAIRS), pp. 230–234 (2000)
25. Mittu, F., et al.: Finezip: pushing the limits of large language models for practical lossless text compression. arXiv preprint arXiv:2409.17141 (2024)
26. Moffat, A.: Implementing the PPM data compression scheme. IEEE Trans. Commun. **38**(11), 1917–1921 (1990)
27. Morris, B.: The components of the wired spanning forest are recurrent. Probab. Theory Relat. Fields **125**(2), 259–265 (2003)
28. Narashiman, S.S., Chandrachoodan, N.: Alphazip: neural network-enhanced lossless text compression. arXiv preprint arXiv:2409.15046 (2024)
29. Navarro, G.: Compact Data Structures: A Practical Approach. Cambridge University Press (2016)
30. Peter, D.: Gzip file format specification version 4.3. Request for Comments: 1952 (1996)
31. Schmidhuber, J., Heil, S.: Sequential neural text compression. IEEE Trans. Neural Networks **7**(1), 142–146 (1996)
32. Seward, J.: bzip2 and libbzip2: a program and library for data compression (2000). https://sourceware.org/pub/bzip2/docs/manual.pdf. Accessed 28 Oct 2025

33. Shannon, C.E.: Prediction and entropy of printed english. Bell Syst. Tech. J. **30**(1), 50–64 (1951)
34. Szewczyk, K.: bzip3: a better, faster and stronger spiritual successor to BZip2 (2022). https://github.com/kspalaiologos/bzip3. Accessed 28 Oct 2025
35. Valmeekam, C.S.K., Narayanan, K., Kalathil, D., Chamberland, J.F., Shakkottai, S.: LLMzip: lossless text compression using large language models. arXiv preprint arXiv:2306.04050 (2023)
36. Vaswani, A., et al.: Attention is all you need. In: Advances in Neural Information Processing Systems, vol. 30 (2017)
37. Witten, I.H., Neal, R.M., Cleary, J.G.: Arithmetic coding for data compression. Commun. ACM **30**(6), 520–540 (1987)

# Accountable FDR Anomaly Detection Through Neuro-Symbolic Runtime Assurance

Anahita Nouri and Matteo Cristani(✉)

Dipartimento di Informatica, Università degli Studi di Verona, Strada Le Grazie 15, 37134 Verona, Italy
{anahita.nouri,matteo.cristani}@univr.it

**Abstract.** This paper presents a two-tier neuro-symbolic runtime-assurance architecture for safety-critical aviation. A learned perception tier maps noisy flight-data streams into symbolic facts, which are then evaluated by a Defeasible Logic reasoning tier derived from aviation regulations and operational guidance. Rather than making the neural component explainable, the architecture places accountability at the perceptual-symbolic boundary, where auditable non-monotonic reasoning governs neural outputs. A three-agent extension translates formal conclusions into graded crew advisories. Evaluation on heterogeneous aviation datasets shows an anomaly-detection $F_1$ of 81.4% on the NASA DASHlink four-class benchmark, compared with a 93.9% unconstrained neural ceiling, while providing named-rule justifications for every detection. The reasoning tier resolves six conflict scenarios constructed from real aviation accident investigations and transfers across datasets without modification. The paper also introduces $\Phi$, an accountability metric measuring the audit burden of the active rule base independently of detection accuracy.

**Keywords:** Neuro-symbolic AI · Flight-data recorder anomaly detection · Defeasible Logic · Runtime assurance · Aviation safety · Knowledge representation

## 1 Introduction

Flight-data recorders (FDRs) contain dense, temporally structured evidence about aircraft behaviour, including the evolution of multiple sensor and operational parameters across different phases of flight. They are therefore a natural substrate for aviation anomaly detection, yet they also expose the central difficulty of applying AI to safety-critical transport: the most sensitive statistical systems are often the least accountable, while fully symbolic monitors are auditable but brittle when applied directly to noisy, high-dimensional sensor data. This tension is particularly acute in aviation, where anomalous behaviour is rarely determined by a single variable in isolation and where the operational


S. Bistarelli et al. (Eds.): AIxIA 2026, LNAI 17131, pp. 481–498, 2027.
https://doi.org/10.1007/978-3-032-40774-0_35

meaning of the same measurement may change with flight phase, surrounding conditions, and the presence of recognised exceptions.

The problem is not merely one of explanation after prediction. In aviation, a safety-relevant conclusion must be connected to an inspectable operational rule, an exception structure, and a reproducible proof path. A model may correctly identify which measurements contributed to a classification, yet this does not by itself establish why the resulting classification should count as an operationally meaningful anomaly. Feature attribution alone does not supply that normative link. What is required is a mechanism capable of connecting statistically detected conditions to explicit safety-relevant rules and of showing how conflicts, exceptions, and priorities affect the final conclusion.

This paper develops a neuro-symbolic runtime-assurance architecture centred on FDR anomaly detection. The first tier learns from flight-data streams and converts continuous sensor windows into symbolic facts. Its role is perceptual: it extracts statistically meaningful patterns from high-dimensional observations without being required to encode the complete safety semantics of those observations internally. The second tier evaluates those facts through a Defeasible Logic theory derived from aviation regulations, guidance material, and operational safety principles. Its role is interpretative and assuring: it determines whether a candidate anomaly should be accepted, defeated, or otherwise qualified in the presence of contextual knowledge and explicit exceptions.

The architectural claim is that accuracy and accountability should be separated rather than forced into a single computational component. Neural and statistical models perform the task for which they are most effective, namely perceptual discrimination over noisy sensor data, while symbolic rules determine whether the perceived condition has safety significance. This division of responsibilities also defines an explicit assurance boundary: the output of the learned component is not treated directly as the final safety conclusion, but as evidence that must pass through a symbolic reasoning layer before acquiring operational meaning.

The best accountable configuration obtains an anomaly-detection $F_1$ of 81.4 above an unusable hand-coded symbolic baseline. Every accountable detection is accompanied by a named-rule justification, making it possible to identify which facts, rules, exceptions, and priorities support the resulting conclusion. The paper therefore treats the performance gap not as a failure of the architecture but as the empirical price of rule-grounded accountability. The relevant comparison is consequently not only between classifiers of different predictive accuracy, but between an unconstrained statistical ceiling and a system whose outputs remain explicitly connected to an inspectable safety-oriented reasoning process.

The contributions are fourfold. First, the paper formulates FDR anomaly detection as a perceptual-symbolic assurance problem, separating the detection of statistically relevant patterns from the determination of their operational safety significance. Second, it gives a compact Defeasible Logic account of the reasoning layer, including strict rules, defeasible rules, defeaters, and priority relations, so that conflicting and exceptional conditions can be represented explicitly. Third, it reports the staged effect of non-monotonic corrections on FDR false positives, showing how successive symbolic refinements alter the behaviour of the accountable detector. Fourth, it introduces Φ, an accountability metric that measures the audit burden of the active rule base independently of predictive accuracy, thereby providing a separate quantitative view of the complexity of the reasoning process that must be inspected.

The rest of this paper is organised as follows. Section 2 reviews prior work on flight-data anomaly detection, runtime assurance, and neuro-symbolic accountability, and introduces the background on Defeasible Logic required by the proposed architecture. Section 3 presents the neuro-symbolic runtime-assurance framework and describes the interface between learned FDR perception and symbolic reasoning. Section 4 details the experimental setting, including the datasets, anomaly classes, learning models, symbolic rule base, and evaluation measures. Section 5 reports the experimental results, including the comparison with the unconstrained neural ceiling, the staged effect of defeasible corrections, and the full-flight FDR analysis. Section 6 discusses accountability, the interpretation of Φ, and the trade-offs between predictive performance, auditability, and rule-base complexity. Finally, Sect. 7 concludes the paper and outlines directions for future work.

# 2 Background and Related Work

## 2.1 Flight-Data Anomaly Detection

Aviation anomaly detection has increasingly moved from the analysis of predefined exceedances toward data-driven identification of unusual or operationally significant patterns in large collections of flight-recorded parameters. Early work in the NASA aviation-safety setting showed how heterogeneous streams containing both discrete operational events and continuous sensor measurements can be analysed jointly to identify abnormal flight behaviour that may not be captured by conventional threshold-based monitoring [7]. This line of research was subsequently extended through scalable data-mining methods over high-dimensional flight data, including the NASA DASHlink setting used in this work [15].

More recent approaches have exploited the ability of machine-learning models to capture complex temporal and multivariate dependencies among FDR parameters. In particular, deep and unsupervised architectures have been applied to flight-data anomaly detection in order to learn nominal operating patterns and identify deviations without requiring an exhaustive catalogue of anomalous events [16]. Related work has also investigated large-scale emergency and safety-event analysis using surveillance and operational aviation data [21]. These approaches are attractive because abnormal behaviour in aviation rarely corresponds to a single isolated variable: its significance commonly depends on combinations of parameters, temporal evolution, and the operational phase in which the observation occurs.

However, detecting statistical abnormality and establishing the operational meaning of an anomaly are distinct tasks. A learned detector can identify that an FDR segment differs from nominal behaviour, but this does not by itself establish whether the deviation represents an unsafe condition, an expected transient, or an operationally justified exception. This distinction is especially important in flight data, where identical values may carry different meanings during climb, cruise, approach, or a phase transition. Consequently, a high anomaly score should not automatically be interpreted as a safety conclusion.

Post-hoc explanation techniques such as LIME and SHAP can identify features that contributed to a model prediction [14,22]. Such methods are useful for exposing the statistical basis of a decision, but they do not necessarily provide the form of justification required in a safety-oriented reasoning process. In high-stakes applications, this distinction between explaining a black-box prediction and obtaining an intrinsically inspectable decision process has been emphasised more generally [24]. For FDR anomaly detection, therefore, the missing element is not merely feature attribution but *rule-grounded justifiability*: the system should be able to state why the detected pattern, in the current flight context, licenses or fails to license a particular safety conclusion.

### 2.2 Runtime Assurance and Safety-Critical AI

Runtime assurance provides a useful architectural precedent for separating high-performance behaviour from safety-critical decision authority. The foundational Simplex architecture introduced the idea that an advanced or potentially complex controller can operate while a simpler and more trustworthy component supervises the system and preserves safety when the advanced component can no longer be relied upon [25]. The general principle is therefore not that every high-performance component must itself be made fully certifiable, but that its behaviour is constrained at a well-defined assurance boundary.

This principle has subsequently developed into runtime-assurance architectures in which a system is monitored during operation and unsafe behaviour is constrained through a verified or otherwise inspectable assurance component [2,17–19]. Such architectures are particularly relevant when advanced algorithms offer performance advantages but are difficult to verify exhaustively. The assurance mechanism provides an independent criterion for determining when the behaviour of the advanced component can be accepted and when an alternative safe response is required.

The architecture proposed here adapts this idea from control to learned interpretation. We do not use runtime assurance to switch between physical aircraft controllers. Instead, the assurance boundary is placed at the interface where neural interpretations of FDR observations become symbolic claims about anomalous or safety-relevant behaviour. The learned component is therefore permitted to exploit complex statistical regularities in the recorded data, while the symbolic tier determines whether the corresponding interpretation is compatible with contextual and domain-level rules.

This adaptation changes the object of assurance from an actuator command to an *inference*. A neural prediction can be treated as a candidate conclusion rather than as an authoritative safety statement. Before that conclusion acquires operational meaning, it is evaluated against explicit rules, exceptions, and priorities. In this sense, the symbolic reasoner plays a role analogous to an assurance component: it defines the conditions under which the output of the high-performance learned component is allowed to propagate into the final interpretation.

### 2.3 Neuro-Symbolic Accountability

The combination of learning and symbolic reasoning is consistent with the broader neuro-symbolic research programme, which seeks to integrate the pattern-learning capabilities of neural models with explicit knowledge representation and logical inference [8]. Neuro-symbolic approaches are motivated in part by the complementary properties of the two paradigms: neural models are effective at extracting regularities from high-dimensional data, whereas symbolic representations provide explicit structures for reasoning, constraints, and inspectable inference.

Our use of this combination is deliberately asymmetric. The neural tier is not required to become transparent in itself, nor do we attempt to translate the complete internal state of the learned model into symbolic form. Instead, its output is made accountable by passing through a symbolic layer that can accept, reject, defeat, or prioritise conclusions. The symbolic component therefore does not merely explain an already finalised prediction; it participates in determining whether that prediction should become the system's final conclusion.

This distinction separates the proposed architecture from purely post-hoc explainability. Feature-attribution techniques explain which inputs were important for a model output, but an attribution does not establish whether that output is permissible or justified under domain knowledge. This limitation is particularly significant in safety-critical applications, where an explanation of how a model reached an erroneous conclusion does not make the conclusion acceptable. More generally, concerns about relying on post-hoc explanations for black-box models in high-stakes settings motivate architectures in which interpretable reasoning is incorporated directly into the decision process [24].

In our setting, accountability is therefore attached to the transition from *detection* to *operational meaning*. A neural model may report that a sequence of FDR measurements resembles anomalous behaviour, but the symbolic tier determines whether contextual facts support that interpretation, whether an exception defeats it, or whether a competing rule has priority. Every final symbolic conclusion can consequently be associated with the facts, rules, and preference relations that supported or defeated it.

The resulting design introduces a normative checkpoint between statistical detection and safety interpretation. Rather than treating the machine-learning prediction as the end of the reasoning pipeline, it becomes one source of evidence within an explicit non-monotonic reasoning process. This allows the system to retain the representational power of learned FDR models while providing a rule-grounded and auditable account of how their outputs acquire safety-relevant meaning.

## 3 A Short Introduction to Defeasible Logic

Defeasible Logic is a non-monotonic rule formalism designed for reasoning with rules, exceptions, and priorities [1,9,20]. A defeasible theory $D = (F, R, >)$ comprises a set of facts $F$, a set of rules $R$, and a superiority relation $>$ ordering rules in conflict. Three rule classes are semantically distinct. Strict rules ($A \rightarrow q$) fire whenever their antecedents hold. Defeasible rules ($A \Rightarrow q$) yield normally valid conclusions that may be overridden. Defeaters ($A \rightsquigarrow q$) block opposing inferences without drawing positive conclusions. The superiority relation $r_i > r_j$ states that $r_i$ prevails over $r_j$ when both are applicable and their conclusions conflict [6,11]. Consequently, conclusions in Defeasible Logic are not determined only by which rules are applicable, but also by the explicit preference structure among competing rules.

This latter property is particularly relevant when symbolic reasoning is used to supervise or correct the behaviour of a learned model. Preferences among defeasible rules need not be regarded as immutable: revising the superiority relation provides a principled mechanism for changing the conclusions supported by a defeasible knowledge base without replacing the knowledge base as a whole [10]. In the setting considered here, this makes rule priorities a natural control point for correcting erroneous or undesirable machine-learning decisions. When observed evidence indicates that a learned prediction is inappropriate in a particular operational context, the symbolic layer can favour an exception rule over the rule supporting the prediction, thereby revising the resulting decision in an explicit and inspectable manner.

This interaction can also be understood as a form of agreement process between two heterogeneous sources of information: the data-driven model and the symbolic knowledge encoded by domain rules. Agreement methods have been studied as processes in which initially different representations or interpretations are progressively reconciled through negotiation [3]. Although the setting here is different from semantic meaning negotiation, the underlying principle is useful: rather than assuming that one source is unconditionally authoritative, conflicting conclusions can be resolved through an explicit process in which contextual evidence and preferences determine which position prevails. In our case, defeasible rules and their priorities provide the formal mechanism implementing this negotiation between the ML prediction and domain-level constraints.

The applicability of this approach is not restricted to aviation. Defeasible reasoning has, for example, been used to control sensor-driven systems for energy efficiency, where operational rules may conflict, admit exceptions, and depend on contextual observations [26]. Such applications illustrate the suitability of non-monotonic rules for translating low-level sensor information into context-dependent operational decisions, a requirement that is closely related to the treatment of FDR data considered here.

For FDR anomaly detection, Defeasible Logic therefore turns sensor-derived facts and machine-learning outputs into auditable conclusions while providing an explicit mechanism for resolving exceptional situations. For example:

$$r_1 : \texttt{airspeed\_high}(t) \wedge \texttt{approach}(t) \Rightarrow \texttt{speed\_high\_anomaly}(t),$$
$$r_2 : \texttt{phase\_transition}(t) \rightsquigarrow \neg\texttt{speed\_high\_anomaly}(t), \quad r_2 > r_1.$$

Rule $r_1$ supports a speed-high anomaly during approach; rule $r_2$ blocks that inference during a phase transition. The superiority relation makes the exception explicit, deterministic, and auditable. More generally, when the output of the learned model conflicts with contextual or domain knowledge, the same preference mechanism can determine whether the learned conclusion is retained or defeated. This separates the statistical identification of potentially anomalous behaviour from the context-sensitive reasoning required to validate or correct that identification, while preserving a traceable account of why the final conclusion was reached.

## 4 Architecture

The architecture contains three agents. Agent 1 performs FDR perception: it consumes windows of sensor data and emits candidate symbolic facts. Agent 2 performs Defeasible Logic reasoning over these facts. Agent 3 translates formal conclusions and proof chains into graded crew advisories (Fig. 1).

### 4.1 Agent 1: FDR Perception and Symbol Grounding

The perception tier bridges continuous FDR streams and discrete rule-based reasoning. Its function is to transform low-level temporal observations into a symbolic representation that can be consumed by the reasoning agent. The architecture therefore combines statistical learning with symbolic reasoning while keeping the boundary between the two components explicit.

Depending on the perception bridge, the learning component may be neural or non-neural, while the symbolic reasoning layer remains unchanged. In the learned bridge, models such as XGBoost [5], BiLSTM [12], or a filtered LSTM map 160-second windows of 20 FDR channels into anomaly probabilities and candidate labels. These outputs provide the intermediate representation through which patterns identified in the continuous flight-data stream become discrete candidate facts for subsequent symbolic evaluation. Class imbalance is handled using standard techniques such as SMOTE [4], so that the perception model can be trained in the presence of comparatively rare anomalous observations.

In the kinematic bridge, by contrast, FAA-inspired thresholds and phase-of-flight information directly instantiate symbolic predicates. Here, symbol grounding does not depend on a learned classifier: observed sensor values are mapped into predicates through explicitly defined kinematic conditions and contextual

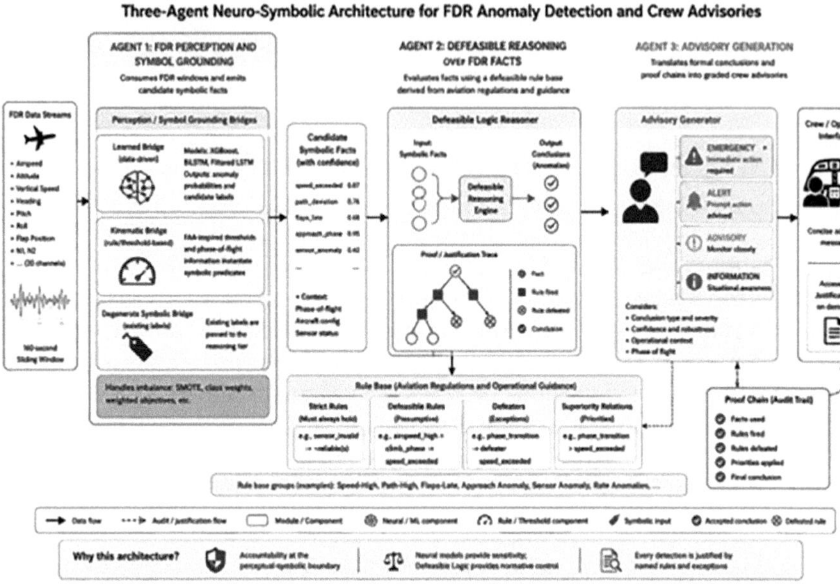


**Fig. 1.** Three-agent neuro-symbolic architecture for FDR anomaly detection and crew advisories. Agent 1 maps multichannel FDR streams into candidate symbolic facts via learned, kinematic, or symbolic bridges. Agent 2 evaluates facts through a Defeasible Logic engine backed by an FAA regulatory rule base (strict rules, defeasible rules, defeaters, and superiority relations), yielding a formal proof tree. Agent 3 translates verified conclusions into graded operational advisories (EMERGENCY, ALERT, ADVISORY, INFORMATION) while maintaining an auditable proof chain.

flight-phase information. The two bridges therefore differ in how symbolic facts are obtained, but not in the form of the facts delivered to the reasoning tier.

This separation makes the perception component replaceable without requiring a corresponding redesign of the symbolic layer. A dataset for which sufficient labelled data are available may use a learned bridge, whereas a setting dominated by explicit operational thresholds may use the kinematic bridge. In either case, the downstream reasoner operates over the same kind of symbolic predicates and applies the same rule-based inference mechanism. This modularity is essential: the perception bridge may vary across datasets, models, or sensing conditions, while the reasoning tier remains fixed.

## 4.2 Agent 2: Defeasible Reasoning over FDR Facts

Agent 2 evaluates symbolic facts against a rule base containing strict rules, defeasible rules, defeaters, and superiority relations. Its role is to interpret the candidate facts produced by the perception tier in the light of explicit operational knowledge, exceptions, and conflict resolution policies. It is therefore not a second classifier; it is a normative filter over classifier outputs.

A neural model may report a high anomaly probability, but Agent 2 determines whether the corresponding symbolic fact can be defended by the active rule base. The learned prediction is consequently treated as an input to the reasoning process rather than as a final safety-relevant conclusion. Depending on the available contextual facts, the corresponding inference may be supported, blocked by a defeater, or overridden by a competing rule with higher priority.

This distinction is important because the same classifier output may have different operational meanings under different flight conditions. Agent 2 makes those contextual dependencies explicit by reasoning over the symbolic representation supplied by Agent 1 and applying the rule structure independently of the internal mechanism of the perception model. The reasoning layer therefore provides a stable interface through which different learned or kinematic perception bridges can be evaluated against the same symbolic knowledge base.

For every conclusion, the proof chain records which facts were used, which rules fired, which rules were defeated, and which priority relation resolved any conflict. The resulting trace makes the final decision reproducible and auditable, because the system can expose not only the accepted conclusion but also the reasoning steps that supported it and the competing rules that failed to prevail. In this way, Agent 2 acts as the explicit assurance layer of the architecture, connecting candidate anomaly detections to rule-grounded and inspectable operational conclusions.

### 4.3 Knowledge Base Construction

The process follows a six-step pipeline. Steps 1 and 4 are the authors' original contributions; the remaining steps use standard tooling.

1. **Source identification.** Relevant FAA documents are identified according to their relevance to the target anomaly classes and segmented at the level of individual regulatory or operational clauses. The principal sources are AC 120-71B, FAA Order 7110.65, and FAA Advisory Circular 00-54. Clause-level segmentation preserves a direct link between each encoded rule and the source provision from which it originates.
2. **LLM-assisted extraction.** Each clause is passed to a large language model using a structured prompt requesting the operative condition, the normal conclusion, and any explicit exception. The LLM produces candidate symbolic rules, but it is used only as an extraction aid. All semantic interpretation and validation remain the responsibility of the author, and no generated rule is accepted automatically.
3. **Schema normalisation.** Candidate rules are mapped to the defeasible schema $(A, q, type)$, where $A$ is the antecedent conjunction, $q$ the consequent literal, and $type \in \rightarrow, \Rightarrow, \rightsquigarrow$. Equivalent natural-language expressions are normalised to a common symbolic vocabulary so that rules originating from different sources can be evaluated consistently.
4. **Expert validation.** The first author, holding a commercial pilot licence, verifies every normalised rule against the corresponding source text. The val-

idation checks that antecedents, conclusions, exceptions, and rule types preserve the intended operational meaning. Rules that cannot be justified by the source document are corrected or discarded.

5. **Superiority encoding.** Potential conflicts among validated rules are identified and, where the source specifies a priority, represented through the superiority relation $r_i > r_j$. For example, the priority of a TCAS advisory over a conflicting ATC instruction is encoded according to FAA Order 7110.65 §2-1-6. This makes regulatory precedence and exception handling explicit in the rule base.
6. **Houdini compilation.** The validated theory is translated into the representation required by the Houdini Defeasible Logic engine [6]. Houdini evaluates rule applicability, resolves conflicts through the encoded superiority relations, and determines whether candidate conclusions are supported or defeated. The use of named rules and explicit priorities preserves traceability from runtime conclusions back to their symbolic justification.

As a worked example, FAA AC 120-71B states: *"An approach is stabilised if airspeed does not exceed the target approach speed by more than 10 knots."* This is extracted as the defeasible rule:

$$r_{\text{stab}} : \texttt{airspeed}_{\texttt{e}}\texttt{xceeds}_{\texttt{t}}\texttt{arget}(t) \wedge \texttt{approach}(t) \Rightarrow \texttt{speed}_{\texttt{h}}\texttt{igh}_{\texttt{a}}\texttt{nomaly}(t).$$

FAA AC 120-71B also notes that during a phase transition from cruise to approach, a brief exceedance is operationally expected. This is encoded as a defeater:

$$r_{\text{trans}} : \texttt{phase}_{\texttt{t}}\texttt{ransition}(t) \rightsquigarrow \neg\texttt{speed}_{\texttt{h}}\texttt{igh}_{\texttt{a}}\texttt{nomaly}(t), \quad r_{\text{trans}} > r_{\text{stab}}.$$

The final knowledge base contains 75 strict rules, 218 defeasible rules, 51 defeaters, and 124 superiority relations, covering approach stabilisation, emergency descent, engine failure, stall risk, electrical failure, and conflict resolution.

### 4.4 Agent 3: Advisory Generation

Agent 3 translates formal conclusions into operational language (information, advisory, alert, or emergency) while preserving the underlying formal justification for later audit.

The architecture intentionally decouples statistical perception from symbolic reasoning. The perception bridge may be implemented using different learning models including BiLSTM, FilteredLSTM, or XGBoost without modifying the symbolic reasoning tier. The bridge maps continuous telemetry into symbolic facts, which are then evaluated against the FAA-derived defeasible theory. This separation allows the accountability mechanism to remain independent of the choice of machine learning model: a tree-based learner such as XGBoost produces the same symbolic interface as a recurrent neural network, and both are subject to the same rule-grounded accountability check.

**Table 1.** Performance on the DASHlink full-flight FDR two-tier evaluation.

| Metric | Before PLA fix | After PLA fix | Final | Mechanism |
|---|---|---|---|---|
| False positives, total | 34,273 | 127 | 528* | ML bridge residual |
| False positives, ground | 0 | 0 | 0 | Phase state machine |
| PLA false alarms | 127 | 0 | 0 | Defeater |
| Recall | 100% | 100% | 100% | — |
| Precision | 31.5% | 99.2% | 99.2% | — |
| $F_1$ | 47.9% | 99.6% | 99.6% | — |

*The 528 residual FPs belong to the learned four-class bridge evaluation, not the kinematic bridge.

# 5 FDR Anomaly Detection as the Core Evaluation

## 5.1 Full-Flight DASHlink Two-Tier Evaluation

The full-flight FDR experiment tests the kinematic bridge across all seven flight phases. The central empirical result of this evaluation is the staged reduction of false positives shown in Table 1: the defeasible reasoning tier reduces 34,273 false positives to zero through two targeted non-monotonic mechanisms, while maintaining 100% recall throughout. This is the clearest demonstration of why symbolic reasoning matters, a purely statistical system would have no mechanism to remove these false alarms without also removing true detections. The symbolic reasoning stage operates in milliseconds on standard hardware and represents a negligible fraction of the perception pipeline latency.

## 5.2 NASA DASHlink Four-Class Benchmark

The four-class benchmark evaluates the learned bridge on 19,968 test flights with nominal, speed-high, path-high, and flaps-late classes. Table 2 reports the binary anomaly-versus-nominal results. The headline result is the FilteredLSTM+DL configuration, which reaches $F_1 = 81.4\%$ while generating a named-rule justification for every detection. The pure neural model achieves 93.9% $F_1$ but has $\Phi = 0$ because it produces no rule-grounded proof chain.

The relevant baseline is not only the neural ceiling. A hand-coded symbolic classifier was operationally unusable on the same data, producing 34,273 false positives and anomaly precision of 3.5%. The neuro-symbolic architecture closes much of the gap between brittle symbolic monitoring and opaque neural classification.

## 5.3 False Negatives and Operational Interpretation

The FilteredLSTM+DL configuration produces 276 false negatives on the four-class benchmark, distributed across three failure modes. Approximately 157 cases

**Table 2.** Aggregate performance on the NASA DASHlink four-class benchmark.

| System | Recall | Precision | $F_1$ | $\Phi$ |
|---|---|---|---|---|
| XGBoost alone | 94.9% | 98.7% | 93.9% | 0.000 |
| BiLSTM alone | 90.6% | 99.6% | 91.0% | 0.000 |
| OR Ensemble + DL | 88.6% | 62.1% | 73.0% | 0.106 |
| XGBoost + DL | 84.9% | 76.1% | 80.3% | 0.106 |
| FilteredLSTM + DL | 86.4% | 76.9% | **81.4%** | 0.106 |

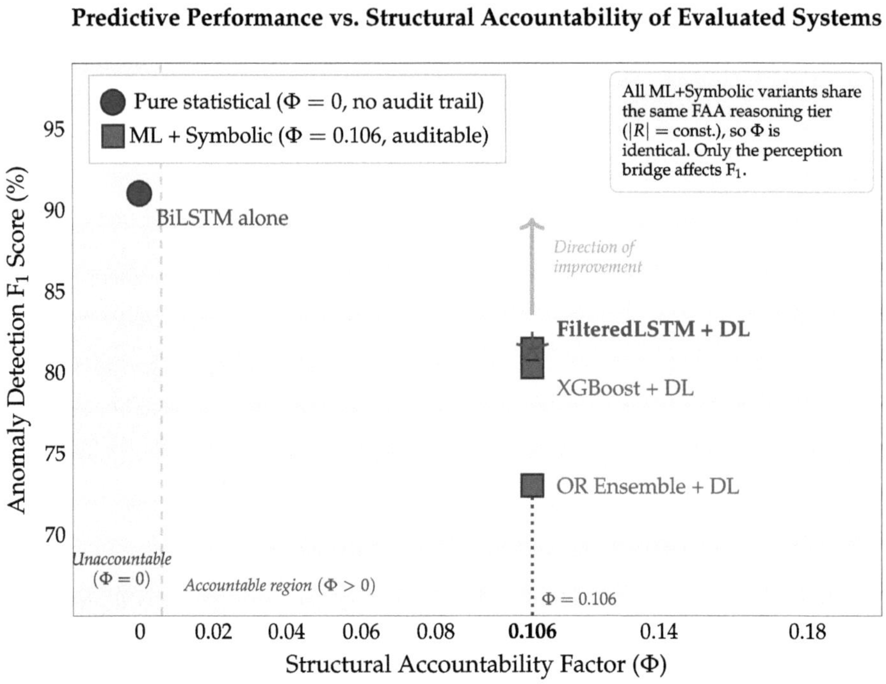


**Fig. 2.** Predictive performance vs. structural accountability $\Phi$ for all systems in Table 2. Pure statistical models (blue circles) achieve high $F_1$ but no structural accountability ($\Phi = 0$, no audit trail). ML+Symbolic configurations (green squares) retain competitive $F_1$ while moving into the accountable region ($\Phi = 0.106$). Since all ML+Symbolic variants use the same FAA-derived reasoning tier ($|R| =$ const.), their $\Phi$ values are identical; only the perception bridge (BiLSTM, FilteredLSTM, or XGBoost) affects $F_1$. The arrow indicates the direction of future improvement: higher $\Phi$ with maintained predictive performance.

(57%) are kinematically ambiguous: the available FDR channels do not distinguish the event cleanly from a normal approach, as reflected in Fig. 3 which shows 9% of Path-High cases misclassified as Nominal. A further 79 cases (29%) are borderline: the event lies close to the operational threshold. The remaining

40 cases (14%) are late-developing: the anomaly emerges near the end of the 160-second window, beyond the attention mechanism's effective temporal horizon. The limitation is primarily in the perceptual evidence and temporal horizon, not in the rule formalism.

## 6 Conflict Resolution and Cross-Dataset Transfer

The Defeasible Logic tier was evaluated on six conflict scenarios constructed from real aviation accident investigations. Each scenario encodes the regulatory conflict that the corresponding accident exposed: a pair of individually valid safety rules whose conclusions are mutually incompatible under the same operational conditions. The scenarios, their accident grounding, and their formal resolution are shown in Table 3.

For illustration, the Überlingen conflict is formalised as:

$$r_{\text{TCAS}} : \texttt{ra\_advisory}(climb, t) \Rightarrow \texttt{climb}(t),$$
$$r_{\text{ATC}} : \texttt{atc\_instruction}(descend, t) \Rightarrow \texttt{descend}(t), \quad r_{\text{TCAS}} > r_{\text{ATC}}.$$

Given the facts $\texttt{ra\_advisory}(climb, t)$ and $\texttt{atc\_instruction}(descend, t)$, the engine derives $+\partial\,\texttt{climb}(t)$ and $-\partial\,\texttt{descend}(t)$, resolving the conflict in favour of the TCAS advisory in accordance with FAA Order 7110.65 §2-1-6. This resolution holds across all 9,600 instances of this scenario.

The system resolves all six scenario types correctly across all 57,600 tested instances. Correctness is a logical property, not a statistical estimate: each scenario has a regulatory ground truth established by the accident investigation record, and the superiority relations in the theory encode exactly those priorities.

Cross-dataset transfer further supports the separation thesis. Across simulation, full-flight FDR data, expert-annotated approach segments, and accident-conflict cases, the perception bridge changes but the reasoning theory remains stable.

## 7 Accountability and Explainability Metric

Predictive metrics do not measure whether a conclusion can be audited. We therefore introduce two quantities: a structural accountability factor $\Phi$, which measures the auditability of the active rule base, and an explainability score $\Xi$, which combines accountability with predictive performance.

Let $R$ be the set of active rules participating in a system conclusion. The structural accountability factor is:

$$\Phi = \begin{cases} \dfrac{1}{\log_2 |R| + 1} & |R| > 0, \\ 0 & |R| = 0. \end{cases} \tag{1}$$

A system with no active rules receives $\Phi = 0$. A system with a single active rule receives $\Phi = 1$, the ideal limit of human auditability. The logarithm models diminishing growth in human audit effort as the number of rules increases: a practitioner reading ten rules does not expend ten times the effort of reading one, because rules share vocabulary and structure. The logarithmic formulation is therefore a first approximation of sublinear audit cost, not a claim to be a universal auditability standard. The explainability score is $\Xi = P \cdot \Phi$, where $P \in [0, 1]$ is any task-appropriate performance measure. In the anomaly-detection setting, $P$ is macro-$F_1$.

## 8 Discussion

The FDR results show that combining statistical learning with symbolic reasoning provides a viable middle ground between brittle symbolic monitoring and opaque statistical detection. The strongest empirical result is the false-positive reduction in Table 1: 34,273 false positives reduced to zero through two targeted

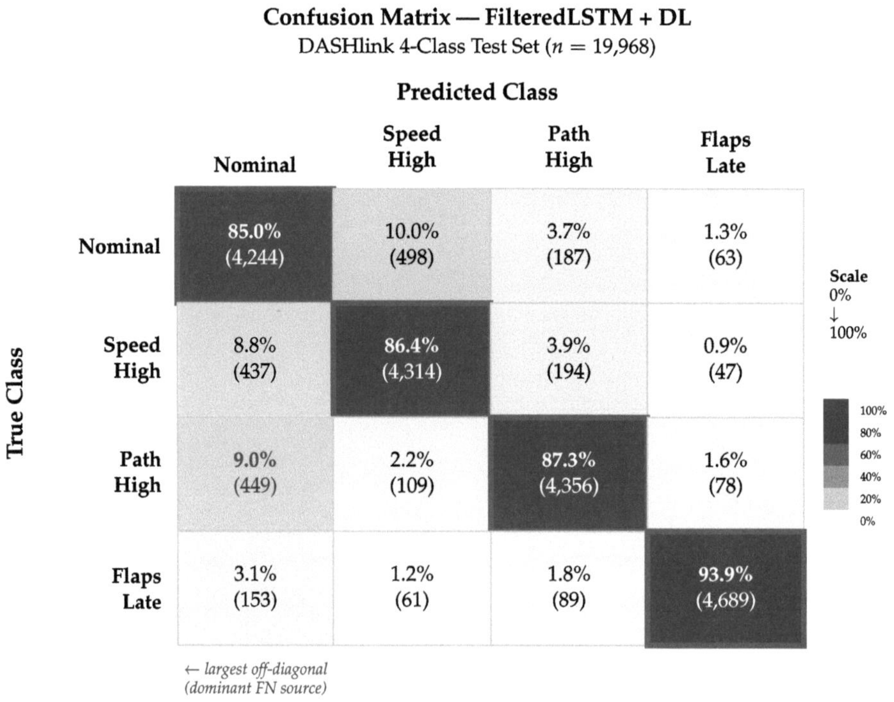


**Fig. 3.** Confusion matrix for the FilteredLSTM+DL system on the DASHlink 4-class test set, normalised by true class (row percentages). Diagonal dominance confirms strong per-class separation. The principal off-diagonal mass lies in the Path High row, where 9% of cases are misclassified as Nominal, the dominant contributor to the 276 false negatives (157 kinematically ambiguous, 79 borderline, 40 late-developing).

**Table 3.** Conflict scenarios constructed from real accident investigations. Each row encodes the regulatory conflict exposed by the accident as a superiority relation; the system resolves all 57,600 instances correctly.

| Accident | Conflict type | Resolution rule | Instances |
|---|---|---|---|
| Überlingen (2002) | TCAS climb vs. ATC descend | TCAS precedence | 9,600 |
| Boeing 737 MAX (2018–19) | MCAS activation vs. manual recovery | Emergency precedence | 9,600 |
| Air France 447 (2009) | Stall warning vs. invalid pitot | Sensor fault masking | 9,600 |
| Atlas Air 3591 (2019) | Go-around trigger vs. pilot pitch | Pilot override | 9,600 |
| US Airways 1549 (2009) | Gear-normal procedure vs. ditching | Emergency override | 9,600 |
| Electrical fire (generic) | Shut off master vs. keep radio | Electrical fire rule | 9,600 |

defeasible mechanisms while recall remains at 100%. This result is more significant than the NASA four-class $F_1$ figures because it demonstrates exactly what non-monotonic reasoning contributes something no purely statistical adjustment could achieve without sacrificing recall. The relationship between predictive performance and accountability across all system configurations is summarised in Fig. 2. Pure neural models cluster at $\Phi = 0$: they achieve the highest unconstrained $F_1$ but provide no rule-grounded proof chain. The accountable configurations occupy $\Phi = 0.106$, sacrificing part of the unconstrained performance in exchange for named-rule justifications.

The architecture also offers a different kind of explainability from post-hoc attribution methods. LIME and SHAP identify influential features but cannot state which operational rule licenses a conclusion or which exception was considered. A defeasible proof chain supplies exactly that: the rule name, its antecedents, the defeater that was checked, and the superiority relation that resolved any conflict precisely the audit trail required by certification-oriented frameworks such as DO-178C [23]. Although the perception bridge may use neural or non-neural models, this accountability property holds regardless of the underlying learner, because it is a property of the symbolic tier rather than the statistical one.

The proposed system is a research prototype and should not be interpreted as certified avionics. Although the reasoning engine is domain-independent, the current rule base is aviation-specific and would require reconstruction for other regulatory frameworks or sensor-grounded domains. Furthermore, the proposed accountability metric, $\Phi$, is an experimental structural measure rather than a settled standard, and future work should investigate richer formulations that account for proof complexity and human audit effort. Finally, the remaining gap between the accountable system and the neural ceiling indicates that continued improvements to the perception bridge are needed, particularly for kinematically ambiguous and late-developing anomalies.

# 9 Conclusion

This paper presented an accountable neuro-symbolic runtime-assurance architecture for FDR anomaly detection in safety-critical aviation. The proposed approach separates statistical detection from safety-relevant interpretation: a neural component identifies potentially anomalous patterns in flight data, while a defeasible symbolic layer determines whether those patterns should be accepted, rejected, or overridden in light of contextual facts, exceptions, and rule priorities.

On the NASA DASHlink four-class benchmark, the best accountable configuration reaches $F_1 = 81.4\%$, compared with a 93.9% unconstrained neural ceiling, while providing named-rule justifications for every detection. This difference highlights an explicit trade-off between maximum predictive performance and accountable decision-making. In the proposed architecture, a reduction in raw classification performance is accepted in exchange for a reasoning process whose conclusions can be inspected, challenged, and traced back to the rules and facts that produced them. For safety-critical applications, this distinction is important because high predictive accuracy alone does not establish that individual decisions are operationally justified.

On the full-flight FDR evaluation, defeaters and phase-of-flight reasoning reduce a large false-positive burden. This result shows the value of treating machine-learning predictions as candidate conclusions rather than final decisions. Contextual information can defeat predictions that are statistically plausible but operationally inappropriate, particularly in transient flight conditions where identical sensor values may have different meanings. The defeasible layer therefore acts not only as an explanation mechanism, but also as an explicit error-correction and assurance mechanism between learned detection and safety interpretation.

The broader lesson is architectural: trustworthy AI for safety-critical environments can combine learned sensor perception with explicit, inspectable defeasible reasoning over normatively meaningful facts. Such an architecture does not require the internal operation of the neural model itself to become fully transparent. Instead, accountability is enforced at the point where its outputs acquire operational meaning, through rules that make assumptions, exceptions, conflicts, and priorities explicit.

Several limitations remain. The present evaluation considers a specific set of anomaly classes and a manually engineered symbolic knowledge layer, and the quality of the final assurance mechanism necessarily depends on the coverage and correctness of those rules. Future work should therefore investigate systematic rule acquisition and validation, richer temporal reasoning over complete flight trajectories, and adaptive revision of rule priorities when recurrent disagreement emerges between learned predictions and domain-level constraints. Extending the approach to additional aircraft, operational conditions, and safety-event datasets would also be necessary to assess its generalisability.

Overall, the results suggest that neuro-symbolic assurance can provide a practical middle ground between opaque high-performance anomaly detection and fully hand-coded safety reasoning. Learned models retain responsibility for extracting complex patterns from high-dimensional FDR data, while defeasible reasoning provides an auditable checkpoint before those patterns are promoted to safety-relevant conclusions. This division of responsibilities offers a promising direction for the deployment of machine learning in aviation and, more generally, in domains where predictive performance must coexist with traceability, contestability, and explicit safety reasoning.

**Declaration on the Use of AI Tools.** ChatGPT 5.3 was used for drafting assistance, language refinement, structural organisation, and condensation of thesis material into conference-paper form. The scientific claims, experimental results, interpretation, and final responsibility for the submitted manuscript remain with the human researcher(s).

## References


1. Antoniou, G., Billington, D., Governatori, G., Maher, M.J.: Representation results for defeasible logic. ACM Trans. Comput. Logic **2**(2), 255–287 (2001)
2. Brat, G., Pai, G.: Runtime assurance of aeronautical products. NASA/TM-20220015734, NASA Ames (2023)
3. Burato, E., Cristani, M.: The process of reaching agreement in meaning negotiation. In: Nguyen, N.T. (ed.) Transactions on Computational Collective Intelligence VII. LNCS, vol. 7270, pp. 1–42. Springer, Heidelberg (2012). https://doi.org/10.1007/978-3-642-32066-8_1
4. Chawla, N.V., Bowyer, K.W., Hall, L.O., Kegelmeyer, W.P.: SMOTE: synthetic minority over-sampling technique. JAIR **16**, 321–357 (2002)
5. Chen, T., Guestrin, C.: XGBoost: a scalable tree boosting system. In: Proceedings of 22nd ACM SIGKDD, pp. 785–794 (2016)
6. Cristani, M., et al.: Houdini (unchained): an effective reasoner for defeasible logic. In: Proceedings of 6th Workshop on Advances in Argumentation in AI. CEUR, vol. 3354 (2022)
7. Das, S., Matthews, B.L., Srivastava, A.N., Oza, N.C.: Multiple kernel learning for heterogeneous anomaly detection: algorithm and aviation safety case study. In: Proceedings of 16th ACM SIGKDD, pp. 47–56 (2010)
8. Garcez, A.d'A., Lamb, L.C.: Neurosymbolic AI: the 3rd wave. Artif. Intell. Rev. **56**(11), 12387–12406 (2023)
9. Governatori, G., Maher, M.J., Antoniou, G., Billington, D.: Argumentation semantics for defeasible logic. J. Logic Comput. **14**(5), 675–702 (2004)
10. Governatori, G., Olivieri, F., Cristani, M., Scannapieco, S.: Revision of defeasible preferences. Int. J. Approx. Reason. **104**, 205–230 (2019)
11. Governatori, G., Olivieri, F., Rotolo, A., Cristani, M.: Stable normative explanations. In: JURIX 2022. Frontiers in AI, vol. 362, pp. 43–52. IOS Press (2022)
12. Hochreiter, S., Schmidhuber, J.: Long short-term memory. Neural Comput. **9**(8), 1735–1780 (1997)
13. Lipton, Z.: The mythos of model interpretability. Queue **16**(3), 31–57 (2018)
14. Lundberg, S.M., Lee, S.I.: A unified approach to interpreting model predictions. In: NeurIPS, vol. 30 (2017)
15. Matthews, B., et al.: Discovering anomalous aviation safety events using scalable data mining algorithms. J. Aerospace Inf. Sys. **10**(10), 467–475 (2013)
16. Memarzadeh, M., Matthews, B., Avrekh, I.: Unsupervised anomaly detection in flight data using convolutional variational autoencoder. Aerospace **7**(8), 115 (2020)

17. Miller, K., Zeitler, C.K., Shen, W., Viswanathan, M., Mitra, S.: RTAEval: a framework for evaluating runtime assurance logic. In: ATVA 2023. LNCS, vol. 14216. Springer (2023)
18. Miller, K., et al.: Optimal runtime assurance via reinforcement learning. In: ICCPS 2024. IEEE (2024)
19. Nagarajan, P., Kannan, S.K., Torens, C., Vukas, M.E., Wilber, G.F.: ASTM F3269 — an industry standard on run time assurance for aircraft systems. In: AIAA Scitech 2021 (2021)
20. Nute, D.: Defeasible logic. In: Handbook of Logic in AI and Logic Programming, vol. 3. Oxford University Press (1994)
21. Olive, X., et al.: OpenSky report 2020: analysing in-flight emergencies using big data. In: Proceedings of 39th IEEE/AIAA DASC (2020)
22. Ribeiro, M.T., Singh, S., Guestrin, C.: Why should I trust you?: explaining the predictions of any classifier. In: Proceedings of 22nd ACM SIGKDD, pp. 1135–1144 (2016)
23. RTCA: Software considerations in airborne systems and equipment certification, DO-178C. Technical report, RTCA, Washington, D.C. (2011)
24. Rudin, C.: Stop explaining black box machine learning models for high stakes decisions and use interpretable models instead. Nat. Mach. Intell. **1**, 206–215 (2019)
25. Seto, D., Krogh, B., Sha, L., Chutinan, A.: The simplex architecture for safe on-line control system upgrades. In: Proceedings of American Control Conference, vol. 6, pp. 3504–3508. IEEE (1998)
26. Tomazzoli, C., Cristani, M., Karafili, E., Olivieri, F.: Non-monotonic reasoning rules for energy efficiency. J. Ambient Intell. Smart Environ. **9**(3), 345–360 (2017)

# Autonomous Skill Development: Neuro-Symbolic Agents that Self-generate Verifiable Tools

Elia Pacioni[1,2](✉), Valerio Crocetti[1,3], Andrei C. Coman[1], Davide Calvaresi[1], Gaetano Manzo[1], and Michael Ignaz Schumacher[1]

[1] HES-SO Valais-Wallis, 3960 Sierre, Switzerland
{elia.pacioni,valerio.crocetti,andrei.coman,davide.calvaresi, gaetano.manzo,michael.schumacher}@hevs.ch
[2] University of Extremadura, 06800 Mérida, Spain
[3] Università Politecnica delle Marche, 60121 Ancona, Italy

**Abstract.** Large language model (LLM)-based agents can address highly heterogeneous tasks. However, their result and justifications are generated through opaque (non-inspectable) sub-symbolic processing. Thus, even a plausible explanation may be post-hoc and unfaithful to the process that produced the answer. Such behavior undermines safety, auditability, and accountability in high-stakes domains such as healthcare and finance. This paper presents Autonomous Skill Development (ASD), a neuro-symbolic agent architecture that separates open-ended language reasoning from deterministic computation. Rather than relying on the LLM to repeatedly solve and explain computational problems, ASD dynamically generates, validates, stores, and reuses explicit symbolic skills. A neuro-symbolic router first determines whether a request contains a deterministic computation that can be extracted and formalized. When such a computation is identified, ASD generates a skill as a pure function exposed through an interoperable Model Context Protocol (MCP) tool. The skill is then evaluated through a layered validation pipeline that combines deterministic tests with an independent LLM judge and, once validated, is stored in a reusable, versioned skill library. Subsequent computations are performed by inspectable code, while the LLM is restricted to interpreting and communicating the resulting output. Each answer is therefore accompanied by explicit provenance identifying the skill executed, the input values provided, and the result produced. Unlike a free-form LLM justification, this trace is faithful by construction because it directly reflects the computation that generated the answer. Dynamic skill generation is essential for scalability, as manually implementing rules for every possible deterministic subtask would be impractical. We evaluate ASD in the nutrition domain by examining the skills it generates and validates, and assessing whether delegating deterministic computation to verified tools allows smaller language models to retain correctness.


S. Bistarelli et al. (Eds.): AIxIA 2026, LNAI 17131, pp. 499–513, 2027.
https://doi.org/10.1007/978-3-032-40774-0_36

**Keywords:** Agentic AI · LLM-based Agents · MCP Tools · Agent Skills · Neuro-Symbolic AI

## 1 Introduction

Large language models (LLMs) increasingly support agents that address heterogeneous tasks by interpreting requests, planning actions, and invoking external tools [19]. However, their flexibility comes with limited process transparency. This limitation is particularly consequential when a request contains a deterministic computation, such as applying formulas, consulting structured tables, or performing unit conversions. Such operations admit reproducible and directly inspectable solutions. Nevertheless, to date, both the result and its justification are produced through non-inspectable sub-symbolic computations. Best-case scenario, an explanation can be produced by post-hoc approaches. However, such explanations (LLM- and post-hoc-based) can reflect the process that produced the answer unfaithfully [11]. In high-stakes domains such as healthcare and finance, this makes incorrect calculations difficult to detect, audit, and contest [18]. A natural response is to separate responsibilities: the LLM can interpret requests and communicate results, while deterministic computations are delegated to explicit executable procedures. Tool-augmented language models already follow this principle by offloading arithmetic, logical, and information-retrieval operations to external resources [19]. However, static tool libraries provide only limited coverage because their developers must anticipate the computations that users will request. Generating tools on demand can address this limitation. However, it introduces a further challenge: a dynamically generated procedure should not be executed or reused unless its behavior has been assessed first. A scalable architecture must therefore determine when a request contains an extractable deterministic component, generate an appropriate procedure, validate it before use, and preserve an inspectable record of its subsequent execution.

This paper presents Autonomous Skill Development (ASD), a neuro-symbolic agent architecture that combines neural language understanding with explicit rule-based computation. Whereas existing tool-making approaches primarily emphasize tool generation and reuse, ASD makes validation a prerequisite for admitting a generated skill to its library. A neuro-symbolic router first determines whether a request contains an extractable deterministic core. When such a core is identified, ASD generates a skill as a pure, typed function exposed through the Model Context Protocol (MCP)[1]. The generated skill is evaluated through a layered validation pipeline comprising deterministic tests (L1), semantic assessment by an LLM judge distinct from the generating model (L2) [29], and optional human review (L3). Skills that fail validation are returned to a repair loop, while accepted skills are stored in a reusable and versioned library. Once a skill has been admitted, the corresponding computation is performed by explicit executable code rather than regenerated through the LLM at each request. The LLM is subsequently used to contextualize and communicate the

[1] https://modelcontextprotocol.io.

result. ASD also records the skill invoked, the input values supplied to it, and the output it produced. This computational provenance is faithful by construction in a precise sense: it describes the function call that actually generated the reported value, rather than reconstructing a possible reasoning process after the fact. The trace is therefore inspectable and reproducible, although its semantic correctness remains dependent on the adequacy of the skill-generation and validation process. We evaluate ASD on a controlled nutrition-domain benchmark containing 38 tasks: 28 deterministic tasks spanning 18 computation families and 10 non-deterministic tasks used to assess routing behavior. The evaluation considers two open-weight model families, Gemma 4 [7] and Qwen 3.5 [22], with different model sizes assigned to routing, skill generation, validation, and execution roles. We assess routing accuracy, generated skill quality, tool selection reliability, end-to-end task correctness, and computational cost. All experiments are conducted with locally hosted models, without external model APIs, demonstrating the architecture's feasibility on a single workstation.

The contribution of this paper is threefold. It presents:

- ASD, a neuro-symbolic agent architecture that identifies deterministic components of user requests and dynamically generates, validates, versions, and reuses executable skills exposed as MCP tools.
- An evaluation that separates routing, skill generation, skill validation, tool selection, and execution, thereby distinguishing failures caused by incorrect skills from those caused by selecting or invoking the wrong skill.
- Evidence that offloading deterministic computation to validated skills preserves correctness for smaller execution models. As execution models shrink, tool selection, rather than skill quality, becomes the dominant bottleneck, motivating tool retrieval for large libraries [20].

## 2 Related Work

Recent studies explore hybrid approaches in which LLMs delegate part of the reasoning process to symbolic or executable components. Faithful CoT [11] shows that explanations are more reliable when the symbolic reasoning chain is the one actually used by a deterministic solver to compute the answer. In a related neuro-symbolic direction, Crocetti and Dragoni [3] connect LLMs with logic programming, using the language model as an interface toward Prolog-based [8] symbolic reasoning.

A growing line of work moves from one-shot symbolic execution to reusable, self-generated tools. VOYAGER [25] builds an ever-growing library of executable skills refined through feedback and self-verification. LATM [2] uses a powerful model to generate reusable Python [24] tools that a cheaper model can later invoke through a functional cache. CRAFT [28] constructs specialized tool sets offline and retrieves the relevant tool at inference time. TroVE [26] induces reusable functions while solving programmatic tasks, keeping a candidate when the solution that uses it executes correctly. APIGen [10] automates the generation of verifiable function-calling data, and ToolVerifier [13] adds a self-verification step that distinguishes between close candidates during tool selection.

ASD builds on these directions but differs in its validation regime. In LATM and CRAFT, a tool is reused once created, and in TroVE, a function is accepted based on its execution inside the generator's loop. Conversely, ASD admits a skill only upon validation of a pipeline external to the generator. Moreover, unlike Tool Verifier's self-verification, the judging model is distinct from the one that produced the skill. Doing so shifts trust from the generator's self-assessment to an independent check, mitigating self-bias in the validation process.

## 3 Methodology

Some requests have a deterministic computational core: a formula, a conversion, a lookup. When a language model enacts these on itself, computation and explanation are fused and non-inspectable. The model's output and justification come from the same opaque process, with no way to verify one against the other. ASD addresses it directly. For requests with a deterministic core, the computation moves out of the model and into verified code. For each request, the agent decides whether a deterministic core exists. If so, it generates, validates, and exposes the corresponding code as a reusable tool.

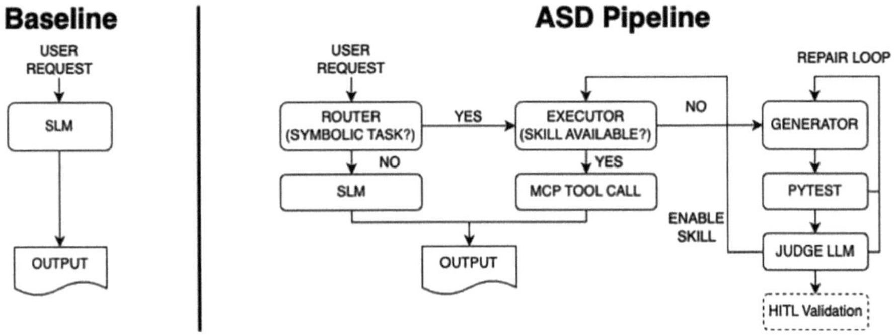


**Fig. 1.** Baseline vs ASD Pipeline. The baseline shows the user making a request to an SLM and receiving a natural-language response. On the right is the ASD Pipeline, where the user's request is analyzed by a first model that determines the nature of the request (symbolic task or not). If the task is not symbolic, the SLM responds; otherwise, the skills are checked, and if no adequate skill is found, one is created. The creation process involves generating Python code, tests, the LLM judge, and, in case of need, a human-in-the-loop (HITL).

### 3.1 Request Pipeline

ASD defines four roles, *router*, *executor*, *generator*, and *judge*. A request is handled in one of two ways. A router first decides whether the request has an extractable deterministic core, a verifiable input-to-output function computable without semantic judgment, like a formula, a table lookup, a unit conversion, or arithmetic, even when it is wrapped in interpretive advice. If the answer is no, the execution model replies directly, as an ordinary assistant would. If yes, the request enters the skill branch.

The agent exposes the trusted library to the execution model as callable tools. Calling one is a reuse, a *hit*, and the computation runs as verified code. Calling none is a *miss* and triggers skill generation. Once generated and validated, the new skill is added to the library, and the execution model is queried again so it can call the skill just created, as shown in Fig. 1. Either way, the model writes the natural-language answer, but on this branch, the reported number comes from inspectable, tested code rather than the model's own arithmetic.

### 3.2 Router: Extractable Deterministic Core

The router is a binary classifier over the request and the highest-risk component in the pipeline. A false negative misses the opportunity to compute deterministically, and a false positive triggers the generation of a task with no verifiable core. A fixed instruction defines the extractable deterministic core and asks for a two-line reply, a yes/no decision, and a one-line reason.

### 3.3 Skill Generation and Layered Validation

When the request is on the skill branch and no existing tool matches, the agent generates a new skill, a single pure, deterministic Python function with its own tests. The generation role returns a fixed set of sections in order, a `snake_case` name, the function signature, a description, a code block with the function, and a code block with `pytest` tests that import the function by name. The function must be pure and typed, with no I/O, no network, no globals, and no randomness. Type annotations matter because the tool's input schema is derived from them (Sect. 3.4). The description drives tool selection in the execution model, so it must state exactly what the function computes and from which inputs, specifically enough not to be chosen for a different quantity. The reply is parsed into a draft of name, signature, description, function code, and test code. A reply that does not follow the section format is not discarded. It is returned with a short reminder of the format, and the model is asked again up to a fixed number of times before a parse failure is raised. A draft must pass the validation pipeline below before it is trusted. Failures are repaired rather than rejected, and a single repair loop interleaves up to three layers.

The first layer (L1) writes the function and tests to a temporary directory and runs them with `pytest` in a separate subprocess under a timeout. It catches functions that do not run, that raise, or that disagree with the values the model itself asserts.

The second layer (L2) is an LLM judge, distinct from the generator. Given the task and the candidate's code and tests, the judge decides whether the function correctly and completely solves the task and whether its tests genuinely verify it. It replies with an approve-or-reject verdict and a one-line reason at temperature zero, and an unparseable verdict counts as a rejection. L2 targets a gap L1 cannot see, a wrong formula paired with weak tests that agree with it. Neither layer compares the skill against an external oracle. L1 checks that code and tests agree, L2 adds an independent opinion on the formula, so together they certify internal consistency rather than ground-truth correctness.

When a layer fails and attempts remain, its failure is fed back to the generator role as repair feedback: the `pytest` output for L1, or the judge's reason for L2. The conversation is then rebuilt from the task, the previous draft, and that feedback, and the generation runs again. The loop runs up to a fixed maximum, and only a draft that passes the active layers is accepted. Every evaluated draft is kept with its code, tests, L1 output, L2 verdict, attempt count, and rejecting layer for analysis.

The third layer (L3) is optional and involves human review. A skill that passed the automatic layers can be flagged as human-validated in its metadata. The flag is recorded and surfaced in provenance rather than enforced, so a reviewed skill is reported as such, but review does not block use.

### 3.4 Library, Reuse, and Provenance

Accepted skills are stored on disk in a versioned library. Each skill is represented by three artifacts: the typed function that implements the tool, the generated tests, and a metadata record. The metadata records the skill status, validation outcomes, human-review flag, and reuse count.

An in-process server turns the library into callable tools. Each trusted skill becomes a tool whose name is the skill's name and whose description is the skill's description, with an input schema automatically derived from the function's type annotations.

On the skill branch, the agent builds the tool server from the current trusted library, lists the tools over an in-memory transport, and converts them to the execution model's format. Through native tool calling, the model decides which tool to invoke and whether to invoke it. A tool call is a reuse, so the verified function computes the result, the reuse count is incremented, and the model comments on the returned value. No tool call is a miss, which triggers generation and one re-entry into the tool loop so the new skill can be called. Selection is left entirely to the execution model.

Every answer in the skill branch has an inspectable provenance: which skill was applied, at which version, and the value it produced. The trust level is computed by code from the skill's metadata, not by the model, which distinguishes a system-validated skill from one that is also human-reviewed. The reported number is taken directly from the function's output, so the explanation reflects the computation that produced it rather than the model's own arithmetic.

# 4 Experimental Setup

This section presents the ASD evaluation: domain and benchmark, model configurations, conditions, metrics, and the run protocol. All experiments are run on a single NVIDIA DGX Spark workstation (GB10 Grace Blackwell, 128 GB unified memory), which hosts models for all four roles simultaneously (see Sect. 3.1), with no external models or APIs in the loop.

## 4.1 Domain and Benchmark

We instantiate the domain-agnostic core on nutrition, a domain where many requests carry a deterministic core (formulas, table lookups, unit conversions, arithmetic) wrapped in interpretive advice, and where a wrong number has real consequences. The benchmark is a single labeled dataset of 38 tasks, 28 deterministic and 10 non-deterministic. The 28 deterministic tasks span 18 families: 10 literature rules (each with 2 cases) and 8 generic conversion and arithmetic tasks (each with 1 case).

At the core of the benchmark are 10 nutrition rules from the literature, each drawn from a peer-reviewed source and instantiated as a family of two cases. Two families come from the Mifflin–St Jeor equation [14], one as a resting energy expenditure rule for men and one as a BMR estimate for women. The remaining eight are body-fat percentage from BMI and age [4], estimated energy requirement (EER) [17], the Digestible Indispensable Amino Acid Score [5], the Body Roundness Index (BRI) [23], the carbohydrate lower bound of the Acceptable Macronutrient Distribution Range (AMDR) [16], A Body Shape Index (ABSI) [9], energy availability [15], and the triglyceride-glucose (TyG) index [21]. These rules span a difficulty gradient. Some are common knowledge for a capable model, such as BMR and TyG. In contrast, others are highly specific, such as the exact 2023 NASEM EER coefficients and the AMDR percentages, so a model that does not know them precisely will miss the value, which is itself informative.

Each request gives only the input data, never the formula or the conversion factor needed to compute the result. Each request specifies the rule or target quantity and provides the inputs, including only the qualifiers needed to fix the ground truth, such as sex, population, and activity level. The generator role must therefore know the formula and implement it correctly. Each deterministic task also carries a verified ground-truth value and a per-task absolute tolerance.

The eight generic conversion and arithmetic tasks, such as kilocalories to kilojoules, Atwater calories [1], and a multi-ingredient meal total, span the easy-to-hard range, so the results show where ASD begins to help. The ten non-deterministic tasks, such as whether a ketogenic diet is preferable, need semantic judgment and have no deterministic core. These form the router's negative class and exercise the direct, non-skilled answer path used by the baseline.

### 4.2 Model Configurations

We evaluate a matrix over two open-weight families, Gemma 4 [7] and Qwen 3.5 [22]. We chose them because they come from two independent providers, are released in a wide range of small sizes suitable for local deployment, and support the native tool calling the executor role requires. This lets us vary model size on one axis at a time. All models are the F16 GGUF builds released by Unsloth[2], served locally with `llama.cpp` [6], one model per role. We set the sampling temperature per role: 0.0 for the router and the judge, 0.2 for generation, and 0.7 for execution. The remaining sampling parameters are left at their default values. Across the entire matrix, the judge is held fixed to a single 31B Gemma instance. Table 1 lists the full matrix. Each role can run with or without explicit chain-of-thought reasoning [27]. We treat reasoning as an ablative axis, comparing it on and off in the baseline and in the generator role, with everything else held constant.

**Table 1.** Model configuration matrix.

| Config | Family | Router | Executor | Generator |
|---|---|---|---|---|
| C1 | Gemma 4 | E2B | E4B | 12B |
| C2 | Gemma 4 | E2B | E4B | 26B-A4B |
| C3 | Gemma 4 | E2B | E2B | 12B |
| C4 | Gemma 4 | E2B | E2B | E4B |
| C5 | Qwen 3.5 | 2B | 4B | 9B |
| C6 | Qwen 3.5 | 0.8B | 2B | 4B |
| C7 | Qwen 3.5 | 0.8B | 0.8B | 4B |
| C8 | Qwen 3.5 | 0.8B | 0.8B | 2B |

### 4.3 Setup

Each task runs under one or more setup, and a run can select any subset of them. The conditions isolate different costs and behaviors of the system.

- **baseline**: the pure-language-model behavior, answering every task directly with no router and no skills. It uses only the executor role.
- **create**: the skill branch with a cold library, generating one skill per family with L1 and L2 validation.
- **reuse**: all skills are preloaded, so every measured request is a hit. This measures the cost and correctness of reuse.

[2] https://huggingface.co/unsloth.

### 4.4 Metrics and Protocol Execution

The following metrics are derived from logs.

- **Correctness**: for a deterministic task, whether the answer contains a number within the task's tolerance of the ground-truth value.
- **Router quality**: the router is a binary classifier over the full benchmark, with the 28 deterministic tasks as the positive class and the 10 non-deterministic tasks as the negative class. We report its accuracy, precision, and recall.
- **Correctness at hit (c@hit)**: correctness restricted to cases where the model invokes a skill from the same family as the task. Requests with no skill invocation or with a skill from a different family are excluded. We compute this metric only on deterministic requests with a graded answer.
- **Tool selection (right, wrong, miss)**: *right*, a same-family skill is invoked; *wrong* a different-family skill is invoked; *miss* no skill is invoked.
- **Latency (lat)**: the operating time for each request.
- **Repair and rejection**: the number of repair attempts driven by each layer (L1 test failures and L2 judge rejections) and the number of skills finally rejected by each layer. These quantify each layer's contribution during a run.

Each setup is repeated 5 times, and we report the mean and standard deviation. A request that fails, for example, on a generation timeout, is recorded as failed, and the run continues.

## 5 Results

This section centers on four questions. (i) How does a pure language model behave on the symbolic core? (ii) How reliably does the router separate deterministic from non-deterministic requests? (iii) What does ASD add when it creates and reuses verified skills, where does it fail, and does reasoning help? And (iv) what do the layered validation and the inspectable artifact contribute beyond accuracy? Tables 2a to 5 report all results, which we discuss in turn below.

**The Sole LLM Setting is Weak and Unstable on the Symbolic Core.** Answering directly, with no router and no skills, yields a weak and inconsistent execution model across families and sizes (Table 2a). Correctness ranges from 29.3% at the smallest executor to 72.9% at the 4B Qwen one, with smaller models at the low end and most configurations well below what a high-stakes setting would require. Chain-of-thought reasoning does not rescue the baseline (Table 2b): the strongest configuration stays flat (72.9% to 73.6%), others drop (39.3% to 25.0% for the Gemma-E4B executor, 47.1% to 38.6% for the 2B Qwen one), and latency roughly doubles. We take the no-reasoning baseline as the reference.

**The Router is Accurate.** The router is accurate and conservative by design (Table 2c). Accuracy is 83–95% and precision is 100% across all configurations;

**Table 2.** (a) Baseline no reasoning, (b) Baseline reasoning, and (c) Router quality.

| c | corr% | lat (s) |
|---|---|---|
| C1,2 | $39.3 \pm 4.4$ | $5.4 \pm 0.4$ |
| C3,4 | $57.9 \pm 3.0$ | $3.4 \pm 0.1$ |
| C5 | $72.9 \pm 5.4$ | $10.8 \pm 5.3$ |
| C6 | $47.1 \pm 1.6$ | $5.9 \pm 2.0$ |
| C7,8 | $29.3 \pm 3.0$ | $2.7 \pm 0.8$ |

(a)

| c | corr% | lat (s) |
|---|---|---|
| C1,2 | $25.0 \pm 4.4$ | $10.5 \pm 0.4$ |
| C3,4 | $57.9 \pm 3.9$ | $7.5 \pm 0.2$ |
| C5 | $73.6 \pm 3.2$ | $22.5 \pm 8.0$ |
| C6 | $38.6 \pm 3.0$ | $16.3 \pm 2.5$ |
| C7,8 | $23.6 \pm 2.0$ | $12.5 \pm 2.6$ |

(b)

| config | acc% | prec% | rec% |
|---|---|---|---|
| C1,2,3,4 | 95 | 100 | 93 |
| C5 | 89 | 100 | 85 |
| C6,7,8 | 83 | 100 | 77 |

(c)

it never routes a non-deterministic request to the skill branch. Its only errors are false negatives, with recall from 77 to 93%, where a genuinely deterministic task is sent to the direct path and loses verification.

**ASD Improves Correctness.** Generating one verified skill per family on a cold library raises correctness over the baseline across the board (Table 3c). We compare the baseline and the per-task results using an exact McNemar [12] test, taking the majority across the 5 repeats per configuration, without pooling. Create wins in every configuration compared, significantly in three (C1, C6, C4; $p = .006, .031, .004$) ranges, and the rest move the same way, with too few discordant pairs to reach significance. When the right skill is invoked, c@hit ranges from 84.9 to 100%, so the generated code is rarely the problem. What limits correctness is the model's ability to call the right skill. The gap between overall correctness (54 to 78%) and c@hit is therefore almost entirely due to the selection, the model failing to call the freshly created tool, rather than the code being wrong. The exception is C8, whose 2B generator is below the size needed to write working code: it yields an accepted skill in only 2.9% of creation attempts and collapses to 23.6% of creation attempts. A generator this small does not benefit from ASD because it cannot reliably write the skill in the first place, a limit of the generator rather than of the approach. Even the capable generators do not pass validation on every attempt, with accepted-skill rates around 60–80%.

**Table 3.** ASD Pipeline: (a) Create no reasoning, (b) Create reasoning

| c | corr% | c@hit | miss% | created% | lat (s) |
|---|---|---|---|---|---|
| C1 | $70.0 \pm 3.2$ | $96.1 \pm 2.2$ | $22.9 \pm 7.8$ | $71.4 \pm 5.1$ | $97 \pm 8.7$ |
| C2 | $73.6 \pm 4.1$ | $93.6 \pm 4$ | $3.5 \pm 3.7$ | $77.9 \pm 3.0$ | $82.3 \pm 10.7$ |
| C3 | $69.3 \pm 3.2$ | $94.9 \pm 5.1$ | $25.2 \pm 5.5$ | $69.3 \pm 3.2$ | $98.6 \pm 13.4$ |
| C5 | $77.9 \pm 1.6$ | $95.7 \pm 3$ | $4.2 \pm 2.9$ | $81.4 \pm 3.0$ | $85.8 \pm 12.1$ |
| C6 | $67.1 \pm 3.0$ | $98.8 \pm 2.8$ | $23.1 \pm 5.9$ | $59.3 \pm 4.8$ | $64.9 \pm 8.5$ |
| C4 | $65.0 \pm 5.3$ | $89.1 \pm 8.5$ | $32.3 \pm 5.2$ | $62.9 \pm 6$ | $73.3 \pm 6.3$ |
| C7 | $54.3 \pm 4.7$ | $84.9 \pm 2.6$ | $27.6 \pm 4.8$ | $68.6 \pm 3.9$ | $64.5 \pm 6.6$ |
| C8 | $23.6 \pm 3.2$ | $100.0 \pm 0.0$ | $96.3 \pm 3.8$ | $2.9 \pm 3.0$ | $21.9 \pm 3.4$ |

(a)

| c | corr% | c@hit | miss% | created% | lat (s) |
|---|---|---|---|---|---|
| C1 | $63.6 \pm 3.0$ | $96.8 \pm 2.9$ | $2.0 \pm 2.7$ | $65.7 \pm 4.1$ | $100.1 \pm 10.1$ |
| C2 | $75.7 \pm 1.6$ | $100 \pm 0.0$ | $0.0 \pm 0.0$ | $75.7 \pm 1.6$ | $90.1 \pm 16.6$ |
| C3 | $65.7 \pm 3.2$ | $100.0 \pm 0.0$ | $1.0 \pm 2.2$ | $65.7 \pm 3.2$ | $90.5 \pm 7.1$ |
| C5 | $62.1 \pm 7.4$ | $94.7 \pm 3.7$ | $3.3 \pm 3.1$ | $66.4 \pm 10$ | $115.2 \pm 22.4$ |
| C6 | $69.3 \pm 4.1$ | $97.9 \pm 2.9$ | $17.3 \pm 5.9$ | $67.9 \pm 4.4$ | $103.4 \pm 17.2$ |
| C4 | $74.3 \pm 1.6$ | $97.2 \pm 4.1$ | $24.6 \pm 3.1$ | $72.1 \pm 4.7$ | $84.9 \pm 8.8$ |
| C7 | $55.7 \pm 4.8$ | $90.7 \pm 6.8$ | $42 \pm 7.1$ | $64.3 \pm 5.1$ | $99.4 \pm 12.1$ |
| C8 | $2.9 \pm 3$ | – | $100 \pm 0$ | $0 \pm 0.0$ | $130.0 \pm 3.9$ |

(b)

**Reasoning Does Not Help Creation.** Repeating create with reasoning on the generation role gives no consistent benefit (Table 3b). The direction is split evenly across configurations, and the paired McNemar test shows no significant difference. The capable 9B Qwen generator drops from 77.9% to 62.1%, the smallest generator falls from 23.6% to 2.9%, and latency increases across the board. We keep no-reasoning as the main configuration.

**Reuse: Given the Right Skills, ASD is Near-Perfect.** With the verified library pre-built and every request a hit, ASD reaches the ceiling (Table 4). c@hit is 100% in every configuration, and overall correctness is 94–100% for every executor but the smallest. Partitioning the routed tasks into right, wrong, and miss, the losses are entirely selection errors, concentrated in the smallest executors (C7 and C8, 12% wrong tool and 13% no tool), while the other executors select 94–100% of the time correctly. This is the paper's central finding, made precise: given the right skills, the dominant failure mode is tool selection, and it worsens as the executor shrinks. Reuse is also the fastest path: a hit answers in about 1 to 2 s, below the baseline, and far below the tens of seconds spent on generation. That cost is paid once per family and then amortized across subsequent requests, so the expensive step occurs only at creation.

**Table 4.** Reuse Task - No Reasoning

| c | right% | wrong% | miss% | corr% | c@hit% | lat(s) |
|---|---|---|---|---|---|---|
| C1,2 | 98 | 2 | 0 | 98 | 100 | $1.4 \pm 0.0$ |
| C3,4 | 100 | 0 | 0 | 100 | 100 | $0.9 \pm 0.0$ |
| C5 | 96 | 4 | 0 | 98 | 100 | $1.8 \pm 0.1$ |
| C6 | 94 | 6 | 0 | 94 | 100 | $1.3 \pm 0.1$ |
| C7,8 | 74 | 12 | 13 | 80 | 100 | $1.1 \pm 0.6$ |

**Validation Layers Contribution.** Table 5 shows the effort the pipeline spends during creation. L1, the deterministic tests, is the workhorse: L1-triggered repairs are common and grow as the generator weakens, from 28% of attempts for the Gemma-12B generator to 84–97% for the small Qwen generators, and almost all final rejections are L1's. The independent judge L2 adds a distinct signal: on the Gemma generators, it triggers a repair in 19 to 30% of attempts and a final rejection in 1 to 9%, catching consistency gaps that L1 had passed, such as a wrong formula paired with agreeing tests, while on the Qwen generators, it rarely fires. Most repairs are recoverable rather than fatal: C2 needs a L1 repair in 56% of attempts but is finally rejected in only 3%, so the loop fixes rather than discards. config8 is again the floor, with 97% of attempts requiring a L1 repair and 94% finally rejected, so below a certain generator size, the layers correctly refuse broken code rather than letting it through. Read together with the *created* column of Table 3a, these rates explain the accepted-skill percentages:

the stronger generators recover most drafts through the repair loop and end around 60–80%. At the same time, C8's 94% rejection leaves almost nothing accepted, the 2.9% reported there.

**Table 5.** Repair Loop Statistics

| c | attempts | L1 rep. (%) | L2 rep. (%) | rej. L1 (%) | rej. L2 (%) |
|---|---|---|---|---|---|
| C1 | $1.7 \pm 0.1$ | $28 \pm 11$ | $25 \pm 5$ | $15 \pm 8$ | $8 \pm 4$ |
| C2 | $1.8 \pm 0.1$ | $56 \pm 6$ | $19 \pm 5$ | $3 \pm 4$ | $1 \pm 2$ |
| C3 | $1.7 \pm 0.1$ | $28 \pm 4$ | $28 \pm 5$ | $16 \pm 5$ | $9 \pm 3$ |
| C4 | $1.9 \pm 0.1$ | $39 \pm 6$ | $30 \pm 4$ | $25 \pm 4$ | $8 \pm 6$ |
| C5 | $1.5 \pm 0.1$ | $39 \pm 8$ | $3 \pm 2$ | $4 \pm 3$ | $0 \pm 0$ |
| C6 | $2.3 \pm 0.1$ | $93 \pm 4$ | $4 \pm 4$ | $22 \pm 5$ | $1 \pm 2$ |
| C7 | $2.1 \pm 0.1$ | $84 \pm 4$ | $4 \pm 4$ | $10 \pm 5$ | $2 \pm 3$ |
| C8 | $2.9 \pm 0.1$ | $97 \pm 4$ | $2 \pm 3$ | $94 \pm 6$ | $2 \pm 3$ |

**Cost in Time: Creation is a One-Time Expense, Reuse is Light.** Creation is expensive, about 65 to 130 s per request (Tables 3a and 3b), since it runs generation, the test subprocess, the judge, and the repair loop. This cost is paid only during creation. During reuse, ASD runs only the router and the executor over an already validated tool, answering in about 1 to 2 s. We therefore do not claim that ASD is cheaper than the baseline for every request. Its value is verifiability: the expensive step is front-loaded, while repeated use remains lightweight.

**Human Inspection.** Beyond accuracy, the create branch leaves behind an artifact: each skill carries its own tests and a provenance record of which rule, inputs, value, and validation produced the answer, as well as whether a human reviewed it. Unlike a black-box answer, it can be read, audited, and corrected by a domain expert. This matters where the pipeline is imperfect: a skill with a subtly wrong formula, which L1 and L2 certify only for internal consistency, can be fixed once, and because skills are versioned and reused, the correction then serves every future request. A single human review thus becomes permanent correctness, the safety and audit advantage that justifies the one-time creation cost in high-stakes domains.

## 6 Conclusion

This study presented ASD, a neuro-symbolic agent that turns the deterministic core of a request into a verified, reusable tool. A router decides whether such a core exists. If so, ASD generates a skill as a pure typed function exposed as an MCP tool, validates it with deterministic tests and an independent LLM judge in a repair loop, and stores it in a versioned library. The computation then runs as inspectable, tested code, and the language model only reports the result. The whole pipeline runs locally on open-weight models on a single workstation.

Across a nutrition benchmark and two open-weight families, the results support three claims. Moving the symbolic core to verified code keeps smaller execution models correct, down to the point where the generator is too small to write a usable skill. Given the right skill, ASD is near-perfect, and the only residual error is in tool selection, which grows as the execution model shrinks. The validation layers do real work: the deterministic tests are the workhorse, and the independent judge catches consistency gaps they miss. Beyond accuracy, each skill is an inspectable, editable, reusable artifact, so a single human review becomes the definitive correctness for every subsequent request.

Several directions follow. Since the main residual error is tool selection, retrieval-based skill indexing, which exposes only a few relevant skills per request, is the natural next step and should also help as the library grows. Our validation checks internal consistency, not ground-truth correctness, so a skill with a subtly incorrect formula can still be admitted. A further open question is whether generator and judge, being trained on partly overlapping corpora, may share blind spots, so that a poorly represented rule could be implemented incorrectly and approved for the same reason. How often this happens and how the model behaves when a skill returns a wrong value are open robustness questions. Finally, the smallest generators mark a floor below which no usable skill is produced, and a stronger generator may widen the range of small execution models that ASD can serve.

**Acknowledgments.** This work was supported by the HES-SO RCSO ISNet Hybrid Ai foR RelIable perSonalized cOachiNg (HARRISON) grant, Swiss AI Initiative (a0138), HES-SO R&I Mind the Gap: Adapting Higher Education to the Age of AI (MTG, 140012/RI-PSTRAT25-06).

## References

1. Atwater, W.O., Benedict, F.G.: An experimental inquiry regarding the nutritive value of alcohol. No. 233, US Government Printing Office (1902)
2. Cai, T., Wang, X., Ma, T., Chen, X., Zhou, D.: Large language models as tool makers. In: International Conference on Learning Representations, vol. 2024, pp. 54067–54089 (2024)
3. Crocetti, V., Dragoni, A.F.: Bridging large language models and logic programming. In: 2025 IEEE International Conference on Metrology for eXtended Reality, Artificial Intelligence and Neural Engineering (MetroXRAINE), pp. 1066–1071 (2025). https://doi.org/10.1109/MetroXRAINE66377.2025.11340308
4. Deurenberg, P., Weststrate, J.A., Seidell, J.C.: Body mass index as a measure of body fatness: age- and sex-specific prediction formulas. Br. J. Nutr. **65**(2), 105–114 (1991). https://doi.org/10.1079/BJN19910073
5. Food and Agriculture Organization of the United Nations: Dietary protein quality evaluation in human nutrition. Technical Report 92, Food and Agriculture

Organization of the United Nations, Rome (2013). https://openknowledge.fao.org/handle/20.500.14283/i3124e, report of an FAO Expert Consultation
6. Gerganov, G., llama.cpp contributors: llama.cpp: LLM inference in C/C++ (2023). https://github.com/ggml-org/llama.cpp. Accessed 19 June 2026
7. Google DeepMind: Gemma 4 model card (2026). https://ai.google.dev/gemma/docs/core/model_card_4. Accessed 28 May 2026
8. Körner, P., et al.: Fifty years of prolog and beyond. Theory Pract. Logic Program. **22**(6), 776–858 (2022). https://doi.org/10.1017/S1471068422000102
9. Krakauer, N.Y., Krakauer, J.C.: A new body shape index predicts mortality hazard independently of body mass index. PLoS ONE **7**(7), e39504 (2012). https://doi.org/10.1371/journal.pone.0039504
10. Liu, Z., et al.: Apigen: automated pipeline for generating verifiable and diverse function-calling datasets. Adv. Neural. Inf. Process. Syst. **37**, 54463–54482 (2024)
11. Lyu, Q., et al.: Faithful chain-of-thought reasoning. In: Park, J.C., et al. (eds.) Proceedings of the 13th International Joint Conference on Natural Language Processing and the 3rd Conference of the Asia-Pacific Chapter of the Association for Computational Linguistics (Volume 1: Long Papers), pp. 305–329. Association for Computational Linguistics, Nusa Dua, Bali (2023). https://doi.org/10.18653/v1/2023.ijcnlp-main.20. https://aclanthology.org/2023.ijcnlp-main.20/
12. McNemar, Q.: Note on the sampling error of the difference between correlated proportions or percentages. Psychometrika **12**(2), 153–157 (1947)
13. Mekala, D., et al.: Toolverifier: generalization to new tools via self-verification. In: Findings of the Association for Computational Linguistics: EMNLP 2024, pp. 5026–5041 (2024)
14. Mifflin, M., St Jeor, S., Hill, L., Scott, B., Daugherty, S., Koh, Y.: A new predictive equation for resting energy expenditure in healthy individuals. Am. J. Clin. Nutr. **51**(2), 241–247 (1990). https://doi.org/10.1093/ajcn/51.2.241
15. Mountjoy, M., et al.: 2023 international olympic committee's (IOC) consensus statement on relative energy deficiency in sport (REDs). Br. J. Sports Med. **57**(17), 1073–1097 (2023). https://doi.org/10.1136/bjsports-2023-106994
16. National Academies of Sciences, Engineering, and Medicine: Dietary Reference Intakes for Energy, Carbohydrate, Fiber, Fat, Fatty Acids, Cholesterol, Protein, and Amino Acids. The National Academies Press, Washington, DC (2005). https://doi.org/10.17226/10490
17. National Academies of Sciences, Engineering, and Medicine: Dietary Reference Intakes for Energy. The National Academies Press, Washington, DC (2023). https://doi.org/10.17226/26818
18. Pacioni, E., Coman, A.C., Calvaresi, D., Manzo, G., Schumacher, M.I.: Agent-based hybrid ai models and technologies: a systematic literature review. IEEE Access **14**, 21148–21166 (2026). https://doi.org/10.1109/ACCESS.2026.3661027
19. Qu, C., et al.: Tool learning with large language models: a survey. Front. Comput. Sci. **19**(8), 198343 (2025)
20. Shi, Z., et al.: Retrieval models aren't tool-savvy: benchmarking tool retrieval for large language models. In: Findings of the Association for Computational Linguistics: ACL 2025, pp. 24497–24524 (2025)
21. Simental-Mendía, L.E., Rodríguez-Morán, M., Guerrero-Romero, F.: The product of fasting glucose and triglycerides as surrogate for identifying insulin resistance in apparently healthy subjects. Metab. Syndr. Relat. Disord. **6**(4), 299–304 (2008). https://doi.org/10.1089/met.2008.0034
22. Team, Q.: Qwen3 technical report (2025). https://arxiv.org/abs/2505.09388

23. Thomas, D.M., et al.: Relationships between body roundness with body fat and visceral adipose tissue emerging from a new geometrical model. Obesity **21**(11), 2264–2271 (2013). https://doi.org/10.1002/oby.20408
24. Van Rossum, G., Drake, F.L.: Python reference manual, vol. 111. Centrum voor Wiskunde en Informatica, Amsterdam (1995)
25. Wang, G., et al.: Voyager: an open-ended embodied agent with large language models. arXiv preprint arXiv:2305.16291 (2023)
26. Wang, Z.Z., Neubig, G., Fried, D.: Trove: inducing verifiable and efficient toolboxes for solving programmatic tasks. In: Proceedings of the 41st International Conference on Machine Learning. ICML 2024. JMLR.org (2024)
27. Wei, J., et al.: Chain-of-thought prompting elicits reasoning in large language models. Adv. Neural. Inf. Process. Syst. **35**, 24824–24837 (2022)
28. Yuan, L., Chen, Y., Wang, X., Fung, Y., Peng, H., Ji, H.: Craft: customizing LLMs by creating and retrieving from specialized toolsets. In: International Conference on Learning Representations, vol. 2024, pp. 40097–40125 (2024)
29. Zheng, L., et al.: Judging LLM-as-a-judge with mt-bench and chatbot arena. Adv. Neural. Inf. Process. Syst. **36**, 46595–46623 (2023)

# The Interplay Between Functionality and Complexity in Neural Network Efficiency

Paolo Pagliuca(✉) and Alessandra Vitanza

Institute of Cognitive Sciences and Technologies (ISTC), National Research Council (CNR), Rome, Italy
{paolo.pagliuca,alessandra.vitanza}@cnr.it

**Abstract.** The design of efficient neural network controllers entails identifying suitable network architectures, which requires a high level of expertise, or defining methods that allow users to evolve connection weights and topology in parallel. Although both approaches are widely used in the literature, they present limitations related either to the criteria used for selecting network architectures or the complexity of co-evolving weights and topology. Moreover, the role of single neurons within neural networks is often overlooked. This work presents an analysis of functional neurons—defined as units that cannot be deleted without producing remarkable performance differences—within neural network controllers, with the aim to provide a general framework for explaining neural network efficiency. Specifically, we investigate a series of benchmark locomotion problems, varying the number of internal neurons to capture potential relationships between functionality and complexity. Our findings show the difficulty of identifying an optimal network configuration. However, we observe that functional neurons play a crucial role in the final performance, hence emphasizing their significance. Moreover, our experiments indicate that the percentage of functional neurons appears to depend on the features of the evolutionary algorithm used. This underscores the existence of complex, intertwined relationships between the chosen optimization method and the resulting properties of neural network controllers.

**Keywords:** Functional Neurons · Neural Network Efficiency · Complexity · Robot Locomotion

## 1 Introduction

In the field of neural network research, the concept of functional neurons represents a critical area of investigation. Functional neurons are defined as those that contribute significantly to the performance and can predict the capabilities of a neural network. In other words, they play an indispensable role in the networks. The importance of these neurons was highlighted in some biological [2,30]


S. Bistarelli et al. (Eds.): AIxIA 2026, LNAI 17131, pp. 514–527, 2027.
https://doi.org/10.1007/978-3-032-40774-0_37

and technical studies [1,17], which emphasized that their removal significantly degrades network functionality. This idea aligns with the concept of network sparsity, where only a subset of the network components actively contributes to its success despite the apparent complexity of the overall system [9]. Furthermore, this concept is similar to the *lottery ticket hypothesis* introduced by [8] and further supported by [12]. This hypothesis suggests that, within a large, randomly initialized feedforward neural network, there exists a sparse sub-network, the so-called "winning ticket", which, if isolated and trained independently, can achieve performance comparable to that of the original network. These findings highlight the intrinsic sparsity and efficiency of neural network structures and emphasize the importance of identifying and exploiting such functional sub-networks. In particular, [12] provided evidence by demonstrating how pruning non-essential components can reveal these crucial sub-networks, highlighting their central role in network performance. To broaden the perspective, some parallelism can be found between functional sparsity in artificial neural networks and organizational principles in biological systems. Indeed, studies in neuroscience have explored the relationship between functional segregation and integration in brain networks by measuring "neural complexity", which reflects how local and distributed interactions jointly guide neural processing [29]. Similarly, identifying functional interactions (i.e., connections) among neurons has been studied as an approach to inferring effective connectivity, providing insights from biological systems into computational feasibility [28]. In particular, these ideas have informed artificial neural network research, particularly the study of the dynamic evolution of connections and topologies. Such biological principles have inspired methods like NeuroEvolution of Augmenting Topologies (NEAT) [27], which demonstrate that evolving both network structure and weights can yield more efficient solutions than static architectures. These approaches move beyond traditional practices based on fixed topologies or predefined numbers of neurons. The authors argued that rigid architectures often lack the adaptability needed to optimize performance across diverse tasks, and the rationale behind architectural choices is frequently underexplored. Despite these advances, significant challenges remain in designing neural networks that balance functionality and complexity. For example, in [18], a fixed number of hidden neurons was used. However, the authors did not provide any justification for their choice of network architectures, leaving gaps in understanding how architecture affects performance. Moreover, while evolutionary algorithms offer promising strategies for co-evolving weights and topologies, they are computationally demanding and often fail to promote sufficient diversity within populations. Building on these works, the present study aims to address these issues by exploring the relationship between functionality and complexity in neural network controllers, with a specific focus on functional neurons. In particular, we investigate the impact of the number of hidden neurons on the final performance of neural networks across a series of benchmark problems. By analyzing the functional contributions of individual neurons, we seek to understand the role of sparsity and structure in enhancing network efficiency, aiming to address open questions in evolutionary design and functional analysis. Lastly, this work contributes to the broader objective of emphasizing the functionality-complexity interplay, with the goal of producing guidelines for designing efficient, high-performing networks.

To sum up, the main contributions of this work are as follows:

- an analysis of the impact of functional neurons on neural network performance is presented;
- the relationship between performance and functionality is investigated specifically in the context of locomotion tasks simulated using PyBullet [7]—an open-source physics engine widely used in robotics and reinforcement learning research, and known for its realistic simulation of rigid body dynamics.
- experiments with different neural network controllers have been performed, varying the number of hidden neurons (referred to as $NH$);
- the optimal value of $NH$ is shown to be task-dependent, hence emphasizing how identifying a general network architecture is far from trivial;
- functional neurons are found to play a crucial role in the considered scenarios;
- the percentage of functional neurons depends on the algorithm used.

## 2 Materials and Methods

In this section, we present the materials and methods used for the analysis. Specifically, we first describe the simulation environment and then present the benchmark problems used for testing. Lastly, we provide a definition of functional neurons and describe the methodology used for their analysis.

### 2.1 PyBullet

PyBullet [7] is the Python library of the Bullet engine [6]. Originally designed for robot manipulation, it has rapidly expanded to provide a broad range of simulation environments and robotic platforms. Moreover, it can be further extended by creating custom simulations. The definition of robot properties, such as the number and size of rigid bodies, the number of joints, and the way they are connected, is provided in an eXtensible Markup Language (XML) file.

The main advantage of PyBullet is its ability to use the Python programming language, which is intuitive but relatively slow, to directly call the Bullet primitives written in C++, which are significantly faster. A shortcoming of PyBullet is represented by its relatively long simulation times [3]. However, PyBullet is a widely used tool for evaluating Evolutionary Algorithms (EAs) [18,22] and Reinforcement Learning (RL) methods [10,11].

### 2.2 Tasks

Of the six problems considered, four belong to the PyBullet locomotor family. In particular, we investigated the Ant, Halfcheetah, Hopper, and Walker2D tasks.

(a) Ant (b) Halfcheetah (c) Hopper (d) Walker2D

**Fig. 1.** PyBullet locomotors.

These problems involve mobile legged robots whose ultimate goal is to travel as far as possible. They are widely used as benchmark tasks in studies exploring EAs and RL [14,18,24,32]. The Ant task (see Fig. 1a) consists of developing successful locomotion behavior in a simulated Ant robot with a spherical body, 4 legs, and 8 joints, capable of moving both frontally and laterally. The Halfcheetah (see Fig. 1b), Hopper (see Fig. 1c) and Walker2D (see Fig. 1d) tasks require simpler robots that can only travel frontally. In particular, these robots consist of 2, 1 and 2 legs, respectively.

**Fig. 2.** BipedalWalker: a two-legged robot with a hull has to locomote as far as possible in a 2D environment.

The performance of the solutions discovered for the PyBullet locomotors is measured according to Eqs. 1–4.

$$F_{ant} = \sum_{i=1}^{N_s}(\Delta x_i + 0.01 - 0.01 \times \overline{a}_i{}^2 - 0.1 \times \hat{J}_i) \tag{1}$$

$$F_{halfcheetah} = \sum_{i=1}^{N_s}(\Delta x_i - 0.1 \times \hat{J}_i) \tag{2}$$

$$F_{hopper} = \sum_{i=1}^{N_s} \Delta x_i \tag{3}$$

$$F_{walker2D} = \sum_{i=1}^{N_s} \Delta x_i \tag{4}$$

Symbols in Eqs. 1–4 are defined as follows: $N_s$ is the number of steps; $\Delta x_i$ is the displacement of the robot in step $i$; $\overline{a}_i$ is the average value of the actions (i.e., motor torques) applied to the robot at step $i$; $\hat{J}_i$ indicates the number of joints in their limits during step $i$.

Additionally, we used the BipedalWalker problem [5,31], in which a two-legged robot with a hull has to locomote toward a target location placed approximately 300 m from the start (see Fig. 2). The robot is endowed with a LIDAR sensor to perceive the frontal part of the environment, particularly the distance from the ground.

**Fig. 3.** Initial configuration of the Embryo robot in the corresponding task environment.

The performance of the solutions discovered for the BipedalWalker task is computed according to Eq. 5:

$$F_{bipedalWalker} = \sum_{i=1}^{N_s} (\Delta x_i - 5.0 \times |h| - 0.028 \times clip(|a_i|)) \tag{5}$$

where $h$ represents the position of the hull and $clip()$ function bounds the penalty in the range $[0, 1]$. The multiplying factors 5.0 and 0.028 are heuristic values defined in the Gymnasium engine [5,31].

Lastly, we used the Embryo problem, a two-dimensional version of the original task introduced in [19] (see also [13]), in which the robot has to locomote toward a target location placed approximately 300 m away from the start (refer to Eq. 6).

$$F_{embryo} = \sum_{i=1}^{N_s} \Delta x_i \tag{6}$$

Unlike the other tasks, this problem involves evolving both the morphological and control parameters of the robot. Consequently, the behavioral strategies of the evolved agents might be diversified. The Embryo robot consists of 7 rigid bodies connected by 6 joints, initially forming a single long body parallel to the terrain (see Fig. 3). Both the length and thickness of each body, as well as the joint angles, are subject to evolution, thereby determining the robot's final appearance and behavior (two examples of evolved robots are provided in Fig. 4). In particular, morphological parameters are varied at a rate of 90%. This value has been set sufficiently high in order to allow the algorithm to freely explore the search space and identify more effective morphologies. The default values of the morphological parameters and the transformation used are illustrated in Table 1.

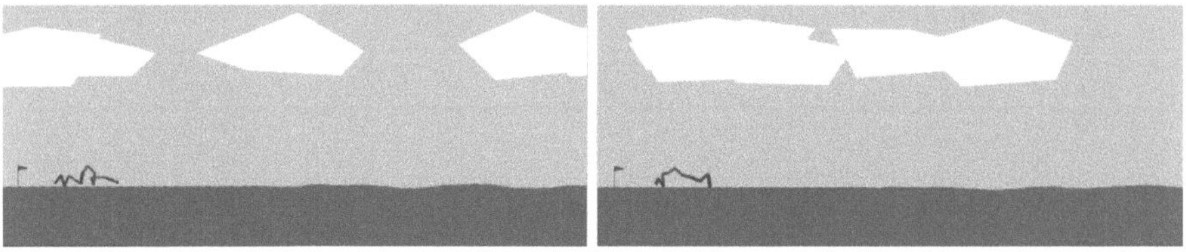

**Fig. 4.** Example of two evolved robots in the Embryo task.

**Table 1.** Default values and transformations used to evolve morphological parameters in the Embryo task. Rigid body values (i.e., size and thickness) are measured in cm, whereas joint angles are expressed in degrees. The symbol $p$ denotes the corresponding evolutionary parameter.

| Morphological Parameter | Default value | Transformation |
|---|---|---|
| Rigid body width ($w$) | 24 | $w \times (1 + (\tanh(p) \times 0.9))$ |
| Rigid body height ($h$) | 6 | $h \times (1 + (\tanh(p) \times 0.9))$ |
| Rigid body thickness ($t$) | 5 | $t + (\tanh(p) \times 0.8)$ |
| Joint angle ($a$) | 0 | $\text{hardtanh}(p) \times (\frac{3}{4} \times \pi)$ |

As an optimization algorithm, we employ the widely used OpenAI-ES algorithm [25], which has demonstrated high effectiveness in the tasks considered (see [18, 20]) and in other collective problems [23]. The algorithm optimizes a set of parameters, referred to as the *centroid*, through a sophisticated mechanism that retains historical information about exploration. Specifically, the OpenAI-ES algorithm tracks previous exploratory steps using two momentum vectors (i.e., mean and variance). In this way, the method directs exploration towards regions of the search space that are more likely to correspond to high performance levels. An illustration of how OpenAI-ES operates can be found in [23, 25].

In all experimental scenarios, robots are controlled by feed-forward neural networks with a single layer containing $NH$ hidden neurons. However, unlike previous works reported in [18, 25], we investigate different networks in which the parameter $NH$ has been varied, with $NH \in [10, 20, 50, 100]$. We considered these network sizes as they represent values allowing to cover adequately the spectrum of effective controllers. In addition, some of these sizes have proved effective in similar experimental settings [20, 21]. Table 2 provides the full set of experimental parameters used in all scenarios considered. We performed a preliminary analysis aimed to identify the best trade-off between time constraints, computational budget and minimum set of data required for statistical evaluation. Based on this investigation, we limited the number of replications to 10 and the evolutionary run length to $5 \times 10^7$ evaluation steps.

The simulations have been run by using *evorobotpy3* [20], a new tool enabling the implementation of experiments and testing Evolutionary Algorithms (EAs). To replicate our simulations, the code can be downloaded from https://github.com/PaoloP84/evorobotpy3.

### 2.3 Methodology

Functional neurons can be defined as follows: let $\mathcal{N} = \{n_i\}$ be the set of neurons of the neural network controller $\mathcal{C}$ evolved by OpenAI-ES. Let $\hat{\mathcal{C}}$ be a modified controller obtained by removing a neuron $n_i$. A neuron $n_i$ is considered "functional" (denoted with $n_i^F$) if the performance difference between $\mathcal{C}$ and $\hat{\mathcal{C}}$ is statistically significant according to the Mann-Whitney U test (see Eq. 7).

$$n_i^F = \begin{cases} 1 & if\ mannWhitneyU(F(\mathcal{C}), F(\hat{\mathcal{C}})) < 0.05 \\ 0 & otherwise \end{cases} \tag{7}$$

With the term "functional network", we refer to the set of functional neurons $\mathcal{N}^F = \{n_i^F\}$ [17]. The importance of identifying functional neurons within a neural network controller lies in the possibility to understand whether the network is sufficiently robust to cope with component failures, or if each component (i.e., neuron) plays a pivotal role for the network operation.

**Table 2.** Task experimental parameters.

| Parameter | # of replications | # of evaluation steps | # of samples | # of episodes | # of episode steps | $NH$ |
|---|---|---|---|---|---|---|
| Value | 10 | $5 \times 10^7$ | 20 | 1 | 1000 | $[10, 20, 50, 100]$ |

According to the definition in Eq. 7, functional neurons might affect the neural network's performance either positively, or negatively. Therefore, to differentiate the two cases, neurons whose removal leads to a performance drop (growth) are defined as "positive functional" ("negative functional").

In order to assess the percentage of functional neurons in the evolved neural network controllers, we have defined a dedicated post-evaluation phase in which the evolved controller $\mathcal{C}$ and the modified controllers $\hat{\mathcal{C}}$ have been evaluated in 10 fixed episodes. The performance comparison between $F(\mathcal{C})$ and $F(\hat{\mathcal{C}})$ is analyzed with the Mann-Whitney U test for each neuron $n_i \in \mathcal{N}$, and the percentage of functional neurons is derived.

## 3 Results

The analysis of performance variation depending on the number of hidden neurons, $NH$, reveals differences between experimental scenarios (see Table 3 and

Fig. 5). In particular, $NH = 50$ represents the optimal choice for the BipedalWalker, Hopper and Walker2D tasks. For the Ant task, the best solution is obtained with $NH = 20$. Regarding the Embryo problem, performance correlates positively with the value of $NH$ (with the best result at $NH = 100$); on the contrary, the opposite is true for the Halfcheetah task (with the best result at $NH = 10$). Overall, identifying an optimal value for $NH$ is far from trivial and closely linked to the specific characteristics of each problem.

**Table 3.** Performance of the neural network controllers evolved with OpenAI-ES across different experimental scenarios. The values represent the average fitness over 10 replications, with standard deviations shown in square brackets. Bold values indicate the best performance (higher is better).

| Task | NH | | | |
|---|---|---|---|---|
| | 10 | 20 | 50 | 100 |
| Ant | 1200.764 [481.983] | **1571.469 [218.883]** | 1492.234 [220.010] | 1550.617 [405.568] |
| BipedalWalker | 232.959 [142.774] | 243.579 [87.107] | **262.806 [114.845]** | 194.358 [135.054] |
| Embryo | 294.596 [52.013] | 303.573 [33.452] | 322.075 [17.188] | **332.298 [8.489]** |
| Halfcheetah | **2710.860 [143.570]** | 2701.864 [304.016] | 2531.258 [337.617] | 2296.310 [339.572] |
| Hopper | 2288.095 [220.338] | 2129.612 [256.141] | **2432.743 [241.061]** | 2429.923 [196.800] |
| Walker2D | 1158.521 [343.440] | 899.189 [356.462] | **1297.084 [556.799]** | 888.098 [351.731] |

In terms of statistical analysis, we found that the condition $NH \in [10, 20]$ outperformed the condition $NH \in [50, 100]$ in the Halfcheetah problem (Kruskal-Wallis H test, $p < 0.05$), whereas the opposite result holds in the Hopper problem (Kruskal-Wallis H test, $p < 0.05$). Lastly, the condition $NH \in [10, 50]$ performed significantly better than the condition $NH \in [20, 100]$ in the Walker2D problem (Kruskal-Wallis H test, $p < 0.05$). No significant differences were found for the Ant, BipedalWalker and Embryo tasks.

**Table 4.** Percentage of functional neurons across different neural network configurations. Data are shown as $[avg, std, min, max]$ (i.e., average, standard deviation, minimum and maximum values, respectively), and have been obtained by running 10 experimental replications for each task.

| | 10 | 20 | 50 | 100 |
|---|---|---|---|---|
| Ant | $[100.0, 0.0, 100.0, 100.0]$ | $[100.0, 0.0, 100.0, 100.0]$ | $[92.0, 10.2, 72.0, 100.0]$ | $[77.9, 28.8, 17.0, 100.0]$ |
| BipedalWalker | $[98.0, 4.0, 90.0, 100.0]$ | $[86.0, 22.3, 45.0, 100.0]$ | $[85.4, 24.2, 18.0, 100.0]$ | $[69.9, 30.0, 5.0, 100.0]$ |
| Embryo | $[84.0, 14.3, 60.0, 100.0]$ | $[41.0, 27.4, 10.0, 100.0]$ | $[36.0, 28.4, 10.0, 94.0]$ | $[43.7, 34.6, 6.0, 91.0]$ |
| Halfcheetah | $[95.0, 10.2, 70.0, 100.0]$ | $[97.5, 7.5, 75.0, 100.0]$ | $[89.8, 19.2, 40.0, 100.0]$ | $[67.5, 33.6, 8.0, 100.0]$ |
| Hopper | $[91.0, 13.7, 60.0, 100.0]$ | $[86.0, 16.7, 55.0, 100.0]$ | $[73.8, 30.4, 2.0, 100.0]$ | $[62.3, 25.8, 31.0, 98.0]$ |
| Walker2D | $[90.0, 17.9, 50.0, 100.0]$ | $[76.0, 33.2, 0.0, 100.0]$ | $[75.0, 30.6, 0.0, 100.0]$ | $[67.7, 34.3, 2.0, 100.0]$ |

We examined the role of the hidden neurons in the computation of the neural network controller during a post-evaluation phase structured as follows: for each

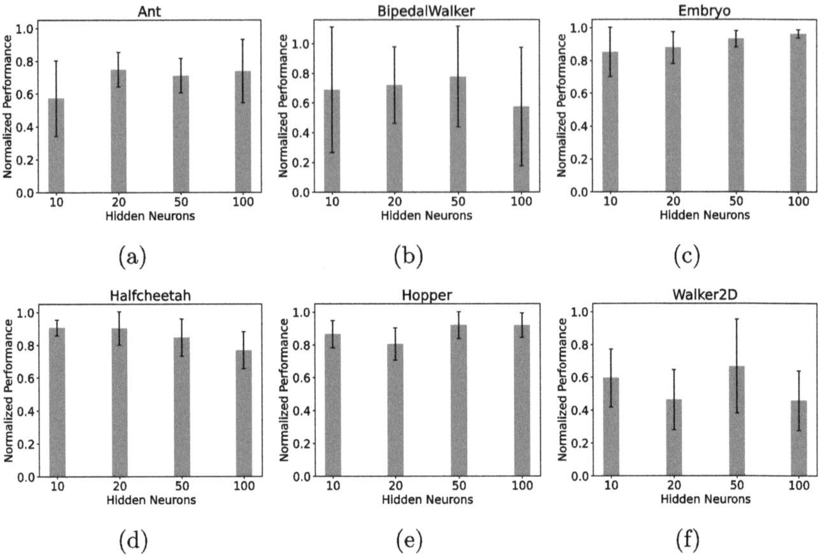


**Fig. 5.** Performance of the OpenAI-ES algorithm with varying numbers of hidden neurons. Values are normalized for each task. Bars represent the average values from 10 replications of the experiment. Error bars denote the standard deviations. **(a)** Ant **(b)** BipedalWalker **(c)** Embryo **(d)** Halfcheetah **(e)** Hopper **(f)** Walker2D

evolved controller, we created a set of variants $\hat{C}$ by removing only one hidden neuron at a time. Both the original neural network and its variants were then evaluated over 10 episodes. We collected the average performance of all the considered controllers and determined how many neurons are functional in the evolved neural network controllers. Our investigation revealed that the percentage of functional neurons is high for all the evolved controllers (see Table 4), but there is substantial variation. In particular, the cases with the highest portion of functional neurons are the Ant with $NH = 10$ and $NH = 20$ (average percentage of functional neurons 100%), followed by the BipedalWalker with $NH = 10$ (average percentage of functional neurons 98.0%) and Halfcheetah with $NH = 20$ (average percentage of functional neurons 97.5%). Upon analyzing the performance, in the case of Ant with $NH = 20$ we observe that the controllers evolved by OpenAI-ES outperform their variants by 100% (see Fig. 6a and Table 4). This suggests that, in this context, functional neurons play a crucial role in final performance: removing these neurons results in less effective network controllers.

The case with the lowest percentage of functional neurons is the Embryo with $NH = 50$ (average percentage of functional neurons 36.0%), in which the controllers evolved by OpenAI-ES are slighlty above the average fitness across the analyzed neural networks (see Fig. 6b). In general, the controllers evolved for the Embryo problem are those with the lowest percentage of functional neurons (see Table 4). This outcome might be due to the different characteristics of the

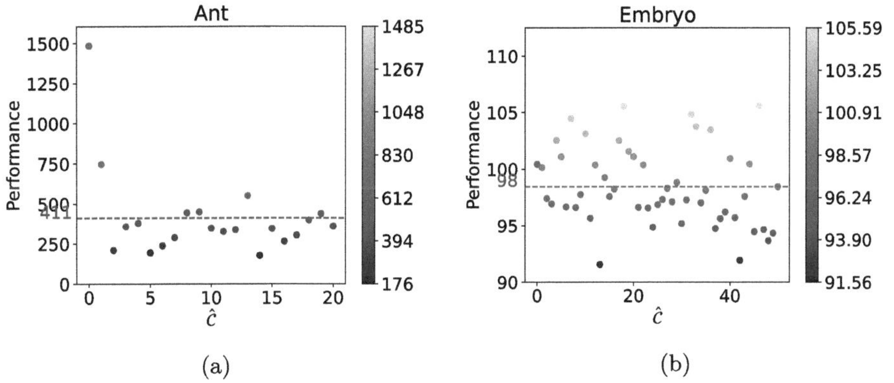


**Fig. 6.** Performance of the original neural network controller $\mathcal{C}$ (red circle) and its variations $\hat{\mathcal{C}}$, obtained by removing one neuron in turn. The purple dashed line represents the average fitness (indicated on the y-axis) of the considered controllers. Data represents the average performance over 10 replications of the experiments. **(a)** Ant with $NH = 20$. **(b)** Embryo with $NH = 50$. (Color figure online)

problem, which entail the need to co-evolve both morphological parameters (e.g., body lengths and thickness, joint angles) and control parameters (e.g., the neural network's connection weights).

A more detailed analysis of the performance of the controllers generated during the post-evaluation phase reveals a general trend for the considered tasks. In fact, among the functional neurons, we see that positive functional neurons are the majority for all tasks except for the Embryo with $NH = 50$ (see Table 5), which corresponds to the case with the lowest percentage of functional neurons (see also Table 4 and Fig. 6b). As we already discussed, the Embryo problem differs from the others with respect to the need to co-evolve body and brain. However, the co-optimization mutually adapts morphological and neural parameters, as highlighted in [19]. Therefore, the effect of neuron removal is unpredictable and might theoretically lead to enhanced performance, as our analysis suggests.

To verify the relationship between functional neurons and the evolutionary algorithm used, we run additional experiments on the Halfcheetah and Hopper problems by using a modified version of Separable Natural Evolution Strategies (sNES) [26] introduced in [15], which exploits symmetric sampling [4] to enhance performance. We refer to this algorithm as "sNES_s". The fitness achieved and the percentage of functional neurons are illustrated in Table 6. Two interesting findings emerge: (i) the performance of sNES_s is notably inferior to OpenAI-ES (Mann-Whitney U test, $p < 0.05$ for each pair of comparisons); (ii) the percentage of functional neurons is significantly lower, with a remarkable drop with $NH \geq 50$. Therefore, depending on the algorithm used, the evolved controllers are characterized by different percentages of functional neurons.

**Table 5.** Analysis of the variants generated during the post-evaluation phase by removing only one hidden neuron from the evolved controllers. Specifically, the data are expressed as $[{n_i}^F, {n_i}^{FP}, {n_i}^{FN}]$ and represent the percentage of functional (${n_i}^F$), positive functional (${n_i}^{FP}$) and negative functional (${n_i}^{FN}$) neurons. Values are averaged over 10 experimental replications.

| | 10 | 20 | 50 | 100 |
|---|---|---|---|---|
| Ant | $[100.0, 100.0, 0.0]$ | $[100.0, 99.5, 0.5]$ | $[92.0, 90.6, 1.4]$ | $[77.9, 77.9, 0.0]$ |
| BipedalWalker | $[98.0, 97.0, 1.0]$ | $[86.0, 85.5, 0.5]$ | $[85.4, 84.8, 0.6]$ | $[69.9, 62.2, 7.7]$ |
| Embryo | $[84.0, 81.0, 3.0]$ | $[41.0, 33.0, 8.0]$ | $[36.0, 14.6, 21.4]$ | $[43.7, 39.2, 4.5]$ |
| Halfcheetah | $[95.0, 95.0, 0.0]$ | $[97.5, 97.5, 0.0]$ | $[89.8, 88.6, 1.2]$ | $[67.5, 57.9, 9.6]$ |
| Hopper | $[91.0, 91.0, 0.0]$ | $[86.0, 86.0, 0.0]$ | $[73.8, 69.0, 4.8]$ | $[62.3, 62.2, 0.1]$ |
| Walker2D | $[90.0, 90.0, 0.0]$ | $[76.0, 76.0, 0.0]$ | $[75.0, 72.2, 2.8]$ | $[67.7, 65.1, 2.6]$ |

**Table 6.** Analysis of the neural network controllers evolved with sNES_s for the Halfcheetah and Hopper problems. Concerning performance, the values represent the average fitness over 10 replications, with standard deviations shown in square brackets. Bold values indicate the best performance (higher is better). With respect to functional neurons, data are shown as $[avg, std, min, max]$ (i.e., average, standard deviation, minimum and maximum values, respectively), and have been obtained by running 10 experimental replications for each task.

| | | NH | | | |
|---|---|---|---|---|---|
| | | 10 | 20 | 50 | 100 |
| Halfcheetah | Performance | 1542.074 [449.459] | 1414.470 [411.304] | **1550.928 [405.987]** | 1410.455 [258.881] |
| | Functional neurons | $[66.0, 22.0, 20.0, 100.0]$ | $[38.5, 32.4, 10.0, 100.0]$ | $[16.4, 28.1, 10.0, 100.0]$ | $[4.6, 6.3, 0.0, 22.0]$ |
| Hopper | Performance | 992.545 [636.620] | 1272.529 [700.504] | **1527.481 [650.057]** | 1022.486 [592.565] |
| | Functional neurons | $[67.0, 30.7, 20.0, 100.0]$ | $[43.5, 37.5, 5.0, 100.0]$ | $[28.6, 29.1, 0.0, 86.0]$ | $[5.0, 5.5, 1.0, 20.0]$ |

# 4 Conclusions

The design of neural network controllers is often task-dependent and requires a high level of expertise from the human designer. However, there is limited understanding of which parts of the network are the most critical. Investigating the role of functional neurons, which cannot be removed without significantly altering controller performance, is paramount to understanding how a neural network operates. Another limitation lies in the use of fixed network architectures, which are not necessarily optimized for the task. Although pioneering attempts have been made in order to evolve both connection weights and network architecture simultaneously, such as those of [27], the complexity of these techniques makes it difficult to understand how individual neurons contribute to network performance.

In this work, we analyze how the number of hidden neurons $NH$ affects the effectiveness of neural network controllers in a set of locomotion benchmark problems. In particular, we assess whether functional neurons play a significant role in the final network performance. To this end, we conduct experiments using OpenAI-ES, a state-of-the-art evolutionary algorithm successfully applied to the domains under study. The fitness evaluation emphasizes the difficulty of identifying a precise optimal value of $NH$ across all tasks, underscoring the limitations of fixed network architectures, which may be sub-optimal. In addition, OpenAI-ES works by evolving a single solution, the *centroid*, and identifying the most promising direction in the search space by preserving information about past progress. Clearly, this approach optimizes exploration and achieves excellent performance, but it might limit diversity of the solutions. Nevertheless, the number of functional neurons is generally high, meaning that the evolved neural network controllers are largely sensitive to the removal of hidden neurons. This indicates that functional neurons play a pivotal role and strongly affect the final performance. Moreover, by varying the evolutionary algorithm, we observe that the percentage of functional neurons changes, thus emphasizing the existence of complex relationships between the algorithm used and the properties of the evolved neural network controllers.

Given the outcomes of this work, a promising direction for future research would be to analyze the existence of sub-functional networks through multiple-neuron pruning [12]. Moreover, further investigations could explore enhancements of OpenAI-ES, such as evolving a population of centroids in parallel as proposed in [16], or extending our analysis to other evolutionary algorithms. Another worthwhile future research direction concerns the evaluation of a broader set of network sizes and configurations, with the aim to expand and generalize the findings illustrated in this work. Finally, the analysis of the relationship between functionality and complexity might be extended to other network architectures, like Recurrent Neural Networks (RNNs) or Convolutional Neural Networks (CNNs).

## References

1. Amjad, R.A., Liu, K., Geiger, B.C.: Understanding neural networks and individual neuron importance via information-ordered cumulative ablation. IEEE Trans. Neural Netw. Learn. Syst. **33**(12), 7842–7852 (2021)
2. Arshavsky, Y.I.: Neurons versus networks: the interplay between individual neurons and neural networks in cognitive functions. Neuroscientist **23**(4), 341–355 (2017)
3. Berrocal, E., Sierra, B., Herrero, H.: Evaluating PyBullet and isaac sim in the scope of robotics and reinforcement learning. In: 2024 7th Iberian Robotics Conference (ROBOT), pp. 1–6. IEEE (2024)
4. Brockhoff, D., Auger, A., Hansen, N., Arnold, D.V., Hohm, T.: Mirrored sampling and sequential selection for evolution strategies. In: International Conference on Parallel Problem Solving from Nature, pp. 11–21. Springer (2010)
5. Brockman, G., et al.: Openai gym. arXiv preprint arXiv:1606.01540 (2016)
6. Coumans, E.: Bullet physics simulation. In: ACM SIGGRAPH 2015 Courses, p. 1 (2015)
7. Coumans, E., Bai, Y.: PyBullet, a python module for physics simulation for games, robotics and machine learning (2016)
8. Frankle, J., Carbin, M.: The lottery ticket hypothesis: finding sparse, trainable neural networks. arXiv preprint arXiv:1803.03635 (2018)

9. Hoefler, T., Alistarh, D., Ben-Nun, T., Dryden, N., Peste, A.: Sparsity in deep learning: pruning and growth for efficient inference and training in neural networks. J. Mach. Learn. Res. **22**(1) (2021)
10. Kaup, M., Wolff, C., Hwang, H., Mayer, J., Bruni, E.: A review of nine physics engines for reinforcement learning research. arXiv preprint arXiv:2407.08590 (2024)
11. Liu, F., Zhang, S.: A reinforcement learning toolkit for quadruped robots with PyBullet. In: 2023 5th International Symposium on Robotics & Intelligent Manufacturing Technology (ISRIMT), pp. 296–299. IEEE (2023)
12. Malach, E., Yehudai, G., Shalev-Schwartz, S., Shamir, O.: Proving the lottery ticket hypothesis: pruning is all you need. In: International Conference on Machine Learning, pp. 6682–6691. PMLR (2020)
13. Nolfi, S.: Behavioral and cognitive robotics: an adaptive perspective (2021)
14. Ohashi, K., Nakanishi, K., Goto, N., Yasui, Y., Ishii, S.: Orthogonal adversarial deep reinforcement learning for discrete-and continuous-action problems. IEEE Access (2024)
15. Pagliuca, P.: Enhancing performance of evolutionary strategies with symmetric sampling (furthermore, weight decay). Algorithms **19**(7), 504 (2026)
16. Pagliuca, P.: Whether, how and when modern evolutionary strategies can be improved. J. Artif. Intell. Auton. Intell. **2**(3), 425–449 (2026)
17. Pagliuca, P., Inglese, D.Y.: The importance of functionality over complexity. a preliminary study on feed-forward neural networks. In: Advanced Neural Artificial Intelligence: Theories and Applications, pp. 447–458. Springer (2025)
18. Pagliuca, P., Milano, N., Nolfi, S.: Efficacy of modern neuro-evolutionary strategies for continuous control optimization. Front. Robot. AI **7**, 98 (2020)
19. Pagliuca, P., Nolfi, S.: The dynamic of body and brain co-evolution. Adapt. Behav. **30**(3), 245–255 (2022)
20. Pagliuca, P., Nolfi, S., Vitanza, A.: Evorobotpy3: a flexible and easy-to-use simulation tool for evolutionary robotics. In: Proceedings of the Genetic and Evolutionary Computation Conference Companion, GECCO 2025 Companion (2025)
21. Pagliuca, P., Trivisano, G., Vitanza, A.: How to evolve aggregation in robotic multi-agent systems. In: Proceedings of the 26th Edition of the Workshop From Object to Agents (WOA25), pp. 140–156 (2025)
22. Pagliuca, P., Vitanza, A.: Enhancing aggregation in locomotor multi-agent systems: a theoretical framework. In: Proceedings of the 25th Edition of the Workshop From Object to Agents (WOA24), vol. 3735, pp. 42–57 (2024)
23. Pagliuca, P., Vitanza, A.: A comparative study of evolutionary strategies for aggregation tasks in robot swarms: macro- and micro-level behavioral analysis. IEEE Access **13**, 72721–72735 (2025)
24. Reda, D., Tao, T., van de Panne, M.: Learning to locomote: understanding how environment design matters for deep reinforcement learning. In: Proceedings of the 13th ACM SIGGRAPH Conference on Motion, Interaction and Games, pp. 1–10 (2020)
25. Salimans, T., Ho, J., Chen, X., Sidor, S., Sutskever, I.: Evolution strategies as a scalable alternative to reinforcement learning. arXiv preprint arXiv:1703.03864 (2017)
26. Schaul, T., Glasmachers, T., Schmidhuber, J.: High dimensions and heavy tails for natural evolution strategies. In: Proceedings of the 13th Annual Conference on Genetic and Evolutionary Computation, pp. 845–852 (2011)
27. Stanley, K.O., Miikkulainen, R.: Evolving neural networks through augmenting topologies. Evol. Comput. **10**(2), 99–127 (2002)

28. Stevenson, I.H., Rebesco, J.M., Miller, L.E., Körding, K.P.: Inferring functional connections between neurons. Curr. Opin. Neurobiol. **18**(6), 582–588 (2008)
29. Tononi, G., Sporns, O., Edelman, G.M.: A measure for brain complexity: relating functional segregation and integration in the nervous system. Proc. Natl. Acad. Sci. **91**(11), 5033–5037 (1994)
30. Tononi, G., Sporns, O., Edelman, G.M.: Measures of degeneracy and redundancy in biological networks. Proc. Natl. Acad. Sci. **96**(6), 3257–3262 (1999)
31. Towers, M., et al.: Gymnasium: a standard interface for reinforcement learning environments. Adv. Neural. Inf. Process. Syst. **38** (2026)
32. Wang, D., Hu, M.: Contrastive learning methods for deep reinforcement learning. IEEE Access (2023)

# Semantic Grounding over Brute-Force Inference: A Symbiotic Evaluation of Text-to-SQL Systems

Michele Paolicelli[1(✉)], Cataldo Musto[1], Giovanni Semeraro[1], Alessandro Crnjar[2], David Landi[2], and Claudio Saccà[2]

[1] Università degli Studi di Bari Aldo Moro, Bari, Italy
m.paolicelli9@phd.uniba.it, {cataldo.musto,giovanni.semeraro}@uniba.it
[2] QuestIT S.r.l., Siena, Italy
{Alessandro.Crnjar,david.landi,claudio.sacca}@vection-technologies.com

**Abstract.** Recent Text-to-SQL systems increasingly improve performance by scaling inference-time computation, for example, through candidate generation, orchestration, and multi-step reasoning. While effective in some settings, these strategies often increase token usage, latency, and deployment costs, and leave open the question of whether observed failures are primarily due to insufficient reasoning or insufficient semantic grounding.

This paper studies this question through a cost-aware symbiotic evaluation framework that jointly considers execution quality, relation-level correctness, token usage, latency, and inference complexity. We analyze conversational Text-to-SQL systems on state-of-the-art benchmarks and compare brute-force candidate generation with compact semantic enrichment of schema information, including lightweight semantic descriptions and disambiguation hints.

Our results indicate that many observed errors arise from semantic underspecification rather than SQL generation failures, including schema ambiguity, entity–event confusion, aggregation ambiguity, value normalization issues, and benchmark-specific annotation artifacts. In our experiments, lightweight semantic enrichment improves execution accuracy from approximately 0.78 to 0.93 with only a modest increase in prompt size, whereas candidate generation yields smaller and less consistent gains despite substantially higher inference cost.

These findings suggest that semantic information quality is a central factor in Text-to-SQL performance and that many apparent reasoning failures may originate from incomplete or underspecified semantic context rather than from limitations in reasoning or brute-force inference strategies.

Code and supplementary material are available at: https://github.com/michelepao1993-dev/semantic-grounding-text2sql.


S. Bistarelli et al. (Eds.): AIxIA 2026, LNAI 17131, pp. 528–541, 2027.
https://doi.org/10.1007/978-3-032-40774-0_38

**Keywords:** Text-to-SQL · Large Language Models · Semantic Grounding · Evaluation Metrics · Hallucination Analysis · Database Interfaces

## 1 Introduction

Text-to-SQL aims to translate natural-language questions into executable SQL queries over relational databases [1]. Recent advances in Large Language Models (LLMs) have significantly improved Text-to-SQL performance, enabling conversational agents to generate increasingly accurate SQL queries [2,3].

Current Text-to-SQL research increasingly relies on inference-time scaling strategies such as candidate generation, orchestration, and multi-step reasoning [4–9]. However, these approaches often incur substantial computational costs while leaving open a more fundamental question: *are current Text-to-SQL failures primarily caused by insufficient reasoning, or by insufficient semantic grounding?*

Motivated by this question, we investigate the role of semantic grounding and information quality in Text-to-SQL systems. Throughout this paper, semantic grounding refers to lightweight schema-level knowledge such as column semantics, aggregation conventions, value normalization rules, and entity–event relationships. In particular, we investigate whether many Text-to-SQL failures commonly attributed to reasoning limitations instead arise from semantic ambiguities, aggregation conventions, entity–event mismatches, and benchmark-specific artifacts. We further investigate whether this is the case and whether improving the semantic information available to the model may yield larger gains than increasing inference complexity alone.

To guide our study, we investigate the following research questions (RQs):
*RQ1*: *How can we evaluate Text-to-SQL systems in a way that simultaneously considers response quality, cost, and inference complexity?*
*RQ2*: *To what extent does the quality of semantic information available to the model influence performance compared to approaches based primarily on inference scaling?*
*RQ3*: *What are the main causes of hallucinations/errors in conversational Text-to-SQL systems?*
While addressing these questions, this paper makes the following main contributions:

1. We introduce a symbiotic evaluation framework that jointly considers relational correctness, execution quality, token usage, latency, and inference complexity, providing a broader assessment of deployment-oriented Text-to-SQL systems.
2. We show that lightweight semantic enrichment can substantially improve Text-to-SQL performance while requiring substantially lower computational overhead than candidate generation and other inference-scaling strategies.

3. We present a qualitative error taxonomy showing that many observed failures originate from semantic ambiguity, entity–event confusion, aggregation misinterpretations, and benchmark-specific artifacts rather than from an inability to generate valid SQL queries.

The rest of this paper is organized as follows. Section 2 introduces the symbiotic evaluation framework and its metrics. Sections 3 and 4 discuss experimental setting and results. Finally, Sects. 5, 6, and 7 discuss related work, limitations, and conclusions.

## 2 Symbiotic Evaluation Framework

This section presents the evaluation framework adopted in this work. We first summarize standard evaluation metrics and discuss their limitations in conversational settings; we then employ complementary relation-level measures and define a cost-aware Symbiosis score to evaluate the quality–efficiency profile of a system over extended interactions.

### 2.1 A Motivating Example: Informative but Non-Exact Outputs

Standard evaluation protocols for Text-to-SQL systems commonly rely on execution-based and structure-based metrics [3,10] such as Component Matching (CM), which measures the overlap between predicted and ground-truth SQL components using F1 score, or Exact Matching (EM), which considers a prediction correct only if it exactly matches the ground-truth SQL query in all its components. Moreover, Execution Accuracy (EX) measures the proportion of query pairs for which the predicted query $\hat{Q}_n$ returns the exact same result as the corresponding ground-truth query $Q_n$ when executed:

$$\mathrm{EX} = \frac{1}{N}\sum_{n=1}^{N} \mathbb{1}\big(\mathrm{Exec}(Q_n) = \mathrm{Exec}(\hat{Q}_n)\big).$$

Although execution-based metrics are widely adopted in Text-to-SQL evaluation, some conversational and deployment-oriented scenarios may not be fully characterized by exact query matching or strict execution equivalence. Recent work has also proposed metrics that incorporate efficiency considerations, such as Valid Efficiency Score (VES) [11]. However, these metrics still assume that benchmark correctness is the primary evaluation target. To illustrate this issue, let us consider an example from *Spider* [10], a large-scale, complex, and cross-domain semantic parsing and Text-to-SQL dataset. The following example has been selected from the Spider database *Concert Singer*.

**User Query**

What are the names of the singers and number of concerts for each person?

The corresponding outputs are shown in Table 1, followed by the corresponding predicted and reference SQL queries.

Predicted vs. Gold SQL

**Predicted:**
```
SELECT s.Name, COUNT(sic.concert_ID) AS Number_of_Concerts
FROM singer s LEFT JOIN singer_in_concert sic ON s.Singer_ID =
sic.Singer_ID GROUP BY s.Name.
```
**Gold:**
```
SELECT T2.name, count(*) FROM singer_in_concert AS T1 JOIN singer
AS T2 ON T1.singer_id = T2.singer_id GROUP BY T2.singer_id.
```

A model may generate a query that starts from the `singer` table and uses a `LEFT JOIN` with `singer_in_concert`, thereby returning all singers, including those with zero concerts. The reference query, instead, starts from the relationship table and excludes singers without concert records. In this case, the predicted relation contains all tuples returned by the reference query and only adds the singer with zero concerts. Thus, although the prediction is marked as execution-incorrect, it is arguably more faithful to the expression "each person" from a user-facing perspective.

**Table 1.** Predicted and gold results for concert counts.

| Predicted | | Gold | |
|---|---|---|---|
| Name | Number_of_Concerts | Name | count(*) |
| Joe Sharp | 0 | Timbaland | 2 |
| John Nizinik | 2 | Justin Brown | 3 |
| Justin Brown | 3 | Rose White | 1 |
| Rose White | 1 | John Nizinik | 2 |
| Timbaland | 2 | Tribal King | 2 |
| Tribal King | 2 | | |

This example illustrates how standard binary metrics can underestimate the utility of modern conversational Text-to-SQL systems and fail to capture subtle aspects of interactive database querying. Although the queries are structurally different, they capture closely related semantics and produce comparable results. However, standard metrics may assign significantly different scores, highlighting their limitations in practical settings. These observations motivate the need for evaluation criteria that better capture the utility of generated outputs. In the next section, we introduce a complementary evaluation framework based on relation-level structure, aiming to provide a more robust and informative assessment of Text-to-SQL systems.

### 2.2 Relation-Level Evaluation

Unlike many natural language processing tasks, the output of Text-to-SQL systems is structured data that can be represented as a two-dimensional table.

In this work, to complement standard execution-based evaluation, we interpret such tables as relations, i.e., subsets of a Cartesian product between non-empty sets, following a standard set-theoretic perspective [12], and adopt relation-level metrics that operate directly on query outputs interpreted as sets of tuples (i.e., relational tables returned by SQL queries).

**Relational Accuracy.** Given nonempty predicted and ground-truth relations $R(t)$ and $R_{\text{gold}}(t)$ at turn $t$, we define the turn-indexed *Relational Accuracy* as

$$A^{\text{rel}}_{\alpha,\beta}(t) := \exp\left(-\alpha\frac{|R_{\text{gold}}(t) \setminus R(t)|}{|R_{\text{gold}}(t)|} - \beta\frac{|R(t) \setminus R_{\text{gold}}(t)|}{|R(t)|}\right), \tag{1}$$

where $\alpha, \beta \in \mathbb{R}$, with $\alpha \geq \beta \geq 0$, control the penalties assigned to missing and additional information (e.g., $\alpha = 2$, $\beta = 1$).

For empty relations, we extend the definition as follows:

$$A^{\text{rel}}_{\alpha,\beta}(t) := \begin{cases} 1 & \text{if } R_{\text{gold}}(t) = \emptyset = R(t), \\ \exp(-\beta) & \text{if } R_{\text{gold}}(t) = \emptyset \neq R(t), \\ 0 & \text{if } R_{\text{gold}}(t) \neq \emptyset = R(t), \\ A^{\text{rel}}_{\alpha,\beta}(t) \text{ from Eq. (1)} & \text{otherwise.} \end{cases}$$

Setting $\beta = 0$ in Eq. (1) yields

$$A^{\text{rel}}_{\alpha,0}(t) := \exp\left(-\alpha\frac{|R_{\text{gold}}(t) \setminus R(t)|}{|R_{\text{gold}}(t)|}\right), \tag{2}$$

which penalizes only missing tuples from the ground-truth relation. We refer to Eq. (2) as *Informational Relational Accuracy.*

*Penalty Interpretation.* This formulation captures both under- and over-generation effects. The exponential function ensures that $A^{\text{rel}}_{\alpha,\beta} \in (0, 1]$ and yields strong decay as the discrepancy between $R$ and $R_{\text{gold}}$ increases, thereby severely penalizing substantially incorrect predictions. The metric is task-sensitive and tunable: by choosing $\alpha$ and $\beta$, developers can decide whether the evaluation should behave like a strict EX or a more permissive relation-level similarity score.

The informational variant defined in Eq. (2) is more permissive, as it does not penalize additional information in $R$. We argue that this setting is meaningful in practical scenarios, where user queries may be ambiguous and returning superset relations can still be useful. Nevertheless, this permissive variant should be interpreted as a diagnostic measure of information coverage rather than as a standalone correctness metric, since additional irrelevant tuples are not penalized. Empirically, we observe that our agents often produce relations that fully cover $R_{\text{gold}}$ while including additional relevant information. In such cases, standard metrics and the full Relational Accuracy (with $\beta \neq 0$) may underestimate the quality of the generated output. For instance, in Table 1, the predicted relation contains all relevant information from the ground truth, despite structural differences in the underlying SQL queries.

### 2.3 Cost-Aware Symbiotic Evaluation

While relation-level metrics address cases where generated outputs remain useful despite deviating from the benchmark, they do not capture the computational resources required to obtain them. Therefore, evaluation should account not only for output quality but also for the cost incurred during generation.

**Symbiosis.** Let $\mathcal{Q} := \{q_1, ..., q_N\}$ be other quantities of interest (e.g. tokens, latency, tool calls, pricing). If $A^{\text{rel}}_{\alpha,\beta}(t) \neq 0$, we can exploit the properties of the exponential function and take into account all desired quantities by subtracting their quadratic mean into the exponential function and set

$$\mathcal{S}(t) := A^{\text{rel}}_{\alpha,\beta}(t) \cdot \exp\left( - \frac{\sqrt{\frac{1}{N}\sum_{i=1}^{N}[q_i(t)/q_{i,\max}]^2}}{\mu} \right) \in [0,1]. \tag{3}$$

where $\mu$ indicates how strong the penalizing effect of the quantities $(q_i)_{1\leq i\leq N}$ is with respect to $A^{\text{rel}}_{\alpha,\beta}$, which is the landmark quantity in this work. Such quantities may have different units and orders of magnitude; therefore, they are normalized to threshold values, which, in turn, should depend on the setup. We chose quadratic mean to weakly penalize quantities in $[0, 1]$ and strongly penalize quantities greater than 1.

We refer to $\mathcal{S}(t)$ as the *Symbiosis score* of the agent at turn $t$.

*Interpretation.* The previous definition is general, because the family $\mathcal{Q} = \{q_1, ..., q_N\}$ is undefined. Once the experimental setup is fixed, it is up to the developer to define $\mathcal{Q}$ and the function $\mathcal{S} = \mathcal{S}(\mathcal{Q}(t))$ accordingly. In this work, we focus on three main quantities: Relational Accuracy ($A^{\text{rel}}_{\alpha,\beta}$), number of tokens ($T$) and latency ($L$), hence $\mathcal{Q} = \{T, L\}$.

In practical terms, higher values of $\mathcal{S}(t)$ indicate a more favorable trade-off between relation-level quality and inference cost. We use "Symbiotic" operationally to denote interactions that jointly favor user-facing response quality and system-side resource efficiency. This formulation allows different evaluation dimensions to be combined into a single deployment-oriented measure without privileging any specific implementation strategy. Symbiosis is therefore intended primarily as a deployment-dependent diagnostic score for comparing configurations under a common resource budget, rather than as an absolute ranking criterion across heterogeneous systems.

## 3 Experimental Setup

Experiments are conducted on *Spider Dev*, which contains 1,034 queries in total, across various databases on general topics; benchmarks are executed using SQLite databases [10].

Since the aim of this work is to propose a novel way of evaluating Text-to-SQL agents, and not to carry out a benchmark analysis, we evaluated our configurations with different temperatures and numbers of generated SQL candidates on a subset of Spider Dev consisting of 108 queries across 3 databases, with different perceived levels of complexity: all 18 questions from *Museum Visit*, 45 from *Concert Singer*, and 45 from *Student Transcript Tracking*, to study candidate generation behavior and compare multiple model configurations under controlled computational cost. The subset was intentionally selected to support detailed qualitative error analysis and semantic-grounding inspection. Since one of the goals of this work is to study the causes of Text-to-SQL failures rather than to report leaderboard results, each query, schema, and gold SQL annotation was manually inspected during the analysis. Accordingly, the results should be interpreted as a controlled exploratory study rather than as a comprehensive evaluation of Spider Dev.

Relation-level evaluation treats query outputs as unordered sets of tuples, making the comparison invariant to row ordering and syntactic variations in queries. For the avoidance of doubt, in this paper, EX does not take into account invariance at the tabular level.

In our experiments, we leverage a standard monolithic Text-to-SQL agent consisting of a single end-to-end model that receives the full database schema and descriptions in the prompt. Since one of the goals of this work is to compare semantic enrichment with inference-scaling strategies, the agent can optionally generate a fixed number $N \geq 1$ of candidate SQL queries. Our preferred configuration uses a single generation $N = 1$, while larger values are used exclusively to study the effect of candidate generation. Among the generated candidates, we assume an idealized oracle selection strategy: if any candidate exactly matches the ground-truth query, it is selected; otherwise, one candidate is chosen at random. This controlled selection procedure isolates exact-reference recovery but may overlook execution-equivalent candidates; candidate-generation results should therefore not be interpreted as a definitive upper bound for candidate-ranking strategies. To promote diversity, candidate queries are generated at a nonzero temperature. Different configurations are evaluated in Sect. 4.

*Semantic enrichment* consists of manually curated textual annotations, which may include column-level and relationship semantics, aggregation conventions, value-normalization hints, and deduplication policies. For example, the following annotation help resolve a common entity–event ambiguity illustrated in Table 1:

System Prompt Chunk

- Use LEFT JOIN only if the question explicitly asks to include entities with no related records.

The annotations were manually curated after inspecting the selected database schemas, natural-language questions, and reference SQL queries. This intentionally simulates a deployment scenario in which developers possess domain knowledge and can specify database semantics and expected interpretation conventions. The enrichment may therefore include database-level rules and FAQ-style clarifications for cases that are difficult to express through general patterns, while not directly exposing the reference SQL to the model at inference time. These additions do not to provide query-specific solutions, but reduce semantically plausible yet unintended interpretations of the database schema.

Prompts are shared across all configurations, with differences encoded only in database descriptions. This design allows the comparison to isolate the impact of semantic information quality while keeping the underlying prompting structure consistent across experiments. For reproducibility purposes, complete prompting details, system instructions, and implementation configurations are available in the accompanying repository. Two Few-shot examples per query are also provided in all configurations, retrieved from the Spider training set using Jaccard Similarity on the query [13].

All agents are implemented in Python, using LangGraph [14] as the primary orchestration framework and OpenAI chat models [15] accessed via the LangChain [16] `ChatOpenAI` interface. Temperature and token limits are controlled through the API. To simulate a conversational setting, our agents maintain a sliding window of the most recent conversation history (user, system, and assistant messages), with a size of $k = 50$. Older messages are truncated using a first-in, first-out (FIFO) policy.

# 4 Results

This section investigates whether Text-to-SQL performance is improved more effectively by inference scaling or by better semantic grounding. We first evaluate candidate generation from a cost-aware perspective using the proposed Symbiotic framework, then compare semantically enriched configurations, and finally analyze the error patterns that explain the observed performance differences.

## 4.1 Symbiotic Evaluation

This subsection addresses *RQ1* by evaluating our agents using novel symbiotic evaluation metrics. Table 2 reports the relationship between candidate generation, execution quality, and inference cost. In this case, we set $\mu = 2$, and $T_{\max} = 10000$, $L_{\max} = 5$ as thresholds for tokens and latencies, respectively, which represent deployment-dependent reference budgets rather than universal constants. The selected values reflect developer-defined resource budgets and are consistent with the token and latency scales observed across the evaluated configurations. Different application scenarios, such as larger databases, agentic workflows, or multi-tool systems, may naturally require different values.

Across all tested models, increasing the number of generated candidates consistently increases token consumption and latency, while providing limited or inconsistent gains in EX and Symbiosis. This suggests that additional inference branches often explore semantically similar solutions rather than correcting the query's underlying interpretation.

**Table 2.** Effect of candidate generation on $\mathcal{S}(t)$ of some of the GPT-family models.

| Model | temperature | Candidates | EX | $A^{\text{rel}}_{2,1}(t)$ | $A^{\text{rel}}_{2,0}(t)$ | Tokens | Latency | $\mathcal{S}(t)$ |
|---|---|---|---|---|---|---|---|---|
| 4o | 0.0 | **1** | 0.83 | 0.90 | 0.91 | **1463.86** | 1.57 | 0.89 |
| 4o | 0.7 | 5 | 0.84 | 0.92 | 0.92 | 7298.55 | 2.02 | 0.84 |
| 4o | 1.0 | 10 | 0.84 | 0.92 | 0.92 | 14543.15 | 3.03 | 0.67 |
| 4o | 0.7 | 20 | 0.83 | 0.90 | 0.91 | 29589.33 | 5.50 | 0.33 |
| 4.1 | 0.0 | **1** | 0.80 | 0.89 | 0.90 | 1488.38 | **1.41** | 0.88 |
| 4.1 | 0.7 | 5 | 0.77 | 0.85 | 0.86 | 7410.09 | 2.38 | 0.77 |
| 4.1 | 1.0 | 10 | 0.78 | 0.88 | 0.89 | 14761.44 | 3.01 | 0.65 |
| **4.1-mini** | 0.0 | **1** | 0.78 | 0.91 | **0.92** | 1496.70 | 1.54 | **0.91** |
| 4.1-mini | 0.7 | 5 | 0.77 | 0.90 | 0.91 | 7418.68 | 2.42 | 0.82 |
| 4.1-mini | 1.0 | 10 | 0.73 | 0.86 | 0.88 | 14968.24 | 3.27 | 0.63 |

### 4.2 Semantic Information Quality vs Inference Scaling

We next study whether Text-to-SQL performance improves more by increasing inference depth or by improving the semantic information available to the model. Table 3 shows the comparison between the candidate generator with the highest Symbiosis score and the enriched model. It also highlights a primary value of the proposed metrics: large gains in EX do not always translate into equally large gains in $A^{\text{rel}}$, while increased performance may come at a computational cost that is not fully reflected by EX alone.

**Table 3.** Best candidate generator vs enriched model

| Model | temperature | Candidates | EX | $A^{\text{rel}}_{2,1}(t)$ | $A^{\text{rel}}_{2,0}(t)$ | Tokens | Latency | $\mathcal{S}(t)$ |
|---|---|---|---|---|---|---|---|---|
| 4o | 0.7 | 5 | 0.84 | 0.92 | 0.92 | 7298.55 | 2.02 | 0.84 |
| **4.1-mini enriched** | 0.0 | **1** | **0.93** | **0.95** | **0.95** | **1732.06** | 3.81 | **0.88** |

In the 4.1-mini setting, which resulted as the most symbiotic setting in Table 2, the compact schema prompt achieves an EX of approximately 0.78 with about 1.5K tokens on average. Adding targeted semantic information raises EX to approximately 0.93, while increasing the prompt size and latency only to about 1.7K tokens and 3.81 seconds. Accordingly, the higher Symbiosis of the compact configuration does not imply that it should always be preferred over the enriched model. Rather, the score exposes the trade-off: the enriched configuration achieves substantially higher EX at a higher measured inference cost, leaving the preferred operating point dependent on deployment priorities.

Moreover, since GPT-4.1-mini is designed as a lower-cost model, the observed improvements are achieved despite using a cheaper underlying model and substantially fewer inference resources [19]. This comparison suggests that semantic information quality can be a more effective optimization target than inference scaling. Candidate generation increases the number of attempts, but it does not necessarily alter the assumptions the model uses to generate SQL. Semantic enrichment, instead, changes the grounding context itself, allowing even a simple monolithic model to generate more appropriate queries.

Interestingly, the enriched configuration achieves a substantially higher EX, while the corresponding increase in $A^{\text{rel}}$ is much smaller. As a consequence, $\mathcal{S}(t)$ slightly decreases despite the large EX improvement, because the gain in relation-level utility is partially offset by the additional inference cost. This observation highlights a limitation of benchmark-oriented metrics: relatively small semantic corrections may produce large changes in EX, even when the generated outputs were already highly informative from a relational perspective. In this sense, the gap between EX and relation-level evaluation provides further evidence that standard benchmarks may overemphasize annotation-specific distinctions and underestimate the utility of semantically meaningful outputs.

Therefore, *RQ2* can be answered as follows: in the analyzed setting, improving semantic grounding has a larger impact on performance-per-token than increasing inference complexity through candidate generation. Beyond a certain point, brute-force inference exhibits diminishing returns, whereas targeted semantic information directly addresses the source of many observed failures.

### 4.3 Recurring Hallucinations and Error Patterns

We now analyze some of the errors observed in the three Spider databases considered in our study: *Concert Singer*, *Museum Visit*, and *Student Transcripts Tracking*. In this work, we use the term *hallucination* in an operational sense: a generated SQL query is considered weakly grounded when it is syntactically valid and superficially plausible, but relies on semantic assumptions that are not supported, or not sufficiently specified, by the database schema and the natural-language question. We identify four recurring patterns.

*Semantic Attribute Ambiguity.* A first class of errors arises when different columns have closely related surface names but distinct semantics. For example, in *Concert Singer*, the question asking for "the name and release year of the song by the youngest singer" requires the column `Song_Name`, while the model may select `Name`, which denotes the singer's name. The generated query is syntactically valid and follows a plausible interpretation, but it is not grounded in the intended column semantics.

*Entity-Event Confusion.* A second pattern concerns the distinction between entities and observed events. Questions such as "What are the names of the singers and number of concerts for each person?" may be interpreted as requiring all singers, including those with zero concerts, leading to a `LEFT JOIN`. However, the Spider reference query counts only singers that actually appear in the `concert` table. Similar phenomena occur when counting stadiums, courses, or enrollments. These failures suggest that models often reason over complete sets of entities, whereas the benchmark expects results to be derived only from entities that participate in recorded events.

*Aggregation and Quantity Ambiguity.* A third source of error concerns whether a quantity should be computed or read as a stored attribute. In *Concert Singer*, the question asking for the "maximum capacity and the average of all stadiums" naturally leads to `AVG(Capacity)`, while the reference query selects the stored column `Average`. Similarly, in *Museum Visit*, the question about visitors who visited museums more than once can be confused with `Num_of_Ticket > 1`, although the intended interpretation is to count visit records per visitor. These cases show that column names alone are often insufficient to determine the intended semantics of aggregation and counting.

*Benchmark and Annotation Artifacts.* Finally, several residual errors are better explained as benchmark artifacts than as genuine model failures. Examples include gold queries that use `<= 2` for questions phrased as "less than 2", unspecified tie-breaking in maximum-count queries, duplicated projected columns, and cases where the gold SQL ignores parts of the natural-language question, such as "in one semester". In such cases, improving EX would require adapting to benchmark-specific conventions rather than improving semantic understanding.

**Table 4.** Representative error categories observed during analysis.

| Category | Examples | Semantic Recovery | Benchmark Adaptation |
|---|---|---|---|
| Attribute ambiguity | Name vs Song_Name | ✓ | |
| Entity–event confusion | LEFT vs INNER JOIN | ✓ | |
| Aggregation & quantity ambiguity | Average vs AVG() | ✓ | |
| | Visits vs tickets | ✓ | |
| Benchmark & annotation artifacts | $\leq 2$ vs $< 2$ | | ✓ |
| | Semester constraints | | ✓ |
| | MAX-count queries | | ✓ |

Table 4 presents representative examples of recurring failure patterns observed during our analysis. These examples naturally group into two broader classes: semantic-recovery failures, which can be mitigated through improved semantic grounding, and benchmark-adaptation failures, which arise from dataset-specific conventions and annotation choices. The taxonomy was derived qualitatively through manual inspection of the analyzed schemas, questions, reference SQL queries, and generated outputs. It is intended to identify recurring failure patterns rather than estimate their frequency or prevalence.

Overall, these observations answer *RQ3* by suggesting that, within the analyzed sample, the main recurring sources associated with hallucinations and errors include semantic ambiguities, entity–event confusion, aggregation misinterpretations, and evaluation artifacts. This supports the view that many Text-to-SQL errors are informational rather than purely inferential, consistent with recent analyses suggesting that hallucinations often emerge when models must commit to an interpretation despite incomplete or underspecified information [20].

## 5 Related Work

Recent Text-to-SQL systems increasingly rely on inference-time scaling strategies to improve the output. Representative approaches combine full-schema prompting, few-shot examples, Chain-of-Thought reasoning, candidate generation, and self-consistency mechanisms [3–5,17]. More generally, retrieval-augmented and agentic paradigms [6,8,9,18] enable models to dynamically access external information and tools during reasoning. These approaches often improve benchmark performance, but may also increase token consumption, latency, and system complexity. A complementary line of research focuses on schema understanding and schema linking, which remain central challenges in Text-to-SQL systems [3,17]. These approaches aim to help models identify the database elements most relevant to a natural-language query. Our work is related to this direction, but focuses on a different question: rather than improving schema linking itself, we study how lightweight semantic information can reduce ambiguity, improve grounding, and explain a substantial fraction of observed Text-to-SQL failures.

Text-to-SQL evaluation traditionally relies on Exact Matching and Execution Accuracy [10], while more recent metrics such as Valid Efficiency Score (VES) additionally consider execution efficiency [11]. Our work complements these evaluation protocols in two ways. First, we adopt relation-level measures that better capture semantically informative outputs when benchmark annotations are ambiguous or incomplete. Second, we propose a cost-aware Symbiotic evaluation framework that jointly considers output quality, latency, and token consumption, enabling a more deployment-oriented assessment of Text-to-SQL systems.

## 6 Limitations

Despite the results obtained, this work has limitations that can serve as starting points for future research. In fact, our experiments rely on a limited set of proprietary LLMs, and the effectiveness of the enrichment may depend on model-specific reasoning capabilities. Moreover, current experiments are mostly based on single-turn benchmarks and therefore only partially capture long-term conversational interaction and clarification behaviors. Future work should extend the current analysis in two complementary directions: quantitatively examining the frequency of the identified error categories and their relationship with relation-level and Symbiosis metrics, and systematically assessing the sensitivity of Symbiosis scores to normalization thresholds and penalty parameters across deployment settings.

## 7 Conclusions

This paper investigated the relationship between semantic grounding, inference complexity, and evaluation in conversational Text-to-SQL systems. We introduced a Symbiotic Evaluation Framework that complements traditional execution-based metrics with relation-level and cost-aware measures, enabling a broader assessment of deployment-oriented systems. Our findings indicate that practical Text-to-SQL systems should be evaluated not only in terms of benchmark accuracy, but also with respect to information quality, efficiency, and deployment cost. More broadly, they suggest that many apparent reasoning failures may originate from limitations in semantic grounding rather than from insufficient reasoning capabilities.

## References

1. Nascimento, E., García, G.M., Feijó, L., et al.: Text-to-SQL meets the real-world. In: Proceedings of the 26th International Conference on Enterprise Information Systems (ICEIS), pp. 61–72 (2024). https://www.scitepress.org/Papers/2024/125552/125552.pdf
2. Minaee, S., et al.: Large Language Models: A Survey. arXiv preprint arXiv:2402.06196 (2025). https://arxiv.org/abs/2402.06196
3. Hong, Z., et al.: Next-generation database interfaces: a survey of LLM-based text-to-SQL. IEEE Trans. Knowl. Data Eng. **37**(12), 7328–7345 (2025). https://doi.org/10.1109/TKDE.2025.3609486
4. He, M., Shen, Y., Zhang, W., Peng, Q., Wang, J., Lu, W.: STAR-SQL: self-taught reasoner for text-to-SQL. In: Proceedings of the 63rd Annual Meeting of the Association for Computational Linguistics (ACL), pp. 24365–24375 (2025). https://aclanthology.org/2025.acl-long.1187/
5. Wei, J., Wang, X., Schuurmans, D., et al.: Chain-of-thought prompting elicits reasoning in large language models. In: Advances in Neural Information Processing Systems (NeurIPS), vol. 35, pp. 24824–24837 (2022). https://proceedings.neurips.cc/paper/2022/hash/9d5609613524ecf4f15af0f7b31abca4-Abstract.html
6. Lewis, P., Perez, E., Piktus, A., et al.: Retrieval-augmented generation for knowledge-intensive NLP tasks. In: Advances in Neural Information Processing Systems (NeurIPS), vol. 33, pp. 9459–9474 (2020). https://proceedings.neurips.cc/paper/2020/hash/6b493230205f780e1bc26945df7481e5-Abstract.html
7. Brown, T., Mann, B., Ryder, N., et al.: Language models are few-shot learners. In: Advances in Neural Information Processing Systems (NeurIPS), vol. 33, pp. 1877–1901 (2020). https://proceedings.neurips.cc/paper/2020/hash/1457c0d6bfcb4967418bfb8ac142f64a-Abstract.html
8. Sapkota, R., Roumeliotis, K.I., Karkee, M.: AI agents vs. agentic AI: a conceptual taxonomy, applications and challenges. Inf. Fusion 103599 (2025). https://doi.org/10.1016/j.inffus.2025.103599

9. Yao, S., Zhao, J., Yu, D.: ReAct: Synergizing Reasoning and Acting in Language Models. arXiv preprint arXiv:2210.03629 (2022)
10. Yu, T., Zhang, R., Yang, K., et al.: Spider: a large-scale human-labeled dataset for complex and cross-domain semantic parsing and text-to-SQL task. In: Proceedings of the 2018 Conference on Empirical Methods in Natural Language Processing (EMNLP), pp. 3911–3921 (2018). https://doi.org/10.18653/v1/D18-1425
11. Li, J., Hui, B., Qu, G., et al.: Can LLM already serve as a database interface? A big bench for large-scale database grounded text-to-SQLs. In: Advances in Neural Information Processing Systems (NeurIPS), vol. 36, pp. 42330–42357 (2023). https://proceedings.neurips.cc/paper_files/paper/2023/hash/83fc8fab1710363050bbd1d4b8cc0021-Abstract-Datasets_and_Benchmarks.html
12. Codd, E.F.: A relational model of data for large shared data banks. Commun. ACM **13**(6), 377–387 (1970). https://doi.org/10.1145/362384.362685
13. Jaccard, P.: Étude Comparative de la Distribution Florale dans une Portion des Alpes et du Jura. Bulletin de la Société Vaudoise des Sciences Naturelles **37**, 547–579 (1901). https://doi.org/10.5169/seals-266450
14. LangChain Team: LangGraph. GitHub repository (2024). https://github.com/langchain-ai/langgraph
15. OpenAI: GPT-4 Technical Report. arXiv preprint arXiv:2303.08774 (2023)
16. LangChain Team: LangChain. GitHub repository (2023). https://github.com/langchain-ai/langchain
17. Li, H., Zhang, J., Li, C., Chen, H.: RESDSQL: decoupling schema linking and skeleton parsing for text-to-SQL. In: Proceedings of the AAAI Conference on Artificial Intelligence, vol. 37, no. 11, pp. 13067–13075 (2023). https://doi.org/10.1609/AAAI.V37I11.26535
18. Schick, T., Dwivedi-Yu, J., Dessì, R., et al.: Toolformer: language models can teach themselves to use tools. In: Advances in Neural Information Processing Systems (NeurIPS), vol. 36, pp. 68539–68551 (2023). https://proceedings.neurips.cc/paper_files/paper/2023/hash/d842425e4bf79ba039352da0f658a906-Abstract-Conference.html
19. OpenAI: API Pricing. https://developers.openai.com/api/docs/pricing
20. Kalai, A.T., Nachum, O., Vempala, S.S., Zhang, E.: Why Language Models Hallucinate. arXiv preprint arXiv:2509.04664 (2025)

# Towards Human-Centric Lighting for Cognitive Tasks in Older Adults: A Multi-timescale Reinforcement Learning Framework

Patrizia Ribino[1(✉)], Maria Mannone[1,3], Giovanni Paragliola[2], and Claudia Di Napoli[2]

[1] ICAR, National Research Council of Italy (CNR), Palermo, Italy
{patrizia.ribino,maria.mannone}@cnr.it
[2] ICAR, National Research Council of Italy (CNR), Naples, Italy
{giovanni.paragliola,claudia.dinapoli}@cnr.it
[3] Potsdam Institute for Climate Impact Research (CNR), Potsdam, Germany

**Abstract.** The global increase in the aging population is driving growing interest in intelligent technologies that support healthy aging and cognitive well-being. Among the environmental factors influencing cognitive activities, lighting has received considerable attention for its effects on visual comfort, alertness, and the overall user experience. However, most adaptive lighting systems rely on predefined control strategies and provide limited support for long-term personalization. This paper presents a multi-timescale reinforcement learning framework for personalizing lighting conditions during cognitive tasks performed by older adults. The framework combines two complementary learning processes operating at different temporal scales. The first regulates lighting conditions during task execution in response to environmental changes, while the second progressively personalizes future lighting targets based on user feedback, including cognitive performance, perceived fatigue, and task duration. An Environmental Lighting Model is used to estimate the effects of possible lighting actions by combining natural and artificial light contributions. The proposed architecture integrates environmental sensing, adaptive lighting control, user feedback, and reinforcement learning within a unified framework designed for real-world deployment. A proof-of-concept evaluation based on two representative simulated scenarios shows that the framework maintained the target illuminance with mean absolute errors of 20.9 lx and 44.3 lx, respectively. The measured illuminance remained within the predefined tolerance in 99.9% of the adaptation cycles in the first scenario and 82.7% in the more challenging second scenario. The proposed framework provides a novel methodological foundation for adaptive cognitive lighting through the integration of multi-timescale reinforcement learning, environmental sensing, and user-centered feedback. A fully functional prototype has been implemented for real-world deployment.


S. Bistarelli et al. (Eds.): AIxIA 2026, LNAI 17131, pp. 542–555, 2027.
https://doi.org/10.1007/978-3-032-40774-0_39

**Keywords:** Healthy Aging · Adaptive Lighting · Reinforcement Learning · Human-Centric Lighting

## 1 Introduction

Population aging represents one of the most significant societal challenges of the coming decades. According to the World Health Organization, promoting healthy aging requires not only healthcare interventions but also environments that support people in maintaining autonomy, well-being, and cognitive functioning [14]. Consequently, increasing attention has been devoted to technologies that can support older adults during everyday activities. In particular, cognitive stimulation activities are widely adopted in residential care facilities and community-based interventions to support attention, memory, executive functions, and other cognitive processes [6]. While the effectiveness of these activities depends primarily on their design and execution, environmental factors may also influence users' experience and engagement. Among these factors, lighting plays a particularly relevant role, affecting visual perception, comfort, alertness, and task execution. Recent studies have investigated the relationship between indoor lighting conditions and measures of brain health in older adults, confirming the growing interest in understanding how environmental illumination may contribute to healthy aging [7,11,12]. This interest has contributed to the emergence of Human-Centric Lighting (HCL) approaches, which move beyond traditional energy-oriented lighting systems by including users' physiological and psychological needs [5]. Research on the non-visual effects of light has also shown that illumination can influence alertness, circadian regulation, sleep quality, and overall well-being [4,10]. More recently, Fani and Sharp [3] reviewed the relationship between lighting, sleep, and cognition in healthy older adults, highlighting both the potential of lighting interventions and the need for more ecologically valid studies conducted in realistic environments.

Several adaptive lighting systems have been proposed to regulate illumination according to daylight, occupancy, circadian cycles, or explicit user preferences. However, most available solutions rely on predefined adaptation strategies and provide limited support for continuous personalization based on users' responses over time. In fact, some of the challenges are constituted by inter- and intra-individual variability, together with progressive degeneration of vision abilities over time. Artificial Intelligence (AI) techniques are increasingly being employed to create environments that learn from user behavior and contextual information. Reinforcement Learning (RL) [1] is particularly attractive in this context, enabling systems to progressively optimize their behavior through interaction with both the environment and the user [9]. RL is typically applied to learn preferred illumination set-points, balance visual comfort and energy consumption, or react to manual corrections and subjective satisfaction [8,13].

Although these approaches show the potential of RL for adaptive lighting, they treat adaptation as a single decision process in which environmental observations and user feedback contribute to the same objective. The framework pro-

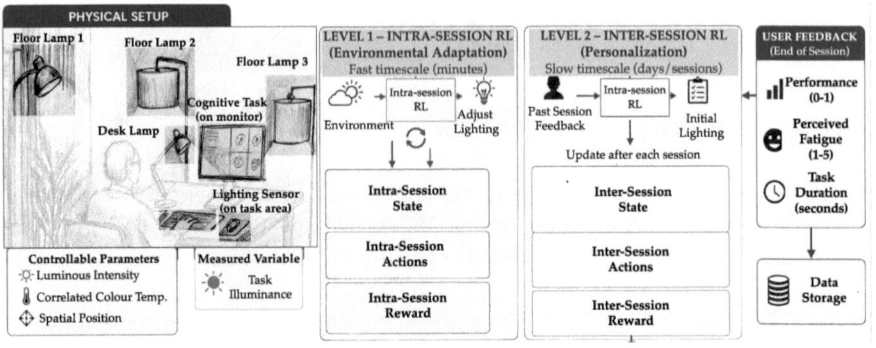


**Fig. 1.** Overview of RL framework. Hand-drawn by M.M.

posed in this work addresses two complementary decision problems, each characterized by distinct objectives and temporal dynamics. The first problem is to select, during the execution of a cognitive task, the lighting action that best balances multiple competing objectives, including maintaining visual comfort (in terms of illuminance and correlated color temperature), minimizing unnecessary energy consumption, and avoiding abrupt lighting variations while compensating for changing daylight conditions. The second problem is to progressively learn personalized lighting targets for a specific user and cognitive task by exploiting performance, perceived fatigue, and task duration collected across repeated task sessions. These two decision problems, relying on different sources of information and evolving over different temporal scales, are formulated as two interacting RL processes. The *Intra-Session* process learns context-dependent lighting actions, whereas the *Inter-Session* process learns long-term personalized lighting targets. Through this dual adaptation strategy, the framework is designed to support the creation of personalized lighting environments that adapt to both environmental conditions and user needs. The personalization process is driven by task-related outcomes rather than only by explicit lighting preferences or manual overrides.

A fully functional prototype has been developed by integrating environmental sensing, adaptive lighting control, user-feedback collection, and the RL layers within a unified architecture. It has been evaluated under two representative simulated scenarios to examine the operational behavior of both adaptation processes. The objective of this paper is to present and provide a preliminary assessment of the proposed multi-timescale learning architecture for future deployment in a residential care facility.

## 2 Framework Overview

The system's physical setup consists of a workstation used to perform cognitive activities (see Fig. 1) organized in consecutive sessions, each one consisting in the execution of a single cognitive task. The lighting environment includes a desk lamp and three floor lamps that can be independently controlled in terms of luminous intensity (dimming) and correlated color temperature (CCT). The position of the desk lamp can also be adjusted. Environmental sensing is performed through illuminance and spectral color sensors positioned near the task area to monitor lighting conditions around the user. At the beginning of a session, the Inter-Session RL process suggests a target lighting configuration based on the previous session feedback. Based on the observed environmental conditions, the Intra-Session RL controls lamp intensity, color temperature, and desk-lamp position to optimize visual conditions, energy consumption, and adaptation smoothness. At the end of each session, information including cognitive performance, perceived fatigue, and task duration is collected and stored together with the adopted lighting configuration. These data are subsequently used to update future lighting recommendations and progressively personalize the environment based on the individual responses. It is worth noting that the framework has been designed to support structured cognitive stimulation sessions routinely administered in residential care facilities, where computerized cognitive exercises are already widely adopted under the supervision of healthcare professionals.

## 3 Multi-timescale Reinforcement Learning Framework

Both the Intra-Session RL and the Inter-Session RL are modeled as Markov Decision Processes (MDPs), defined by $M = \langle S, A, P, R \rangle$ where $S$ denotes the state space, $A$ the action space, $P$ the state-transition function, and $R$ the reward function. Both learning processes adopt a Q-learning strategy [2].

### 3.1 Environmental Lighting Model

The Intra-Session process relies on an Environmental Lighting Model to estimate the effects of possible lighting actions before they are applied to the physical environment. To model the spatial relationship between the luminaries and the working area, a Cartesian coordinate system is defined with its origin at the center of the task area, where illuminance and CCT are evaluated, and the cognitive task is performed. The coordinates $(x_i, y_i, z_i)$ specify the position of lamp $i$ with respect to this reference point. For each lamp $i$, the illuminance contribution is estimated as:

$$E_i = \frac{\Phi_i D_i k_i z_i}{d_i^3}, \tag{1}$$

where $\Phi_i$ denotes the maximum luminous flux, $D_i$ is its dimming level, $k_i$ is a calibration coefficient, $z_i$ is the height of the lamp relative to the task area, and $d_i$ is the distance between the lamp and the task area. The total illuminance at the task area is then computed as:

$$E^{task-area} = E^{nat} + \sum_{i \in \mathcal{L}} E_i, \tag{2}$$

where $E^{nat}$ is the natural-light contribution and $\mathcal{L}$ is the set of controllable lamps. The model also predicts the resulting CCT at the task area using an illuminance-weighted color-mixing formulation that accounts for the combined contribution of natural and artificial light:

$$CCT^{task-area} = \frac{E^{task-area}}{\frac{E^{nat}}{CCT^{nat}} + \sum_{i \in \mathcal{L}} \frac{E_i}{CCT_i}}, \tag{3}$$

with $CCT^{nat}$ denoting daylight and $CCT_i$ the $i^{th}$ lamp colors, respectively.

### 3.2 Intra-session Reinforcement Learning

The Intra-Session RL relies on an MDP with the state at time $t$ is defined as:

$$s_t^{Intra-S} = (e_t^{lux}, e_t^{cct}, d_t^{desk}, d_t^{bl}, d_t^{br}, d_t^{fs}, c_t^{desk}, c_t^{bl}, c_t^{br}, c_t^{fs}, x_t^{desk}, y_t^{desk}, z_t^{desk}), \tag{4}$$

where $e_t^{lux} = E^{target} - E_t^{task-area}$ is the illuminance error between the target illuminance level and the illuminance currently measured or estimated at the task area, while $e_t^{cct} = CCT^{target} - CCT_t^{task-area}$ is the color temperature error between the target CCT and the resulting CCT at the task area. The variables $d_t^{desk}$, $d_t^{bl}$, $d_t^{br}$, and $d_t^{fs}$ denote the dimming levels of the desk, back-left floor, back-right floor, and front-side floor lamps. The variables $c_t^{desk}$, $c_t^{bl}$, $c_t^{br}$ and $c_t^{fs}$ denote the CCT settings of the lamps. Finally, $(x_t^{desk}, y_t^{desk}, z_t^{desk})$ denotes the spatial position of the desk lamp.

The action space consists of modifications to the lighting configuration:

$$a_t^{Intra-S} = \{\pm\delta_{d_i}, \pm\delta_{c_i}, \pm\delta_{x^{desk}}, \pm\delta_{y^{desk}}, \pm\delta_{z^{desk}}\}, \tag{5}$$

where $\pm\delta_{d_i}$ and $\pm\delta_{c_i}$ denote the intensity and CCT variation of the $i^{th}$ lamp, and $\pm\delta_{x^{desk}}$, $\pm\delta_{y^{desk}}$, and $\pm\delta_{z^{desk}}$ its displacement along the three axes. The reward is formulated as a weighted combination of illuminance accuracy, color accuracy, energy efficiency, and adaptation smoothness:

$$R_t^{Intra-S} = \beta - w_I P_t^{ill} - w_C P_t^{cct} - w_E P_t^{energy} - w_S P_t^{smooth}. \tag{6}$$

where illuminance, CCT, and energy penalties are defined as:

$$P_t^{ill} = \left(\frac{E_t^{task} - E^{target}}{E^{target}}\right)^2, P_t^{cct} = \left(\frac{CCT_t^{task} - CCT^{target}}{CCT^{target}}\right)^2, P_t^{energy} = \sum_{i \in \mathcal{L}} \left(D_t^i\right)^2. \tag{7}$$

and $D_t^i$ is the dimming level of lamp $i$ at time $t$ and $\beta$ is a positive offset. $P_t^{smooth}$ is introduced to penalize sudden changes in lighting that may be distracting or uncomfortable for users. It is computed as $P_t^{smooth} = P_t^{dim} + P_t^{cct} + P_t^{pos}$, where

$$P_t^{dim} = \sum_{i \in \mathcal{L}} \left|D_t^i - D_{t-1}^i\right|, \; P_t^{cct} = \sum_{i \in \mathcal{L}} \frac{\left|CCT_t^i - CCT_{t-1}^i\right|}{F_C^{norm}}, \; P_t^{pos} = \frac{\left\|\mathbf{X}_t^{desk} - \mathbf{X}_{t-1}^{desk}\right\|_2}{F_X^{norm}}. \tag{8}$$

In Eq. (8), $\mathbf{X}_t^{desk} = (x_t, y_t, z_t)$ represents the position of the desk lamp. The constants $F_C^{norm}$ and $F_X^{norm}$ are normalization factors used to make color temperature and positional variations comparable with dimming changes.

### 3.3 Inter-session Reinforcement Learning

The Inter-Session RL relies on an MDP with the state at session $k$ defined as:

$$s_k^{Inter-S} = (p_{k-1}, f_{k-1}, d_{k-1}, E_{k-1}, C_{k-1}), \tag{9}$$

where $p_{k-1}$, $f_{k-1}$, and $d_{k-1}$ denote, respectively, the cognitive performance, perceived fatigue, and task duration, while $E_{k-1}$ and $C_{k-1}$ are the target illuminance and correlated color temperature of the previous session.

Unlike the Intra-Session process, the Inter-Session process modifies the characteristics of the initial lighting scenario for the next session. The action space is defined as: $a_k^{Inter-S} \in \{\pm\delta E_k, \pm\delta C_k\}$, including fixed increases or decreases of target illuminance ($\delta E_k$), color temperature ($\delta C_k$), or combined modifications of both parameters. The reward function is defined as: $R_k^{Inter-S} = w_P P_k - w_F F_k - w_D D_k$. It combines cognitive performance, perceived fatigue, and task duration with relative weights ($w_P$, $w_F$, $w_D$). The performance term ($P_k$) represents the task-specific performance score computed by the cognitive application. Depending on the adopted cognitive activity, this score may reflect indicators such as accuracy, number of correct responses, completion rate, or other task-dependent performance measures. The fatigue term ($F_k$) is obtained through a self-reported assessment collected at the end of each cognitive task session. Finally, $D_k$ represents the normalized task duration, indicating the effort required to complete the activity, and it is computed as: $D_k = \tau_k/\tau_{expected}$, where $\tau_k$ and $\tau_{expected}$ are the actual and the expected duration for the task. Performance contributes positively to the reward, while perceived fatigue and long execution time are penalization terms.

## 4 Simulation-Based Demonstration

To illustrate the behavior of the proposed framework, two scenarios have been simulated. The first one (see Fig. 2) considers a sustained-attention task performed in the morning under progressively increasing natural daylight conditions. As natural illumination rises during the session, task illuminance exceeds the target level. The Intra-Session RL compensates for this variation by gradually reducing lamp intensity while preserving the desired lighting conditions. At the end of the session, the user reports high performance and high perceived fatigue. Since this combination may indicate an overstimulating lighting configuration, the Inter-Session RL explores a less activating setting for the next session by reducing both the target illuminance and the target CCT.
The second scenario (see Fig. 3) considers a working-memory task performed under decreasing daylight conditions. As natural illumination declines during the session, task illuminance falls below the target level. The Intra-Session RL compensates for this by increasing the contribution of artificial lighting. At the end of the session, low performance and prolonged task duration are observed that may indicate insufficient environmental stimulation. So, the Inter-Session RL explores a brighter and cooler lighting configuration for subsequent sessions.

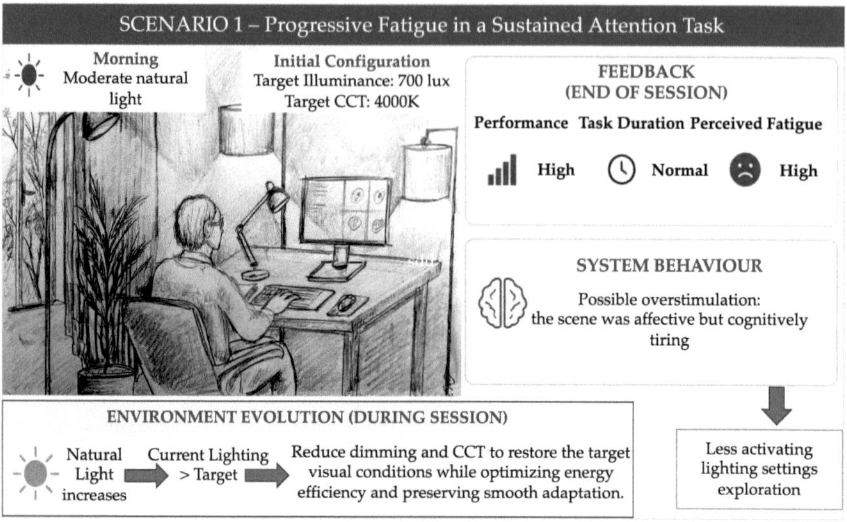


**Fig. 2.** Scenario 1

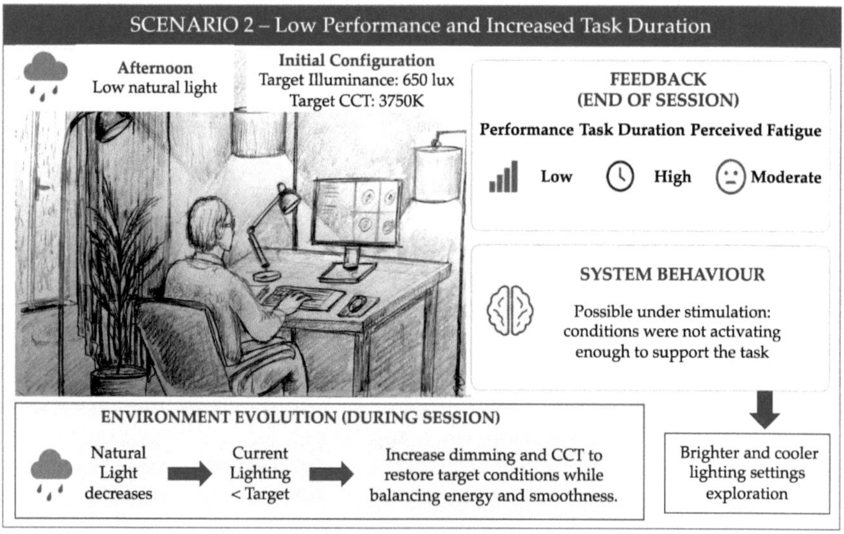


**Fig. 3.** Scenario 2

The prototype was evaluated using fixed parameters for actions (i.e., 0.05 for lamp dimming, 50 K for CCT adjustments, 0.10 m for desk-lamp positioning during the Intra-Session process, ±50 lx for target illuminance and ±250 K for target CCT during the Inter-Session process). The reward parameters were empirically selected during prototype development and kept constant for all experiments. In the current implementation, fatigue is expressed using a five-point Likert scale.

### 4.1 Prototype Behavior Under Simulated Conditions

The evaluation presented here aims to verify that the prototype behaves consistently with the intended adaptation strategy under controlled conditions.

**Scenario 1 Intra-session RL Behavior.** During the simulated cognitive task, both daylight illuminance and correlated color temperature vary substantially, reaching their highest values around the middle of the session. As shown in Fig. 4, the Intra-Session RL continuously adjusts the artificial lighting contribution to compensate for the environmental variations, evaluated within a time range we refer to as an *environmental step*. As daylight increases, artificial illuminance is progressively reduced; when daylight decreases during the second part of the session, artificial lighting increases accordingly. Consequently, the measured illuminance remains close to the target value of 700 lx despite significant environmental fluctuations. Figure 4 shows the corresponding color-temperature adaptation. To maintain the target CCT, the Intra-Session RL dynamically regulates the CCT of the artificial lighting system. When daylight becomes cooler and exceeds 6000 K, the Intra-Session RL lowers the artificial-light CCT; conversely, when daylight becomes warmer, the artificial-light CCT increases. The results also reveal an important physical limitation of the system. Around the middle of the session, daylight is both highly intense and characterized by very high CCT values. Under these conditions, the system reduces the artificial-light CCT to its minimum allowable value. However, the target CCT cannot be perfectly maintained because the daylight contribution dominates the overall lighting mixture. As a result, the task-area CCT temporarily deviates from the target value. This behavior reflects the physical constraints of the lighting hardware rather than a limitation of the proposed approach.

**Scenario 1 Inter-session RL Behavior.** The behavior of the Inter-Session RL during successive sessions of the cognitive task described in Scenario 1 is reported in Fig. 5. As shown in the left panel, starting from a relatively bright and moderately cool lighting configuration, the RL progressively explores less activating lighting settings by reducing both target illuminance and target CCT. While illuminance decreases gradually, CCT is reduced more aggressively, leading to warmer lighting conditions. The right panel reports the corresponding user feedback throughout the simulated sessions, showing that cognitive performance remains high, perceived fatigue is initially elevated, and task duration shows only minor fluctuations and remains substantially stable. Since high performance and high fatigue may be due to overstimulation, the RL progressively explores less stimulating lighting configurations while monitoring the resulting feedback. Unlike the Intra-Session RL, which prioritizes smooth transitions during task execution, the Inter-Session process operates across independent sessions and

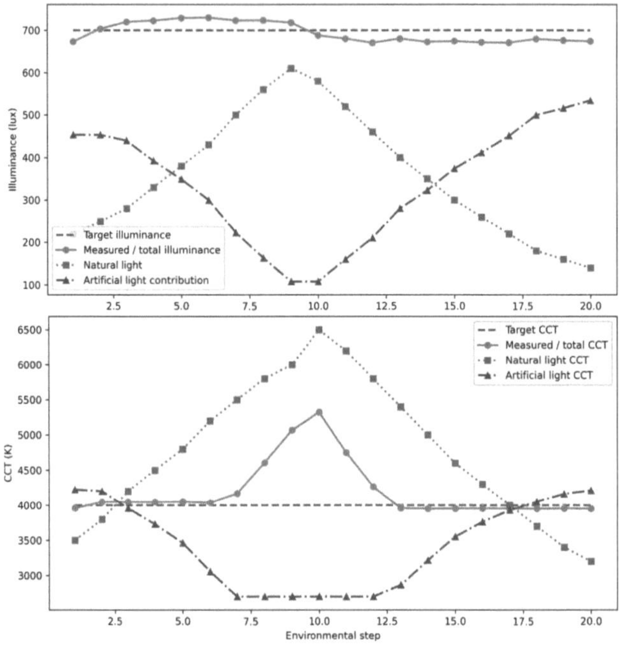


**Fig. 4.** Intra-Session environmental adaptation in Scenario 1.

can therefore introduce larger adjustments without affecting user experience. As adaptation progresses, fatigue gradually decreases while cognitive performance and task duration remain largely unchanged. This may suggest that reducing environmental stimulation does not impair task-execution efficiency, indicating that the RL successfully identifies lighting configurations that reduce fatigue while preserving satisfactory performance. After several sessions, both target illuminance and target CCT show a stabilization trend toward the lower end of their admissible ranges, and no further adaptations are required. Under the simulated conditions, the resulting configuration maintains high task performance while reducing perceived fatigue, demonstrating the ability of the RL Inter-Session to personalize future lighting conditions based on user feedback.

**Scenario 2 Intra-session RL Behavior.** The behavior of the Intra-Session RL under Scenario 2 is illustrated in Fig. 6. During the simulated task, daylight progressively decreases in both illuminance and color temperature, reproducing a situation in which environmental lighting conditions become progressively less supportive for task execution. As shown in Fig. 6, the RL compensates for the reduction of daylight by progressively increasing the artificial light, so allowing the measured illuminance to remain close to the target value throughout the sessions despite the substantial decrease in environmental illumination. Fig. 6 also shows the corresponding color-temperature adaptation. As daylight becomes

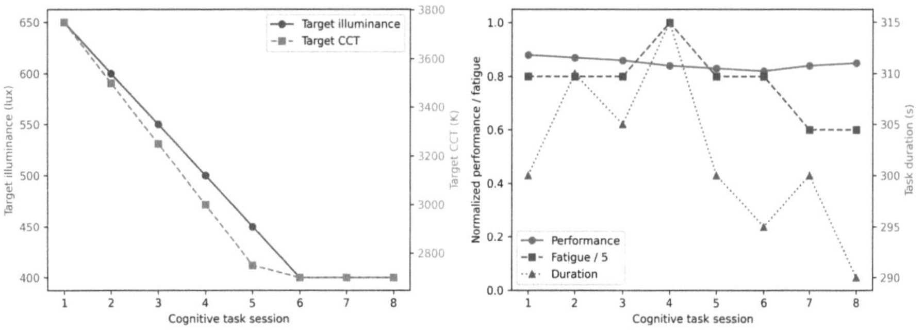


**Fig. 5.** Inter-Session personalization behavior in Scenario 1.

warmer and its CCT decreases, the RL increases the CCT of the artificial lighting system to counterbalance the environmental variation. As a result, the task-area CCT remains close to the desired target value during the entire session. Unlike Scenario 1, no saturation effects are observed. The operating range of the artificial lighting system is sufficient to compensate for both illuminance and CCT variations introduced in the environment, enabling simultaneous regulation of the two lighting parameters without reaching hardware limits.

**Scenario 2 Inter-session RL Behavior.** The behavior of the Inter-Session RL in Scenario 2 is reported in Fig. 7. In this scenario, the initial sessions are characterized by relatively low performance levels and prolonged execution times, while perceived fatigue remains moderate. The left panel shows the evolution of the target illuminance and correlated color temperature selected by Inter-Session RL. Starting from a relatively dim and warm lighting configuration, the RL progressively explores more activating settings by increasing both target illuminance and target CCT. The two parameters follow similar trajectories because the current adaptation strategy treats illuminance and CCT as complementary indicators of environmental activation. The right panel reports the corresponding user feedback. During the initial sessions, low performance and prolonged task duration suggest that the selected lighting configuration provides insufficient support for the cognitive activity, whereas perceived fatigue remains relatively stable. Based on this feedback, the RL progressively increases environmental activation by selecting brighter and cooler lighting conditions. As adaptation progresses, task performance steadily improves while task duration gradually decreases. The fatigue remains largely stable and decreases during the final sessions. After several sessions, both target illuminance and target CCT reach the upper limits allowed by the physical operating range of the lighting devices and remain stable. Under the simulated conditions, no further increases can be explored despite the continued improvement observed in the feedback variables. The stabilization of the target parameters, therefore, reflects the limits imposed on the personalization space rather than a lack of system responsiveness. Unlike Scenario 1, where environmental stimulation was progressively

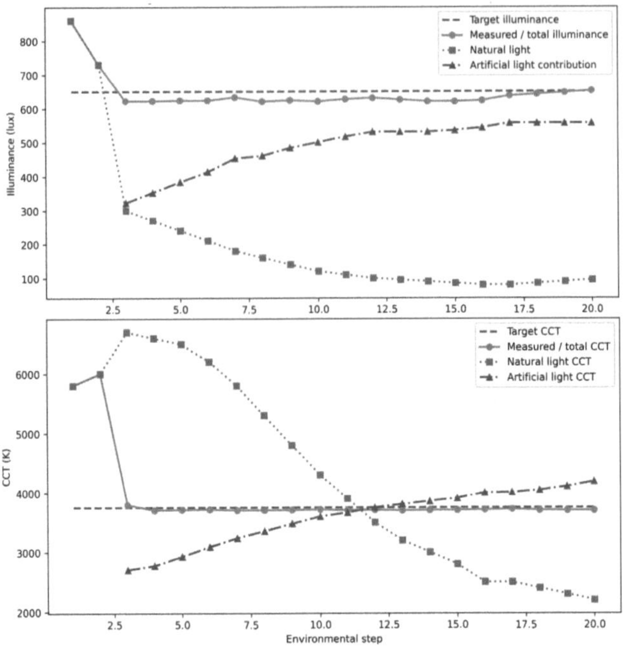


**Fig. 6.** Intra-Session RL behavior in Scenario 2.

reduced in response to elevated fatigue, Scenario 2 exhibits the opposite trend. Here, the RL increases both illuminance and CCT in response to low performance and prolonged task duration, demonstrating the ability of the proposed framework to personalize future lighting conditions based on user feedback.

**Performance Comparison.** Table 1 shows the results of the Intra-Session process. Scenario 2 resulted in larger illuminance errors and required more recovery cycles than Scenario 1, reflecting the greater difficulty in compensating progressively decreasing daylight. The larger number of learned environmental states also indicates that the process explored a broader portion of the state space under the more demanding environmental conditions. Unlike the Intra-Session process, the Inter-Session process does not solve a reference-tracking problem. Its objective is not to minimize the error with respect to a predefined target, but to progressively adapt the target lighting conditions based on user-related feedback collected across successive cognitive task sessions. So, classical metrics such as MAE or RMSE are not applicable. Instead, the evaluation focuses on the evolution of the learned lighting targets and on the behaviour of the personalization process under representative feedback patterns.

Table 2 shows the behavior of the Inter-Sessionprocess in terms of initial and final target configurations. In Scenario 1, high task performance combined with high perceived fatigue led the system to progressively reduce both target illumi-

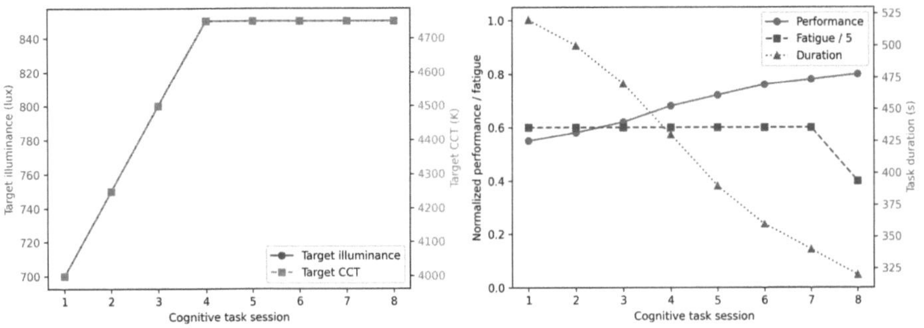


**Fig. 7.** Inter-Session personalization behavior in Scenario 2.

**Table 1.** Performance of the Intra-Session RL in the two simulated scenarios.

| Metric | Scenario 1 | Scenario 2 |
|---|---|---|
| MAE (lx) | 20.9 | 44.3 |
| RMSE (lx) | 21.7 | 73.8 |
| Cycles within tolerance (%) | 99.9 | 82.7 |
| Learned environmental states | 358 | 626 |

nance and CCT, resulting in a less activating lighting configuration. Conversely, in Scenario 2, lower performance and prolonged task duration led the system towards progressively brighter and cooler lighting targets. The larger number of learned personalization states in Scenario 2 also reflects the broader exploration of the personalization policy under more demanding feedback conditions.

**Table 2.** Performance of the Inter-Session RL in the two simulated scenarios.

| Metric | Scenario 1 | Scenario 2 |
|---|---|---|
| Initial target illuminance (lx) | 650 | 650 |
| Final target illuminance (lx) | 400 | 850 |
| Initial target CCT (K) | 3750 | 3750 |
| Final target CCT (K) | 2700 | 4750 |
| Learned personalization states | 8 | 16 |

## 5 Conclusions and Future Work

This paper presented a multi-timescale RL framework for personalizing lighting conditions during the execution of cognitive tasks. The proposed approach combines two RL processes. The Intra-Session process optimizes visual comfort, energy consumption, and adaptation smoothness in response to environmental changes. The Inter-Session process adapts lighting configurations based on user feedback concerning performance, perceived fatigue, and task duration for successive cognitive task sessions. From a methodological perspective, the framework addresses both environmental regulation and long-term lighting personalization through two different and hierarchically interleaved RL processes.

A prototype evaluation based on simulated scenarios demonstrated the expected behavior of both RL processes. The results also highlighted the influence of physical lighting-system constraints on achievable CCT compensation under specific environmental conditions. The reward formulation of the two RL processes introduces several terms to capture multiple aspects regarding environmental factors and users' performance in the cognitive task. The relative contribution of each term has not yet been optimized systematically. Future work will include sensitivity analyses and ablation studies to quantify the influence of individual reward components and identify the most effective weighting configuration for real-world deployment.

The proposed approach provides a general methodology for adaptive environments that continuously learn from both environmental dynamics and user feedback. The current prototype constitutes the basis for the forthcoming real-world deployment and longitudinal validation. Future work will focus on validating the proposed approach under real-world conditions, assessing the robustness of the adaptation mechanisms, and investigating the relationship among personalized lighting configurations, user experience, task performance, and well-being. Although no conclusions regarding cognitive benefits can be drawn at this stage, the proposed framework provides a foundation for future research on adaptive and personalized lighting environments to support healthy ageing. Finally, although the present work has been designed for cognitive stimulation activities in older adults, the framework is application-independent so it could potentially be extended to other contexts involving prolonged computer-based activities, such as office environments or educational settings.

**Acknowledgments.** This work is supported by the Project "Ecosistema uRbano per l'invecchiaMEnto attivo e in Salute (ERMES)" Traiettoria 1 del Piano Operativo Salute "Active & Healthy Ageing - Tecnologie per l'invecchiamento attivo e l'assistenza domiciliare" funded by the Italian Ministry of Health (Project code n. T1-MZ-24; CUP B83C22004520001).

**Code Availability.** The code supporting the findings of this study is available from the corresponding author upon reasonable request.

## References

1. Barto, A.G.: Reinforcement learning: an introduction. SIAM Rev. **6**(2), 423 (2021)
2. Clifton, J., Laber, E.: Q-learning: theory and applications. Ann. Rev. Stat. Appl. **7**(1), 279–301 (2020)

3. Fani, M., Sharp, N.: Exploring methodological considerations: a literature review on how lighting affects the sleep and cognition in healthy older adults. J. Daylighting **11**(1), 97–118 (2024)
4. Figueiro, M., Nagare, R., Price, L.: Non-visual effects of light: how to use light to promote circadian entrainment and elicit alertness. Light. Res. Techn. **50**(1), 38–62 (2018)
5. Houser, K.W., Esposito, T.: Human-centric lighting: foundational considerations and a five-step design process. Front. Neurol. **12**, 630553 (2021)
6. Livingston, G., et al.: Dementia prevention, intervention, and care: 2024 report of the lancet standing commission. Lancet **404**(10452), 572–628 (2024)
7. Mazurek, K.A., et al.: Investigating the effects of indoor lighting on measures of brain health in older adults: protocol for a cross-over randomized controlled trial. BMC Geriatr. **24**(1), 816 (2024)
8. Park, J.Y., Dougherty, T., Fritz, H., Nagy, Z.: Lightlearn: an adaptive and occupant centered controller for lighting based on reinforcement learning. Build. Environ. **147**, 397–414 (2019)
9. Potenza, G., Baglivo, C., Bonomolo, M., Ribino, P.: Self-adaptive and self-learning lighting system: integrating LSTM and RL for energy efficiency and personalized visual comfort. Adv. Signal Process. Art. Int. 125 (2025)
10. Rea, M.S., Figueiro, M.: Light as a circadian stimulus for architectural lighting. Lighting Res. Techn. **50**(4), 497–510 (2018)
11. Shi, T., Chen, B.: Association between ambient illumination and cognitive impairment: a population-based study of older. Behav. Neur. **2023**(1), 4131377 (2023)
12. Shishegar, N., Boubekri, M.: Lighting up living spaces to improve mood and cognitive performance in older adults. J. Environ. Psych. **82**, 101845 (2022)
13. Vashishtha, K., Saad, A., Faieghi, R., Xi, F.: Intelligent adaptive lighting algorithm: integrating reinforcement learning and fuzzy logic for personalized interior lighting. Eng. Appl. Artif. Intell. **133**, 108512 (2024)
14. World Health Organization: Decade of healthy ageing 2021–2030 (2021). https://www.who.int/initiatives/decade-of-healthy-ageing. Accessed 10 June 2026

# A Decision Framework for Inter-agent Communication Protocol Selection

Andrea Salzillo, Yuriy Moskovchuk, Ciro Panariello, Giuseppe Gambino, Domenico Alfano(✉), and Roberto Abbruzzese

Eustema S.p.A, Rome, Italy
{a.salzillo,y.moskovchuk,c.panariello,g.gambino,d.alfano, r.abbruzzese}@eustema.it

**Abstract.** Enterprise adoption of multi-agent systems for knowledge-intensive work demands interoperability across agents built on heterogeneous stacks. Since 2024 a fragmented ecosystem of framework-agnostic inter-agent communication protocols has emerged, each with distinct capability trade-offs, leaving enterprise architects without a principled way to choose among them. We propose a transparent, auditable and extensible decision framework grounded in Multi-Criteria Decision Analysis (MCDA). We decompose every inter-agent interaction into four lifecycle macro-features (Presentation, Discovery, Authentication, Communication) and build a comparative matrix mapping the capabilities of eight protocols onto their sub-features. The architect classifies each sub-feature as a hard constraint, a soft preference, an exclusion criterion or irrelevant; the framework combines this profile with the matrix through conjunctive screening and a Simple Additive Weighting aggregation whose weights are elicited by a hierarchical Analytic Hierarchy Process (AHP), returning a ranked list of candidate protocols. We illustrate the framework on three knowledge-enterprise scenarios. No single specification universally dominates, and structured selection makes the dependence of the choice on operational context explicit. The scenarios are worked examples of how the framework operates rather than an empirical validation: in particular, the AHP pairwise judgments are produced by the authors and are not elicited from independent enterprise architects.

**Keywords:** Inter-Agent Communication · Agent Protocols · Multi-Agent Systems · Knowledge Enterprise · Decision Framework · MCDA · AHP

## 1 Introduction

Large language models have evolved from text generation into agentic systems that retrieve information, invoke tools and orchestrate multi-step workflows [1,2]. In the enterprise, the natural next step is to let specialised third-party agents collaborate across organisational and vendor boundaries (the vision of the *Internet*


S. Bistarelli et al. (Eds.): AIxIA 2026, LNAI 17131, pp. 556–571, 2027.
https://doi.org/10.1007/978-3-032-40774-0_40

*of Agents* (IoA) [3,4]), reviving at enterprise scale the open-interoperability problem that KQML and FIPA-ACL first standardised [5,6]. To let agents on different stacks interoperate without hard-coded, ecosystem-specific pipelines [3,7], a generation of *framework-agnostic* inter-agent protocols has emerged in under two years [8,9]. Their proliferation, however, is itself a source of fragmentation: which protocol best fits a given use case, regulatory perimeter, identity infrastructure and integration stack is a strongly context-dependent choice that no protocol-centric, transparent and auditable instrument has so far supported. This paper treats protocol selection as a first-class decision in the engineering of multi-agent systems, owned by the enterprise architect, whose requirements, judgments and accountability the framework makes explicit, auditable and reproducible.

*Contributions.* We make three contributions: (i) four recurring lifecycle macro-features characterising every agent-to-agent interaction, *Presentation, Discovery, Authentication* and *Communication*; (ii) a reproducible qualitative analysis of the eight in-scope protocols across their fine-grained sub-features, grounded in public specifications; (iii) a protocol-agnostic, extensible MCDA-based decision framework that screens hard and exclusion constraints conjunctively [10] and ranks the feasible protocols through a SAW aggregation with weights elicited by a hierarchical AHP [11,12]. The MCDA machinery is deliberately standard: the novelty lies in the domain formalisation (the lifecycle taxonomy, the support matrix and the requirement encoding) that turns protocol selection into a tractable, auditable decision problem.

## 2 Related Work

*Protocol Surveys and Comparisons.* Recent surveys map the ecosystem and propose taxonomies [7,13]; security studies characterise threat models [14,15]; position papers argue for standardisation [8]; the closest comparative study [9] contrasts four protocols qualitatively. All stop at description: to our knowledge, no prior decision framework targets inter-agent protocol selection (Sect. 6 contrasts the candidate decision paradigms). Ours covers a broader, heterogeneous set of protocol families and adds a decision layer translating an explicit enterprise requirement into a justified, reproducible choice.

*Agent Communication Languages.* Standardising agent communication is not new: KQML introduced a performative-based message layer [5], and FIPA-ACL standardised speech-act semantics [6] within the FIPA Abstract Architecture [16], operationalised by JADE [17]. That architecture prefigures our decomposition (its Agent Management System maps to Presentation, its Directory Facilitator to Discovery, its ACL layer across Authentication and Communication): we inherit FIPA's lifecycle decomposition and specialise it to the LLM era, whose signed self-descriptions, decentralised identity and meta-protocol negotiation were not normative in FIPA.

*Multi-criteria Selection of Software and Frameworks.* Choosing among competing options under multiple, partially conflicting criteria is the canonical setting of MCDA, the dominant paradigm in enterprise software-package and ERP/CRM selection [18,19]. Within MCDA, AHP elicits weights from structured pairwise comparisons [11] and is often paired with SAW [20]; closest to our setting, a fuzzy AHP-TOPSIS model has been applied to IoT protocol selection [21], outside the inter-agent, LLM-era scope we target.

## 3 Inter-sgent Communication Protocols

Our scope is the agent-to-agent channel only: of the protocols catalogued by recent surveys [7,9,14], we retain *every* specification that explicitly targets inter-agent communication, is publicly documented and is mutually distinct in design, eight in total. We exclude tool-use standards such as the Model Context Protocol (MCP) [22,23], which standardises how an agent consumes external tools rather than how two agents interact (Sect. 9).

**ACP-AGNTCY (Agent Connect Protocol)** [24–26] is a REST/RPC stack in the AGNTCY ecosystem, with an OASF-based descriptor, an external Agent Directory Service for capability-indexed lookup, and synchronous, polled and streaming interactions with thread-based state. **ACP-IBM (Agent Communication Protocol)** [27] is a REST-native, asynchronous-first specification centred on an `Agent` object exposed via registry or offline metadata, with runs of MIME-typed message parts and an `Await` primitive for human-in-the-loop suspension. **ACP-AgentUnion** [28,29] mediates an *Agent Internet* through Access Points (APs) that handle identity, authentication, routing, sessions, public metadata and message delivery for the domain-style Agent Identifiers they host, with certificate-backed identity and real-time transport. **A2A (Agent-to-Agent)** [30–32] is an enterprise reference protocol built around a cryptographically signed *Agent Card* discoverable via well-known URI or curated registries, with a mature enterprise security stack and a *Task* lifecycle of typed *Parts* over synchronous, streaming and webhook interactions.

**ANP (Agent Network Protocol)** [33–35] targets the agentic Web: a JSON-LD *Agent Description* with cryptographic proof, identity anchored to decentralised identifiers (DIDs) with per-request signatures, end-to-end encryption and verifiable-credential audit logs. **AITP (Agent Interaction & Transaction Protocol)** [36–38] is an agentic-commerce protocol of conversational *Threads* carrying typed, schema-declared *Capabilities*; it delegates discovery and authentication to the deployment context and natively supports wallet-signed transactions and inter-agent payments. **ACN (Agent Communication Network)** [39,40] is a permissionless peer-to-peer overlay where the agent address is the hash of its public key, resolved through a distributed hash table [41], with direct, relayed, delegate and mailbox delivery. **Agora** [42] is a *Layer Zero* meta-protocol standardising only how two agents agree on a protocol: an LLM negotiates a *Protocol Document* for each exchange, transported in a minimal HTTPS envelope and addressed by hash for caching and reuse via shared Protocol Databases.

None of these specifications dominates: each trades off interoperability, governance, identity assurance and communication expressiveness; maturity also differs sharply, from A2A, a Linux Foundation project with production deployments [30,31], to early-stage drafts such as ACP-AgentUnion and AITP [28,37]. This heterogeneity motivates the comparative analysis that follows.

## 4 Protocol Features Description

A protocol *natively supports* a sub-feature when its normative specification defines or mandates the corresponding mechanism, rather than leaving it to the deployment context or an optional extension: native support is a property of the specification, not of implementations, and underpins every cell of the matrix of Sect. 5. Kong et al. [14] survey agent-to-agent communication along a layered functional axis (connection, identity, application semantics); we cut the design space along a complementary *lifecycle* axis: an agent first *describes itself*, then *is located*, then *proves its identity* and finally *exchanges task-level information*. For enterprise selection the lifecycle axis is more directly actionable: the layered view collapses identity establishment and self-description into discovery and communication, obscuring decisive design choices, whereas each lifecycle macro-feature isolates exactly one architectural decision. Every mechanism we encountered maps onto exactly one phase, so the macro-features form an exhaustive grid; a delegated phase (as discovery and authentication in AITP) is recorded as zero cells. We therefore adopt **Presentation**, **Discovery**, **Authentication** and **Communication** as the four *macro-features*, articulated into the sub-features forming the columns of the comparative matrix [7,9].

**Presentation** captures *what an agent declares about itself* before any exchange. ***Standard Agent Card format***: a normative self-descriptive document exposing identity, endpoint, capabilities and security schemes (the Agent Card in A2A, the Agent Description in ANP, analogous descriptors in the three ACPs) [32,33]. ***Agent Card authenticity***: a cryptographic binding of the descriptor to the agent identity to prevent spoofing, via signed cards, signed registry artifacts or DID-based proofs [32,34]. ***Extended Agent Card***: a richer descriptor revealed only after authentication, so that sensitive metadata is not leaked to anonymous discoverers (A2A; analogous policies in ANP) [32,33].

**Discovery** answers how an agent is made reachable, the dimension along which protocols differ most sharply. ***Active discovery***: direct lookup against a conventional endpoint or identity-derived address, with no capability catalogue as mediator, through the well-known URI convention [43] (A2A, ANP, Agora) or a domain-style identity endpoint (ACP-AgentUnion). ***Passive discovery***: indexed lookup through catalogues searchable by capability, from centralised registries to directory services [26], AP-indexed search and peer-to-peer stores; it scales better to heterogeneous ecosystems at the cost of an infrastructural dependency (Agora is excluded here: its Protocol Databases index *protocols*, not agents).

**Authentication** establishes mutual identity, one of the most discriminating dimensions for security-sensitive deployments [15]. ***Self-authentication (DID-based)***: the agent proves control of its identity through cryptographic primitives anchored to a decentralised identifier, with no central authority (ANP; ACN, whose identifier derives from the public key) [44,45]. ***Centralised authentication***: credentials issued by a trusted authority, at the HTTP layer or through a certificate-backed infrastructure, dominant in enterprise-oriented protocols because it integrates with governed IAM [27,32]. ***Human authentication***: explicit, attestable proof that a human principal approved a high-stakes operation, distinct from generic human-in-the-loop suspension such as ACP-IBM's `Await` (ANP's human-authorisation keys; AITP's wallet-signing and form capabilities) [33,37].

**Communication** captures the task-level exchange, the richest macro-feature. ***Secure communication channel***: confidentiality and integrity on the wire, mandated as TLS-based transport by all eight protocols and variously extended up to end-to-end encryption (ANP) [32,33]. ***Polling***: synchronous request/response, virtually universal. ***Streaming***: progressive-output primitives for incremental responses. ***Webhook/push***: server-initiated callbacks or persistent push channels (A2A webhooks; ACP-AgentUnion AP-routed messaging). ***Long-running and stateful communication***: first-class lifecycle primitives such as task state machines, sessions, threads and credential hash chains; ACN deliberately stays stateless [27,32,37]. ***Structured payload***: schema-typed message bodies, almost universal. ***Raw bytes payload***: direct support for binary payloads or binary-framed transport. ***Multimodal payload***: text, image, audio and file content via extensible MIME types. ***Artifact handling***: first-class artifacts or managed files attached to a task, run or session [27,32]. ***Negotiation***: the ability to dynamically agree on *how* to communicate when no contract is assumed a priori, from static version headers to fully dynamic meta-protocols [7,42].

## 5 Communication Protocols Evaluation

Table 1 projects the eight protocols of Sect. 3 onto the sub-features of Sect. 4, grouped by macro-feature; the grid is stable, so current and future protocols alike can be projected onto it, and each cell summarises a systematic study of the corresponding public documentation.

*Coding Protocol.* The cells of Table 1 were coded against the public documentation cited in Sect. 3 by two of the authors independently. Each cell was assessed against the native-support definition above, with disagreements adjudicated by joint re-reading of the normative text. The initial inter-coder agreement was Cohen's $\kappa = 0.85$, computed over the $8 \times 18 = 144$ (protocol, sub-feature) cells. The most frequent sources of disagreement were (i) whether optional non-normative extensions count as native support (they do not) and (ii) whether a primitive instantiated through a normatively specified external dependency counts as native (it does). The matrix is dated to its access snapshot of June 2026; living specifications require periodic re-coding, and a deprecated protocol is simply removed: by construction (Sect. 6) the scores of the remaining candidates are unaffected.

**Table 1.** Comparative matrix. AGN = ACP (AGNTCY), IBM = ACP (IBM), UNI = ACP (AgentUnion), A2A = A2A, ANP = ANP, AIT = AITP, ACN = ACN, AGR = Agora; ✔ natively supported, ✗ not natively supported.

| Sub-feature | AGN | IBM | UNI | A2A | ANP | AIT | ACN | AGR |
|---|---|---|---|---|---|---|---|---|
| *Presentation* | | | | | | | | |
| Standard Agent Card | ✔ | ✔ | ✔ | ✔ | ✔ | ✗ | ✗ | ✗ |
| Agent Card authenticity | ✔ | ✗ | ✔ | ✔ | ✔ | ✗ | ✔ | ✗ |
| Extended Agent Card | ✗ | ✗ | ✗ | ✔ | ✗ | ✗ | ✗ | ✗ |
| *Discovery* | | | | | | | | |
| Active discovery | ✗ | ✔ | ✔ | ✔ | ✔ | ✗ | ✗ | ✔ |
| Passive discovery | ✔ | ✔ | ✔ | ✔ | ✔ | ✗ | ✔ | ✗ |
| *Authentication* | | | | | | | | |
| Self-authentication | ✗ | ✗ | ✗ | ✗ | ✔ | ✗ | ✔ | ✗ |
| Centralised authentication | ✔ | ✔ | ✔ | ✔ | ✗ | ✔ | ✗ | ✗ |
| Human authentication | ✗ | ✗ | ✗ | ✗ | ✔ | ✔ | ✗ | ✗ |
| *Communication* | | | | | | | | |
| Secure channel | ✔ | ✔ | ✔ | ✔ | ✔ | ✔ | ✔ | ✔ |
| Polling | ✔ | ✔ | ✔ | ✔ | ✔ | ✔ | ✗ | ✔ |
| Streaming | ✔ | ✔ | ✔ | ✔ | ✗ | ✗ | ✗ | ✗ |
| Webhook/push | ✗ | ✗ | ✔ | ✔ | ✗ | ✗ | ✗ | ✗ |
| Long-running/stateful | ✔ | ✔ | ✔ | ✔ | ✗ | ✔ | ✗ | ✗ |
| Structured payload | ✔ | ✔ | ✔ | ✔ | ✔ | ✔ | ✗ | ✔ |
| Raw bytes payload | ✗ | ✔ | ✔ | ✔ | ✗ | ✗ | ✔ | ✗ |
| Multimodal payload | ✗ | ✔ | ✗ | ✔ | ✔ | ✗ | ✗ | ✗ |
| Artifact handling | ✗ | ✔ | ✔ | ✔ | ✔ | ✗ | ✗ | ✗ |
| Negotiation | ✗ | ✗ | ✗ | ✗ | ✔ | ✗ | ✗ | ✔ |

The matrix confirms the diverse design philosophies of Sect. 3: **A2A** retains the broadest surface, lacking only self-authentication, human authentication and negotiation, yet breadth is not dominance, since different trust assumptions are served by alternative designs: **ANP** uniquely combines DID-anchored self and human authentication with verifiable-credential audit logs, **AITP** centres on conversational threads with wallet signing, **ACN** is a permissionless key-derived overlay, **Agora** a negotiation-only envelope. Each cell is binary, enabling the formal treatment of the next section; graded support is discussed in Sect. 8.

# 6 Decision Framework

*Comparison with Alternative Decision Paradigms.* Table 1 states *which* sub-features each protocol supports, but not *which protocol to adopt*: use-case needs must be translated into a requirement profile and combined with the matrix. Selecting one option from a finite set evaluated against multiple, partially conflicting criteria is the canonical MCDA formulation [12,46], which natively distinguishes admissibility filters from preference aggregation; alternative paradigms (utility theory, decision tables, expert systems, cost–benefit analysis) require global utility functions, exhaustive tables or monetary inputs typically unavailable in the early architectural phase [47–50], while constraint satisfaction [10] captures feasibility but not preference. We adopt the two-level schema of the enterprise software-selection literature [18,19]: *conjunctive screening* of hard requirements and exclusion constraints, followed by a SAW ranking of the feasible protocols with weights elicited by a hierarchical AHP [11,20]. We prefer SAW to TOPSIS and to outranking schemes [51,52] because, with binary support values, a protocol's SAW score is simply the total weight of the soft requirements it supports, so every contribution traces back to one explicit architect judgment and is independent of the candidate set, whereas TOPSIS suffers rank reversal when the pool is extended [53] and its distance-to-ideal geometry, like outranking thresholds, degenerates on binary data. The framework is thereby *protocol-agnostic*, *extensible* (new protocols and sub-features enlarge the matrix), *monotone* (added support never lowers a score) and *auditable* (every output traces back to an architect choice).

## 6.1 Formal Model and Selection Procedure

Let $\mathcal{P}$ denote the candidate protocols, the eight of Sect. 3 or any protocol projectable onto the same grid, and $\mathcal{F} = \bigcup_{k=1}^{4} \mathcal{F}_k$ the sub-features grouped under the four macro-features. The cells of Table 1 map onto a binary *support matrix* $S \in \{0,1\}^{|\mathcal{P}|\times|\mathcal{F}|}$, with $S_{p,f} = 1$ if and only if protocol $p$ natively supports sub-feature $f$. A use case is encoded as a triple $\mathcal{R} = (\mathcal{W}, \mathcal{H}, \mathcal{X})$ of pairwise disjoint subsets of $\mathcal{F}$: the architect assigns each sub-feature exactly one label $\ell(f) \in \{\textsc{Hard}, \textsc{Soft}, \textsc{Exclude}, \textsc{Irrelevant}\}$, so that $\mathcal{H}$ (mandatory native support), $\mathcal{W}$ (desirable sub-features) and $\mathcal{X}$ (native adoption to be avoided) collect the correspondingly labelled sub-features, while Irrelevant ones affect neither feasibility nor scoring.

*Feasibility Predicate.* A protocol is feasible if it natively supports all hard requirements and does not natively instantiate any excluded sub-feature (each condition vacuous when the set is empty):

$$\Phi(p, \mathcal{R}) \equiv \big(\mathcal{H} = \emptyset \vee \forall f \in \mathcal{H} : S_{p,f} = 1\big) \wedge \big(\mathcal{X} = \emptyset \vee \forall f \in \mathcal{X} : S_{p,f} = 0\big). \quad (1)$$

*Soft-Requirement Weights.* The soft requirements are weighted by a two-level AHP. Within each macro-feature $\mathcal{F}_k$ the architect compares pairwise the soft requirements it contains, $\mathcal{W}_k = \mathcal{W} \cap \mathcal{F}_k$, and the local priorities $v_f \geq 0$ ($\sum_{f \in \mathcal{W}_k} v_f = 1$) are the principal eigenvector of the comparison matrix; at the upper level, the macro-features containing at least one soft requirement are compared pairwise, yielding macro priorities $u_k \geq 0$ summing to one. The global weight of $f \in \mathcal{W}_k$ is

$$w_f = u_k \, v_f, \qquad \sum_{f \in \mathcal{W}} w_f = 1. \tag{2}$$

Each comparison matrix is accepted only if its consistency ratio is below the usual 0.10 threshold [11]; comparing sub-features before macro-features keeps every judgment local.

*Suitability Function.* Given $\mathcal{R}$ and the weights of Eq. (2), the suitability of $p \in \mathcal{P}$ is its weighted support over the soft-requirement set, conditioned on feasibility, i.e. a SAW score with binary criterion values and AHP weights:

$$\sigma(p \mid \mathcal{R}) = \begin{cases} \sum_{f \in \mathcal{W}} w_f \, S_{p,f} & \text{if } \Phi(p, \mathcal{R}) = \text{true} \\ -\infty & \text{otherwise.} \end{cases} \tag{3}$$

The score lies in $[0, 1]$ for feasible protocols and is $-\infty$ otherwise, separating *admissibility* from *preference.*

*Elicitation and Selection.* Operationally, HARD marks a mandatory capability, SOFT a desirable but non-disqualifying property, EXCLUDE a property to be avoided when natively adopted, and IRRELEVANT a sub-feature with no material impact. The framework then operates through four steps: (i) the architect labels each sub-feature, yielding $\mathcal{H}$, $\mathcal{W}$ and $\mathcal{X}$; (ii) the architect performs the hierarchical AHP comparisons over $\mathcal{W}$, yielding the consistency-checked weights of Eq. (2); (iii) the feasibility predicate of Eq. (1) prunes the infeasible protocols; (iv) the suitability of Eq. (3) is computed on the survivors and returned as a ranked list, with the top-ranked protocol as the recommendation and the second as a natural fallback. Labels and weights keep the profile auditable; the procedure can be repeated whenever deployment assumptions change.

## 7 Knowledge-Enterprise Use Cases

We instantiate the framework on three knowledge-enterprise scenarios with markedly different operational, security and identity perimeters, reporting for each the architect's classification (Table 2), the induced AHP weights (Table 3) and the rankings of Table 4 obtained through Eqs. (1) and (3). All comparison matrices of dimension $\geq 3$ have consistency ratio (CR) below the 0.10 Saaty threshold (Appendix A). These scenarios are worked examples, not an empirical validation: the AHP judgments are the authors' own, not elicited from independent enterprise architects.

**Table 2.** Sub-feature classification for the three use cases. H = Hard, S = Soft, X = Exclude, I = Irrelevant.

| Sub-feature | UC1 Intra | UC2 Regulated | UC3 Cross-org |
|---|---|---|---|
| Standard Agent Card | S | I | S |
| Agent Card authenticity | I | S | H |
| Extended Agent Card | I | I | S |
| Active discovery | S | I | I |
| Passive discovery | S | I | H |
| Self-authentication | X | I | H |
| Centralised authentication | H | S | X |
| Human authentication | I | H | I |
| Secure channel | H | H | H |
| Polling | S | S | S |
| Streaming | S | I | I |
| Webhook/push | S | I | I |
| Long-running/stateful | S | S | I |
| Structured payload | S | S | S |
| Raw bytes payload | I | I | S |
| Multimodal payload | S | I | S |
| Artifact handling | S | S | S |
| Negotiation | I | I | I |

**Table 3.** Macro-feature priorities $u_k$ (italic rows) and global soft-requirement weights $w_f = u_k v_f$. A dash marks a sub-feature that is not a soft requirement in that scenario; each column sums to one up to rounding.

| Soft sub-feature | UC1 Intra | UC2 Regulated | UC3 Cross-org |
|---|---|---|---|
| *Presentation* ($u_k$) | *0.10* | *0.29* | *0.50* |
| Standard Agent Card | 0.10 | – | 0.38 |
| Agent Card authenticity | – | 0.29 | – |
| Extended Agent Card | – | – | 0.13 |
| *Discovery* ($u_k$) | *0.25* | – | – |
| Active discovery | 0.14 | – | – |
| Passive discovery | 0.11 | – | – |
| *Authentication* ($u_k$) | – | *0.14* | – |
| Centralised authentication | – | 0.14 | – |
| *Communication* ($u_k$) | *0.65* | *0.57* | *0.50* |
| Polling | 0.05 | 0.08 | 0.07 |
| Streaming | 0.19 | – | – |
| Webhook/push | 0.03 | – | – |
| Long-running/stateful | 0.11 | 0.15 | – |
| Structured payload | 0.05 | 0.08 | 0.07 |
| Raw bytes payload | – | – | 0.14 |
| Multimodal payload | 0.11 | – | 0.07 |
| Artifact handling | 0.11 | 0.26 | 0.14 |

*UC1 – Intra-perimeter Knowledge Orchestration.* This scenario orchestrates specialised agents *within the corporate perimeter* for legal, finance, HR and customer operations, up to the progressive synthesis of long-form deliverables. Identity is governed by the corporate IAM and decentralised self-authentication is excluded by compliance policy [15]: column UC1 of Table 2 yields $\mathcal{H}$ = {centralised authentication, secure channel}, $\mathcal{X}$ = {self-authentication}, $|\mathcal{W}| = 10$. Since identity is already governed, the discriminating factor is the richness of the task-level exchange (upper-level matrix in Appendix A): within Communication Streaming dominates for progressive synthesis (3 over Polling and Structured payload, 2 over Long-running state, Multimodal payload and Artifact handling), with Webhook least relevant, concentrating the weights on Streaming (0.19) and the two discovery modes. The filter prunes ANP and ACN (excluded self-authentication) and Agora (no centralised authentication); the ranking (Table 4) places A2A first ($\sigma = 1.00$), then ACP-IBM (0.97), ACP-AgentUnion (0.89), ACP-AGNTCY (0.61) and AITP (0.21): A2A is recommended, with ACP-IBM as a strong fallback.

*UC2 – Regulated Workflows with Human-in-the-Loop Authorisation.* Regulated domains (financial reporting, healthcare, legal review, compliance attestations) require that high-stakes operations be *explicitly and verifiably* approved by a human principal, with an end-to-end auditable decision trail [4,15]: column UC2 yields $\mathcal{H}$ = {human authentication, secure channel}, $\mathcal{X} = \emptyset$, $|\mathcal{W}| = 6$. Only ANP and AITP pass the filter, tying at 4/6 under uniform weights. The AHP comparisons resolve the tie around the verifiable evidence trail (upper-level matrix in Appendix A): within Communication the evidence-carrying Artifact handling dominates (3 over Polling and Structured payload, 2 over Long-running state). The weights concentrate on Agent Card authenticity (0.29) and Artifact handling (0.26), so ANP, which signs its descriptor and emits verifiable-credential audit chains [33,35], scores $\sigma = 0.71$ and is recommended ahead of AITP (0.45). An IAM-dominant profile prioritising centralised authentication and stateful threading would invert the ordering in favour of AITP [37]; making this dependence explicit is precisely the role of the weighting step.

*UC3 – Cross-Organisational Agent Collaboration.* Workflows crossing organisational boundaries, such as multi-vendor supply chains and federated procurement, require agents from distinct legal entities to discover one another, prove their identity and exchange auditable evidence *without a shared IAM authority* [3,4,8]. Centralised authentication is structurally non-viable, while DID-anchored self-authentication, signed Agent Cards and capability-based registries are required for trustworthy cross-domain discovery [14]: column UC3 yields $\mathcal{H}$ = {Agent Card authenticity, passive discovery, self-authentication, secure channel}, $\mathcal{X}$ = {centralised authentication}, $|\mathcal{W}| = 7$. Presentation and Communication weigh equally at the macro level; within Presentation the Standard Agent Card leads the Extended Card (3), open self-description being the precondition for cross-organisational discovery, and within Communication the evidence-bearing Raw-bytes and Artifact payloads lead the remaining primitives

(2), concentrating the weights on the self-description card (0.38) and the two evidence payloads (0.14 each). Only ANP and ACN satisfy the filter: ANP scores $\sigma = 0.73$ and is recommended, with ACN (0.14) as fallback [39,40].

**Table 4.** Suitability rankings derived by the framework for the three use cases. Each cell reports the AHP-weighted SAW score $\sigma(p \mid \mathcal{R})$, rounded to two decimals, followed by the protocol's rank in parentheses; protocols pruned by the feasibility predicate of Eq. (1) are marked "n.f." (not feasible).

| Protocol | UC1 Intra | UC2 Regulated | UC3 Cross-org |
|---|---|---|---|
| A2A | **1.00** (1st) | n.f. | n.f. |
| ACP-IBM | 0.97 (2nd) | n.f. | n.f. |
| ACP-AgentUnion | 0.89 (3rd) | n.f. | n.f. |
| ACP-AGNTCY | 0.61 (4th) | n.f. | n.f. |
| AITP | 0.21 (5th) | 0.45 (2nd) | n.f. |
| Agora | n.f. | n.f. | n.f. |
| ANP | n.f. | **0.71** (1st) | **0.73** (1st) |
| ACN | n.f. | n.f. | 0.14 (2nd) |

*Sensitivity Analysis.* We sampled, for each use case, 10,000 weight vectors from a Dirichlet $\mathrm{Dir}(K \cdot \mathbf{w}_{\mathrm{AHP}})$ centred on the elicited weights, with $K \in \{10, 50, 200\}$ (larger $K$, tighter perturbation), and from a uniform $\mathrm{Dir}(1, \ldots, 1)$ as the uninformed worst case (Table 5; seed 42). UC1 and UC3 are stable: A2A supports all ten soft requirements of UC1 and Pareto-dominates the feasible set, remaining top-ranked in 100% of samples, and in UC3 ANP remains top-ranked in 96.9% even under uniform sampling. UC2 is robust to small perturbations but materially sensitive to the architect's judgments: under uninformed sampling its top-1 frequency drops to 50.3%, and the IAM-dominant profile (the elicited judgments with the Presentation/Authentication macro-priorities and the Artifact/Long-running local priorities swapped) inverts the scores, exactly mirroring the elicited ones (ANP 0.45, AITP 0.71). The framework records this fragility explicitly through the weights rather than concealing it inside an aggregate score.

**Table 5.** Fraction of samples in which the protocol recommended by the elicited weights remained top-ranked under Dirichlet perturbation (10,000 samples per setting, seed 42); the Unif. column samples from $\mathrm{Dir}(1, \ldots, 1)$.

| Use case | Top-1 (AHP) | $K = 10$ | $K = 50$ | $K = 200$ | Unif. | Note |
|---|---|---|---|---|---|---|
| UC1 | A2A ($\sigma = 1.00$) | 100% | 100% | 100% | 100% | A2A Pareto-dominates the feasible set |
| UC2 | ANP ($\sigma = 0.71$) | 82.5% | 98.0% | 100% | 50.3% | IAM-dominant profile → AITP wins |
| UC3 | ANP ($\sigma = 0.73$) | 98.7% | 100% | 100% | 97.1% | rank stable even under uniform weights |

## 8 Limitations

First, the case studies *illustrate* how the framework operates, not an empirical validation: profiles and rankings have not been confronted with field deployments. Second, the support matrix is *qualitative and binary*: a cell records whether a capability is normatively specified, not how mature, performant or widely implemented it is; a graded schema with $S \in [0, 1]$ (e.g. "specified but optional") is a natural extension, with implementation maturity and adoption as its first dimensions, but eliciting and calibrating such values is left open. Ties between feasible protocols supporting the same soft requirements can be partially resolved by deterministic tie-breakers (broader overall support, then fewer deployment assumptions), beyond which the choice escalates to non-technical criteria (Sect. 9). Third, the weights are only as reliable as the architect's judgments: AHP makes them explicit and consistency-checked, different architects may legitimately weight the same scenario differently, and the framework records this subjectivity; the sensitivity analysis quantifies its impact. Finally, the framework scores only *technical* native support, leaving out the non-technical criteria that often decide real enterprise procurement.

## 9 Conclusion and Future Works

We have addressed inter-agent protocol selection for knowledge-intensive enterprise scenarios across a fragmented ecosystem of eight competing specifications: four lifecycle macro-features decomposed into sub-features; a binary support matrix built from systematic documentation analysis; and, grounded on this evidence, an MCDA-based framework combining conjunctive screening with an AHP-weighted SAW aggregation, returning a transparent, auditable ranking from an explicit architect requirement profile. As the IoA matures, such a protocol-agnostic, extensible and auditable instrument becomes a strategic asset for architects, security teams and procurement functions.

*Future works.* Fuzzy AHP and SAW could propagate the imprecision of the architect's judgments to the ranking [19,21]; the matrix could move to graded values (Sect. 8), enriched with implementation maturity and vendor support; non-technical criteria (licensing, vendor lock-in, community traction, security audits, total cost of ownership) could enter as further weighted criteria or filters; and extending the framework to *extra-agent* protocols, such as tool-use standards like MCP [22,23], would apply the same lifecycle reasoning to the full agent-system surface.

## A Hierarchical AHP Comparison Matrices

For auditability we report the upper-level AHP matrices of the worked examples, narrated in Sect. 7 and verified computationally (matrices of dimension $\leq 2$ are trivially consistent and omitted):

| UC1 | Pres | Disc | Comm |
|---|---|---|---|
| Pres | 1 | 1/3 | 1/6 |
| Disc | 3 | 1 | 1/3 |
| Comm | 6 | 3 | 1 |

| UC2 | Pres | Auth | Comm |
|---|---|---|---|
| Pres | 1 | 2 | 1/2 |
| Auth | 1/2 | 1 | 1/4 |
| Comm | 2 | 4 | 1 |

with principal-eigenvector weights $(0.10, 0.25, 0.65)$ for UC1 ($CR = 0.016$) and $(0.29, 0.14, 0.57)$ for UC2 ($CR = 0$), the macro priorities of Table 3; the lower-level Communication matrices have dimension 7, 4 and 5, all with $CR < 0.10$.

## References


1. Schick, T., et al.: Toolformer: language models can teach themselves to use tools. In: Advances in Neural Information Processing Systems, NeurIPS 2023, vol. 36 (2023). https://proceedings.neurips.cc/paper_files/paper/2023/hash/d842425e4bf79ba039352da0f658a906-Abstract-Conference.html
2. Hu, J., Zhong, M., Chen, K., Bai, X., Zhang, M.: Agentic tool use in large language models. arXiv preprint arXiv:2604.00835 (2026)
3. Chen, W., et al.: Internet of agents: weaving a web of heterogeneous agents for collaborative intelligence. In: International Conference on Learning Representations (ICLR), Spotlight (2025). arXiv preprint arXiv:2407.07061 (2024). https://openreview.net/forum?id=o1Et3MogPw
4. Wibowo, J.A., Polyzos, G.C.: Toward a Safe Internet of Agents. arXiv preprint arXiv:2512.00520 (2025)
5. Finin, T., Fritzson, R., McKay, D., McEntire, R.: KQML as an agent communication language. In: Proceedings of the Third International Conference on Information and Knowledge Management (CIKM 1994), pp. 456–463. ACM, New York (1994). https://doi.org/10.1145/191246.191322
6. Foundation for Intelligent Physical Agents (FIPA): FIPA ACL Message Structure Specification. FIPA Standard SC00061G, Geneva, Switzerland (2002). http://www.fipa.org/specs/fipa00061/. https://ppgia.pucpr.br/~fabricio/ftp/Aulas/Mestrado/AS/Aula3/SC00061G_FIPA_ACL.pdf. Accessed 04 June 2026
7. Yang, Y., et al.: A survey of AI agent protocols. arXiv preprint arXiv:2504.16736 (2025)
8. Li, X., Liu, M., Yuen, C.: LLM agent communication protocol (LACP) requires urgent standardization: a telecom-inspired protocol is necessary. arXiv preprint arXiv:2510.13821 (2025). Accepted at NeurIPS 2025 AI4NextG Workshop
9. Ehtesham, A., Singh, A., Gupta, G.K., Kumar, S.: A survey of agent interoperability protocols: model context protocol (MCP). In: Agent Communication Protocol (ACP), Agent-to-Agent Protocol (A2A), and Agent Network Protocol (ANP). arXiv preprint arXiv:2505.02279 (2025)
10. Bistarelli, S., Montanari, U., Rossi, F.: Semiring-based constraint satisfaction and optimization. J. ACM **44**(2), 201–236 (1997). https://doi.org/10.1145/256303.256306
11. Saaty, T.L.: The Analytic Hierarchy Process: Planning, Priority Setting, Resource Allocation. McGraw-Hill, New York (1980)
12. Hwang, C.-L., Yoon, K.: Multiple Attribute Decision Making: Methods and Applications. A State-of-the-Art Survey. LNEMS, vol. 186. Springer, Heidelberg (1981)

13. Ray, P.P.: A review on agent-to-agent protocol: concept, state-of-the-art, challenges and future directions. TechRxiv preprint, posted 1 May 2025. https://doi.org/10.36227/techrxiv.174612014.42157096/v1
14. Kong, D., et al.: A survey of LLM-driven AI agent communication: protocols, security risks, and defense countermeasures. arXiv preprint arXiv:2506.19676 (2025)
15. Anbiaee, Z., et al.: Security threat modeling for emerging AI-agent protocols: a comparative analysis of MCP, A2A, Agora, and ANP. arXiv preprint arXiv:2602.11327 (2026)
16. Foundation for Intelligent Physical Agents (FIPA): FIPA Abstract Architecture Specification. FIPA Standard SC00001L, Geneva, Switzerland (2002). http://www.fipa.org/specs/fipa00001/. Accessed 04 June 2026
17. Bellifemine, F., Caire, G., Greenwood, D.: Developing Multi-Agent Systems with JADE. Wiley Series in Agent Technology. Wiley, Chichester (2007). https://doi.org/10.1002/9780470058411
18. Jadhav, A.S., Sonar, R.M.: Evaluating and selecting software packages: a review. Inf. Softw. Technol. **51**(3), 555–563 (2009). https://doi.org/10.1016/j.infsof.2008.09.003
19. Lin, H.-Y., Hsu, P.-Y., Sheen, G.-J.: A fuzzy-based decision-making procedure for data warehouse system selection. Expert Syst. Appl. **32**(3), 939–953 (2007). https://doi.org/10.1016/j.eswa.2006.01.031
20. Kurniawati, D., Lenti, F.N., Nugroho, R.W.: Implementation of AHP and SAW methods for optimization of decision recommendations. In: Journal of International Conference Proceedings, vol. 4, no. 1, pp. 254–265 (2021). https://doi.org/10.32535/jicp.v4i1.1152
21. Abdelkarim, M., Al-Hubaishi, M.: A novel fuzzy AHP-TOPSIS model for IoT protocol selection in smart air quality monitoring systems. In: 2025 5th International Conference on Pervasive Computing and Social Networking (ICPCSN), pp. 194–201. IEEE (2025). https://doi.org/10.1109/ICPCSN65854.2025.11034858
22. Anthropic: Model Context Protocol (MCP) Documentation. https://modelcontextprotocol.io/. Accessed 04 June 2026
23. Hou, X., Zhao, Y., Wang, S., Wang, H.: Model context protocol (MCP): landscape, security threats, and future research directions. arXiv preprint arXiv:2503.23278 (2025)
24. AGNTCY: Agent Connect Protocol – Documentation. AGNTCY Documentation (2025). https://docs.agntcy.org/. See also the archived specification https://github.com/agntcy/acp-spec and the ACP SDK documentation https://agntcy.github.io/acp-sdk/html/index.html. Accessed 04 June 2026
25. AGNTCY Collective: Agent Connect Protocol Specification. Archived GitHub repository/OpenAPI specification (2025). https://github.com/agntcy/acp-spec. See also the current AGNTCY documentation https://docs.agntcy.org/. Accessed 04 June 2026
26. Muscariello, L., Pandey, V., Polic, R.: The AGNTCY agent directory service: architecture and implementation. arXiv preprint arXiv:2509.18787 (2025)
27. Besen, S., Gutowska, A.: What is Agent Communication Protocol (ACP)? IBM Think (2025). https://www.ibm.com/think/topics/agent-communication-protocol. Accessed 04 June 2026. Note: ACP is being realigned with the A2A project under the Linux Foundation; see https://a2a-protocol.org/latest/
28. AgentUnion: ACP Protocol Full Documentation. AgentUnion Documentation (2026). early-stage project source. https://www.agentunion.cn/introduction/llms-full.txt. For a more established standard, cf. the A2A Protocol https://a2a-protocol.org/latest/. Accessed 04 June 2026

29. AgentUnion: AgentCP – Agent Communication Protocol SDK. GitHub repository (2026), early-stage project source. https://github.com/auliwenjiang/agentcp. For a more established standard, cf. the A2A Protocol https://a2a-protocol.org/latest/. Accessed 04 June 2026
30. The Linux Foundation: Linux Foundation Launches the Agent2Agent Protocol Project to Enable Secure, Intelligent Communication Between AI Agents. Press release, 23 June 2025. https://www.linuxfoundation.org/press/linux-foundation-launches-the-agent2agent-protocol-project-to-enable-secure-intelligent-communication-between-ai-agents. Accessed 04 June 2026
31. Surapaneni, R., Segal, T., Vakoc, M.: Google Cloud Donates A2A to Linux Foundation. Google Developers Blog, 23 June 2025. https://developers.googleblog.com/en/google-cloud-donates-a2a-to-linux-foundation/. Accessed 04 June 2026
32. A2A Project: Agent2Agent (A2A) Protocol Documentation. Linux Foundation/A2A Project (2026). https://a2a-protocol.org/latest/. Accessed 04 June 2026
33. Chang, G., et al.: Agent network protocol technical white paper. arXiv preprint arXiv:2508.00007 (2025)
34. Agent Network Protocol Community: ANP Agent Description Protocol Specification. Project specification (2025). https://agent-network-protocol.com/specs/agent-description. Accessed 04 June 2026
35. Agent Network Protocol Community: ANP – Agent Network Protocol. Project website (2025). https://agent-network-protocol.com/. Accessed 04 June 2026
36. NEAR AI: Introducing AITP: Agent Interaction & Transaction Protocol to Enable Inter-Agent Payments & Communication. NEAR AI, AITP official documentation (2025). https://aitp.dev/. See also the official repository https://github.com/nearai/aitp. Accessed 04 June 2026
37. AITP Project: AITP – Agent Interaction & Transaction Protocol, version 0.1.0 (Draft). Specification website (2025). https://aitp.dev/. See also the official repository https://github.com/nearai/aitp. Accessed 04 June 2026
38. NEAR AI: AITP: Agent Interaction & Transaction Protocol. GitHub repository (2025). https://github.com/nearai/aitp. Accessed 04 June 2026
39. Fetch.ai: Agent Communication Network (ACN). AEA Framework Documentation, GitHub repository (2025). https://github.com/fetchai/agents-aea/blob/main/docs/acn.md. Accessed 04 June 2026
40. Olas Network: ACN Internals. Olas Stack Developer Documentation (2025). https://stack.olas.network/open-aea/acn-internals/. Accessed 04 June 2026
41. Baumgart, I., Mies, S.: S/Kademlia: a practicable approach towards secure key-based routing. In: 2007 International Conference on Parallel and Distributed Systems (ICPADS), pp. 1–8. IEEE (2007). https://doi.org/10.1109/ICPADS.2007.4447808
42. Marro, S., et al.: A scalable communication protocol for networks of large language models. arXiv preprint arXiv:2410.11905 (2024)
43. Nottingham, M.: Well-Known Uniform Resource Identifiers (URIs). RFC 8615, Internet Engineering Task Force (IETF) (2019). https://www.rfc-editor.org/rfc/rfc8615. Accessed 04 June 2026
44. Sporny, M., Longley, D., Sabadello, M., Reed, D., Steele, O., Allen, C.: Decentralized Identifiers (DIDs) v1.0. W3C Recommendation, 19 July 2022. https://www.w3.org/TR/did-core/. Accessed 04 June 2026
45. Sporny, M., Longley, D., Chadwick, D., Steele, O.: Verifiable Credentials Data Model v2.0. W3C Recommendation, 15 May 2025. https://www.w3.org/TR/vc-data-model-2.0/. Accessed 04 June 2026

46. Triantaphyllou, E.: Multi-criteria Decision Making Methods: A Comparative Study. Applied Optimization, vol. 44. Springer, Boston (2000)
47. Keeney, R.L., Raiffa, H.: Decisions with Multiple Objectives: Preferences and Value Tradeoffs. Wiley, New York (1976)
48. Quinlan, J.R.: Induction of decision trees. Mach. Learn. **1**(1), 81–106 (1986). https://doi.org/10.1007/BF00116251
49. Liao, S.-H.: Expert system methodologies and applications: a decade review from 1995 to 2004. Expert Syst. Appl. **28**(1), 93–103 (2005). https://doi.org/10.1016/j.eswa.2004.08.003
50. Boardman, A.E., Greenberg, D.H., Vining, A.R., Weimer, D.L.: Cost-Benefit Analysis: Concepts and Practice, 5th edn. Cambridge University Press, Cambridge (2018)
51. Roy, B.: The outranking approach and the foundations of ELECTRE methods. Theory Decis. **31**(1), 49–73 (1991). https://doi.org/10.1007/BF00134132
52. Brans, J.-P., Vincke, P., Mareschal, B.: How to select and how to rank projects: the PROMETHEE method. Eur. J. Oper. Res. **24**(2), 228–238 (1986). https://doi.org/10.1016/0377-2217(86)90044-5
53. García-Cascales, M.S., Lamata, M.T.: On rank reversal and TOPSIS method. Math. Comput. Model. **56**(5–6), 123–132 (2012). https://doi.org/10.1016/j.mcm.2011.12.022

# Multi-valued Estimation of Distribution Algorithms for RNA Design

Roberto Santana(✉)

Intelligent Systems Group, University of the Basque Country, San Sebastian, Spain
roberto.santana@ehu.eus

**Abstract.** The RNA design problem is an NP-hard combinatorial challenge with critical applications in mRNA vaccine development and synthetic biology. In this paper, we propose an enhanced multi-valued Univariate Marginal Distribution Algorithm (UMDA) to address this problem. The enhanced UMDA incorporates a more effective representation that leverages pairing relationships between nucleotides and other structural features of RNA conformations. We demonstrate that while the classical multi-valued UMDA lacks the capacity to model higher-order variable dependencies, the enhanced version is capable of navigating the RNA design landscape by exploiting known variable interactions. We evaluate the proposed algorithm against state-of-the-art methods using the Eterna100 RNA design benchmark and the Vienna RNA package (RNAfold). The introduced algorithm achieves competitive results with the other methods, in particular when considering the ensemble defect metric.

**Keywords:** optimization · estimation of distribution algorithms · RNA design · probabilistic graphical models · bioinformatics

## 1 Introduction

The RNA design problem, also known as the RNA inverse folding problem, seeks to determine a nucleotide sequence that will spontaneously fold into a prescribed target structure, whether at the secondary or tertiary level. The ability to solve this problem is fundamental to harnessing RNA for a rapidly expanding array of biotechnological and therapeutic applications. For instance, RNA is a core component in mRNA vaccine design [7], serves as the crucial guide molecule (guide RNA) within the CRISPR-Cas9 gene-editing system [25], and forms the functional basis for the emerging field of RNA enzyme (ribozyme) design and synthetic biology [9].

In its straightforward formulation, the RNA design problem can be posed as finding the right assignment, among four possible nucleotides, to each element of the RNA sequence. Given that the search space grows exponentially with the length of the sequence, the problem is known to be NP-hard. A variety of


S. Bistarelli et al. (Eds.): AIxIA 2026, LNAI 17131, pp. 572–585, 2027.
https://doi.org/10.1007/978-3-032-40774-0_41

optimization approaches have been used to address the problem, including Evolutionary Algorithms (EAs) [5,6]. While EAs provide a robust and adaptable framework for RNA inverse folding, they struggle to capture and exploit the regularities that arise in this domain. Some researchers have tried to circumvent this limitation by using approaches that incorporate structural decomposition [18,19], advanced mutation sampling [15], and dynamic objective weighting [13]. In this paper we propose the application of model-building EAs that automatically learn the most important features of the problem during the search using probabilistic models.

Estimation of Distribution Algorithms (EDAs) [10] are a well known class of model-building EAs that learn probabilistic models and use them for sampling new solutions. Although they have been mainly applied to binary optimization problems, a number of recent works investigate their application to multi-valued problems where the cardinality of the variables is higher than two [1,3]. Multi-valued problems represent a challenge for EDAs since the storage requirements needed by the probabilistic models significantly increase with the cardinality of the variables. Due to this limitation, EDAs that use simpler probabilistic models are the preferred choice for this problem.

In this paper we propose ways to enhance the behavior of the Univariate Estimation of Distribution Algorithm (UMDA) [16] for the RNA inverse folding problem by using compound variables. Our aims are two-fold: First, to advance research on the use of evolutionary algorithms for the RNA design problem; Second, we would like to investigate the performance of the multi-valued UMDA, an algorithm that in principle is not able to model higher order dependencies, on a challenging RNA design benchmark with known variable interactions.

The paper is organized as follows: The next section presents the necessary background for the paper. Section 3 describes the main characteristics of the model-based algorithm used in the paper. Section 4 briefly reviews work related to our proposal. The experimental framework and the results of our experiments are introduced in Sect. 5. We present our conclusions and some lines for future research in Sect. 6.

## 2 Background

### 2.1 RNA Design

The canonical secondary structure of an RNA sequence of length $n$ can be described compactly in *Dot-Bracket Notation* (DBN): a string $s$ of length $n$ over the alphabet { "(", ")", "."}, where "(" and ")" mark the left and right sides of a Watson–Crick pair, respectively, and "." denotes an unpaired position. For example:

```
Sequence: A C G U A C G U
Structure: ( ( . . . . ) )
```

indicates that positions 1 and 8 form one base pair and positions 2 and 7 form another, while positions 3–6 are unpaired.

Standard RNA forward folding takes a nucleotide sequence as input and predicts its minimum free-energy (MFE) secondary structure using a nearest-neighbor thermodynamic model [8,30]. Let $\mathcal{S}(\mathbf{x})$ denote the set of all valid secondary structures of $\mathbf{x}$, that is, the sets of base pairs in which every position is paired at most once, each pair joins complementary (Watson–Crick or wobble) nucleotides, the pairs are properly nested (no pseudoknots), and a minimum hairpin-loop size is respected. The Turner nearest-neighbor model assigns to each structure $S \in \mathcal{S}(\mathbf{x})$ a free energy $\Delta G(S, \mathbf{x})$ obtained by summing tabulated contributions of its loops (stacked pairs, hairpins, bulges, internal loops, and multiloops). The MFE structure is the single valid structure that minimizes this energy,

$$s(\mathbf{x}) = \mathcal{F}(\mathbf{x}) = \arg\min_{S \in \mathcal{S}(\mathbf{x})} \Delta G(S, \mathbf{x}).$$

The Vienna RNA package computes $s(\mathbf{x})$ exactly with the cubic-time Zuker dynamic-programming algorithm [30]; the result is therefore a single, well-formed (feasible) secondary structure, and not a superposition or ensemble of conformations. The inverse problem, also called RNA design or RNA inverse folding, is the reverse: given a target secondary structure $s^*$, find one or more nucleotide sequences $\mathbf{x}$ such that the MFE structure predicted for $\mathbf{x}$ is $s^*$ (or as close to it as possible).

**Definition 1 (RNA Inverse Folding).** *Let $s^* \in \{\text{“(”}, \text{“)”}, \text{“.”}\}^n$ be a target secondary structure of length $n$. The RNA inverse folding problem is to find a sequence of nucleotides $\mathbf{x} \in \{\mathrm{A}, \mathrm{C}, \mathrm{G}, \mathrm{U}\}^n$ such that*

$$\mathcal{F}(\mathbf{x}) = s^*,$$

*where $\mathcal{F}(\mathbf{x})$ denotes the MFE secondary structure predicted for sequence $\mathbf{x}$ by a thermodynamic folding algorithm.*

**Objective Functions.** In the literature, three main objective functions are used to measure the quality of a sequence. Each one measures a distinct aspect of how well a designed sequence $\mathbf{x}$ achieves the target structure $s^*$. All three are formulated as maximization objectives by negating their natural cost.

Let $s(\mathbf{x}) = \mathcal{F}(\mathbf{x})$ be the MFE secondary structure predicted for sequence $\mathbf{x}$ by the Vienna RNA package (`RNAfold`) [12]. Both $s(\mathbf{x})$ and the target $s^*$ are valid structures written in dot-bracket notation, so we quantify their dissimilarity by the *positional (Hamming) distance* between the two dot-bracket strings,

$$d_{\mathrm{H}}(\mathbf{x},\, s^*) \;=\; \sum_{i=1}^{n} \mathbb{1}[\, s(\mathbf{x})_i \neq s_i^* \,],$$

that is, the number of positions whose dot-bracket symbol (“(”, “)”, or “.”) differs between the predicted MFE structure and the target. The corresponding maximization objective is the negative distance, $f_1(\mathbf{x}) = -d_{\mathrm{H}}(\mathbf{x},\, s^*)$, and a solution with $f_1(\mathbf{x}) = 0$ reproduces the target exactly and has thus solved the design problem.

Another criterion used is the *probability of the target structure*, where given a sequence $\mathbf{x}$, the Boltzmann partition function $Z(\mathbf{x})$ sums the Boltzmann weights of all possible secondary structures

$$Z(\mathbf{x}) = \sum_{s} \exp\left(-\frac{\Delta G(s,\mathbf{x})}{RT}\right),$$

where $\Delta G(s,\mathbf{x})$ is the free energy of structure $s$ folded from sequence $\mathbf{x}$, $R$ is the gas constant, and $T$ is the absolute temperature. The probability of the target structure $s^*$ under the Boltzmann ensemble is

$$p(s^* \mid \mathbf{x}) = \frac{\exp(-\Delta G(s^*,\mathbf{x}) \,/\, RT)}{Z(\mathbf{x})}.$$

Then, the optimization objective is the log-probability of the target:

$$f_2(\mathbf{x}) = \log p(s^* \mid \mathbf{x}) = -\frac{\Delta G(s^*,\mathbf{x})}{RT} - \log Z(\mathbf{x}).$$

Finally, another objective function is the *ensemble defect* [28] which quantifies the expected number of incorrectly paired nucleotides when a structure is drawn at random from the Boltzmann ensemble:

$$D(\mathbf{x},\, s^*) = n \;-\; \sum_{i=1}^{n}\sum_{j=0}^{n} \mathbb{1}[s^*_{ij}]\, p_{ij}(\mathbf{x}),$$

where $p_{ij}(\mathbf{x})$ is the base-pair probability between positions $i$ and $j$ (with $j = 0$ denoting the unpaired state), and $\mathbb{1}[s^*_{ij}]$ is 1 if positions $i$ and $j$ are paired (or i unpaired if j=0) in $s^*$. The negative *normalized ensemble defect* is the negative normalized D divided by $n$: $f_3(\mathbf{x}) = -\tilde{D}(\mathbf{x},\, s^*)$. A value of $f_3(\mathbf{x}) = 0$ means that, on average, every nucleotide adopts its target pairing state across the Boltzmann ensemble.

## 2.2 Multi-valued UMDA

Algorithm 1 shows the pseudocode of UMDA [16]. The algorithm can start from a random or seeded population and in each iteration it evaluates the newly generated solutions, selects a subset of them according to the objective values, learns the model and samples new solutions from it. UMDA assumes complete statistical independence among the $n$ variables. The model factorizes as a product of univariate marginals:

$$\hat{p}_t(\mathbf{x}) = \prod_{i=1}^{n} p_t(x_i),$$

where each $p_t(x_i)$ is estimated by frequency counting over the selected population $D_t^S$:

$$p_t(x_i = v) = \frac{|\{s \in D_t^S : s_i = v\}|}{|D_t^S|}, \quad v \in \{0, 1, 2, \ldots, K_i - 1\}.$$

**Algorithm 1.** Estimation of distribution algorithm

1: Set $t \leftarrow 0$. Generate $N$ solutions randomly.
2: **repeat**
3: Evaluate the solutions using the fitness function.
4: Select a population $D_t^S$ of $K \leq N$ solutions according to a selection method.
5: Learn the univariate probabilistic model of $D_t^S$.
6: Generate $N$ new solutions sampling from the model.
7: Combine the new solutions with the current population.
8: $t \leftarrow t + 1$
9: **until** Termination criteria are met.

and $K_i$ is the number of discrete values variable $X_i$ can take.

While in most literature of multi-valued EDAs it is assumed that the cardinality of all variables is the same, in the most general case, and in several realistic scenarios, as one of those treated in this paper, variables can take different number of values.

Laplace smoothing with parameter $\alpha \geq 0$ is usually applied to prevent zero probabilities [14]:

$$\hat{p}_t(x_i = v) = \frac{\sum_i I(x_i, v) + \alpha}{|D_t^S| + K_i \alpha}, \text{where } I \text{ is the indicator function.}$$

While UMDA is computationally cheap and robust to small population sizes, a straightforward problem representation (four possible values for each variable corresponding to nucleotide assignments) would violate the independence assumption in RNA design: base pairs by definition couple two positions, and the nucleotide at a paired position is severely constrained by the complementarity rules (A–U, G–C, G–U). It is expected that ignoring these dependencies when modeling would yield suboptimal solutions.

# 3 Multi-valued UMDA for RNA Design

The RNA design problem belongs to the class of *gray-box optimization* problems [22]: the target structure is known a priori and encodes, in explicit form, the structural relationships among the variables. Specifically, a base pair $(i, j)$ in $s^*$ tells us unambiguously that nucleotides at positions $i$ and $j$ are strongly coupled: the identity of $x_i$ severely constrains the set of admissible values for $x_j$ (complementarity rules). Moreover, consecutive positions share stacking interactions and backbone geometry constraints. Both types of information are available before the EDA runs a single generation.

## 3.1 Problem Representation

We use two problem representations to evaluate the performance of UMDA. The *full representation* and the *reduced representation*.

In the full representation, each candidate solution is a discrete vector $\mathbf{x} = (x_1, x_2, \ldots, x_n) \in \{0, 1, 2, 3\}^n$, where each component $x_i$ encodes the nucleotide at position $i$ of the RNA sequence using the mapping

$$0 \leftrightarrow \mathrm{A}, \quad 1 \leftrightarrow \mathrm{C}, \quad 2 \leftrightarrow \mathrm{G}, \quad 3 \leftrightarrow \mathrm{U}.$$

Variable $x_i$ has cardinality 4 for all $i$. The EDA population is an $N \times n$ integer matrix.

Different authors have previously proposed the possibility of using the pairing relationships between nucleotides and other structural characteristics of the RNA conformations to propose a more efficient implementation [5,24,27]. We follow the same approach and use a reduced representation where the target secondary structure is exploited to group strongly coupled positions into compound variables, substantially shrinking the search space while guaranteeing that every sampled solution is structurally valid. The grouping rules are as follows [24]:

- **Base-pair variables.** Each base pair $(i, j)$ in $s^*$ is merged into a single variable that ranges over the six valid Watson-Crick and wobble pairs $\{\texttt{CG}, \texttt{GC}, \texttt{AU}, \texttt{UA}, \texttt{GU}, \texttt{UG}\}$, giving a cardinality of 6 instead of the $4 \times 4 = 16$ unconstrained combinations.
- **Mismatch variables (2-position).** Positions immediately adjacent to a base pair on the inward side, specifically $(i+1, j-1)$ for a hairpin pair $(i, j)$ and for $1 \times 1$ internal loops, are coupled into a single variable with $4^2 = 16$ feasible values. These positions correspond to hairpin-loop or symmetric internal-loop mismatches that co-evolve with adjacent stacking pairs in the Turner energy model.
- **Trimismatch variables (3-position).** For asymmetric $1 \times k$ internal loops (one unpaired nucleotide on the left, $k > 1$ unpaired nucleotides on the right) or $k \times 1$ loops, three positions are coupled into a single trimismatch variable with $4^3 = 64$ feasible values. Specifically, for a $1 \times k$ loop enclosed by the outer pair $(i, j)$ and inner pair $(p, q)$, the variable covers positions $\{i+1, q+1, j-1\}$; for an $n \times 1$ loop it covers $\{i+1, p-1, j-1\}$.
- **Unpaired variables.** All remaining positions that are not covered by any of the above groups are retained as individual variables with cardinality 4 ($\{\mathrm{A}, \mathrm{C}, \mathrm{G}, \mathrm{U}\}$).

The result of applying these rules is a reduced vector of length $m \leq n$ with a heterogeneous cardinality profile because every compound variable encodes only biologically admissible combinations. When randomly sampling the initial population, each compound variable is uniformly sampled from its range of values. In addition to capturing problem information, the reduced representation allows UMDA, which in the straightforward approach ignores interactions, to implicitly deal with interactions between variables of the original representation. Some compound variables will actually represent building blocks of the RNA sequences.

### 3.2 Biasing the Distribution of Nucleotides in the Population

One of the enhancements we have applied to UMDA is biasing the initial population according to nucleotide distributions that have been previously shown to better characterize solutions conformal with the structure. Three initialization strategies are used in the experiments.

In the *Uniform initialization* each variable is drawn independently and uniformly at random from its feasible alphabet. For pair variables this means any of the six valid Watson-Crick/wobble pairs is equally probable; for unpaired variables each of the four nucleotides is equally probable. In the *Targeted initialization*, all unpaired positions are set to `A`; each base-pair variable is initialized to `CG` or `GC` with equal probability. This scheme, previously used in [24] exploits the fact that long complementary GC stacks are the most stable motif in the Turner energy model. Finally, the *ε-targeted initialization* is a mixture strategy introduced in [24], in which 80% of the individuals in the initial population are generated by the targeted rule and 20% are drawn uniformly.

### 3.3 Other Changes to Typical EDA Settings

In addition, we use the best elitism method, a variant of elitism where all the selected population (selected by means of truncation selection) is passed to the next generation. Since UMDA sampling is highly disruptive, this method tries to keep in the population a large proportion of the best solutions found so far.

A further non-standard feature of the implementation is a random-reset mutation operator applied to every newly sampled population before evaluation. For the full (4-letter) representation the operator is the multivalue generalization of bit-flip mutation: each position is independently mutated with probability $p_m$ to a uniformly drawn different nucleotide. For the reduced representation the same operator is extended to heterogeneous cardinality: with probability $p_m$, the current value of reduced variable $j$ with cardinality $c_j$ is replaced by a value drawn uniformly from the remaining $c_j - 1$ alternatives.

## 4 Related Work

There exist a variety of optimization approaches for RNA design and we focus the analysis of related work on evolutionary approaches and other state of the art optimizers that we use as baselines for our experiments.

Some existing approaches explicitly optimize for thermodynamic stability by minimizing the free energy of the sequence folding into the target structure. However, it is rarely used alone [13,26]. Instead, it is frequently combined with other metrics or constraints. For example, the MODENA algorithm, a multi-objective genetic algorithm (based on NSGA-II), utilizes a multi-objective genetic algorithm that simultaneously optimizes a structure stability score (based on free energy) and a structure similarity score [23].

Other advanced EAs for RNA design include the Multiobjective Metaheuristic to Design RNA Sequences (M2dRNAs) [19], a multi-objective approach that evaluates candidate sequences by simultaneously optimizing the partition function, ensemble diversity, and nucleotide composition. The enhanced M2dRNAs (eM2dRNAs) [19] is a development of M2dRNAs, in which a recursive decomposition of the target structure into substructures is computed. Substructures are then independently solved. Since these structures are smaller and consequently easier to solve, eM2dRNAs produces better solutions than M2dRNAs.

The Structure-Aware Multifrontier Ensemble Optimization (SAMFEO) framework [29] is a multifrontier iterative search method that optimizes RNA ensemble objectives (equilibrium probability or ensemble defect) while collecting MFE solutions as by-products of the optimization. The algorithm maintains a priority queue of the $k$ best sequences found so far, the multifrontier. Starting from a targeted initialization (unpaired positions set to `A`; base-paired positions set to `CG` or `GC` at random), SAMFEO is able to design thousands of RNA sequences satisfying the MFE criterion for all 100 puzzles of the Eterna100 benchmark.

The SamplingDesign algorithm [24] reformulates RNA design as a continuous optimization problem over probability distributions of candidate sequences. Rather than searching for a single sequence, SamplingDesign maintains a coupled-variable distribution defined on the valid design space, where pair positions use a distribution over the six valid Watson-Crick-wobble pairs and mismatch-trimismatch positions are also coupled (as described in Sect. 3.1). Gradient descent is applied to minimize the expected value of an arbitrary objective function. SamplingDesign consistently outperforms state-of-the-art methods, including SAMFEO and NEMO [17].

In comparison to problems with binary representations, there are few applications of multi-valued EDAs in the bioinformatics domains [21]. In [4], multi-valued EDAs based on Markovian models, where each variable depends on its k previous variables, are applied to a simplified protein problem. In the multi-valued representation all variables have cardinality 3. In [20], a multi-valued UMDA is applied to the protein side chain placement problem in which each variable can have a different cardinality. With the exception of [20], we have not found any previous application of EDAs to problems with variables of different cardinality.

# 5 Experiments

## 5.1 Experimental Framework

For evaluating the introduced algorithms, we use the *Eterna100* [2,11] dataset, which is a widely adopted benchmark suite for RNA design algorithms. It consists of 100 RNA secondary structure puzzles. The benchmark was introduced specifically to evaluate computational design algorithms under conditions that reflect real-world difficulty.

In the evaluation of the methods, we use the following evaluation protocol:

- An algorithm is given the target structure $s_k^*$ for puzzle $k \in \{1, \ldots, 100\}$.

- The algorithm returns a candidate sequence $\hat{\mathbf{x}}_k$.
- The sequence is folded with the Vienna RNA package (`RNAfold`); if the predicted MFE structure equals $s_k^*$ (i.e., base-pair distance = 0), the puzzle is counted as solved.
- We also compute the Boltzmann distribution for the obtained solution.

**Table 1.** UMDA variant comparison: mean across the 100 puzzles of the per-instance best value over 20 seeds. Arrows indicate the direction of improvement. The best value in each column is shown in bold. log(NED), DIST, and BOLTZ respectively refer to functions $f_3$, $f_1$, and $f_2$.

| Init | Rep | log(NED) ↓ | DIST ↓ | BOLTZ ↑ |
|---|---|---|---|---|
| $\varepsilon$-targeted | full | −7.408 | 5.260 | 0.4434 |
| $\varepsilon$-targeted | reduced | **−7.630** | 7.200 | **0.5008** |
| targeted | full | −7.415 | **5.320** | 0.4481 |
| targeted | reduced | −7.626 | 7.260 | 0.5024 |
| uniform | full | −5.919 | 57.620 | 0.1131 |
| uniform | reduced | −7.297 | 14.760 | 0.4139 |

For each puzzle, and each algorithm variant, we run 20 experiments. The total number of experiments conducted is $100 \times 2 \times 3 \times 20 = 12,000$. For evaluating the behavior of the algorithm we consider the solve rate (number of puzzles solved out of 100) as the primary performance metric, as well as the average objective value for each of the objectives.

We compare multi-valued UMDA with other state of the art algorithms. In particular, we compare to eM2dRNAs, one of the most advanced EAs for the RNA design problem, SAMFEO [29], and SamplingDesign method (See Sect. 4 for more details on these algorithms). When comparing with the results achieved by these methods, we use the results provided by the authors of the papers. Due to the different nature of the algorithms (decomposition strategies, continuous representation, sampling methods, etc.) the algorithms cannot be directly compared in terms of the number of fitness evaluations.

In all the experiments, the multi-valued UMDA was run with a population size of 1000, 100 generations, truncation selection keeping the top 30% of the population, $p_m = 0.05$, Laplace parameter $\alpha_{\text{Lap}} = 0.05$, and best elitism. We evaluate the two representations (full and reduced) of Sect. 3.1, each combined with the three initialization strategies (uniform, targeted, and $\varepsilon$-targeted), yielding six UMDA variants. Each variant is independently optimized for each of the three objective functions of Sect. 2.1.

### 5.2 Comparison Among Multi-valued UMDA Variants

In the first set of experiments, we compare the six UMDA variants. Table 1 reports, for each variant, the mean across the 100 puzzles of the per-instance best value attained over the 20 seeds, for the three objectives.

From the analysis of Table 1, two clear trends emerge. First, the initialization strategy plays an important role in the performance of the algorithm: the uniform initialization is consistently the worst, and with the full representation it essentially fails (mean distance of 57.6 versus 5.3 for the targeted variants). The targeted and $\varepsilon$-targeted strategies, which bias the initial population toward stable `GC` stacks and `A`-rich loops, perform almost identically and dominate the uniform one across all objectives. This confirms that an informed initialization of the marginals is essential to counteract the rapid genetic drift that affects multi-valued UMDA.

Second, the two representations exhibit a complementary behavior. The full representation attains the lowest base-pair distance (best 5.26 with $\varepsilon$-targeted initialization), whereas the reduced representation attains the best ensemble metrics, i.e., Boltzmann probability (0.50 versus 0.44) and normalized ensemble defect. This is consistent with the design of each encoding: the reduced representation guarantees structurally valid base pairs by construction and therefore concentrates on stabilizing the target structure within the Boltzmann ensemble, while the full representation explores nucleotide assignments more freely and occasionally reaches the exact MFE target at the price of weaker ensemble stability. The reduced representation makes the algorithm more robust to a poor (uniform) initialization, reducing the mean distance from 57.6 to 14.8.

### 5.3 Comparison with Other Algorithms

In the second set of experiments we compare the multi-valued UMDA against the three state-of-the-art baselines (SAMFEO, SamplingDesign, and eM2dRNAs). For each puzzle we take the best sequence found by UMDA across all variants and seeds and compare its three objective values against the sequence reported by each baseline. Table 2 reports the mean values together with the UMDA win rate (percentage of puzzles on which UMDA is strictly better).

The analysis of the results reveals that the multi-valued UMDA clearly outperforms eM2dRNAs, the strongest of the evolutionary baselines, on all three metrics: it wins on 95.7% of the puzzles in NED, on 81.7% in Boltzmann probability, and roughly halves the mean base-pair distance (3.06 versus 6.47). This is a relevant result given that UMDA uses a strictly univariate model with no problem-specific decomposition. Against the two specialized ensemble-based designers, SAMFEO and SamplingDesign, UMDA is competitive on the normalized ensemble defect. In fact, it is actually slightly better on average, winning on 50–56% of the puzzles. However, the multi-valued UMDA is outperformed on the base-pair distance and the Boltzmann probability, where SamplingDesign in particular reaches a much lower mean distance (1.90). This is the expected outcome:

**Table 2.** Multi-valued UMDA versus the state-of-the-art baselines. For each metric we report the mean UMDA value, the mean baseline value, and the UMDA win rate (% of puzzles where UMDA is strictly better). NED and distance are minimized; Boltzmann probability is maximized. eM2dRNAs reports results for 93 of the 100 puzzles. Bold marks the better mean of the two.

| Baseline | Metric | UMDA | Baseline | UMDA win % |
|---|---|---|---|---|
| SAMFEO | NED ↓ | $\mathbf{4.56 \times 10^{-4}}$ | $4.93 \times 10^{-4}$ | 56.0 |
| | DIST ↓ | 4.56 | **4.26** | 8.0 |
| | BOLTZ ↑ | 0.540 | **0.581** | 30.0 |
| SamplingDesign | NED ↓ | $\mathbf{4.56 \times 10^{-4}}$ | $4.92 \times 10^{-4}$ | 50.0 |
| | DIST ↓ | 4.56 | **1.90** | 4.0 |
| | BOLTZ ↑ | 0.540 | **0.595** | 28.0 |
| eM2dRNAs | NED ↓ | $\mathbf{4.61 \times 10^{-4}}$ | $1.02 \times 10^{-3}$ | 95.7 |
| | DIST ↓ | **3.06** | 6.47 | 25.8 |
| | BOLTZ ↑ | **0.580** | 0.418 | 81.7 |

SAMFEO and SamplingDesign are highly engineered, gradient- or multifrontier-based methods, whereas UMDA is a general-purpose probabilistic baseline.

The aggregate means hide a strong dependence on puzzle size. Figure 1 stratifies the per-instance UMDA advantage (positive bars mean UMDA is better) into four size bins. On the small and medium puzzles (lengths up to 104), UMDA is competitive with, and on several metrics better than, SAMFEO and SamplingDesign, and it dominates eM2dRNAs across the whole range. The disadvantage against SAMFEO and SamplingDesign concentrates on the large and very large puzzles (lengths above 213), and for the largest bin SamplingDesign attains a much lower distance. Against eM2dRNAs, by contrast, the UMDA advantage grows with size, reaching the largest gaps precisely on the hardest puzzles. It is important to notice that UMDA uses the same population size and number of evaluations for all sequence sizes. However, harder problems may require a higher number of evaluations in order to find the optimal solutions. Further research in this direction is required.

Finally, Fig. 2 reports, for every (baseline, UMDA variant) combination, the number of Eterna100 puzzles for which the UMDA-designed sequence matches the solving criterion of the baseline. The information displayed in the figure is consistent with the variant analysis: the reduced representation produces more exact matches than the full one (up to 9 puzzles for the SamplingDesign comparison under $\varepsilon$-targeted initialization, versus at most 4 for any full-representation variant). This pattern confirms that exploiting the known base-pairing structure through compound variables, even within a purely univariate model, is the single most effective enhancement of the algorithm.

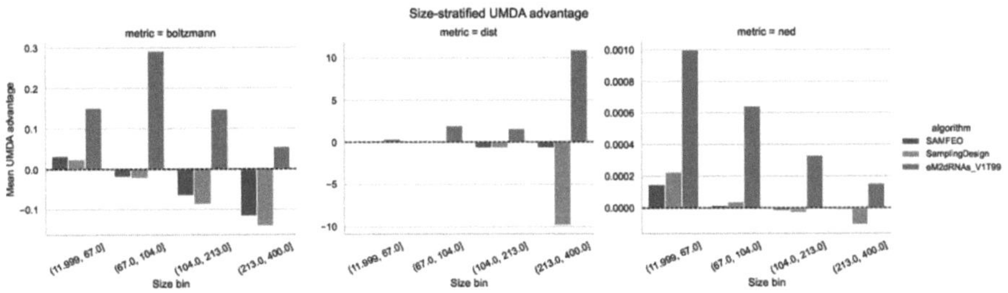


**Fig. 1.** Size-stratified mean UMDA advantage per puzzle-length bin against each baseline. Positive bars indicate that UMDA outperforms the baseline on that metric.

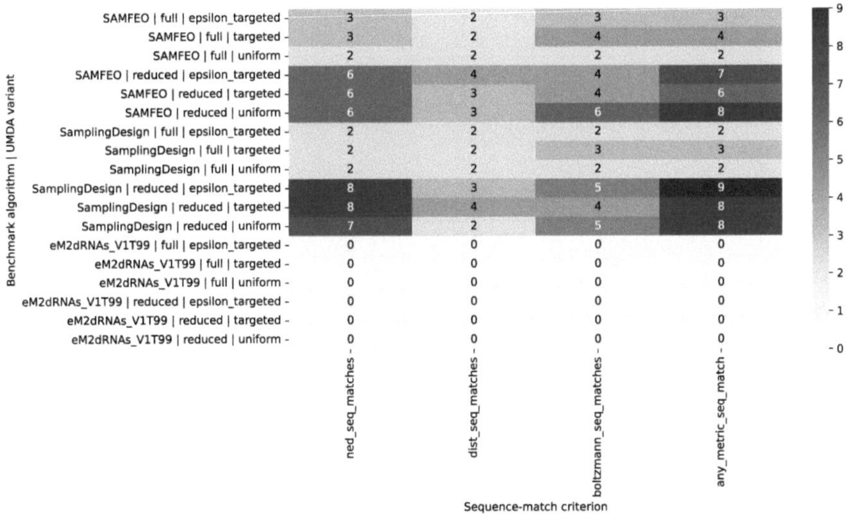


**Fig. 2.** Number of Eterna100 puzzles for which the UMDA-designed sequence matches the baseline solving criterion, per (baseline, UMDA variant) combination and per metric.

## 6 Conclusions

In this paper, we have investigated the use of an enhanced multi-valued UMDA for the RNA inverse-folding problem. Our experiments on the Eterna100 suite show that the multi-valued UMDA is able to achieve the best ensemble metrics and the largest number of exactly solved puzzles. UMDA clearly outperforms eM2dRNAs across all three objectives and remains competitive with the highly specialized SAMFEO and SamplingDesign on the normalized ensemble defect and on small-to-medium structures. These results establish multi-valued UMDA as a competitive baseline for RNA design.

More research is needed to determine whether the limited budget of function evaluations or the lack of explicit dependency modeling drives the deterioration of the algorithm's performance for the largest puzzles. As future work, we plan to investigate the behavior of EDAs that capture higher-order dependencies, such as tree- or Markov-network-based models [4,21], and to validate the reduced representation and adaptive initialization on longer and harder target structures.

**Acknowledgments.** We acknowledge support from the Spanish Ministry of Science, Innovation and Universities (Projects ID2023-149195NB-I00 and PID 2022-137442NB-I00), and the Basque Government (Projects KK-2026/00055 and IT2109-26). This work benefited from the Dagstuhl Seminar 25092 "Estimation-of-Distribution Algorithms: Theory and Applications" held at Schloss Dagstuhl– Leibniz Zentrum für Informatik in [February, 2025]. Roberto Santana thanks Schloss Dagstuhl - Leibniz-Zentrum für Informatik for their support and hospitality.

We have used Claude and Copilot AI programming assistants as a support for code design and implementation for the Experimental section. Gemini and Deepseek AI assistants have been used for grammar and style correction of the paper.

## References

1. Adak, S., Witt, C.: Mathematical runtime analysis of a multi-valued estimation of distribution algorithm. Artif. Intell. 104501 (2026)
2. Anderson, E., Das, R.: Eterna100 benchmark for RNA inverse folding (2016), gitHub repository: https://github.com/eternagame/Eterna100-benchmarking
3. Ben Jedidia, F., Doerr, B., Krejca, M.S.: Estimation-of-distribution algorithms for multi-valued decision variables. In: Proceedings of the Genetic and Evolutionary Computation Conference, pp. 230–238 (2023)
4. Chen, B., Li, L., Hu, J.: A novel EDAs based method for HP model protein folding. In: Proceedings of the 2009 Congress on Evolutionary Computation CEC-2009, pp. 309–315. IEEE Press, Norway (2009)
5. Churkin, A., Drory Retwitzer, M., Reinharz, V., Ponty, Y., Waldispühl, J., Barash, D.: Design of RNAs: comparing programs for inverse RNA folding. Brief. Bioinform. **19**(2), 350–358 (2018)
6. Cole, J., Li, F., Wu, L., Li, K.: RNAInvbench: benchmark for the RNA inverse design problem. In: ICML 2024 AI for Science Workshop (2024)
7. Corbett, K.S., et al.: SARS-CoV-2 mRNA vaccine design enabled by prototype pathogen preparedness. Nature **586**(7830), 567–571 (2020)
8. Hofacker, I.L., Fontana, W., Stadler, P.F., Bonhoeffer, L.S., Tacker, M., Schuster, P.: Fast folding and comparison of RNA secondary structures. Monatshefte für Chemie/Chem. Monthly **125**(2), 167–188 (1994)
9. Isaacs, F.J., Dwyer, D.J., Collins, J.J.: RNA synthetic biology. Nat. Biotechnol. **24**(5), 545–554 (2006)
10. Larrañaga, P., Lozano, J.A. (eds.): Estimation of Distribution Algorithms. A New Tool for Evolutionary Computation. Kluwer Academic Publishers (2002)
11. Lee, J., et al.: RNA design rules from a massive open laboratory. Proc. Natl. Acad. Sci. **111**(6), 2122–2127 (2014)
12. Lorenz, R., et al.: ViennaRNA package 2.0. Algorithms Mol. Biol. **6**(1), 26 (2011)
13. Lozano-García, N., Rubio-Largo, Á., Granado-Criado, J.M.: A simple yet effective greedy evolutionary strategy for RNA design. IEEE Trans. Evol. Comput. (2024)

14. Mahnig, T., Mühlenbein, H.: Optimal mutation rate using Bayesian priors for estimation of distribution algorithms. In: Steinhöfel, K. (ed.) SAGA 2001. LNCS, vol. 2264, pp. 33–48. Springer, Heidelberg (2001). https://doi.org/10.1007/3-540-45322-9_2
15. Merleau, N.S., Smerlak, M.: aRNAque: an evolutionary algorithm for inverse pseudoknotted RNA folding inspired by lévy flights. BMC Bioinform. **23**(335) (2022)
16. Mühlenbein, H., Paaß, G.: From recombination of genes to the estimation of distributions I. Binary parameters. In: Voigt, H.M., Ebeling, W., Rechenberg, I., Schwefel, H.P. (eds.) Parallel Problem Solving from Nature - PPSN IV. LNCS, vol. 1141, pp. 178–187. Springer, Berlin (1996)
17. Portela, F.: An unexpectedly effective Monte-Carlo technique for the RNA inverse folding problem. BioRxiv, p. 345587 (2018)
18. Rubio-Largo, Á., Escobar-Encinas, L., Lozano-García, N., Granado-Criado, J.M.: Evolutionary strategy to enhance an RNA design tool performance. IEEE Access **12**, 15582–15593 (2024)
19. Rubio-Largo, Á., Lozano-García, N., Granado-Criado, J.M., Vega-Rodríguez, M.A.: Solving the RNA inverse folding problem through target structure decomposition and multiobjective evolutionary computation. Appl. Soft Comput. **147**, 110779 (2023)
20. Santana, R., Larrañaga, P., Lozano, J.A.: Side chain placement using estimation of distribution algorithms. Artif. Intell. Med. **39**(1), 49–63 (2007). http://dx.doi.org/10.1016/j.artmed.2006.04.004
21. Santana, R., Larrañaga, P., Lozano, J.A.: Protein folding in simplified models with estimation of distribution algorithms. IEEE Trans. Evol. Comput. **12**(4), 418–438 (2008). https://doi.org/10.1109/TEVC.2007.906095
22. Santana, R.: Gray-box optimization and factorized distribution algorithms: where two worlds collide. CoRR abs/1707.03093 (2017). https://arxiv.org/abs/1707.03093
23. Taneda, A.: MODENA: a multi-objective RNA inverse folding. Adv. Appl. Bioinforma. Chem. **4**, 1–12 (2011)
24. Tang, W.Y., Dai, N., Zhou, T., Mathews, D.H., Huang, L.: Samplingdesign: RNA design via continuous optimization with coupled variables and Monte-Carlo sampling. Nat. Commun. (2026)
25. Wang, S.W., et al.: Current applications and future perspective of CRISPR/Cas9 gene editing in cancer. Mol. Cancer **21**(1), 57 (2022)
26. Ward, M., Courtney, E., Rivas, E.: Fitness functions for RNA structure design. Nucleic Acids Res. **51**(7), e40 (2023)
27. Yang, X., Yoshizoe, K., Taneda, A., Tsuda, K.: RNA inverse folding using Monte Carlo tree search. BMC Bioinform. **18**(1), 468 (2017)
28. Zadeh, J.N., et al.: NUPACK: analysis and design of nucleic acid systems. J. Comput. Chem. **32**(1), 170–173 (2011)
29. Zhou, T., Dai, N., Li, S., Ward, M., Mathews, D.H., Huang, L.: RNA design via structure-aware multifrontier ensemble optimization. Bioinformatics **39**(Supplement_1), i563–i571 (2023)
30. Zuker, M., Stiegler, P.: Optimal computer folding of large RNA sequences using thermodynamics and auxiliary information. Nucleic Acids Res. **9**(1), 133–148 (1981)

# GatGCN: Attention-Driven Graph Convolution for Accurate and Diverse Recommendation

Luigi Sauro(✉) and Carmine Vanacore

D.I.E.T.I., University of Naples Federico II, Naples, Italy
luigi.sauro@unina.it

**Abstract.** Graph Convolutional Networks (GCNs) have achieved state-of-the-art performance in collaborative filtering by modeling high-order connectivity patterns. However, recent advanced baselines like LightGCN++ still rely primarily on static, degree-based weighting schemes, failing to dynamically capture pair-specific affinities and the varying relational importance of neighboring nodes. To bridge this gap, we propose GatGCN, a novel framework that integrates a Graph Attention Network (GAT) mechanism into the structurally enhanced LightGCN++ architecture. By replacing static neighbor aggregation with learnable attention coefficients, GatGCN adaptively weighs local interactions to significantly improve representation quality while preserving optimized layer-wise pooling and decoupled user-item degree scaling. Empirical results demonstrate that GatGCN outperforms state-of-the-art baselines in ranking accuracy, measured by Recall@20 and NDCG@20. Crucially, GatGCN exhibits a decisive advantage in recommendation diversity, increasing Intra-List Diversity (ILD@20) by up to 35% w.r.t. LightGCN++.

## 1 Introduction

In an era of information overload, recommender systems have become essential tools for personalized information filtering [1]. A central technique underlying many of these systems is Collaborative Filtering (CF), which predicts user preferences from historical user–item interactions [12,18,25]. More recently, Graph Convolutional Networks (GCNs) have proven particularly effective for recommendation, achieving state-of-the-art performance by exploiting high-order connectivity patterns. However, early graph-based recommenders largely inherited architectural components from conventional graph classification tasks, including nonlinear activations and feature transformations [21]. Since nodes in collaborative filtering typically do not have rich semantic attributes and are instead represented by one-hot identifiers, these complex operations turned out to be unnecessary or, in some cases, even detrimental.

LightGCN was introduced to overcome these limitations by substantially simplifying the graph convolution process, removing both feature transformations and nonlinear activations. Its design relies only on linear neighborhood


S. Bistarelli et al. (Eds.): AIxIA 2026, LNAI 17131, pp. 586–599, 2027.
https://doi.org/10.1007/978-3-032-40774-0_42

aggregation and a weighted combination of embeddings from different layers, establishing a strong balance between efficiency and recommendation accuracy [9]. Despite its broad adoption, recent analyses have shown that LightGCN can exhibit unexpected rigidity and inconsistency when applied to real-world datasets. In particular, its fixed strategy for embedding norm scaling tends to produce nearly uniform neighbor weights and may introduce inconsistencies across convolutional layers. To address these issues, LightGCN++ was proposed, introducing flexible norm scaling, adjustable layer-wise embedding pooling, and decoupled neighbor weighting to better capture the structural heterogeneity of real-world bipartite graphs [13].

Although LightGCN++ mitigates these structural inconsistencies, its aggregation mechanism still relies primarily on static degree-based weighting. As a result, it cannot dynamically assess the relational importance of different neighbors. In practice, neighboring nodes may contribute unequally to the representation of a central node. Weighting interactions mainly as a function of topological popularity, it may overlook the pair-specific affinities between users and items. To bridge this gap, we propose `GatGCN` (Gat Graph Convolution Network), a novel framework that incorporates a Graph Attention Network mechanism into the enhanced LightGCN++ architecture [20]. By replacing static neighborhood aggregation with learnable attention coefficients, `GatGCN` adaptively assigns importance to neighboring nodes, thereby improving representation quality by emphasizing the most relevant topological interactions.

We evaluate `GatGCN` through an extensive experimental assessment on five benchmark datasets: LastFM, MovieLens-1M, Gowalla, Yelp, and Amazon-Book. The empirical results show that `GatGCN` dominates state-of-the-art baselines in the LastFM and MovieLens-1M test cases, achieving substantial improvements in accuracy as measured by Recall@20 and NDCG@20. In contrast, LightGCN++ still outperforms our approach in fragmented datasets such as Gowalla and Yelp. In addition, `GatGCN` also demonstrates clear advantages in recommendation diversity, increasing Intra-List Diversity (ILD@20) by up to 35% w.r.t. LightGCN++. Finally, a comprehensive design analysis further confirms the role of the attention mechanism in GatGCN. Ablation studies show that adding a standard GAT linear transformation brings negligible gains, while the proposed lightweight attention formulation, the decoupled degree-scaling factors, and the stronger contribution of initial embeddings provide a better accuracy–diversity trade-off. Moreover, even when LightGCN++ is retrained with the same embedding dimensionality, GatGCN remains superior, especially in terms of recommendation diversity.

The paper is structured as follows: Sect. 2 discusses related work on GCNs in the context of recommender systems, Sect. 3 introduces our GCN-based framework `GatGCN`, including its convolution model (including the attention-based aggregation function), the pooling mechanism, and the training process. Section 4 concerns the experiments and design analysis. Conclusions end the paper with final remarks and future works.

## 2 Related Work

Graph convolution pioneered an innovative paradigm for representation learning on graph-structured data. As delineated in the comprehensive survey by Bacciu et al. [2], the primary objective of graph convolution is to generate a representative feature vector for each node through neural networks or Bayesian inference. Typical applications include node classification (i.e. classifying users, papers, or web pages), link prediction in knowledge graphs, and recommender systems.

LightGCN and LightGCN++ has gained widespread acclaim in recommender systems due to its simplicity, omitting feature transformations and non-linear activations [9,13]. Several recent works build directly upon its paradigm. Dual-LightGCN [10] splits user interactions into positive and negative sub-graphs based on a rating threshold, training parallel LightGCN models to subtract disliked items from the final top-$k$ recommendation list. Lee et al. [14] identified that embedding magnitudes decay across consecutive layers and that uniform average pooling causes over-smoothing; they propose introducing a layer-wise scalar multiplication and utilizing only the final layer's output as the definitive embedding. Furthermore, the definition of a node's neighborhood can be expanded beyond immediate topological ties, as demonstrated by MotifGCN [27]. This framework leverages recurring sub-graph patterns (motifs) to capture high-order connectivities and define alternative adjacency matrices for message propagation. UltraGCN [16] represents a radical architectural departure by skipping explicit message-passing entirely. It optimizes a constraint loss function that analytically approximates the convergence of an infinite-layer graph convolution, significantly accelerating training while improving accuracy.

Generally, Graph Convolutional Networks (GCNs) suffer from data sparsity, popularity bias, and interaction noise. To mitigate these vulnerabilities, Wu et al. [22] proposed SGL (Self-supervised Graph Learning), which augments the supervised recommendation objective with an auxiliary contrastive learning task. SGL generates multiple structural views via node/edge dropout and random walks, ensuring the model learns invariant node representations that are robust to noise and popularity bias. NCL extends LightGCN by incorporating neighborhood-enriched contrastive learning [15]. The notion of neighborhood includes both *structural neighbors*, namely nodes connected through high-order paths, and *semantic neighbors*, namely nodes that exhibit feature-level similarity even when they are not directly reachable in the graph. NCL exploits these two forms of neighborhood information to complement the standard BPR loss with additional contrastive learning objectives similar to InfoNCE loss. Another prominent framework extending LightGCN via contrastive learning is XSimGCL [26]. Its predecessor, SimGCL, minimizes an InfoNCE loss using contrastive views generated via structure-based graph dropout; however, constructing these augmented graphs often introduces severe computational bottlenecks. To mitigate this, XSimGCL derives contrastive node representations directly by pairing embeddings across two distinct convolutional layers (typically the final layer and an intermediate one). This architectural shift completely bypasses explicit graph augmentations, preventing the training process from incurring significant computational overhead.

The broader literature has been extensively systematized by Wu et al. [23], who studies GCN-based recommendation systems in different contexts: user-item, sequential, social, and knowledge graph paradigms. Each context requires a specific design in both graph representation and message aggregation and propagation. A more detailed analysis can be found in [6] where Gao et al. provide classified frameworks based on operational objectives (matching vs. ranking) and evaluation dimensions (such as diversity, explainability, fairness). Both surveys emphasize that managing massive real-world graphs remains a critical bottleneck. Addressing this, LightGNN [4] leverages knowledge distillation and adaptive pruning to remove redundant edges and embedding entries, employing a hierarchical framework to compress the model without sacrificing structural information. Finally, industrial scalability is exemplified by PinSage [24], a framework deployed by Pinterest to operate over massive bipartite graphs of pins and boards. To handle the computational challenge of massive node neighborhoods, PinSage introduces a neighborhood selection method driven by random walks and employs a hard negative sampling strategy to refine the model's discriminative capabilities.

## 3 The GatGCN Framework

This section describes the architectural design of the GatGCN model, detailing the implementation of each constituent module. As other GCN methods, we start from a bipartite graph $\mathcal{G} = \langle U, V, E \rangle$, where $U$ and $V$ serves as user and item nodes, respectively, and $E$ is a set of symmetric edges $\{u, v\}$, with $u \in U$ and $v \in V$, representing user-item iterations. The execution pipeline of GatGCN in Fig. 1 can be summarized as follows: each node in $U \cup V$ is initially assigned a trainable parameter vector as its base representation. These initial node embeddings serve as input to the first convolutional layer, which outputs an updated embedding for each node. These representations are sequentially propagated through a stacking of $K$ convolutional layers, where each layer refines a node's embedding by aggregating features from its localized neighborhood. Finally, a pooling function combines the initial embeddings with the representations generated at each intermediate layer to yield the definitive node embeddings. Recommendations are subsequently generated by computing the dot product between these final user and item embeddings to produce personalized rankings.

The integration of a Graph Attention Network (GAT) mechanism into the aggregation phase stems from the limitation of the LightGCN++ graph convolution, which assigns uniform weights to all adjacent nodes. Intuitively, neighboring nodes exert varying degrees of influence on a central node; dynamically weighting these neighbors can significantly enhance representation quality by prioritizing the most relevant topological interactions. Consequently, we incorporate this attentional paradigm to compute the updated representation of each node $i$ from its local neighborhood based on optimally learned weights.

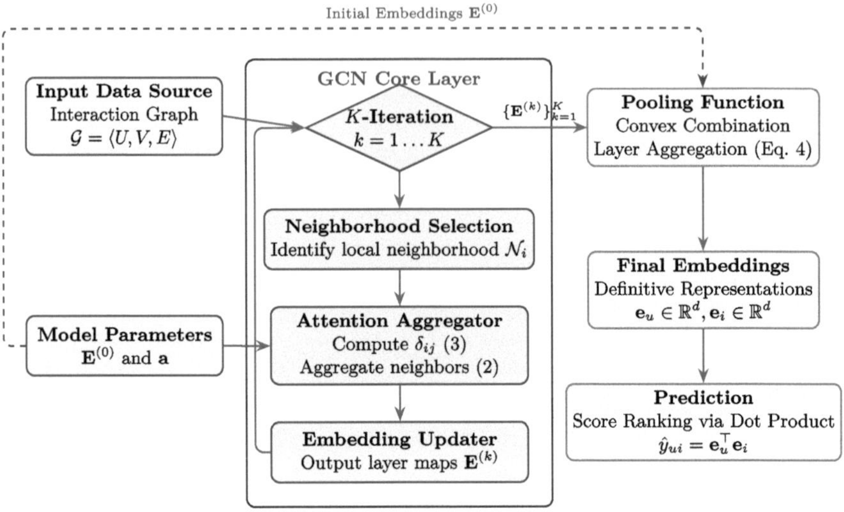


**Fig. 1.** `GatGCN` Model Architecture.

*Convolutional Layer.* The convolutional layer constitutes the core of the framework, operationalizing the attention-driven neighborhood aggregation. In the baseline LightGCN++ architecture, the convolutional propagation rule is formulated as:

$$\mathbf{e}_i^{(k+1)} = \frac{1}{|\mathcal{N}_i|^\alpha} \sum_{j \in \mathcal{N}_i} \frac{1}{|\mathcal{N}_j|^\beta} \frac{\mathbf{e}_j^{(k)}}{\left\| \mathbf{e}_j^{(k)} \right\|} \tag{1}$$

where $\mathbf{e}_i^{(k+1)}$ denotes the embedding of node $i$ at layer $k+1$, $\mathcal{N}_h$ represents the neighborhood set of node $h$, and $\alpha$ and $\beta$ are hyperparameters regulating embedding normalization based on node degrees. This formulation normalizes the previous-layer embeddings of adjacent nodes to unit length, scales them by $\frac{1}{|\mathcal{N}_i|^\alpha \cdot |\mathcal{N}_j|^\beta}$, and computes their sum. Normalizing the embeddings $\mathbf{e}_j^{(k)}$ to a unit norm ensures that scale discrepancies across representations do not disproportionately affect the aggregation.

To incorporate the GAT mechanism, the convolutional update rule in `GatGCN` is modified as follows:

$$\mathbf{e}_i^{(k+1)} = \sum_{j \in \mathcal{N}_i} \frac{\delta_{ij}}{|\mathcal{N}_j|^\beta} \frac{\mathbf{e}_j^{(k)}}{\left\| \mathbf{e}_j^{(k)} \right\|} \tag{2}$$

Compared to Eq. (1), this formulation omits the node-degree normalization term $\frac{1}{|\mathcal{N}_i|^\alpha}$ and introduces the learnable attention weight $\delta_{ij}$ between nodes $i$ and $j$. The factor $\frac{1}{|\mathcal{N}_i|^\alpha}$ was omitted because the attention coefficients $\delta_{ij}$ are normalized via a softmax function (summing to 1 over $j \in \mathcal{N}_i$), inherently providing a localized normalization for node $i$.

Furthermore, we decouple the neighbor scaling hyperparameter $\beta$ into two distinct variables: $\beta_{user}$ when $j$ represents a user, and $\beta_{item}$ when $j$ represents an item. This accounts for structural asymmetries in user-item bipartite graphs, as popular items often possess massive interaction degrees, whereas individual users rarely interact with a comparable volume of items.

The attention coefficient $\delta_{ij}$ is computed as follows:

$$\delta_{ij} = \frac{\exp(\text{LeakyReLU}(\mathbf{a}^\top [\mathbf{e}_i \,\|\, \mathbf{e}_j]))}{\sum_{k \in \mathcal{N}_i} \exp(\text{LeakyReLU}(\mathbf{a}^\top [\mathbf{e}_i \,\|\, \mathbf{e}_k]))} \tag{3}$$

where $\mathbf{a}$ denotes a learnable parameter vector. Following [19], we employ the LeakyReLU activation function with a negative slope of 0.2. This choice prevents the vanishing gradient problem during backpropagation when the input values are negative (a known limitation of the standard ReLU activation), ensuring continuous parameter updates.

*Pooling.* The pooling operation aggregates the intermediate representations to generate the final embeddings used to compute user-item affinity scores. Following LightGCN++ , the final embedding for a given node $i$ is defined:

$$\mathbf{e}_i = \gamma \, \mathbf{e}_i^{(0)} + (1 - \gamma) \, \frac{1}{K} \sum_{k=1}^{K} \mathbf{e}_i^{(k)} \tag{4}$$

where $\gamma \in [0, 1]$ is a balancing hyperparameter and $K$ represents the total number of convolutional layers. The pooling operation corresponds to a convex combination of the initial embeddings ($\mathbf{e}_i^{(0)}$) and the arithmetic mean of the embeddings generated across all sequential convolutional layers.

*Model Training.* The training parameters of `GatGCN` are the initial embeddings $\mathbf{e}_i^{(0)}$ and the vector $\mathbf{a}$ in (3). We adopt the Bayesian Personalized Ranking (BPR) loss [17], utilized by baseline frameworks such as LightGCN [9], LightGCN++ [13], and NGCF [21]. Roughly, the BPR loss encourages the prediction of an observed entry (represented as the dot product $\hat{y}_{ui}$ between a user $u$ embedding and an item $i$ embedding for which $\{u, i\} \in E$) to be higher than its unobserved counterparts. Formally, BPR loss is defined as:

$$L_{\text{BPR}} = -\sum_{u=1}^{M} \sum_{i \in N_u} \sum_{j \notin N_u} \log \sigma(\hat{y}_{ui} - \hat{y}_{uj}) \; + \; \lambda \left\| \mathbf{E}^{(0)} \right\|^2 \tag{5}$$

where $\mathbf{E}^{(0)}$ represents the initial embedding matrix, which encompasses the non-attentional trainable parameters of the model, and $\lambda$ is a $L_2$ regularization coefficient (we use 0.000148 in our framework).

## 4 Experiments

This section details the setup of our experiments and reviews the results that support the effectiveness of `GatGCN`.

**Table 1.** Statistics of the evaluated datasets.

| Dataset | User # | Item # | Interaction # |
|---|---|---|---|
| Gowalla | 29,858 | 40,981 | 1,027,370 |
| Yelp2018 | 31,668 | 38,048 | 1,561,406 |
| Amazon-Book | 52,643 | 91,599 | 2,704,860 |
| LastFM | 1,885 | 17,388 | 91,779 |
| MovieLens-1M | 6,039 | 3,628 | 836,478 |

### 4.1 Experimental Settings

*Datasets.* To ensure a fair comparison, we adopted the exact five benchmark datasets provided and preprocessed by the authors of LightGCN++ [13]:

LastFM [3], MovieLens-1M [8], Gowalla [5], Yelp2018, and Amazon-Book. Table 1 summarizes the dataset statistics.

*Parameter Initialization.* As LightGCN and LightGCN++, we use the the Xavier method [7] to initialize all model parameters. This method samples initial weights uniformly at random over an interval $[-h, h]$, where $h$ is calculated as:

$$h = \text{gain} \times \sqrt{\frac{6}{n_{in} + n_{out}}}, \tag{6}$$

where *gain* is a hyperparameter that we have set to 1 as in [13], whereas $n_{in}$ and $n_{out}$ denote, respectively, the fan-in and fan-out of the parameter tensors. In `GatGCN`, the only model parameters are the base node embeddings $\mathbf{e}_i^{(0)}$ and the projection vectors $\mathbf{a}$ for each convolutional layer. For the base embeddings, $n_{out}$ corresponds to the total number of nodes in the graph, and $n_{in}$ is the embedding dimension. For the attention vectors $\mathbf{a}$, $n_{in}$ equals twice the embedding dimension (due to the concatenation of two embeddings), and $n_{out}$ equals 1.

*Evaluation Metrics.* To evaluate the accuracy of top-$k$ recommendations, we use Recall@$k$ and NDCG@$k$, which are standard ranking metrics widely adopted in baseline frameworks such as NGCF, LightGCN, and LightGCN++ [9,13, 21]. Additionally, we computed ILD@$k$ to assess the diversity of the generated recommendations.

Recall@$k$, NDCG@$k$, and ILD@$k$ are calculated as the average across all users of the following user specific metrics:

*Recall@$k(u)$.* This metric quantifies the fraction of relevant items successfully retrieved in the top-$k$ recommendation list of a user $u$. It is defined as:

$$\text{Recall@}k(u) = \frac{|R(u) \cap Topk(u)|}{|R(u)|} \tag{7}$$

where $R(u) = \{v \in V \mid (u, v) \in E\}$ is the set of items user $u$ interacted with, and $Topk(u)$ is the set of items recommended by the system.

*NDCG@k(u).* Unlike Recall, NDCG accounts for the position of relevant items within the top-$k$ list, assigning higher weights to items ranked at the top. Given the top-$k$ list of a user $u$, let $v_i$ denote the item in position $1 \leq i \leq k$. Then, $rel_i(u) = \mathbb{I}[(u, v_i) \in E]$ is a binary value that yields 1 if $u$ actually interacted with $v_i$, while $rel_i^*(u) = \mathbb{I}[i \leq |R(u)|]$ denotes the ideal relevance. Then, $NDCG@k(u)$ is computed as:

$$\text{NDCG@}k(u) = \frac{\text{DCG@}k(u)}{\text{IDCG@}k(u)} \tag{8}$$

where DCG@$k$ and IDCG@$k$ (Ideal DCG) are formulated as:

$$\text{DCG@}k(u) = \sum_{i=1}^{k} \frac{2^{rel_i(u)} - 1}{\log_2(i+1)} \qquad \text{IDCG@}k(u) = \sum_{i=1}^{k} \frac{2^{rel_i^*(u)} - 1}{\log_2(i+1)}. \tag{9}$$

*ILD@k(u).* Intra-List Diversity evaluates a system's ability to recommend a diverse set of items, avoiding homogeneous suggestions. It is defined as:

$$ILD@k(u) = \frac{1}{k(k-1)} \sum_{\substack{i,j \in Topk(u) \\ j \neq i}} (1 - sim(i,j)) \tag{10}$$

where $sim(i, j)$ represents the cosine similarity between items $i$ and $j$.

*Learning Process.* The original datasets were pre-split into three subsets: a training graph (containing all nodes and 70% of the original interactions) used for learning; a validation graph (all nodes and 10% of interactions) used for model selection based on Recall, NDCG, and ILD metrics; and a test graph (all nodes and the remaining 20% of interactions) used for final evaluation.

Parameter optimization is handled by the Adam optimizer [11], using mimibatch of size 4096, learning rate 0.0031, and a maximum number of epochs equal to 1000.

*Hyperparameter Tuning.* To streamline the optimization, only $\beta_{user}$, $\beta_{item}$, and $\gamma$ were fine-tuned individually for each dataset. The remaining hyperparameters, i.e. the number of convolutional layers and the embedding dimention, were kept fixed across all datasets, as preliminary tests indicated that their optimal values did not fluctuate significantly. More specifically, we followed the prescription of LightGCN and LightGCN++, setting the number $K$ of convolutional layers to 2, this low value is preferred to prevent over-smoothing. However, whereas LightGCN and LightGCN++ set the embedding dimension to 64, we found during our tuning process that GatGCN framework benefits from larger embeddings with size 256.

Similarly to [13], we tuned the remaining parameters $\beta_{user}$, $\beta_{item}$, and $\gamma$ for each dataset, using the Bayesian optimization framework Optuna. The tuning values are shown in Table 2.

**Table 2.** Dataset-specific hyperparameter tuning.

| Hyperparameter | LastFM | MovieLens | Gowalla | Yelp | Amazon-Book |
|---|---|---|---|---|---|
| $\beta_{user}$ | 0.1322 | 0.2423 | −0.4242 | 0.3563 | −0.1552 |
| $\beta_{item}$ | 0.1316 | 0.1201 | 0.1448 | 0.6180 | 0.0491 |
| $\gamma$ | 0.7028 | 0.7471 | 0.4778 | 0.5694 | 0.5653 |

**Table 3.** Performance comparison based on Recall@20 and NDCG@20.

| Dataset | LastFM | | MovieLens | | Gowalla | | Yelp | | Amazon-Book | |
|---|---|---|---|---|---|---|---|---|---|---|
| Metric | Recall | NDCG | Recall | NDCG | Recall | NDCG | Recall | NDCG | Recall | NDCG |
| BPRMF | 0.2014 | 0.1891 | 0.2098 | 0.2692 | 0.1335 | 0.1040 | 0.0367 | 0.0301 | 0.0296 | 0.0223 |
| NeuMF | 0.2182 | 0.2064 | 0.2167 | 0.2737 | 0.1231 | 0.0991 | 0.0375 | 0.0296 | 0.0236 | 0.0178 |
| NGCF | 0.2334 | 0.2190 | 0.2280 | 0.2894 | 0.1364 | 0.1081 | 0.0462 | 0.0369 | 0.0318 | 0.0236 |
| LR-GCCF | 0.1980 | 0.1919 | 0.1651 | 0.2252 | 0.0967 | 0.0829 | 0.0392 | 0.0322 | 0.0167 | 0.0136 |
| HCCF | 0.2242 | 0.2128 | 0.2198 | 0.2881 | 0.1328 | 0.1152 | 0.0627 | 0.0510 | 0.0338 | 0.0256 |
| UltraGCN | 0.2494 | 0.2528 | 0.2551 | 0.3172 | 0.1702 | 0.1408 | 0.0625 | 0.0507 | 0.0367 | 0.0278 |
| LightGCL | 0.2525 | 0.2428 | 0.2344 | 0.2951 | 0.1703 | 0.1425 | 0.0623 | 0.0506 | 0.0418 | 0.0316 |
| ALGCN | 0.2408 | 0.2318 | 0.2404 | 0.3050 | 0.1635 | 0.1376 | 0.0538 | 0.0435 | 0.0349 | 0.0259 |
| AdjNorm | 0.2532 | 0.2434 | 0.2419 | 0.3054 | 0.1635 | 0.1344 | 0.0554 | 0.0448 | 0.0379 | 0.0282 |
| SSM-GNN | 0.2612 | 0.2523 | 0.2515 | 0.3124 | 0.1639 | 0.1380 | 0.0602 | 0.0491 | 0.0373 | 0.0278 |
| LightGCN | 0.2523 | 0.2427 | 0.2392 | 0.3010 | 0.1683 | 0.1426 | 0.0553 | 0.0449 | 0.0367 | 0.0274 |
| LightGCN++ | 0.2715 | 0.2624 | 0.2616 | 0.3275 | 0.1739 | 0.1469 | 0.0650 | 0.0529 | 0.0394 | 0.0294 |
| NCL | 0.2548 | 0.2453 | 0.2401 | 0.3027 | 0.1704 | 0.1430 | 0.0584 | 0.0475 | 0.0393 | 0.0293 |
| NCL++ | 0.2721 | 0.2632 | 0.2621 | 0.3285 | **0.1759** | **0.1478** | **0.0678** | **0.0553** | 0.0424 | 0.0315 |
| SimGCL | 0.2602 | 0.2494 | 0.2584 | 0.3217 | 0.1703 | 0.1424 | 0.0650 | 0.0528 | 0.0415 | 0.0314 |
| SimGCL++ | 0.2723 | 0.2617 | 0.2615 | 0.3276 | 0.1704 | 0.1431 | 0.0657 | 0.0536 | 0.0444 | 0.0334 |
| XSimGCL | 0.2614 | 0.2508 | 0.2600 | 0.3245 | 0.1678 | 0.1400 | 0.0651 | 0.0528 | 0.0397 | 0.0298 |
| XSimGCL++ | 0.2738 | 0.2638 | 0.2613 | 0.3270 | 0.1705 | 0.1432 | 0.0674 | 0.0549 | **0.0454** | **0.0342** |
| `GatGCN` | **0.2946** | **0.2902** | **0.2955** | **0.4122** | 0.1472 | 0.1153 | 0.0583 | 0.0484 | 0.0394 | 0.0298 |
| Impr. | 7% | 9% | 11% | 20% | −16% | −21% | −14% | −12% | −13% | −12% |

## 4.2 Experimental Comparison

In this section, we analyze the results of our experiments, which include a comparison bewteen `GatGCN` and state-of-art methods. To ensure a comprehensive evaluation, `GatGCN` was tested on the same five datasets as LightGCN++. Table 3 presents the Recall@20 and NDCG@20 results reported in [13], alongside the results achieved by `GatGCN` and, in the last row, the relative improvement of `GatGCN` with respect to the best competitor.

Observing the results, `GatGCN` dominates all its competitors in the LastFM test. This superiority is even more pronounced on MovieLens-1M where the relative improvements for Recall@20 and NDCG@20 are 11% and 20%, respectively.

On Amazon-Book GatGCN outperforms by a narrow margin LightGCN++, however it is dominated by SimGCL and its variants. Finally, NCL++ excels on the Gowalla and Yelp datasets, where GatGCN runs after its predecessor LightGCN++.

To give a possible justification to the contrastive performance of our framework, we use UMAP to visualize the embeddings that results from the different datasets (see Fig. 2). The UMAP projections suggest that GatGCN is most effective when user and item embeddings lie on compact and mutually aligned manifolds, as observed in MovieLens-1M and LastFM. In these cases, attention-based aggregation can exploit meaningful local affinity patterns, assigning higher weights to informative neighbors without introducing excessive variance. Conversely, in Gowalla and Yelp, and partially in Amazon-Book, the embedding spaces are more fragmented, with several isolated clusters and weak user-item overlap. Under these conditions, the local softmax attention mechanism may over-emphasize sparse or noisy neighborhood relations, whereas degree-based smoothing appears more robust. This provides a possible explanation for why GatGCN improves ranking accuracy on LastFM and MovieLens but underperforms on the more fragmented datasets.

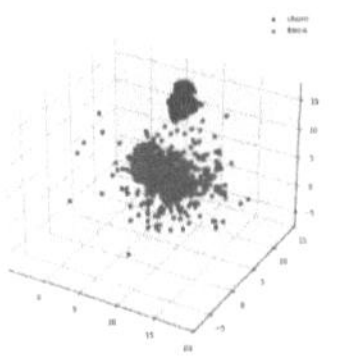

(a) LastFM

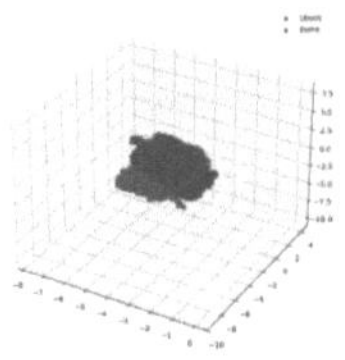

(b) MovieLens-1M

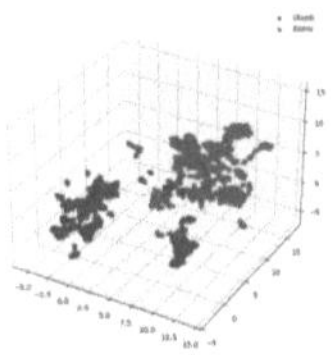

(c) Gowalla

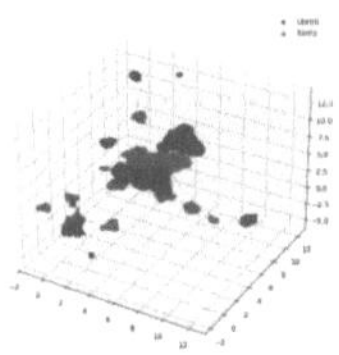

(d) Yelp2018

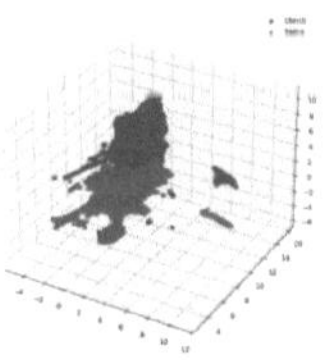

(e) Amazon-Book

**Fig. 2.** Three-dimensional UMAP projections of user and item embeddings produced by GatGCN across the five benchmark datasets. Blue points represent users, while red points represent items. (Color figure online)

We further compared `GatGCN` and its predecessor LightGCN++ using the ILD@20 metric (Table 4). Since [13] did not report ILD values, we re-implemented and trained LightGCN++ under the same conditions to obtain these measurements. `GatGCN` demonstrates decisive superiority in this regard, proving its capability to recommend more diverse items.

**Table 4.** Performance comparison based on ILD@20.

| Dataset | LastFM | MovieLens | Gowalla | Yelp | Amazon-Book |
|---|---|---|---|---|---|
| LightGCN++ | 0.3565 | 0.4581 | 0.3785 | 0.3642 | 0.4402 |
| `GatGCN` | **0.6721** | **0.8994** | **0.4571** | **0.6808** | **0.6198** |

### 4.3 Design Analysis

To dissect the impact of individual structural components, we conducted several ablation studies on the MovieLens-1M dataset. These included: introducing a linear transformation $\mathbf{W}$ in the attention mechanism, utilizing a unified $\beta$ coefficient, heavily reducing $\gamma$, and matching the embedding dimensions between architectures.

`GatGCN` *with Linear Transformation W.* Standard GAT uses a trainable linear transformation matrix $\mathbf{W}$ to project embeddings before computing attention coefficients. `GatGCN` omits this operation. To evaluate its necessity, we temporarily reintroduced $\mathbf{W}$:

$$\delta_{ij} = \frac{\exp(\text{LeakyReLU}(\mathbf{a}^\top [\mathbf{W}\mathbf{e}_i \parallel \mathbf{W}\mathbf{e}_j]))}{\sum_{k \in \mathcal{N}_i} \exp(\text{LeakyReLU}(\mathbf{a}^\top [\mathbf{W}\mathbf{e}_i \parallel \mathbf{W}\mathbf{e}_k]))} \tag{11}$$

Compared to Table 3, the inclusion of $\mathbf{W}$ yielded a negligible performance variance: Recall@20 0.2958, NDCG@20 0.4138, ILD@20 0.8999. Then, given the substantial computational overhead introduced by the additional parameters, we conclude that the transformation matrix $\mathbf{W}$ is unnecessary.

`GatGCN` *with a Unified β.* LightGCN++ employs a single $\beta$ coefficient. To validate the efficacy of decoupling it into $\beta_{user}$ and $\beta_{item}$, we evaluated a unified $\beta$ (the average of the two decoupled values). The decoupled configuration (NDCG 0.4122) performed pretty much the same as the unified one (NDCG 0.4123) on MovieLens-1M, but earlier tests on LastFM showed more pronounced benefits. Consequently, the dual-$\beta$ approach was retained.

*Impact of γ Reduction.* Both LightGCN and LightGCN++ generally use small $\gamma$, shifting the balance toward the aggregated convolutional contribute. Conversely, Optuna suggested higher values for $\gamma$, granting dominant weight to the initial embeddings (see Table 2). To disambiguate this discrepancy we lowered $\gamma$ from

0.74 to 0.2 on MovieLens-1M. This adjustment caused a slight degradation of Recall@20 (about 1%) and NDCG (about 3%). ILD decreased more severely by approximately 25%. This confirms that heavily weighting initial embeddings is more profitable, in particular for diversity.

*LightGCN++ with 256-Dimensional Embeddings.* The original LightGCN++ experiments used an embedding dimension of 64, while GatGCN utilized 256. To isolate the gains provided by the attention mechanism from those provided by higher dimensionality, we retrained LightGCN++ using 256-dimensional embeddings. While scaling the embedding size improved LightGCN++, it remained visibly inferior to GatGCN across all metrics. Specifically, GatGCN retained a +35% advantage in ILD over the scaled LightGCN++. These findings empirically validate that the integration of the attention mechanism drives substantial and genuine improvements in recommendation accuracy and diversity (Table 5).

**Table 5.** Impact of embedding dimensionality between baseline and proposed framework.

| Model | Recall@20 | NDCG@20 | ILD@20 |
|---|---|---|---|
| GatGCN | **0.2955** | **0.4122** | **0.8994** |
| LightGCN++(256) | 0.2893 | 0.3800 | 0.5457 |
| LightGCN++(64) | 0.2616 | 0.3275 | 0.4581 |

## 5 Conclusions

In this work, we introduced GatGCN, a graph-based collaborative filtering framework designed to enhance the LightGCN++ architecture with an attention-driven aggregation mechanism. The core idea behind GatGCN is to move beyond static degree-based neighborhood weighting by allowing the model to learn pair-specific importance coefficients between connected users and items. In this way, the contribution of each neighbor is not determined only by its topological degree, but also by its learned relevance to the target node. This design preserves the lightweight propagation philosophy of LightGCN-style recommenders while introducing a more adaptive mechanism for capturing user–item relations.

The experimental results over five benchmark datasets show that GatGCN is particularly effective on datasets where user and item representations exhibit a compact and well-aligned structure. In particular, GatGCN achieves its strongest improvements on LastFM and MovieLens-1M, where it clearly outperforms the considered baselines in terms of Recall and NDCG. Moreover, the model consistently improves recommendation diversity, as measured by ILD, across all evaluated datasets. This suggests that the attention mechanism is beneficial not only for ranking accuracy in favorable settings, but also for promoting more diverse recommendation lists. At the same time, the results also reveal that `GatGCN` is outperformed by stronger competing methods on datasets such as Gowalla and Yelp2018. The UMAP visualizations suggest that these datasets induce more dispersed embedding structures, where local attention may over-emphasize noisy neighborhood relations rather than producing globally robust representations.

We provide a design analysis aimed at isolating the contribution of the main architectural choices, including the attention mechanism, the decoupled degree-scaling factors, the pooling coefficient, and the embedding dimensionality. This analysis showed that the lightweight attention formulation is the main driver of GatGCN's gains, especially in terms of recommendation diversity.

Future work will focus on better understanding how attention-based graph recommender models can deal with fragmented user–item spaces. Promising directions include cluster-aware propagation, attention regularization, and contrastive learning techniques.

## References


1. Aggarwal, C.C.: Recommender Systems: The Textbook. Springer, Cham (2016)
2. Bacciu, D., Errica, F., Micheli, A., Podda, M.: A gentle introduction to deep learning for graphs. Neural Netw. **129**, 203–221 (2020)
3. Bertin-Mahieux, T., Ellis, D.P.W., Whitman, B., Lamere, P.: The million song dataset. In: Proceedings of the 12th International Conference on Music Information Retrieval (ISMIR 2011) (2011)
4. Chen, G., Xia, L., Huang, C.: LightGNN: simple graph neural network for recommendation. In: Proceedings of the Eighteenth ACM International Conference on Web Search and Data Mining, pp. 549–558 (2025)
5. Cho, E., Myers, S.A., Leskovec, J.: Friendship and mobility: user movement in location-based social networks. In: Proceedings of the 17th ACM SIGKDD International Conference on Knowledge Discovery and Data Mining, pp. 1082–1090 (2011)
6. Gao, C., et al.: A survey of graph neural networks for recommender systems: challenges, methods, and directions. ACM Trans. Recommender Syst. **1**(1), 1–51 (2023)
7. Glorot, X., Bengio, Y.: Understanding the difficulty of training deep feedforward neural networks. In: Proceedings of the Thirteenth International Conference on Artificial Intelligence and Statistics, pp. 249–256. JMLR Workshop and Conference Proceedings (2010)
8. Maxwell Harper, F., Konstan, J.A.: The movielens datasets: history and context. ACM Trans. Interact. Intell. Syst. (TIIS) **5**(4), 1–19 (2015)
9. He, X., Deng, K., Wang, X., Li, Y., Zhang, Y., Wang, M.: LightGCN: simplifying and powering graph convolution network for recommendation. In: Proceedings of the 43rd International ACM SIGIR Conference on Research and Development in Information Retrieval, pp. 639–648 (2020)
10. Huang, W., et al.: Dual-lightgcn: dual light graph convolutional network for discriminative recommendation. Comput. Commun. **204**, 89–100 (2023)
11. Kingma, D.P., Ba, J.: Adam: a method for stochastic optimization. arXiv preprint arXiv:1412.6980 (2014)
12. Koren, Y., Bell, R., Volinsky, C.: Matrix factorization techniques for recommender systems. Computer **42**(8), 30–37 (2009)

13. Lee, G., Kim, K., Shin, K.: Revisiting lightgcn: unexpected inflexibility, inconsistency, and a remedy towards improved recommendation. In: Proceedings of the 18th ACM Conference on Recommender Systems, pp. 957–962 (2024)
14. Lee, S., Ahn, J., Kim, N.: Embedding enhancement method for lightgcn in recommendation information systems. Electronics **13**(12), 2282 (2024)
15. Lin, Z., Tian, C., Hou, Y., Zhao, W.X.: Improving graph collaborative filtering with neighborhood-enriched contrastive learning. In: Laforest, F., et al. (eds.) WWW 2022: The ACM Web Conference 2022, Virtual Event, Lyon, France, 25–29 April 2022, pp. 2320–2329. ACM (2022)
16. Mao, K., Zhu, J., Xiao, X., Lu, B., Wang, Z., He, X.: UltraGCN: ultra simplification of graph convolutional networks for recommendation. In: Proceedings of the 30th ACM International Conference on Information & Knowledge Management, pp. 1253–1262 (2021)
17. Rendle, S., Freudenthaler, C., Gantner, Z., Schmidt-Thieme, L.: BPR: Bayesian personalized ranking from implicit feedback. arXiv preprint arXiv:1205.2618 (2012)
18. Sarwar, B., Karypis, G., Konstan, J., Riedl, J.: Item-based collaborative filtering recommendation algorithms. In: Proceedings of the 10th International Conference on World Wide Web, pp. 285–295 (2001)
19. Veličković, P., Cucurull, G., Casanova, A., Romero, A., Lio, P., Bengio, Y.: Graph attention networks. arXiv preprint arXiv:1710.10903 (2017)
20. Velickovic, P., Cucurull, G., Casanova, A., Romero, A., Liò, P., Bengio, Y.: Graph attention networks. In: 6th International Conference on Learning Representations, ICLR 2018, Vancouver, BC, Canada, 30 April–3 May 2018, Conference Track Proceedings. OpenReview.net (2018)
21. Wang, X., He, X., Wang, M., Feng, F., Chua, T.-S.: Neural graph collaborative filtering. In: Proceedings of the 42nd International ACM SIGIR Conference on Research and Development in Information Retrieval, pp. 165–174 (2019)
22. Wu, J., et al.: Self-supervised graph learning for recommendation. In: Proceedings of the 44th International ACM SIGIR Conference on Research and Development in Information Retrieval, pp. 726–735 (2021)
23. Wu, S., Sun, F., Zhang, W., Xie, X., Cui, B.: Graph neural networks in recommender systems: a survey. ACM Comput. Surv. **55**(5), 1–37 (2022)
24. Ying, R., He, R., Chen, K., Eksombatchai, P., Hamilton, W.L., Leskovec, J.: Graph convolutional neural networks for web-scale recommender systems. In: Proceedings of the 24th ACM SIGKDD International Conference on Knowledge Discovery & Data Mining, pp. 974–983 (2018)
25. Yu, H.-F., Hsieh, C.-J., Si, S., Dhillon, I.: Scalable coordinate descent approaches to parallel matrix factorization for recommender systems. In: 2012 IEEE 12th International Conference on Data Mining, pp. 765–774. IEEE (2012)
26. Yu, J., et al.: XSimGCL: towards extremely simple graph contrastive learning for recommendation. IEEE Trans. Knowl. Data Eng. **36**(2), 913–926 (2024)
27. Zhang, Y., et al.: Improving graph collaborative filtering with network motifs. Neural Comput. Appl. **37**(16), 9413–9432 (2025)

# *Path-Jaccard*: A Logic-Based Similarity Measure for RDF Resources

Verdiana Schena[1(✉)], Simona Colucci[1], Francesco M. Donini[2], and Floriano Scioscia[1]

[1] Polytechnic University of Bari, Bari, Italy
v.schena@phd.poliba.it, {simona.colucci,floriano.scioscia}@poliba.it
[2] University of Tuscia, Viterbo, Italy
donini@unitus.it

**Abstract.** Semantic similarity measures are essential for comparing entities according to the knowledge encoded in a given representation. In RDF knowledge graphs, this task is particularly challenging because resources are described not only by direct features, but also by multi-hop relational structures involving heterogeneous predicates. Existing set-based measures, such as Jaccard similarity, are often applied to direct or shallow descriptions and may therefore miss semantic commonalities emerging at larger graph depths. In this paper, we propose *path-Jaccard*, a logic-based semantic similarity measure for groups of RDF resources. The measure builds on the Jaccard intuition of comparing shared and non-shared descriptions, applying it to RDF path-based descriptions. By relying on the logic-based notion of Common Subsumer of RDF resources which uses blank nodes to denote generic resources, *path-Jaccard* captures both exact shared paths and generalized structural commonalities. We further illustrate one possible application of *path-Jaccard*: assessing whether knowledge graph embeddings reflect semantic similarity in the original knowledge graph. Experiments are conducted on DrugBank (around 3,6M triples) with several embedding models and extended to SemOpenAlex (around 7.7M triples) for a subset of them.

**Keywords:** Similarity Measures · Knowledge Graphs · Knowledge Graph Embeddings · RDF Semantic Similarity

## 1 Introduction

Semantic similarity (SemSim) is a central topic in several domains, supporting applications such as biomedical research [36], ontology matching [6], and information retrieval [39]. It aims to quantify how close two or more entities are according to the knowledge encoded in a given representation. However, there is no single universally accepted SemSim measure [23], since different measures may emphasize different aspects of the underlying representation [46]. This issue is particularly relevant in the analysis of RDF knowledge graphs (KGs), where


S. Bistarelli et al. (Eds.): AIxIA 2026, LNAI 17131, pp. 600–616, 2027.
https://doi.org/10.1007/978-3-032-40774-0_43

resources are described not only by direct features, but also by relational structures involving heterogeneous predicates and paths of varying length. In this paper, we propose *path-Jaccard*, a logic-based SEMSIM measure for groups of RDF resources. The measure builds on Jaccard's intuition of balancing shared and non-shared descriptions, but extends it from shallow feature overlap to RDF path-based descriptions extracted up to a given depth. While previous Jaccard-based approaches have been applied to shallow graph features [14,23] or to sets of terms derived from ontology annotations [36], our approach accounts for richer relational structures encoded in RDF KGs. By relying on Common Subsumers (CSs) computed over RDF resources and by using blank nodes to represent generalized descriptions [15], *path-Jaccard* captures not only semantic commonalities emerging from longer relational structures, but also distinguishes exact shared paths from general structural commonalities. We further illustrate one possible application of *path-Jaccard* to the analysis of knowledge graph embeddings (KGEs). Building on recent studies questioning whether KGEs preserve graph semantics [17,23,25,30,41], we address this problem from the perspective of RDF path-based SEMSIM. Specifically, we use the proposed measure to assess whether geometrically close RDF resources in the embedding space also share coherent path-based descriptions in the original KG.

## 2 Related Work

### 2.1 Semantic Similarity Measures

SEMSIM measures quantify how similar two or more resources are with respect to a given background knowledge. They usually rely on the idea that similarity increases with shared information and decreases with distinguishing aspects. Accordingly, some measures focus mainly on commonalities, while others balance shared and non-shared information [46]. In the context of ontologies and KGs, SEMSIM is usually assessed by exploiting the entities, relations, and descriptive information encoded in the graph. Over the years, several SEMSIM measures have been proposed for these settings. They are commonly [1,21,36] classified into node-based, edge-based, and hybrid approaches. Node-based measures compare node properties or ontology annotations, and include feature-based [24,47] and information-content-based [27,28,37,40] measures. Edge-based measures [38,53] rely on the structure of the ontology, for example by considering path length or the depth of the least common ancestor, while hybrid approaches [33,49] combine both types of evidence. However, many information-content-based and edge-based measures are mainly designed for ontologies organized around taxonomic hierarchical relations. This makes their direct application to RDF KGs less straightforward, since RDF KGs often contain heterogeneous predicates and relational structures that go beyond hierarchical relations. In this context, feature-based measures such as Jaccard similarity [24] provide a flexible alternative. It compares the amount of shared information among resources with respect to the total amount of information considered for them, making it suitable when resources are described by sets of features, annotations, triples or graph-based descriptions. For instance, Jaccard similarity has been applied to taxonomic representations by comparing ontology annotations of resources [36]. It has also been used in RDF KGs to compare local graph features, as in Hubert et al. [23], where similarity is computed over 1-hop and 2-hop neighborhood descriptions.

### 2.2 Semantic Similarity and Knowledge Graph Embeddings

Recent studies [23,25,30,41] question whether knowledge graph embedding models (KGEMs) preserve the semantic encoded in the original KG, arguing that strong link prediction (LP) performance does not necessarily imply that geometric proximity reflects SEMSIM among entities. Jain et al. [25] analyze this issue through classification and clustering tasks, investigating whether entities can be grouped or predicted according to their classes in the embedding space. Their results show that the semantic capability of KGEMs depends on both the model and the dataset. Hubert et al. [23] adopt a pairwise perspective by comparing semantic and geometric $k$-nearest neighbors, using Jaccard over 1-hop and 2-hop entity descriptions and cosine similarity in the embedding space, respectively. Their results show that geometric proximity and LP performance do not necessarily reflect graph-based SEMSIM. Along the same line of research, Schena et al. [41] further investigate this issue by using clustering to inspect the commonalities among geometrically close resources. Their results show that such resources often share only limited information, further questioning whether embedding proximity reliably reflects SEMSIM. Finally, Méroué et al. [30] analyze KGEMs from a stability perspective, showing that standard LP metrics may remain stable across random seeds while hiding substantial variability in individual predictions and in the organization of the embedding space. Their findings further support the need for complementary evaluation perspectives beyond LP performance, especially when KGEs are reused for downstream tasks such as similarity assessment or clustering.

## 3 *Path-Jaccard* Measure

We here define *path-Jaccard*, a logic-based semantic similarity measure that builds on the Jaccard [24] intuition of comparing shared and non-shared descriptions. Recall that the standard Jaccard similarity between two sets $A$ and $B$ is defined as $J(A, B) = |A \cap B| \ / \ |A \cup B|$. We extend this definition to compute *path-Jaccard* over a set $R = \{r_1, \ldots, r_n\}_{n \geq 2}$ of RDF resources to be compared; in Sect. 3.1 we recall past research, and in Sect. 3.2 we introduce our novel definitions. Definitions are accompanied by a running example (Fig. 1) that for simplicity, focuses on two resources, but our definitions naturally apply to sets $R$ of any arity.

### 3.1 Background Definitions

The syntax of RDF-graphs [22] allows IRIs to occur both as names of nodes and as names of arcs (predicates), and previous research [14,15] took this pecu-

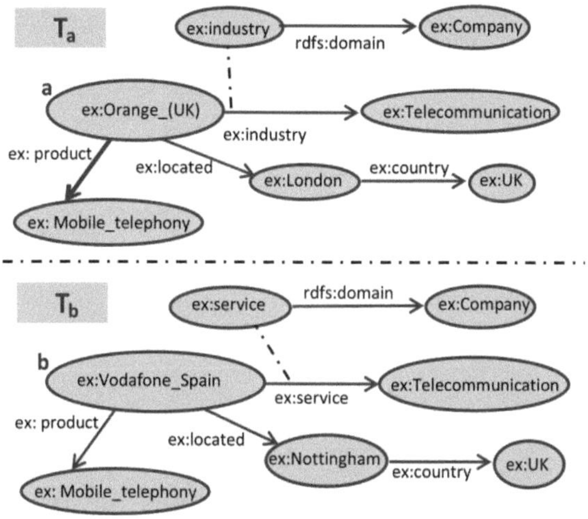


**Fig. 1.** KG of the RDF resources in the running example. To ease readability, in the text, resources `ex:Orange_(UK)` and `ex:Vodafone_(Spain)` are abbreviated as $a$ and $b$.

liarity into account in the definition of connection between resources. For self-containment, we recall those definitions of RDF *-path* and RDF *-connection*, adding here a notion of *length* of an RDF-path.

**Definition 1 (RDF-path, -connection, length).** *Given a set of triples* $T$, *define an* RDF*-path* $P \subseteq T$, *its length, and the resources it connects as:*

- *A resource* $r$ *is always* RDF*-connected to itself by the empty* RDF*-path* $\emptyset$ *of length 0 (independently of* $T$*).*
- *A resource* $r$ *is* RDF*-connected to another resource* $p$ *by an* RDF*-path* $P$ *of length* $n+1$ *if (1)* $r$ *is connected to a resource* $s$ *with an* RDF*-path* $S$ *of length* $n > 0$, *and either (2a) a triple* $\langle s\ p\ t\rangle \in T$ *and* $P = S \cup \langle s\ p\ t\rangle$, *or (2b) a triple* $\langle s\ q\ p\rangle \in T$ *and* $P - S \cup \langle s\ q\ p\rangle$.
- *A* cycle *is a non-empty* RDF*-path that* RDF*-connects a resource* $r$ *to itself.*
- *An* RDF*-path is* simple *if it does not contain cycles for any of the resources in the path.*

*A resource* $r$ *is [simply]* RDF-connected *to a resource* $p$ *in* $T$ *if there is a [simple]* RDF*-path from* $r$ *to* $p$.

From now on, we consider only simple RDF-paths and connections, and we omit to specify the word "simple".

*Example 1.* Considering the resource a (`ex:Orange_(UK)`) in Fig. 1, an example of an RDF path of length 2 rooted in a is:

$$(\langle \texttt{a}, \texttt{ex:located}, \texttt{ex:London}\rangle, \langle \texttt{ex:London}, \texttt{ex:country}, \texttt{ex:UK}\rangle).$$

We say that both `ex:country` and `ex:UK` are connected to a with an RDF-path of length 2. □

Now, we recall the representation of an RDF resource $r$ in terms of its descriptive triples as *rooted-graph* [14].

**Definition 2 (Rooted RDF-Graph (r-graph)).** *A* Rooted RDF-Graph *(*r-graph *for short) is a pair* $\langle r, T_r \rangle$*, where:*

1. $r$ *is either the IRI of a resource, or a blank node*
2. $T_r$ *is a set of* RDF *triples, whose resources are all* RDF*-connected to* $r$.

We now recall entailment between rooted graphs as defined by Colucci *et al.* [14], which is at the basis of our logic-based method for computing commonalities among RDF resources. We denote by $G[x \mapsto y]$ the substitution in a graph $G$ of all occurrences of a resource $x$ with a resource $y$. Next definition is based on Simple Entailment between RDF-graphs $G, H$ denoted by $G \models H$ as usual [34].

**Definition 3 (Rooted Entailment).** *Let* $\langle r, T_r \rangle, \langle s, T_s \rangle$ *be two r-graphs. We say that* $\langle r, T_r \rangle$ entails $\langle s, T_s \rangle$*—denoted by* $\langle r, T_r \rangle \models_{\mathcal{R}} \langle s, T_s \rangle$*—in exactly these cases:*

1. $s$ *is a blank node and either*
   1. $r$ *is not a blank node and* $T_r \models T_s[s \mapsto r]$ *holds; or*
   2. $r$ *is a blank node and, for a new IRI* $u$ *occurring neither in* $T_r$ *nor in* $T_s$, $T_r[r \mapsto u] \models T_s[s \mapsto u]$ *holds;*
2. $s$ *is not a blank node,* $s = r$*, and* $T_r \models T_s$ *holds.*

*In all other cases* $\langle r, T_r \rangle \not\models_{\mathcal{R}} \langle s, T_s \rangle$.

Below we redefine the CS—originally introduced in Description Logics [13]—to meet RDF peculiarities[1]

**Definition 4 (Common Subsumer).** *Let* $\langle a, T_a \rangle$, $\langle b, T_b \rangle$ *be two r-graphs. An r-graph* $\langle x, T_x \rangle$ *is a Common Subsumer of* $\langle a, T_a \rangle$, $\langle b, T_b \rangle$ *iff both* $\langle a, T_a \rangle \models_{\mathcal{R}} \langle x, T_x \rangle$ *and* $\langle b, T_b \rangle \models_{\mathcal{R}} \langle x, T_x \rangle$.

Definition 4 (and the computation of a CS) was directly extended to groups of RDF resources [16]. Intuitively, a CS collects in an r-graph the commonalities of pairs/groups of resources, by abstracting differences with blank nodes[2]. Similar structures were independently proposed by other researchers [3,11]—but not used for SemSim as in this paper—proving the ubiquity of the general idea.

*Example 2.* Considering the resource $\langle a, T_a \rangle$ and $\langle b, T_b \rangle$ in Fig. 1, a CS for them is show in Fig. 2, as an r-graph rooted in the blank node `_:x` □

[1] Actually both the original [13] and the RDF-adapted [14] definitions focused on *the Least* Common Subsumer, which is unique up to logical equivalence, but too detailed to be of use (it can even be composed by all blank nodes). CSs are not unique; however, once an algorithm for computing a CS is fixed (as we do), its uniform application to all sets of resources allows to deterministically compare resources.

[2] A blank node is always denoted by the prefix "`_:`", *e.g.* `_:x`, `_:y`.

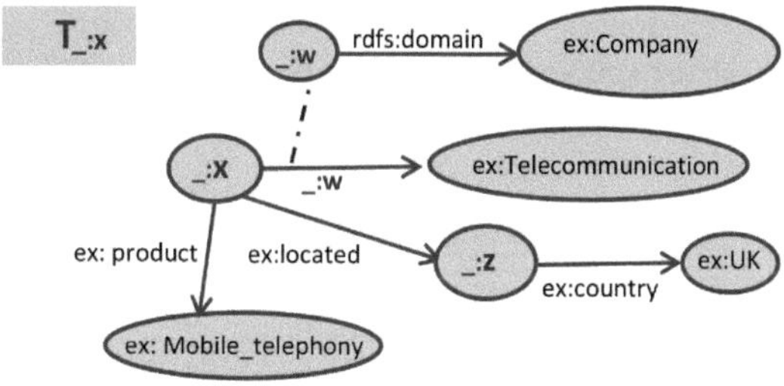


**Fig. 2.** CS of the RDF resources in the running example. Note that blank nodes preserve the structure of the connections, while abstracting different resources.

### 3.2 Novel Definitions

In this work, we need a representation *by path* of r-graphs, defined below.

**Definition 5 (Path-based description of r-graphs).** *Let* $\langle r, T_r\rangle$ *be an r-graph; the path-based description of length d for* $\langle r, T_r\rangle$ *denoted by* $P_d(\langle r, T_r\rangle)$*, is the subset of* RDF*-paths in* $T_r$ *rooted in r, such that no path in* $P_d(\langle r, T_r\rangle)$ *is entirely contained in another path in* $P_d(\langle r, T_r\rangle)$*, and having length at most d. We call* depth *such a maximal length d.*

*Example 3.* Let $\langle a, T_a\rangle$ and $\langle b, T_b\rangle$ denote the two r-graphs in Fig. 1. The RDF path-based description of depth 2 for $\langle a, T_a\rangle$ (with $a=$ `ex:Orange_(UK)`) and $\langle b, T_b\rangle$ (with $b=$`ex:Vodafone_Spain`) is given below, where each RDF-path is enclosed in round parentheses:

$$P_2(\langle a, T_a\rangle) = \{(\langle \texttt{a}, \texttt{ex:industry}, \texttt{ex:Telecommunication}\rangle, \langle \texttt{ex:industry}, \texttt{rdfs:domain}, \texttt{ex:Company}\rangle), (\langle \texttt{a}, \texttt{ex:located}, \texttt{ex:London}\rangle, \langle \texttt{ex:London}, \texttt{ex:country}, \texttt{ex:UK}\rangle), (\langle \texttt{a}, \texttt{ex:product}, \texttt{ex:Mobile\_telephony}\rangle)\}.$$

$$P_2(\langle b, T_b\rangle) = \{(\langle \texttt{b}, \texttt{ex:service}, \texttt{ex:Telecommunication}\rangle, \langle \texttt{ex:service}, \texttt{rdfs:domain}, \texttt{ex:Company}\rangle), (\langle \texttt{b}, \texttt{ex:located}, \texttt{ex:Nottingham}\rangle, \langle \texttt{ex:Nottingham}, \texttt{ex:country}, \texttt{ex:UK}\rangle), (\langle \texttt{b}, \texttt{ex:product}, \texttt{ex:Mobile\_telephony}\rangle)\}.$$

□

We notice that Definition 5 applies to any r-graph, including the ones representing Common Subsumers. For the sake of conciseness, we denote by $P_d(CS(R))$, the path-based description of a $CS$ for the set $R$ up to depth $d$. $|P_d(CS(R))|$ denotes the number of paths in the CS. From now on, we refer to $P_d(CS(R))$ as a non-redundant set, assuming that no path in it is simply entailed by any other path.

*Example 4.* Let $\langle x, T_x \rangle$ denote a CS of the set $R$, including $\langle a, T_a \rangle$ and $\langle b, T_b \rangle$. Here, $T_{\_:\mathtt{x}}$ is the RDF graph describing the commonalities between $T_\mathtt{a}$ and $T_\mathtt{b}$, while `_:x` is a blank node that generalizes the root resources `a` and `b`. Accordingly, $P_2(CS(R))$ is the set of RDF paths occurring in $T_{\_:\mathtt{x}}$:

$$P_2(CS(R)) = \{(\langle \_\mathtt{:x}, \_\mathtt{:w}, \mathtt{ex:Telecommunication} \rangle, \langle \_\mathtt{:w}, \mathtt{rdfs:domain}, \mathtt{ex:Company} \rangle), (\langle \_\mathtt{:x}, \mathtt{ex:located}, \_\mathtt{:z} \rangle, \langle \_\mathtt{:z}, \mathtt{ex:country}, \mathtt{ex:UK} \rangle), (\langle \_\mathtt{:x}, \mathtt{ex:product}, \mathtt{ex:Mobile\_telephony} \rangle).$$

Hence, $CS(R)$ contains three paths, i.e., $|P_2(CS(R))| = 3$. The blank nodes `_:z` and `_:w` denote generalizations introduced by the CS. In particular, `_:z` generalizes the resources `ex:London` and `ex:Nottingham`, occurring respectively in the descriptions of `a` and `b`. Similarly, `_:w` generalizes the properties `ex:industry` and `ex:service`, occurring respectively in the descriptions of `a` and `b`. □

In what follows, we introduce a specific form of union of r-graphs, applied to their path-based descriptions (see Definition 5).

**Definition 6 (Path-based Union of r-graphs).** *Let $R$ be a set of $k$ r-graphs $\langle r_i, T_{r_i} \rangle$ such that $T_{r_i} \neq \emptyset$ for all $i \in \{1, \ldots, k\}$, and let $\sigma$ be a substitution on their path-based descriptions replacing all root nodes with the same new blank node _:y, i.e. $\sigma(P_d(r_i)) = P_d(r_i)[r_i \leftarrow \_:y]$ for all $i \in \{1, \ldots, k\}$. The* path-based union of length $d$ for $R$ *is defined as:*

$$U(R) = \bigcup_{r_i \in R} \sigma(P_d(r_i)). \tag{1}$$

Note that when computing this union, all starting root nodes are substituted by the same blank node `_:y`, so that two paths whose only difference is in their root node are considered equal and added just once in the union. Hence, the cardinality $|U(R)|$ denotes the number of maximal paths occurring in at least one r-graph in $R$, which are distinct but for their root node.

*Example 5.* Let $R = \{\langle a, T_a \rangle, \langle b, T_b \rangle\}$, $P_2(\langle a, T_a \rangle)$ and $P_2(\langle b, T_b \rangle)$ be two path-based descriptions, and the root nodes `a` and `b` be both represented by the blank node `_:y` when computing the union. Therefore, the path-based union of $R$ is:

$$U(R) = P_2(\langle a, T_a \rangle) \cup P_2(\langle b, T_b \rangle) = \{(\langle \_\mathtt{:y}, \mathtt{ex:industry}, \mathtt{ex:Telecommunication} \rangle, \langle \mathtt{ex:industry}, \mathtt{rdfs:domain}, \mathtt{ex:Company} \rangle), (\langle \_\mathtt{:y}, \mathtt{ex:located}, \mathtt{ex:London} \rangle, \langle \mathtt{ex:London}, \mathtt{ex:country}, \mathtt{ex:UK} \rangle), (\langle \_\mathtt{:y}, \mathtt{ex:service}, \mathtt{ex:Telecommunication} \rangle, \langle \mathtt{ex:service}, \mathtt{rdfs:domain}, \mathtt{ex:Company} \rangle), (\langle \_\mathtt{:y}, \mathtt{ex:located}, \mathtt{ex:Nottingham} \rangle, \langle \mathtt{ex:Nottingham}, \mathtt{ex:country}, \mathtt{ex:UK} \rangle), (\langle \_\mathtt{:y}, \mathtt{ex:product}, \mathtt{ex:Mobile\_telephony} \rangle)\}.$$

Hence, the union contains five distinct paths, *i.e.* $|U(R)| = 5$. □

**Definition 7 (Path-Jaccard similarity).** *The path-Jaccard similarity of depth d for the* RDF *resources in a set R is defined as:*

$$PJ_d(R) = \frac{|P_d(CS(R))|}{|U(R)|} \tag{2}$$

*Example 6.* $PJ_2(R) = \frac{|P_2(CS(R))|}{|U(R)|} = \frac{3}{5} = 0.6$ □

*Path-Jaccard* returns a value in the interval $[0, 1]$. A value close to 1 indicates that the resources share most of their path-based descriptions, while a value close to 0 indicates that they have few or no common paths. We notice that $P_2(CS(R))$ in the numerator is always simply entailed by $U(R)$ in the denominator, making Path-Jaccard a logic extension of its standard version. Unlike standard Jaccard similarity computed over shallow features, *path-Jaccard* compares RDF path-based descriptions and can therefore capture commonalities emerging at larger graph depths. A key aspect of the measure is the use of CSs, which capture not only exact path matches, but also generalized commonalities represented through blank nodes. This allows *path-Jaccard* to assign a non-zero score when the compared resources share the same structural pattern, even if entities occurring in the corresponding paths are not identical.

*Example 7.* The path involving `ex:product` and `ex:Mobile_telephony` is an exact commonality, since it occurs in both descriptions after replacing the roots with the blank node `_:x`:

$$(\langle \texttt{\_:x}, \texttt{ex:product}, \texttt{ex:Mobile\_telephony}\rangle).$$

By contrast, the two location paths, for `a` and `b` respectively, are not exactly identical:

$$(\langle \texttt{a}, \texttt{ex:located}, \texttt{ex:London}\rangle, \langle \texttt{ex:London}, \texttt{ex:country}, \texttt{ex:UK}\rangle) \subseteq P_2(\langle a, T_a\rangle)$$
$$(\langle \texttt{b}, \texttt{ex:located}, \texttt{ex:Nottingham}\rangle, \langle \texttt{ex:Nottingham}, \texttt{ex:country}, \texttt{ex:UK}\rangle) \subseteq P_2(\langle b, T_b\rangle)$$

However, the CS computed in *Example 4* generalizes resources `ex:London` and `ex:Nottingham` through the blank node `_:z`, producing the generalized path:

$$(\langle \texttt{\_:x}, \texttt{ex:located}, \texttt{\_:z}\rangle, \langle \texttt{\_:z}, \texttt{ex:country}, \texttt{ex:UK}\rangle).$$

Therefore, these two non-identical paths add 1 to the numerator through their generalized commonality. At the same time, they remain distinct paths in the union, adding 2 to the denominator. As a consequence, *path-Jaccard* rewards their shared structure, but less strongly than if the two paths were exactly identical. Similarly, the paths involving `ex:industry` and `ex:service` are not identical, because they use different predicates. This behavior differs from computing exact path intersection of paths with blank-substituted roots, in which only paths that are identical after root replacement would contribute to the numerator. Applying such exact path intersection to our running example, the only exactly shared path is the one involving `ex:product` and `ex:Mobile_telephony`. The two location paths would not be counted, because they involve different intermediate resources, namely `ex:London` and `ex:Nottingham`. Similarly, the paths involving `ex:industry` and `ex:service` would not be counted, because they use different predicates. Therefore, exact path intersection would have numerator 1 and denominator 5, yielding $\frac{1}{5} = 0.2 < 0.6 = PJ_2(R)$ obtained previously. □

# 4 Application Scenario

This section presents one possible application scenario for the proposed *path-Jaccard* measure. Building on the literature discussed in Sect. 2.2, we consider KGEs as a case study and investigate whether groups of resources that are geometrically close in the embedding space also exhibit semantic coherence in terms of path-based descriptions in the original RDF KG.

## 4.1 Experimental Settings

**Datasets.** We consider two RDF KGs from different domains: *DrugBank*[3] [52], a biomedical KG of 3,649,531 triples, from which we focus on 7,678 drug resources[4], and *SemOpenAlex* [19], a scholarly KG of 7,733,754 triples from which we focus on 4,747 works about *business*.[5]

**Knowledge Graph Embedding Models.** KGEs are generated using PyKEEN [2] (version 1.11.1). For DrugBank, we consider a broad selection of KGEMs: *CrossE* [56], *DistMA* [43], *DistMult* [55], *HolE* [31], *MuRE* [4], *NTN* [44], *PairRE* [12], *ProjE* [42], *RESCAL* [32], *SE* [9], *TorusE* [18], *TransD* [26], *TransE* [8], *TransF* [20], *TransH* [51], *TransR* [29], *TuckER* [5], and *UM* [7]. For SemOpenAlex, due to the larger size of the dataset and the higher computational cost of computing CSs [16] and the subsequent *path-Jaccard* scores, we restrict the analysis to a smaller subset of representative models: *CrossE*, *DistMA*, *PairRE*, *ProjE*, *TorusE*, and *TransD*. This subset ensures heterogeneity by covering the main KGEM families introduced by [50]: *translational-distance-based* (*e.g. TransD*), *semantic information-based* (*e.g. CrossE*), and *neural network-based models*(*e.g. ProjE*). Since, in our setting, KGEs are not evaluated in terms of LP performance, but are used to obtain latent-space representations of the resources, models are trained by splitting both datasets into training, validation, and test sets with a 90%, 5%, and 5% ratio. This choice allows us to use most triples for training, while keeping small validation and test sets required by the PyKEEN pipeline. We also ensure that each entity occurs at least once in every split, so that KGEs can be learned for all resources considered in the evaluation. We fix the random seed to 1 and set the embedding dimensionality to 100, a common choice in the literature [12,26,45,54], providing a reasonable trade-off between expressiveness and computational cost, since both time and space

[3] https://download.bio2rdf.org/#/current/drugbank/.

[4] SPARQL queries are in Supplementary Material (https://doi.org/10.5281/zenodo.21704117), Appendix A.

[5] Version and subset details are provided in Supplementary Material, Appendix B.

requirements depend on this hyperparameter [10]. Unless otherwise specified, all hyperparameters are left at their default values.

**Clustering.** We adopt Hierarchical Agglomerative Clustering[6] with cosine distance and average linkage, keeping all other hyperparameters at their default values. Since cosine distance is used, embeddings are L2-normalized before clustering so that comparisons depend on angular proximity rather than vector magnitude. Average linkage is selected because it considers all pairwise distances between resources in two clusters, providing a balanced criterion for building groups of geometrically close entities. The number of clusters $k$ is selected using the Calinski–Harabasz index over predefined ranges, namely $[80, 570]$ for DrugBank and $[50, 350]$ for SemOpenAlex. These ranges are chosen to avoid both overly coarse partitions, where most resources are grouped into a few large clusters, and overly fragmented partitions, where clusters contain only very few resources. For each resulting cluster, we compute two cohesion measures: geometric cohesion in the embedding space, defined as the mean pairwise cosine similarity among the resources in the cluster, and semantic cohesion, measured by *path-Jaccard*. Hierarchical clustering, the Calinski–Harabasz index, and cosine similarity are computed using the corresponding scikit-learn [35] functions.

***Path-Jaccard* computation.** To compute *path-Jaccard*, for each model and for each of the 10 most geometrically cohesive clusters, we first run SPARQL queries over the datasets to extract the subgraphs rooted in the clustered resources[7]. We then filter out triples considered irrelevant for the comparison, hereafter referred to as *stop-patterns*. From each filtered subgraph, we extract RDF paths up to a maximum depth of 4 and use them to compute the path-based union. For each cluster, we also compute a CS up to the same depth. During CS computation, dataset-specific *uninformative triples* are additionally filtered out, as they are not relevant for characterizing meaningful commonalities[8]. Hardware and implementation details are reported in the Supplementary Material.

### 4.2 Results

Tables 1 and 2 report the *path-Jaccard* scores of the top 10 most geometrically cohesive clusters for each model on DrugBank and SemOpenAlex, respectively. In each row, values are ordered from left to right by decreasing geometric cohesion. Thus, a clear agreement between the embedding space and the RDF graph would correspond to higher *path-Jaccard* scores in the leftmost columns and lower scores toward the right. However, this trend is not generally observed across models and

[6] Clustering is used here to group resources in the latent space under common settings, rather than to optimize performance for each model and dataset.

[7] Resources and CSs used to compute the *path-Jaccard* scores for the 10 most cohesive clusters of each model are reported in the Supplementary Material.

[8] *Stop-patterns* and *uninformative triples* adopted for DrugBank and SemOpenAlex are reported in Supplementary Material, Appendix C and Appendix D, respectively.

datasets. In several cases, the most geometrically cohesive clusters obtain low or even zero *path-Jaccard* scores, suggesting that resources can be close in the latent space without sharing many path-based descriptions in the original RDF graph. On DrugBank, this is especially visible for models such as *DistMA*, *SE*, *NTN*, *PairRE*, *TorusE*, and *UM*, whereas *TransE*, *TransD*, *HolE*, *MuRE*, and *DistMult*, show higher values for some clusters. A similar behavior is observed on SemOpenAlex in Table 2: *DistMA*, *PairRE*, and *TorusE* consistently obtain very low *path-Jaccard* scores, while higher values are reached by *ProjE* and *TransD*, with 0.5556 and 0.8477, respectively. Nevertheless, also in this dataset, scores do not decrease regularly from left to right, indicating that the most geometrically cohesive clusters are not necessarily the most semantically cohesive ones.

**Table 1.** *Path-Jaccard* scores on DrugBank for the top 10 most geometrically cohesive clusters obtained from each KGEM. Columns are ordered from left to right from the most to the least geometrically cohesive cluster among the selected top 10.

| ***Path-Jaccard scores on DrugBank*** | | | | | | | | | | |
|---|---|---|---|---|---|---|---|---|---|---|
| *CrossE* | 0.4348 | 0.0857 | 0.0333 | 0 | 0.0385 | 0 | 0 | 0 | 0 | 0.0175 |
| *DistMA* | 0 | 0 | 0 | 0 | 0 | 0 | 0 | 0 | 0 | 0 |
| *DistMult* | 0 | 0.3333 | 0.0294 | 0.2500 | 0.1053 | 0.5278 | 0.0526 | 0.0270 | 0.0312 | 0.0149 |
| *HolE* | 0.0312 | 0.0066 | 0.2000 | 0.3438 | 0.0238 | 0.3556 | 0.5000 | 0.0500 | 1 | 0.1558 |
| *MuRE* | 0.3056 | 0.0714 | 0.1846 | 0.3125 | 0.0083 | 0.1705 | 0.1000 | 0.5000 | 0.0446 | 0.0244 |
| *NTN* | 0 | 0.0006 | 0 | 0 | 0 | 0 | 0 | 0 | 0.0008 | 0 |
| *PairRE* | 0 | 0 | 0 | 0 | 0 | 0.0008 | 0 | 0 | 0 | 0 |
| *ProjE* | 0.0400 | 0 | 0.0656 | 0.1233 | 0.1000 | 0.0164 | 0.0123 | 0.0294 | 0 | 0.0058 |
| *RESCAL* | 0 | 0 | 0.4030 | 0 | 0.0417 | 0.0204 | 0.1899 | 0.2609 | 0.2000 | 0.0588 |
| *SE* | 0 | 0 | 0 | 0 | 0 | 0 | 0 | 0 | 0 | 0 |
| *TorusE* | 0 | 0 | 0.0005 | 0 | 0 | 0.0004 | 0 | 0 | 0 | 0.0004 |
| *TransD* | 0.3529 | 0.5556 | 0 | 0 | 0.5000 | 0.1964 | 0.0109 | 0.3542 | 0.0147 | 0.1356 |
| *TransE* | 0.0588 | 0.5000 | 0.1728 | 1 | 1 | 0.0213 | 1 | 0.0556 | 0 | 1 |
| *TransF* | 0.0067 | 0 | 0.0022 | 0.0039 | 0 | 0 | 0 | 0 | 0.0015 | 0 |
| *TransH* | 0 | 0.0185 | 0.5000 | 0 | 0.0500 | 0.1250 | 0 | 0 | 0.5000 | - |
| *TransR* | 0 | 0 | 0.3636 | 0 | 0.2979 | 0.0024 | 0.0036 | 0 | 0 | 0 |
| *TuckER* | 0.5000 | 0 | 0.2273 | 0 | 0.1250 | 0.0556 | 0.1176 | 0.0286 | 0 | 0 |
| *UM* | 0 | 0 | 0 | 0 | 0 | 0.0009 | 0 | 0 | 0 | 0 |

Furthermore, the cases where *path-Jaccard* is equal to 1 on DrugBank may initially appear as positive examples, since they indicate that the resources within the cluster share all the path-based descriptions. However, a qualitative inspection suggests a more cautious interpretation: all these clusters contain only two resources, whose common information is limited to the fact that they are described as small molecules with no other characteristic in common. Although this confirms that *path-Jaccard* correctly captures full semantic overlap, these semantically equivalent pairs appear in separate small clusters. This example suggests that the KGEs are poorly distributed, causing the clustering algorithm to produce this kind of partition. A similar behavior can be observed for *TransH*, for which Table 1 reports only 9 clusters out of 10, since the remaining clusters are singletons.

**Table 2.** *Path-Jaccard* scores on SemOpenAlex for the top 10 most geometrically cohesive clusters obtained from each KGEM. Columns are ordered from left to right from the most to the least geometrically cohesive cluster among the selected top 10.

| ***Path-Jaccard scores on SemOpenAlex*** | | | | | | | | | | |
|---|---|---|---|---|---|---|---|---|---|---|
| *CrossE* | 0.0110 | 0.0785 | 0.0075 | 0.0046 | 0.0720 | 0.0152 | 0.2821 | 0.3486 | 0.1070 | 0.0047 |
| *DistMA* | 0.0031 | 0.0030 | 0.0009 | 0.0001 | 0.0018 | 0.0002 | 0.0010 | 0.0003 | 0.0003 | 0.0002 |
| *PairRE* | 0.0475 | 0.0022 | 0.0002 | 0.0029 | 0.0003 | 0.0026 | 0.0019 | 0.0004 | 0.0018 | 0.0001 |
| *ProjE* | 0.3211 | 0.5556 | 0.2481 | 0.1921 | 0.0094 | 0.1509 | 0.0175 | 0.0007 | 0.1773 | 0.0207 |
| *TorusE* | 0.0021 | 0.0005 | 0.0006 | 0.0014 | 0.0004 | 0.0008 | 0.0002 | 0.0003 | 0.0005 | 0.0003 |
| *TransD* | 0.1913 | 0.0137 | 0.2576 | 0.8477 | 0.0019 | 0.2086 | 0.1039 | 0.0725 | 0.0928 | 0.0771 |

To further assess the agreement between geometric cohesion and *path-Jaccard* we conducted a correlation analysis using Kendall's Tau[9]. Since each correlation is computed over only the 10 most geometrically cohesive clusters for each model, the sample size is too small to draw strong statistical conclusions[10]. Accordingly, the only statistically significant cases ($p < 0.05$) are *CrossE* on DrugBank and *ProjE* on SemOpenAlex, with Kendall's Tau values of 0.5292 and 0.5556, respectively. These are also the highest correlation values obtained for the datasets across all models, further indicating that the agreement between geometric and semantic cohesion is limited and model-dependent.

## 5 Conclusion and Future Work

In this work, we introduced *path-Jaccard*, a logic-based SemSim measure for groups of RDF resources. The measure extends Jaccard similarity to RDF path-based descriptions. By relying on the notion of CS, *path-Jaccard* can capture both exact shared paths and generalized structural commonalities represented through blank nodes. We also illustrated one possible use of the measure by analyzing whether resources that are geometrically close in the KGE space share coherent path-based descriptions in the original RDF graph. The

[9] Relying on its SciPy [48] implementation.
[10] Complete similarity and correlation results are in the Supplementary Material.

results on DrugBank and SemOpenAlex show that this agreement is limited and model-dependent. This finding is in line with previous studies that, although from related but different perspectives, question whether geometric proximity in embedding spaces reliably reflects SemSim in the original KG. With respect to such previous studies, our path-based measure is more accurate in considering all long-distance commonalities, and still suggests that KGEMs should be used with caution in SemSim tasks, especially when similarity is expected to reflect explicit graph-based descriptions. As future work, we plan to extend the evaluation to all clusters produced by the considered models, to obtain a broader view of the alignment between geometric and semantic cohesion and to extend to user-defined weights as is possible for standard Jaccard similarity.

**Acknowledgments.** This work is co-funded by the Italian aerospace technological district "Distretto Tecnologico Aerospaziale S.C.a.r.l." and by project "LIFE: the itaLian system wIde Frailty nEtwork" founded by Ministry of Health (CUP D93C22000640001).

## References

1. Adhikari, A., Dutta, B., Dutta, A.: Finding most informative common ancestor in cross-ontological semantic similarity assessment: an intrinsic information content-based approach. Expert Syst. Appl. **192**, 116281 (2022). https://doi.org/10.1016/j.eswa.2021.116281
2. Ali, M., et al.: PyKEEN 1.0: a Python library for training and evaluating knowledge graph embeddings. J. Mach. Learn. Res. **22**(1) (2021)
3. Amendola, G., Manna, M., Ricioppo, A.: A logic-based framework for characterizing nexus of similarity within knowledge bases. Inf. Sci. **664** (2024). https://doi.org/10.1016/j.ins.2024.120331
4. Balažević, I., Allen, C., Hospedales, T.: Multi-relational Poincaré Graph Embeddings. Curran Associates Inc., Red Hook (2019)
5. Balazevic, I., Allen, C., Hospedales, T.: TuckER: tensor factorization for knowledge graph completion. In: Inui, K., Jiang, J., Ng, V., Wan, X. (eds.) Proceedings of the 2019 Conference on Empirical Methods in Natural Language Processing and the 9th International Joint Conference on Natural Language Processing (EMNLP-IJCNLP), pp. 5185–5194. Association for Computational Linguistics, Hong Kong, China (2019). https://doi.org/10.18653/v1/D19-1522
6. Banerjee, S., Chakravarthi, B.R., McCrae, J.P.: Cross-lingual ontology matching using structural and semantic similarity. In: Chiarcos, C., et al. (eds.) Proceedings of the 9th Workshop on Linked Data in Linguistics @ LREC-COLING 2024, pp. 11–21. ELRA and ICCL, Torino, Italia (2024)
7. Bordes, A., Glorot, X., Weston, J., Bengio, Y.: A semantic matching energy function for learning with multi-relational data. Mach. Learn. **94**(2), 233–259 (2014). https://doi.org/10.1007/s10994-013-5363-6
8. Bordes, A., Usunier, N., Garcia-Durán, A., Weston, J., Yakhnenko, O.: Translating embeddings for modeling multi-relational data. In: Proceedings of the 27th International Conference on Neural Information Processing System, NIPS 2013, vol. 2, pp. 2787–2795. Curran Associates Inc., Red Hook (2013)

9. Bordes, A., Weston, J., Collobert, R., Bengio, Y.: Learning structured embeddings of knowledge bases. In: Proceedings of the Twenty-Fifth AAAI Conference on Artificial Intelligence, AAAI 2011, pp. 301–306. AAAI Press (2011)
10. Cao, J., Fang, J., Meng, Z., Liang, S.: Knowledge graph embedding: a survey from the perspective of representation spaces. ACM Comput. Surv. **56**(6) (2024). https://doi.org/10.1145/3643806
11. Cebiric, S., Goasdoué, F., Manolescu, I.: Query-oriented summarization of RDF graphs. Proc. VLDB Endow. **8**(12), 2012–2015 (2015)
12. Chao, L., He, J., Wang, T., Chu, W.: PairRE: knowledge graph embeddings via paired relation vectors. In: Zong, C., Xia, F., Li, W., Navigli, R. (eds.) Proceedings of the 59th Annual Meeting of the Association for Computational Linguistics and the 11th International Joint Conference on Natural Language Processing (Volume 1: Long Papers), pp. 4360–4369. Association for Computational Linguistics, Online (2021). https://doi.org/10.18653/v1/2021.acl-long.336
13. Cohen, W.W., Borgida, A., Hirsh, H.: Computing least common subsumers in description logics. In: Swartout, W.R. (ed.) Proceedings of the 10th National Conference on Artificial Intelligence, San Jose, CA, USA, 12–16 July 1992, pp. 754–760. AAAI Press/The MIT Press (1992)
14. Colucci, S., Donini, F., Giannini, S., Di Sciascio, E.: Defining and computing least common subsumers in RDF. Web Semant. **39**(C), 62–80 (2016). https://doi.org/10.1016/j.websem.2016.02.001
15. Colucci, S., Donini, F.M., Di Sciascio, E.: Common subsumbers in RDF. In: Baldoni, M., Baroglio, C., Boella, G., Micalizio, R. (eds.) AI*IA 2013: Advances in Artificial Intelligence, pp. 348–359. Springer, Cham (2013)
16. Colucci, S., Donini, F.M., Di Sciascio, E.: Computing the commonalities of clusters in resource description framework: computational aspects. Data **9**(10) (2024). https://doi.org/10.3390/data9100121
17. Domingues, A., Jain, N., Peñuela, A.M., Simperl, E.: Bringing back semantics to knowledge graph embeddings: an interpretability approach. In: Besold, T.R., d'Avila Garcez, A., Jimenez-Ruiz, E., Confalonieri, R., Madhyastha, P., Wagner, B. (eds.) Neural-Symbolic Learning and Reasoning, pp. 192–203. Springer, Cham (2024)
18. Ebisu, T., Ichise, R.: Toruse: knowledge graph embedding on a lie group. In: Proceedings of the Thirty-Second AAAI Conference on Artificial Intelligence and Thirtieth Innovative Applications of Artificial Intelligence Conference and Eighth AAAI Symposium on Educational Advances in Artificial Intelligence, AAAI 2018/IAAI 2018/EAAI 2018. AAAI Press (2018)
19. Färber, M., Lamprecht, D., Krause, J., Aung, L., Haase, P.: SemOpenAlex: the scientific landscape in 26 billion RDF triples. In: The Semantic Web - ISWC 2023: 22nd International Semantic Web Conference. Athens, Greece, 6–10 November 2023, Proceedings, Part II, pp. 94–112. Springer, Heidelberg (2023)
20. Feng, J., Huang, M., Wang, M., Zhou, M., Hao, Y., Zhu, X.: Knowledge graph embedding by flexible translation. In: Proceedings of the Fifteenth International Conference on Principles of Knowledge Representation and Reasoning, KR 2016, pp. 557–560. AAAI Press (2016)
21. Harispe, S., Sánchez, D., Ranwez, S., Janaqi, S., Montmain, J.: A framework for unifying ontology-based semantic similarity measures: a study in the biomedical domain. J. Biomed. Inform. **48**, 38–53 (2014). https://doi.org/10.1016/j.jbi.2013.11.006

22. Hartig, O., Champin, P.A., Kellogg, G., Seaborne, A.: RDF 1.2 concepts and abstract syntax, w3c working draft (2024). https://www.w3.org/TR/rdf12-concepts/
23. Hubert, N., Paulheim, H., Brun, A., Monticolo, D.: Do similar entities have similar embeddings? In: Meroño Peñuela, A., et al. (eds.) The Semantic Web, pp. 3–21. Springer, Cham (2024)
24. Jaccard, P.: Distribution de la flore alpine dans le bassin des dranses et dans quelques régions voisines. Bull. Soc. Vaudoise Sci. Nat. **37**, 241–272 (1901)
25. Jain, N., Kalo, J.C., Balke, W.T., Krestel, R.: Do embeddings actually capture knowledge graph semantics? In: Verborgh, R., et al. (eds.) The Semantic Web, pp. 143–159. Springer, Cham (2021)
26. Ji, G., He, S., Xu, L., Liu, K., Zhao, J.: Knowledge graph embedding via dynamic mapping matrix. In: Zong, C., Strube, M. (eds.) Proceedings of the 53rd Annual Meeting of the Association for Computational Linguistics and the 7th International Joint Conference on Natural Language Processing (Volume 1: Long Papers), pp. 687–696. Association for Computational Linguistics, Beijing, China (2015). https://doi.org/10.3115/v1/P15-1067
27. Jiang, J.J., Conrath, D.W.: Semantic similarity based on corpus statistics and lexical taxonomy. In: Chen, K.J., Huang, C.R., Sproat, R. (eds.) Proceedings of the 10th Research on Computational Linguistics International Conference, pp. 19–33. The Association for Computational Linguistics and Chinese Language Processing (ACLCLP), Taipei, Taiwan (1997)
28. Lin, D.: An information-theoretic definition of similarity. In: Proceedings of the Fifteenth International Conference on Machine Learning, ICML 1998, pp. 296–304. Morgan Kaufmann Publishers Inc., San Francisco (1998)
29. Lin, Y., Liu, Z., Sun, M., Liu, Y., Zhu, X.: Learning entity and relation embeddings for knowledge graph completion. In: Proceedings of the Twenty-Ninth AAAI Conference on Artificial Intelligence, AAAI 2015, pp. 2181–2187. AAAI Press (2015)
30. Méroué, G., Gandon, F., Monnin, P.: Link prediction or perdition: the seeds of instability in knowledge graph embeddings. In: Acosta, M., et al. (eds.) The Semantic Web, pp. 198–216. Springer, Cham (2026)
31. Nickel, M., Rosasco, L., Poggio, T.: Holographic embeddings of knowledge graphs. In: Proceedings of the Thirtieth AAAI Conference on Artificial Intelligence, AAAI 2016, pp. 1955–1961. AAAI Press (2016)
32. Nickel, M., Tresp, V., Kriegel, H.P.: A three-way model for collective learning on multi-relational data. In: Proceedings of the 28th International Conference on International Conference on Machine Learning, ICML 2011, pp. 809–816, Omnipress, Madison, WI, USA (2011)
33. Othman, R.M., Deris, S.B., Illias, R.M.: A genetic similarity algorithm for searching the gene ontology terms and annotating anonymous protein sequences. J. Biomed. Inform. **41**(1), 65–81 (2008)
34. Patel-Schneider, P., Arndt, D., Haudebourg, T.: RDF 1.2 semantics, W3C recommendation (2023). https://www.w3.org/TR/rdf12-semantics/
35. Pedregosa, F., et al.: Scikit-learn: machine learning in Python. J. Mach. Learn. Res. **12**, 2825–2830 (2011)
36. Pesquita, C., Faria, D., Falcão, A.O., Lord, P., Couto, F.M.: Semantic similarity in biomedical ontologies. PLOS Comput. Biol. **5**(7), 1–12 (2009). https://doi.org/10.1371/journal.pcbi.1000443
37. Pirró, G., Euzenat, J.: A feature and information theoretic framework for semantic similarity and relatedness. In: Patel-Schneider, P.F., et al. (eds.) The Semantic Web - ISWC 2010, pp. 615–630. Springer, Heidelberg (2010)

38. Rada, R., Mili, H., Bicknell, E., Blettner, M.: Development and application of a metric on semantic nets. IEEE Trans. Syst. Man Cybern. **19**(1), 17–30 (1989). https://doi.org/10.1109/21.24528
39. Rathee, P., Malik, S.K.: An analysis of semantic similarity measures for information retrieval. In: Dutta, P., Bhattacharya, A., Dutta, S., Lai, W.C. (eds.) Emerging Technologies in Data Mining and Information Security, pp. 665–673. Springer, Singapore (2023)
40. Resnik, P.: Using information content to evaluate semantic similarity in a taxonomy. In: Proceedings of the 14th International Joint Conference on Artificial Intelligence, IJCAI 1995, vol. 1, pp. 448–453. Morgan Kaufmann Publishers Inc., San Francisco, CA, USA (1995)
41. Schena, V., Colucci, S., Scioscia, F., Donini, F.M.: Human-in-the-loop refinement of knowledge graph embeddings for semantic similarity. In: Camarinha-Matos, L.M., Ferrada, F. (eds.) Technological Innovation to Tackle Societal Challenges, pp. 358–369. Springer, Cham (2027)
42. Shi, B., Weninger, T.: Proje: embedding projection for knowledge graph completion. In: Proceedings of the Thirty-First AAAI Conference on Artificial Intelligence, AAAI 2017, pp. 1236–1242. AAAI Press (2017)
43. Shi, X., Xiao, Y.: Modeling multi-mapping relations for precise cross-lingual entity alignment. In: Inui, K., Jiang, J., Ng, V., Wan, X. (eds.) Proceedings of the 2019 Conference on Empirical Methods in Natural Language Processing and the 9th International Joint Conference on Natural Language Processing (EMNLP-IJCNLP), pp. 813–822. Association for Computational Linguistics, Hong Kong, China (2019). https://doi.org/10.18653/v1/D19-1075
44. Socher, R., et al.: Reasoning with neural tensor networks for knowledge base completion. In: Weinberger, K. (ed.) Advances in Neural Information Processing Systems, vol. 26. Curran Associates, Inc. (2013)
45. Socher, R., et al.: Reasoning with neural tensor networks for knowledge base completion. In: Weinberger, K. (ed.) Advances in Neural Information Processing Systems, NeurIPS 2013, vol. 26. Curran Associates, Inc. (2013)
46. Szmeja, P., Ganzha, M., Paprzycki, M., Pawłowski, W.: Dimensions of semantic similarity. In: Gawęda, A.E., Kacprzyk, J., Rutkowski, L., Yen, G.G. (eds.) Advances in Data Analysis with Computational Intelligence Methods. SCI, vol. 738, pp. 87–125. Springer, Cham (2018). https://doi.org/10.1007/978-3-319-67946-4_3
47. Tversky, A.: Features of similarity. Psychol. Rev. **84**(4), 327–352 (1977). https://doi.org/10.1037/0033-295X.84.4.327
48. Virtanen, P., et al.: Fundamental algorithms for scientific computing in Python. Nat. Methods **17**, 261–272 (2020). https://doi.org/10.1038/s41592-019-0686-2
49. Wang, J.Z., Du, Z., Payattakool, R., Yu, P.S., Chen, C.F.: A new method to measure the semantic similarity of go terms. Bioinformatics **23**(10), 1274–81 (2007)
50. Wang, M., Qiu, L., Wang, X.: A survey on knowledge graph embeddings for link prediction. Symmetry **13**(3) (2021). https://doi.org/10.3390/sym13030485
51. Wang, Z., Zhang, J., Feng, J., Chen, Z.: Knowledge graph embedding by translating on hyperplanes. In: Proceedings of the Twenty-Eighth AAAI Conference on Artificial Intelligence, AAAI 2014, pp. 1112–1119. AAAI Press (2014)
52. Wishart, D.S., et al.: DrugBank: a comprehensive resource for in silico drug discovery and exploration. Nucleic Acids Res. **34**(suppl_1), D668–D672 (2006)
53. Wu, Z., Palmer, M.: Verb semantics and lexical selection. In: 32nd Annual Meeting of the Association for Computational Linguistics, pp. 133–138. Association for

Computational Linguistics, Las Cruces, New Mexico, USA (1994). https://doi.org/10.3115/981732.981751
54. Yang, B., Yih, W., He, X., Gao, J., Deng, L.: Embedding entities and relations for learning and inference in knowledge bases. In: International Conference on Learning Representations (2014)
55. Yang, B., Yih, W., He, X., Gao, J., Deng, L.: Embedding entities and relations for learning and inference in knowledge bases (2015)
56. Zhang, W., Paudel, B., Zhang, W., Bernstein, A., Chen, H.: Interaction embeddings for prediction and explanation in knowledge graphs. In: Proceedings of the Twelfth ACM International Conference on Web Search and Data Mining, WSDM 2019, pp. 96–104. Association for Computing Machinery, New York (2019). https://doi.org/10.1145/3289600.3291014

# Rotary Informational Embeddings for Symbolic Music Generation

Felix Schön(✉) and Hans Tompits

Institute of Logic and Computation E192-03, Technische Universität Wien, Favoritenstraße 9–11, 1040 Vienna, Austria
felix.schoen@alumni.tuwien.ac.at, tompits@kr.tuwien.ac.at

**Abstract.** Rotary positional embeddings (RoPE) encode relative token position through rotations, but do not directly account for other discrete attributes of structured data. We introduce *rotary informational embeddings* (RotIE), a RoPE generalisation that rotates query and key components according to integer-valued musical attributes such as pitch, absolute time, and intra-bar position. We define four assignment strategies and evaluate them for Transformer-based symbolic music generation on the Lakh MIDI and POP909 datasets. RotIE improves perplexity over RoPE in several settings without additional learned parameters and with negligible runtime overhead in our matched benchmark, while distributional and user-study analyses suggest that musical quality is retained.

**Keywords:** Attention · RoPE · Symbolic Music Generation

## 1 Introduction

Since the introduction of the *Transformer* architecture by Vaswani et al. [20], the field of machine learning has undergone a profound shift, impacting a wide variety of fields, including, e.g., natural language processing (NLP) [3,4,12] and computer vision [5,9].

At the heart of the Transformer architecture lies the *attention module* [1,20], which computes similarity scores between pairs of vector representations of input tokens. Here, degrees of influence of source tokens are assigned to a current sequence representation. As shown by Shaw et al. [17], adding learned terms based on the relative distances between positions of tokens to this influence matrix can positively impact the performance of a model. Huang et al. [6] improved upon this concept, greatly reducing its computational requirements, and applied it to the task of *symbolic music generation*. In this field, music is represented using discrete tokens, which can mark, e.g., the start and end of a

A preliminary version of this work appeared as an extended abstract in the proceedings of the 39th Canadian Conference on Artificial Intelligence (Canadian AI 2026) [16]. The current paper substantially extends it with the complete RotIE framework, all four assignment strategies, imputation, and additional evaluations.


S. Bistarelli et al. (Eds.): AIxIA 2026, LNAI 17131, pp. 617–630, 2027.
https://doi.org/10.1007/978-3-032-40774-0_44

note. As in the broader machine-learning domain, Transformer-based approaches have shown particular promise for this application [8,10,11,19,22].

Recently, Su et al. [18] introduced a multiplicative approach for relative attention in the form of the *rotary positional embedding* (RoPE) architecture and realised it within the RoFormer system. Here, absolute token positions are encoded using rotations of subvectors such that the inner product of two such vectors is dependent on the difference of their encoded positions. While RoPE has seen wide adoption across various domains [2], it remains fundamentally limited to encoding a single type of information: sequential token positions. However, in structured domains such as music, tokens carry rich semantic attributes beyond their position, e.g., a note has a pitch, occurs at a specific point in time, and occupies a position within a bar. Existing approaches either ignore these attributes in the attention mechanism or require additional learned embeddings, thereby increasing model complexity.

In this paper, we address this limitation by extending RoPE to handle arbitrary integer-valued information. We introduce *rotary informational embeddings* (RotIE), a generalisation of rotary embeddings that allows encoding multiple types of information such as pitch values, temporal positions, or intra-bar timings directly into the attention computation. Here, RotIE preserves the efficiency of RoPE by encoding information through rotations rather than learned embeddings. The approach thus incurs no need for additional learned parameters and, in our matched benchmark, adds only negligible runtime overhead relative to RoPE. As a result, the attention mechanism becomes dependent not only on relative token positions but also on relative differences in the embedded musical attributes.

We provide a general description of our RotIE approach and introduce four concrete strategies for applying rotary informational embeddings. A key advantage of RotIE over RoPE is the ability to include an arbitrary number of different information types in the same attention step, enabling the model to jointly consider multiple musical dimensions. In particular, we introduce

(i) a *per-layer approach*, which uses a single type of information per Transformer layer,
(ii) a *per-head approach*, which uses different information per attention head,
(iii) a *consecutive pairwise approach*, where each head includes all types of information consecutively, and
(iv) an *interleaved pairwise approach*, which interleaves information throughout the embedded vectors.

In an experimental evaluation, we trained a number of Transformer models making use of the different strategies of our RotIE approach and compared them to a regular Transformer, the Music Transformer [6], and a RoFormer baseline [18]. Here, our models show promise, with many outperforming the baselines on perplexity with statistical significance. To complement the perplexity evaluation, we conducted a distributional analysis comparing the statistical properties of generated music to ground truth data. This analysis suggests that RotIE variants better capture the analysed distributions, achieving the smallest distances across all four metrics. Furthermore, we conducted an exploratory small-scale user study which suggests that perceived musical quality is retained alongside the objective improvements.

The paper is organised as follows. In Sect. 2, we recapitulate the basics of the attention mechanism and conventional rotary positional embeddings. Section 3 introduces our general RotIE approach along with four specific strategies. The results of our experiments are outlined in Sect. 4, where we also discuss the advantages of including RotIE in a musical context. Finally, the paper concludes with a brief summary in Sect. 5.

## 2 Background

Unless stated otherwise, all indices used throughout this paper are zero-based. That is, the first element of an indexed object has index 0, and an indexed object of length $d$ has indices $\{0, \ldots, d-1\}$.

### 2.1 Scaled Dot-Product Attention

At the heart of the Transformer [20] lies the *scaled dot-product attention* mechanism, which computes similarity scores between query and key representations and uses the resulting weights to combine values. Given query and key matrices $Q, K \in \mathbb{R}^{l_{seq} \times d_k}$ and a value matrix $V \in \mathbb{R}^{l_{seq} \times d_v}$, scaled dot-product attention is defined as follows:

$$sdpa(Q, K, V) := softmax\Big(\frac{1}{\sqrt{d_k}} QK^\intercal\Big)V. \tag{1}$$

Here, $l_{seq}$ is the sequence length, $d_k$ is the query/key dimensionality, and $d_v$ is the value dimensionality. In multi-head attention, $Q$ and $K$ are split into $n_{head}$ equally sized head matrices $Q^h$ and $K^h$, where $0 \leq h < n_{head}$, with dimensionality $d_{head} = d_k / n_{head}$. The value matrix $V$ is split analogously into matrices $V^h$ with value-head dimensionality $d_v / n_{head}$. Each head performs attention in parallel, and the resulting head outputs are concatenated and projected back to the model dimension.

For the remainder of the paper, we use bracket notation to avoid ambiguity between names and indices: $v_{[i]}$ denotes a scalar element of a vector, $M_{[i,j]}$ denotes a scalar element of a matrix, $M_{[i]}$ denotes the row vector at index $i$, and $Q^h_{[i,2k]}$ denotes the corresponding scalar in the $h$th attention head. Moreover, we use "$\|$" for vector concatenation. Batching and causal masking are applied in the implementation but omitted from the notation.

### 2.2 Rotary Positional Embedding

Following the introduction of *additive relative attention* by Shaw et al. [17], relative-attention mechanisms have been widely used for Transformer-based symbolic music generation. Such approaches modify the attention computation by adding scores derived from relative token positions. For example, Huang et al. [6] reformulated scaled dot-product attention as follows:

$$sdpa_{adrel}(Q, K, V, S) := softmax\Big(\frac{QK^{\intercal} + S}{\sqrt{d_k}}\Big)V,$$

where $S \in \mathbb{R}^{l_{seq} \times l_{seq}}$ contains relative positional scores depending on token-position differences.

In contrast to these additive approaches, Su et al. [18] introduced *rotary position embeddings* (RoPE), a multiplicative mechanism for relative positional information. Let $v = (v_{[0]}, v_{[1]})$ be a vector, $s$ a position to encode, and $\theta$ a predefined rotation parameter. Then, the rotary positional embedding is defined as follows:

$$RoPE(v, s, \theta) := \begin{pmatrix} \cos(s\theta) & -\sin(s\theta) \\ \sin(s\theta) & \cos(s\theta) \end{pmatrix} \begin{pmatrix} v_{[0]} \\ v_{[1]} \end{pmatrix}.$$

This operation rotates $v$ by the angle $s\theta$. For two vectors rotated with the same $\theta$, their inner product depends on the difference between the encoded values:

$$\langle RoPE(u, s, \theta), RoPE(v, t, \theta)\rangle = \langle RoPE(u, 0, \theta), RoPE(v, t - s, \theta)\rangle.$$

We refer to Su et al. [18] for the full derivation.

By applying this procedure to consecutive pairs of query and key values, RoPE makes the attention score between positions $s$ and $t$ depend on the relative position $(t - s)$. For an even query/key dimension $d$, let

$$\Theta_d = (\theta_0, \ldots, \theta_{d/2-1}), \text{ with } \theta_k = 10000^{-2k/d}.$$

An auxiliary *rotate* function can be used to apply RoPE to all consecutive pairs of an input matrix $M$:

$$rotate(M, \Theta_d) := \begin{pmatrix} \|_{k=0}^{d/2-1} RoPE((M_{[0,2k]}, M_{[0,2k+1]}), 0, \theta_k) \\ \vdots \\ \|_{k=0}^{d/2-1} RoPE((M_{[l_{seq}-1,2k]}, M_{[l_{seq}-1,2k+1]}), l_{seq} - 1, \theta_k) \end{pmatrix}.$$

The corresponding rotary version of scaled dot-product attention is then

$$sdpa_{mulrel}(Q, K, V, \Theta_{d_k}) := softmax\left(\frac{1}{\sqrt{d_k}} rotate(Q, \Theta_{d_k})(rotate(K, \Theta_{d_k}))^{\intercal}\right)V.$$

In contrast to additive approaches, RoPE does not require an additional learned table of relative-position weights and has since been adopted across a range of applications [2].

## 3 Rotary Informational Embeddings

We now introduce our *rotary informational embedding* (*RotIE*) approach. In contrast to the rotary positional embeddings, which encode positions of tokens within an input sequence only, we are interested in a relative attention procedure that takes distances of more general information into account. For example, in the field of symbolic music generation, where we use tokens to represent musical elements like notes, we can assign additional values to elements of a sequence, representing, e.g., the pitch of a note, its velocity, or its temporal position within a bar.

### 3.1 General Description

Formally, given an input sequence $S_{inp} = (t_0, \ldots, t_{l_{seq}-1})$ of length $l_{seq}$, the embedded values $S_{emb} = (t_0^{emb}, \ldots, t_{l_{seq}-1}^{emb})$, where $t_i^{emb} \in \mathbb{R}^{d_{mod}}$ for any $t_i^{emb} \in S_{emb}$, we require an additional *information vector* $S_{nfo} = (n_0, \ldots, n_{l_{seq}-1})$, which assigns *information values* to the (embedded) input tokens.

The exact nature of these information values is dependent on the context. For instance, if the values represent note pitches they would range, e.g., from 0 to 87. We denote the minimal possible value of $S_{nfo}$ with $v_{min}$ and the maximal possible value with $v_{max}$. Furthermore, we shift $S_{nfo}$ by $-v_{min}$, to ensure all values fall in the range $[0, v_{max} - v_{min}]$.

We can then use these values to inject information into the embedded queries and keys by rotating consecutive pairs of query and key components,

$$(Q^h_{[i,2k]}, Q^h_{[i,2k+1]}) \quad \text{and} \quad (K^h_{[j,2k]}, K^h_{[j,2k+1]}),$$

where $0 \leq k < \frac{d_{head}}{2}$. The rotations are based on their respective information values $n_i$ and $n_j$, as discussed in Sect. 2.2. During the attention process, the dot product will then depend on the injected information values, as is the case with the positional values for the conventional RoPE procedure.

In order to support information assignments for which not all tokens can be assigned information from $S_{nfo}$ (e.g., rest tokens do not have a pitch value), we propose and compare between two different "imputation" strategies:

(i) As $RoPE(v, 0) = v$ for any vector $v$, simply not applying rotational information embedding to such tokens is a valid option.
(ii) In order to encode information about the incompatibility of these "invalid" tokens, we propose to rotate these invalid tokens of the queries $Q$ with $-(v_{max} - v_{min})$, and the invalid tokens of the keys $K$ with $2(v_{max} - v_{min})$. This way, the absolute distance values between a valid and an invalid token will always be greater than or equal to $(v_{max} - v_{min})$, indicating a lack of similarity for these tokens.

### 3.2 RotIE Approaches

In contrast to RoPE, which uses the same "information" (in the form of absolute positions of tokens within a sequence), with RotIE we support both freely-selectable integer information, and an arbitrary amount of different information

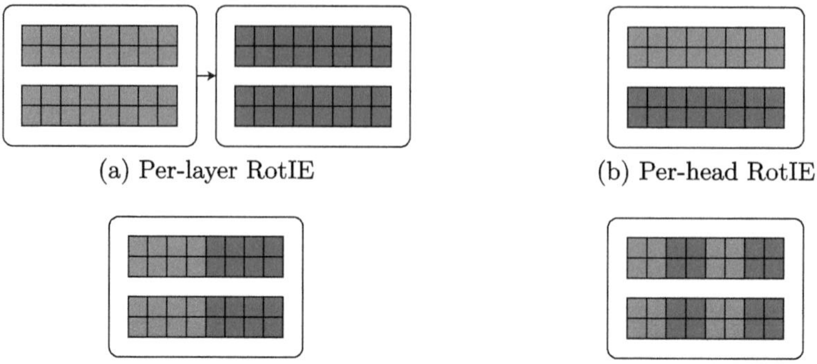

(a) Per-layer RotIE (b) Per-head RotIE

(c) Consecutive pairwise RotIE (d) Interleaved pairwise RotIE

**Fig. 1.** Simplified representations of the four RotIE approaches using two types of information (coloured in blue and orange, respectively). The panels show a single layer each, with the exception of the per-layer case in (a), and two attention heads with two embedded tokens (blocks of $2 \times 8$ cells), with a dimensionality of 8. (Color figure online)

vectors $S^{0}_{nfo}, \dots, S^{n_{nfo}-1}_{nfo}$. As a result, the need for a procedure to include these different types of information arises.

In this paper, we introduce four different approaches for RotIE: (i) a *per-layer approach*, discussed in Sect. 3.2, which uses exactly one type of information per Transformer layer, (ii) a *per-head approach*, outlined in Sect. 3.2, which uses different kinds of information for each attention head, (iii) a *consecutive pairwise approach*, where each head includes all types of information consecutively, and (iv) an *interleaved pairwise approach*, which interleaves information throughout the embedded vectors. These latter two approaches are covered in Sect. 3.2. In the following definitions, $\widetilde{Q}$ denotes the rotated query tensor; the keys are rotated analogously. Moreover, $\theta_k$ denotes the element at index $k$ of $\Theta_{d_{head}}$.

**Per-Layer RotIE.** Figure 1(a) shows a simplified version of our per-layer RotIE approach. Here, each Transformer layer (represented by the rectangles around the coloured blocks) receives a different information vector $S^{y}_{nfo}$. In our implementation, we use a cyclic approach for the distribution of information values, i.e., the layer at index $\ell$ receives the information vector $S^{\ell \bmod n_{nfo}}_{nfo}$.

For a given layer $\ell$ and its respective queries $Q$ and keys $K$, we then rotate the query values as follows:

$$\begin{aligned} \widetilde{Q}^{h}_{[i,2k]} &= v_{[0]}, \\ \widetilde{Q}^{h}_{[i,2k+1]} &= v_{[1]}, \text{ where } v = RoPE((Q^{h}_{[i,2k]}, Q^{h}_{[i,2k+1]}), S^{y}_{nfo\,[i]}, \theta_k), \end{aligned}$$

for $0 \leq i < l_{seq}$, $0 \leq k < \frac{d_{head}}{2}$, and where $y = \ell \bmod n_{nfo}$. As a result, the information of $S^{y}_{nfo}$ is injected into the queries and keys, and during the matrix multiplication of the attention mechanisms, the relative distances are implicitly computed.

**Per-Head RotIE.** In contrast to the per-layer approach, for the following approaches the information embeddings are computed in the same way for each layer. We thus drop the layer index for clarity.

Figure 1(b) shows a simplified version of our per-head approach. Here, one type of information is used per attention head, cycling through the information types should the number of heads exceed the number of different information sources. We can then define the per-head approach for the queries (analogously for keys):

$$\widetilde{Q}^h_{[i,2k]} = v_{[0]},$$
$$\widetilde{Q}^h_{[i,2k+1]} = v_{[1]}, \text{ where } v = RoPE((Q^h_{[i,2k]}, Q^h_{[i,2k+1]}), S^y_{nfo\,[i]}, \theta_k),$$

where for $i$ and $k$ the same constraints as with the per-layer approach hold, $0 \leq h < n_{head}$, and $y = h \bmod n_{nfo}$.

In this way, every layer can consider all information types, while individual heads may specialise in different types of information. We conjecture that this contributes to its strong perplexity performance and user-study ratings.

**Consecutive and Interleaved Pairwise RotIE.** For the pairwise RotIE approaches, we embed all information values within the queries (respectively the keys) of any single attention head. The difference between the consecutive pairwise and interleaved pairwise approaches stems from the order of the information values used.

Figures 1(c) and 1(d) visualise these differences. Here, the order of information values within an attention head is clear to see. For the consecutive approach all embeddings of a specific information type are grouped together, while for the interleaved approach the embedded information type changes with every pair of values.

Formally, we can define the consecutive approach as follows:

$$\widetilde{Q}^h_{[i,2k]} = v_{[0]},$$
$$\widetilde{Q}^h_{[i,2k+1]} = v_{[1]}, \text{ where } v = RoPE((Q^h_{[i,2k]}, Q^h_{[i,2k+1]}), S^y_{nfo\,[i]}, \theta_k),$$

where $i$ and $k$ are as defined previously, and

$$y = \left\lfloor \frac{2\, n_{nfo} k}{d_{head}} \right\rfloor.$$

This assigns pair indices to contiguous blocks of information sources. In our configurations, $d_{head}/2 \geq n_{nfo}$, so each source receives at least one pair.

We can define the interleaved pairwise approach in a similar fashion. Here, we simply use a value of

$$y = k \bmod n_{nfo},$$

ensuring that a different type of information is used for each consecutive pair, effectively interleaving the embedded information over the pairs.

# 4 Experiments and Evaluation

In order to evaluate the impact of RotIE, we trained a total of seven Transformer models using (i) the regular Transformer model as introduced by Vaswani et al. [20], (ii) the Music Transformer [6], (iii) the RoFormer [18] approach making use of regular rotary positional embeddings, (iv) per-layer RotIE, (v) per-head RotIE, (vi) consecutive pairwise RotIE, and (vii) interleaved pairwise RotIE, respectively. We then compared these models based on objective metrics and conducted a small-scale user study, evaluating the perceived quality of the output of the models.

## 4.1 Experimental Settings

**Datasets and Hyperparameters.** We conducted our experiments on both the widely used Lakh MIDI dataset [13] and the smaller POP909 dataset [21], comprising about 175,000 and 909 MIDI files, respectively.

We applied data deduplication techniques [23] to eliminate duplicate pieces and removed invalid pieces with empty tracks or unsupported time signatures. We then quantised MIDI messages to a predefined grid and assigned tracks to one of six instruments (piano, guitar, bass, strings, synth, and drums). The dataset was augmented by transposing each piece by a random half-tone value in the range $[-5, +6]$, and pieces were split into 16-bar excerpts for training. For the length-extrapolation evaluation, we additionally construct 32-bar test sequences, i.e., sequences twice as long as those seen during training.

We used our large-vocabulary note-like tokenisation approach [14], which is comparable to REMI [7], to transform the MIDI data into machine-readable input tokens. Here, MIDI data is represented using a combination of (among others) *play*, *duration*, and *pause* tokens, indicating the start, duration, and temporal position of notes within a bar.

The final training dataset consists of a total of 729,062 16-bar long sequences, with an average ($\pm$ standard deviation) of 910 $\pm$ 520 tokens per sequence, 57 $\pm$ 36 tokens per bar on average, and an average of 3.15 $\pm$ 1.56 instruments per piece.

For all models, we used a model dimensionality of 512, 2,048 neurons per feed-forward layer, 4 attention heads, a dropout rate of 0.1, and a total of 4 layers. Models were trained using half precision, gradient clipping of 1.0, and beta, epsilon, and weight decay values as used by Vaswani et al. [20]. We trained the models for 16 epochs each, using eight NVIDIA Ampere GPUs.

**Imputation Strategy.** For the four RotIE variants of the practical evaluation, we used the first strategy described in Sect. 3.1, leaving tokens without an assigned information value unrotated.

**Table 1.** Perplexity results for the different approaches compared for different sequence lengths (lower is better).

| Model/Dataset | 16 Bars (Lakh MIDI) | 32 Bars (Lakh MIDI) | 16 Bars (POP909) | 32 Bars (POP909) |
|---|---|---|---|---|
| Regular Transformer | 2.53 | >999 | 5.86 | >999 |
| Music Transformer | 2.46 | 2.77 | 5.64 | 6.28 |
| RoFormer | 2.51 | 2.94 | 5.83 | 7.01 |
| RotIE (per-layer) | 2.44 | 2.87 | 5.50 | 6.08 |
| RotIE (per-head) | 2.42 | **2.47** | 5.42 | **5.30** |
| RotIE (consecutive pairwise) | 2.45 | 3.91 | 5.61 | 9.43 |
| RotIE (interleaved pairwise) | **2.40** | 3.04 | **5.37** | 6.41 |

**Choice of Information.** The selection of which information types to embed is an important design decision. In companion work on additive relative attention for symbolic music [15], we evaluated different information combinations, showing that temporal information (absolute time and intra-bar positions) consistently improved model performance, while pitch information exhibited mixed results. Building on these results, we tested similar configurations with RotIE, including combinations of positional, pitch, temporal, and intra-bar temporal information. Although several configurations showed promise in perplexity evaluations, preliminary assessments of output quality revealed issues with musical validity. Here, pieces would often have repetitive phrases, disharmonious passages, or lack rhythmic coherence. We settled on a configuration including token positions (as with regular RoPE), absolute time, and intra-bar positions, as this produced the most musically coherent results.

### 4.2 Perplexity Evaluation

A common measure of the ability of a model to correctly predict future tokens in a sequence is its *perplexity*, which is calculated on a test set using

$$\exp\Big(-\frac{1}{N}\sum_{i=0}^{N-1}\log(P(t_i \mid t_{<i}))\Big),$$

where $t_{<i}$ abbreviates the prefix $(t_0, \ldots, t_{i-1})$, which is empty for $i = 0$. Thus, the expression exponentiates the average negative log-likelihood. Here, lower values indicate a model that makes more correct predictions in which it is more certain.

Table 1 shows the results of this evaluation. Our RotIE approaches show clear improvements over the conventional rotary positional embedding approach when it comes to the 16 bar case. To confirm this, we first checked the distributions of the per-batch losses using D'Agostino-Pearson tests. As normality was rejected for most model and condition combinations (21 of 28; $p < 0.05$), we used one-sided Mann-Whitney $U$ tests to compare each RotIE approach against each of the three baselines, applying Holm correction within each condition and using a significance level of $p < 0.01$. In the 16-bar cases, all RotIE approaches achieve lower perplexity than all baselines, and all comparisons are significant except those between the consecutive pairwise approach and the Music Transformer. In order to evaluate the ability of the models to generalise to longer sequences, we conducted the same analysis on musical pieces of 32 bars in length, twice as long compared to the sequences seen during training. Here, the pairwise approaches showed less promise, although all four RotIE approaches significantly outperformed the regular Transformer for both datasets. Significant improvements were also observed for the per-layer approach relative to the RoFormer on both datasets and the Music Transformer on POP909. The same held for the per-head approach against all three baselines for both datasets, and for the interleaved pairwise approach against the RoFormer for POP909. No other comparisons reached the corrected significance level. Together with the 16-bar results, this suggests that the per-head approach serves as a good compromise between the regular cases and extending to longer sequence lengths than seen during training.

In addition to these promising results, the rotations used by RotIE are linear in the sequence length and head dimension, whereas attention matrix multiplication is quadratic in the sequence length. The asymptotic runtime is therefore still dominated by the attention matrix multiplication. Empirically, including RotIE has negligible impact on the overall model runtime in our matched forward-pass benchmark.

### 4.3 Distribution Analysis

While perplexity measures the ability of a model to predict tokens, it does not directly capture whether the generated music exhibits realistic musical properties. To address this, we conducted a distributional analysis comparing the statistical properties of generated outputs to ground truth data from the held-out test set.

Specifically, we analysed the distributions of relative distances between notes within segments of four consecutive bars. For each note and the notes preceding it within the segment, we computed: (i) the relative pitch distance, i.e., the difference in MIDI pitch values, (ii) the relative time distance, measuring the temporal offset between note onsets, (iii) the relative time-in-bar distance, capturing differences in intra-bar positions, and (iv) the distance on the circle of fifths, a measure of harmonic relatedness based on the shortest path on the circle of fifths. These metrics capture fundamental aspects of rhythmic structure and harmonic relationships.

We generated up to 250 pieces per model and compared their distributions against those of the full deduplicated held-out test set using the Wasserstein distance, which quantifies how much "effort" is required to transform one distribution into another. Lower values indicate closer similarity to the ground truth distribution.

**Table 2.** Wasserstein distances between distributions of generated and ground truth sequences (lower is better).

| Model | Rel. Pitch | Rel. Time | Rel. Bar Time | Circle of Fifths |
|---|---|---|---|---|
| Regular Transformer | 0.474 | 0.234 | 0.079 | 0.032 |
| Music Transformer | 1.615 | 0.516 | 0.078 | 0.047 |
| RoFormer | 0.586 | 0.995 | 0.082 | 0.054 |
| RotIE (per-layer) | 0.458 | 0.083 | 0.105 | **0.031** |
| RotIE (per-head) | 0.455 | 0.280 | 0.088 | 0.066 |
| RotIE (consecutive pairwise) | **0.431** | **0.074** | **0.066** | 0.032 |
| RotIE (interleaved pairwise) | 0.870 | 0.308 | 0.068 | 0.054 |

Table 2 shows the results for this analysis. Our RotIE models demonstrate strong performance across multiple metrics. Notably, the consecutive pairwise RotIE approach achieves the best results for relative pitch distance, relative time distance, and relative time-in-bar distance, while the per-layer approach achieves the best result for the circle-of-fifths distance.

Overall, the consecutive pairwise RotIE approach achieves the best mean rank across all metrics, followed by the per-layer approach and the regular Transformer. These Wasserstein distances and mean ranks provide a descriptive comparison of how closely each model matches the held-out test set. We use this distribution-level view because distances within the same piece are related.

### 4.4 User Study

To complement the objective evaluation with an assessment of perceived musical quality, we conducted an exploratory small-scale user study. We received 14 submissions, each rating eight pieces randomly drawn from a selection of the output of the RotIE approaches, the GPT-like regular Transformer model, the Music Transformer [6], RoFormer [18], and the ground truth stemming from the test dataset, across five evaluation metrics. Participants were asked to rate the 16-bar long samples on a scale from 1 (lowest) to 5 (highest) based on the perceived quality of the harmony, the validity of the rhythm, the variedness of the pieces, the believed genuineness or authenticity of the pieces, and their overall quality. The result of this study is shown in Table 3, where we report the average results for each metric and their standard deviation.

Here, our RotIE models show good promise, with higher mean ratings than the baselines on many metrics. Still, we want to emphasise that music is highly subjective, and evaluations often reduce to personal preferences rather than objective measures of quality. Furthermore, all models tend to produce failure samples lacking musical variedness, or overall structure. For this study, we selected five representative pieces per class, deliberately excluding clear failures such as overly repetitive or incoherent samples. This keeps the survey focused on typical usable outputs, but means that the ratings should be read

**Table 3.** Results (mean ± standard deviation) of the user study per model and metric (higher is better).

| Model/Metric | Harmony | Rhythm | Variedness | Genuineness | Quality |
|---|---|---|---|---|---|
| Ground Truth | 4.14 ± 0.83 | 4.00 ± 1.13 | 3.43 ± 1.12 | 4.00 ± 1.07 | 3.79 ± 0.94 |
| Regular Transformer | 3.21 ± 1.01 | 3.14 ± 1.30 | 2.71 ± 1.10 | 2.71 ± 1.03 | 2.71 ± 0.88 |
| Music Transformer | 2.71 ± 0.96 | 2.79 ± 1.01 | 3.00 ± 0.93 | 2.43 ± 1.05 | 2.71 ± 1.28 |
| RoFormer | 2.64 ± 1.23 | 3.07 ± 1.39 | 2.43 ± 0.82 | 2.64 ± 1.29 | 2.43 ± 1.05 |
| RotIE (per-layer) | 3.36 ± 1.23 | 3.43 ± 1.12 | 3.43 ± 1.12 | **3.36 ± 1.23** | 3.14 ± 1.36 |
| RotIE (per-head) | **3.71 ± 1.16** | 3.79 ± 1.15 | 3.14 ± 1.30 | **3.36 ± 1.44** | **3.43 ± 1.50** |
| RotIE (consecutive pairwise) | 3.43 ± 1.35 | **3.93 ± 1.22** | **3.50 ± 1.30** | 3.14 ± 1.51 | 3.36 ± 1.11 |
| RotIE (interleaved pairwise) | 3.00 ± 1.46 | 3.57 ± 1.18 | 2.86 ± 1.36 | 2.93 ± 1.58 | 2.71 ± 1.44 |

as representative-quality estimates rather than unconditional generation-quality estimates.

The per-head approach performs particularly well. It achieves higher mean ratings than every generated baseline in harmony and quality, ties in genuineness, and remains competitive for rhythm and variedness. We note that the ground truth itself shows reduced variedness, as the training dataset often contains overly-repetitive pieces. Interestingly, the interleaved pairwise approach falls a bit short of expectations, showing weaker evaluations across all five metrics. We again note that this may be due to the small-scale nature of the survey.

Overall, the study suggests that RotIE retains the perceived musical quality of the generated pieces. Taken together, the statistically significant objective improvements of RotIE over the baseline metrics in the perplexity evaluation suggest that RotIE is a promising approach for symbolic music generation.

## 5 Conclusion

In this paper, we introduced RotIE, a generalisation of rotary embeddings that incorporates diverse types of information such as timing or pitch directly into the attention mechanism. We introduced four strategies for integrating multiple information types and evaluated them on symbolic music generation.

Experimental results demonstrate statistically significant improvements in perplexity over baseline models in several settings, with the per-head approach performing particularly well in the 32-bar setting that tests generalisation to longer sequences than those seen during training. A descriptive distributional analysis further shows that RotIE variants achieve the smallest distances for all four analysed metrics, with the consecutive pairwise approach achieving the best mean rank. Importantly, these gains come with negligible runtime overhead in our matched benchmark. An exploratory small-scale user study suggests that perceived musical quality is retained alongside the objective improvements, although a larger study is needed to confirm this. These results suggest that the approaches have different strengths: per-head performs best in length extrapolation and achieves the highest mean harmony and quality ratings among the generated models, while consecutive and per-layer provide the closest matches to the analysed ground-truth distributions. We therefore recommend per-head RotIE as a practical default, given its strong perplexity results and high mean user-study ratings. Overall, RotIE establishes a flexible and efficient framework for enriching Transformer-based models with domain-specific information. While we demonstrated its effectiveness for symbolic music generation, we conjecture that the approach can be generalised to other structured domains where tokens carry meaningful integer-valued attributes. Evaluating this remains future work.

## References

1. Bahdanau, D., Cho, K., Bengio, Y.: Neural machine translation by jointly learning to align and translate. In: Bengio, Y., LeCun, Y. (eds.) Proceedings of the 3rd International Conference on Learning Representations (ICLR 2015) (2015)
2. Barbero, F., Vitvitskyi, A., Perivolaropoulos, C., Pascanu, R., Velickovic, P.: Round and round we go! What makes rotary positional encodings useful? In: Proceedings of the 13th International Conference on Learning Representations (ICLR 2025). OpenReview.net (2025)
3. Brown, T.B., et al.: Language models are few-shot learners. In: Larochelle, H., Ranzato, M., Hadsell, R., Balcan, M., Lin, H. (eds.) Proceedings of the 33rd Annual Conference on Neural Information Processing Systems (NeurIPS 2020) (2020)
4. Devlin, J., Chang, M., Lee, K., Toutanova, K.: BERT: pre-training of deep bidirectional Transformers for language understanding. In: Burstein, J., Doran, C., Solorio, T. (eds.) Proceedings of the 2019 Conference of the North American Chapter of the Association for Computational Linguistics: Human Language Technologies (NAACL-HLT 2019), pp. 4171–4186. Association for Computational Linguistics (2019)
5. Dosovitskiy, A., et al.: An image is worth 16x16 words: transformers for image recognition at scale. In: Proceedings of the 9th International Conference on Learning Representations (ICLR 2021) (2021). OpenReview.net
6. Huang, C.A., et al.: Music transformer: generating music with long-term structure. In: Proceedings of the 7th International Conference on Learning Representations (ICLR 2019) (2019). OpenReview.net
7. Huang, Y., Yang, Y.: Pop Music transformer: beat-based modeling and generation of expressive pop piano compositions. In: Proceedings of the 28th International Conference on Multimedia, pp. 1180–1188. ACM (2020)
8. Liu, J., et al.: Symphony generation with permutation invariant language model. In: Proceedings of the 23rd International Society for Music Information Retrieval Conference (ISMIR 2022), pp. 551–558 (2022)
9. Liu, Z., et al.: Swin transformer: hierarchical vision transformer using shifted windows. In: Proceedings of the 2021 IEEE/CVF International Conference on Computer Vision (ICCV 2021), pp. 9992–10002. IEEE (2021)
10. Lu, P., et al.: MuseCoco: generating symbolic music from text. CoRR abs/2306.00110 (2023)
11. Payne, C.: MuseNet (2019). https://openai.com/blog/musenet. Accessed 5 May 2025

12. Radford, A., Wu, J., Child, R., Luan, D., Amodei, D., Sutskever, I.: Language models are unsupervised multitask learners. OpenAI Blog (2019). openAI Technical Report
13. Raffel, C.: Learning-based methods for comparing sequences, with applications to audio-to-MIDI alignment and matching. Ph.D. thesis, Columbia University, USA (2016)
14. Schön, F., Tompits, H.: On different symbolic music representations for algorithmic composition approaches based on neural sequence models. In: Artale, A., Cortellessa, G., Montali, M. (eds.) Proceedings of the 2024 Conference of the Italian Association for Artificial Intelligence (AIxIA 2024). LNCS, vol. 15450, pp. 274–287. Springer (2024). https://doi.org/10.1007/978-3-031-80607-0_21
15. Schön, F., Tompits, H.: Efficient additive relative information attention for transformer-based symbolic music composition. In: Proceedings of the 39th Canadian Conference on Artificial Intelligence, vol. 318, Canadian AI (2026). Proceedings of Machine Learning Research
16. Schön, F., Tompits, H.: Rotary informational embeddings for symbolic music generation. In: Proceedings of the 39th Canadian Conference on Artificial Intelligence, vol. 318, Canadian AI 2026. Proceedings of Machine Learning Research (2026)
17. Shaw, P., Uszkoreit, J., Vaswani, A.: Self-attention with relative position representations. In: Walker, M.A., Ji, H., Stent, A. (eds.) Proceedings of the 2018 Conference of the North American Chapter of the Association for Computational Linguistics: Human Language Technologies (NAACL-HLT 2018), pp. 464–468. Association for Computational Linguistics (2018)
18. Su, J., Ahmed, M.H.M., Lu, Y., Pan, S., Bo, W., Liu, Y.: RoFormer: enhanced transformer with rotary position embedding. Neurocomputing **568**, 127063 (2024)
19. Thickstun, J., Hall, D.L.W., Donahue, C., Liang, P.: Anticipatory music Transformer. Trans. Mach. Learn. Res. (2024)
20. Vaswani, A., et al.: Attention is all you need. In: Proceedings of the 30th Annual Conference on Neural Information Processing Systems (NIPS 2017) (2017)
21. Wang, Z., et al.: POP909: a pop-song dataset for music arrangement generation. In: Proceedings of the 21st International Society for Music Information Retrieval Conference (ISMIR 2020) (2020)
22. Wu, S., Yang, Y.: Musemorphose: full-song and fine-grained piano music style transfer with one transformer VAE. IEEE ACM Trans. Audio Speech Lang. Process. **31**, 1953–1967 (2023)
23. Zeng, M., Tan, X., Wang, R., Ju, Z., Qin, T., Liu, T.: MusicBERT: symbolic music understanding with large-scale pre-training. In: Proceedings of the 59th Annual Meeting of the Association for Computational Linguistics (ACL 2021), pp. 791–800. Association for Computational Linguistics (2021)

# Operationalising the AI Act in Italy: A Governance Framework for the National Regulatory Sandbox

Nadia Spatari[1,2](✉)

[1] IMT School for Advanced Studies, Lucca, Italy
nadia.spatari@imtlucca.it
[2] CINI - Consorzio Interuniversitario Nazionale per l'Informatica, Rome, Italy

**Abstract.** The EU AI Act mandates Member States to establish at least one operational AI Regulatory Sandbox (AIRS) by August 2, 2026, facilitating innovation while ensuring safety and compliance with fundamental rights. In Italy, this framework relies on a dual-authority model, with the Agency for Digital Italy (AgID) and the National Cybersecurity Agency (ACN) designated as joint managers of national experimentation spaces. Drawing on lessons from previous initiatives such as "Sperimentazione Italia," this study identifies critical governance challenges, including technical capacity constraints, regulatory fragmentation, and the risk of regulatory arbitrage among market participants. The paper also examines how the Italian institutional framework can support the implementation of the AI Act while promoting innovation in a secure and trustworthy environment. To address these issues, the research proposes a methodological framework for the Italian AIRS that balances the "dilemma of control" by integrating cybersecurity-by-design principles with fundamental rights impact assessments. By providing a structured compliance roadmap, the proposed model aims to reduce legal uncertainty for SMEs and startups entering the European single market. This analysis offers actionable insights for policymakers, regulators, and developers navigating the complex intersection of AI innovation and European digital regulation.

**Keywords:** AI Act · Regulatory Sandbox · Law 132/2025 · Italy · AgID · ACN · Cybersecurity · Fundamental Rights

## 1 Introduction

The adoption of the European Regulation on Artificial Intelligence, known as the AI Act [9], represents one of the most significant legislative attempts to regulate the development and deployment of AI systems within the European Union. In this context, Article 57 introduces a particularly relevant tool for the relationship between technological innovation and legal regulation: AI regulatory sandboxes. The provision requires Member States to establish at least one operational regulatory sandbox by August 2, 2026, with the aim of enabling the development,


S. Bistarelli et al. (Eds.): AIxIA 2026, LNAI 17131, pp. 631–644, 2027.
https://doi.org/10.1007/978-3-032-40774-0_45

testing, and validation of AI systems in an environment controlled and supervised by competent authorities [9]. Regulatory sandboxes are experimental governance mechanisms designed to foster responsible innovation, allowing companies, startups, research centers, and public administrations to test AI-based solutions before launching them on the market. This approach reflects a paradigm shift in European technology regulation: no longer exclusively ex-post regulation, based on sanctions and subsequent controls, but rather collaborative and preventive regulation, geared toward co-designing regulatory compliance (compliance by design) [12]. However, the implementation of sandboxes is part of a well-known theoretical and practical tension in the technology governance literature: the so-called "Collingridge dilemma." Formulated by David Collingridge, this dilemma highlights the difficulty of effectively intervening in the regulation of emerging technologies [10]. In the early stages of development, the technology is still sufficiently malleable to be regulatoryly guided, but the social and economic impacts are difficult to predict. Conversely, by the time the technologyes consequences become clear, it is already widespread, economically consolidated, and therefore more difficult to modify or regulate without high costs. In the case of artificial intelligence, this tension manifests itself in the need to ensure security, transparency, and the protection of fundamental rights without hindering the technological competitiveness and innovative capacity of European operators. In this context, regulatory sandboxes emerge as a governance tool aimed at mitigating this dilemma through experimental, iterative, and collaborative approaches to regulation. Rather than rigid and immediate regulatory imposition, sandboxes create institutional spaces in which regulators, businesses, researchers, and other stakeholders can interact throughout the technology development cycle. This allows for the combination of regulatory learning, regulatory adaptability, and technological experimentation, while simultaneously promoting compliance with the AI Act requirements and reducing legal uncertainty. In light of this framework, Italy faces a significant institutional and strategic challenge. Implementing Article 57 of the AI Act requires not only fulfilling a European obligation, but also defining a national governance model capable of coordinating multiple authorities, ensuring transparency and accountability, supporting innovation actors, and ensuring consistency with constitutional principles and EU law. The risk is twofold: on the one hand, excessive fragmentation or bureaucracy in the system could hinder innovation; on the other, an overly permissive approach could compromise the regulation's protective and guaranteeing function.

## 2 Objective

This paper examines the implementation of Article 57 AI Act within the Italian legal and institutional framework and addresses a gap in the current literature concerning the operational governance of national AI regulatory sandboxes. While existing studies have primarily focused on the regulatory rationale and comparative experiences of AI sandboxes across Europe, limited attention has been devoted to the institutional challenges arising from the Italian dual-authority model established by Law No. 132/2025. The paper therefore proposes a governance framework aimed at balancing innovation, cybersecurity, fundamental rights protection, and regulatory certainty through a coordinated multi-agency approach. This raises three interconnected questions:

- How the Italian "dual authority" model (AgID and ACN) can ensure effective coordination for the national sandbox?
- What critical issues that have emerged from initiatives like "Sperimentazione Italia" must be overcome to ensure that the new sandbox truly attracts businesses and SMEs?
- How can cybersecurity-by-design and rights-by-design principles be operationalised within the Italian AI Regulatory Sandbox to support both innovation and compliance?

## 3 State of Art: AI Regulatory Sandbox in Europe

In the panorama of European AI governance, AI regulatory sandboxes are taking on an increasingly central role as "anticipatory regulation" tools, designed to accompany technological development through experimental and collaborative mechanisms between public authorities and private operators [12]. In general terms, a regulatory sandbox can be defined as a controlled regulatory experimentation environment in which companies, startups, research centers, and public administrations can test innovative AI systems under the supervision of competent authorities, benefiting from direct interaction with the regulator and temporary flexibility regarding certain regulatory obligations. The primary purpose of this tool is to reduce legal uncertainty, foster responsible innovation, and enable institutions to acquire technical and operational knowledge on the emerging risks associated with new algorithmic systems. As highlighted in the scientific literature, sandboxes represent a form of adaptive and experimental governance, capable of integrating the protection of fundamental rights with the need to support European technological competitiveness [11]. According to some scholars, these tools also foster forms of mutual learning between regulators and businesses, contributing to the development of shared technical and interpretative standards [5]. Sandboxes, therefore, not only represent a mechanism to support economic innovation, but also constitute an institutional laboratory in which to experiment with new regulatory methods based on cooperation, continuous risk assessment, and the empowerment of the actors involved. In the European context, different national AI sandbox models are emerging, characterised by different regulatory priorities and institutional structures. Spain is widely considered a pioneer in Europe thanks to the launch of the first pilot project aimed at the practical implementation of the European AI Act. The initiative was jointly presented by the Spanish government and the European Commission as the first European regulatory sandbox dedicated to artificial intelligence, with the aim of testing the application of future regulatory requirements to high-risk AI systems.

The Spanish initiative [14], promoted by the Ministry for Digital Transformation in collaboration with the European Commission, aimed to concretely test the requirements applicable to high-risk AI systems, involving businesses and developers in a guided compliance process. This model stands out for its strong operational focus and its desire to transform the sandbox into a tool for preparing ahead of the AI Act's entry into force, allowing economic operators to understand and experimentally apply the obligations relating to risk management, transparency, data governance, and human oversight. In the European AI regulatory sandbox landscape, Norway represents one of the most established models for regulatory experimentation applied to artificial intelligence. The initiative was developed by the Norwegian Data Protection Authority (Datatilsynet) with the aim of encouraging the development of AI systems compliant with the principles of personal data protection and fundamental rights, while also promoting technological innovation [20]. The Norwegian sandbox is characterized by the absence of exemptions from existing regulatory provisions and by an approach based on cooperation between regulators and economic operators. Rather than being a testing environment exempt from legal obligations, it is a forum for discussion in which businesses, public bodies, and competent authorities collaborate to identify concrete ways of applying regulations in technologically complex contexts. A distinctive element of the Norwegian model is its strong emphasis on mutual learning: on the one hand, participants receive interpretative guidance useful for designing systems compliant with regulatory requirements; on the other, regulators acquire technical and operational knowledge that contributes to improving their supervisory capacity and ability to adapt to new technologies. Projects are selected based on their social relevance and potential to generate knowledge transferable to other stakeholders, with a view to maximizing the public value of the experiment. Particular attention is also paid to transparency, through the publication of the results and recommendations developed during the projects [17]. The literature highlights how the Norwegian model gives great importance to the ethical dimension of experimental regulation, considering the sandbox not only as a technical testing environment, but also as a space for normative reflection on the social and moral values incorporated in AI systems [18]. Also particularly significant is the French model developed by the CNIL, the national data protection authority, which has adopted an approach based on "thematic cohorts." In this system, projects admitted to the sandbox are selected based on specific application areas deemed strategic or with a high social impact, such as digital healthcare, education, public services, or online child protection. Organizing into cohorts facilitates the exchange of experiences among participants, identifies common issues, and develops sector-specific interpretative guidelines. In particular, some French initiatives have focused on creating safe digital environments for children, exploring the role of sandboxes in testing AI tools compatible with the principles of safety, accountability, and the protection of vulnerable individuals [20]. This model is therefore characterized by a strong collaborative dimension and the use of the sandbox as a mechanism for the progressive production of shared regulatory standards. The comparative analysis of different

European regulatory sandbox models highlights a significant heterogeneity in implementation strategies, reflecting the still evolving stage of artificial intelligence governance within the European Union. While some jurisdictions favor an approach oriented toward compliance readiness with the AI Act, others adopt more cooperative or sector-specific models, in which the sandbox functions as a space for regulatory dialogue and the gradual development of shared interpretative standards. This plurality, while representing an element of experimental enrichment, also underscores the need for greater institutional coordination at the European level in order to avoid regulatory fragmentation and ensure coherence in the implementation of the digital single market.

## 4 The Italian Landscape: Legal and Institutional Framework

The Italian regulatory sandbox was introduced by Decree-Law No. 34/2019 (the so-called Decreto Crescita) and further regulated by Ministerial Decree No. 100/2021 with the aim of fostering innovation in the fintech sector by allowing the controlled testing of innovative products, services, and business models in the banking, financial, and insurance industries. The framework involves the participation of several public authorities, including the Bank of Italy, CONSOB, IVASS, the Data Protection Authority, AgID, the Italian Competition Authority (AGCM), and the Revenue Agency, all coordinated through the FinTech Committee established within the Ministry of Economy and Finance. Access to the sandbox is granted to technologically innovative projects that are at an advanced stage of development, financially sustainable, and capable of generating benefits for end users, improving system efficiency, or facilitating a more effective application of existing regulations. The procedure consists of a preliminary support phase, the submission of an application, an assessment and authorization process, and ongoing monitoring by the competent authority, which may approve, amend, or revoke the testing arrangement. At the end of the experimentation period, the results are evaluated and may lead to proposals for regulatory adjustments where necessary. The Italian model is characterized by a particularly complex and multi-level governance structure, in which coordination and dialogue between innovators and public institutions are primarily entrusted to the executive branch and the FinTech Committee, while direct involvement of Parliament and regional authorities is notably absent [23]. With Sperimentazione Italia, introduced by Article 36 of Decree-Law No. 76 of 16 July 2020 (Urgent Measures for Simplification and Digital Innovation), subsequently converted into Law No. 120 of 11 September 2020, Italy established a cross-sectoral regulatory sandbox. Under this framework, entities seeking to test an innovative solution may submit an application to the Department for Digital Transformation and the Ministry of Enterprises and Made in Italy. Following a thorough assessment procedure, these authorities may authorize the experimentation and define its operational conditions. At the conclusion of the testing period, the applicant is required to submit a report outlining the results achieved, as well as the economic and social benefits generated by the initiative [6]. Official documentation indicates that Sperimentazione Italia has authorised a limited number of pilot projects, mainly focused on the field of autonomous mobility. In particular, two main experiments have been carried out: the autonomous shuttle project developed by the Gruppo Torinese Trasporti (GTT) within the European SHOW programme in Turin, and the Yape project, involving autonomous delivery robots developed by the e-Novia group and tested in Milan. The Turin experiment concerned the use of autonomous shuttles on public roads along a 5 km urban route, structured in an initial phase without passengers followed by a second phase open to the public. The Milan project, by contrast, involved testing a fleet of autonomous delivery robots for last-mile logistics, with the aim of assessing safety, urban navigation capabilities, obstacle detection, and the operational sustainability of the service. The analysis of the legal framework and of the experiments conducted so far highlights several structural limitations of Sperimentazione Italia. First, no systematic final reports evaluating the outcomes and critical issues of the projects have been made publicly available, despite the legal obligation to submit them, resulting in a lack of transparency regarding results. Moreover, the number of authorised experiments appears to be very limited, suggesting a still restricted use of the instrument. Rather than a literal 'automatic' change, the framework should implement a structured feedback loop where sandbox results trigger a mandatory 'Regulatory Review Requirement.' This would compel the Ministry of Enterprises and Made in Italy to issue a public report every six months, stating whether experimental findings necessitate specific regulatory updates or circulars to clarify existing norms. Law No. 132/2025 represents the first comprehensive national framework governing artificial intelligence in Italy, adopted in coordination with the European AI Act. The law is based on a distinctly human-centric approach, placing human beings at the centre of automated decision-making processes and subordinating the development and deployment of AI systems to the protection of fundamental rights, human dignity, non-discrimination, and transparency. From this perspective, artificial intelligence is conceived as a tool capable of fostering economic and social progress, provided that meaningful human oversight over relevant decision-making processes is maintained [16]. Alongside this value-based framework, the law assigns a central role to cybersecurity, which is regarded as a cross-cutting requirement throughout the entire lifecycle of AI systems. The design, development, and deployment of AI technologies must comply with standards of cybersecurity, resilience, and risk management, following a risk-based approach proportionate to the level of criticality of the system concerned. Cybersecurity therefore assumes not only a technical but also a legal function, serving as an essential safeguard for the reliability of AI systems, the protection of users, and the stability of socio-technical environments. The national governance framework for artificial intelligence is further characterised by the adoption of a dual-authority model, designed to ensure an effective balance between digital innovation and security. In particular, the Italian Digital Agency (AgID) serves as the notifying authority, responsible for activities related to conformity assessment procedures and relations with notified bodies. The National Cybersecurity Agency(ACN) acts as the market surveillance authority, overseeing compliance with the applicable regulatory framework, investigating potential violations, and adopting the measures necessary to ensure the safety, security, and trustworthiness of AI systems placed on the market. This division of responsibilities reflects the legislator's intention to integrate technological development with national security considerations and the protection of individuals. Within this framework, the law also provides for the establishment of regulatory sandboxes, intended to enable the controlled testing of innovative AI solutions under temporary and limited regulatory derogations. The management of these experimentation environments is entrusted to a coordinated set of public authorities. In particular, the Department for Digital Transformation and the Ministry of Enterprises and Made in Italy (MIMIT) are responsible for assessing applications, authorising pilot projects, and defining the operational conditions of experimentation. AgID and ACN may also contribute, within their respective areas of competence, to the assessment of technical, compliance, and cybersecurity requirements of the solutions being tested [16]. The competent authorities are further entrusted with monitoring the experimentation process and evaluating its outcomes on the basis of the final reports submitted by participating entities. This institutional framework seeks to promote continuous dialogue between regulators and market actors, enabling innovative technologies to be tested in a controlled environment while generating evidence that may inform future regulatory developments, in line with the experimental and adaptive regulatory approach promoted by the AI Act.

## 5 Proposed Framework for the Italian AI Sandbox

To maximise the effectiveness of the Italian AI Regulatory Sandbox (AIRS) and ensure consistency with the European regulatory framework, a structured methodological approach should be adopted. Such a framework should combine technological innovation, regulatory compliance, cybersecurity, and the protection of fundamental rights within a coherent governance architecture. Four key pillars can be identified: the integration of cybersecurity-by-design principles, the systematic implementation of Fundamental Rights Impact Assessments (FRIAs), the establishment of a multi-agency governance model, and the definition of a clear sandbox lifecycle.

- *Cybersecurity-by-Design.* A first pillar of the proposed framework concerns the incorporation of cybersecurity-by-design principles throughout the entire experimentation process. In line with the objectives of the Cyber Resilience Act (CRA), AI systems admitted to the sandbox should be required to demonstrate the adoption of appropriate cybersecurity measures from the earliest stages of development rather than as ex post compliance mechanisms [1]. This approach would enable developers to identify vulnerabilities, assess cyber risks, and implement mitigation measures before market deployment. Integrating CRA requirements into the sandbox environment would not only

strengthen the resilience and trustworthiness of AI systems but would also facilitate future compliance with European cybersecurity obligations, thereby reducing regulatory uncertainty and compliance costs. In particular, the experimentation phase should be aligned with the principles of cybersecurity-by-design and security-by-default enshrined in the Cyber Resilience Act, especially Article 13 and Annex I of Regulation (EU) 2024/2847, which require the integration of cybersecurity risk assessment and essential security requirements throughout the entire product lifecycle. Moreover, reference to Article 12 CRA would enable effective coordination between the cybersecurity requirements applicable to high-risk AI systems and those established under the AI Act, thereby ensuring greater coherence between the two pillars of the European regulatory framework governing artificial intelligence and digital security [24].
- *Fundamental Rights Impact Assessments (FRIAs).* A second pillar concerns the systematic integration of FRIAs for high-risk AI systems. Although the AI Act requires providers and deployers to consider the impact of certain systems on fundamental rights, the sandbox provides an ideal environment in which such assessments can be operationalised and tested in practice [5]. Participants should therefore be required to conduct preliminary, intermediate, and final FRIAs, assessing potential risks related to privacy, non-discrimination, freedom of expression, due process, and other fundamental rights protected under the legal order. In this perspective, the Italian sandbox should encourage the adoption of a "Rights-by-Design" approach from the earliest stages of system development, thereby embedding fundamental rights protection directly into the technical and functional architecture of algorithms [22]. This orientation is fully consistent with the European model of anticipatory governance, which seeks to prevent the harmful effects of technological innovation through ex ante regulatory tools rather than ex post corrective interventions. Evidence in the literature shows that post-development adaptation (retrofitting) is often costly, complex, and technically limited, leading to inefficiencies for both operators and regulators [19].
- *Multi-Agency Governance Model.* Given the multidimensional nature of AI regulation, an effective AIRS should be based on a multi-agency governance model capable of overcoming institutional fragmentation [13]. In this regard, a structured coordination mechanism should be established among the Italian Digital Agency (AgID), the National Cybersecurity Agency (ACN), and the Italian Data Protection Authority (Garante per la protezione dei dati personali). AgID could provide expertise on conformity assessment and digital governance; ACN could oversee cybersecurity, resilience, and risk-management requirements; while the Data Protection Authority could assess compliance with privacy and data protection rules. To operationalise this form of coordination, a Joint Steering Committee (JSC) should be established, comprising technical representatives from AgID and ACN. The Committee would serve as a single point of entry for applicants, managing a unified digital portal designed to prevent administrative duplication. Conflict resolution would be handled through a consensus-based protocol: AgID would have the final

say on matters concerning compliance and interoperability standards, while ACN would retain veto power over any architecture presenting significant risks to national cybersecurity or critical infrastructure. Resource allocation would follow a "shared-expert" model, whereby specialised personnel from both Agencies would be organised into cross-functional task forces to assess high-risk AI projects.

- *Sandbox Lifecycle.* The effectiveness of the AIRS would also depend on the adoption of a clearly defined sandbox lifecycle, structured into three main phases: pre-testing, testing, and post-testing. During the pre-testing phase, applicants would undergo an admission process based on predefined eligibility criteria, including the innovative nature of the project, its technological maturity, its potential societal benefits, and the adequacy of proposed risk-mitigation measures. This stage should also include a preliminary assessment of cybersecurity requirements and fundamental rights implications. The testing phase would involve the controlled deployment of the AI system under regulatory supervision [15]. During this period, participants would receive technical guidance from the competent authorities and would be required to comply with agreed testing protocols, reporting obligations, and monitoring procedures. Continuous interaction between regulators and innovators would facilitate the identification of legal, technical, and ethical issues emerging during experimentation. Finally, the post-testing phase would focus on the evaluation of outcomes through a comprehensive final report documenting the results achieved, the risks identified, the mitigation measures adopted, and the lessons learned. Based on this assessment, successful projects could enter a graduation phase, enabling their transition from the experimental environment to full market deployment. At the same time, the evidence collected during experimentation could inform future regulatory adjustments, thereby contributing to a more adaptive and evidence-based governance of artificial intelligence.

In addition to this general framework, the Italian sandbox should explicitly include dedicated pathways for high social-impact sectors, in which the use of artificial intelligence raises particularly sensitive ethical, legal, and societal issues. In this regard, priority should be given to areas such as education and smart toys, given their direct impact on minors and vulnerable users [4]. These sectors require enhanced safeguards due to information asymmetries, the potential for behavioural influence, and the sensitivity of the data involved. The introduction of dedicated sectoral tracks would enable regulators and innovators to address contextual risks more effectively while simultaneously developing tailored compliance methodologies. Furthermore, beyond the AI Act, the sandbox framework should integrate existing national regulatory instruments in order to ensure a coherent and multi-layered regulatory approach. In particular, reference should be made to AGCOM Resolution No. 9/23/CONS on the protection of minors in digital environments, which establishes principles and safeguards relevant to online content and services accessible to minors [2]. Aligning sandbox experimentation with such sector-specific instruments would strengthen coherence across different regulatory domains, avoid regulatory fragmentation, and ensure that AI innovation in sensitive sectors is guided not only by European requirements but also by existing national standards.

# 6 Risks and Mitigation Implementation

The successful implementation of an Italian AIRS depends not only on the adequacy of its legal and institutional design but also on its capacity to address a number of operational and strategic challenges. While regulatory sandboxes have the potential to foster innovation and facilitate compliance with complex regulatory requirements, their effectiveness ultimately depends on the availability of technical expertise, the ability to prevent regulatory distortions, and the creation of appropriate incentives for market participants, particularly small and medium-sized enterprises (SMEs) and startups.

## 6.1 Technical Capacity and Resource Allocation

One of the most significant challenges facing the implementation of an AIRS concerns the availability of adequate human and financial resources. The assessment of AI systems requires highly specialised expertise spanning multiple disciplines, including computer science, cybersecurity, data protection, ethics, and administrative law. Regulatory authorities must therefore be capable of evaluating not only the technical functioning of algorithms, but also their compliance with legal requirements, their potential impact on fundamental rights, and the adequacy of risk mitigation measures [1]. In practice, this implies the need to recruit and retain professionals with hybrid skill sets, combining technological knowledge with legal and regulatory expertise. Such profiles are often scarce and highly sought after by the private sector, creating a risk that public authorities may face difficulties in attracting and retaining qualified personnel. Beyond technical recruitment, the sandbox must prioritize the development of 'hybrid' human skills—competencies that blend legal reasoning with algorithmic auditing. This involves moving from a purely ex ante compliance checklist to a continuous monitoring model, where regulators and developers co-evolve their understanding of the AI system's social impact throughout its operational lifecycle. To address this challenge, Italy could adopt a multidisciplinary model based on dedicated expert pools, inter-agency cooperation mechanisms, partnerships with universities and research centres, and targeted training programmes for public officials. Without adequate investment in technical capacity, there is a risk that the sandbox may become a merely formal mechanism, unable to provide meaningful guidance to innovators or to effectively supervise experimentation.

## 6.2 Preventing Regulatory Arbitrage (Forum Shopping)

Another critical issue concerns the possibility of regulatory arbitrage, whereby companies seek access to the most permissive regulatory environment available within the European Union. Since the AI Act allows Member States to establish their own regulatory sandboxes, significant divergences in admission criteria, supervisory practices, or regulatory expectations could encourage developers to engage in "forum shopping," selecting jurisdictions that impose lower compliance burdens rather than those offering the most effective regulatory oversight [13]. To avoid a potential race to the bottom, the Italian AIRS should maintain high standards of safety, transparency, cybersecurity, and fundamental rights protection while simultaneously offering legal certainty and efficient administrative procedures. Rather than competing through regulatory leniency, the Italian model should seek to differentiate itself through the quality of regulatory support provided to participants, the expertise of supervisory authorities, and the integration of cybersecurity and ethical assessment mechanisms [3]. Close cooperation with other national authorities and the European AI Office could further contribute to the harmonisation of practices and reduce the risk of regulatory fragmentation across the Union.

### 6.3 Incentives for SMEs and Startups

The AI Act and Italian Law No. 132/2025 place SMEs and innovative startups at the centre of their regulatory framework, recognising that compliance costs could otherwise hinder the development and deployment of AI systems. In this context, regulatory sandboxes serve not only as supervisory tools but also as instruments of industrial policy aimed at fostering innovation. They provide controlled environments where operators can test and validate AI systems while engaging directly with regulators and receiving support in meeting AI Act requirements. A key advantage of sandboxes is the reduction of compliance costs. Access is free for startups and SMEs, with only exceptional costs potentially recovered on a proportional basis by competent authorities. This is particularly relevant given the complexity of AI regulation, which often requires specialised legal and technical expertise. Direct interaction with regulators reduces reliance on external consultancy and supports a more efficient compliance process. At the same time, the framework allows for simplified administrative procedures for micro-enterprises and grants national authorities some discretion to reduce bureaucratic burdens further [15]. Participation in sandboxes also provides strategic benefits beyond compliance. Although no formal certification is issued, the final sandbox report is expected to be positively considered in subsequent conformity assessments, potentially accelerating time-to-market. This can also improve access to investment, as reduced legal uncertainty lowers perceived risk for venture capital and institutional investors. In addition, participation enhances reputational value by demonstrating responsible AI practices within a supervised environment, strengthening trust among stakeholders [21]. Sandboxes further facilitate access to essential technical resources, including high-quality datasets, synthetic data, and advanced computing infrastructure through integration with initiatives such as AI Factories and Testing and Experimentation Facilities (TEFs) [8]. This is particularly valuable for SMEs that would otherwise lack access to such resources. Moreover, continuous interaction with regulators promotes regulatory learning and enables companies to embed compliance requirements early in the design process, operationalising the principle of compliance by design. Finally, the AI Act introduces a safe harbour mechanism, whereby operators acting in good faith in line with the sandbox testing plan are exempt from administrative fines for infringements occurring during experimentation. This reduces legal risk and encourages innovation in high-risk or uncertain regulatory environments [15].

## 7 Conclusion and Future Work

The strategic success of the Italian AIRS will depend on its ability to balance innovation and regulation through strong technical expertise, effective safeguards against regulatory arbitrage, and targeted support for SMEs and startups.

The analysis shows that adopting a by-design approach, encompassing privacy by design, security by design, and rights by design, should be viewed not only as a legal and ethical requirement, but also as a competitive advantage. Embedding compliance requirements from the earliest design stages reduces retrofitting costs, accelerates development processes, and enhances the sustainability of innovation. The scientific community also plays a crucial role. As highlighted by the Italian Strategy for Artificial Intelligence, cooperation among academia, research centres, and public institutions is essential to promote innovation oriented toward social good and aligned with European values [7]. Equally important is the active involvement of stakeholders. Regulatory sandboxes should not be closed technical environments but participatory spaces that include developers, fundamental rights experts, and, where appropriate, vulnerable groups such as minors, thereby bridging the gap between technological development and societal needs. At the same time, clear governance mechanisms and transparent operational guidelines are necessary to prevent underutilisation and regulatory arbitrage. From a broader governance perspective, AI regulatory sandboxes can be seen as tools for addressing the Collingridge dilemma. By fostering interaction between regulators and innovators during the early stages of technological development, they enable risks to be identified and managed before AI systems become deeply embedded in society. In this way, sandboxes transform regulation from a reactive process into a proactive and adaptive form of governance. Future research should evaluate the practical implementation of the Italian sandbox, focusing on inter-agency coordination, participation by SMEs and startups, and the impact of experimentation outcomes on future regulatory developments. Comparative studies with other European experiences may further contribute to identifying best practices for the evolution of AI regulatory sandboxes across the European Union.

## References

1. Ahern, D.: Operationalising AI regulatory sandboxes under the EU AI act: the triple challenge of capacity, coordination and attractiveness to providers. Cambridge Forum AI: Law Gov. **1**, 1–25 (2025). https://doi.org/10.1017/cfl.2025.10023

2. Autorità per le Garanzie nelle Comunicazioni: Adozione delle linee guida finalizzate all'attuazione dell'articolo 7-bis del decreto-legge 30 aprile 2020, n. 28 in materia di "sistemi di protezione dei minori dai rischi del cyberspazio" (2023). https://www.agcom.it/documents/10179/29648921/Delibera+9-23-CIR/51108184-df9e-45fc-9bab-52280c0bbb09?version=1.1
3. Bagni, F.: Regulatory sandboxes as a bridge between AI and cybersecurity: Exploring the interplay between the AI act and the cyber resilience act. In: Regulatory sandboxes for AI and Cybersecurity. Questions and Answers for Stakeholders, pp. 54–69. Cybersecurity National Lab (2025)
4. Charisi, V., Dignum, V.: Operationalizing AI Regulatory Sandboxes for Children's Rights and Well-Being, pp. 231–249. Chapman and Hall/CRC (2024). https://doi.org/10.1201/9781003320791-25
5. Cirone, E.: Gli spazi di sperimentazione normativa nell'unione europea: regolamentare l'innovazione tra principi e prassi applicative. Rivista italiana di diritto pubblico comunitario **34**(1), 53–88 (2024)
6. Dipartimento per la trasformazione digitale: Sperimentazione Italia. https://innovazione.gov.it. accesso 17 giugno 2026
7. Dipartimento per la trasformazione digitale, AgID – Agenzia per l'Italia Digitale: Strategia italiana per l'intelligenza artificiale 2024-2026. Documento strategico istituzionale, Presidenza del Consiglio dei Ministri (2024). https://assets.innovazione.gov.it/1721376223-01-strategia-italiana-per-l-intelligenza-artificiale-2024-2026.pdf
8. European Commission: Sectorial AI testing and experimentation facilities under the digital Europe Programme. Shaping Europe's digital future (2025). https://digital-strategy.ec.europa.eu/en/policies/testing-and-experimentation-facilities. Accessed 11 Sep 2026
9. European parliament and council: Artificial intelligence act. Regulation (EU) 2024/1689 of the European Parliament and of the Council (13 June 2024). http://data.europa.eu/eli/reg/2024/1689/oj
10. Genus, A., Stirling, A.: Collingridge and the dilemma of control: Towards responsible and accountable innovation. Res. Policy **47**(1), 61–69 (2018). https://doi.org/10.1016/j.respol.2017.09.012
11. Gumbo, L., Chude-Okonkwo, U.A.K.: Regulatory sandbox as a frontier for innovation and sustainability: a systematic review. Cogent Bus. Manage. **12**(1), 2510555 (2025). https://doi.org/10.1080/23311975.2025.2510555
12. Lanamaki, A., Vayrynen, K., Hietala, H., Sky, N.: Sociotechnical imaginaries of upcoming AI act regulatory sandboxes. In: Proceedings of the 16th Scandinavian Conference on Information Systems, vol. 15 (2025). https://aisel.aisnet.org/scis2025/15
13. Longo, E., Bagni, F., Seferi, F.: Unboxing the complexity of the ai regulatory sandboxes' ecosystem: Policy challenges and strategic lines. Cambridge Forum AI: Law Gov. **1** (2025). https://doi.org/10.1017/cfl.2025.10031
14. Ministerio de Asuntos Económicos y Transformación Digital: Real decreto 817/2023, de 8 de noviembre, por el que se establece un entorno controlado de pruebas para el ensayo del cumplimiento de la propuesta de reglamento del parlamento europeo y del consejo por el que se establecen normas armonizadas en materia de inteligencia artificial. Real Decreto 817/2023 BOE-A-2023-22767 (9 nov 2023). https://www.boe.es/eli/es/rd/2023/11/08/817
15. Novelli, C., Hacker, P., McDougall, S., Morley, J., Rotolo, A., Floridi, L.: Getting regulatory sandboxes right: design and governance under the AI act. Eur. J. Risk Regul., 1–27 (2026). https://doi.org/10.1017/err.2026.10096

16. Parlamento Italiano: Legge 23 settembre 2025, n. 132 (2025). https://www.gazzettaufficiale.it/eli/id/2025/09/25/25G00143/sg
17. Paul, R., Åm, H.: From watchdogs to partners in tech innovation: navigating regulatory roles in Norway's AI sandbox. Cambridge Forum AI: Law Gov. **1**, 33 (2025). https://doi.org/10.1017/cfl.2025.10014
18. Ranchordas, S.: Experimental regulations for AI: sandboxes for morals and mores. Morals Mach. **1**(1), 86–100 (2021). https://doi.org/10.2139/ssrn.3839744
19. Spatari, N.: Exploring regulatory sandboxes: safeguarding AI-based software for minors. In: Proceedings of the 2024 International Conference on Information Technology for Social Good, pp. 158–162. GoodIT 2024, ACM (2024). https://doi.org/10.1145/3677525.3678656
20. Spatari, N.: Building safe digital environments for children: AI regulatory sandbox and pilot project insights. In: 2025 12th International Conference on Future Internet of Things and Cloud (FiCloud), pp. 459–466 (2025). https://doi.org/10.1109/FiCloud66139.2025.00070
21. Tibidò, S., Spatari, N., Lilli, S., Zucca, M.V.: A story of and for children: the lifecycle loop of child rights-based AI. Opinio Juris in Comparatione **2** (2025). https://hdl.handle.net/20.500.11771/37738
22. Tibidò S., Spatari N., R.A.: Children and artificial intelligence. Towards an Italian discussion on artificial intelligence, children's rights and regulatory sandboxes. Joint National Conferenceon Cybersecurity (ITASEC & SERICS 2025), February 03-8, 2025, Bologna, IT (2025)
23. Trapani, M.: L'utilizzo delle sandboxes normative: una ricognizione comparata delle principali esperienze di tecniche di produzione normativa sperimentali e il loro impatto sull'ordinamento. Osservatorio sulle fonti (3), (2022)
24. Unione Europea: Regolamento (UE) 2024/2847 del Parlamento europeo e del Consiglio, del 23 ottobre 2024, relativo ai requisiti orizzontali di sicurezza informatica per i prodotti con componenti digitali (Cyber Resilience Act). Gazzetta ufficiale dell'Unione europea, L del 20.11.2024 (2024). https://eur-lex.europa.eu/eli/reg/2024/2847/oj, ultimo accesso: 18 giugno 2026

# Escaping the Holistic Trap: Probing Linguistic Phenomena in Quantized LLMs for Machine Translation

Dhairya Suman[1,2(✉)], Marco Gaido[2], and Matteo Negri[2]

[1] University of Trento, Trento, Italy
[2] Fondazione Bruno Kessler, Trento, Italy
{dsuman,mgaido,negri}@fbk.eu

**Abstract.** Despite growing interest in quantization as an efficiency enabler for deploying Large Language Models (LLMs) in Machine Translation (MT), its evaluation remains largely restricted to aggregate metrics on general-purpose benchmarks. This can create a "holistic trap", in which stable global scores can mask localized failures in specific linguistic phenomena. To address this gap, we reorient the analysis towards targeted probing of post-training quantization (PTQ) methods against individual linguistic phenomena. In addition to general translation accuracy, we consider five dimensions: gender bias, named entity translation, robustness to noisy user-generated text, terminology translation, and translation consistency. For each linguistic phenomenon, we examine how different quantization methods (AWQ, GPTQ, BnB, GGUF) and bit-width reduction levels (8-bit, 4-bit, and 2-bit) impact each phenomenon across varying model scales and families. We find that the holistic trap is narrow: 8-bit quantization largely preserves baseline behavior and 4-bit introduces only moderate drift, while at 2-bit, degradation becomes more severe and uneven across phenomena. At the same time we observe, robustness at even 4-bit is not consistent across models, methods, or benchmarks, implying that stability observed in one configuration cannot be assumed to hold in another. Overall, our results indicate that 8 and 4-bit quantization are broadly safe for MT deployment, but that reliable use of aggressive 2-bit compression, and even generally safe 4-bit compression in edge cases, requires phenomenon-level evaluation rather than relying on purely aggregate metrics.

**Keywords:** Quantization · Machine Translation · Large Language Models · Model Compression

## 1 Introduction

Large Language Models (LLMs) have significantly advanced the state of the art in Machine Translation (MT), achieving high translation quality and demonstrating strong zero-shot linguistic proficiency across a wide range of languages


S. Bistarelli et al. (Eds.): AIxIA 2026, LNAI 17131, pp. 645–661, 2027.
https://doi.org/10.1007/978-3-032-40774-0_46

[37]. However, these gains are closely tied to a massive increase in parameter count, which imposes prohibitive computational requirements for real-world deployment. Although modern model families offer various scales, maintaining a fleet of task-specific models remains computationally expensive. This challenge has catalyzed research into model compression, with Post-Training Quantization (PTQ) emerging as the de facto standard for democratizing access to large-scale models [10]. By transforming high-precision weights into lower-bitwidth representations without requiring extensive retraining, PTQ has become the most practical paradigm for sustainable deployment.

Despite its prevalence, the evaluation of quantization remains largely holistic. Standard protocols typically assess performance degradation using aggregate automatic metrics on generic benchmarks [10,21,23]. While these explorations provide a coarse-grained view of model quality, they offer an incomplete picture of the multifaceted factors influencing performance. This can create what we define a "holistic trap": a scenario where stable global scores may mask significant failures in specific linguistic or social phenomena. Furthermore, preliminary evidence suggests that the impact of quantization is not uniform across languages, with low-resource and structurally diverse settings being disproportionately affected [21,23]. However, there is still a lack of systematic investigations into how compression affects specific linguistic constructs, as most studies remain focused on aggregate evaluations.

To fill this gap, we investigate whether quantization-induced degradation manifests uniformly across translation tasks or selectively erodes robustness on specific linguistic phenomena. We move beyond holistic evaluations by probing the interaction between model scale and quantization aggressiveness (from 8-bit down to 2-bit) across diverse PTQ methods. We question whether evaluations on general-purpose MT test sets act as reliable proxies for task-specific robustness or mask hidden failures in nuances such as gender bias, named entity translation, and domain-specific terminology translation, robustness to noise and document-level consistency. By exploring these neglected dimensions, our main contribution is **the first multi-dimensional evaluation of PTQ in MT**. Our framework encompasses state-of-the-art architectures subjected to PTQ with different methods and varying degrees of compression intensity. Through extensive analyses on both general-purpose and specialized test suites covering a diverse set of language pairs, we aim to determine the conditions under which compression compromises linguistic accuracy and model reliability, ultimately informing whether aggressive quantization is safe for MT production or risks introducing subtle but critical biases. To this aim, we probe quantization effects across five targeted dimensions beyond general translation accuracy, spanning two model families, two scales, four quantization methods, and bit-widths from 8-bit down to 2-bit. The results of our extensive empirical evaluation indicate that *i)* aggregate MT quality is largely preserved under moderate quantization, with meaningful degradation happening only at aggressive 2-bit compression, *ii)* despite this apparent stability, there exists a "holistic trap", where stable aggregate scores mask phenomenon-specific failures that emerge unpredictably across specific language pairs and model-method configurations, *iii)* the degree and nature of this degradation cannot be extrapolated across models, methods, or tasks, meaning robustness in one setting offers no guarantee of similar robustness in another.

## 2 Related Works

The ascent of LLMs has fundamentally redefined the MT landscape, with decoder-only architectures such as the Llama, Qwen3, and Aya Expanse series demonstrating remarkable zero-shot proficiency [33,36]. Several studies have shown that these models can surpass traditional supervised neural MT systems in terms of multilingual flexibility and stylistic fluency [2,3,5,15,17,20,34,35,37]. However, **the bulk of this literature remains primarily concerned with maximizing performance as a function of parameter scale**, often treating computational efficiency as a secondary concern [27]. This leaves a critical gap in our understanding of how such models can be sustainably deployed in real-world, resource-constrained environments without relying on massive, full-parameter configurations.

To address these sustainability challenges, PTQ has emerged as the pragmatic standard for democratizing access to large-scale models due to its ability to preserve the original model architecture while enabling the execution of 30B+ parameter models on consumer-grade hardware. Unlike pruning or knowledge distillation, which typically require retraining, PTQ strategies such as GPTQ [9] and AWQ [19] offer a scalable path to efficiency by transforming weights into lower-bitwidth representations ranging from 8 down to 2 bits.

Nevertheless, **existing research in this area frequently validates the success of compression almost exclusively through aggregate metrics** like BLEU [28] or COMET [30] **on generic benchmarks** like FLORES [12] and WMT24++ [8]. While these metrics provide a proxy for general quality, such black box evaluations remain blind to whether quantization compromises specific phenomena, such as gender bias or the translation of named entities and technical terminology.

Recent investigations have begun to highlight the "uneven impact" of compression, suggesting that the burden of quantization is not distributed equally across languages. While performance may remain stable for high-resource languages, it often disproportionately penalizes morphologically rich or structurally diverse ones [21,23–25]. Despite these insights, **the literature still lacks a systematic diagnostic of granular linguistic phenomena**, leaving it unclear whether quantization induces a general decline in quality or a specific collapse of certain linguistic constructs.

Our work is positioned as a direct extension of the WMT 2025 Shared Task on Model Compression [10],[1] the first collective effort specifically dedicated to benchmarking LLM efficiency in MT. While this task established crucial baselines, its primary findings highlighted a troubling trade-off between compression

[1] https://www2.statmt.org/wmt25/model-compression.html.

and stability. However, because such shared tasks are inherently designed for competitive ranking, they often lack the granular perspective needed to diagnose the root causes of linguistic degradation beyond leaderboard performance. We bridge this gap by transitioning from a leaderboard-centric view to a diagnostic-oriented framework that combines holistic evaluation with specialized test suites and their respective scorers. This allows us to provide the first comprehensive analysis that sheds light on the risk that specific linguistic phenomena and application domains are sacrificed on the altar of computational efficiency, ultimately identifying the boundary between sustainable optimization and the erosion of task-specific robustness.

## 3 Experimental Setting

In this section, we detail the technical framework of our study, covering the quantization methods, the model architectures, the linguistic phenomena under investigation, and the evaluation metrics.

### 3.1 Quantization Techniques

**BitsandBytes** [6,7]. We employ the Hugging Face integration[2] of the BitsandBytes library to evaluate models in 8-bit and 4-bit configurations. For 8-bit quantization, we use the LLM.int8() algorithm, which isolates outlier features in full precision and quantizes the rest to 8-bit; matrix multiplications are computed separately for each component. For 4-bit, we test three formats: FP4 (E2M1: 1 sign, 2 exponent, 1 mantissa bit), NF4 (weights mapped to a normal-distribution-optimized scale), and NF4 with Double Quantization (NF4-2Q), where scaling factors are themselves quantized to 8-bit to further reduce memory.

**GPTQ** [9]. We use the GPTQModel implementation[3] to evaluate models at 8-bit, 4-bit, and 2-bit precision. GPTQ is a layer-wise PTQ method that minimizes each layer's squared reconstruction error, using an approximate inverse Hessian to capture second-order weight interactions and preserve fidelity at low bit-widths. It requires a calibration dataset to estimate activation statistics; we use C4 dataset [29] for this purpose.

**AWQ** [18]. We use the AutoAWQ library[4] to evaluate models in a 4-bit precision. AWQ is an activation-aware quantization method that identifies salient channels from calibration activation statistics and applies per-channel scaling to redistribute dynamic range before quantization, reducing reconstruction error while preserving functional equivalence without mixed-precision storage overhead. We use a group size of 128, asymmetric zero-point quantization, and the C4 dataset [29] for calibration, consistent with our other experiments.

[2] https://huggingface.co/docs/bitsandbytes/.
[3] https://github.com/ModelCloud/GPTQModel.
[4] https://github.com/casper-hansen/AutoAWQ.

**GGUF Quantization.** We use the `llama.cpp` framework[5] to evaluate models in 4-bit and 2-bit precision using two GGUF quantization families. K-Quants apply block-wise scalar quantization with per-block scaling factors, combined with mixed-precision allocation across tensors, sensitive layers (e.g., attention and output projections) are kept at higher bit-widths while less critical layers are quantized more aggressively—requiring no calibration data; we use the Q4_K_M and Q2_K variants. I-Quants (Importance-aware Quantization) instead use lookup-table-based quantization guided by an Importance Matrix (I-Matrix), which weights reconstruction error by empirical activation magnitudes from a calibration set rather than treating all weights equally; we use IQ4_NL and IQ2_M. This importance weighting improves the rate–distortion trade-off over uniform quantization schemes, particularly at the lowest bit-widths.

### 3.2 Models

To investigate the interaction between model capacity and compression robustness, we select four models from two state-of-the-art decoder-only families, namely Aya Expanse and Qwen3 in the 8B and 32B sizes. These families were chosen for their permissive licenses, specifically CC-BY-NC 4.0 and Apache 2.0 respectively, which enable reproducible research and open deployment. Beyond licensing, our selection is motivated by their varying degrees of multilingual support (respectively covering 23 and 119 languages). Furthermore, these families offer a critical architectural and optimization contrast: while Aya Expanse is explicitly instruction-tuned for massively multilingual operations, Qwen3 balances standard dense language modeling with an integrated native inference thinking paradigm. This choice is also strategically aligned with the model compression tasks that have scrutinized the effects of quantization in translation at recent evaluation campaigns, such as machine translation at WMT 2025 [10] and speech translation at IWSLT 2025 [1]. By selecting these specific scales of 8B and 32B, we establish a controlled experimental framework where both families are evaluated at comparable parameter counts. This "square" design compares two different architectures across two identical size tiers to ensure maximum comparability. Such a setup allows us to isolate whether quantization robustness is primarily a function of model scale or family-specific training and design choices, providing a clearer understanding of how different multilingual training paradigms respond to aggressive bit-width reduction.

### 3.3 Evaluation Benchmarks and Metrics

To assess the impact of LLM quantization on translation quality, we employ a diverse array of benchmarks comprising a general-purpose evaluation set alongside targeted diagnostic suites to evaluate granular linguistic stability across specific phenomena.

[5] https://github.com/ggml-org/llama.cpp.

**General-Purpose Evaluation Set.** To anchor our analysis to established benchmarks, we initially evaluate the models on the test data released for the "constrained" track of the WMT 2025 Shared Task on Model Compression [10].[6] These sets cover three language directions (English→Arabic, Japanese→Chinese, and Czech→German) that represent a sufficiently diverse linguistic landscape for validating our models against official findings. General quality is tracked using the XCOMET-XL[7] [13] and MetricX-24-Hybrid-XL[8] [16] scores.

In the second and core stage of our evaluation, we probe model robustness on targeted diagnostic suites representative of five specialized dimensions. For these sets, we either rely on the general quality metrics or, where available, we adopt the specialized scoring frameworks provided by each suite.

**Gender Bias.** We evaluate gender bias on WinoMT [32],[9] a 3,888-sentence challenge set for gender coreference and stereotypical bias in MT, covering eight grammatically gendered target languages (Arabic, French, German, Hebrew, Italian, Russian, Spanish, and Ukrainian). Each sentence pairs two gender-neutral occupations with a gendered pronoun, designed to pit masculine or feminine pronouns against stereotypical/anti-stereotypical occupations. We report two metrics: *Accuracy*, the fraction of instances where the source gender is correctly preserved in translation, and $\Delta_g$, the difference in F1 scores between correctly translated male and female entities, where higher values indicate greater gender bias.

**Robustness to Noisy User-Generated Content.** We evaluate MT robustness using RoCS-MTv2[10] [4], a benchmark of 1,922 English sentences sourced from Reddit featuring real-world noise such as spelling errors, devowelling, acronyms, and expressive punctuation, with professional translations into French, German, Czech, Ukrainian, and Russian. As a WMT 2025 General Translation Task test suite, it serves as a stress-test for whether quantization-induced capacity reduction disproportionately impairs generalization across linguistic irregularities inherent in social media discourse. Performance is tracked via chrF and COMET.

**Terminology Translation.** We evaluate terminology translation using the WMT 2025 Terminology Translation Task benchmark [31][11], comprising 500 sentences across IT and Finance domains for English→German/Russian/Spanish. Unlike the original constrained task, we operate in a zero-shot setting without

[6] https://www2.statmt.org/wmt25/model-compression.html.
[7] https://huggingface.co/Unbabel/XCOMET-XL.
[8] https://huggingface.co/google/metricx-24-hybrid-xl-v2p6-bfloat16.
[9] https://github.com/gabrielStanovsky/mt_gender.
[10] https://huggingface.co/datasets/rbawden/RoCS-MT-v2.
[11] https://github.com/wmt-conference/wmt25-terminology.

external terminology dictionaries, assessing each model's native ability to correctly translate specialized lexicon under compression. Performance is tracked via chrF and COMET.

**Translation Consistency.** We evaluate using the WMT 2024 Biomedical Translation Task [26],[12] covering 12 translation directions across French, German, Italian, Portuguese, Russian, and Spanish (both to and from English). Each test set comprises 50 PubMed title-abstract paragraphs, making it a document-level benchmark that subsumes several sentence-level phenomena, including named entity preservation, terminology translation, and numerical expressions, while additionally exposing paragraph-level failures such as sentence omissions or hallucinations under compression. Performance is tracked via chrF and COMET.

**Named Entity Translation.** We evaluate named entity translation using NEuRoparl-ST [11],[13] a multilingual benchmark derived from the Europarl-ST corpus of European Parliament speeches [14] and annotated with NEs and terminology. Its English → Spanish/French/Italian triplets comprise approximately 1,200 sentences per language pair, manually NE-annotated based on the 18-tag OntoNotes scheme, covering a wide range of entities from frequent classes to rarer, more complex categories. This unbalanced distribution, combined with the inherent difficulty of translating specific entity types, makes the benchmark well-suited for stress-testing quantized models. Performance is tracked via per-category Named Entity Accuracy, measuring the proportion of entities correctly preserved in translation.

## 4 Results and Discussion

All models, in both their base and compressed configurations, are evaluated using a zero-shot approach with the standardized prompt from the WMT 2025 Shared Task on Model Compression:

`Translate the following text from` *src* `to` *tgt*. `\n` *text* `\n`

To isolate the impact of quantization, we report $\Delta$ scores relative to the uncompressed (FP16/BF16) models. This differential approach allows us to pinpoint whether a decrease in aggregate performance reflects a uniform decline across all capabilities or a catastrophic failure within specific linguistic dimensions, effectively filtering out the inherent performance variations between different model architectures. Given space constraints, only tables relevant to the scores discussed are included; the remaining results are omitted.

Before delving into the experimental results, a distinction should be made regarding the scope of our evaluation. While system-level performance, such as

[12] https://github.com/cgrozea/wmt24biomed-ref.
[13] https://mt.fbk.eu/neuroparl-st/.

inference throughput (tokens/s) or wall-clock time, is critical for production-ready deployment, it is often contingent on specific hardware configurations and software optimizations. Consequently, in this work, and in contrast to the evaluation framework of the WMT 2025 model compression task, we deliberately focus on the relationship between model capacity and translation quality, following the simpler yet quality-centric protocol established for the analogous task at IWSLT 2025. By using model size and bit-width as proxies for efficiency, we prioritize an information-theoretic perspective, isolating how the compression of the weight space impacts the preservation of complex linguistic structures independently of hardware-specific acceleration.

### 4.1 General-Purpose Benchmarking

The performance for both the model sizes and families is nearly indistinguishable from the original baselines at 8-bit. At 4-bit, the impact on output quality is more evident, although the larger models (32B) are more resistant to degradation. Moving to 2-bit, Aya Expanse 32B is more robust to GGUF-Q2_K quantization than other models. Quantizing the model using GPTQ at the 2-bit level renders the model non-functional across all language pairs and the drop in quality becomes catastrophic. Table 1 reports the change in COMET-XL and MetricX scores for all the models quantized to 4 bits using all the methods averaged across the language pairs. **Our results on the WMT25 benchmark broadly confirm that translation quality remains largely intact under moderate (8- and 4-bit) quantization, with substantial degradation only emerging at more extreme compression levels, consistent with the pattern reported by** [10,21,23].

**Table 1.** $\Delta COMET - XL$ and $\Delta MetricX$ across Qwen3 and AyaExpanse model families averaged across all the languages for the WMT25 benchmark.

| | Qwen3 8B | | Qwen3 32B | | Aya 8B | | Aya 32B | |
|---|---|---|---|---|---|---|---|---|
| Method | C-XL | M-X | C-XL | M-X | C-XL | M-X | C-XL | M-X |
| AWQ-4bit | −0.01 | 0.46 | 0.00 | 0.05 | 0.00 | −0.04 | 0.00 | 0.02 |
| GPTQ-4bit | −0.01 | 0.33 | −0.01 | 0.11 | 0.00 | −0.04 | 0.00 | 0.02 |
| BnB-fp4 | −0.02 | 0.45 | −0.01 | 0.29 | −0.01 | 0.05 | 0.00 | 0.06 |
| BnB-nf4 | 0.00 | 0.13 | 0.00 | 0.01 | 0.00 | −0.01 | 0.00 | 0.02 |
| BnB-nf4-2q | 0.00 | 0.15 | 0.00 | 0.01 | 0.00 | −0.01 | 0.00 | 0.02 |
| Q4_K_M | 0.00 | 0.01 | 0.00 | −0.20 | −0.06 | 0.56 | −0.02 | 0.00 |
| IQ4_NL | 0.00 | 0.08 | 0.01 | −0.15 | −0.05 | 0.47 | −0.03 | 0.10 |
| Q2_K | −0.20 | 4.68 | −0.21 | 6.95 | −0.08 | 0.99 | **−0.05** | **0.42** |
| IQ2_M | −0.06 | 1.73 | −0.03 | 0.75 | −0.09 | 1.34 | −0.03 | 0.34 |
| **Average** | −0.03 | 0.89 | −0.03 | 0.87 | −0.03 | 0.38 | **−0.01** | **0.11** |

Note: AyaExpanse is shortened to Aya. C-XL stands for COMET-XL and M-X stands for MetricX.

## 4.2 Targeted Benchmarking

**Gender Bias.** Similarly to the findings of [22], moderate quantization leaves gender bias largely stable across both model families and sizes, with a change of less than 2 points in $\Delta_g$ on average under all 4-bit methods as shown in Table 2. However, the effect is neither directionally consistent nor language-independent: en→ru and en→uk (which carry the highest baselines across all models) suffer greater degradation than other language pairs under compression for Qwen3, however, this pattern does not generalise to Aya Expanse. Under aggressive compression, bias increases through female F1 degradation: Qwen3-32B under GGUF IQ2_M sees $\Delta_g$ rise to 15.7, while Aya Expanse 32B rises more sharply to 19.6 (from 14.6). Aya Expanse 8B under GGUF IQ2_M shows the opposite pattern, with $\Delta_g$ apparently dropping to 13.5. However, this is not a genuine fairness gain: both male and female F1 drop simultaneously. The model loses the capacity to handle gendered entities altogether, producing a reduction in the gap through symmetric degradation. **Gender bias is a phenomenon where metrics can provide unrealiable signals, $\Delta_g$ reductions under aggressive compression can reflect model's inability to handle gendered entities rather than genuine fairness improvement.**

**Table 2.** WinoMT evaluation metrics: Average across all languages and (ru + uk).

| | | All Languages (Avg.) | | | ru + uk | |
|---|---|---|---|---|---|---|
| Model | Method | $\Delta_g$ | $\Delta$ F1-F | $\Delta_{\Delta_g}$ | $\Delta_g$ | $\Delta_{\Delta_g}$ |
| Qwen3 32B | Baseline | 14.0 | — | — | 28.4 | — |
| | Avg-4bit | 14.4 | 0.5 | −0.4 | 29.8 | 0.7 |
| | GGUF Q2_K | 17.2 | −2.0 | −2.3 | 33.8 | 5.5 |
| | GGUF IQ2_M | 15.7 | 1.7 | −1.6 | 33.8 | 5.5 |
| Qwen3 8B | Baseline | 24.8 | — | — | 29.9 | — |
| | Avg-4bit | 25.1 | −0.6 | −0.3 | 29.1 | 1.91 |
| | GGUF Q2_K | 24.2 | −2.2 | 0.6 | 24.90 | 5 |
| | GGUF IQ2_M | 26.7 | −2.7 | −1.2 | 33.6 | 2.8 |
| Aya 32B | Baseline | 14.6 | — | — | 27.0 | — |
| | Avg-4bit | 15.6 | 1.1 | −0.1 | 29.1 | 0.7 |
| | GGUF Q2_K | 18.6 | −6.6 | −4.1 | 29.5 | 2.5 |
| | GGUF IQ2_M | 19.6 | −7 | −5 | 33.8 | 4.3 |
| Aya 8B | Baseline | 16.5 | — | — | 24.7 | — |
| | Avg-4bit | 17.8 | −1.8 | −1.3 | 26.2 | 1.6 |
| | GGUF Q2_K | 24.2 | −11.4 | −7.2 | 31.8 | 7.2 |
| | GGUF IQ2_M | 13.5 | 1.54 | 3.0 | 25.9 | 1.2 |

**Robustness to Noisy User-Generated Content.** Similar to the findings in the general test set, we see that the 32B models are highly robust to moderate quantization [23]. However, for 8B models, the picture changes: Aya Expanse 8B suffers from disproportionate degradation in the chrf scores under the GGUF 4 bit quantized models (Table 3), while remaining stable for every other 4-bit method. This contrasts the findings of [22] that state that quantization effects are largely consistent across model architectures. At 2-bit precision, degradation becomes severe across both families at 8B. **While the findings are similar to the evaluation for general MT, the deviations observed at 4-bit and 2-bit compression levels suggest that robustness to this benchmark cannot be extrapolated from the general benchmark alone for all possible model-method settings.**

**Table 3.** $\Delta$ chrF from baseline on RoCsMTv2.

| Model | Method | en-cs | en-de | en-fr | en-ru | en-uk |
|---|---|---|---|---|---|---|
| Qwen3 8B | AWQ-4bit | −0.5 | −0.6 | −0.5 | −0.1 | −0.2 |
| | BnB-nf4 | −0.7 | −0.8 | −0.2 | −0.5 | −0.8 |
| | GPTQ-4bit | −1.1 | −0.9 | −0.6 | −0.8 | −0.9 |
| | GGUF Q4_K_M | −0.5 | −0.4 | −0.2 | −0.6 | −0.2 |
| | **GGUF IQ2_M** | **−6.8** | **−3.7** | **−2.3** | **−2.6** | **−6.1** |
| Qwen3 32B | AWQ-4bit | −0.4 | −0.4 | −0.2 | −0.5 | −0.4 |
| | BnB-nf4 | −0.4 | −0.3 | 0.0 | −0.3 | −0.4 |
| | GPTQ-4bit | −0.6 | −0.3 | −0.3 | −0.2 | −0.3 |
| | GGUF Q4_K_M | 0.0 | 0.0 | −0.2 | −0.2 | −0.2 |
| | GGUF IQ2_M | −2.5 | −1.8 | −0.9 | −1.6 | −3.1 |
| Aya 8B | AWQ-4bit | −0.4 | −0.4 | 0.0 | −0.4 | −0.7 |
| | BnB-nf4 | +0.1 | −0.1 | +0.3 | +0.5 | −0.2 |
| | GPTQ-4bit | −0.7 | −0.8 | +0.2 | −0.2 | −0.5 |
| | **GGUF Q4_K_M** | **−3.6** | **−8.6** | **−5.1** | **−1.4** | **−4.9** |
| | **GGUF IQ2_M** | **−8.6** | **−14.2** | **−8.4** | **−5.3** | **−11.5** |
| Aya 32B | AWQ-4bit | 0.5 | 0.24 | 0.6 | 0.2 | 0.8 |
| | BnB-nf4 | 0.1 | 1.1 | 0.6 | 0.1 | 0.5 |
| | GPTQ-4bit | −0.2 | 0.9 | 0.9 | 0.3 | −0.3 |
| | GGUF Q4_K_M | −0.5 | −0.3 | 0.1 | −0.5 | −2 |
| | GGUF IQ2_M | −2.7 | −1.2 | −0.6 | −0.8 | −4.8 |

**Terminology Translation.** Consistent with the findings from the general benchmarking and the RoCsMTv2 test set, the 32B models prove highly stable under moderate quantization. Additionally, the disproportionate degradation of

Aya Expanse 8B with GGUF Q4_K_M quantization is consistent with the results in 4.2, and is even more pronounced in this case. However, the degradation on this test set is lower than that shown in the RoCsMTv2 benchmark for the Qwen3 models. While the overall pattern of findings is consistent with the 4.1 and 4.2 evaluations, the amount of degradation varies from both test sets: while it increases for Aya Expanse 8B, the reverse is seen for the Qwen3 model. **This inconsistency in both the direction and magnitude further confirms that while the broad pattern of robustness holds, the impact and the degree of degradation caused by quantization cannot be extrapolated reliably across all possible settings** (Table 4).

**Table 4.** $\Delta$ chrF from baseline on Terminology Translation WMT25.

| Model | Method | en-de | en-es | en-ru |
|---|---|---|---|---|
| Qwen3 8B | AWQ-4bit | −0.2 | +0.1 | −0.8 |
| | BnB-nf4 | −0.2 | −0.7 | −0.5 |
| | GPTQ-4bit | 0.0 | −0.3 | −0.6 |
| | GGUF Q4_K_M | 0.0 | +0.1 | −0.3 |
| | GGUF IQ2_M | −1.2 | −1.1 | −2.0 |
| Aya 8B | AWQ-4bit | −0.3 | −0.2 | −2.5 |
| | BnB-nf4 | −0.5 | −0.1 | +1.0 |
| | GPTQ-4bit | −0.3 | −0.8 | −0.9 |
| | **GGUF Q4_K_M** | **−13.7** | **−12.7** | **−8.6** |
| | GGUF IQ2_M | −19.8 | −18.4 | −14.5 |

**Translation Consistency.** A notable and consistent finding is that translation into English (xx→en) and translation out of English (en→xx) respond very differently to 4 bit GGUF quantization. As seen in Table 5, for Qwen3-32B under GGUF 4 bit quantization the English-output directions are largely preserved, while the English-input directions lose an average of 3.90 chrF points. Moreover, Qwen3 32B quantized to 4 bits using BnB-fp4 degrades specifically in the xx→en directions (−19.74 points), while the en→xx directions are comparatively spared (average loss of 3.5 points). This drop in accuracy aligns with the findings in [23], who suggest the performance of BnB degrades at larger scales. **This indicates that in this line of linguistic inquiry, the impact of quantization may depend as much on translation direction and numeric format.**

**Named Entity Translation.** At 4-bit, both 32B models are highly stable, all the methods produce average absolute changes of less than 0.04 across all entity types and language pairs, with the main exceptions being isolated and not statistically significant drops in low-frequency entity types such as EVENT

**Table 5.** $\Delta$ chrF comparison across model quantization methods on WMT24 Biomedical.

| Model | Method | en → xx $\Delta$ chrF | xx → en $\Delta$ chrF |
|---|---|---|---|
| Qwen3 8B | avg 4bit | −1.04 | −0.43 |
| | GGUF 4bit | −3.48 | −1.31 |
| Qwen3 32B | avg 4bit | −1.86 | −4.14 |
| | GGUF 4bit | −3.90 | −1.76 |
| | **BnB-fp4** | **−3.52** | **−19.74** |
| Aya 8B | avg 4bit | −0.57 | −0.67 |
| | GGUF 4bit | −1.51 | −1.52 |
| Aya 32B | avg 4bit | −0.52 | −0.98 |
| | GGUF 4bit | −1.35 | −2.11 |

and QUANTITY. The 8B models are similarly stable at 4 bit under non-GGUF methods, with both Qwen3-8B and Aya Expanse 8B showing entity-level changes within ±0.03 for the majority of entity types under AWQ and GPTQ-4bit. Aya Expanse 8B, which suffered considerable degradation on RoCsMTv2 and the terminology benchmark, performs comparably to Qwen3-8B on NER under GGUF Q4_K_M and IQ4_NL, with only LAW and ORG showing marginally larger drops. We see that the entity type determines sensitivity far more than the size of the model or the family. LANGUAGE and PRODUCT achieve perfect accuracy (1.00) in all four base models and remain essentially unaffected by any quantization method, including aggressive 2-bit-class formats. PERSON and GPE are similarly robust, with baseline accuracies of 0.85–0.93 and changes rarely exceeding ±0.02 under any 4-bit method. LAW and ORDINAL show moderate but consistent degradation under aggressive GGUF formats across both model families. While the change in scores after quantization is not statistically significant for most categories across models, some categories, such as LAW, show moderate degradation under extreme compression to 2-bit for the smaller models. **Unlike the other phenomenon examined, named entity translation is uniformly resilient to quantization, with any meaningful degradation only emerging under the most aggressive compression settings** (Table 6).

**Table 6.** $\Delta$ accuracy per entity type under GGUF Q2_K on NEuRoparl-ST (average across the language pairs).

| Model | LANG | PER | GPE | ORG | LAW | ORD | EVT | PCT | QTY |
|---|---|---|---|---|---|---|---|---|---|
| Qwen3 32B | 0.00 | −0.02 | −0.02 | −0.05 | −0.06 | −0.13 | −0.22 | −0.33 | −0.67 |
| Aya Expanse 8B | 0.00 | −0.01 | −0.02 | −0.06 | −0.08 | −0.11 | −0.18 | −0.15 | −0.21 |

## 5 Conclusion

In this study we presented a comprehensive evaluation about the effects of PTQ on MT quality. More specifically, we examined whether aggregate scores on general-purpose MT benchmarks can create a "holistic trap" by masking systematic, phenomenon-specific failures invisible to standard evaluation. Our results suggest this trap is narrow: while quantizing down to 8 and 4 bits is generally safe, going beyond this to 2-bit compression can induce failures. At the same time, while the degradation caused by compressing to 4 bits is minimal, it is not uniform, its severity depends on the linguistic phenomenon under study, the language pair, the quantization method and the model size and family. In particular, these patterns do not transfer cleanly across settings; a model–method combination that shows robust behaviour on one benchmark or for one linguistic phenomenon may still exhibit a different degree or pattern of degradation on another. Hence, relying on general benchmarks and aggregate metrics alone, while informative, risks obscuring these configuration-specific failures, creating a "holistic trap" for evaluation practices that do not incorporate targeted, phenomenon-level testing.

## 6 Limitations

While this study provides a multifaceted evaluation of quantization effects on LLM-based MT, several constraints merit acknowledgment. We focus exclusively on PTQ, leaving quantization-aware training for future work. For methods requiring a calibration set, we consistently used C4; ignoring the influence of calibration data diversity. A methodological asymmetry exists in our inference backends: while GGUF models run through llama.cpp, the other methods are executed via HuggingFace Transformers, a difference that may introduce confounding factors beyond quantization itself. Our five diagnostic benchmarks cover a broad range of MT phenomena but cannot represent their full inventory and may carry data contamination risk; however, since our analysis focuses on PTQ-induced degradation relative to uncompressed baselines this does not undermine our conclusions. Finally, we use a fixed, untuned prompt, and multilingual results are often aggregated, which may obscure language-specific behavior.

**Acknowledgments.** This paper has received funding from the European Union's Horizon Europe programme grant agreement No. 101213369 (project DVPS) and European Union's Digital Europe Programme (DIGITAL) under grant agreement No. 101198470 (project LLMs4EU). We also acknowledge the CINECA award under the ISCRA initiative (project MAP-MT), for the availability of high-performance computing resources and support.

**Disclosure of Interests.** The authors declare no competing interests.

## References

1. Abdulmumin, I., et al.: Findings of the IWSLT 2025 evaluation campaign. In: Salesky, E., Federico, M., Anastasopoulos, A. (eds.) Proceedings of the 22nd International Conference on Spoken Language Translation (IWSLT 2025), pp. 412–481. Association for Computational Linguistics, Vienna, Austria (in-person and online) (2025). https://doi.org/10.18653/v1/2025.iwslt-1.44
2. Ahuja, S., et al.: MEGAVERSE: benchmarking large language models across languages, modalities, models and tasks. In: Duh, K., Gomez, H., Bethard, S. (eds.) Proceedings of the 2024 Conference of the North American Chapter of the Association for Computational Linguistics: Human Language Technologies (Volume 1: Long Papers), pp. 2598–2637. Association for Computational Linguistics, Mexico City, Mexico (2024). https://doi.org/10.18653/v1/2024.naacl-long.143
3. Ataman, D., Birch, A., Habash, N., Federico, M., Koehn, P., Cho, K.: Machine translation in the era of large language models: a survey of historical and emerging problems. Information **16**(9) (2025). https://doi.org/10.3390/info16090723
4. Bawden, R., Sagot, B.: RoCS-MT v2 at WMT 2025: robust challenge set for machine translation. In: Haddow, B., Kocmi, T., Koehn, P., Monz, C. (eds.) Proceedings of the Tenth Conference on Machine Translation, pp. 834–849. Association for Computational Linguistics, Suzhou, China (2025). https://doi.org/10.18653/v1/2025.wmt-1.58
5. Cui, M., Gao, P., Liu, W., Luan, J., Wang, B.: Multilingual machine translation with open large language models at practical scale: An empirical study. In: Chiruzzo, L., Ritter, A., Wang, L. (eds.) Proceedings of the 2025 Conference of the Nations of the Americas Chapter of the Association for Computational Linguistics: Human Language Technologies (Volume 1: Long Papers), pp. 5420–5443. Association for Computational Linguistics, Albuquerque, New Mexico (2025). https://doi.org/10.18653/v1/2025.naacl-long.280
6. Dettmers, T., Lewis, M., Belkada, Y., Zettlemoyer, L.: Llm.int8(): 8-bit matrix multiplication for transformers at scale. In: Proceedings of the 36th International Conference on Neural Information Processing Systems. NIPS 2022, Curran Associates Inc., Red Hook, NY, USA (2022)
7. Dettmers, T., Pagnoni, A., Holtzman, A., Zettlemoyer, L.: QLORA: efficient finetuning of quantized LLMS. In: Proceedings of the 37th International Conference on Neural Information Processing Systems. NIPS 2023, Curran Associates Inc, Red Hook, NY, USA (2023)
8. Deutsch, D., et al.: WMT24++: expanding the language coverage of WMT24 to 55 languages & dialects (2025). https://arxiv.org/abs/2502.12404
9. Frantar, E., Ashkboos, S., Hoefler, T., Alistarh, D.: GPTQ: accurate post-training quantization for generative pre-trained transformers (2023). https://arxiv.org/abs/2210.17323
10. Gaido, M., Grundkiewicz, R., Gowda, T., Negri, M.: Findings of the WMT 2025 shared task on model compression: Early insights on compressing LLMs for machine translation. In: Haddow, B., Kocmi, T., Koehn, P., Monz, C. (eds.) Proceedings of the Tenth Conference on Machine Translation, pp. 484–494. Association for Computational Linguistics, Suzhou, China (2025). https://doi.org/10.18653/v1/2025.wmt-1.25
11. Gaido, M., Rodríguez, S., Negri, M., Bentivogli, L., Turchi, M.: Is "moby dick" a whale or a bird? Named entities and terminology in speech translation. In: Moens, M.F., Huang, X., Specia, L., Yih, S.W.t. (eds.) Proceedings of the 2021 Conference

on Empirical Methods in Natural Language Processing, pp. 1707–1716. Association for Computational Linguistics, Online and Punta Cana, Dominican Republic (2021). https://doi.org/10.18653/v1/2021.emnlp-main.128
12. Goyal, N., et al.: The Flores-101 evaluation benchmark for low-resource and multilingual machine translation. Trans. Assoc. Comput. Linguist. **10**, 522–538 (2022). https://doi.org/10.1162/tacl_a_00474
13. Guerreiro, N.M., Rei, R., Stigt, D., Coheur, L., Colombo, P., Martins, A.F.T.: XCOMET: transparent machine translation evaluation through fine-grained error detection. Trans. Assoc. Comput. Linguist. **12**, 979–995 (2024). https://doi.org/10.1162/tacl_a_00683
14. Iranzo-Sánchez, J., et al.: Europarl-ST: a multilingual corpus for speech translation of parliamentary debates. In: ICASSP 2020 - 2020 IEEE International Conference on Acoustics, Speech and Signal Processing (ICASSP), pp. 8229–8233 (2020). https://doi.org/10.1109/ICASSP40776.2020.9054626
15. Iyer, V., Chen, P., Birch, A.: Towards effective disambiguation for machine translation with large language models. In: Koehn, P., Haddow, B., Kocmi, T., Monz, C. (eds.) Proceedings of the Eighth Conference on Machine Translation, pp. 482–495. Association for Computational Linguistics, Singapore (2023). https://doi.org/10.18653/v1/2023.wmt-1.44
16. Juraska, J., Deutsch, D., Finkelstein, M., Freitag, M.: MetricX-24: the Google submission to the WMT 2024 metrics shared task. In: Haddow, B., Kocmi, T., Koehn, P., Monz, C. (eds.) Proceedings of the Ninth Conference on Machine Translation, pp. 492–504. Association for Computational Linguistics, Miami, Florida, USA (2024). https://doi.org/10.18653/v1/2024.wmt-1.35
17. Kocmi, T., et al.: Findings of the WMT24 general machine translation shared task: the LLM era is here but MT is not solved yet. In: Haddow, B., Kocmi, T., Koehn, P., Monz, C. (eds.) Proceedings of the Ninth Conference on Machine Translation, pp. 1–46. Association for Computational Linguistics, Miami, Florida, USA (2024). https://doi.org/10.18653/v1/2024.wmt-1.1
18. Lin, J., et al.: AWQ: Activation-aware weight quantization for LLM compression and acceleration (2024). https://arxiv.org/abs/2306.00978
19. Lin, J., et al.: AWQ: Activation-aware weight quantization for on-device LLM compression and acceleration. In: Gibbons, P., Pekhimenko, G., Sa, C.D. (eds.) Proceedings of Machine Learning and Systems, vol. 6, pp. 87–100 (2024)
20. Lyu, C., et al.: A paradigm shift: the future of machine translation lies with large language models. In: Calzolari, N., Kan, M.Y., Hoste, V., Lenci, A., Sakti, S., Xue, N. (eds.) Proceedings of the 2024 Joint International Conference on Computational Linguistics, Language Resources and Evaluation (LREC-COLING 2024), pp. 1339–1352. ELRA and ICCL, Torino, Italia (2024). https://aclanthology.org/2024.lrec-main.120/
21. Marchisio, K., et al.: How does quantization affect multilingual LLMS? (2024). https://arxiv.org/abs/2407.03211
22. Marcuzzi, F., Ning, X., Schwartz, R., Gurevych, I.: How quantization shapes bias in large language models. In: Demberg, V., Inui, K., Marquez, L. (eds.) Proceedings of the 19th Conference of the European Chapter of the Association for Computational Linguistics (Volume 1: Long Papers), pp. 363–404. Association for Computational Linguistics, Rabat, Morocco (2026). https://doi.org/10.18653/v1/2026.eacl-long.17
23. Marie, B., Fujita, A.: The uneven impact of post-training quantization in machine translation (2025). https://arxiv.org/abs/2508.20893

24. Mekala, A., Atmakuru, A., Song, Y., Karpinska, M., Iyyer, M.: Does quantization affect models' performance on long-context tasks? In: Christodoulopoulos, C., Chakraborty, T., Rose, C., Peng, V. (eds.) Proceedings of the 2025 Conference on Empirical Methods in Natural Language Processing, pp. 9422–9470. Association for Computational Linguistics, Suzhou, China (2025). https://doi.org/10.18653/v1/2025.emnlp-main.479
25. Mohammadshahi, A., Nikoulina, V., Berard, A., Brun, C., Henderson, J., Besacier, L.: What do compressed multilingual machine translation models forget? In: Goldberg, Y., Kozareva, Z., Zhang, Y. (eds.) Findings of the Association for Computational Linguistics: EMNLP 2022, pp. 4308–4329. Association for Computational Linguistics, Abu Dhabi, United Arab Emirates (2022). https://doi.org/10.18653/v1/2022.findings-emnlp.317
26. Neves, M., et al.: Findings of the WMT 2024 biomedical translation shared task: Test sets on abstract level. In: Haddow, B., Kocmi, T., Koehn, P., Monz, C. (eds.) Proceedings of the Ninth Conference on Machine Translation, pp. 124–138. Association for Computational Linguistics, Miami, Florida, USA (2024). https://doi.org/10.18653/v1/2024.wmt-1.6
27. Pang, J., et al.: Salute the classic: revisiting challenges of machine translation in the age of large language models. Trans. Assoc. Comput. Linguist. **13**, 73–95 (2025). https://doi.org/10.1162/tacl_a_00730
28. Papineni, K., Roukos, S., Ward, T., Zhu, W.J.: Bleu: a method for automatic evaluation of machine translation. In: Isabelle, P., Charniak, E., Lin, D. (eds.) Proceedings of the 40th Annual Meeting of the Association for Computational Linguistics, pp. 311–318. Association for Computational Linguistics, Philadelphia, Pennsylvania, USA (2002). https://doi.org/10.3115/1073083.1073135, https://aclanthology.org/P02-1040/
29. Raffel, C., et al.: Exploring the limits of transfer learning with a unified text-to-text transformer (2023). https://arxiv.org/abs/1910.10683
30. Rei, R., Stewart, C., Farinha, A.C., Lavie, A.: COMET: A neural framework for MT evaluation. In: Webber, B., Cohn, T., He, Y., Liu, Y. (eds.) Proceedings of the 2020 Conference on Empirical Methods in Natural Language Processing (EMNLP), pp. 2685–2702. Association for Computational Linguistics, Online (2020). https://doi.org/10.18653/v1/2020.emnlp-main.213
31. Semenov, K., et al.: Findings of the WMT25 terminology translation task: Terminology is useful especially for good MTs. In: Haddow, B., Kocmi, T., Koehn, P., Monz, C. (eds.) Proceedings of the Tenth Conference on Machine Translation, pp. 554–576. Association for Computational Linguistics, Suzhou, China (2025). https://doi.org/10.18653/v1/2025.wmt-1.30
32. Stanovsky, G., Smith, N.A., Zettlemoyer, L.: Evaluating gender bias in machine translation. In: Korhonen, A., Traum, D., Màrquez, L. (eds.) Proceedings of the 57th Annual Meeting of the Association for Computational Linguistics, pp. 1679–1684. Association for Computational Linguistics, Florence, Italy (2019). https://doi.org/10.18653/v1/P19-1164
33. Vilar, D., Freitag, M., Cherry, C., Luo, J., Ratnakar, V., Foster, G.: Prompting PaLM for translation: assessing strategies and performance. In: Rogers, A., Boyd-Graber, J., Okazaki, N. (eds.) Proceedings of the 61st Annual Meeting of the Association for Computational Linguistics (Volume 1: Long Papers), pp. 15406–15427. Association for Computational Linguistics, Toronto, Canada (2023). https://doi.org/10.18653/v1/2023.acl-long.859

34. Wang, L., et al.: Document-level machine translation with large language models. In: Bouamor, H., Pino, J., Bali, K. (eds.) Proceedings of the 2023 Conference on Empirical Methods in Natural Language Processing, pp. 16646–16661. Association for Computational Linguistics, Singapore (2023). https://doi.org/10.18653/v1/2023.emnlp-main.1036
35. Wang, Y., Zhang, J., Shi, T., Deng, D., Tian, Y., Matsumoto, T.: Recent advances in interactive machine translation with large language models. IEEE Access **12**, 179353–179382 (2024). https://doi.org/10.1109/ACCESS.2024.3487352
36. Wassie, A.K., Molaei, M., Moslem, Y.: Domain-specific translation with open-source large language models: resource-oriented analysis (2025). https://arxiv.org/abs/2412.05862
37. Zhu, W., et al.: Multilingual machine translation with large language models: Empirical results and analysis. In: Duh, K., Gomez, H., Bethard, S. (eds.) Findings of the Association for Computational Linguistics: NAACL 2024, pp. 2765–2781. Association for Computational Linguistics, Mexico City, Mexico (2024). https://doi.org/10.18653/v1/2024.findings-naacl.176

# A Large Language Model-Based Framework for Human State Estimation from Wearable Sensors

Christian Tamantini[1(✉)], Alessandro Umbrico[1], Francesca Fracasso[1], Gabriella Cortellessa[1], Francesca Cordella[2], and Andrea Orlandini[1]

[1] National Research Council of Italy, Institute of Cognitive Sciences and Technologies, 00196 Rome, Italy
christian.tamantini@cnr.it

[2] Research Unit of Advanced Robotics and Human-Centred Technologies, Università Campus Bio-Medico di Roma, Rome, Italy

**Abstract.** Wearable sensors enable continuous monitoring, supporting the estimation of human states. Conventional supervised and rule-based approaches often provide limited support for user-accessible explanations linking the estimated state to the underlying physiological evidence.

This work proposes a minimal, structured Large Language Model (LLM)-based framework for human state estimation from wearable physiological data, with human-readable rationales. The framework uses the LLM as a reasoning layer that receives only a task specification, a physiological feature vector, and a constrained output schema, returning both a numerical estimate and a concise LLM-generated rationale grounded in the provided features. The approach was validated in a physical workload estimation case study using wearable-derived measurements. LLM-based workload scores were compared with subjective physical-demand ratings derived from NASA-TLX.

Results showed positive, statistically significant, moderate-to-strong correlations between LLM-based estimates and perceived workload ratings ($\rho \geq 0.70$). In addition, all LLM responses complied with the requested structured output format and were generated in $0.87 \pm 0.17$ s on average. These findings suggest that LLMs can support human state estimation by transforming wearable-derived physiological features into structured outputs accompanied by human-readable LLM-generated rationale.

**Keywords:** Large Language Models · Wearable Sensors · Human State Estimation · Human-Readable Rationales · Physical Workload · Multimodal Monitoring

## 1 Introduction

Human state monitoring is becoming increasingly relevant in domains where interactions among humans, technologies, and environments require continuous


S. Bistarelli et al. (Eds.): AIxIA 2026, LNAI 17131, pp. 662–674, 2027.
https://doi.org/10.1007/978-3-032-40774-0_47

awareness of the user's psychophysiological state [1]. The growing availability of wearable sensors enables the unobtrusive acquisition of physiological and movement-related signals in real-world and semi-controlled settings, including cardiac activity, respiration, electrodermal activity, and body acceleration [2]. These signals provide indirect but informative markers of autonomic regulation, physical effort, cognitive demand, and behavioral activation, supporting the development of systems capable of estimating the user's state over time [3]. Such capability is particularly important in applications such as human-computer interaction [4], occupational safety [5], rehabilitation [6], sport and physical training [7], where timely information about the user's condition can support more personalized and responsive interventions.

Several approaches have been proposed to infer human state from wearable-derived physiological features, addressing dimensions such as mental and physical workload, fatigue, stress, affective state, and psychophysiological arousal [8,9]. Most systems rely on supervised learning or rule-based/fuzzy-logic approaches. Supervised models, including classical machine learning classifiers, regression methods, and deep learning architectures, learn mappings between physiological features and labels collected during experimental protocols [10,11]. Although these methods can achieve good predictive performance and capture nonlinear relationships among multimodal signals, they require labeled datasets and are sensitive to the conditions under which training data are collected. As a result, their performance may decrease across different subjects, tasks, sensors, or application scenarios. Moreover, many models are not inherently interpretable, making it difficult for non-expert users to understand how physiological patterns contributed to the final estimate.

Rule-based and fuzzy-logic systems offer a more transparent alternative, mapping physiological parameters to user-state estimates through predefined rules and membership functions [12,13]. However, their performance depends on expert knowledge, manual rule design, and task-specific assumptions, making their adaptation to new users, signals, or target states difficult. Overall, while supervised and fuzzy-logic approaches are valuable for human state estimation, they present complementary limitations: supervised models often lack user-accessible LLM-generated rationale, whereas fuzzy systems require extensive manual design. Both may therefore be limited when the goal is not only to estimate a user's state, but also to provide an understandable rationale grounded in physiological evidence.

Recent studies have started to investigate the use of Large Language Models (LLMs) for sensor-based human state estimation. In a recent survey, [14] highlighted the growing role of LLMs in human activity recognition, health monitoring, and behavior modeling from sensor data, emphasizing their ability to integrate heterogeneous information, operate in zero-shot or few-shot settings, and generate context-aware interpretations. This perspective suggests that LLMs may complement traditional data-driven models by providing not only predictions, but also natural-language explanations and reasoning over sensor derived representations. Following this direction, LLMs have been explored in different human-state monitoring scenarios. Affective-state prediction from passive smartphone sensing data was investigated in [15], showing that behavioral features transformed into natural-language descriptions can be used by LLMs to infer mood-related states, especially under few-shot prompting strategies. Similarly, StressLLM evaluated the use of LLMs for stress prediction from wearable datasets, showing that prompting strategies and feature selection can influence the ability of the model to identify stress-related biomarkers [16]. Other works have explored hybrid strategies, combining classical machine learning models with LLM-based reasoning for fatigue prediction [17], or using structured prompts to estimate multiple wellbeing-related dimensions such as stress, fatigue, readiness, and sleep quality from multimodal wearable features [18]. Overall, these studies suggest that LLMs can be effectively used to reason over sensor-derived information and support the interpretation of human psychophysiological states.

However, despite these promising results, existing LLM-based approaches still leave three aspects only partially addressed. Firstly, prompt construction is not always formalized to clearly separate the desired human-state estimation task, the input physiological evidence, and the required response format. Since prompts directly influence the model output, their design should be explicitly motivated and reported in a simple, understandable way to support reproducibility and future research. Second, many studies include contextual or behavioral information in the prompt, making it difficult to assess whether the estimate is grounded in physiological signals alone. From this perspective, it is relevant to investigate whether a minimal input set, limited to the monitored physiological parameters, is sufficient to obtain reliable and interpretable human-state estimates.

The objective of this work is to propose and evaluate a minimal and structured LLM-based framework for human state estimation from wearable physiological data accompanied by human-readable rationales. The framework uses the LLM as a reasoning layer that receives only a task specification, a physiological feature vector, and a constrained output schema, returning both a numerical estimate and a concise LLM-generated rationale grounded in the provided features. The core innovation of the proposed approach lies in using the LLM as a semantic interface rather than as a conventional predictor. By excluding contextual task information, the framework specifically evaluates whether LLMs can reason over physiological evidence alone while producing structured outputs and human-readable explanations grounded in wearable-derived parameters.

The contribution of this paper is threefold:

- we introduce a general framework for LLM-based human state estimation from wearable-derived physiological features;
- we formalize a minimal prompt-generation strategy that separates the target estimation task, the physiological feature vector, and the required structured output;
- we validate the approach in a physical workload estimation case study.

By focusing on physiological features rather than contextual task descriptions, the proposed approach aims to isolate the contribution of wearable-derived signals and to assess the potential of LLMs as a human-readable interface between sensor-based monitoring and user-accessible state interpretation.

## 2 Proposed Approach

The proposed approach aims to use Large Language Models (LLMs) as a human-readable reasoning layer for human state estimation from wearable sensor data. Rather than processing raw biosignals directly, the framework relies on physiological and movement-related parameters extracted from wearable recordings and organized into a structured feature vector. This vector is then embedded into a task-specific prompt that defines the target state to be estimated and constrains the expected output format.

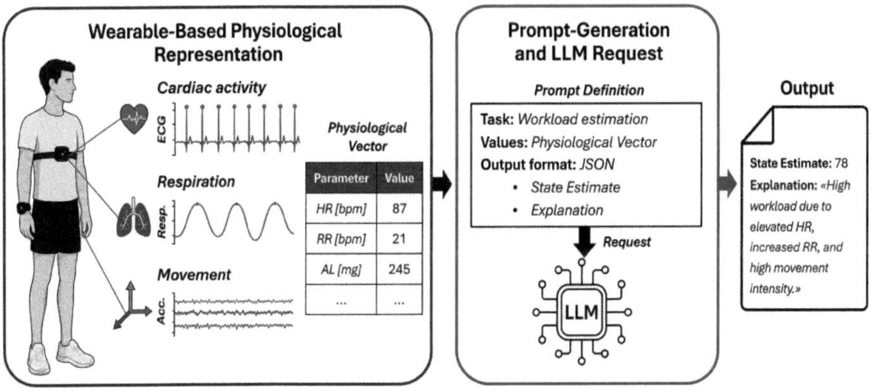


**Fig. 1.** Overview of the proposed LLM-based framework for human state estimation. Multimodal wearable signals are acquired from cardiorespiratory and movement sensors, processed to extract a task-relevant physiological vector, and provided to an LLM through a structured prompt. The LLM returns both a state estimate and a concise LLM-generated rationale grounded in the extracted physiological parameters.

As illustrated in Fig. 1, the LLM returns both a state estimate and a concise LLM-generated rationale grounded in the provided physiological evidence. This structure allows the framework to be adapted to different human-state estimation tasks while preserving a transparent link between sensor-derived features, model output, and human-readable interpretation.

### 2.1 Wearable-Based Physiological Representation

Wearable sensors can be used to continuously monitor different physiological and behavioral processes related to the user, including cardiac activity, respiration, electrodermal activity, body movement, skin temperature, and other autonomic or motor responses. Depending on the target state to be estimated, these signals can provide complementary information about psychophysiological activation, physical effort, stress, fatigue, cognitive demand, or emotional arousal.

In the proposed framework, raw wearable signals are not directly provided to the LLM. Instead, they are first preprocessed and transformed into a structured set of physiological parameters. This step may include signal filtering, artifact removal, segmentation into temporal windows, and the extraction of task-relevant descriptors.

The selection of the physiological parameters depends on the specific state estimation task. For instance, physical workload estimation may require features related to cardiorespiratory activation and movement intensity, while cognitive workload or emotional-state estimation may benefit from autonomic indices such as heart rate variability or electrodermal activity. Therefore, for each target state, the framework requires the definition of a task-relevant physiological feature vector:

$$\mathbf{x}_i = [x_{i,1}, x_{i,2}, \ldots, x_{i,d}], \tag{1}$$

where $\mathbf{x}_i$ represents the set of wearable-derived parameters extracted from the $i$-th analysis window and $d$ is the number of selected features.

This representation provides a compact and interpretable description of the user's physiological state over time. The resulting feature vector is then used as the input evidence for the LLM-based reasoning module, which generates both the state estimate and its LLM-generated rationale.

### 2.2 Prompt Generation and LLM Request

The proposed framework uses the LLM as a semantic reasoning layer that receives a structured physiological representation and returns a human-readable LLM-generated rationale of the computed human state. The prompt is generated to explicitly define three elements: the state-estimation task, the physiological feature vector extracted from wearable data, and the expected output format.

For each analysis window, the LLM request can be formally represented as:

$$\mathcal{R}_i = \{I_s,\ P_i\}, \tag{2}$$

where $I_s$ denotes the system instruction and $P_i$ is the structured user payload associated with the $i$-th physiological window. The system instruction constrains the model to estimate the requested human state using only the provided wearable-derived features and to return a valid JSON object without additional text.

The structured payload is defined as:

$$P_i = \begin{cases} \texttt{task}: & \mathcal{T}, \\ \texttt{features}: & \mathbf{x}_i, \\ \texttt{output}: & \mathcal{O}. \end{cases}$$

Here, $\tau$ represents the target state-estimation task, $\mathbf{x}_i$ is the physiological feature vector extracted from the $i$-th time window, and $\mathcal{O}$ defines the required output schema. In the general framework, $\tau$ can be adapted to different human-state estimation targets, such as physical workload, cognitive workload, psychophysiological activation, or emotional state, depending on the application.

The output schema requires the LLM to return both a state estimate and a concise LLM-generated rationale grounded only in the input features. This design allows the framework to produce not only a numerical or categorical assessment, but also a human-readable rationale linking the estimated state to the physiological evidence provided as input.

# 3 Experimental Validation

The proposed framework was experimentally validated in a physical workload estimation scenario using physiological and movement data collected from wearable sensors. The goal of this validation was to assess whether the LLM could generate workload estimates consistent with subjective workload perception, while also producing structured and interpretable outputs. Specifically, the analysis focused on three aspects: the agreement between LLM-based workload scores and user perception of the physical workload, the compliance of the model responses with the requested JSON format, and the presence of concise LLM-generated rationale grounded in the provided physiological features.

## 3.1 Experimental Setup

The experimental setup was designed to collect multimodal physiological and movement data during physical training. Cardiorespiratory activity, as well as body acceleration, were acquired using the Zephyr BioHarness 3.0, a wearable chest belt integrating a capacitive sensor, a stretch sensor, and a tri-axial accelerometer. The capacitive sensor detects electrical cardiac activity at 250 Hz, while the stretch sensor captures ribcage deformations associated with breathing at 20 Hz. The accelerometer, operating at 100 Hz, captures movement data from the bodies of the enrolled participants. The device was worn directly against the skin at sternum height to optimize signal acquisition.

Heart rate (HR) and respiration rate (RR) were computed from the cardiac and respiratory signals using the `BioSPPy` library. Specifically, peaks were identified from the corresponding signals, and the instantaneous frequency was derived from the inter-beat or inter-breath interval as $60/IBI(t)$, where $IBI(t)$ denotes the time interval between two consecutive detected peaks. HR was expressed in beats per minute (bpm), while RR was expressed in breaths per minute. Movement intensity was quantified through the Activity Level (AL), defined as the Euclidean norm of the three acceleration components expressed in [g]:

$$AL(t) = \sqrt{a_x(t)^2 + a_y(t)^2 + a_z(t)^2}. \quad (3)$$

To obtain a compact and temporally consistent representation of the participant's physiological state, HR, RR, and AL were averaged over non-overlapping 5 s windows. Each window, therefore, produced one representative physiological feature vector, corresponding to a sampling rate of 0.2 Hz. These feature vectors were then provided as input to the LLM for physical workload estimation.

The LLM-based estimation was performed using `gpt-4.1-nano`. For each physiological vector, a structured request was generated and submitted to the model, consisting of two components: a system instruction and a user message encoded as a JSON payload. The system instruction constrained the model to estimate the requested human state using only the provided wearable-derived features and to return a valid JSON object without additional text. The user message contained three elements: the target estimation task, the physiological feature vector, and the expected output schema.

For the experimental validation, the general prompt-generation strategy was instantiated for the specific task of physical workload estimation. Accordingly, the target task $\tau$ was defined as the estimation of physical workload, while the physiological feature vector was defined as $\mathbf{x}_i = [HR_i, RR_i, AL_i]$, with the three parameters extracted from each 5 s window. The required output schema $\mathcal{O}$ consisted of two fields: `workload_score`, defined as an integer value between 0 and 100, and `explanation`, defined as a short sentence grounded only in the provided physiological features.

### 3.2 Experimental Protocol

The experiments were conducted involving 14 healthy participants (6 males and 8 females, $35.3 \pm 18.2$ years). They were asked to carry out physical exercises selected to elicit increasing levels of physical demand, together with non-physical conditions used as resting. More in detail, the physical exercises administered to the participants were:

- **Shoulder Flexion/Extension**: participants performed repeated forward and backward arm movements. This low-intensity exercise was intended to elicit minimal physical exertion while involving controlled upper-limb motion.
- **Walking in Place**: participants performed rhythmic lower-limb movements while maintaining a steady pace. This task was intended to induce a moderate level of physical effort and cardiorespiratory activation.
- **Squat**: participants performed repeated squat movements. This high-intensity exercise engaged lower-body muscles and required greater physical effort and coordination.

Each task lasted 1 min and 30 s and was followed by at least a 3 min resting period, namely **RECOVERY**. Each activity included in the protocol was repeated four times for each participant in a random order. This structure was adopted to allow physiological variables to progressively return toward baseline before the subsequent task administration, while providing multiple repetitions of each workload condition. At the end of each condition, participants rated their perceived physical demand using a 1–10 scale derived from the NASA Task Load Index (NASA-TLX) methodology. These ratings were used as subjective reference values for perceived physical workload and were subsequently normalized to the range $[0, 1]$ to improve comparability across participants.

### 3.3 Data Analysis

The analysis was designed to evaluate both the numerical workload estimates generated by the LLM and the reliability of the structured output format. More in detail, the following key performance indicators were computed:

- **Estimation time:** the computational responsiveness of the LLM-based estimation process was assessed by measuring the inference time required to generate each workload estimate. Inference time was computed as the elapsed time between the submission of the structured LLM request and the reception of the corresponding response. The average inference time was reported as mean $\pm$ standard deviation.
- **JSON compliance and output validity:** the robustness of the structured prompting strategy was evaluated by verifying whether the LLM responses could be automatically parsed as JSON and contained the required fields, namely `workload_score` and `explanation`. In addition, we checked whether the workload score was a numerical value within the expected range from 0 to 100 and whether the LLM-generated rationale field was non-empty. These metrics were computed as a safety check to assess whether the model consistently respected the requested output structure and constraints.
- **Correlation:** the numerical validity of the LLM-based workload estimation was assessed by comparing the generated workload scores with the subjective physical-demand ratings derived from the NASA-TLX questionnaire. Since NASA-TLX ratings were collected at the condition level, LLM estimates generated over the corresponding 5 s windows were aggregated for each condition before correlation analysis. The association between aggregated LLM estimates and NASA-TLX ratings was quantified using Spearman's rank correlation coefficient, assessing the monotonic relationship between estimated and perceived physical workload.

## 4 Results and Discussion

Figure 2 shows a representative example of the collected data and the estimations obtained for one participant. The first three panels report the physiological and movement-related parameters extracted from the wearable recordings. The shaded areas indicate the experimental conditions, distinguishing recovery periods from the three physical exercises considered in the validation protocol. As expected, physical workload conditions are generally associated with visible increases in HR and AL, with more pronounced peaks during higher-intensity

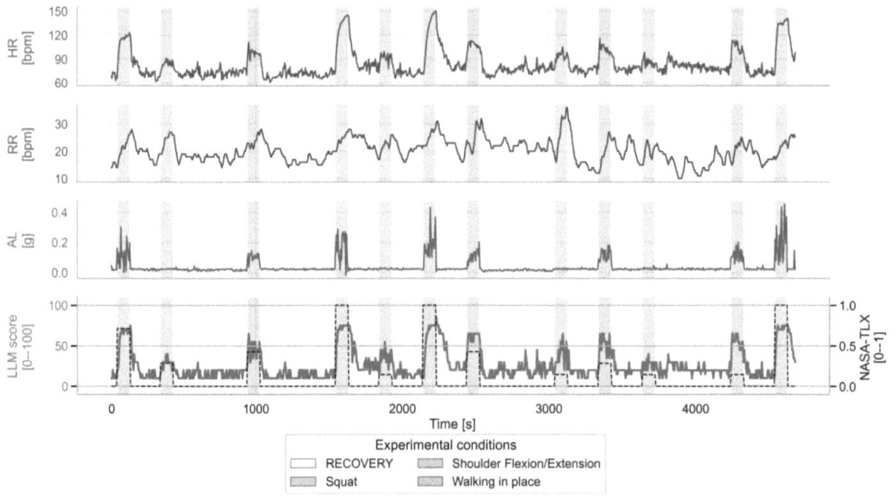


**Fig. 2.** Representative time series of physiological parameters and workload estimates obtained for one participant. The upper panels show heart rate (HR), respiration rate (RR), and Activity Level (AL), while the bottom panel reports the workload score generated by the proposed LLM-based framework together with the corresponding NASA-TLX physical-demand ratings. Shaded areas indicate the experimental conditions performed during the protocol.

movements such as squats and walking in place. RR also shows task-dependent modulations, although with a smoother and more variable temporal pattern.

The bottom panel reports the workload score estimated by the proposed LLM-based framework, together with the corresponding NASA-TLX physical-demand ratings used as subjective reference values. The estimated workload score generally follows the main variations induced by the experimental conditions, increasing during physically demanding segments and decreasing during recovery or low-load periods. A short temporal delay can be observed around some activity transitions. This behavior should be interpreted considering both the use of non-overlapping 5 s averaging windows and the different temporal dynamics of the input parameters. In particular, AL can decrease rapidly when movement stops, whereas HR and RR may remain elevated during the initial recovery phase. Therefore, workload estimates persisting briefly after the end of an exercise may reflect residual cardiorespiratory activation rather than solely a delayed recognition of activity cessation. Indeed, the proposed framework estimates the participant's physiological workload and is not intended to detect the exact onset and offset of the performed activity.

Table 1 reports representative examples of the outputs generated by the proposed framework for different physiological configurations. Low HR and RR values, together with minimal movement intensity, were associated with low workload scores and LLM-generated rationale referring to reduced physiological activation. Conversely, the highest workload estimate was produced for a vector characterized by markedly increased HR and RR, despite negligible acceleration. This suggests that the LLM did not interpret movement intensity alone as the main determinant of physical workload, but assigned substantial relevance to the cardiorespiratory response when estimating the current physiological effort. Overall, these examples show that the model generated concise LLM-generated rationale explicitly linking the estimated workload score to the physiological evidence provided as input.

**Table 1.** Examples of LLM-based workload estimation and explanation from representative physiological feature vectors.

| Physiological feature vector | | | LLM output | |
|---|---|---|---|---|
| HR [bpm] | RR [bpm] | AL [g] | Score | Explanation |
| 66 | 14 | 0.02 | 10 | The low heart rate, normal respiration rate, and minimal acceleration suggest a very low physical workload. |
| 74 | 15 | 0.02 | 20 | The heart rate of 74 bpm, respiration rate of 15 breaths per minute, and low acceleration level suggest a low physical workload. |
| 149 | 30 | 0.00 | 85 | The high heart rate of 149 bpm and respiration rate of 30 breaths per minute indicate a high physical workload. |

The computational responsiveness of the proposed framework was assessed by measuring the inference time required to generate each workload estimate. The LLM-based estimation required on average $0.83 \pm 0.17$ s per sample, with a median inference time of 0.80 s. The observed values ranged from 0.47 s to 1.36 s, indicating that the system was able to provide workload estimates within approximately one second for most physiological windows. Considering that the input feature vectors were generated every 5 s, these results suggest that the proposed framework is compatible with near-real-time human state monitoring applications.

All LLM responses complied with the requested structured output format. Specifically, all 13,453 responses were correctly parsed as JSON and contained the required fields, namely `workload_score` and `explanation`. In addition, all generated workload scores were valid numerical values within the expected range from 0 to 100, and all responses included a non-empty explanation. Therefore, JSON compliance, score validity, explanation availability, and fully valid output rate were all equal to 100%. This result indicates that the structured prompting strategy was highly reliable for automatic parsing and downstream quantitative analysis.

Figure 3 reports the subject-level association between the condition-level LLM workload estimates and the corresponding NASA-TLX physical-demand ratings. Condition-level LLM estimates were obtained by averaging the workload scores generated over the 5 s windows belonging to each condition. Overall, positive Spearman correlations were observed for all participants included in the analysis, indicating that higher perceived physical demand was generally associated with higher LLM-based workload estimates. All computed correlations were statistically significant, as indicated by the asterisks, and several subjects showed strong associations, with $\rho \geq 0.7$.

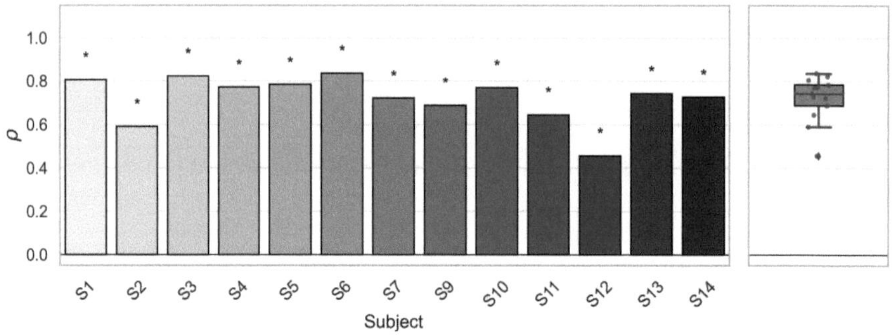


**Fig. 3.** Subject-level Spearman correlations between condition-level LLM-based workload estimates and NASA-TLX physical-demand ratings. The left panel reports the correlation coefficient for each participant, with asterisks indicating statistically significant correlations. The right panel shows the distribution of correlation coefficients across participants included in the analysis.

The boxplot on the right summarizes the distribution of subject-level correlation coefficients. The median correlation was high, suggesting a consistent relationship between the LLM estimates and subjective workload ratings across participants. Although some inter-subject variability was observed, the distribution remained predominantly in the positive and moderate-to-strong range. These results support the ability of the proposed framework to generate workload estimates that are coherent with participants' perceived physical demand.

## 5 Conclusions

This paper proposes a minimal and structured LLM-based framework for human state estimation from wearable physiological data. The main objective was to investigate whether an LLM could act as a semantic interface between wearable-derived physiological features and user-accessible state interpretation, returning both a numerical estimate and a concise explanation grounded in the provided input features.

The framework was validated in a physical workload estimation case study. Physiological and movement-related parameters, extracted from wearable recordings, were provided to the LLM without contextual information about the performed task or experimental condition. The generated workload estimates were compared with subjective physical-demand ratings derived from the NASA-TLX questionnaire. Results showed positive, moderate to strong, statistically significant correlations between condition-level LLM estimates and perceived workload ratings across all the enrolled participants. Moreover, all LLM responses were returned in the requested structured JSON format, contained valid workload scores and non-empty LLM-generated rationale, and had estimation times compatible with near-real-time monitoring.

These findings should be interpreted as evidence of the feasibility of using LLMs for human state estimation rather than as a comparative assessment against conventional supervised or rule-based approaches. The objective of this study was to explore whether an LLM could serve as a semantic, human-readable reasoning layer between wearable-derived physiological features and human-state estimates. In this role, LLMs offer potential advantages, including reduced reliance on manually encoded rules, flexibility in adapting the estimation task and output specification, and the ability to generate structured estimates together with concise LLM-generated rationale. However, the present study was not designed to determine whether the proposed approach outperforms existing human-state estimation methods.

Future work will broaden the validation to additional human-state estimation tasks and include systematic comparisons with conventional supervised, rule-based, and fuzzy-logic approaches, as well as across different LLMs and prompting configurations. It will also investigate the inclusion of subject-specific information, such as age, sex, fitness level, and individual physiological baselines, to account for inter-individual variability in the interpretation of heart rate and respiration. Particular attention will be devoted to explanation quality through human evaluation and quantitative grounding metrics, since the current analysis is limited to a small set of illustrative examples and does not establish whether the generated rationales are genuinely supported by the physiological evidence.

**Acknowledgments.** This work was supported partially by the Italian Ministry of Research, under the complementary actions to the NRRP "Fit4MedRob - Fit for Medical Robotics" Grant (#PNC0000007) and partially by the EU's Horizon Europe research and innovation programme under grant agreement No. 101168042 (TRIFFID).

**Disclosure of Interests.** The authors have no competing interests to declare that are relevant to the content of this article.

## References

1. Yamashita, A., Maeda, H., Jouh, Y., Chew, K., Amano: Internal state estimation via physiological data and its modulation by environmental context during social activity. J. Cogn. Neurosci. **37**(8), 1364–1380 (2025)
2. Zhang, T., et al:. Physiological measurements of situation awarcness: a systematic review. Hum. Factors **65**(5), 737–758 (2023)

3. Tamantini, C., Cordella, F., Scotto di Luzio, F., et al.: A fuzzy-logic approach for longitudinal assessment of patients' psychophysiological state: an application to upper-limb orthopedic robot-aided rehabilitation. J. NeuroEng. Rehabil. **21**(1), 202 (2024). https://doi.org/10.1186/s12984-024-01501-y
4. Hou, Y., Xie, Q., Zhang, N., Lv, J.: Cognitive load classification of mixed reality human computer interaction tasks based on multimodal sensor signals. Sci. Rep. **15**(1), 13732 (2025)
5. Ozobu, C.O., Adikwu, F.E., Odujobi, N.O., Onyekwe, F.O., Nwulu, E.O.: Advancing occupational safety with AI-powered monitoring systems: a conceptual framework for hazard detection and exposure control. World J. Innov. Mod. Technol. **9**(1), 186–213 (2025)
6. Molle, R., Tamantini, C., Lauretti, C., Romano, E.M., Zollo, L.: An online reinforcement learning method to improve control adaptability in robot-aided rehabilitation. Eng. Appl. Artif. Intell. **161**, 112248 (2025)
7. Chen, F., et al.: Wearable physiological monitoring of physical exercise and mental health: a systematic review. Intell. Sports Health **1**(1), 11–21 (2025)
8. Tamantini, C., et al.: Physiological sensor technologies in workload estimation: a review. IEEE Sensors J. (2025)
9. Stephen, P.J., et al.: Marino: approaches to inducing mental fatigue: a systematic review and meta-analysis of (neuro) physiologic indices. Behav. Res. Methods **57**(4), 102 (2025)
10. Fenoglio, D., et al.: Federated learning for privacy-aware cognitive workload estimation. In: Proceedings of the 22nd International Conference on Mobile and Ubiquitous Multimedia, pp. 25–36 (2023)
11. Liu, C., Zhang, C., Sun, L., Liu, K., Liu, H., Zhu, W., Jiang, C.: Detection of pilot's mental workload using a wireless EEG headset in airfield traffic pattern tasks. Entropy **25**(7), 1035 (2023)
12. Wang, D., Lin, Y., Hong, L., Zhang, C., Bai, Y., Bi, Z.Z.: Detection of the driver's mental workload level in smart and autonomous systems using physiological signals. Math. Probl. Eng. **2022**(1), 5233257 (2022)
13. Tamantini, C., et al.: A data-driven fuzzy logic method for psychophysiological assessment: an application to exoskeleton-assisted walking. IEEE Trans. Med. Robot. Bion. (2024)
14. Ferrara, E.: Large language models for wearable sensor-based human activity recognition, health monitoring, and behavioral modeling: a survey of early trends, datasets, and challenges. Sensors **24**(15), 5045 (2024)
15. Zhang, T., Teng, S., Jia, H., D'Alfonso, S.: Leveraging LLMS to predict affective states via smartphone sensor features. In: Companion of the 2024 on ACM International Joint Conference on Pervasive and Ubiquitous Computing, pp. 709–716 (2024)
16. Thapa, B., Rivas, M., Griffith, H., Rathore, H.: StressLLM: large language models for stress prediction via wearable sensor data. In: 2025 IEEE International Conference on Consumer Electronics (ICCE), pp. 1–6. IEEE (2025)
17. Ha, S., Lee, T., Seo, H., Yoon, S., Lee, H.: A selective rag-enhanced hybrid ML-LLM framework for efficient and explainable fatigue prediction using wearable sensor data. Bioengineering **13**(1), 58 (2026)
18. Cheng-Huan, Yu., Masum, M.: Hybridsense-LLM: a structured multimodal framework for large-language-model-based wellness prediction from wearable sensors with contextual self-reports. Bioengineering **13**(1), 120 (2026)

# TriQA: A Multilingual, Multi-KB Question-Answer Dataset Generated from Knowledge Graph Triples and LLMs

Alessandro Temperoni(✉) and Beatrice Turano

Almawave, Rome, Italy
{a.temperoni,b.turano}@almawave.it

**Abstract.** Creating high-quality question-answer (QA) datasets is expensive, yet essential for knowledge-intensive NLP systems. We present **TriQA**, a pipeline that combines structured knowledge from multiple knowledge bases with the generative capabilities of large language models (LLMs) to produce QA datasets controllable along three axes: *topic*, *difficulty*, and *language*. By grounding generation in knowledge graph triples, every generated answer is traceable to its source facts, substantially reducing hallucination risk compared to unconstrained LLM generation. Our approach extracts triples from eight heterogeneous knowledge sources—Wikidata, Freebase, DBpedia, ConceptNet, GeoNames, ArCo, OpenFoodFacts, and Italian parliamentary open data—and over 10 million Wikipedia abstracts from DBpedia, covering domains from general knowledge to cultural heritage, commonsense reasoning, geography, nutrition, and politics. The pipeline supports six languages through a scalable architecture that processes compressed dumps locally, producing 292 million triples and over 28 million QA pairs. A hybrid difficulty scoring mechanism combines heuristic signals with LLM-as-judge ratings, and a *property classification benchmark* evaluates relational schema understanding across sources, achieving 96–100% zero-shot accuracy with Gemma-4-31B on most knowledge bases. (A representative subset of the dataset and the pipeline code will be made publicly available).

**Keywords:** Question answering · Knowledge graphs · Multilingual NLP · Dataset generation · Large language models

## 1 Introduction

Question answering (QA) is a crucial task in NLP, underpinning applications from search engines to conversational AI [11,15]. Automated QA generation has emerged as a promising alternative to labor-intensive manual dataset construction, progressing from template-based methods [16] and neural question generation [7] to LLM-based synthesis [14]. Yet most approaches lack fine-grained control over three properties that practitioners frequently need: *topical domain*, *difficulty level*, and *output language*. Template-based KG methods [3,20] offer


S. Bistarelli et al. (Eds.): AIxIA 2026, LNAI 17131, pp. 675–688, 2027.
https://doi.org/10.1007/978-3-032-40774-0_48

topical control but produce stilted questions; neural generators produce fluent questions but cannot easily control difficulty or domain coverage, and the vast majority of pipelines are English-only.

Knowledge graphs provide an ideal foundation for controllable, multilingual QA generation, but no single KB covers all domains or languages equally well. Commonsense knowledge is richly represented in ConceptNet [17] but absent from Wikidata [21]; Italian cultural heritage exists in ArCo [4] but not in general-purpose KBs; nutritional data, geographic detail, and entertainment metadata each reside in specialized sources. By combining multiple KBs, we can produce QA datasets with unprecedented topical diversity. Crucially, grounding generation in structured triples means the generated QA pairs can be automatically checked against their source facts, substantially reducing the manual effort required for quality assurance. While this does not eliminate all hallucination risk, it provides a tractable verification path that unconstrained generation lacks.

In this paper, we present **TriQA**, a pipeline with four stages:

1. **Multi-source triple extraction**: We extract subject–predicate–object triples from eight knowledge bases spanning diverse domains, formats, and languages, using a scalable local processing architecture that streams compressed dumps without requiring full decompression.
2. **Multilingual QA generation**: We prompt an LLM with entity-grouped batches of triples using language-specific prompt templates to produce natural-language question-answer pairs in six languages.
3. **Difficulty scoring**: We apply a hybrid scoring mechanism combining heuristic features (entity popularity, property commonality) with LLM-as-judge ratings.
4. **Property classification**: We construct a multiple-choice benchmark from the generated questions, where the task is to identify which knowledge base property a question queries, with distractors drawn from multiple ontologies.

Our contributions are:

1. A fully automated, multi-source pipeline that extracts triples from eight heterogeneous knowledge bases and text-grounded abstracts from six DBpedia language editions, producing 292 million triples and 10.4 million abstracts across domains including factual knowledge, commonsense reasoning, cultural heritage, geography, nutrition, and politics.
2. A scalable extraction architecture based on local dump streaming with label caching, resume support, and single-scan multi-language processing, eliminating dependence on rate-limited APIs.
3. A multilingual QA generation framework with fully translated prompt templates, entity-grouped batching, and provenance tracking.
4. A property classification benchmark with semantically aware distractor selection from multiple ontologies, achieving 96–100% zero-shot accuracy with Gemma-4-31B across most knowledge bases, demonstrating that the generated questions are reliably property-specific.
5. A hybrid difficulty scoring mechanism combining structural knowledge graph features with LLM-based judgment.

## 2 Related Work

*Question Generation.* QA generation has evolved from rule-based [10] and template-based methods [16], through neural sequence-to-sequence models [7,27] with answer-aware conditioning [18] and reinforcement learning [24], to LLM-based synthesis for domain adaptation [14], data augmentation [23], and roundtrip consistency filtering [1]. Our work differs by grounding generation in structured KG triples from multiple sources, providing stronger factual guarantees and cross-domain diversity.

*Knowledge Graphs for QA.* KG-based QA benchmarks include SimpleQuestions [3] (Freebase single-relation questions), LC-QuAD [20] (SPARQL templates), and LC-QuAD 2.0 [8] (complex Wikidata patterns). [12] proposed difficulty-controllable multi-hop generation, and [6] showed that combining multiple knowledge sources improves answer coverage. These approaches typically rely on a single source. TriQA extends this direction by combining eight KBs, leveraging instruction-following LLMs for multilingual generation, and introducing a hybrid difficulty mechanism over heterogeneous sources.

*Multilingual QA and Question Difficulty.* Multilingual benchmarks [2,5,13] highlight the need for language diversity but rely on translation or crowdsourcing. Our pipeline generates QA pairs natively in six languages. For difficulty, [12] relies on entity popularity; our hybrid approach adds structural KG features and LLM-based judgment across heterogeneous sources.

*Relation Classification and Schema Understanding.* Relation classification [25, 26] has been evaluated with LLMs on benchmarks like FewRel [9,22], revealing struggles with fine-grained distinctions. [19] showed that KG triples can enrich relation extraction via OpenIE decompositions. Our property classification benchmark frames this as a controlled multiple-choice task with distractors drawn from multiple ontologies.

## 3 Approach

Figure 1 illustrates the TriQA pipeline. We describe each stage below.

### 3.1 Multi-source Triple Extraction

A central design decision in TriQA is to draw triples from multiple, complementary knowledge bases rather than relying on a single source. This yields broader topical coverage, richer domain diversity, and stronger multilingual support. Table 1 summarizes the eight knowledge sources we integrate.

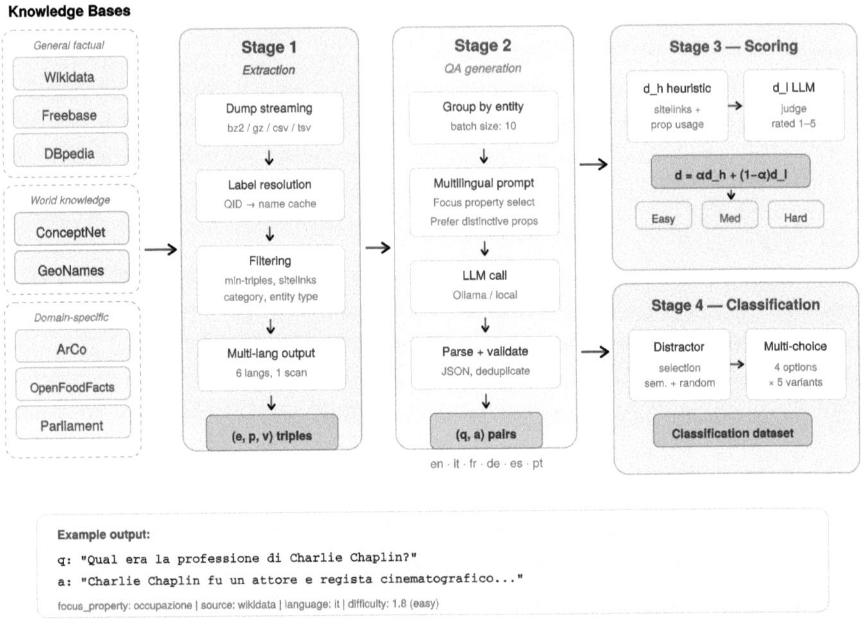


**Fig. 1.** The TriQA pipeline. Eight knowledge bases, grouped by domain, feed into a multi-source extractor (Stage 1) that streams compressed dumps, resolves labels, and applies configurable filters to produce standardized $(e, p, v)$ triples in six languages. Stage 2 groups triples by entity and prompts an LLM with multilingual templates to generate QA pairs. The output branches into Stage 3 (hybrid difficulty scoring combining heuristic and LLM signals) and Stage 4 (property classification with semantically aware distractors). An example Italian QA pair is shown at the bottom.

**Table 1.** Knowledge sources integrated in TriQA. "Size" refers to the compressed dump size. Languages indicates how many of our six target languages are supported. The bottom row represents a text-grounded source (Wikipedia abstracts) rather than structured triples.

| Source | Domain | Format | Size | Langs | Key Properties |
|---|---|---|---|---|---|
| Wikidata | General factual | JSON dump | 90 GB | 6 | birth, occupation, award, ... |
| Freebase | Entertainment, sports | N-Triples | 30 GB | 6 (EN) | genre, director, team, ... |
| DBpedia | Italian Wikipedia | Turtle | 260 MB | IT | infobox fields |
| ConceptNet | Commonsense | CSV | 330 MB | 6 | UsedFor, CapableOf, Causes |
| GeoNames | Geography | TSV | 650 MB | 6 | population, elevation, timezone |
| ArCo | Italian cult. heritage | N-Triples | 3.7 GB | IT | material, technique, author |
| OpenFoodFacts | Nutrition | CSV | 900 MB | 6 | ingredients, nutriscore, allergens |
| Parliament | Italian politics | SPARQL | — | IT | deputies, bills, votes |
| DBpedia Abs. | Wikipedia abstracts | Turtle | 500 MB | 6 | text-grounded descriptions |

*Label Resolution.* Knowledge bases use internal identifiers, so we build reusable *label caches* by scanning each dump once to extract human-readable labels for all six languages. For Wikidata, this one-time process produces approximately 92 million English labels. For Freebase, a two-stream approach collects labels in the first pass and resolves triples in the second, keeping memory manageable at 10.5 GB despite 3.1 billion input lines. For RDF sources (ArCo, DBpedia), labels are extracted from `rdfs:label` predicates; for tabular sources (GeoNames, OpenFoodFacts, ConceptNet), labels are provided directly. For multilingual sources, all six languages are processed in a single scan, writing to six output files simultaneously. It is important to note that TriQA does not perform cross-source entity alignment: each knowledge base is processed independently, and entities appearing in multiple sources (e.g., "Leonardo da Vinci" in both Wikidata and ArCo) are treated as separate entries with their own triples. This is a deliberate design choice: since each source contributes different properties and schemas, the generated QA pairs are complementary rather than redundant. Homonymous labels referring to different entities (e.g., multiple cities named "Springfield") are disambiguated within each source by tracking unique entity identifiers (QIDs for Wikidata, MIDs for Freebase) rather than labels. Cross-source entity linking remains an avenue for future work that could enable multi-hop questions spanning knowledge bases.

### 3.2 Multilingual QA Generation

We group triples by entity and send each group (up to $B$ triples, the batch size) to an instruction-following LLM to generate one question-answer pair per batch. The prompt instructs the model to (1) select one property as the question's focus, preferring distinctive properties over generic ones, (2) phrase the question naturally without using the property name or close synonyms, and (3) produce a fluent 2–3 sentence answer that primarily addresses the focus question but may incorporate related facts from other triples in the batch.

*Entity-Grouped Batching.* Rather than generating one question per individual triple, we group all triples for the same entity and send them together. This allows the LLM to produce richer answers that weave multiple facts together. For an entity with 15 triples and a batch size of 10, the system produces two QA pairs: one from the first 10 triples and one from the remaining 5. The batch size thus controls a tradeoff: larger batches give the LLM more context to produce richer, multi-fact answers, but yield fewer QA pairs per entity; smaller batches produce more QA pairs but with thinner answers grounded in fewer facts.

*Provenance Tracking.* Each generated QA pair records (1) the focus property selected by the LLM, (2) the specific triples used to compose the answer (`used_triples`), (3) the source KB, and (4) the language. This fine-grained provenance supports factual verification: the answer can be checked against its source triples, making quality more tractable than for unconstrained generation, though manual inspection remains valuable for detecting subtle errors.

We evaluate multiple LLMs for generation, including Gemma-4-31B and Qwen3-8B, served locally. We apply post-hoc deduplication by removing QA pairs with identical questions after normalization.

*Abstract-Based QA Generation.* In addition to the triple-based approach, we extract short abstracts (the first paragraph of each Wikipedia article) from DBpedia for all six target languages, yielding 10.4 million abstracts total. Each abstract is a dense natural-language description containing multiple facts about an entity. We prompt the LLM with a dedicated abstract-based template that instructs it to identify the most distinctive fact in the description and generate one natural question-answer pair grounded in the text. This complements the triple-based approach: triples produce precise, property-focused questions ("What is the population of Florence?"), while abstracts produce richer, contextual questions ("In which historical period did Florence become a major cultural center?"). The output format is identical to the triple-based pipeline, enabling seamless integration with the downstream scoring and classification stages.

### 3.3 Hybrid Difficulty Scoring

We score each QA pair on a 1–5 difficulty scale using a two-layer mechanism. The *heuristic layer* computes $d_h$ from three signals: entity popularity (the ratio of an entity's sitelink count $s_e$ to the dataset median $\tilde{s}$, mapped through $\Delta_e = -1.5 \cdot \tanh(\ln(s_e/\tilde{s})/\ln 3)$ so that popular entities score easier and obscure ones harder), property commonality (usage frequency across the dataset, similarly mapped), and answer complexity. For domain-specific sources without prominence metadata, a default offset reflects their inherently specialized content. The *LLM-as-judge layer* prompts a model to rate difficulty on a 1–5 rubric from "common knowledge" to "expert knowledge." The final score combines both:

$$d = \alpha \cdot d_h + (1 - \alpha) \cdot d_l \tag{1}$$

discretized into EASY ($d \leq 2$), MEDIUM ($2 < d \leq 3.5$), and HARD ($d > 3.5$). The multi-source design provides a natural difficulty gradient without explicit tuning.

### 3.4 Property Classification

From the generated QA pairs, we construct a multiple-choice classification benchmark. Given a natural-language question, the task is to identify which knowledge base property the question queries, selecting from four options.

*Distractor Selection.* For each question with correct property $p^*$, we select three distractor properties using a mixed strategy. Properties are first categorized into semantic groups (person, location, temporal, organization, media, science, etc.) using multilingual keyword matching. We then sample distractors as a configurable mix of *semantically similar* properties (from the same category as

$p^*$, making the task harder) and *random* properties (from different categories, providing easier contrasts). This enables controlled difficulty for the classification task itself.

*Option Enrichment.* When available, each option is enriched with a description from the source knowledge base: "*occupation—position held by a person.*" For Wikidata properties, we query descriptions via SPARQL (cached locally). For all other sources, we build a *unified property description cache*: we use Gemma-4-31B to generate one-line multilingual descriptions for over 13,000 unique properties across all non-Wikidata knowledge bases, stored in a single JSON file. This cache is constructed once and reused across all downstream classification and evaluation tasks.

*Multilingual Support.* Category keywords for semantic grouping are provided in English, Italian, French, German, and Spanish. The system auto-detects the dominant language from input QA pairs and selects the appropriate keyword set, with English as a fallback.

# 4 Experimental Setup

## 4.1 Dataset Construction

We constructed the multi-source QA dataset by executing the extraction pipeline across all eight knowledge bases. For Wikidata, we streamed the full JSON dump (~90 GB compressed) with minimum sitelink threshold of 10 and minimum triple count of 10, extracting all six languages in a single scan using pre-built label caches. For Freebase, a two-pass architecture (labels then triples) processed the 30 GB dump with 10.5 GB peak memory. Smaller sources (ConceptNet, GeoNames, OpenFoodFacts, DBpedia Italian) completed in under 15 min each; ArCo used a simplified extraction with only direct literal values. The Italian Parliament data was queried via SPARQL endpoints.

QA generation used a batch size of 10 triples per entity with fully translated prompt templates. For abstract-based QA, 10.4 million short abstracts were extracted from DBpedia across all six languages. For property classification, each QA pair generated 5 variants with different distractor sets; property descriptions for non-Wikidata sources were generated using Gemma-4-31B, covering over 13,000 properties.

We evaluate the pipeline along three axes: (1) QA quality via factual correctness, naturalness, and answerability ratings on a stratified sample; (2) property classification accuracy in a zero-shot setting; and (3) difficulty calibration against human judgments. All scripts run on consumer hardware (64 GB RAM) with LLMs served locally via vLLM and Ollama.

**Table 2.** Triple counts per knowledge base and language (in thousands). Cells marked "—" indicate that the source does not provide data in that language. Italian-only sources (ArCo, DBpedia, Parliament) contribute exclusively to the IT column. The total exceeds 292 million triples across eight knowledge sources and six languages.

| Source | EN | IT | FR | DE | ES | PT | Total |
|---|---|---|---|---|---|---|---|
| Wikidata | 11,690 | 13,273 | 14,921 | 13,501 | 13,595 | 11,243 | 78,223 |
| Freebase | 37,611 | 4,327 | 5,219 | 4,790 | 4,019 | 3,454 | 59,419 |
| DBpedia | — | 16,729 | — | — | — | — | 16,729 |
| ConceptNet | 1,097 | 60 | 473 | 550 | 39 | 103 | 2,322 |
| GeoNames | 361 | 361 | 361 | 361 | 361 | 361 | 2,165 |
| ArCo | — | 1,337 | — | — | — | — | 1,337 |
| OpenFoodFacts | 21,920 | 21,920 | 21,920 | 21,920 | 21,920 | 21,920 | 131,518 |
| Parliament | — | 1,089 | — | — | — | — | 1,089 |
| **Total** | **72,678** | **59,096** | **42,893** | **41,121** | **39,934** | **37,080** | **292,802** |

# 5 Results

## 5.1 Dataset Statistics

Table 2 summarizes the extraction results across all knowledge bases and six languages, and Table 3 reports the number of generated QA pairs.

Table 4 places TriQA in the context of existing QA benchmarks. While prior datasets excel at specific evaluation tasks, TriQA is distinguished by its scale (28M+ QA pairs), multilingual coverage (6 languages), multi-source knowledge grounding (8 KBs spanning 8+ domains), and integrated difficulty scoring. To our knowledge, no prior dataset combines all four of these properties.

## 5.2 QA Quality Analysis

We present a qualitative analysis of the generated QA pairs, highlighting how multi-source extraction produces diverse question types that no single knowledge base could provide alone.

Table 5 shows representative QA pairs from five knowledge bases, illustrating how each source contributes a distinct question style.

Native-language prompting produces idiomatic phrasing across all six languages. The two generation modes are complementary: triple-based QA yields precise, property-focused questions, while abstract-based QA produces contextual, inferential questions from narrative paragraphs.

## 5.3 Difficulty Distribution

The multi-source design produces a natural difficulty gradient: Wikidata questions about famous entities tend toward easy, domain-specific questions (ArCo,

**Table 3.** Generated QA pairs per source for English and Italian (in thousands). Abstract-based QA is also available for FR (1,505K), DE (1,610K), ES (1,118K), and PT (784K), bringing the total across all six languages to over 28 million QA pairs.

| Source | EN QA | IT QA |
|---|---|---|
| *Triple-based QA:* | | |
| Wikidata | 2,100 | 2,670 |
| Freebase | 4,540 | 533 |
| DBpedia | — | 2,123 |
| OpenFoodFacts | 2,800 | 2,800 |
| ConceptNet | 200 | — |
| ArCo | — | 164 |
| Parliament | — | 130 |
| GeoNames | — | 50 |
| *Abstract-based QA:* | | |
| DBpedia Abs. | 4,524 | 855 |
| **Total** | **14,164** | **9,325** |

Parliament) toward hard, and OpenFoodFacts and Freebase span the full range depending on entity prominence. This yields a well-distributed difficulty spectrum without explicit tuning.

### 5.4 Property Classification

We evaluate the property classification task using zero-shot prompting with Gemma-4-31B on 200 randomly sampled examples per knowledge base and language combination. The model receives a question and four property options and must select the correct one. The random baseline is 25%. As a concrete example, given the question "What was Charlie Chaplin's profession?," the four options might be: (A) *occupation*, (B) *country of citizenship*, (C) *genre*, (D) *elevation*—where (B) and (C) are semantically similar distractors and (D) is random.

*Results.* Table 6 reports classification accuracy across knowledge bases and languages. The model achieves near-perfect accuracy on most sources, with an overall average of 94.9% across all evaluated conditions. Wikidata English achieves 100%, indicating that questions generated from Wikidata triples are highly property-specific and the enriched option descriptions provide sufficient disambiguation. The outlier is OpenFoodFacts English (74%): nutritional properties ("fat per 100g," "sugars per 100g") are semantically too similar for reliable discrimination. Italian OpenFoodFacts reaches 97.5%, suggesting more distinctive Italian descriptions.

*Description Coverage.* The property description cache achieves high coverage: 96.2% of options in DBpedia Italian and 100% in Freebase English include

**Table 4.** Comparison with existing QA benchmarks. TriQA is distinguished by its scale (two orders of magnitude larger than most benchmarks), native multilingual generation (not translated), multi-source knowledge grounding, and integrated difficulty scoring. "Domains" counts the number of distinct topical domains covered.

| Dataset | Year | QA Pairs | Langs | Sources | Generation | Difficulty | Domains |
|---|---|---|---|---|---|---|---|
| SQuAD 1.1 | 2016 | 100K | 1 | Wikipedia text | Crowdsourced | No | General |
| TriviaQA | 2017 | 650K | 1 | Web + Wikipedia | Trivia fans | No | Trivia |
| SimpleQuestions | 2015 | 108K | 1 | Freebase | Crowdsourced | No | General |
| LC-QuAD | 2017 | 5K | 1 | DBpedia | Template | No | General |
| LC-QuAD 2.0 | 2019 | 30K | 1 | Wikidata+DBpedia | Template | No | General |
| XQuAD | 2020 | 1.2K | 11 | Wikipedia text | Translated | No | General |
| MLQA | 2020 | 12K | 7 | Wikipedia text | Parallel | No | General |
| TyDi QA | 2020 | 204K | 11 | Wikipedia text | Native | No | General |
| **TriQA** | 2026 | **28M+** | **6** | **8 KBs + abstracts** | **LLM** | **Yes** | **8+** |

descriptions alongside property names. This enrichment is critical: without descriptions, options like "track" or "region" are ambiguous, while "track—a musical piece on an album" provides the semantic context needed for informed selection.

*Cross-source Classification.* The distractor pool draws from all knowledge bases simultaneously, so a Freebase question may include Wikidata and DBpedia properties as distractors. This cross-source design tests whether a model can distinguish relational semantics across heterogeneous schemas, where naming conventions vary (e.g., "birth place" in Wikidata vs. "luogo di nascita" in ArCo). The consistently high accuracy (96–100% on most sources) suggests that despite schema heterogeneity, the questions generated by our pipeline are sufficiently property-specific to enable reliable classification. This result supports the value of KG-grounded generation: because each question is derived from a specific triple, the LLM tends to produce questions that target identifiable relational properties, though this does not guarantee that all answer content is free from hallucinated details beyond the source triple.

## 6 Discussion

### 6.1 Multi-source Tradeoffs

Each knowledge base contributes a distinct piece: Wikidata provides broad factual coverage, Freebase adds entertainment and sports depth (frozen at 2015), DBpedia Italian offers infobox properties with no Wikidata equivalent (e.g., "capoluogo," "sindaco"), and ConceptNet contributes commonsense knowledge after aggressive filtering (30 whitelisted relations from 34M assertions). The domain-specific Italian sources—ArCo and Parliament—contribute inherently harder questions by virtue of their specialized content.

**Table 5.** Representative QA pairs from five knowledge sources, illustrating domain diversity. CN = ConceptNet, OFF = OpenFoodFacts.

| Source | Question | Answer |
|---|---|---|
| Wikidata | Qual era la professione di Charlie Chaplin? *(What was Charlie Chaplin's profession?)* | Charlie Chaplin fu un attore comico e regista cinematografico britannico... *(Charlie Chaplin was a British comic actor and filmmaker...)* |
| Freebase | What musical pieces are featured on the third disc of the Classic FM Hall of Fame? | The third disc features orchestral works including pieces by Beethoven, Mozart, and Tchaikovsky, curated from the annual listener poll. |
| DBpedia | Quanti abitanti ha la località di Lhota nell'area di Olomouc? *(How many inhabitants does Lhota have in the Olomouc area?)* | La località di Lhota... circa 1.200 abitanti. *(The town of Lhota... approx. 1,200 inhabitants.)* |
| CN | What is a bicycle typically used for? | A bicycle is used for transportation, exercise, and recreation. |
| OFF | What allergens does Nutella contain? | Nutella contains milk and nuts as allergens, with potential traces of soy. |

Non-English coverage varies dramatically: Freebase English yielded 31.5 million triples versus 3.6 million Italian (9:1 ratio); ConceptNet is even more skewed. This gap motivated the inclusion of Italian-specific sources (DBpedia Italian, ArCo, Parliament), which collectively contribute millions of triples in domains that general-purpose multilingual KBs cover poorly. The resulting Italian emphasis is by design: TriQA was developed to support Italian-centered NLP research, and the inclusion of domain-specific Italian sources (cultural heritage, parliamentary data) reflects this priority.

### 6.2 Limitations

Data staleness affects Freebase (2015) and DBpedia Italian (2016–2017); Wikidata dumps are updated weekly. The fixed batch size $B$ for entity-grouped QA generation introduces a segmentation that does not reflect natural property groupings; alternative strategies such as property-based clustering or adaptive batch sizes could yield different question distributions and are worth exploring in future work. Entity overlap across Wikidata, Freebase, and DBpedia may introduce partial redundancy. The simplified ArCo extraction retains only direct literal values, sacrificing properties behind intermediate RDF nodes. The LLM-as-judge difficulty scoring is inherently nondeterministic and version-dependent;

**Table 6.** Property classification accuracy (%) by knowledge base and language, evaluated with Gemma-4-31B in a zero-shot setting ($n = 200$ per cell). Random baseline is 25%. DBpedia and GeoNames lack EN entries because DBpedia was extracted only from the Italian edition and GeoNames QA generation was performed only in Italian in the current pipeline configuration.

| Source | EN | IT |
|---|---|---|
| Wikidata | 100.0 | 97.5 |
| Freebase | 98.0 | 98.5 |
| DBpedia | — | 96.0 |
| OpenFoodFacts | 74.0 | 97.5 |
| GeoNames | — | 98.0 |
| **Average** | **90.7** | **97.5** |

we mitigate this by combining it with deterministic heuristic signals (the $\alpha$-weighted hybrid in Eq. 1, but reproducibility across LLM versions remains an open challenge shared by all LLM-based evaluation approaches. The current evaluation relies on a single model (Gemma-4-31B) and covers only English and Italian for property classification; extending evaluation to additional models and languages would strengthen the findings. Similarly, the QA quality analysis is primarily qualitative; a systematic human evaluation with inter-annotator agreement metrics is a natural next step.

## 7 Conclusion

We have presented TriQA, a pipeline for generating multilingual, multi-source question-answer datasets from knowledge graph triples, Wikipedia abstracts, and large language models. By integrating eight heterogeneous knowledge bases and text-grounded abstracts from six DBpedia language editions, the pipeline produces QA datasets with unprecedented scale and topical diversity: 292 million triples, 10.4 million abstracts, and over 28 million QA pairs across six languages, spanning domains from general factual knowledge to commonsense reasoning, cultural heritage, geography, nutrition, and politics. The system operates entirely on consumer hardware through a scalable architecture based on local dump streaming, multilingual label caching, and native-language generation prompts. By anchoring generation to verifiable knowledge graph triples, TriQA enables automatic validation of generated answers against their source facts, substantially reducing the manual effort needed for quality assurance compared to unconstrained LLM generation.

The pipeline further introduces a property classification benchmark with semantically aware distractor selection, achieving 96–100% zero-shot classification accuracy across most knowledge bases with Gemma-4-31B, and a hybrid difficulty scoring mechanism that combines structural knowledge graph signals with LLM-based judgment. A unified multilingual property description cache, generated automatically for over 13,000 properties across all integrated sources, enables enriched classification options across heterogeneous schemas.

Future work includes evaluating downstream QA training value using the abstract-based data (where Wikipedia paragraphs provide natural extractive contexts), extending language coverage beyond the current six languages, developing more memory-efficient intermediate node resolution for deeply nested knowledge graphs, and investigating difficulty-stratified curriculum learning strategies.

**Acknowledgments.** We are deeply grateful to Federico Wolenski, Cristina Giannone, Andrea Favalli and Raniero Romagnoli who generously contributed their time, ideas and effort to this work, and without whom it would not have taken the shape it has today.

## References

1. Alberti, C., Andor, D., Pitler, E., Devlin, J., Collins, M.: Synthetic QA corpora generation with roundtrip consistency. In: Proceedings of ACL, pp. 6168–6173 (2019)
2. Artetxe, M., Ruder, S., Yogatama, D.: On the cross-lingual transferability of monolingual representations. In: Proceedings of ACL, pp. 4623–4637 (2020)
3. Bordes, A., Usunier, N., Chopra, S., Weston, J.: Large-scale simple question answering with memory networks. arXiv preprint arXiv:1506.02075 (2015)
4. Carriero, V.A., Gangemi, A., Mancinelli, M.L., Nuzzolese, A.G., Presutti, V., Veninata, C.: ArCo: The Italian cultural heritage knowledge graph. In: Proceedings of ISWC, pp. 36–52 (2019)
5. Clark, J.H., et al.: TyDi QA: a benchmark for information-seeking question answering in typologically diverse languages. Trans. Assoc. Comput. Linguist. **8**, 454–470 (2020)
6. Das, R., Zaheer, M., Reddy, S., McCallum, A.: Question answering on knowledge bases and text using universal schema and memory networks. In: Proceedings of ACL, pp. 358–365 (2017)
7. Du, X., Shao, J., Cardie, C.: Learning to ask: neural question generation for reading comprehension. In: Proceedings of ACL, pp. 1342–1352 (2017)
8. Dubey, M., Banerjee, D., Abdelkawi, A., Lehmann, J.: LC-QuAD 2.0: a large dataset for complex question answering over Wikidata and DBpedia. In: Proceedings of ISWC, pp. 69–78 (2019)
9. Han, X., et al.: Fewrel: a large-scale supervised few-shot relation classification dataset with state-of-the-art evaluation. In: Proceedings of EMNLP, pp. 4803–4809 (2018)
10. Heilman, M., Smith, N.A.: Good question! statistical ranking for question generation. In: Proceedings of NAACL-HLT, pp. 609–617 (2010)
11. Joshi, M., Choi, E., Weld, D., Zettlemoyer, L.: TriviaQA: a large scale distantly supervised challenge dataset for reading comprehension. In: Proceedings of ACL, pp. 1601–1611 (2017)
12. Kumar, V., Hua, Y., Ramakrishnan, G., Qi, G., Gao, L., Li, Y.F.: Difficulty-controllable multi-hop question generation from knowledge graphs. In: Proceedings of ISWC, pp. 382–398 (2019)

13. Lewis, P., Oğuz, B., Rinott, R., Riedel, S., Schwenk, H.: MLQA: evaluating cross-lingual extractive question answering. In: Proceedings of ACL, pp. 7315–7330 (2020)
14. Puri, R., Spring, R., Shoeybi, M., Patwary, M., Catanzaro, B.: Training question answering models from synthetic data. In: Proceedings of EMNLP, pp. 5811–5826 (2020)
15. Rajpurkar, P., Zhang, J., Lopyrev, K., Liang, P.: SQuAD: 100,000+ questions for machine comprehension of text. In: Proceedings of EMNLP, pp. 2383–2392 (2016)
16. Serban, I.V., et al.: Generating factoid questions with recurrent neural networks: The 30M factoid question-answer corpus. In: Proceedings of ACL, pp. 588–598 (2016)
17. Speer, R., Chin, J., Havasi, C.: ConceptNet 5.5: an open multilingual graph of general knowledge. In: Proceedings of AAAI, pp. 4444–4451 (2017)
18. Sun, X., Liu, J., Lyu, Y., He, W., Ma, Y., Wang, S.: Answer-focused and position-aware neural question generation. In: Proceedings of EMNLP, pp. 3930–3939 (2018)
19. Temperoni, A., Biryukov, M., Theobald, M.: Enriching relation extraction with OPENIE. In: Proceedings of the 12th International Conference on Data Science, Technology and Applications, pp. 359–366 (2023)
20. Trivedi, P., Maheshwari, G., Dubey, M., Lehmann, J.: LC-QuAD: a corpus for complex question answering over knowledge graphs. In: Proceedings of ISWC, pp. 210–218 (2017)
21. Vrandečić, D., Krötzsch, M.: Wikidata: a free collaborative knowledgebase. Commun. ACM **57**(10), 78–85 (2014)
22. Wadhwa, S., Amir, S., Wallace, B.C.: Revisiting relation extraction in the era of large language models, pp. 15566–15589 (2023)
23. Yoo, K.M., Park, D., Kang, J., Lee, S.W., Park, W.: GPT3Mix: leveraging large-scale language models for text augmentation. In: Findings of EMNLP, pp. 2225–2239 (2021)
24. Yuan, X., et al.: Machine comprehension by text-to-text neural question generation. In: Proceedings of the 2nd Workshop on Representation Learning for NLP, pp. 15–25 (2017)
25. Zeng, D., Liu, K., Lai, S., Zhou, G., Zhao, J.: Relation classification via convolutional deep neural network. In: Proceedings of COLING, pp. 2335–2344 (2014)
26. Zhang, Y., Zhong, V., Chen, D., Angeli, G., Manning, C.D.: Position-aware attention and supervised data improve slot filling. In: Proceedings of EMNLP, pp. 35–45 (2017)
27. Zhao, Y., Ni, X., Ding, Y., Ke, Q.: Paragraph-level neural question generation with maxout pointer and gated self-attention networks. In: Proceedings of EMNLP, pp. 3901–3910 (2018)

# On Learning Neural Policies for FOND Planning via Transformers

Massimiliano Tummolo(✉), Nicholas Rossetti, Luca Putelli, Ivan Serina, and Alfonso Emilio Gerevini

Dipartimento di Ingegneria dell'Informazione, Università degli Studi di Brescia, Via Branze 38, Brescia, Italy
massimiliano.tummolo@unibs.it

**Abstract.** Neural Networks have been successfully applied to learn domain-dependent policies for deterministic planning, yet their use in Fully Observable Non-Deterministic (FOND) planning remains largely unexplored. This paper introduces a Transformer-based architecture, PlanGPT-ND, that predicts the next action to execute given the current state and goal in a non-deterministic environment. Training relies on a dataset of state–action pairs that, in our experiments, are extracted from PRP-generated policies across four benchmark FOND domains. The architecture incorporates an action masking mechanism enforcing applicability constraints by dynamically filtering out invalid actions during generation. We evaluate the resulting neural policies by simulating the agent's behaviour in the environment: starting from the initial state, the agent queries PlanGPT-ND for the next action to execute; the state resulting from executing this action, sampled according to the non-determinism of the action, is then fed back to the model, and this process continues until the goal is reached or a stopping condition is encountered.

**Keywords:** Generalised planning · FOND · language models

## 1 Introduction

Recent advances in neural networks have demonstrated their effectiveness in learning domain-dependent policies for deterministic planning. In particular, Transformer architectures [2,8] and graph neural networks [1,13] have shown strong performance on tasks where the environment exhibits fully predictable transitions and the policy can be learned from action trajectories.

Despite these successes, the application of neural models to Fully Observable Non-Deterministic (FOND) planning [4] remains largely unexplored. FOND domains introduce an additional layer of complexity: executing an action may

M. Tummolo was enrolled in the National Doctorate on AI conducted by Sapienza, University of Rome with the University of Brescia.


S. Bistarelli et al. (Eds.): AIxIA 2026, LNAI 17131, pp. 689–699, 2027.
https://doi.org/10.1007/978-3-032-40774-0_49

lead to multiple successor states, and a policy must account for these outcomes to guide the agent toward its objective.

Inspired by [11], we address this gap by introducing PLANGPT-ND, the first Transformer-based model that learns an implicit policy for non-deterministic planning. Once trained, the model predicts the next action to execute given the current state and the goal. The model is trained from scratch on a supervised dataset constructed from policies generated by the Planner-for-Relevant-Policies (PRP) planner [3,7] over four standard FOND benchmark domains. Each training instance pairs a state and a goal, with the action recommended by PRP's policy, allowing PlanGPT-ND to approximate expert behaviour.

A key component of our approach is the action-masking mechanism, which enforces applicability constraints at generation time. By dynamically filtering out actions whose preconditions are not satisfied in the current state, the mechanism prevents invalid outputs. In addition, we introduce a novelty-based exploitation mechanism that encourages the model to explore previously unvisited states, further improving the model's ability to progress toward the goal.

To evaluate the learned policies, we simulate the agent's execution in each domain. Starting in the initial state, the agent repeatedly queries PlanGPT-ND for its next action, applies it in the environment, and observes one of the possible non-deterministic outcomes. This new state is then provided to the model, which selects the next action, and the process continues until either the goal is reached or a stopping condition is encountered. Through this evaluation, we show that the learned policies achieve promising performance to approximate expert behaviour in FOND domains.

## 2 Background

### 2.1 Generative Pretrained Transformer (GPT)

Transformer-based architectures [15] revolutionised sequence modelling by introducing the self-attention mechanism. Among them, the Generative Pre-trained Transformer (GPT) [9] has become a standard choice for many Natural Language Processing (NLP) tasks.

GPT processes text by first tokenising the input and mapping each token to a continuous vector through an embedding layer. The core of the architecture is the self-attention mechanism, which enables each token to incorporate contextual information from all other tokens in the sequence. Formally, token embeddings are projected into query, key, and value vectors, and attention is computed as:

$$\mathrm{softmax}\left(\frac{QK^\top}{\sqrt{d_k}}\right)V$$

GPT models use only the decoder portion of the Transformer and are trained with causal language modelling, whose objective is to predict the next token given all preceding ones. This autoregressive setup enables GPT to generate coherent sequences token by token, making it well-suited for tasks requiring sequential reasoning, such as automated planning.

### 2.2 FOND Planning

Following the formalism of [7], we consider a fully-observable non-deterministic (FOND) planning task as a tuple $<\mathcal{V}, s0, s^*, \mathcal{A}>$, where $\mathcal{V}$ is a set of finite domain variables, $s0$ is the initial state (complete assignment to $V$), $s^*$ is the goal condition (partial assignment to $V$), and $\mathcal{A}$ is the set of (possibly non-deterministic) actions. Each action $a \in \mathcal{A}$ is described by a pair $<Pre_a, Eff_a>$ where $Pre_a$ is a partial assignment to $\mathcal{V}$ that determines when $a$ is applicable, and $Eff_a$ is a set of possible outcomes. Each outcome $o \in Eff_a$ is a partial assignment to $\mathcal{V}$ that indicates how the state is modified when that outcome occurs. Given an initial state $s_0$ and a set of actions $\mathcal{A}$, the FOND task induces a set of states reachable from $s_0$. A policy $\pi$ is a function that assigns to each state an action to execute; we regard a plan as a policy that is guaranteed to achieve the goal under suitable assumptions on how non-determinism is resolved.

## 3 PlanGPT

PlanGPT is a recent GPT-2 model that is trained from scratch for learning general planning policies [6,12] achieving SoTA results on various classical planning domains [10,11,14]. Within this framework, the input of PlanGPT is a set of fluents describing the initial state and the goal of the problem. During training, the completion sentence is the solution plan for the input problem obtained by a planner. The dataset is built using thousands of planning problems for each domain, obtaining multiple solutions using the LPG planner [5]. Furthermore, they perform a randomisation on the object names to avoid biases related to specific names in the training problems and plans. During the tokenisation, they split each fluent (and each action) into its components (the tokens), comprising the fluent (or action) name and its associated objects. After the generation of the plan by PlanGPT, the validator unites the tokens into actions and checks the validity of the plan.

## 4 PlanGPT-ND

Our objective is to compute a policy for a FOND planning domain by training a domain-specific GPT model from scratch. Each model is trained on examples that pair an initial state and a set of goal fluents with the corresponding action chosen by a reference planner. In the following, we detail the architecture and the training procedure, the auto-regressive action-generation process with action masking, and the simulation-based methodology used to evaluate our policies.

### 4.1 Architecture, Training and Generation

For each FOND planning domain, we develop a custom GPT model (**PlanGPT-ND**) trained from scratch to act as a generalised policy capable of solving previously unseen domain instances. Given the current state and the goal of a planning problem, PLANGPT-ND generates a pool of candidate actions that progress towards the goal.

Following the training setup proposed in [11], our training process mimics the behaviour of the policies computed by PRP. Each dataset sample is first converted into a sequence of tokens suitable for PLANGPT-ND: a pre-processing step splits every fluent and action into its parameters (predicate or action names and objects), and the tokeniser maps each parameter into integer tokens drawn from a fixed vocabulary. During training, the model receives the tokenised state and goal as input and generates the tokens corresponding to an action. The predicted action is then compared with the action selected by PRP for the same state–goal pair, and the discrepancy, measured by the cross-entropy loss, is used to update the model's parameters. Training proceeds for a fixed number of epochs, with the model evaluated on a validation set after each epoch; the final model is the checkpoint achieving the lowest validation loss.

Once trained, PLANGPT-ND can be applied to previously unseen problems. The initial state and goal are tokenised and provided as input to the model, which then generates a set of candidate actions. In standard GPT decoding, greedy generation selects the token with the highest probability at each step, appends it to the prompt, and feeds the extended prompt back into the model until a complete action is produced. However, relying solely on greedy decoding may cause the model to repeatedly select the same actions, potentially falling into loops. To mitigate this issue, PLANGPT-ND employs sampling-based generation to produce a pool of $N$ diverse action candidates. At each decoding step, we retain the smallest set of tokens whose cumulative probability exceeds a predefined threshold $p$ (default at 0.90), renormalise the probabilities over this set, and sample a token; repeating the procedure $N$ times yields a diverse set of action proposals.

### 4.2 Action Masking Generation

Sampling-based generation may still produce inapplicable actions, which interrupt the simulation when their preconditions are violated. To overcome this limitation, we introduce **Action Masking Generation (am-g)**, which prevents the model from generating inapplicable actions in the first place. At each decoding step, AM-G computes the set of applicable actions in the current state and encodes them as a tree of valid token sequences, each consisting of an action name followed by its arguments. A binary mask of vocabulary size is then constructed to restrict the model's output distribution: tokens that do not correspond to a valid continuation in the tree are assigned zero probability. The mask is applied to the final layer logits before sampling. Once a complete grounded action has been generated, it is executed to update the state, and the procedure repeats. This guarantees that every action produced by PLANGPT-ND is applicable in the current state, ensuring local soundness throughout decoding.

### 4.3 Simulation and Novelty Exploitation Mechanism

To evaluate the performance of our Transformer-based policies, we simulate a non-deterministic environment. Given the initial state and goal of a FOND problem, we query PlanGPT-ND using either sampling (samp) or action-masking generation (am-g) to obtain a pool of candidate valid actions, each associated with a heuristic value. We select the one with the highest heuristic value and, using the simulator, sample uniformly at random one of the action's successor states, using it as the new current state. This process repeats until the goal is reached or a maximum number of simulation steps is exceeded.

To prevent loops and promote exploration of novel states, we introduce a **novelty exploitation n-exp** mechanism. The idea is to penalise any candidate action all of whose successors have already been visited, by reducing its heuristic value by a factor $\alpha$. The action to execute is then selected as the one with the highest heuristic value; in case of ties, it is sampled uniformly from the set of highest-valued actions. This penalty lowers the probability of selecting a fully-visited action without excluding it, thereby biasing the search towards actions that lead to previously unvisited states. The heuristic value is normalised to lie in $[0, 1)$, and $\alpha$ is set to a default of 1.0, so that fully-visited actions are strongly, but not absolutely, disfavoured. When all candidate actions are penalised by n-exp, the novelty mechanism is disabled and the action with the highest heuristic value is selected.

### 4.4 Dataset Generation

This section describes the procedure used to construct the dataset for training our GPT-based models. First, we develop custom problem generators for each selected domain, following the benchmarks used by the PRP [7] planner. By varying the number of objects, the generators produce problem instances of differing difficulty. To reduce naming biases, object identifiers are randomised in every generated instance.

For each problem, a policy is computed using PRP, yielding a sequence of partial states paired with the corresponding action to execute. Starting from the initial state, we follow the policy and expand all non-deterministic effects until either the goal is reached or the execution enters a cycle. At every expansion step, we record a dataset sample consisting of the current state, the goal, and the action prescribed by the PRP policy. These samples will be used to train PlanGPT-ND.

## 5 Experimental Results

We trained a custom GPT model, named PlanGPT-ND, for each of the four domains (blocksworld, first-response, elevators, tireworld) using GPT-2 Small, which consists of 12 transformer blocks with 12 attention heads each, for a total of approximately 83M parameters. All models were trained on an NVIDIA A100 GPU with 40 GB of memory. For every domain, we generated 10,000 planning problems for training, 100 for validation, and 1,000 for testing.

To support our analysis, we compare two action-generation mechanisms: sampling generation (SAMP), which draws an action directly from the model's distribution, and action masking generation (AM-G), which removes inapplicable actions before selecting the most probable one. During simulation, we evaluate the contribution of the **Novelty Exploitation** mechanism (N-EXP), along with alternative heuristics, in guiding the action selection performed by PLANGPT-ND. We report results using two metrics: accuracy, which quantifies the agreement between the model's output and PRP's reference action, and coverage, defined as the percentage of solved problems during simulation.

### 5.1 PRP Similarity and Training Analysis

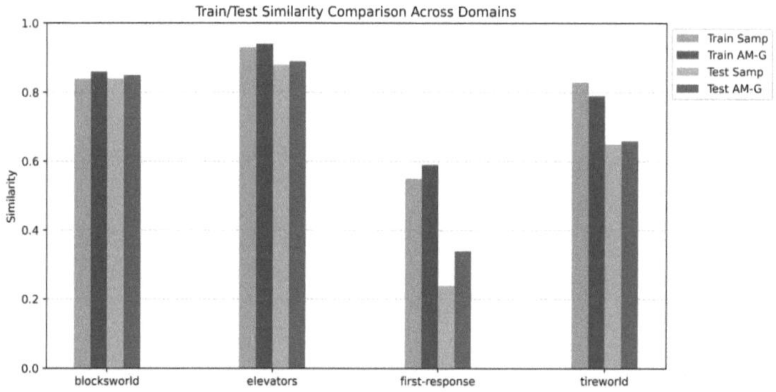


**Fig. 1.** Accuracy (similarity) between the action obtained from action masking (AM-G) and sampling (SAMP) generations compared to the action obtained in PRP policies.

The similarity experiment measures how closely the actions generated by the model match those selected by PRP, providing a measure of how accurately PLANGPT-ND approximates expert policies. Given a state and the goal condition, we consider a generated action equal if each of its tokens corresponds to the action computed by PRP. The accuracy metric is computed as the quotient of the equal generated actions compared to the total actions in the test set. Our test set is composed of 100 problems extracted from the train and test set: for each problem we tested the state and action pairs to compare the action provided by PLANGPT-ND with the one from PRP. To give an estimate, the number of evaluated states ranges from $3k$ to $10k$ states for each domain.

Overall, the results in Fig. 1 show that AM-G achieves similarity equal to or higher than SAMP to PRP on the more challenging domains. Both mechanisms obtain high scores in testing accuracy on BLOCKSWORLD (0.86 vs. 0.84) and ELEVATORS (0.89 vs. 0.88), indicating that PLANGPT-ND closely reproduces the policies computed by PRP in these domains. A similar trend holds for the training split, with BLOCKSWORLD (0.86 vs. 0.85) and ELEVATORS (0.94 vs. 0.93) achieving close accuracy scores. In TIREWORLD, AM-G marginally outperforms SAMP (0.66 vs. 0.65), though both mechanisms achieve lower accuracy compared to BLOCKSWORLD and ELEVATORS. The gap between training accuracy (0.84 for AM-G and 0.80 for SAMP) and testing accuracy suggests that overfitting may partially account for this degradation in performance. Finally, in FIRST-RESPONSE, both mechanisms struggle to approximate PRP, with AM-G achieving a testing accuracy of only 0.34, although higher than the 0.24 obtained by SAMP. As observed in TIREWORLD, the training accuracy exceeds the testing accuracy (0.59 vs. 0.55), further indicating a higher degree of overfitting in this domain.

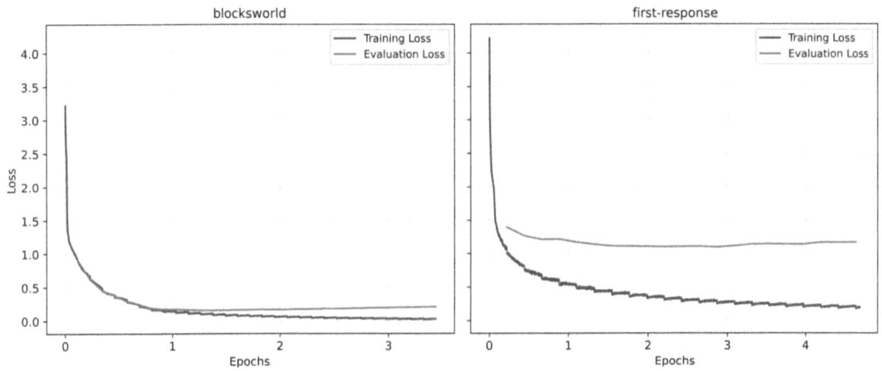


**Fig. 2.** Comparison of training and evaluation loss over epochs for BLOCKSWORLD and FIRST-RESPONSE domains.

To further investigate the overfitting observed in TIREWORLD and FIRST-RESPONSE, Fig. 2 compares the training and evaluation loss across epochs for BLOCKSWORLD and FIRST-RESPONSE, the two domains exhibiting the most divergent behaviour. In BLOCKSWORLD, the two curves remain close throughout training, with only a slight increase in evaluation loss after the first epoch: by the end of training, the training loss reaches 0.02 while the evaluation loss reaches 0.21. ELEVATORS follows a similar pattern, with a training loss of 0.02 and an evaluation loss below 0.1. In FIRST-RESPONSE, instead, the evaluation loss decreases only marginally and remains far from the training loss throughout training, a further indication of overfitting in this domain: the training loss reaches a minimum of 0.20, while the evaluation loss starts at 1.39 and only reaches a minimum of 1.16. This behaviour may stem from the higher number of actions in the FIRST-RESPONSE (9) domain compared to BLOCKSWORLD (7), as well as from a richer state representation involving multiple typed objects (locations, victims, fire-units, medical-units) and their interactions, compared to the single-type, block-stacking structure of BLOCKSWORLD. Finally, in TIREWORLD there is a comparably large gap, with a training loss around 0.1 and an evaluation loss around 0.5, consistent with the overfitting trend observed in this domain.

**Table 1.** Coverage of solved problems in simulation using AM-G and SAMP, with and without the N-EXP mechanism.

| | – | | N-EXP | |
|---|---|---|---|---|
| **Domain** | SAMP | AM-G | SAMP | AM-G |
| BLOCKSWORLD | 0.31 | 0.47 | 0.33 | **0.51** |
| ELEVATORS | 0.92 | 0.94 | 0.94 | **0.94** |
| FIRST-RESPONSE | 0.13 | 0.55 | 0.13 | **0.57** |
| TIREWORLD | 0.33 | 0.39 | 0.34 | **0.39** |

### 5.2 Simulation

The simulation experiment evaluates the system under non-deterministic effects, executing the model's actions in a stochastic environment to determine whether PLANGPT-ND solves the problem. At each step, the model generates up to 3 candidate actions using SAMPLING or AM-G, selected according to a selected heuristic, which lets us assess how well the model guides the simulation as described above. We also experimented with more than 4 actions but observed no significant performance improvements, suggesting that increasing the number of candidate actions is less beneficial than focusing on those in which the model has the highest confidence. Each simulation is stopped after 500 actions.

Table 1 compares SAMP and AM-G, both with and without the N-EXP mechanism. In this experiment we tested as a heuristic the probabilities of the generated tokens by PLANGPT-ND. Overall, AM-G consistently improves the percentage of solved problems over SAMP across all domains, and enabling N-EXP further enhances performance in every domain.

Focusing on the configurations with N-EXP enabled, in BLOCKSWORLD, AM-G substantially increases coverage over SAMP (0.51 vs. 0.33). Despite the high similarity to PRP, as shown in Sect. 5.1, coverage remains moderate, suggesting that the model has captured much, though not all, of the underlying structure of this domain. In ELEVATORS, both AM-G and SAMP attain high testing accuracy (0.94 for both methods), indicating that both mechanisms closely reproduce PRP's policy even in the presence of non-deterministic actions (e.g., `move-left-gate` and `move-right-gate`) whose outcomes can reset the agent's position to (`f1`, `p1`). In FIRST-RESPONSE, AM-G outperforms sampling (0.57 vs. 0.13) and demonstrates solid problem-solving performance, despite its relatively low similarity to PRP, indicating that masking and novelty exploitation recover part of what the model was not able to learn during training. TIREWORLD remains the most challenging, yet AM-G obtains better results compared to sampling (0.39 vs. 0.34).

While masking prevents mistakes that generate inapplicable actions, the low coverage is due to the dead-end states (a flat tire without having collected a spare tire that prevents the car from moving further) that AM-G could not prevent.

Comparing AM-G with and without N-EXP, the benefit of novelty exploitation is most pronounced in BLOCKSWORLD (0.51 vs. 0.47), and in FIRST-RESPONSE (0.57 vs. 0.55), indicating that N-EXP prevents the repetition of actions that are not useful for achieving the goal, and encourages the exploration of alternative actions following failures due to the non-deterministic nature of the problem. In ELEVATORS, by contrast, there is no increase in coverage (both at 0.94), consistent with the model having already learned this domain very effectively, so that novelty exploitation yields limited additional benefit. Lastly, in TIREWORLD, the use of N-EXP does not help in avoiding the dead-ends in the domain therefore reaching the same results.

**Table 2.** Coverage of solved problems in simulation using AM-G, with the N-EXP mechanism, using different heuristics.

| **Domain** | R | G | P | $\mu$(P,G) |
|---|---|---|---|---|
| BLOCKSWORLD | **0.52** | **0.52** | 0.51 | 0.51 |
| ELEVATORS | **0.96** | **0.96** | 0.94 | 0.95 |
| FIRST-RESPONSE | 0.58 | **0.60** | 0.57 | 0.55 |
| TIREWORLD | 0.42 | **0.46** | 0.39 | 0.45 |

Table 2 reports the performance of PLANGPT-ND when paired with different heuristics during simulation. We evaluate four heuristics: **random** (R), which selects an action uniformly at random from the candidate set; **goals** (G), which generates, for each candidate, the fraction of goal fluents solved in the successor state, **probs** (P), which averages, for each candidate, the probabilities that PLANGPT-ND assigns to each action token (already shown in Table 1); and $\mu(\mathbf{P}, \mathbf{G})$, which takes the average of the **goals** (G) and **probs** (P) heuristics.

The goals heuristic (G) is the strongest heuristic overall: it attains the highest coverage in every domain, tying with random selection in BLOCKSWORLD (0.52) and ELEVATORS (0.96) and leading in FIRST-RESPONSE (0.60) and TIREWORLD (0.46). Selecting the action whose best successor satisfies the largest fraction of goal fluents thus provides the most informative criterion, and it improves on the corresponding N-EXP configurations of Table 1 in every domain. The strong performance of the random selection in the two easier domains shows that the candidate set confined to the applicable, high-probability actions produced by AM-G is sufficient to solve the problem. The remaining heuristics are less effective. The probs heuristic (P), which ranks candidates by the probabilities that PLANGPT-ND assigns to their successors, is consistently among the weakest, with ELEVATORS (0.94) and TIREWORLD (0.39) obtaining the worst score, indicating that using the model probabilities again in selecting actions constrains that selection to the best already sampled, reducing the exploration of the approach. Finally, averaging the two scores in $\mu(\mathrm{P}, \mathrm{G})$ never improves on G alone, and in FIRST-RESPONSE it falls below P (0.55 vs. 0.57), overall degrading the results.

Analysing the contrast between the higher PRP accuracy and the lower percentage of solved simulations in BLOCKSWORLD indicates that reproducing the expert action at individual states does not, alone, solve problems under non-determinism. We attribute part of this gap to the way PLANGPT-ND is queried during simulation. The original PLANGPT generates an entire plan, conditioning each action on the full sequence produced so far, whereas PLANGPT-ND is invoked at every state and emits a single action as a short sequence of tokens, conditioned only on the current state and the goal. A policy is, in principle, a memory-less mapping from states to actions, so this formulation is a natural one; in practice, however, we hypothesise that, without any record of the trajectory, this Transformer-based architecture cannot recognise when it is repeating unproductive actions, or when an unfavourable non-deterministic outcome has driven it into an unhelpful region of the state space.

## 6 Conclusions

We have investigated the use of Transformer architectures to learn implicit neural policies for non-deterministic planning. We propose PLANGPT-ND, a system that acquires domain-specific policies by imitating the action choices produced by PRP for individual problems. In addition, we introduced action masking generation, which constrains the model to generate only applicable actions, ensuring sound solution trajectories, and a novelty exploitation mechanism, which promotes exploration by encouraging the model to select actions that lead to previously unvisited states.

Our experiments show that PLANGPT-ND learns FOND policies that solve non-deterministic problems while remaining inferior to the PRP planner. Across the four domains, action masking consistently improves coverage over plain sampling, novelty exploitation yields further gains, and the goals heuristic is the most informative selection criterion, achieving the highest coverage in every domain. The results are modest: coverage is elevated only in ELEVATORS, and modest in BLOCKSWORLD, FIRST-RESPONSE and TIREWORLD. Agreement with PRP follows a related pattern, ranging from high values in BLOCKSWORLD and ELEVATORS to modest in TIREWORLD and low in FIRST-RESPONSE. These results show that committing to individual actions in isolation is insufficient for these domains, and that representing and generating longer action sequences may be required to capture the structure that PLANGPT-ND currently reproduces only locally.

As future work, we plan to remove the dependence on PRP for generating training policies, to study how to integrate the sequence of previously generated actions into PLANGPT-ND and to exploit symbolic planning strategies to enhance the action generation process.

**Acknowledgments.** This work has been partly supported by the Italian Ministry of University and Research within the PRIMA 2024 programme project "Optimizing Water Resources in Coastal Areas using Artificial Intelligence" (AI4WATER – D53C25000510006), by project FAIR under the NRRP MUR program funded by the EU - NGEU (B53C22003980006), and by project SERICS (PE00000014) under the NRRP MUR program funded by the EU - NGEU.

## References

1. Chen, D.Z., Thiébaux, S., Trevizan, F.W.: Learning domain-independent heuristics for grounded and lifted planning. In: AAAI, pp. 20078–20086. AAAI Press (2024)
2. Chiari, M., Putelli, L., Rossetti, N., Serina, I., Gerevini, A.E.: On planning through LLMs (2025)
3. Cimatti, A., Pistore, M., Roveri, M., Traverso, P.: Weak, strong, and strong cyclic planning via symbolic model checking. Artif. Intell. **147**(1–2), 35–84 (2003)
4. Daniele, M., Traverso, P., Vardi, M.Y.: Strong cyclic planning revisited. ECP. Lecture Notes in Computer Science **1809**, 35–48 (1999). Springer
5. Gerevini, A., Serina, I.: LPG: a planner based on local search for planning graphs with action costs. In: AIPS, pp. 13–22. AAAI Press (2002)
6. Hu, Y., De Giacomo, G.: Generalized planning: synthesizing plans that work for multiple environments. In: IJCAI, pp. 918–923 (2011). IJCAI Org
7. Muise, C.J., McIlraith, S.A., Beck, J.C.: Improved non-deterministic planning by exploiting state relevance. In: ICAPS. AAAI (2012)
8. Pallagani, V., et al.: On the prospects of incorporating large language models (LLMs) in automated planning and scheduling (APS). In: ICAPS, pp. 432–444. AAAI Press (2024)
9. Radford, A., Narasimhan, K.: Improving language understanding by generative pre-training, p. preprint (2018). api.semanticscholar.org/CorpusID:49313245
10. Rossetti, N., Tummolo, M., Gerevini, A.E., Olivato, M., Putelli, L., Serina, I.: Enhancing GPT-based planning policies by model-based plan validation. In: NeSy (2). Lecture Notes in Computer Science, vol. 14980, pp. 328–337. Springer (2024)
11. Rossetti, N., et al.: Learning general policies for planning through GPT models. In: ICAPS, pp. 500–508. AAAI Press (2024)
12. Srivastava, S., Immerman, N., Zilberstein, S.: Learning generalized plans using abstract counting. In: AAAI, pp. 991–997. AAAI Press (2008)
13. Ståhlberg, S., Bonet, B., Geffner, H.: Learning general optimal policies with graph neural networks: Expressive power, transparency, and limits. In: ICAPS, pp. 629–637. AAAI Press (2022)
14. Tummolo, M., Rossetti, N., Chrpa, L., Serina, I., Gerevini, A.E.: Exploiting macro-actions in learning GPT-based general planning policies. In: ICTAI, pp. 915–919. IEEE (2025)
15. Vaswani, A., et al.: Attention is all you need. In: NIPS, pp. 5998–6008 (2017)

# Pareto-Based Heuristic Search for Timelines

Alessandro Umbrico(✉), Riccardo Rasconi, and Andrea Orlandini

CNR - Institute of Cognitive Sciences and Technologies, Rome, Italy
alessandro.umbrico@cnr.it

**Abstract.** Designing effective heuristics is essential for improving the performance of general-purpose planning frameworks. While heuristic research has largely focused on classical planning, alternative paradigms such as timeline-based planning have received comparatively little attention. Moreover, most existing approaches optimize a single objective, whereas real-world domains require balancing multiple criteria such as makespan, safety, and resource availability. This paper presents a multi-objective heuristic framework for timeline-based planning that combines multiple evaluation metrics to guide search. Implemented in an open-source planner and evaluated on a realistic Human-Robot Collaboration scenario, the proposed approach improves both planning efficiency and solution quality.

**Keywords:** Automated Planning and Scheduling · Timeline-based Planning · Heuristic Search · Multi-objective Optimization

## 1 Introduction

Artificial Intelligence (AI) planning systems typically rely on carefully designed heuristics to guide search and improve efficiency. Heuristic search has long been a cornerstone of automated planning research, particularly in the action-based community [12,22]. Heuristics often rely on some relaxations of a planning specification that enable *quick* insights about qualities of plans (e.g., the *estimated distance* to a solution). Prominent examples include $h_{add}$ and $h_{max}$ [3], which assume sub-goal independence, and $h^{FF}$ [19], based on relaxed GRAPHPLAN [2] running on a planning task without delete lists (*delete-relaxation*). Another notable contribution is [18], which introduces *multi-valued planning tasks* to support alternative representations of a planning problem, using hierarchical decomposition graphs. Most contributions have focused on optimizing a single objective (plan cost or makespan), while real-world problems often account for multiple conflicting objectives (e.g., balancing makespan and robot velocity for safety). Several works have addressed multi-objective extensions to classical planners. For example, the work in [26] extends the single-objective classical planner GRT [25] to A*-based multi-objective search. Nodes are associated with *vector states*


S. Bistarelli et al. (Eds.): AIxIA 2026, LNAI 17131, pp. 700–714, 2027.
https://doi.org/10.1007/978-3-032-40774-0_50

that encapsulate an arbitrary number of evaluated criteria. The work [10] proposes a metric temporal planner called *Sapa* which pursues a multi-objective solving approach. The framework implements an A* forward chaining algorithm where a multi-objective evaluation function assesses both makespan and action cost. The work [21] presents an evolutionary planner enriching the search process of YAHSP [30] with Pareto-based optimization. These approaches highlight the potential of *Pareto dominance* for managing trade-offs among competing objective functions.

A planning paradigm particularly suited for multi-objective reasoning is *timeline-based planning* [20,24]. Unlike action-based formalisms, it is inherently temporal and synthesizes envelopes of valid temporal behaviors by combining planning and scheduling decisions. Timeline-based planners such as EUROPA [1], APSI [13], IxTeT [14], PLATINUm [29], and oRatio [9] have shown success in complex real-world domains [4,5,8,28]. The work [7] has proposed a rigorous formalization of timelines, enabling new theoretical insights [15–17]. Nevertheless, the absence of standard benchmarks and the structural differences from classical planning have limited progress on domain-independent heuristics. The work in [9] investigates the adoption of action-based heuristics in timeline reasoning, but is confined to the single-objective case.

This paper extends timeline-based planning to multi-objective heuristic search by investigating the following directions: (i) propose a general framework for time-aware multiple optimization; (ii) structure domain-independent graph-based heuristic search; and (iii) implement a search procedure guided by Pareto dominance to approximate the Pareto-optimal set of plans. The approach complies with and extends the formalization presented in [7]. Experiments on a realistic Human-Robot Collaboration (HRC) scenario demonstrate that our framework effectively balances efficiency, safety, and robustness. Notably, our contribution builds on the effective integration of classical heuristics within a controllability-aware, multi-objective timeline-based setting.

## 2 The Timeline-Based Formalism

A timeline-based specification describes the temporal behaviors of the domain features to be controlled [24]. The planning process synthesizes valid and flexible temporal trajectories (timelines) describing *how* domain features should behave to accomplish complex tasks (*objectives*). A timeline defines *what* states and actions the associated domain feature assumes or executes, and *when*. According to [7], *state variables* (SVs) model domain features by specifying valid sequences of *state variable values*.

**Definition 1.** *A* State Variable *is a tuple* $SV = \langle V, T, D, \gamma \rangle$ *describing valid behaviors of a domain feature:*

- $V$ *is a set of* values $v_i \in V$ *representing states of actions the feature can perform or assume over time.*
- $T : V \rightarrow 2^V$ *is a* state transition function *describing for each value* $v_i \in V$ *possible successors on a timeline and thus valid transitions.*

- $D : V \rightarrow \mathbb{T} \times \mathbb{T}$ *is a* duration function *specifying for each value* $v_i \in V$ *its expected duration bounds, expressed in some temporal domain* $\mathbb{T}$ *(typically* $\mathbb{N}^+$*).*
- $\gamma : V \rightarrow \{c, pc, u\}$ *is a* controllability tagging function *that specifies the controllability property of a value.*

Controllability properties characterize the interactions of SVs' values with the environment at execution time. Information about controllability and temporal flexibility accounts for *temporal uncertainty*, allowing a planner to synthesize plans with execution properties [6,23].

**Definition 2.** *A value* $v_i \in V$ *of a state variable* $SV = \langle V, T, D, \gamma \rangle$ *is:*

- Controllable *(*$\gamma(v_i) = c$*) if the control system can decide both the start and end times for its execution.*
- Partially-controllable *(*$\gamma(v_i) = pc$*) if it can only be started by the control system, while its end time and, i.e., its actual duration, can be only observed.*
- Uncontrollable *(*$\gamma(v_i) = u$*) the control system can neither decide its start nor its end times.*

A *flexible timeline* for a state variable $SV_i$ is a sequence of (flexible) temporal intervals called *tokens* that encapsulate an *envelope* of valid temporal behaviors.

**Definition 3.** *If* $SV_i = (V, T, \gamma, D)$ *is a state variable, a* token $x_j$ *for the variable is:*

$$x_j = (v_k, [e_j, e_j^{'}], [d_j, d_j^{'}], \gamma(v_k))$$

*where* $v_k \in V$ *is the value assumed by the token* $x_j$*,* $[e_j, e_j^{'}]$ *is the end-time interval of* $x_j$ *(with* $e_j \leq e_j^{'}$*) and* $[d_j, d_j^{'}]$ *is the minimum and maximum duration of* $x_j$ *(with* $d_j \leq d_J^{'}$*).*

A token $x_j$ represents the instantiation of a value $v_k \in V$ over a certain (flexible) temporal interval. The duration of a token must be consistent with the duration bound of $v_k$. A *timeline* is a *continuous sequence of tokens* $x_i$ from a *temporal origin* to (at least) a *planning horizon* $\mathtt{H} \in \mathbb{T}$.

*Synchronization rules* specify additional constraints between state variable values, necessary to synthesize valid plans (i.e., valid schedules of timelines).

**Definition 4.** *A* synchronization rule *has the form*

$$a_0[SV_0 = v_0] \rightarrow a_1[SV_1 = v_1], ..., a_n[SV_n = v_n].\mathcal{C}$$

*where* $a_i[SV_i = v_i]$ *is a* token variable *denoting a temporal interval in which a state variable* $SV_i$ *assumes the value* $v_i$*. The left-hand part of the synchronization rule is the* trigger*. The set* $C$ *specifies* temporal relations *between token variables.*

Token variables and temporal relations within the body (right-hand side) of a synchronization rule are treated as conjunctions. Instead, synchronization rules with the same trigger are treated as disjunctions, and related bodies are interpreted as disjunctions.

### 2.1 Iterative Refinement of Timelines

Given a set of state variables ($\mathcal{SV}$) and synchronization rules ($\mathcal{S}$), a partial plan $\pi$ is initialized from *facts* (i.e., partial timelines) and *goals* of a planning problem. A partial plan consists of a set of timelines characterized by *flaws* that denote either tokens to be added (i.e., planning flaws - completeness issues) or tokens to be scheduled (i.e., scheduling flaws - validity issues). Each iteration of a planning process detects the set of flaws in the current plan $\pi$ (stored in a planning *agenda*), selects the "most promising flaw" and computes its solutions, i.e., *plan refinements*. Alternative refinements expand the search space and are analyzed in the next iterations. A solution is found when no flaw is detected in the plan $\pi$ selected for the current iteration. The algorithm takes into account partial plan validity as well as *controllability properties*, thus synthesizing *pseudo-controllable* plans [23] (i.e., plans that do not make *hypotheses* on the actual duration of non-controllable tokens). Algorithm 1 summarizes this procedure.

**Algorithm 1.** Timeline-based plan synthesis

**Require:** $\mathcal{SV}$, $\mathcal{S}$, $\mathcal{H}_\pi$, $\mathcal{H}_\phi$
**Ensure:** $\pi = (FTL, R)$
1: $\Pi \leftarrow \emptyset$
2: $\pi \leftarrow$ initialize $(\mathcal{SV}, \mathcal{S})$
3: **while** $\neg$isSolution $(\pi, \mathcal{SV}, \mathcal{S})$ **do**
4: $\quad \Phi \leftarrow$ flaws $(\pi, \mathcal{SV}, \mathcal{S})$
5: $\quad \Phi^* \leftarrow$ choose $(\Phi, \mathcal{H}_\phi)$
6: $\quad$ **for** $\phi \in \Phi^*$ **do**
7: $\quad\quad \Pi \leftarrow$ refine $(\pi$, resolvers $(\phi))$
8: $\quad \pi \leftarrow$ choose $(\Pi, \mathcal{H}_\pi)$
9: **return** $\pi$

Algorithm 1 presents two decision points within the solving process. The first choice selects the flaw to solve for plan refinement (line 5). Similarly to CSP, this is not a backtracking decision (all the flaws must be solved) but strongly affects the *efficiency* of the solving procedure. Heuristic $\mathcal{H}_\phi$ encapsulates evaluation criteria supporting this choice. The second choice selects the most promising (partial) plan to visit in the next iteration (line 8), according to heuristic $\mathcal{H}_\pi$. This is a backtracking decision affecting the *qualities* of synthesized plans.

## 3 The Search Problem

Heuristic search focuses on the second decision point in Algorithm 1 (line 8), which determines how the planner explores the search space by encapsulating the comparison criteria for alternative partial plans. A key aspect of such heuristics is estimating future refinements of a plan with respect to one or more metrics. This section describes heuristic functions designed to support multi-objective search with timelines.

### 3.1 Value Decomposition Graph

A heuristic function $h : \Pi \rightarrow \mathbb{R}_0^+$, given a plan $\pi \in \Pi$, returns a real number $h(\pi) \in \mathbb{R}_0^+$ that estimates the *quality* of $\pi$ with respect to some *metric*. Taking inspiration from classical approaches such as [2,3,19], a graph-based representation of a *domain specification* is used to perform *reachability analysis* and compute the expected *cost/value* of reachable solutions with respect to some metrics.

The *value decomposition graph* is automatically built from the synchronization rules and state variable definitions of a timeline-based specification. The assumption behind the definition (and use) of this graph is that a synchronization rule establishes a "causal relationship" among state variable values. Timelines do not explicitly define preconditions and effects. However, considering the semantics of synchronization rules, every time a state variable $SV_i$ assumes a value $v_j$ during a certain temporal interval (denoted by token variable $a_0$, the trigger of the rule) the state variables $sv_1$, ..., $sv_n$ should assume, respectively, the values $v_1$, ..., $v_n$ during some temporal intervals (denoted by token variables $a_1$, ..., $a_n$), and the temporal constraints $c \in \mathcal{C}$ should hold between them. Namely, there is a dependency relationship between the behaviors of the state variables referred to in the body of a synchronization rule and the behavior of the state variable referred to by the head of a rule.

**Algorithm 2.** Value Decomposition Graph Extraction

**Require:** $\mathcal{SV}$, $\mathcal{S}$
**Ensure:** $\mathcal{G_V}$
$\mathcal{G_V} \leftarrow \emptyset$
**for** $v_i \in \mathcal{SV}$ **do**
  $\mathcal{R}_{v_i} \leftarrow \text{rules}(\mathcal{S}, v_i)$
  **if** $\mathcal{R}_{v_i} \neq \emptyset$ **then**
    $n_{v_i} \leftarrow \text{NODE}(v_i, \mathcal{G_V})$
    **if** $|\mathcal{R}_{v_i}| > 1$ **then**
      $n_{v_i}^{\vee} \leftarrow \text{OR}(n_{v_i}, \mathcal{G_V})$
      **for** $r \in \mathcal{R}_{v_i}$ **do**
        $n_{v_i}^{\wedge} \leftarrow \text{AND}(n_{v_i}^{\vee}, \mathcal{G_V})$
        **for** $v_j \in \text{body}(r)$ **do**
          $n_{v_j} \leftarrow \text{NODE}(v_j, n_{v_i}^{\wedge}, \mathcal{G_V})$
    **else**
      $n_{v_i}^{\wedge} \leftarrow \text{AND}(n_{v_i}, \mathcal{G_V})$
      **for** $v_j \in \text{body}(\mathcal{R})$ **do**
        $n_{v_j} \leftarrow \text{NODE}(v_j, n_{v_i}^{\wedge}, \mathcal{G_V})$
**return** $\mathcal{G_V}$

Algorithm 2 builds the *value decomposition graph* $\mathcal{G_V}$ from a timeline-based specification. Three types of nodes compose the graph: i) *value nodes* ($n_{v_i}$); ii) `OR` *nodes* ($n_{v_i}^{\vee}$) and; iii) `AND` *nodes* ($n_{v_i}^{\wedge}$). Each node $n_{v_i}$ is associated with a grounded state variable value occurring as a trigger in some synchronization rule (line 5). In case of rules with the same triggerer (i.e., $|\mathcal{R}_{v_i}| > 1$), a node $n_{v_i}$ is associated with an `OR` *node* $n^{\vee}_{v_i}$ (lines 6–11). The rules $r \in \mathcal{R}_{v_i}$ describe alternative decompositions of a value and are represented as disjunctions of `AND` *nodes* ($n^{\wedge}_{v_i}$) into $\mathcal{G}_{\mathcal{V}}$. The body of a rule $r \in \mathcal{R}_{v_i}$ specifies a particular decomposition of value $v_i$ in terms of a *conjunction* of (grounded) values $v_j$ that should be added to a plan (i.e., *sub-goals*). The *causal relationship* is maintained by associating each value node $n_{v_i}$ (or its `OR` *node* $n^{\vee}_{v_i}$) with an `AND` *node* $n^{\wedge}_{v_i}$ connecting $n_{v_i}$ to all the *value nodes* $n_{v_j}$ of the (grounded) values that appear in the body of the rule (lines 8–9 and lines 13–15). Cycles are checked after each introduction of an edge to keep the graph $\mathcal{G}_{\mathcal{V}}$ acyclic. The procedure discards edges that generate cycles when added to the structure.

### 3.2 Heuristic Search of Plan Metrics

The *value decomposition graph* compactly represents all possible refinements of a partial plan. The heuristic performs a reachability analysis over this graph to identify sub-goals (i.e., plan refinements) and estimate lower/upper bounds of metrics for reachable plans. Following an A* formulation, the general evaluation function $f_i$ for a plan $\pi$ with respect to a metric $i$ is defined as:

$$f_i(\pi) = g_i(\pi) + h_i(\pi), \tag{1}$$

where $g_i(\pi)$ estimates the contribution of tokens already part of $\pi$, and $h_i(\pi)$ estimates the contribution of future tokens derived from the graph. The computation of $h_i(\pi)$ takes inspiration from $h_{max}$ [3] and relies on the graph $\mathcal{G}_{\mathcal{V}}$ to

**Algorithm 3.** Heuristic evaluation of plan metrics

**Require:** $\mathcal{G}_{\mathcal{V}}, \pi$
**Ensure:** $h_i(\pi)$
$\Phi_{goal}(\pi) \leftarrow$ goals (agenda ($\pi$))
$h_i(\pi) \leftarrow 0$
**for** $\phi_{goal} \in \Phi_{goal}(\pi)$ **do**
    $v_j \leftarrow value(\phi_{goal})$
    **if** leaf($\mathcal{G}_{\mathcal{V}}, v_j$) **then**
        $h_i(\pi) \leftarrow m_i(\pi, v_j) + h_i(\pi)$
    **else**
        $h_{i,j} \leftarrow \infty$
        $\{\mathcal{V}^1, ..., \mathcal{V}^n\} \leftarrow$ decomposition($\mathcal{G}_{\mathcal{V}}, v_j$)
        **for** $\mathcal{V}^k \in \{\mathcal{V}^1, ..., \mathcal{V}^n\}$ **do**
            $h^k_{i,j} \leftarrow 0$
            **for** $v^k_t \in V^k$ **do**
                $h^k_{i,j} \leftarrow m_i\left(\pi, v^k_t\right) + h^k_{i,j}$
            $h_{i,j} \leftarrow \min\left(h_{i,j}, h^k_{i_j}\right)$
        $h_i(\pi) \leftarrow h_{i,j} + m_i(\pi, v_j)$
**return** $h_i(\pi)$

compute sub-goals/refinements. Algorithm 3 computes the heuristic estimation $h_i(\pi)$ for a plan $\pi$ with respect to a metric $i$.

Algorithm 3 evaluates a partial plan $\pi$ by considering both tokens already in the plan and tokens that could be added in future refinements. The computation relaxes the complexity of plan refinements by specifically considering only *planning flaws* of the *agenda* of $\pi$. For each planning flaw $\phi_{goal}$, the associated state variable value $v_j$ is checked in the graph. If $v_j$ is a leaf, $h_i(\pi)$ is incremented by $m_i(\pi, v_j)$, representing the cost or duration to introduce that token. Otherwise, all possible decompositions of $v_j$ are considered, and the minimum expected evaluation among these alternatives is selected. This ensures that the heuristic remains optimistic, providing a *lower bound* on the true cost/makespan of the plan (*admissibility condition*).

### 3.3 Heuristic Evaluation Function

Algorithm 3 assumes the use of a *metric evaluation function* $m_i : \Pi \times \mathcal{V} \rightarrow \mathbb{R}_0^+$, each estimating the *minimum expected* value of metric $m_i$ for a plan $\pi \in \Pi$ and a state variable value $v_j$The specific set of metrics to be optimized may depend on the application domain. Two metrics are domain-independent and always relevant: (i) the *planning cost*, and (ii) the *makespan*.

The *planning cost* is computed as the cost of the operations performed to build the partial plan $\pi$, plus the *minimum expected remaining cost* derived from possible refinements. Let $A(\pi) = \{a_1, ..., a_n\}$ be the set of token variables, denoting the tokens that compose the timelines of the current plan $\pi$. Let $\Omega(\pi) = \{\Omega^1, ..., \Omega^m\}$ be the subset of *planning-flaw refinements* of $\pi$, extracted from the decomposition graph $\mathcal{G}_\mathcal{V}$. Each $\Omega^j \in \Omega$ represents an alternative set of token variables $\Omega^j = \{\omega_1^j, ..., \omega_k^j\}$ that could complete the partial plan $\pi$. The cost evaluation function is then defined as:

$$f_c(\pi) = \sum_{a_i \in A(\pi)} \text{cost}(a_i) + \min_{\Omega^j \in \Omega(\pi)} \sum_{\omega_k^j \in \Omega^j} \text{cost}\left(\omega_k^j\right) \tag{2}$$

The function cost () returns the cost of the planning operation required to introduce the corresponding token. The relaxation defined by $\Omega(\pi)$ ensures that the heuristic estimation of cost is a lower bound on the true remaining cost, thus preserving admissibility.

The *plan makespan* is computed by considering the *maximum* total duration across all timelines[1]. Let $\mathcal{SV}$ be the set of state variables, and for each $sv_i \in \mathcal{SV}$, let $A^i(\pi) \subseteq A(\pi)$ denote the tokens of timelines $i$. Each relaxed refinement $\Omega^i \in \Omega(\pi)$ includes sets $\Omega^{j,i} \subseteq \Omega^j$, denoting tokens $\omega_k^{j,i} \in \Omega^{j,i}$ that could appear in the timeline of $sv_i$. The makespan evaluation function is thus:

[1] Timelines are parallel execution of components, thus the overall plan duration is determined by the lower bound of the longest one.

$$f_d(\pi) = \max_{sv_i \in \mathcal{SV}} \Bigg( \sum_{a_j^i \in A^i(\pi)} \text{duration}\left(a_j^i\right) + \min_{\Omega^j \in \Omega(\pi)} \min_{\Omega^{j,i} \in \Omega^j} \sum_{\omega_k^{j,i} \in \Omega^{j,i}} \text{duration}\left(\omega_k^{j,i}\right) \Bigg) \tag{3}$$

The function duration () returns the lower-bound duration of the corresponding token variable. Taking the minimum over all possible relaxed refinements ensures that the estimated remaining duration per timeline is optimistic.

### 3.4 Evaluating Plan Risk

In complex domains like HRC, collaborative plans should account for efficient simultaneous behaviors of humans and robots and safe interactions. In addition to the evaluation function $f_c$, defined in Eq. 2 and $f_d$ defined in Eq. 3, the evaluation function $f_r$ estimates the *collision risk* of a plan. It estimates the expected physical proximity and interactions during the simultaneous execution of human and robot tasks. A *risk matrix* $C^{R-H}$ provides the risk index associated with pairs of human and robot tasks in a give deployment [11,27]. Although the data of $C^{R-H}$ are strictly correlated with the layout of a collaborative scenario and the geometric constraints of the tasks, the evaluation methodology is general to any planning problem accounting for positive or negative synergies between parallel tasks.

Token variables $a_i^R \in \mathcal{A}^R$ refer to tokens whose values $v_i^R \in \mathcal{V}^R$ denote tasks assigned to the robot. Similarly, token variables $a_i^H \in \mathcal{A}^H$ refer to tokens whose values $v_i^H \in \mathcal{V}^H$ denote tasks assigned to the human. Let $\Psi\left(a_i^R, \pi\right) = \{a_1^H, ..., a_k^H\}$ be the set of token variables denoting human tasks $a_j^H \in \mathcal{A}^H$ that could overlap with the robot token $a_i^R$ in a plan $\pi$. A *risk function* $\rho : \mathcal{A}^R \times \mathcal{A}^H \rightarrow \mathbb{R}^+$ returns a positive number representing the collision risk estimated by the matrix $C^{R-H}$. The risk evaluation function $f_r$ is then defined as follows:

$$f_r(\pi) = \sum_{a_i^R \in A^R(\pi)} \sum_{a_j^H \in \Psi(a_i^R, \pi)} \rho\left(a_i^R, a_j^H\right) + \min_{\Omega^{R,k} \in \Omega^R(\pi)} \sum_{\omega_i^{R,k} \in \Omega^{R,k}} \rho\left(\omega_i^{R,k}, *\right) \tag{4}$$

The cost part of $f_r(\pi)$ computes the consolidated collision risk resulting from the assigned human and robot tasks and their overlaps $\Psi\left(a_i^R, \pi\right) = \{a_1^H, ..., a_k^H\}$, according to the flexible schedule of $\pi$. For each pair of tokens $a_i^R$ and $a_j^H$, the risk is the sum of the associated risk indices $\rho\left(a_i^R, a_j^H\right)$. The heuristic part of the function $h(\pi)$ computes the expected minimum collision risk according to the possible refinements of $pi$, $\Omega^R(\pi)$. For each alternative set of robot token variables $\Omega^{R,k} \in \Omega^R(\pi)$, the expected collision risk is the sum of the *minimum risk* associated with the robot token $\rho\left(\omega_i^{R,k}, *\right)$. The function considers the minimum risk associated with $\omega_i^{R,k}$, according to the matrix $C^{R-H}$, to optimistically estimate the risk and preserve admissibility (worst synergies might occur depending on the overlapping human tasks).

# 4 Pareto-Based Search

Given a set of metrics $\mathcal{I}$, a timeline-based planning problem can be seen as a multi-objective optimization problem for a set of functions $\mathcal{F} = \{f_1, .., f_n\}$ where each element $f_i \in \mathcal{F}$ is the evaluation function of a plan $\pi$ with respect to a specific metric $i \in \mathcal{I}$. Multi-objective evaluation is proposed here through the concept of *Pareto dominance* to compare partial plans and identify those that best balance the objective functions $f_i \in \mathcal{F}$.

**Definition 5.** *Given a set of evaluation functions $\mathcal{F} = \{f_1, ..., f_n\}$, where each function $f_t$ is associated with a distinct metric $t$, a partial plan $\pi_i$ is said to* dominate *another partial plan $\pi_j$ (with $i \neq j$) if:*

- $\forall f_k \in \mathcal{F}, f_k(\pi_i) \leq f_k(\pi_j)$
- $\exists f_h \in \mathcal{F}, f_h(\pi_i) < f_h(\pi_j)$

A plan $\pi_i$ thus dominates a plan $\pi_j$ (with $i \neq j$) if and only if, for each function $f_k \in \mathcal{F}$ the evaluation of $\pi_i$ with respect to the considered metric $k$ (i.e., $f_k(\pi_i)$) is not worse than the evaluation of $\pi_j$ with respect to the same metric (i.e., $f_k(\pi_j)$), and there exists at least one metric $h$ for which the evaluation of $\pi_i$ (i.e., $f_h(\pi_i)$) is strictly better than $\pi_j$ (i.e., $f_h(\pi_j)$). The heuristic would thus guide the search towards exploring non-dominated plans belonging to the *Pareto set* portion of the search space fringe.

## 4.1 Plan Polarization

The Pareto-dominance criteria would not select a specific partial plan among the non-dominated ones. To further guide the search, a *preference-based mechanism* helps the planner select the partial plan to explore, allowing also to *tailor* the qualities of desired solution plans. A *priority function* is a function $\sigma : \mathcal{I} \rightarrow \mathbb{R}^+$, such that $\forall i, j \in \mathcal{I}, \sigma(i) \neq \sigma(j)$ (with $i \neq j$). Let $\mathcal{F}^*$ be a list of evaluation functions $f_i \in \mathcal{F}$ ordered according to $\sigma$, $f_i \prec f_j$ in $\mathcal{F}^*$ (with $i \neq j$) if and only if $\sigma(i) > \sigma(j)$. According to Algorithm 4, the search relies on Pareto dominance to find balanced plans, and then specializes its choice by *prioritizing* the set of metrics $\mathcal{I}$.

If plan $\pi_i$ is better than plan $\pi_j$ with respect to the current evaluation function $f_k \in \mathcal{F}^*$ (lines 3) then the procedure returns $\pi_i$ (line 4). If plan $\pi_j$ is better than $\pi_i$ with respect to $f_k \in \mathcal{F}^*$ (line 5) then the procedure returns $\pi_j$ (line 6). Otherwise, the procedure checks the next function in $\mathcal{F}^*$ (line 8), or makes a random choice if no preference emerges (line 9).

**Algorithm 4.** Plan Polarization

**Require:** $\mathcal{F}^*$, $\pi_i$, $\pi_j$
**Ensure:** $\pi^*$
$\pi^* \leftarrow \emptyset$
**for** $f_k \in \mathcal{F}^*$ **do**
    **if** $f_k(\pi_i) < f_k(\pi_j)$ **then**
        **return** $\pi^* \leftarrow \pi_i$
    **else if** $f_k(\pi_j) < f_k(\pi_i)$ **then**
        **return** $\pi^* \leftarrow \pi_j$
    **else**
        $\pi^* \leftarrow \emptyset$
**return** $\pi^* \leftarrow \text{random}(\pi_i, \pi_j)$

## 5 Experimental Assessment

Experiments consider a collaborative manufacturing scenario in which a worker and a *cobot* share the workspace performing an assembly task. The planner must optimize the process while keeping the collaboration safe. The work-piece is a *mosaic*, which can be seen as a matrix with N rows and M columns. The task requires the *pick & place* of several boxes to assemble the mosaic. Boxes should be picked from different areas of the environment and placed into target positions [11,27].

The timeline-based specification models the collaborative process and the tasks the human and the robot can perform. Three state variables $\{sv_P, sv_H, sv_R\}$ model the production process at different levels of abstraction. The values $\mathcal{V}^P$ of $sv_P$ characterize the low-level production tasks needed to build the mosaic. The values $\mathcal{V}^R$ of $sv_R$ and $\mathcal{V}^H$ of $sv_H$ respectively characterize the pick-and-place tasks that the robot and the human can perform. Robot values $v_i^R \in \mathcal{V}^R$ are *partially-controllable*, since the end time of each pick-and-place can be delayed due to the presence of the human operator. Human values $v_i^H \in \mathcal{V}^H$ are *fully uncontrollable* since the planner cannot decide when the operator starts/ends tasks. Both human and robot values are associated with lower and upper bounds. Synchronization rules hierarchically decompose the procedure by associating Production tasks with lower-level human/robot tasks. Temporal relations constrain the execution of tasks within the decomposition.

The evaluation of the proposed multi-objective heuristic search relies on the open-source timeline-based planning framework PLATINUm [29][2]. Five planning configurations are evaluated, comparing the multi-objective heuristics against classical single-objective heuristics. Specifically, the comparison concerns: (i) `MHS` - Multi-objective Heuristic Search; (ii) `GHS` - Greedy Single-objective Heuristic Search; (iii) `MBS` - Multi-objective Blind Search; (iv) `AHS` - A* Single-objective Heuristic Search; (v) `DBS` - Depth Blind Search. The configurations `MHS` and `MBS` implement the multi-objective approach with and without the heuristic component of Eq. 1. In both cases, the *risk* has the highest priority while the *plan*

[2] https://github.com/pstlab/PLATINUm.git.

*cost* has the lowest. The configurations GHS and AHS implement classical single-objective heuristic search based on plan cost, replicating the behavior of state-of-the-art classical action-based planners. The configuration DBS implements a blind search. All planners run with the same solving timeout (150 s) and the same flaw selection heuristics.

Several problem instances have been defined by varying the mosaic size from a minimum of 2 rows and 2 columns to a maximum of 10 rows and 10 columns. Each cell of a mosaic entails a pick-and-place task by the human or the robot. For evaluation purposes, a risk matrix $C^{R-H}$ has been generated for each problem instance by assigning random risk indices to pairs of human and robot tasks. Each planner configuration has been run 3 times on each problem instance for a total of 1500 runs[3].

**Table 1.** Average results by problem size. Time is reported in seconds; the remaining metrics retain their original units. The final row reports averages over all successful runs. The best value for each metric and problem size is shown in bold.

| | AHS | | | | GHS | | | | MHS | | | |
|---|---|---|---|---|---|---|---|---|---|---|---|---|
| Rows | Time | Cost | Risk | Makespan | Time | Cost | Risk | Makespan | Time | Cost | Risk | Makespan |
| 2 | **1** | 250 | 473 | 75 | 4 | 251 | 466 | **70** | 1 | **247** | **66** | 135 |
| 3 | **3** | **374** | 728 | **112** | 8 | 379 | 751 | 115 | 4 | 381 | **57** | 242 |
| 4 | **8** | 505 | 944 | 351 | 9 | **501** | 957 | **153** | 11 | 510 | **83** | 325 |
| 5 | **20** | **637** | 1208 | 190 | 23 | 639 | 1170 | **184** | 29 | 648 | **103** | 397 |
| 6 | **42** | **770** | 1412 | 241 | 48 | **770** | 1423 | **235** | 70 | 784 | **116** | 504 |
| 7 | 83 | 903 | 1657 | 252 | **53** | **831** | 1528 | **242** | **53** | 841 | **104** | 541 |
| 8 | 62 | 868 | 1638 | **253** | 65 | 870 | 1560 | 259 | **60** | **795** | **107** | 476 |
| 9 | 72 | 889 | 1611 | **245** | **69** | **884** | 1620 | 251 | 95 | 901 | **123** | 551 |
| 10 | **66** | **884** | 1489 | 248 | 67 | 887 | 1567 | **242** | 90 | 899 | **143** | 560 |
| Overall | 40 | 676 | 1240 | 219 | **38** | 668 | 1227 | **195** | 46 | **667** | **100** | 414 |

Table 1 summarizes the results of the different planning configurations on the defined problem instances. All configurations solve the entire set of problem instances and are compared according to efficiency and plan qualities, specifically: *Time* (i.e., planning time; *Risk* (i.e., average cumulative risk of plans); *Makespan* (i.e., average duration of plans). Concerning reasoning efficiency, GHS achieves the lowest overall average solving time, requiring 38 seconds, followed by AHS with 40 seconds and MHS with 46 seconds. The additional computational cost of MHS is therefore limited to approximately 21% with respect to GHS and 15% with respect to AHS. This overhead is consistent with the more demanding search strategy implemented by MHS: Pareto dominance evaluates partial plans according to multiple criteria and can retain several mutually non-dominated

[3] Runs made on a 2.8 GHz quad-core CPU with 16 GB RAM.

alternatives, whereas GHS and AHS guide the search using a single cost-oriented evaluation function.

The configurations obtain broadly comparable plan costs. The overall average cost is 667 for MHS, 668 for GHS, and 676 for AHS. This indicates that explicitly accounting for risk does not result in a relevant degradation of the cost metric. Namely, it does not affect the number of planning choices necessary to generate a plan (i.e., the depth of the search space). Rather, the main differences concern the temporal organization and safety properties of the generated plans. The single-objective configurations produce the shortest plans. Their overall average makespan is 195 for GHS and 219 for AHS, whereas MHS obtains an average makespan of 414. This increase results from the priority assigned to risk by the multi-objective configuration. To avoid unsafe concurrent execution, MHS reduces the overlap between human and robot activities and may assign tasks differently, thereby limiting parallelism and extending the overall plan duration. Conversely, GHS and AHS optimize cost without explicitly accounting for the negative synergies that may arise from simultaneous human and robot operations. The difference is particularly evident in the aggregated risk. The average risk of the plans generated by MHS is 100, compared with 1227 for GHS and 1240 for AHS. Hence, MHS reduces risk by approximately 92% with respect to both single-objective configurations. This gap is consistently observed across all problem sizes: while the risk of GHS and AHS rapidly increases as the instances become larger, the values obtained by MHS remain between 57 and 143. The result confirms that the Pareto-based heuristic effectively steers the search towards plans that satisfy the

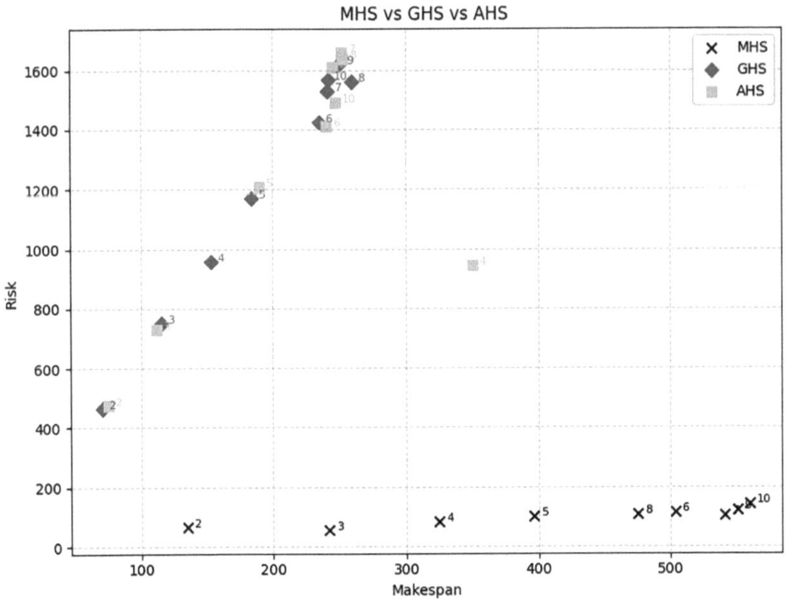


**Fig. 1.** Comparison of plan quality.

safety-oriented objective, rather than treating risk as an incidental property of the final solution.

Figure 1 highlights the resulting trade-off between aggregated makespan and risk. GHS and AHS prefer shorter plans, but their solutions occupy a substantially higher-risk region. In contrast, MHS accepts a higher makespan to maintain risk at a lower level. This view confirms the greater *awareness* of MHS, whose plans best balance makespan and risk. Plans provided by GHS and AHS instead entail a non-negligible or even high level of risk. The proposed method should therefore not be interpreted as optimizing makespan alone, but as identifying solutions that better reflect the safety and operational priorities of human–robot collaboration. The results show that this improvement in solution quality is obtained without a significant increase in plan cost and with only a moderate increase in average solving time.

## 6 Conclusions and Final Remarks

This work introduced a multi-objective heuristic search for timeline-based planning. It adapts key contributions from classical planning and extends heuristic search principles to timelines in a multi-objective setting. Experiments on a realistic collaborative scenario demonstrate the ability of the approach to handle heterogeneous quality criteria and synthesize effective plans. Future work are to extend the multi-objective framework and conduct a broader evaluation campaign. An open challenge concerns the benchmarking of timeline-based formalisms and their empirical comparison with temporal action-based planners. Furthermore, we plan to develop a mapping encoding (based, e.g., on [16]) enabling fair and meaningful comparisons between these different planning paradigms.

**Disclosure of Interests.** The authors have no competing interests to declare that are relevant to the content of this article.

## References

1. Barreiro, J., et al.: EUROPA: a platform for AI planning, scheduling, constraint programming, and optimization. In: ICKEPS 2012: the 4th International Competition on Knowledge Engineering for Planning and Scheduling (2012)
2. Blum, A.L., Furst, M.L.: Fast planning through planning graph analysis. Artif. Intell. **90**(1), 281–300 (1997)
3. Bonet, B., Geffner, H.: Planning as heuristic search: new results. In: Proceedings of the 5th European Conference on Planning: Recent Advances in AI Planning, pp. 360–372. Springer-Verlag, Berlin, Heidelberg (1999)
4. Cesta, A., Cortellessa, G., Fratini, S., Oddi, A.: Developing an end-to-end planning application from a timeline representation framework. In: IAAI-09. Proceedings of the $21^{st}$ Innovative Application of Artificial Intelligence Conference,, Pasadena, CA, USA (2009)

5. Chien, S., Tran, D., Rabideau, G., Schaffer, S., Mandl, D., Frye, S.: Timeline-based space operations scheduling with external constraints. In: ICAPS-10. Proceedings of the $20^{th}$ International Conference on Automated Planning and Scheduling (2010)
6. Mayer, C., Orlandini, M., A.: An executable semantics of flexible plans in terms of timed game automata. In: The 22nd International Symposium on Temporal Representation and Reasoning (TIME), IEEE (2015)
7. Cialdea Mayer, M., Orlandini, A., Umbrico, A.: Planning and execution with flexible timelines: a formal account. Acta Informatica **53**(6–8), 649–680 (2016)
8. De Benedictis, R., Beraldo, G., Cesta, A., Cortellessa, G.: Incremental timeline-based planning for efficient plan execution and adaptation. In: Dovier, A., Montanari, A., Orlandini, A. (eds.) AIxIA 2022 - Advances in Artificial Intelligence, pp. 225–240. Springer International Publishing, Cham (2023)
9. De Benedictis, R., Cesta, A.: Lifted heuristics for timeline-based planning. In: Giacomo, G.D., et al. (eds.) ECAI 2020 - 24th European Conference on Artificial Intelligence. Frontiers in Artificial Intelligence and Applications, vol. 325, pp. 2330–2337. IOS Press (2020)
10. Do, M., Kambhampati, S.: Sapa: a multi-objective metric temporal planner. J. Artif. Intell. Res. **20**, 155–194 (2003)
11. Faroni, M., Umbrico, A., Beschi, M., Orlandini, A., Cesta, A., Pedrocchi, N.: Optimal task and motion planning and execution for multiagent systems in dynamic environments. IEEE Trans. Cybern. **54**(6) (2024). https://doi.org/10.1109/TCYB.2023.3263380
12. Fox, M., Long, D.: PDDL2.1: an extension to PDDL for expressing temporal planning domains. J. Artif. Intell. Res. (JAIR) **20**, 61–124 (2003)
13. Fratini, S., Cesta, A., De Benedictis, R., Orlandini, A., Rasconi, R.: APSI-based deliberation in Goal Oriented Autonomous Controllers. In: ASTRA-11. 11th Symposium on Advanced Space Technologies in Robotics and Automation (2011)
14. Ghallab, M., Laruelle, H.: Representation and control in IxTeT, a temporal planner. In: 2nd International Conference on Artificial Intelligence Planning and Scheduling (AIPS) (1994)
15. Gigante, N., Montanari, A., Cialdea Mayer, M., Orlandini, A.: Complexity of timeline-based planning. In: ICAPS. The 27th International Conference on Automated Planning and Scheduling (2017)
16. Gigante, N., Montanari, A., Cialdea Mayer, M., Orlandini, A.: Timelines are expressive enough to capture action-based temporal planning. In: The 23rd International Symposium on Temporal Representation and Reasoning (TIME). IEEE (2016)
17. Gigante, N., Montanari, A., Orlandini, A., Cialdea Mayer, M., Reynolds, M.: On timeline-based games and their complexity. Theoret. Comput. Sci. **815**, 247–269 (2020)
18. Helmert, M.: The fast downward planning system. J. Artif. Int. Res. **26**(1), 191–246 (2006)
19. Hoffmann, J., Nebel, B.: The ff planning system: fast plan generation through heuristic search. J. Artif. Int. Res. **14**(1), 253–302 (2001)
20. Jonsson, A., Morris, P., Muscettola, N., Rajan, K., Smith, B.: Planning in interplanetary space: theory and practice. In: AIPS-00. Proceedings of the Fifth International Conference on AI Planning and Scheduling, (2000)
21. Khouadjia, M., Schoenauer, M., Vidal, V., Dréo, J., Savéant, P.: Pareto-based multiobjective ai planning. In: Proceedings of the Twenty-Third International Joint Conference on Artificial Intelligence, pp. 2321–2327. AAAI Press (2013)

22. Mcdermott, D., et al.: PDDL - The Planning Domain Definition Language, Yale Center for Computational Vision and Control (1998). rep., CVC TR-98-003/DCS TR-1165 Tech
23. Morris, P.H., Muscettola, N., Vidal, T.: Dynamic control of plans with temporal uncertainty. In: International Joint Conference on Artificial Intelligence (IJCAI), pp. 494–502 (2001)
24. Muscettola, N.: HSTS: integrating planning and scheduling. In: Zweben, M., Fox, M.S. (ed.) Intelligent Scheduling. Morgan Kauffmann (1994)
25. Refanidis, I., Vlahavas, I.: The GRT planning system: backward heuristic construction in forward state-space planning. J. Artif. Int. Res. **15**(1), 115–161 (2001)
26. Refanidis, I., Vlahavas, I.: Multiobjective heuristic state-space planning. Artif. Intell. **145**(1), 1–32 (2003)
27. Sandrini, S., Faroni, M., Pedrocchi, N.: Learning and planning for optimal synergistic human-robot coordination in manufacturing contexts. Robot. Comput.-Integr. Manufact. **95**, 103006 (2025). https://doi.org/10.1016/j.rcim.2025.103006
28. Umbrico, A., et al.: Combining clinical and spatial constraints into temporal planning to personalize physical rehabilitation. In: Proceedings International Conference on Automated Planning and Scheduling, ICAPS, vol. 33 (2023). https://doi.org/10.1609/icaps.v33i1.27234
29. Umbrico, A., Cesta, A., Cialdea Mayer, M., Orlandini, A.: PLATINUm: a new framework for planning and acting. Lect. Notes Comput. Sci. 498–512 (2017)
30. Vidal, V., Geffner, H.: Branching and pruning: an optimal temporal POCL planner based on constraint programming. Artif. Intell. **170**(3), 298–335 (2006)

# CA-WM: Learning Cellular Automaton World Models via LLM Rule Induction and Online Correction

Cesare Zavattari, Alessandro Tommasi, and Giuseppe Prencipe(✉)

Dipartimento di Informatica, Università di Pisa, Pisa, Italy
{cesare.zavattari,alessandro.tommasi}@phd.unipi.it,
giuseppe.prencipe@unipi.it

**Abstract.** We present CA-WM, a world model for grid-based agents in which an LLM induces action-conditional transition rules over $3 \times 3$ local neighborhoods, stored in a persistent rule bank. Locality and determinism are enforced by construction, yielding position-independent rules that transfer to unseen layouts where covered; completeness is validated after every LLM call. The correction mechanism is the core contribution: when a predicted transition mismatches the observed outcome, the wrong rule is evicted and re-learned from a single example within the same step. This allows CA-WM to override an incorrect prior in the tested setting—on ForwardDoorKey, a MiniGrid variant where FORWARD opens a locked door, CA-WM achieves 100% planning success on five out-of-distribution layouts against 0% for a physics oracle that cannot update its assumptions. On standard DoorKey-5×5 the bank saturates after one accumulation episode: subsequent episodes require zero LLM calls while exactly predicting every changed cell—a ≈25,000× reduction in marginal prediction cost. A greedy lookahead planner over the bank reaches BFS-optimal solutions on all out-of-distribution seeds. All results use `Qwen3-Next-80B-A3B-Instruct` (3B active per token) served locally via vLLM at zero API cost.

**Keywords:** World models · LLM agents · Neuro-symbolic learning · Rule induction · Out-of-distribution generalization

## 1 Introduction

LLM-based planning agents typically simulate futures via autoregressive generation [5], paying a full forward pass per rollout step and compounding errors across the horizon; neural world models such as DreamerV3 [4] avoid per-step LLM queries but embed dynamics in opaque weights with no targeted correction. Recent neuro-symbolic systems [2,16] instead induce explicit symbolic rules from trajectories under LLM guidance, but rely on the LLM's prior being broadly correct or revise rules *episodically*—a full-episode lag before a wrong rule is fixed.


S. Bistarelli et al. (Eds.): AIxIA 2026, LNAI 17131, pp. 715–727, 2027.
https://doi.org/10.1007/978-3-032-40774-0_51

We present **CA-WM**, a world model for environments with *locally factorizable*, fully observable, deterministic dynamics. In this regime transitions decompose into a finite set of local rules over $3 \times 3$ neighborhoods and world modeling reduces to rule induction and lookup; the regime captures grid worlds, cellular systems, object-centric interactions, and discretized physical processes.

*Role of the LLM.* The LLM is not used for trajectory reasoning. It serves as a *structured prior over local transition functions*, mapping a neighborhood context and action directly to a candidate rule—replacing sample-based discovery with compositional generalization. CA-WM stores rules in a persistent *rule bank* $\mathcal{B}$, indexed by $(action, 3 \times 3\text{-neighborhood})$ tuple; because rules are indexed by neighborhood pattern, a rule learned at one location applies anywhere the same pattern appears—including unseen layouts. (We retain CA terminology although our rules are action-conditional.)

The correction mechanism is the core contribution: at each step CA-WM applies the bank, and on any mismatch the offending rule is evicted and re-learned via one LLM call with the true transition as a correction example, before the next step. A single corrected transition induces a rule that generalizes across all states sharing the same $3 \times 3$ pattern—one-shot structure learning over an equivalence class. In our experiments this correction converges in a single step (an empirical observation, not a theorem; Sect. 4).

*Discriminating Result.* On ForwardDoorKey (a MiniGrid variant where FORWARD opens a locked door, contradicting standard physics) a physics oracle loops indefinitely on TOGGLE and solves 0/5 layouts; CA-WM learns the correct rule from a single mismatch and solves all 5 at BFS-optimal step counts—despite the LLM's own prior also predicting FORWARD as blocked.

*Contributions.* We contribute in four ways: (1) A world-model architecture based on action-conditional CA rules with structurally enforced locality and determinism and runtime-validated completeness, yielding position-independent OOD transfer (Sects. 4, 6). (2) An online correction loop that evicts wrong rules and re-learns from a single example, amortizing LLM cost to zero after one accumulation episode on DoorKey-5×5 and to a residual call floor on larger grids (Exp 1–2). (3) A greedy lookahead planner over the bank with a physics fallback, achieving BFS-optimal solutions on out-of-distribution layouts at zero LLM-call cost (Exp 5). (4) An empirical demonstration that the correction mechanism can override the LLM's prior on non-standard physics, outperforming a physics oracle 100% vs. 0% (Exp 6).

## 2 Related Work

*Neural and LLM-as-World-Model Approaches.* DreamerV3 [4] predicts latent next states with a recurrent state-space model; errors compound across the horizon and dynamics live in opaque weights with no targeted correction. RAP [5] prompts the LLM itself to simulate transitions, preserving interpretability at a per-step latency cost. CA-WM addresses both: rules are explicit and correctable, and inference is constant-time lookup after accumulation.

*Neuro-Symbolic World Models.* WALL-E 2.0 [16] extracts symbolic action rules and knowledge graphs from trajectories, compiles them to code, and combines them with an aligned LLM and MPC, reaching 98% on ALFWorld [10]. CA-WM differs in predicting the full next grid state directly (enabling lookahead without environment interaction), enforcing locality and determinism by construction, correcting per-step rather than episodically, and running on a local 80B MoE rather than GPT-4. NeSyC [2] shares the closed-loop correction philosophy but uses generic symbolic tools; CA-WM specializes to CA neighborhoods, gaining single-step convergence (Sect. 4). [15] use a wake–sleep habit library with offline consolidation; CA-WM amortizes similarly but fully online. LLM-Modulo [6] pairs an LLM with an external PDDL verifier; CA-WM uses the environment itself as verifier and corrects within the same step.

*LLM Agents and Locally-Factored Models.* ReAct [14] interleaves reasoning and actions without an explicit world model; Reflexion [9] adds verbal self-correction across episodes but accumulates no structured model. RAFA [8] combines LLM world modeling with tree-search planning; CA-WM is complementary and could serve as its transition model. [3] model object interactions via time-varying graphs, mirroring our local factorization; CA-WM makes the factorization *explicit and enumerable* as an auditable lookup table. [11] treat CA rule induction as a benchmark for active information gathering; we invert this, using CA as the world model's representational language.

## 3 Background and Problem Setup

### 3.1 MiniGrid Environments

MiniGrid [1] is a fully observable 2D-grid RL suite; our tasks use six of its seven discrete actions (LEFT, RIGHT, FORWARD, PICKUP, DROP, TOGGLE). We map each cell to a single integer folding object type, door state, and agent overlap into one code (0 = empty, 1 = wall, 2 = agent, 3 = goal, 4 = door_open, 5 = door_locked, 6 = key, 7 = agent_on_door_open, 8 = agent_on_goal), so a $3 \times 3$ neighborhood is a 9-tuple of integers. We evaluate on standard **DoorKey** ($5{\times}5/8{\times}8/16{\times}16$: pick up key, toggle locked door, reach goal) and on **ForwardDoorKey-5**$\times$**5**, a custom variant where FORWARD into a locked door opens and enters it, TOGGLE is a no-op, and no key is placed—the discriminating environment for Exp 6.

### 3.2 Rule Representation

We represent environment dynamics as a finite set of *action-conditional local rules*, drawing on the cellular automaton formalism [12]. A rule maps a $3 \times 3$ Moore neighborhood and an agent action to a new center-cell value:

$$f_a : \{0, \ldots, K\}^9 \rightarrow \{0, \ldots, K\}, \tag{1}$$

where the 9-tuple $(n_0, \dots, n_8)$ lists the neighborhood cells in row-major order (NW to SE) with $n_4$ as the center, and $a \in \mathcal{A}$ is the agent action. Rules are collected into a *rule bank* $\mathcal{B} = \{a \mapsto \{(n_0, \dots, n_8) \mapsto v\}\}$, implemented as a per-action dictionary; writing $N(c, s)$ for the 9-tuple of cell $c$ in state $s$, a rule applied to $c$ under action $a$ is $\mathcal{B}[a][N(c, s)]$.

The bank maintains three structural properties; the first two are enforced by construction, the third is validated at runtime: **(1) Locality.** Every key is a 9-tuple drawn from the $3 \times 3$ Moore neighborhood of the cell being predicted. **(2) Determinism.** The bank is a dictionary: the same neighborhood under the same action always produces the same output. **(3) Completeness.** Every dynamic cell type (all codes except wall, code 1) must appear as $n_4$ in at least one rule in $\mathcal{B}[a]$ for each action $a$. Unlike the first two, completeness is not structurally guaranteed: omitted cell types persist as bank misses and are re-prompted later; on larger grids a few remain uncovered—the residual LLM-call floor.

Locality is the key property enabling out-of-distribution transfer: because a rule is indexed by neighborhood pattern rather than absolute grid position, a rule learned at coordinates $(r, c)$ applies identically wherever the same $3 \times 3$ pattern appears—including unseen layouts and grid sizes.

### 3.3 Problem Statement

At each step $t$ the agent observes $s_t \in \{0, \dots, K\}^{H \times W}$, selects $a_t \in \mathcal{A}$, and receives $s_{t+1}$. The *world-modeling problem* is to maintain $\mathcal{B}$ such that applying $\mathcal{B}[a_t]$ to $s_t$ produces $\hat{s}_{t+1}$ matching $s_{t+1}$ on all changed cells; the *planning problem* is to pick the action sequence reaching the goal in minimum steps using $\mathcal{B}$ as the transition model (zero environment queries at inference).

## 4 CA-WM Architecture

### 4.1 Overview

CA-WM operates in a closed loop—predict from the bank, act, observe, correct before the next step—through the four phases of Fig. 1: *induction* (LLM generates rules for unseen neighborhoods), *prediction* (bank produces $\hat{s}_{t+1}$), *correction* (mismatched rules evicted and re-learned), and *planning* (greedy lookahead over the bank).

### 4.2 Rule Induction

On a *bank miss* (bank does not cover all neighborhoods of $s_t$ under $a_t$), CA-WM calls the LLM with an *inverted prompt*: the $3 \times 3$ neighborhood tuple of every non-wall cell is extracted and presented as `CELL r,c: value | neighborhood: n0..n8`; the LLM responds with `CELL r,c: old -> new` per cell, and rules are read off the observed tuples—the LLM never computes geometry. A pre-computed hint (agent position, direction, forward-cell PASSABLE/BLOCKED) is intended to reduce wrong-destination errors without revealing the outcome. The

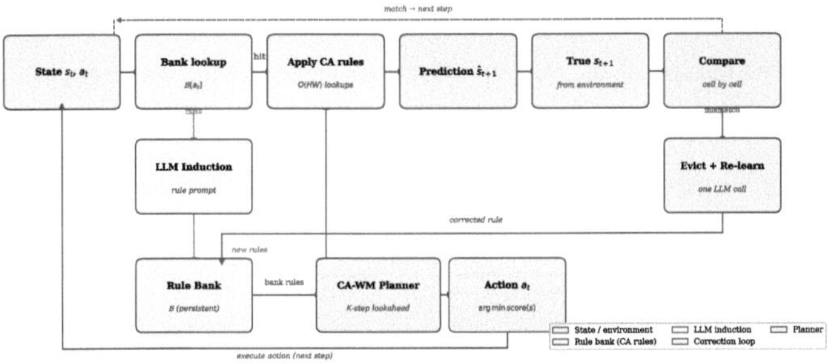


**Fig. 1.** CA-WM pipeline. **Prediction loop** (top): on a bank hit, CA rules produce $\hat{s}_{t+1}$ in $O(HW)$ lookups (green); a miss (orange) triggers an LLM call and merges new rules; a mismatch (red) evicts and re-learns the wrong rule. **Planning loop** (bottom, purple): $K$-step lookahead over $\mathcal{B}$ selects $a_t$. (Color figure online)

parser checks each `old` against the actual cell value, falling back to identity on mismatch; grid dimensions prevent out-of-bounds hallucination; the last three correction examples (Sect. 4.4) are appended as in-context demonstrations.

### 4.3 Bank Management

On a *hit* (all neighborhoods of $s_t$ under $a_t$ covered), each cell $c$ is updated to $\mathcal{B}[a_t][N(c, s_t)]$ in $O(HW)$ lookups with no LLM call; on a *miss*, the LLM is called and the returned rules merged. On conflict the new observation wins: determinism makes any conflict an encoding error, not genuine ambiguity.

### 4.4 Online Correction

After acting and observing $s_{t+1}$, CA-WM compares the prediction $\hat{s}_{t+1}$ with the true outcome cell by cell. For each mismatched cell $c$, the entry $\mathcal{B}[a_t][N(c, s_t)]$ is **evicted** and the LLM is **re-called immediately in the same step** with the observed mismatch appended as a correction example; the corrected rule enters the bank before the next step.

Because rules are indexed by local neighborhood rather than absolute position, a single corrected transition induces a rule that applies to all states sharing the same $3 \times 3$ pattern. Single-step convergence arises from (i) local factorization, (ii) deterministic dynamics, and (iii) the LLM's ability to produce a consistent rule from a single correction example.

*Proposition 1 (Informal).* Under (i)–(iii), once a neighborhood type has been corrected the corresponding rule produces the true transition for every grid state in which that neighborhood appears. Empirically, acc_changed = 1.000 from episode 2 on every seed across all evaluated environments (Tables 1, 2) implies no rule is re-evicted after its initial correction; we report this as an observed consequence rather than a formal guarantee.

In the tested setting this holds regardless of whether the LLM's prior is correct: on ForwardDoorKey the eviction–re-learn cycle produces the true rule on the first mismatch even though the prior predicts FORWARD as blocked.

### 4.5 CA-WM Planner

At inference time, CA-WM runs a greedy $K$-step lookahead ($K = 3$) over the rule bank, with a physics fallback for uncovered neighborhoods and zero LLM calls.

*State Scoring.* A candidate state $s$ reached after a hypothetical action sequence is scored by the following equation:

$$\text{score}(s) = h(s) + \lambda \cdot \mathbb{1}[\text{bank-miss}(s, a)],$$

where $h(s)$ is a direction-aware heuristic (Manhattan distance to the next sub-goal: key → door → goal) and $\lambda = 5.0$ penalizes actions whose lookup is not yet covered—discouraging the planner from committing to transitions it cannot simulate.

*Physics Fallback.* For states that still incur a bank miss after penalization, a lightweight physics predictor provides a fallback: FORWARD moves the agent if the target is passable, PICKUP collects an adjacent key, and TOGGLE opens a door if the agent carries a key. Key possession is inferred from a global scan of the grid (key code absent ⇒ key held)—a deliberate asymmetry with the strictly local rule bank, sound under DoorKey's single-key, fully-observable setting. After accumulation the planner runs entirely from dictionary lookups, the heuristic, and the fallback—no LLM calls, ≈10–11 ms per step.

### 4.6 Evaluation Metrics

**acc_changed**: fraction of cells that actually changed between $s_t$ and $s_{t+1}$ that are correctly predicted. The primary metric; trivial steps (no cell changes, e.g., agent bumps a wall) are excluded. **acc**: fraction of all cells correctly predicted; less discriminative because the grid is sparse. **bank_hit_pct**: fraction of steps served entirely from the bank with no LLM call. **false_changes**: cells predicted to change on a trivial step—a pure hallucination measure. Across all canonical runs (Exp 1–2, incl. 16×16) it is zero except an episode-2 transient of at most one per seed as freshly-corrected rules first generalize.

## 5 Experimental Setup

### 5.1 Environments and Model

DoorKey-5×5/8×8/16×16 (BFS-optimal sequences of 7–14, 11–22, 26–40 steps; the rollout cap exceeds the longest BFS length, so each episode runs in full) and ForwardDoorKey-5×5 (Sect. 3). All experiments use `Qwen3-Next-80B-A3B-Instruct` [13] (3B active per token, MoE), served locally via vLLM [7] at temperature 0. LLM calls fire only on bank misses and corrections.

### 5.2 Evaluation Protocol

*Action Sequences.* Exp 1–4 follow BFS-optimal action sequences, computed by state-space search over ($p_{\text{agent}}$, *has_key*, *door_open*) triples and verified by environment replay; seeds vary layouts.

*Multi-episode Protocol.* Episode 1 is the *accumulation episode* (bank starts empty); episodes 2–$E$ test bank reuse on the same seed (Exp 1–3) or unseen seeds (Exp 4).

*Seeds.* Exp 1–4 use $N = 10$ accumulation seeds (mean $\pm$ std across seeds). Exp 5 plans on OOD seeds 200–209 after 1-seed (seed 4) or 10-seed ({4,7,42,100,13,99,1,2,3,5}) accumulation; Exp 6 uses ForwardDoorKey accumulation seeds {4,7,42,13} and five held-out OOD seeds.

*Baselines.* **Autoregressive (Exp 3)**: the LLM predicts the full next grid state directly, with no CA structure or persistent bank. **Physics-only (Exp 6)**: the CA-WM planner with an empty bank, falling through to the physics fallback (Sect. 4), which hardcodes standard MiniGrid dynamics.

### 5.3 Experiment Overview

Experiments 1–4 evaluate CA-WM as a *predictive world model* along a fixed BFS-optimal action sequence, isolating dynamics learning from exploration: the correction ablation (Exp 1), bank accumulation across grid sizes (Exp 2), the autoregressive baseline (Exp 3), and OOD generalization (Exp 4). Experiments 5–6 close the loop, with the planner (Sect. 4.5) selecting actions autonomously from the bank—on standard DoorKey (Exp 5) and against the physics oracle on ForwardDoorKey (Exp 6), the discriminating experiment.

## 6 Results

### 6.1 Exp 1 — In-Context Correction Ablation

Table 1 compares WITH vs. WITHOUT correction examples in the prompt, across $N = 10$ seeds and $E = 5$ episodes on DoorKey-5×5 and 8×8.

On DoorKey-5×5 both conditions start at acc_changed $= 0.855 \pm 0.062$: the LLM knows standard MiniGrid semantics but errs systematically on the non-standard cell codes 7 and 8 (agent_on_door_open, agent_on_goal). From episode 2 the WITH condition converges to $1.000 \pm 0.000$ and stays there; WITHOUT remains at $0.855 \pm 0.062$—it never degrades, and never learns.

On DoorKey-8×8 the same pattern holds: episode 1 is $0.923 \pm 0.023$ for both conditions (Table 2's $0.926 \pm 0.026$ comes from the Exp 2 runner; each re-derives from its own log); from episode 2 WITH converges to $1.000 \pm 0.000$.

**Table 1.** Exp 1—acc_changed (mean ± std, $N = 10$ seeds).

| Environment | Condition | Episode 1 | Episodes 2–5 |
|---|---|---|---|
| DoorKey-5×5 | WITH corrections | $0.855 \pm 0.062$ | **$1.000 \pm 0.000$** |
| | WITHOUT corrections | $0.855 \pm 0.062$ | $0.855 \pm 0.062$ |
| DoorKey-8×8 | WITH corrections | $0.923 \pm 0.023$ | **$1.000 \pm 0.000$** |
| | WITHOUT corrections | $0.923 \pm 0.023$ | $0.923 \pm 0.023$ |

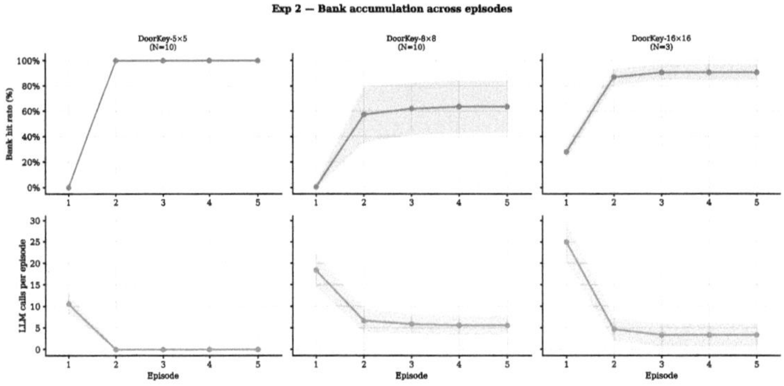


**Fig. 2.** Exp 2—bank hit rate (%) and LLM calls per episode (mean ± std; $N = 10$ seeds for 5×5 and 8×8, $N = 3$ for 16×16). 5×5 saturates fully after episode 1; 8×8 and 16×16 plateau below 100%.

**Finding.** In these tasks, in-context corrections are necessary and sufficient for convergence: one correction example per novel encoding type eliminates the error from episode 2.

## 6.2 Exp 2 — Bank Accumulation

Figure 2 and Table 2 summarize. On DoorKey-5×5, episode 1 requires $10.6 \pm 2.2$ LLM calls (all neighborhoods unseen). From episode 2 onward: hit rate = 100% ± 0%, LLM calls = $0.0 \pm 0.0$, acc_changed = $1.000 \pm 0.000$—the bank saturates in exactly one episode on every seed. Episode-1 accuracy matches Exp 1 (Table 1): the first encounter with each novel encoding type still errs once before the correction loop fires.

On DoorKey-8×8 coverage is uneven: seeds whose BFS trajectory misses certain neighborhoods stall at 18–60% hit rate while others saturate to ≈85% (mean ≈64%, residual calls 2–9 per episode); acc_changed = 1.000 from episode 2 regardless—the larger vocabulary affects cost, not accuracy.

On DoorKey-16×16 ($N = 3$ seeds) episode 1 requires 20–31 LLM calls (23–35% bank hit rate); three first-pass mismatches occur across the three seeds, all on FORWARD transitions, and the correction loop evicts and re-learns each within the same episode. From episode 2 the bank stabilises at 82–96% hit rate, with 1–7 residual calls per episode and acc_changed = 1.000 on every seed; the three corrected neighborhoods are never re-evicted. Aggregate episode-1 acc_changed rises with grid size (Table 2); we report this as an empirical trend.

**Finding.** The bank fully amortizes LLM cost on 5×5 and plateaus at a residual call floor on 8×8 and 16×16; acc_changed = 1.000 from episode 2 in all three regimes.

**Table 2.** Exp 2—bank accumulation summary across grid sizes.

| Environment | $N$ | ep1 acc_ch | ep1 hits | ep2+ hits | ep2+ LLM calls |
|---|---|---|---|---|---|
| DoorKey-5×5 | 10 | $0.855 \pm 0.062$ | 0% | **100%** | 0.0 |
| DoorKey-8×8 | 10 | $0.926 \pm 0.026$ | 0% | ≈64% | ≈5.6 |
| DoorKey-16×16 | 3 | $0.990 \pm 0.007$ | 23–35% | 82–96% | 1–7 |

**Latency.** Mean LLM call latency is ≈2,500 ms (vLLM served locally); mean CA bank apply is ≈0.1 ms (dict lookup): ≈25,000× on bank-hit steps. This is the marginal cost of a prediction versus the LLM query it replaces, not a comparison against an optimised rollout model.

### 6.3 Exp 3 — CA-WM vs. Autoregressive Baseline

In episode 1 the baseline beats CA-WM ($0.980 \pm 0.030$ vs. $0.855 \pm 0.062$) by exploiting Qwen3's MiniGrid knowledge directly. From episode 2 CA-WM reaches $1.000 \pm 0.000$ at zero LLM cost while the baseline remains at ≈ 0.980 with a full LLM call per step.

**Finding.** The baseline's advantage is episode-1 only; CA-WM's exact-prediction-at-zero-cost advantage compounds thereafter.

### 6.4 Exp 4 — Out-of-Distribution Generalization

Single-seed accumulation gives mean OOD acc_changed 0.931 with a bimodal distribution: 6 of 10 accumulation seeds yield 0.938–1.000, 4 yield 0.800–0.833—the low-band seeds are those whose BFS path never visits a cell adjacent to the goal or door, so codes 7/8 never get corrected. Multi-seed accumulation (seeds 4 + 13) covers all transition types: OOD acc_changed = 1.000 on all five OOD seeds (Fig. 3).

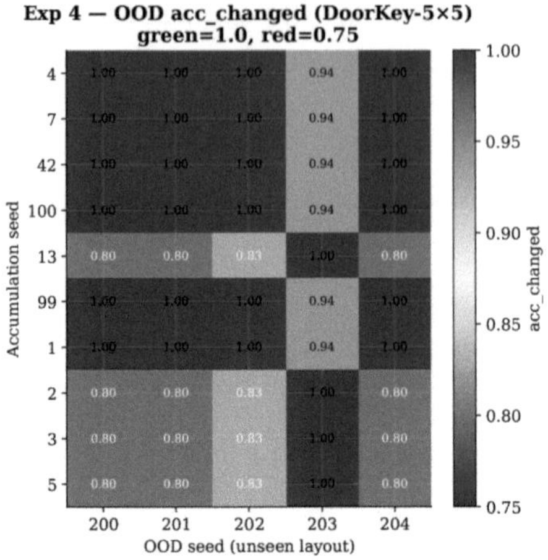


**Fig. 3.** Exp 4—OOD acc_changed heatmap (accumulation seed × OOD seed, DoorKey-5×5). Bimodal: 4 accumulation seeds miss the code-7 transition, degrading all their OOD seeds.

**Finding.** Locality gives position-independence; full OOD transfer additionally requires every transition type to be observed during accumulation—a property of the accumulation trajectory, not of the OOD layout. The BFS-optimal path is the least exploratory trajectory, so the bimodal result is a near-worst-case lower bound on coverage.

## 6.5 Exp 5 — CA-WM Planner

Both the 1-seed (8 LLM calls, hit = 52%) and 10-seed (38 calls, 88.3%) conditions solve all 10 OOD seeds at BFS-optimal step counts, with zero LLM calls at inference. More accumulation increases coverage but not solution quality; on seeds 203 and 208 the 1-seed bank contributes zero hits and the planner succeeds entirely via the physics fallback.

## 6.6 Exp 6 — CA-WM vs. Physics Oracle on Non-standard Physics

Figure 4 is the discriminating result. On ForwardDoorKey-5×5 (4 accumulation seeds, 18 LLM calls), **CA-WM** solves 5/5 OOD seeds at BFS-optimal steps (bank hit 89.2%); **physics-only** solves 0/5, exhausting the 50-step episode limit on every seed.

The physics predictor hardcodes FORWARD-into-locked-door as blocked and tries TOGGLE—a no-op in this variant—so the planner loops indefinitely. The LLM's prior is wrong in the same way, but on the first FORWARD-into-door step the observed mismatch triggers eviction and re-learning within the same step; the planner thereafter prefers FORWARD (bank hit) over TOGGLE (miss, penalty $\lambda$).

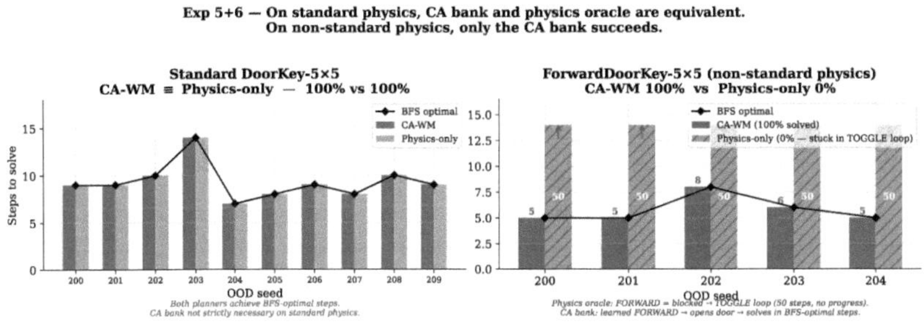


**Fig. 4.** Exp 5+6 comparison. *Left*: standard DoorKey-5×5—CA-WM and physics-only both 100% at BFS-optimal. *Right*: ForwardDoorKey-5×5—CA-WM 5/5 at BFS-optimal; physics-only exhausts the 50-step limit on every seed.

**Finding.** The correction mechanism overrides an incorrect prior in the tested setting; the evaluated transition classes were learned from a single observed mismatch. The physics oracle has no update mechanism and so cannot.

# 7 Discussion

## 7.1 LLM Prior as a Starting Point, Not a Prerequisite

In Exp 3 the autoregressive baseline wins episode 1 by exploiting standard MiniGrid semantics; CA-WM starts from the same prior but must discover codes 7 and 8 through correction, surpassing the baseline from episode 2 at zero LLM-call cost. In Exp 6 the LLM's prior matches the physics oracle's wrong answer, and the correction loop overrides both from the first mismatch. The LLM is a generator of candidate rules enabling zero-shot completion of unseen neighborhoods, not a knowledge oracle—a purely tabular alternative would have to visit every neighborhood type before predicting it. CA-WM trades compression for explicit, verifiable, editable dynamics.

*Complementary Mechanisms.* Where the bank lacks coverage (Exp 5) the physics fallback still reaches the goal; where the physics is wrong (Exp 6) the correction loop overrides it. A failure requires both to be unavailable at once—a regime not observed in our experiments.

## 7.2 Scalability

The three grid sizes span three operating regimes of increasing vocabulary (Table 2): full saturation on 5×5, uneven per-seed coverage on 8×8, and a stable 82–96% plateau on 16×16—variation reflecting accumulation coverage, not grid size. No 16×16 seed saturates within five episodes: the LLM occasionally omits cell types, so a few (action, direction) tuples retain uncovered neighborhoods—the residual LLM-call floor (Sect. 3). In all three regimes acc_changed = 1.000 from episode 2: scale affects efficiency, not correctness; residual calls are bounded by the task vocabulary, far below an autoregressive rollout's $O(N)$ calls per step.

### 7.3 Limitations

*Greedy Decoding and Phase 1 Only.* All results use greedy decoding (temperature 0) and in-context learning only; sampling non-determinism would mainly affect episode 1.

*Accumulation Coverage.* OOD transfer holds only for neighborhood types observed during accumulation; uncovered transitions fall back to the physics predictor. The generalization boundary is explicit: failures arise from missing coverage, not model uncertainty.

*Deterministic, Fully Observable Dynamics Only.* The correction loop's "new observation wins" policy is sound only because transitions are deterministic (a single mismatch proves the stored rule wrong). Under stochastic dynamics the same neighborhood may legitimately yield different outcomes, so eviction-on-mismatch would discard correct rules; the bank would need distributional entries and a statistical test in place of exact matching. Under partial observability the $3 \times 3$ neighborhood no longer determines the next cell value, breaking locality itself. Both extensions change the correction mechanism qualitatively; we do not claim the present results transfer to either setting.

*2D Grid Environments Only.* The $3 \times 3$ Moore neighborhood is natural for 2D grids; continuous, 3D, or larger-context settings would require a different factorization primitive.

*Model Capability Requirements.* CA-WM needs no frontier API model but does need reliable structured output: `Qwen2.5-7B-Instruct` fails to converge on DoorKey-5×5 (acc_changed oscillates 0.0–0.5) because it cannot produce well-formed `CELL` responses, while `Qwen3-Next-80B-A3B-Instruct` (3B active per token) converges on a single A100-class GPU. "Local" means adequate instruction-following on one research-grade GPU, not commodity hardware.

## 8 Conclusions and Future Work

We presented CA-WM: an LLM induces action-conditional CA rules over $3 \times 3$ neighborhoods, stored in a persistent bank and corrected from single observed transitions. The experiments establish that in-context correction is necessary for convergence (Exp 1); that the bank amortizes LLM cost to zero on DoorKey-5×5 ($\approx$25,000× lower marginal prediction cost; Exp 2); and, most importantly, that the correction mechanism is independent of the LLM's prior: on Forward-DoorKey, where that prior is incorrect, CA-WM achieves 100% planning success against 0% for a physics oracle that cannot update its assumptions (Exp 6).

Future work: *LoRA fine-tuning* on accumulated corrections, which could eliminate episode-1 errors; *active accumulation* to maximize coverage (addressing Exp 4's bimodal result); an *adaptive neighborhood radius* for longer-range interactions; and *richer cell representations* (color, state, orientation) for multiple object instances.

**Acknowledgements.** This work has been partially supported by the project FISA2023-00323 RehAI, funded by the Italian MUR, and by the Italian National Group for Scientific Computation (GNCS-INdAM).

## References

1. Chevalier-Boisvert, M., et al.: Minigrid & Miniworld: modular & customizable reinforcement learning environments for goal-oriented tasks. In: Advances in Neural Information Processing Systems. vol. 36 (2023). datasets and Benchmarks Track
2. Choi, W., Park, J., Ahn, S., Lee, D., Woo, H.: NeSyC: a neuro-symbolic continual learner for complex embodied tasks in open domains. In: International Conference on Learning Representations (2025)
3. Feng, F., Lippe, P., Magliacane, S.: Learning interactive world model for object-centric reinforcement learning. In: Advances in Neural Information Processing Systems, vol. 38 (2025)
4. Hafner, D., Pasukonis, J., Ba, J., Lillicrap, T.: Mastering diverse control tasks through world models. Nature (2025). https://doi.org/10.1038/s41586-025-08744-2
5. Hao, S., et al.: Reasoning with language model is planning with world model. In: Proceedings of the 2023 Conference on Empirical Methods in Natural Language Processing, pp. 8154–8173. Association for Computational Linguistics, Singapore (2023)
6. Kambhampati, S., et al.: LLMs can't plan, but can help planning in LLM-modulo frameworks. In: Proceedings of the 41st International Conference on Machine Learning. PMLR, vol. 235 (2024)
7. Kwon, W., et al.: Efficient memory management for large language model serving with PagedAttention. In: Proceedings of the 29th Symposium on Operating Systems Principles. SOSP, p. 23 (2023). https://doi.org/10.1145/3600006.3613165
8. Liu, Z., et al.: Reason for future, act for now: a principled framework for autonomous LLM agents with provable sample efficiency. In: Proceedings of the 41st International Conference on Machine Learning. PMLR, vol. 235 (2024)
9. Shinn, N., Cassano, F., Berman, E., Gopinath, A., Narasimhan, K., Yao, S.: Reflexion: language agents with verbal reinforcement learning. In: Advances in Neural Information Processing Systems, vol. 36 (2023)
10. Shridhar, M., Yuan, X., Côté, M.A., Bisk, Y., Trischler, A., Hausknecht, M.: ALFWorld: aligning text and embodied environments for interactive learning. In: International Conference on Learning Representations (2021)
11. Tajwar, F., et al.: Training a generally curious agent (2025). https://arxiv.org/abs/2502.17543
12. Wolfram, S.: A New Kind of Science. Wolfram Media (2002)
13. Yang, A., et al.: Qwen3 technical report. Tech. rep, Alibaba Cloud (2025)
14. Yao, S., et al.: ReAct: synergizing reasoning and acting in language models. In: International Conference on Learning Representations (2023)
15. Zhiren, G., Yang, C., Ren, W., Li, S.: Learning human habits with rule-guided active inference. In: The Fourteenth International Conference on Learning Representations (2026). https://openreview.net/forum?id=FZXwkBH6s7
16. Zhou, S., et al.: WALL-E 2.0: World alignment by NeuroSymbolic learning improves world model-based LLM agents. arXiv preprint arXiv:2504.15785 (2025)

# Preserving Computer Music Heritage Through RAG-Based Interpretation of Historical Source Code

Anna Zuccante(✉) and Sergio Canazza

Centro di Sonologia Computazionale, Department of Information Engineering, University of Padova, Padova, Italy
anna.zuccante@phd.unipd.it, sergio.canazza@unipd.it

**Abstract.** The preservation of computer music heritage requires methods capable of recovering not only audio outputs, but also the historical programming languages and manuals, through which such works were created. Music V, an early and highly influential computer music language, is available only through historical manuals that are fragmented, not natively machine-readable, and difficult to interpret without specialist expertise. Although modern large language models are increasingly capable of interpreting complex code, they remain unreliable when applied to niche and domain-specific languages such as those used in early computer music, often producing incorrect explanations or hallucinated interpretations. To overcome this limitation, we propose a Retrieval-Augmented Generation (RAG) system grounding LLMs in the historical computer music manuals through a hybrid lexical (BM25) and semantic (FAISS) retrieval pipeline. The proposed system is evaluated against zero-shot large language model baselines using BERT-based similarity metrics, cosine similarity, and RAGAS metrics. Results show that the RAG-based approach improves the interpretation of Music V code with respect to zero-shot LLMs, demonstrating the importance of grounding language models in domain-specific historical documentation.

**Keywords:** Retrieval-Augmented Generation · Cultural Heritage · Computer Music · Software Preservation · Large Language Models

## 1 Introduction

The birth of computer music can be dated to the 1950s, when the advent of the first computers led composers to regard the computer as a new medium for experimenting with sound synthesis [16]. To this end, they began developing programming languages, built upon existing ones, designed to represent sound synthesis processes while remaining simple and intuitive enough to be used by people without a computer science background, once the underlying grammar had been learned. In particular, the family of Music N languages, created by Max Mathews starting in 1957, was the most representative and influential, to


S. Bistarelli et al. (Eds.): AIxIA 2026, LNAI 17131, pp. 728–742, 2027.
https://doi.org/10.1007/978-3-032-40774-0_52

the point of being adopted by numerous computer music centers worldwide, including several across Europe [5].

These languages are distinguished by the combination of two paradigms, the orchestra and the score, which operate jointly [8]: the former defines the set of instruments, represented as unit generators, while the latter defines the sequence of sound events that trigger those instruments to produce the final sound. Among these, the most important was the fifth version, Music V [20], which in turn paved the way for more modern languages such as Csound [18], implemented in C. Despite their importance and role in inspiring more intuitive languages closer to natural language, this very success led to their gradual abandonment and obsolescence. If they are not soon recovered and understood, a significant part of the cultural heritage of computer music, and, to some extent, history of software, risks being lost [37].

This problem cannot be reduced to simply manually consulting a manual. Even when the relevant manual is found, correct interpretation demands knowledge of Music V syntax, score structure, and historical computer music practice that is increasingly rare. A model is therefore needed to interpret these languages automatically, preserving them and making them accessible to non-experts, such as musicologists and archivists without prior familiarity with Music V.

Therefore, in this paper: (i) we present, to the best of our knowledge, the first RAG-based system for interpreting a historical, low-resource computer music language, grounded in a historical institutional manual not originally available in structured machine-readable form; (ii) we adapt an established hybrid lexical-semantic retrieval strategy to the challenges of computer music documentation, namely short, cryptic instruction tokens and structurally heterogeneous manual content (text, tables, and code); and (iii) we provide a critical, empirically grounded analysis of evaluation metrics compared with zero-shot LLMs.

To this end, the paper is structured as follows: Sect. 2 reviews the state of the art on large language models for code understanding, their application to low-resource and historical programming languages, and the use of retrieval-augmented approaches in digital humanities, Sect. 3 presents the proposed retrieval augmented generation (RAG) model, Sect. 4 presents the results, and Sect. 5 provides discussion and conclusions.

## 2 Related Work

Large language models have rapidly become a standard tool for code-related tasks, spanning everything from code generation [17,29] to program repair [1,30]. At the same time, an increasing amount of research is investigating how well these models truly comprehend the code they process, rather than reproducing surface-level patterns acquired during pretraining. Xie et al. [31] present CORE, a large-scale benchmark that spans data, control, and information-flow dependencies in C/C++, Java, and Python. They find that while reasoning-oriented models perform well on basic dependency classification, they systematically struggle with tasks that demand multi-step reasoning, such as producing full dependency traces, with accuracy dropping significantly in the presence of complex control structures or backward dependencies. Similarly, Maveli et al. [21] introduce RTCE, an evaluation method that assesses code understanding via round-trip invertibility on compression algorithms. Their results indicate that models frequently manage the forward and reverse executions in isolation, yet fail to sustain a single, coherent internal representation that remains consistent in both directions, a gap that neither fine-tuning nor iterative self-reflection fully remedies. Taken together, these studies show that even for programming languages that are heavily represented in pretraining data, current LLMs still lack the compositional and coherent understanding of code semantics required for reliable interpretation.

If LLMs already exhibit fragile reasoning on languages with rich training data, the problem can be expected to be more severe for languages that are scarcely represented, or entirely absent, from training corpora, an issue receiving growing attention in the context of low-resource and legacy programming languages. Cassano et al. [3] show that Code LLMs perform substantially worse in low-resource languages such as OCaml and Racket than in high-resource ones, proposing a knowledge-transfer strategy based on semi-synthetic data; Giagnorio et al. [14] similarly find that no single technique reliably closes this gap. More specifically related to our work, recent research has examined RAG as an adaptation strategy for low-resource languages [19]. This approach reduces LLMs' knowledge gaps and hallucinations by supplementing their internal memory with external retrieval from dedicated knowledge bases. It has been demonstrated that this substantially enhances LLM performance, and the authors further propose a distillation-based knowledge base construction method that streamlines the RAG pipeline and balances effectiveness with computational cost.

For low-resource languages, the problem is intensified by the fact that LLM performance depends heavily on the availability and quality of documentation, and degrades when documentation is missing, outdated, or inconsistent with the code. This is especially true for historical computer music languages such as Music V, which have minimal presence in modern online corpora, no active user community, and no digitized, structured documentation beyond scanned historical manuals, conditions that, to our knowledge, remain unexplored.

Beyond the technical issues of an under-represented language, early computer music languages add a cultural dimension linking this work to digital heritage preservation. In parallel, digital humanities researchers increasingly use LLMs for retrieving and interpreting historical, non-standardized textual material, showing that retrieval-augmented methods grounded in original sources can substantially improve the reliability of LLM-based analysis over reliance on parametric knowledge alone [10,23,34–36].

While prior studies have benchmarked the limits of LLM code reasoning on common programming languages, examined adaptation strategies for low-resource languages, and applied LLMs to historical document interpretation in other humanities domains, to the best of our knowledge, no existing work addresses the interpretation of historical computer music languages through

Retrieval-Augmented Generation (RAG) grounded in their original technical manuals. This paper aims to fill this gap, proposing Music V as a historically significant case study for the broader problem of preserving and reactivating obsolete domain-specific programming languages of cultural significance. In this work, preservation refers specifically to preserving and making operationally accessible the technical knowledge required to interpret historical source code, rather than to emulating or executing the original software environment.

# 3 Methodology: The Proposed RAG Framework

The architecture of the proposed RAG system is designed to bridge the gap between historical computer music syntax and modern LLM understanding, enabling more reliable interpretation of Music V syntax. The overall pipeline is organized into two main stages, illustrated in Fig. 1 and Fig. 3: Knowledge Base Preparation (offline), in which the historical Music V manual is processed, and Contextual Retrieval and Generation (online), in which a code line submitted by a user is passed to an LLM together with the most relevant manual passages to generate a grounded interpretation. The remainder of this section describes each stage in detail.

## 3.1 Knowledge Base Preparation (Offline)

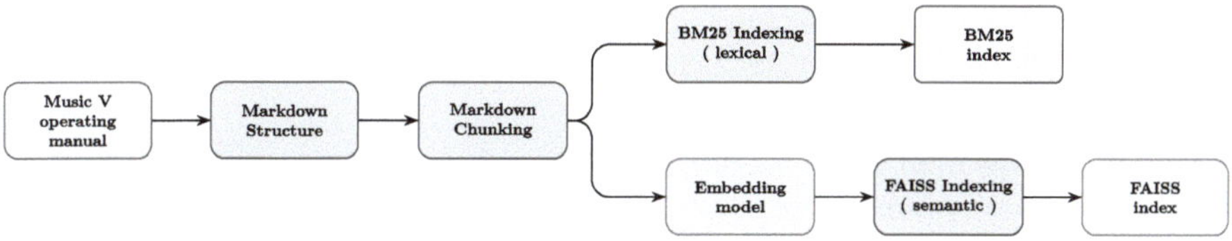


**Fig. 1.** Knowledge Base Preparation (offline) pipeline: document segmentation, chunking, and Dual-Layer (BM25 + FAISS) indexing of the Music V manual.

The reliability of the system depends strictly on the authority of its knowledge base. We ingested the Italian-translated Music V documentation preserved at the Centro di Sonologia Computazionale (CSC) of the University of Padova [2,9]. We used the Italian-translated manual since it represents an authentic instance of institutionally archived, non-English historical documentation, though this could introduce an additional layer of complexity. Although no obvious retrieval failures could be attributed to the language of the manual during our qualitative inspection, we did not conduct a controlled comparison with the English version; this remains future work. As shown in Fig. 2, the manual is structured into chapters, subsections, tables, and code examples, all of which must be preserved when fragmenting the document. For this reason, the document is first segmented by content type (text, code, or table) preventing tables and code blocks from being split across chunks. The text segments are then further split using Langchain's MarkdownTextSplitter [4], which keeps each section as intact as possible by using Markdown headers as semantic boundaries. To retain as much contextual information as possible, each chunk is additionally annotated with metadata recording its chapter, section, and subsection, its content type (text, code, or table), and a unique identifier. This approach preserves the structural integrity of the source documents containing dense technical tables describing Unit Generator parameters (e.g., inputs, outputs, and, controls), and keeps code blocks intact as atomic units within their context, avoiding the fragmentation that often causes RAG failures in technical domains [28].

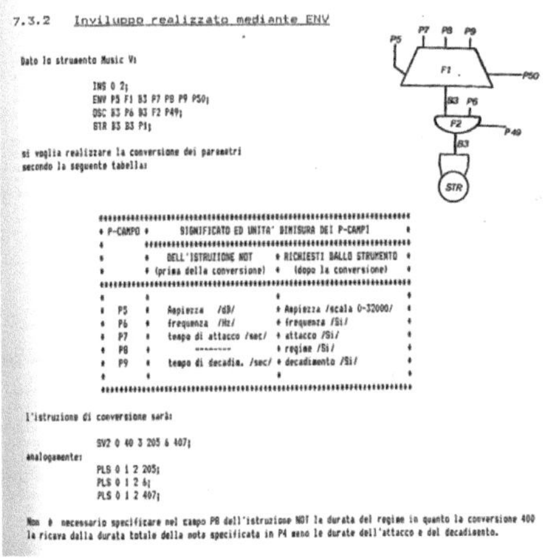
7.3.2 Inviluppo realizzato mediante ENV

Dato lo strumento Music V:

```
INS 0 2;
ENV P5 F1 B3 P7 P8 P9 P50;
OSC B3 P6 B3 F2 P49;
STR B3 B3 P1;
```



si voglia realizzare la conversione dei parametri secondo la seguente tabella:

| P-CAMPO | SIGNIFICATO ED UNITA' DIMISURA DEI P-CAMPI | |
|---|---|---|
| | DELL'ISTRUZIONE NOT (prima della conversione) | RICHIESTI DALLO STRUMENTO (dopo la conversione) |
| P5 | Ampiezza /dB/ | Ampiezza /scala 0-32000/ |
| P6 | frequenza /Hz/ | frequenza /Si/ |
| P7 | tempo di attacco /sec/ | attacco /Si/ |
| P8 | -------- | regime /Si/ |
| P9 | tempo di decadim. /sec/ | decadimento /Si/ |

l'istruzione di conversione sarà:

```
SV2 0 40 3 205 6 407;
```

analogamente:

```
PLS 0 1 2 205;
PLS 0 1 2 6;
PLS 0 1 2 407;
```

Non è necessario specificare nel campo P8 dell'istruzione NOT la durata del regime in quanto la conversione 400 la ricava dalla durata totale della nota specificata in P4 meno le durate dell'attacco e del decadimento.

**Fig. 2.** An excerpt from the Music V manual [9]. As can be seen, the manual features various types of structures, including titles, text, tables, and code.

The chunking procedure produced 429 chunks in total, with an average length of 382 tokens, distributed across 283 text chunks, 138 code chunks, and 8 table chunks. To assess chunking quality, the authors manually checked that each chunk retained enough surrounding context to support its intended retrieval and interpretation.

Following the schematic in Fig. 1, the resulting chunks are then indexed. Because Music V syntax relies on short, cryptic tokens (e.g., OSC, NOT, OUT), dense vector embeddings alone often fail to capture the exact syntactic intent, leading to false positives. To mitigate this, we developed a Dual-Layer Indexing mechanism combining two complementary retrieval paradigms:

- Lexical Layer (Sparse Retrieval): implemented using the BM25 algorithm [25] to index exact keyword tokens. BM25 scores document relevance based on exact string matching, ensuring that when a specific Music V instruction is queried, the manual page describing that instruction is prioritized.

- Semantic Layer (Dense Retrieval): implemented using the FAISS (Facebook AI Similarity Search) index [11], a data structure for efficient similarity search and clustering of dense vectors. Each chunk is embedded into a high-dimensional vector space using a pre-trained Qwen3 embedding model [33]. This layer captures the semantic meaning of architectural descriptions, matching synonyms, and conceptual explanations that lexical matching alone would miss.

These two indices are then used during the online stage.

### 3.2 Answer Generation (Online)

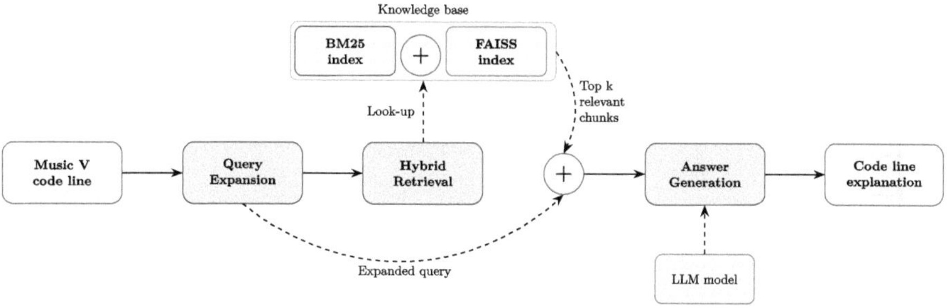


**Fig. 3.** Contextual Retrieval and Generation (online): query validation, expansion, hybrid retrieval via RRF, and LLM-based answer generation.

During the online phase, the system processes the user's query against the knowledge base built in the previous stage. The user submits a code line written in Music V, which first passes through a verification layer ensuring that it follows the correct syntax, raising an error otherwise; this check is performed using a set of regular expressions derived from the Music V grammar [9]. The validated line goes through a Query Expansion step, in which the raw snippet is pre-processed to prioritize its first token, which in Music V represents the function being invoked [20]. This step is essential to ensure the correct chunks are retrieved.

At this point, the system begins the retrieval phase, comparing the query against both indices. For BM25, the query is compared against all chunks in the lexical index, and a score is computed for each query-document pair $(D, Q)$ according to the formula:

$$score(D,Q) = \sum_{i=1}^{n} IDF(q_i) \cdot \frac{f(q_i, D) \cdot (k_1 + 1)}{f(q_i, D) + k_1 \cdot (1 - b + b \cdot \frac{|D|}{avgdl})} \quad (1)$$

where,

- $IDF(q) = \ln((N - n(q) + 0.5)/(n(q) + 0.5))$ measures how often a term appears across the entire collection, where $q$ is a query term, $N$ the total number of documents in the corpus, and $n(q)$ the number of documents containing the query term;
- $f(q_i, D)$ is the frequency of a query word inside the document;
- $k_1$ is a saturation parameter, set by default to 1.2;
- $b$ is the length parameter, set by default to 0.75;
- $avgdl$ is the average document length of the corpus.

The 20 highest-scoring chunks are retained from this step.

At the same time, the query is embedded using the same Qwen3 embedding model employed during the offline stage. The embedded query is compared against the embedded chunks in the FAISS index by computing the Euclidean distance, and, analogously to the lexical search, the 20 nearest neighbours are retrieved.

To combine the results of the two retrieval methods into a single ranking, we use Reciprocal Rank Fusion (RRF) [7], defined as:

$$RRF(d) = \sum_{r \in R} \frac{1}{(k + r(d))} \quad . \tag{2}$$

where $d$ is a document, $R$ is the set of rankers (retrievers), $k$ is a smoothing constant, set to 60, following the original paper, and $r(d)$ is the rank of document $d$ according to a given ranker.

Using this formula, the top 10 chunks are retrieved, representing the best combined results of the lexical and semantic searches. These chunks, together with the expanded query, form the context provided to the LLM for answer generation. The full prompt for answer generation is as follows:

**Prompt.** "You are a technical documentation assistant of MUSIC V code. Explain what the given line of code *[CodeLine]* does based only on the provided context from the technical manual *[Context]*, without making up any new information. Use the manual's terminology and be precise and concise in your explanation. Return the syntax, the parameters and the meaning of the code line, based only on the provided context. Don't make up any new information and don't explain acronyms. If you don't know the answer, say you don't know."

Finally, the model returns the interpretation of the code line to the user, following the manual's terminology and the structure specified in the prompt.

## 4 Results and Discussion

To evaluate the proposed retrieval-augmented approach, we used three large language models deployed locally through Ollama: Qwen3.5:9B and Qwen3.5:35B [24], two models from the same family differing in scale, and DeepSeek-Coder:6.7B [15], a code-specialized model. This selection allows us to assess whether the benefit of retrieval augmentation depends on model scale or on code-specific pretraining. For each model, we compared a zero-shot baseline against our RAG-based configuration, isolating the contribution of grounding the model in historical documentation from that of model scale or architecture. We evaluated both configurations using two complementary metric families. First, we computed BERTScore [32] between each generated answer and its reference, since it captures contextual semantic similarity rather than exact lexical overlap, important here, as correct Music V explanations can be phrased in different but equivalent ways that n-gram metrics such as BLEU or ROUGE would unfairly penalize. Second, we used RAGAS (Retrieval Augmented Generation Assessment) [12], a suite of metrics for retrieval-augmented systems, all normalized between 0 and 1 with higher values indicating better performance:

- *Answer Correctness*: measures how closely the generated answer matches the ground truth.
- *Answer Similarity*: calculates the semantic similarity between the generated answer and the ground truth.
- *Answer Relevancy*: measures how closely a response addresses the intent of the user's original question, regardless of factual correctness, penalizing answers that are incomplete or contain extraneous information. It is computed by generating synthetic questions from the response, computing the cosine similarity between each synthetic question's embedding and the original user input, and averaging these similarities.
- *Faithfulness*: evaluates how well a response's claims are supported by the retrieved context; a response is faithful only if every claim can be traced back to the retrieved passages.
- *Context Recall*: measures the proportion of relevant information that was successfully retrieved, capturing whether important content was overlooked.
- *Context Precision*: measures whether relevant chunks are ranked above irrelevant ones within the retrieved context.

Since RAGAS relies on an LLM-as-judge, we used Llama3.1:8B [22], deliberately chosen from a different model family than the three evaluated models to avoid self-preference bias. We report the full set of RAGAS metrics for the RAG configuration, but restrict the zero-shot evaluation to Answer Relevancy, Answer Correctness, and Answer Similarity, since the remaining metrics require retrieved context that is absent in that setting. Given the absence of any existing benchmark for Music V question answering, we constructed a dedicated evaluation set of 100 query-answer pairs, generated with Gemini 3.1 Pro from the available Music V manuals and subsequently reviewed and corrected by the authors against the original sources, ensuring the final references are grounded in authoritative historical documentation rather than unsupervised LLM output.

Table 1 reports BERTScore, Answer Correctness, Answer Similarity, and Answer Relevancy for both configurations, together with Faithfulness, Context Recall, and Context Precision for RAG only, since these require retrieved context unavailable in the zero-shot setting.

**Table 1.** Zero-shot and RAG performance of the three evaluated models on the Music V interpretation task, averaged over 100 query–answer pairs. Reported metrics are BERTScore (BERTs), Answer Correctness (AnsCor), Answer Similarity (AnsSim), Answer Relevancy (AnsRel), Faithfulness (FaiFul), Context Recall (ConRec), and Context Precision (ConPrec). Although all models share the same retrieval module, context metrics (ConRec and ConPrec) show minor differences due to stochasticity in the LLM-as-a-judge RAGAS evaluations, which are run separately for each model pipeline.

| Models | *BERTs* | *AnsCor* | *AnsSim* | *AnsRel* | *FaiFul* | *ConRec* | *ConPrec* |
|---|---|---|---|---|---|---|---|
| Qwen3.5:9B | 0.8403 | 0.5670 | 0.5904 | 0.6552 | – | – | – |
| Qwen3.5:35B | 0.8483 | 0.5694 | 0.6480 | 0.6276 | – | – | – |
| DeepSeek-Coder:6.7B | 0.7998 | 0.4398 | 0.4687 | 0.4578 | – | – | – |
| Qwen3.5:9B + RAG | 0.8808 | **0.7029** | 0.8872 | 0.5824 | 0.7231 | 0.9154 | 0.7986 |
| Qwen3.5:35B + RAG | **0.8879** | 0.6787 | **0.8995** | 0.5630 | **0.7801** | 0.9181 | 0.7982 |
| DeepSeek-Coder:6.7B + RAG | 0.8450 | 0.5693 | 0.7443 | **0.6558** | 0.7323 | 0.9157 | 0.7957 |

Overall, the results show that the RAG architecture improves performance for all three models on three of the four metrics shared between configurations, BERTScore, Answer Correctness, and Answer Similarity, supporting our initial hypothesis that grounding the model in domain-specific historical documentation improves its ability to interpret Music V code. The one exception is Answer Relevancy, which decreases under RAG for both Qwen models while improving for DeepSeek-Coder; we discuss this result separately below. The largest and most consistent gains are observed for Answer Similarity, which increases substantially for all three models once retrieval augmentation is introduced (from 0.590 to 0.887 for Qwen3.5:9B, from 0.648 to 0.900 for Qwen3.5:35B, and from 0.469 to 0.744 for DeepSeek-Coder:6.7B). Since this metric directly measures how closely the generated answer matches the ground-truth reference, this result indicates that RAG answers are more aligned with the content of the historical manuals than zero-shot answers, which are instead generated purely from their internal knowledge. A similar trend is observed for the BERTScore. Even in the zero-shot setting, BERTScore values are already comparatively high across all three models (0.80–0.85). We attribute this high baseline primarily to how the metric is computed: rather than evaluating whether the logical content of an answer matches the reference, BERTScore performs token-level matching based on cosine similarity between contextual embeddings and aggregates these matches into a single score.

In our domain, many tokens in any answer, numeric values, parameter names, unit identifiers, and common connectives—are essentially fixed by the question's structure and recur across candidate and reference answers, since both zero-shot and RAG systems are prompted to use the same format. Because these tokens match almost perfectly or have very similar embeddings, BERTScore can stay high even when the logical relations between them, the actual content, are partly or entirely incorrect. Thus, an answer can be structurally well-formed and use the right technical vocabulary while being logically incorrect, without this error being fully captured by BERTScore. This is a further instance of a broader limitation of cosine-similarity-based metrics, a point we return to below in relation to Answer Relevancy.

Despite this fact, RAG still yields a consistent improvement of 4 to 6 points in BERTScore across all three models.

Answer Correctness follows a similar pattern, improving for all three models under RAG, with Qwen3.5:9B showing the strongest absolute gain (from 0.567 to 0.703), while DeepSeek-Coder:6.7B remains the weakest performer on this metric even with retrieval augmentation (0.440 zero-shot, 0.569 with RAG).

Taking into account only RAG configurations, Qwen3.5:35B achieves the best score on four of the seven metrics reported (BERTScore, Answer Similarity, and Faithfulness), making it the model with the highest consistent strength overall. However, Qwen3.5:9B outperforms its larger counterpart on Answer Correctness, suggesting that increased model size primarily benefits fluency and grounding quality rather than factual correctness per se. DeepSeek-Coder:6.7B, despite being the smallest model in our comparison and the only one specialized in source code rather than general-purpose language understanding, remains the weakest performer on BERTScore, Answer Correctness, and Answer Similarity even with RAG. Nevertheless, it achieves the best Answer Relevancy (0.656) among all three RAG setups, indicating that it generates responses that stay closely aligned with the topic, even though it is relatively weaker at turning this grounded context into fluent and fully accurate explanations.

The decrease in Answer Relevancy observed for both Qwen models under RAG deserves further discussion, as it appears to contradict the otherwise consistent improvement observed across the other shared metrics. We identify two complementary explanations, one methodological and one related to model behavior. From a methodological point of view, this metric depends more heavily on the underlying LLM of the judge than the other RAGAS metrics we report. As Roychowdhury et al. point out, Answer Relevancy is computed by having the judge model generate a small set of synthetic questions from the candidate answer and then measuring their cosine similarity to the embedding of the original question [26]; this makes the metric sensitive both to the specific questions generated by the judge model and, more fundamentally, to the well-documented limitations of cosine similarity as an absolute measure of semantic relatedness [6,13,27]. For this reason, we consider the absolute Answer Relevancy values reported here to be less reliable than the other evaluation metrics and we consider the study of this specific metric as a relevant direction for future work, for instance, by explicitly measuring answer length and conciseness alongside relevancy.

To complement the quantitative findings presented above with a qualitative example, in Fig. 4 we show the zero-shot and RAG responses generated by the Qwen3.5:35B model for the same Music V code line, `NOT 6.5 13 2.3 66 440 ;`. The RAG answer correctly identifies the statement as a note instruction, the construct in Music V used to trigger a sound event, recognizing the standard parameter structure T1 NUM DUR PAR... (start time, instrument number, duration, and instrument-specific parameters) and correctly relating the values 66 and 440 to the instrument's P-fields. In contrast, the zero-shot answer misinterprets the NOT keyword as a logical negation opcode that "performs a logical inversion operation on the specified control signals", treating the five values that follow as generic, undifferentiated arguments rather than recognizing their distinct functional roles as time, instrument, duration, and parameter fields. This example also offers a concrete qualitative confirmation of the Answer Relevancy paradox discussed above. Despite being factually incorrect, the zero-shot answer obtains a higher Answer Relevancy score (0.6262) than the correct, well-grounded RAG answer (0.5994), while the RAG answer scores substantially higher on the metrics more directly tied to factual correctness (Answer Similarity: 0.9636 vs. 0.5061; Answer Correctness: 0.8409 vs. 0.4795). This single example illustrates, at the level of an individual query, the broader pattern observed across the full evaluation set: Answer Relevancy, as computed by RAGAS, can reward an answer for confidently and narrowly addressing the surface form of the question even when its content is incorrect, while penalizing a more accurate, detailed, and properly grounded answer for its added explanatory length.

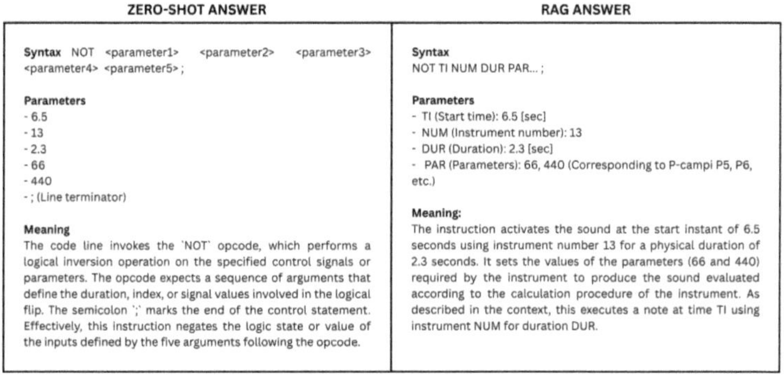


**Fig. 4.** Example of a result for the query: `NOT 6.5 13 2.3 66 440 ;`. On the left the zero shot answer of the model Qwen3.5:35B, on the right the answer of the RAG + Qwen3.5:35B model.

## 5 Conclusions

This paper addressed the problem of preserving and interpreting early computer music programming languages, focusing on Music V as a representative case of a fragile, undocumented form of digital cultural heritage. We proposed a retrieval-augmented generation system that grounds large language models in historical Music V manuals through a hybrid BM25 and dense (FAISS) retrieval pipeline, with the goal of improving the reliability of automated interpretation of Music V code beyond what zero-shot LLMs can currently achieve. Our evaluation across three open-weight models of different scale and specialization, Qwen3.5:9B, Qwen3.5:35B, and DeepSeek-Coder:6.7B, shows that grounding the models in the original historical documentation yields consistent improvements in Answer Correctness, Answer Similarity, and BERTScore across all three models, confirming that retrieval augmentation substantially improves the factual accuracy of generated interpretations compared to relying on the models' parametric knowledge alone, which is necessarily limited for a language likely to be severely underrepresented in modern pretraining corpora. Qwen3.5:35B emerged as the most consistently strong model when paired with retrieval, though our results also show that scaling within the same model family does not uniformly translate into better performance across all metrics, and that DeepSeek-Coder, despite being specialized for source code, did not transfer this specialization advantageously to a historical, non-standard language such as Music V. We further showed that commonly used automatic evaluation metrics based on cosine similarity, including BERTScore and Answer Relevancy, can be misleading in this domain, since they are sensitive to surface-level lexical overlap arising from the small, recurring technical vocabulary of Music V, and can in some cases reward confidently incorrect answers over correct, well-grounded ones. We consider this methodological observation a contribution in its own right, relevant to future evaluations of LLMs on niche, domain-specific programming languages more generally. While our study focuses on Music V, we hypothesize that the dual-layer indexing strategy can be adapted to other historical languages with different syntax, given some retuning. Music V's short, cryptic, keyword-like symbols (e.g., OSC, NOT, OUT) motivated our use of exact lexical matching (BM25) with semantic retrieval to reduce false positives from dense embeddings. For more verbose historical languages, such as COBOLs, semantic retrieval would likely assume a larger role, as longer constructs provide richer embedding contexts, while lexical retrieval would focus on reserved keywords and fixed-format clauses. The key parameters to adjust are the relative weights of the two retrieval layers in the RRF combination and the chunk size used for indexing. Empirically testing this generalization across additional historical languages is an important direction for future research.

This work has several limitations. Our evaluation set, while carefully constructed and manually verified, includes only 100 query–answer pairs, limiting statistical robustness and preventing a more detailed assessment of performance across different Music V constructs. Our experiments are restricted to Music V; while we anticipate that the same challenges apply to the broader Music N family and to other obsolete, domain-specific languages, this assumption has yet to be empirically confirmed. In addition, our evaluation relies exclusively on automatic metrics; given the constraints of cosine-similarity-based measures described above, a human study involving musicologists or composers experienced with Music V would provide stronger and more dependable validation. Finally, the current model operates only on a single line of code, since reliable interpretation of individual statements is necessary for both accessibility and higher-level analysis of Music V scores.

Future work will generalize the method to handle multiple lines of code, with the goal of enhancing the system's effectiveness for interpreting historical scores. We also intend to broaden the evaluation to other languages in the Music N family, including Music IV and Music 360, and more generally to additional domain-specific historical programming languages at risk of digital obsolescence. Moreover, we plan to carry out a human evaluation with domain experts to supplement and validate our automatic metrics, and to investigate whether the approach can be extended beyond interpretation towards the reactivation of historical computer music works. We believe that combining retrieval-augmented generation with carefully preserved historical documentation provides a promising and broadly applicable strategy for protecting the fragile, often poorly documented knowledge embodied in early computer music languages and, more generally, in obsolete software systems of cultural and historical importance.

**Disclosure of Interests.** The authors have no competing interests to declare that are relevant to the content of this article.

## References

1. Bouzenia, I., Devanbu, P., Pradel, M.: RepairAgent: an autonomous, LLM-based agent for program repair. In: 2025 IEEE/ACM 47th International Conference on Software Engineering (ICSE), pp. 2188–2200. IEEE (2025)
2. Canazza, S., De Poli, G.: Four decades of music research, creation, and education at Padua's Centro di Sonologia Computazionale. Comput. Music. J. **43**(4), 58–80 (2020)
3. Cassano, F., et al.: Knowledge transfer from high-resource to low-resource programming languages for code LLMs. Proc. ACM Program. Lang. **8**(OOPSLA2) (2024). https://doi.org/10.1145/3689735
4. Chase, H.: LangChain (2022). https://github.com/langchain-ai/langchain
5. Collins, N.: Introduction to computer music. John Wiley & Sons (2010)
6. Connor, R.: A tale of four metrics. Lecture Notes in Computer Science, pp. 210–217 (2016). https://doi.org/10.1007/978-3-319-46759-7_16
7. Cormack, G.V., Clarke, C.L., Buettcher, S.: Reciprocal rank fusion outperforms Condorcet and individual rank learning methods. In: Proceedings of the 32nd International ACM SIGIR Conference on Research and Development in Information Retrieval, pp. 758–759 (2009)
8. Dannenberg, R.B.: Languages for computer music. Front. Digital Humanit. **5**, 26 (2018)
9. De Poli, G., Vidolin, A.: Music v: manuale operativo (1983). collection of Centro di Sonologia Computazionale. Padova
10. Di Pasqua, F., Merialdo, P., Torlone, R.: Generative AI for ancient insights: leveraging LLMs and rag for ancient world studies. In: 2025 IEEE International Conference on Cyber Humanities (IEEE-CH), pp. 1–6 (2025). https://doi.org/10.1109/IEEE-CH65308.2025.11279339
11. Douze, M., et al.: The Faiss library. IEEE Trans. Big Data **12**(2), 346–361 (2026). https://doi.org/10.1109/TBDATA.2025.3618474
12. Es, S., James, J., Espinosa Anke, L., Schockaert, S.: RAGAs: automated evaluation of retrieval augmented generation. In: Aletras, N., De Clercq, O. (eds.) Proceedings of the 18th Conference of the European Chapter of the Association for Computational Linguistics: System Demonstrations, pp. 150–158. Association for

Computational Linguistics, St. Julians, Malta (2024). https://doi.org/10.18653/v1/2024.eacl-demo.16
13. Ethayarajh, K.: How contextual are contextualized word representations? Comparing the geometry of BERT, ELMo, and GPT-2 embeddings. In: Inui, K., Jiang, J., Ng, V., Wan, X. (eds.) Proceedings of the 2019 Conference on Empirical Methods in Natural Language Processing and the 9th International Joint Conference on Natural Language Processing (EMNLP-IJCNLP), pp. 55–65. Association for Computational Linguistics, Hong Kong, China (2019). https://doi.org/10.18653/v1/D19-1006
14. Giagnorio, A., Martin-Lopez, A., Bavota, G.: Enhancing code generation for low-resource languages: no silver bullet. In: 2025 IEEE/ACM 33rd International Conference on Program Comprehension (ICPC), pp. 478–488. IEEE Press (2025). https://doi.org/10.1109/ICPC66645.2025.00058
15. Guo, D., et al.: DeepSeek-coder: When the large language model meets programming-the rise of code intelligence. arXiv preprint arXiv:2401.14196 (2024)
16. Hiller, L.A.: Computer music. Sci. Am. **201**(6), 109–121 (1959)
17. Jiang, J., Wang, F., Shen, J., Kim, S., Kim, S.: A survey on large language models for code generation. ACM Trans. Softw. Eng. Methodol. **35**(2), 1–72 (2026)
18. Lazzarini, V., Yi, S., Heintz, J., Brandtsegg, Ø., McCurdy, I., et al.: Csound: a sound and music computing system. Springer (2016)
19. Lin, J., Zhang, Y., Li, C., Zou, W., Ge, J., Luo, B.: Retrieval-augmented code generation of low-resource programming languages. In: 2025 32nd Asia-Pacific Software Engineering Conference (APSEC), pp. 927–931 (2025). https://doi.org/10.1109/APSEC66846.2025.00106
20. Matthews, M.V., Miller, J.E., Moore, F., Pierce, J.R., Risset, J.: The Technology of Computer Music, The MIT Press (1969)
21. Maveli, N., Vergari, A., Cohen, S.B.: Can LLMs compress (and decompress)? Evaluating code understanding and execution via invertibility (2026). https://arxiv.org/abs/2601.13398
22. Meta AI: Llama 3.1: Our most capable models to date (2024). https://ai.meta.com/blog/meta-llama-3-1/
23. Murugaraj, K., Lamsiyah, S., During, M., Theobald, M.: Topic-RAG for historical newspapers: enhancing information retrieval in humanities research through topic-based retrieval-augmented generation. Comput. Humanit. Res. **1**, e15 (2025). https://doi.org/10.1017/chr.2025.10018
24. Qwen Team: Qwen3.5: Towards native multimodal agents (2026). https://qwen.ai/blog?id=qwen3.5
25. Robertson, S., Zaragoza, H.: The probabilistic relevance framework: BM25 and beyond. Found. Trends Inf. Retr. **3**(4), 333–389 (2009). https://doi.org/10.1561/1500000019
26. Roychowdhury, S., Soman, S., Ranjani, H., Gunda, N., Chhabra, V., Bala, S.K.: Evaluation of rag metrics for question answering in the telecom domain. arXiv preprint arXiv:2407.12873 (2024)
27. Timkey, W., van Schijndel, M.: All bark and no bite: rogue dimensions in transformer language models obscure representational quality. In: Moens, M.F., Huang, X., Specia, L., Yih, S.W.t. (eds.) Proceedings of the 2021 Conference on Empirical Methods in Natural Language Processing, pp. 4527–4546. Association for Computational Linguistics, Online and Punta Cana, Dominican Republic (2021). https://doi.org/10.18653/v1/2021.emnlp-main.372

28. Widiiswa, R.A.N., Henry, M.M., Imani, A., Pardamean, B.: Retrieval-augmented generation chunking strategies for financial document analysis: a systematic literature review. In: 2026 30th International Conference on Information Technology (IT), pp. 1–4 (2026). https://doi.org/10.1109/IT67293.2026.11435730
29. Wong, M.F., Guo, S., Hang, C.N., Ho, S.W., Tan, C.W.: Natural language generation and understanding of big code for AI-assisted programming: a review. Entropy **25**(6), 888 (2023)
30. Xia, C.S., Wei, Y., Zhang, L.: Automated program repair in the era of large pre-trained language models. In: 2023 IEEE/ACM 45th International Conference on Software Engineering (ICSE), pp. 1482–1494. IEEE (2023)
31. Xie, D., et al.: CoRe: Benchmarking LLMs code reasoning capabilities through static analysis tasks (2026). https://arxiv.org/abs/2507.05269
32. Zhang, T., Kishore, V., Wu, F., Weinberger, K.Q., Artzi, Y.: BERTScore: Evaluating text generation with BERT. arXiv preprint arXiv:1904.09675 (2019)
33. Zhang, Y., et al.: Qwen3 embedding: Advancing text embedding and reranking through foundation models. arXiv preprint arXiv:2506.05176 (2025)
34. Zhou, J., Si, L., Hou, W.: Humanities-in-the-loop: using close reading as a method for retrieval-augmented generation (RAG). Proc. Assoc. Inf. Sci. Technol. **62**(1), 1185–1189 (2025). https://doi.org/10.1002/pra2.1355
35. Zhou, X., Lin, J.: Multimodal rag for cultural heritage: a technical exploration based on Jino traditional knowledge. Digital Sch. Humanit. **41**(2), 1138–1153 (2026). https://doi.org/10.1093/llc/fqag042
36. Zou, J., Cai, Y.: A human-AI hybrid framework for stylistic analysis: bridging AI and humanities education. In: Proceedings of the 2025 3rd International Conference on Information Education and Artificial Intelligence, pp. 909–915. ICIEAI'25, Association for Computing Machinery, New York, NY, USA (2026). https://doi.org/10.1145/3799457.3799607
37. Zuccante, A., Canazza, S.: Software nostalgia: state of the art on software preservation. In: 2025 IEEE History of Electrotechnology Conference (HISTELCON), pp. 1–6 (2025). https://doi.org/10.1109/HISTELCON64051.2025.11285955

# Author Index




S. Bistarelli et al. (Eds.): AIxIA 2026, LNAI 17131, pp. 743–745, 2027.
https://doi.org/10.1007/978-3-032-40774-0

MIX
Papier aus verantwortungsvollen Quellen
Paper from responsible sources
FSC® C105338

If you have any concerns about our products,
you can contact us on
**ProductSafety@springernature.com**

In case Publisher is established outside the EU,
the EU authorized representative is:
**Springer Nature Customer Service Center GmbH**
**Europaplatz 3, 69115 Heidelberg, Germany**

Printed by Libri Plureos GmbH
in Hamburg, Germany